Volume 1 • 2011

WHAT DO I READ NEXT?

A Reader's Guide to Current Genre Fiction

- Fantasy
- Popular Fiction
- Popular Romances
- Horror
- Mystery
- Science Fiction
- Historical
- Inspirational

ISSN 1052-2212

Volume 1 • 2011

WHAT DO I READ NEXT?

A Reader's Guide
to Current
Genre Fiction

- Fantasy
- Popular Fiction
- Popular Romances
- Horror
- Mystery
- Science Fiction
- Historical
- Inspirational

DANIEL S. BURT

DON D'AMMASSA

NATALIE DANFORD

ANGIE KIESLING

CLAIR LAMB

KRISTIN RAMSDELL

GALE
CENGAGE Learning

Detroit • New York • San Francisco • New Haven, Conn • Waterville, Maine • London

GALE
CENGAGE Learning™

What Do I Read Next 2011, Volume 1

Project Editors: Dana Ferguson, Michelle Kazensky

Composition and Electronic Prepress: Gary Leach, Evi Seoud

Manufacturing: Rita Wimberley

For product information and technology assistance, contact us at
Gale Customer Support, 1-800-877-4253.
For permission to use material from this text or product,
submit all requests online at **www.cengage.com/permissions.**
Further permissions questions can be emailed to
permissionrequest@cengage.com

While every effort has been made to ensure the reliability of the information presented in this publication, Gale, a part of Cengage Learning, does not guarantee the accuracy of the data contained herein. Gale accepts no payment for listing; and inclusion in the publication of any organization, agency, institution, publication, service, or individual does not imply endorsement of the editors or publisher. Errors brought to the attention of the publisher and verified to the satisfaction of the publisher will be corrected in future editions.

Gale
27500 Drake Rd.
Farmington Hills, MI, 48331-3535

LIBRARY OF CONGRESS CONTROL NUMBER 82-15700

ISBN-13: 978-1-4144-6136-6
ISBN-10: 1-4144-6136-4

ISSN: 1052-2212

Printed in Mexico
1 2 3 4 5 6 7 15 14 13 12 11

Contents

Introduction

Thousands of books are published each year intended for devoted fans of genre fiction. Dragons, outlaws, lovers, murderers, monsters, and aliens abound on our own world or on other worlds, throughout time—all featured in the pages of fantasy, romance, mystery, horror, science fiction, historical, inspirational, and popular fiction. Given the huge variety of titles available each year, added to the numbers from previous years, readers can be forgiven if they're stumped by the question "What do I read next?" And that's where this book comes in.

Designed as a tool to assist in the exploration of genre fiction, *What Do I Read Next?* guides the reader to both current and classic recommendations in eight widely read genres: Mystery, Romance, Fantasy, Horror, Science Fiction, Historical, Inspirational, and Popular Fiction. *What Do I Read Next?* allows readers quick and easy access to specific data on recent titles in these popular genres. Plus, each entry provides alternate reading selections, thus coming to the rescue of librarians and booksellers, who are often unfamiliar with a genre, yet must answer the question frequently posed by their patrons and customers, "What do I read next?"

Details on Titles

Volume 1 of this year's edition of *What Do I Read Next?* contains entries for titles published primarily in late 2010. These entries are divided into sections for Mystery, Popular Romances, Fantasy, Horror, Science Fiction, Historical, Inspirational, and Popular Fiction. Experts in each field compile the entries for their respective genres. The experts also discuss topics relevant to their genres in essays that appear at the beginning of each section.

The criteria for inclusion of specific titles vary somewhat from genre to genre. In genres such as Romance and Mystery, where large numbers of titles are published each year, the inclusion criteria are more selective, with the experts attempting to select the recently published books that they consider best. In genres such as Horror, where the amount of new material is relatively small, a broader range of titles is represented, including many titles published by small or independent houses and some young adult books.

The entries are listed alphabetically by main author in each genre section. Most provide the following information:

- **Author or editor's** name and real name if a pseudonym is used. Co-authors, co-editors, and illustrators are also listed where applicable.
- **Book title.**
- **Date and place of publication; name of publisher.**
- **Series name.**
- **Story type:** Specific categories within each genre, identified by the compiling expert. Definitions of these types are listed in the "Key to Genre Terms" section.
- **Subject(s):** Gives the subject matter covered by the title.
- **Major character(s):** Names and brief descriptions of up to three characters featured in the title.
- **Time period(s):** Tells when the story takes place.
- **Locale(s):** Tells where the story takes place.
- **What the book is about:** A brief plot summary.
- **Where it's reviewed:** Citations to reviews of the book, including the source of the review, date of the source, and the page on which the review appears. Reviews are included from genre-specific sources such as *Locus* and *Affaire de Coeur*, as well as more general reviewing sources such as *Booklist* and *Publishers* Weekly.
- **Other books by the author:** Titles and publication dates of other books the author has written, useful for those wanting to read more by a particular author.
- **Other books you might like:** Titles by other authors written on a similar theme or in a similar style. These titles further the reader's exploration of the genre.

Indexes Answer Readers' Questions

The nine indexes in *What Do I Read Next?* used separately or in conjunction with each other, create many pathways to the featured titles, answering general questions or locating specific titles. For example:

"Are there any new Maisie Dobbs books?"

The SERIES INDEX lists entries by the name of the series of which they are a part.

"I like Regency Romances. Can you recommend any new ones?"

The GENRE INDEX breaks each genre into story types or more specialized areas. In the Romance genre for example, there is a story type heading "Regency." For the definitions of story types, see the "Key to Genre Terms."

"I'm looking for a story set in Paris."

The GEOGRAPHIC INDEX lists titles by their locale. This can help readers pinpoint an area in which they may have a particular interest, such as their home town, another country, or even Cyberspace.

"Do you know of any science fiction stories set during the 22nd century?"

The TIME PERIOD INDEX is a chronological listing of the time settings in which the main entry titles take place.

"What books are available that feature teachers?"

The CHARACTER DESCRIPTION INDEX identifies the major characters by occupation (e.g. Accountant, Editor, Librarian) or persona (e.g. Cyborg, Noble woman, Stowaway).

"Has anyone written any new books with Sherlock Holmes in them?"

The CHARACTER NAME INDEX lists the major characters named in the entries. This can help readers who remember some information about a book, but not an author or title.

"What has Laurell K. Hamilton written recently?"

The AUTHOR INDEX contains the names of all authors featured in the entries and those listed under "Other books you might like."

The TITLE INDEX includes all main entry titles and all titles recommended under "Other books by the author" and "Other books you might like" in one alphabetical listing. Thus a reader can find a specific title, new or old, then go to that entry to find out what new titles are similar.

"I'm interested in books that depict military life."

The SUBJECT INDEX is an alphabetical listing of all the subjects covered by the main entry titles.

The indexes can also be used together to narrow down or broaden choices. A reader interested in Mysteries set in New York during the 19th century would consult the TIME PERIOD INDEX and GEOGRAPHIC INDEX to see which titles appear in both. Time Travel is a common theme in Science Fiction but occasionally appears in other genres such as Fantasy and Romance. Searching for this theme in other genres would enable a reader to cross over into previously unknown realms of reading experiences. And with the AUTHOR and TITLE indexes, which include all books listed under "Other books by the author" and "Other books you might like," it is easy to compile an extensive list of recommended reading, beginning with a recently published title or a classic from the past.

Also Available Online

The entries in this book can also be found online in Gale's *Books & Authors* database. This electronic product encompasses over 169,000 books, including genre fiction, mainstream fiction, and nonfiction. All the books included in the online version are recommended by librarians or other experts, award winners, or appear on bestseller lists. The user-friendly functionality allows users to refine their searching by using several criteria, while making it easy to identify similar titles for further research and reading. *Books & Authors* is updated with new information weekly. For more information about *Books & Authors*, please visit Gale online at gale.cengage.com.

Suggestions Are Welcome

The editors welcome any comments and suggestions for enhancing and improving *What Do I Read Next?* Please address correspondence to the Editor, *What Do I Read Next?*, at the following address:

Gale, Cengage Learning

27500 Drake Rd.

Farmington Hills, MI 48331-3535

Phone: 248-699-GALE

Toll-free: 800-347-GALE

Fax: 248-699-8054

About the Genre Experts

Daniel S. Burt (Historical Fiction) Burt is a writer and college professor who has taught undergraduate courses at Trinity College and graduate literature courses at Wesleyan University, where he was a dean for nine years. He is the author of *The Chronology of American Literature* (Houghton Mifflin, 2004), *What Historical Novel Do I Read Next?* Volumes 1-3 (Gale, 1997-2003), *The Novel 100* (Facts on File, 2003), *The Literary 100* (Facts on File, 2001), *The Biography Book* (Greenwood/Oryx, 2001), *Drama 100* (Facts on File, 2007). He is the academic director for an annual series of educationally-based workshops held in Ireland (www.discoverytours.ws). When not teaching and traveling to Ireland, he lives with his wife on Cape Cod, Massachusetts.

Don D'Ammassa (Science Fiction, Horror, and Fantasy) D'Ammassa was the book reviewer for *Science Fiction Chronicle* for almost thirty years. He has had fiction published in fantastic magazines and anthologies and has contributed essays to a variety of reference books dealing withfantastic literature. D'Ammassa is the author of the novels *Blood Beast* (Windsor, 1988), *Servants of Chaos* (Leisure, 2002), *Scarab* (Five Star, 2004), *Haven* (Five Star, 2004), *Narcissus* (Five Star, 2007), and the nonfiction works *Encyclopedia of Science Fiction* (Facts on File, 2005), the *Encyclopedia of Fantasy and Horror* (Facts on File, 2006), and the *Encyclopedia of Adventure Fiction* (Facts on File, 2008).

Natalie Danford (Popular Fiction) Danford is the author of *Inheritance*, a novel published by St. Martin's Press. She is also coeditor of the annual *Best New American Voices* anthology series, which introduces emerging writers. An experienced freelance writer and book critic, Natalie has published articles and reviews in *People, The Los Angeles Times, Salon,* and many other publications.

Angie Kiesling (Inspirational) Angie Kiesling has worked in the publishing industry since 1985 as a writer and editor, authoring numerous books along the way, including the novel *Skizzer*. She has worked as a magazine staff editor, website editor, and small press editorial manager, and she formerly covered religion and spirituality trends for Publishers Weekly. A fiction judge for a national awards contest, today she works as a freelance writer/editor, author consultant, and writing retreat leader

Clair Lamb (Mystery) is a writer, editor and researcher whose clients include award-winning, bestselling authors and first-time novelists. She is a regular contributor to Crimespree magazine, has written The Mystery Bookstore http://www.mystery-bookstore.com 's weekly and monthly newsletters since 2000, and maintains a personal blog at www.answergirlnet.blogspot.com http://www.answergirlnet. blogspot.com.

Kristin Ramsdell (Romance Fiction) Ramsdell is a librarian at California State University, East Bay and is a nationally known speaker and consultant on the subject of romance fiction. Besides writing articles about the romance genre, she writes a romance review column for *Library Journal* and is the author of *Romance Fiction: A Guide to the Genre* (Libraries Unlimited, 1999) and its predecessor, *Happily Ever After: A Guide to Reading Interests in Romance Fiction* (Libraries Unlimited, 1987). She was named Librarian of the Year by Romance Writers of America in 1996 and received in 2007 the Melinda Helfer Fairy Godmother Award from *Romantic Times* Magazine.

John Charles (Romance Fiction) Charles, a reference librarian and retrospective fiction selector for the Scottsdale Public Library, was named 2002 Librarian of the Year by the Romance Writers of America. Charles reviews books for *Library Journal, Booklist,* the *Chicago Tribune,* and *VOYA(Voice of Youth Advocates)* and co-authors VOYA's annual "Clueless: Adult Mysteries with Young Adult Appeal" column. John Charles is co-author of *The Mystery Readers' Advisory: The Librarian's Clues to Murder and Mayhem* (ALA, 2001). Along with co-author Shelley Mosley, Charles has twice been the recipient of the Romance Writers of America's Veritas Award.

Shelley Mosley (Romance Fiction) Retired library manager Shelley Mosley has co-authored several nonfiction books: The Suffragists in Literature for Youth; Romance Today: An A-to-Z Guide to Contemporary American Romance Writers; The Complete Idiot's Guide to the Ultimate Reading List;and Crash Course in Library Supervision. With John Charles, she has won two Romance Writers of America's Veritas awards. Mosley, Romance Writers of America's 2001 Librarian of the Year, reviews books for both Booklist and Library Journal. She also writes romantic comedies with Deborah Mazoyer under the pen name Deborah Shelley. Their novels have been published by Kensington and, most recently, Avalon Books.

Key to Genre Terms

The following is a list of terms used to classify the story type of each novel included in What Do I Read Next? along with brief definitions of the terms. To find books that fall under a particular story type heading, see the Genre Index.

Action/Adventure ▮ Minimal detection; not usually espionage, but can contain rogue police or out of control spies.

Adult ▮ Fiction dealing with adult characters and mature, developed ideas.

Adventure ▮ The character(s) must face a series of obstacles, which may include monsters, conflict with other travelers, war, interference by supernatural elements, interference by nature, and so on.

Alternate History ▮ A story dealing with how society might have evolved if a specific historical event had happened differently, e.g., if the South had won the American Civil War.

Alternate Intelligence ▮ Story featuring an entity with a sense of identity and able to self-determine goals and actions. The natural or manufactured entity results from a synergy, generally unpredictable, of individual elements. This subgenre frequently involves a computer-type intelligence.

Alternate Universe ▮ More accurately, in most cases, alternate history, in which the South won the Civil War, the Nazis triumphed, etc. The idea is a venerable one in SF.

Alternate World ▮ The story starts out in the everyday world, but the main character is transported to an alternate/parallel world by supernatural means.

Amateur Detective ▮ Detective work is performed by a non-professional rather than by police or a private detective.

Americana ▮ A romance set in the present that features themes that are particularly American; often focuses on small-town life.

Ancient Evil Unleashed ▮ The evils may take familiar forms, like vampires undead for centuries, or malevolent ancient gods released from bondage by careless humans, or ancient prophecies wreaking havoc on today's world. The so-called *Cthulhu Mythos* originated by H.P. Lovecraft, in which *Cthulhu* is prominent among a pantheon of ancient evil gods, is a specific variation of this.

Anthology ▮ A collection of short stories by different authors, usually sharing a common theme.

Apocalyptic Horror ▮ Traditionally, horrors that signal or presage the end of the world, or the world of the characters, and the establishment of a new, possibly very sinister order.

Arts ▮ Fiction that incorporates some aspect of the arts, whether it be music, painting, drama, etc.

Biblical Fiction ▮ Novels that take their plots or characters from the Bible.

Black Magic ▮ Magic directed toward malevolent ends, as distinct from white magic, which is directed toward benevolent ends. Witchcraft is commonly thought of as a black art. Voodoo consists of mysterious rites and practices, including sorcery, magic and conjuration, and often has evil goals.

Carnival-Circus Horror ▮ Derived from its setting, especially the freakish world of the sideshow, in which the distorted or horrific is the norm and is sometimes used as a distorting mirror to reveal hidden selves.

Chase ▮ A traditional Western in which the action of the plot is based on some form of pursuit.

Child-in-Peril ▮ The innocence of childhood is often used to heighten the intensity and unpredictability of evil.

Collection ▮ A book of short stories by a single author.

Coming-of-Age ▮ A story in which the primary character is a young person, usually a teenager. The growth of maturity is chronicled.

Contemporary ▮ A story set in the present.

Contemporary/Exotic ▮ Set in the present but with an especially unusual or exotic setting, e.g., the tent of a desert sheik or a boat on the Amazon.

Contemporary/Fantasy ▮ A contemporary story that makes use of fantasy or supernatural elements.

Contemporary/Innocent ▮ Story set in the present that contains little or no sex.

Contemporary/Mainstream ▮ A story set in the present that would be more properly categorized as general fiction rather than a work in a specific genre.

Contemporary Realism ▮ An accurate representation of characters, settings, ideas, themes in the present day. Not idealistic in nature.

Cozy Mystery ▮ Most often "gentle" reads that frequently downplay graphic violence, profanity, and sex.

Curse ▮ Words said when someone wishes evil or harm on someone or something, such as a witch's or prophet's curse.

Cyberpunk | Usually applied to the stories by a group of writers who became prominent in the mid-1980s, such as William Gibson and his *Necromancer* (1984). The "cyber" is derived from cybernetics, nominally the study of control and communications in machines. These books also feature a downbeat, punk sensibility reminiscent of the hardboiled school of detective fiction writers.

Disaster | A tale recounting some event or events seriously disruptive of the social fabric but not as serious as a holocaust.

Domestic | Fiction relating to household and family matters. Concerned with psychological and emotional needs of family members.

Doppelganger | A double or alter ego, popularized in the works of E.T.A. Hoffmann, Edgar Allan Poe, and Robert Louis Stevenson.

Dystopian | The antonym of utopian, sometimes called anti-utopian, in which traditionally positive utopian themes are treated satirically or ironically and the mood is downbeat or satiric.

End of the World | A story that concerns the last events following some sort of disaster.

Erotic Horror | Sexuality and horror are often argued to be inextricably linked, as in Bram Stoker's *Dracula* and Sheridan Le Fanu's "Carmilla," although others have argued that they are antithetical. Sexuality became increasingly explicit in the 1980s, sometimes verging on the pornographic, as in Brett Easton Ellis' *American Psycho.*

Espionage | Involving the CIA, KGB, or other organizations whose main focus is the collection of information from the other side. Can be either violent or quiet.

Espionage Thriller | Plot contains a high level of action and suspense relating to espionage.

Ethnic | A work in which the ethnic background of the characters is integral to the story. Usually the focus is on an American ethnic minority group (e.g., African American, Asian American, Native American, Latino) and the two main characters are members of this group.

Evil Children | The presumed innocence of a child is replaced with adult-like malevolence and cunning, contradicting the reader's usual expectations.

Family Saga | Stories focusing on the problems or concerns of a family; estrangement and reunion are common themes.

Fantasy | A story that contains some fantasy or supernatural elements.

Femme Fatale | A seductress for whom men abandon careers, families, and responsibilities and who feels no pity or compunction in return; a common figure in history and literature.

First Contact | Any story about the initial meeting or communication of humans with extraterrestrials or aliens. The term may take its name from the eponymous 1945 story by Murray Leinster.

Future Shock | A journalistic term derived from Alvin Toffler's 1970 book and which refers to the alleged disorientation resulting from rapid technological change.

Futuristic | A story with a science fiction setting. Often these stories are set on other planets, aboard spaceships or space stations, or on Earth in an imaginary future or, in some cases, past.

Gay/Lesbian Fiction | Stories portraying homosexual characters or themes.

Generation Starship | If pseudoscientific explanations involving faster-than-light drives are rejected, then the time required for interstellar travel will encompass many human generations.

Genetic Manipulation | Sometimes called genetic engineering, this assumes that the knowledge exists to shape creatures, human or otherwise, using genetic means, as in *Brave New World* (1932).

Ghost Story | The spirits of the dead, who can be benevolent, as in Charles Dickens, or malevolent, as in the tales of M.R. James.

Gothic | A story with a strong mystery suspense plot that emphasizes mood, atmosphere, and/or supernatural or paranormal elements. Unexplained events, ancient family secrets, and a general feeling of impending doom often characterize these tales. These stories are most often set in the past.

Gothic Family Chronicle | A story often covering several generations of a family, many of whose members are typically evil, perverted, or loathsome, and in which family violence is common. The family may live in a decaying mansion suggestive of those in 18th century Gothic novels.

Hard Science Fiction | Stories in which the author adheres with varying degrees of rigor to scientific principles believed to be true at the time of writing, principles derived from hard (physical, biological) rather than soft (social) sciences.

Haunted House | Literally, a house visited by ghosts, usually with evil intentions in horror fiction, but sometimes the subject of comedy.

Historical | Set in an earlier time frame than the present.

Historical/American Civil War | Set during the American Civil War, 1861-1865.

Historical/American Revolution | Set during the American Revolutionary period.

Historical/American West | Set in the Western portion of the United States, usually during the second half of the 19th century. Stories often involve the hardships of pioneer life (Indian raids, range wars, climatic disasters, etc.) and the main characters (most often the hero) can be of Native American extraction.

Historical/American West Coast | Set in the American Far West (California, Oregon, Washington, or Alaska). Stories often focus on the Gold Rush and the tension between Spanish Land Grant families and immigrants from the Pacific Rim, usually China.

Historical/Americana | A story dealing with themes unique to the American experience.

Historical/Ancient Egypt | A novel set during the time of the pharaohs from the fourth century B.C. to the first century A.D. and the absorption of Egypt into the Roman Empire.

Historical/Ancient Greece ▌ Set during the flowering of the ancient Greek civilization, particularly during the age of Pericles in the 5th century B.C.

Historical/Ancient Rome ▌ Covering the history of Rome from its founding and the Roman Republic before Augustus through the decline and fall of the Roman Empire in the fifth century.

Historical/Antebellum American South ▌ Set in the American Old South (prior to the Civil War).

Historical/Canadian West ▌ Set in the western or frontier portions of Canada, usually during the 19th century. Stories most often revolve around the hardships of frontier life.

Historical/Colonial America ▌ Set in America before the American Revolution, 1620-1775. Stories featuring the Jamestown Colony, the Salem Witch Trials, and the French and Indian Wars are especially popular.

Historical/Depression Era ▌ Set mainly in America during the period of economic hardship brought on by the 1929 Stock Market Crash that continued throughout the 1930s.

Historical/Edwardian ▌ Set during the reign of Edward VII of England, 1901-1910.

Historical/Eighteenth Century ▌ A work of fiction set during the eighteenth century.

Historical/Elizabethan ▌ A novel set during the reign of Elizabeth I of England (1558-1603). There is some overlap with the last part of the Historical Renaissance category but the emphasis is British.

Historical/Exotic ▌ Setting is an unusual or exotic place.

Historical/Fantasy ▌ A historical work that makes use of fantasy or supernatural elements.

Historical/French Revolution ▌ Set during the French Revolution, 1789-1795.

Historical/Georgian ▌ Set during the reigns of the first three "Georges" of England. Roughly corresponds to the 18th century. Stories often focus on the Jacobite Rebellions and the escapades of Bonnie Prince Charlie.

Historical/Mainstream ▌ Historical fiction that would be more properly categorized as fiction rather than a specific genre.

Historical/Medieval ▌ Set during the Middle Ages, approximately the fifth through the fifteenth centuries. Stories feature battles, raids, crusades, and court intrigues; plotlines associated with the Battle of Hastings (1066) are especially popular.

Historical/Napoleonic Wars ▌ Set between 1803-1815 during the wars waged by and against France under Napoleon Bonaparte.

Historical/Post-American Civil War ▌ Set in the years following the Civil War/War Between the States, generally from 1865 into the 1870s.

Historical/Post-American Revolution ▌ Set in the years immediately following the Civil War, 1865-1870s.

Historical/Post-French Revolution ▌ Set during the years immediately following the French Revolution; stories usually take place in France or England.

Historical/Pre-History ▌ Set in the years before the Middle Ages.

Historical/Regency ▌ A novel that is set during the Regency period (1811-1820).

Historical/Renaissance ▌ Novel set in the years of the Renaissance in Europe, generally lasting from the 14th through the 17th centuries.

Historical/Roaring Twenties ▌ Usually has an American setting and takes place in the 1920s.

Historical/Russian Revolution ▌ These stories are set around and during the 1917 Russian Revolution.

Historical/Seventeenth Century ▌ A work of fiction set during the 17th century. Stories of this type often center around the clashes between the Royalists and the Cromwellians and the Restoration.

Historical/Tudor Period ▌ A novel set during the Tudor dynasty in England (1485-1603). Roughly corresponds to the Renaissance, but the emphasis is British. Overlaps with the Elizabethan period, which is marked by the reign of Elizabeth Tudor.

Historical/Victorian ▌ Set during the reign of Queen Victoria, 1837-1901. This designation does not include works with a predominately American setting.

Historical/Victorian America ▌ Set in America, usually the Eastern part, during the Victorian Period, 1837-1901.

Historical/War of 1812 ▌ Set during the British-U.S. conflict which lasted from 1812 to 1814.

Historical/World War I ▌ Set during the First World War, 1914-1918.

Historical/World War II ▌ Set in the years of the Second World War, 1939-1945.

Holiday Themes ▌ Fiction that focuses on or is set during a particular holiday or holiday season (e.g., Christmas, Valentine's Day, Mardi Gras).

Horror ▌ Refers to stories in which interest in the events, the intellectual puzzle characteristic of much of SF, is subordinated to a feeling of terror or horror by the reader, which could result from a variety of causes, including a disaster or an invasion of earth.

Humor ▌ Story with an amusing story line.

Immortality ▌ Usually includes extreme longevity, resulting from fountains of youth, elixirs, or something with a pseudoscientific basis.

Indian Culture ▌ These novels center on the lives, customs, and cultures of characters who are American Indians or who lived among the Indians.

Indian Wars ▌ Often traditional Westerns, these stories are set during the period of the Indian wars and rely on this warfare for plots, characters, and themes.

Inspirational ▌ A novel with an uplifting, often Christian theme, and usually considered "innocent."

Invasion of Earth ▌ An extremely common theme, often paralleling historical events and reflecting fears of the time. Most invasions are depicted as malign, only occasionally benign.

Legal ▌ Main focus is on a lawyer, though it does not always involve courtroom action.

Legend ▮ A story based on a legend, myth, or fairy tale that has been rewritten.

Lesbian/Contemporary ▮ A story with lesbian protagonists set in the present.

Lesbian/Historical ▮ Historical fiction with lesbian protagonists.

Light Fantasy ▮ There is a great deal of humor throughout the story and it is almost guaranteed to have a happy ending.

Literary ▮ Relates to the nature and knowledge of literature; can be applied to setting or characters.

Lost Colony ▮ Stories centering around a colony on another world that loses contact with or is abandoned by its parent civilization and the type of society that evolves under those conditions. Conflict usually arises when contact is re-established between the colony and its home world.

Magic Conflict ▮ The main conflict of the story stems from magical interference. Protagonists may be caught in the middle of a conflict between sorcerers or may themselves be engaged in conflict with other sorcerers.

Magic Realism ▮ A style of prose fiction writing in which the author blends the realism of describing ordinary places and incidents with fantastic, dreamlike, or mythical events and does not differentiate between the real and the magical.

Man Alone ▮ A lone man, alienated from the society that would normally support him, faces overwhelming dangers.

Medical ▮ Stories in which medical themes are dominant.

Military ▮ Stories have a military theme; may deal with life in the armed forces or military battles.

Modern ▮ Reflection of the present time period.

Mountain Man ▮ Any story in which the principal characters are mountain men and women, living in mountain areas remote from civilization and depending upon their own resourcefulness for survival.

Multicultural ▮ A romance in which the ethnic background of the characters is integral to the story.

Mystery ▮ Usually a story where a crime occurs or a puzzle must be solved.

Mystical ▮ Fiction dealing with spiritual elements. Miraculous or supernatural characteristics of events, characters, settings, and themes.

Nature in Revolt ▮ Tales in which normally docile plants or animals suddenly turn against humankind, sometimes transformed (giant crabs resulting from radioactivity, predatory rats, plagues, blobs that threaten London or Miami, etc.).

Occult ▮ An adjective suggesting fiction based on a mystical or secret doctrine, but sometimes referring to supernatural fiction generally. Implies that there is a reality beyond the perceived world that only adepts can penetrate.

Paranormal ▮ Novel contains supernatural elements. Story may include ghosts, UFOs, aliens, demons, and haunted houses among other unexplained phenomena.

Parody ▮ A narrative that follows the form of the original but usually changes its sense to nonsense, thus making fun of the original or its ideas.

Police Procedural ▮ A story in which the action is centered around a police officer.

Political ▮ The novel deals with political issues that are skewed by the use and presence of fantastic elements.

Possession ▮ Domination, usually of humans, by evil spirits, demons, aliens, or other agencies in which one's own volition is replaced by an outside force.

Post-Disaster ▮ Story set in a much degraded environment, frequently involving a reduction in population and the resulting loss of access to processes, resources, technology, etc.

Post-Holocaust ▮ The events following a world-wide disaster, often the result of human folly rather than natural events (collision with a meteor, etc.).

Post-Nuclear Holocaust ▮ The events following a world-wide nuclear disaster.

Private Detective ▮ Usually detection, involving a professional for hire.

Psychic Powers ▮ Parapsychological or paranormal powers.

Psychological ▮ Fiction dealing with mental or emotional responses.

Psychological Suspense ▮ Tales in which the psychological exploration and quirks of characters generate suspense and plot.

Quest ▮ The central characters are on a journey filled with dangers to reach some worthwhile goal.

Ranch Life ▮ The basic cowboy story, in which the plot and characters are inextricably bound up in the workings of a ranch.

Regency ▮ A light romance involving the British upper classes, set during the Regency Period, 1811-1820. During this time, the Prince of Wales acted as Prince Regent because of the incapacity of his father, George III. In 1820, "Prinny" became George IV. These stories, in the style of Jane Austen, are essentially comedies of manners and the emphasis is on language, wit, and style. Georgette Heyer set the standard for the modern version of this genre. This designation is also given to stories of similar type that may not fit precisely within the Regency time period.

Reincarnation ▮ A tale in which the horror arises in connection with the reincarnation of one of the characters.

Religious ▮ Religion of any sort plays a primary role in the plot.

Revenge ▮ A character who has suffered an unjust loss returns to take vengeance. This is one of the most common traditional themes.

Robot Fiction ▮ From the Jewish Golem to the traditional clanking bucket of bolts to the human-like android, robots in various guises have been among us for centuries. The term comes from Karl Capek's play, *R.U.R.*, which stands for Rossum's Universal Robots. Robots are often surrogates for humans and may be treated seriously or comically.

Romance ▮ Stories involving love affairs and love stories; deals with the emotional attachments of the characters.

Romantic Suspense ▌ Romance with a strong mystery suspense plot. This is a broad category including works in the tradition of Mary Stewart, as well as the newer women-in-jeopardy tales by writers such as Mary Higgins Clark. These stories usually have contemporary settings but some are also set in the past.

Saga ▌ A multi-generational story that usually centers around one particular family and its trials, tribulations, successes, and loves.

Satanism ▌ Suggests worship of evil rather than benevolent gods, the antithesis of conventional theism, whether Christianity or other religions. Evil demons are Satan writ small and usually lack the awful majesty of their parent.

Satire ▌ Fiction written in a sarcastic and ironic way to ridicule human vices or follies; usually using an exaggeration of characteristics to stress a point.

Science Fantasy ▌ A somewhat vague term in which there are "rational" elements from SF and "magical" or "fanciful" elements from fantasy, which hopefully cohere in a plausible story.

Science Fiction ▌ Although the story has been classified in another genre, there are strong elements of science fiction.

Serial Killer ▌ A multiple murderer, going back to Bluebeard and up to Ed Gein, who inspired Robert Bloch's *Psycho*.

Series ▌ A number of books united either by continuing characters and situations or by a common theme. Series books may appear under a single author's name or each book in the series may be by a different author.

Small Town Horror ▌ The coziness and intimacy of a small community is disrupted by some sort of horrific happening, suggesting an unjustified placidity and complacency on the part of the citizens.

Space Colony ▌ A permanent space station, usually orbiting Earth but in principal located in deep space or near other planets or stars.

Space Opera ▌ Intergalactic adventures; westerns in space; a specialized form of the genre type Adventure.

Supernatural Vengeance ▌ Punishment inflicted by God or a godlike creature, whether justly or capriciously.

Sword and Sorcery ▌ Often a muscle-bound swordsman, who is innocent of thought and common sense, up against evil sorcerers and sorceresses, who naturally lose in the end because they are evil.

Techno-Horror ▌ Suggests a catastrophe with horrific elements resulting from a scientific miscalculation or technological hubris; Victor Frankenstein's unnamed monster or a plague resulting from a laboratory mishap.

Techno-Thriller ▌ Stories in which a technological development, such as an invention, is linked to a series of suspenseful (thrilling) events.

Theological ▌ Stories in which religion or religious belief plays an important role.

Time Travel ▌ A story in which characters from one time are transported either literally or in spirit to another time period. The time shifts are usually between the present and another historical period.

Traditional ▌ Traditional stories may deal with virtually any time period or situation, but they are related by shared conventions of setting and characterization.

Trail Drive ▌ Any story in which a cattle drive (or, more rarely, a drive of sheep or horses) is a major plot component.

UFO ▌ Unidentified Flying Objects, literally, although sometimes used more generally to refer to any object of mysterious origin or intent.

Urban ▌ Stories set in large cities; usually the tone of the novel is gritty and realistic and may involve issues such as drugs and gangs.

Utopia ▌ A large, often influential, story type that takes its name from Thomas More's 1516 book. Usually refers to a society considered better by the author, even if not perfect. Aldous Huxley's *Island* (1962) is a utopia, whereas his more famous *Brave New World* (1932) is a dark twin, a dystopia.

Vampire Story ▌ Based on mythical bloodsucking creatures possessing supernatural powers and various forms, both animal and human. The concept can be traced far back in history, long before Bram Stoker's famous novel, *Dracula*.

Wagon Train ▌ A book that deals with wagon trains traveling across the American West.

Werewolf Story ▌ Were is Old English for man, suggesting the ancient lineage of a creature that once dominated a world in which witches and sorcerers were equally feared. Sometimes used to refer to any shape shifter, whether wolves or other animals.

Wild Talents ▌ The phrase comes from Charles Fort's writings and usually refers to parapsychological powers such a telepathy, psychokinesis, and precognition, collectively called psychic or psi phenomena.

Witchcraft ▌ Characters either profess to be or are stigmatized as witches or warlocks, and practitioners of magic associated with witchcraft. This can include black magic or white magic (e.g., Wicca).

Young Adult ▌ A marketing term for publishers; one or more of the central characters is a teenager often testing his or her skills against adversity to achieve a greater degree of maturity and self-awareness. A category used by librarians to shelve books of likely appeal to teenage readers.

Young Readers ▌ A novel with characters, plot, and vocabulary primarily aimed at juveniles.

Zombie ▌ A creature that is typically a reanimated corpse or a human being who is being controlled by someone else by use of magic or voodoo.

Award Winners

Fantastic Fiction Awards
By Don D'Ammassa

Several organizations present awards for science fiction, fantasy, and horror fiction, usually on an annual basis, sometimes with open balloting, and in some cases assigning the final decision to a group of judges. These awards typically cover short fiction of varying lengths, dramatic presentations, and other categories in addition to those involving a specific book as shown below. Since these awards are all presented retroactively, the individual titles that follow will have been covered in earlier editions of *What Do I Read Next?*.

Hugo Awards: The Hugo Awards, named in honor of Hugo Gernsback for his pioneering work in creating science fiction magazines, are presented at the World Science Fiction convention which takes place annually on a rotating regional schedule. This year's convention took place in Melbourne, Australia. This is the fantastic fiction's oldest award originating in 1953. Anyone who purchases a membership is entitled to nominate and vote for all of the awards. The 2010 winners are as follows:

Best Novel (tie): *The City and the City* by China Mieville, and *The Windup Girl* by Paolo Bacigalupi

Runners Up: *Wake* by Robert J. Sawyer, *Boneshaker* by Cherie Priest, *Julian Comstock: A Story of 22nd Century America* by Robert Charles Wilson, *Palimpsest* by Catherynne Valente

Best Related Book: *This Is Me, Jack Vance! (Or, More Properly, This Is "I")* by Jack Vance

Runners Up: *The Intergalactic Playground: A Critical Study of Children's and Teens' Science Fiction* by Farah Mendlesohn, *The Secret Feminist Cabal: A Cultural History of SF Feminisms* by Helen Merrick, *Hope-in-the-Mist: The Extraordinary Career and Mysterious Life of Hope Mirrlees* by Michael Swanwick, *Canary Fever: Reviews* by John Clute, *On Joanna Russ* by Farah Mendlesohn

Locus Awards: The Locus Awards are presented to winners of *Locus Magazine*'s annual readers' poll, which was established in the early '70s specifically to provide recommendations and suggestions to Hugo Awards voters.

In recent years Locus Awards are presented at an annual banquet, and unlike any other award, explicitly honor publishers of winning works with certificates. The 2010 winners in the categories involving book length works are as follows:

Best Science Fiction Novel: *Boneshaker* by Cherie Priest

Best Fantasy Novel: *The City and the City* by China Mieville

Best First Novel: *The Windup Girl* by Paolo Bacigalupi

Best Young Adult Book: *Leviathan* by Scott Westerfeld

Best Anthology: *The New Space Opera 2* edited by Gardner Dozois and Jonathan Strahan

Best Collection: *The Best of Gene Wolfe* by Gene Wolfe

Best Non-Fiction Book: *Cheek by Jowl: Essays* by Ursula K. Le Guin

Nebula Awards: The Nebula Awards are presented by the Science Fiction and Fantasy Writers of America at their annual meeting. Only full members are entitled to vote for the final selection. This year's meeting was held in Washington, D.C. The award has been presented annually since 1965.

Best Novel: *The Windup Girl* by Paolo Bacigalupi

Runners Up: *The Love We Share Without Knowing* by Christopher Barzak, *Flesh and Fire* by Laura Anne Gilman, *The City and the City* by China Mieville, *Boneshaker* by Cherie Priest, Finch by Jeff VanderMeer

The Andre Norton Award: *The Girl Who Circumnavigated Fairyland in a Ship of Her Own Making* by Catherynne M. Valente

Bram Stoker Awards: This award is presented by the Horror Writers of America at their annual meeting. Named after the author of *Dracula*, it has been presented since 1987. Awards this year were presented in Brighton, England. The 2009 winners are as follows:

Best Novel: *Audrey's Door* by Sarah Langan

Runners Up: *Patient Zero* by Jonathan Maberry,

Quarantined by Joe McKinney, *Cursed* by Jeremy Shipp

Best First Novel: *Damnable* by Hank Schwaeble

Runners Up: *Breathers* by S.G. Browne, *Solomon's Grave* Daniel G. Keohane, *The Little Sleep* by Paul Tremblay

Best Collection: *A Taste of Tenderloin* by Gene O'Neill

Runners Up: *Martyrs and Monsters* by Robert Dunbar, *Got to Kill Them All and Other Stories* by Dennis Etchison, *In the Closet, Under the Bed* by Lee Thomas

Best Non-Fiction: *Writer's Workshop of Horror* edited by Michael Knost

Runners Up: *Cinema Knife Fight* by L.L. Soares and Michael Arruda, *The Stephen King Illustrated Companion* by Bev Vincent, *Stephen King: The Non-Fiction* by Rocky Wood and Justin Brook

Best Anthology: *He Is Legend* edited by Christopher Conlon

Runners Up: *Lovecraft Unbound* edited by Ellen Datlow, *Poe* edited by Ellen Datlow, *Midnight Walk* edited by Lisa Morton

World Fantasy Awards: Readers nominate a list of potential winners for this annual award but the final decision is made by a panel of judges. This year's awards were presented at the World Fantasy Convention in Columbus, Ohio. The 2010 winners are as follows:

Best Novel: *The City and the City* by China Mieville

Runners Up: *Blood of Ambrose* by James Enge, *The Red Tree* by Caitlin R. Kiernan, *Finch* by Jeff Vander-Meer, *In Great Waters* by Kit Whitfield

Best Anthology: *American Fantastic Tales: Terror and the Uncanny: From Poe to the Pulps/From the 1940s to Now* edited by Peter Straub

Runners Up: *Poe* edited by Ellen Datlow, *Songs of the Dying Earth: Stories in Honor of Jack Vance* edited by George R.R. Martin and Gardner Dozois, *Exotic Gothic 3: Strange Visitations* edited by Danel Olson, *Eclipse Three* edited by Jonathan Strahan, *The Very Best of Fantasy & Science Fiction: Sixtieth Anniversary Collection* edited by Gordon Van Gelder

Best Collection (tie): *There Once Lived a Woman Who Tried to Kill Her Neighbor's Baby: Scary Fairy Tales* by Ludmilla Petrushevskaya, and *The Very Best of Gene Wolfe* by Gene Wolfe

Runners Up: *We Never Talk About My Brother* by Peter S. Beagle, *Fugue State* by Brian Evenson, *Northwest Passages* by Barbara Roden, *Everland and Other Stories* by Paul Witcover

Historical Awards
by Dana Ferguson

Scott O'Dell Award for Historical Fiction: In 1982, Scott O'Dell established The Scott O'Dell Award for Histori-
cal Fiction. The annual award of $5,000 goes to a meritorious book published in the previous year for children or young adults. Scott O'Dell established this award to encourage other writers—particularly new authors—to focus on historical fiction. He hoped in this way to increase the interest of young readers in the historical background that has helped to shape their country and their world.

2011 Winner: *One Crazy Summer* by Rita Williams-Garcia

Walter Scott Prize: The Walter Scott Prize is a British literary award for historical fiction founded in 2010. The award was created by the Duke and Duchess of Buccleuch, whose ancestors were closely linked to Scottish author Sir Walter Scott, who is generally considered the originator of historical fiction with the novel *Waverley* in 1814. The winner was announced June 19, 2010 as part of the Brewin Dolphin Borders Book Festival which took place at Sir Walter Scott's historic home Abbotsford House in Scotland.

2010 Winner: *Wolf Hall* by Hilary Mantel

2011 Mystery Award Winners
by Clair Lamb, for Bookreporter.com

The Anthony Awards: The Anthony Awards The award, like the convention itself, is named for the late mystery editor, reviewer and writer Anthony Boucher. Nominations and final voting are by the convention's registrants. Winners were announced at Bouchercon in in San Francisco, California, in October 2010, for books published in 2009. The 2010 winners are as follows:

Best Novel: *The Brutal Telling* by Louise Penny

Best First Novel: *A Bad Day for Sorry* by Sophie Littlefield

Best Paperback Original: *Starvation Lake* by Bryan Gruley

Best Critical/Non-Fiction Work: *Talking About Detective Fiction* by P.D. James

The Barry Award: The Barry Award is named for the late fan reviewer Barry Gardner. Voting is by subscribers to *Deadly Pleasures*. Winners were announced at Bouchercon in San Francisco, California, in October 2010, honoring books published during the previous year. The 2010 winners are as follows:

Best Novel: *The Last Child* by John Hart

Best First Novel: *The Sweetness at the Bottom of the Pie* by Alan Bradley

Best British Crime Novel: *If the Dead Rise Not* by Philip Kerr

Best Thriller: *Running from the Devil* by Jamie Freveletti

Best Paperback Original: *Starvation Lake* by Bryan Gruley

Best Mystery/Crime Novel of the Decade: *The Girl with the Dragon Tattoo* by Stieg Larsson

The Left Coast Crime Convention Awards: The Left Coast Crime Convention was held in Santa Fe, New Mexico, in March 2011. Several awards were bestowed at the conference. The 2010 individual awards, along with a brief description and their winners, are as follows:

The Dilys Award is named for Dilys Winn, the founder of Murder Ink, the world's first brick-and-mortar mystery bookstore, and is awarded by members of the Independent Mystery Booksellers Association to the book they "most enjoyed" selling in the previous year.

Winner: *Bury Your Dead* by Louise Penny

The Lefty Award recognizes the best humorous mystery published during the previous year.

Winner: *The Pot Thief Who Studied Einstein* by J. Michael Orenduff

The Bruce Alexander Memorial Historical Mystery Award is presented to the best historical mystery award published during the previous year.

Winner: *The Mapping of Love and Death* by Jacqueline Winspear

The Hillerman Sky Award recognizes the mystery (short story or novel) that best captures the landscape of the Southwest.

Winner: *The Spider's Web* by Margaret Coel

The Watson Award honors the mystery novel that features the best sidekick.

Winner: *Junkyard Dogs* by Craig Johnson

The Edgar Awards: The Edgar Awards may be the best-known and most prestigious awards given within the mystery world, bestowed by the Mystery Writers of America at an annual banquet in April. Named after Edgar Allan Poe, the Edgar Awards are peer-bestowed, determined by judging panels composed of active MWA members. The Edgars were awarded at a banquet at the Grand Hyatt in New York City on April 29, 2010. The 2010 winners are as follows:

Best Novel: *The Last Child* by John Hart

Best First Novel: *In the Shadow of Gotham* by Stefanie Pintoff

Best Paperback Original: *Body Blows* by Marc Strange

Best Short Story: "Amapola" by Luis Alberto Urrea, from Phoenix Noir

Best Fact Crime: *Columbine* by Dave Cullen

Best Critical/Biographical Work: *The Lineup: The World's Greatest Crime Writers Tell the Inside Story of their Greatest Detectives* edited by Otto Penzler

Best Young Adult: *Reality Check* by Peter Abrahams

Best Juvenile: *Closed for the Season* by Mary Downing Hahn

The Hammett Prize: The Hammett Prize is given by the North American Branch of the International Association of Crime Writers, with nominees chosen by the organization's nominating committee. A rotating panel of outside judges makes the final selection. The 2010 award, for books published in 2009, was presented at the Bloody Words X Mystery Conference in Toronto, Canada, in May 2010:

Winner: *The Manual of Detection* by Jedediah Berry

The Macavity Award: The Macavity Award, named for the "mystery cat" in T.S. Eliot's *Old Possum's Book of Practical Cats*, is nominated and voted on by members of Mystery Readers International. Winners were announced at Bouchercon in San Francisco, California, in October 2010, for books published in 2009. The 2010 winners are as follows:

Best Mystery Novel: *Tower* by Ken Bruen & Reed Farrel Coleman

Best First Mystery: *The Sweetness at the Bottom of the Pie* by Alan Bradley

Best Nonfiction/Critical: *Talking About Detective Fiction* by P.D. James

Sue Feder Memorial Historical Mystery: *A Trace of Smoke* by Rebecca Cantrell

The Nero Award: The Nero Award is presented annually to an author for literary excellence in the mystery genre by the Wolfe Pack, the Nero Wolfe Society. It is presented at the Black Orchid Banquet, traditionally held on the first Saturday in December in New York City. The 2010 winner is as follows:?

Winner: *Faces of the Gone* by Brad Parks

Popular Fiction Awards
by Natalie Danford

Man Booker Prize: The Man Booker Prize, Great Britain's major literary prize, is awarded annually to the author of a full-length novel. The prize was established in 1968 by Booker PLC, an international food company, and the Book Trust and Publishers Association. The Man Group took over sponsorship for the prize in 2002. The 2010 winner is as follows:

Winner: *The Finkler Question* by Howard Jacobson

Finalists: *Parrot and Olivier in America* by Peter Carey, *Room* by Emma Donoghue, *In a Strange Room by Damon Galgut*, *The Long Song* by Andrea Levy, and *C* by Tom McCarthy

National Book Awards: The National Book Award for Fiction, sponsored by the National Book Foundation, was established in 1950. The award is given out each year for a work judged to be commendable. Nominees are submitted by publishers and the winner is determined by a panel of independent judges. The 2010 winner is as follows:

Winner: *Lord of Misrule* by Jaimy Gordon

Finalists: *Parrot and Olivier in America* by Peter Carey, *Great House by Nicole Krauss*, *So Much for That* by Lionel Shriver, and *I Hotel* by Karen Tei Yamashita

The Medal for Distinguished Contribution to American Letters: This award is sponsored by the National Book Foundation and is given out annually to an author whose total body of work has made a significant contribution to American literature. The 2010 winner is as follows:

Winner: Tom Wolfe

Nobel Prize: The Nobel Prize for Literature recognizes a person who has produced the most distinguished work of an idealistic nature in the field of literature. Authors, regardless of nationality, are considered for their complete body of work. A monetary prize, paid in Swedish kronor, a gold medal, and a diploma are awarded annually. The 2010 winner is as follows:

Winner: Mario Vargas Llosa

Inspirational Awards
by Angie Kiesling, for FaithfulReader.com

ECPA Christian Book Awards: Since 1978 the Evangelical Christian Publishers Association has recognized quality and encouraged excellence by presenting the ECPA Christian Book Awards (formerly known as Gold Medallion) each year. After a rigorous judging process, five finalists are selected in each of six categories. Out of 226 entries of books and Bibles published in the past year, five finalists in six categories were chosen to represent Christian publishing's finest books and Bibles for 2011. Many of the titles have enjoyed the success of industry bestseller lists—with four appearing in the past year on the New York Times bestseller list—while other titles and authors are receiving the industry's highest award attention for the first time. This year's winners will be announced at the upcoming ECPA Awards Banquet held May 2nd in Colorado Springs in conjunction with the ECPA Executive Leadership Summit. The finalists for the 2011 Christian Book Awards are:

Bibles: *HCSB Study Bible* edited by Jeremy Royal Howard and Ed Blum, *The Lucado Life Lessons Study Bible, NKJV* by Max Lucado, *Apologetics Study Bible for Students* edited by Sean McDowell, and *The Case for Christ Study Bible, NIV* by Lee Strobel

Fiction: *Secrets of Harmony Grove* by Mindy Starns Clark, *Almost Heaven* by Chris Fabry, *Petra* by T.L. Higley, *Crossing Oceans* by Gina Holmes, and *The Twelfth Imam* by Joel C. Rosenberg

Children: *Asking For Trouble* by Sandra Byrd, *Between God and Me* by Vicki Courtney, *This Little Prayer of Mine* by Anthony DeStefano; illustrated by Mark Elliott, *A Girl After God's Own Heart* by Elizabeth George, and *The Action Bible* edited by Doug Mauss; illustrated by Sergio Cariello

Inspiration: *Amish Proverbs* by Suzanne Woods Fisher, *Life Saver: The Ultimate Devotional Handbook for Teens* by Todd Hafer, Vicki Kuyper, Michael Klassen and Vicki Caruana, *Prayers For Those Who Grieve* by Jill Kelly, *You Changed My Life* by Max Lucado, and

Praying Through Your Pregnancy by Jennifer Polimino, Carolyn Warren

Bible Reference: *Crossway ESV Bible Atlas* by John D. Currid and David P. Barrett, *A Visual Guide to Gospel Events* by James C. Martin, John A. Beck, and David G. Hansen, *Zondervan Atlas of the Bible* by Carl G. Rasmussen, *The Story of the Bible* by Larry Stone, and *Zondervan Illustrated Bible Backgrounds Commentary* edited by John H. Walton

Non-fiction: *God Girl* by Hayley DiMarco, *Outlive Your Life: You Were Made to Make a Difference* by Max Lucado, *Bonhoeffer* by Eric Metaxas, *A Place of Healing* by Joni Eareckson Tada, and *Son of Hamas* by Mosab Hassan Yousef with Ron Brackin

The Romance Writers of America Awards

The Romance Writers of America (RWA) annually presents RITA Awards, named after RWA co-founders Rita Gallagher and Rita Clay Estrada, for published novels in 12 categories, including Inspirational Romance. In addition, the organization presents Golden Heart Awards for unpublished manuscripts in 10 categories, also including Inspirational Romance. Winners will be announced on July 1, 2011, at the RITA and Golden Heart Awards Ceremony at RWA's 31st Annual National Conference in New York, New York. The finalists for the 2010 awards are as follows:

RITA: Inspirational Romance: *Within My Heart* by Tamera Alexander, *Doctor in Petticoats* by Mary Connealy, *Maid to Match* by Deeanne Gist, *Finding Her Way Home* by Linda Goodnight, *The Wedding Garden* by Linda Goodnight, *In Harm's Way* by Irene Hannon, *Whisper on the Wind* by Maureen Lang, *Shades of Morning* by Marlo M. Schalesky, and *A Convenient Wife* by Anna Schmidt

Golden Heart: Inspirational Romance: *Stealing Jake* by Pam Hillman, *At His Command* by Ruth Kaufman, *Pinch-Hit Dad* by Laurie Kellogg, and *Love Thy Neighbor* by Cheryl Nagro

Audies Awards: Winners of the Audio Publishers Association's annual Audies Awards for spoken word entertainment will be announced on May 24, 2011, at The Times Center in New York City. Awards will be presented in 28 categories, including Inspirational/Faith-Based Fiction. The finalists for the 2011 awards are as follows:

Unlocked: A Love Story by Karen Kingsbury; narrated by Roxanne Hernandez, *Edge of Apocalypse: The End Series, Volume 1* by Tim LaHaye, Craig Parshall, narrated by Stefan Rudnicki, *The Gathering Storm* by Bodie Thoene and Brock Thoene; narrated by Bodie Thoene, *Fireflies in December* by Jennifer Erin Valent; narrated by Kate Forbes and *Missing Max* by Karen Young; narrated by Laural Merlington

The Year in Fantasy: 2010
by
Don D'Ammassa

There was something of a paradox in fantasy this year. On the one hand, the movement away from traditional and Tolkienesque fantasy adventure to contemporary urban adventures and paranormal romance has not only continued but intensified. Although vampires and were-wolves continue to dominate among them, this year saw a resurgence of ghosts and fairies. Zombies, which are generally associated with horror fiction, also began to appear in fantasy novels, including a new series about a zombie detective. On the other hand, there were quite a few novels in 2010 that made use of original or at least less popular themes, and the appearance of a number of new and innovative writers certainly bodes well for the future.

While fantasy novels are doing well, short fantasy continues to lag behind, even more so than in science fiction or horror. *The Magazine of Fantasy & Science Fiction* went from monthly to bi-monthly, and the future of *Realms of Fantasy* magazine is at this point uncertain. Online fantasy at shorter length is not as healthy as in the other two genres, and original anthologies of fantasy fiction, once quite numerous, have dropped noticeably in quantity for the past two years. Single-author fantasy collections are almost unknown except in the small press.

Young adult fantasy fiction remains popular, although with the conclusion of the Harry Potter series, the romantic vampire novels of Stephenie Meyer, and the Olympians series by Rick Riordan, it is unclear who will be the dominant authors for the next few years. Most of the major writers of adult fantasy have been relatively unproductive for the past two years as well. George R.R. Martin's long awaited new novel in the A Song of Fire and Ice sequence has not appeared and Robert Jordan died, although the Wheel of Time series will be completed by Brandon Sanderson, emerging as a major talent in his own right.

Fantasy was dominated by a surprisingly large percent of relatively new writers, most notably China Mieville whose first novel appeared in 1999, although Mieville perhaps has reached the point where he can no longer be considered new. After producing the award winning *The City and the City* in 2009, Mieville has written an even more intricately plotted novel, although the complexity of the story may put off some readers. The setting is an alternate London where a variety of magical creatures—unique to this novel—co-exist more or less peacefully. When a stuffed giant squid is stolen from a museum, the curator finds himself involved with animated tattoos, talking statues, and a variety of other unusual beings.

Danielle Trussoni's *Angelology* similarly creates a complex fantasy world so interesting that it occasionally distracts the reader from the actual plot. It is based largely on some mildly obscure Christian mythology about the Nephilim, the offspring of angels who live secretly among humans. A young woman seeking information about the research conducted by her late parents becomes involved with the Nephilim, who turn out to be more than just mythological fantasies.

Historical settings—real or modified—were very popular this year. In *A Star Shall Fall* by Marie Brennan, the throne of the kingdom of Faerie exists hidden beneath the city of London during the 18th Century. A powerful dragon was imprisoned on a comet to save the world, but the comet is returning and disaster looms. This is the third in the Onyx Court series, although it is complete in itself. *Shades of Milk and Honey* by Mary Robinette Kowal bears some resemblance to a Regency romance, except that magic is a common device used in polite society. There is little of the melodramatic conflict that characterizes most fantasy and despite some minor awkwardness common to first novels, it manages to be likeable, convincing, and sometimes genuinely funny.

Tongues of Serpents by Naomi Novik is the sixth in the Temeraire series, set against the backdrop of an alternate history in which the Napoleonic Wars are fought using flying dragons and other magical elements. The series moves in a new direction this time with our disgraced heroes exiled to Australia. There they find a revolution brewing and must once again choose sides with care. Although somewhat slower paced and less inventive than the earlier books in the series, the story is still compelling and Novik's fans should be pleased.

Dave Duncan turns to an alternate version of 15th Century Europe for a political struggle revolving around the control of those few people who can interpret magical communications. It's the first in a series and promises to be among Duncan's best work.

At the Queen's Command by Michael A. Stackpole, also first in a projected series, is not technically an historical fantasy, but it closely resembles one because it is patterned in part on Europe's colonization of the New World and roughly parallels the French and Indian War with the walking dead and other magical elements in place of historical enemies and artifacts. Stackpole has improved dramatically since starting his career writing game related adventure stories and this promises to be his second major fantasy sequence. *Lady Lazarus* by Michele Lang is set just before the onset of World War II. The story is as much a secret history as it is an alternate world. The protagonist is a young Jewish witch who seeks to secure a magical artifact before it can fall into the hands of the Nazis. Angels and vampires make an appearance in a story that includes elements of urban as well as historical fantasy.

Although high fantasy was not as dominant as it has been in the past, that doesn't mean it wasn't a good year for this sub-genre as well. Steven Brust continued his story of Taltos in *Iorich*, with our somewhat flawed hero dodging assassins at every turn. Although intended as a standalone adventure, the novel contains references to earlier events, which may be confusing to readers not already familiar with the series. J.V. Jones added to the Sword of Shadows series with *Watcher of the Dead*, which advances the numerous plots developed in the earlier volumes. Although the stories are complex and involve a large cast of characters, the author provides a detailed summary of what went before, although it would still be more rewarding to read the earlier volumes in the series first.

Tad Williams brought his epic Shadowrise tetralogy to a conclusion with *Shadowheart*, which opens with a crisis coming to a head. Various contending forces are all headed for Southmarch where a series of surprise revelations, confrontations, and transformations brings the various plot threads to a conclusion. As with the Jones novel above, the author has provided a comprehensive summary of the previous three books. Michelle West offers readers the sequel to *The Hidden City*. *City of Night* is a very long and ambitious novel that deals in large part with a group of orphan children in a fantasy world metropolis who struggle to survive, and later with the efforts of a demon hunter who hopes to expose the fact that demons are living secretly among humans. This could have used a summary as well, and readers who have not read the first book may find it tough going.

There were also several excellent novels this year that don't fit quite so neatly into a category. New writer Felix Gilman borrows somewhat from steampunk in *The Half-Made World*, but instaed of an alternate version of the past the story is set in an entirely different universe. The human civilization is split into two cultures, roughly based on science and the supernatural, which have been at war for generations. When rumors arise that a weapon might exist which could tilt the balance of power in either direction, agents of both sides obviously hope to acquire it. Gilman's first two novels were noted for their imaginative settings and well-drawn characters and his third reflects those same qualities.

Patricia A. McKillip is almost a sub-genre by herself, *The Bards of Bone Plain* being a case in point. It contains elements of the quest story, but more of an intellectual than physical one. A newly trained bard must write a learned treatise so he chooses the Bone Plain, supposedly the place that forms the origin of all poetry. His efforts overlap with those of others and an old legend suddenly takes on new life. Beautifully written and free of the more melodramatic elements that predominate in fantasy, this is certainly one of the author's best novels. Kage Baker's *The Bird of the River*, published posthumously, has much of the same dreamy, low key atmosphere. The protagonist is a young girl who supports herself and her younger brother by working on a river barge. She gets involved in a murder investigation, encounters assassins, and the captain of her ship has a supernatural secret, but there is little melodrama and the story will leave readers feeling content and uplifted.

Jay Lake introduced his clockwork version of Earth in *Mainspring* and conducts a third tour for his readers in *Pinion*. A woman with the power to affect the outcome of the power struggle between nations in this innovative setting is on the run and readers follow her adventures in another unexplored part of Lake's singularly fascinating creation.

Contemporary urban fantasy is so homogeneous that it is difficult to single out individual novels, but the twelfth Harry Dresden novel by Jim Butcher, *Changes*, continues the author's string of successful magical adventures, this time suggesting that the series may take a new direction in the future thanks to the introduction of a daughter for the protagonist. A collection of shorter Dresden stories, *Side Jobs*, also appeared this year. Laura Resnick re-introduced Esther Diamond in *Doppelgangster*, a nicely crafted magical mystery in which she has to figure out how and why New York City gangsters are being duplicated. Unlike most similar series, Resnick does not rely on a single character to carry the story and the supporting cast is excellent. A third adventure, *Unsympathetic Magic* also appeared in 2010.

Humorous fantasy is making something of a comeback after years of declining popularity. Jasper Fforde's *Shades of Grey* is set in a society where social position is determined by one's ability to perceive nuances of color. As is the case with most of the author's previous books, the ensuing romp is not necessarily realistic but is inevitably entertaining. A.J. Hartley's *Will Power*, sequel to *Act of Will*, also mixes wild humor with high adventure. There's a war brewing between the fairies and the goblins and our heroes find themselves smack in the middle.

The most notable young adult fantasy of the year was

Factotum, by D.M. Cornish, part three of The Foundling's Tale. Cornish spends more time on setting and description than is common for this form, but his prose is elegant and his characters are compelling.

Recommended Titles

The movement away from high fantasy, novels of kings and castles and dragons, has continued this year. The flood of urban fantasy and paranormal romances continues to dominate the genre, with well over a hundred different series underway. The good news is that there have been quite a few very original fantasy novels in 2010, which bodes well for the future. The vast majority of titles continue to be entries in ongoing series, but this year has seen a surprisingly large number of first rate, standalone novels. Note that some 2010 titles were covered in the previous volume in this series.

The Bird of the River by Kage Baker

A Star Shall Fall by Marie Brennan

Iorich by Steven Brust

Changes by Jim Butcher

Factotum by D.M. Cornish

Speak to the Devil by Dave Duncan

Shades of Grey by Jasper Fforde

The Half-Made World by Felix Gilman

Will Power by A.J. Hartley

Watcher of the Dead by J.V. Jones

Shades of Milk and Honey by Mary Robinette Kowal

Pinion by Jay Lake

Lady Lazarus by Michelle Lang

The Bards of Bone Plain by Patricia A. McKillip

Kraken by China Mieville

Tongues of Serpents by Naomi Novik

Doppelgangster by Laura Resnick

At the Queen's Command by Michael A. Stackpole

Angelology by Danielle Trussoni

City of Night by Michelle West

Shadowheart by Tad Williams

Fantasy Fiction

TIM AKERS

The Horns of Ruin
(Amherst, New York: Pyr, 2010)

Story type: Historical - Victorian; Occult
Subject(s): Cults; Fantasy; Revenge
Major character(s): Eva Forge, Warrior, Cult Member
Locale(s): Ash, Fictional Location

Summary: *The Horns of Ruin* is a steampunk fantasy novel from author, Tim Akers. Three competitive brothers, Morgan, Amon, and Alexander, are worshiped as gods. Each oversees his own dedicated cult of followers. Constantly at war, the brothers are determined to destroy one another. Amon's followers have wiped out or kidnapped nearly every one of the Morganites, save one: Eva Forge. Eva is the only remaining warrior and she's determined to avenge her god and restore her people. Traveling to the strange city of Ash, Eva searches for assistance and answers to her deep questions about life and faith.

Where it's reviewed:
Library Journal, November 15, 2010, page 62
Publishers Weekly, September 27, 2010, page 41

Other books by the same author:
Heart of Veridon, 2009

Other books you might like:
Lynn Abbey, *The Nether Scroll*, 2000
James Enge, *The Wolf Age*, 2010
Paul Kearney, *Corvus*, 2010
Jon Sprunk, *Shadow's Son*, 2010
Matthew Sturges, *Midwinter*, 2009

ANDREW FOSTER ALTSCHUL

Lady Lazarus: A Novel
(Orlando, Florida: Harcourt, 2008)

Subject(s): Suicide; Rock music; Family sagas
Major character(s): Calliope Bird Morath, Daughter (of Brandt and Penny), Writer (poet); Brandt Morath, Musician, Father (of Calliope, deceased), Spouse (of Penny); Penny "Power" Morath, Musician, Mother (of Calliope), Spouse (of Brandt); Andrew, Writer (Calliope's biographer)

Summary: Calliope Bird Morath was destined for stardom from the day she was born. The only child of rock superstars Brandt Morath and Penny Power, Calliope's life was filled with eager reporters and photographers from day one. Things only got more chaotic after Calliope's father committed suicide in front of her, an event that left the little girl mute for several years. The media frenzy continues when an adult Calliope publishes a collection of poems about her father's death. Told from the perspectives of both Calliope and her biographer, Andrew, *Lady Lazarus* explores the public's strange fascination with celebrity. This is the first novel from author Andrew Foster Altschul.

Where it's reviewed:
Booklist, September 1, 2010, page 56
Library Journal, September 15, 2010, page 65
Locus, October 2010, page 54
Publishers Weekly, July 12, 2010, page 32

Other books by the same author:
Netherwood, 2008
Ms. Pendragon, 2006

Other books you might like:
Barbara Hambly, *The Magicians of Night*, 1991
Katherine Kurtz, *Lammas Night*, 1983
Mercedes Lackey, *The Serpent's Shadow*, 2001
Graham Masterton, *The Devils of D-Day*, 1978
Michael Moorcock, *The Dragon in the Sword*, 1986

3

M.T. ANDERSON

The Suburb Beyond the Stars
(New York: Scholastic Press, 2010)

Series: Game of Sunken Places Series. Book 2
Story type: Series; Young Readers
Subject(s): Fantasy; Games; Supernatural
Major character(s): Brian, Boy; Gregory, Friend (of Brian); Prudence, Cousin (of Gregory); Kalgrash, Mythical Creature (troll)
Time period(s): 21st century; 2010s
Locale(s): Vermont, United States

Summary: In *The Suburb Beyond the Stars* by M.T. Anderson, best friends, Brian and Gregory return to the scene of their first adventure—a Vermont neighborhood that is undergoing mysterious changes. When the boys journey to Gregory's cousin Prudence's house, an eerie scene awaits them—a cat hair-covered chair sitting in a vandalized room. Outside, the house's surroundings have been transformed by an encroaching suburb. But despite the increase in houses, the human population is gradually diminishing. To rescue Prudence, Brian and Gregory must face magical villains from the past. *The Suburb Beyond the Stars* is the second book in the Game of Sunken Places series.

Where it's reviewed:
Booklist, June 1, 2010, page 80
Horn Book Guide, Fall 2010, page 329
School Library Journal, July 2010, page 80

Other books by the same author:
The Game of Sunken Places, 2010
Burger Wuss, 2008
Thirsty, 2008
Whales on Stilts, 2005
Feed, 2002

Other books you might like:
Pamela Dean, *The Secret Country*, 1985
Edward Eager, *Magic by the Lake*, 1957
Alan Garner, *The Weirdstone of Brisingamen*, 1960
Roderick Gordon, *Deeper*, 2009
Andre Norton, *Lavender-Green Magic*, 1974

ALEX ARCHER

Rogue Angel: Tribal Ways

(Don Mills, Ontario, Canada; New York: Gold Eagle/Worldwide Library, 2010)

Series: Rogue Angel Series. Book 25
Story type: Contemporary
Subject(s): Witchcraft; Revenge; Archaeology
Major character(s): Annja Creed, Archaeologist
Time period(s): 21st century; 2010s
Locale(s): United States

Summary: An archaeological dig for Native American artifacts takes a bloody turn. When the violence finally ends, archaeologist Annja Creed learns—from the lips of the last survivor on his deathbed—who is responsible for the slaughter. She sets out to avenge the deaths of her comrades, but Annja is not prepared for the truths she is about to stumble upon. Witchcraft, shape-shifting, and deadly lore soon take over her mission, and Annja soon finds herself in mortal danger. *Rogue Angel: Tribal Ways* is the 25th book in Alex Archer's Rogue Angel series.

Other books by the same author:
The Bone Conjurer, 2010
The Dragon's Mark, 2010
Phantom Prospect, 2010
Eternal Journey, 2009
Footprints, 2009

Other books you might like:
James Axler, *Desert Kings*, 2008
Mark Frost, *The List of Seven*, 1993
E.E. Knight, *Lara Croft Tomb Raider: The Lost Cult*, 2004
Mike Resnick, *The Amulet of Power*, 2003
James Rollins, *Sandstorm*, 2004

5

ALEX ARCHER

Rogue Angel: The Dragon's Mark

(New York: Worldwide Library, 2010)

Series: Rogue Angel Series. Book 26
Story type: Adventure; Series
Subject(s): Adventure; Violence; Weapons
Major character(s): Annja Creed, Archaeologist; The Dragon, Warrior
Time period(s): 21st century; 2010s
Locale(s): United States

Summary: Archaeologist Annja Creed returns for another sword-slinging adventure. In this outing, Annja discovers an ancient story regarding a coveted sword—a sword that requires the finesse of a particularly ruthless handler known only as the Dragon. Now the Dragon is after Annja, and he constructs an elaborate house of cards designed to terrify and intimidate her. But Annja isn't that quick to frighten, and she is more than prepared to meet the challenge of a duel with the mighty Dragon. *Rogue Angel: The Dragon's Mark* is the 26th book in Alex Archer's adventure series.

Other books by the same author:
The Bone Conjurer, 2010
Phantom Prospect, 2010
Tribal Ways, 2010
Eternal Journey, 2009
Footprints, 2009

Other books you might like:
James Axler, *Remember Tomorrow*, 2007
James Alan Gardner, *Lara Croft Tomb Raider: The Man of Bronze*, 2005
E.E. Knight, *Lara Croft Tomb Raider: The Lost Cult*, 2004
James Rollins, *Map of Bones*, 2005
Lilith Saintcrow, *Dead Man Rising*, 2006

6

ALEX ARCHER

Rogue Angel: Phantom Prospect

(New York: Worldwide Library, 2010)

Series: Rogue Angel Series. Book 27
Story type: Adventure; Series
Subject(s): Shipwrecks; Sharks; Adventure
Major character(s): Annja Creed, Archaeologist
Time period(s): 21st century; 2010s
Locale(s): Nova Scotia, Canada

Summary: In *Rogue Angel: Phantom Prospect*, author Alex Archer presents the 27th volume in his fantasy series featuring the adventures of sword-wielding archeologist Annja Creed. This installment finds Annja setting out with a friend to recover a treasure aboard a sunken ship. What they find, however, is a different matter entirely. There is a band of sharks—long considered extinct—keeping watch over the shipwreck, and someone, or something, wants to ensure Annja doesn't acquire the buried loot.

Other books by the same author:
The Bone Conjurer, 2010
The Dragon's Mark, 2010
Eternal Journey, 2009
Footprints, 2009
Tribal Ways, 2010

Other books you might like:
James Axler, *Pantheon of Vengeance*, 2008
James Alan Gardner, *Lara Croft Tomb Raider: The Man of Bronze*, 2005
Mike Resnick, *The Amulet of Power*, 2003
James Rollins, *The Last Oracle*, 2008
Lilith Saintcrow, *Redemption Alley*, 2009

7

CAMILLE BACON-SMITH

A Legacy of Daemons

(New York: DAW, 2010)

Series: Daemons Series. Book 3
Story type: Urban
Subject(s): Demons; Adventure; Detective fiction
Major character(s): Evan Davis, Supernatural Being (half-daemon), Son (of Brad), Detective; Brad, Father (of Evan), Detective; Lily, Detective
Time period(s): 21st century

Summary: Camille Bacon-Smith's *A Legacy of Daemons* is the third novel in a series featuring a trio of supernatural detectives. Evan Davis is the half-daemon son of Brad, and together with Lily, the three tackle all manner of problems related to anything mystical. Their latest case takes them into a perilous web of dark magic, leading them to a confrontation with droves of daemon warriors.

Other books by the same author:
Daemon Eyes, 2007
Eyes of the Empress, 1998
Eye of the Daemon, 1996

Other books you might like:
Ilona Andrews, *Magic Strikes*, 2009
Yasmine Galenorn, *Bone Magic*, 2010
Laurell K. Hamilton, *Flirt*, 2010
Seanan McGuire, *An Artificial Night*, 2010
Rob Thurman, *The Grimrose Path*, 2010

8

KAGE BAKER

The Bird of the River

(New York: Tor, 2010)

Subject(s): Orphans; Pirates; Adventure
Major character(s): Eliss, Stepsister (of Alder), Worker (lookout); Alder, Stepbrother (of Eliss); Krelan, Assassin
Time period(s): Indeterminate

Summary: Set on a river barge, Kage Baker's *The Bird of the River* charts the adventures of half-siblings Eliss and Alder, who become assets to the crew of the barge after their diver-mother unexpectedly dies. Eliss becomes an ace lookout and can spot trouble miles in advance. When she meets Krelan on board the vessel, she becomes involved in his search for the severed head of a dead man. As she investigates Krelan's case, trouble is plaguing the cities along the shore, and it's up to Eliss to stop the rampant looting—and find the severed head.

Where it's reviewed:
Booklist, July 1, 2010, page 43
Library Journal, June 15, 2010, page 66
Locus, August 2010, page 25
Publishers Weekly, May 3, 2010, page 35

Other books by the same author:
The Empress of Mars, 2009
The House of the Stag, 2008
Gods and Pawns, 2007
The Children of the Company, 2005
The Anvil of the World, 2003

Other books you might like:
Gayle Greeno, *Sunderlies Seeking*, 1998
Robin Hobb, *Ship of Magic*, 1998
Andre Norton, *Lost Lands of Witch World*, 2004
Robert V.S. Redick, *The Red Wolf Conspiracy*, 2008
Lawrence Watt-Evans, *Taking Flight*, 1993

9

DANIELLE BENNETT
JAIDA JONES, Co-Author

Dragon Soul

(New York: Spectra/Ballantine Books, 2010)

Series: Metal Dragon Series. Book 3
Story type: Alternate World; Series
Subject(s): Dragons; Brothers; Fantasy
Major character(s): Rook, Military Personnel (dragon rider); Thom, Military Personnel (dragon rider), Brother (of Rook)
Time period(s): Indeterminate
Locale(s): Ke-Han Kingdom, Fictional Location; Volstov Kingdom, Fictional Location

Summary: In *Dragon Soul* by Jaida Jones and Danielle Bennett, the method of warfare in the embattled kingdoms of Vostov and Ke-Han is dragon power, with specially trained human riders to guide them. The boldest rider, Rook, is paired with the dragon, Havemercy, which is the mightiest mechanical beast in the Vostov force until the Ke-Han bring her down. With Havemercy gone, Rook grows more aloof, forsaking even the attention of his brother, Thom. When the siblings learn that there is a market for dragon remains, they unite to protect the beloved Havemercy, even in death. *Dragon Soul* is the third book in the Havemercy series.

Other books by the same author:
Shadow Magic, 2009
Havemercy, 2008

Other books you might like:
Joanne Bertin, *The Last Dragonlord*, 1998
Barbara Hambly, *Dragonshadow*, 1999
Mercedes Lackey, *Sanctuary*, 2005
Dennis L. McKiernan, *Dragondoom*, 1990
Alan F. Troop, *A Host of Dragons*, 2006

10

HOLLY BLACK

White Cat

(New York: Margaret K. McElderry Books, 2010)

Series: Curse Workers Series. Book 1
Story type: Young Adult
Subject(s): Memory; Criminals; Brothers
Major character(s): Cassel Sharpe, Teenager
Time period(s): 21st century; 2010s
Locale(s): United States

Summary: *White Cat* is the first installment in Holly Black's Curse Workers series. This volume introduces teenager Cassel Sharpe, who belongs to a family that possesses the dark power to alter the memories and emotions of others. But Cassel doesn't have this same ability, and he's something of a black sheep among the Sharpes. Cassel is also struggling with his guilt over murdering his best friend, Lila, several years ago. Soon a series of strange events prompts Cassel to investigate the magical powers of his family, leading him to question his role in Lila's death—and if there's a chance she could still be alive.

Where it's reviewed:
Locus, July 2010, page 27
School Library Journal, October 2010, page 60

Other books by the same author:
The Poison Eaters: And Other Stories, 2010
Ironside, 2008
Valiant, 2006
Tithe, 2002

Other books you might like:
Eoin Colfer, *Artemis Fowl*, 2001
Charlie Fletcher, *Silvertongue*, 2009
Diana Wynne Jones, *Archer's Goon*, 1984
Rick Riordan, *The Lightning Thief*, 2005
Vivian Vande Velde, *Magic Can Be Murder*, 2000

11

ANNETTE BLAIR

Death by Diamonds

(New York: Berkley Books, 2010)

Series: Vintage Magic Series. Book 3
Subject(s): Mystery; Magic; Fantasy
Major character(s): Madeira Cutler, Store Owner (vintage clothing), Psychic; Dominique Delong, Actress
Time period(s): 21st century; 2010s
Locale(s): Mystick Falls, Connecticut; New York, New York

Summary: *Death by Diamonds* by Annette Blair is the story of Madeira Cutler, a vintage clothing shop owner who possesses the power to see secrets about each piece of clothing and the previous owner who wore it. When a piece from famous actress and longtime pal Dominique Delong is consigned to her, she is excited to see that it is the very dress she designed for her old friend. When she sees into the dress's past, however, she finds some unsettling truths. First of all, Dominique recently passed away after a performance; worse yet, it seems that she may have been murdered. Can Madeira get to the bottom of this mystery in time to bring justice for her friend? *Death by Diamonds* is the third novel in the Vintage Magic Mystery series.

Other books by the same author:
Bedeviled Angel, 2010
Naked Dragon, 2010
Larceny and Lace, 2009
Gone with the Witch, 2008
My Favorite Witch, 2005

Other books you might like:
Madelyn Alt, *A Witch in Time*, 2010
Rebecca Kent, *Murder Has No Class*, 2010
Chaz McGee, *Angel Interrupted*, 2010
Wendy Roberts, *Dead and Kicking*, 2009
Mary Stanton, *Angel's Advocate*, 2009

12

ERIN BOW

Plain Kate

(New York: Arthur A. Levine Books, 2010)

Story type: Young Adult
Subject(s): Witchcraft; Orphans; Outcasts
Major character(s): Kate, Orphan, Witch (suspected), Outcast
Time period(s): Indeterminate

Summary: Plain Kate, the orphaned daughter of a wood carver, is definitely an outcast in her strange, superstitious village. Her impressive knife-wielding and wood-carving skills have even caused some to speculate that she might be a witch, a dangerous accusation in the small community. When a supernatural sickness befalls the town, Kate becomes the chief suspect. In an attempt to save her own life, Kate agrees to sell her shadow to a stranger in exchange for freedom and her "heart's desire." Making her new home with a gypsy group known as the Roamers, Kate discovers that she can't live without her shadow and must fight to get it back. First novel.

Where it's reviewed:
Horn Book Magazine, September-October 2010, page 72
Locus, December 2010, page 29
Publishers Weekly, August 16, 2010, page 54
School Library Journal, October 2010, page 108

Other books you might like:
Bruce Coville, *Dark Whispers*, 2008
Alan Garner, *Elidor*, 1965
C.S. Lewis, *The Lion, the Witch and the Wardrobe*, 1950
William Nicholson, *Jango*, 2006
Pamela F. Service, *Being of Two Minds*, 1991

13

MARIE BRENNAN

A Star Shall Fall

(New York: Tor, 2010)

Story type: Historical; Magic Conflict
Subject(s): Magic; Fairies; Dragons
Time period(s): 18th century; 1750s
Locale(s): London, England

Summary: Set in London in the 1750s, *A Star Shall Fall* follows the parallel existence of an underground faerie world and the Royal Society of London, a group of brilliant academics and scientists determined to disprove the existence of magic. Nearly a century before, in 1666, 80% of London burned to the ground from a fire started by a ferocious dragon. The faes harnessed their magical powers to banish the dragon to a distant comet, but according to a scientist named Sir Edmond Halley, the comet is set to return in 1759. The faeries know they aren't strong enough to stop the dragon on their own. If they hope to succeed, they'll need assistance from the Royal Society, but can scientists and magical creatures ever work together in unity?

Where it's reviewed:
Library Journal, September 15, 2010, page 64
Locus, September 2010, page 19
Publishers Weekly, July 19, 2010, page 117

Other books by the same author:
In Ashes Lie, 2009
Midnight Never Comes, 2008
Doppelganger, 2006
Warrior and Witch, 2006

Other books you might like:
Emma Bull, *War for the Oaks*, 1987
Laurell K. Hamilton, *A Kiss of Shadows*, 2000
Mercedes Lackey, *The Wizard of London*, 2005
Karen Marie Moning, *Dreamfever*, 2009
Sarban, *Ringstones*, 1951

14

PETER V. BRETT

The Warded Man

(New York: Ballantine Books, 2009)

Series: Demon Trilogy. Book 1
Story type: Ancient Evil Unleashed; Coming-of-Age
Subject(s): Demons; Magic; Good and evil
Major character(s): Arlen, Hero (wants to become a brave Messenger); Leesha, Healer (apprentice to Bruna); Rojer, Musician; Bruna, Sorceress (and healer)
Locale(s): Cutter's Hollow, Fictional Location; Krasia, Fictional Location; Tibbet's Brook, Fictional Location

Summary: Thousands of years ago, the Deliverer discovered powerful symbols called "wards" that could fend off demons from the planet's core, called "corelings," and keep people safe. Over time, however, people began to take the magical wards' protection for granted. Then one night, the corelings rose again and decimated much of the human population. Now, each night when darkness arrives, the corelings ascend in a mysterious fog and devour anyone who lacks the protection of a magical ward. It's up to three young people with troubled pasts to save the world from the ruthless corelings. Brave Arlen, who has an innate ability to draw wards, left home at the age of eleven after a coreling attack left his mother dead. Arlen dreams of defeating the corelings and freeing the people from their fear. Lies and betrayal shattered Leesha's perfect life, so she becomes the apprentice of a powerful sorceress and healer. And Rojer was just a child when corelings crippled him and killed everyone else in his town, but he became a talented musician with a surprising power. Together, they must find the strength and courage to stand up to the night. Originally published in the United Kingdom as *The Painted Man*, *The Warded Man* is the first volume in author Peter V. Brett's Demon trilogy.

Where it's reviewed:
Booklist, February 1, 2009, page 36

Other books by the same author:
The Desert Spear, 2010
The Great Bazaar and Other Stories, 2010
The Painted Man, 2008

Other books you might like:
Dave Duncan, *Children of Chaos*, 2006
David Gemmell, *Dark Prince*, 1993
R.A. Salvatore, *The Orc King*, 2007
Elizabeth Vaughan, *Warprize*, 2005

15

PETER V. BRETT

The Desert Spear

(New York: Del Rey-Ballantine Books, 2010)

Subject(s): Demons; Good and evil; Horror
Major character(s): Ahmann Jardir, Warrior, Hunter (of

demons); Arlen "Warded Man", Hunter (of demons), Warrior

Time period(s): Indeterminate

Summary: *The Desert Spear* is a horror novel from author Peter V. Brett. The world is in chaos and gripped with fear as demons wreak havoc every night murdering innocent people. Desperate for a savior, the people remind themselves of the ancient tales of the Deliverer, a man strong enough to slay the demons and set the people free. When Ahmann Jardir comes from the desert, leading an army of demon slayers and wielding ancient weapons, the people rejoice at the return of their Deliverer, but Jardir's old friend, known simply as the Warded Man, challenges the claim. Both men possess unusual strength and the ability to kill demons, but which one is the true Deliverer?

Where it's reviewed:
Booklist, April 1, 2010, page 30
Locus, June 2010, page 23
Publishers Weekly, February 8, 2010, page 34
School Library Journal, March 15, 2010, page 96

Other books by the same author:
The Great Bazaar and Other Stories, 2010
The Warded Man, 2010
The Painted Man, 2008

Other books you might like:
Dave Duncan, *Mother of Lies*, 2007
David Gemmell, *White Wolf*, 2003
R.A. Salvatore, *The Ancient*, 2008
Elizabeth Vaughan, *Dagger-Star*, 2008
Lawrence Watt-Evans, *Touched by the Gods*, 1997

16

TERRY BROOKS

Bearers of the Black Staff

(New York: Ballantine Books, 2010)

Series: Legends of Shannara Series. Book 1
Subject(s): Adventure; Apocalypse; Magic
Major character(s): Sider Ament, Warrior; Panterra Qu, Teenager (Tracker); Prue Liss, Teenager (Tracker)
Time period(s): Indeterminate Past
Locale(s): Shannara, Fictional Location

Summary: In the centuries that have passed since the near-annihilation of the United States, survivors have struggled to piece their lives back together, now residing in a picturesque area protected by magical powers. Lately, however, these powers seem to be faltering. Sider Ament, two seasoned Trackers, and a determined elf set out to inform the nation of the possible threats they are facing. There are, however, other forces at work—forces that want to ensure the destruction of the entire planet. *Bearers of the Black Staff* is the first novel in Terry Brooks's Legends of Shannara series.

Where it's reviewed:
Library Journal, November 15, 2010, page 34
Publishers Weekly, July 5, 2010, page 32

Other books by the same author:
The Gypsy Morph, 2008

The Elves of Cintra, 2007
Armageddon's Children, 2006
Tanequil, 2004
Antrax, 2001

Other books you might like:
Stephen R. Donaldson, *Lord Foul's Bane*, 1977
David Gemmell, *Stormrider*, 2002
Robin Hobb, *Forest Mage*, 2006
J.V. Jones, *Watcher of the Dead*, 2010
R.A. Salvatore, *The Bear*, 2010

17

ELIZABETH C. BUNCE

Star Crossed

(New York: Arthur A. Levine Books, 2010)

Story type: Young Adult
Subject(s): Fantasy; Politics; Theft
Major character(s): Digger, 16-Year-Old, Orphan, Thief, Magician
Time period(s): Indeterminate

Summary: Digger is a teenage orphan with a gift of magic and a penchant for stealing. When Digger and her lover/partner, Tegen, are caught in the middle of a major heist, Digger manages to escape and fears that Tegen is dead. Desperate to get away, Digger finds herself aboard a boat with a group of young aristocrats heading for their mountain home. During her stay with the young nobles, Digger crosses paths with an ambitious lord who knows her secret. He blackmails Digger to find out political secrets about the royal family, forcing her to choose between her own protection and the far-reaching danger the secrets could invoke.

Where it's reviewed:
Booklist, November 15, 2010, page 44
Bulletin of the Center for Children's Books, October 2010, page 66
School Library Journal, January 2011, page 102

Other books by the same author:
A Curse as Dark as Gold, 2008

Other books you might like:
Carol Berg, *The Spirit Lens: A Novel of the Collegia Magica*, 2010
Anne Bishop, *The Shadow Queen*, 2009
Stephen R. Donaldson, *A Man Rides Through*, 1987
Mindy L. Klasky, *The Glasswright's Master*, 2004
Mercedes Lackey, *The Wizard of London*, 2005

18

JIM BUTCHER

Side Jobs: Stories from the Dresden Files

(New York: Roc/New American Library, 2010)

Story type: Urban
Subject(s): Wizards; Detective fiction; Short stories

Major character(s): Harry Dresden, Detective—Private, Wizard
Time period(s): 21st century; 2010s
Locale(s): Chicago, Illinois
Summary: Urban fantasy author Jim Butcher brings together a collection of his short fiction, which includes a short novel starring Butcher's most famous character, wizard and private detective Harry Dresden. *Side Jobs: Stories from the Dresden Files* contains a series of short cases tackled by Harry and his various colleagues as they confront the forces of evil that threaten the citizens of Chicago. This collection includes some of Jim Butcher's first short stories.

Where it's reviewed:
Booklist, December 1, 2010, page 37
Publishers Weekly, September 20, 2010, page 52

Other books by the same author:
Changes, 2010
Turn Coat, 2009
Small Favor: A Novel of the Dresden Files, 2008
White Night, 2007
Proven Guilty, 2006

Other books you might like:
Harry Connolly, *Game of Cages*, 2010
Charles de Lint, *Mulengro: A Romany Tale*, 1985
Simon R. Green, *Hell to Pay*, 2007
Tanya Huff, *The Enchantment Emporium*, 2009
S. Andrew Swann, *The Dragons of the Cuyahoga*, 2001

19

JACQUELINE CAREY

Naamah's Curse

(New York: Grand Central Publishing, 2010)

Series: Naamah Trilogy. Book 2
Story type: Alternate World; Series
Subject(s): Fantasy; Alternative worlds; Magicians
Major character(s): Moirin, Servant; Bao, Companion (soulmate of Moirin); Great Khan, Relative (father-in-law of Bao)
Time period(s): Indeterminate Past
Locale(s): Tatar Territory, Fictional Location

Summary: In *Naamah's Curse* by Jacqueline Carey, a servant sets out on a mystical journey in Tatar territory—a re-imagined Asian landscape. Moirin has been dutiful to the goddess in her care, but knows that she is missing a vital component of her being. Bao, a Ch'in fighter who lives far away, possesses a portion of Moirin's ancestors' soul-spark, and Moirin knows that she must retrieve it to assume her full powers. But Moirin soon learns that quest holds many challenges, including would-be killers and Bao's marriage to another. *Naamah's Curse* is the second book in Naamah's trilogy.

Where it's reviewed:
Booklist, May 15, 2010, page 30
Library Journal, June 15, 2010, page 68

Other books by the same author:
Naamah's Kiss, 2009
Kushiel's Mercy, 2008

Kushiel's Justice, 2007
Kushiel's Scion, 2006
Kushiel's Dart, 2001

Other books you might like:
Leah R. Cutter, *Paper Mage*, 2003
Kara Dalkey, *Genpei*, 2001
Lian Hearn, *Across the Nightingale Floor*, 2002
Richard A. Lupoff, *Sword of the Demon*, 1976
E. Hoffmann Price, *The Jade Enchantress*, 1982

20

LEE CARROLL

Black Swan Rising

(New York: Tor, 2010)

Subject(s): Magic; Good and evil; Vampires
Major character(s): Garet James, Designer (jewelry)
Time period(s): 21st century; 2010s
Locale(s): New York, New York

Summary: In Lee Carroll's *Black Swan Rising*, Garet James is a successful Manhattan jewelry designer who happens upon a beautiful antique box in a local shop. The design on the box is identical to one emblazoned on a precious family heirloom. When Garet opens the delicate silver box, however, strange things begin to happen. The box eventually disappears, and as Garet investigates the situation, she is pulled into a world of supernatural beings who are out to destroy all she knows and loves.

Where it's reviewed:
Publishers Weekly, June 28, 2010, page 114

Other books you might like:
Lynn Abbey, *Behind Time*, 2001
Elaine Bergstrom, *The Door through Washington Square*, 1998
Richard Grant, *Kaspian Lost*, 1999
Tanya Huff, *The Enchantment Emporium*, 2009
Tim Powers, *Earthquake Weather*, 1997

21

HARRY CONNOLLY

Game of Cages

(New York: Del Ray, 2010)

Series: Twenty Palaces Series. Book 2
Story type: Urban
Subject(s): Crime; Magic; Theft
Major character(s): Ray Lilly, Thief, Clerk (stock boy); Catherine Little, Sorcerer
Time period(s): 21st century; 2000s
Locale(s): North Cascades, Fictional Location

Summary: In Harry Connolly's *Game of Cages*, Ray Lilly is growing tired of his boring life. He used to be a wooden man and then lived his life as a car thief. Now, the ex-convict simply works as a stock boy in a North Cascades supermarket. Ray believes adventure and excitement may come back to his life when he's contacted by Catherine, a powerful sorcerer who heads the magical Twenty Palace Society. She wants him to help her purchase a predator at the upcoming auction. The task seems easy, but when the predator escapes, Ray must rely on his brute strength and the sole spell he knows to help Catherine capture the being.

Where it's reviewed:
Booklist, August 1, 2010, page 36
Locus, August 2010, page 27
Publishers Weekly, July 5, 2010, page 33

Other books by the same author:
Child of Fire, 2009

Other books you might like:
Jim Butcher, *Small Favor: A Novel of the Dresden Files*, 2008
Charles de Lint, *Mulengro: A Romany Tale*, 1985
Simon R. Green, *Just Another Judgement Day*, 2009
Tanya Huff, *Smoke and Mirrors*, 2005
S. Andrew Swann, *The Dwarves of Whiskey Island*, 2005

22

D.M. CORNISH

Factotum

(New York: G. P. Putnam's Sons, 2010)

Series: Foundling's Tale Trilogy. Book 3
Story type: Young Adult
Subject(s): Monsters; Fantasy; Orphans
Major character(s): Rossamund Bookchild, Orphan, Monster, Human; Europe, Hunter (monster), Friend (of Rossamund)
Time period(s): Indeterminate
Locale(s): Brandenbrass, Fictional Location

Summary: *Factotum* is the third and final installment in the Foundling's Tale Trilogy (formerly known as the Monster Blood Tattoo Series). Rossamund Bookchild cannot escape dangerous accusations, regardless of how far he travels or with whom he associates. The young orphan has been dogged by allegations that he's a monster disguised as a human. Befriending Europe, one of the most revered monster-hunters in the area, doesn't do much to help Rossamund's case. Together, Rossamund and Europe travel to Brandenbrass where Rossamund is forced to confront his heritage and identity, finding out for himself whether or not all monsters are truly evil. The book includes more than 100 pages of maps, charts, and vocabulary to supplement the story.

Where it's reviewed:
Locus, December 2010, page 21

Other books by the same author:
Lamplighter, 2008
Foundling, 2007

Other books you might like:
Bruce Coville, *The Last Hunt*, 2010
Neil Gaiman, *Coraline*, 2002
Ursula K. Le Guin, *A Wizard of Earthsea*, 1968

China Mieville, *Un Lun Dun*, 2007
Philip Pullman, *The Golden Compass*, 1995

23

BRUCE COVILLE

The Last Hunt

(New York: Scholastic Press, 2010)

Series: Unicorn Chronicles. Book 4
Story type: Young Readers
Subject(s): Fantasy; Good and evil; Unicorns
Major character(s): Cara, Teenager, Unicorn (half), Human (half); Beloved, Hunter, Murderer (of unicorns)
Time period(s): Indeterminate
Locale(s): Luster, Fictional Location

Summary: *The Last Hunt* is an exciting, adventurous, and imaginative fantasy novel for young readers from author Bruce Coville. The fourth and final installation in the Unicorn Chronicles series, *The Last Hunt* centers on an epic struggle that could bring about the end of the world. In the magical land of Luster, the unicorns are facing extinction. For centuries, they've been hunted and killed by the revenge-bent Beloved whose father was murdered by a unicorn. The fate of the world rests on the shoulders of Cara, a teenaged half-unicorn, half-human orphan whose bloodline is connected with Beloved. With the help of an unstable dragon, Cara seeks to defeat Beloved and the Hunters and save the world in the process.

Where it's reviewed:
Horn Book Guide, Fall 2010, page 334
School Library Journal, July 2010, page 85

Other books by the same author:
Dark Whispers, 2007
Odds Are Good, 2006
Thor's Wedding Day, 2005
Song of the Wanderer, 2001
Oddly Enough, 1994

Other books you might like:
Peter S. Beagle, *The Last Unicorn*, 1968
Michael Bishop, *Unicorn Mountain*, 1988
Terry Brooks, *The Black Unicorn*, 1987
David Lee Jones, *Unicorn Highway*, 1992
Elizabeth Ann Scarborough, *The Unicorn Creed*, 1983

24

J.A. CULLUM

Cinkarion: The Heart of Fire

(Calgary, Alberta, Canada: EDGE, 2010)

Series: Chronicles of the Karionin Trilogy. Book 2
Story type: Alternate World
Subject(s): Fantasy; Wars; Magic
Major character(s): Saranith Kamrasi, Royalty, Magician, Sister (of Nathan), Tiger (folk); Nathan Kamrasi, Tiger (folk), Wizard, Brother (of Saranith), Exile
Time period(s): Indeterminate
Locale(s): Tamar, Fictional Location

Summary: *Cinkarion: The Heart of Fire* is a fantasy novel from author J.A. Cullum. The book is the second installment in the Chronicles of the Karionin trilogy. Tamar's inhabitants include nine humanoid races, each fueled by their own hostility, ambition, and prejudice toward others. On the continent of Cibata, one human nation remains, the Cassinga, but their future is uncertain. The tiger folk, rulers of the Senangan Empire, are desperate to destroy Cassinga once and for all. Leading the Senangan charge is Saranith Kamrasi, a member of the Empire's royal family, who is being empowered by a living crystal known as Cinkarion. The Wizard Nathan, Saranith's estranged brother, is determined to save Cassinga, even if it means fighting against his own flesh and blood.

Other books by the same author:
Lyskarion: The Song of the Wind, 2001

Other books you might like:
Robin Wayne Bailey, *Brothers of the Dragon*, 1993
Stephen R. Donaldson, *The Runes of the Earth*, 2004
Craig Shaw Gardner, *Dragon Sleeping*, 1994
China Mieville, *The Scar*, 2002
Mickey Zucker Reichert, *The Beasts of Barakhai*, 2001

25

CHRIS D'LACEY

Dark Fire

(New York: Orchard Books, 2010)

Series: Last Dragon Chronicles. Book 5
Story type: Young Readers
Subject(s): Dragons; Father-daughter relations; Adventure
Major character(s): David Rain, Writer, Father (of Alexa); Alexa, Daughter (of David)
Time period(s): Indeterminate

Summary: Writer, David Rain has just come back home after spending five years working with dragons in the Arctic. As he attempts to rebuild his relationship with his daughter Alexa, David begins to realize that Alexa just might possess a unique magical ability that could eradicate the mortal foes of the dragons. *Dark Fire* is the fifth installment in Chris D'Lacey's Last Dragon Chronicles.

Where it's reviewed:
Horn Book Guide, Fall 2010, page 336

Other books by the same author:
The Dragons of Wayward Crescent, 2009
Gruffen, 2009
The Fire Eternal, 2007
Fire Star, 2007
Ice Fire, 2006

Other books you might like:
Piers Anthony, *Dragon on a Pedestal*, 1983
Robert N. Charrette, *Never Deal with a Dragon*, 1990
Gordon R. Dickson, *The Dragon and the Fair Maid of Kent*, 2000
E.E. Knight, *Dragon Champion*, 2005
Jo Walton, *Tooth and Claw*, 2003

26

ROWENA CORY DANIELLS

The Uncrowned King

(Oxford, England: Solaris, 2010)

Series: King Rolen's Kin Series. Book 2
Story type: Alternate World
Subject(s): Fantasy; Royalty; Father-son relations
Major character(s): Piro, 13-Year-Old, Daughter (of King Rolen), Royalty, Sister (of Bryen); Bryen, Son (of King Rolen), Heir, Royalty, Brother (of Piro); Rolen, Royalty (King of Rolencia), Father (of Piro and Bryen)
Time period(s): Indeterminate
Locale(s): Rolencia, Fictional Location

Summary: *The Uncrowned King* is a fantasy novel by Rowena Cory Daniells. The book is the second installment in the King Rolen's Kin series. In *The Uncrowned King*, King Rolen's castle is being stormed by Rolencia's longtime enemies, Merofynia. King Rolen's 13-year-old daughter, Piro, is shocked to hear the vicious rumors circulating about her brother, Bryen, the king's second son and potential heir to the throne. Even more shocking than the rumors is the fact that the King starts to believe them. Bryen must prove his commitment and loyalty to his father, even if it means braving the advancing army in hopes of finding a way to protect his family's castle.

Other books by the same author:
The King's Bastard, 2010
The Usurper, 2010

Other books you might like:
Anne Bishop, *Shalador's Lady*, 2010
Katherine Kurtz, *Childe Morgan*, 2006
Juliet E. McKenna, *Irons in the Fire*, 2009
Joel Shepherd, *Petrodor*, 2010
Freda Warrington, *The Sapphire Throne*, 2000

27

ROWENA CORY DANIELLS

The King's Bastard

(Oxford: Solaris, 2010)

Series: King Rolen's Kin Series. Book 1
Story type: Adventure; Series
Subject(s): Fantasy; Adventure; Epics
Major character(s): Fyn, Son (of king)
Time period(s): Indeterminate Past
Locale(s): Kingdom of Rolencia, Fictional Location

Summary: In *The King's Bastard* by Rowena Cory Daniells, the Kingdom of Rolencia is plagued by a strange affliction known as Affinity. The king has ordered all of his subjects infected with Affinity to place themselves in the service of the Abbey. The punishment for disobedience is execution. When the king's own son, Fyn, is forced to go to the Abbey, he prepares for the increasing unrest by learning the skills of the monk and the warrior. Beyond the Abbey, other victims of Affinity struggle to preserve their lives. *The King's Bastard* is the first book in the King Rolen's Kin series.

Other books by the same author:
The Uncrowned King, 2010
The Usurper, 2010

Other books you might like:
Anne Bishop, *Dreams Made Flesh*, 2005
Katherine Kurtz, *Childe Morgan*, 2006
Juliet E. McKenna, *Banners in the Wind*, 2010
Joel Shepherd, *Sasha*, 2009
Freda Warrington, *The Sapphire Throne*, 2000

28

ROWENA CORY DANIELLS

The Usurper
(London: Solaris, 2010)

Series: King Rolen's Kin Series. Book 3
Subject(s): Adventure; Slavery; Royalty
Major character(s): Piro, Slave; Bryen, Royalty; Fyn, Brother (of Bryen)
Time period(s): Indeterminate

Summary: Piro is enslaved at the Merofynian Palace, and she must watch every step or risk having her identity exposed, which could lead to her death. She struggles to keep the secret of her identity securely under wraps. Bryen is about to be named king, but he is far from thrilled about the prospect. His brother Fyn sets out to save Bryen from the league of rebels who want to ensure he does not take the throne. These fantasy-adventure dramas unfold in Rowena Cory Daniell's *The Usurper*, the third novel in the King Rolen's Kin series.

Other books by the same author:
The King's Bastard, 2010
The Uncrowned King, 2010

Other books you might like:
Anne Bishop, *Sebastian*, 2006
Katherine Kurtz, *In the King's Service*, 2003
Juliet E. McKenna, *Irons in the Fire*, 2009
Joel Shepherd, *Sasha*, 2009
Janny Wurts, *To Ride Hell's Chasm*, 2004

29

JAMES P. DAVIS

Circle of Skulls
(Renton, Washington: Wizards of the Coast, 2010)

Series: Forgotten Realms: Waterdeep Series. Book 6
Story type: Horror; Young Adult
Subject(s): Angels; Demons; Supernatural
Major character(s): Jinn, Angel, Warrior
Time period(s): Indeterminate
Locale(s): Waterdeep, Fictional Location

Summary: *Circle of Skulls* is the sixth and final installment in the Forgotten Realms: Waterdeep series. Jinn is an angel tasked with living in a human body to fight against evil. Over his various human lifetimes, he has become hell-bent on seeking revenge against the demon responsible for killing his lover, the dark angel of Asmodeus. A series of occult murders give Jinn the knowledge he needs to track down his enemy, leading him into the final battle for Waterdeep. When the two come face-to-face, can Jinn find the strength, courage, and motivation he needs to destroy the dark angel once and for all, or will he fail like he has so many times in the past?

Other books by the same author:
The Restless Shore, 2009
The Shield of Weeping Ghosts, 2008
Bloodwalk, 2006

Other books you might like:
Richard Awlinson, *Waterdeep*, 1989
Eric Scott de Bie, *Downshadow*, 2009
Erin M. Evans, *The God Catcher*, 2010
Mel Odom, *The Sea Devil's Eye*, 2000
R.A. Salvatore, *The Orc King*, 2007

30

STEPHEN R. DONALDSON

Against All Things Ending
(New York: G.P. Putnams Sons, 2010)

Series: Last Chronicles of Thomas Covenant Series. Book 3
Story type: Alternate World; Series
Subject(s): Fantasy; Epics; Alternative worlds
Major character(s): Linden Avery, Young Woman; Jeremiah, Son (of Linden); Thomas Covenant, Writer, Lover (of Linden); Despiser, Villain
Time period(s): Indeterminate
Locale(s): The Land, Fictional Location

Summary: In *Against All Things Ending* by Stephen R. Donaldson, Linden Avery continues her quest that began in the previous volumes of this tetralogy. Although she has successfully released her lover, Thomas Covenant, from the Arch of Time, Linden's actions threaten to stir the Worm of the World's End. The dreaded Worm has the power to annihilate the Land, unless Linden and Thomas can summon enough assistance to defeat it. Linden's son, Jeremiah, could be their most useful weapon, but he needs to be rescued before he can join their battle. *Against All Things Ending* is the third book in the Last Chronicles of Thomas Covenant series.

Where it's reviewed:
Library Journal, September 15, 2010, page 64
Publishers Weekly, August 2, 2010, page 34

Other books by the same author:
Fatal Revenant, 2007
The Runes of the Earth, 2004
Reave the Just, 1998
The Mirror of Her Dreams, 1986
Lord Foul's Bane, 1977

Other books you might like:
Jim Butcher, *Furies of Calderon*, 2004
Jacqueline Carey, *Godslayer*, 2005
Robert Jordan, *The Eye of the World*, 1990

Brandon Sanderson, *The Hero of Ages*, 2008
Tad Williams, *Shadowmarch: Volume 1*, 2004

`31`

P.N. ELROD

Dark and Stormy Knights

(New York: St. Martin's Griffin, 2010)

Story type: Collection; Urban
Subject(s): Vampires; Supernatural; Magic

Summary: *Dark and Stormy Knights*, edited by P.N. Elrod, includes nine never-before-published urban fantasy stories featuring the most respectable knights in the paranormal world. Each story follows a supernatural human or creature who performs dark duties in the name of good, love, or both. They may be intimidating as they shift shapes or command ancient magic, but each hero uses his or her powers to battle a threatening evil. This collection includes "God's Creatures" by Carrie Vaughn, "A Questionable Client" by Ilona Andrews, and "Even Hand" by Jim Butcher. Sharon K. Butcher, Rachel Caine, and Deidre Knight also contributed stories to this collection.

Where it's reviewed:
Booklist, June 1, 2010, page 46
Publishers Weekly, June 14, 2010, page 39

Other books by the same author:
Song in the Dark, 2005
Cold Streets, 2003
Lady Crymsyn, 2000
The Dark Sleep, 1999
Dance of Death, 1996

Other books you might like:
Ilona Andrews, *Bayou Moon*, 2010
Jim Butcher, *First Lord's Fury*, 2009
Rachel Caine, *Ill Wind*, 2003
Vicki Pettersson, *The Touch of Twilight: The Third Sign of the Zodiac*, 2008
Lilith Saintcrow, *Night Shift*, 2008

`32`

JAMES ENGE

The Wolf Age

(Amherst, New York: Pyr, 2010)

Series: Morlock Series. Book 3
Story type: Sword and Sorcery; Werewolf Story
Subject(s): Fantasy; Werewolves; Magic
Major character(s): Morlock Ambrosius, Sorcerer, Prisoner; Rokhlenu, Werewolf, Prisoner
Time period(s): Indeterminate
Locale(s): Wuruyaaria, Fictional Location

Summary: *The Wolf Age* is an action-packed fantasy novel from author James Enge. The book is the third installment in the Morlock series. Morlock Ambrosius, a powerful sorcerer from the south, winds up being captured and imprisoned in Wuruyaaria, a city overrun with werewolves. In an attempt to block Morlock's magic, the werewolves hammer a glass spike into his skull while he's in jail. Morlock soon befriends his cell-mate, a werewolf named Rokhlenu, whose life was saved by Morlock. As the two prisoners bond, the city of Wuruyaaria is at war with itself, as the werewolves fight for more power. When Morlock and Rokhlenu escape, they find themselves at the center of the tumultuous battle, carrying more power than they ever dreamed possible.

Where it's reviewed:
Library Journal, October 15, 2010, page 72
Locus, November 2010, page 27
Publishers Weekly, August 23, 2010, page 34

Other books by the same author:
Blood of Ambrose, 2009
This Crooked Way, 2009

Other books you might like:
Rowena Cory Daniells, *The King's Bastard*, 2010
Paul Kearney, *This Forsaken Earth*, 2006
Richard A. Knaak, *Beastmaster: Myth*, 2009
Joel Shepherd, *Sasha*, 2009
Matthew Sturges, *The Office of Shadow*, 2010

`33`

JENNIFER FALLON

The Palace of Impossible Dreams

(New York: Tor, 2010)

Series: Tide Lords Series. Book 4
Subject(s): Slavery; Immortality; Magic
Major character(s): Arkady, Slave; Stellan, Spouse (of Arkady); Declan Hawkes, Spy, Friend (of Arkady)
Time period(s): Indeterminate

Summary: The evil Immortals are taking over the world in Jennifer Fallon's *The Palace of Impossible Dreams*, the fourth novel in The Tide Lords series. Mortal Arkady has become a slave and is wracked with grief over the presumed loss of her husband Stellan. The only person she can rely on now is her friend and royal spymaster Declan Hawkes, who, she realizes with dread, isn't even aware of her current circumstances. As this drama unfolds, more and more Immortals are emerging to once again wield their power over the seemingly helpless mortal population.

Where it's reviewed:
Booklist, June 1, 2010, page 47
Library Journal, June 15, 2010, page 66

Other books by the same author:
The Gods of Amyrantha, 2009
The Immortal Prince, 2007
Warlord, 2007
Warrior, 2006
Treason Keep, 2004

Other books you might like:
Raymond E. Feist, *Flight of the Nighthawks*, 2006
David Gemmell, *Ravenheart*, 2001
Elizabeth Haydon, *The Assassin King*, 2006

Dennis L. McKiernan, *Red Slippers*, 2004
Janny Wurts, *Grand Conspiracy*, 2000

34

LISA ROWE FRAUSTINO

The Hole in the Wall

(Minneapolis, Minnesota: Milkweed Editions, 2010)

Story type: Young Readers
Subject(s): Fantasy; Children; Mining
Major character(s): Sebastian "Sebby" Daniels, 11-Year-Old, Twin, Child of an Alcoholic; Barbie Daniels, 11-Year-Old, Twin, Child of an Alcoholic
Time period(s): 21st century; 2010s

Summary: Sebastian "Sebby" Daniels's family is a mess, forcing the 11-year-old boy to find a way to escape from the everyday chaos. Sebby discovers the hole in the wall, a private cave on the edge of the family's property where he can be alone with his imagination. Shortly after discovering the hole in the wall, bizarre things start happening in Sebby's life. From his mother's disappearing chickens to his strange stomachaches, Sebby knows something isn't right. Along with his twin sister, Barbie, Sebby follows the tunnels and paths stretching out from the hole in the wall to the hidden lair of astrophysicist, Stanley Odum, an unusual man with a surprising secret.

Where it's reviewed:
Booklist, December 15, 2010, page 52

Other books by the same author:
The Hickory Chair, 2001

Other books you might like:
James P. Blaylock, *The Knights of the Cornerstone*, 2008
Eoin Colfer, *Artemis Fowl: The Opal Deception*, 2005
Peter Dickinson, *The Changes: A Trilogy*, 1986
Diana Wynne Jones, *Hexwood*, 1993
Vivian Vande Velde, *User Unfriendly*, 1991

35

DAVE FREER
ERIC FLINT , Co-Author
MERCEDES LACKEY , Co-Author

Much Fall of Blood

(Riverdale, New York: Baen, 2010)

Series: Heirs of Alexandria Series. Book 3
Story type: Alternate History
Subject(s): Knights; Wars; Adventure
Major character(s): Prince Manfred, Diplomat; Erik, Bodyguard (of Prince Manfred); Elizabeth Batholdy, Noblewoman (countess); Prince Vlad, Nobleman (duke)
Time period(s): 16th century
Locale(s): Asia; Europe

Summary: In *Much Fall of Blood*, authors Mercedes Lackey, Eric Flint, and Dave Freer present the third

installment in the Heirs of Alexandria series. This outing finds Prince Manfred, his Icelandic bodyguard Erik, and their army of knights escorting a band of Mongol warriors to the Golden Horde leader. But once they arrive, the intentions for a noble mission are destroyed, and the group finds itself embroiled in a civil war that could threaten the future of humanity.

Other books by the same author:
Trio of Sorcery, 2010
Foundation, 2008
Fortune's Fool, 2007
Exile's Valor, 2003
Brightly Burning, 2000

Other books you might like:
Marion Zimmer Bradley, *The Forest House*, 1993
Sara Douglass, *The Nameless Day*, 2004
Barbara Hambly, *Bride of the Rat God*, 1994
Talbot Mundy, *Tros of Samothrace*, 1934
Chelsea Quinn Yarbro, *Ariosto*, 1980

36

IAN GIBSON

Stuff of Legends

(New York: Ace, 2010)

Story type: Legend
Subject(s): Legends; Humor; Fantasy
Major character(s): Elliot, 15-Year-Old; Jordan "Jordan the Red", Hero, Retiree; Kess, Guardian (of Elliot)
Time period(s): Indeterminate

Summary: In Ian Gibson's *Stuff of Legends*, retired hero Jordan the Red is enjoying his time off after a life jam-packed with quests, sword fights, and world travels. While playing chess with a friend, he is approached by 15-year-old Elliot and his Elvish caregiver Kess. Elliot wishes for Jordan the Red to come out of retirement and embark on a quest with him, but Jordan makes it clear that days of rescuing damsels and slaying dragons are in his past—where he really wishes them to remain. Elliot does not take Jordan's rejection lightly and soon, Jordan finds himself on the road again with Elliot and Kess. Gibson details the trios adventures in *Stuff of Legends*.

Where it's reviewed:
Locus, August 2010, page 27

Other books you might like:
Dave Duncan, *Paragon Lost: Tales of the King's Blades*, 2002
David Gemmell, *The Hawk Eternal*, 1996
Barb Hendee, *In Shade and Shadow*, 2009
Paul Kearney, *Corvus*, 2010
Joel Shepherd, *Tracato*, 2010

37

FELIX GILMAN

The Half-Made World

(New York: Tor, 2010)

Story type: Alternate World
Subject(s): Fantasy; Epics; Technology

Major character(s): Dr. Liv Alverhuysen, Psychologist; John Creedmoor, Agent (Agent of the Gun); General, Mentally Ill Person
Time period(s): 19th century
Locale(s): American West

Summary: In *The Half-Made World* by Felix Gilman, a re-imagined American West is populated by opposing forces battling for dominance in an atmosphere of strange technology. The people of the Gun arm themselves with weapons that hold demonic powers. The people of the Line coexist with machines capable of thought. The General—the man who knows how to build a device that would bring peace to the region—is a longtime patient in an asylum. Dr. Liv Alverhuysen, a practitioner of the fledgling field of psychology, may be able to release the General's secrets, but only if she can escape the clutches of a dangerous Gun agent.

Where it's reviewed:
Booklist, September 15, 2010, page 38
Bookmarks, January-February 2010, page 45
Locus, October 2010, page 18
Publishers Weekly, August 23, 2010, page 33

Other books by the same author:
Gears of the City, 2009
Thunderer, 2008

Other books you might like:
Alan Campbell, *God of Clocks*, 2009
Jay Lake, *Mainspring*, 2007
Michael Moorcock, *The Dreamthief's Daughter*, 2001
Michael Swanwick, *The Dragons of Babel*, 2008
Tad Williams, *River of Blue Fire*, 1998

38

LAURA ANNE GILMAN

Weight of Stone

(New York: Gallery Books, 2010)

Series: Vineart War Series. Book 2
Story type: Alternate World
Subject(s): Magic; Voyages and travels; Wars
Major character(s): Jerzy, Apprentice, Slave (former); Ao, Trader; Mahault, Refugee; Kainam, Heir
Time period(s): Indeterminate
Locale(s): Lands Vin, Fictional Location

Summary: The second book of the Vineart War series, Laura Anne Gilman's *Weight of Stone* continues the epic story of four travelers on a mission to find the truth behind the strange war destroying their world. The Lands Vin is a world of magic that enjoys a tenuous peace. Now, the land is threatened by strange outbreaks of violence and terror. Jerzy, Ao, Mahault, and Kainam are about to walk away from all they know and love in order to confront a force of pure evil that will stop at nothing to exact a twisted revenge.

Where it's reviewed:
Library Journal, October 15, 2010, page 72
Publishers Weekly, August 23, 2010, page 34

Other books by the same author:
Blood from Stone, 2009

Flesh and Fire, 2009
Free Fall, 2008
Burning Bridges, 2007
Morgain's Revenge, 2006

Other books you might like:
Sara Douglass, *The Serpent Bride*, 2007
Jennifer Fallon, *The Gods of Amyrantha*, 2009
Elizabeth Haydon, *The Assassin King*, 2006
Katharine Kerr, *The Shadow Isle*, 2008
Juliet Marillier, *Daughter of the Forest*, 2000

39

SIMON R. GREEN

From Hell with Love

(New York: Roc Books, 2010)

Series: Secret Histories Series. Book 4
Story type: Family Saga; Urban
Subject(s): Family history; Murder; Mystery
Major character(s): Eddie Drood, Boyfriend (of Molly); Molly Metcalf, Girlfriend (of Eddie)
Time period(s): Indeterminate

Summary: In Simon Green's *From Hell With Love*, the Droods are anticipating the arrival of Doctor Delirium, an evil man who has vocalized his intentions of purchasing a powerful item at an upcoming auction. The Droods, who have kept humans safe for centuries, are distracted by Delirium's plans when their matriarch is killed. The family immediately takes sides, causing feelings of anger and betrayal to spread throughout the entire group. They have two suspects in the death of their matriarch: Eddie Drood and his girlfriend, Molly Metcalf. Eddie knows he didn't do it, and he also knows exactly how powerful and headstrong Molly can be. This is the fourth book in Green's Secret Histories series.

Where it's reviewed:
Publishers Weekly, April 26, 2010, page 94

Other books by the same author:
Ghost of a Chance, 2010
The Spy Who Haunted Me, 2009
The Unnatural Inquirer, 2008
Guards of Haven, 2007
The Man with the Golden Torc, 2007

Other books you might like:
Glen Cook, *Gilded Latten Bones*, 2010
Dave Duncan, *The Alchemist's Apprentice*, 2007
J. Michael Reaves, *Darkworld Detective*, 1982
Mike Resnick, *Stalking the Unicorn*, 1987
Michelle Sagara, *Cast in Shadow*, 2005

40

JESS HAINES

Hunted by the Others

(New York: Zebra, 2010)

Story type: Mystery; Vampire Story
Subject(s): Vampires; Werewolves; Supernatural

Major character(s): Shiarra Waynest, Detective—Private, Girlfriend (ex, of Chaz); Alec Royce, Vampire; Chaz, Werewolf; Sara, Friend (and business partner, of Shiarra); Arnold, Supernatural Being (mage)
Time period(s): 21st century; 2010s
Locale(s): New York, New York

Summary: In Jess Haines's debut novel, *Hunted by the Others*, a desperate private investigator accepts business from a mage, an Other. Ever since the fall of the Twin Towers in 2001, supernatural and magical beings have swarmed the city, waging endless wars between good and evil. The Others consist of vampires, werewolves, mages, and many other creatures. Although Shiarra Waynest has had experience holding a relationship with an Other—her ex, Chaz, is a werewolf—she's never worked with them until now. The mage asks her to hunt down an artifact and promises to pay her handsomely. When Shiarra finds that the artifact is in the possession of sexy vampire Alec Royce, she turns to Chaz, her partner Sara, and mage Arnold for help.

Where it's reviewed:
Locus, August 2010, page 27
Publishers Weekly, March 1, 2010, page 40

Other books by the same author:
Taken by the Others, 2010

Other books you might like:
Cat Adams, *Siren Song*, 2010
Jeannie Holmes, *Blood Law*, 2010
Adrian Phoenix, *Beneath the Skin*, 2009
Lilith Saintcrow, *To Hell and Back*, 2008

41

LAURELL K. HAMILTON

Bullet

(New York: Berkley Books, 2010)

Series: Anita Blake: Vampire Hunter Series. Book 19
Story type: Horror; Romance
Subject(s): Vampires; Werewolves; Fantasy
Major character(s): Anita Blake, Supernatural Being (necromancer); Jean-Claude, Vampire; Richard Zeeman, Werewolf
Time period(s): 21st century; 2000s
Locale(s): St. Louis, Missouri

Summary: *Bullet* is the nineteenth book in the Anita Blake: Vampire Hunter series by Laurell K. Hamilton. Anita Blake, a necromancer, has been working with Jean-Claude, a very powerful vampire, and Richard Zeeman, a werewolf. Jean-Claude is becoming more powerful every day, bringing back memories of Belle Morte's powers in Europe, despite the fact that Jean-Claude's motives are good. The team learns that assassins are coming to St. Louis to kill them all and must stop the plan before it is too late.

Other books by the same author:
Flirt, 2010
The Harlequin, 2007
Danse Macabre, 2006
Incubus Dreams, 2004
Midnight Cafe, 1996

Other books you might like:
Ilona Andrews, *On the Edge*, 2009
Patricia Briggs, *Cry Wolf*, 2008
Jim Butcher, *Changes*, 2010
Harry Connolly, *Child of Fire*, 2009
Rob Thurman, *Deathwish*, 2009

42

TRACY HICKMAN

Song of the Dragon

(New York: DAW, 2010)

Series: Annals of Drakis Series. Book 1
Subject(s): Dwarfs; Magic; Adventure
Major character(s): Drakis, Slave, Warrior
Time period(s): Indeterminate Past
Locale(s): Rhonas Empire, Fictional Location

Summary: The first book in Tracy Hickman's Annals of Drakis series, *Song of the Dragon* centers on a ruthless slave warrior named Drakis who finds his mission—and his life—forever altered. After capturing a powerful dwarf who practices a unique magic on Drakis, the warrior's eyes are opened to the brutality of his existence and the nefarious plans of his masters. Now Drakis must take on those to whom he was previously allied, and this battle will summon all the forces of good and evil—and all the wits Drakis possesses.

Other books by the same author:
Mystic Empire, 2006
Mystic Quest, 2005
Mystic Warrior, 2004
The Immortals, 1996
Requiem of Stars, 1996

Other books you might like:
Elaine Cunningham, *The Blood Red Harp*, 2006
Troy Denning, *The Siege*, 2001
Richard A. Knaak, *The Black Talon*, 2007
R.A. Salvatore, *The Dame*, 2009
Margaret Weis, *Master of Dragons*, 2005

43

JIM C. HINES

Red Hood's Revenge

(New York: DAW, 2010)

Series: Princess Novel Series. Book 3
Subject(s): Adventure; Fairies; Fairy tales
Major character(s): Roudette, Assassin; Talia, Royalty (princess); Danielle, Royalty (princess); Snow, Royalty (princess)
Time period(s): Indeterminate Past
Locale(s): Arathea, Fictional Location

Summary: In *Red Hood's Revenge*, author Jim C. Hines offers the third outing in the Princess series of reworked fairy tales. This installment centers on the story of Roudette, otherwise known as Little Red Riding Hood, who has transcended her legendary victim status to become a feared warrior and hired assassin. She is recruited to kill a rogue young princess who has escaped her homeland, but when Roudette meets Talia—whom popular legend refers to as Sleeping Beauty—the two join forces with other exiled princesses to fight the evils of the fairies.

Where it's reviewed:
Publishers Weekly, May 31, 2010, page 33

Other books by the same author:
The Mermaid's Madness, 2009
The Stepsister Scheme, 2009
Goblin War, 2008
Goblin Hero, 2007
Goblin Quest, 2004

Other books you might like:
Piers Anthony, *Knot Gneiss*, 2010
Esther M. Friesner, *Elf Defense*, 1988
Craig Shaw Gardner, *A Bad Day for Ali Baba*, 1992
Tom Holt, *The Portable Door*, 2003
Terry Pratchett, *Making Money*, 2007

44

M.K. HOBSON

The Native Star

(New York: Spectra/Ballantine Books, 2010)

Story type: Historical - American West; Witchcraft
Subject(s): Western fiction; Witches; Magic
Major character(s): Emily Edwards, Witch; Dreadnought Stanton, Warlock, Exile
Time period(s): 19th century; 1870s (1876)
Locale(s): Lost Pine, United States

Summary: *The Native Star* is set in the Wild West in 1876. A young witch, Emily Edwards, is slowly losing business now that the villagers of Lost Pine have discovered mail-order magics. In an effort to turn things around, Emily dabbles with a love spell that has disastrous consequences. When Emily finds a magical relic, her life is put in danger by the wicked warlocks desperate to get their hands on it. With her safety at risk, Emily must depend on Dreadnought Stanton, an arrogant warlock from New York who has been exiled to Lost Pine. Together, the pair race across the country in search of the man who can unleash the artifact's power, overwhelmed along the way by their affection for one another.

Where it's reviewed:
Locus, September 2010, page 21

Other books you might like:
James P. Blaylock, *Homunculus*, 1986
Susanna Clarke, *Jonathan Strange & Mr. Norrell*, 2004
Gordon Dahlquist, *The Glass Books of the Dream Eaters: A Novel*, 2006
Cherie Priest, *Boneshaker*, 2009
Jean Rabe, *Steampunk'd*, 2010

45

ANTHONY HOROWITZ

Battles and Quests

(New York: Kingfisher, 2010)

Series: Legends Series. Book 1
Story type: Young Readers
Subject(s): Mythology; Wars; Short stories

Summary: In *Battles and Quests*, author Anthony Horowitz presents an installment in the Legends series, which breathes new life into some of the most famous—and little-known—myths of all time. This collection of short stories focuses on the mythology and folklore surrounding legendary warriors, historic battles, and epic searches for truth and redemption. Among the characters featured in these tales are The Minotaur, King Arthur, and Theseus. Accompanied by Thomas Yeates's illustrations, *Battles and Quests* also contains a quiz to test readers' mythological IQ.

Where it's reviewed:
Horn Book Guide, Fall 2010, page 400

Other books by the same author:
Beasts and Monsters, 2010
Nightrise, 2007
The Silver Citadel, 1986
The Night of the Scorpion, 1985
The Devil's Door-Bell, 1983

Other books you might like:
Patrick H. Adkins, *Lord of the Crooked Paths*, 1987
K.A. Applegate, *Gateway to the Gods*, 2000
Adele Geras, *Troy*, 2000
Diana Wynne Jones, *Castle in the Air*, 1991
Rick Riordan, *The Lightning Thief*, 2005

46

ANTHONY HOROWITZ

Beasts and Monsters

(New York: Kingfisher, 2010)

Story type: Young Readers
Subject(s): Mythology; Monsters; Short stories

Summary: The stories of mythology's greatest ghouls are retold in this collection of short fiction by Anthony Horowitz. Monsters ranging from gorgons to dragons, from Medusa's snake-infested hair to the famed riddle of The Sphinx, are highlighted in this installment of the Legends series. *Beasts and Monsters* includes illustrations by Thomas Yeates and a quiz on mythological weapons.

Where it's reviewed:
School Librarian, Winter 2010, page 229

Other books by the same author:
Battles and Quests, 2010
Nightrise, 2007
The Silver Citadel, 1986
The Night of the Scorpion, 1985

The Devil's Door-Bell, 1983

Other books you might like:
Piers Anthony, *Hasan*, 1969
Toby Bishop, *Airs Beneath the Moon*, 2007
Alan Dean Foster, *Clash of the Titans*, 1981
L. Ron Hubbard, *Slaves of Sleep*, 1948
Katherine Kurtz, *St. Patrick's Gargoyle*, 2001

47

ANTHONY HUSO

The Last Page

(New York: Tor, 2010)

Subject(s): Royalty; Witches; Spies
Major character(s): Caliph Howl, Royalty (King of the Duchy of Stonehold); Sena, Lover (former love of Caliph), Spy
Time period(s): Indeterminate
Locale(s): Duchy of Stonehold, Fictional Location

Summary: In Anthony Huso's *The Last Page*, the land of Stronghold is rife with monsters, corruption, and long-suppressed conspiracies. When young Caliph Howl becomes king, he is far from thrilled about the dark-sided happenings plaguing the Hold. As he attempts to find his way through the problems gripping his homeland, his ex-love Sena returns to him. But Sena, too, has dark secrets of her own: she is now a double agent, and she has come back to Caliph so she can spy on him. First novel.

Where it's reviewed:
Locus, October 2010, page 18
Publishers Weekly, June 28, 2010, page 115

Other books you might like:
Alan Campbell, *Iron Angel*, 2008
Ian R. MacLeod, *The House of Storms*, 2005
China Mieville, *The Scar*, 2002
Michael Swanwick, *The Dragons of Babel*, 2008
Catherynne M. Valente, *Palimpsest*, 2009

48

STACIA KANE

Unholy Magic

(New York: Random House, 2010)

Series: Downside Ghosts. Book 2
Story type: Series; Urban
Subject(s): Fantasy; Mystery; Magic
Major character(s): Chess Putnam, Agent (Church of Real Truth)
Time period(s): Indeterminate Future
Locale(s): Downside, Fictional Location

Summary: In *Unholy Magic* by Stacia Kane, the reanimation of the world's dead has created an atmosphere of violence and terror. Chess Putnam is an agent of the world's new governing body, the Church of the Real Truth. She is also a drug addict. Her latest case involves the brutal killings of Downside's prostitutes. Though members of the undead ranks are the presumed suspects in the murders, Chess believes that the perpetrator is human, but just as dangerous. As she seeks evidence to support her theory, Chess is drawn deeper into Downside's underworld. *Unholy Magic* is the second book in the Downside Ghosts series.

Other books by the same author:
City of Ghosts, 2010
Unholy Ghosts, 2010
Personal Demons, 2008

Other books you might like:
Anya Bast, *Witch Fury*, 2009
Jennifer Estep, *Karma Girl*, 2010
Faith Hunter, *Bloodring*, 2006
Seanan McGuire, *Rosemary and Rue: An October Daye Novel*, 2009
Rob Thurman, *The Grimrose Path*, 2010

49

PAUL KEARNEY

Hawkwood and the Kings

(Oxford, England: Solaris, 2010)

Series: Monarchies of God Series. Book 1
Story type: Alternate World
Subject(s): Fantasy; Religion; Wars
Time period(s): Indeterminate
Locale(s): Normannia, Fictional Location

Summary: *Hawkwood and the Kings* is the first installment in The Monarchies of God series. The entire world has spun into chaos as each region wrestles with its own issues, too busy to care about the affairs of the rest of the world. The ruthless Merduks, disciples of Prophet Ahrimuz, have seized control of the eastern holy city of Aekir, but no one seems to mind. The western kingdoms are battling among themselves and the Church is focused on finding heretics. In a land where magic is forbidden, wars are inevitable, and fantastical beings like were-wolves and sorcerers roam the land, two powerful religions will go head-to-head for ultimate control and domination.

Other books by the same author:
Corvus, 2010
The Ten Thousand, 2008
The Mark of Ran, 2005
Ships from the West, 2002
The Heretic Kings, 1996

Other books you might like:
James Barclay, *Noonshade*, 2000
Dave Duncan, *The Gilded Chain: A Tale of the King's Blades*, 1998
David Gemmell, *Ironhand's Daughter: A Novel of the Hawk Queen*, 1995
Fritz Leiber, *The First Book of Lankhmar*, 2001
Jack Vance, *Cugel's Saga*, 1983

50

PAUL KEARNEY

Corvus

(Oxford, United Kingdom: Solaris, 2010)

Story type: Alternate World; Series
Subject(s): Adventure; Wars; Violence
Major character(s): Rictus, Military Personnel (captain); Corvus, Leader (who wants to take over the Empire)
Time period(s): Indeterminate Past
Locale(s): Macht, Fictional Location

Summary: In Paul Kearney's *Corvus*, a power-hungry warrior rumored to be half-man and half-god is taking over the Asurian Empire one kingdom at a time. His army slaughters the villages they pass through; the survivors immediately bow to their new king—King Corvus. In Macht, a worn military captain named Rictus hears of Corvus's destruction and knows the tyrant will soon come his way. More than 20 years ago, Rictus led ten thousand men to victory—the Macht army had never been stronger than it was under his control. Corvus has heard the stories of Rictus's victory and knows that with Rictus on his side, he would soon take control of the entire Empire, including Macht.

Other books by the same author:
Hawkwood and the Kings, 2010
The Ten Thousand, 2008
The Mark of Ran, 2005
Ships from the West, 2002
The Heretic Kings, 1996

Other books you might like:
Steven Brust, *The Phoenix Guards*, 1991
Dave Duncan, *The Jaguar Knights*, 2004
James Enge, *The Wolf Age*, 2010
David Gemmell, *Midnight Falcon*, 1999
Joel Shepherd, *Petrodor*, 2010

51

MARY ROBINETTE KOWAL

Shades of Milk and Honey

(New York: Tor, 2010)

Story type: Romance
Subject(s): Sisters; Magic; Love
Major character(s): Jane Ellsworth, Sister (of Melody); Melody Ellsworth, Sister (of Jane); Mr. Vincent, Artist
Time period(s): 19th century
Locale(s): United Kingdom

Summary: Two sisters in Regency-era England struggle with the vagaries of love and the power of magic in Mary Robinette Kowal's *Shades of Milk and Honey*. Jane Ellsworth is an ordinary girl with a particular penchant for magic. Her sister Melody is ravishingly beautiful but lacks Jane's prowess with the mystical arts. In the hopes of finding suitable men for marriage, the sisters become involved with the goings-on of their neighbors—and love, heartbreak, and magical fantasy ensue. First novel.

Where it's reviewed:
Booklist, August 1, 2010, page 36
Library Journal, June 15, 2010, page 68
Locus, August 2010, page 25
Publishers Weekly, June 14, 2010, page 40

Other books you might like:
Jonathan Barnes, *The Somnambulist*, 2007
Susanna Clarke, *Jonathan Strange & Mr. Norrell*, 2004
Gordon Dahlquist, *The Dark Volume*, 2009
Neil Gaiman, *Neverwhere*, 1997
China Mieville, *Kraken*, 2010

52

NICK KYME

Grimblades

(Nottingham, United Kingdom: The Black Library, 2010)

Story type: Alternate World
Subject(s): Adventure; Wars; Violence
Major character(s): Prince Wilhelm, Leader (of the Grimblades); Emperor Dieter IV, Leader (Emperor)
Time period(s): Indeterminate Past

Summary: In Nick Kyme's *Grimblades*, the Empire is under attack and the Grimblades appear to be the only group fighting to defend their home. The orcs and goblins have declared war on the entire Empire. Having never received word from Emperor Dieter IV as to how to defend their territory, Grimblades leader, Prince Wilhelm, decides it's up to him and his men to save the Empire. While they fight, the men discover the greenskins—and possibly men within their own kingdom—are planning to execute the prince. Can the courageous Grimblades save their prince and the Empire, or will one suffer as they fight for the other?

Other books by the same author:
Firedrake, 2010
Honourkeeper, 2009
Salamander, 2009
Oathbreaker, 2008
Back from the Dead, 2006

Other books you might like:
Robert Earl, *Ancient Blood*, 2008
Anthony Reynolds, *Knight of the Realm*, 2009
Aaron Rosenberg, *Hour of the Daemon*, 2007
C.L. Werner, *Wulfrik*, 2010
Chris Wraight, *Dark Storm Gathering*, 2009

53

MERCEDES LACKEY

Finding the Way and Other Tales of Valdemar

(New York: DAW, 2010)

Subject(s): Magic; Adventure; Short stories
Locale(s): Valdemar, Fictional Location

Summary: In *Finding the Way and Other Tales of Valdemar*, author and editor Mercedes Lackey compiles a series of tales set in the mythical land of Valdemar. The stories that comprise this volume continue to illuminate the multifaceted world, spotlighting its diverse history, unique characters, and intricate social customs and traditions. Authors contributing to this volume include Tanya Huff, Fiona Patton, and Judith Tarr.

Other books by the same author:
Trio of Sorcery, 2010
Foundation, 2008
Fortune's Fool, 2007
Exile's Valor, 2003
Brightly Burning, 2000

Other books you might like:
Jacqueline Carey, *Naamah's Kiss*, 2009
Sara Douglass, *The Infinity Gate*, 2010
Lynn Flewelling, *The White Road*, 2009
Lois McMaster Bujold, *The Sharing Knife: Horizon*, 2009
Diana L. Paxson, *Ancestors of Avalon*, 2004

54

MERCEDES LACKEY

Intrigues

(New York: DAW Hardcover, 2010)

Series: Collegium Chronicles Series. Book 2
Story type: Series
Subject(s): Adventure; Alternative worlds; Children
Major character(s): Magpie, Boy, 13-Year-Old, Orphan
Time period(s): Indeterminate Future
Locale(s): Haven, Fictional Location

Summary: Shortly after young Magpie is orphaned, he finds himself being whisked away by a Companion horse of Valdemar in *Intrigues*. Magpie is taken to the land of Haven, where he will train to be a herald. However, no one knows about his secret power of telepathy. Just when things start looking up, Magpie finds himself in trouble. Soon, people in the kingdom begin to suspect Magpie of being a spy. Now, Magpie must find a way to prove his innocence before it's too late. This is the second book in author Mercedes Lackey's Collegium Chronicles series.

Where it's reviewed:
Locus, November 2010, page 29

Other books by the same author:
Trio of Sorcery, 2010
Foundation, 2008
Fortune's Fool, 2007
Exile's Valor, 2003
Brightly Burning, 2000

Other books you might like:
Kate Elliott, *Traitor's Gate*, 2009
Elizabeth Haydon, *Rhapsody: Child of Blood*, 1999
Katharine Kerr, *The Spirit Stone*, 2007
Juliet Marillier, *Cybele's Secret*, 2008
Michelle West, *City of Night*, 2010

55

DAWN LAIRAMORE

Ivy's Ever After

(New York: Holiday House, 2010)

Story type: Young Readers
Subject(s): Dragons; Royalty; Fairy tales
Major character(s): Ivy, Royalty (princess), 14-Year-Old
Time period(s): Indeterminate Past
Locale(s): Ardendale, Fictional Location

Summary: Dawn Lairamore's *Ivy's Ever After* chronicles the story of 14-year-old Princess Ivy, who, in keeping with an ancient ritual, is sentenced to imprisonment in a tower until her prince rescues her. Guarded by a dragon, Ivy is determined to do anything it takes to avoid marriage to an evil prince. With the help of her dragon-guard Eldridge, Ivy escapes the tower and flees. But she soon uncovers a plan that could put the fate of the entire kingdom in jeopardy—and she may be the only one who can stop it.

Where it's reviewed:
Booklist, May 15, 2010, page 53
Horn Book Guide, Fall 2010, page 345
School Library Journal, August 2010, page 106

Other books you might like:
Gillian Bradshaw, *The Land of Gold*, 1992
Bryan Buchan, *The Dragon Children*, 1975
Jackie French Koller, *The Dragonling*, 1990
Mercedes Lackey, *Joust*, 2003
Shirley Rousseau Murphy, *Nightpool*, 1985

56

L. JAGI LAMPLIGHTER

Prospero in Hell

(New York: Tor, 2010)

Subject(s): Father-daughter relations; Magic; Hell
Major character(s): Miranda, Daughter (of Prospero); Prospero, Sorcerer, Hostage
Time period(s): 21st century; 2010s

Summary: In *Prospero in Hell*, author L. Jagi Lamplighter continues the mythic adventures first begun in *Prospero Lost*. The legendary sorcerer Prospero has vanished into hell after one of his magical spells went dangerously amiss. Now his daughter Miranda must locate her father and rescue him from the powerful forces of evil that hold him hostage. In order to do so, she will have to investigate her own family's dark history and come face to face with a startling truth about her heritage.

Where it's reviewed:
Library Journal, June 15, 2010, page 66
Publishers Weekly, June 14, 2010, page 37

Other books by the same author:
Prospero Lost, 2009

Other books you might like:
Dave Duncan, *Ill Met in the Arena*, 2008
Jennifer Fallon, *The Immortal Prince*, 2008

Lynn Flewelling, *Shadows Return*, 2008
Simon R. Green, *Blue Moon Rising*, 1991
Ken Scholes, *Antiphon*, 2010

57

GLENDA LARKE

Stormlord Rising

(New York: Hachette, 2010)

Series: Stormlord Series. Book 2
Story type: Alternate World; Series
Subject(s): Fantasy; Deserts; Epics
Major character(s): Shale, Outcast; Terelle, Slave
Time period(s): Indeterminate
Locale(s): The Quartern, Fictional Location

Summary: In *Stormlord Rising* by Glenda Larke, the cities of the Quartern are suffering under drought and their only hope for survival lies with the Stormlord. But now that the last of the Stormlords is dead, the population faces a violent struggle. Shale, once a misfit, has developed powers that could help the cities' plight, but he is attacked and turned over to his opponent. Terelle, who has fled to find a source of water, is drawn back to the Quartern to help Shale in his quest to save the cities' residents as the next Stormlord. *Stormlord Rising* is the second book in the Stormlord series.

Other books by the same author:
The Last Stormlord, 2010
Gilfeather, 2004
The Tainted, 2004
The Aware, 2003

Other books you might like:
Lynn Abbey, *Rifkind's Challenge*, 2006
Jennifer Fallon, *Treason Keep*, 2004
Lynn Flewelling, *Hidden Warrior*, 2003
Maggie Furey, *Echo of Eternity*, 2003
Tanith Lee, *Anackire*, 1983

58

MARJORIE M. LIU

A Wild Light

(New York: Ace, 2010)

Series: Hunter Kiss Series. Book 3
Story type: Mystery; Romance
Subject(s): Demons; Romances (Fiction); Murder
Major character(s): Maxine Kiss, Hunter (of demons), Demon; Grant Cooperon, Lover (of Maxine)
Time period(s): 21st century; 2010s

Summary: In Marjorie M. Liu's *A Wild Light*, exorcist and demon hunter, Maxine Kiss receives the worst birthday present she could ever imagine: waking up covered in her own grandfather's blood. She cannot remember what happened, but she fears that she might be responsible for his death. Being part demon herself, Maxine knows that evil lurks inside of her, but she has always been able to control her powers and use them to save humans from demons like her and her family members. Maxine searches for clues that point her to a suspect other than herself and calls on her long time love interest, Grant Cooperon, for help. The two grow close as they hunt for the murderer. This is the third book in the Hunter Kiss series.

Other books by the same author:
The Fire King, 2009
The Wild Road, 2008
Soul Song, 2007
Eye of Heaven, 2006
The Red Heart of Jade, 2006

Other books you might like:
Lynn Abbey, *Rifkind's Challenge*, 2006
Jennifer Fallon, *Medalon*, 2000
Violette Malan, *The Sleeping God*, 2007
Diana L. Paxson, *The Golden Hills of Westria*, 2006
Elizabeth Vaughan, *Destiny's Star*, 2010

59

TOM LLOYD

The Ragged Man

(Amherst, New York: Pyr, 2010)

Series: Twilight Reign Series. Book 4
Subject(s): Wars; Adventure; Magic
Major character(s): King Emin, Royalty; Count Vesna, Nobleman; Tila, Girlfriend (of Count Vesna)
Time period(s): Indeterminate
Locale(s): The Land, Fictional Location

Summary: After the death of Lord Isak, King Emin is forced to continue waging war against enemies of the Land. One solider, Count Vesna, is filled with personal turmoil over the lack of support he has received from those closest to him. And as these dramas play out, an even darker threat is looming on the horizon—a threat that could escalate the war-torn Land into sheer chaos. *The Ragged Man* is the fourth book in Tom Lloyd's Twilight Reign series.

Where it's reviewed:
Library Journal, August 2010, page 72

Other books by the same author:
The Grave Thief, 2008
The Twilight Herald, 2007
The Stormcaller, 2006

Other books you might like:
James Barclay, *Cry of the Newborn*, 2005
Anne Bishop, *Shalador's Lady*, 2010
Eric Flint, *The Philosophical Strangler*, 2001
Juliet E. McKenna, *Irons in the Fire*, 2009
Jon Sprunk, *Shadow's Son*, 2010

Fantasy Fiction

60

NATHAN LONG

Bloodborn

(Lenton, Nottingham, England: Black Library, 2010)

Subject(s): Vampires; Crime; Murder
Major character(s): Ulrika, Vampire, Investigator; Gabriella, Vampire, Investigator
Time period(s): Indeterminate
Locale(s): Nuln, Fictional Location

Summary: Nathan Long's *Bloodborn* is a horror novel set in the Warhammer universe. Ulrika is still adjusting to her new life as a newly made vampire when she becomes involved in dangerous investigation. When a fellow vampire is murdered in Nuln, Ulrika accompanies her mentor, Gabriella, to the crime scene. It doesn't take long for the vampires to discover that the murder was much more than a random crime. Someone, or something, is hoping to destroy the Lahmian lineage for good. Despite the fact that their very existence is at stake, Ulrika and Gabriella will stop at nothing to find out who is responsible.

Other books by the same author:
Shamanslayer, 2009
Elfslayer, 2008
Blackhearts, 2007
Orcslayer, 2006
The Broken Lance, 2005

Other books you might like:
Nick Kyme, *Grimblades*, 2010
Graham McNeill, *Empire*, 2009
Gav Thorpe, *Malekith*, 2009
C.L. Werner, *Wulfrik*, 2010
Chris Wraight, *Sword of Justice*, 2010

61

JAMES LOVEGROVE

The Age of Zeus

(London: Solaris, 2010)

Subject(s): Adventure; Mythology; Wars
Major character(s): Sam Akehurst, Police Officer (former police officer)
Time period(s): 21st century; 2010s

Summary: In James Lovegrove's *The Age of Zeus*, the immortal Greek Gods have come back to Earth in human form, ready to once again exert their power over the masses. Once they have achieved this end, humanity lives under the oppression of the Gods...until a rogue band of warriors decides to take them on. Ex-police officer Sam Akehurst is recruited to join the group, which calls itself the Titans and is preparing to engage in an epic battle with the Olympians.

Other books by the same author:
The Age of Ra, 2009
Provender Gleed, 2005
Worldstorm, 2004

Untied Kingdom, 2003
Imagined Slights, 2002

Other books you might like:
Peter Dickinson, *The Changes: A Trilogy*, 1986
Edmond Hamilton, *A Yank at Valhalla*, 1973
Thorne Smith, *The Night Life of the Gods*, 1931
S.M. Stirling, *Dies the Fire*, 2004
Roger Zelazny, *Lord of Light*, 1967

62

ALEXANDRA MACKENZIE

Immortal Quest: The Trouble with Mages

(Kentwood, Louisiana: EDGE, 2010)

Story type: Urban
Subject(s): Fantasy; Urban life; Crime
Major character(s): Nick Watson, Detective—Police; Marlen, Thief
Time period(s): 21st century; 2010s
Locale(s): London, England

Summary: In *Immortal Quest: The Trouble with Mages* by Alexandra MacKenzie, London police detective, Nick Watson takes a case that is much more complicated than it first seems. When Watson meets a thief named Marlen, the small-time crook tries to convince the detective that he is a centuries-old magician on a mission to recover a powerful object. He also says that Watson himself is an amnesiac who has forgotten their long-term relationship. Practical Watson doesn't want to believe Marlen's claims, but when he becomes a British secret agent, he learns that the government is very interested in the mage's fantastic story.

Other books you might like:
Jim Butcher, *Side Jobs: Stories from the Dresden Files*, 2010
Harry Connolly, *Game of Cages*, 2010
Charles de Lint, *Mulengro: A Romany Tale*, 1985
Simon R. Green, *Hell to Pay*, 2007
Tanya Huff, *Smoke and Mirrors*, 2005

63

VIOLETTE MALAN

Path of the Sun

(New York: DAW Books, 2010)

Series: Dhulyn and Parno Series. Book 4
Story type: Alternate World
Subject(s): Missing persons; Royalty; Fantasy
Major character(s): Dhulyn, Mercenary; Parno, Mercenary
Time period(s): Indeterminate
Locale(s): Menoin, Fictional Location

Summary: *Path of the Sun* is the fourth installment in the Dhulyn and Parno series. The two mercenaries are sent out on a mission by the Mercenary Brotherhood, but their responsibility is greater than they know. They think they're supposed to escort Princess of Arderon to Menoin for her upcoming nuptials with their Tarkin, but really the Brotherhood wants them to investigate the disappearance of two mercenaries from Menoin. When Dhulyn and Parno arrive, they soon discover that a series of brutal murders might be connected to the brothers' disappearance. When the princess's mutilated body is found, Dhulyn and Parno must follow the killer to a dangerous labyrinth known as the Path of the Sun, a mysterious place from where they might never return.

Other books by the same author:
The Storm Witch, 2009
The Soldier King, 2008
The Mirror Prince, 2007

Other books you might like:
Simon R. Green, *Haven of Lost Souls*, 1999
Robin Hobb, *Assassin's Quest*, 1997
Fritz Leiber, *Farewell to Lankhmar*, 1998
Marjorie M. Liu, *Tiger Eye*, 2005
Jennifer Roberson, *Sword-Dancer*, 1986

64

LYN MCCONCHIE

The Questing Road

(New York: Tor, 2010)

Story type: Alternate World
Subject(s): Fantasy; Demons; Alternative worlds
Time period(s): Indeterminate

Summary: When a young horse disappears, several farmers embark on a quest to find it. During their search, they inadvertently enter a portal into another world. A short time later, a cat also disappears, sending its Lord and Lady through the same portal. The two groups meet in the strange new land only to discover a terrible truth. The foal and cat have been taken as part of a supernatural ritual to unleash an army of demons on the world. The two groups must work together to foil the plan, lest the dark and powerful forces destroy the world.

Where it's reviewed:
Library Journal, August 2010, page 72

Other books you might like:
Elizabeth H. Boyer, *Keeper of Cats*, 1995
P.N. Elrod, *The Adventures of Myhr*, 2003
Esther M. Friesner, *Majyk by Accident*, 1993
Mercedes Lackey, *Reserved for the Cat*, 2007
Tad Williams, *Tailchaser's Song*, 1986

65

L.J. MCDONALD

The Shattered Sylph

(New York: Leisure Books, 2010)

Series: Sylph Series. Book 3
Subject(s): Alternative worlds; Slavery; Romances (Fiction)

Major character(s): Ril, Supernatural Being (sylph); Lizzy Petrule, Young Woman, Slave

Summary: *The Shattered Sylph* is the sequel to fantasy romance author L.J. McDonald's *The Battle Sylph*. It is years after Ril the Sylph faced that treacherous battle with Eferem upon the rocky cliffs. Now he is free, but in his mind he still feels just as much a slave as ever. However, when he learns that Lizzy Petrule has been enslaved and taken away, he vows to save her—even if he isn't allowed to love her.

Other books by the same author:
The Battle Sylph, 2009

Other books you might like:
Alyssa Day, *Atlantis Rising*, 2007
Sherrilyn Kenyon, *Born of Ice*, 2009
Marjorie M. Liu, *The Fire King*, 2009
Nalini Singh, *Bonds of Justice*, 2010
Elizabeth Vaughan, *Warprize*, 2005

66

SEANAN MCGUIRE

An Artificial Night

(New York: DAW Books, 2010)

Series: October Daye Series. Book 3
Story type: Urban
Subject(s): Fantasy; Fairies; Kidnapping
Major character(s): October "Toby" Daye, Supernatural Being (half-human, half-fae), Knight; Blind Michael, Villain
Time period(s): 21st century; 2010s
Locale(s): United States

Summary: *An Artificial Night* is a suspenseful urban fantasy novel from author Seanan McGuire. The book is the third installation in the October Daye series, focusing on the girl of half-human/half-fae descent. October "Toby" Daye has tried to leave behind her faerie heritage to no avail. Now, she's been knighted and is a respected leader in her community. When fae and mortal children are kidnapped, all signs point to the villainous Blind Michael. It's up to Toby to confront Blind Michael and try to rescue the children, but there are only three magical roads that lead to Michael's realm and each one can only be traveled once. If Toby makes a mistake on her journey, she could end up trapped among Blind Michael and the Wild Hunt forever.

Where it's reviewed:
Locus, October 2010, page 25
Publishers Weekly, July 26, 2010, page 58

Other books by the same author:
A Local Habitation, 2010
Rosemary and Rue: An October Daye Novel, 2009

Other books you might like:
Ilona Andrews, *On the Edge*, 2009
Yasmine Galenorn, *Darkling*, 2008
Devon Monk, *Magic at the Gate*, 2010
Laura Resnick, *Doppelgangster*, 2010
Kat Richardson, *Labyrinth*, 2010

67

JULIET E. MCKENNA

Banners in the Wind

(Oxford: Solaris, 2010)

Series: Chronicles of the Lescari Revolution Series. Book 3
Story type: Alternate World; Series
Subject(s): Alternative worlds; Fantasy; Epics
Time period(s): Indeterminate
Locale(s): Vanam, Fictional Location

Summary: In *Banners in the Wind* by Juliet McKenna, the world of Vanam is plagued by war. The Lescar have enacted a plan to depose the current rulers, hoping the subsequent revolution will eventually bring harmony. But during the days of turmoil that follow the Lescari exile, they realize how complicated—and dangerous—their world has become. While they fight for their original goal, they know that all will not live to see the realization of their vision. *Banners in the Wind* is the third book in the Chronicles of the Lescari Revolution series.

Other books by the same author:
Blood in the Water, 2009
Irons in the Fire, 2009
Southern Fire, 2005
The Assassin's Edge, 2002
The Gambler's Fortune, 2000

Other books you might like:
Jacqueline Carey, *Banewreaker*, 2004
Jennifer Fallon, *Harshini*, 2005
Robin Hobb, *Renegade's Magic: Book Three of the Soldier Son Trilogy*, 2008
J.V. Jones, *A Cavern of Black Ice*, 1999
Mickey Zucker Reichert, *The Return of Nightfall*, 2004

68

PATRICIA A. MCKILLIP

The Bards of Bone Plain

(New York: Ace Books, 2010)

Subject(s): Poetry; Adventure; Magic
Major character(s): Phelan Cle, Student; Princess Beatrice, Archaeologist; Nairn, Wanderer
Time period(s): Indeterminate Past
Locale(s): Bone Plain, Fictional Location

Summary: In Patricia A. McKillip's *The Bards of Bone Plain*, Phelan Cle is a student preparing for a career as a bard. With his studies nearly complete, he must now write his thesis. He chooses what seems like an easy enough topic to research: the story of Bone Plain, where, legend has it, the world of poetry first began. But the more Phelan learns about Bone Plain, the more mysterious the place seems to him, and he sets out to uncover the truth about this fabled locale and its magical history.

Where it's reviewed:
Booklist, December 15, 2010, page 28

Library Journal, December 2010, page 107
Publishers Weekly, October 25, 2010, page 34

Other books by the same author:
The Bell at Sealey Head, 2008
Cygnet, 2007
Harrowing the Dragon, 2005
Od Magic, 2005
Ombria in Shadow, 2003

Other books you might like:
Raymond E. Feist, *King of Foxes*, 2004
L.E. Modesitt, *Mage-Guard of Hamor*, 2008
R.A. Salvatore, *The Highwayman*, 2004
Freda Warrington, *The Court of the Midnight King*, 2010
Lawrence Watt-Evans, *Above His Proper Station*, 2010

69

KELLY MEDING

As Lie the Dead

(New York: Dell, 2010)

Series: Dreg City Series. Book 2
Story type: Series; Urban
Subject(s): Fantasy; Urban life; Vampires
Major character(s): Evangeline Stone, Bounty Hunter
Time period(s): 21st century; 2010s
Locale(s): United States

Summary: In *As Lie the Dead* by Kelly Meding, a bounty hunter has been afflicted with the ability to resurrect herself again and again in different host bodies. Though Evangeline Stone's existence is unpleasant, her survival is necessary if the recent slaughter of shapeshifters is to be avenged. One of the few remaining shapeshifters, a pregnant woman, convinces Evangeline to join her quest for justice. But while Evangeline deals with increasing unrest among the werewolf, vampire, and gremlin populations, she also realizes that she is being targeting by a killer. *As Lie the Dead* is the second book in the Dreg City series.

Other books by the same author:
Three Days to Dead, 2009

Other books you might like:
Joanne Bertin, *The Last Dragonlord*, 1998
Louise Cooper, *The Sleep of Stone*, 1991
Sarah A. Hoyt, *Draw One in the Dark*, 2006
Jennifer Roberson, *The Lion Throne*, 2001
Fred Saberhagen, *Dancing Bears*, 1996

70

CHINA MIEVILLE

Kraken

(New York: Tor, 2010)

Subject(s): Squid; Adventure; Cults
Major character(s): Billy Harrow, Museum Curator, Scientist; Dane Parnell, Warrior, Cult Member; Leon,

Friend (of Billy); Marge, Friend (of Billy); Goss, Murderer; Subby, Murderer; The Tattoo, Criminal; Wati, Spirit, Labor Leader
Time period(s): Indeterminate Future
Locale(s): London, United Kingdom

Summary: In *Kraken*, award-winning fantasy author China Mieville tells the story of Billy Harrow, a museum curator in London, who finds himself at the center of an eerie adventure when a massive four-ton giant squid he helped preserve disappears from his museum. After a series of unusual happenings land Billy in trouble with both the authorities and the increasingly agitated cults of London - some of whom worship the now-missing squid - he goes on the run with former squid cult member Dane through London's secret underworld of magic to find the missing "kraken". As the two make their way across London, they encounter a bizarre series of magicians, policemen, assassins, supernatural labor leaders, and other macabre undesirables - and the distinct possibility of that the Apocalypse (or several Apocalypses) may be right around the corner.

Where it's reviewed:
Locus, June 2010, page 14

Other books by the same author:
The City & the City, 2009
Un Lun Dun, 2007
Looking for Jake, 2005
Iron Council, 2004
The Scar, 2002

Other books you might like:
James P. Blaylock, *The Paper Grail*, 1991
John Crowley, *Aegypt*, 1987
Mark Frost, *The List of Seven*, 1993
Andrew Klavan, *The Uncanny*, 1998
Tim Powers, *Three Days to Never*, 2006

| 71 |

L.E. MODESITT

Imager's Intrigue
(New York: Tor Books, 2010)

Series: Imager Portfolio Series. Book 3
Story type: Alternate World; Political
Subject(s): Alternative worlds; Supernatural; Wars
Major character(s): Rhennthyl, (Imager), Spouse, Father; Seliora, Spouse (wife of Rhennthyl)
Time period(s): Indeterminate
Locale(s): L'Excelcis, Fictional Location

Summary: In L.E. Modesitt Jr.'s *Imager's Intrigue: The Third Book of the Imager Portfolio*, Rhennthyl has finally found comfort in his life. He's a husband, a father, and an Imager. He also has a comfortable working relationship with the local law officials. This is all threatened, however, when a war begins and two of the most powerful Imagers in the world are killed. Now, Rhen is the single most powerful Imager and he has become a target. His skills—which include imagining items into different shapes and, possibly, existence—are in high demand. If he refuses to use his skills for his enemy's gain, he faces a death sentence.

Where it's reviewed:
Booklist, June 1, 2010, page 4

Other books by the same author:
Imager, 2009
Imager's Challenge, 2009
Mage-Guard of Hamor, 2008
Natural Ordermage, 2007
Ordermaster, 2005

Other books you might like:
Raymond E. Feist, *Into a Dark Realm*, 2007
L. Jagi Lamplighter, *Prospero Lost*, 2009
George R.R. Martin, *A Game of Thrones*, 1996
Brandon Sanderson, *Mistborn*, 2006
Lawrence Watt-Evans, *The Wizard Lord*, 2006

| 72 |

DEVON MONK

A Cup of Normal
(Auburn, Washington: Fairwood Press, Inc., 2010)

Story type: Alternate World
Subject(s): Alternative worlds; Monsters; Robotics

Summary: In the short-fiction collection *A Cup of Normal*, author Devon Monk blends the normal with the fantastical to create a world that readers will find both recognizable and unfamiliar. In these stories, apparently normal human girls walk the streets, and vampires work as seamstresses. Robots and monsters search for love and trust, and humans continue to struggle with keeping secrets that could tear apart families and end friendships with other humans and evolving creatures. Monk's humor is dark, but his characters are full of life and energy. He is also the author of *Magic to the Bone* and *Magic in the Blood*.

Where it's reviewed:
Locus, October 2010, page 19
Publishers Weekly, July 26, 2010, page 56

Other books by the same author:
Magic at the Gate, 2010
Magic in the Blood, 2009
Magic in the Shadows, 2009
Magic to the Bone, 2008

Other books you might like:
Jeffrey Ford, *The Empire of Ice Cream*, 2006
Charlaine Harris, *A Touch of Dead: Sookie Stackhouse: The Complete Stories*, 2009
Nina Kiriki Hoffman, *Past the Size of Dreaming*, 2001
Tanya Huff, *Finding Magic*, 2007
Pamela Sargent, *Eye of Flame and Other Fantasies*, 2004

| 73 |

ERIC NYLUND

All That Lives Must Die
(New York: Tor, 2010)

Series: Mortal Coils Series. Book 2
Subject(s): Twins; High schools; Angels

Major character(s): Eliot Post, Twin (of Fiona), 15-Year-Old; Fiona Post, 15-Year-Old, Twin (of Eliot); Henry, Uncle (of Eliot and Fiona); Miss Weston, Administrator (headmistress); Mr. Ma, Teacher
Time period(s): 21st century; 2010s
Summary: 15-year-olds Eliot and Fiona Post are not typical twins. They are the progeny of the goddess Atropos and the evil angel Lucifer. They have also just discovered they possess rare magical powers. Now Eliot and Fiona are attending the cutthroat Paxington School, where their newfound mystical abilities will be put to the ultimate test. *All That Lives Must Die* is the second book in Eric Nylund's Mortal Coils series.

Where it's reviewed:
Booklist, July 1, 2010, page 43
Library Journal, June 15, 2010, page 67
Publishers Weekly, May 24, 2010, page 40

Other books by the same author:
Mortal Coils, 2009
A Game of Universe, 2007
Ghosts of Onyx, 2006
Dry Water, 1997
Pawn's Dream, 1995

Other books you might like:
Charlie Fletcher, *Stoneheart*, 2007
Katherine Kurtz, *St. Patrick's Gargoyle*, 2001
Rick Riordan, *The Lightning Thief*, 2005
J.K. Rowling, *Harry Potter and the Sorcerer's Stone*, 1998
John C. Wright, *Orphans of Chaos*, 2005

74

PATTI O'SHEA

In the Darkest Night
(New York: Tor, 2010)

Series: Light Warriors Series. Book 4
Story type: Romance
Subject(s): Demons; Magic; Love
Major character(s): Kel Andrews, Troubleshooter; Farran, Young Woman (novice mage)
Time period(s): 21st century; 2010s
Locale(s): Seattle, Washington

Summary: *In the Darkest Night* is the fourth installment in Patti O'Shea's Light Warriors series of fantasy romances. This novel follows Kel Andrews as he deals with the emotional fallout from his time spent as a tortured hostage. Into his world of night terrors and rampant pain comes Farran, a young woman on the run from a demon. She has come seeking Kel's help, but are his fighting spirit and wounded heart up to this latest challenge?

Where it's reviewed:
Publishers Weekly, February 15, 2010, page 120

Other books by the same author:
Edge of Dawn, 2009
In Twilight's Shadow, 2008
In the Midnight Hour, 2007
Through a Crimson Veil, 2007
Ravyn's Flight, 2002

Other books you might like:
Patricia Briggs, *Bone Crossed*, 2009
Rachel Caine, *Undone*, 2009
Kim Harrison, *Black Magic Sanction*, 2010
Marjorie M. Liu, *The Wild Road*, 2008
Elizabeth Vaughan, *White Star*, 2009

75

NNEDI OKORAFOR

Who Fears Death
(New York: Penguin, 2010)

Story type: Futuristic
Subject(s): Fantasy; Magic; Genocide
Major character(s): Onyesonwu, Sorceress
Time period(s): Indeterminate Future
Locale(s): Africa

Summary: In *Who Fears Death* by Nnedi Okorafor, a young woman conceived by her mother's rape works to assume her role in a futurist Africa dominated by violence. Onyesonwu (her name means "who fears death?") is the child of two races but is welcomed by neither. But the strong-willed girl recognizes her magical powers at an early age and follows her destiny despite the obstacles posed by her ethnicity and sex. Amidst threats of genocide and female suppression that have endured on the continent for centuries, Onyesonwu embarks on a journey that could save her people but take her own life.

Where it's reviewed:
Library Journal, June 15, 2010, page 68
Locus, June 2010, page 14
Publishers Weekly, April 5, 2010, page 51

Other books by the same author:
Long Juju Man, 2009
The Shadow Speaker, 2009
Zahrar the Windseeker, 2008

Other books you might like:
Tananarive Due, *The Living Blood*, 2001
Elizabeth Haydon, *The Floating Island*, 2006
Lee Killough, *The Leopard's Daughter*, 1987
Nancy Springer, *Plumage*, 2000
Amos Tutuola, *The Palm-Wine Drinkard and his Dead Palm-Wine Tapster in the Dead's Town*, 1984

76

PIERRE PEVEL

The Cardinal's Blades
(Amherst, New York: Pyr, 2010)

Story type: Alternate History
Subject(s): Fantasy; Dragons; Spies
Major character(s): Richelieu, Religious (cardinal), Leader
Time period(s): 17th century
Locale(s): Paris, France

Summary: *The Cardinal's Blades* is a fantasy novel from award-winning French author, Pierre Pevel. The people of 17th-century Paris are no strangers to dragons. Harmless dragonets wander their streets like stray animals, while domesticated wyverns are ridden and flown by men through the skies of Paris, but the Spain's Black Claw cult are a dangerous breed of dragons posing a threat to France's peace. Cardinal Richelieu must reunite the Cardinal's Blades, an elite army of skilled warriors, to fight the enemy. As the nation's last hope, the Cardinal's Blades must fight against the terrifying Black Claws and uproot traitorous spies from within Paris.

Where it's reviewed:
Library Journal, September 15, 2010, page 65
Publishers Weekly, August 30, 2010, page 34

Other books you might like:
Gael Baudino, *Branch and Crown*, 1996
Sara Douglass, *The Nameless Day*, 2004
Jasper Kent, *Twelve*, 2010
Mike Mignola, *Baltimore, or, the Steadfast Tin Soldier and the Vampire*, 2007
Chelsea Quinn Yarbro, *Tempting Fate*, 1982

77

J.A. PITTS

Black Blade Blues

(New York: Tor, 2010)

Subject(s): Adventure; Magic; Dragons
Major character(s): Sarah Beauhall, Warrior, Lesbian
Time period(s): 21st century; 2010s
Locale(s): Seattle, Washington

Summary: In J.A. Pitts's *Black Blade Blues*, Sarah Beauhall is the quintessential anti-heroine: a tough lesbian warrior with a powerful sword that is imbued with a rich history. But as Sarah tries to navigate her very modern life, ancient forces of evil have come after her in order to get their hands on the sword. Even as her personal life falls apart around her, Sarah engages in an epic battle to keep the storied weapon—and to maintain her own fighting spirit. First novel.

Where it's reviewed:
Library Journal, April 1, 2010, page 68
Publishers Weekly, February 15, 2010, page 119

Other books you might like:
Poul Anderson, *Three Hearts and Three Lions*, 1961
Greg Van Eekhout, *Norse Code*, 2009
Guy Gavriel Kay, *The Last Light of the Sun*, 2004
Juliet Marillier, *Wolfskin*, 2003
Mickey Zucker Reichert, *Flight of the Renshai*, 2009

78

PHILIP REEVE

No Such Things As Dragons

(New York: Scholastic Press, 2010)

Story type: Young Readers
Subject(s): Fantasy; Dragons; Suspense

Major character(s): Ansel, Boy, Servant (to Brock); Brock, Dragon (slayer)
Time period(s): Indeterminate

Summary: *No Such Things As Dragons* is a fantasy chapter book for young readers. Young Ansel is a mute boy who's been sold as a servant to the mighty dragon slayer, Brock. Although Brock has countless tales of his brave and heroic deeds killing dragons, Ansel has his doubts about whether or not dragons really exist. Is Brock simply capitalizing on the fear of his fellow villagers? Just when Ansel thinks he's discovered the truth, he's shocked to find a ferocious man-eating monster dwelling in the haunted caves of Dragon Mountain. Do he and Brock have what it takes to slay a real-life dragon?

Where it's reviewed:
Booklist, August 1, 2010, page 51
Horn Book Magazine, September-October 2010, page 92
Locus, November 2010, page 49
Publishers Weekly, July 19, 2010, page 130
School Library Journal, September 2010, page 163

Other books by the same author:
Fever Crumb, 2010
Here Lies Arthur, 2008
Infernal Devices, 2005
Predator's Gold, 2004
Mortal Engines, 2002

Other books you might like:
Bruce Coville, *Dark Whispers*, 2008
Chris D'Lacey, *Dark Fire*, 2010
Philip Pullman, *The Amber Spyglass*, 2000
Vivian Vande Velde, *The Changeling Prince*, 1998
Jane Yolen, *Cards of Grief*, 1984

79

WARREN ROCHELLE

The Called

(Urbana, Illinois: Golden Gryphon Press, 2010)

Subject(s): Fairies; Adventure; Magic
Major character(s): Malachi, Mythical Creature (half-human, half-faerie); Jeff, Mythical Creature (half-human, half-faerie); Russell, Mythical Creature (half-human, half-faerie); Hazel, Mythical Creature (half-human, half-faerie)
Time period(s): Indeterminate
Locale(s): Earth

Summary: Warren Rochelle's *The Called* continues the adventures of a group of magically gifted youngsters first begun in *A Harvest of Changelings* (2007). In this sequel, the evil Fomorrii are putting in motion a dastardly plan to turn the human world against anything magical. Determined to stop this chain of events, Malachi, Jeff, Hazel, and Russell come back to Earth to take on the Fomorrii. But things soon grow increasingly more sinister once Malachi is abducted, and the ultimate battle for the soul of humanity commences.

Other books by the same author:
Harvest of Changelings, 2007

The Wild Boy, 2001

Other books you might like:
Diane Duane, *Stealing the Elf-King's Roses*, 2002
Kenneth C. Flint, *Cromm*, 1990
Laurell K. Hamilton, *A Caress of Twilight*, 2002
Karen Marie Moning, *Faefever*, 2008
Tim Powers, *Last Call*, 1992

80

KEN SCHOLES

Antiphon

(New York: Tor, 2010)

Series: Psalms of Isaak Series. Book 3
Subject(s): Wars; Prophecy; Magic
Major character(s): Nebios, Young Man; Jin Li Tam, Royalty (queen of the Ninefold Forest), Mother (of Jakob); Jakob, Son (of Jin Li Tam)
Time period(s): Indeterminate Past
Locale(s): Windwir, Fictional Location

Summary: The city of Windwir has been destroyed in battle, and now an even larger war looms on the horizon. As the threat grows ever closer, a series of characters deal with the impending doom. Nebios is being pursued by a group of ruthless female fighters, while the queen of the Ninefold Forest, Jin Li Tam, hears word of an ancient prophesy regarding her son Jakob. In the meantime, magical music is being emitted from a recently unearthed silver crescent—music that could herald either a new beginning...or a vicious end. *Antiphon* is the third book in The Psalms of Isaak series.

Where it's reviewed:
Publishers Weekly, July 12, 2010, page 33

Other books by the same author:
Diving Mimes, Weeping Czars and Other Unusual Suspects, 2010
Lamentation, 2009
Canticle, 2008
Long Walks, Last Flights, and Other Strange Journeys, 2008
Last Flight of the Goddess, 2006

Other books you might like:
Alan Campbell, *Scar Night*, 2007
Mary Gentle, *Rats and Gargoyles*, 1990
Tim Lebbon, *Echo City*, 2010
China Mieville, *Iron Council*, 2004
Tad Williams, *Shadowmarch: Volume 1*, 2004

81

MARK SEBANC
JAMES G. ANDERSON, Co-Author

Darkling Fields of Arvon

(Riverdale, New York: Baen, 2010)

Series: Legacy of the Stone Harp Series. Book 2
Subject(s): Adventure; Royalty; Voyages and travels

Major character(s): Kalaquinn "Kal" Wright, Leader (High Bard); Prince Starigan, Royalty
Time period(s): Indeterminate Past
Locale(s): Arvon, Fictional Location

Summary: Kalaquinn Wright has just been named High Bard of the realm and sets off to find the displaced prince who is the rightful heir to the nation's throne. In order to accomplish his mission, however, Kal will have to face a number of deadly adversaries and track down the Talmadh, an enchanted harp that has the power to once again unite the people of the warring lands. *Darkling Fields of Arvon* is the second book in James G. Anderson and Mark Sebanc's Legacy of the Stone Harp series.

Where it's reviewed:
Library Journal, April 15, 2010, page 78
Publishers Weekly, April 5, 2010, page 51

Other books by the same author:
The Stoneholding, 2009

Other books you might like:
Greg Bear, *The Infinity Concerto*, 1984
Alan Dean Foster, *Spellsinger*, 1983
Mercedes Lackey, *Four & Twenty Blackbirds*, 1997
L.E. Modesitt, *The Soprano Sorceress*, 1997
Keith Taylor, *Bard II*, 1984

82

JONI SENSEL

The Farwalker's Quest

(New York: Bloomsbury, 2009)

Story type: Adventure; Young Readers
Subject(s): Fantasy; Adventure; Identity
Major character(s): Ariel, 12-Year-Old; Zeke, Friend (of Ariel)
Time period(s): Indeterminate Past
Locale(s): Fictional Location

Summary: In *The Farwalker's Quest* by Joni Sensel, two children discover an ancient object that could hold the secret to their destiny. With Namingfest approaching, Ariel and Zeke anticipate which of the village's 12 trades will be assigned to them. When they find a telling dart—a device not employed for many years—Ariel feels she is the target of its message. When two travelers come to the village in search of the dart, Ariel realizes its power. Though the dart's meaning seems obscured, Ariel believes that she is being called to be a Farwalker, not a Healtouch, which was the trade of her mother.

Other books by the same author:
The Timekeeper's Moon, 2010
The Humming of Numbers, 2008

Other books you might like:
Sharon Green, *Convergence*, 1996
Mindy L. Klasky, *The Glasswright's Apprentice*, 2000
Juliet E. McKenna, *Southern Fire*, 2005
William Nicholson, *Noman: Book Three of the Noble Warriors*, 2008
Mickey Zucker Reichert, *The Flightless Falcon*, 2000

83

JOEL SHEPHERD

Tracato

(Amherst, New York: Orbit, 2010)

Series: Trial of Blood and Steel Series. Book 3
Story type: Series
Subject(s): Wars; Family; Love
Major character(s): Sasha, Royalty (former princess); Errollyn, Lover (of Sasha); Kessligh, Teacher (of Sasha)
Time period(s): Indeterminate Past
Locale(s): Rhodia, Fictional Location

Summary: Set in the land of Rhodia, this volume finds the human and serrin populations on the precipice of an all-out war. Now, one-time princess, Sasha, works alongside her teacher, Kessligh, to ensure the survival of Tracato, their beloved home and a mecca of thought and progress in Rhodia. Sasha's challenges are about to compound, however, when matters of family, love, and loyalty threaten to divide her allegiances. *Tracato* is the third novel in Joel Shepherd's Trial of Blood and Steel series.

Other books by the same author:
Petrodor, 2010
Sasha, 2009
Crossover, 2006
Killswitch, 2004
Breakaway, 2003

Other books you might like:
James Barclay, *Dawnthief*, 1999
Paul Kearney, *Corvus*, 2010
Juliet E. McKenna, *The Thief's Gamble*, 1999
R.A. Salvatore, *The Highwayman*, 2004
Matthew Sturges, *The Office of Shadow*, 2010

84

ALISON SINCLAIR

Lightborn

(New York: New American Library, 2010)

Series: Darkborn Trilogy. Book 2
Subject(s): Magic; Adventure; Family
Major character(s): Telmaine Hearne, Heroine (Lightborn); Balthasar, Spouse (of Telmaine)
Time period(s): Indeterminate Past
Locale(s): Minhorne, Fictional Location

Summary: The intricate relationships between the Darkborn—those allergic to light—and the Lightborn—those allergic to darkness—continue to play out in Alison Sinclair's *Lightborn*, the second novel in the Darkborn Trilogy. This outing finds Lady Telmaine Hearne, a Lightborn, struggling to keep her mystical gifts a secret, fearing repercussions from the ruling Darkborn, who seek to eradicate all forms of magic. But when she is recruited to stop a possible assassination attempt against members of the nobility, Telmaine may be forced to use the magic that could spell her doom.

Where it's reviewed:
Locus, June 2010, page 17
Publishers Weekly, April 5, 2010, page 51

Other books by the same author:
Darkborn, 2009
Cavalcade, 1998
Blueheart, 1996
Legacies, 1995

Other books you might like:
Carol Berg, *Flesh and Spirit*, 2007
Jacqueline Carey, *Kushiel's Dart*, 2001
Stephen R. Donaldson, *The Mirror of Her Dreams*, 1986
Mindy L. Klasky, *Season of Sacrifice*, 2002
Paula Volsky, *The Grand Ellipse*, 2000

85

NALINI SINGH

Archangel's Kiss

(New York: Berkley Sensation, 2010)

Series: Guild Hunter Series. Book 2
Story type: Contemporary; Vampire Story
Subject(s): Angels; Vampires; Fantasy
Major character(s): Elena Deveraux, Vampire Hunter, Angel; Raphael, Angel, Lover (of Elena); Lijuan, Angel
Time period(s): 21st century; 2010s
Locale(s): Beijing, China

Summary: *Archangel's Kiss* is the second novel in the Guild Hunter fantasy series by Nalini Singh. In the book, vampire hunter Elena Deveraux has been in a coma for a year. When she wakes, she learns that she has become an angel; her lover, the dangerous yet handsome archangel Raphael, is pleased to finally be able to control her. Elena soon learns that she must get on a plane to Beijing to attend a party thrown by the archangel Lijuan; far more dangerous than Raphael, Lijuan has power over the dead, and has interesting plans for Elena as soon as she arrives.

Other books by the same author:
Bonds of Justice, 2010
Angels' Blood, 2009
Blaze of Memory, 2009
Branded by Fire, 2009
Hostage to Pleasure, 2009
Mine to Possess, 2008

Other books you might like:
Kresley Cole, *Pleasure of a Dark Prince*, 2010
Larissa Ione, *Desire Unchained*, 2009
Gena Showalter, *Jewel of Atlantis*, 2006
J.R. Ward, *Lover Mine: A Novel of the Black Dagger Brotherhood*, 2010
Eileen Wilks, *Night Season*, 2008

86

NALINI SINGH

Bonds of Justice

(New York: Berkley, 2010)

Series: Psy-Changelings Series. Book 8
Subject(s): Supernatural; Psychokinesis; Psychics
Major character(s): Max Shannon, Police Officer
Time period(s): Indeterminate
Locale(s): New York, New York

Summary: *Bonds of Justice* is an installment in author Nalini Singh's Psy-Changeling series. New York enforcement officer Max Shannon has the ability to guard his mind from intrusions by those with psychic abilities—people known as "Psys." Unfortunately, in a world dominated by Psys, this also limits Max's chances of being promoted. As he investigates the murders of several people connected to a Psy councilor, Max realizes that his partner is on the brink of breakdown. Can Max save her before it is too late?

Where it's reviewed:
Romantic Times, July 2010, page 96

Other books by the same author:
Angels' Blood, 2009
Blaze of Memory, 2009
Branded by Fire, 2009
Hostage to Pleasure, 2008
Mine to Possess, 2008
Caressed by Ice, 2007

Other books you might like:
Meljean Brook, *The Iron Duke*, 2010
Christine Feehan, *Hidden Currents*, 2009
Charlaine Harris, *Definitely Dead*, 2006
Lora Leigh, *Styx's Storm*, 2010
Maggie Shayne, *Angel's Pain*, 2008

87

SHERWOOD SMITH

Coronets and Steel

(New York: Penguin, 2010)

Story type: Paranormal
Subject(s): Fantasy; Fencing (Sport); Romances (Fiction)
Major character(s): Kim Murray, Student—Graduate; Alec Ysvorod, Royalty (prince)
Time period(s): 21st century; 2010s
Locale(s): Dobrenica, Europe; California, United States

Summary: In *Coronets and Steel* by Sherwood Smith, a California grad student finds adventure and love in the imaginary country of Dobrenica. Kim Murray longs for the romance of the past and eagerly embarks on a European journey where she hopes to learn about her family's history. When Kim is taken captive by a prince (in a case of mistaken identity), she finds herself in an enchanted land where time seems to have stopped. In Dobrenica, Kim puts her fencing skills to work as she deals with mysterious pursuers. Meanwhile, Kim discov-

ers that she also has a knack of communicating with the spirit world.

Where it's reviewed:
Booklist, September 15, 2010, page 37
Library Journal, September 15, 2010, page 65
Locus, October 2010, page 25

Other books by the same author:
Treason's Shore, 2009
King's Shield, 2008
The Fox, 2007
Inda, 2006
Journey to Otherwhere, 2000

Other books you might like:
Dave Duncan, *Impossible Odds*, 2003
Ian Gibson, *Stuff of Legends*, 2010
J.C. Hendee, *Dhampir*, 2003
Paul Kearney, *Corvus*, 2010
Jennifer Roberson, *Sword-Sworn*, 2002

88

JON SPRUNK

Shadow's Son

(Amherst, New York: Pyr, 2010)

Story type: Alternate World
Subject(s): Assassination; Orphans; Revenge
Major character(s): Caim, Murderer (assassin), Friend (of Josephine); Josephine, Daughter (of assassinated nobleman), Friend (of Caim); Kit, Spirit
Time period(s): Indeterminate
Locale(s): Othir, Fictional Location

Summary: In Jon Sprunk's *Shadow's Son*, assassin-for-hire Caim arrives at a kill only to find that someone else beat him to it. Instead of his intended victim, he finds the nobleman's daughter, Josephine, and the two immediately form an impenetrable bond. She is the only woman he can trust other than Kit, a spirit who helps him twist shadows in the night to work in his favor. Together, Caim and Josephine set out to find her father's killer, the man who stole Caim's kill. On the way, they discover that the holy city is more corrupt than they ever imagined. Each must come clean about his or her past and who they really are if they wish to survive the dark alleys of Othir. This is Sprunk's debut novel.

Where it's reviewed:
Booklist, June 1, 2010, page 47

Other books you might like:
James Barclay, *Dawnthief*, 1999
Jennifer Fallon, *The Lion of Senet*, 2004
Mindy L. Klasky, *The Glasswright's Apprentice*, 2000
L.E. Modesitt, *Darknesses*, 2003

89

MICHAEL A. STACKPOLE

At the Queen's Command

(San Francisco, California: Night Shade Books, 2010)

Series: Crown Colonies Series. Book 1
Story type: Alternate History; Series

Subject(s): History; Zombies; Fantasy
Major character(s): Owen Strake, Military Personnel (captain, the Queen's Own Wurms); Nathaniel Woods, Scout; Kamiskwa, Royalty (prince); Guy du Malphias, Villain; Vladimir, Royalty (prince)
Time period(s): 18th century; 1760s (1763)
Locale(s): Mystria, Fictional Location

Summary: In *At the Queen's Command* by Michael Stackpole, the imaginary colonial world of Mystria is the setting for political scheming, human-zombie battles, and a mysterious plot involving dragon eggs. Captain Owen Strake is on her majesty's duty, mapping new territories in advance of an approaching war, when he is taken captive and confronted by the necromancer Guy du Malphias. Meanwhile, Vladimir, a nephew of the queen who holds limited political clout, keeps close watch of his collection of "wurm" eggs—one of which is about to reveal its magical contents. *At the Queen's Command* is the first book in the Crown Colonies series.

Where it's reviewed:
Publishers Weekly, September 27, 2010, page 43

Other books by the same author:
The New World, 2007
Perchance to Dream and Other Stories, 2005
A Secret Atlas, 2005
The Grand Crusade, 2004
Talion Revenant, 1997

Other books you might like:
Poul Anderson, *Operation Chaos*, 1971
Diane Duane, *To Visit the Queen*, 1999
Paul Park, *A Princess of Roumania*, 2005
Roger Zelazny, *A Dark Traveling*, 1987

⬛ **90**

GABI STEVENS

The Wish List
(New York: Tom Doherty Associates, 2010)

Series: Time of Transition Trilogy. Book 1
Story type: Paranormal; Series
Subject(s): Parapsychology; Romances (Fiction); Magic
Major character(s): Kristin Montgomery, Accountant; Tennyson Ritter, Historian
Time period(s): 21st century; 2010s
Locale(s): San Diego, California

Summary: In *The Wish List* by Gabi Stevens, a California accountant receives a magic wand and a surprising legacy from three aunts who reveal themselves to be fairy godmothers. Before Kristin Montgomery's aunts depart on a long-awaited vacation, they dub her a fairy godmother in training and leave her to sort out her emerging powers. The bookish but good-looking Tennyson Ritter is dispatched by the Arcani authorities to supervise the new fairy's progress. Though Tennyson is initially bored with his assignment, Kristen's charms soon win him over. *The Wish List* is the first book in the Time of Transition trilogy. First novel.

Where it's reviewed:
Publishers Weekly, March 15, 2010, page 42

Other books you might like:
Ilona Andrews, *Bayou Moon*, 2010
Tanya Huff, *The Enchantment Emporium*, 2009
Mercedes Lackey, *The Fairy Godmother*, 2004
Seanan McGuire, *A Local Habitation*, 2010
Devon Monk, *Magic to the Bone*, 2008

⬛ **91**

S.M. STIRLING

A Taint in the Blood
(New York: New American Library, 2010)

Series: Shadowspawn Series. Book 1
Subject(s): Werewolves; Brothers and sisters; Adventure
Major character(s): Adrian Breze, Werewolf; Ellen, Girlfriend (ex-girlfriend of Adrian), Kidnap Victim
Time period(s): 21st century
Locale(s): United States

Summary: *A Taint in the Blood* is the first installment in S.M. Stirling's series continuing the world of the Shadowspawn, werewolves who live among humans all over the world. Adrian Breze is a Shadowspawn who spends his life battling his desire for flesh and blood. His sister, however, is not concerned with such formalities. When she abducts and tortures Adrian's ex-girlfriend Ellen, Adrian sets out to rescue his ex—but are his dark urges about to take over once and for all?

Where it's reviewed:
Library Journal, April 15, 2010, page 80
Publishers Weekly, March 29, 2010, page 44

Other books by the same author:
The Scourge of God, 2008
The Sunrise Lands, 2007
The Protector's War, 2005
The High King of Montival, 2010
The Sword of the Lady, 2009

Other books you might like:
Don Bassingthwaite, *Breathe Deeply*, 1994
Patricia Briggs, *Moon Called*, 2006
Richard Lee Byers, *Netherworld*, 1995
Cathy Clamp, *Serpent Moon*, 2010
David Niall Wilson, *Lasombra*, 2003

⬛ **92**

S.M. STIRLING

The High King of Montival
(New York: Roc, 2010)

Series: Emberverse Series. Book 7
Subject(s): Science fiction; History; Dystopias
Major character(s): Rudi Mackenzie, Warrior, Young Man
Time period(s): Indeterminate Future
Locale(s): Pacific Northwest

Summary: In *The High King of Montival* by S.M. Stirling, a catastrophic event known as "The Change" has set the world on an alternate path through history—a path where there is no electricity, internal combustion engines, explosives, or guns. In this post-apocalyptic landscape, Rudi Mackenzie—a descendant of the Mackenzie clan and a skilled swordsman—prepares to confront a dangerous enemy. At Montival, in a re-imagined Pacific Northwest, the legions of the Prophet await Rudi's return as the young warrior leads a force of former rivals to defend his native soil. *The High King of Montival* is the seventh book in the Emberverse series.

Other books by the same author:
A Taint in the Blood, 2010
The Sword of the Lady, 2009
The Scourge of God, 2008
The Sunrise Lands, 2007
The Protector's War, 2005

Other books you might like:
Peter Dickinson, *The Changes: A Trilogy*, 1986
Karen Marie Moning, *Darkfever*, 2006
Madeleine E. Robins, *The Stone War*, 1999
Justina Robson, *Chasing the Dragon*, 2009
Rudy Rucker, *Hylozoic*, 2009

93

MATTHEW STOVER
ROBERT E. VARDEMAN, Co-Author

God of War

(New York: Del Rey, 2010)

Subject(s): Mythology; Slavery; Adventure
Major character(s): Kratos, Slave, Warrior
Time period(s): Indeterminate Past
Locale(s): Greece

Summary: Based on the popular video game, Matthew Stover and Robert E. Vardeman's *God of War* follows the adventures of Kratos, a young man enslaved to the Olympian gods. Kratos is desperate to attain his freedom, but in order to do so, he will have to carry out one final mission that could destroy himself—and humanity. Ares, the God of War, must be killed. But Kratos is a mortal with limited abilities. Can he take on the most powerful god in the world?

Other books by the same author:
Caine Black Knife, 2008
Blade of Tyshalle, 2001
Heroes Die, 1998
Jericho Moon, 1998
Iron Dawn, 1997

Other books you might like:
Doug Beyer, *Alara Unbroken*, 2009
Geary Gravel, *The Dreamwright*, 1994
J. Robert King, *Legions*, 2003
Richard A. Knaak, *Birthright*, 2006
Mel Odom, *The Black Road*, 2002

94

MATTHEW STURGES

The Office of Shadow

(Amherst, New York: Pyr, 2010)

Subject(s): Prisoners; Adventure; Magic
Major character(s): Silverdun, Spy; Ironfoot, Military Personnel (ex-soldier); Sela, Empath
Time period(s): Indeterminate

Summary: Matthew Sturges's *The Office of Shadow* is the sequel to 2009's *Midwinter*. In this fantasy adventure, Silverdun has become a priest, but he finds himself uninterested in the monastic life. He is soon asked to become a spy for the government and is paired with Ironfoot and Sela on a dangerous new mission. The trio must uncover the truth about a cache of weapons that possesses the power to destroy the world.

Where it's reviewed:
Publishers Weekly, April 26, 2010, page 93

Other books by the same author:
Midwinter, 2009

Other books you might like:
Dave Duncan, *The Jaguar Knights*, 2004
Raymond E. Feist, *Exile's Return*, 2004
George R.R. Martin, *A Game of Thrones*, 1996
L.E. Modesitt Jr., *Imager*, 2009
Jon Sprunk, *Shadow's Son*, 2010

95

BENJAMIN TATE

Well of Sorrows

(New York: DAW, 2010)

Subject(s): Magic; Adventure; Good and evil
Major character(s): Colin Harten, Young Man
Time period(s): Indeterminate
Locale(s): Portstown, Fictional Location

Summary: Benjamin Tate's *Well of Sorrows* is set in a fictional world, where Colin Harten relocates with his family from their war-torn home to a new land on the other side of the ocean. After facing prejudice from the locals in their new community, Colin and his family journey into the dark forests—where everyone but Colin meets a gruesome end. Now Colin has drunk from the fabled Well of Sorrows and realizes he is suddenly in possession of some highly coveted secret powers—powers that could either change the world for the better or lead him to the same fate as his family. First novel.

Other books you might like:
Orson Scott Card, *The Crystal City*, 2003
Raymond E. Feist, *Rage of a Demon King*, 1997
Elizabeth Haydon, *Requiem for the Sun*, 2002
Jennifer Roberson, *Karavans*, 2006
Elizabeth Vaughan, *Warprize*, 2005

96

ADRIAN TCHAIKOVSKY

Dragonfly Falling

(Amherst, New York: Pyr, 2010)

Series: Shadows of the Apt Series. Book 2
Story type: Science Fantasy
Subject(s): Insects; Science fiction; Fantasy
Time period(s): Indeterminate
Locale(s): Collegium, Fictional Location

Summary: *Dragonfly Falling* is a fantasy novel from author Adrian Tchaikovsky. The second book in the Shadows of the Apt series, *Dragonfly Falling* is about an alternate world where insect tribes reign. The book focuses on the inhabitants of the city of Collegium as they face a menacing threat from their enemy. The Wasp army continues to grow in power, posing a threat to the innovative people of the Lowlands, but many are still naive to the true danger. As the Wasp army attacks the imperial city of Collegium, a small group of individuals must come together and use their unusual gifts to fight off their powerful foe.

Where it's reviewed:
Booklist, April 1, 2010, page 31
Publishers Weekly, February 8, 2010, page 35

Other books by the same author:
Blood of the Mantis, 2010
Empire in Black and Gold, 2010
Salute the Dark, 2010

Other books you might like:
James Barclay, *Elfsorrow*, 2002
Ed Greenwood, *Dark Vengeance*, 2008
John Holm, *The Hammer and the Cross*, 1993
Stan Nicholls, *The Righteous Blade*, 2005
Matthew Sturges, *Midwinter*, 2009

97

ADRIAN TCHAIKOVSKY

Blood of the Mantis

(Amherst, New York: Pyr, 2010)

Series: Shadows of the Apt Series. Book 3
Story type: Sword and Sorcery
Subject(s): Fantasy; Supernatural; Wars
Time period(s): Indeterminate
Locale(s): Lowlands, Fictional Location

Summary: *Blood of the Mantis* is a fantasy novel from author Adrian Tchaikovsky. The third book in the Shadows of the Apt series, *Blood of the Mantis* follows the residents of the Lowlands as the wicked Wasp Empire struggles to maintain its leadership. The Wasps have abused their power, creating factions and strife among the people, and now they're facing threats from outside armies. If they want to keep their authority and continue to control the Lowlands, the Wasp Empire will need the assistance of the mysterious Shadow Box. The box promises power to whoever possesses it, but it also car-

ries a frightening and ominous force.

Where it's reviewed:
Booklist, May 15, 2010, page 27
Library Journal, May 15, 2010, page 71
Publishers Weekly, March 22, 2010, page 57

Other books by the same author:
Dragonfly Falling, 2010
Empire in Black and Gold, 2010
Salute the Dark, 2010

Other books you might like:
Glen Cook, *The Tyranny of the Night*, 2005
Elaine Cunningham, *The Magehound*, 2000
David Gemmell, *Bloodstone*, 1994
Paul Kearney, *Corvus*, 2010
Joel Shepherd, *Petrodor*, 2010

98

ADRIAN TCHAIKOVSKY

Salute the Dark

(Amherst, New York: Tor Books, 2010)

Series: Shadows of the Apt Series. Book 4
Story type: Futuristic
Subject(s): Insects; Technology; Alternative worlds
Major character(s): Stenwold Maker, Insect

Summary: *Salute the Dark* is the fourth installment from Adrian Tchaikovsky's Shadows of the Apt series. In this book, the malevolent Wasp Empire continues to threaten the peaceful Lowlands as Stenwold Maker, a beetle-human hybrid, defends his homeland against their impending takeover. Yet, those who once swore their allegiance to Stenwold's cause have long since moved on from the campaign, and Maker is no longer sure if he can rely on his former allies. Tchaikovsky tells the ongoing saga of the Wasp Empire's quest for domination, as well as the interwoven stories of those humanistic insects that stand in the wasps' path.

Where it's reviewed:
Booklist, August 1, 2010, page 36
Publishers Weekly, July 5, 2010, page 31
Realms of Fantasy, December 2010, page 59

Other books by the same author:
Blood of the Mantis, 2010
Dragonfly Falling, 2010
Empire in Black and Gold, 2010

Other books you might like:
Elaine Bergstrom, *Baroness of Blood*, 1995
Jo Clayton, *Drinker of Souls*, 1986
J.C. Hendee, *Child of a Dead God*, 2008
William King, *Vampireslayer*, 2001
Meredith Ann Pierce, *The Pearl of the Soul of the World*, 1990

99

RAY VUKCEVICH

Boarding Instructions
(Auburn, Washington: Fairwood Press, Inc., 2010)

Story type: Alternate World; Collection
Subject(s): Fantasy; Short stories; Vampires

Summary: In *Boarding Instructions*, Ray Vukcevich's stories take place in an unfamiliar world riddled with fire starters, vampires, and indescribable smells. Secret pathways and hidden doorways lead characters to rooms where they experience events unlike any other in the world with which readers are familiar. Vukcevich is known for his odd and original works, and this collection contains 33 unique stories, including "Intercontinental Ballistic Missile Boy" and "Miles and Miles of Broccoli." His other works have appeared in collections such as *Is Anybody Out There?* and *Tales of Wonder and Imagination* and on many online forums and Web sites.

Other books by the same author:
Meet Me in the Moon Room, 2010

Other books you might like:
Harlan Ellison, *Deathbird Stories*, 1975
Jeffrey Ford, *The Fantasy Writer's Assistant and Other Stories*, 2002
Jay Lake, *Dogs in the Moonlight*, 2004
Ursula K. Le Guin, *Tales from Earthsea*, 2001

100

FREDA WARRINGTON

Midsummer Night
(New York: Tor, 2010)

Summary: Two sisters in Regency-era England struggle with the vagaries of love and the power of magic in Mary Robinette Kowal's *Shades of Milk and Honey*. Jane Ellsworth is an ordinary girl with a particular penchant for magic. Her sister Melody is ravishingly beautiful but lacks Jane's prowess with the mystical arts. In the hopes of finding suitable men for marriage, the sisters become involved with the goings-on of their neighbors—and love, heartbreak, and magical fantasy ensue. First novel.

Where it's reviewed:
Booklist, November 15, 2010, page 27
Library Journal, November 15, 2010, page 63
Locus, November 2010, page 20
Publishers Weekly, September 20, 2010, page 53

Other books by the same author:
The Court of the Midnight King, 2003
Dark Cathedrall, 1996
Darker Than the Storm, 1991
A Blackbird in Twilight, 1988
A Blackbird in Darkness, 1986

Other books you might like:
Storm Constantine, *Sea Dragon Heir*, 1999
Jay Lake, *Escapement*, 2008

Michael Moorcock, *The War Amongst the Angels*, 1997
Sharon Shinn, *Dark Moon Defender*, 2006
Catherynne M. Valente, *Palimpsest*, 2009

101

C.L. WERNER

Temple of the Serpent
(Nottingham, England: Black Library, 2011)

Series: Thanquol and Boneripper Series. Book 2
Story type: Alternate World
Subject(s): Fantasy; Assassination; Islands
Major character(s): Thanquol, Psychic
Time period(s): Indeterminate
Locale(s): Lustria, Fictional Location

Summary: The second installment in the Thanquol and Boneripper series and part of the Warhammer collection, *Temple of the Servant* follows the adventures of Skaven Grey Seer Thanquol as he sets out to find redemption for his past mistakes. After failing time and time again, Thanquol is tasked with the arduous job of murdering the Prophet of Sotek. Thanquol must travel to Lustria, an island inhabited by huge lizard men, to complete the task and redeem himself once and for all. If Thanquol hopes to survive the harsh jungles, terrifying lizards, and determined assassins, he must utilize his own craftiness and magical skills against his powerful foes.

Other books by the same author:
Forged by Chaos, 2009
Grey Seer, 2009
Blood for the Blood God, 2008
Palace of the Plague Lord, 2007
Witch Finder, 2005

Other books you might like:
Ben Counter, *Crimson Tears*, 2005
Darius Hinks, *Warrior Priest*, 2010
Nick Kyme, *Oathbreaker*, 2008
Nathan Long, *Manslayer*, 2007
Anthony Reynolds, *Dark Creed*, 2010

102

MIKE WILD

Engines of the Apocalypse
(London: Abaddon Books, 2010)

Series: Twilight of Kerberos Series. Book 7
Subject(s): Machinery; Wars; Magic
Major character(s): Kali Hooper, Warrior
Time period(s): Indeterminate
Locale(s): Twilight, Fictional Location

Summary: In the land known as Twilight, giant machines have spewed forth from the ground and heralded an end to all magical practices. Kali Hooper finds herself targeted as the person behind the emergence of the machines, and she is soon fighting for both her honor and her life. In order to clear her name, Kali will have to take on an evil autocrat and join forces with those she never dreamed she would have to fight alongside. *Engines of the Apocalypse* is the seventh novel in Mike Wild's Twilight of Kerberos series.

Other books by the same author:
Crucible of the Dragon God, 2009

Other books you might like:
Alan Campbell, *God of Clocks*, 2009
Ian R. MacLeod, *The Light Ages*, 2003
China Mieville, *Iron Council*, 2004
Andre Norton, *Witch World*, 1963
Michael Swanwick, *The Iron Dragon's Daughter*, 1994

103

CHRIS WRAIGHT

Sword of Justice

(Nottingham, United Kingdom: The Black Library, 2010)

Series: Warhammer Series. Book 1
Story type: Quest; Series
Subject(s): Wars; Violence; Politics
Major character(s): Ludwig Schwarzhelm, Warrior
Time period(s): Indeterminate
Locale(s): Averland, Fictional Location

Summary: In Chris Wraight's *Sword of Justice*, Ludwig Schwarzhelm, the Emperor's champion, travels to Averland, where he will perform a simple task: ensure the successful induction of the new elector count. At first, the warrior welcomes this errand, as he has just left battlegrounds in the North that claimed the lives of many of his fellow warriors and needs to rest. When he reaches Averland, he discovers that gathering his strength and resting are not in his future. The province is disheveled; everyone has taken sides and as hard as Schwarzhelm tries, he cannot bring them back together. To make matters worse, it does not appear that any of his allies wants to see the province succeed. As the atmosphere in Averland becomes violent, the Emperor's champion must take action—the fall of Averland may mean the fall of the entire empire.

Other books by the same author:
Dark Storm Gathering, 2009
Iron Company, 2009
Masters of Magic, 2008

Other books you might like:
Darius Hinks, *Warrior Priest*, 2010
Mike Lee, *Nagash the Unbroken*, 2010
Nathan Long, *Zombieslayer*, 2010
C.L. Werner, *Forged by Chaos*, 2009
Richard Williams, *Reiksguard*, 2009

The Year in Historical Fiction
by
Daniel S. Burt

Philosopher George Santayana famously warned that "Those who cannot remember the past are condemned to repeat it." Readers of historical fiction might respond: What's so terrible about repeating the past, even if you remember it well? In other words, the past, for readers of historical fiction, is not to be avoided by remembering but embraced by re-encountering it. Santayana's declaration is also problematic on the grounds of the challenge of fully remembering the past: Can the past ever be remembered sufficiently to resist repeating history's lessons? And is repeating the past in any way a bad thing? Readers of historical fiction at least are attentive enough to the problems of fully recalling the past to be endlessly fascinated by its re-enactment in stories, suggesting that the past is complex and deep enough for an ongoing effort of remembering. In the context of historical fiction, repeating the past is no condemnation but a delight and an illumination.

Considering the elusive nature of the past and the countless ways we fail to remember it sufficiently, try the following brief quiz to test your knowledge of the past (the answers are to found in the historical novels collected here, published in the second half of 2010):

1. What do you know about life in Yemen during the 1930s? (ans. Nadifa Mohamed's *Black Mamba Boy*)

2. What about the Armenian massacre, the historical event that confirmed Hitler's "Final Solution"? (ans. Mark T. Mustian's *The Gendarme*)

3. How about polygamy among the Mormons in the nineteenth century? (ans. Diane Noble's *The Sister Wife*)

4. The important Penobscot Expedition of 1779 during the Revolutionary War? (ans. Bernard Cornwell's *The Fort*)

5. The Rock Springs Massacre in Wyoming in 1885? (ans. Brian Leung's *Take Me Home*)

Not so easy, were they? So, here is the past unremembered but waiting for the reader to repeat, at least imaginatively through the remarkable agency of historical fiction in the novels collected here.

Selection Criteria

More so than any other fictional genre, it is necessary to define exactly what constitutes a historical novel to justify my selections. All novels deal with the past, except science fiction that is set in the future, or most fantasy novels set in an imagined, alternative world outside historical time. Yet not all novels are truly historical. Central to any workable definition of historical fiction is the degree to which the writer attempts not to recall the past but to recreate it. In some cases the time frame, setting, and customs of a novel's era are merely incidental to its action and characterization. In other cases, period details function as little more than a colorful backdrop for characters and situations that could as easily be played out in a different era with little alteration. So-called historical "costume dramas" could to a greater or lesser degree work as well with a change of costume in a different place and time. The novels that we can identify as truly historical, however, attempt much more than incidental period surface details or interchangeable historical eras. What justifies a designation as a historical novel is the writer's efforts at providing an accurate and believable representation of a particular historical era. The writer of historical fiction shares with the historian a verifiable depiction of past events, lives, and customs. In historical fiction, the past itself becomes as much a subject for the novelist as the characters and action.

Most of us use the phrase "historical novel" casually, never really needing an exact definition to make ourselves understood. We just know it when we see it. This listing, however, requires a set of criteria to determine what's in and what's out. Otherwise the list has no boundaries. If the working definition of historical fiction is too loose, every novel set in a period before the present qualifies, and nearly every novel becomes a historical novel immediately upon publication. If the definition is so strict that only books set in a time before the author's birth, for example, make the cut, then countless works that critics, readers, librarians, and the authors themselves think of as historical novels would be excluded.

The challenge here, therefore, has been to fashion a definition or set of criteria flexible enough to include novels that pass what can be regarded as the litmus test for historical fiction: Did the author use his or her imagination—and often quite a bit of research—to evoke another and earlier time than the author's own? Walter Scott, who is credited with "inventing" the historical novel in English during the early nineteenth century, provides a useful criterion in the subtitle of *Waverley*, his initial historical novel, the story of Scottish life at the time of the Jacobite Rebellion of 1745: "'Tis Sixty Years Since." This supplies a possible formula for separating the created past from the remembered past. What is unique and distinctive about the so-called historical novel is its attempt to imagine a distant period of time before the novelist's lifetime. Scott's sixty-year span between a novel's composition and its imagined era offers an arbitrary but useful means to distinguish between the personal and the historical past. The distance of two generations or nearly a lifetime provides a necessary span for the past to emerge as history and forces the writer to rely on more than recollection to uncover the patterns and textures of the past. I have, therefore, adopted Scott's formula but adjusted it to fifty years, including those books in which the significant portion of their plots is set in a period fifty years or more before the novel was written.

Because a rigid application of this fifty-year rule might disqualify quite a few books intended by their authors and regarded by their readers to be historical novels, another test has been applied to books written about more recent eras: Did the author use actual historical figures and events while setting out to recreate a specific, rather than a general or incidental, historical period? Although it is, of course, risky to speculate about a writer's intention, it is possible by looking at the book's approach, its use of actual historical figures, and its emphasis on a distinctive time and place that enhances the reader's knowledge of past lives, events, and customs to detect when a book conforms to what most would consider a central preoccupation of the historical novel.

I have tried to apply these criteria for the historical novel thoughtfully, and have allowed some exceptions when warranted by special circumstances. I hope I have been able to anticipate what most readers would consider historical novels, but I recognize that I may have overlooked some worthy representations of the past in the interest of dealing with a manageable list of titles. Finally, not every title in the Western, historical mystery, or historical romance genres has been included to avoid unnecessary duplication with the other sections of this book. I have included those novels that share characteristics with another genre—whether fantasy, Western, mystery, or romance—that seem to put the strongest emphasis on historical interest, detail, and accuracy.

Historical Fiction Highlights in the Second Half of 2010

Represented in this selection are worthy novels from all the popular sub-genres of the form, including historical mystery, biography, and fantasy, which I will survey in turn below. Here, I would like to call attention to the rich crop of first-time historical novelists. The form continues to attract important writers of high literary distinction, such as Jay Parini (*The Passage of H.M.*) and Philip Roth (*Nemesis*), as well as established masters of the form such as Bernard Cornwell, Philippa Gregory (*The Red Queen*), and Cecelia Holland (*Kings of the North*), but the future of historical fiction and the health of the genre can best be judged by the quality of the first-time novelists it attracts. The second half of 2010 has a particularly strong roster of impressive debuts, with first historical novels constituting more than twenty percent of the novels collected here.

Having surveyed historical fiction for more years than I care to admit, I am continually impressed by how often, just when you think you have read about every conceivable historical event or different angle on a familiar subject, fresh material and original approaches keep appearing. This is particularly true of the works of these first-time historical novelists. Examples include Mark Keating's eighteenth-century pirate adventure (*The Pirate Devlin*), Adrienne McDonnell's story about an early twentieth-century obstetrician (*The Doctor and the Diva*), Anne Fortier's retelling of Shakespeare's *Romeo and Juliet* (*Juliet*), Michael Sledge's fictional biography of poet Elizabeth Bishop and her relationship with Lola de Macedo Soares (*The More I Owe You*), Paul Grossman's mystery featuring a Jewish detective in 1932 Berlin (*The Sleepwalkers*), and Bruce Machart's account of a horse race in Texas during 1910 (*The Wake of Forgiveness*).

As in the full listing, there is a wide and deep range of time periods represented by these first timers, from Ancient Greece (Gary Corby's *The Pericles Commission* and Annabel Lyon's *The Golden Mean*) through Ancient Rome (Bruce McBain's *Roman Games*) and the Elizabethan period (Ted Bacino's *The Shakespeare Conspiracy*, the Victorian era (Alastair Sim's *The Unbelievers* and D.E. Meredith's *Devoured*), and the crucial events of the twentieth century, including World War I (Nigel Farndale's *The Blasphemer*) and World War II (Patricia Friedberg's *21 Aldgate*, Kate Walbert's *The Gardens of Kyoto*, and Phil Ward's *Those Who Dare*).

These are just a few of the imaginative and original work represented here by first novelists. If you value historical fiction and want to encourage it to thrive, support some of these debuts by buying their books and spreading the word about them.

One of the more interesting recent trends in historical fiction, exploited by both first-time and long-time historical novelists, are literary subjects: representing the life and times of a well-known or lesser known literary figure or reimagining a famous literary work. Examples of the former include, beside the aforementioned depictions of Shakespeare (and Christopher Marlowe) in Ted Bacino's *The Shakespeare Conspiracy* and poet Elizabeth Bishop in Michael Sledge's *The More I Owe You*, a fictional biography of nineteenth-century English poet John Clare in Adam Foulds's *The Quickening Maze*, and Herman Melville (Jay Parini's *The Passage of H.M.*), a depiction of Victorian poet Algernon Swinburne (and travel writer and adventurer Sir Richard Burton) as sleuth in Mark Hodder's mystery *The Strange Affair of Spring Heeled Jack*. Writers as sleuths also appear in Joanna Challis's *Peril at Sumner House* (Daphne de Maurier), Michael Atkinson's *Hemingway Cutthroat* (Ernest Hemingway), and Susan Wittig Albert's *The Tale of Oat Cake Crag* (Beatrix Potter).

Examples of re-imaginings of classic literary works include, besides Anne Fortier's retelling of Shakespeare's *Romeo and Juliet*, Myrlin A. Hermes's *The Lunatic, the Love, and the Poet*, a version of *Hamlet*. Libby Sternberg re-imagines Charlotte Bronte's *Jane Eyre* in *Sloane Hall*, and Karen Essex writes her way into Bram Stoker's classic in *Dracula in Love*.

Jane Austen is practically a sub-genre on her own, and there are no fewer than five Austen-inspired novels, including Allyn C. Pierson's *Mr. Darcy's Little Sister*, Abigail Reynold's *Mr. Darcy's Obsession*, both extending treatment of Austen's *Pride and Prejudice*. There is a mystery involving characters from a Jane Austen novel: Lynn Shepherd's *Murder at Mansfield Park*, and Jane herself puts in an appearance in Lauren Willig's suspense thriller *The Mischief of the Mistletoe*.

Austen is also featured in one of the most recent trends in historical fiction: the mash-up of history/literature/fantasy/horror. It all started with 2009's *Pride and Prejudice and Zombies* by Seth Grahame-Smith, and the mashing continues with Wayne Josephson's *Emma and the Vampires* (Austen's Emma Woodhouse as vampire) and Janet Mullany's *Jane and the Damned* (Jane Austen as a vampire).

Other literary mash-ups collected here are Ben H. Winters's retooling of Tolstoy's *Anna Karenina* with robots in *Android Karenina* and Sarah Gray's populating Emily Bronte's *Wuthering Heights* with the undead in *Wuthering Bites*. It's too soon to tell whether the literary/fantasy mash-up has played out or even more classic texts and historical figures will collide with vampires, androids, and zombies. At this stage, however, I would be in favor of a moratorium on Jane Austen sequels and send-ups. It's time to give Mr. Darcy and company a rest and get on to other worthy literary sources.

Historical Mysteries

As in past listings of historical fiction, the largest single sub-set of historical novels is historical mysteries. Who dunnit still provides the narrative focus of multiple recreations of past eras and historical figures. Mysteries animate depiction of the ancient worlds of Egypt (Nick Drake's *Tuthankhamun*), Greece (Marilyn Todd's *Still Waters*), and Rome (Lindsey Davis's *Nemesis*). The leading era for sleuthing appears to be the Middle Ages, and examples include Alys Clare's *Music of the Distant Stars*, Priscilla Royal's *Valley of Dry Bones*, Jeri Westerson's *The Demon's Parchment*, and, my favorite title, Pat McIntosh's *A Pig of Cold Poison*. The medieval world is also represented on the other side of the globe in I.J. Parker's *The Masuda Affair*, about medieval Japan.

More contemporary sleuthing is being done in and around the two great wars of the twentieth century: World War I in Graham Ison's *Hardcastle's Soldiers* and Charles Todd's *An Impartial Witness* and World War II in James R. Benn's *Rag and Bone* and Aileen G. Barron's *The Scorpion's Bite*.

Among the more unusual settings for mysteries are William Ryan's *The Holy Thief*, set in Russia during the 1930s; Africa in the 1920s in Suzanne Arruda's *The Crocodile's Last Embrace*; ancient Ireland in Peter Tremayne's *The Dove of Death*; and aboard a post-World War II passenger train in Sheldon Russell's *The Insane Train*, another favorite title.

Fictional Biographies

The lives of historical figures—verifiable or invented—come as a close second to historical mysteries in popularity. Collected here are full-scale fictional biographies, treatment of significant portions of historical figures' lives, or invented scenes and situations featuring real figures. Among those depicted are Genghis Khan in Conn Iggulen's *Khan: Empire of Silver*, a further installment in a biographical series; two depictions of Eleanor of Aquitaine (Alison Weir's *Captive Queen* and Samek Norton Hana's *The Sixth Surrender*; another queen, Margaret of Scotland, in Susan Fraser King's *Queen Hereafter*; and Renaissance royalty, Catherine Sforza, in Jeanne Kalogridis's *The Scarlet Contessa*. Alexander the Great's schooling under Aristotle is depicted in *The Golden Mean*, and Lincoln's assassin John Wilkes Booth is given an alternative career in Barnaby Conrad's *The Second Life of John Wilkes Booth*.

Several novels consider lesser-known historical figures in full-scale or partial treatments. They include French romantic poet and actress Marceline Desbordes-Valmore in Anne Plantagenet's *The Last Rendezvous*, seventeenth-century entomologist Eleanor Glanville in Fiona Mountain's *Lady of the Butterflies*, Ethelred II in Cecelia Holland's *Kings of the North*, and Emma, queen consort of Canute I in Helen Hollick's *The Forever Queen*. Other royalty or nobility include Elizabeth I's cousin Lettice Knollys, her rival for the love of Sir Robert Dudley; seventeenth-century Contess Erzebet Bathory in Rebecca Johns's *The Countess*; and Anne Neville, queen to Richard III, in Anne O'Brien's *The Virgin Widow*. Eighteenth century scientists—Peter Artedi and Carl Linnaeus—are featured in Theodore W. Pietsch's *The Curious Death of Peter Artedi*, and one of the great American Indian chiefs—Quanah Parker—is the subject of Jan Reid's *Comanche Sundown*.

Finally, even a famous dog gets biographical treatment: Marilyn Monroe's dog in Andrew O'Hagan's *The Life and Opinions of Maf the Dog, and His Friend Marilyn Monroe*, yet another favorite title!

Historical Fantasy

One of the more recent trends in historical fiction has been tampering with the historical record by fantastical means and injecting the past with fanciful manipulations, with time travel, alternate realities, and supernatural occurrences. The conjunction of history and fantasy has served to resuscitate the dead facts of history and find new and fresh inspiration in the familiar figures and stories from the past. Already mentioned were the several literary mash-ups in which the fantastical is added to well-known works of literature. Other uses of historical fantasy include Jacqueline Lepore's Victorian vampire tale, *Descent into Dust*; Naomi Novik's account of the Napoleonic Wars that includes dragons in the arsenal; *Tongues of Serpents*, an installment of Eric Flint's time-travel series in which a contemporary West Virginia community finds itself transported into the middle of the Thirty Years' War in *1635: The Eastern Front*; and Camille DeAngelis's account of another war—World War II—that features witchcraft: *Petty Magic*. Another World War II fantasy is the wildly inventive *Heidegger's Glasses* by Thaisa Frank.

Historical Fact

Historical fantasy is the exception to the rule that usually applies to historical fiction. Fact not fantasy is the more expected fare for the historical novelist who specializes in introducing the reader to unfamiliar places and events, or showing new or unusual vantage points on the familiar. Let me conclude my round-up of historical novels that appeared in the second half of 2010 with mention of a few of the intriguing stops in the past by the historical imagination in this selection.

The early American colony of Jamestown is a locale for suspense in Marilyn J. Clay's *Deceptions*. An African American woman's life on a South Dakota ranch is depicted in Ann Weisgarber's *The Personal History of Rachel DuPree*. Bo Caldwell's *City of Tranquil Light* treats missionaries in early twentieth-century China. Quakers and orphans during World War I are the subject of Kim Vogel Sawyer's *In Every Heartbeat*. The Tripolitan War against the Barbary Pirates is the subject of William C. Hammond's *For Love of Country*, and a polio outbreak in the summer of 1944 is the occasion for Philip Roth's *Nemesis*.

Want to know what it was like to be in a postwar Glasgow dance band? Try Anne Douglas's *The Melody Girls*. Cairo, Egypt, in 1167? See Scott Oden's *The Lion of Cairo*. What was it like in a European brothel in the nineteenth century? Check out Kathe Koja's *Under the Poppy*.

All to say that there is a good deal to remember about the past in the works collected here as well as much to repeat.

Recommendations

Here are my selections of the 25 most accomplished and intriguing historical novels for the second half of 2010:

City of Tranquil Light by Bo Caldwell

The Fort: A Novel of the Revolutionary War by Bernard Cornwell

Rival to the Queen by Carolly Erickson

Dracula in Love by Karen Essex

Fall of Giants by Ken Follett

Juliet by Anne Fortier

The Red Queen by Philippa Gregory

Kings of the North by Cecelia Holland

Khan: Empire of Silver by Conn Iggulden

The Scarlet Contessa by Jeanne Kalogridis

The Wolves of Andover by Kathleen Kent

Queen Hereafter: A Novel of Margaret of Scotland by Susan Fraser King

The Typist by Michael Knight

A Lily of the Field by John Lawton

Take Me Home by Brian Leung

Daniel by Henning Mankell

Black Mamba Boy by Nadifa Mohamed

The Gendarme by Mark T. Mustian

The Passages of H.M.: A Novel of Herman Melville by Jay Parini

Pirates of the Levant by Arturo Perez-Reverte

Nemesis by Philip Roth

Empire: The Novel of Imperial Rome by Steven Saylor

The True Memoirs of Little K by Adrienne Sharp

Captive Queen: A Novel of Eleanor of Aquitaine by Alison Weir

The Personal History of Rachel DuPree by Ann WeisgarberFor More Information about Historical Fiction-Printed Sources

Lynda G. Adamson, *American Historical Fiction: An Annotated Guide to Novels for Adults and Young Adults*. Phoenix: Oryx Press, 1999.

Lynda G. Adamson, *World Historical Fiction: An Annotated Guide to Novels for Adults and Young Adults*. Phoenix: Oryx Press, 1999.

Daniel S. Burt, *What Historical Fiction Do I Read Next?* Detroit: Gale, Vols. 1-3, 1997-2003.

Daniel S. Burt, *The Biography Book*. Westport: Oryx/Greenwood Press, 2001.

Mark C. Carnes, *Novel History: Historians and Novelists Confront America's Past (and Each Other)*. New York: Simon & Schuster, 2001.

Donald K Hartman, *Historical Figures in Fiction*. Phoenix: Oryx Press, 1994.Electronic Sources

The Historical Novel Society (http//www.historicalnovel society.org): Includes articles, interviews, and reviews of historical novels.

Of Ages Past: The Online Magazine of Historical Fiction (http://www.angelfire.com/il/ofagespast/): Includes novel excerpts, short stories, articles, author profiles, and reviews.

Soon's Historical Fiction Site (http://uts.cc.utexas.edu/~soon/histfiction/): A rich source of information on the historical novel genre, including links to more specialized sites on particular authors and types of historical fiction.

Historical Fiction

104

LEILA ABOULELA

Lyrics Alley

(London, England: Weidenfeld & Nicolson, 2011)

Story type: Family Saga
Subject(s): History; Family; Tradition
Major character(s): Mahmoud Bey Abuzeid, Businessman, Spouse (of Waheeba & Nabilah), Father (of Nur); Nur Abuzeid, Son (of Mahmoud), Accident Victim; Waheeba Abuzeid, Spouse (of Mahmoud), Religious; Nabilah Abuzeid, Spouse (of Mahmoud), Young Woman
Time period(s): 20th century; 1950s
Locale(s): Sudan

Summary: *Lyrics Alley* is a historical novel from author Leila Aboulela. Set in Sudan during a tumultuous, political time in the 1950s, *Lyrics Alley* follows the lives and setbacks of the Abuzeid family. Mahmoud Bey, the patriarch of the family, has built a prosperous business for the family in the form of a trading firm. His favorite son, Nur, is slated to take over the family business, but everything changes when Nur is seriously injured in a horrific accident. The future of the Abuzeids is uncertain, especially in light of the changing political climate happening around them as Britain begins losing its power in Sudan and the nation struggles between moving forward and staying grounded in the past. Adding to the conflict is the differing viewpoints of Mahmoud's two wives, the traditional and reserved Waheeba, and the young and modern Nabilah who wishes to return to Egypt.

Where it's reviewed:
Booklist, February 15, 2011, page 57
Library Journal, October 15, 2010, page 63
The Middle East, January 2011, page 65

Other books by the same author:
Minaret, 2005
Coloured Lights, 2001
The Translator, 1999

Other books you might like:
Chimamanda Ngozi Adichie, *Half of a Yellow Sun: A Novel*, 2006
Teju Cole, *Open City*, 2011
Aminatta Forna, *The Memory of Love*, 2011
Tea Obreht, *The Tiger's Wife*, 2011

105

JOHN ADDIEGO

Tears of the Mountain

(Denver, Colorado: Unbridled Books, 2010)

Subject(s): History; Western fiction; Mystery
Major character(s): Elijah Applewood, Professor; Morris, Political Figure (senator); Jeremiah McKinley, Friend (of Elijah)
Time period(s): 19th century; 1870s (1876)

Summary: In *Tears of the Mountain* by John Addiego, July 4, 1876, proves to be a life-changing day for a Sonoma County man. Jeremiah McKinley had anticipated Santa Rosa's Independence Day celebration as an occasion to visit with family and friends. His friend Elijah Applewood, an educator, is on hand to join in the festivities. But when the outspoken Senator Morris, also in town for the celebration, is murdered and Professor Applewood is arrested for the crime, the day takes a dark turn. McKinley must exonerate his friend before he is executed. Meanwhile, surprising threats place McKinley's immediate family in danger.

Where it's reviewed:
Booklist, September 1, 2010, page 55
Publishers Weekly, July 5, 2010, page 27

Other books by the same author:
The Islands of Divine Music, 2008

Other books you might like:
David Ebershoff, *Pasadena*, 2002
Robert Goolrick, *A Reliable Wife: A Novel*, 2009
Garth Murphy, *The Indian Lover*, 2002
Heather Parkinson, *Across Open Ground*, 2002
Guy Vanderhaeghe, *The Englishman's Boy*, 1996

106

SUSAN WITTIG ALBERT

The Tale of Oat Cake Crag

(New York: Berkley Prime Crime, 2010)

Series: Cottage Tales of Beatrix Potter Series. Book 7
Subject(s): Writers; Human-animal relationships; Animals
Major character(s): Beatrix Potter, Writer, Detective—

Amateur; Will Heelis, Fiance(e) (of Beatrix); Fred Baum, Architect (airplane designer); Grace Lythecoe, Friend (of Beatrix)

Time period(s): 20th century; 1910s
Locale(s): United Kingdom

Summary: Beatrix Potter has come to the Lake District to be with her beloved fiancee, Will, and get a small respite from her ever-nagging parents. Beatrix shares an enchanted union with the animals of the region—all of whom are more than a little angered by the sudden emergence of a strange airplane over Lake Windemere. Meanwhile, one of the plane's original architects, Fred Baum, has been critically hurt, and Beatrix herself gets ensnared in another mystery involving her friend Grace Lythecoe, who has been receiving menacing letters. Could the aggravating airplane, Fred Baum's injury, and Grace's being bullied be somehow connected? *The Tale of Oat Cake Crag* is the seventh book in the Cottage Tales of Beatrix Potter series by Susan Wittig Albert.

Where it's reviewed:
Library Journal, April 1, 2010, page 65
Publishers Weekly, July 5, 2010, page 30

Other books by the same author:
The Tale of Applebeck Orchard, 2009
The Tale of Briar Bank, 2008
The Tale of Hawthorn House, 2007
The Tale of Cuckoo Brow Wood, 2006
The Tale of Holly How, 2005
The Tale of Hill Top Farm, 2004

Other books you might like:
Stephanie Barron, *Jane and the Madness of Lord Byron*, 2010
Emily Brightwell, *The Inspector and Mrs. Jeffries*, 1993
Richard Maltby, *Miss Potter*, 2006
Robin Paige, *Death at Gallows Green*, 1995
Diane Setterfield, *The Thirteenth Tale*, 2006

107

SUSAN WITTIG ALBERT

The Darling Dahlias and the Cucumber Tree

(New York: Berkley Books, 2010)

Subject(s): Americana; Detective fiction; Mystery
Major character(s): Mrs. Dahlia Blackstone, Wealthy; Verna Tidwell, Clerk (probate), Widow(er); Elizabeth "Lizzy" Lacy, Journalist, Secretary (legal); Bunny Scott, Crime Victim; Ophelia Snow, Spouse (of the town's mayor)
Time period(s): 20th century; 1910s-1930s
Locale(s): Darling, Alabama

Summary: *The Darling Dahlias and the Cucumber Tree* is a mystery novel by Susan Wittig Albert. The Darling Dahlias are a group of ladies-who-lunch from Darling, Alabama, who seem oblivious to the ongoing Depression that has hit the rest of the country, including their own hometown. Rather than acknowledge the Depression, the women have set to work beautifying the town by planting new flower gardens and hosting small garden parties.

They are all enthusiastic about their newest inheritance: an estate from the wealthy Dahlia Blackstone, which includes a clubhouse and a garden with a haunted cucumber tree and possible treasure. Their excitement is short-lived, however, when one of the most scandalous women in town is found dead. Lizzy, Ophelia, and Verna decide it is up to them to investigate the murder and possibly even track down a prisoner who has escaped from the local jail. Albert is also the author of *Holly Blues: A China Bayles Mystery* and *The Tale of Oat Cake Crag*.

Where it's reviewed:
Booklist, July 1, 2010, page 36
Kirkus Reviews, June 1, 2010, page 494
Publishers Weekly, May 10, 2010, page 31

Other books by the same author:
Nightshade, 2008
Spanish Dagger, 2007
Bleeding Hearts, 2006
Dead Man's Bones, 2005
A Dilly of a Death, 2004

Other books you might like:
Katie Fforde, *Second Thyme Around*, 2001
Jean Hager, *Blooming Murder*, 1994
Rosemary Harris, *Pushing Up Daisies*, 2008
Jo-Ann Mapson, *Bad Girl Creek*, 2001
Ann Ripley, *Death in the Orchid Garden*, 2006

108

TASHA ALEXANDER

Dangerous to Know

(New York: Minotaur Books, 2010)

Series: Lady Emily Mysteries. Book 5
Subject(s): Murder; Suspense; Detective fiction
Major character(s): Emily Hargreaves, Noblewoman, Detective—Amateur, Spouse (of Colin); Colin Hargreaves, Spouse (of Emily)
Time period(s): 19th century-20th century; 1830s-1900s (1837-1901)
Locale(s): Rouen, France

Summary: *Dangerous to Know*, the fifth installment in Tasha Alexander's Lady Emily Mysteries, finds the sleuthing noblewoman home from her honeymoon, where she almost lost her life solving a crime. Resting at her mother-in-law's home in France, Emily soon stumbles upon another case, this one involving the discovery of a murdered young woman in the nearby woods. The markings on the corpse bear uncanny resemblances to those left on Jack the Ripper's victims and now Emily refuses to rest until she finds out if the killings are connected.

Where it's reviewed:
Library Journal, June 1, 2010, page 72
Publishers Weekly, September 20, 2010, page 46

Other books by the same author:
Tears of Pearl, 2009
A Fatal Waltz, 2008

A Poisoned Season, 2007
And Only To Deceive, 2005

Other books you might like:
Rhys Bowen, *Royal Blood*, 2010
Kenneth M. Cameron, *The Frightened Man*, 2008
Charles Finch, *A Beautiful Blue Death*, 2007
D.E. Meredith, *Devoured*, 2010
Lauren Willig, *The Mischief of the Mistletoe*, 2010

109

SUZANNE ARRUDA

The Crocodile's Last Embrace

(New York: Obsidian, 2010)

Series: Jade del Cameron Mystery Series. Book 6
Story type: Mystery; Series
Subject(s): Mystery; Adventure; History
Major character(s): Jade del Cameron, Journalist, Adventurer; Sam Featherstone, Boyfriend (of Jade); Lilith Worthy, Prisoner (escaped), Mother (of David); David Worthy, Spouse (of Jade, deceased); Pili, Son (of David); Lord Avery Dunbury, Nobleman, Friend (of Jade); Lady Avery Dunbury, Spouse (of Lord Dunbury), Friend (of Jade)
Time period(s): 20th century; 1920s (1921)
Locale(s): Kenya

Summary: In *The Crocodile's Last Embrace* by Suzanne Arruda, photojournalist Jade del Cameron returns to Kenya in 1921 after a European trip. Jade lost her fiance David, a World War I veteran, and is now involved with Sam Featherstone. David's mother, Lilith Worthy, has been serving a sentence in an English prison but has escaped to hunt down Jade. Meanwhile, Jade begins receiving accusing messages from David, even though she witnessed his death. As Jade tries to outrun wily Lilith, she must also do battle with a crocodile. *The Crocodile's Last Embrace* is the sixth book in the Jade Del Cameron mystery series.

Where it's reviewed:
Kirkus Reviews, July 15, 2010, page 648
Publishers Weekly, July 19, 2010, page 115

Other books by the same author:
The Leopard's Prey, 2009
Treasure of the Golden Cheetah, 2009
The Serpent's Daughter, 2008
Stalking Ivory, 2007
Mark the Lion, 2006

Other books you might like:
Michael Bowen, *Act of Faith*, 1993
Dennis Casley, *Death Underfoot*, 1994
Alexander McCall Smith, *The Good Husband of Zebra Drive*, 2007
Karin McQuillan, *Elephants' Graveyard*, 1993
Tracy Price-Thompson, *A Woman's Worth*, 2004

110

MICHAEL ATKINSON

Hemingway Cutthroat

(New York: Minotaur Books, 2010)

Story type: Mystery
Subject(s): Writers; Murder; Detective fiction
Major character(s): Ernest Hemingway, Writer, Detective—Amateur; Jose Robles Pazos, Crime Victim, Volunteer
Time period(s): 20th century; 1930s (1937)
Locale(s): Madrid, Spain

Summary: It is 1937, and the Spanish Civil War is in full swing. Death and dying is everywhere in Madrid, but one particular killing—the demise of a volunteer and suspected spy—has American writer, Ernest Hemingway especially perplexed. In Spain to cover the war, Hemingway is drawn into his own investigation into the killing of Jose Robles Pazos. But he soon finds there are some very dangerous individuals intent on keeping Robles Pazos's death a secret—no matter the cost. Michael Atkinson's *Hemingway Cutthroat* is the sequel to *Hemingway Deadlights*.

Where it's reviewed:
Booklist, May 1, 2010, page 30
Publishers Weekly, May 3, 2010, page 33

Other books by the same author:
Hemingway Deadlights, 2009

Other books you might like:
Clancy Carlile, *The Paris Pilgrims*, 1999
Joe Haldeman, *The Hemingway Hoax*, 1990
William McCranor Henderson, *I Killed Hemingway*, 1993
Craig McDonald, *Print the Legend*, 2010
Dan Simmons, *The Crook Factory*, 1999

111

TED BACINO

The Shakespeare Conspiracy

(Bloomington, Indiana: AuthorHouse, 2010)

Subject(s): Murder; Writers; Plays
Major character(s): Christopher Marlowe, Writer (playwright); William Shakespeare, Writer (playwright)
Time period(s): 16th century; 1590s
Locale(s): London, United Kingdom

Summary: Set in Elizabethan England, Tony Bacino's *The Shakespeare Conspiracy* chronicles two of the literary world's most enduring mysteries. Christopher Marlowe was the reigning playwright of the day, but when he was found guilty of treason and sentenced to death, his status was usurped by a young horse guard named William Shakespeare. Bacino fictionalizes the story behind this duel set of mysteries: Marlowe's sudden, politically motivated death and Shakespeare's quick ascension to the status of the day's most legendary playwright. First novel.

Other books you might like:
Anthony Burgess, *A Dead Man in Deptford*, 1993
Bruce Cook, *Young Will*, 2004
George Garrett, *Entered from the Sun*, 1990
Leslie Silbert, *The Intelligencer*, 2004
Martin Stephen, *The Conscience of the King*, 2003

112

MIGNON F. BALLARD

Miss Dimple Disappears

(New York: Minotaur Books, 2010)

Story type: Cozy Mystery; Historical - World War II
Subject(s): World War II, 1939-1945; Missing persons; Mystery
Major character(s): Charlie Carr, Teacher, Detective—Amateur; Annie, Friend (of Charlie), Detective—Amateur
Time period(s): 20th century; 1940s (1942)
Locale(s): Elderberry, Georgia

Summary: *Miss Dimple Disappears* is a historical cozy mystery from author Mignon F. Ballard. Charlie Carr already has her hands full when the school janitor ends up dead in the storage closet: World War II is raging on, people in the small town of Elderberry, Georgia, are overcome with tragedy, Charlie's beau is fighting in the conflict, and she can't stop thinking about her best friend's boyfriend. But when a beloved first-grade teacher, Miss Dimple Kirkpatrick, vanishes in the middle of the night, Charlie begins to take notice. Charlie knows Miss Dimple would never run away, so what could have happened to the elderly lady? The police don't seem all that concerned, leading Charlie, along with her best pal, Annie, to do some sleuthing of their own.

Where it's reviewed:
Booklist, November 1, 2010, page 30
Kirkus Reviews, October 15, 2010, page 1029
Publishers Weekly, October 4, 2010, page 30

Other books by the same author:
The Angel and the Jabberwocky, 2006
The Angel Whispered Danger, 2003
Final Curtain, 1992
Deadly Promise, 1989
Raven Rock, 1986

Other books you might like:
James R. Benn, *Rag and Bone*, 2010
Garrison Keillor, *Leaving Home: A Collection of Lake Wobegon Stories*, 1987
Helen Hooven Santmyer, *And Ladies of the Club*, 1984
Mary Helen Stefaniak, *The Cailiffs of Baghdad, Georgia*, 2010
Jack Todd, *Come Again No More: A Novel*, 2010

113

AILEEN G. BARON

Scorpion's Bite

(Scottsdale, Arizona: Poisoned Pen Press, 2010)

Series: Lily Sampson Series. Book 3
Subject(s): Middle East; Murder; Archaeology
Major character(s): Lily Sampson, Archaeologist, Detective—Amateur; Gideon Weil, Archaeologist, Crime Suspect
Time period(s): 19th century; 1940s (1943)
Locale(s): Middle East

Summary: In *Scorpion's Bite*, Aileen G. Baron spins a tale of mystery, suspense, and espionage in the Middle East during World War II. Lily Sampson, an archeologist with the Office of Strategic Services (OSS), is summoned to survey the Trans-Jordanian desert with Gideon Weil, the head of Jerusalem's American School of Archeological Research. When the man serving as their guide turns up dead, Gideon stands accused of the murder. As Lily tries to help her colleague, she finds two pipelines running through the desert—a discovery that could have major repercussions on the safety and security on the entire Middle East. *Scorpion's Bite* is the third novel in the Lily Sampson series.

Where it's reviewed:
Publishers Weekly, July 26, 2010, page 56

Other books by the same author:
The Gold of Thrace, 2007
The Torch of Tangier, 2006
A Fly Has a Hundred Eyes, 2002

Other books you might like:
James R. Benn, *Rag and Bone*, 2010
Iris Johansen, *Deadlock*, 2009
Raymond Khoury, *The Last Templar*, 2006
Steve Shagan, *The Discovery*, 1984
Barbara Wood, *The Prophetess: A Novel*, 1996

114

STEPHANIE BARRON

Jane and the Madness of Lord Byron

(New York: Bantam Books, 2010)

Series: Jane Austen Mystery Series. Book 9
Story type: Mystery; Series
Subject(s): Murder; History; Grief
Major character(s): Jane Austen, Writer, Sister (of Harry); George "Lord Byron" Gorda, Writer (poet); Harry Austen, Brother (of Jane), Widow(er)
Time period(s): 19th century; 1810-1820 (1813)
Locale(s): Brighton Beach, England

Summary: In Stephanie Barron's *Jane and the Madness of Lord Byron*, novelist Jane Austen travels to Brighton Beach with her brother, Henry, to relax and hopefully cope with the death of her sister-in-law. When they arrive, they are advised that the maddening poet Lord Byron is also in Brighton. If Lord Byron's temper isn't enough to scare people away, rumors that have spread throughout Brighton that the poet is responsible for the death of a beautiful young woman certainly will. When curiosity gets the best of Jane, she begins to investigate these claims herself. Could Lord Byron really be responsible for the woman's death? And will Jane be his next victim? This is the ninth book in the Being A Jane Austen Mystery series.

Where it's reviewed:
Kirkus Reviews, June 15, 2010, page 542
Library Journal, June 15, 2010, page 70
Publishers Weekly, August 23, 2010, page 31

Other books by the same author:
Jane and His Lordship's Legacy, 2005
Jane and the Ghosts of Netley, 2003
Jane and the Prisoner of Wool House, 2001
Jane and the Man of the Cloth, 1997
Jane and the Unpleasantness at Scargrave Manor, 1996

Other books you might like:
John Crowley, *Lord Byron's Novel*, 2005
Tracy Kiely, *Murder at Longbourn: A Mystery*, 2009
Jude Morgan, *Passion*, 2005
Lauren Willig, *The Mischief of the Mistletoe*, 2010

115

SIMON BEAUFORT

The Bloodstained Throne

(New York: Severn House, 2010)

Series: Sir Geoffrey Mappestone Series. Book 7
Story type: Historical - Medieval; Series
Subject(s): History; Middle Ages; Mystery
Major character(s): Geoffrey Mappestone, Knight (crusader, former); Roger, Knight (crusader, former), Friend (of Geoffrey Mappestone); Philippa, Passenger (ship); Juhel, Passenger (ship); Paisnel, Passenger (ship); Vitalis, Passenger (ship)
Time period(s): 21th century; 1100s (1103)
Locale(s): England

Summary: In *The Bloodstained Throne* by Simon Beaufort, Geoffrey Mappestone and Roger of Durham, both former knights of the Crusades, are sailing from England toward Jerusalem when their vessel, the *Patrick*, is shipwrecked in a storm. Two passengers are killed—not by the weather but at the hand of an unknown murderer on board—forcing Geoffrey and Roger to recognize the precariousness of their situation. The two knights join the party of survivors as they make their way to a local abbey, fearing for their lives in the company of pirates and killers. *The Bloodstained Throne* is the seventh book in the Sir Geoffrey Mappestone series.

Where it's reviewed:
Booklist, October 15, 2010, page 22
Kirkus Reviews, October 15, 2010, page 10354
Publishers Weekly, September 6, 2010, page 27

Other books by the same author:
Deadly Inheritance, 2009
A Head for Poisoning, 2009

The Coiners' Quarrel, 2004
The Bishop's Brood, 2003
The King's Spies, 2003

Other books you might like:
Elizabeth Chadwick, *The Conquest*, 1997
Alys Clare, *Music of the Distant Stars*, 2010
Paul Doherty, *The Waxman Murders*, 2010
Ellis Peters, *An Excellent Mystery*, 1985
Priscilla Royal, *Valley of Dry Bones*, 2010

116

ANN BELL

Rebekah's Journey: An Historical Novel

(Georgetown, Texas: Kathy Crossing Press, 2010)

Story type: Religious
Subject(s): History; Religion; Quakers
Major character(s): Rebekah Bradford, Young Woman
Time period(s): 18th century
Locale(s): London, England; Philadelphia, Pennsylvania

Summary: In *Rebekah's Journey: An Historical Novel* by Ann Bell, a young woman comes to America from England as an indentured servant when her family suffers a devastating tragedy. In Philadelphia, Rebekah Bradford works for a Quaker family and learns firsthand about their unique way of life. Although it is the 18th century, Quaker women are valued members of the community. In that positive atmosphere, Rebekah is able to escape a life of servitude, marry, have children, and establish her own career. Rebekah's personal journey parallels the daunting journey of all Quakers as they try to establish their position in the fledgling nation.

Other books by the same author:
Mended Wheels, 2002
Love Abounds, 2000
Love Remembered, 1999
Distant Love, 1995
Inspired Love, 1995

Other books you might like:
Helen C. Barney, *Green Rose of Furley*, 1953
Margaret Elphinstone, *Voyageurs*, 2004
Evie Yoder Miller, *Eyes at the Window*, 2003
Mary Pope Osborne, *Standing in the Light: The Captive Diary of Catharine Carey Logan*, 1998
Joanne Sundell, *Hearts Persuaded*, 2010

117

JAMES R. BENN

Rag and Bone

(New York: Soho Press, 2010)

Series: Billy Boyle World War II Mystery Series. Book 5
Story type: Historical - World War II
Subject(s): Detective fiction; Murder; Russians
Major character(s): Billy Boyle, Military Personnel,

Detective; Dwight Eisenhower, Military Personnel
Time period(s): 20th century; 1940s (1943)
Locale(s): London, United Kingdom

Summary: Set amidst the chaos of the Second World War, James R. Benn's *Rag and Bone* is the fifth novel in the Billy Boyle World War II Mystery series. This outing finds Billy called back early from leave to investigate the murder of a Russian security officer. As Billy probes the details of the case, he slowly realizes the implications of the Russian's murder, which, Billy suspects, was committed in revenge for the mass killings of thousands of Poles.

Where it's reviewed:
Booklist, August 1, 2010, page 33
Publishers Weekly, July 19, 2010, page 116

Other books by the same author:
Evil for Evil, 2009
Blood Alone, 2008
The First Wave, 2007
Billy Boyle, 2006

Other books you might like:
Rennie Airth, *The Dead of Winter*, 2009
Aileen G. Baron, *Scorpion's Bite*, 2010
Sebastian Faulks, *Charlotte Gray*, 1998
Jill Paton Walsh, *A Presumption of Death*, 2003
Sarah Waters, *The Night Watch*, 2006

118

MAGGIE BENNETT

Strangers and Pilgrims

(New York: Severn House, 2010)

Story type: Historical - Medieval
Subject(s): History; Middle Ages; Religious life
Major character(s): Ralph "Friar Valerian" de Courcy, Lawyer; Cecily Wynstede, Daughter (of knight)
Time period(s): 14th century; 1340s (1340)
Locale(s): England

Summary: In *Strangers and Pilgrims* by Maggie Bennett, a successful law and medical professional in 1340 England assumes a new vocation when his beloved wife dies in childbirth. Master Ralph de Courcy, now Friar Valerian, roams the countryside offering help to those in need. Believing that he can never love again, Valerian is surprised by his immediate attraction to Cecily Wynstede, a young woman he meets on his travels whom he feels is the embodiment of his patron saint, Cecelia. Cecily has feelings for Valerian as well, but is bound to honor the betrothal that has been arranged by her parents.

Where it's reviewed:
Booklist, November 1, 2010, page 33

Other books by the same author:
The Unchanging Heart, 2007
The Tailor's Daughter, 2006
For Love of Lily, 2005
A Carriage for the Midwife, 2003
A Child at the Door, 2002

Other books you might like:
Bernard Cornwell, *The Archer's Tale*, 2001
Paul Harding, *Murder Most Holy*, 1992
Paul Harding, *Red Slayer: Being the Second of the Sorrowful Mysteries of Brother Athelstan*, 1992
Karen Maitland, *Company of Liars*, 2008
Judith Merkle Riley, *A Vision of Light*, 1989

119

JAMES D. BEST

Tempest at Dawn

(Tucson, Arizona: Wheatmark, 2011)

Story type: Historical - Post-American Revolution
Subject(s): United States history; Law; Military science
Major character(s): Roger Sherman, Historical Figure; James Madison, Historical Figure; George Washington, Historical Figure; Thomas Jefferson, Historical Figure; Charles Pinckney, Historical Figure; Pierce Butler, Historical Figure
Time period(s): 18th century; 1780s
Locale(s): Philadelphia, Pennsylvania

Summary: In *Tempest at Dawn*, author James D. Best presents a fictionalized account of the 1787 meeting that led to the establishment of America as a republic. With the United States suffering from economic, military, and diplomatic instability in the wake of the revolution, a group of 55 influential leaders agree to meet in Philadelphia to amend the Articles of Confederation. The players include Roger Sherman, James Madison, George Washington, Thomas Jefferson, Charles Pinckney, Pierce Butler, and other familiar historical figures. Their clandestine mission results in the founding of the world's most steadfast republic.

Other books you might like:
Ellen Cooney, *Gun Battle Hill*, 2004
David Liss, *The Whiskey Rebels*, 2008
William Martin, *The Lost Constitution*, 2007
Gordon Ryan, *A Question of Consequence: A Novel*, 2003
R.W. Stone, *Trail Hand*, 2006

120

WILLIAM PETER BLATTY

Crazy

(New York: Forge, 2010)

Story type: Historical - World War II; Mystery
Subject(s): World War II, 1939-1945; Friendship; Mystery
Major character(s): Joey El Bueno, Writer; Jane Bent, Friend (of Joey)
Time period(s): 20th century; 1940s
Locale(s): New York, New York

Summary: Joey El Bueno, Peruvian-American screenwriter, reminisces on his childhood in New York City during World War II. While a student at St. Stephen's middle school, Joey first encountered the eccentric and enigmatic Jane Bent. Drawn to Jane's quirky charm and her carefree attitude, Joey spends a day with her and quickly forms a bond with the unusual girl, but no one seems to know anything about her. Jane continues to pop up in Joey's life sporadically in mysterious ways, fueling Joey's intrigue about the mystery surrounding this fascinating girl.

Where it's reviewed:
Booklist, November 1, 2010, page 22
Publishers Weekly, July 26, 2010, page 42

Other books by the same author:
Dimiter, 2010
Elsewhere, 2009
Legion, 1983
The Ninth Configuration, 1978
The Exorcist, 1971

Other books you might like:
Amram Ducovny, *Coney*, 2000
R.J. Ellory, *A Quiet Belief in Angels*, 2009
Kathryn Miller Haines, *The Winter of Her Discontent*, 2008
Jay Neugeboren, *1940*, 2008
Sheila York, *A Good Knife's Work*, 2010

121

RHYS BOWEN

Royal Blood

(New York: Berkley Prime Crime, 2010)

Series: Royal Spyness Mystery Series. Book 4
Subject(s): Vampires; Humor; Weddings
Major character(s): Georgiana "Georgie" Rannoch, Noblewoman, Detective—Amateur; Queenie Hepplewhite, Servant (of Georgie)
Time period(s): 20th century; 1930s
Locale(s): Transylvania, Romania

Summary: The fourth book in Rhys Bowen's Royal Spyness Mystery series, *Royal Blood* finds poor noblewoman Lady Georgiana Rannoch dispatched to a wedding in Romania as a favor to the Queen. With her hapless maid Queenie Hepplewhite in tow, Georgie travels to the isolated castle in the hills of Transylvania. There she happens upon a murder mystery involving the strange death of a Bulgarian field marshal. Georgie once again puts her sleuthing skills to the test and embarks upon her own investigation into the grisly event.

Where it's reviewed:
Booklist, September 1, 2010, page 52
Kirkus Reviews, July 15, 2010, page 649
Publishers Weekly, July 19, 2010, page 116

Other books by the same author:
Royal Flush, 2009
A Royal Pain, 2008
Tell Me, Pretty Maiden, 2008
Her Royal Spyness, 2007
In Dublin's Fair City, 2007
Oh Danny Boy, 2006
Murphy's Law, 2001
Evans Above, 1997

Other books you might like:
Carole Nelson Douglas, *Castle Rouge*, 2002
Barbara Hambly, *Renfield: Slave of Dracula*, 2006
Jeanne Kalogridis, *Covenant with the Vampire: The Diaries of the Family Dracul*, 1994
Elizabeth Kostova, *The Historian*, 2005
Barbara Sjoholm, *Trouble in Translyvania*, 1993

122

PAULA BRACKSTON

The Witch's Daughter

(New York: Thomas Dunne Books, 2011)

Story type: Witchcraft
Subject(s): Witches; History; Fantasy
Major character(s): Elizabeth Anne Hawksmith, Witch, Orphan; Gideon Masters, Warlock
Time period(s): Multiple Time Periods; 17th century-21st century; 1620s-2010s
Locale(s): England

Summary: *The Witch's Daughter* is a fantasy novel from author Paula Brackston. In 1628, Elizabeth Anne Hawksmith watches in horror as her mother is hanged for witchcraft. Now an orphan, after losing the rest of her family the previous year to the plague, and fearing for her own life, Elizabeth seeks refuge from a mysterious warlock named Gideon Masters. Gideon instructs Elizabeth in the ways of witchcraft, revealing dark and surprising powers and equipping her to live forever. In modern-day England, Elizabeth continues to discreetly practice the craft, all the while avoiding being hunted by Gideon who is eager for payment after saving her life so many years earlier. When a quirky teenager begins hanging around, Elizabeth begins teaching her about the Craft and, in the process, unlocks dark and powerful secrets of her past.

Where it's reviewed:
Booklist, November 15, 2010, page 26
Kirkus Reviews, November 1, 2010, page 1072
Library Journal, December 1, 2010, page 102
Publishers Weekly, October 4, 2010, page 31

Other books by the same author:
Lamp Black, Wolf Grey, 2010
Book of Shadows, 2009

Other books you might like:
Nina Bawden, *The Witch's Daughter*, 1966
Susan Fletcher, *Corrag*, 2010
Sheri Holman, *The Witches on the Road Tonight*, 2011
Kathleen Kent, *The Heretic's Daughter*, 2008
Mary Sharratt, *Daughters of the Witching Hill*, 2010

123

BO CALDWELL

City of Tranquil Light

(New York: Henry Holt and Co., 2010)

Story type: Inspirational
Subject(s): Missionaries; China; Wars

Major character(s): Will Kiehn, Spouse (husband of Katherine), Volunteer (Missionary), Farmer; Katherine, Volunteer (Missionary), Spouse (wife of Will)
Time period(s): 20th century
Locale(s): Kuang P'ing Ch'eng, China

Summary: Bo Caldwell's *City of Tranquil Light* shares the story of Will and Katherine, missionaries in China in the early 20th century. Will has lived his entire life as a farmer, but now he believes that his presence is necessary elsewhere. Taking a leap of faith, he becomes a missionary in China, where he meets Katherine, who is also a missionary. The two connect instantly and eventually wed. Their lives take a dramatic turn, however, as they find themselves caught in the middle of a civil war. The nation they've been aiding seems to be crashing down around them, and the two must hold on tightly to their faith and each other. *City of Tranquil Light* was inspired by the lives of real missionaries in China during the first half of the 20th century.

Where it's reviewed:
Booklist, September 15, 2010, page 36
Kirkus Reviews, September 1, 2010, page 811
Library Journal, June 1, 2010, page 75
Publishers Weekly, August 2, 2010, page 27

Other books by the same author:
The Distant Land of My Father, 2001

Other books you might like:
David W. Ball, *China Run*, 2002
James Brady, *Warning of War*, 2002
John Hersey, *The Call*, 1985
Judith Michael, *A Certain Smile*, 1999
Anchee Min, *Pearl of China: A Novel*, 2009

124

CHRISTIAN CAMERON

Killer of Men

(London: Orion, 2010)

Subject(s): Ancient Greek civilization; Revenge; Violence
Major character(s): Arimnestos, Slave
Locale(s): Greece

Summary: Christian Cameron's *Killer of Men* chronicles the adventures of Arimnestos, a young farmer-turned-soldier who eventually ends up a slave. After a brutal battle with the forces of Thebes, Arimnestos wakes from unconsciousness to find he has been sold into slavery. As he struggles to escape his new, suffocating existence, Arimnestos's true calling is kindled, and he discovers his own voracious appetite and skill for vengeance and killing.

Other books by the same author:
Funeral Games, 2010
Storm of Arrows, 2009
Tyrant, 2008
Washington and Caesar, 2004

Other books you might like:
Steve Berry, *The Venetian Betrayal*, 2007
Scott Oden, *Men of Bronze*, 2005

Steven Pressfield, *Gates of Fire*, 1998
Mary Renault, *Fire from Heaven*, 1969
Gene Wolfe, *Soldier of the Mist*, 1986

125

EMMA CAMPION

The King's Mistress: A Novel

(New York: Crown Publishers, 2010)

Story type: Historical - Medieval
Subject(s): British history, 1066-1688; Royalty; Mother-daughter relations
Major character(s): Alice Perrers, Lover (mistress of Edward III), Spouse (of Janyn); Janyn Perrers, Spouse (of Alice); Edward III, Royalty (king of England); Isabella, Royalty (queen of England)
Time period(s): 14th century
Locale(s): United Kingdom

Summary: Emma Campion's *The King's Mistress: A Novel* is set in 14th century England. Alice Salisbury is married off to Janyn Perrers, a wealthy businessman favored by Queen Isabella. When fate disrupts their conventional lifestyle, Alice is forced to take up residence at the royal court. There she falls under the eye of Edward III, who soon makes his feelings for her quite plain. Now Alice must sacrifice her own interests in order to save her daughter from meeting the same doom. First novel.

Where it's reviewed:
Library Journal, July 1, 2010, page 72
Publishers Weekly, May 17, 2010, page 29

Other books you might like:
Vanora Bennett, *The People's Queen*, 2010
Bernard Cornwell, *The Archer's Tale*, 2001
Maurice Druon, *The Lily and the Lion*, 1961
Jean Plaidy, *The Vow on the Heron*, 1980
Judith Merkle Riley, *A Vision of Light*, 1989

126

REBECCA CANTRELL

A Night of Long Knives

(New York: Forge, 2010)

Series: Hannah Vogel Series. Book 2
Subject(s): Germans; Kidnapping; Suspense
Major character(s): Hannah Vogel, Journalist, Mother (of Anton); Anton, Son (of Hannah), Kidnap Victim; Ernst Rohm, Worker (head of the SA)
Time period(s): 20th century; 1930s (1934)
Locale(s): Germany

Summary: It is 1934, and Germany is in the iron grip of the Nazis. Hannah Vogel and her son, Anton, are en route to Switzerland when the zeppelin in which they are traveling makes an unexpected stop in Hannah's native Germany. There, Anton is whisked away by SA officers headed by Ernst Rohm, who claims to be the boy's father. After escaping Rohm's dangerous clutches, Hannah sets out to find her son, bringing her face to face with the most terrifying figures of the Nazi regime. *A Night of Long Knives* is the second novel in Rebecca Cantrell's Hannah Vogel series.

Where it's reviewed:
Booklist, June 1, 2010, page 41
Kirkus Reviews, May 1, 2010, page 394
Publishers Weekly, April 26, 2010, page 92

Other books by the same author:
A Trace of Smoke, 2009

Other books you might like:
Richard Hughes, *The Wooden Shepherdess*, 1973
Hans Hellmut Kirst, *The Nights of the Long Knives*, 1976
John Lawton, *A Lily of the Field*, 2010
Daniel Silva, *A Death in Vienna*, 2004
Gordon Zuckerman, *The Sentinels: Fortunes of War*, 2009

127

JOANNA CHALLIS

Peril at Somner House

(New York: Minotaur Books, 2010)

Series: Daphne du Maurier Mystery Series. Book 2
Story type: Mystery
Subject(s): Mystery; Murder; Vacations
Major character(s): Daphne du Maurier, Detective—Amateur, Writer (aspiring); Max Trevalyan, Nobleman (Lord), Crime Victim; Angela du Maurier, Sister (of Daphne), Detective—Amateur
Time period(s): Indeterminate Past
Locale(s): Cornwall, England

Summary: *Peril at Somner House*, the second installment in the Daphne du Maurier Mystery series, is a suspenseful historical mystery from author Joanna Challis. Aspiring writer Daphne du Maurier agrees to accompany her sister, Angela, to Somner House, a picturesque coastal estate in Cornwall owned by Lord and Lady Trevalyan, for a brief winter vacation. No sooner has a threatening winter storm rolled in than Lord Max Trevalyan is found murdered and his wife is discovered in an illicit affair with another man. A chance encounter with a sexy and mysterious stranger fuels Daphne to do some amateur sleuthing in an attempt to find the cold-hearted killer.

Where it's reviewed:
Booklist, October 15, 2010, page 25
Kirkus Reviews, September 15, 2010, page 896
Library Journal, November 1, 2010, page 49
Publishers Weekly, September 13, 2010, page 26

Other books by the same author:
Murder on the Cliffs, 2009

Other books you might like:
Sally Beauman, *Rebecca's Tale*, 2001
Sam Llewellyn, *The Sea Garden*, 1999
Justine Picardie, *Daphne: A Novel*, 2008
Diane Setterfield, *The Thirteenth Tale*, 2006
Charles Todd, *Wings of Fire*, 1998

128

JACQUES CHESSEX

A Jew Must Die

(London: Bitter Lemon Press, 2010)

Subject(s): Jews; Murder; World War II, 1939-1945
Major character(s): Fernand Ischi, Religious (pastor); Arthur Bloch, Dealer (cattle)
Time period(s): 20th century; 1940s (1942)
Locale(s): Payerne, Switzerland

Summary: The malicious violence of World War II is illustrated in one case of anti-Semitic crime in Jacques Chessex's *A Jew Must Die*. In the rural town of Payerne, Switzerland, minister Fernand Ischi gathers his group of henchman to terrorize local Jew and cattle businessman Arthur Bloch. Ischi's aim: to murder Bloch as a tribute to Adolf Hitler. This volume is translated from the Swiss by Charles Wilson.

Where it's reviewed:
Booklist, April 15, 2010, page 37
Publishers Weekly, February 15, 2010, page 114

Other books by the same author:
The Vampire of Ropraz, 2008
A Father's Love, 1975

Other books you might like:
Maria Angels Anglada, *The Auschwitz Violin*, 2010
Paul Grossman, *The Sleepwalkers*, 2010
Frank Moorhouse, *Dark Palace*, 2000
Natasha Solomons, *Mr. Rosenblum Dreams in English: A Novel*, 2010
Sarah Waters, *The Night Watch*, 2006

129

ALYS CLARE

Music of the Distant Stars

(New York: Severn House Publishers, 2010)

Series: Aelf Fen Series. Book 3
Subject(s): Supernatural; Mysticism; Murder
Major character(s): Lassair, Healer, Young Woman
Time period(s): 11th century-12th century; 1080-1100 (1087-1100)
Locale(s): Aelf Fen, Fictional Location

Summary: Alys Clare's *Music of the Distant Stars* is the third book in the Aelf Fen series. In this installment, Lassair, a healer who has recently discovered her mystical powers, sneaks out of her house one night to visit her grandmother's grave. When she reaches the cemetery, however, she stumbles across the body of the local seamstress. The girl is young and pregnant and Lassair can immediately tell she was strangled. As the authorities work to track down the seamstress's killer, Lassair uses her own strengths and powers to try to solve the mystery around the woman's death. As time passes, another body is discovered and Lassair fears the killer is on her trail.

Where it's reviewed:
Booklist, November 15, 2010, page 5
Kirkus Reviews, October 1, 2010, page 962
Library Journal, November 1, 2010, page 49
Publishers Weekly, October 11, 2010, page 29

Other books by the same author:
Mist Over the Water, 2009
Out of the Dawn Light, 2009
The Joys of My life, 2008
Ashes of the Elements, 2001
Fortune Like the Moon, 2000

Other books you might like:
Simon Beaufort, *The Bloodstained Throne*, 2010
Paul Doherty, *The Waxman Murders*, 2010
Pat McIntosh, *A Pig of Cold Poison*, 2010
Priscilla Royal, *Valley of Dry Bones*, 2010
Peter Tremayne, *The Dove of Death*, 2010

130

MARILYN J. CLAY

Deceptions: A Jamestown Novel

(Waterville, Maine: Five Star, 2010)

Subject(s): Love; Adventure; Marriage
Major character(s): Catherine Parke, Young Woman; Noah Colton, Fiance(e) (of Catherine); Adam, Brother (of Catherine); Pocahontas, Diplomat
Time period(s): 17th century; 1610s (1617-1619)
Locale(s): Virginia, United States

Summary: Marilyn J. Clay's *Deceptions: A Jamestown Novel* follows Englishwoman, Catherine Parke on her adventures through the New World. Six years prior, Catherine's father, brother, and betrothed all set sail for America, and now she has received word that she can join them. Those looking after her, however, have other ideas, and Catherine is soon engaged to another. With a little help from visiting diplomat Pocahontas, Catherine is able to ditch the arranged marriage and make it to the New World, where an unexpected heartbreak lies in store: her betrothed, Noah, has married another.

Where it's reviewed:
Booklist, June 1, 2010, page 44

Other books by the same author:
Miss Darby's Debut, 1999
Miss Eliza's Gentleman Caller, 1998
Felicity's Folly, 1997
The Unsuitable Suitor, 1997
Brighton Beauty, 1996

Other books you might like:
Virginia Bernhard, *A Durable Fire*, 1990
Philippa Gregory, *Virgin Earth*, 1999
Karleen Koen, *Now Face to Face*, 1995
George Robert Minkoff, *The Weight of Smoke*, 2006
William T. Vollmann, *Argall*, 2001

131

BARNABY CONRAD

The Second Life of John Wilkes Booth

(San Francisco, California: Oak Books, 2010)

Story type: Alternate History
Subject(s): Assassination; Murder; History
Major character(s): John Wilkes Booth, Murderer, Criminal, Historical Figure, Actor; Robert E. Lee, Historical Figure, Military Personnel
Time period(s): 19th century; 1860s
Locale(s): Washington, District of Columbia; Montana, United States

Summary: *The Second Life of John Wilkes Booth* is a historical novel from critically acclaimed author Barnaby Conrad. In Conrad's alternative history, John Wilkes Booth still assassinates Abraham Lincoln at Ford Theater but manages to escape capture. Following the assassination, Booth travels south to find General Robert E. Lee, a man Booth assumes will be happy to hear the news. Lee's outrage and hostility toward Booth drive the assassin out west to start a quiet new life deep in Montana. Booth manages to start afresh, assuming the identity of John Richard Marlowe, but a curious and committed reporter, eager to get the story of a lifetime, won't let Booth get too comfortable before busting the story wide open.

Where it's reviewed:
Kirkus Reviews, October 1, 2010, page 953

Other books by the same author:
Last Boat to Cadiz, 2003
Endangered, 1978
Dangerfield, 1961
Matador, 1952
The Innocent Villa, 1948

Other books you might like:
Jan Jordan, *Dim the Flaring Lamps*, 1972
Benjamin King, *A Bullet for Lincoln*, 1993
John J. Miller, *The First Assassin*, 2009
David Robertson, *Booth*, 1998
Pamela Redford Russell, *The Woman Who Loved John Wilkes Booth*, 1978

132

GARY CORBY

The Pericles Commission

(New York: Minotaur Books, 2010)

Story type: Mystery
Subject(s): Ancient Greek civilization; Murder; Mystery
Major character(s): Nicolaos, Son (of a sculptor), Detective; Pericles, Political Figure
Time period(s): 5th century B.C.
Locale(s): Athens, Greece

Summary: *The Pericles Commission* is a historical mystery from debut author Gary Corby. Nicolaos, a sculptor's son expected to assume his father's trade, is given a new career direction when he discovers the dead body of Ephialtes, the politician who introduced democracy to ancient Athens. When Ephialtes's friend, Pericles, shows up to the crime scene moments later, he offers Nicolaos a job tracking down the person responsible for the killing. Nicolaos sets out on an investigation through classic Athens, hunting for clues and looking for suspects, but Nicolaos's first job as detective isn't going so well. Someone is killing off the witnesses, Nicolaos's 12-year-old brother Socrates is irritating to no end, and Nicolaos can't keep his mind off the beautiful virgin priestess, Diotima. First novel.

Where it's reviewed:
Kirkus Reviews, September 15, 2010, page 897
Publishers Weekly, August 9, 2010, page 33

Other books you might like:
Barbara Cleverly, *A Darker God*, 2010
Margaret Doody, *Aristotle Detective*, 1980
Annabel Lyon, *The Golden Mean: A Novel of Aristotle and Alexander the Great*, 2009
Steven Pressfield, *Tides of War*, 2000
Rex Warner, *Pericles the Athenian*, 1963

133

BERNARD CORNWELL

The Fort: A Novel of the Revolutionary War
(New York: Harper, 2010)

Story type: Historical - American Revolution
Subject(s): United States history; Military life; Wars
Major character(s): Solomon Lovell, Military Personnel; Dudley Saltonstall, Military Personnel; Paul Revere, Military Personnel
Time period(s): 18th century; 1770s (1779)
Locale(s): Massachusetts, United States

Summary: In *The Fort: A Novel of the Revolutionary War*, best-selling historical novelist Bernard Cornwell presents a fictionalized account of the Penobscot Expedition, an often-overlooked, 18th-century military battle. The seeds of revolution have been sown, and the Americans are waging war against the British. General Solomon Lovell, Commander Dudley Saltonstall, and Paul Revere are among the cast of American military personnel hatching a poorly conceived attack on a British fort. The resulting chaos brings together an epic clash of personalities, culminating on a cannon- and musket-filled battleground.

Where it's reviewed:
Booklist, July 1, 2010, page 7
Publishers Weekly, August 2, 2010, page 29

Other books by the same author:
Agincourt, 2009
Sword Song, 2008
The Pale Horseman, 2006
The Last Kingdom, 2005
Rebel, 1993

Other books you might like:
Jimmy Carter, *The Hornet's Nest: A Novel of the Revolutionary War*, 2003
William R. Forstchen, *Valley Forge: George Washington and the Crucible of Victory*, 2010
Charles F. Price, *Nor the Battle to the Strong*, 2008
Kenneth Roberts, *Arundel*, 1930
Willard M. Wallace, *East to Bagaduce*, 1963

134

J.D. DAVIES

Gentleman Captain
(Boston, Massachusetts: Houghton Mifflin Harcourt, 2010)

Story type: Mystery
Subject(s): Ships; Mystery; Rebellion
Major character(s): Matthew Quinton, 21-Year-Old, Gentleman, Sea Captain
Time period(s): 17th century; 1660s (1662)
Locale(s): England; Scotland

Summary: *Gentleman Captain* is a historical, nautical-themed novel from award-winning author J.D. Davies. Matthew Quinton, a 21-year-old gentleman captain, got a rocky start to his nautical career. His first ship was caught in a storm off the coast of Ireland and sank. Fortunately for Matthew, the newly reinstated King Charles II is giving him another ship and a chance to earn some respect and honor. A rebellion is brewing in Scotland and the King sends Matthew aboard the ship Jupiter, but Matthew's crew is hardly supportive. As the men get closer to the wild shores of Scotland, Matthew begins to earn their trust, but a greater threat is at hand: rumors that the Jupiter's previous captain was murdered and the killer might still be at large.

Where it's reviewed:
Booklist, September 15, 2010, page 37
Kirkus Reviews, July 15, 2010, page 643
Publishers Weekly, June 28, 2010, page 108

Other books you might like:
Alex Beecroft, *False Colors*, 2009
Naomi Novik, *Throne of Jade*, 2006
Patrick O'Brian, *The Hundred Days*, 1998
Dudley Pope, *Drumbeat*, 1968
Julian Stockwin, *Victory*, 2010

135

LINDSEY DAVIS

Nemesis
(New York: Minotaur Books, 2010)

Series: Marcus Didius Falco Series. Book 20
Subject(s): Mystery; Murder; History
Major character(s): Marcus Didius Falco, Detective; Geminus, Father (of Falco); Petronius, Friend (of Falco); Anacrites, Spy
Time period(s): 1st century; 70s (77)
Locale(s): Rome, Italy

Summary: In *Nemesis* by Lindsey Davis, a Roman informant dealing with the death of his son and father in 77 A.D. Rome distracts himself by investigating a murder. When Marcus Didius Falco is asked to work on a case involving the killing of a local art dealer, he calls on his friend, Petronius, for assistance. As Falco uncovers a connection between the victim and a brutish band of freedmen, the Claudii, the trail of dead bodies grows, leading him into the treacherous Pontine Marshes. In addition to the Claudii and the disease-infested swamps, Falco and Petronius also encounter another nemesis in the form of Anacrites, a spy. *Nemesis* is the 20th book in the Marcus Didius Falco series.

Where it's reviewed:
Booklist, September 15, 2010, page 34
Publishers Weekly, July 19, 2010, page 115

Other books by the same author:
Alexandria, 2009
Saturnalia, 2007
See Delphi and Die, 2006
The Accusers, 2003
Three Hands in the Fountain, 1999

Other books you might like:
Ruth Downie, *Medicus*, 2007
Robert Harris, *Conspirata: A Novel of Ancient Rome*, 2010
Bruce Macbain, *Roman Games*, 2010
Steven Saylor, *Empire: The Novel of Imperial Rome*, 2010
Marilyn Todd, *Still Waters*, 2010

136

PABLO DE SANTIS

Voltaire's Calligrapher

(New York: Harper Perennial, 2010)

Story type: Mystery
Subject(s): Enlightenment (Cultural movement); Mystery; Religion
Major character(s): Dalessius, Assistant (to Voltaire), Writer (calligrapher), Detective—Amateur; Voltaire, Historical Figure, Philosopher
Time period(s): 18th century; 1760s
Locale(s): France

Summary: *Voltaire's Calligrapher* is a historical mystery novel from author Pablo De Santis. As the printing press rises in popularity, calligraphy is becoming a lost art and a dying profession. Fortunately, a young scribe named Dalessius catches a lucky break when he's offered a job working for Voltaire, one of the Enlightenment's most famous philosophers. It seems that Voltaire has more for Dalessius to do than write when he sends the young man to Paris to spy on the Church's activities. Dalessius soon finds himself caught up in a murder investigation, as a man has been accused of killing his son before he could convert to Catholicism. The dead boy's followers insist he's still performing miracles from beyond the grave and demand his father's execution, forcing Dalessius to illegally search for the truth.

Other books by the same author:
The Paris Enigma: A Novel, 2008

Other books you might like:
Christophe Bataille, *Hourmaster*, 1998
Rosalind Laker, *To Dance with Kings*, 1988
Vonda N. McIntyre, *The Moon and the Sun*, 1997
Janine Montupet, *The Lacemaker*, 1988
Judith Rock, *The Rhetoric of Death*, 2010

137

CAMILLE DEANGELIS

Petty Magic: Being the Memoirs and Confessions of Miss Evelyn Harbinger, Temptress and Troublemaker

(New York: Crown Publishers, 2010)

Story type: Witchcraft
Subject(s): Witchcraft; Witches; World War II, 1939-1945
Major character(s): Evelyn Harbinger, Witch; Justin, Antiques Dealer
Time period(s): Multiple Time Periods; 20th century; (1930s-1940s); 21st century; 2010s

Summary: *Petty Magic: Being the Memoirs and Confessions of Miss Evelyn Harbinger, Temptress and Troublemaker* is a witty supernatural novel from author Camille DeAngelis. Being 149 years old isn't going to stop Evelyn Harbinger from having a good time, especially when she possesses the powers to transform herself into a beautiful young woman who captures the eye of nearly every passing male. Evelyn's been warned about the dangers of witch-human romances, but she's so convinced that her new guy, Justin, is the reincarnation of her former lover, Jonah, she throws all caution to the wind. Despite the increasing warnings from her coven and shocking accusations against her sister, Evelyn is only focused on one thing: proving that Justin is really Jonah, the man who fought alongside Evelyn in World War II.

Where it's reviewed:
Booklist, September 15, 2010, page 29
Library Journal, August 1, 2010, page 66
Publishers Weekly, August 2, 2010, page 35

Other books by the same author:
Mary Modern, 2007
The Second Life of Mary Morrigan, 2007

Other books you might like:
Stephen Hunter, *Hot Springs*, 2000
Hillary Jordan, *Mudbound*, 2008
James Lehrer, *The Special Prisoner*, 2000
James Michael Pratt, *Ticket Home*, 2001
Scott Turow, *Ordinary Heroes*, 2005

138

CATHERINE DELORS

For the King

(New York: Dutton, 2010)

Subject(s): Napoleonic Wars, 1800-1815; Assassination; Detective fiction
Major character(s): Roch Miquel, Police Officer, Detective—Amateur; Blanche Coudert, Lover (of Miquel); Fouche, Police Officer (Minister of Police)
Time period(s): 19th century; 1800s (1800)
Locale(s): France

Summary: In *For the King*, Catherine Delors charts the investigations of a determined young police officer intent on finding those responsible for an assassination attempt on the life of Napoleon. Roch Miquel meets obstacles at every phase of his inquiry, most notably from police commissioner Fouche, who, for some reason, does not want Miquel to succeed. Miquel diverts himself by spending time with his mistress, Blanche Coudert, but she has some secrets of her own about the assassination attempt—secrets that could compromise her lover's investigation.

Where it's reviewed:
Kirkus Reviews, June 1, 2010, page 484
Publishers Weekly, May 3, 2010, page 28

Other books by the same author:
Mistress of the Revolution, 2008

Other books you might like:
Susanne Alleyn, *The Cavalier of the Apocalypse*, 2009
Peter Carey, *Parrot and Olivier in America*, 2010
Dean Fuller, *A Death in Paris*, 1992
Sheila Kohler, *Bluebird, or the Invention of Happiness*, 2007
Marge Piercy, *City of Darkness, City of Light*, 1996

139

J.M. DILLARD

The Scarlet Contessa: A Novel of the Italian Renaissance

(New York: St. Martin's Press, 2010)

Story type: Historical - Renaissance
Subject(s): Marriage; Women; History
Major character(s): Caterina Sforza, Widow(er) (of Count Girolamo Riario), Daughter (of Duke of Milan); Dea, Narrator
Time period(s): 15th century-16th century; 1460-1510
Locale(s): Italy

Summary: In *The Scarlet Contessa: A Novel of the Italian Renaissance*, J.M. Dillard tells a fictionalized version of Caterina Sforza's influential life during Italy's Renaissance. Caterina, the daughter of Duke of Milan, was married to Count Girolamo Riario, a man known to be sneaky, but oftentimes dimwitted. After her husband's death, Caterina should have lost the family's land, but she single-handedly fought off those who came to claim

it. In this story, Caterina's lady-in-waiting, Dea, tells of Caterina's numerous personal victories as she managed her own land and made a name for herself without a husband. Although she had many suitors, Caterina was a strong judge of character and enjoyed her independence too much to accept them. Dillard combines fact with fiction to produce this historical novel.

Where it's reviewed:
Library Journal, June 15, 2010, page 62
Publishers Weekly, May 24, 2010, page 35

Other books by the same author:
The Devil's Queen, 2009
I, Mona Lisa, 2006
The Burning Times, 2001
Lord of the Vampires, 1996
Covenant with the Vampire, 1994

Other books you might like:
Bridget Boland, *Caterina*, 1975
Matt Chamings, *The Medici Curse*, 2007
Genevieve Davis, *A Passion in the Blood*, 1977
Elle Newmark, *The Book of Unholy Mischief*, 2008
Sara Poole, *Poison: A Novel of the Renaissance*, 2010

140

MARGARET DILLOWAY

How to Be an American Housewife

(New York: G.P. Putnam's Sons, 2010)

Subject(s): Mother-daughter relations; Japanese Americans; Family
Major character(s): Shoko, Mother (of Sue), Spouse (of Charlie), Daughter (of Taro); Sue, Daughter (of Shoko and Charlie), Granddaughter (of Taro); Charlie Morgan, Spouse (of Shoko), Father (of Sue); Taro, Father (of Shoko), Grandfather (of Sue)
Time period(s): 20th century-21st century; 1940s-2010s
Locale(s): Japan; United States

Summary: Margaret Dilloway's *How to Be an American Housewife* is a moving tale of a mother and daughter and the turbulent relationship they share. After World War II has ended, Japanese clerk Shoko marries American solider Charlie Morgan, much to the ire of Shoko's father, Taro. The newlyweds return to the United States, where they begin a family. Shoko feels isolated in her new surroundings and struggles to fit in with the American wives, prompting her to channel her hopes and dreams into her daughter, Sue. Not surprisingly, this places an intense strain on the mother-daughter bond. Sue grows up under her mother's exacting eye, but when Shoko becomes ill, it is Sue who returns to Japan to mend her mother's ties with Taro. First novel.

Where it's reviewed:
Kirkus Reviews, June 1, 2010, page 485
Library Journal, July 2010, page 69
Publishers Weekly, June 21, 2010, page 32

Other books you might like:
Jane Hamilton, *The Book of Ruth*, 1988
Anna Quindlen, *One True Thing*, 1994
Christina Schwarz, *Drowning Ruth: A Novel*, 2000

Alice Sebold, *The Almost Moon: A Novel*, 2007
Amy Tan, *The Joy Luck Club*, 1989

141

PAUL DOHERTY

The Waxman Murders

(London: Headline Book Publishing, 2010)

Series: Hugh Corbett Series. Book 15
Subject(s): Mystery; Detective fiction; Crime
Major character(s): Hugh Corbett, Spy, Detective—
Amateur
Time period(s): 14th century
Locale(s): England, United Kingdom

Summary: The year is 1300. The Hanseatic League of northern Germany holds a trade monopoly in northern Europe and rules the sea-lanes. An English vessel, the Waxman, is taken by two Hansa warships, a tragedy for England, because the English vessel was carrying a cask of the most accurate maps and charts known to man. These charts could mean the difference between life and death, between enormous fortune and penury, for any ship. Several years later, an emissary from the Hansa arrives in England, and rumor has it that he wants to negotiate the return of the charts to England. But murder interrupts diplomacy, and master spy Sir Hugh Corbett must investigate.

Where it's reviewed:
Kirkus Reviews, October 15, 2010, page 1030
Publishers Weekly, September 13, 2010, page 25

Other books by the same author:
The Magician's Death, 2009
Corpse Candle, 2002
The Demon Archer, 2001
The Devil's Hunt, 1998
The Death of a King, 1985

Other books you might like:
Simon Beaufort, *The Bloodstained Throne*, 2010
Elizabeth Chadwick, *The Conquest*, 1997
Alys Clare, *Music of the Distant Stars*, 2010
Ellis Peters, *An Excellent Mystery*, 1985
Priscilla Royal, *Valley of Dry Bones*, 2010

142

DAVID DONACHIE

Blown off Course

(London: Allison & Busby, 2011)

Series: John Pearce Series. Book 7
Story type: Adventure; Series
Subject(s): History; Sea stories; Military life
Major character(s): John Pearce, Military Personnel
(lieutenant); Ralph Barclay, Military Personnel
(captain); Emily, Spouse (of John Pearce, estranged)
Time period(s): 18th century; 1790s
Locale(s): England

Summary: In *Blown Off Course* by David Donachie, Lieutenant John Pearce tries to salvage his naval career as his nemesis, Captain Ralph Barclay, conspires against him. In London, Pearce visits the Pelican Tavern where he and a crew of misfits were forcibly enlisted into the Royal Navy. The Pelicans, as the group has come to be known, have shared many adventures but now face an uncertain future. As Pearce searches for a way to prove that Barclay lied under oath, he accepts a risky mission for his crew that could lead them to riches or ruin. *Blown Off Course* is the seventh book in the John Pearce series.

Other books by the same author:
The Admirals' Game, 2008
A Flag of Truce, 2008
An Awkward Commission, 2006
A Shot Rolling Ship, 2005
A Game of Bones, 1997

Other books you might like:
Max Hennessy, *The Dangerous Years*, 1979
Seth Hunter, *The Tide of War*, 2010
Julian Stockwin, *Victory*, 2010
Edwin Thomas, *Treason's River*, 2006
Jay Worrall, *Sails on the Horizon*, 2005

143

ANNE DOUGHTY

Shadow on the Land

(London: Severn House Publishers, 2010)

Story type: Historical - World War II
Subject(s): Irish (European people); Ireland; Family
Major character(s): Alex Hamilton, Spouse (of Emily),
Father (of Cathy, Jane, Lizzie, and Johnny); Emily
Hamilton, Spouse (of Alex), Mother (of Cathy, Jane,
Lizzie, and Johnny); Cathy, Teacher, Daughter (of
Alex and Emily), Sister (of Jane, Lizzie, and
Johnny); Jane Hamilton, Nurse, Daughter (of Alex
and Emily), Sister (of Cathy, Lizzie, and Johnny);
Lizzie Hamilton, Military Personnel, Daughter (of
Alex and Emily), Sister (of Cathy, Jane, and
Johnny); Johnny Hamilton, Military Personnel, Son
(of Alex and Emily), Brother (of Cathy, Jane, and
Lizzie)
Time period(s): 20th century; 1930s-1940s
Locale(s): Ulster, Ireland

Summary: Anne Doughty's *Shadow on the Land* is an un-numbered installment in the Hamilton Saga. This outing centers on Alex and Emily Hamilton, a married couple who, during the Second World War, deal with life in war-affected Ireland. Both orphaned when they were children, Alex and Emily have built a solid relationship and have four devoted children: teacher Cathy, nurse Jane, and soldiers Lizzie and Johnny. But as the horrors of war hit close to home, the Hamilton family's bonds are tested like never before.

Where it's reviewed:
Booklist, April 15, 2010, page 39

Other books by the same author:
For Many a Long Day, 2009
A Girl Called Rosie, 2008

The Woman from Kerry, 2003
Beyond the Green Hills, 2002
On a Clear Day, 2001

Other books you might like:
James R. Benn, *Evil for Evil*, 2009
Benjamin Black, *Elegy for April*, 2010
Jack Higgins, *The Eagle Has Flown*, 1991
Brian Moore, *The Emperor of Ice-Cream*, 1965
Chris Petit, *The Psalm Killer*, 1997

144

ANNE DOUGLAS

The Melody Girls

(Sutton, Surrey, England: Severn House, 2010)

Story type: Historical - World War II
Subject(s): Music; Scotland; Women
Major character(s): Lorna Fernie, Musician, Postal Worker; Rod Warren, Musician, Lover (of Lorna)
Time period(s): 20th century
Locale(s): Glasgow, Scotland

Summary: Shortly after World War II, Scottish postal worker and saxophonist, Lorna Fernie enters a talent contest. Although she doesn't take home the grand prize, she secures a job playing in an orchestra for Glasgow dance halls. It's not long until her new gig leads to love with the handsome and amiable trumpet player, Rod Warren. Her good fortune doesn't last long though and soon Lorna finds herself out of a job and out of love. Determined to create a brighter future for herself, Lorna decides to start an orchestra of her own, made entirely of female players known as The Melody Girls, but her new endeavor isn't enough to fill the void in her heart.

Where it's reviewed:
Booklist, November 1, 2010, page 34

Other books by the same author:
Starlight, 2010
The Kilt Maker, 2009
The Girl form Wish Lane, 2008
A Song in the Air, 2008
The Road to the Sands, 2006

Other books you might like:
Stella Cameron, *Tell Me Why*, 2001
Joyce Hackett, *Disturbance of the Inner Ear*, 2002
Jane Hamilton, *Disobedience*, 2000
Sarah Smith, *The Knowledge of Water*, 1996
Lisa Tucker, *Shout Down the Moon*, 2004

145

RUTH DOWNIE

Caveat Emptor

(New York: Bloomsbury Press, 2010)

Series: Roman Empire Series. Book 4
Story type: Mystery

Subject(s): Roman Empire, 30 BC-476 AD; Murder; Mystery
Major character(s): Gaius Petreius Ruso, Doctor, Detective; Julius Asper, Collector (tax), Crime Victim
Time period(s): 2nd century
Locale(s): England

Summary: *Caveat Emptor*, a historical mystery novel, is the fourth installment in the Roman Empire series from best-selling author Ruth Downie. When a tax collector named Julius Asper goes missing, along with a great deal of Emperor Hadrian's money, physician-turned-detective Gaius Petreius Ruso is assigned to investigate. Traveling between Londinium to the northern city of Verulamium, Gaius concludes that Asper, along with his brother, have been murdered while either fleeing with or transferring the cash. Gaius's missing-person investigation has turned into a full-blown murder case, made more difficult by Asper's pregnant wife and her hostile and bold accusations.

Where it's reviewed:
Library Journal, November 1, 2010, page 54
Publishers Weekly, October 25, 2010, page 27

Other books by the same author:
Persona Non Grata, 2009
Terra Incognita, 2008
Medicus, 2007

Other books you might like:
Gillian Bradshaw, *Island of Ghosts*, 1998
Lindsey Davis, *A Body in the Bathhouse*, 2001
William Dietrich, *Hadrian's Wall*, 2004
Manda Scott, *Dreaming the Eagle*, 2003
Jack Whyte, *The Skystone*, 1996

146

NICK DRAKE

Tutankhamun: The Book of Shadows

(New York: Harper, 2010)

Series: Rai Rahotep Trilogy. Book 2
Subject(s): Egyptian history, to 642 (Ancient period); Murder; Detective fiction
Major character(s): Rahotep, Detective—Police; Tutankhamun, Royalty
Time period(s): 14th century B.C.; 1330s B.C.-1320s B.C.
Locale(s): Thebes, Egypt

Summary: Set in ancient times, during the reign of the young Egyptian king, *Tutankhamun* finds police detective Rahotep summoned to a grisly murder scene. A man has been tortured, killed, and—Rahotep suspects—drugged in the process. After another killing of similar barbarism is committed, the detective debates the possibility that the murders may be tied to a rogue group of dissenters attempting to overthrow King Tutankhamun. Rahotep's investigation brings him face to face with the king's deadliest adversaries, forcing him into the most dangerous confrontations of his career and impelling him to protect himself and his loved ones at all cost. *Tutankhamun* is the second novel in Nick Drake's ancient Egyptian mystery trilogy.

Where it's reviewed:
Booklist, June 1, 2010, page 42
Kirkus Reviews, June 1, 2010, page 495
Publishers Weekly, May 3, 2010, page 29

Other books by the same author:
Nefertiti: The Book of the Dead, 2007

Other books you might like:
P.C. Doherty, *The Year of the Cobra*, 2006
Cecelia Holland, *Valley of the Kings*, 1977
William Klein, *The Woman Who Would Be Pharaoh*, 2009
Lee Levin, *King Tut's Private Eye*, 1996
Linda S. Robinson, *Murder at the God's Gate*, 1995

147

STEPHANIE DRAY

Lily of the Nile

(New York: Berkley Books, 2011)

Story type: Historical - Pre-history
Subject(s): Egyptian history, to 642 (Ancient period); Royalty; Roman Empire, 30 BC-476 AD
Major character(s): Selene, Historical Figure, Royalty, Daughter (of Cleopatra), Prisoner (of Rome), Twin (of Helios); Helios, Royalty, Prisoner (of Rome), Son (of Cleopatra), Prisoner (of Rome), Historical Figure
Time period(s): 3rd century B.C.
Locale(s): Egypt

Summary: *Lily of the Nile* is a historical novel from author Stephanie Dray. Selene Ptolemy, daughter of Cleopatra and Marc Antony, will stop at nothing to preserve her family's name and earn her rightful inheritance. After her mother's death, Selene and her two brothers are captured by Rome and taken in by the emperor Octavian. Selene's twin brother, Helios, rebels against Octavian's rule, but the Egyptian princess strives to be compliant, all the while struggling to formulate a plan to guarantee their safety. When the goddess Isis begins speaking to Selene through magical manifestations, the young woman develops the strength and courage needed to endure Rome's harsh treatment and maintain her Egyptian identity.

148

KATE EMERSON (Pseudonym of Kathy Lynn Emerson)

Secrets of the Tudor Court: By Royal Decree

(New York: Gallery Books, 2010)

Series: Secrets of the Tudor Court Series. Book 3
Story type: Romance
Subject(s): British history, 1066-1688; Royalty; Politics
Major character(s): Elizabeth "Bess" Brooke, Young Woman, Lover (of William), Noblewoman; William Parr, Historical Figure, Courtier, Brother (in-law to King Henry VIII), Lover (of Elizabeth); Henry VIII, Royalty (king), Historical Figure

Time period(s): 16th century
Locale(s): England

Summary: The third book in the Secrets of the Tudor Court series, *Secrets of the Tudor Court: By Royal Decree* is a historical romance novel from author Kate Emerson. For the first time in her life, Elizabeth "Bess" Brooke's captivating beauty might work against her. She's been summoned to the court of King Henry VIII, an aging king currently married to his sixth wife, Kathryn Parr, where she's fallen in love with Parr's brother, Will. Unfortunately for Bess, Will already has a wife and divorce is unlawful by anyone other than the King himself. Desperate for King Henry's favor, but loathing his attraction, Bess trickily navigates the political maze of the Tudor House in hopes of finding true love and living happily ever after.

Where it's reviewed:
Booklist, November 15, 2010, page 25
Publishers Weekly, October 25, 2010, page 28

Other books by the same author:
Secrets of the Tudor Court: Between Two Queens, 2010
Secrets of the Tudor Court: The Pleasure Palace, 2009

Other books you might like:
Suzannah Dunn, *The Queen of Subtleties*, 2004
Margaret George, *The Autobiography of Henry 8*, 1986
Philippa Gregory, *The Constant Princess*, 2005
Hilary Mantel, *Wolf Hall*, 2009
Robin Maxwell, *The Secret Diary of Anne Boleyn*, 1997

149

CAROLLY ERICKSON

Rival to the Queen

(New York: St. Martin's Press, 2010)

Story type: Family Saga; Romance
Subject(s): Cousins; Royalty; Family history
Major character(s): Queen Elizabeth I, Royalty (Queen of England); Robert Dudley, Royalty (Earl of Leicester), Lover (of Lettice); Lettice Knollys, Cousin (of Queen), Lover (of Robert)
Time period(s): 16th century
Locale(s): England

Summary: In Carolly Erickson's *Rival to the Queen*, fact and fiction come together to tell the story of Queen Elizabeth I's fight for one of the only men she ever trusted. Everyone knew the Virgin Queen had an especially deep relationship with her consort, Robert Dudley, Earl of Leicester. Dudley loved the Queen so much, in fact, that it was believed he had his own wife killed so he could be available to fulfill the Queen's every request. The relationship turns sour, however, when Elizabeth hears of Dudley's relationship with her very own cousin, Lettice Knollys, in *Rival to the Queen*. Hurt and betrayed, Elizabeth takes immediate steps to ensure that her cousin's life would be as utterly miserable as her own.

Where it's reviewed:
Kirkus Reviews, September 1, 2010, page 812
Library Journal, October 15, 2010, page 65
Publishers Weekly, August 16, 2010, page 812

Other books by the same author:
The Memoirs of Mary Queen of Scots, 2009
The Secret Life of Josephine, 2007
The Last Wife of Henry VIII, 2006
The Hidden Diary of Marie Antoinette, 2005
The Tsarina's Daughter, 2008

Other books you might like:
Philippa Gregory, *The Virgin's Lover*, 2004
Victoria Holt, *My Enemy the Queen*, 1978
Robin Maxwell, *The Queen's Bastard*, 1999
Jean Plaidy, *Gay Lord Robert*, 1955
Alison Weir, *The Lady Elizabeth: A Novel*, 2008

150

KAREN ESSEX

Dracula in Love

(New York: Doubleday, 2010)

Summary: In *The Personal History of Rachel DuPree: A Novel*, author Ann Weisgarber tells the story of a young black woman's search for identity in the remote stretches of South Dakota during the early years of the 20th century. Rachel meets Isaac while they are both working in Chicago. Later, the two marry and take advantage of the 160 acres offered by the Homestead Act. Relocating to rural South Dakota, they struggle to build a successful farm. Years pass and their family grows, but their lives are still difficult. Rachel soon learns that finding her own sense of self is the only way she will endure the hardships of such a challenging life on the prairie. First novel.

Where it's reviewed:
Booklist, August 1, 2010, page 36

Other books by the same author:
Stealing Athena, 2008
Leonardo's Swans, 2006
Pharaoh, 2002
Kleopatra, 2001

Other books you might like:
Roderick Anscombe, *The Secret Life of Laszlo, Count Dracula*, 1994
Barbara Hambly, *Renfield: Slave of Dracula*, 2006
Jeanne Kalogridis, *Covenant with the Vampire: The Diaries of the Family Dracul*, 1994
Allen C. Kupfer, *The Journal of Professor Abraham Van Helsing*, 2004
Kim Newman, *Anno Dracula*, 1993

151

LOREN D. ESTLEMAN

Roy & Lillie

(New York: Forge Books, 2010)

Subject(s): Western fiction; Actors; Love
Major character(s): Roy Bean, Judge; Lillie Langtry, Actress

Time period(s): 19th century
Locale(s): United Kingdom; Texas, United States

Summary: In *Roy & Lillie*, award-winning author, Loren D. Estleman spins a tale of romance based on the real-life relationship between a legendary Texas judge and a famed British actress. Roy Bean is the most revered judge of his day and one of the most powerful men in the Old West. He has a very public yen for Lillie Langtry, the world's most famous and lauded actress. The two never cross paths, but their correspondence illuminates their very different lives—and a very unorthodox love affair.

Where it's reviewed:
Kirkus Reviews, July 1, 2010, page 587

Other books by the same author:
The Branch and the Scaffold, 2009
The Undertaker's Wife, 2005
The Master Executioner, 2001
Sudden Country, 1991
Bloody Season, 1988

Other books you might like:
David Butler, *Lillie*, 1978
Susann Cokal, *Breath and Bones*, 2005
Larry McMurtry, *Telegraph Days*, 2006
Joseph O'Connor, *Redemption Falls*, 2007
Robert B. Parker, *Gunman's Rhapsody*, 2001

152

NIGEL FARNDALE

The Blasphemer

(New York: Crown, 2010)

Subject(s): Courage; World War I, 1914-1918; Interpersonal relations
Major character(s): Daniel, Young Man; Nancy, Girlfriend (of Daniel); Andrew Kennedy, Grandfather (great-grandfather of Daniel), Military Personnel
Time period(s): 21st century; (2010s); 20th century; 1910s
Locale(s): London, United Kingdom

Summary: Nigel Farndale's *The Blasphemer* follows one family as they struggle with issues of honor and duty. Immediately after the crash of their plane, Daniel leaves his girlfriend and chooses instead to save himself from the wreckage. Though he returns to save Nancy as well, his instinctual action throws their relationship into upheaval. As this drama plays out, the story of Daniel's great-grandfather, Andrew Kennedy, is relayed as he deals with his own struggles with personal duty and faith during the First World War.

Where it's reviewed:
Kirkus Reviews, July 1, 2010, page 588
Publishers Weekly, June 28, 2010, page 102

Other books you might like:
A.S. Byatt, *The Children's Book*, 2009
Nelson DeMille, *Night Fall*, 2004
Katherine McMahon, *The Rose of Sebastopol*, 2007
Jill Paton Walsh, *The Bad Quarto*, 2007
Anita Shreve, *The Pilot's Wife*, 1998

153

CHARLES FINCH

A Stranger in Mayfair

(New York: Minotaur Books, 2010)

Series: Charles Lenox Mysteries Series. Book 4
Story type: Mystery
Subject(s): England; Mystery; Murder
Major character(s): Charles Lenox, Detective, Government Official (Parliament member); Ludovic Starling, Client (of Charles)
Time period(s): 19th century; 1860s
Locale(s): England

Summary: *A Stranger in Mayfair*, a Victorian mystery, is the fourth installment in the Charles Lenox Mystery series from author Charles Finch. Things are going rather well for gentleman detective, Charles Lenox. He's recently wed his beautiful longtime pal Lady Jane Grey and he's been elected to Parliament. Shortly after returning from his honeymoon, Charles finds himself on yet another complex investigation, this time looking into the death of an associate's servant. The victim, footman to Ludovic Starling, was beaten to death with a brick. Charles is hesitant about taking on the case, especially so close to the opening of Parliament, but once he begins sleuthing he realizes that the murder and the Starling family are not at all what they seem.

Where it's reviewed:
Booklist, October 15, 2010, page 25
Kirkus Reviews, October 1, 2010, page 963
Library Journal, November 1, 2010, page 49
Publishers Weekly, September 20, 2010, page 51

Other books by the same author:
Bleeding Heart Square, 2009
An Unpardonable Crime, 2004
The Office of the Dead, 2000
An Air that Kills, 1995
An Old School Tie, 1986

Other books you might like:
Stephanie Barron, *Jane and the Madness of Lord Byron*, 2010
Tracy Kiely, *Murder at Longbourn: A Mystery*, 2009
Anne Perry, *Death of a Stranger*, 2002
Lynn Shepherd, *Murder at Mansfield Park*, 2010
Lauren Willig, *The Mischief of the Mistletoe*, 2010

154

KEN FOLLETT

Fall of Giants

(New York: Dutton, 2010)

Series: Century Trilogy. Book 1
Story type: Historical - World War I
Subject(s): Epics; Family; Russian Revolution, 1917-1921
Major character(s): Billy Williams, 13-Year-Old, Miner, Brother (of Ethel); Ethel Williams, Housekeeper, Sister (of Billy); Gus Dewar, Political Figure; Grigori Peshkov, Brother (of Lev); Lev Peshkov, Brother (of Grigori); Maud Fitzherbert, Noblewoman; Walter von Ulrich, Spy
Time period(s): 20th century; 1910s-1920s
Locale(s): Germany; Russia; United Kingdom; United States

Summary: Celebrated author Ken Follett turns his lens on the 20th century in the sprawling epic *Fall of Giants*. The triumphs and tragedies of five families are chronicled in this monumental story, which encompasses World War I, the Russian Revolution, and the women's rights movement. The players in this tempestuous historical drama include a young man who lands an unlikely job in American politics; a teenage miner and his sister; Russian brothers whose lives take divergent roads; and a noblewoman who falls for a mysterious double agent. *Fall of Giants* is the first installment in the Century Trilogy.

Where it's reviewed:
Booklist, July 1, 2010, page 6
Kirkus Reviews, June 15, 2010, page 643
Library Journal, July 1, 2010, page 70
New York Times Book Review, October 3, 2010, page 22
Publishers Weekly, July 12, 2010, page 27

Other books by the same author:
World Without End, 2007
Jackdaws, 2001
The Third Twin, 1996
A Place Called Freedom, 1995
Pillars of the Earth, 1989
On Wings of Eagles, 1983
The Key to Rebecca, 1980
Eye of the Needle, 1978

Other books you might like:
Robert Alexander, *The Kitchen Boy*, 2003
Rebecca Cantrell, *A Trace of Smoke*, 2009
John Dos Passos, *U.S.A.*, 1930
Robert Littell, *The Revolutionist: A Novel of Russia*, 1988
Robert Vaughan, *Over There*, 1992

155

WILLIAM R. FORSTCHEN
NEWT GINGRICH, Co-Author

Valley Forge: George Washington and the Crucible of Victory

(New York: Thomas Dunne Books, 2010)

Series: George Washington Series. Book 2
Story type: Historical - American Revolution
Subject(s): American Revolution, 1775-1783; History; Valley Forge, Pennsylvania
Major character(s): George Washington, Political Figure, Military Personnel (General); Baron Friederich von Steuben, Friend (of George Washington)
Time period(s): 18th century; 1770s (1777)
Locale(s): Valley Forge, Pennsylvania

Summary: Newt Gingrich and William R. Forstchen's *Valley Forge: George Washington and the Crucible of Vic-*

tory is the second book in the George Washington series of historical fiction novels, following *To Try Men's Souls*. *Valley Forge* picks up where *To Try Men's Souls* ends. The year is 1777 and the Revolutionary War is in full swing. George Washington and his troops have retreated to Valley Forge, Pennsylvania, to prepare for the harsh winter. Lacking basic necessities such as food and warm clothing, however, things look dismal for the general and his soldiers. Although the odds are stacked against them, the men persevere. Help eventually arrives in the form of a German ally, Baron Friederich von Steuben, who aids Washington by helping him rebuild and strengthen his troops to fight the British once more.

Where it's reviewed:
Booklist, September 15, 2010, page 37
Kirkus Reviews, September 15, 2010, page 886
Library Journal, September 15, 2010, page 59

Other books by the same author:
To Try Men's Souls, 2009
Days of Infamy, 2008
Never Call Retreat, 2005
Grant Comes East, 2004
Gettysburg, 2003

Other books you might like:
Burke Boyce, *Man from Mt. Vernon*, 1961
Christian Cameron, *Washington and Caesar*, 2003
Howard Fast, *The Unvanquished*, 1942
Michael Kilian, *Major Washington*, 1998
William Martin, *Citizen Washington*, 1999

156

ANNE FORTIER

Juliet
(New York: Ballantine Books, 2010)

Subject(s): Family history; Love; Italy
Major character(s): Julie Jacobs, Young Woman; Giulietta Tomei, Relative (ancestor of Julie)
Time period(s): 21st century; 2010s
Locale(s): Siena, Italy

Summary: In *Juliet*, author Anne Fortier crafts a unique tale blending history, fantasy, romance, and the world of Shakespeare. Julie Jacobs travels to Siena, Italy, after the death of her much-loved aunt. She hopes to find out more about her family history, but she isn't prepared for the ancestral treasure she uncovers: one of her descendants was Giulietta Tomei, the young woman who inspired Shakespeare's greatest heroine. As Julie dives into the sordid details of her family's past, she must also confront the barrage of problems affecting her family in the present—problems resulting from a curse placed on them by a heartbroken friar. First novel.

Where it's reviewed:
Booklist, July 1, 2010, page 31
Entertainment Weekly, August 20, 2010, page 127
Library Journal, June 15, 2010, page 1
Library Journal, May 15, 2010, page 67
Publishers Weekly, May 31, 2010, page 22

Other books you might like:
Bridget Boland, *Caterina*, 1975
Matt Chamings, *The Medici Curse*, 2007
Jeanne Kalogridis, *The Scarlet Contessa: A Novel of the Italian Renaissance*, 2010
Elle Newmark, *The Book of Unholy Mischief*, 2008
Sara Poole, *Poison: A Novel of the Renaissance*, 2010

157

ADAM FOULDS

The Quickening Maze
(London: Jonathan Cape, 2009)

Subject(s): Poetry; Writers; Mental health
Major character(s): John Clare, Writer (poet), Mentally Ill Person; Alfred Tennyson, Brother (of Septimus Tennyson), Writer (poet); Dr. Matthew Allen, Businessman (owner of High Beach), Doctor; Septimus Tennyson, Mentally Ill Person, Brother (of Alfred Tennyson); Hannah Allen, Daughter (of Dr. Matthew Allen)
Time period(s): 19th century
Locale(s): Epping Forest, London, England

Summary: *The Quickening Maze*, by Adam Foulds, is a historical novel that centers on two very real poets— John Clare and Alfred Tennyson. Clare, an alcoholic suffering from depression, checks himself into an asylum called High Beach near Epping Forest, London. Poet Alfred Tennyson moves near the asylum when his brother, Septimus, is admitted. Clare's and Tennyson's lives never really become intertwined. Clare leaves the asylum from time to time seeking the company of gypsies. Tennyson becomes close with the hospital's owner, Dr. Matthew Allen, while Allen's daughter, Hannah, becomes infatuated with Tennyson and tries to get him to marry her.

Where it's reviewed:
Booklist, July 1, 2010, page 32
Kirkus Reviews, June 1, 2010, page 486
Publishers Weekly, May 17, 2010, page 29

Other books you might like:
Judith Allnatt, *The Poet's Wife*, 2010
Joan Lock, *Dead Letters*, 2003
Matthew Pearl, *The Last Dickens*, 2009
Dan Simmons, *Drood: A Novel*, 2008
Sara Stockbridge, *Grace Hammer: A Novel of the Victorian Underworld*, 2009

158

PATRICIA FRIEDBERG

21 Aldgate
(Highland City, Florida: Rainbow Books, Inc., 2010)

Story type: Historical - World War II
Subject(s): Love; Jews; Artists
Major character(s): Clara Simon, Secretary; Paul Maze, Artist

Time period(s): 20th century; 1930s
Locale(s): London, United Kingdom

Summary: Patricia Friedberg's *21 Aldgate* takes place in London just before the commencement of World War II. Secretary Clara Simon is outraged by her boss's attitude toward Jews, and she quits her job. Unsure where to find support in the chaotic days before the Second World War, Clara is led to artist Paul Maze, who is seeking an assistant to help him write his autobiography. The sparks fly between the two immediately, and an intense affair begins, jeopardizing Clara's status, safety, and her marriage.

Other books you might like:
Elizabeth Bowen, *The Heat of the Day*, 1948
Francis Cottam, *The Fire Fighter*, 2001
David Stuart Davies, *Without Conscience: A Johnny Hawke Novel*, 2008
John E. Gardner, *The Streets of Town*, 2003
Sarah Waters, *The Night Watch*, 2006

159

KATE FURNIVALL

The Jewel of St. Petersburg

(New York: Berkley Books, 2010)

Story type: Historical - Russian Revolution
Subject(s): History; Russian history; Romances (Fiction)
Major character(s): Valentina Ivanova, 17-Year-Old; Jens Friis, Engineer; Viktor Arkin, Political Figure (Bolshevik leader); Katya, Sister (of Valentina)
Time period(s): 20th century; 1910s (1910)
Locale(s): Russia

Summary: In *The Jewel of St. Petersburg* by Kate Furnivall, a privileged Russian family struggles with internal conflicts as their nation moves closer to revolution in 1910. A Bolshevik bombing has damaged the Ivanovas' country home and left young Katya an invalid. Katya's 17-year-old sister, the beautiful and independent Valentina, challenges the wishes of her family and pursues a career as a nurse. But Valentina's choice of men is even more controversial. Rather than marry a wealthy nobleman (and solve her family's financial problems), Valentina falls in love with Jens Friis, the Danish man who serves as the czar's engineer.

160

JANE GARDAM

God on the Rocks

(London, England: Abacus, 2010)

Story type: Coming-of-Age
Subject(s): Family; History; England
Major character(s): Margaret Marsh, 8-Year-Old; Lydia, Nurse, Child-Care Giver
Time period(s): 20th century; 1930s
Locale(s): England

Summary: Growing up in England between the wars, eight-year-old Margaret Marsh is the only child of a religious zealot father and a quiet, submissive mother. When her parents have another child, they hire a brash but caring maid named Lydia who opens up Margaret to life outside her sheltered home. Lydia begins taking Margaret on day trips where she encounters a slew of unique, shocking, and interesting people, including the patients at a home for the insane. As Margaret becomes aware of the world around her, she makes startling discoveries about her own parents and their so-called moral behavior.

Where it's reviewed:
Booklist, October 15, 2010, page 25
Library Journal, September 1, 2010, page 99
Publishers Weekly, August 8, 2010, page 28

Other books by the same author:
The Man in the Wooden Hat, 2009
Old Filth, 2006
Faith Fox, 2003
The Flight of the Maidens, 2001
The Queen of the Tambourine, 1995

Other books you might like:
Julian Barnes, *Arthur & George*, 2006
Catherine Cookson, *The Parson's Daughter*, 1987
Beverly Lewis, *The Preacher's Daughter*, 2005
Marilynne Robinson, *Gilead*, 2004
Nicholas Sparks, *A Walk to Remember*, 1999

161

ELIZABETH GILL

Snow Hall

(New York: Severn House, 2010)

Story type: Historical - Edwardian
Subject(s): History; England; Women
Major character(s): Lorna Robson, Worker (hat shop)
Time period(s): 20th century; 1900s (1907)
Locale(s): County Durham, England

Summary: In *Snow Hall* by Elizabeth Gill, a young woman struggling to make a living in Edwardian England finds her life transformed by a mysterious inheritance. Though Lorna Robson is grateful for the job she holds at her aunt's hat store, she resents the difficult working conditions. When Lorna learns that a distant relation has left her a house called Snow Hall, she leaves her aunt's employ—on less than amicable terms—and moves into her new home. As Lorna soon realizes, Snow Hall is in dire need of repair and upkeep beyond the financial means of a single woman in 1907 County Durham.

Where it's reviewed:
Booklist, December 15, 2010, page 27

Other books by the same author:
Dream Breakers, 2009
Paradise Lane, 2009
Sweet Wells, 2008
The Secret, 2007
Swan Island, 2007

The Foxglove Tree, 2006
The Preacher's Son, 2005

Other books you might like:
Catherine Cookson, *The Maltese Angel*, 1992
Abigail De Witt, *Lili*, 2000
Ruth Hamilton, *The Judge's Daughter*, 2007
Una Horne, *The Ironmaster's Girl*, 2003
Gwen Kirkwood, *A Home of Our Own*, 2010

162

MICHAEL GOLDMAN

Vision in the Forest

(Bloomington, Indiana: Trafford Publishing, 2010)

Subject(s): Vikings; Adventure; Tribalism
Major character(s): Thorfinn Oakenshield, Viking
Time period(s): 11th century; 1000s
Locale(s): Vinland, Fictional Location

Summary: In *Vision in the Forest*, author Michael Goldman tells the story of Thorfinn Oakenshield, a Viking who makes a courageous voyage to the New World land of Vinland. There he meets the native peoples living in the forest and becomes fascinated by their way of life. When Thorfinn's fellow travelers suddenly die, the adventurer takes to the woods, determined to live with the forest tribes and learn the customs, traditions, and daily events that define their lives. As he becomes a part of them, Thorfinn sets out to stop the constant wars being waged between enemy tribes. First novel.

Other books you might like:
Bernard Cornwell, *Lords of the North*, 2006
Cecelia Holland, *The Soul Thief*, 2002
Jeff Janoda, *Saga: A Novel of Medieval Iceland*, 2005
Robert Low, *The Prow Beast*, 2010
Henry Treece, *Viking's Dawn*, 1956

163

KERRY GREENWOOD

Dead Man's Chest

(Scottsdale, Arizona: Poisoned Pen Press, 2010)

Series: Phryne Fisher Series. Book 18
Story type: Mystery; Series
Subject(s): Mystery; History; Detective fiction
Major character(s): Phryne Fisher, Detective—Private;
  Dot, Servant (maid); Jane, Daughter (of Phryne
  (adopted)); Ruth, Daughter (of Phryne (adopted));
  Lin Chung, Fiance(e) (of Phryne), Police Officer;
  Mrs. Mason, Neighbor (of Phryne); Tinker, Neighbor
  (of Phryne)
Time period(s): 20th century; 1920s
Locale(s): Queenscliff, Australia

Summary: In *Dead Man's Chest* by Kerry Greenwood, socialite and private detective, Phryne Fisher leaves behind her hectic life for a stay in a beach house in Queenscliff. When Phryne arrives in the Australian coastal community with her maid and two adopted children, a mystery presents itself immediately. The resident maid and butler are nowhere to be found and the pantry is empty. When the Queenscliff authorities prove themselves incompetent, Phryne initiates her own investigation. The case is complicated by an assortment of quirky neighbors and a local pirate legend. *Dead Man's Chest* is the 18th book in the Phryne Fisher series.

Where it's reviewed:
Booklist, November 15, 2010, page 24
Kirkus Reviews, October 15, 2010, page 1030
Publishers Weekly, October 11, 2010, page 28

Other books by the same author:
Murder in the Dark, 2009
Murder on a Midsummer Night, 2009
Death Before Wicket, 2008
Queen of the Flowers, 2008
Away with the Fairies, 2005

Other books you might like:
Caroline Carver, *Dead Heat*, 2004
Carola Dunn, *The Bloody Tower*, 2007
Diana Haviland, *Death on the Ladies Mile*, 2006
Gillian Linscott, *Nell Bray Series*, 1991
Catriona McPherson, *After the Armistice Ball*, 2005

164

PHILIPPA GREGORY

The Red Queen

(New York: Touchstone Books, 2010)

Series: Cousins' War Series. Book 2
Story type: Family Saga
Subject(s): Royalty; Family; Wars
Major character(s): Margaret Beaufort, Widow(er); Henry
  VII, Son (of Margaret)
Time period(s): 15th century; 1450s-1480s
Locale(s): England

Summary: *The Red Queen* by Philippa Gregory is a fictionalized account of the War of the Roses in 15th-century England, told from the point of view of Margaret Beaufort, mother of Henry VII. Margaret, the cousin of Henry VI, is widowed and the mother of a young son before she is fourteen years old. She remarries by the time she is fifteen and is separated from her son, whom she names Henry VII, believing that her house of Lancaster is the true heir to the throne of England. Widowed again, Margaret stops at nothing to see her son take his rightful place on the throne; she marries Thomas, Lord Stanley, makes dangerous alliances, and brings about a political rebellion—all for her son and the future of England.

Where it's reviewed:
Booklist, June 1, 2010, page 5
Kirkus Reviews, June 15, 2010, page 535
Library Journal, May 15, 2010, page 68
Publishers Weekly, October 25, 2010, page 43

Other books by the same author:
The White Queen, 2009
The Other Queen, 2008
The Boleyn Inheritance, 2006

The Constant Princess, 2005
The Virgin's Lover, 2004

Other books you might like:
Alice Walworth Graham, *The Summer Queen*, 1973
Rosemary Hawley Jarman, *The King's Grey Mare*, 1973
Robin Maxwell, *To the Tower Born*, 2005
Jean Plaidy, *The Sun in Splendour*, 1982
Jan Westcott, *The White Rose*, 1969

165

KATHLEEN GRISSOM

The Kitchen House

(New York: Simon & Schuster, 2010)

Story type: Historical - Post-American Revolution
Subject(s): History; Slavery; Southern United States
Major character(s): Lavinia, 7-Year-Old, Servant; Belle, Slave
Time period(s): 18th century
Locale(s): American South

Summary: In *The Kitchen House* by Kathleen Grisson, a harrowing 1790 sea voyage from Ireland to America claims the life of a woman and leaves her seven-year-old daughter an orphan. When the ship lands, young Lavinia is sent to work on a tobacco plantation. Living with the slaves, the white girl learns the laws of plantation life from the servant girl who was fathered by the master. When Lavinia is moved from the kitchen house, she discovers that the rules in the big house are very different. As she deals with the opium-addicted lady of the house, Lavinia becomes privy to a potentially devastating secret.

166

LISA GRUNWALD

The Irresistible Henry House

(New York: Random House, 2010)

Story type: Psychological
Subject(s): Teachers; Orphans; Home economics
Major character(s): Henry House, Orphan ("practice baby"); Martha Gaines, Caregiver (to Henry); Dr. Benjamin Spock, Historical Figure; Walt Disney, Historical Figure; John Lennon, Historical Figure
Time period(s): 20th century; 1940s-1960s
Locale(s): England; United States

Summary: In *The Irresistible Henry House* by Lisa Grunwald, Wilton College believes in giving its Home Economics students hands-on experience. The campus Practice House is home to orphan baby Henry House, whose physical and emotional needs are met by the attentive students and program director Martha Gaines. Martha adopts Henry, but eventually sends him to a facility for difficult teenagers in Connecticut when he stops talking as a form of protest. When he finally ventures into the real world in the 1960s, Henry takes a takes a position with Disney studios where he draws penguins for *Mary Poppins* and the Beatles' *Yellow Submarine*.

167

ERICH HACKL

The Wedding in Auschwitz

(London: Serpent's Tail, 2010)

Story type: Historical - World War II
Subject(s): Weddings; Holocaust, 1933-1945; Jews
Major character(s): Rudi Friemel, Prisoner (concentration camp); Marga, Spouse (of Rudi)
Time period(s): 20th century; 1930s-1940s
Locale(s): Auschwitz, Poland

Summary: Based on a real-life incident, Erich Hackl's *The Wedding in Auschwitz* tells the story of the marriage between a concentration-camp prisoner and the Spanish-born Austrian woman he loves. In the throes of World War II, with more and more Jews being transported to Auschwitz, camp officials are determined to put a decidedly false face on the horrors taking place within the camp. They allow Rudi Friemel to wed Marga, the mother of his child, within the camp. Marga, their son, and Rudi's family are all brought into Auschwitz for the propaganda of a wedding, which changes all of their lives forever. *The Wedding in Auschwitz* is translated by Martin Chalmers.

Where it's reviewed:
Booklist, April 15, 2010, page 39

Other books by the same author:
Farewell Sidonia, 1991
Aurora's Motive, 1989

Other books you might like:
John Boyne, *The Boy in the Striped Pajamas*, 2006
Jacques Chessex, *A Jew Must Die*, 2010
Arnost Lustig, *Lovely Green Eyes: A Novel*, 2002
D.M. Thomas, *Pictures at an Exhibition*, 1993
Fred Wander, *The Seventh Well: A Novel*, 2008

168

RUTH HAMILTON

Sugar and Spice

(Sutton, Surrey, England: Severn House, 2010)

Story type: Family Saga
Subject(s): Sisters; World War II, 1939-1945; Twins
Major character(s): Anna McRae, Child, Sister (of twins)
Time period(s): Multiple Time Periods; 20th century; 1940s
Locale(s): England

Summary: Set in the mid-20th century in England, Ruth Hamilton's historical novel *Sugar and Spice* recounts the challenges and complexities of family dynamics. At the age of five, with a father fighting in the war and a mother dead from childbirth, Anna McRae finds herself primary caregiver for her infant twin sisters. The three children are sent to live in the English countryside until World War II is over, but things quickly go from bad to worse. Although Anna is a remarkable and compassionate young girl, her twin sisters are malevolent and wicked, constantly launching coldhearted attacks on their unsuspecting big sister. As a grown woman, Anna is terrified when she has twins of her own, wondering if history will repeat itself.

Where it's reviewed:
Booklist, December 15, 2010, page 27

Other books by the same author:
Mercy View, 2010
A Parallel Life, 2010
A Parallel Life, 2010
The Reading Room, 2009
The Judge's Daughter, 2007
The Bell House, 2005
Dorothy's War, 2005
Chandlers Green, 2003
Matthew & Son, 2002

Other books you might like:
Anne Douglas, *The Melody Girls*, 2010
Annie Gower, *The Grafton Girls*, 2007
Jeannie Johnson, *Secret Sins*, 2007
Margaret Mayhew, *Those in Peril*, 2006
Rowena Summers, *The Caldwell Girls*, 2002

169

WILLIAM C. HAMMOND

For Love of Country

(Annapolis, Maryland: Naval Institute Press, 2010)

Series: Cutler Family Chronicles Series. Book 2
Story type: Historical - Post-American Revolution; Series
Subject(s): History; Sea stories; Ships
Major character(s): Richard Cutler, Sea Captain; Caleb Cutler, Sea Captain, Brother (of Richard); Anne-Marie Helevetian, Friend (of Richard); John Paul Jones, Military Personnel (naval commander), Historical Figure
Time period(s): 18th century; 1780s
Locale(s): Algeria; Paris, France; Hingham, Massachusetts

Summary: In *For Love of Country* by William C. Hammond, the Cutler family of Massachusetts tries to protect its shipping enterprise as its newly founded nation struggles to secure its position in the international arena. When Caleb Cutler is taken hostage by pirates and held in Algiers, older brother Richard brings the required ransom to his captors. After successfully defeating the pirates, Richard voyages to France—a country rocked by revolution—to meet with John Paul Jones. When he learns that a former lover has been sentenced to death by guillotine, Richard risks his life to rescue her. *For Love of Country* is the second book in the Cutler Family Chronicles.

Other books by the same author:
A Matter of Honor, 2007

Other books you might like:
William Dietrich, *The Barbary Pirates*, 2010
Edwin P. Hoyt, *Against Cold Steel*, 1974
John Edward Jennings, *The Salem Frigate*, 1946
F. van Wyck Mason, *Captain Judas*, 1956
William H. White, *The Greater Honor*, 2003

170

RICHARD HARVELL

The Bells

(New York: Shaye Areheart Books, 2010)

Story type: Saga
Subject(s): Singing; Love; Operas
Major character(s): Moses Froben, Singer, Lover (of Amalia); Amalia Duft, Lover (of Moses)
Time period(s): 18th century
Locale(s): Vienna, Italy; Switzerland

Summary: In the novel *The Bells* by Richard Harvell, Moses Froben is born in a valley in the Swiss Alps in the 18th century to a deaf-mute mother. As a boy, Moses listens to the bells his mother rings in the belfry day after day. When Moses is forced to leave his home, he travels to Vienna to join a choir and learns he has a beautiful singing voice. The choirmaster turns Moses into a "musico," or a castrated male soprano, so his voice will never deepen. When in Vienna, Moses meets and falls in love with the crippled Amalia Duft, a woman from a very wealthy family who is being forced into an arranged marriage. Moses and Amalia fall in love, but their affection for one another will ultimately lead to tragedy.

Where it's reviewed:
Booklist, September 1, 2010, page 53
Kirkus Reviews, June 15, 2010, page 535
Library Journal, July 1, 2010, page 71
Publishers Weekly, July 19, 2010, page 112

Other books you might like:
Rita Charbonnier, *Mozart's Sister*, 2007
Stephanie Cowell, *Marrying Mozart*, 2004
Susanne Dunlap, *The Musician's Daughter*, 2009
Carolyn Meyer, *In Mozart's Shadow: His Sister's Story*, 2008
Beverle Graves Myers, *Cruel Music*, 2006

171

MYRLIN A. HERMES

The Lunatic, the Lover, and the Poet

(New York: Harper Perennial, 2010)

Subject(s): Shakespeare, William; Royalty; Revenge
Major character(s): Horatio, Friend (of Hamlet); Hamlet, Royalty (prince); Lady Adriane, Noblewoman; William "Will" Shakespeare, Writer
Time period(s): 14th century-18th century
Locale(s): Europe

Summary: In *The Lunatic, the Lover, and the Poet*, author Myrlin A. Hermes presents an imaginative prelude to Shakespeare's classic play, *Hamlet*. Years before the action in *Hamlet* begins, Hamlet and Horatio are students at Wittenberg University. As they get to know one another, Horatio slowly becomes enchanted with the charismatic young Hamlet. Into their increasingly close friendship comes noblewoman Lady Adriane, as well as a spirited young writer named Will Shakespeare, both of whom also begin to show an interest in Hamlet—much to Horatio's chagrin.

Where it's reviewed:
Booklist, February 1, 2010, page 28
Publishers Weekly, December 7, 2009, page 36

Other books by the same author:
Careful What You Wish For, 1999

Other books you might like:
Alan Gordon, *An Antic Disposition*, 2004
Graham Holderness, *The Prince of Denmark*, 2002
John Marsden, *Hamlet: A Novel*, 2009
Jeremy Trafford, *Ophelia*, 2001
John Updike, *Gertrud and Claudius*, 2000

172

HEIKKI HIETALA

Tulagi Hotel

(United Kingdom: Dragon International Independent Arts, 2010)

Story type: Historical - World War II
Subject(s): World War II, 1939-1945; Veterans; Interpersonal relations
Major character(s): Jack McGuire, Veteran (World War II); Kay Wheeler, Widow(er) (of Jack's friend)
Time period(s): 20th century; 1940s
Locale(s): Solomon Islands

Summary: In *Tulagi Hotel* by Heikki Hietala, a World War II veteran has trouble readjusting to civilian life after the war ends. When Jack McGuire returns to his Midwest hometown, he realizes that his heart is still in the Pacific Islands that once served as landmarks on his bombing runs. Rather than waiting to inherit his family's farm, Jack moves to the Solomon Islands where he builds a hotel. Jack still carries bad war memories, including the combat death of his wingman. His plans to create an isolated island refuge are complicated by the appearance of Kay Wheeler, the dead man's widow.

173

SUSAN HIGGINBOTHAM

The Queen of Last Hopes: The Story of Margaret of Anjou

(Naperville, Illinois: Sourcebooks, 2011)

Story type: Historical - Medieval
Subject(s): Wars of the Roses, 1455-1485; Royalty; History
Major character(s): Margaret, Royalty (queen of England), Spouse (of Henry VI), Mother (of Edward); Henry VI, Royalty (king of England), Spouse (of Margaret), Father (of Edward), Mentally Ill Person; Edward, Son (of Margaret & Henry VI), Heir, Royalty
Time period(s): 15th century; 1450s-1480s
Locale(s): England

Summary: *The Queen of Last Hopes: The Story of Margaret of Anjou* is a historical novel about the War of the Roses from author Susan Higginbotham. Margaret of Anjou, wife of Henry VI and queen of England, is desperate to save her family's legacy despite the number of obstacles standing in her way. Her husband, the king, is struggling with his mental health, going madder with each passing day. As the king-maker, Warwick, plots with the Duke of York to overthrow King Henry and take his throne, Margaret knows she must act swiftly and surely if she hopes to restore her husband, protect the future of their son, Edward, and save the House of Lancaster.

174

JOYCE HINNEFELD

Stranger Here Below

(Columbia, Missouri; Lakewood, Colorado: Unbridled Books, 2010)

Subject(s): Women; Family; Identity
Major character(s): Amazing Grace "Maze" Jansen, Artist (weaver); Mary Elizabeth Cox, Friend (of Maze); Georginea "Sister Georgia" Ward, Religious
Time period(s): 20th century; 1960s (1961)
Locale(s): Kentucky, United States

Summary: Joyce Hinnefeld's *Stranger Here Below* chronicles the experiences of three different women united by their desire for family and belonging. It is 1961, and weaver, Amazing Grace "Maze" Jansen has just crossed paths with Mary Elizabeth Cox, the African-American daughter of a preacher. The two women find solace in their unexpected friendship, which eventually leads them to Georginea Ward, a local woman whose relationship with a black man decades prior all but blacklisted her from the community. Now the resident of a tiny Shaker village, "Sister Georgia" inspires Maze and Mary Elizabeth to create their own families in order to find the love they seek.

Where it's reviewed:
Library Journal, September 1, 2010, page 100

Other books by the same author:
In Hovering Flight, 2008

Other books you might like:
C.E. Morgan, *All the Living: A Novel*, 2009
Toni Morrison, *Love*, 2003
James Sherburne, *Hacey Miller*, 1971
Kathryn Stockett, *The Help*, 2009
Ann Weisgarber, *The Personal History of Rachel DuPree: A Novel*, 2010

175

CECELIA HOLLAND

Kings of the North

(New York: Tor, 2010)

Subject(s): Vikings; Fantasy; Adventure
Major character(s): Raef Corbanson, Viking; Leif the

Icelander, Sidekick (of Raef); Laissa, Sidekick (of Raef)

Time period(s): 11th century
Locale(s): United Kingdom

Summary: Cecelia Holland's *Kings of the North* is the sequel to *The High City* and continues the adventures of Viking Raef Corbanson, who now finds himself in the middle of a royal power struggle. Raef and his companions are intent on making it back to Raef's home village, but along the way, they get sidetracked into an epic battle for the throne of England. And Raef, it seems, may be the only one who can stop the increasingly brutal power play before it's too late.

Where it's reviewed:
Kirkus Reviews, June 1, 2010, page 487
Publishers Weekly, May 31, 2010, page 28

Other books by the same author:
The Serpent Dreamer, 2005
The Witches' Kitchen, 2004
The Soul Thief, 2002
The Angel and the Sword, 2000
Pillar of the Sky, 1985

Other books you might like:
Bernard Cornwell, *The Last Kingdom*, 2004
Michael Crichton, *Eaters of the Dead*, 1976
Heather Graham, *Lord of the Wolves*, 1993
Harry Harrison, *King and Emperor*, 1996
Juliet Marillier, *Foxmask*, 2004

176

HELEN HOLLICK

The Forever Queen

(Naperville, Illinois: Sourcebooks Landmark, 2010)

Story type: Political
Subject(s): England; History; Royalty
Major character(s): Emma, Royalty (Queen), Spouse (of Aethelred & Cnut), Mother; Aethelred, Royalty (king), Spouse (of Emma); Cnut, Viking, Royalty (king), Spouse (of Emma)
Time period(s): 11th century; 1000s-1050s
Locale(s): England

Summary: Set in the early 11th century, Helen Hollick's historical novel, *The Forever Queen*, offers a fictionalized life account of Emma, the Queen of Saxon England, who reigned for 50 years through one of the nation's most turbulent eras in history. In 1002, Emma of Normandy is forced into marrying the harsh and brutal King Aetherland, a malevolent man deeply flawed by insecurity and fear. After Aetherland's death, Cnut, a Danish Viking, usurps his throne, taking over the kingdom and claiming Emma as his wife. Surprisingly, Emma finds love and happiness with Cnut, but political unrest and disloyalty among their people forces Emma to step up, with bravery and boldness, to protect her husband, her family, and her crown.

Where it's reviewed:
Booklist, October 15, 2010, page 25
Publishers Weekly, Septeber 6, 2010, page 23

Other books by the same author:
Harold the King, 2000
Shadow of the King, 1997
Pendragon's Banner, 1996
The Kingmaking, 1995

Other books you might like:
Melvyn Bragg, *The Sword and the Miracle*, 1997
Gene Farrington, *The Breath of Kings*, 1982
Harry Harrison, *King and Emperor*, 1996
Cecelia Holland, *Kings of the North*, 2010
Joan Wolf, *Born of the Sun*, 1989

177

CONN IGGULDEN

Khan: Empire of Silver

(New York: Delacorte Press, 2010)

Series: Genghis Khan: Conqueror Series. Book 4
Story type: Adventure
Subject(s): History; Mongol Empire, 1206-1502; Sibling rivalry
Major character(s): Ogedai, Son (of Genghis Khan), Heir; Chagetai, Brother (of Ogedai), Warrior
Time period(s): 13th century
Locale(s): Mongolia

Summary: *Khan: Empire of Silver*, an action-packed historical novel, is the fourth installment in the best-selling Genghis Khan: Conqueror Series from author Conn Iggulden. With Genghis Khan now dead, his three sons and four grandsons fight to take over his empire. Ogedai is the rightful heir, but his peculiar decisions are fostering impatience among his siblings and the Mongol warriors. On the brink of being crowned the new Khan, Ogedai has delayed his coronation in order to finish construction on Karakorum, a glorious new city. His unusual plans infuriate his prideful brother, Chagetai, who tries to overthrow him, causing their honorable brother Tolui to be caught in the middle and the entire empire to hang in the balance.

Where it's reviewed:
Library Journal, November 1, 2010, page 55
Publishers Weekly, October 11, 2010, page 24

Other books by the same author:
Genghis: Bones of the Hills, 2009
Genghis: Lords of the Bow, 2008
Genghis: Birth of an Empire, 2007
Emperor: The Death of Kings, 2004
Emperor: The Gates of Rome, 2003

Other books you might like:
Taylor Caldwell, *The Earth Is the Lord's: A Tale of the Rise of Genghis Khan*, 1941
Don Dandrea, *Orlok*, 1986
Homeric, *The Blue Wolf*, 2003
Yasushi Inoue, *The Blue Wolf: A Novel of the Life of Chinggis Khan*, 2008

178

GLYN ILIFFE

The Armour of Achilles

(New York: Macmillan, 2010)

Series: Adventures of Odysseus Series. Book 3
Subject(s): Friendship; Wars; Ancient Greek civilization
Major character(s): Odysseus, Military Personnel; Agamemnon, Royalty (king); Eperitus, Military Personnel
Locale(s): Greece

Summary: In *The Armour of Achilles*, author Glyn Iliffe presents the third installment in the Adventures of Odysseus series. This effort continues the wartime escapades of the legendary hero, who pines for his home of Ithaca while waging war with some of Troy's most hostile and powerful men. Odysseus has a dependable but beleaguered army at his side, including his cohort Eperitus, and they are about to face the wrath of Agamemnon—a wrath that could mean doom for them all.

Other books you might like:
Elizabeth Cook, *Achilles*, 2002
Sarah B. Franklin, *Daughter of Troy*, 1998
Margaret George, *Helen of Troy*, 2006
David Malouf, *Ransom: A Novel*, 2010
Barry Unsworth, *The Songs of the Kings*, 2003

179

GRAHAM ISON

Hardcastle's Soldiers

(London: Severn House Publishers, 2010)

Series: Hardcastle Series. Book 8
Story type: Mystery
Subject(s): Detective fiction; Murder; World War I, 1914-1918
Major character(s): Ernest Hardcastle, Detective—Police; Charles Marriott, Sidekick (of Hardcastle)
Time period(s): 20th century; 1910s (1914)
Locale(s): London, United Kingdom

Summary: *Hardcastle's Soldiers* is the eighth novel in Graham Ison's Hardcastle series. In this installment, police detective Ernest Hardcastle investigates the murder of a railway station attendant. World War I is holding London in its steely grip, but that isn't enough to keep Hardcastle and his trusted assistant, Charles Marriott, from delving into the dark details of their latest case. The more deeply entrenched they become, however, the more dead ends they encounter. The eponymous detective soon realizes this latest case will take all of his considerable skill and cunning.

Where it's reviewed:
Booklist, February 15, 2010, page 41

Other books by the same author:
Hardcastle's Mandarin, 2009
Hardcastle's Burglar, 2008
Hardcastle's Actress, 2007

Hardcastle's Airmen, 2006
Hardcastle's Conspiracy, 2005

Other books you might like:
Michael Lowenthal, *Charity Girl*, 2007
Barbara Nadel, *Sure and Certain Death*, 2009
Anne Perry, *No Graves as Yet*, 2003
Jody Shields, *The Crimson Portrait*, 2006
Charles Todd, *An Impartial Witness*, 2010

180

CLAUDE IZNER

The Montmartre Investigation

(New York: Minotaur Books, 2010)

Series: Victor Legris Series. Book 3
Subject(s): Detective fiction; Murder; Books
Major character(s): Victor Legris, Store Owner (bookseller), Detective—Amateur; Joseph Pignot, Assistant (of Legris); Tasha, Lover (of Legris)
Time period(s): 19th century; 1890s
Locale(s): Paris, France

Summary: Bookshop owner and amateur private detective, Victor Legris launches headlong into a thrilling new case when a single red shoe shows up at his Parisian bookstore. That same day, he hears word of a young woman, dressed in red, who has been brutally murdered. Convinced the shoe belonged to the dead woman, Victor follows the twists and turns of his investigation, which eventually lead him to other unsolved, savage killings. Claude Izner's *The Montmartre Investigation*, translated from French by Lorenza Garcia and Isabel Reid, is the third novel in the Victor Legris Mysteries series.

Where it's reviewed:
Booklist, September 1, 2010, page 51
Kirkus Reviews, August 1, 2010, page 703

Other books by the same author:
The Disappearance of Pere-Lachaise, 2009
Murder on the Eiffel Tower, 2008

Other books you might like:
Jonathan Barnes, *The Somnambulist*, 2007
Pablo De Santis, *The Paris Enigma: A Novel*, 2008
Denis Guedj, *The Parrot's Theorem*, 2001
Kate Horsley, *Black Elk in Paris*, 2006
Will Thomas, *The Limehouse Text*, 2006

181

MICHAEL JECKS

The Oath

(London: Simon & Schuster UK, 2010)

Series: Knights Templar Mystery Series. Book 29
Story type: Alternate History
Subject(s): Royalty; Betrayal; Wars
Major character(s): Simon Puttock, Investigator; King Edward II, Spouse (of Queen Isabella); Roger Mortimer, Knight, Lover (of Queen Isabella); Queen Isa-

bella, Spouse (of King Edward II), Lover (of Sir Roger Mortimer); Baldwin de Furnshill, Knight, Investigator

Time period(s): 14th century; 1320-1330 (1326)

Locale(s): England; France

Summary: In Michael Jecks's *The Oath*, the 29th book in the Knights Templar series, bailiff Simon Puttock's strengths and talents are called upon to investigate a series of brutal slayings in 14th-century England. While King Edward II decides whether to go to war with the queen's lover, Sir Roger Mortimer of France, his kingdom suffers a great loss when an entire family, including a newborn child, is murdered. Puttock teams with Sir Baldwin de Furnshill to track down the murderer as the execution of Sir Hugh le Despenser—the king's supposed lover—draws near. Jecks combines factual historical events with dramatic fiction throughout this series.

Where it's reviewed:
Publishers Weekly, October 4, 2010, page 31

Other books by the same author:
The Bishop Must Die, 2009
No Law in the Land, 2009
The King of Thieves, 2008
The Chapel of Bones, 2004
The Mad Monk of Gidleigh, 2002

Other books you might like:
P.C. Doherty, *The Poison Maiden*, 2007
Susan Higginbotham, *The Traitor's Wife*, 2009
Karen Maitland, *The Owl Killers*, 2009
Ian Morson, *William Falconer Series*, 1994
Sharon Kay Penman, *Cruel as the Grave*, 1998

182

BEVERLY JENSEN

The Sisters from Hardscrabble Bay

(New York: Viking, 2010)

Subject(s): Sisters; Rural life; Family

Major character(s): Avis Hillock, Sister (of Idella); Idella Hillock, Sister (of Avis)

Time period(s): 20th century; 1910s (1916)

Locale(s): New Brunswick, Canada

Summary: Beverly Jensen's *The Sisters from Hardscrabble Bay* is a collection of short stories centering on the lives, loves, and heartbreaks of the Hillock sisters. It is 1916, and Avis and Idella Hillock are living in their native New Brunswick. Here, the sisters endure a series of unique experiences that have profound effects on their lives. This volume includes the story "Wake," which was nominated for the Pushcart Prize. First book.

Where it's reviewed:
Booklist, April 15, 2010, page 39
Kirkus Reviews, May 15, 2010, page 433
Library Journal, April 15, 2010, page 74
New York Times Book Review, August 1, 2010, page 48
Publishers Weekly, May 2, 2010, page 28

Other books you might like:
Margaret Atwood, *The Blind Assassin*, 2000

Sue Monk Kidd, *The Secret Life of Bees*, 2002
Ian McEwan, *Atonement*, 2002
Christina Schwarz, *Drowning Ruth: A Novel*, 2000
Amy Tan, *The Hundred Secret Senses*, 1995

183

REBECCA JOHNS

The Countess

(New York: Crown Publishers, 2010)

Story type: Serial Killer

Subject(s): History; Serial murders; Royalty

Major character(s): Erzsebet Bathory, Noblewoman (countess), Serial Killer

Time period(s): 17th century; 1610s (1611)

Locale(s): Hungary

Summary: *The Countess* is a dark historical thriller from author Rebecca Johns. In 1611, Countess Erzsebet Bathory helplessly observes as she's walled into her castle tower, sentenced to live in solitary confinement for the rest of her days. Erzsebet, also known as the Blood Countess, is being punished for the murder of dozens of young women, servants who were disobedient or disrespectful to her over the years. Outraged at the accusations and the subsequent punishment, Erzsebet sets out to write her life story as both a letter to her son and an explanation of her behavior. As she relives the events of her tragic childhood and her loveless marriage, Erzsebet matter-of-factly exposes the dark and sinister motives that caused the serial murders.

Where it's reviewed:
Publishers Weekly, August 9, 2010, page 29

Other books by the same author:
Icebergs, 2005

Other books you might like:
Elaine Bergstrom, *Daughter of the Night*, 1992
Rhys Bowen, *Royal Blood*, 2010
James Brownley, *A Picture of Guilt*, 2007
Andrei Codrescu, *The Blood Countess*, 1995
Frances Gordon, *Blood Ritual*, 1995

184

MELISSA JONES

Emily Hudson

(New York: Viking, 2010)

Subject(s): Literature; Cousins; England

Major character(s): Emily Hudson, 19-Year-Old, Orphan; William, Cousin (of Emily), Writer; James Lindsay, Fiance(e) (of Emily), Military Personnel (Captain); Lord Firle, Friend (of Emily)

Time period(s): 19th century; 1860s

Locale(s): London, England; Rome, Italy; Newport, Rhode Island

Summary: In *Emily Hudson* by Melissa Jones, a young woman orphaned by consumption becomes an unwelcome addition to her uncle's family. With the Civil War under way, Emily Hudson has left her Rochester boarding school for her relatives' Newport home. While Emily's uncle discourages her artistic pursuits, cousin William—a sickly writer—takes an interest in the free-spirited girl. An engagement to Captain Lindsay seems to fulfill the uncle's wish to get rid of Emily, but when the relationship falters, she travels with William to London. In England, William's attentions become overbearing and Emily seeks adventure elsewhere. Originally published in the United Kingdom by Sphere as *The Hidden Heart of Emily Hudson*.

Where it's reviewed:
Kirkus Reviews, August 15, 2010, page 752
Library Journal, August 2010, page 69
Publishers Weekly, July 19, 2010, page 111

Other books by the same author:
Sick at Heart, 1999
Cold in Earth, 1998

Other books you might like:
Robert J. Begiebing, *The Adventures of Allegra Fullerton*, 1999
Emma Donoghue, *The Sealed Letter*, 2008
Denise Girardina, *Fallam's Secret*, 2003
Margaret Mayhew, *I'll Be Seeing You*, 2006
Barry Unsworth, *Land of Marvels: A Novel*, 2009

185

BEN KANE

The Road to Rome

(New York: St. Martin's Press, 2010)

Series: Forgotten Legion Series. Book 3
Subject(s): Ancient Roman civilization; Twins; Adventure
Major character(s): Fabiola, Twin (of Romulus); Romulus, Twin (of Fabiola); Tarquinius, Friend (of Romulus)
Locale(s): Rome, Italy

Summary: The adventurous lives of a set of twins in Ancient Rome are the spotlight of *The Road to Rome*, the third novel in Ben Kane's Forgotten Legion series. This installment finds Fabiola caught between her position as Brutus's lover and the affections of his rival, Marcus Antonius. Meanwhile, her brother Romulus and his comrade Tarquinius engage in brutal military battles in their quest to return home. The vibrant world of ancient Rome is brought to life as Fabiola and Romulus make their respective journeys to find one another again.

Other books by the same author:
The Silver Eagle, 2010
The Forgotten Legion, 2009

Other books you might like:
Taylor Caldwell, *A Pillar of Iron*, 1965
Robert Harris, *Imperium: A Novel of Ancient Rome*, 2006
Conn Iggulden, *Emperor: The Gates of Rome*, 2003
Colleen McCullough, *The Grass Crown*, 1991
Steven Saylor, *Empire: The Novel of Imperial Rome*, 2010

186

LARRY KARP

The Ragtime Fool

(Scottsdale, Arizona: Poisoned Pen Press, 2010)

Series: Ragtime Series. Book 3
Story type: Mystery
Subject(s): Music; Musicians; Diaries
Major character(s): Brun Campbell, Musician, Detective—Amateur; Alan Chandler, 17-Year-Old, Friend (of Brun); Rudi Blesh, Writer, Historian
Time period(s): 20th century; 1950s (1951)
Locale(s): Sedalia, Missouri

Summary: In 1951 Sedalia, Missouri, two ragtime music fans are meeting at a convention honoring ragtime musician Scott Joplin. Brun Campbell and Alan Chandler are both thrilled to learn that Joplin's widow has brought along her late husband's journal for the crowds to peruse. But several people in attendance are determined to get their hands on this highly prized diary and use it for their own questionable intentions. Can Brun and his pal stop them in time? *The Ragtime Fool* is the third and final novel in Larry Karp's Ragtime Trilogy.

Where it's reviewed:
Booklist, February 15, 2010, page 43
Kirkus Reviews, January 15, 2010, page 65
Publishers Weekly, January 25, 2010, page 100

Other books by the same author:
The King of Ragtime, 2008
The Ragtime Kid, 2006
First, Do No Harm, 2004
The Midnight Special, 2001
The Music Box Murders, 1999

Other books you might like:
Ace Atkins, *Crossroad Blues*, 1998
Robert Greer, *The Devil's Red Nickel*, 1997
John Lutz, *The Right to Sing the Blues*, 1986
Bill Moody, *Bird Lives!*, 1999
Julie Smith, *Jazz Funeral*, 1993

187

MARK KEATING

The Pirate Devlin

(New York: Grand Central Publishing, 2010)

Subject(s): Pirates; Adventure; Sea stories
Major character(s): Patrick Devlin, Pirate; John Coxon, Military Personnel (Royal Navy Captain)
Time period(s): 18th century

Summary: Mark Keating's *The Pirate Devlin* chronicles the seagoing adventures of pirate, Patrick Devlin as he attempts to make his way across the high seas to a buried treasure on a Caribbean island. But Devlin's journey will not be a smooth one. Enemies are lurking at virtually every bend in the water. Among them is John Coxon, Devlin's former Navy commander, who is determined to see that his old subordinate is put in his proper place. First novel.

Where it's reviewed:
Kirkus Reviews, June 15, 2010, page 537
Publishers Weekly, May 17, 2010, page 28

Other books you might like:
Philip Caveney, *Sebastian Darke: Prince of Pirates*, 2009
Michael Crichton, *Pirate Latitudes: A Novel*, 2009
William Dietrich, *The Barbary Pirates*, 2010
Laurie Lawlor, *Dead Reckoning: A Pirate Voyage with Captain Drake*, 2005
Arturo Perez-Reverte, *Pirates of the Levant*, 2010

188

LAURIE R. KING

The God of the Hive

(New York: Bantam Books, 2010)

Series: Mary Russell/Sherlock Holmes Series. Book 10
Subject(s): Detective fiction; Murder; Religion
Major character(s): Sherlock Holmes, Detective—Private; Mary Russell, Detective—Private, Spouse (of Sherlock Holmes); Thomas Brothers, Religious (Reverend); Damian Adler, Son (of Sherlock Holmes)
Time period(s): 20th century; 1920s (1924)
Locale(s): London, England

Summary: *The God of the Hive* is the tenth novel in Laurie R. King's detective series featuring Mary Russell and her husband, famous detective Sherlock Holmes, and is also the follow-up to 2009's *The Language of Bees*. After his son, Damian Adler, has been shot by a religious zealot named Rev. Thomas Brothers, Holmes must figure out a way to get Damian from England to Holland. Meanwhile, Mary must safeguard Damian's daughter from Brothers and his cronies. To make things worse, they learn that Brothers was once married to Damian's wife, who was recently murdered. Now the duo must figure out a way to protect their family while figuring out how to stop Brothers from his quest to unleash psychic abilities through human sacrifice.

Where it's reviewed:
Booklist, February 15, 2010, page 5
Library Journal, April 15, 2010, page 122
Publishers Weekly, March 8, 2010, page 32

Other books by the same author:
The Art of Deduction, 2006
Locked Rooms, 2005
The Game, 2004
Keeping Watch, 2003
Justice Hall, 2002

Other books you might like:
Caleb Carr, *The Italian Secretary*, 2005
Michael Chabon, *The Final Solution*, 2004
Jamyang Norbu, *Sherlock Holmes—The Missing Years*, 2001
Anita Janda, *The Secret Diary of Dr. Watson*, 2001

Barrie Roberts, *Sherlock Holmes and the Crosby Murder*, 2002

189

SUSAN FRASER KING

Queen Hereafter: A Novel of Margaret of Scotland

(New York: Crown, 2010)

Subject(s): Royalty; Scotland; Love
Major character(s): Margaret, Royalty (Queen of Scotland), Spouse (of Malcolm); Malcolm, Royalty (King of Scotland), Spouse (of Margaret); Eva, Companion (bard), Spy; Lady Macbeth, Widow(er)
Time period(s): 11th century
Locale(s): Scotland

Summary: In *Queen Hereafter: A Novel of Margaret of Scotland*, Susan Fraser King presents a fictionalized account of the reign of the Scottish queen. From her position as a Saxon princess, Margaret marries the much-older Malcolm and helps transform him into a powerful monarch. Along the way, she strikes an unexpected friendship with royal bard Eva, a young woman taken hostage to anger Lady Macbeth, whose famous husband was killed by Malcolm. Royal intrigue, personal passions, and divided loyalties soon divide the two women, setting them on very different courses through 11th-century Scottish life.

Where it's reviewed:
Booklist, November 15, 2010, page 26
Library Journal, November 1, 2010, page 56
Publishers Weekly, October 18, 2010, page 26

Other books by the same author:
Lady Macbeth, 2008
Kissing the Countess, 2003
Waking the Princess, 2003
The Sword Maiden, 2001
The Stone Maiden, 2000

Other books you might like:
Dorothy Dunnett, *Queen's Play*, 1964
Carolly Erickson, *The Memoirs of Mary Queen of Scots*, 2009
Elisabeth McNiell, *Blood Royal*, 2008
Jean Plaidy, *The Thistle and the Rose*, 1963
Jan Westcott, *The Tower and the Dream*, 1974

190

PEG KINGMAN

Original Sins: A Novel of Slavery & Freedom

(New York: W. W. Norton and Company, 2010)

Subject(s): Slavery; Missing persons; Family history
Major character(s): Grace MacDonald Pollocke, Artist (portrait painter), Friend (of Anibaddh); Anibaddh

Lyngdoh, Slave (former slave), Friend (of Grace)
Time period(s): 19th century
Locale(s): United States

Summary: Set in the United States during the 19th century, Peg Kingman's *Original Sins: A Novel of Slavery & Freedom* finds Grace MacDonald Pollocke investigating the true intentions of her friend, a former slave named Anibaddh Lyngdoh. Anibaddh attained her freedom nearly 20 years prior, but now she has returned to America to set up her own silk business. Grace suspects, however, that Anibaddh has other reasons for coming home, especially when slavery is still the rule and her freedom could be snatched away from her at any moment. Determined to help her friend, Grace looks into Anibaddh's past—only to find horrific connections with Grace's own family.

Where it's reviewed:
Kirkus Reviews, June 15, 2010, page 537
Library Journal, June 1, 2010, page 80
Publishers Weekly, June 28, 2010, page 102

Other books by the same author:
Not Yet Drown'd, 2007

Other books you might like:
Jon Clinch, *Finn*, 2007
James McBride, *Song Yet Sung*, 2008
Dolen Perkins-Valdez, *Wench: A Novel*, 2010
Ann Weisgarber, *The Personal History of Rachel DuPree: A Novel*, 2010
Michael C. White, *Soul Catcher*, 2007

191

P.F. KLUGE

A Call from Jersey
(New York: Overlook Press, 2010)

Subject(s): Immigrants; Father-son relations; Writers
Major character(s): Hans Greifinger, Immigrant, Father (of George and Heinz); George Griffin, Son (of Hans), Brother (of Heinz), Writer; Heinz Greifinger, Son (of Hans), Brother (of George)
Time period(s): 20th century; 1920s-1980s
Locale(s): New Jersey, United States

Summary: P.F. Kluge's *A Call from Jersey* charts the experiences of the men in the Greifinger family as they come of age and grow into adulthood. Widower, Hans Greifinger immigrates to America from Germany and works hard to become a homeowner and raise his sons. One son, George, goes to college, changes his last name, and becomes a world-famous travel writer. His other son, Heinz, returns to Germany at the onset of the Second World War to fight for his ancestral homeland—and is never seen again. The stories of these three men are told through the unfolding of family dramas, personal struggles, and major 20th-century events.

Where it's reviewed:
Library Journal, September 1, 2010, page 102
Publishers Weekly, May 24, 2010, page 32

Other books by the same author:
Gone Tomorrow, 2008

Biggest Elvis, 1996
MacArthur's Ghost, 1987
Season for War, 1984
Eddie and the Cruisers, 1980

Other books you might like:
Louise Erdrich, *The Master Butchers Singing Club*, 2003
Elizabeth Gaffney, *Metropolis*, 2005
Dorothy Garlock, *The Moon Looked Down*, 2010
Ursula Hegi, *The Vision of Emma Blau*, 2000
John Jakes, *Homeland*, 1993

192

DEWEY LAMBDIN

The Invasion Year
(New York: Thomas Dunne Books, 2011)

Series: Alan Lewrie Series. Book 17
Story type: Military
Subject(s): Wars; British history, 1714-1815; Armed forces
Major character(s): Alan Lewrie, Sea Captain, Military Personnel, Widow(er); Lydia Stangbourne, Young Woman, Socialite
Time period(s): 19th century; 1800s (1803)
Locale(s): England; Haiti

Summary: *The Invasion Year*, a historical military novel, is the 17th installment in the Alan Lewrie Naval series from Dewey Lambdin. It's the fall of 1803. Alan Lewrie, a captain in England's Royal Navy, begins his latest adventure off the coast of Haiti while waiting for the surrender of French refugees. After inadvertently rescuing the French men, whom he hates more than anything on earth, Lewrie returns to England where King George III has prepared a lavish celebration in his honor. Lewrie suspects that his new knighthood has to do more with pity over his wife's murder than honor for his service, but the gala leads him to the beautiful Lydia Stangbourne, the first woman to catch his eye since his wife's passing. Just as Lewrie begins exploring his feelings for this new woman, he's sent on yet another assignment: testing a controversial new war weapon in preparation of an attack from Napoleon Bonaparte.

Where it's reviewed:
Kirkus Reviews, December 1, 2010, page 1180
Publishers Weekly, November 15, 2010, page 40

Other books by the same author:
King, Ship, and Sword, 2010
Troubled Waters, 2008
Havoc's Sword, 2003
King's Captain, 2000
The King's Privateer, 1992

Other books you might like:
David Donachie, *Blown off Course*, 2011
Max Hennessy, *The Dangerous Years*, 1979
Julian Stockwin, *Victory*, 2010
Edwin Thomas, *Treason's River*, 2006
Jay Worrall, *Sails on the Horizon*, 2005

193

JOHN LAWTON

A Lily of the Field

(Washington, D.C.: Atlantic Monthly Press, 2010)

Series: Frederick Troy Series. Book 7
Story type: Mystery; Series
Subject(s): History; Mystery; Detective fiction
Major character(s): Frederick Troy, Inspector (Scotland Yard); Meret Voytek, 10-Year-Old, Musician (cellist); Karel Szabo, Scientist (physicist); Andre Skolnik, Artist; Viktor Rosen, Musician, Teacher (of Meret)
Time period(s): 20th century; 1930s-1940s (1934-1948)
Locale(s): Vienna, Austria; London, England; Poland; Los Alamos, New Mexico

Summary: In *A Lily of the Field* by John Lawton, a murder in post-war London draws Scotland Yard's Inspector Frederick Troy into a case that reaches back to 1934 Vienna. In this intricate novel's first part, "Audacity," a 10-year-old cellist named Meret Voytek is sent to Auschwitz even though she is not Jewish. In the second part—"Austerity," set in 1948—Troy investigates the shooting of an artist, Andre Skolnik, who may have been a Soviet spy. As Lawton weaves together the stories of Voytek and Skolnik, a complex tale of espionage and politics is revealed. *A Lily of the Field* is the seventh book in the Inspector Troy series.

Where it's reviewed:
Booklist, August 1, 2010, page 34
Kirkus Reviews, August 15, 2010, page 753
Library Journal, September 1, 2010, page 102
New York Times Book Review, October 17, 2010, page 30
Publishers Weekly, August 2, 2010, page 29

Other books by the same author:
Second Violin, 2008
A Little White Death, 2006
Bluffing Mr. Churchill, 2004
Old Flames, 2003
Black Out, 1995

Other books you might like:
Rebecca Cantrell, *A Night of Long Knives*, 2010
Paul Grossman, *The Sleepwalkers*, 2010
Philip Kerr, *If the Dead Rise Not*, 2009
Robert Wilson, *The Company of Strangers*, 2001

194

JACQUELINE LEPORE

Descent into Dust

(New York: HarperCollins 2010)

Summary: In *The Last Rendezvous*, Anne Plantagenet creates a fictionalized chronicle of the life of 19th-century French actress and poet, Marceline Desbordes. A contemporary of Paul Verlaine, Charles Baudelaire, Victor Hugo, and Alfred de Vigny, Desbordes held a place of prominence in French literary society—an uncommon accomplishment for a woman in the early 1800s. Plan-

tangenet's account finds Desbordes the wife of handsome (and younger) actor Prosper Valmore. Still emotionally unsettled at the age of 33, Marceline embarks on an intense love affair with Henri de Latouche—a union that has a lasting and profound effect on her personal life and her work.

Where it's reviewed:
Booklist, March 15, 2010, page 27
Library Journal, March 15, 2010, page 98
Publishers Weekly, February 1, 2010, page 38

Other books by the same author:
Immortal with a Kiss, 2010

Other books you might like:
Charlotte Bronte, *Jane Slayre*, 2010
Michel Faber, *The Crimson Petal and the White*, 2002
Elizabeth Kostova, *The Historian*, 2005
Lynn Messina, *Little Vampire Women*, 2010
Anne Perry, *Buckingham Palace Gardens: A Novel*, 2008

195

ELIZABETH LORD

All That We Are

(Sutton, Surrey, England: Severn House, 2010)

Story type: Family Saga
Subject(s): World War I, 1914-1918; Family sagas; England
Major character(s): Maggie Taylor, Sister (to Nora), Fiance(e) (of Robert); Nora Taylor, Sister (of Maggie), Lover (of Robert); Robert, Widow(er), Single Father
Time period(s): Multiple Time Periods; 20th century
Locale(s): England

Summary: *All That We Are* is a family saga from author Elizabeth Lord loosely based on her own family background. In the early 20th century, Jack and Moira Taylor juggle their attentions between their booming business and their six children in London's East End. Things are blissful and harmonious for the clan until a sibling feud disrupts the family's peace. When 18-year-old Maggie's fiance, Robert, an older widow with a son, meets and falls in love with Maggie's older sister, Nora, the sisters sever their bond. The family division continues through World War I and the outbreak of the Spanish flu, ultimately affecting the next generation of Taylors.

Where it's reviewed:
Booklist, September 15, 2010, page 36

Other books by the same author:
Julia's Way, 2009
A Secret Inheritance, 2007
To Cast a Stone, 2007
Company of Rebels, 2004
Shadow of the Protector, 2002

Other books you might like:
Tishani Doshi, *Pleasure Seekers*, 2010
Roopa Farooki, *Bitter Sweets*, 2007
Philippa Gregory, *Fallen Skies*, 1993

Claire Rayner, *Gower Street*, 1973
Sally Worboyes, *At the Mile End Gate*, 2001

196

ELIZABETH LOUPAS

The Second Duchess

(New York: New American Library, 2011)

Story type: Historical - Renaissance
Subject(s): Italian history; Royalty; Murder
Major character(s): Alfonso d'Este, Nobleman (duke of Ferrara), Widow(er), Crime Suspect, Spouse (of Barbara), Historical Figure; Barbara, Historical Figure, Noblewoman (duchess of Ferarra), Spouse (of Alfonso)
Time period(s): 16th century; 1560s
Locale(s): Italy

Summary: In Renaissance Italy, Alfonso d'Este, the duke of Ferrara, has married a new wife after the untimely death of his previous one. Although his new bride, Barbara of Austria, is quite smart, she's not nearly as beautiful as Lucrezia, the duke's first wife. As Barbara and Alfonso settle into their new life together, the new duchess can't ignore the growing rumors and whispered murmurs surrounding the details of Lucrezia's death. Many suspect the duke murdered her, but no one is courageous enough to accuse him. As the gossip persists, Barbara is determined to uncover the truth, regardless of the risk it poses to her own life and future.

197

ANNABEL LYON

The Golden Mean: A Novel of Aristotle and Alexander the Great

(Toronto, Ontario, Canada: Random House Canada, 2009)

Subject(s): Alexander the Great; Philosophy; Ancient history
Major character(s): Aristotle, Philosopher, Teacher (of Alexander), Friend (of King Philip); Alexander, Warrior, Student (of Aristotle), 13-Year-Old, Son (of King Philip), Heir; King Philip, Royalty (king of Macedonia), Father (of Alexander), Friend (of Aristotle)
Time period(s): 4th century BC
Locale(s): Pella, Greece

Summary: In Annabel Lyon's *The Golden Mean*, Aristotle is asked to stay in Pella and teach Alexander, the son of King Philip of Macedonia. Aristotle agrees to help his old friend and put his dreams of succeeding Plato on hold to teach the boy who would one day become the next great warrior. He knows he must teach him the golden mean—a balance or compromise between two extremes. He tries to instill ethics and conduct in Alexander, but finds that he is too jaded by his father's bullying and behavior—behavior that will later affect Aristotle's relationship with King Philip. First novel.

Where it's reviewed:
Booklist, September 15, 2010, page 37
Kirkus Reviews, September 15, 2010, page 890
Library Journal, June 15, 2010, page S2
Publishers Weekly, July 26, 2010, page 49

Other books by the same author:
The Best Thing for You, 2004
Oxygen, 2000

Other books you might like:
L. Sprague de Camp, *An Elephant for Aristotle*, 1958
Nikos Kazantzakis, *Alexander the Great*, 1982
Harold Lamb, *Alexander of Macedon: The Journey to World's End*, 1946
Steven Pressfield, *The Virtues of War: A Novel of Alexander the Great*, 2004
Mary Renault, *Fire from Heaven*, 1969

198

BRUCE MACBAIN

Roman Games

(Brookline, Massachusetts: Jesselton Books, 2010)

Series: Plinius Secundus Series. Book 1
Subject(s): Ancient Roman civilization; Murder; Detective fiction
Major character(s): Plinius "Pliny" Secundus, Lawyer, Political Figure (senator), Detective—Amateur; Martial, Detective—Amateur, Writer, Friend (of Pliny); Sextus Verpa, Crime Victim
Time period(s): 1st century; 90s (96)
Locale(s): Rome, Italy

Summary: In Ancient Rome, lawyer and statesman Plinius Secundus is summoned to investigate the murder of Sextus Verpa, an infamous snitch working within the government. Pliny and his sidekick, the sometime-poet Martial, delve into the strange circumstances surrounding Verpa's murder, of which his slaves stand accused. The entire city of Rome has gone on a 15-day holiday due to the festivities of the Roman Games, and in that stretch of time, Pliny and Martial must unlock the key to this puzzling mystery—or Verpa's slaves will be burned alive by the authorities. *Roman Games* is the first installment in the Plinius Secundus series by Bruce Macbain. First novel.

Where it's reviewed:
Booklist, October 1, 2010, page 35
Library Journal, September 1, 2010, page 94
Publishers Weekly, June 28, 2010, page 112

Other books you might like:
Albert Bell, *The Blood of Caesar*, 2008
Lindsey Davis, *Nemesis*, 2010
Robert Harris, *Conspirata: A Novel of Ancient Rome*, 2010
Steven Saylor, *Empire: The Novel of Imperial Rome*, 2010
Marilyn Todd, *Still Waters*, 2010

199

BRUCE MACHART

The Wake of Forgiveness

(Boston, Massachusetts: Houghton Mifflin Harcourt, 2010)

Story type: Family Saga
Subject(s): Death; Love; Family
Major character(s): Karel, Young Man (horse racer)
Time period(s): 19th century-20th century; 1890s-1900s
Locale(s): Texas, United States

Summary: *The Wake of Forgiveness*, by Bruce Machart, focuses on the life of a horse racer. Karel loses his mother when he is born. Karel's father is devastated at the loss and takes it out on his sons, forcing them to work on the family's farm. Karel feels guilty and knows that his father resents him by the way he beats him with his belt. He longs for his father's love and forgiveness, while he's haunted by the memory of a mother he never knew. One day he gets on a horse and everything changes. He feels strong and confident on top of the majestic beast. Years later in 1910, Karel prepares for the race of his life against a Spanish patriarch—with his fate, his father's fortune, and his brothers' futures dangling before him.

Where it's reviewed:
Kirkus Reviews, September 1, 2010, page 816
Library Journal, July 1, 2010, page 76
New York Times Book Review, October 31, 2010, page 12
Publishers Weekly, June 28, 2010, page 101

Other books you might like:
Tessa Dare, *One Dance with a Duke*, 2010
Lisa Jackson, *High Stakes*, 2008
William Kinsolving, *Bred to Win: A Novel*, 1990
Heather Reed, *A Secret Design*, 2006
Arabella Seymour, *A Passion in the Blood*, 1985

200

SARITA MANDANNA

Tiger Hills: A Novel

(New York: Grand Central Publishing, 2011)

Story type: Romance
Subject(s): History; Romances (Fiction); Epics
Major character(s): Devi, Girl; Devanna, Boy; Machu, Cousin (of Devanna)
Time period(s): 19th century
Locale(s): India

Summary: In *Tiger Hills* by Sarita Mandanna, 19th-century India provides the setting for a story of friendship, love, and heartache. Devi is born into a life of privilege, a beloved daughter in a family dominated by males. Her childhood friend, Devanna, has no immediate family to speak of. His mother abandoned him and his father killed himself. Through the years, Devanna's feelings for Devi grow from friendship to romance, but Devi has lost her heart at an early age to Devanna's cousin Machu—a famed tiger hunter. Devanna goes to university to study

medicine but abruptly returns home, desperate to be with Devi. First novel.

201

HENNING MANKELL

Daniel

(New York: The New Press, 2010)

Story type: Literary
Subject(s): History; Africa; Sweden
Major character(s): Hans Bengler, Scientist (entomologist); Daniel, Orphan
Time period(s): 19th century; 1870s
Locale(s): Africa; Sweden

Summary: In *Daniel* by Henning Mankell, an entomologist searching for new insect species in Africa finds an orphan who will become his adopted son. Hans Bengler names the boy Daniel and brings him to his native Sweden. In 1870s Sweden, Daniel's dark skin and textured hair make him an oddity. Since Bengler's Africa trip was unsuccessful scientifically and financially, he decides to make money by exhibiting the boy, who struggles to adapt to a new environment and culture. Eventually, Daniel is orphaned once again when Bengler leaves him in the care of a rural Swedish family. Translated from the Swedish by Steven T. Murray.

Where it's reviewed:
Booklist, November 1, 2010, page 33
Library Journal, September 15, 2010, page 61
New York Times Book Review, December 26, 2010, page 20
Publishers Weekly, September 13, 2010, page 23

Other books by the same author:
The Man from Beijing, 2010
The Eye of the Leopard, 2008
The Man Who Smiled, 2006
Before the Frost, 2005
The Fifth Woman, 2000

Other books you might like:
Tony Eprile, *The Persistence of Memory*, 2004
Lynn Freed, *The Servants' Quarters*, 2009
Nadine Gordimer, *My Son's Story*, 1990
Malla Nunn, *A Beautiful Place to Die*, 2009
Michael Stanley, *The Second Death of Goodluck Tinubu*, 2009

202

JULIET MARILLIER

Seer of Sevenwaters

(New York: Roc, 2010)

Series: Sevenwaters Trilogy. Book 5
Story type: Adventure
Subject(s): History; Druids; Love
Major character(s): Sibeal, Young Woman, Religious; Felix, Amnesiac, Accident Victim (shipwreck)

Time period(s): Indeterminate Past
Locale(s): Europe

Summary: *Seer of Sevenwaters*, a historical novel, is the fifth installment in the Sevenwaters series from best-selling author Juliet Marillier. Before making her final vow as a druid, the young soothsayer Sibeal pays a visit to an island of powerful warriors where she meets Felix, an intelligent Viking shipwreck survivor suffering from amnesia. The pair have an easy and quick connection, but Sibeal, out of commitment to her calling, is careful to guard her heart from feeling anything too strongly for Felix. As Felix's memories begin to return, Sibeal has a vision that Felix is meant to go on a dangerous journey and she's supposed to accompany him. As they face fearsome creatures and turbulent waters, Sibeal's biggest obstacle is her own heart and whether she will give up her faith to follow it.

Where it's reviewed:
Booklist, November 15, 2010, page 28
Library Journal, December 1, 2010, page 107
Publishers Weekly, October 18, 2010, page 29

Other books by the same author:
Heir of Sevenwaters, 2008
Foxmask, 2004
Child of the Prophecy, 2002
Son of the Shadows, 2001
Daughter of the Forest, 2000

Other books you might like:
Roberta Gellis, *Ill Met by Moonlight*, 2005
Morgan Llywelyn, *Red Branch*, 1989
Nora Roberts, *Key of Valor*, 2004
Edward Rutherfurd, *The Princes of Ireland*, 2004
Alexander McCall Smith, *Dream Angus*, 2006

203

EDWARD MARSTON

Under Siege

(London, England: Allison and Busby, 2010)

Story type: Military
Subject(s): Wars; Military life; History
Major character(s): Daniel Rawson, Military Personnel (captain)
Time period(s): 18th century
Locale(s): France

Summary: *Under Siege* is an action-packed historical novel from author Edward Marston. After a decisive victory in the Battle of Oudenarde, the Allied forces are making a strong push to invade further into France. Playing a crucial part in the military maneuver is career soldier, Captain Daniel Rawson. Unbeknownst to Rawson, his proximity to fellow soldier, Duke of Marlborough, is putting him in danger. Back in England, unscrupulous politicians are plotting the Duke's downfall, threatening his safety on the battlefield. Making matters more complicated, Rawson must rescue his dear friend and soldier, Henry Welbeck, fight a worthy rival for the hand of the beautiful Amalia Janssen, and avoid capture by the French.

Other books by the same author:
Fire and Sword, 2009
Drums of War, 2008
Soldier of Fortune, 2008
The Princess of Denmark, 2006
The Railway Detective, 2004

Other books you might like:
Josephine Bell, *A Question of Loyalties*, 1974
Bass Blake, *A Lady's Honour*, 1902
Daniel Defoe, *Memoir of a Cavalier*, 1720
G.A. Henty, *The Cornet of Horse*, 1890
F.W. Kenyon, *The Glory and the Dream*, 1963

204

CAROLYN MCCRAY

30 Pieces of Silver

(Hollywood, California: Off Our Meds Multimedia, 2010)

Story type: Adventure
Subject(s): History; Science; Religion
Major character(s): Dr. Rebecca Monroe, Scientist (geneticist); Dr. Archibald Lochum, Scientist
Time period(s): 21st century; 2010s
Locale(s): Europe

Summary: In *30 Pieces of Silver* by Carolyn McCray, two scientists on different quests are brought together when they become the targets of government agents and a secret society known as the Knot. Dr. Rebecca Monroe, a geneticist, has been searching around the globe for the elusive "smart gene." At the same time, her mentor and one-time love interest, Dr. Archibald Lochum, is on an aggressive search for Jesus Christ's bones. Although Monroe had believed that Lochum was dead, she now joins him as he attempts to reveal a mystery that has endured since the day of Christ's death.

205

ADRIENNE MCDONNELL

The Doctor and the Diva

(New York: Pamela Dorman Books/Viking, 2010)

Subject(s): Operas; Singing; Physicians
Major character(s): Dr. Ravell, Doctor (obstetrician); Erika, Singer (opera)
Time period(s): 20th century; 1900s (1903)
Locale(s): Italy; Trinidad and Tobago; Boston, Massachusetts

Summary: In *The Doctor and the Diva* by Adrienne McDonnell, a woman must choose between her marriage and her career at the turn of the 20th century. Erika, a gifted opera singer, is desperate to have a child with her husband and seeks the help of obstetrician Dr. Ravell. A Harvard graduate with an impressive list of Boston patients, Dr. Ravell seems Erika's last chance. When even his efforts fail, Erika throws herself into her singing career, but her relationship with Ravell has grown beyond that of patient and doctor. Leaving her husband behind, Erika's new life takes her to Trinidad and Italy. First novel.

Where it's reviewed:
Booklist, June 1, 2010, page 30
Kirkus Reviews, June 1, 2010, page 489
Publishers Weekly, April 26, 2010, page 83

Other books you might like:
Margaret Cuthbert, *The Silent Cradle*, 1998
Janice Kaplan, *The Whole Truth*, 1997
Elizabeth Letts, *Quality of Care*, 2005
Ann Patchett, *Bel Canto*, 2001
Katherine Stone, *Island of Dreams*, 2000

206

PAT MCINTOSH

A Pig of Cold Poison
(New York: Soho Press, 2010)

Series: Gil Cunningham Series. Book 7
Subject(s): Scots (British people); Detective fiction; Murder
Major character(s): Gil Cunningham, Detective—Police; Dan "Danny" Gibson, Crime Victim, Actor; Nanty Bothwell, Actress, Crime Suspect
Time period(s): 15th century
Locale(s): Glasgow, Scotland

Summary: *A Pig of Cold Poison* is the seventh book in Pat McIntosh's Gil Cunningham Murder Mystery series. Set in 15th-century Glasgow, this volume follows constable Gil on a perplexing new case. A string of poisonings is plaguing the community, starting with an actor in a production Gil attends. What he first thinks is simply a case of love gone wrong quickly turns into an all-out attack on the city's innocent residents—and only the determination and cunning of Constable Cunningham can stop it.

Where it's reviewed:
Booklist, May 1, 2010, page 39
Publishers Weekly, March 29, 2010, page 41

Other books by the same author:
The Stolen Voice, 2009
St. Mungo's Robin, 2007
The Merchant's Mark, 2006
The Nicholas Feast, 2005
The Harper's Quine, 2004

Other books you might like:
P.F. Chisholm, *A Surfeit of Guns*, 1997
Sharan Newman, *Cursed in the Blood*, 1998
C.J. Sansom, *Heartstone*, 2010
Kate Sedley, *The Green Man*, 2008
Bertrice Small, *The Captive Heart*, 2008

207

D.E. MEREDITH

Devoured
(New York: Minotaur Books, 2010)

Story type: Mystery
Subject(s): History; Mystery; Murder
Major character(s): George Adams, Inspector (Scotland Yard); Adolphus Hatton, Scientist (pathologist); Katherine Bessingham, Noblewoman; Albert Roumande, Assistant (to Hatton); Benjamin Broderig, Scientist (botanist)
Time period(s): 19th century; 1850s (1856)
Locale(s): Borneo, Asia; England

Summary: In *Devoured* by D.E. Meredith, the murder of a female patron of science in Victorian England draws attention to the contentious subject of evolution. When Lady Bessingham's battered body is discovered, Scotland Yard's Inspector George Adams is assigned to the case. While searching for Bessingham's murderer, Adams and medical consultant Adolphus Hatton follow a series of clues that include some missing letters that originated in Borneo. Apparently, Lady Bessingham had been corresponding with a botanist who was collecting samples there. Meanwhile, Adams and Hatton investigate another seemingly unrelated case involving the killing of a group of young girls. First novel.

Where it's reviewed:
Booklist, September 15, 2010, page 32
Kirkus Reviews, September 15, 2010, page 899
Library Journal, November 1, 2010, page 49
Publishers Weekly, September 13, 2010, page 26

Other books you might like:
Tasha Alexander, *Dangerous to Know*, 2010
Charles Finch, *A Beautiful Blue Death*, 2007
Robin Paige, *Death at Whitechapel*, 2000
Anne Perry, *Death of a Stranger*, 2002
Will Thomas, *The Limehouse Text*, 2006

208

JOHN J. MILLER

The First Assassin
(Woodbridge, Virginia: Woodbridge Press, 2009)

Story type: Historical - American Civil War
Subject(s): History; Presidents (Government); Assassination
Major character(s): Charles P. Rook, Military Personnel (colonel); Abraham Lincoln, Historical Figure (president elect); Portia, Slave
Time period(s): 19th century; 1860s (1861)
Locale(s): Washington, District of Columbia

Summary: In *The First Assassin* by John J. Miller, the inauguration of Abraham Lincoln brings tension and danger to the nation's capital. As the man responsible for the president's—and the city's—safety, Colonel Charles P. Rook uses all available resources to thwart the assassin who has threatened to strike. Despite the presence of guards and snipers in Washington, a killer lurks among the crowd, but Rook doesn't know who it could be. A young escaped slave, Portia, has taken the secret to the assassin's identity with her. To catch the would-be assassin, Rook must find Portia, whose journey has taken her far from Washington.

Where it's reviewed:
Booklist, September 1, 2010, page 49

Other books you might like:
Barnaby Conrad, *The Second Life of John Wilkes Booth*, 2010
Jan Jordan, *Dim the Flaring Lamps*, 1972
Benjamin King, *A Bullet for Lincoln*, 1993
David Robertson, *Booth*, 1998
Pamela Redford Russell, *The Woman Who Loved John Wilkes Booth*, 1978

209

JUDITH MILLER

More Than Words

(Bloomington, Minnesota: Bethany House, 2010)

Series: Daughters of Amana Series. Book 2
Subject(s): Amish; Christian life; Love
Major character(s): Gretchen Kohler, Writer; Allen Finley, Salesman
Time period(s): 19th century; 1880s
Locale(s): Homestead Village, Iowa

Summary: Gretchen Kohler is a young Amish woman in the late-19th century Amana Colonies. She juggles caring for her brother and grandmother with working long hours at her father's store. An avid writer, Gretchen also struggles to find the time to pursue her literary passion. When she meets salesman Allen Finley, she feels she's met a kindred spirit who understands her artistic interest. But a romance with Allen would mean sacrificing her precious time with family and her work. Now, Gretchen must make some tough decisions about her future. *More Than Words* is the second novel in Judith Miller's Daughters of Amana series.

Other books you might like:
Suzanne Woods Fisher, *The Waiting: A Novel*, 2010

210

NADIFA MOHAMED

Black Mamba Boy

(New York: Farrar, Straus and Giroux, 2010)

Subject(s): Fathers; Family; Voyages and travels
Major character(s): Jama, 11-Year-Old
Time period(s): 20th century; 1930s (1935)
Locale(s): Aden, Yemen

Summary: In *Black Mamba Boy*, Nadifa Mohamed tells the heart-wrenching tale of a boy in search of his father. After his father leaves the family, 11-year-old Jama and his mother go to stay with relatives in a nearby city. Jama, however, is not welcomed by his kinfolk and

spends his days on the streets. When his mother unexpectedly dies, she leaves him a small amount of money, which he uses to seek out the one person he feels can save him: his father. First novel.

Where it's reviewed:
Booklist, July 1, 2010, page 26
Kirkus Reviews, June 15, 2010, page 538
New York Times Book Review, August 29, 2010, page 19
Publishers Weekly, May 24, 2010, page 33

Other books you might like:
Tatiana de Rosnay, *Sarah's Key*, 2007
Jamie Ford, *Hotel on the Corner of Bitter and Sweet: A Novel*, 2009
Kate Morton, *The Forgotten Garden: A Novel*, 2009
Adam Thorpe, *Pieces of Light: A Novel*, 1998
Abraham Verghese, *Cutting for Stone: A Novel*, 2009

211

CONNIE MONK

Beyond the Shore

(London: Severn House Publishers, 2010)

Story type: Historical - World War II
Subject(s): Love; Family; Marriage
Major character(s): Georgie Franklyn, Artist; James, Spouse (of Georgie); Muriel, Stepmother (of Georgie)
Time period(s): 20th century; 1930s
Locale(s): London, United Kingdom

Summary: Affairs of the heart just before the onset of the Second World War are the focus of Connie Monk's *Beyond the Shore*. Aspiring artist Georgie Franklyn is crushed when her father unexpectedly dies, leaving his wife—Georgie's stepmother Muriel—in Georgie's care. With nowhere to turn, Georgie marries her best friend James to better provide for herself and her stepmother. As the darkness of war looms ever thicker over London, Georgie fights her attraction to the building landlord, and Muriel struggles with her own attraction...to James.

Where it's reviewed:
Booklist, June 1, 2010, page 28

Other books by the same author:
A Promise Fulfilled, 2009
Hunter's Lodge, 2008
Mistress of Mannington, 2002
From this Day Forward, 2000
Season of Change, 1984

Other books you might like:
Suzanne Goodwin, *A Change of Season*, 1992
Ian McEwan, *Atonement*, 2002
Linda Sole, *A Promise Made*, 2009
Penny Vincenzi, *Something Dangerous*, 2004
Sarah Waters, *The Night Watch*, 2006

212

FIONA MOUNTAIN

Lady of the Butterflies

(New York: G. P. Putnam's Sons, 2009)

Subject(s): Science; Love; Marriage
Major character(s): Eleanor Glanville, Scientist (lepidopterist); Edmund Ashfield, Spouse (of Eleanor); Richard Glanville, Spouse (of Eleanor)
Time period(s): 17th century
Locale(s): London, United Kingdom

Summary: Fiona Mountain's *Lady of the Butterflies* chronicles the work, passion, and love life of legendary butterfly scholar, Eleanor Glanville. From a young age, Eleanor studies butterflies and the natural lands of her family's estate. Her devotion to her work is not quelled by her relationships with two very different husbands, but it is her romance with a London pharmacist that rivals the main passion in Eleanor's life.

Where it's reviewed:
Booklist, June 1, 2010, page 31
Publishers Weekly, April 15, 2010, page 42

Other books by the same author:
Bloodline, 2006
Pale as the Dead, 2004
Isabella, 1999

Other books you might like:
Lynn Cullen, *The Creation of Eve*, 2010
J.M. Dillard, *The Scarlet Contessa: A Novel of the Italian Renaissance*, 2010
Carolly Erickson, *Rival to the Queen*, 2010
Paula Reed, *Hester: The Missing Years of The Scarlet Letter: A Novel*, 2010
Alison Weir, *The Captive Queen: A Novel of Eleanor of Aquitaine*, 2010

213

JANET MULLANY

Jane and the Damned

(New York: HarperCollins, 2010)

Story type: Series; Vampire Story
Subject(s): Fantasy; History; Romances (Fiction)
Major character(s): Jane Austen, Historical Figure, Writer; William Smith, Gentleman, Vampire; Reverend Austen, Father (of Jane); Cassandra Austen, Sister (of Jane)
Time period(s): 18th century; 1790s (1797)
Locale(s): England

Summary: In *Jane and the Damned*, author Janet Mullany provides a fictional account of Jane Austen's life casting the novelist as a reluctant vampire. Here, Austen's 18th-century England is home to a mannerly band of vampires known as the Damned. Though the Austen sisters know that proper ladies don't mingle with the Damned, Jane nonetheless surrenders to the temptations of William Smith and is unwillingly turned into a vampire. When

Reverend Austen takes his family to Bath so that Jane can be cured, an invasion by the French calls the Damned to royal duty.

Where it's reviewed:
Booklist, September 1, 2010, page 55
Kirkus Reviews, August 1, 2010, page 697
Library Journal, August 1, 2010, page 73
Publishers Weekly, August 9, 2010, page 34

Other books by the same author:
Improper Relations, 2010
The Rules of Gentility, 2007
Dedication, 2005

Other books you might like:
Jane Austen, *Emma and the Vampires*, 2010
Jane Austen, *Pride and Prejudice and Zombies*, 2009
Jane Austen, *Sense and Sensibility and Sea Monsters*, 2009
Arielle Eckstut, *Pride and Promiscuity*, 2001
Sarah Gray, *Wuthering Bites*, 2010

214

BRUCE MURKOFF

Red Rain

(New York: Knopf, 2010)

Story type: Historical - American Civil War
Subject(s): Civil war; Rural life; Interpersonal relations
Major character(s): Will Harp, Doctor; Jane, Spouse (of missing soldier); Mickey Blessing, Sea Captain (former shipping captain); Coley Hinds, 13-Year-Old
Time period(s): 19th century; 1860s (1864)
Locale(s): Rondout, New York

Summary: In Bruce Murkoff's *Red Rain*, it's been ten years since Will Harp has been home. With his time in the Army now over and the Civil War looming in the South, Will sets out to revive his medical practice in his small hometown of Rondout, New York. As he does so, the lives of several townspeople orbit his own, including those of Jane, a young woman grieving the disappearance of her soldier husband; Jane's brother, former captain, Mickey Blessing; and teenage alcoholic, Coley Hinds.

Where it's reviewed:
Booklist, May 1, 2010, page 22
Kirkus Reviews, June 1, 2010, page 489
Library Journal, February 15, 2010, page 90
Publishers Weekly, March 15, 2010, page 34

Other books by the same author:
Waterborne, 2004

Other books you might like:
Ken Follett, *Fall of Giants*, 2010
Julia Glass, *The Widower's Tale*, 2010
Michelle Hoover, *The Quickening*, 2010
Robin Oliveira, *My Name Is Mary Sutter*, 2010
Ann Weisgarber, *The Personal History of Rachel DuPree: A Novel*, 2010

215

MARK T. MUSTIAN

The Gendarme

(New York: G.P. Putnam's Sons, 2010)

Subject(s): Dreams; History; Old age
Major character(s): Emmett Conn, Aged Person, Veteran (World War I); Carol, Spouse (of Emmett); Araxie, Young Woman
Time period(s): 20th century; 1980s
Locale(s): Georgia, United States

Summary: In *The Gendarme* by M.T. Mustian, a World War I veteran's suppressed memories are restored after he has surgery to remove a brain tumor. Emmett Conn, now 92, recollects little of his war activities. Wounded at Gallipoli, Conn eventually married the American nurse who took care of him and moved to Georgia with her after the war. But recent neurosurgery has triggered vivid dreams in which Conn cruelly and brutally carries out his duty. Gradually, Conn realizes that the nightmares are revealing the truth about his wartime activities—sins that can only be reconciled by finding an Armenian girl that was one of his victims. First novel.

Where it's reviewed:
Kirkus Reviews, July 15, 2010, page 645
Library Journal, June 1, 2010, page 82
New York Times Book Review, October 10, 2010, page 25
Publishers Weekly, July 19, 2010, page 111

Other books by the same author:
The Mask of God, 2000
The Return, 2000

Other books you might like:
Adam Bagdasarian, *Forgotten Fire*, 2000
Carol Edgarian, *Rise the Euphrates*, 1994
Sonia Levitin, *The Return*, 1987
Micheline Aharonian Marcom, *Three Apples Fell from Heaven*, 2001
Elif Shafak, *The Bastard of Istanbul*, 2007

216

DIANE NOBLE

The Sister Wife

(New York: Avon Inspire, 2010)

Series: Brides of Gabriel Series. Book 1
Story type: Religious
Subject(s): Mormons; Marriage; Faith
Major character(s): Mary Rose, Spouse (of Gabriel), Religious; Gabriel, Spouse (of Mary Rose & Bronwyn), Religious; Bronwyn, Spouse (of Gabriel), Religious
Time period(s): 19th century
Locale(s): United States

Summary: *The Sister Wife* is a historical novel about polygamy from award-winning author Diane Noble. The book is the first installment in the Brides of Gabriel series. Mary Rose and her husband, Gabriel, are devout followers of the Prophet Joseph Smith and his new religious sect known as the Saints, but when the Prophet orders Gabriel to take another wife, Mary Rose is put to the ultimate test. The bride in question happens to be her best friend, Bronwyn. Devastated by the order, Mary Rose tries earnestly to make the marriage work, but sharing a husband with her best friend proves too challenging and painful to bear. As Mary Rose and Bronwyn question their God, their faith, and their beloved husband, they must make a critical choice about what's most important in life.

Where it's reviewed:
Booklist, June 1, 2010, page 34

Other books by the same author:
The Last Storyteller, 2004
Heart of Glass, 2002
Come My Little Angel, 2001
Distant Bells, 1999
When the Far Hills Bloom, 1999

Other books you might like:
Natalie R. Collins, *Wives and Sisters*, 2004
John Gates, *Sister Wife*, 2001
Cleo Jones, *Sister Wives*, 1984
Laura Kalpakian, *These Latter Days*, 1985
Betty Webb, *Desert Wives*, 2003

217

HANA SAMEK NORTON

The Sixth Surrender

(New York: Plume, 2010)

Story type: Romance
Subject(s): Romances (Fiction); History; Wars
Major character(s): Alienor, Royalty (queen-duchess); Juliana de Charnais, Religious (nun), Bride (of Guerin); Guerin de Lasalle, Mercenary, Bridegroom (of Juliana)
Time period(s): 13th century; 1200s (1200-1204)
Locale(s): France

Summary: *The Sixth Surrender* is a historical romance from author Hana Samek Norton. With only a few years left to live, queen-duchess Alienor of Aquitaine, mother of King John, makes a few more political plays in an effort to expand her son's dynasty to include rule over England and Normandy. To succeed in her plan, Alienor arranges the marriage of an unlikely couple: Juliana de Charnais, a bookish woman hoping to regain possession of her family property, and Guerin de Lasalle, a trouble-making mercenary vowing loyalty to King John. The pair make suitable partners in war, if not in love, but the grueling challenges of battle begin to soften their hearts and increase their desire.

Where it's reviewed:
Booklist, April 15, 2010, page 39
Library Journal, July 1, 2010, page 72

Other books you might like:
Margaret Ball, *Duchess of Aquitaine*, 2006

Ellen Jones, *Beloved Enemy: The Passions of Eleanor of Aquitaine*, 1994
Pamela Kaufman, *The Book of Eleanor*, 2002
Jean Plaidy, *The Courts of Love*, 1987
Alison Weir, *The Captive Queen: A Novel of Eleanor of Aquitaine*, 2010

218

NAOMI NOVIK

Tongues of Serpents

(New York: Del Rey/Ballantine Books, 2010)

Series: Temeraire Series. Book 6
Subject(s): Fantasy; History; Dragons
Major character(s): Will Laurence, Military Personnel (Captain); Temeraire, Dragon
Time period(s): 18th century-19th century; 1790s-1810s (1799-1815)
Locale(s): Australia

Summary: In *Tongues of Serpents* by Naomi Novik, a reimagined account of the Napoleonic age populates England's military with dragons and dragon riders. In this adventure, Captain Will Laurence and his mixed-breed dragon, Temeraire, have been sentenced to a penal colony in Australia for treasonous actions. Despite their status as prisoners, Laurence and Temeraire manage to smuggle three dragon eggs into Australia where they plan to hatch them secretly. Amidst the colony's unrest, one of the eggs disappears, setting off a perilous mountain search for its recovery. *Tongues of Serpents* is the sixth book in the Temeraire series.

Where it's reviewed:
Booklist, June 1, 2010, page 5
Library Journal, June 15, 2010, page 67
Locus, June 2010, page 23
Publishers Weekly, May 17, 2010, page 34

Other books by the same author:
Victory of Eagles, 2008
Empire of Ivory, 2007
Black Powder War, 2006
His Majesty's Dragon, 2006
Throne of Jade, 2006

Other books you might like:
Kate Grenville, *The Lieutenant*, 2009
Anne McCaffrey, *Dragonseye*, 1997
Colleen McCullough, *Morgan's Run*, 2000
Jane Rogers, *Promised Lands*, 1997
Julian Stockwin, *Command*, 2007

219

ANNE O'BRIEN

The Virgin Widow

(New York: New American Library, 2010)

Story type: Romance
Subject(s): History; Biographies; Romances (Fiction)

Major character(s): Richard Neville, Nobleman (Earl of Warwick); Anne Neville, Daughter (of Richard); Isobel Neville, Daughter (of Richard); Edward, Royalty (King of England); Richard, Brother (of Edward); Clarence, Brother (of Edward)
Time period(s): 15th century
Locale(s): England

Summary: In *The Virgin Widow*, author Anne O'Brien creates a fictional account of Anne Neville's life during the War of the Roses. The daughter of the Earl of Warwick, Anne is caught in political maneuvers that would ally the Nevilles with royal family. At first, the earl devises a plan that would make Anne the wife of King Edward's brother, Richard. When the king objects to the arrangement, the earl is accused of treason and the Nevilles are forced to leave England and move to France. As the war rages on to determine who will rule England, Anne maintains her love for Richard of Gloucester.

Where it's reviewed:
Booklist, November 1, 2010, page 33
Publishers Weekly, September 6, 2010, page 29

Other books by the same author:
Compromised Man, 2009
Conquering Knight, Captive Lady, 2009
The Enigmatic Rake, 2006
The Outrageous Debutante, 2005
The Puritan Bride, 2004

Other books you might like:
Philippa Gregory, *The Red Queen*, 2010
Rosemary Hawley Jarman, *We Speak No Treason*, 1971
Robin Maxwell, *To the Tower Born*, 2005
Lesley J. Nickell, *The White Queen*, 1978
Jean Plaidy, *The Reluctant Queen: The Story of Anne of York*, 1990

220

CHARLES O'BRIEN

False Patriots

(London: Severn House Publishers, 2010)

Series: Anne Cartier Series. Book 9
Subject(s): Detective fiction; Murder; Deafness
Major character(s): Anne Cartier, Detective—Amateur, Teacher; Patrick O'Fallon, Crime Suspect, Student (of Anne); Paul de Saint-Martin, Crime Victim, Political Figure
Time period(s): 18th century; 1790s (1791)
Locale(s): Paris, France

Summary: In 18th-century Paris, Anne Cartier is a teacher of deaf students and an amateur detective. When a famous do-gooder politician is killed, the authorities suspect Patrick O'Fallon, one of Anne's students. Determined to clear Patrick's name, Anne launches her own investigation into the events surrounding the death of Colonel Paul de Saint-Martin. What she finds, however, reveals a shocking connection between the mob and the crown. Charles O'Brien's *False Patriots* is the ninth novel in the Anne Cartier Mysteries series.

Where it's reviewed:
Booklist, June 1, 2010, page 39
Publishers Weekly, May 10, 2010, page 31

Other books by the same author:
Deadly Quarrel, 2009
Assassins' Rage, 2008
Cruel Choices, 2007
Fatal Carnival, 2006
Lethal Beauty, 2005

Other books you might like:
Jane Borodale, *The Book of Fires: A Novel*, 2010
Kathryn Davis, *Versailles*, 2002
Carolly Erickson, *The Hidden Diary of Marie Antoinette*, 2005
David Liss, *A Conspiracy of Paper*, 2000
Kate Sedley, *Wheel of Fate*, 2010

221

ANDREW O'HAGAN

The Life and Opinions of Maf the Dog, and of His Friend Marilyn Monroe

(London: Faber, 2010)

Subject(s): Dogs; Entertainment industry; Human-animal relationships
Major character(s): Mafia Honey "Maf", Dog (pet of Marilyn); Marilyn Monroe, Actress, Friend (of Frank); Frank Sinatra, Friend (of Marilyn), Singer
Time period(s): 20th century; 1960s
Locale(s): Hollywood, California; New York, New York

Summary: In *The Life and Opinions of Maf the Dog, and of His Friend Marilyn Monroe*, award-winning author Andrew O'Hagan presents a one-of-a-kind tale about dogs, devotion, and celebrity. Mafia Honey, Maf for short, is a scrappy little dog given to screen siren Marilyn Monroe as a Christmas present from legendary crooner Frank Sinatra. In the book, Maf chronicles his life as the beloved companion of the famous movie star while offering unique insights into the people who surround him and the demons that consume his talented but troubled owner. Andrew O'Hagan is the author of the novels *Our Fathers* and *Be Near Me*.

Where it's reviewed:
Booklist, October 1, 2010, page 28
Library Journal, October 15, 2010, page 68
New York Times Book Review, January 2, 2011, page 12
Publishers Weekly, August 2, 2010, page 1

Other books by the same author:
Be Near Me, 2006
Personality, 2003
Our Fathers, 1999

Other books you might like:
Michael Korda, *The Immortals*, 1992
Wendy Leigh, *The Secret Letters of Marilyn Monroe and Jackie Kennedy*, 2003
Joyce Carol Oates, *Blonde: A Novel*, 2000

John Rechy, *Marilyn's Daughter*, 1988
Sam Toperoff, *Queen of Desire: A Novel*, 1992

222

SCOTT ODEN

The Lion of Cairo

(New York: Thomas Dunne Books, 2010)

Story type: Adventure; Historical - Medieval
Subject(s): Egyptians; History; Wars
Major character(s): Caliph Rashid al-Hasan, Leader (of Cairo), Young Man
Time period(s): Multiple Time Periods
Locale(s): Cairo, Egypt

Summary: *The Lion of Cairo* is a gripping, suspenseful, and adventurous tale from author Scott Oden. In *The Lion of Cairo*, Oden breathes life into medieval Cairo, a desperate, deteriorating place in need of a hero. Caliph Rashid al-Hasan rules over the failing empire, but all around him, men and rulers are scheming to take over. In his own streets and alleys, mutinies are forming, men are dying, and the desire for power is overtaking everyone. As the empire caves in on itself, neighboring enemies are eager to seize the opportunity to take Cairo for themselves. An elderly man from a faraway place decides to help Caliph resume control of his kingdom by sending the strongest weapon in Egypt: a powerful and deadly man known as the Emir of the Knife.

Other books by the same author:
Memnon, 2006
Men of Bronze, 2005

Other books you might like:
Bartle Bull, *A Cafe on the Nile*, 1998
Jan Guillou, *The Road to Jerusalem*, 2009
Jean-Christophe Rufin, *The Abyssinian*, 1999
Diane Whiteside, *The Devil She Knows*, 2010
Robyn Young, *The Fall of the Templars*, 2009

223

I.J. PARKER

The Masuda Affair

(Sutton, Surrey, England: Severn House, 2010)

Series: Sugawara Akitada Series. Book 7
Story type: Mystery
Subject(s): Japanese history; Mystery; Murder
Major character(s): Sugawara Akitada, Government Official, Detective—Amateur; Tora, Servant (of Sugawara)
Time period(s): 11th century
Locale(s): Japan

Summary: *The Masuda Affair* is the seventh installment in the Sugawara Akitada Mystery series from author I.J. Parker. Sugawara Akitada, a government official in 11th-century Japan, is traveling home from a mission when he encounters a young mute boy in the forest. Still mourning the loss of his own young son, Sugawara takes the boy in and decides to help him find his parents. Meanwhile, Sugawara's loyal servant Tora is having romance issues: a powerful man with a ruthless penchant for beautiful women has taken Tora's new bride. The two incidents seem unrelated, but clues from both lead Sugawara and Tora into the midst of a murder investigation in the seedy entertainment district.

Where it's reviewed:
Booklist, October 1, 2010, page 34
Kirkus Reviews, September 15, 2010, page 899
Publishers Weekly, September 13, 2010, page 26

Other books by the same author:
The Fires of the Gods, 2011
The Convict's Sword, 2009
Island of Exiles, 2007
The Hell Screen, 2003
Rashomon Gate, 2002

Other books you might like:
Liza Dalby, *The Tale of Murasaki*, 2000
Alison Fell, *The Pillow Boy of Lady Onogoro*, 1994
Julith Jedamus, *The Book of Loss*, 2006
Katherine Paterson, *The Sign of the Chrysanthemum*, 1976
Ann Woodward, *The Exile Way*, 1996

224

MICHAEL PEARCE

A Dead Man in Malta

(New York: Soho Constable, 2010)

Series: Sandor Seymour Series. Book 7
Story type: Mystery
Subject(s): Mystery; Murder; History
Major character(s): Sandor Seymour, Investigator, Troubleshooter
Time period(s): 20th century; 1910s (1913)
Locale(s): Malta

Summary: *A Dead Man in Malta*, a historical mystery novel, is the seventh installment in the Sandor Seymour series from award-winning author Michael Pearce. It's 1913 and Scotland Yard problem-solver and investigator, Sandor Seymour, is assigned a case on the island of Malta. Three seemingly healthy individuals mysteriously die shortly after being checked into a naval hospital on the island. Two of the victims are British sailors, one of whom was visited by a stranger shortly before expiring, and one was a hot-air balloonist who made a routine visit to the hospital after a surprise landing. When witnesses begin reporting the presence of a visiting stranger near the victims shortly before their deaths, Sandor concludes that these deaths were no accident, but rather the work of a murderer.

Where it's reviewed:
Kirkus Reviews, September 15, 2010, page 899
Publishers Weekly, September 27, 2010, page 41

Other books by the same author:
A Dead Man in Naples, 2010
A Dead Man in Barcelona, 2008
A Dead Man in Tangier, 2007

A Dead Man in Athens, 2006
A Dead Man in Trieste, 2005

Other books you might like:
Boris Akunin, *The Death of Achilles*, 2005
John Le Carre, *The Constant Gardener*, 2001
James Melville, *Diplomatic Baggage*, 1994
Mark Mills, *The Information Officer: A Novel*, 2009
Joanna Trollope, *The Brass Dolphin*, 1999

225

ARTURO PEREZ-REVERTE

Pirates of the Levant

(New York: G.P. Putnam's Sons, 2010)

Series: Captain Alatriste Series. Book 6
Story type: Adventure; Series
Subject(s): Pirates; Spaniards; Adventure
Major character(s): Diego Alatriste, Pirate, Mercenary; Inigo Alatriste, Son (of Diego), Mercenary, Pirate
Time period(s): 17th century
Locale(s): Algeria; Malta; Morocco

Summary: Captain Diego Alatriste and his teenage son, Inigo, make their living as vigilante pirates. Set in the 17th century, this volume charts their adventures aboard a notorious Spanish ship that takes them to some of the most exotic locales in the world. Diego, who is preparing for retirement, will now have to face the most brutal battle of his life, testing his mettle and sword-fighting prowess like no other match of his long and storied career. *Pirates of the Levant* is the sixth and final novel in Arturo Perez-Reverte's Captain Alatriste series, translated from Spanish by Margaret Jull Costa.

Where it's reviewed:
Booklist, August 1, 2010, page 27
Kirkus Reviews, August 15, 2010, page 892
Library Journal, August 1, 2010, page 71
Publishers Weekly, June 28, 2010, page 108

Other books by the same author:
The Painter of Battles, 2008
Purity of Blood, 2006
Captain Alatriste, 2005
The Queen of the South, 2004
The Fencing Master, 1999

Other books you might like:
Isabel Allende, *Zorro*, 2005
Shirlee Busbee, *The Spanish Rose*, 1986
Michael Crichton, *Pirate Latitudes: A Novel*, 2009
Wilbur Smith, *Birds of Prey*, 1997
Liliane Webb, *The Marranos*, 1980

226

C. ALLYN PIERSON

Mr. Darcy's Little Sister

(Naperville, Illinois: Sourcebooks Landmark, 2010)

Story type: Romance
Subject(s): History; Romances (Fiction); Brothers and sisters

Major character(s): Georgina Darcy, Sister (to Mr. Darcy), Young Woman; Mr. Fitzwilliam Darcy, Brother (to Georgina)
Time period(s): 19th century
Locale(s): England

Summary: In the historical novel *Mr. Darcy's Little Sister*, C. Allyn Pierson carries on the tale of Jane Austen's *Pride and Prejudice* with a story about the dashing Mr. Darcy's shy and beloved younger sibling, Georgina. As an older brother, Mr. Darcy is loyal, committed, and fiercely overprotective. Now that Georgina has grown into a beautiful young woman, she naturally longs to find a romance like the one shared by her brother and the strong-willed Elizabeth Bennet. Unfortunately, Mr. Darcy is far too concerned about his sister's safety and protection to ever allow some irresponsible or undeserving young man to enter the picture, leaving Georgina to fear that she'll never find love.

Where it's reviewed:
Booklist, September 1, 2010, page 54

Other books you might like:
Julia Barrett, *Presumption*, 1993
Linda Berdoll, *Mr. Darcy Takes a Wife*, 2004
Janet Mullany, *Jane and the Damned*, 2010
Abigail Reynolds, *Mr. Darcy's Obsession*, 2010
Emma Tennant, *Pemberley*, 1993

227

THEODORE W. PIETSCH

The Curious Death of Peter Artedi: A Mystery in the History of Science

(New York: Scott and Nix, 2010)

Story type: Mystery
Subject(s): Enlightenment (Cultural movement); Death; Science
Major character(s): Peter Artedi, Historical Figure, Scientist; Carl Linnaeus, Historical Figure, Scientist
Time period(s): 18th century; 1720s-1730s
Locale(s): Amsterdam, Netherlands

Summary: Set in Old Amsterdam in the spring of the 18th century, Theodore W. Pietsch's *The Curious Death of Peter Artedi: A Mystery in the History of Science* reimagines the friendship and rivalry of Age of Enlightenment thinkers, Artedi, a budding ichthyologist, and Carl Linnaeus, a promising botanist and taxonomist. When the pair meet in 1729 as students, they develop a quick and powerful connection as friends, intellectuals, rivals, and maybe lovers. Working together, they develop a new classification system for plants and animals, but in 1735, shortly before Artedi is slated to publish his work, he drowns in the canal, leaving Linnaeus to take the credit and fame for their collective work.

Where it's reviewed:
Booklist, October 15, 2010, page 30

Other books you might like:
Tracy Chevalier, *Girl with a Pearl Earring*, 1999
Rosalind Laker, *The Golden Tulip*, 1991
David Liss, *The Coffee Trader*, 2003

Gladys Schmitt, *Rembrandt*, 1961
Daniel Silva, *The Secret Servant*, 2007

228

ANNE PLANTAGENET

The Last Rendezvous

(New York: Other Press, 2010)

Story type: Historical - Post-French Revolution
Subject(s): Biographies; Writers; Women
Major character(s): Marceline Desbordes-Valmore, Historical Figure, Writer; Prosper Valmore, Spouse (of Marceline), Historical Figure; Henri de Latouche, Lover (of Marceline)
Time period(s): 18th century-19th century; 1780s-1850s
Locale(s): France

Summary: In *The Last Rendezvous*, Anne Plantagenet creates a fictionalized chronicle of the life of 19th-century French actress and poet, Marceline Desbordes-Valmore. A contemporary of Paul Verlaine, Charles Baudelaire, Victor Hugo, and Alfred de Vigny, Desbordes held a place of prominence in French literary society—an uncommon accomplishment for a woman in the early 1800s. Plantagenet's account finds Desbordes the wife of handsome (and younger) actor Prosper Valmore. Still emotionally unsettled at the age of 33, Marceline embarks on an intense love affair with Henri de Latouche—a union that has a lasting and profound effect on her personal life and her work.

Where it's reviewed:
Booklist, March 15, 2010, page 21
Kirkus Reviews, January 15, 2010, page 62
Library Journal, March 2, 2010, page 79

Other books you might like:
Pat Barker, *Life Class: A Novel*, 2008
Sheramy Bundrick, *Sunflowers*, 2009
Stacy Cohen, *The Last Train from Paris*, 2009
Stephanie Cowell, *Claude and Camille: A Novel of Monet*, 2010
Jennifer Cody Epstein, *The Painter from Shanghai*, 2008

229

JAN REID

Comanche Sundown

(Fort Worth, Texas: Texas Christian University Press, 2010)

Story type: Western
Subject(s): History; Western fiction; Native Americans
Major character(s): Bose Ikard, Slave (former), Cowboy/Cowgirl, Captive (of Quanah); Quanah, Indian (Commanche), Chieftain
Time period(s): 19th century; 1860s
Locale(s): American Southwest

Summary: *Comanche Sundown* is an action-packed historical Western from acclaimed author Jan Reid. Born the son of a mighty Indian warrior and a white slave, Quanah is shunned by the Comanches for his impure bloodline. When he's denied the right to marry Weck-eah, the woman he loves, Quanah leaves his community for another group of Comanches, eventually earning a noble position as their war chief. Bose Ikard, a former slave and wild cowboy, is captured by the Comanches during a longhorn ride in New Mexico. Sworn enemies at first, Quanah and Bose slowly build a solid friendship founded on mutual respect and admiration, but Bose's budding attraction to Quanah's stunning wife poses a threat to their hard-earned trust.

Other books by the same author:
Deerinwater, 1984

Other books you might like:
Bill Dugan, *Quanah Parker*, 1993
David Anthony Durham, *Gabriel's Story*, 2001
Walter Lucas, *Blood Red River*, 2000
Larry McMurtry, *Comanche Moon*, 1997
Lucia St. Clair Robson, *Ride the Wind: The Story of Cynthia Ann Parker and the Last Days of the Comanche*, 1982

230

JOANNE RENDELL

Out of the Shadows

(New York: New American Library, 2010)

Story type: Literary
Subject(s): Writers; Family relations; Genealogy
Major character(s): Clara Fitzgerald, Professor, Researcher; Mary Shelley, Writer, Historical Figure
Time period(s): 21st century; (2010s); 19th century
Locale(s): United States

Summary: *Out of the Shadows* is a literary novel from author Joanne Rendell. Struggling with her mother's recent death, her fiance's booming career, and her own apathetic approach to work, Clara Fitzgerald is desperate for something new to distract her from the woes of life. Recalling childhood stories her mother used to tell about a distant relation to *Frankenstein* author Mary Shelley, Clara decides to conduct an amateur investigation into her ancestry to see if there's any truth to the tale. As Clara, along with her sister and a Shelley scholar, search for Shelley's lost diaries and letters, she makes a shocking discovery about both her past and her future.

Where it's reviewed:
Booklist, September 1, 2010, page 54

Other books by the same author:
The Professors' Wives' Club, 2008

Other books you might like:
Peter Ackroyd, *The Casebook of Victor Frankenstein*, 2008
Frederico Andahazi, *The Merciful Women*, 2000
Judith Chernaik, *Love's Children*, 1992
Anne Edwards, *Haunted Summer*, 1972
Jude Morgan, *Passion*, 2005

231

ABIGAIL REYNOLDS

Mr. Darcy's Obsession

(Naperville, Illinois: Sourcebooks, 2010)

Series: Pemberley Variations Series. Book 6
Story type: Literary; Series
Subject(s): Literature; England; Social class
Major character(s): Elizabeth Bennett, Gentlewoman; Jane Bennett, Sister (of Elizabeth); Fitzwilliam Darcy, Gentleman; Uncle Gardiner, Uncle (of Elizabeth); Aunt Gardiner, Aunt (of Elizabeth); Lydia Bennett, Sister (of Elizabeth)
Time period(s): 19th century; 1800s
Locale(s): England

Summary: In *Mr. Darcy's Obsession*, author Abigail Reynolds re-imagines Jane Austen's *Pride and Prejudice* by scripting a premature demise for the father of Elizabeth Bennett. Upon the death of Mr. Bennett, the remaining family members are forced to leave their home at Longbourn. Jane marries a working man many years her elder; young Lydia takes up with a soldier who leaves her when she becomes pregnant. Elizabeth moves in with her aunt and uncle and though Fitzwilliam Darcy finds her there, their relationship seems doomed by the family's changed social situation. *Mr. Darcy's Obsession* is the sixth book in the Pride and Prejudice Continues series.

Where it's reviewed:
Booklist, September 1, 2010, page 54

Other books by the same author:
The Man Who Loved Pride & Prejudice, 2010
Mr. Fitzwilliam Darcy: the Last Man in the World, 2010
To Conquer Mr. Darcy, 2010
Impulse & Initiation, 2008
Pemberley by the Sea, 2008

Other books you might like:
Elizabeth Aston, *Mr. Darcy's Daughters*, 2003
Linda Berdoll, *Darcy & Elizabeth: Nights and Days at Pemberley*, 2006
Janet Mullany, *Jane and the Damned*, 2010
C. Allyn Pierson, *Mr. Darcy's Little Sister*, 2010
Emma Tennant, *An Unequal Marriage*, 1994

232

ANN RONALD

Friendly Fallout 1953

(Reno, Nevada: University of Nevada Press, 2010)

Story type: Post-Nuclear Holocaust
Subject(s): Nuclear weapons; Nuclear literature; United States
Time period(s): 20th century; 1950s (1953)
Locale(s): Nevada, United States

Summary: *Friendly Fallout 1953* is a historical novel from author Ann Ronald. Using factual information as the backdrop, Ronald tells the fictional tale of individuals caught in the consequences of atomic-bomb testing in the Nevada desert in 1953. Throughout the year, nearly a dozen above-ground atomic bomb tests were conducted in the desert, affecting thousands of people with radiation and nuclear fallout. Ronald chronicles the lives of 12 random individuals who were impacted by the government's attempt at protection, including a Las Vegas showgirl, a visiting journalist, a local Mormon mother, and a radiation specialist, to give readers insight into a terrifying time in American history and the high price of freedom and safety.

Other books you might like:
Doug Beason, *Fallout*, 1997
Tracy Daugherty, *What Falls Away*, 1996
Brian Freemantle, *Bomb Grade*, 1996
David Ignatius, *The Increment*, 2009
Kyle Mills, *The Second Horseman*, 2006

233

PRISCILLA ROYAL

Valley of Dry Bones

(Scottsdale, Arizona: Poisoned Pen Press, 2010)

Series: Medieval Mysteries Series. Book 7
Story type: Mystery; Series
Subject(s): History; Mystery; Detective fiction
Major character(s): Eleanor, Religious (Prioress, Tyndal Priory); Baron Otes, Agent (emissary); Thomas, Religious (Brother)
Time period(s): 13th century; 1270s (1274)
Locale(s): England

Summary: In *Valley of Dry Bones* by Priscilla Royal, a royal pilgrimage in the 13th century brings mystery and murder to Tyndal Priory. When Prioress Eleanor learns that King Edward's wife has planned a journey of thanksgiving to her priory, she prepares for the scrutiny the monarch's visit will bring. But problems arise early when the advance team of envoys arrives and a member of their party is murdered near Brother Thomas's hermitage. Eleanor, with the aid of Brother Thomas, works to solve the murder and expose the sinister plot that threatens the priory's peace. *Valley of Dry Bones* is the seventh book in the Medieval Mystery series.

Where it's reviewed:
Booklist, October 1, 2010, page 36
Publishers Weekly, August 30, 2010, page 32

Other books by the same author:
Chambers of Death, 2009
Forsaken Soul, 2008
Justice for the Damned, 2007
Sorrow Without End, 2006

Other books you might like:
Simon Beaufort, *The Bloodstained Throne*, 2010
Alys Clare, *Music of the Distant Stars*, 2010
Paul Doherty, *The Waxman Murders*, 2010
Ariana Franklin, *Mistress of the Art of Death*, 2007
Peter Tremayne, *The Dove of Death*, 2010

234

S. THOMAS RUSSELL

A Battle Won

(New York: G. P. Putnam's Sons, 2010)

Subject(s): Ships; Sea stories; Wars
Major character(s): Charles Hayden, Military Personnel
Time period(s): 18th century; 1790s (1793)
Locale(s): Corsica, Europe

Summary: In 1793, British and French forces are vying for dominance over the island of Corsica. Master and Commander Charles Hayden is called into the fray as leader of the ship known as *Themis*. But as soon as the vessel hits the turbulent seas, Hayden realizes this will be no ordinary battle: it will entail all the might of two of the world's strongest fighting forces—and one of them will have to lose. S. Thomas Russell's *A Battle Won* is the sequel to *Under Enemy Colors*.

Where it's reviewed:
Kirkus Reviews, July 1, 2010, page 592
Publishers Weekly, June 28, 2010, page 108

Other books by the same author:
Under Enemy Colors, 2007
The Shadow Roads, 2004
The Isle of Battle, 2002
The One Kingdom, 2001
The Compass of the Soul, 1998

Other books you might like:
David Donachie, *An Ill Wind*, 2010
Alexander Kent, *Stand into Danger*, 1981
Dewey Lambdin, *King, Ship, and Sword*, 2010
Julian Stockwin, *Kydd*, 2001
Jay Worrall, *Any Approaching Enemy*, 2006

235

WILLIAM RYAN

The Holy Thief

(New York: Minotaur Books, 2010)

Subject(s): Russians; Murder; Detective fiction
Major character(s): Alexei Korolev, Detective—Police
Time period(s): 20th century; 1930s (1936)
Locale(s): Moscow, Russia

Summary: In *The Holy Thief*, author William Ryan tells the story of Alexei Korolev, a detective with the Moscow Militia. It is 1936, Stalin's power is just beginning to take hold throughout the country, and Korolev is called in to investigate a brutal murder. The body of a young woman has been found in a local church. With a little investigative work, Korolev learns the woman is an American—a finding that puts the detective under immediate suspicion from the government. Now Korolev will have to infiltrate the dark criminal world of Moscow in order to solve this murder, save his reputation, and avoid being sent to a forced labor camp. First novel.

Where it's reviewed:
Booklist, September 15, 2010, page 32

New York Times Book Review, September 19, 2010, page 17
Publishers Weekly, June 14, 2010, page 34

Other books you might like:
Sam Eastland, *Shadow Pass*, 2011
Alan Furst, *Kingdom of Shadows*, 2000
Donald James, *Monstrum*, 1997
Stuart M. Kaminsky, *The Dog Who Bit a Policeman*, 1998
Martin Cruz Smith, *Gorky Park*, 1981

236

VANITHA SANKARAN

Watermark: A Novel of the Middle Ages

(New York: Avon, 2010)

Story type: Historical - Medieval
Subject(s): History; Middle Ages; Women
Major character(s): Auda, Girl, Handicapped (mute); Martin, Father (of Auda)
Time period(s): 14th century; 1300s
Locale(s): France

Summary: In *Watermark* by Vanitha Sankaran, an albino girl born in 1320 is the subject of suspicion and fear. After her mother dies in childbirth, the pale infant is identified as a devil's child and subsequently has her tongue removed by a medical apprentice. The girl's father, a skilled papermaker, names her Auda and teaches her his trade from an early age. Though mute, Auda shows an affinity for working with words and eventually becomes a scribe. When Auda begins to put her own thoughts on paper, she is accused as a heretic but finds refuge and love with an artist.

237

C.J. SANSOM

Heartstone

(New York: Viking Adult, 2010)

Series: Matthew Shardlake Series. Book 5
Story type: Mystery; Series
Subject(s): Mystery; Crime; England
Major character(s): Matthew Shardlake, Lawyer, Investigator; Jack Barak, Sidekick, Investigator
Time period(s): 16th century; 1540-1550 (1545)
Locale(s): England

Summary: In C.J. Sansom's *Heartstone*, attorney Matthew Shardlake is approached by one of the Queen's former servants. She tells Shardlake that a serious wrongdoing has taken place involving a young ward. As a favor to the woman, Shardlake agrees to investigate these claims and takes off for Portsmouth with his assistant, Jack Barak. While the two men search for evidence of the alleged wrongdoing, their country is on the brink of war with France. As men rush to enlist, Shardlake and Barak hurry to unmask a criminal. Their search takes them

aboard Henry VIII's ships and right into the heart of the upcoming war. This is the fifth book in the Matthew Shardlake series.

Where it's reviewed:
Publishers Weekly, November 1, 2010, page 30

Other books by the same author:
Revelation, 2009
Winter in Madrid, 2008
Sovereign, 2007
Dark Fire, 2005
Dissolution, 2003

Other books you might like:
Philippa Gregory, *The Boleyn Inheritance*, 2006
Hilary Mantel, *Wolf Hall*, 2009
Robin Maxwell, *The Secret Diary of Anne Boleyn*, 1997
Jean Plaidy, *Murder Most Royal*, 1949
Judith Merkle Riley, *The Serpent Garden*, 1996

238

KIM VOGEL SAWYER

In Every Heartbeat

(Minneapolis, Minnesota: Bethany House, 2010)

Subject(s): Friendship; College environment; Christian life
Major character(s): Petey, Student—College, Religious; Libby, Student—College; Bennett, Student—College
Time period(s): 20th century; 1910s (1914)
Locale(s): Missouri, United States

Summary: Kim Vogel Sawyer's *In Every Heartbeat* follows three friends through their first year at college, circa 1914. Petey wants to be a minister, but first he will have to reconcile his own demons and learn to forgive the parents that abandoned him. Creative-minded Libby must discover how to harness the strengths of her imagination to build a career as a journalist. And Bennett, still haunted by the ghosts of his past, has to figure out how to transcend his penchants for violence and vice. Each draws strength from his or her friends and from faith in God to confront the challenges of college life.

Other books by the same author:
A Promise for Spring, 2009
Blessings, 2008
My Heart Remembers, 2008
Beginnings, 2007
Bygones, 2007

Other books you might like:
Irene Allen, *Quaker Witness*, 1993
Jan De Hartog, *The Lamb's War*, 1980
Hallie Ephron, *Never Tell a Lie: A Novel of Suspense*, 2009
Paulette Jiles, *The Color of Lightning: A Novel*, 2010
Daisy Newman, *Indian Summer of the Heart*, 1982

239

STEVEN SAYLOR

Empire: The Novel of Imperial Rome

(New York: St. Martin's Press, 2010)

Story type: Family Saga
Subject(s): Ancient Roman civilization; Family history; Success
Major character(s): Lucius Pinarius, Father; Lucius Pinarius, Son
Time period(s): 1st century-2nd century; 10s-140s (14-141)
Locale(s): Rome, Italy

Summary: In *Empire: The Novel of Imperial Rome*, the sequel to *Roma*, Steven Saylor documents the initial success and eventual fall of the Pinarius family between 14 AD and 141 AD. The men and women in this family, though not royalty, spent over a century serving the many Roman emperors. While the eldest Pinarius served the emperors directly, he trained his first son, Lucius, to speak well enough to impress the emperors and the Roman people simultaneously. Lucius gains the attention of many and is held in high regards wherever he goes. While the Pinarius family serve under the reign of Augustus, Trajan, and Hadrian happily, they fear for their lives when Tiberius, Caligula, Nero, and Domitian come in to power.

Where it's reviewed:
Library Journal, August 1, 2010, page 74
Publishers Weekly, July 5, 2010, page 26

Other books by the same author:
The Triumph of Caesar, 2008
Roma, 2007
The Judgment of Caesar, 2004
A Mist of Prophecies, 2002
Rubicon, 1999

Other books you might like:
Robert Harris, *Imperium: A Novel of Ancient Rome*, 2006
Ursula K. Le Guin, *Lavinia*, 2008
Colleen McCullough, *The First Man in Rome*, 1990
Gore Vidal, *Julian*, 1964
Thornton Wilder, *The Ides of March*, 1948

240

LYNN SHEPHERD

Murder at Mansfield Park

(New York: St. Martin's Griffin, 2010)

Subject(s): Mystery; Murder; History
Major character(s): Fanny Price, Wealthy, Heiress, Crime Victim; Mary Crawford, Detective—Amateur
Time period(s): 19th century; 1810s
Locale(s): England

Summary: *Murder at Mansfield Park* is an engaging, entertaining, and clever historical mystery novel from debut author Lynn Shepherd. The book reinvents the story and characters of Jane Austen's classic novel, *Mansfield Park*, infusing elements of mystery, murder, and intrigue. In *Murder at Mansfield Park*, Fanny Price is an entitled, unbearable wealthy snob who finds pleasure in making sweet and humble Mary Crawford's life miserable. Despite Fanny's cruel behavior toward her, Mary becomes determined to find the person responsible for Fanny's murder after her body is discovered in Mansfield Park. Mary plays amateur sleuth alongside a private investigator from London to track down the killer. First novel.

Where it's reviewed:
Kirkus Reviews, June 1, 2010, page 497
Library Journal, June 15, 2010, page 70
Publishers Weekly, June 14, 2010, page 36

Other books you might like:
Marsha Altman, *The Darcys and the Bingleys: A Tale of Two Gentlemen's Marriages to Two Most Devoted Sisters*, 2008
Stephanie Barron, *Jane and the Madness of Lord Byron*, 2010
Carrie Bebris, *The Matters at Mansfield: Or, the Crawford Affair*, 2008
Rebecca Ann Collins, *Netherfield Park Revisited*, 2008
Emma Tennant, *Pemberley*, 1993

241

HARRY SIDEBOTTOM

King of Kings

(London: Michael Joseph Books, 2009)

Series: Warrior of Rome Series. Book 2
Story type: Historical - Pre-history
Subject(s): Ancient Roman civilization; Christianity; Wars
Major character(s): Ballista, Military Personnel (general in the Roman Army)
Locale(s): Rome, Italy

Summary: The second novel in Harry Sidebottom's Warrior of Rome series, *King of Kings* continues the adventures of General Ballista as he returns home from yet another bloody battle. But life in Rome is not as he left it. Christian zeal has spread throughout the Empire, and Rome's enemies want nothing more than to see the great city fall. It isn't long before Ballista is drawn into the fight to keep Rome the way she was, a battle that thrusts the general squarely into the heart of an epic religious war. Can the Warrior of Rome save the city from the religious fundamentalists bent on changing it forever?

Other books by the same author:
Fire in the East, 2009

Other books you might like:
Gillian Bradshaw, *Island of Ghosts*, 1998
Robert Harris, *Imperium: A Novel of Ancient Rome*, 2006
Conn Iggulden, *Emperor: The Gates of Rome*, 2003
Ursula K. Le Guin, *Lavinia*, 2008

Steven Saylor, *Empire: The Novel of Imperial Rome*, 2010

242

ALASTAIR SIM

The Unbelievers

(New York: Minotaur Books, 2010)

Subject(s): Social class; Scotland; Detective fiction
Major character(s): Inspector Allerdyce, Detective—Police; Sergeant McGillivray, Detective—Police; Duke of Dornoch, Wealthy, Crime Victim
Time period(s): 19th century
Locale(s): Scotland

Summary: In Alastar Sim's *The Unbelievers*, the Duke of Dornoch is the wealthiest man in Scotland—and he's just been murdered. Inspector Allerdyce and Sergeant McGillivray are called in to investigate the much-despised tycoon's demise, and they find a laundry list of suspects who all had good reason to want the Duke dead. But the question remains: who, among this ever-growing list, could have actually done the deed?

Where it's reviewed:
Kirkus Reviews, August 1, 2010, page 705
Library Journal, September 1, 2010, page 94

Other books you might like:
M.C. Beaton, *Death of a Maid*, 2007
Kate Morton, *The Distant Hours*, 2010
Ian Rankin, *The Naming of the Dead*, 2006
Helen Simonson, *Major Pettigrew's Last Stand: A Novel*, 2010
Charles Todd, *Legacy of the Dead*, 2000

243

JOSEPH SKIBELL

A Curable Romantic

(Chapel Hill, North Carolina: Algonquin Books, 2010)

Subject(s): Jews; Picaresque literature; Psychology
Major character(s): Jakob Sammelsohn, Doctor; Sigmund Freud, Psychologist (psychoanalyst), Historical Figure; Ita, Spirit; Dr. Ludovik Leyzer Zamenhof, Inventor; Loe Bernfeld, Socialite
Time period(s): 19th century-20th century; 1890s-1940s
Locale(s): Vienna, Austria; Warsaw, Poland

Summary: Set in Eastern Europe, Joseph Skibell's *A Curable Romantic* spans the 1890s to the 1940s. A young doctor, Jakob Sammelsohn, embarks on a series of adventures that takes him from a face-to-face meeting with Sigmund Freud to the World War II ghettos of Warsaw. Along the way, he encounters a string of unforgettable characters, including a tortured ghost, a language inventor, and a rich socialite.

Where it's reviewed:
Library Journal, July 1, 2010, page 79

Library Journal, July 1, 2010, page 79
Publishers Weekly, May 31, 2010, page 22

Other books by the same author:
The English Disease, 2003
A Blessing on the Moon, 1997

Other books you might like:
Alan Furst, *The Spies of Warsaw: A Novel*, 2008
John Hersey, *The Wall*, 1950
Carol De Chellis Hill, *Henry James' Midnight Song*, 1993
Daniel Silva, *A Death in Vienna*, 2004
D.M. Thomas, *The White Hotel*, 1981

244

MICHAEL SLEDGE

The More I Owe You: A Novel

(Berkeley, California: Counterpoint, 2010)

Subject(s): Biographies; Poetry; Writers
Major character(s): Elizabeth Bishop, Writer (poet), Lesbian; Lota de Macedo Soares, Daughter (of a Brazilian politician), Lesbian
Time period(s): 20th century; 1940s-1970s
Locale(s): Brazil; Nova Scotia, Canada; United States

Summary: *The More I Owe You* is a fictional account of American poet Elizabeth Bishop's life. Referring to real events, perspectives, and opinions that Bishop recorded in letters and diaries, author Michael Sledge is able to bring concrete facts and tales into the mix. Bishop's poetic success took her all over the world, and Sledge incorporates many of these travels in *The More I Owe You*. Bishop's relationship with Lota de Macedo Soares while living secluded in Brazil was a reoccurring subject in her diaries and letters. Sledge takes care to represent Soares's perspective throughout this book, as he depicts her as the woman she really was: a woman who just wanted to be loved and appreciated, and who happened to depend more on alcohol than she did on those around her. In *The More I Owe You*, Sledge depicts the struggle he imagined Soares and Bishop lived through as they fought for their relationship despite social norms, Soares's political family, and Bishop's international success.

Where it's reviewed:
Booklist, June 1, 2010, page 31
New York Times Book Review, July 11, 2010, page 14
Publishers Weekly, April 5, 2010, page 48

Other books you might like:
Brian Hall, *Fall of Frost*, 2008
Jodi Picoult, *Sing You Home*, 2011
Jane Rule, *Memory Board*, 1987
Vernor Vinge, *Rainbow's End*, 2006
Richard Yates, *Young Hearts Crying*, 1984

245

LINDA SOLE

All My Sins

(London: Severn House Publishers, 2010)

Subject(s): Family; Father-daughter relations; Forgiveness
Major character(s): Maggie Bailey, 16-Year-Old
Time period(s): 20th century; 1920s
Locale(s): London, United Kingdom

Summary: Linda Soles's *All My Sins* follows 16-year-old Maggie Bailey as she struggles to survive in 1920s London. Her brute of a father terrorizes the family, and Maggie is forced to work two hardscrabble jobs to contribute to the family's support. Finally fed up with her father's bullying, she commits a single act that forever changes the course of her life. As Maggie searches for forgiveness in her own heart, her journey of discovery leads her somewhere she never expected—to her true self.

Other books by the same author:
A Different Kind of Justice, 2008
Justice Is Served, 2007
A Rose in Winter, 2002
The Last Summer of Innocence, 1992
The Shadow Players, 1992

Other books you might like:
Philippa Gregory, *Fallen Skies*, 1993
Elizabeth Lord, *Julia's Way*, 2009
Claire Lorrimer, *Infatuation*, 2007
Katherine Stone, *Island of Dreams*, 2000
Janet Woods, *Hearts of Gold*, 2009

246

ROZ SOUTHEY

Sword and Song

(Chesterfield, Pennsylvania: Creme de la Crime, 2010)

Series: Charles Patterson Series. Book 4
Story type: Mystery
Subject(s): Mystery; Murder; History
Major character(s): Charles Patterson, Musician, Detective—Amateur
Time period(s): 18th century
Locale(s): England

Summary: *Sword and Song* is the fourth installment in the Charles Patterson series from author Roz Southey. A teenage prostitute is murdered, and musician turned amateur sleuth, Charles Patterson, starts up an immediate investigation when he realizes he knows the victim. Prior to her demise, the victim had been asked by a mysterious client to protect a book of unknown origins. Shortly after getting the case, Charles has to take a break from the murder investigation to provide entertainment at a party. Little does he know, the party and its many eccentric guests, including the book's heir, prove to be exactly what he needs to get his investigation off the ground.

Where it's reviewed:
Booklist, November 1, 2010, page 32
Library Journal, November 1, 2010, page 49
Publishers Weekly, September 27, 2010, page 41

Other books by the same author:
Secret Lament, 2009
Chords and Discords, 2008
Broken Harmony, 2007

Other books you might like:
Edward Cline, *Sparrowhawk—Jack Frake*, 2001
Diana Gabaldon, *Lord John and the Private Matter*, 2003
Geneva Stephenson, *Melody in Darkness*, 1943
Patricia Veryan, *The Tyrant*, 1987
Daisy Vivian, *Rose White, Rose Red*, 1986

247

SALLY SPENCER

Blackstone and the Wolf of Wall Street

(Sutton, Surrey, England: Severn House, 2010)

Series: Inspector Sam Blackstone Series. Book 8
Story type: Mystery
Subject(s): Kidnapping; Murder; Mystery
Major character(s): Sam Blackstone, Investigator; William Holt, Businessman, Wealthy, Kidnap Victim
Time period(s): 20th century; 1900s (1900)
Locale(s): New York, New York

Summary: *Blackstone and the Wolf of Wall Street*, a historical mystery novel, is the eighth installment in the Inspector Sam Blackstone series from author Sally Spencer. At the turn of the 20th century, Scotland Yard investigator Sam Blackstone is still visiting New York City after his previous assignment brought him to the United States when a wealthy mogul is kidnapped. After the brutal murders of his two bodyguards, William Holt, a reclusive millionaire, is taken hostage by captors demanding a huge ransom. With Holt's sons scrambling to get the cash and the local police unable to be trusted, Blackstone is put in charge of the investigation, but he'll need to work fast to outwit the crazed kidnappers before they murder the tycoon.

Where it's reviewed:
Booklist, September 15, 2010, page 33
Kirkus Reviews, September 1, 2010, page 826
Publishers Weekly, August 23, 2010, page 33

Other books by the same author:
Blackstone and the New World, 2009
Blackstone and the Heart of Darkness, 2007
Blackstone and the Balloon of Death, 2006
Blackstone and the Firebug, 2005
Blackstone and the Golden Egg, 2004

Other books you might like:
Tasha Alexander, *And Only to Deceive*, 2005
Rhys Bowen, *In Dublin's Fair City*, 2007
Anne Perry, *William Monk Series*, 1990

Deanna Raybourn, *Silent in the Grave*, 2007
Roberta Rogow, *Dodgson and Doyle Series*, 1998

248

MARY HELEN STEFANIAK

The Cailiffs of Baghdad, Georgia

(New York: W.W. Norton & Co, 2010)

Subject(s): Teacher-student relations; Great Depression, 1929-1934; Middle East
Major character(s): Gladys Cailiff, 11-Year-Old; Miss Grace Spivey, Teacher; Force Cailiff, Brother (of Gladys); May Cailiff, Sister (of Gladys); Theo Boykin, Neighbor (of Gladys)
Time period(s): 20th century; 1930s (1938)
Locale(s): Threestep, Georgia

Summary: In *The Cailiffs of Baghdad, Georgia* by Mary Helen Stefaniak, an unconventional teacher brings adventure and controversy to 1938 Threestep, Georgia. Unencumbered by the boundaries of her one-room schoolhouse, Miss Grace Spivey uses *The Thousand and One Nights* for inspiration and transforms the small town into old Baghdad. With Gladys Cailiff, a young student, serving as narrator, the story mirrors the original Arabian tales with Threestep's own convoluted accounts of family relationships, intolerance, violence, and magic. But while Miss Spivey's methods inspire some residents, they raise the suspicions of others—especially when the town's Arabian bazaar coincides with a tragedy.

Where it's reviewed:
Booklist, August 1, 2010, page 21
Kirkus Reviews, July 15, 2010, page 646
Library Journal, September 1, 2010, page 104
Publishers Weekly, July 19, 2010, page 110

Other books by the same author:
The Turk and My Mother, 2004
Self Storage and Other Stories, 1997

Other books you might like:
E.L. Doctorow, *City of God*, 2000
Kent Haruf, *Plainsong*, 1999
Garrison Keillor, *Leaving Home: A Collection of Lake Wobegon Stories*, 1987
Larry McMurtry, *Texasville*, 1987
Helen Hooven Santmyer, *And Ladies of the Club*, 1984

249

LIBBY STERNBERG

Sloane Hall

(Waterville, Maine: Five Star, 2010)

Subject(s): Movie industry; Actors; Love
Major character(s): John Doyle, Chauffeur (of Pauline); Pauline Sloane, Actress
Time period(s): 20th century; 1920s
Locale(s): Hollywood, California

Summary: Libby Sternberg's *Sloane Hall* offers an inventive retelling of the classic, *Jane Eyre* set in Hollywood during the 1920s. John Doyle is working as a cinematographer when a careless blunder gets him fired. Desperate for money, he takes a job as chauffeur to a once-famous actress named Pauline Sloane, who resides in a towering Hollywood palazzo known as Sloane Hall. John eventually falls head over heels in love with Pauline, and he is thrilled when the feelings appear to be mutual. As the two move toward building a life together, however, long-buried secrets are about to resurface—and they are more shocking than any movie script could imagine.

Other books by the same author:
Recovering Dad, 2008
The Case Against My Brother, 2007
Finding the Forger, 2004
Uncovering Sadie's Secret, 2003

Other books you might like:
Jennifer Crusie, *Welcome to Temptation*, 2000
John Jakes, *American Dreams*, 1998
Joyce Carol Oates, *Blonde: A Novel*, 2000
Thomas Tryon, *All That Glitters*, 1996
Stuart Woods, *Dead Eyes: A Novel*, 1994

250

JULIAN STOCKWIN

Victory

(Ithaca, New York: McBooks Press, 2010)

Series: Kydd Sea Adventures Series. Book 11
Story type: Military; Series
Subject(s): History; Napoleonic Wars, 1800-1815; Sea stories
Major character(s): Thomas Kydd, Military Personnel (commander); Horatio Nelson, Military Personnel (admiral); Napoleon Bonaparte, Historical Figure
Time period(s): 19th century; 1800s (1805)
Locale(s): Atlantic Ocean; England

Summary: In *Victory* by Julian Stockwin, the 1805 Battle of Trafalgar provides the backdrop for a high-seas adventure that follows the career of Commander Thomas Kydd. After a bit of political jostling that tests his loyalty, Kydd is assigned to a frigate in the fleet of Admiral Lord Horatio Nelson and assumes his role in the complex maneuvers that will outwit and overpower the French and Spanish forces. Though not directly involved in the historic battle, Kydd and his crew provide crucial intelligence to the ships engaged in combat at sea. *Victory* is the 11th book in the Thomas Kydd series.

Where it's reviewed:
Booklist, September 15, 2010, page 30
Publishers Weekly, August 2, 2010, page 30

Other books by the same author:
Invasion, 2009
Quarterdeck, 2005
Seaflower, 2003
Artemis, 2002
Kydd, 2001

Other books you might like:
Bernard Cornwell, *Sharpe's Trafalgar*, 2001
J.D. Davies, *Gentleman Captain*, 2010
William P. Mack, *Commodore Kilburnie*, 2002
Dudley Pope, *Ramage at Trafalgar*, 1986
Richard Woodman, *1805*, 1985

251

ANDREW TAYLOR

The Anatomy of Ghosts
(London, England: Michael Joseph, 2011)

Story type: Ghost Story; Mystery
Subject(s): Ghosts; Mystery; College environment
Major character(s): Frank Oldershaw, Student—College; John Holdsworth, Writer, Scholar
Time period(s): 18th century; 1780s (1786)
Locale(s): Cambridge, England

Summary: *The Anatomy of Ghosts* is a haunting historical mystery from award-winning author Andrew Taylor. In 1786, Frank Oldershaw, a student at Jerusalem College in Cambridge, insists he's encountered the ghost of Sylvia Whichcote roaming the school grounds, and his subsequent reaction is both violent and disturbing, resulting in his institutionalization. His mother, Lady Anne Oldershaw, is determined to clear his name so she hires John Holdsworth, a ghost scholar who teaches that sightings are nothing more than delusion. Holdsworth's presence at the privileged school ruffles feathers, but none more than his own when he begins being haunted by the ghost of his dead wife and harassed by the schoolmaster's living wife. Holdsworth knows he must find Sylvia's murderer or the ghostly visitations will never stop violently changing everyone who encounters them.

Where it's reviewed:
Kirkus Reviews, December 1, 2010, page 1188
New York Times Book Review, February 27, 2011, page 23
Publishers Weekly, November 15, 2010, page 38

Other books by the same author:
Bleeding Heart Square, 2009
An Unpardonable Crime, 2004
The Office of the Dead, 2000
An Air that Kills, 1995
An Old School Tie, 1986

Other books you might like:
Sophie Gee, *The Scandal of the Season*, 2007
Elizabeth Hoyt, *To Desire a Devil*, 2009
Eloisa James, *Potent Pleasures*, 1999
Christopher Nicholson, *The Elephant Keeper*, 2009
Jill Paton Walsh, *The Bad Quarto*, 2007

252

DONALD THOMAS

Sherlock Holmes and the Ghosts of Bly
(New York: Pegasus Books, 2010)

Story type: Mystery
Subject(s): Mystery; Ghosts; Murder
Major character(s): Sherlock Holmes, Detective—Private; Watson, Doctor; Victoria Temple, Mentally Ill Person, Governess, Crime Victim
Time period(s): 19th century; 1890s (1898)
Summary: *Sherlock Holmes and the Ghosts of Bly* is a historical mystery from author Donald Thomas. It's 1898 and the great detective, Sherlock Holmes, is at the peak of his career when he is approached by Victoria Temple, a governess recently found guilty, yet insane, for the murder of one of her charges. Temple insists that the house of Bly, where she was employed, was haunted by ghosts trying to lure the children into evil. Holmes and Watson agree to take the case and soon find themselves thrust into a haunting world filled with supernatural phenomena, occult practices, and deceptive conspiracy.

Where it's reviewed:
Booklist, November 1, 2010, page 32
Kirkus Reviews, October 15, 2010, page 1035
Library Journal, November 15, 2010, page 66
Publishers Weekly, September 27, 2010, page 39

Other books by the same author:
Sherlock Holmes and the King's Evil, 2009
The Execution of Sherlock Holmes, 2007
Sherlock Holmes and the Running Noose, 2002
Sherlock Holmes and the Voice from the Crypt, 2002
The Secret Cases of Sherlock Holmes, 1997

Other books you might like:
Caleb Carr, *The Italian Secretary*, 2005
Michael Chabon, *The Final Solution*, 2004
Anita Janda, *The Secret Diary of Dr. Watson*, 2001
Laurie R. King, *The God of the Hive*, 2010

253

CHARLES TODD   (Pseudonym of Caroline Todd and Charles Todd)

An Impartial Witness
(New York: William Morrow, 2010)

Series: Bess Crawford Series. Book 2
Subject(s): Nursing; Murder; Detective fiction
Major character(s): Bess Crawford, Nurse, Detective—Amateur; Meriwether Evanson, Military Personnel; Marjorie Evanson, Spouse (of Meriwether), Crime Victim
Time period(s): 20th century; 1910s (1917)
Locale(s): France; United Kingdom

Summary: Nurse Bess Crawford returns in *An Impartial Witness*, the second installment in Charles Todd's mystery series of the same name. In this novel, the caregiver/amateur sleuth returns to England to escort a soldier who has been seriously burned in World War I. While at the train station, she spots the soldier's wife in the arms of a mysterious stranger. When she returns to the front, Bess learns that the solider has killed himself and his wife has been murdered, prompting Bess to set out to find the identity of the mystery man she saw at the train station. Charles Todd is the penname of the mother-son writing team Caroline and Charles Todd. *An Impartial Witness* follows *A Duty to the Dead,* published in 2009.

Where it's reviewed:
Kirkus Reviews, June 15, 2010, page 545
New York Times Book Review, September 15, 2010, page 26
Publishers Weekly, July 5, 2010, page 29

Other books by the same author:
A Duty to the Dead, 2009
The Red Door, 2009
A Pale Horse, 2008
A False Mirror, 2007
A Long Shadow, 2006
Search the Dark, 1999
Wings of Fire, 1998
A Test of Wills, 1996

Other books you might like:
A.S. Byatt, *The Children's Book,* 2009
Katherine McMahon, *The Rose of Sebastopol,* 2007
Jill Paton Walsh, *The Bad Quarto,* 2007
Anne Perry, *A Funeral in Blue,* 2001
Jacqueline Winspear, *Pardonable Lies,* 2005

254

JACK TODD

Come Again No More: A Novel

(New York: Simon & Schuster, 2010)

Subject(s): Great Depression, 1929-1934; Family; Grandfathers
Major character(s): Eli Paint, Rancher; Emaline, Granddaughter (of Eli); Jake, Spouse (of Emaline)
Time period(s): 20th century; 1930s
Locale(s): Nebraska, United States

Summary: In *Come Again No More,* a novel by Jack Todd set during the Great Depression, the Paint clan was once a strong and stable family with a great deal of land; however, the events of the Depression and a rift between two generations of the family have destroyed them, and they are now struggling to survive. When Eli Paint, the patriarch of the family, is involved in an accident that nearly kills him, he is forced to examine the events and the choices he made that separated him from his daughter. He sees a potential second chance to make things right with his granddaughter, Emaline, who is married to Jake, a man who makes a lot of promises to Emaline but does not often keep them.

Where it's reviewed:
Booklist, September 1, 2010, page 40
Kirkus Reviews, July 15, 2010, page 647

Publishers Weekly, July 12, 2010, page 26

Other books by the same author:
Sun Going Down, 2008

Other books you might like:
Pamela Carter Joern, *The Plain Sense of Things,* 2008
Ron Hansen, *Atticus,* 1996
Shelton Johnson, *Gloryland,* 2009
Jonathan Segura, *Occupational Hazards,* 2008

255

MARILYN TODD

Still Waters

(Sutton, Surrey, England: Severn House, 2010)

Series: High Priestess Iliona Greek Mysteries Series. Book 3
Subject(s): Greek history, to 330 (Ancient period); Mystery; Murder
Major character(s): Iliona, Religious (high priestess), Detective—Amateur; Lysander, Detective, Police Officer; Gregos, Detective, Crime Victim (possible)
Time period(s): 5th century
Locale(s): Greece

Summary: *Still Waters* is a historical mystery novel from author Marilyn Todd. The third book in the High Priestess Iliona Greek Mysteries series finds Iliona pulled into solving another unusual crime. Set in the 5th century B.C., the story begins with Lysander, head of the Spartan secret police, recruiting Iliona's help on an investigation. Police agent Gregos was tracking a case involving stolen gold dust when he disappeared. Lysander fears Gregos has been killed and wants Iliona to find the person responsible. As she dives into the case, an Olympic wrestler dies under unusual and suspicious circumstances, leading Iliona to believe the two cases are related. When Iliona uncovers a shocking secret that both men knew, she fears that she might be the next target of the murderer.

Where it's reviewed:
Booklist, June 1, 2010, page 42
Publishers Weekly, May 24, 2010, page 39

Other books by the same author:
Blood Moon, 2009
Blind Eye, 2007
Scorpion Rising, 2006
Widow's Pique, 2004
Second Act, 2003

Other books you might like:
Christian Cameron, *Funeral Games,* 2010
Lindsey Davis, *Nemesis,* 2010
Robert Harris, *Conspirata: A Novel of Ancient Rome,* 2010
Ben Kane, *The Silver Eagle,* 2010
Bruce Macbain, *Roman Games,* 2010

256

PETER TREMAYNE (Pseudonym of Peter Berresford Ellis)

The Dove of Death

(London: Headline, 2010)

Series: Sister Fidelma Series. Book 20
Story type: Mystery; Series
Subject(s): History; Mystery; Religious life
Major character(s): Sister Fidelma, Religious; Brother Eadulf, Spouse (of Sister Fidelma); Murchad, Sea Captain
Time period(s): 7th century; 670s (670)
Locale(s): Ireland

Summary: In *The Dove of Death* by Peter Tremayne, 7th-century legal adviser Sister Fidelma and her husband, Brother Eadulf, are sailing on the *Barnacle Goose* toward Ireland when their vessel is boarded by pirates. Fidelma and Eadulf throw themselves into the sea to escape the brutal attack but the captain and an imperial emissary on board are killed. Rescued by a small boat nearby, Fidelma and Eadulf are brought to a small island where the violence seems to follow them. As Sister Fidelma works to solve the murders, she realizes that the case may have political implications. *The Dove of Death* is the 20th book in the Sister Fidelma series.

Where it's reviewed:
Booklist, October 1, 2010, page 33
Kirkus Reviews, October 1, 2010, page 967
Library Journal, September 1, 2010, page 94
Publishers Weekly, September 6, 2010, page 26

Other books by the same author:
The Council of the Cursed, 2009
Dancing with Demons, 2008
A Prayer for the Damned, 2007
The Leper's Bell, 2006
Master of Souls, 2006

Other books you might like:
Cecelia Holland, *The Kings in Winter*, 1968
Kate Horsley, *Confessions of a Pagan Nun*, 2001
Morgan Llywelyn, *Pride of Lions*, 1996
Juilene Osborne-McKnight, *Daughter of Ireland*, 2002
Edward Rutherfurd, *The Princes of Ireland*, 2004

257

PENNY VINCENZI

Forbidden Places

(London: Orion, 1996)

Story type: Family Saga; Historical - World War II
Subject(s): Family Saga; Marriage; Infidelity
Major character(s): Grace Marchant, Spouse (of Charles); Charles Bennett, Spouse (of Grace); Florence, Sister (of Charles); Clarissa, Friend (of Florence)
Time period(s): 20th century; 1930s-1940s
Locale(s): United Kingdom

Summary: Penny Vincenzi's *Forbidden Places* is set in England during World War II. Grace Marchant becomes drawn into the drama surrounding her husband's relatives. Her sister-in-law Florence is unbearably snobbish, but Grace soon learns that Florence may be hiding a dark secret about her marriage. Meanwhile, Florence's friend Clarissa is a newlywed who embarks on an illicit love affair. The lives of these three women soon collide, revealing the fragile underpinnings of a seemingly perfect family.

Where it's reviewed:
Booklist, September 15, 2010, page 27

Other books by the same author:
The Best of Times, 2009
Sheer Abandon, 2007
Something Dangerous, 2005
No Angel, 2003
Old Sins, 1989

Other books you might like:
Shirley Hazzard, *The Great Fire*, 2003
Alexander McCall Smith, *La's Orchestra Saves the World: A Novel*, 2009
Rosamunde Pilcher, *The Shell Seekers*, 1987
Daniel Silva, *The Unlikely Spy*, 1996
Sarah Waters, *The Night Watch*, 2006

258

PHIL WARD

Those Who Dare

(Austin, Texas: Greenleaf Book Group Press, 2010)

Series: Second World War Fiction Series. Book 1
Story type: Historical - World War II
Subject(s): Military life; History; Wars
Major character(s): John Randal, Military Personnel; Jane Seaborn, Noblewoman; "Geronimo Joe" McKoy, Military Personnel; David Niven, Military Personnel
Time period(s): 20th century; 1940s
Locale(s): Europe

Summary: It is the spring of 1940, and World War II is in full force. Lieutenant John Randal heads a squadron of highly skilled, highly courageous fighters who carry out a series of stealthy attacks on Hitler's troops. This volume follows Randal and his crew as they navigate the terrain of wars both in the larger world and within themselves. *Those Who Dare* is the first installment in Phil Ward's Second World War Fiction series.

Other books you might like:
Stephen D. Becker, *Dog Tags*, 1973
Thomas Fleming, *Loyalties: A Novel of World War II*, 1994
Greg Iles, *Black Cross*, 1995
Milena McGraw, *After Dunkirk*, 1998
Jeff Shaara, *The Steel Wave: A Novel of World War II*, 2008

259

ALISON WEIR

The Captive Queen: A Novel of Eleanor of Aquitaine

(New York: Ballantine Books, 2010)

Story type: Historical - Medieval
Subject(s): England; Biographies; History
Major character(s): Eleanor of Aquitaine, Spouse (of King Louis VII), Spouse (of King Henry II), Noblewoman; King Louis VII, Royalty (king of France), Spouse (of Eleanor); King Henry II, Spouse (of Eleanor), Royalty (king of England); Richard, Son (of Eleanor and Henry); John, Son (of Eleanor and Henry)
Time period(s): 12th century
Locale(s): England; France

Summary: Alison Weir's *The Captive Queen: A Novel of Eleanor of Aquitaine* is a historical novel about one of the most dynamic women of the High Middle Ages. Eleanor of Aquitaine, wife of France's King Louis VII, is frustrated with her husband and her failure to produce a male heir. When she meets Henry of Anjou—the man who will be King of England—Eleanor is immediately smitten and launches a plan to escape her current discontent. Soon after she wins an annulment, Eleanor marries the young and exciting Henry. The couple's passionate marriage and hunger for power spawns an abundance of children and far-reaching political influence. But the intensity of their relationship proves its undoing as jealousy and deceit undermine their empire and destroy their family.

Where it's reviewed:
Booklist, May 15, 2010, page 4
Library Journal, July 1, 2010, page 72
Publishers Weekly, June 28, 2010, page 101

Other books by the same author:
The Lady Elizabeth: A Novel, 2008
Innocent Traitor, 2006

Other books you might like:
Margaret Ball, *Duchess of Aquitaine*, 2006
Ellen Jones, *Beloved Enemy: The Passions of Eleanor of Aquitaine*, 1994
Pamela Kaufman, *The Book of Eleanor*, 2002
Sharon Kay Penman, *Dragon's Lair*, 2003
Jean Plaidy, *The Plantagenet Prelude*, 1976

260

ANN WEISGARBER

The Personal History of Rachel DuPree: A Novel

(New York: Viking, 2010)

Story type: Family Saga
Subject(s): Identity; African Americans; Rural life
Major character(s): Rachel DuPree, Farmwife, Spouse (of Isaac); Isaac, Farmer, Spouse (of Rachel)
Time period(s): 20th century; 1900s
Locale(s): South Dakota, United States

Summary: In *The Personal History of Rachel DuPree: A Novel*, author Ann Weisgarber tells the story of a young black woman's search for identity in the remote stretches of South Dakota during the early years of the 20th century. Rachel meets Isaac while they are both working in Chicago. Later, the two marry and take advantage of the 160 acres offered by the Homestead Act. Relocating to rural South Dakota, they struggle to build a successful farm. Years pass and their family grows, but their lives are still difficult. Rachel soon learns that finding her own sense of self is the only way she will endure the hardships of such a challenging life on the prairie. First novel.

Where it's reviewed:
Kirkus Reviews, May 15, 2010, page 437
Library Journal, June 15, 2010, page 69
Publishers Weekly, June 14, 2010, page 35

Other books you might like:
Ernest J. Gaines, *The Autobiography of Miss Jane Pittman*, 1971
Sue Monk Kidd, *The Secret Life of Bees*, 2002
Toni Morrison, *Love*, 2003
Lalita Tademy, *Cane River*, 2001
Alice Walker, *Possessing the Secret of Joy*, 1992

261

JERI WESTERSON

The Demon's Parchment

(New York: Minotaur Books, 2010)

Series: Crispin Guest Medieval Mystery Series. Book 3
Story type: Historical - Medieval; Mystery
Subject(s): History; Mystery; Serial murders
Major character(s): Crispin Guest, Detective, Knight (former); Jack Tucker, Orphan, Streetperson, Thief, Apprentice (to Crispin); Jacob, Doctor, Religious (Jewish), Client (of Crispin)
Time period(s): 14th century
Locale(s): London, England

Summary: Set in 14th-century London, Jeri Westerson's historical mystery, *The Demon's Parchment*, is the third installment in the Crispin Guest Medieval Mystery series. Former knight Crispin Guest has fallen from grace, losing his title and property in the process, and is forced to rely on his tracking and sleuthing skills to earn a living. Accompanied by Jack Tucker, his orphaned and thieving apprentice, there's no puzzle that Crispin can't solve, but there are some he'd prefer not to even try. When Jacob of Provencal, a Jewish doctor working for the King, approaches Crispin about missing Hebrew manuscripts, Crispin is reluctant to get involved in a case with such strong religious and political implications, but a seemingly unrelated case, the serial killings of several young men, leads the detective on a trail that seems to end with the stolen scrolls.

Where it's reviewed:
Booklist, September 15, 2010, page 33
Kirkus Reviews, July 1, 2010, page 598
Publishers Weekly, July 19, 2010, page 114

Other books by the same author:
Serpent in the Thorns, 2009
Veil of Lies, 2008

Other books you might like:
Simon Beaufort, *The Bloodstained Throne*, 2010
Alys Clare, *Music of the Distant Stars*, 2010
Paul Doherty, *The Waxman Murders*, 2010
Ariana Franklin, *Mistress of the Art of Death*, 2007
Priscilla Royal, *Valley of Dry Bones*, 2010

262

RICHARD S. WHEELER

The Owl Hunt

(New York: Forge, 2010)

Series: Skye's West Series. Book 18
Story type: Western
Subject(s): Native Americans; Western fiction; History
Major character(s): Dirk, Teacher, Indian; Waiting Wolf, 15-Year-Old, Student (of Dirk's), Indian
Time period(s): 19th century; 1870s (1878)
Locale(s): Wyoming, United States

Summary: *The Owl Hunt*, a historical Western, is the 18th installment in the Skye's West series from award-winning author Richard S. Wheeler. Set in 1878, the story focuses on the late Barnabay Skye's son, Dirk, a half-white, half-Shoshone man who teaches school on the reservation. Waiting Wolf, a 15-year-old student of Dirk's, claims that an owl, a dreaded bird feared by the Shoshones, gave him a vision about a future free from the rule of white people. Waiting Wolf changes his name to Owl and becomes a prophet among a small band of followers known as the Dreamers. The Indian agent and the army fear an uprising, despite Dirk's attempts to calm them down, and lash out harshly against the Shoshones, putting Dirk in a desperate place warring between his two heritages.

Where it's reviewed:
Booklist, December 15, 2010, page 29
Publishers Weekly, October 11, 2010, page 25

Other books by the same author:
Virgin River, 2008
The Canyon of Bones, 2007
Downriver, 2001
Rendezvous, 1997
Sierra, 1996

Other books you might like:
Isabel Allende, *Zorro*, 2005
Will Baker, *Track of the Giant*, 1990
Dee Brown, *Creek Mary's Blood*, 1980
Charles Frazier, *Thirteen Moons: A Novel*, 2006
Scott O'Dell, *Streams to the River, River to the Sea: A Novel of Sacagawea*, 1986

263

LAUREN WILLIG

The Mischief of the Mistletoe

(New York: Dutton, 2010)

Series: Pink Carnation Series. Book 7
Subject(s): Romances (Fiction); Suspense; Spies
Major character(s): Reginald "Turnip" Fitzhugh, Detective; Arabella Dempsey, Teacher, Friend (of Jane); Jane Austen, Friend (of Arabella)
Locale(s): Bath, United Kingdom

Summary: The seventh novel in Lauren Willig's Pink Carnation Mysteries, *The Mischief of the Mistletoe* finds Reginald "Turnip" Fitzhugh, a popular secondary character in the series, and newly minted teacher Arabella Dempsey embarking on a holiday-themed adventure. When Turnip, who is mistaken for the famous Pink Carnation spy, and Arabella find a strange note attached to a Christmas pudding, they embark on an epic quest to discover the message's puzzling meaning.

Where it's reviewed:
Booklist, December 1, 2010, page 35
Booklist, September 15, 2010, page 50
Kirkus Reviews, August 15, 2010, page 758
Publishers Weekly, September 6, 2010, page 24
Romantic Times, December 2010, page 33

Other books by the same author:
The Betrayal of the Blood Lily, 2010
The Temptation of the Night Jasmine, 2009
The Seduction of the Crimson Rose, 2008
The Deception of the Emerald Ring, 2006
The Masque of the Black Tulip, 2005
The Secret History of the Pink Carnation, 2005

Other books you might like:
Stephanie Barron, *Jane and the Madness of Lord Byron*, 2010
Rhys Bowen, *Royal Blood*, 2010
Tracy Kiely, *Murder at Longbourn: A Mystery*, 2009
Anne Perry, *A Christmas Odyssey*, 2010
Lynn Shepherd, *Murder at Mansfield Park*, 2010

264

SANDRA WORTH

Pale Rose of England

(New York: Berkley Books, 2011)

Story type: Historical - Renaissance
Subject(s): History; Biographies; Romances (Fiction)
Major character(s): Richard Plantagenet, Nobleman (Duke of York), Historical Figure; James IV, Royalty (King of Scotland), Historical Figure; Henry VII, Royalty (King of England)
Time period(s): 15th century; 1490s (1497)
Locale(s): England

Summary: In *Pale Rose of England*, author Sandra Worth presents a fictionalized account of Richard Plantagenet's attempt to take the throne from Henry VII. In 1497 Richard Plantagenet, Duke of York, arrives in England very much alive, despite rumors of his demise. Richard's wife, Lady Catherine Gordon, supports her husband's campaign to win back his lawful position in the house of Tudor. When the Duke's plan fails, Richard is jailed, accused as a traitor, and sentenced to death. Although Catherine, who has gained the attention of the king, is safe in the court, she is determined to forge her own future.

The Year in Horror: 2010
by
Don D'Ammassa

The taste of the reading public changes unpredictably at times. Although horror fiction seemed viable as a separate genre within mainstream publishing during the 1980s, its popularity with most of its readers was clearly transitory. Since then the number of publishers with dedicated horror publishing program has declined steadily, a trend that has probably reached its end this year with the demise of Leisure Books as a regular horror publisher. Although Stephen King and Dean R. Koontz still make the bestseller lists with regularity, their popularity essentially transcends genre and in fact many of their recent books have been marginally horror at best. Other horror novels appear intermittently if at all and some of the most successful names of a few years ago—Ramsay Campbell, Thomas F. Monteleone, and others—have been relatively silent.

This doesn't mean that there is less horror fiction being published in absolute terms. Indeed in total numbers of new titles it may be at its high point. There are more than a dozen small press publishers who deal only with horror titles including Bad Moon Books, Dark Regions Press, Damnation Books, CD Publications, and Permuted Press. The average number of readers per book, on the other hand, may have reached a record low. Occasionally novels from the small press are picked up and re-issued by major imprints, but this is extremely rare. The short story situation is even more skewed toward the small press. The closest thing to a professional horror magazine is *Cemetery Dance*, which has been appearing with diminishing frequency. There are, however, dozens of online and print on demand venues for short horror fiction, and occasional original anthologies. Again, only a handful of these appear from the major publishers.

Horror fiction has long masqueraded in other guises, sometimes as science fiction, sometimes as contemporary thriller or mystery novel. In recent years there has been considerable overlap with fantasy thanks to the popularity of urban fantasy and the rise of the vampire as a romantic figure rather than an object of dread. Those who wish to draw a clear line of demarcation between the genres are on very shaky ground here but the selective reader can still find chills and carnage cleverly or not so cleverly disguised.

Another recent trend that will probably continue for the next few years is the advent of the zombie as subject matter. Zombies in this case are not the historical figures associated with voodoo rites but the shambling, flesh-eating creatures George Romero introduced in his classic low budget horror film, *Night of the Living Dead*. These usually mindless and always unpleasant creatures seem to have filled the void left when vampires moved from villain to hero. Initially novels published in this area closely resembled the movie, notably *The Rising* by Brian Keene and *Black Tide* by Del Stone Jr. It has only been this year that we have started to see some experimentation on the part of authors of zombie fiction.

Unfortunately, one of the side effects of the zombie's rise in popularity was initiated by the appearance of Seth Grahame-Smith's *Pride and Prejudice and Zombies*, which took the actual text of the Jane Austen novel and interspersed it with zombie attacks. The floodgates opened soon after. Eric S. Brown offered us *The War of the Worlds, Plus Blood, Guts and Zombies*, W. Bill Czolgosz produced *Adventures of Huckleberry Finn and Zombie Jim*, and Ryan C. Thomas added *The Undead World of Oz*. Associated with these but at least mostly original are skewed versions of classic stories or alternative lives of historical figures. Among these are *Robin Hood and Friar Tuck: Zombie Killers* by Paul A. Freeman, *Queen Victoria, Demon Hunter* by A.E. Moorat, and *Romeo & Juliet & Vampires* by Claudia Gabel.

Only one zombie novel stood out this year, *Dust* by Joan Frances Turner, although *The Loving Dead* by Amelia Beamer and *The Zombies of Lake Woebegotten* by the pseudonymous Harrison Geillor provide amusing spoofs of the theme. Turner's novel is told from the point of view of one of the zombies, who has considerably more depth than Romero's shamblers, and the contrasts between the gross physical descriptions and the emotions of the protagonist are startling and entertaining.

Several of the year's best horror novels overlapped with urban fantasy. Closest to fantasy is *Black Magic*

Sanction by Kim Harrison, the eighth adventure of Rachel Morgan. Morgan has now been revealed as partly demon and interpersonal relationships are as important as physical confrontations this time. Chris Marie Green's Vampire Babylon series is closer in spirit to *Buffy the Vampire Slayer*. The sixth installment, *Deep in the Woods*, has vampire hunter Dawn Madison and her team in London where a master vampire sends minions against our heroes. There are no new directions for the series this time but the plot is focused and the atmosphere tense.

Kat Richardson's Harper Blaine series falls somewhere between these two. In *Labyrinth* Blaine is trying to free her father's ghost from thrall while simultaneously dodging the evil intentions of vampires and a variation of an Egyptian mummy. Blaine, a private investigator specializing in the paranormal, is one of the best drawn of the urban fantasy/horror protagonists. *Kitty's House of Horrors* by Carrie Vaughn, seventh in the Kitty Norville series, pits the benevolent werewolf/radio personality against an interesting group of potential enemies this time. As part of a television reality show featuring the paranormal, she agrees to spend several days at a remote location where the contestants begin dying for real in short order. This one is more serious in tone than the earlier volumes in the series.

Joe Hill mixes fantasy and horror in *Horns*. A man wakes up after an apparent drunken blackout to discover that he has grown horns and acquired the ability to compel other people to confess their inner secrets. Because he is currently grieving over the murder of his girlfriend, a crime for which many people believe him responsible, he decides to use his new ability to track down the real culprit, accomplishing this amidst mildly frightening and occasionally grimly funny events. Graham Joyce, known for his intelligent and complex horror fiction, returned to print with a somewhat similar novel, *How to Make Friends with Demons*. His protagonist is an alcoholic, an unsavory man who is also psychic; he can see demons including those possessing other humans. Several interlocking stories are resolved in an atmosphere that is alternately frightening and funny.

Sandman Slim by Richard Kadrey bears some resemblance to urban fantasy, but is more properly a supernatural noir detective story. James Stark is a violent and not particularly admirable character trying to track down the people, or unpeople, who killed his girlfriend. He also has to deal with an old enemy and discovers a strange underworld of fallen angels, monsters, and monstrous humans. Kadrey writes overtly violent action sequences and there is a grim undertone throughout. Although not labeled as the first in a series, it clearly has that potential.

M.J. Rose's Reincarnationist series moved from fantasy adventure toward the supernatural with the third title, *The Hypnotist*. This one features a struggle for control of an art object imbued with occult powers that can be absorbed by its possessor. The series is the inspiration for a new television show, *Past Life*. Occult adventure also figures prominently in *The Iron Khan* by Liz Williams, wherein Inspector Chen must locate a magical book that has the power to alter the course of history. The Inspector Chen novels are set in an alternate version of China and would appeal to fans of fantasy as well as horror.

Three of the most familiar names in horror had significant new novels published in 2010. Dan Simmons takes a new and original look at Custer's Last Stand in *Black Hills*: Custer's ghost possesses the body of a young Sioux who has paranormal powers and remains as a kind of powerless spectator throughout the man's life, which culminates in an attempt to sabotage the construction of the Mount Rushmore memorial. F. Paul Wilson reaches the brink of the conclusion of his Repairman Jack series in *Fatal Error*, in which Jack's arch enemies, the Order of Septimus, hope to open a gateway between realities so that the world will be overrun by monsters. Meanwhile other forces gather on both sides and the stage is set for the final confrontation, due out in 2011. Peter Straub's latest is *A Dark Matter*, which involves a group of students who fall under the sway of a charismatic figure who has genuinely discovered a way to use meditation to gain access to another reality, but by doing so he causes the death of one of his followers. The novel explores the lingering effects on each of the survivors individually before gathering them once again for the climax.

There were some notable new names in horror fiction this year. Jasper Kent's *Twelve* is set during Napoleon's invasion of Russia in 1812 and mixes historical adventure with horror as a pack of vampires takes advantage of the carnage. A sequel, *Thirteen Years Later*, is scheduled for release in 2011. Ronald Malfi's first horror novel, *Snow*, is reminiscent of Stephen King. A group of travelers find themselves stranded in a small town in the middle of winter. The town is largely deserted except for a handful of people who are clearly terrified. The newcomers discover that enigmatic creatures who manifest themselves as clouds of snow are preying on the humans, possessing or destroying them.

Although most short horror fiction had limited distribution in 2010, two excellent anthologies appeared from major imprints. *He Is Legend* edited by Christopher Conlon was conceived as an homage to Richard Matheson, one of the most highly respected writers in horror, particularly at shorter length. The second was *Darkness: Two Decades of Modern Horror* edited by Ellen Datlow, a retrospective look at the genre that mixes well- and lesser-known writers, a diverse range of themes and styles, but always maintains a high overall quality level. The best single author collection of the year was *The Best of Joe R. Lansdale* by Joe R. Lansdale. Mercedes Lackey revived her series about Diana Tregarde, a contemporary good witch whose earlier adventures anticipated current urban fantasy, in *Trio of Sorcery*, which consists of three original novelettes. *Dark Dimensions* by William F. Nolan, another well respected short story writer with a long career, is also noteworthy.

Recommended Titles

Two major trends have affected horror fiction this year, both of which have been changing the nature of the genre for some time. The first is the rise of paranormal or urban fantasies and romances, which frequently make use of horror tropes, notably vampires and werewolves. The second is the move from major publishers to small presses, particularly for short fiction. A third and presumably temporary phenomenon is the flood of classic novels by Jane Austen, Mark Twain, and others, which have been altered to include passages involving supernatural beings, mostly but not exclusively zombies. None of these latter have proven to be interesting in their own right. Note that some 2010 titles were covered in the previous volume in this series.

He Is Legend edited by Christopher Conlon

Darkness: Two Decades of Modern Horror edited by Ellen Datlow

Deep in the Woods by Chris Marie Green

Black Magic Sanction by Kim Harrison

Horns by Joe Hill

How to Make Friends with Demons by Graham Joyce

Sandman Slim by Richard Kadrey

Twelve by Jasper Kent

The Best of Joe R. Lansdale by Joe R. Lansdale

Trio for Sorcery by Mercedes Lackey

Snow by Ronald Malfi

Dark Dimensions by William F. Nolan

Labyrinth by Kat Richardson

The Hypnotist by M.J. Rose

Black Hills by Dan Simmons

A Dark Matter by Peter Straub

Dust by Joan Frances Turner

Kitty's House of Horrors by Carrie Vaughn

The Iron Khan by Liz Williams

Fatal Error by F. Paul Wilson

Horror Fiction

265

KEVIN J. ANDERSON

Blood Lite II: Overbite

(New York: Gallery, 2010)

Subject(s): Terror; Humor; Short stories

Summary: Editor Kevin J. Anderson compiles a collection of terrifying short stories that may send chills up the spine—but may also bring a smile to the face. The tales of *Blood Lite II: Overbite* focus on the dark and twisted humor of the modern horror story, encompassing the escapades of a variety of ghosts, monsters, ghouls, and other assorted bad guys. Authors contributing to this volume include Janis Ian, Edward Bryant, Aaron Polson, Eric James Stone, Jordan Summers, and Anderson.

Other books by the same author:
Ashes of Worlds, 2008
Metal Swarm, 2007
Landscapes, 2006
Of Fire and Night, 2006
Scattered Suns, 2005

Other books you might like:
Harrison Geillor, *The Zombies of Lake Woebegotten*, 2010
Julie Kenner, *Deja Demon*, 2008
Victoria Laurie, *Death Perception: A Psychic Eye Mystery*, 2008
Richard Laymon, *Resurrection Dreams*, 1988
A. Lee Martinez, *Gil's All Fright Diner*, 2005

266

JANE AUSTEN
WAYNE JOSEPHSON, Co-Author

Emma and the Vampires

(Naperville, Illinois: Sourcebooks, 2010)

Story type: Romance
Subject(s): Horror; History; Vampires
Major character(s): Emma Woodhouse, Young Woman; George Knightley, Vampire

Time period(s): 19th century
Locale(s): Highbury, England

Summary: In *Emma and the Vampires*, author Wayne Josephson retells the Jane Austen classic, retaining the novel's mannerly tone but casting the main characters as vampires and vampire hunters. In the proper community of 19th-century Highbury, England, Emma Woodhouse is skilled at fending off the marauding undead with a sharpened stake, but she and her naive friends are slow to recognize the true identity of the dashing George Knightley. Attributing the coarse behavior and strange appetites of Knightley and his cohorts to typical male vulgarity, Emma harbors romantic feelings for George even as his symptomatic bloodless complexion and distinctive teeth begin to raise suspicions. First novel.

Where it's reviewed:
First for Women, October 18, 2010, page 110

Other books you might like:
Charlotte Bronte, *Jane Slayre*, 2010
Lori Handeland, *Shakespeare Undead*, 2010
Adam Rann, *Emma and the Werewolves*, 2010

267

L. FRANK BAUM
RYAN C. THOMAS, Co-Author

The Undead World of Oz: L. Frank Baum's The Wonderful Wizard of Oz Complete with Zombies and Monsters

(Winnipeg: Coscom Entertainment, 2010)

Subject(s): Zombies; Adventure; Monsters
Major character(s): Dorothy, Girl; Toto, Dog; Scarecrow, Sidekick (of Dorothy); Cowardly Lion, Sidekick (of Dorothy), Lion; Tin Man, Sidekick (of Dorothy); Wicked Witch of the West, Witch; The Wizard, Leader (of Oz)
Time period(s): Indeterminate
Locale(s): Oz, Fictional Location

Summary: In *The Undead World of Oz: L. Frank Baum's The Wonderful Wizard of Oz Complete with Zombies and Monsters*, author Ryan C. Thomas presents Baum's classic fantasy with a twist. When Dorothy and Toto arrive in Kansas, the Wicked Witch of the West has wrapped the land of Oz in a dark curse: The dead will rise and once again walk the earth. Now Dorothy, Toto, the Scarecrow, the Tin Man, and the Cowardly Lion must get to The Wizard as soon as possible in order to stop the monsters—or they just might risk becoming zombie meat.

Other books you might like:

Jane Austen, *Emma and the Vampires*, 2010

Porter Grand, *Little Women and Werewolves*, 2010

Vera Nazarian, *Mansfield Park and Mummies: Monster Mayhem, Matrimony, Ancient Curses, True Love, and Other Dire Delights*, 2010

Adam Rann, *Emma and the Werewolves*, 2010

Leo Tolstoy, *Android Karenina*, 2010

268

AMELIA BEAMER

The Loving Dead

(San Francisco: Night Shade Books, 2010)

Story type: Contemporary
Subject(s): Zombies; Adventure; Humor
Major character(s): Kate, Roommate (of Michael); Michael, Roommate (of Kate)
Time period(s): 21st century; 2010s
Locale(s): San Francisco, California

Summary: Amelia Beamer's *The Loving Dead* is a zombie-filled farce following the exploits of roommates Kate and Michael, who throw a party that turns into a nightmare of the undead. During the course of their fete, a terrifying new STD ravages the partygoers—and eventually the entire San Francisco Bay area—and transforms the afflicted into sexually ravenous zombies. Kate and Michael are thrust into the greatest adventure of their lives, setting out to both escape and outwit the hungry dead ravaging the city. First novel.

Where it's reviewed:
Library Journal, July 2010, page 76
Publishers Weekly, May 24, 2010, page 40

Other books you might like:

Mario Acevedo, *Jailbait Zombie*, 2009

J.L. Bourne, *Day by Day Armageddon: Beyond Exile*, 2010

Brian Hodge, *The Darker Saints*, 1993

Joe R. Lansdale, *Dead in the West*, 1986

Joan Frances Turner, *Dust*, 2010

269

J.K. BECK

When Blood Calls

(New York: Bantam, 2010)

Story type: Contemporary
Subject(s): Romances (Fiction); Demons; Supernatural
Major character(s): Sara Constantine, Lawyer; Lucius "Luke" Dragos, Demon, Crime Suspect

Time period(s): 21st century; 2010s
Locale(s): United States

Summary: In J.K. Beck's *When Blood Calls*, Sara Constantine is a lawyer who has landed what she thinks is a dream gig as a prosecuting attorney. She soon learns, however, that those she will be prosecuting are demons, and she wonders if she has what it takes to handle the requirements of the job. Lucius Dragos is a demon with whom Sara spent one fiery night, but when they come face to face in the courtroom, Sara must decide between her devotion to her job and her passion for this mysterious stranger. First novel.

Where it's reviewed:
Library Journal, June 15, 2010, page S16

Other books by the same author:
When Pleasure Rules, 2010
When Wicked Craves, 2010
Demons Are Forever, 2007
Good Ghouls Do, 2007
California Demon, 2006

Other books you might like:
Keri Arthur, *Deadly Desire*, 2009
Anya Bast, *Witch Fury*, 2009
Elle Jasper, *Afterlight*, 2010
Gena Showalter, *The Vampire's Bride*, 2009
Susan Sizemore, *I Hunger for You*, 2005

270

J.K. BECK

When Wicked Craves

(New York: Bantam, 2010)

Series: Shadow Keepers Series. Book 3
Story type: Romance
Subject(s): Vampires; Demons; Love
Major character(s): Petra Lang, Young Woman; Nicholas Monteguev, Vampire
Time period(s): 21st century; 2010s
Locale(s): United States

Summary: Beautiful Petra Lang is afflicted with an unusual curse: She can never be touched. If she is, demons will be summoned forth. When she meets vampire Nicholas Montegue, Petra feels a desire like nothing she's ever before experienced. After Nicholas saves her from the bounty placed on her head by the unforgiving Shadow Alliance, the two find it increasingly difficult to hold their passions in check. But one touch from Nicholas could spell doom for all humankind—unless a cure can be found. *When Wicked Craves* is the third book in J.K. Beck's Shadow Keepers series.

Other books by the same author:
When Blood Calls, 2010
When Pleasure Rules, 2010
Demons Are Forever, 2007
Good Ghouls Do, 2007
California Demon, 2006

Other books you might like:
Jeaniene Frost, *One Foot in the Grave*, 2008
Larissa Ione, *Passion Unleashed*, 2009
Michelle Rowen, *The Demon in Me*, 2010

Gena Showalter, *The Darkest Night*, 2008
Jeanne C. Stein, *Chosen*, 2010

271

J.K. BECK

When Pleasure Rules

(New York: Random House, 2010)

Story type: Romance
Subject(s): Horror; Werewolves; Supernatural
Major character(s): Lissa Monroe, Demon (succubus);
    Vincent Rand, Werewolf
Time period(s): 21st century; 2010s
Locale(s): Los Angeles, California

Summary: In *When Pleasure Rules* by J.K. Beck, Los Angeles is the battleground for a violent dispute between the resident vampires and werewolves. Though the Shadow Alliance has investigated recent killings in the city, the cases remain unsolved. The organization recruits a secret agent—Lissa Monroe, a beautiful succubus—who possesses unique skills of persuasion. Lissa is assigned to pry information from the dominant werewolf Vincent Rand, but finds that her opponent has talents of his own. With the blood feud coming to a boil in Los Angeles, Lissa and Vincent must work together to avert a catastrophe and save their own lives.

Other books by the same author:
When Blood Calls, 2010
When Wicked Craves, 2010
Demons Are Forever, 2007
Good Ghouls Do, 2007
California Demon, 2006

Other books you might like:
Keri Arthur, *Deadly Desire*, 2009
Anya Bast, *Witch Fury*, 2009
Elle Jasper, *Afterlight*, 2010
Gena Showalter, *The Vampire's Bride*, 2009
Susan Sizemore, *I Hunger for You*, 2005

272

TOM BECKER

Lifeblood

(New York: Orchard, 2008)

Series: Darkside Series. Book 2
Story type: Mystery; Young Adult
Major character(s): Jonathan Starling, Teenager; Elias Carnegie, Werewolf, Detective—Private; Humphrey Glanville, Criminal
Time period(s): 19th century
Locale(s): London, England

Summary: Jonathan Starling explores more of the Darkside, a part of Victorian London where the supernatural is real, in his quest to find his missing mother. Unfortunately, his plans are disrupted by a series of murders, and the continued interest of two men who don't necessarily wish him the best.

Where it's reviewed:
School Library Journal, March 2009, page 55

Other books by the same author:
Timecurse, 2009
Nighttrap, 2008

Other books you might like:
Tony Abbott, *City of the Dead*, 2009
Bruce Coville, *Eyes of the Tarot*, 1996
Simon Lake, *Death Cycle*, 1993
Joseph Locke, *Kiss of Death*, 1992
Darren Shan, *Dark Calling*, 2009

273

HEIDI BETTS

The Bite Before Christmas

(New York: Kensington Publishing Corporation, 2010)

Story type: Romance
Subject(s): Horror; Romances (Fiction); Christmas
Major character(s): Angelina Ricci, Matchmaker
Time period(s): 21st century; 2010s
Locale(s): Boston, Massachusetts

Summary: *The Bite Before Christmas* by Heidi Betts collects three holiday romances that center around a vampire dating service in Boston. In *Vampire in Her Stocking*, Angelina Ricci, owner of the Love Bites agency, saves the terminally ill love interest of a client by transforming him into a vampire. In *All I Vant for Christmas*, a party planner finds a chance at romance when she decorates a vampire's mansion for the holidays. In *It's a Wonderful Bite*, Angelina the matchmaker is seeking a match of her own. Her wish for a solid commitment from her boyfriend Sergio conjures an eggnog-fueled Christmas dream.

Where it's reviewed:
Publishers Weekly, August 16, 2010, page 40

Other books by the same author:
Knock Me for a Loop, 2010
Loves Me, Loves Me Knot, 2009
Tangled Up in Love, 2009
Seven-Year Seduction, 2006
Bought By a Millionaire, 2005

Other books you might like:
Katie MacAlister, *Even Vampires Get the Blues*, 2006
Michelle Rowen, *The Demon in Me*, 2010
Maggie Shayne, *Bloodline*, 2009
Susan Squires, *One with the Night*, 2007

274

ALEX BLEDSOE

The Girls with Games of Blood

(New York: Tor, 2010)

Subject(s): Vampires; Fantasy; Sisters
Major character(s): Rudolfo Vladimir Zginski, Vampire;

Horror

Patience Bolade, Singer; Prudence Bolade, Sister (of Patience)
Time period(s): 19th century; 1970s (1975)
Locale(s): Memphis, Tennessee

Summary: In *The Girls with Games of Blood*, author Alex Bledsoe continues the adventures of vampire Rudolfo Zginski, first begun in 2010's *Blood Grove*. It is the mid-1970s in Memphis, Tennessee, and Rudolfo and his crew have come to wreak their particular brand of havoc on the city. But he soon meets a vampire cabaret singer who lures him into a centuries-old quarrel involving sibling rivalry, revenge, and the unquenchable desires of the heart.

Where it's reviewed:
Booklist, July 1, 2010, page 40
Locus, August 2010, page 20
Publishers Weekly, May 24, 2010, page 40

Other books by the same author:
Blood Groove, 2009
Burn Me Deadly, 2009
The Sword-Edge Blonde, 2009

Other books you might like:
Suzy McKee Charnas, *The Vampire Tapestry*, 1980
Andrew Fox, *Fat White Vampire Blues*, 2002
Ray Garton, *Live Girls*, 1987
Cherie Priest, *Dreadful Skin*, 2007
Jeff Rice, *The Night Stalker*, 1973

275

J.L. BOURNE

Day by Day Armageddon: Beyond Exile

(New York: Pocket Books, 2010)

Series: Day by Day Armageddon Series. Book 2
Story type: Contemporary
Subject(s): Apocalypse; Military life; Diaries
Major character(s): Anonymous, Military Personnel (Navy), Narrator
Locale(s): Texas, United States

Summary: *Beyond Exile*, the second outing in J.L. Bourne's Day by Day Armageddon series, continues the diary of a military officer who is now facing a terrifying new set of challenges. Zombies have invaded the United States, and in the heart of Texas, a rogue group of survivors struggles to rise up and save the country. Among them is the novel's unnamed hero, a Navy officer chronicling the daily challenges of the survivors as they attempt to face the undead.

Other books by the same author:
Day by Day Armageddon, 2007

Other books you might like:
Mario Acevedo, *Jailbait Zombie*, 2009
S.G. Browne, *Breathers: A Zombie's Lament*, 2009
Brian Keene, *The Rising*, 2003
Jonathan Maberry, *Patient Zero*, 2009
Philip Nutman, *Wet Work*, 1993

276

CHARLOTTE BRONTE
SHERRI BROWNING ERWIN, Co-Author

Jane Slayre

(New York: Gallery Books, 2010)

Subject(s): Literature; Vampires; Werewolves
Major character(s): Jane Slayre, Governess, Orphan; Mr. Rochester, Employer (of Jane); John Reed, Uncle (of Jane), Vampire; Mrs. Reed, Spouse (of John Reed); Bertha Rochester, Werewolf
Time period(s): 19th century
Locale(s): England

Summary: In *Jane Slayre*, Sherri Browning Erwin adapts Charlotte Bronte's classic tale of romance and manners to a thrilling story of horror. In keeping with the original plot, Jane leaves the home of her uncle to work as a governess at the manor of Mr. Rochester. In this version, however, the Reeds are vampires, Jane is a vampire slayer, and her new employer keeps his werewolf-wife Bertha hidden in the attic. Amidst the onslaught of the undead, Jane and Mr. Rochester find the beginnings of true love. But in order to secure a future with Rochester, Jane Slayre must do battle with opponents both human and paranormal.

Where it's reviewed:
Library Journal, April 1, 2010, page 5

Other books you might like:
Porter Grand, *Little Women and Werewolves*, 2010
Vera Nazarian, *Mansfield Park and Mummies: Monster Mayhem, Matrimony, Ancient Curses, True Love, and Other Dire Delights*, 2010
Adam Rann, *Emma and the Werewolves*, 2010
Leo Tolstoy, *Android Karenina*, 2010

277

DAVID BURTON

Blood Justice

(Pepperell, Massachusetts: By Light Unseen Media, 2010)

Story type: Contemporary
Subject(s): Vampires; Revenge; Adventure
Major character(s): Justine Kroft, Mother; Simone Gireaux, Vampire; Teresa Diaz, Friend (of Justine); Harry Frazer, Detective; Stephan Sinakov, Vampire
Time period(s): 21st century; 2010s
Locale(s): United States

Summary: In *Blood Justice*, author David Burton tells the story of a mother's unquenchable desire for revenge against those responsible for killing her daughter. After an unsuccessful attempt at retribution, Justine Kroft is saved by a centuries-old vampire named Simone. Together Justine and Simone set out to exact a brutal vengeance on the individuals who murdered Justine's child. With the help of her trusted friends and her immortal sidekick, Justine discovers the truth behind her daughter's death, leading her into a violent showdown that forces her to make the biggest decision of her life.

Other books you might like:
Douglas Clegg, *The Priest of Blood*, 2005
P.N. Elrod, *Cold Streets*, 2003
Charlaine Harris, *All Together Dead*, 2007
Paul Lake, *Among the Immortals: A Novel*, 1994
Michael Romkey, *The Vampire's Violin*, 2003

278

SYDNEY CROFT

Tempting the Fire

(New York: Bantam, 2010)

Series: ACRO Series. Book 4
Story type: Contemporary
Subject(s): Occultism; Erotica; Psychics
Major character(s): Sela Kahne, Agent (ACRO); Logan
  Mills, Rescuer (of Chance); Marlena West, Agent
  (ACRO); Chance McCormack, Military Personnel
  (Navy SEAL)
Time period(s): 21st century; 2010s
Locale(s): Amazonas, Brazil

Summary: Sela Kahne and her colleague Marlena West
are undercover specialists with the Agency for Covert
Rare Operatives (ACRO), a government-run organization whose agents possess supernatural gifts. Sela and
Marlena have been assigned to a brutal jungle locale,
where they are told to track down and eradicate a long-
feared monster. But the two women soon cross paths
with Navy SEAL Chance McCormack and his rescuer,
Logan Mills. Sela realizes she will have to put her
psychic abilities—and her heart—to the test in order to
find out just how Logan Mills can help her investigation.
Tempting the Fire is the fourth book in Sydney Croft's
ACRO series.

Other books you might like:
Peter Benchley, *White Shark*, 1994
John Darnton, *Neanderthal*, 1996
Douglas Preston, *Reliquary*, 1997
Jack Rogan, *The Ocean Dark*, 2010
James Rollins, *Amazonia*, 2002

279

HEATHER DAVIS

Never Cry Werewolf

(New York: HarperTeen, 2009)

Subject(s): Werewolves; Camps (Recreation);
  Interpersonal relations
Major character(s): Shelby Locke, 16-Year-Old; Austin
  Bridges III, Werewolf
Time period(s): 21st century; 2000s
Locale(s): United States

Summary: In Heather Davis's *Never Cry Werewolf*, Shelby
Locke is a troubled 16-year-old whose parents threaten
to send her to boot camp for the summer. After a little
negotiating, Shelby convinces them to send her to an
arts camp instead. Shortly after her arrival, Shelby grows

bored. But everything changes when Austin Bridges III
arrives at Camp Crescent. He's sweet, handsome, and
seems to be harboring a scandalous secret. As he and
Shelby grow closer, she learns the truth about Austin's
heritage. With the full moon just around the corner,
Shelby must now decide if she can give her heart to a
werewolf. First novel.

Where it's reviewed:
Horn Book Guide, Spring 2010, page 93
School Library Journal, December 2009, page 112

Other books by the same author:
The Clearing, 2010

Other books you might like:
Cathy Clamp, *Serpent Moon*, 2010
Susan Krinard, *Secret of the Wolf*, 2001
Mari Mancusi, *Bad Blood*, 2010
Donna Lee Simpson, *Awaiting the Fire*, 2007
Jennifer St. Giles, *Kiss of Darkness*, 2009

280

BENJAMIN KANE ETHRIDGE

Black and Orange

(Garden Grove, California: Bad Moon Books, 2010)

Subject(s): Halloween; Good and evil; Demons
Major character(s): Martin, Nomad; Teresa, Nomad
Time period(s): 21st century; 2010s
Locale(s): United States

Summary: Benjamin Kane Ethridge's *Black and Orange*
takes place on Halloween, when a portal is opened
between the worlds of good and evil. On this particular
All Hallow's Eve, the forces of darkness are demanding
a sacrifice. For Martin and Teresa, this means safeguard-
ing the proposed sacrifice, but the two world-weary
travelers have no idea what they're in for. Teresa is getting sicker every day, and Martin is losing his grip on
reality. What could this mean for the eternal battle
between good and evil? This volume includes illustrations by Zach McCain. First novel.

Other books you might like:
Jack Martin, *Halloween II*, 1982
Paul Melniczek, *A Haunted Halloween*, 2010
David Robbins, *Prank Night*, 1994
Al Sarrantonio, *Horrorween*, 2006

281

JOHN EVERSON

Siren

(New York: Leisure Books, 2010)

Story type: Contemporary
Subject(s): Mythology; Marriage; Suspense
Major character(s): Evan, Spouse (of Sarah); Ligeia,
  Mythical Creature (siren); Sarah, Spouse (of Evan)
Time period(s): 21st century; (2010s); 19th century; 1880s
Locale(s): Delilah, California

Summary: John Everson's *Siren* is set in the town of Delilah, California, where local man Evan is struggling with the collapse of his marriage to Sarah. While Sarah spends her evenings at the bar, Evan wanders a lonely stretch of beach and encounters an alluring, naked woman. Her name is Ligeia, and she is one of the legendary Sirens. Her power soon entrances the broken, water-phobic Evan, who gradually becomes drawn closer and closer to the surf—and toward his own ruin.

Other books by the same author:
The 13th, 2009
Sacrifice, 2007
Failure, 2006
Covenant, 2004
Cage of Bones & Other Deadly Obsessions, 2000

Other books you might like:
Richard Laymon, *The Traveling Vampire Show*, 2000
Tim Powers, *The Stress of Her Regard*, 1989
Ray Russell, *Incubus*, 1975
John Saul, *Comes the Blind Fury*, 1990
J.N. Williamson, *Death-Angel*, 1981

282

PAUL FINCH

Stronghold

(Oxford, United Kingdom: Abaddon, 2010)

Story type: Historical
Subject(s): Knights; Zombies; Welsh history
Major character(s): Ranulf, Knight
Time period(s): 13th century; 1290s (1295)
Locale(s): Wales, United Kingdom

Summary: Set in the latter years of the 13th century, Paul Finch's *Stronghold* finds the British conquering Wales with ferocity and violence. Ranulf is an English knight torn between duty to his country and moral doubts about the intensity of the British occupation. But the Welsh have had enough abuse at the hands of the enemy. They summon the forces of an ancient, evil power that draws hordes of zombies from their graves. Now Ranulf and his men must not only contend with the fate of the living—but also with the brutal vengeance of the dead.

Other books by the same author:
Ghost Realm, 2008
Stains, 2007
Darker Ages, 2004
Cape Wrath, 2002
Aftershocks, 2001

Other books you might like:
Amelia Beamer, *The Loving Dead*, 2010
J.L. Bourne, *Day By Day Armageddon*, 2007
Gary Brandner, *Carrion*, 1986
Joe McKinney, *Apocalypse of the Dead*, 2010
Kim Paffenroth, *Dying to Live: A Novel of Life Among the Undead*, 2008

283

BRIAN JAMES FREEMAN

The Painted Darkness

(Forest Hill, Maryland: Cemetery Dance Publications, 2010)

Subject(s): Artists; Suspense; Psychology
Major character(s): Henry, Artist, Spouse (of Sarah), Father (of Dillon); Sarah, Spouse (of Henry), Mother (of Dillon); Dillon, Son (of Henry and Sarah)
Time period(s): 21st century; 2010s
Locale(s): United States

Summary: In Brian James Freeman's *The Painted Darkness*, Henry is an artist who has found both solace and escape in his dark, perverse artwork. Now, Henry, his wife, and their son have moved into a new home, and they soon realize there is something not right about the basement of the charming old farmhouse. Henry is drawn into the creepy cellar, where he comes face to face with a monster beyond his wildest artistic imaginings—and the unresolved issues of his own traumatic history.

Where it's reviewed:
Locus, June 2010, page 57
Publishers Weekly, September 20, 2010, page 52

Other books you might like:
Randall Boyll, *After Sundown*, 1989
Stephen King, *Bag of Bones*, 1998
Dean R. Koontz, *The Bad Place*, 1990
Graham Masterton, *The House That Jack Built*, 1996
Sheri S. Tepper, *The Bones*, 1987

284

CLAUDIA GABEL

Romeo and Juliet and Vampires

(New York: HarperTeen, 2010)

Story type: Romance
Subject(s): Horror; Romances (Fiction); Vampires
Major character(s): Juliet Capulet, 15-Year-Old, Vampire; Romeo Montague, Vampire Hunter; Prince Radu, Royalty; Tybalt, Cousin (of Juliet); Mercutio, Friend (of Romeo); Laurence, Religious (Friar)
Time period(s): 16th century
Locale(s): Transylvania, Hungary

Summary: In *Romeo and Juliet and Vampires*, Claudia Gabel retells Shakespeare's most famous romance, complicating the young lovers' family feud by casting the Capulets as vampires and the Montagues as vampire hunters. In this version, the Capulets are favored relatives of Vlad the Impaler, and live a life of privilege in a Transylvania castle. As Juliet prepares for her transformation rite, she is smitten with handsome Romeo, even though he and his family have been killing off her vampire relatives since their feud began centuries ago. When a series of vengeful killings forces Romeo to flee, the couple considers drastic measures to preserve their eternal love.

Where it's reviewed:
School Library Journal, January 2011, page 104

Other books by the same author:
Friends Close, Enemies Closer, 2008
Sweet and Vicious, 2008
Inn or Out, 2007
Loves Me, Loves Me Not, 2007

Other books you might like:
Jane Austen, *Emma and the Vampires*, 2010
Charlotte Bronte, *Jane Slayre*, 2010
Porter Grand, *Little Women and Werewolves*, 2010
Vera Nazarian, *Mansfield Park and Mummies: Monster Mayhem, Matrimony, Ancient Curses, True Love, and Other Dire Delights*, 2010
Adam Rann, *Emma and the Werewolves*, 2010

285

W.D. GAGLIANI

Wolf's Bluff

(New York: Leisure Books, 2010)

Series: Nick Lupo Series. Book 3
Story type: Contemporary
Subject(s): Werewolves; Detective fiction; Violence
Major character(s): Nick Lupo, Detective—Private, Werewolf
Time period(s): 21st century; 2010s
Locale(s): United States

Summary: In *Wolf's Bluff*, author W.D. Gagliani presents the third installment in the Nick Lupo series, chronicling the investigative exploits of a werewolf detective. A string of brutal animal assaults has the entire city living in fear, and it's up to Nick and the investigators at Wolfpaw Security to figure out who—or what—is behind the violence. But Nick soon learns there is more to this case than meets the eye—and, if he's not careful, it could spell the end of his sleuthing adventures.

Other books by the same author:
Wolf's Gambit, 2009
Wolf's Trap, 2003

Other books you might like:
Gary Brandner, *The Howling*, 1977
Lee Killough, *Wilding Nights*, 2002
Robert R. McCammon, *The Wolf's Hour*, 1989
Melanie Tem, *Wilding*, 1992
Thomas Tessier, *The Nightwalker*, 1979

286

KELLY GAY

The Darkest Edge of Dawn

(New York: Pocket, 2010)

Series: Charlie Madigan Series. Book 2
Story type: Urban
Subject(s): Fantasy; Adventure; Detective fiction
Major character(s): Charlie Madigan, Detective; Hank, Sidekick (of Charlie)
Locale(s): Atlanta, Georgia

Summary: A plague of darkness has wrapped the city of Atlanta in eternal night. Against this backdrop, Charlie Madigan and her sidekick Hank fight the forces of evil and are now faced with their deadliest challenge yet. A mysterious enemy is targeting a band of angels, but the unknown foe isn't content to stop there: Charlie and Hank may well be the next victims. *The Darkest Edge of Dawn* is the second book in Kelly Gay's Charlie Madigan series.

Other books by the same author:
The Better Part of Darkness, 2009

Other books you might like:
Karen Chance, *Curse the Dawn*, 2009
Seanan McGuire, *Rosemary and Rue: An October Daye Novel*, 2009
Devon Monk, *Magic at the Gate*, 2010
Cherie Priest, *Four and Twenty Blackbirds*, 2005
Kat Richardson, *Labyrinth*, 2010

287

HARRISON GEILLOR

The Zombies of Lake Woebegotten

(San Francisco: Night Shade Books, 2010)

Story type: Contemporary
Subject(s): Zombies; Rural life; Humor
Major character(s): Daniel Inkfist, Religious (minister); Father Edsel, Religious (priest); Mr. Levitt, Serial Killer; Julie Olafson, Companion (dominatrix)
Time period(s): 21st century; 2010s
Locale(s): Lake Woebegotten, Minnesota

Summary: Harrison Geillor's *The Zombies of Lake Woebegotten* is a zombie-themed spoof of Garrison Keillor's classic *Lake Woebegone* stories. Set in a rural Minnesota community, this volume follows minister Daniel Inkfist and priest Father Edsel as they join forces to take on the undead. Meanwhile, the townspeople of Lake Woebegotten have their own responses to the zombie threat, which could spell doom for Inkfist and Edsel's mission. First novel.

Where it's reviewed:
Entertainment Weekly, November 5, 2010, page 74
Locus, October 2010, page 27
Publishers Weekly, July 26, 2010, page 57

Other books you might like:
Jim Butcher, *Blood Lite: An Anthology of Humorous Horror Stories Presented by the Horror Writers Association*, 2008
Julie Kenner, *Deja Demon*, 2008
Victoria Laurie, *Death Perception: A Psychic Eye Mystery*, 2008
Richard Laymon, *Resurrection Dreams*, 1988
A. Lee Martinez, *Gil's All Fright Diner*, 2005

Horror

288

CHRISTOPHER GOLDEN
TIM LEBBON, Co-Author

The Chamber of Ten

(New York: Spectra, 2010)

Series: Hidden Cities Series. Book 3
Subject(s): Italy; Psychics; Archaeology
Major character(s): Geena Hodge, Archaeologist; Nico, Lover (of Geena), Psychic
Time period(s): 21st century; 2010s
Locale(s): Venice, Italy

Summary: In *The Chamber of Ten*, the writing team of Christopher Golden and Tim Lebbon present the third novel in the Hidden Cities series. This outing follows archeologist Geena Hodge to the city of Venice, where she and her crew are launching an investigation into the location's past. But a series of strange events unleashes the dark side of the sinking city's history, and Geena's telepathic lover Nico becomes inhabited by the spirit of a controlling magician.

Where it's reviewed:
Booklist, July 1, 2010, page 43

Other books by the same author:
The Lost Ones, 2008
The Borderkind, 2007
The Myth Hunters, 2006
The Bones of Giants, 2004
The Gathering Dark, 2003

Other books you might like:
Robert Masello, *Bestiary*, 2006
Graham Masterton, *The Doorkeepers*, 2001
Robert R. McCammon, *Usher's Passing*, 1984
Jack Rogan, *The Ocean Dark*, 2010
John Saul, *The Presence*, 1997

289

CHRISTOPHER GOLDEN

The New Dead: A Zombie Anthology

(New York: St. Martin's Griffin, 2010)

Subject(s): Zombies; Adventure; Short stories

Summary: Award-winning author Christopher Golden presents a collection of 19 zombie stories penned by some of modern literature's most lauded writers. From tales of human survival during zombie ambushes to accounts of life and love among the undead, this volume encompasses the terror, humor, and fascination of the popular ghouls. Authors contributing to *The New Dead: A Zombie Anthology* include John Connolly, David Liss, Kelley Armstrong, Aimee Bender, and Brian Keene.

Other books by the same author:
The Lost Ones, 2008
The Borderkind, 2007
The Myth Hunters, 2006

The Bones of Giants, 2004
The Gathering Dark, 2003

Other books you might like:
Mario Acevedo, *Jailbait Zombie*, 2009
S.G. Browne, *Breathers: A Zombie's Lament*, 2009
Brian Keene, *The Rising*, 2003
Jonathan Maberry, *Patient Zero*, 2009
Philip Nutman, *Wet Work*, 1993

290

SETH GRAHAME-SMITH

Abraham Lincoln: Vampire Hunter

(New York: Grand Central Publishing, 2010)

Story type: Alternate History; Historical - American Civil War
Subject(s): Vampires; History; Presidents (Government)
Major character(s): Abraham Lincoln, Hunter (of vampires), Historical Figure
Time period(s): 19th century; 1860s
Locale(s): United States

Summary: People admire Abraham Lincoln. People are fascinated by vampires. For Seth Grahame-Smith, it only made sense to combine these two unrelated concepts. In the historical fiction comedy *Abraham Lincoln: Vampire Hunter*, Grahame-Smith takes a history of Lincoln's life and the Civil War and inserts vampires. He explains that vampires killed Lincoln's mother and that the future president vowed revenge. According to the book, Lincoln had to kill vampires with his bare hands. Grahame-Smith jokes that vampires encouraged slavery, and even presents well-known period photographs and pretends that they portray vampires. Grahame-Smith also wrote *Pride and Prejudice and Zombies*.

Where it's reviewed:
Booklist, January 1, 2010, page 18
Entertainment Weekly, March 5, 2010, page 91
Kirkus Reviews, February 15, 2010, page 103
Library Journal, March 15, 2010, page 98
New York Times, March 18, 2010, page C6

Other books by the same author:
Pride and Prejudice and Zombies, 2009

Other books you might like:
Claudia Gabel, *Romeo and Juliet and Vampires*, 2010
Sarah Gray, *Wuthering Bites*, 2010
Lori Handeland, *Shakespeare Undead*, 2010
Steve Hockensmith, *Pride and Prejudice and Zombies: Dawn of the Dreadfuls*, 2010
A.E. Moorat, *Queen Victoria, Demon Hunter*, 2009

291

PORTER GRAND
LOUISA MAY ALCOTT, Co-Author

Little Women and Werewolves

(New York: Ballantine Books, 2010)

Story type: Historical
Subject(s): Werewolves; Adventure

Major character(s): Jo March, Sister (of Amy, Beth, and Meg); Amy March, Sister (of Jo, Beth, and Meg); Beth March, Sister (of Jo, Amy, and Meg); Meg March, Sister (of Jo, Amy, and Beth); Laurie Laurence, Friend (of Jo)
Time period(s): 19th century
Locale(s): Concord, Massachusetts

Summary: Author Porter Grand presents a new take on Louisa May Alcott's classic tale in *Little Women and Werewolves*. In Civil War-era New England, the March sisters—Jo, Amy, Beth, and Meg—are coming of age and learning about the world around them. But this is no ordinary vision of Concord, Massachusetts; this small, sleepy town is overrun with werewolves, and any one of the March sisters could be the next victim of a ravenous hound. First novel.

Other books you might like:

Jane Austen, *Emma and the Vampires*, 2010

Jane Austen, *Sense and Sensibility and Sea Monsters*, 2009

Charlotte Bronte, *Jane Slayre*, 2010

Vera Nazarian, *Mansfield Park and Mummies: Monster Mayhem, Matrimony, Ancient Curses, True Love, and Other Dire Delights*, 2010

Adam Rann, *Emma and the Werewolves*, 2010

292

MIRA GRANT

Feed

(New York: Orbit, 2010)

Subject(s): Zombies; Science fiction; Diseases
Major character(s): Georgia Mason, Journalist, Twin (of Shaun); Shaun Mason, Journalist, Twin (of Georgia); Buffy, Friend (of Georgia and Shaun); Peter Ryman, Political Figure
Time period(s): 21st century; 2030s (2039)

Summary: Mira Grant's *Feed* is set is 2039, and the planet has somehow managed to endure a violent apocalypse. Twins Shaun and Georgia Mason are bloggers drawn into the dark side of what has become modern life. During their story-hunting, they learn that a lethal virus is spreading among humanity—but in order to tackle this story, the Masons are going to have to take on a trove of people and institutions opposed to revealing the truth.

Where it's reviewed:
Publishers Weekly, March 8, 2010, page 41

Other books you might like:

J.L. Bourne, *Day By Day Armageddon*, 2007

Ray Garton, *Zombie Love*, 2003

Brian Keene, *The Rising*, 2003

S.D. Perry, *Nemesis*, 2000

David Wellington, *Monster Island*, 2006

293

SARAH GRAY

Wuthering Bites

(New York: Kensington Books, 2010)

Story type: Alternate History; Vampire Story
Subject(s): Vampires; Literature; Romances (Fiction)
Major character(s): Heathcliff, Vampire, Orphan; Catherine Earnshaw, Teenager, Human; Edgar Linton, Neighbor, Wealthy
Time period(s): 18th century; 1770-1780 (1771)
Locale(s): Yorkshire, England

Summary: *Wuthering Bites* is Sarah Gray's supernatural twist on Emily Bronte's classic, *Wuthering Heights*. In this book, Catherine Earnshaw's father invites Heathcliff, a young orphan, to Wuthering Heights. Upon meeting Heathcliff, Catherine discovers his secret: He's a vampire, a product of a vampire father and a vampire-slaying gypsy mother. Although Heathcliff scares her at first, Catherine finds herself drawn to him. He's a monster with a kind heart, and he proves it by risking it all to protect her. At night, Heathcliff roams the perimeter of Wuthering Heights, destroying the monsters that lurk in the shadows and hope to prey on the mansion's more innocent residents. Although Catherine is attracted to Heathcliff, she can't help but wonder what life would be like with Edgar Linton, her wealthy next-door neighbor. As she struggles with the decision to choose one of the young men, each risks her love when he shows his true self.

Where it's reviewed:
Kirkus Reviews, August 1, 2010, page 694
Publishers Weekly, July 12, 2010, page 32

Other books you might like:
Claudia Gabel, *Romeo and Juliet and Vampires*, 2010
Lori Handeland, *Shakespeare Undead*, 2010
Steve Hockensmith, *Pride and Prejudice and Zombies: Dawn of the Dreadfuls*, 2010
A.E. Moorat, *Queen Victoria, Demon Hunter*, 2009
Lucy Weston, *The Secret History of Elizabeth Tudor, Vampire Slayer*, 2011

294

AMY GRECH

Blanket of White

(Santa Rosa, California: Damnation Books, 2010)

Subject(s): Fantasy; Sexuality; Short stories

Summary: Amy Grech's *Blanket of White* is a collection of spine-tingling short stories with a dark undercurrent of eerie sensuality. Whether set in the future or in the present day, Grech's tales profile ordinary individuals who find themselves trapped in terrifying, psychologically complex situations. Titles in this volume include "Ashes to Ashes," "Crosshairs," "Prevention Mother," and "Apple of My Eye."

Other books by the same author:
Apple of My Eye, 2006
The Art of Deception, 2000

Other books you might like:
Gary A. Braunbeck, *Home Before Dark*, 2005
Caitlin R. Kiernan, *Alabaster*, 2006
Jeffrey Thomas, *Nocturnal Emissions*, 2010
Scott Thomas, *Quill and Candle*, 2010
Lisa Tuttle, *Ghosts and Other Lovers*, 2002

295

SUSAN GRIFFITH
CLAY GRIFFITH, Co-Author

The Greyfriar

(Amherst, New York: Pyr, 2010)

Series: Vampire Empire Series. Book 1
Story type: Alternate History
Subject(s): Vampires; Royalty; Wars
Major character(s): Adele, Royalty (Princess of Equatorian Empire); The Greyfriar, Warrior
Time period(s): 19th century; (1870s); 21st century; 2020s (2020)
Locale(s): Equatorian Empire, Fictional Location

Summary: Susan and Clay Griffith's *The Greyfriar* is the first installment in the Vampire Empire series. This opening volume tells of the 19th-century vampire occupation that redistributed the populations of Earth. Now, in the year 2020, Princess Adele is in line to take the British throne, but first she will have to contend with a fierce new faction of bloodsuckers bent on world dominance. Her main ally is an enigmatic rogue named The Greyfriar—and he is the only person standing between human survival and absolute vampire control.

Where it's reviewed:
Library Journal, October 15, 2010, page 62
Publishers Weekly, September 13, 2010, page 28

Other books you might like:
Steven Brust, *The Book of Taltos*, 2002
Christie Golden, *Vampire of the Mists*, 1991
Barb Hendee, *In Shade and Shadow*, 2009
Jasper Kent, *Twelve*, 2010
Chelsea Quinn Yarbro, *Dark Light*, 1999

296

TATE HALLAWAY

Almost to Die For

(New York: New American Library, 2010)

Series: Vampire Princess of St. Paul Series. Book 1
Story type: Young Adult
Subject(s): Vampires; Witches; Adolescent interpersonal relations
Major character(s): Anastasija "Ana" Ramses Parker, 16-Year-Old, Vampire, Witch; Bea, Friend (of Ana); Nikolai, Vampire Hunter

Time period(s): 21st century; 2010s
Locale(s): St. Paul, Minnesota

Summary: In *Almost to Die For*, author Tate Hallaway presents the first novel in the Vampire Princess of St. Paul series. This inaugural volume follows 16-year-old Anastasija Ramses Parker, the daughter of a powerful witch, as she struggles with teenage life and magical dilemmas. Not only can Ana not perform any actual magic, but now she's learned she might be part vampire. To further compound the issue, her friend's new crush is a vampire hunter, and he has his eyes—or, more appropriately, his stake—set on Ana.

Where it's reviewed:
Publishers Weekly, June 21, 2010, page 35

Other books by the same author:
Dead If I Do, 2009
Dead Sexy, 2007
Tall, Dark & Dead, 2006
Apocalypse Array, 2004
Messiah Node, 2003

Other books you might like:
Michele Bardsley, *Over My Dead Body*, 2009
Julie Kenner, *Carpe Demon*, 2005
Sherrilyn Kenyon, *Bad Moon Rising*, 2009
Katie MacAlister, *In the Company of Vampires*, 2010
Chloe Neill, *Firespell*, 2010

297

LORI HANDELAND

Shakespeare Undead

(New York: St. Martin's Griffin, 2010)

Subject(s): Vampires; Magic; Adventure
Major character(s): William "Will" Shakespeare, Writer, Vampire; Katherine, Hunter (zombie hunter)
Time period(s): 16th century; 1590s (1592)
Locale(s): London, England

Summary: In *Shakespeare Undead*, bestselling author Lori Handeland crafts an inventive tale revolving around an immortal William Shakespeare and his attempts to stop a hoard of zombies from decimating 16th century London. In his quest to destroy the undead, Will teams up with Katherine, a beautiful zombie slayer who captures his heart and imagination.

Where it's reviewed:
Kirkus Reviews, April 15, 2010, page 329
Library Journal, June 1, 2010, page 84
Publishers Weekly, April 26, 2010, page 94

Other books by the same author:
Chaos Bites, 2010
Marked by the Moon, 2010
Apocalypse Happens, 2009
Any Given Doomsday, 2008
Hidden Moon, 2007
Crescent Moon, 2006
Hunter's Moon, 2005
Blue Moon, 2004

Other books you might like:
P.N. Elrod, *Quincey Morris, Vampire*, 2001
Claudia Gabel, *Romeo and Juliet and Vampires*, 2010
Seth Grahame-Smith, *Abraham Lincoln: Vampire Hunter*, 2010
Sarah Gray, *Wuthering Bites*, 2010
A.E. Moorat, *Queen Victoria, Demon Hunter*, 2009

298

LORI HANDELAND

Marked by the Moon

(New York: St. Martin's Press, 2010)

Series: Nightcreature Series. Book 9
Story type: Romance
Subject(s): Werewolves; Love; Adventure
Major character(s): Alexandra "Alex" Trevalyn, Werewolf; Julian Barlow, Werewolf
Time period(s): 21st century; 2010s
Locale(s): United States

Summary: The ninth book in the Nightcreature series, Lori Handeland's *Marked by the Moon* follows the werewolf-slaying adventures of lycanthrope warrior Alexandra Trevalyn. When she kills werewolf Julian Barlow's wife, she has no idea that the grieving beast is coming to exact revenge. After he tracks her down, Julian transforms Alex into her most despised enemy: a werewolf. And soon she can no longer deny her animalistic instincts—or her desire for Julian.

Other books by the same author:
Chaos Bites, 2010
Doomsday Can Wait, 2009
Hidden Moon, 2007
Crescent Moon, 2006
Blue Moon, 2004

Other books you might like:
Cat Adams, *Blood Song*, 2010
Emma Holly, *Saving Midnight*, 2009
Marjorie M. Liu, *The Iron Hunt*, 2008
Kerrelyn Sparks, *The Undead Next Door*, 2008
Christine Warren, *Walk on the Wild Side*, 2008

299

LORI HANDELAND

Chaos Bites

(New York: St. Martin's Press, 2010)

Series: Phoenix Chronicles Series. Book 4
Story type: Romance
Subject(s): Demons; Love; Adventure
Major character(s): Elizabeth "Liz" Phoenix, Warrior (demon slayer); Sawyer, Witch, Shape-Shifter, Shaman, Sorcerer; Faith, Baby
Time period(s): 21st century; 2010s
Locale(s): United States

Summary: Demon hunter Liz Phoenix is dealing with the death of Sawyer, a mysterious man who had captured her heart. Compounding her grief is the fact that Liz herself is responsible for his death; Sawyer was a witch, and she felt obligated as a demon slayer to fulfill her duty and kill him. But now Sawyer is visiting her dreams, and as the underworld's darkest demons rally their strength to battle her one last time, Liz receives a very unexpected gift: a baby. *Chaos Bites* is the fourth novel in Lori Handeland's Phoenix Chronicles series.

Other books by the same author:
Marked by the Moon, 2010
Doomsday Can Wait, 2009
Hidden Moon, 2007
Crescent Moon, 2006
Blue Moon, 2004

Other books you might like:
C.T. Adams, *Cold Moon Rising*, 2009
Katie MacAlister, *Even Vampires Get the Blues*, 2006
Lynsay Sands, *The Renegade Hunter*, 2009
Nalini Singh, *Angels' Blood*, 2009
Rebecca York, *Eternal Moon*, 2009

300

RHODI HAWK

A Twisted Ladder

(New York: Forge, 2009)

Story type: Psychological
Subject(s): Horror; Psychology; Family history
Major character(s): Dr. Madeleine LeBlanc, Psychologist; Daddy Blank, Father (of Madeleine); Marc LeBlanc, Brother (of Madeleine); Chloe, Grandmother (of Madeleine)
Time period(s): 21st century; 2000s
Locale(s): New Orleans, Louisiana

Summary: In *A Twisted Ladder* by Rhodi Hawk, a psychologist searches for the source of her family's mental illness and uncovers wicked secrets about her psychic grandmother. Madeleine LeBlanc, a psychologist at Tulane University, lost her brother, Marc, to schizophrenia when he killed himself. Her father is also schizophrenic. As Madeleine studies the LeBlanc family tree for evidence of the disease, she begins to question her own mental health. While her colleague, Ethan Manderleigh, assists Madeleine in her pursuit, visions of an evil, otherworldly child and disturbing truths about her family's Louisiana plantation bring Madeline to her mysterious grandmother, Chloe. First novel.

Where it's reviewed:
Booklist, August 1, 2009, page 41
Publishers Weekly, July 13, 2009, page 32

Other books you might like:
Stephen King, *Duma Key*, 2008
Elizabeth Massie, *Southern Discomfort: Selected Works of Elizabeth Massie*, 1993
Robert R. McCammon, *Gone South*, 1992
Michael McDowell, *Cold Moon over Babylon*, 1980
Cherie Priest, *Wings to the Kingdom*, 2006

301

BARB HENDEE

Memories of Envy

(New York: Roc, 2010)

Series: Vampire Memories Series. Book 3
Story type: Urban
Subject(s): Vampires; Adventure; Rehabilitation
Major character(s): Eleisha Clevon, Vampire; Simone Stratford, Vampire; Julian Ashton, Vampire; Philip, Vampire
Time period(s): 21st century; 2010s
Locale(s): Portland, Oregon

Summary: Eleisha Clevon is a vampire who has mastered the art of bloodsucking without killing. She is anxious to teach her fellow vamps this valuable skill, but not all are willing to comply. One such vampire is Simone, whom Eleisha becomes determined to track down and rehabilitate. But Eleisha is in for a bit of a surprise when she slowly learns that even her closest allies are not willing to follow her example and refrain from killing. *Memories of Envy* is the third novel in Barb Hendee's Vampire Memories series.

Where it's reviewed:
Booklist, October 1, 2010, page 38
Publishers Weekly, August 30, 2010, page 35

Other books by the same author:
Hunting Memories, 2009
In Shade and Shadow, 2009
Child of a Dead God, 2008
Rebel Fay, 2007
Thief of Lives, 2004

Other books you might like:
Patricia Briggs, *Blood Bound*, 2007
Rachel Caine, *Ghost Town*, 2010
Chris Marie Green, *A Drop of Red*, 2009
Charlaine Harris, *Dead and Gone*, 2009
Kim Harrison, *For a Few Demons More*, 2007

302

JOE HILL

Horns: A Novel

(New York: William Morrow, 2010)

Subject(s): Crime; Good and evil; Devil
Major character(s): Ignatius Perrish, Young Man (who loses his girlfriend Merrin), Outcast (possibly possessed by devil); Merrin Williams, Girlfriend (of Ignatius), Crime Victim (murdered)
Time period(s): 21st century
Locale(s): United States

Summary: *Horns: A Novel* by Joe Hill is a story about evil incarnate. Ignatius Perrish was a very privileged man, with a wealthy family, popularity, and a true love named Merrin Williams. Suddenly, his illusion of blessings all came tumbling down when Merrin is raped and killed. Ignatius enters a daze of drinking and foul deeds, and one day he wakes up to find that horns have grown on his head. Can it be that he has been inhabited by the devil? Joe Hill is also the author of *Heart-Shaped Box* and the short story collection *20th Century Ghosts*.

Where it's reviewed:
Booklist, May 15, 2010, page 56
Library Journal, February 1, 2010, page 57
New York Times, February 25, 2010, page C1
Publishers Weekly, January 25, 2010, page 91

Other books by the same author:
Heart-Shaped Box: A Novel, 2007
20th Century Ghosts, 2006

Other books you might like:
Jack Cady, *The Well*, 1980
Stephen King, *From a Buick 8*, 2002
Joe R. Lansdale, *Lost Echoes*, 2007
Thomas F. Monteleone, *The Reckoning*, 1999
Thomas Tessier, *Fog Heart*, 1998

303

STEVE HOCKENSMITH

Pride and Prejudice and Zombies: Dawn of the Dreadfuls

(Philadelphia: Quirk Books, 2010)

Story type: Historical
Subject(s): Zombies; Adventure; Humor
Major character(s): Elizabeth Bennet, Hunter (zombie hunter)
Time period(s): 19th century
Locale(s): Meryton, United Kingdom

Summary: Steve Hockensmith's *Pride and Prejudice and Zombies: Dawn of the Dreadfuls* is the prequel to Seth Grahame-Smith's *Pride and Prejudice and Zombies*. The events of this volume take place five years earlier, in which strange events start plaguing the town of Meryton. The Bennet sisters, headed by Elizabeth Bennet, set out to become adept at demon-fighting in order to take on the zombie threat poised to take over the community.

Where it's reviewed:
Booklist, March 1, 2010, page 3

Other books by the same author:
The Crack in the Lens, 2009
On the Wrong Track, 2008
Holmes on the Range, 2007

Other books you might like:
P.N. Elrod, *Quincey Morris, Vampire*, 2001
Claudia Gabel, *Romeo and Juliet and Vampires*, 2010
Seth Grahame-Smith, *Abraham Lincoln: Vampire Hunter*, 2010
Sarah Gray, *Wuthering Bites*, 2010
A.E. Moorat, *Queen Victoria, Demon Hunter*, 2009

304

MARK HODDER

The Strange Affair of Spring Heeled Jack

(Amherst, New York: Pyr, 2010)

Series: Burton and Swinburne Series. Book 1
Story type: Fantasy
Subject(s): Mystery; Technology; Time travel
Major character(s): Richard Francis Burton, Explorer; Algernon Swinburne, Writer, Sidekick (of Burton); Spring Heeled Jack, Monster
Time period(s): 19th century; 1860s
Locale(s): London, United Kingdom

Summary: Explorer Sir Richard Francis Burton and poet Algernon Swinburne team up in 19th-century England to battle a potentially deadly new form of technology. Between the infamous rabble-rouser Spring Heeled Jack and the rogue werewolves assaulting the citizens of London, however, Burton and Swinburne face a series of challenges in their quest to save the city—and the world—from possible destruction. *The Strange Affair of Spring Heeled Jack* is the first novel in Mark Hodder's Burton and Swinburne series. First novel.

Where it's reviewed:
Booklist, September 1, 2010, page 54
Library Journal, September 15, 2010, page 65
Publishers Weekly, July 19, 2010, page 117

Other books by the same author:
The Curious Case of the Clockwork Man, 2011

Other books you might like:
Karl Alexander, *Time After Time*, 1979
Robert Bloch, *The Night of the Ripper*, 1984
Gardner Fox, *Terror Over London*, 1957
Lee Hunt, *The Vampire of New York*, 2007
Colin Wilson, *Ritual in the Dark*, 1960

305

JEANNIE HOLMES

Blood Law

(New York: Dell, 2010)

Series: Alexandra Sabian Series. Book 1
Story type: Contemporary
Subject(s): Vampires; Supernatural; Detective fiction
Major character(s): Alexandra "Alex" Sabian, Vampire, Detective; Varik Baudelaire, Fiance(e) (ex-fiancee of Alex), Vampire, Detective
Time period(s): 21st century; 2010s
Locale(s): Jefferson, Mississippi

Summary: Jeannie Holmes's *Blood Law* is the first installment in a supernatural mystery series starring vampire private eye Alexandra Sabian and set in Jefferson, Mississippi. Alex works for the Federal Bureau of Preternatural Investigation, and her new case is calling back memories of her own father's savage killing. Sud-

denly confronted with an all-too-personal case, Alex joins forces with her former boyfriend Varik Baudelaire to track down the vampire mutilators wreaking havoc on Jefferson. First novel.

Where it's reviewed:
Analog, December 2010, page 106
Booklist, May 1, 2010, page 16
Publishers Weekly, May 3, 2010, page 36

Other books you might like:
Cat Adams, *Blood Song*, 2010
Yasmine Galenorn, *Bone Magic*, 2010
Chris Marie Green, *Deep in the Woods*, 2010
Stacia Kane, *City of Ghosts*, 2010
Adrian Phoenix, *Beneath the Skin*, 2009

306

ELLE JASPER

Afterlight

(New York: Signet, 2010)

Series: Dark Ink Chronicles Series. Book 1
Story type: Contemporary
Subject(s): Romances (Fiction); Vampires; Love
Major character(s): Riley Poe, Artist (tattoo artist), Sister (of Seth); Eli Dupre, Overseer (protector of Riley); Seth, Brother (of Riley)
Time period(s): 21st century; 2010s
Locale(s): United States

Summary: The first book in Elle Jasper's Dark Ink Chronicles, *Afterlight* follows tattoo artist Riley Poe through a vampire-themed adventure set in the Deep South. When Riley's younger brother, Seth, whom she looks after, starts behaving strangely, Riley launches an investigation into the local forces of evil that she suspects have claimed him. Her exploration of the dark side leads her to Eli Dupre, a sexy stranger who claims to be Riley's protector as she takes on the evil all around her. First novel.

Where it's reviewed:
Booklist, November 1, 2010, page 34
Locus, November 2010, page 29
Publishers Weekly, September 13, 2010, page 29

Other books you might like:
Cat Adams, *Siren Song*, 2010
Charlaine Harris, *Dead in the Family: A Sookie Stackhouse Novel*, 2010
Christina Henry, *Black Wings*, 2010
Allyson James, *Stormwalker*, 2010
Lynsay Sands, *Love Bites*, 2004

307

RICHARD KADREY

Sandman Slim

(New York: Eos, 2009)

Series: Sandman Slim Series. Book 1
Story type: Contemporary; Series

Subject(s): Horror; Devil; Fantasy
Major character(s): James Stark, Gladiator (sideshow)
Time period(s): 21st century; 2000s
Locale(s): Los Angeles, California

Summary: In *Sandman Slim* by Richard Kadrey, James Stark has spent 11 years in hell where he entertained Lucifer by slaughtering opponents in the gladiator ring. Finally free, Stark has come to Los Angeles where he hopes to use his lethal skills against his girlfriend's murderer and Mason Faim, the magician who arranged his stint in hell. As Stark navigates L.A.'s shadowy underworld of violence and pleasure, he deals with suspicious government agents, spirits both good and evil, and a conjurer whose severed head subsequently accompanies Stark on his quest. *Sandman Slim* is the first book in the Sandman Slim series.

Where it's reviewed:
Booklist, July 1, 2009, page 42
Publishers Weekly, June 8, 2009, page 31

Other books by the same author:
Kill the Dead, 2010
Butcher Bird, 2007
Kamikaze L'Amour, 1995
Metrophage, 1988

Other books you might like:
Jim Butcher, *Small Favor: A Novel of the Dresden Files*, 2008
Harry Connolly, *Game of Cages*, 2010
Simon R. Green, *From Hell with Love*, 2010
Lilith Saintcrow, *Dead Man Rising*, 2006
Anton Strout, *Dead Matter*, 2010

308

RICHARD KADREY

Kill the Dead

(New York: Eos, 2010)

Series: Sandman Slim Series. Book 2
Story type: Contemporary; Series
Subject(s): Horror; Devil; Fantasy
Major character(s): James Stark, Bodyguard; Lucifer, Demon
Time period(s): 21st century; 2010s
Locale(s): Los Angeles, California

Summary: In *Kill the Dead* by Richard Kadrey, James Stark has escaped his imprisonment in hell and settled in Los Angeles, where his supernatural skills land him a job with a branch of the Homeland Security department known as the Golden Vigil. As Stark stalks the city's evil creatures, his former boss, Lucifer, arrives in L.A. to supervise production of a biographical film. Lucifer engages Stark as his bodyguard, but the job is complicated by a sudden surge in Hollywood's zombie population. If Stark can't get the problem under control, he may be making a return trip to hell. *Kill the Dead* is the second book in the Sandman Slim series.

Where it's reviewed:
Locus, October 2010, page 23
Publishers Weekly, August 30, 2010, page 34

Other books by the same author:
Sandman Slim, 2010
Butcher Bird, 2007
Kamikaze L'Amour, 1995
Metrophage, 1988

309

BRIAN KEENE

A Gathering of Crows

(New York: Leisure Books, 2010)

Story type: Contemporary
Subject(s): Birds; Adventure; Suspense
Major character(s): Levi Stoltzfus, Magician
Time period(s): 21st century; 2010s
Locale(s): United States

Summary: In Brain Keene's *A Gathering of Crows*, magician and former Amish Levi Stoltzfus must face his most deadly adversaries yet. A flock of ravenous crows has attacked a small, rural community, and Levi gets caught up in the chaos. But he soon learns this is no random act of nature. Something truly evil is behind this bizarre event—and Levi may be the only one with the wiles to find the truth.

Other books by the same author:
The Darkness on the Edge of Town, 2010
Castaways, 2009
Dark Hollow, 2008
Ghost Walk, 2008
Dead Sea, 2007

Other books you might like:
Jack Ketchum, *She Wakes*, 1988
Stephen King, *Insomnia*, 1994
Richard Laymon, *The Beast House*, 1986
Harry Shannon, *Daemon*, 2008
Bryan Smith, *The Killing Kind*, 2010

310

TONI L.P. KELNER
CHARLAINE HARRIS, Co-Editor

Death's Excellent Vacation

(New York: Ace Books, 2010)

Subject(s): Short stories; Vacations; Humor

Summary: In *Death's Excellent Vacation*, editors Charlaine Harris and Toni L.P. Kelner present a collection of 13 short stories centering on macabre vacations and sinister holidays. Blending humor and horror, the tales of this volume include works by Jeaniene Frost, Lilith Saintcrow, Katie MacAlister, A. Lee Martinez, Jeff Abbott, and more, as well as a story by Harris featuring her iconic heroine Sookie Stackhouse.

Other books by the same author:
Dead in the Family: A Sookie Stackhouse Novel, 2010
Dead and Gone, 2009
From Dead to Worse, 2008

Grave Surprise, 2006
Grave Sight, 2005

Other books you might like:
Jennifer Ashley, *Just One Sip*, 2006
L.A. Banks, *Cursed to Death*, 2009
Jeaniene Frost, *At Grave's End: A Night Huntress Novel*, 2008
Christopher Golden, *The Lost Ones*, 2008
Lilith Saintcrow, *Night Shift*, 2008

311

HIDEYUKI KIKUCHI

The Scarlet Clan

(New York: Tor, 2010)

Series: Wicked City Series. Book 3
Story type: Young Adult
Subject(s): Demons; Fantasy; Pregnancy
Major character(s): Taki, Human; Makie, Demon
Locale(s): Japan

Summary: Human Taki and demon Makie are about to have a child. The landmark event heralds a new dawn in human-demon relations, but not everyone is thrilled about the impending arrival. A gang of rogue demons wants nothing more than for Taki and Makie's child to remain unborn, and they set out to stop the baby's arrival at all costs. *The Scarlet Clan* is the third novel in Hideyuki Kikuchi's Wicked City series.

Other books by the same author:
The Black Guard, 2010
The Other Side, 2010

Other books you might like:
Camille Bacon-Smith, *Daemon Eyes*, 2007
Laurell K. Hamilton, *Bloody Bones*, 1996
Kim Harrison, *The Outlaw Demon Wails*, 2008
Ted Lebbon, *Unnatural Selection*, 2006
Graham Masterton, *Tengu*, 1983

312

HIDEYUKI KIKUCHI

The Other Side

(New York: Tor, 2010)

Series: Wicked City Series. Book 2
Story type: Young Adult
Subject(s): Demons; Good and evil; Adventure
Major character(s): Taki, Human; Makie, Demon; Miyuki, Agent (Black Guard)
Locale(s): Japan

Summary: Hideyuki Kikuchi's *The Other Side* is the second installment in the Wicked City series. This sophomore outing finds human Taki and his demon partner Makie fighting a force of pure evil. But in order to win this battle, they will first have to join forces with the ruthless Miyuki, an agent with the powerful Black Guard.

Other books by the same author:
The Black Guard, 2010
The Scarlet Clan, 2010

Other books you might like:
Yasmine Galenorn, *Demon Mistress*, 2009
Christopher Golden, *The Bones of Giants*, 2004
Kim Harrison, *Dead Witch Walking*, 2004
Graham Masterton, *Night Wars*, 2006
Roger Zelazny, *Lord Demon*, 1999

313

HIDEYUKI KIKUCHI

The Black Guard

(New York: Tor, 2009)

Series: Wicked City Series. Book 1
Story type: Contemporary; Series
Subject(s): Horror; Fantasy; Science fiction
Major character(s): Renzaburo Taki, Guard (member of Black Guard); Makie, Demon; Giuseppe Mayart, Sorcerer
Time period(s): 21st century; 2010s
Locale(s): Tokyo, Japan

Summary: In *Black Guard* by Hideyuki Kikuchi, a tenuous treaty between Tokyo's human and demon populations is set to expire, and two agents from the Black Guard are charged with guarding a key signer. Giuseppe Mayart, a powerful sorcerer, arrives in Tokyo under the protection of Black Guard agent Renzaburo Taki and his partner, Makie, a demon who has joined the human side. Taki and Makie don't realize that Mayart has come to the treaty signing with his own agenda. As the agents fall victim to their charge's diversion tactics, time is running out on the truce. *Black Guard* is the first book in the Wicked City series.

Where it's reviewed:
Library Journal, September 15, 2009, page 53

Other books by the same author:
The Other Side, 2010
The Scarlet Clan, 2010

Other books you might like:
Camille Bacon-Smith, *Daemon Eyes*, 2007
Laurell K. Hamilton, *Circus of the Damned*, 1994
Kim Harrison, *The Outlaw Demon Wails*, 2008
Ted Lebbon, *Unnatural Selection*, 2006
Graham Masterton, *Tengu*, 1983

314

STEPHEN KING

Blockade Billy

(Forest Hill, Maryland: Cemetery Dance Publications, 2010)

Subject(s): Baseball; Violence; Suspense
Major character(s): Billy Blakely, Baseball Player; George Granny Grantham, Coach

Time period(s): 20th century; 1950s
Locale(s): United States

Summary: In *Blockade Billy*, author Stephen King crafts a dark tale of mystery, suspense, and baseball. Told from the point of view of coach George "Granny" Grantham, this volume tells the story of powerhouse catcher Billy Blakely, who rises to fame in the world of 1950s baseball. Billy's prowess on the field becomes legendary, as does his penchant for violence. As his story unfolds, readers are taken into the twisted mind of Blockade Billy and the volatile secrets he holds.

Where it's reviewed:
Booklist, May 1, 2010, page 6
Publishers Weekly, April 5, 2010, page 50

Other books by the same author:
Full Moon, No Stars, 2010
Duma Key, 2008
Just After Sunset, 2008
Cell, 2006
Lisey's Story, 2006

Other books you might like:
Michael Bishop, *Brittle Innings*, 1994
Karen Joy Fowler, *The Sweetheart Season*, 1996
Frank King, *Southpaw*, 1988
Douglass Wallop, *The Year the Yankees Lost the Pennant*, 1954
Nancy Willard, *Things Invisible to See*, 1984

315

STEPHEN KING

Full Dark, No Stars

(New York: Scribner, 2010)

Subject(s): Short stories; Marriage; Murder

Summary: In *Full Dark, No Stars*, renowned author Stephen King returns to the short story format with four tales of mayhem and madness. "1922" chronicles the horrific fallout that occurs when a long-married couple contemplates putting their home up for sale and relocating to Omaha, Nebraska. In "Big Driver," a writer is attacked and nearly killed, awakening a startling thirst for vengeance. A woman unearths some shocking truths about her husband in "A Good Marriage." "Fair Extension" tells the story of a man who strikes an unusual bargain with the devil so that he may be cured of his terminal illness.

Where it's reviewed:
Booklist, September 15, 2010, page 38
Bookmarks, January-February 2011, page 44
Locus, December 2010, page 26
New York Times Book Review, November 28, 2010,, page 19
Publishers Weekly, September 27, 2010, page 34

Other books by the same author:
Blockade Billy, 2010
Duma Key, 2008
Just After Sunset, 2008

Cell, 2006
Lisey's Story, 2006

Other books you might like:
Charles L. Grant, *Nightmare Seasons*, 1982
Joe Hill, *20th Century Ghosts*, 2005
Bentley Little, *The Collection*, 2002
Peter Straub, *Magic Terror: 7 Tales*, 2000
F. Paul Wilson, *Aftershocks & Others: 19 Oddities*, 2009

316

MERCEDES LACKEY

Trio of Sorcery

(New York: Tor, 2010)

Subject(s): Supernatural; Ghosts; Witchcraft

Summary: In *Trio of Sorcery*, author Mercedes Lackey presents three short novels featuring empowered women blessed with magical abilities. These contemporary sorceresses deal with vitriolic ghosts, psychic investigations, and technological monsters. Titles in this volume are "Arcanum 101," "Ghost in the Machine," and "Drums."

Where it's reviewed:
Booklist, December 15, 2010, page 29
Library Journal, October 15, 2010, page 73

Other books by the same author:
Fortune's Fool, 2007
Sacred Ground, 2004
Jinx High, 1991
Children of the Night, 1990
Burning Water, 1989

Other books you might like:
Marie Brennan, *Doppelganger*, 2006
Yasmine Galenorn, *Demon Mistress*, 2009
Charlaine Harris, *Grave Secret*, 2009
Karen Marie Moning, *Dreamfever*, 2009
Kat Richardson, *Labyrinth*, 2010

317

DAVID LUBAR

The Big Stink

(New York: Tor, 2010)

Series: Nathan Abercrombie, Accidental Zombie. Book 4
Story type: Series; Young Readers
Subject(s): Horror; Zombies; Schools
Major character(s): Nathan Abercrombie, 5th Grader, Supernatural Being (zombie), Spy; Ridley, Bully; Rodney, Bully; Abigail, Friend (of Nathan); Mookie, Friend (of Nathan)
Time period(s): 21st century; 2010s
Locale(s): Fictional Location

Summary: In *The Big Stink* by David Lubar, a fifth-grade zombie deals with his own increasing odor and the stench caused by mold that has invaded Belgosi Upper Elementary School. When Nathan Abercrombie and his friends find themselves sharing a classroom with older students, Nathan realizes that he may not be able to keep his ailment a secret—especially when his limbs threaten to come loose. While Nathan fights the big stink and the school bullies, he also dabbles in espionage with the Bureau of Useful Misadventures. *The Big Stink* is the fourth book in the Nathan Abercrombie, Accidental Zombie series.

Other books by the same author:
Dead Guy Spy, 2010
Goop Soup, 2010
My Rotten Life, 2009
True Talents, 2007
Hidden Talents, 1999

Other books you might like:
Damien Graves, *Voices*, 2006
Andrew Newbound, *Demon Strike*, 2010
Christopher Pike, *The Thing in the Closet*, 1997
R.L. Stine, *The Wizard of Ooze*, 2010
Tom B. Stone, *The Gator Ate Her*, 1997

318

JONATHAN MABERRY

The Wolfman
(New York: Tor Books, 2010)

Story type: Werewolf Story
Subject(s): Werewolves; History; Movies
Major character(s): Lawrence Talbot, Young Man
Time period(s): 19th century; 1890s (1891)
Locale(s): Blackmoor, England

Summary: *The Wolfman* by Jonathan Maberry is a novelization of the movie of the same. Set in Blackmoor, England, in 1891, the novel focuses on Lawrence Talbot, a young man who escaped to London after the death of his mother many years prior. When his brother's fiancee contacts him and asks him to come back to Blackmoor, he learns that his brother is missing. He soon finds out that an incredibly strong creature has been slaughtering the villagers. As he searches for his brother, Lawrence learns about a curse that transforms men into werewolves. Talbot sets out to find the creature himself, and to protect the woman with whom he has fallen in love with.

Other books by the same author:
The Dragon Factory, 2010
Patient Zero, 2009
Bad Moon Rising, 2008
Dead Man's Song, 2007
Ghost Road Blues, 2006

Other books you might like:
P.D. Cacek, *Canyons*, 2000
David Case, *Wolf Tracks*, 1980
Guy Endore, *The Werewolf of Paris*, 1992
Brian Hodge, *Nightlife*, 1991
Whitley Strieber, *The Wild*, 1991

319

JONATHAN MABERRY

The Dragon Factory
(New York: St. Martin's Press, 2010)

Series: Joe Ledger Series. Book 2
Subject(s): Detective fiction; Fantasy; Horror
Major character(s): Joe Ledger, Military Personnel; John Andrews, FBI Agent
Time period(s): 21st century; 2010s
Locale(s): Baltimore, Maryland

Summary: In Jonathan Maberry's *The Dragon Factory*, Joe Ledger and his Echo Team from the Department of Military Sciences set out to stop two separate plots to gain global dominance through genetic engineering. Following in the footsteps of Josef Mengele, one organization is working to fulfill the Nazi vision of a master race. Another band of scientists is producing hybrid fighting forces that combine multi-species traits. As Ledger and his team face biological warfare, ancient beasts of legend, and modern manmade creatures, they must also deal with the prophetic arrival of mysterious albino twins. *The Dragon Factory* is the second book in the Joe Ledger series.

Where it's reviewed:
Booklist, January 1, 2010, page 49
Publishers Weekly, January 4, 2010, page 31

Other books by the same author:
The Wolfman, 2010
Patient Zero, 2009
Bad Moon Rising, 2008
Dead Man's Song, 2007
Ghost Road Blues, 2006

Other books you might like:
Mario Acevedo, *Jailbait Zombie*, 2009
S.G. Browne, *Breathers: A Zombie's Lament*, 2009
Brian Keene, *Dead Sea*, 2007
John Richard Stephens, *The Book of the Living Dead*, 2010
Del Stone Jr., *Black Tide*, 2007

320

KATIE MACALISTER

In the Company of Vampires
(New York: Penguin, 2010)

Series: Dark Ones Series. Book 8
Story type: Occult; Series
Subject(s): Horror; Occultism; Vampires
Major character(s): Francesca Ghetti, Psychic; Loki, Supernatural Being (god); Benedikt, Vampire; David, Shape-Shifter, Brother (of Benedikt)
Time period(s): 21st century; 2010s
Locale(s): Germany

Summary: In *In the Company of Vampires* by Katie MacAlister, a young woman betrothed to a vampire faces betrayal and supernatural threats when she searches for

Horror

her missing mother in Germany. Francesca has been promised to Benedikt since she was a teenager, charged with ensuring his immortality. But when she travels to Gothfaire she discovers that during their time apart he has taken another lover—the wicked Naomi. While Fran tries to win Ben back, she deals with Norse gods, her mother's mysterious past, and Ben's brother David, a troubled shape-shifter. *In the Company of Vampires* is the eighth book in the Dark Ones series.

Where it's reviewed:
Publishers Weekly, September 27, 2010, page 44

Other books by the same author:
Confessions of a Vampire's Girlfriend, 2010
Crouching Vampire, Hidden Fang, 2009
The Last of the Red Hot Vampires, 2007
Even Vampires Get the Blues, 2006
Sex, Lies, and Vampires, 2005

Other books you might like:
Jeaniene Frost, *Halfway to the Grave*, 2007
Michelle Rowen, *Something Wicked*, 2010
Kerrelyn Sparks, *Vamps and the City*, 2006
Jeanne C. Stein, *Chosen*, 2010
Carrie Vaughn, *Kitty Raises Hell*, 2009

321

KATIE MACALISTER

Confessions of a Vampire's Girlfriend

(New York: Penguin, 2010)

Story type: Occult; Series
Subject(s): Horror; Occultism; Vampires
Major character(s): Francesca Ghetti, Psychic; Benedikt, Vampire
Time period(s): 21st century; 2010s
Locale(s): Europe

Summary: *Confessions of a Vampire's Girlfriend* collects two previously published novels by Katie MacAlister. In *Got Fangs*, Francesca Ghetti, a 16-year-old psychic, journeys with her mother to Europe's Gothfaire where she has a fateful encounter with the vampire, Benedikt. Though handsome Benedikt wins Francesca's heart, the teenager struggles to find a place among Gothfaire's misfits. In *Circus of the Darned*, Francesca adjusts to life as a vampire's girlfriend as she deals with a time traveler's advice and a legion of Viking spirits she accidentally summons from the dead.

Other books by the same author:
The Company of Vampires, 2010
Crouching Vampire, Hidden Fang, 2009
The Last of the Red Hot Vampires, 2007
Even Vampires Get the Blues, 2006
Sex, Lies, and Vampires, 2005

Other books you might like:
Nina Bangs, *Night Bites*, 2005
J.K. Beck, *When Blood Calls*, 2010
Heidi Betts, *The Bite Before Christmas*, 2010

Karen Chance, *Embrace the Night*, 2008
Jeanne C. Stein, *The Becoming*, 2006

322

TRISH J. MACGREGOR

Esperanza

(New York: Tor, 2010)

Subject(s): Supernatural; Ghosts; Love
Major character(s): Tess Livingston, Agent (FBI); Ian Ritter, Professor; Dominica, Shape-Shifter, Spirit
Time period(s): 21st century; (2010s); 20th century; 1960s (1968)
Locale(s): Esperanza, South America; Minnesota, United States

Summary: Trish J. MacGregor's *Esperanza* chronicles the time-traveling adventures of FBI agent Tess Livingston and professor Ian Ritter, whose journeys begin when they become stuck at a bus depot deep in the Andes Mountains. After leaving the depot, Livingston and Ritter find their way to the mysterious town of Esperanza, which hosts a ghostly shape-shifter named Dominica. Dominica learns that both Tess and Ian are lynchpins in a longstanding war between good and evil, between the dead and the living, between restless ghosts and at-rest spirits. Soon Ian is traveling back in time to curtail some of the biggest tragedies in the modern world in order to stop the impending battle between darkness and light.

Where it's reviewed:
Publishers Weekly, August 2, 2010, page 32

Other books you might like:
Charles de Lint, *Trader*, 1997
Stephen Dedman, *The Art of Arrow Cutting*, 1997
Stephen Gallagher, *Valley of Lights*, 1987
Roger Manvell, *The Dreamers*, 1958
Graham Masterton, *Night Plague*, 1991

323

NICK MAMATAS
ELLEN DATLOW, Co-Editor

Haunted Legends

(New York: Tor, 2010)

Subject(s): Ghosts; Supernatural; Short stories

Summary: In *Haunted Legends*, editors Ellen Datlow and Nick Mamatas present an anthology of stories centering on ghostly hauntings. The 20 tales of this volume cover the gamut of supernatural adventures, from mass murders to demon-possessed locales. Authors contributing to this collection include Laird Barron, Jeffrey Ford, Catherynne M. Valente, Ekaterina Sedia, and Joe Lansdale.

Other books by the same author:
Best Horror of the Year Volume 2, 2010
Best Horror of the Year Volume 1, 2009
Poe, 2009
The Dark, 2003
Sirens, 1998

Other books you might like:
Rick Hautala, *Dead Voices*, 1990
James Herbert, *Haunted*, 1988
Shirley Jackson, *The Haunting of Hill House*, 1959
Graham Masterton, *The House That Jack Built*, 1996
Peter Straub, *Ghost Story*, 1979

324

JOE MCKINNEY

Apocalypse of the Dead

(New York: Pinnacle, 2010)

Subject(s): Zombies; Survival; Cults
Major character(s): Ed Moore, Retiree (former U.S. Marshal); Jasper, Leader (of a cult)
Time period(s): Indeterminate Future
Locale(s): North Dakota, United States

Summary: In Joe McKinney's *Apocalypse of the Dead*, the sequel to 2010's *Dead City*, a group of survivors has lived through a zombie attack of epidemic proportions. Headed by former U.S. Marshal Ed Moore, the band arrives at a remote settlement for zombie-attack survivors in rural North Dakota. But Ed isn't so sure this community is the best place for his group to settle down. The leader of the settlement is a zealous preacher proclaiming one way to salvation: mass suicide.

Other books by the same author:
Dead City, 2006

Other books you might like:
Bob Fingerman, *Pariah*, 2010
Jonathan Maberry, *Patient Zero*, 2009
Andrew Neiderman, *After Life*, 1993
Al Sarrantonio, *Skeletons*, 1992
Del Stone Jr., *Black Tide*, 2007

325

D. SCOTT MEEK

Dying Light

(Ingraham, Iowa: Canonbridge LLC, 2010)

Story type: Futuristic
Subject(s): Vampires; Dystopias; Politics
Major character(s): Charlotte, Vampire; Michael, Vampire
Time period(s): 25th century

Summary: D. Scott Meek's *Dying Light* is set in a 25th-century dystopia, where vampires and humans live uneasily among one another—though the emerging world government is doing everything in its power to eliminate all traces of vampires on Earth. Into this fold develops a very personal story revolving around Charlotte, who is dispatched to kill Michael, a traitor to the vamps. But Charlotte has some secrets of her own concerning Michael—secrets that, if discovered, could spell her doom. First novel.

Other books you might like:
Suzy McKee Charnas, *The Vampire Tapestry*, 1980

Les Daniels, *Yellow Fog*, 1986
C.S. Friedman, *The Madness Season*, 1990
Tanith Lee, *Sabella, or the Blood Stone*, 1980
Lois Tilton, *Vampire Winter*, 1990

326

PAUL MELNICZEK

Mischief Night

(Garden Grove, California: Bad Moon Books, 2010)

Subject(s): Haunted houses; Adventure; Fear
Major character(s): Rusty, Young Man; Berger, Aged Person
Time period(s): 21st century; 2010s
Locale(s): United States

Summary: In the novella *Mischief Night*, author Paul Melniczek tells the frightening story of Rusty and his friends, whose haunted house adventure takes an ominous turn. What started out as fun and games quickly spills over into a terrifying new reality as Rusty and his pals fall under the control of elderly Berger and his henchmen, who are intent on using the trespassers in their evil schemes. This volume includes illustrations by Caroline O'Neal.

Other books by the same author:
Monsters, 2010
Restless Shades, 2002

Other books you might like:
Benjamin Kane Ethridge, *Black and Orange*, 2010
Ashley McConnell, *Days of the Dead*, 1992
Lisa Morton, *The Samhanach*, 2010
David Robbins, *Prank Night*, 1994
Al Sarrantonio, *Halloweenland*, 2007

327

PAUL MELNICZEK

Monsters

(Colusa, California: Dark Regions Press, 2010)

Subject(s): Monsters; Fantasy; Suspense

Summary: Paul Melniczek's *Monsters* brings together a collection of the author's most spine-tingling, bone-chilling prose. Each of the eight short stories in this volume tells an eerie tale of a monster, ghoul, or other creepy-crawly that both entertains and terrifies. Titles include "Purgatory Calling," "Twilight's Embrace," "Where Trails Sometimes Lead," and "In the Night, Heels Clicking."

Other books by the same author:
Mischief Night, 2010
Restless Shades, 2002

Other books you might like:
Stephen King, *Skeleton Crew*, 1985
Richard Matheson, *Button, Button: Uncanny Stories*, 2008
Scott Nicholson, *Scattered Ashes*, 2008

Lucy Taylor, *Unnatural Acts and Other Stories*, 1994
Jeffrey Thomas, *Thirteen Specimens*, 2008

328

LYNN MESSINA

Little Vampire Women

(New York: HarperTeen, 2010)

Story type: Historical; Vampire Story
Subject(s): Literature; Vampires; Sisters
Major character(s): Jo March, Vampire, Young Woman; Meg March, Vampire, Young Woman; Amy March, Vampire, Young Woman; Beth March, Vampire, Young Woman; Margaret "Marmee" March, Mother, Vampire; Theodore "Laurie" Laurence, Human, Young Man
Time period(s): 19th century; 1860-1870
Locale(s): Concord, Massachusetts
Summary: *Little Vampire Women* is Lynn Messina's supernatural interpretation of Louisa May Alcott's classic, *Little Women*. In this book, Marmee raises her daughters—Meg, Jo, Amy, and Beth—to be upstanding vampire women. This means resisting the urge to feed on humans and wreak havoc in town. It takes a while, but the sisters accept the challenge and soon conquer their bloodlust. In the meantime, their lack of feeding makes them irritable, and they are constantly at each other's throats. Marmee convinces them to direct their supernatural energy to improving society and staying away from angry vampire hunters. While many humans wish to send all vampires to Hell, others, like Laurie, are interested in the vampire lifestyle. Laurie, a mere human, has worshipped the March women for years and will do just about anything to become a vampire himself. The Marches are faced with a difficult decision: go against their moral codes and turn Laurie or lose their very best friend to a mortal death.

Where it's reviewed:
Bulletin for the Center for Children's Books, July-August 2010, page 470
School Library Journal, July 2010, page 93

Other books by the same author:
Savvy Girl, 2008
Fashionistas, 2003

Other books you might like:
Claudia Gabel, *Romeo and Juliet and Vampires*, 2010
Sarah Gray, *Wuthering Bites*, 2010
Lori Handeland, *Shakespeare Undead*, 2010
Steve Hockensmith, *Pride and Prejudice and Zombies: Dawn of the Dreadfuls*, 2010
A.E. Moorat, *Queen Victoria, Demon Hunter*, 2009

329

LENA MEYDAN

Twilight Forever Rising

(New York: Tor, 2010)

Series: Vampire Clan Series. Book 1
Story type: Contemporary
Subject(s): Vampires; Gangs; Love
Major character(s): Darel Ericson, Vampire
Time period(s): 21st century; 2000s

Summary: In *Twilight Forever Rising*, author Lena Meydan presents the first novel in the Vampire Clan series. Rival vampire clans had been vying for power for hundreds of years, but an uneasy ceasefire called a tentative end to the violence. Now, powerful Darel Ericson of the Dahanavar clan is faced with the possibility of an enemy clan taking power and jeopardizing humanity. With the human female who has claimed his heart, Darel must contend with an adversary whose plans for domination just might destroy lives—both human and vampire. This book is translated from Russian by Andrew Bromfield. First novel.

Where it's reviewed:
Booklist, October 1, 2010, page 38

Other books you might like:
Shannon Drake, *Dead by Dusk*, 2005
Charlaine Harris, *Dead in the Family: A Sookie Stackhouse Novel*, 2010
Sherrilyn Kenyon, *Dream Warrior*, 2009
Lynn Viehl, *Stay the Night*, 2009
J.R. Ward, *Lover Mine: A Novel of the Black Dagger Brotherhood*, 2010

330

A.E. MOORAT

Queen Victoria, Demon Hunter

(London: Hodder and Stoughton, 2009)

Story type: Historical
Subject(s): Royalty; Demons; Adventure
Major character(s): Victoria, Royalty (Queen of England)
Time period(s): 19th century
Locale(s): United Kingdom

Summary: In A.E. Moorat's *Queen Victoria, Demon Hunter*, the legendary queen takes on bloodsuckers and ghouls in 19th-century England. After her coronation, Victoria learns that any number of demons is out to control the country—and it's up to her to stop them. Banding together with her group of trusted sidekicks, Victoria launches a campaign to save her nation from the onslaught of vampires, zombies, werewolves, and more. First novel.

Other books you might like:
P.N. Elrod, *Quincey Morris, Vampire*, 2001
Claudia Gabel, *Romeo and Juliet and Vampires*, 2010
Seth Grahame-Smith, *Abraham Lincoln: Vampire Hunter*, 2010
Sarah Gray, *Wuthering Bites*, 2010
Steve Hockensmith, *Pride and Prejudice and Zombies: Dawn of the Dreadfuls*, 2010

⬛ **331**

LISA MORTON

The Samhanach

(Garden Grove, California: Bad Moon Books, 2010)

Subject(s): Demons; Family history; Single parent family
Major character(s): Merran McCafferty, Single Mother; Samhanach, Demon
Time period(s): 21st century; 2010s

Summary: In *The Samhanach*, author Lisa Morton tells the terrifying tale of Merran McCafferty, a single mother whose Halloween plans are destroyed by the appearance of a centuries-old demon. But this isn't a run-of-the-mill spook; this demon has had his eyes on Merran's family for hundreds of years. And, this time, he's come for blood. This volume includes illustrations by Frank Walls.

Other books by the same author:
The Castle of Los Angeles, 2010
The Lucid Dreaming, 2009

Other books you might like:
Benjamin Kane Ethridge, *Black and Orange*, 2010
Richard Laymon, *All Hallow's Eve*, 1986
James A. Moore, *Harvest Moon*, 2006
Al Sarrantonio, *Horrorween*, 2006

⬛ **332**

VERA NAZARIAN
JANE AUSTEN, Co-Author

Mansfield Park and Mummies: Monster Mayhem, Matrimony, Ancient Curses, True Love, and Other Dire Delights

(Winnetka, California: Norilana Books, 2010)

Story type: Romance
Subject(s): Horror; Romances (Fiction); England
Major character(s): Fanny Price, Young Woman; Henry Crawford, Bachelor; Edmund, Cousin (of Fanny); Mrs. Norris, Aunt (of Fanny)
Time period(s): 19th century
Locale(s): England

Summary: In *Mansfield Park and Mummies: Monster Mayhem, Matrimony, Ancient Curses, True Love, and Other Dire Delights*, author Vera Nazarian puts an ancient Egyptian spin on Jane Austen's classic romance. In this adaptation, heroine Fanny Price attracts the affection of Henry Crawford as well as an Egyptian pharaoh, Aunt Norris has become a werewolf, and cousin Edmund is testing his skills as an exorcist. With its collection of Egyptian art and relics, this version of Mansfield Park has become a proper English haven for old spirits and young love. Footnotes and appendices guide readers through this humorous, historical parody.

Other books by the same author:
After the Sundial, 2010
The Duke in His Castle, 2008

Lords of the Rainbow, 2003
Dreams of the Compass Rose, 2002

Other books you might like:
Jane Austen, *Emma and the Vampires*, 2010
Charlotte Bronte, *Jane Slayre*, 2010
Porter Grand, *Little Women and Werewolves*, 2010
Adam Rann, *Emma and the Werewolves*, 2010
Lucy Weston, *The Secret History of Elizabeth Tudor, Vampire Slayer*, 2011

⬛ **333**

ANDREW NEWBOUND

Ghoul Strike!

(New York: The Chicken House, 2010)

Story type: Young Readers
Subject(s): Monsters; Adventure; Supernatural
Major character(s): Alannah Malarra, Psychic (ghost hunter), 12-Year-Old; Wortley, Sidekick (of Alannah)
Time period(s): 21st century; 2010s

Summary: Andrew Newbound's *Ghoul Strike!* follows the adventures of 12-year-old ghost expert Alannah and her trusty sidekick Wortley. During a routine ghost hunt, the two are shocked to find the house they are in is actually a gateway to other planes of existence. They soon learn the creatures that live on the other side are not intent on staying there, and now it's up to Alannah and Wortley to thwart the ghouls who are determined to take over the world.

Where it's reviewed:
School Library Journal, January 2011, page 113

Other books by the same author:
Demon Strike, 2010

Other books you might like:
Lynn Beach, *Curse of the Claw*, 1993
Bruce Coville, *Waiting Spirits*, 1984
David Lubar, *The Big Stink*, 2010
Christopher Pike, *Attack of the Killer Crabs*, 1997
R.L. Stine, *Escape from Horrorland*, 2009

⬛ **334**

ANDREW NEWBOUND

Demon Strike

(Somerset, U.K.: The Chicken House, 2010)

Story type: Contemporary
Subject(s): Horror; Demons; Ghosts
Major character(s): Alannah Malarra, 12-Year-Old, Psychic; Worley Flint, Thief; Flhi Swift, Inspector (police), Angel; Yell, Police Officer, Angel; Gloom, Police Officer, Angel
Time period(s): 21st century; 2010s
Locale(s): Earth

Summary: In *Demon Strike* by Andrew Newbound, a young clairvoyant finds herself at the center of a battle between the forces of heaven and hell. Evil spirits have found a path from the Dark Dimension through a wall into Pittingham Manor where they are discovered by 12-year-old Alannah Malarra. Alannah and her thieving friend Worley Flint are skilled at tracking greedy spirits but are unprepared for the demons that threaten them now. Luckily, Flhi Swift, an inspector from the angel police force, is on a scheduled visit to Earth and recruits angelic officers Yell and Gloom to join the fight against the invading demons. First novel.

Where it's reviewed:
Magpies, September 2010, page S36

Other books by the same author:
Ghoul Strike!, 2010

Other books you might like:
Lynn Beach, *Dead Man's Secret*, 1992
Bruce Coville, *Waiting Spirits*, 1984
David Lubar, *The Big Stink*, 2010
Christopher Pike, *Howling Ghost*, 1995
R.L. Stine, *My Friends Call Me Monster*, 2009

335

JONATHAN OLIVER

The End of the Line

(Nottingham, United Kingdom: Solaris, 2010)

Subject(s): Transportation; Terror; Short stories

Summary: In *The End of the Line*, editor Jonathan Oliver brings together a collection of "underground" horror tales written by both emerging and established authors of the genre. The pieces of this anthology are predominantly set in subway systems around the globe, from London to New York. Authors contributing to this volume include Christopher Fowler, Gary McMahon, and Mark Morris.

Other books you might like:
Christopher Fowler, *Roofworld*, 1988
Stephen Laws, *Ghost Train*, 1985
William F. Nolan, *Helltracks*, 2000
Douglas Preston, *Reliquary*, 1997
Kat Richardson, *Underground*, 2008

336

OTTO PENZLER

Fangs

(New York: Vintage, 2010)

Series: Vampire Archives Series. Book 2
Subject(s): Vampires; Terror; Short stories

Summary: The second installment in a series of short stories, *Fangs*, contains 20 tales of terror, gore, and bloodsucking mayhem. Anne Rice, Arthur Conan Doyle, H.P. Lovecraft, and Clive Barker are among the notable authors who contributed pieces to this collection. Editor Otto Penzler provides an introduction to the immortal adventures.

Other books by the same author:
Agents of Treachery, 2010

Blood Suckers, 2010
Christmas at the Mysterious Bookshop, 2010
The Black Lizard Big Book of Pulps, 2007
Dangerous Women, 2005

Other books you might like:
Mario Acevedo, *X-Rated Bloodsuckers*, 2006
Nina Bangs, *Wicked Nights*, 2005
Les Daniels, *No Blood Spilled*, 1991
P.N. Elrod, *Cold Streets*, 2003
Barbara Hambly, *Those Who Hunt the Night*, 1988

337

TIM PRATT

Sympathy for the Devil

(San Francisco: Nightshade Books, 2010)

Subject(s): Devil; Terror; Short stories

Summary: Editor Tim Pratt offers a volume of short stories centered around the Devil in all his forms. *Sympathy for the Devil* brings together 36 tales penned by some of literature's most esteemed authors. Pieces by modern maestros Stephen King, Michael Chabon, and Kage Baker are interspersed with classic works by Dante, Mark Twain, and Nathaniel Hawthorne. This wide-ranging anthology includes "The Bottle Imp," "The Man in the Black Suit," "The Professor's Teddy Bear," and excerpts from "The Inferno."

Where it's reviewed:
Library Journal, July 2010, page 75
Publishers Weekly, June 21, 2010, page 35

Other books by the same author:
The Strange Adventures of Rangergirl, 2005
Little Gods, 2003

Other books you might like:
Robert Bloch, *Hell on Earth*, 2000
John Collier, *Fancies and Goodnights*, 1951
William Hjortsberg, *Falling Angel*, 1978
Kelly Link, *Pretty Monsters: Stories*, 2008
China Mieville, *Looking for Jake*, 2005

338

ROBERT M. PRICE

The Tindalos Cycle

(New York: Hippocampus Press, 2010)

Subject(s): Poetry; Short stories

Summary: In *The Tindalos Cycle*, editor Robert M. Price brings together a collection of short fiction and poetry inspired by Frank Belknap Long's classic "The Hounds of Tindalos." The nearly 30 pieces of this volume continue Long's tradition and style, offering more entertaining adventures of the Cthulhu Mythos, an eerie alternative universe originally created by H.P. Lovecraft. Authors contributing to this collection include Ambrose Bierce, Ann K. Schwader, Michael Cisco, Adrian Cole, and Long himself.

Other books by the same author:
The Book of Eibon, 2002
Acolytes of Cthulhu, 2001
The Antarktos Cycle, 1999
The Cthulhu Cycle, 1996
The Azathoth Cycle, 1995

Other books you might like:
Robert Bloch, *Strange Eons*, 1978
Don D'Ammassa, *Servants of Chaos*, 2002
Frank Belknap Long, *The Hounds of Tindalos*, 1946
H.P. Lovecraft, *Necronomicon: The Best Weird Tales of H. P. Lovecraft*, 2008
William Browning Spencer, *Resume with Monsters*, 1995

339

ADAM RANN

Emma and the Werewolves

(Winnipeg, Manitoba, Canada: Coscom Entertainment, 2010)

Story type: Werewolf Story
Subject(s): Werewolves; Murder; Literature
Major character(s): Emma Woodhouse, Matchmaker; George Knightley, Wealthy, Werewolf
Time period(s): 19th century
Locale(s): Highbury, England

Summary: *Emma and the Werewolves* is author Adam Rann's paranormal twist on the classic story by Jane Austin. In this book, Emma Woodhouse is well on her way to being a successful matchmaker, but terror in her town of Highbury is hurting her business. Many young people have put thoughts of their love lives on hold and are focusing on a recent rash of grisly murders. A monster is brutally murdering townspeople and must be caught, but no one knows what type of creature they are up against. Emma suspects that Mr. Knightley, her neighbor and the owner of one of the estates where the murders have occurred, knows something about the mysterious murders. Mr. Knightley refuses to share his secrets with Emma, but he assures her that the death and destruction won't last much longer. Emma, however, isn't so sure.

Other books you might like:
Jane Austen, *Emma and the Vampires*, 2010
Porter Grand, *Little Women and Werewolves*, 2010
Vera Nazarian, *Mansfield Park and Mummies: Monster Mayhem, Matrimony, Ancient Curses, True Love, and Other Dire Delights*, 2010
Leo Tolstoy, *Android Karenina*, 2010

340

MICHELLE ROWEN

Something Wicked

(New York: Berkley, 2010)

Series: Living in Eden Series. Book 2
Story type: Romantic Suspense

Subject(s): Demons; Supernatural; Romances (Fiction)
Major character(s): Eden Riley, Supernatural Being (possessed); Darrak, Demon
Time period(s): 21st century; 2010s
Locale(s): United States

Summary: *Something Wicked* is a supernatural thriller from author Michelle Rowen. The book is the second installment in the Living in Eden series. Because of a curse, Eden Riley has been possessed by a demon named Darrak and she doesn't know what to do about it. The situation is made worse when Eden's psychic abilities give Darrak the ability to take physical form during the day and Eden is dangerously attracted to him. Unfortunately, the curse stipulates the only way to find freedom is for one of them to die. With their newfound attraction and affection for one another, the pair must work together to break the curse and spare their lives.

Other books by the same author:
The Demon in Me, 2010
Stakes & Stilletos, 2009
Lady and the Vamp, 2008
Fanged and Fabulous, 2007
Bitten & Smitten, 2006

Other books you might like:
Michele Bardsley, *Over My Dead Body*, 2009
Dakota Cassidy, *Accidentally Dead*, 2008
Alyssa Day, *Atlantis Unmasked*, 2009
Lynn Viehl, *Evermore*, 2008
Christine Warren, *Howl at the Moon*, 2007

341

JAIME RUSH

Touching Darkness

(New York: Avon, 2010)

Series: Offspring Series. Book 3
Story type: Romance
Subject(s): Supernatural; Love; Psychics
Major character(s): Nicholas Braden, Psychic; Olivia, Assistant (of Darkwell); Darkwell, Employer (of Nicholas and Olivia)
Time period(s): 21st century; 2010s
Locale(s): United States

Summary: *Touching Darkness* is the third novel in Jaime Rush's Offspring series. This paranormal romance tells the story of psychically gifted Nicholas Braden, who is hired by the government to work on a top-secret project aimed at nabbing terrorists. His superior, Darkwell, is an unusual figure, and Darkwell's assignments impel him into increasingly dangerous and bizarre situations. Darkwell's beautiful assistant, Olivia, is working closely with Nicholas, and the sparks are soon flying between the two. As the two follow their hearts and give into passion, they begin to question the intentions of their assignment—and their boss.

Other books by the same author:
Out of the Darkness, 2009
A Perfect Darkness, 2009

Other books you might like:
Christina Dodd, *Touch of Darkness*, 2007

Allyson James, *Firewalker*, 2010
Lynsay Sands, *The Immortal Hunter*, 2009
Kerrelyn Sparks, *Secret Life of a Vampire*, 2009
Lynn Viehl, *Dreamveil: A Novel of the Kyndred*, 2010

342

CAROL SERLING

More Stories from the Twilight Zone

(New York: Tor, 2010)

Subject(s): Fantasy; Television programs; Short stories

Summary: When *The Twilight Zone* first debuted on television, it set an all-new standard for the term "creepy." Now, in *More Stories from the Twilight Zone*, editor Carol Serling—widow of the show's creator—presents a collection of short stories that continue the tradition set forth by the iconic television program. These 19 tales touch upon several eerie aspects of the supernatural, including futuristic societies, psychic abilities, and soul-snatching. Authors contributing to this volume include John Farris, David Black, Jean Rabe, and M. Tara Crowl.

Other books by the same author:
Journeys to the Twilight Zone, 2003
Adventures in the Twilight Zone, 1995
Return to the Twilight Zone, 1994

Other books you might like:
Charles Beaumont, *A Touch of the Creature*, 1999
Peter Crowther, *Lonesome Roads*, 1999
John Farris, *Elvisland*, 2004
Richard Matheson, *Bloodlines*, 2006
Kristine Kathryn Rusch, *The Devil's Churn*, 1996

343

DARREN SHAN

Procession of the Dead

(Glasgow: HarperVoyager, 2008)

Series: City Trilogy. Book 1
Subject(s): Gangs; Urban life; Crime
Major character(s): Capac Raimi, Young Man; the Cardinal, Leader; Uncle Theo, Uncle (of Capac), Gang Member
Time period(s): Indeterminate
Locale(s): The City, Fictional Location

Summary: *Procession of the Dead* is the first book in The City Trilogy by D.B. Shan (otherwise known as Darren Shan). The publishers of the book have billed it as a "noirish, gritty urban fantasy for adults." It takes readers to the stark, brutal world of the City. A young man named Capac Raimi comes to the City to seek his future and fortune. Under the guidance of his uncle, Capac enters into the underworld of the City and begins learning the finer points of gangster activities. All is going well until he meets the Cardinal. The Cardinal is like the beating heart of the City, and he controls all of the power. As

Capac is drawn further into the Cardinal's circle of influence, his thirst for power increases, making him question his own morals and wonder how far he is really willing to go. As Capac enmeshes himself in the inner workings of the City, he learns the price that he will have to pay for his ambition.

Other books by the same author:
A Living Nightmare, 2009
Death's Shadow, 2008
Demon Apocalypse, 2008
Bec, 2006
Demon Thief, 2006

Other books you might like:
James Herbert, *Once*, 2002
Joe R. Lansdale, *The Drive-In (a B-Movie with Blood and Popcorn, Made in Texas)*, 1988
Edward Lee, *City Infernal*, 2001
Graham Masterton, *Mirror*, 1988
Robert R. McCammon, *Usher's Passing*, 1984

344

HARRY SHANNON

A Host of Shadows

(Colusa, California: Dark Regions Press, 2010)

Subject(s): Fear; Suspense; Short stories

Summary: In *A Host of Shadows*, Harry Shannon presents a collection of short horror fiction written with the author's trademark style and flair for the macabre. The 25 stories of this volume encompass a spectrum of psychologically terrifying scenarios, featuring indelible characters and bone-chilling situations. This collection includes an introduction by author Rick Hautula.

Other books by the same author:
Daemon, 2008
Dead and Gone, 2008
One of the Wicked, 2008
Memorial Day, 2004
Night of the Beast, 2002

Other books you might like:
Dennis Etchison, *Fine Cuts*, 2004
Rick Hautala, *Four Octobers*, 2006
Brian Keene, *Unhappy Endings*, 2009
Scott Nicholson, *Scattered Ashes*, 2008
David J. Schow, *Havoc Swims Jaded*, 2006

345

DAN SIMMONS

Black Hills

(New York: Reagan Arthur Book/Little, Brown and Company, 2010)

Subject(s): Native Americans; United States history; Ghosts
Major character(s): Paha Sapa, Indian, Psychic
Time period(s): 19th century-20th century; 1870s-1930s
Locale(s): United States

Summary: In *Black Hills*, acclaimed author Dan Simmons crafts a tale of supernatural suspense and Native American history. After General Custer is killed at Little Big Horn, his ghost inhabits the body of a Sioux boy named Paha Sapa. The story follows Paha Sapa as he comes of age, witnessing the birth of the American West and the dying of the Native American way of life. The action culminates in Paha Sapa's plans to detonate Mount Rushmore in honor of President Roosevelt's visit to the historic landmark in 1936.

Where it's reviewed:
Booklist, February 1, 2010, page 25
Entertainment Weekly, February 26. 2010, page 77
Kirkus Reviews, January 1, 2010, page 63
Publishers Weekly, December 21, 2009, page 35

Other books by the same author:
Drood: A Novel, 2009
The Terror, 2007
Ilium, 2003
A Winter Haunting, 2002
Darwin's Blade, 2000
Fires of Eden, 1994
Lovedeath, 1993
Summer of Night, 1991

Other books you might like:
Charles de Lint, *Trader*, 1997
Stephen Dedman, *The Art of Arrow Cutting*, 1997
Stephen Gallagher, *Valley of Lights*, 1987
James Herbert, *Fluke*, 1977
David Seltzer, *Prophecy*, 1979

346

BRYAN SMITH

The Killing Kind
(New York: Leisure Books, 2010)

Subject(s): Students; Violence; Suspense
Major character(s): Robert, Murderer; Roxie, Murderer; Julie Cosgrove, Murderer; Zeb, Murderer
Time period(s): 21st century; 2010s
Locale(s): Myrtle Beach, South Carolina

Summary: Bryan Smith's *The Killing Kind* takes place at an ocean-side rental home in Myrtle Beach, South Carolina, where a group of college friends is throwing a days-long bash in celebration of spring break. What they don't know is that a band of crazed, otherworldly killers is about to make sure their party ends a bit earlier than expected.

Other books by the same author:
Depraved, 2009
Soultaker, 2009
Queen of Blood, 2008
The Freakshow, 2007
Deathbringer, 2006

Other books you might like:
Brian Keene, *Urban Gothic*, 2009
Dean R. Koontz, *Intensity*, 1995
Richard Laymon, *Once upon a Halloween*, 2000

Edward Lee, *Creekers*, 1994
John Saul, *Black Lightning*, 1995

347

MATTHEW SMITH
AL EWING, Co-Author
REBECCA LEVENE, Co-Author

The Best of Tomes of the Dead
(Nottingham, United Kingdom: Abaddon, 2010)

Subject(s): Zombies; Terror; Short stories
Summary: In *The Best of Tomes of the Dead*, authors Matthew Smith, Al Ewing, and Rebecca Levene present an anthology of zombie-themed short fiction. The stories that comprise this volume offer a multifaceted glimpse into the adventures of the undead as they roam the earth, hungry for flesh and retribution. Stories previously appearing in *The Words of Their Roaring*, *I Zombie*, and *Anno Mortis* are collected in this single volume.

Other books you might like:
Amelia Beamer, *The Loving Dead*, 2010
J.L. Bourne, *Day By Day Armageddon*, 2007
Gary Brandner, *Carrion*, 1986
Joe McKinney, *Apocalypse of the Dead*, 2010
Kim Paffenroth, *Dying to Live: A Novel of Life Among the Undead*, 2008

348

JEANNE C. STEIN

Chosen
(New York: Penguin, 2010)

Series: Anna Strong Series. Book 6
Story type: Paranormal; Series
Subject(s): Horror; Parapsychology; Romances (Fiction)
Major character(s): Anna Strong, Bounty Hunter, Vampire; Warren Williams, Police Officer (chief, former)
Time period(s): 21st century; 2010s
Locale(s): United States

Summary: In *Chosen* by Jeanne Stein, a bounty hunter-turned-vampire deals with her emerging impulses and threats to her life. Anna Strong was transformed into a vampire when she was attacked one night a year ago by an unseen assailant. Though she has adapted to her new existence, she is increasingly troubled by instincts that continue to reveal themselves. When Anna is the target of a failed murder attempt, she must find out who wants her dead and why. As the chosen savior of the mortal and undead realms, Anna's life must be preserved. *Chosen* is the sixth book in the Anna Strong Chronicles series.

Other books by the same author:
Retribution, 2009
Legacy, 2008
The Watcher, 2007
The Becoming, 2006
Blood Drive, 2006

Horror

Other books you might like:
Karen Chance, *Claimed by Shadow*, 2007
Yasmine Galenorn, *Bone Magic*, 2010
Chris Marie Green, *Break of Dawn*, 2008
Charlaine Harris, *A Touch of Dead: Sookie Stackhouse: The Complete Stories*, 2009
Kat Richardson, *Vanished*, 2009

349

JOHN RICHARD STEPHENS

The Book of the Living Dead

(New York: Berkley, 2010)

Subject(s): Terror; Fear; Short stories

Summary: In *The Book of the Living Dead*, editor John Richard Stephens compiles a collection of traditional horror tales written by some of the genre's best-loved authors. Edgar Allan Poe, Mary Shelley, H.P. Lovecraft, Guy de Maupassant, Jack London, Mark Twain, and William Butler Yeats are among the acclaimed authors whose short stories appear in this volume. The pieces gathered here offer unparalleled insight into the roots of modern horror storytelling and showcase both the famous and little-known works of various masters of the craft.

Other books you might like:
Amelia Beamer, *The Loving Dead*, 2010
J.L. Bourne, *Day by Day Armageddon: Beyond Exile*, 2010
Jonathan Maberry, *The Dragon Factory*, 2010
Kim Paffenroth, *Dying to Live: A Novel of Life Among the Undead*, 2008
Joan Frances Turner, *Dust*, 2010

350

R.L. STINE

The Wizard of Ooze

(New York: Scholastic, 2010)

Series: HorrorLand Series. Book 17
Story type: Young Readers
Subject(s): Comic books; Adventure; Suspense
Major character(s): Marco Gonzales, Friend (of Gabriella); Gabriella Smith, Friend (of Marco)
Time period(s): 21st century; 2010s
Locale(s): United States

Summary: The 17th installment in R.L. Stine's Goosebumps HorrorLand series, *The Wizard of Ooze*, follows the adventures of Marco Gonzales and Gabriella Smith, two young friends who come upon a highly coveted edition of a popular comic book. Their acquisition of the comic makes them the envy of fellow collectors—so much so that Marco and Gabriella find themselves on the run from comic book enthusiasts who are out to nab their precious copy. If only Marco could find a way to harness the same superhuman powers as the comic's hero.

Where it's reviewed:
Owl, October 2010, page 38

Other books by the same author:
Heads, You Lose!, 2010
Escape from Horrorland, 2009
Say Cheese and Die Screaming, 2009
Little Camp of Horrors, 2004
One Night in Doom House, 2004

Other books you might like:
Tony Abbott, *Bayou Dogs*, 2009
M.T. Coffin, *Curse of the Cheerleaders*, 1997
Damien Graves, *The Catch*, 2007
Christopher Pike, *The Evil House*, 1997
Tom B. Stone, *Don't Tell Mummy*, 1997

351

R.L. STINE

Slappy New Year

(New York: HarperCollins Children's Books, 2010)

Series: HorrorLand Series. Book 3
Story type: Young Readers
Subject(s): Ventriloquism; Fear; Adventure
Major character(s): Slappy, Toy (dummy)
Time period(s): 21st century; 2000s
Locale(s): United States

Summary: *Slappy New Year*, the third volume in R.L. Stine's HorrorLand series, centers on Slappy the Dummy. Slappy springs to life after hearing a particularly ominous chant, and he sets out to terrorize the young people around him—just in time for the New Year celebration.

Other books by the same author:
Help! We Have Strange Powers, 2009
My Friends Call Me Monster, 2009
Monster Blood for Breakfast, 2008
Freaks and Shrieks, 2005
Don't Forget Me, 2000

Other books you might like:
Tony Abbott, *The Ghost Road*, 2009
M.T. Coffin, *Camp Crocodile*, 1997
Damien Graves, *End Game*, 2005
Christopher Pike, *The Haunted Cave*, 1995
Tom B. Stone, *The Spider Beside Her*, 1999

352

S.A. SWANN

Wolf's Cross

(New York: Spectra/Ballantine Books, 2010)

Story type: Historical
Subject(s): Werewolves; Fantasy; Monks
Major character(s): Maria, Servant, 16-Year-Old, Werewolf; Darien, Werewolf; Josef, Religious (monk)
Time period(s): 14th century; 1350s (1353)
Locale(s): Poland

Summary: In *Wolf's Cross*, author S.A. Swann offers a sequel to 2009's *Wolfbreed*. This episode is set in 14th-century Poland, where teenage servant girl, Maria is looking after a monk who has been injured in a werewolf attack. But when fate introduces her to werewolf Darien, Maria's long-hidden birthright is finally revealed to her: She, too, is a member of the wolfbreed. Now Maria's loyalties are divided between the monk she pines for and the wolf who is her destiny.

Where it's reviewed:
Booklist, July 1, 2010, page 43
Library Journal, May 15, 2010, page 71
Publishers Weekly, June 14, 2010, page 39

Other books by the same author:
Wolfbreed, 2009
The Dwarves of Whiskey Island, 2005
Broken Crescent, 2004
The Dragons of Cuyahoga, 2001
Fearful Symmetries, 1999

Other books you might like:
Keri Arthur, *Full Moon Rising*, 2006
Crosland Brown, *Tombley's Walk*, 1991
Michael Cadnum, *Saint Peter's Wolf*, 1991
Nancy A. Collins, *Walking Wolf*, 1995
Charles L. Grant, *The Dark Cry of the Moon*, 1986

353

DIANNE SYLVAN

Queen of Shadows

(New York: Penguin, 2010)

Series: Shadow World Series. Book 1
Story type: Contemporary; Series
Subject(s): Horror; Fantasy; Parapsychology
Major character(s): Miranda Grey, Musician, Psychic; David Solomon, Vampire
Time period(s): 21st century; 2010s
Locale(s): Austin, Texas

Summary: In *Queen of Shadows* by Dianne Sylvan, an Austin musician with psychic powers finds an unlikely mentor in a southern vampire lord. Miranda Grey knows that her music possesses a supernatural quality that affects her audiences, but she doesn't know how to direct it. The strength of her skills becomes evident when she kills the men who rape her by controlling their thoughts. When vampire leader David Solomon takes an interest in Miranda, a romance grows between them. Meanwhile, David deals with the growing strife among his vampire underlings. *Queen of Shadows* is the first novel in the Shadow World series. First novel

Other books you might like:
Patricia Briggs, *Blood Bound*, 2007
Shannon Drake, *Realm of Shadows*, 2002
Susan Krinard, *Chasing Midnight*, 2007
Marjorie M. Liu, *A Wild Light*, 2010
Susan Sizemore, *I Thirst for You*, 2004

354

TERENCE TAYLOR

Blood Pressure

(New York: St. Martin's Griffin, 2010)

Series: Vampire Testament Series. Book 2
Subject(s): Vampires; Interpersonal relations; Love
Major character(s): Christopher Jude Miller, Young Man; Joie, Young Woman
Time period(s): 21st century; 2000s
Locale(s): New York, New York

Summary: Christopher Miller has an ability that makes him startlingly unique; he can cure vampires of their immortality. After arriving in New York, he meets Joie, a beautiful young woman who possesses the same hidden talent. With vampires running rampant, a government organization is intent on getting rid of the creatures once and for all. When Christopher and Joie join forces, their powers are extraordinary, and before long they are questioning the true intentions of the government's vampire-hunting organization. *Blood Pressure* is the second novel in Terence Taylor's Vampire Testament series.

Where it's reviewed:
Publishers Weekly, February 1, 2010, page 37

Other books by the same author:
Bite Marks, 2009

Other books you might like:
Stephen Dedman, *Shadows Bite*, 2002
Stephen King, *Salem's Lot*, 1975
Robert R. McCammon, *They Thirst*, 1981
Judith Reeves-Stevens, *Nightfeeder*, 1991
Lucius Shepard, *The Golden*, 1993

355

JEFFREY THOMAS

Nocturnal Emissions

(Colusa, California: Dark Regions Press, 2010)

Subject(s): Fantasy; Science fiction; Short stories

Summary: In *Nocturnal Emissions*, author Jeffrey Thomas presents a collection of original stories, novellas, and poems. From extraterrestrials to bloodsucking sea creatures, from evil puppets to plague-riddled humans, the topics covered in these works run the gamut from fantasy and sci-fi to straight-out horror. Titles in this volume include "The Night Swimmers," "Godhead Dying Downwards," and "The Possessed."

Where it's reviewed:
Publishers Weekly, August 30, 2010, page 35

Other books by the same author:
Thirteen Specimens, 2008
Doomsdays, 2007
The Dream Dealers, 2006
Terra Incognita, 2000
Avatars of the Old Ones, 1999

Other books you might like:
Gary A. Braunbeck, *Destinations Unknown*, 2006
Dennis Etchison, *The Death Artist*, 2000
Brian Keene, *Unhappy Endings*, 2009
Tim Lebbon, *As the Sun Goes Down*, 2000
Harry Shannon, *A Host of Shadows*, 2010

356

JONATHAN THOMAS

Tempting Providence and Other Stories

(New York: Hippocampus Press, 2010)

Story type: Collection
Subject(s): Horror; Short stories

Summary: In *Tempting Providence and Other Stories*, horror writer Jonathan Thomas presents a collection of 12 short stories. "Tempting Providence" explores strange doings from the past and present that transpire in Providence, Rhode Island. Also set in Providence are a tale about a "Lord of the Animals" with an affinity for communicating with a variety of creatures and the story of a music-obsessed man's search for a hard-to-find vinyl LP. Thomas is also the author of *Midnight Call and Other Stories* (2008). Horror author Sherry Austin provides the book's foreword.

Other books by the same author:
Midnight Call and Other Stories, 2008
Stories from the Big Black House', 1992

Other books you might like:
Gary A. Braunbeck, *Things Left Behind*, 1997
Tim Lebbon, *Fears Unnamed*, 2004
H.P. Lovecraft, *Necronomicon: The Best Weird Tales of H. P. Lovecraft*, 2008
Alan Ryan, *The Bones Wizard*, 1988
Scott Thomas, *The Garden of Ghosts*, 2008

357

LEO TOLSTOY
BEN H. WINTER, Co-Author

Android Karenina

(Philadelphia, Pennsylvania: Quirk Books, 2010)

Subject(s): Literature; Robots; Alternative worlds
Time period(s): 19th century; 1800s
Locale(s): Russia

Summary: What if one of Leo Tolstoy's most celebrated novels was set in an alternate reality, where robots reign supreme? In *Android Karenina*, author Ben H. Winter takes Tolstoy's master literary work and turns it on its head by adding robot maids and butlers, evil scientists, half-android love interests, aliens, and more. Winter writes *Android Karenina* in the steam punk tradition, which messes the anachronistic with the historical, and reworks a classic by an author who was best known for his realistic elements.

Where it's reviewed:
Booklist, June 1, 2010, page 4

Other books by the same author:
Sense and Sensibility and Sea Monsters, 2010

Other books you might like:
Jane Austen, *Emma and the Vampires*, 2010
Charlotte Bronte, *Jane Slayre*, 2010
Porter Grand, *Little Women and Werewolves*, 2010
Vera Nazarian, *Mansfield Park and Mummies: Monster Mayhem, Matrimony, Ancient Curses, True Love, and Other Dire Delights*, 2010
Adam Rann, *Emma and the Werewolves*, 2010

358

MARIE TREANOR

Blood on Silk

(New York: Signet Eclipse, 2010)

Series: Awakened by Blood Series. Book 1
Story type: Contemporary
Subject(s): Vampires; Scots (British people); Erotica
Major character(s): Elizabeth Silk, Student—Graduate; Saloman, Vampire
Time period(s): 21st century; 2010s
Locale(s): Scotland

Summary: Elizabeth Silk is working on her PhD thesis about vampire lore when she opens the door to a dangerous world—and an irresistible vamp named Saloman. Elizabeth's studying inadvertently brings Saloman into her life, and she is simultaneously repulsed and fascinated by the immortal bloodsucker. Even the aid of a group of vampire hunters can't help Elizabeth get Salmon—or his seductive powers—out of her head. Marie Treanor's *Blood on Silk* is the first novel in the Awakened by Blood series.

Where it's reviewed:
Publishers Weekly, July 19, 2010, page 117

Other books by the same author:
The Devil and Via, 2009
Gothic Dragon, 2009
Magic Man, 2009

Other books you might like:
J.K. Beck, *When Wicked Craves*, 2010
Heidi Betts, *The Bite Before Christmas*, 2010
Katie MacAlister, *In the Company of Vampires*, 2010
Chloe Neill, *Twice Bitten*, 2010
Maggie Shayne, *Lover's Bite*, 2008

359

JOAN FRANCES TURNER

Dust

(New York: Ace Books, 2010)

Story type: Contemporary
Subject(s): Zombies; Gangs; Diseases
Major character(s): Jessica "Jessie" Anne Porter,

Reanimated Dead (zombie), 15-Year-Old
Time period(s): 21st century; 2010s
Locale(s): Illinois, United States

Summary: In Joan Frances Turner's *Dust*, Jessica "Jessie" Porter, a 15-year-old zombie, is part of a rambunctious gang of the undead. But there is an evil lurking on the horizon: an illness that could spell the end of zombies and humans alike. Now it's up to Jessie to rally her strength and prevent the advance of a terrifying disease. First novel.

Where it's reviewed:
Booklist, September 1, 2010, page 55
Publishers Weekly, July 26, 2010, page 57

Other books you might like:
Bob Fingerman, *Pariah*, 2010
Brian Keene, *The Rising*, 2003
Joe McKinney, *Dead City*, 2006
Jeffrey Sackett, *Candlemas Eve*, 1988
David Wellington, *Monster Island*, 2006

360

TIM WAGGONER

Nekropolis

(Nottingham, United Kingdom: Angry Robot, 2010)

Series: Matt Richter Series. Book 1
Subject(s): Zombies; Vampires; Detective fiction
Major character(s): Matt Richter, Reanimated Dead (zombie), Detective—Private
Time period(s): 21st century; 2010s
Locale(s): Nekropolis, Fictional Location

Summary: Matt Richter isn't a typical private detective; he's a zombie. Matt patrols the streets of Nekropolis, a city populated by the souls of the dead. For centuries, vampires have been controlling the region, but recently the bloodsuckers' intentions have turned ever sinister. Now it's up to Matt to protect Nekropolis from the evil plans being hatched by the immortal overlords. *Nekropolis* is the first book in Tim Waggoner's Matt Richter series.

Where it's reviewed:
Publishers Weekly, November 9, 2009, page 35

Other books by the same author:
Darkness Wakes, 2006
Pandora Drive, 2006
Like Death, 2005
Protege, 2005
Gangrel, 2004

Other books you might like:
Mario Acevedo, *The Nymphos of Rocky Flats*, 2006
P.N. Elrod, *Lady Crymsyn*, 2000
Tanya Huff, *Blood Debt*, 1997
Lee Killough, *Blood Hunt*, 1987
S.A. Swiniarski, *Blood and Rust*, 2007

361

DAVID WELLINGTON

Overwinter: A Werewolf Tale

(New York: Three Rivers Press, 2010)

Story type: Contemporary
Subject(s): Werewolves; Adventure; Fear
Major character(s): Cheyenne "Chey" Clark, Werewolf; Powell, Werewolf
Time period(s): 21st century; 2010s
Locale(s): Arctic Circle

Summary: Set in the frigid reaches of the Arctic Circle, David Wellington's *Overwinter: A Werewolf Tale* follows Cheyenne "Chey" Clark and her cohort Powell as they attempt to track down a cure for their lycanthropic condition. Their journey, however, is not a smooth one. Werewolf hunters are on their track, but Chey and Powell's innate sense of disgust for all things human keep them on top of their game. Chey is desperate to find a cure for her unusual affliction, and time is working against her. With each passing hour, she slowly becomes more and more werewolf and less and less human. *Overwinter* is the sequel to *Frostbite*.

Other books by the same author:
23 Hours, 2009
Frostbite: A Werewolf Tale, 2009
99 Coffins, 2007
13 Bullets, 2006
Monster Island, 2006

Other books you might like:
Ray Garton, *Bestial*, 2009
Dean R. Koontz, *Midnight*, 1989
Jeffrey Sackett, *Mark of the Werewolf*, 1990
Thomas Tessier, *The Nightwalker*, 1979
Leslie H. Whitten, *Moon of the Wolf*, 1967

362

DAN WELLS

Mr. Monster

(New York: Tor, 2010)

Story type: Young Adult
Subject(s): Demons; Supernatural; Good and evil
Major character(s): John Wayne Cleaver, Teenager
Time period(s): 21st century; 2010s
Locale(s): Clayton County, United States

Summary: Dan Wells's *Mr. Monster*, the sequel to 2010's *I Am Not a Serial Killer*, finds teenager John Wayne Cleaver taking on a new supernatural enemy. As John tries to curb his own appetite for violence and mayhem, a demon has been unleashed on Clayton County. And John may be the only one with the chutzpah—and the demonic power—to take on the evil face to face.

Horror

Where it's reviewed:
Publishers Weekly, August 30, 2010, page 35
School Library Journal, November 2010, page 132

Other books by the same author:
I Am Not a Serial Killer, 2010

Other books you might like:
John Farris, *The Axman Cometh*, 1989
Kim Harrison, *The Good, the Bad, and the Undead*, 2005
Stephen King, *It*, 1986
Joe R. Lansdale, *Lost Echoes*, 2007
Graham Masterton, *A Terrible Beauty*, 2003

363

CONNIE CORCORAN WILSON

Hellfire and Damnation

(Cedar Rapids, Iowa: Sam's Dot Publishing, 2010)

Subject(s): Fear; Terror; Short stories

Summary: In *Hellfire and Damnation*, author Connie Corcoran Wilson presents a series of short stories based on the concepts set forth by Dante's classic work, "The Inferno." Drawn from both imaginative setups and real-life situations, the tales of this volume run the gamut of human emotion, from fear and psychological terror to the poignant and powerful.

Other books by the same author:
Ghostly Tales of Rout 66 Arkansas to Arizona, 2009
Both Sides Now, 2003

Other books you might like:
Jim Cain, *Hard Boiled Vampire Killers*, 2010
Richard Gavin, *Charnel Wine*, 2010
Paul Melniczek, *Monsters*, 2010
Harry Shannon, *A Host of Shadows*, 2010
Jeffrey Thomas, *Avatars of the Old Ones*, 1999

364

F. PAUL WILSON

Fatal Error

(New York: Tor, 2010)

Series: Repairman Jack Series. Book 14
Story type: Supernatural Vengeance
Subject(s): Horror; Supernatural; Good and evil
Major character(s): Jack, Repairman (supernatural); Munir Habib, Crime Victim; Dawn Pickering, Mother
Time period(s): 21st century; 2010s
Locale(s): United States
Summary: *Fatal Error* is a supernatural horror novel from bestselling author F. Paul Wilson. The book is the 14th installment in the Repairman Jack series about a man's quest to save Earth from evil forces. Repairman Jack has been tasked with protecting the Lady, the Earth's consciousness, from the Order of Septimus and their occult force known as the Otherness. Jack agrees to take on a case with Munir Habib, a man who has been threatened about going to the police to report his family's kidnapping. Jack is convinced that Munir's family is connected with a new wicked plot by the Order of Septimus. When Dawn Pickering's horrific newborn baby is taken away from her, she suspects someone—or something—evil is at work. Jack agrees, realizing the cases are connected.

Where it's reviewed:
Publishers Weekly, August 30, 2010, page 28

Other books by the same author:
Aftershocks & Others: 19 Oddities, 2009
Ground Zero, 2009
By the Sword, 2008
Bloodline, 2007
All the Rage, 2000
Conspiracies, 2000
Legacies, 1998
The Tomb, 1984

Other books you might like:
James Blish, *Black Easter*, 1968
Dean R. Koontz, *Fear Nothing*, 1998
Robert R. McCammon, *Mystery Walk*, 1983
John Shirley, *Demons*, 2002
Dennis Wheatley, *The Devil Rides Out*, 1935

The Mystery Genre in 2011: Embracing the Electronic
by
Clair Lamb, for Bookreporter.com

The mystery world's biggest news in Spring 2011 may have been bestselling novelist Barry Eisler's announcement that he was walking away from a "major" handshake deal with a mainstream publisher, St. Martin's, to self-publish his own books electronically.

Eisler described the decision in a conversation with self-publishing guru Joe Konrath on Konrath's blog in March:

"My wife and daughter and I were sitting around the dinner table, talking about what kind of contract I would do next, and with what publisher. And my then eleven-year-old daughter said, Daddy, why don't you just self-publish?

"And I thought, wow, no one would have said something like that even a year ago . . . But I realized from that one innocent comment from my daughter that the new generation was looking at self-publishing differently. And that the question—"Should I self-publish?"—was going to be asked by more and more authors going forward. And that, over time, more and more of them were going to be answering the question, Yes.

"Paper is dying while digital is exploding," Eisler added.

Is paper dying? Is digital exploding? And what does that mean for mystery novels, in particular?

The Association of American Publishers (AAP) announced on April 14th that sales of e-books had tripled between February 2010 and February 2011. Sales of e-books are now higher than sales of any other format of books, outpacing paperbacks for the first time. So yes, it would appear that digital publishing is exploding. Does it follow, then, that paper is dying, as vinyl died in the music business and VCR tapes disappeared from the video industry?

Not yet, says Tom Allen, President and CEO of AAP. While sales of e-books surged by 202.3 percent between February 2010 and February 2011, sales of traditionally published books (hardcover, paperback, and mass market) declined by 34.4 percent. New revenue from e-books did not offset the lost revenue from the decline in traditionally published books, but because e-books tend to be priced well below hardcovers (and in many cases even below mass market books), the trends suggest that the appetite for books among readers remains unchanged, or might even be growing.

Lee Goldberg, author of a series of mystery novels based on the "Monk" television series, as well as an earlier series based on "Diagnosis: Murder" and several standalone novels, sees e-publishing as a natural fit for the type of books that used to be published as "pulp fiction." Between June 2009 and February 2010, he republished his back catalog of out-of-print titles—nine novels and two nonfiction books. Earlier this year, Goldberg estimated that he would sell 3,100 copies of his previously out-of-print books in electronic format on Amazon alone.

Announcing his plan to self-publish his next book electronically, Goldberg wrote, "The Kindle offers mid-list writers a real option to consider before they sign their next . . . contract extension . . . and it has given new opportunity to every mid-list author who has been dropped." Meanwhile, Goldberg has joined forces with a cadre of acclaimed mystery, horror, and Western novelists on The Dead Man, a series of short novels to be published in electronic format, in the tradition of 1940s-era pulp fiction. Nine titles have already been introduced, from authors including David McAfee, James Reasoner, Jude Hardin, Harry Shannon, Mel Odom, Burl Barer, William Rabkin, and Goldberg himself.

Mystery veterans Lise McClendon and Katy Munger have launched Thalia Press, an independent electronic publisher that will start publishing new short story collections in late 2011, in addition to bringing out-of-print titles back into print in electronic format. Thalia's books will be available in print format for order by bookstores, but the primarily electronic platform supports the press's credo: "Not all books need appeal to the masses." Thalia focuses on crime, contemporary fiction, and women's fiction, beginning with McClendon and Munger's own out-of-print titles but looking to expand to include other authors as well.

Whereas most traditional publishers are now offering new titles simultaneously in print and electronic format, some have been curiously slow to reissue out-of-print titles in electronic format, and none has yet announced plans to publish new titles in electronic format only. This seems likely to change, with speculation that Little Brown's new imprint, Mulholland Books, will be the first to embrace an electronic-only model—in addition to the books they plan to publish in traditional print formats.

The surge in e-books in the first quarter of 2011 happened simultaneously with the closure and restructuring of two major bookstore chains: Borders, which closed more than 200 stores nationwide; and the smaller Midwestern chain Joseph-Beth, which closed four stores and will auction off its remaining five stores. Whether those stores will continue to operate or be closed remains unclear. One of the nation's oldest and most prominent independent mystery bookstores, Los Angeles's Mystery Bookstore, closed its doors at the end of January, although San Diego's Mysterious Galaxy will open a second location in Redondo Beach, California, this summer.

Amidst the turmoil, mystery lovers can still count on some things. Mary Higgins Clark published her 43rd book, *I'll Walk Alone,* on April 5th, and has plans to publish two more books before the end of the year; all seem guaranteed to be bestsellers. Stuart Woods's 46th novel, *Bel-Air Dead,* is also out this month, with the 47th, *Son of Stone,* due in September. Michael Connelly's fourth Mickey Haller novel, *The Fifth Witness,* currently stands atop bestseller lists, cheek by jowl with new titles from Harlan Coben (*Live Wire,* the 10th Myron Bolitar novel) and Lisa Scottoline (*Save Me*). Lee Child's 15th Jack Reacher novel, *Worth Dying For,* is due on April 26th. James Patterson's 10th Women's Murder Club mystery, co-written with Maxine Paetro, will be out on May 2nd. All of these books will be published the old-fashioned way, in hardcover—although the first 30 chapters of Patterson and Paetro's book have been available as a free electronic download since early March.

Perhaps most interesting, mystery fiction's institutions have not yet come to grips with electronic-only publishing. Active membership in the Mystery Writers of America, which bestows the industry's Edgar Awards, requires that authors of books have been "paid at least 1,000 dollars in advances, royalties, or a combination of advances and royalties" by an approved publisher, with an initial print run of at least 500 copies for book-length works of fiction or nonfiction. (Screenwriters are eligible for MWA membership under separate guidelines). Making the list of approved publishers requires the publishers to make these initial print runs of at least 500 copies "widely available in brick-and-mortar stores (not "special order" titles). In other words, print-on-demand publishers and Internet-only publishers do *not* qualify." Books published in electronic format only are not currently eligible for Edgar Awards.

It remains to be seen, furthermore, what impact the surge in publishing and republishing electronic titles will have on the publishing of new mystery titles in print. The most recent data available from Bowker show a 15 percent drop in the number of general fiction titles published between 2008 and 2009, from 53,058 to 45,181—but that 2009 figure is still 80 percent higher than the 25,102 fiction titles published in 2002. The adoption of new media and new publishing strategies seem to mean more titles available in absolute terms, meaning more choices for readers in content as well as format.

Mystery Fiction

365

CATHERINE AIRD (Pseudonym of Kinn Hamilton McIntosh)

Past Tense

(New York: Minotaur Books, 2011)

Series: Inspector Sloan Series. Book 23
Story type: Police Procedural
Subject(s): Mystery; Murder; Detective fiction
Major character(s): Sloan, Detective; Crosby, Detective
Time period(s): 21st century; 2010s
Locale(s): England

Summary: *Past Tense*, a suspenseful police procedural, is the 23rd installment in the Sloan and Crosby Mystery series from author Catherine Aird. When a lonely, elderly woman dies in a nursing home, her great-nephew, who never knew her, organizes the funeral to which there are few attendees, including a mysterious man claiming to be a grandson of the deceased. A few days later, the late elderly woman's room at the Berebury Nursing Home is vandalized and a young woman who attended the funeral is found murdered in the river. Detective Inspector Sloan and his pal, Detective Constable Crosby, team up to uncover the truth behind the young woman's murder and the elderly lady's life, finding a shocking connection between the two.

Where it's reviewed:
Publishers Weekly, Dec. 20, 2010, page 37

Other books by the same author:
Losing Ground, 2007
The Religious Body, 1996
A Late Phoenix, 1970
The Complete Steel, 1969
Henrietta Who?, 1968

Other books you might like:
Deborah Crombie, *A Share in Death*, 1993
Christopher Fowler, *Full Dark House*, 2003
Elizabeth George, *A Great Deliverance*, 1988
Ann Granger, *Mud, Muck and Dead Things*, 2009
Ann Granger, *Say It with Poison*, 1991

366

BARBARA ALLAN

Antiques Knock-Off

(New York: Kensington Publishing Corp., 2011)

Series: Trash 'n' Treasures Series. Book 5
Story type: Contemporary; Series
Subject(s): Mystery; Crime; Antiques
Major character(s): Brandy Borne, Antiques Dealer; Vivian, Mother (of Brandy); Tony Cassato, Police Officer (chief)
Time period(s): 21st century; 2010s
Locale(s): Serenity, United States

Summary: In *Antiques Knock-Off* by Barbara Allan, the Midwest town of Serenity is shocked by the murder of one of its nosiest residents, Connie Grimes. Vivian Borne—the mentally ill mother of the town's antique dealer, Brandy Borne—admits to the crime and is quickly jailed. Despite the fact that her mother had means and motive, Brandy knows that Vivian is innocent. Incarcerated with a collection of real criminals, Vivian makes friends as Brandy (a seven-months-pregnant surrogate mother) tries to find the real killer with help from her police-chief boyfriend. *Antiques Knock-Off* is the fifth book in the Trash 'n' Treasures series.

Where it's reviewed:
Publishers Weekly, Jan. 24, 2011, page 135

Other books by the same author:
Antiques Bizarre, 2010
Antiques Flee Market, 2008
Antiques Maul, 2007
Antiques Roadkill, 2006

Other books you might like:
Mary Kay Andrews, *Savannah Blues*, 2002
Jane K. Cleland, *Consigned to Death*, 2006
Sharon Fiffer, *Killer Stuff*, 2001
Jonathan Gash, *The Judas Pair*, 1977
Susan Holtzer, *Something to Kill For*, 1994

367

SUSANNE ALLEYN

Palace of Justice

(New York: Minotaur Books, 2010)

Series: Aristide Ravel Series. Book 4
Story type: Historical - French Revolution
Subject(s): Detective fiction; Serial murders; French Revolution, 1789
Major character(s): Aristide Ravel, Detective
Time period(s): 18th century; 1790s
Locale(s): Paris, France

Summary: The city of Paris is in an uproar. The King is dead, and Marie-Antoinette is about to be tried in court. As the drama of the Revolution plays out, one madman is exerting his own type of perverted vigilante justice on the innocent men and women of Paris. Now it's up to detective Aristide Ravel to thwart a psychopath's plans for destroying the City of Light. *Palace of Justice* is the fourth novel in Susanne Alleyn's Aristide Ravel series.

Where it's reviewed:
Booklist, December 1, 2010, page 31
Houston Chronicle, December 19, 2010, page 16
Library Journal, December 2010, page 91
Publishers Weekly, October 4, 2010, page 30

Other books by the same author:
The Cavalier of the Apocalypse, 2009
A Treasury of Regrets, 2007
Game of Patience, 2006
A Far Better Rest, 2000

Other books you might like:
Louis Bayard, *The Black Tower*, 2008
C.S. Harris, *What Angels Fear*, 2005
Charles O'Brien, *Mute Witness*, 2001
Baroness Emma Orczy, *The Scarlet Pimpernel*, 1905
Dan Simmons, *Drood: A Novel*, 2008

368

MARK ALPERT

The Omega Theory

(New York: Touchstone, 2011)

Story type: Child-in-Peril; Psychological Suspense
Subject(s): Kidnapping; Missing persons; Science
Major character(s): Michael Gupta, Adoptee (of David and Monique); Monique Reynolds, Scientist (physicist), Spouse (of David), Mother (adoptive, of Michael); David Swift, Scientist, Historian, Spouse (of Monique), Father (adoptive, of Michael)

Summary: *The Omega Theory* is the sequel to author Mark Alpert's novel *Final Theory*, which introduced readers to scientific historian David Swift. In this novel, Swift and his wife Monique must track down their kidnapped son Michael. Michael, who is autistic, has memorized Einstein's unified field theory—a theory that cult leaders see as a crucial key to their plot for heavenly glory. As David and Monique try to find the cult that has taken Michael,

they learn more and more about the cult's plans—and realize that its success could destroy the entire Universe.

Where it's reviewed:
Booklist, Jan. 1, 2011, page 50
Publishers Weekly, Dec. 13, 2010, page 36

Other books by the same author:
Final Theory: A Novel, 2008

Other books you might like:
Steve Berry, *The Templar Legacy*, 2006
Chris Kuzneski, *Secret Crown*, 2010
Douglas Preston, *Blasphemy*, 2008
Matthew Reilly, *Ice Station*, 1999
James Rollins, *Sandstorm*, 2004

369

DAVID ANTHONY

Something for Nothing

(New York: Algonquin Books, 2011)

Story type: Contemporary
Subject(s): Economic depressions; Drugs; Law
Major character(s): Martin Anderson, Pilot, Dealer (airplane dealer); Val Desmond, Horse Trainer
Time period(s): 20th century; 1970s (1974)
Locale(s): Oakland, California

Summary: In *Something for Nothing*, author David Anthony tells the story of Martin Anderson, an airplane dealer who was living high on the hog until the economic recession of the 1970s. When he was flush, he spent his money on fancy cars, a luxurious swimming pool, and most of all a stable of racing horses. Now broke and facing bankruptcy, not to mention the unraveling of his marriage and family, Martin is desperate. That's when his horse trainer, Val, comes to him with an offer he can't refuse: use his planes to transport drugs across the border from Mexico. Now Martin is struggling to keep up with his creditors and keep his family together, but will discovery of his illegal operation bust everything apart?

Other books you might like:
Lou Berney, *Gutshot Straight*, 2010
Martin Clark, *The Many Aspects of Mobile Home Living*, 2000
Harry Dolan, *Bad Things Happen*, 2009
Sean Doolittle, *The Cleanup*, 2006
Don Winslow, *The Death and Life of Bobby Z*, 1997

370

WAYNE ARTHURSON

Fall from Grace

(New York: Tom Doherty Associates LLC, 2011)

Story type: Serial Killer
Subject(s): Native Americans; Prostitution; Murder
Major character(s): Leo Desroches, Journalist
Locale(s): Edmonton, Alberta

Summary: *Fall from Grace* is the debut novel from author and journalist, Wayne Arthurson. Canadian newspaper reporter Leo Desroches is surprised when he arrives on the scene of a dead Native prostitute, only to be told by the police that he may investigate the girl's death as much as he'd like. The more Leo digs into the mystery surrounding the prostitute's death the more he sees signs pointing to a serial killer at work, yet when he reveals his conclusions to the cops, they brush off his findings. Does the Edmonton police department, the very people who should be investigating the murder, have a larger role in the prostitute's death? Leo must find out before the serial killer strikes again. First book.

Where it's reviewed:
Publishers Weekly, Feb. 7, 2011, page 37

Other books by the same author:
Final Season, 2002

Other books you might like:
Giles Blunt, *Forty Words for Sorrow*, 2001
Margaret Coel, *The Eagle Catcher*, 1995
Sean Doolittle, *The Cleanup*, 2006
James D. Doss, *The Shaman Sings*, 1994
Louise Penny, *The Brutal Telling*, 2009

371

NANCY ATHERTON

Aunt Dimity and the Family Tree

(New York: Viking, 2011)

Series: Aunt Dimity Series. Book 16
Story type: Cozy Mystery; Paranormal
Subject(s): Mystery; Parapsychology; Haunted houses
Major character(s): Lori Shepard, Mother, Detective—Amateur, Psychic; Dimity, Aunt, Spirit, Detective; William Willis Sr., Lawyer, Retiree, Wealthy, Father (in-law to Lori)
Time period(s): 21st century; 2010s
Locale(s): Finch, England

Summary: *Aunt Dimity and the Family Tree*, a paranormal cozy mystery, is the 16th installment in the best-selling Aunt Dimity series from author Nancy Atherton. After an adventurous tour of Australia, Lori Shephard has returned to her quiet life in the Cotswolds, but things get turned upside down once again for the amateur detective when her wealthy father-in-law purchases a nearby estate. William Sr., recently retired from managing the family law firm, has decided to settle down in the village of Finch to be near his son, daughter-in-law, and grandchildren. As Lori helps William renovate his new home, she notices strange behavior in the aged estate, like moving furniture and eerie sounds. Determined to find the cause of the spooky happenings and out of answers, Lori channels the otherworldly Aunt Dimity for help on the case.

Where it's reviewed:
Publishers Weekly, December 13, 2010, page 40

Other books by the same author:
Aunt Dimity Down Under, 2010
Aunt Dimity Digs In, 1998
Aunt Dimity's Good Deed, 1996

Aunt Dimity and the Duke, 1994
Aunt Dimity's Death, 1992

Other books you might like:
Sneaky Pie Brown, *Wish You Were Here*, 1990
Carolyn G. Hart, *Ghost at Work: A Mystery*, 2008
Sue Ann Jaffarian, *Ghost a la Mode*, 2009
Maggie Sefton, *Knit One, Kill Two*, 2005
Thorne Smith, *Topper*, 1926

372

MICHAEL AYOOB

In Search of Mercy

(New York: Minotaur Books, 2010)

Story type: Contemporary
Subject(s): Detective fiction; Missing persons; Alcoholism
Major character(s): Dexter Bolzjak, Detective—Amateur; Lou Kashon, Alcoholic; Mercy Carnahan, Actress
Time period(s): 21st century; 2010s
Locale(s): Pittsburgh, Pennsylvania

Summary: Dexter Bolzjak was once a popular high-school athlete who is now struggling with mental illness while working a low-paying job in a warehouse. He soon meets Lou Kashon, an alcoholic who offers Dexter a tidy sum of cash to track down a missing starlet who hasn't been seen in half a century. Dexter's investigation leads him into a terrifying new terrain that challenges both his talent and his sanity. Michael Ayoob's *In Search of Mercy* was awarded the Private Eye Writers of America Best First Private Eye Novel prize. First novel.

Where it's reviewed:
Booklist, September 1, 2010, page 50
Publishers Weekly, August 16, 2010, page 37

Other books you might like:
Richard Aleas, *Little Girl Lost*, 2004
Lawrence Block, *Mona*, 1961
Bryan Gruley, *Starvation Lake*, 2009
Duane Swierczynski, *Expiration Date*, 2010
Edward Wright, *While I Disappear*, 2004

373

SANDRA BALZO

A Cup of Jo

(Surrey, United Kingdom: Severn House Publishers, 2010)

Series: Maggy Thorsen Series. Book 6
Story type: Contemporary
Subject(s): Detective fiction; Murder; Suspense
Major character(s): Maggy Thorsen, Businesswoman, Detective—Amateur; Jake Pavlik, Police Officer (sheriff), Boyfriend (of Maggy); JoLynne Penn-Williams, Crime Victim
Time period(s): 21st century; 2010s
Locale(s): Brookhills, Wisconsin

Summary: In Brookhills, Wisconsin, Maggy Thorsen is thrilled that she is finally able to reopen her coffee shop

Mystery

after it was leveled by a near-catastrophic blizzard. The grand reopening is planned to occur in tandem with the unveiling of a new railway line between Milwaukee and Brookhills, but the event turns decidedly bitter when a body is found during the festivities. Maggy launches her own investigation into the murder, which seems to have one prime suspect: Maggy's boyfriend, sheriff Jake Pavlik. *A Cup of Jo* is the sixth book in Sandra Balzo's Maggy Thorsen Mysteries.

Where it's reviewed:
Booklist, September 1, 2010, page 49
Publishers Weekly, August 16, 2010, page 39

Other books by the same author:
From the Grounds Up, 2010
Brewed, Crude and Tattooed, 2009
Bean There, Done That, 2008
Grounds for Murder, 2008
Uncommon Grounds, 2004

Other books you might like:
Lorna Barrett, *Murder Is Binding*, 2008
Jessica Beck, *Glazed Murder: A Donut Shop Mystery*, 2010
Laura Childs, *Death by Darjeeling*, 2001
Laura Childs, *Eggs in Purgatory*, 2008
Cleo Coyle, *On What Grounds*, 2003

374

MAGGIE BARBIERI

Third Degree

(New York: Minotaur Books, 2011)

Series: Murder 101 Series. Book 5
Story type: Amateur Detective; Cozy Mystery
Subject(s): Teachers; Murder; Mystery
Major character(s): Alison Bergeron, Professor, Detective—Amateur; Bobby Crawford, Detective, Boyfriend (of Alison)
Time period(s): 21st century; 2010s
Locale(s): New York, United States

Summary: *Third Degree* is the fifth book in the Murder 101 series, following the adventures of New York English professor and sometimes sleuth, Alison Bergeron. It's a big moment in the relationship of Alison and her NYPD detective boyfriend, Bobby Crawford. He's just proposed, she hasn't answered, and they're going to meet his parents. En route to the meeting, Alison stops for a coffee and witnesses a fatal fistfight between a local blogger and his enemy. The case seems straightforward, especially since Alison witnessed the entire assault, but things are never as easy as they seem. When Alison's car explodes moments later, she begins to suspect the incidents are connected and someone has planned the attacks very carefully.

Where it's reviewed:
Publishers Weekly, October 11, 2010, page 29

Other books by the same author:
Final Exam, 2010
Quick Study, 2008

Extracurricular Activities, 2007
Murder 101, 2006

Other books you might like:
J.S. Borthwick, *The Case of the Hook-Billed Kites*, 1982
Gail Bowen, *Deadly Appearances*, 1990
Sarah Caudwell, *Thus Was Adonis Murdered*, 1981
Bill Crider, *Murder Is an Art*, 1999
Amanda Cross, *Death in a Tenured Position*, 1981

375

JEFFERSON BASS

The Bone Yard

(New York: William Morrow, 2011)

Series: Body Farm Series. Book 6
Story type: Police Procedural
Subject(s): Suspense; Mystery; Murder
Major character(s): Dr. Bill Brockton, Researcher, Detective (forensic); Angie St. Claire, Researcher (forensic analyst)
Time period(s): 21st century; 2010s
Locale(s): Florida, United States

Summary: *The Bone Yard* is a forensic mystery novel from best-selling author, Jefferson Bass. The book is the sixth installment in the Body Farm series following the harrowing adventures of Dr. Bill Brockton, a forensic expert specializing in the study of decomposing human bodies. Brockton agrees to travel to Florida to help a fellow forensic analyst, Angie St. Claire, with a personal investigation. Their case leads them to something much bigger and more sinister when they discover the skulls of two young boys and a decades-old diary. The clues lead them to the site of North Florida Boys' Reformatory, a juvenile detention center that burned to the ground four decades prior. Using the diary as their guide, Brockton and St. Claire discover a grave of adolescent human remains known as the Bone Yard. As the investigation heats up, Brockton meets strong opposition from local authorities who seem desperate to keep the secrets of the past buried in the Bone Yard.

Other books by the same author:
The Bone Thief, 2010
Bones of Betrayal, 2009
The Devil's Bones, 2008
Flesh and Bone, 2007
Carved in Bone, 2006

Other books you might like:
Patricia Cornwell, *Postmortem*, 1990
Kathryn Fox, *Malicious Intent*, 2006
Tess Gerritsen, *Harvest*, 1996
Paul Lindsay, *Witness to the Truth*, 1992
Kathy Reichs, *Deja Dead*, 1997

376

LOUIS BAYARD

The School of Night

(New York: Henry Holt and Company, 2011)

Story type: Historical
Subject(s): Mystery; History; Academia
Major character(s): Henry Cavendish, Scholar; Bernard Styles, Antiquarian; Clarissa Dale, Assistant (to Henry)
Time period(s): 21st century; (2010s); 16th century
Locale(s): England; Washington, District of Columbia

Summary: In the late 1500s, the School of Night, a group of five academics, would hold clandestine meetings to discuss religion, politics, science, and magic. For fear of punishment by the Queen, the club was a secret, but one of the members, Thomas Harriot, shared this secret and many more with his servant and lover. In present-day Washington DC, a sinister antiquarian, Bernard Styles, hires Henry Cavendish, a student of Elizabethan culture, to track down a missing letter that had been stolen by the now-deceased Alonzo Wax. As Henry begins his quest, accompanied by the mysterious Clarissa Dale, he learns that many others are seeking the letter as well, hoping to use its contents to uncover a hidden treasure and an ancient alchemy formula.

Where it's reviewed:
Booklist, January 1, 2011, page 52
Library Journal, December 2010, page 99
Publishers Weekly, February 7, 2011, page 35

Other books by the same author:
The Black Tower, 2008
The Pale Blue Eye, 2007
Mr. Timothy, 2003
Endangered Species, 2001
Fool's Errand, 1999

Other books you might like:
Dan Brown, *The Da Vinci Code*, 2003
Ian Caldwell, *The Rule of Four*, 2004
Deborah Harkness, *A Discovery of Witches*, 2011
Katherine Neville, *The Eight*, 1988
Douglas Preston, *Thunderhead*, 1999

377

SEAN BEAUDOIN

You Killed Wesley Payne

(New York: Little, Brown, 2011)

Story type: Amateur Detective; Young Adult
Subject(s): Mystery; Murder; Detective fiction
Major character(s): Dalton Rev, 17-Year-Old, Student—High School, Detective—Amateur; Macy Payne, Student—High School, Client (of Dalton), Crime Victim
Time period(s): 21st century; 2010s
Locale(s): United States

Summary: *You Killed Wesley Payne* is a humorous mystery novel for young adult readers from author Sean Beaudoin. Seventeen-year-old amateur detective Dalton Rev can't refuse the opportunity to investigate a murder, especially not when the inquiry comes from an adorable classmate like Macy Payne. Macy wants Dalton to find out who's responsible for killing her brother and affixing his body to the football goalposts with duct tape. Dalton, following cues by his fictional sleuthing hero, Lexington Cole, throws himself into the investigation, viewing every pupil at Salt River High as a possible suspect. Dalton makes his way through the school's many cliques (outlined and flowcharted in the book's introduction) in hopes of catching the killer and getting the girl.

378

ALEX BERENSON

The Secret Soldier

(New York: Penguin USA, 2011)

Series: John Wells Series. Book 5
Subject(s): Espionage; Terrorism; Muslims
Major character(s): John Wells, Spy; Brett Gaffan, Spy; Abdullah bin Abdul-Aziz, Royalty, Brother (of Saaed); Saaed bin Abdul-Aziz, Brother (of Abdullah bin Abdul-Aziz)
Locale(s): Saudi Arabia

Summary: *The Secret Soldier* is the fifth installment in Alex Berenson's John Wells series of novels. In this book, Wells has left the CIA and is working for himself. He takes on an assignment for the king of Saudi Arabia, who needs Wells to find out if his brother is trying to overthrow him. Meanwhile, King Abdullah bin Abdul-Aziz's brother, Saaed, plots to begin a war that will tear the Middle East apart. Can Wells and his partner, Brett, stop the king's brother in time to save the world? Berenson is also the author of *The Faithful Spy*, *The Ghost War*, and *The Midnight House*.

Where it's reviewed:
Library Journal, Feb. 15, 2011, page 100

Other books by the same author:
The Midnight House, 2010
The Silent Man, 2009
The Ghost War, 2008
The Faithful Spy, 2006
The Number, 2003

Other books you might like:
Noah Boyd, *The Bricklayer*, 2010
Vince Flynn, *Transfer of Power*, 1999
Mike Lawson, *The Second Perimeter*, 2006
Gene Riehl, *Sleeper*, 2005
Daniel Silva, *The Kill Artist*, 2000

379

MARK BILLINGHAM

Bloodline

(Toronto, Ontario, Canada: McArthur and Co, 2009)

Series: Tom Thorne Series. Book 8
Story type: Contemporary

Subject(s): Serial murders; Detective fiction; Suspense
Major character(s): Tom Thorne, Detective—Police
Time period(s): 21st century; 2000s
Locale(s): London, United Kingdom

Summary: The eighth book in Mark Billingham's Tom Thorne mystery series, *Bloodline* finds Thorne following the tracks of a ruthless serial killer. After investigating a routine murder scene, Thorne finds the shard of an x-ray clasped in the hand of the victim. This clue convinces Thorne that the case he's dealing with is far from routine. After some probing, he comes to learn that the victim was the daughter of a woman who was killed 15 years ago by serial murder Raymond Garvey. And now someone is out to kill the children of Garvey's victims. Each new murder brings another scrap of x-ray, and Thorne is working against the clock to put the pieces of this mysterious puzzle together before the killer strikes again.

Other books by the same author:
Death Message, 2007
The Burning Girl, 2005
Lazybones, 2004
Scaredy Cat, 2003
Sleepyhead, 2002

Other books you might like:
John Harvey, *Lonely Hearts*, 1989
Peter James, *Dead Simple*, 2006
Ian Rankin, *Strip Jack*, 1992
Peter Robinson, *Gallows View*, 1987
Martyn Waites, *The Mercy Seat*, 2006

380

CARA BLACK

Murder in Passy

(New York: Soho Press, 2011)

Series: Aimee Leduc Series. Book 11
Story type: Private Detective
Subject(s): Detective fiction; French (European people); Murder
Major character(s): Aimee Leduc, Investigator, Detective—Private; Morbier, Godfather (of Aimee), Crime Suspect, Boyfriend (of Xavierre), Police Officer; Xavierre, Girlfriend (of Morbier), Crime Victim
Time period(s): 21st century; 2010s
Locale(s): Paris, France

Summary: *Murder in Passy*, a murder mystery, is the eleventh installment in the Aimee Leduc series from author Cara Black. Parisian Private Investigator Aimee Leduc pays a visit to Passy, a posh and affluent Paris neighborhood, at the request of her godfather, Police Commissaire Morbier. Morbier asks Aimee to check on his girlfriend Xavierre, but moments after Aimee arrives, Xavierre is strangled to death in the garden while an unknowing Aimee waits inside. The initial evidence points to Morbier, much to Aimee's disbelief and dismay. Certain that her godfather is innocent, Aimee sets out on her own private investigation to find the real killer and exonerate Morbier's name.

Where it's reviewed:
Publishers Weekly, January 24, 2011, page 134

Other books by the same author:
Murder in the Palais Royal, 2010
Murder in the Bastille, 2003
Murder in the Sentier, 2002
Murder in Belleville, 2000
Murder in the Marais, 1998

Other books you might like:
Linda Barnes, *A Trouble of Fools*, 1987
Donna Leon, *Death at La Fenice*, 1992
Marcia Muller, *Edwin of the Iron Shoes: A Novel of Suspense*, 1977
Georges Simenon, *The Crime of Inspector Maigret*, 1932
Fred Vargas, *The Chalk Circle Man*, 2009

381

LISA BLACK

Trail of Blood

(New York: William Morrow, 2010)

Series: Theresa MacLean Series. Book 3
Story type: Contemporary
Subject(s): Serial murders; Suspense; Detective fiction
Major character(s): Theresa MacLean, Scientist (forensic), Detective; James Miller, Detective—Police, Crime Victim; Kim Hammond, Prostitute, Crime Victim
Time period(s): 21st century; 2010s
Locale(s): Cleveland, Ohio

Summary: Lisa Black's novel *Trail of Blood* follows forensic scientist Theresa MacLean as she investigates the grisly murder of a local police detective. Theresa is called in to help investigate the death of police detective James Miller, whose body is dismembered. The horrible crime reminds Theresa of the stories her grandfather told her about a serial killer who stalked the area 75 years earlier and was never identified. During her investigation, Theresa learns that Miller was investigating that very cold case when he was killed. Now, with the appearance of another maimed body, Theresa wonders if she's dealing with a copycat murderer. This volume is the third installment in the Theresa MacLean series.

Where it's reviewed:
Booklist, July 1, 2010, page 9
Library Journal, August 2010, page 65
Publishers Weekly, July 12, 2010, page 26

Other books by the same author:
Evidence of Murder, 2009
Takeover, 2008

Other books you might like:
Robin Burcell, *The Face of a Killer*, 2008
Kathryn Fox, *Malicious Intent*, 2006
Tess Gerritsen, *The Surgeon*, 2001

382

LAWRENCE BLOCK

A Drop of the Hard Stuff

(New York: Mulholland Books, 2010)

Series: Matthew Scudder Series. Book 17
Story type: Contemporary
Subject(s): Alcoholism; Detective fiction; Friendship
Major character(s): Matthew Scudder, Detective—Private; "High-Low" Jack Ellery, Crime Victim, Friend (of Scudder)
Time period(s): 21st century; 2010s
Locale(s): New York, New York

Summary: The 17th novel in Lawrence Block's Matthew Scudder series, *A Drop of the Hard Stuff* finds Matthew living a newly sober life. As he navigates the world without drink for the first time in decades, he is shocked when a blast from the past—the hard-drinking "High-Low" Jack Ellery—reenters his life. Scudder decides to help Ellery get his life back in order, but, unfortunately, that life is cut short when Ellery is murdered. Now Scudder is on the trail for a killer, not only threatening his newfound sobriety—but also his life.

Where it's reviewed:
Library Journal, Jan. 2011, page 80

Other books by the same author:
All the Flowers are Dying, 2005
Hit Man, 1998
Burglars Can't Be Choosers, 1977
The Sins of the Fathers, 1976
The Thief Who Couldn't Sleep, 1966

Other books you might like:
Richard Barre, *The Innocents*, 1995
Michael Harvey, *The Chicago Way*, 2007
Robert B. Parker, *The Godwulf Manuscript*, 1973
S.J. Rozan, *China Trade*, 1994
Peter Spiegelman, *Black Maps*, 2003

383

RHYS BOWEN

Bless the Bride

(New York: Minotaur Books, 2011)

Series: Molly Murphy Series. Book 10
Story type: Historical; Series
Subject(s): Mystery; Detective fiction; Irish Americans
Major character(s): Molly Murphy, Detective—Private; Daniel Sullivan, Police Officer (NYPD captain), Fiance(e) (of Molly); Lee Sing Tai, Businessman
Time period(s): 20th century; 1900s (1903)
Locale(s): New York, New York

Summary: In *Bless the Bride* by Rhys Bowen, Molly Murphy's approaching marriage to Daniel Sullivan—Captain of the New York Police Department—may mean the end of her career as a private detective. Though she told her husband-to-be that her crime-solving days will end once they are married, Molly gets drawn into another case even as she prepares her trousseau. Lee Sing Tai, a Chinese businessman, needs her assistance in tracking down a piece of jade and his new wife. When Lee dies under suspicious circumstances, Molly hunts for his killer as well. *Bless the Bride* is the tenth book in the Molly Murphy series.

Where it's reviewed:
Booklist, February 1, 2011, page 34

Other books by the same author:
The Last Illusion, 2010
In Like Flynn, 2005
For the Love of Mike, 2003
Death of Riley, 2002
Murphy's Law, 2001

Other books you might like:
Carola Dunn, *Death at Wentwater Court*, 1994
C.S. Harris, *What Angels Fear*, 2005
Carol McCleary, *The Alchemy of Murder*, 2010
Stefanie Pintoff, *In the Shadow of Gotham*, 2009
Victoria Thompson, *Murder on Astor Place*, 1999

384

C.J. BOX

Cold Wind

(New York: G. P. Putnam's Sons, 2011)

Series: Joe Pickett Series. Book 11
Story type: Contemporary; Series
Subject(s): Mystery; Detective fiction; Murder
Major character(s): Joe Pickett, Government Official (game warden); Marybeth, Spouse (of Joe); Missy Alden, Mother (of Marybeth); Earl Alden, Spouse (of Missy); Kyle McLanahan, Lawman (sheriff); Lisa Rich, Lawyer; Nate Romanowski, Friend (of Joe)
Time period(s): 21st century; 2010s
Locale(s): Twelve Sleep County, Wyoming

Summary: In *Cold Wind* by C.J. Box, the discovery of a dead body hanging from a wind turbine attracts the attention of the Twelve Sleep County sheriff and attorney. Though both Kyle McLanahan and Lisa Rich believe that Missy Alden is likely the murderer of her husband Earl, Joe Pickett—Wyoming game warden, amateur detective, and son-in-law of Missy—has his doubts. Though he has no affection for his wife's mother, Joe can't accept the theory that 60-something Missy could lift Earl's corpse up the turbine. Joe needs his friend Nate's assistance, but Nate is on the run from a woman who wants him dead. *Cold Wind* is the 11th book in the Joe Pickett series.

Where it's reviewed:
Booklist, February 15, 2011, page 54
Publishers Weekly, January 31, 2011, page 29

Other books by the same author:
Nowhere to Run, 2010
Trophy Hunt, 2004
Winterkill, 2003
Savage Run, 2002
Open Season, 2001

Mystery

Other books you might like:
Lori Armstrong, *No Mercy*, 2009
Nevada Barr, *High Country*, 2004
Craig Johnson, *The Cold Dish*, 2005
William Kent Krueger, *Iron Lake*, 1998
Lise McClendon, *The Bluejay Shaman*, 1994

385

NOAH BOYD

Agent X

(New York: William Morrow Publishers, 2011)

Series: Steve Vail Series. Book 2
Story type: Espionage
Subject(s): Russians; Espionage; Political crimes
Major character(s): Steve Vail, Agent (former); Kate Bannon, Agent (assistant director)

Summary: *Agent X* is the sequel to author Noah Boyd's 2009 novel *The Bricklayer* featuring former FBI agent Steve Vail. In this novel, Vail has returned to D.C. to accompany his sweetheart, Kate Bannon, to an embassy party. As assistant director to the FBI, Kate is the first to be contacted when a member from the Russian embassy announces he will reveal the names of American double agents who are spying for the Russian government. Soon, the Russian is whisked away to Moscow, and Kate and Vail suspect a leak in FBI intelligence. Can they get to the Russian before the enemies do?

Where it's reviewed:
Library Journal, February 1, 2011, page 50

Other books by the same author:
The Bricklayer, 2010

Other books you might like:
Alex Berenson, *The Faithful Spy*, 2006
Vince Flynn, *Transfer of Power*, 1999
Mike Lawson, *The Second Perimeter*, 2006
Gene Riehl, *Sleeper*, 2005
Daniel Silva, *The Kill Artist*, 2000

386

SARAH BRAUNSTEIN

The Sweet Relief of Missing Children

(New York: W.W. Norton & Co., 2011)

Story type: Psychological
Subject(s): Suspense; Mystery; Psychology
Major character(s): Leonora, 12-Year-Old, Kidnap Victim; Paul, 16-Year-Old, Runaway; Judith, Teenager, Runaway
Time period(s): 21st century; 2010s
Locale(s): United States

Summary: In *The Sweet Relief of Missing Children*, author Sarah Braunstein chronicles the lives of three young people who go missing under different circumstances. Leonora is just 12 when she is kidnapped on the street by a stranger pretending to need help. As Leonora's family searches desperately for her, she learns that she must abandon her well-mannered demeanor if she is to survive. Though Paul, 16, willingly runs away from his dysfunctional family, his life situation improves little as he wanders through young adulthood with no direction. Party girl Judith's quest for a good time leads her to a sleazy life of abuse and disillusionment. First novel.

Where it's reviewed:
Booklist, Dec. 1, 2010, page 28
Library Journal, Dec. 2010, page 99

Other books you might like:
Laura Benedict, *Calling Mr. Lonely Hearts: A Novel*, 2008
Gillian Flynn, *Dark Places*, 2009
Heather Gudenkauf, *The Weight of Silence: A Novel*, 2009
John Hart, *The Last Child*, 2009
Donna Tartt, *The Little Friend*, 2002

387

ALLISON BRENNAN

Love Me to Death

(New York: Ballantine Books, 2010)

Story type: Contemporary
Subject(s): Crime; Suspense; Love
Major character(s): Lucy Kincaid, Crime Victim; Sean Rogan, Detective—Private
Time period(s): 21st century; 2010s
Locale(s): United States

Summary: Allison Brennan's *Love Me to Death* tells the story of Lucy Kincaid, a young woman intent on ridding the world of online predators. Lucy herself survived a particularly brutal attack by one such predator, who ended up dead, and now she spends her days helping law enforcement officers nab other cyber criminals. But when the men she's luring into the arms of the law start being killed, suspicion is cast on Lucy. Private eye Sean Rogan just might be the only one who can help her maintain her innocence—and help her learn to trust men again.

Where it's reviewed:
Library Journal, June 15, 2010, page S17
Publishers Weekly, November 8, 2010, page 48

Other books by the same author:
Carnal Sin, 2010
Original Sin, 2010
Cutting Edge, 2009
Fatal Secrets, 2009
Sudden Death, 2009

Other books you might like:
Peter Abrahams, *End of Story*, 2006
Dianne Emley, *The First Cut: A Novel*, 2006
Lisa Gardner, *Alone*, 2005
Tess Gerritsen, *The Surgeon*, 2001
Cody McFadyen, *Shadow Man*, 2006

388

P.J. BROOKE

A Darker Night

(London: Soho Constable, 2010)

Series: Max Romero Series. Book 2
Story type: Contemporary
Subject(s): Detective fiction; Murder; Romanies
Major character(s): Max Romero, Detective—Police;
Paco, Gypsy, Crime Victim
Time period(s): 21st century; 2010s
Locale(s): Grenada

Summary: P.J. Brooke's *A Darker Night* is the second novel in the Max Romero series, set in modern-day Grenada and featuring the adventures of a resolute yet sensitive police detective. This installment finds Max investigating the murder of a man who had recently been released from prison for killing his wife. The man was a gypsy, and the rest of the police department couldn't be less interested in taking on the case. But Max is determined to find justice for the dead man—even if that means being unpopular with his colleagues. His investigation into the gypsy's death soon leads him into a dark world of religion, money, and conspiracy.

Where it's reviewed:
New York Times Book Review, October 3, 2010, page 34

Other books by the same author:
Blood Wedding, 2008

Other books you might like:
Andrea Camilleri, *The Shape of Water*, 2002
Roderic Jeffries, *Unseemly End*, 1981
Donna Leon, *Death at La Fenice*, 1992
Rebecca Pawel, *Death of a Nationalist*, 2003
Robert Wilson, *The Blind Man of Seville*, 2003

389

MARY BURTON

Senseless

(New York: Kensington Publishers, 2010)

Story type: Romantic Suspense; Serial Killer
Subject(s): Serial murders; Mystery; Romances (Fiction)
Major character(s): Eva Rayburn, Crime Suspect, Crime Victim, Prisoner (former); Deacon Garrison, Detective
Time period(s): 21st century; 2010s
Locale(s): Virginia, United States

Summary: Ten years ago, Eva Rayburn was partying with her sorority sisters at the end of another school year when their fun-filled night turned dark and terrifying. After spending a decade in prison, Eva has returned to her childhood hometown in Virginia to discover that the nightmare of the past is far from over. A serial killer is on the loose, branding his victims with a star before stabbing them in the heart. The circumstances of the murders are too reminiscent of that fateful night ten years ago and each of the victims is somehow connected to Eva. The detective assigned to the case, Deacon Gar-

rison, tries to ignore his attraction to Eva long enough to decide if she's a suspect or a target.

Where it's reviewed:
Library Journal, October 1, 2010, page 65

Other books by the same author:
Dying Scream, 2009
Dead Ringer, 2008
I'm Watching You, 2007
Wise Moves, 2006
In Dark Waters, 2005

Other books you might like:
Chelsea Cain, *Heartsick*, 2007
J.T. Ellison, *All the Pretty Girls*, 2007
Alex Kava, *A Perfect Evil*, 2001
Cody McFadyen, *Shadow Man*, 2006
Karin Slaughter, *Blindsighted*, 2001

390

CHELSEA CAIN

The Night Season

(New York: Minotaur Books, 2011)

Series: Archie and Gretchen Series. Book 4
Story type: Serial Killer; Series
Subject(s): Mystery; Journalism; Law enforcement
Major character(s): Archie Sheridan, Detective—Police;
Gretchen Lowell, Serial Killer; Susan Ward, Journalist
Time period(s): 21st century; 2010s
Locale(s): Portland, Oregon

Summary: In *The Night Season* by Chelsea Cain, the rising Willamette River has claimed several drowning victims in Portland, Oregon. When detective Archie Sheridan is called to the scene of another death in the city, he is surprised when the coroner rules the case a homicide. A strange puncture wound on the body reveals that the victim was killed with octopus venom. Through further investigation, Archie learns that several other apparent drowning victims were killed the same way. As Portland faces the threat of a serial killer, the city also braces for the worst flooding since 1948. *The Night Season* is the fourth book in the Archie and Gretchen series.

Where it's reviewed:
Library Journal, November 1, 2010, page 54
New York Times Book Review, February 27, 2011, page 9

Other books by the same author:
Evil at Heart, 2009
Sweetheart, 2008
HeartSick, 2007
Confessions of a Teen Sleuth, 2004

Other books you might like:
J. T. Ellison, *Judas Kiss*, 2009
Lisa Gardner, *Alone*, 2005
Alex Kava, *A Perfect Evil*, 2001
Karin Slaughter, *Blindsighted*, 2001
Eleanor Woods, *Above Suspicion*, 1990

Mystery

391

PAMELA CALLOW

Indefensible

(New York: Mira, 2010)

Series: Kate Lange Series. Book 2
Story type: Contemporary
Subject(s): Family; Law; Murder
Major character(s): Kate Lange, Lawyer, Detective—Amateur; Randall Barrett, Lawyer, Crime Suspect; Elise Vanderzell, Crime Victim
Time period(s): 21st century; 2010s
Locale(s): United States

Summary: Attorney and amateur sleuth, Kate Lange returns in *Indefensible*, the second novel in Pamela Callow's Kate Lange series. This outing finds Kate charged with defending one of her colleagues on a murder rap, and she soon lands in the dark details of this very unusual case. Randall Barrett stands accused of murdering his former wife, and their teenage son is the one who claims to have seen his father commit the heinous act. But the more Kate unearths about that fateful night, the more she begins to wonder whose stories are true and whom—if anyone—she can trust.

Where it's reviewed:
Publishers Weekly, November 15, 2010, page 40

Other books by the same author:
Damaged, 2010

Other books you might like:
Allison Brennan, *Love Me to Death*, 2010
Jonnie Jacobs, *Shadow of Doubt*, 1996
Perri O'Shaughnessy, *Motion to Suppress*, 1995
Lisa Scottoline, *Everywhere That Mary Went*, 2003
Erica Spindler, *Last Known Victim*, 2007

392

KATE CARLISLE

The Lies that Bind

(New York: Signet, 2010)

Series: Bibliophile Mystery Series. Book 3
Story type: Contemporary
Subject(s): Detective fiction; Books; Murder
Major character(s): Brooklyn Wainwright, Expert (book restoration expert), Detective—Amateur; Layla Fontaine, Crime Victim
Time period(s): 21st century; 2010s
Locale(s): San Francisco, California

Summary: The third novel in Kate Carlisle's Bibliophile Mysteries series, *The Lies that Bind* continues the investigations of book expert and amateur private eye, Brooklyn Wainwright. Brooklyn returns to her native San Francisco to lead a class in bookbinding, but the woman hosting the class, Layla Fontaine, proves to be more than a handful. When the high-maintenance Layla is murdered, Brooklyn sets out to find the killer, even as she herself could well become the next victim.

Other books by the same author:
If Books Could Kill, 2010
Homicide in Hardcover, 2009

Other books you might like:
Lawrence Block, *Burglars Can't Be Choosers*, 1977
John Dunning, *Booked to Die*, 1992
Joan Hess, *Strangled Prose*, 1986
Julie Kaewert, *Unsolicited*, 1994
Marianne Macdonald, *Death's Autograph*, 1997

393

CAROL K. CARR

India Black

(New York: Berkley Prime Crime, 2011)

Story type: Historical; Romance
Subject(s): Mystery; Romances (Fiction); British history, 1815-1914
Major character(s): India Black, Prostitute, Madam; Archibald Latham, Government Official, Knight; Mr. French, Spy
Time period(s): 19th century; 1870s (1876)
Locale(s): London, England

Summary: *India Black* is a historical romance novel from debut author Carol K. Carr. India Black runs the Lotus House, a London brothel catering to high-profile clients, like Sir Archibald Latham of the War Office. When Sir Archibald dies from a heart attack during a visit to the Lotus House, India plans to dispose of his body to protect her business. Her task is thwarted by a mysterious man known as Mr. French who offers to get rid of the corpse in exchange for a favor. He needs India to retrieve some top-secret government papers that were with Archibald at the time of his death. India agrees and soon finds herself fighting off Russian spies and a growing attraction to the mysterious and sexy Mr. French. First novel.

Where it's reviewed:
Booklist, December 15, 2010, page 23
Library Journal, January 2011, page 80
Publishers Weekly, November 8, 2010, page 46

Other books you might like:
Tasha Alexander, *And Only to Deceive*, 2005
Michel Faber, *The Crimson Petal and the White*, 2002
Sheri Holman, *The Dress Lodger*, 2000
Fidelis Morgan, *Unnatural Fires*, 2000
Deanna Raybourn, *Silent in the Grave*, 2007

394

PHILIP CARTER (Pseudonym of Penelope Williamson)

Altar of Bones

(New York: Simon and Schuster, 2011)

Story type: Psychological Suspense
Subject(s): Prisons; Murder; Suspense
Major character(s): Zoe Dmitroff, Lawyer; Ry O'Malley, Bodyguard
Locale(s): Siberia, Russia; San Francisco, California

Summary: *Altar of Bones* is a thriller by author Phillip Carter. In it, Carter tells the story of an ages-old mystery surrounding a Siberian cave. Known as the Altar of Bones, the cave is rumored to contain the powers of the Fountain of Youth. When San Francisco attorney Zoe Dmitroff receives a note from her murderer grandmother, she learns that she is now the keeper of these secrets, and that she must protect them at all costs. Unfortunately, the long list of people willing to risk Zoe's life to obtain the secrets includes the Russian mob as well as Zoe's own mother. Now Zoe must put her trust in bodyguard Ry O'Malley to keep her safe, but can she trust even him?

Where it's reviewed:
Library Journal, Feb. 1, 2011, page 51
Publishers Weekly, Jan. 24, 2011, page 132

Other books you might like:
Dan Brown, *The Da Vinci Code*, 2003
Chris Kuzneski, *Sign of the Cross*, 2006
Katherine Neville, *The Eight*, 1988
Douglas Preston, *The Codex*, 2004
James Rollins, *Map of Bones*, 2005

395

C.S. CHALLINOR

Murder on the Moor

(Woodbury, Minnesota: Midnight Ink, 2011)

Series: Rex Graves Series. Book 4
Story type: Amateur Detective
Subject(s): Murder; Mystery; Scotland
Major character(s): Rex Graves, Lawyer, Detective—Amateur; Helen D'Arcy, Girlfriend (of Rex)
Time period(s): 21st century; 2010s
Locale(s): Scotland

Summary: *Murder on the Moor*, a suspenseful mystery novel, is the fourth installment in the Rex Graves series from author C.S. Challinor. Rex Graves, along with his girlfriend Helen D'Arcy, decides to assemble a random group of friends that includes a lawyer, hotelier, and freelance journalist, for a quiet party at his new Scotland lakeside cottage. What begins as a relaxing gathering soon turns into a puzzling mystery when Graves' ex-girlfriend arrives, a torrential downpour forces the guests to stay overnight, and a killer strikes. When a body is discovered the next morning and every way of escape and communication has been destroyed, it's up to Graves to investigate and determine which of his so-called friends is actually a deranged murderer.

Where it's reviewed:
Publishers Weekly, Dec. 13, 2010, page 40

Other books by the same author:
Phi Beta Murder, 2010
Murder in the Raw, 2009
Christmas is Murder, 2008

Other books you might like:
M.C. Beaton, *Death of a Gossip*, 1985
Rhys Bowen, *Evans Above*, 1997
Simon Brett, *Cast in Order of Disappearance*, 1975

Ann Granger, *Say It with Poison*, 1991
Hazel Holt, *Mrs. Malory Investigates*, 1989

396

LINCOLN CHILD
DOUGLAS PRESTON, Co-Author

Gideon's Sword

(New York: Grand Central Publishing, 2011)

Story type: Contemporary
Subject(s): Mystery; Murder; Revenge
Major character(s): Gideon Crew, Agent (government)
Time period(s): 21st century; 2010s
Locale(s): United States

Summary: In *Gideon's Sword* by Douglas Preston and Lincoln Child, a quest for vengeance holds unexpected consequences for Gideon Crew. When he was just 12, Gideon saw his father—a government mathematician—killed by a sniper. Gideon's mother waited until she was on the verge of death 12 years later to tell him the truth about his father's death and to ask him to get revenge. When Gideon finally finds and kills his father's murderer, his actions earn him a mission with a government subcontractor. Gideon's assignment is to retrieve weapons plans from a Chinese scientist. But when the mission fails, Gideon is on his own with only a cryptic list of numbers to guide him.

Where it's reviewed:
Library Journal, Jan. 2011, page 89

Other books by the same author:
Fever Dream, 2010
Still Life with Crows, 2004
Cabinet of Curiosities, 2002
Reliquary, 1997
Relic, 1995

Other books you might like:
Lee Child, *Killing Floor*, 1997
Joseph Finder, *Vanished*, 2009
Matthew Reilly, *Ice Station*, 1999
James Rollins, *Sandstorm*, 2004
Brad Thor, *The Lions of Lucerne*, February 27, 2007

397

TOM CLANCY
GRANT BLACKWOOD, Co-Author

Dead or Alive

(New York: Putnam Adult, 2010)

Story type: Adventure
Subject(s): Adventure; Terrorism; Mystery
Major character(s): Jack Ryan Jr., Agent (CIA Agent), Cousin (of Dominick and Brian); Dominick Caruso, Cousin (of Jack); Brian Caruso, Cousin (of Jack)
Time period(s): 21st century; 2010s
Locale(s): United States

Mystery

Summary: *Dead or Alive*, written by Tom Clancy and Grant Blackwood, is a thriller featuring Jack Ryan Jr., who is still working as a member of the Campus, a secret anti-terrorism agency. In this novel, Ryan and his team, which includes his cousins Dominick and Brian Caruso and the rest of the Campus members, are attempting to bring in a terrorist known as the Emir. This madman has planned and executed some of the deadliest attacks on Western soil, yet the government has not been able to capture him. Ryan and his team are determined to do whatever it takes to put a stop to these terror attacks and take the Emir out once and for all.

Where it's reviewed:
The Bookseller, September 3, 2010, page 25
Library Journal, February 1, 2011, page 52
Swiss News, January 2011, page 68

Other books by the same author:
The Teeth of the Tiger, 2003
Without Remorse, 1993
The Cardinal of the Kremlin, 1988
Red Storm Rising, 1986
The Hunt for Red October, 1984

Other books you might like:
Alex Berenson, *The Faithful Spy*, 2006
Dan Fesperman, *The Warlord's Son*, 2004
Frederick Forsyth, *The Afghan*, 2006
Brad Thor, *The Apostle*, 2009
Thomas W. Young, *The Mullah's Storm*, 2010

398

CAROL HIGGINS CLARK
Mobbed
(New York: Scribner, 2011)

Series: Regan Reilly Series. Book 14
Story type: Contemporary; Series
Subject(s): Mystery; Detective fiction; Suspense
Major character(s): Regan Reilly, Detective—Private; Jack Reilly, Detective—Police, Spouse (of Regan); Nora Regan Reilly, Writer, Mother (of Regan); Hayley Patton, Planner (event), Friend (of Regan); Scott, Boyfriend (of Hayley); Karen Frawley Fulton, Friend (of Regan)
Time period(s): 21st century; 2010s
Locale(s): Bay Head, New Jersey

Summary: In *Mobbed* by Carol Higgins Clark, private investigator Regan Reilly and her police detective husband, Jack, plan to escape New York for a Jersey shore vacation with her novelist mother, Nora Regan Reilly. When Nora's friend Karen Frawley Fulton calls from California with the news that her mother has suddenly decided to sell her New Jersey beach house, Regan is summoned to the shore early to help sort matters out. Meanwhile, Edna Frawley (Karen's mother) has started selling the contents of the house—family possessions as well as those that belonged to the celebrity renter who disappeared mysteriously. *Mobbed* is the 14th book in the Regan Reilly series.

Where it's reviewed:
Library Journal, Nov. 15, 2010, page 44

Other books by the same author:
Wrecked, 2010
Twanged, 1998
Iced, 1995
Snagged, 1993
Decked, 1992

Other books you might like:
Janet Evanovich, *Wicked Appetite*, 2010
Rhonda Pollero, *Knock Off*, 2007
Nora Roberts, *Public Secrets*, 1990
Hank Phillippi Ryan, *Prime Time*, 2007
Laura Van Wormer, *Expose*, 1999

399

MARCIA CLARK
Guilt by Association
(New York: Little, Brown and Co., 2011)

Story type: Legal
Subject(s): Mystery; Law; Murder
Major character(s): Rachel Knight, Lawyer (district attorney); Jake Pahlmeyer, Lawyer; Susan Densmore, 15-Year-Old; Bailey Keller, Detective—Police
Time period(s): 21st century; 2010s
Locale(s): Los Angeles, California

Summary: In *Guilt by Association* by Marcia Clark, L.A. District Attorney Rachel Knight is shocked by the death of a colleague, Jake, in an apparent murder-suicide in a motel room. Certain that her friend was not capable of murder, Knight decides to play private investigator to learn the true circumstances of Jake's death. Before he died, Jake was working on a case involving the sexual assault of a teenage girl, Susan Densmore. Now, that case is Rachel Knight's. Susan's father, a physician who made contributions to the District Attorney's campaign, claims to know the attacker's identity. First novel.

Where it's reviewed:
Booklist, Feb. 15, 2011, page 56
Library Journal, Feb. 15, 2011, page 98
Publishers Weekly, Jan. 31, 2011, page 26
USA Today, Feb. 17, 2011, page 03D

Other books by the same author:
Without a Doubt, 1997

Other books you might like:
Rose Connors, *Absolute Certainty*, 2002
David Ellis, *Line of Vision*, 2001
Linda Fairstein, *Final Jeopardy*, 1996
Dick Lochte, *The Trials of Nikki Hill*, 1999
Lisa Scottoline, *Everywhere That Mary Went*, 2003

400

MARY HIGGINS CLARK
I'll Walk Alone
(New York: Simon & Schuster, 2011)

Story type: Contemporary
Subject(s): Mystery; Suspense; Missing persons

Major character(s): Alexandra "Zan" Moreland, Interior Decorator; Matthew, Son (of Zan); Alvirah Meehan, Detective—Amateur; Aiden O'Brien, Religious (priest)
Time period(s): 21st century; 2010s
Locale(s): New York, New York

Summary: In *I'll Walk Alone* by Mary Higgins Clark, a New York interior designer is dealing with the kidnapping of her son two years ago when she learns that she is the victim of identity theft. Alexandra "Zan" Moreland still believes that her son, Matthew, may be alive. Though she is grief-stricken by his abduction, Zan has continued to build her career. That career is put in jeopardy when someone starts running up charges on her credit cards. Then, on the day of Matthew's fifth birthday, Zan learns that the person who stole her identity is also trying to frame her for the kidnapping of her son.

Where it's reviewed:
Library Journal, Nov. 15, 2010, page 44

Other books by the same author:
The Shadow of Your Smile, 2010
A Cry in the Night, 1982
The Cradle will Fall, 1980
A Stranger is Watching, 1977
Where are the Children?, 1975

Other books you might like:
Carol Higgins Clark, *Decked*, 1992
Lisa Gardner, *The Survivors Club*, 2001
Judith Kelman, *Prime Evil*, 1986
Barbara Michaels, *Someone in the House*, 1981
Phyllis A. Whitney, *Listen for the Whisperer*, 1972

401

MARY JANE CLARK

To Have and To Kill: A Wedding Cake Mystery

(New York: HarperCollins, 2011)

Story type: Cozy Mystery
Subject(s): Food; Weddings; Crime
Major character(s): Piper Donovan, Actress, Baker, Friend (of Glenna), Detective—Amateur; Glenna Brooks, Actress, Friend (of Piper)
Locale(s): New York, New York

Summary: *To Have and To Kill* is the first novel in author Mary Jane Clark's Wedding Cake Mystery series. When Piper Donovan returns home to her parents' after breaking up with her fiance, she decides to put her dreams on hold and instead work in the family's cake business. There Piper finds some success as a wedding-cake decorator, especially after her friend Glenna, a star on a popular soap opera, requests that Piper design her wedding cake. Glenna's own nuptials are put at risk when her character is cut from the show and her former co-star turns up dead. Can Piper turn from baker to amateur sleuth in time to find the killer and keep Glenna safe?

Where it's reviewed:
Library Journal, Oct. 15, 2010, page 74
Publishers Weekly, Sept. 27, 2010, page 39

Other books by the same author:
It Only Takes a Moment, 2008
When Day Breaks, 2007
Let Me Whisper in Your Ear, 2000
Do You Promise Not to Tell, 1999
Do You Want to Know a Secret?, 1998

Other books you might like:
Sheryl J. Anderson, *Killer Heels*, 2004
Jessica Beck, *Glazed Murder: A Donut Shop Mystery*, 2010
Diane Mott Davidson, *Catering to Nobody*, 1990
Julie Hyzy, *State of the Onion*, 2008
Jenn McKinlay, *Sprinkle with Murder*, 2010

402

JANE K. CLELAND

Deadly Threads

(New York: St. Martin's Minotaur, 2011)

Series: Josie Prescott Antiques Mystery Series. Book 6
Story type: Cozy Mystery; Series
Subject(s): Mystery; Murder; Detective fiction
Major character(s): Josie Prescott, Antiques Dealer; Riley Jordan, Antiques Dealer (speaker); Ellis Hunter, Police Officer (chief)
Time period(s): 21st century; 2010s
Locale(s): Rocky Point, New Hampshire

Summary: In *Deadly Threads* by Jane Cleland, a New Hampshire antique dealer's popular shop becomes a crime scene when a visiting lecturer is strangled. Riley Jordan had been scheduled to appear at Josie Prescott's Rocky Point shop to lecture on vintage fashion accessories. When Riley runs late, Josie proceeds to start the presentation without her, then finds Riley's dead body stashed under a table. Josie reports the crime to local police chief Ellis Hunter. With help from *Seacoast Star* journalist Wes Smith, Josie and Ellis follow a collection of tasteful clues to find Riley Jordan's killer. *Deadly Threads* is the sixth book in the Josie Prescott Antiques Mystery series.

Where it's reviewed:
Publishers Weekly, Feb. 14, 2011, page 40

Other books by the same author:
Silent Auction, 2010
Killer Keepsakes, 2009
Antiques to Die For, 2008
Deadly Appraisal, 2007
Consigned to Death, 2006

Other books you might like:
Barbara Allan, *Antiques Knock-Off*, 2011
Mary Kay Andrews, *Savannah Blues*, 2002
Sharon Fiffer, *Killer Stuff*, 2001
Jonathan Gash, *The Judas Pair*, 1977
Susan Holtzer, *Something to Kill For*, 1994

Mystery

403

BLAIZE CLEMENT

Cat Sitter Among the Pigeons

(New York: Minotaur Books, 2010)

Series: Dixie Hemingway Mystery Series. Book 6
Story type: Cozy Mystery
Subject(s): Pets; Mystery; Kidnapping
Major character(s): Dixie Hemingway, Animal Lover, Babysitter (pet), Detective—Amateur
Time period(s): 21st century; 2010s
Locale(s): United States

Summary: *Cat Sitter Among the Pigeons* is the sixth book in the Dixie Hemingway series. Dixie has been hired by an ailing, elderly man to care for his orange cat, Cheddar. The job seems simple enough until Dixie is mistaken for the man's granddaughter, Ruby, and kidnapped by unsavory businessmen in the area. It turns out Ruby, mother of a precious baby girl, is privy to some damning information about the kidnappers and she plans to testify to it in court. The kidnappers release Dixie, but they're determined to silence Ruby, no matter what it takes. Desperate to protect Ruby and her daughter, Dixie starts secretly sleuthing in hopes of uncovering the truth and protecting the innocent.

Where it's reviewed:
Publishers Weekly, November 29, 2010, page 33

Other books by the same author:
Raining Cat Sitters and Dogs, 2010
Cat Sitter on a Hot Tin Roof, 2009
Even Cat Sitters Get the Blues, 2008
Curiosity Killed the Cat Sitter, 2007
Duplicity Dogged the Dachshund, 2007

Other books you might like:
Lydia Adamson, *A Cat in the Manger*, 1990
Barbara Block, *Chutes and Adders*, 1994
Sneaky Pie Brown, *Wish You Were Here*, 1990
Linda O. Johnston, *Sit, Stay, Slay*, 2005
Leann Sweeney, *The Cat, the Quilt and the Corpse*, 2009

404

HARLAN COBEN

Live Wire

(New York: Dutton, 2011)

Series: Myron Bolitar Series. Book 10
Story type: Amateur Detective
Subject(s): Sports; Family; Mystery
Major character(s): Myron Bolitar, Agent (sports), Detective—Amateur; Suzze Tervantino, Tennis Player, Client (of Myron)
Time period(s): 21st century; 2010s
Locale(s): New York, New York

Summary: *Live Wire* is a mystery novel from award-winning author, Harlan Coben. The book is the tenth installment in the Myron Bolitar series about a former athlete turned sports agent. In *Live Wire*, Bolitar finds himself in the midst of a heated paternity battle, the search for a missing client, and questions surrounding his own family's dark past. Former tennis pro, Suzze T, is eight months pregnant and can't find her husband, rock star Lex Ryder. After an online tabloid questioned Lex's paternity of Suzze's unborn child, the rocker disappeared and Suzze is desperate for Bolitar to track him down. Bolitar accepts the case, but his investigation leads to unexpected results as Bolitar stumbles upon his own brother, Brad, whom he hasn't seen in 16 years.

Where it's reviewed:
Library Journal, Feb. 15, 2011, page 99

Other books by the same author:
Long Lost, 2009
Back Spin, 1997
Drop Shot, 1996
Fade Away, 1996
Deal Breaker, 1995

Other books you might like:
Robert Crais, *Stalking the Angel*, 1989
Chris Grabenstein, *Mind Scrambler: A John Ceepak Mystery*, 2009
Dennis Lehane, *Sacred*, 1997
Laura Lippman, *Another Thing to Fall*, 2008
Randy Wayne White, *Captiva*, 1996

405

GABRIEL COHEN

The Ninth Step

(New York: Minotaur Books, 2010)

Series: Jack Leightner Series. Book 4
Story type: Police Procedural
Subject(s): Murder; Mystery; Terrorism
Major character(s): Jack Leightner, Detective—Homicide
Time period(s): 21st century; 2010s
Locale(s): New York, New York

Summary: *The Ninth Step*, a suspenseful mystery novel, is the fourth installment in the Jack Leightner series from author Gabriel Cohen. Four decades after witnessing his brother's murder, Brooklyn homicide detective Jack Leightner is shocked when the killer, who was never caught, shows up at his front door. Darnel Teague Jr. visits Jack to make amends for the past as part of a 12-step process and reveals shocking details about the tragedy. Jack is distracted when a murder takes place at a local deli and Homeland Security suggests the random killing might be part of a larger terrorist plot. As Jack hunts down the Pakistani-American killer, he's forced to confront his family's dark past and the mystery surrounding his brother's murder.

406

MICHAEL CONNELLY

The Fifth Witness

(New York: Little, Brown and Company, 2010)

Series: Mickey Haller Series. Book 4
Story type: Legal; Series

Subject(s): Mystery; Law; Trials
Major character(s): Mickey Haller, Lawyer; Lisa Trammel, Client (of Haller); Mitchell Bondurant, Banker
Time period(s): 21st century; 2010s
Locale(s): Losn Angeles, California

Summary: In *The Fifth Witness* by Michael Connelly, a woman about to lose her Los Angeles home in foreclosure is suspected of murder when a bank official is bludgeoned to death with a hammer. Lisa Trammel's aggressive protests against her pending foreclosure prompt her mortgage holder to file for a restraining order. When she is accused of Mitchell Bondurant's murder, eccentric but brilliant attorney Mickey Haller comes to her defense. Working out of his car, Haller counters the evidence against his client with an ingenious defense (featuring a fifth witness) that indicts the mortgage industry. *The Fifth Witness* is the fourth book in the Mickey Haller series.

Where it's reviewed:
Library Journal, February 15, 2011, page 99

Other books by the same author:
The Reversal, 2010
The Brass Verdict, 2008
The Lincoln Lawyer, 2005
The Poet, 1996
The Black Echo, 1992

Other books you might like:
Richard Barre, *The Innocents*, 1995
Robert Crais, *L.A. Requiem*, 1999
Terrill Lee Lankford, *Earthquake Weather*, 2004
William Lashner, *Hostile Witness*, 1995
John Shannon, *The Concrete River*, 1996

407

SHEILA CONNOLLY

Fundraising the Dead

(New York: Berkley Prime Crime, 2010)

Series: Museum Mystery Series. Book 1
Story type: Amateur Detective; Cozy Mystery
Subject(s): Mystery; Antiques; Letters (Correspondence)
Major character(s): Eleanor "Nell" Pratt, Antiquarian, Detective—Amateur
Time period(s): 21st century; 2010s
Locale(s): Pennsylvania, United States

Summary: *Fundraising the Dead* is the first book in the Museum Mystery series from best-selling author Sheila Connolly. The cozy mystery follows the adventures of Nell Pratt, fundraising director for The Society for the Preservation of Pennsylvania Antiques. She's also an occasional amateur sleuth. A series of incredibly valuable documents is missing, including letters from President George Washington, and the archivist who discovered their absence is found dead. It seems obvious to Nell that the two incidents must be connected, but strangely, the Society isn't requesting an investigation. Nell, certain that something is afoot, conducts her own investigation and uncovers a shocking history of criminal activity.

Where it's reviewed:
Publishers Weekly, August 9, 2010, page 36

Other books by the same author:
A Killer Crop, 2010
Red Delicious Death, 2010
Rotten to the Core, 2009
One Bad Apple, 2008

Other books you might like:
Lorna Barrett, *Bookmarked for Death*, 2009
Simon Brett, *Murder in the Museum*, 2003
Kate Carlisle, *Homicide in Hardcover*, 2009
Jane K. Cleland, *Consigned to Death*, 2006
Jo Dereske, *Miss Zukas and the Library Murders*, 1994

408

DEBORAH COONTS

Lucky Stiff

(New York: Forge Books, 2011)

Series: Lucky O'Toole Series. Book 2
Story type: Series
Subject(s): Murder; Friendship; Detective fiction
Major character(s): Lucky O'Toole, Public Relations (head of hotel); Jeremy Whitlock, Investigator
Time period(s): 21st century; 2010s
Locale(s): Las Vegas, Nevada

Summary: In Deborah Coonts's *Lucky Stiff*, Lucky O'Toole assumes the crazy events happening in her Vegas hotel, The Babylon, are part of the typical Vegas nightlife. People are angry, drunk, and ready to gamble their lives away—at the blackjack tables and in the hundreds of private rooms the hotel offers. When her friend and investigator, Jeremy Whitlock, fights with gambler Numbers Neidermeyer, Lucky thinks nothing of it—until Numbers turns up dead in the shark's tank at Mandalay Bay. Vegas police immediately retrace Numbers's footsteps from the night before and Jeremy becomes their prime suspect. Lucky is confident Jeremy didn't hurt Numbers and vows to look back at the hectic night with a better eye to see if she can spot the real killer.

Where it's reviewed:
Booklist, February 1, 2011, page 36
Publishers Weekly, December 6, 2010, page 31

Other books by the same author:
Wanna Get Lucky?, 2010

Other books you might like:
Janet Evanovich, *One for the Money*, 1994
Sophie Littlefield, *A Bad Day for Sorry*, 2009
Karen E. Olson, *The Missing Ink*, 2009
James Swain, *Grift Sense*, 2001
Vince Van Patten, *The Picasso Flop*, 2007

409

PATRICIA CORNWELL

Port Mortuary

(New York: G.P. Putnam's Sons, 2010)

Series: Kay Scarpetta Series. Book 18
Story type: Contemporary; Military

Subject(s): Terrorism; Detective fiction; Medical professions

Major character(s): Kay Scarpetta, Doctor (Chief Medical Examiner), Detective

Time period(s): 21st century; 2010s

Locale(s): Delaware, United States; Cambridge, Massachusetts

Summary: Medical examiner/PI Kay Scarpetta is drawn into the top secret world of the United States military. Long ago, Scarpetta accepted an Air Force scholarship to pay off her student loans, and now she is back at Dover Air Force Base to train new recruits. She is soon promoted to head of a new unit—sponsored by the government and the country's most renowned institutions of higher learning—that studies forensics. But a shocking case could threaten Scarpetta's new position, and she must rally all her skills and cunning to thwart this latest menace.... *Port Mortuary* is the 18th novel in Patricia Cornwell's Scarpetta series.

Where it's reviewed:
Library Journal, January 2011, page 80

Other books by the same author:
The Scarpetta Factor, 2009
Cruel and Unusual, 1993
All That Remains, 1992
Body of Evidence, 1991
Postmortem, 1990

Other books you might like:
Jefferson Bass, *Carved in Bone*, 2006
Lisa Black, *Takeover*, 2008
Beverly Connor, *One Grave Too Many*, 2003
Kathryn Fox, *Malicious Intent*, 2006
Kathy Reichs, *Deja Dead*, 1997

410

MILES CORWIN

Kind of Blue

(Longboat Key, Florida: Oceanview Publishing, 2010)

Story type: Contemporary
Subject(s): Detective fiction; Law enforcement; Murder
Major character(s): Ash Levine, Detective—Police
Time period(s): 21st century; 2010s
Locale(s): Los Angeles, California

Summary: In Miles Corwin's *Kind of Blue*, police detective Ash Levine was kicked off the force for providing inadequate protection to an imperiled witness. Now, nearly a year later, Ash is called back to work to help solve the murder of a former cop. What he finds, however, is rife corruption within the LAPD—and superior officers who are determined to keep the murderer's identity a secret.

Where it's reviewed:
Booklist, September 1, 2010, page 50
Library Journal, September 1, 2010, page 94
Publishers Weekly, September 13, 2010, page 26

Other books by the same author:
Homicide Special, 2003

And Still We Rise, 2000
The Killing Season, 1997

Other books you might like:
Stephen J. Cannell, *The Tin Collectors*, 2001
Michael Connelly, *The Black Echo*, 1992
Faye Kellerman, *The Ritual Bath*, 1986
Jonathan Kellerman, *The Murder Book*, 2002
Joseph Wambaugh, *Hollywood Station: A Novel*, 2006

411

JACK COUGHLIN
DONALD A. DAVIS, Co-Author

An Act of Treason

(New York: St. Martin's Press, 2011)

Series: Sniper Series. Book 4
Subject(s): Suspense; Armed forces; Deception
Major character(s): Kyle Swanson, Military Personnel (Marine sniper); Lauren Carson, Agent (CIA), Girlfriend (of Kyle); Jim Hall, Agent (CIA), Traitor
Time period(s): 21st century; 2010s
Locale(s): Pakistan; United States

Summary: *An Act of Treason* is a novel filled with action, treason, and political intrigue from authors, Jack Coughlin and Donald A. Davis. The book is the fourth installment in the Sniper series. In *An Act of Treason*, Marine sniper Swanson and his CIA agent girlfriend, Lauren Carson, are en route to a mission in Pakistan when Swanson is arrested and imprisoned and Carson is accused of being a double agent. The only person who can prove their innocence is Jim Hall, the former CIA agent who trained Swanson, dated Carson, and sent them both on the black op. Unfortunately, Hall has become a traitor, selling America's political secrets to a terrorist organization. It's up to Swanson to find Hall and stop him, but tracking down his former mentor and killing him is the hardest assignment Swanson has ever had to face.

Other books by the same author:
Clean Kill, 2010
Dead Shot, 2009
Kill Zone, 2007
Shooter, 2005

Other books you might like:
Mark Berent, *Rolling Thunder*, 1989
Dale Brown, *Flight of the Old Dog*, 1987
Jim DeFelice, *Stephen Coonts' Deep Black*, 2003
W.E.B. Griffin, *Semper Fi*, 1986
David Poyer, *The Med*, 1988

412

ROBERT CRAIS

The Sentry

(New York: G.P. Putnam's Sons, 2011)

Series: Joe Pike Series. Book 3
Story type: Contemporary

Subject(s): Suspense; Detective fiction; Family
Major character(s): Joe Pike, Military Personnel (former marine), Detective; Elvis Cole, Detective; Dru Rayne, Young Woman
Time period(s): 21st century; 2010s
Locale(s): Los Angeles, California

Summary: Former marine Joe Pike and his crime-solving partner Elvis Cole team up to protect a young woman and her uncle from a murderous gang that wants them dead. Dru Rayne and her uncle leave hurricane-ravaged New Orleans for the security of Los Angeles, but they soon find themselves the target of some very determined thugs. When Pike and Cole try to help, Dru and her uncle don't seem to want their protection. Now, it's up to the two investigators to get to the bottom of the case, unearthing secrets that reveal who Dru and her uncle really are. *The Sentry* is the third novel in Robert Crais's Joe Pike series.

Where it's reviewed:
Booklist, December 1, 2010, page 32
Library Journal, December 2010, page 99
Publishers Weekly, November 22, 2010, page 42

Other books by the same author:
The First Rule, 2010
Chasing Darkness, 2008
The Watchman, 2007
L.A. Requiem, 1999
The Monkey's Raincoat, 1987

Other books you might like:
Jan Burke, *Kidnapped*, 2006
Harlan Coben, *The Final Detail*, 1999
Michael Connelly, *Blood Work*, 1998
T. Jefferson Parker, *L.A. Outlaws*, 2008
John Shannon, *The Concrete River*, 1996

413

CHARLES CUMMING

The Trinity Six

(New York: St. Martin's Press, 2011)

Story type: Espionage
Subject(s): Cold War, 1945-1991; Spies; Suspense
Major character(s): Sam Gaddis, Researcher
Time period(s): 21st century; 2000s
Locale(s): England

Summary: *The Trinity Six* is a suspenseful spy novel from best-selling author, Charles Cumming. In 1992, 76-year-old "career diplomat" Edward Crane is pronounced dead in London. Fifteen years later, academic Sam Gaddis makes a shocking discovery about Crane's true identity and his involvement in a major Cold War scandal. Gaddis is desperately in need of money when a journalist friend asks for his help on a story. The journalist is researching the identity of a possible sixth member of the Cambridge Five, a notorious group of traitorous British spies who shared political secrets with the Soviet Union during and after World War II. When the journalist ends up dead, Gaddis decides to continue the investigation alone, unaware of the dangerous truth he's about to uncover.

Where it's reviewed:
Library Journal, Dec. 2010, page 99

Other books by the same author:
Typhoon, 2008
The Spanish Game, 2006
The Hidden Man, 2003
A Spy by Nature, 2001

Other books you might like:
Alan Furst, *The Foreign Correspondent: A Novel*, 2006
Graham Greene, *The Human Factor*, 1978
John Le Carre, *The Honourable Schoolboy*, 1977
Olen Steinhauer, *The Tourist*, 2009
Kevin Wignall, *Who Is Conrad Hirst?*, 2007

414

CLIVE CUSSLER
JACK DU BRUL, Co-Author

The Jungle

(New York: G. P. Putnam's Sons, 2011)

Series: Oregon Files Series. Book 8
Subject(s): Terrorism; Ships; Suspense
Major character(s): Juan Cabrillo, Mercenary, Shipowner, Leader
Time period(s): 21st century; 2010s

Summary: *The Jungle* is an action-packed novel from best-selling authors, Clive Cussler and Jack Du Brul. The book is the eighth installment in the Oregon Files series about a group of mercenaries working from aboard their state-of-the-art ship called the Oregon. In this latest novel, Juan Cabrillo and the Oregon crew face the threat of a power-obsessed madman and a plot that could destroy the United States. After rescuing a kidnapped Indonesian boy from an Afghan community, Cabrillo and his men are pleased to add a new member to their midst, former U.S. Army Ranger MacD Lawless. When a mysterious and powerful man, hellbent on taking over the world, discovers a strange 13th-century Chinese weapon, he holds the power to take down the United States. It's up to Cabrillo and his men to stop him on a quest that leads them around the world through treacherous conditions and impossible obstacles.

Where it's reviewed:
Publishers Weekly, January 24, 2011, page 132

Other books by the same author:
The Silent Sea, 2010
Skeleton Coast, 2006
Dark Watch, 2005
Sacred Stone, 2004
Golden Buddha, 2003

Other books you might like:
David Angsten, *Dark Gold*, 2006
Steve Berry, *The Templar Legacy*, 2006
Chris Kuzneski, *The Plantation*, 2009
Douglas Preston, *The Codex*, 2004
James Rollins, *Amazonia*, 2002

415

BARBARA D'AMATO

Other Eyes

(New York: Forge, 2011)

Story type: Amateur Detective
Subject(s): Drugs; Mystery; Archaeology
Major character(s): Blue Eriksen, Archaeologist, Professor
Time period(s): 21st century; 2010s
Locale(s): Chicago, Illinois

Summary: *Other Eyes* is a suspenseful mystery novel from award-winning author Barbara D'Amato. Blue Eriksen, world famous forensic archaeologist and professor at Northwestern University, had long been researching the use of hallucinogens in ancient civilizations when she stumbled on an amazing possibility: psilocybin, a mushroom-derived hallucinogen, might cure drug addiction. The startling realization scares Leeuwarden Associates, a powerful secret organization that facilitates drug sales around the world, so much that they hire an assassin to eliminate Blue. When Blue's ex-husband is violently murdered during a home invasion, she suspects that she was actually the intended target, but can she uncover the truth about Leeuwarden before they're successful in eliminating her?

Where it's reviewed:
Booklist, Dec. 15, 2010, page 24
Publishers Weekly, Nov. 15, 2010, page 39

Other books by the same author:
Death of a Thousand Cuts, 2004
White Male Infant, 2002
Killer.app, 1996
Hardball, 1989
The Hands of Healing Murder, 1980

Other books you might like:
Steve Berry, *The Templar Legacy*, 2006
Chris Kuzneski, *The Prophecy*, 2010
Douglas Preston, *The Codex*, 2004
Douglas Preston, *Dinosaur Canyon*, 2005
M.J. Rose, *The Reincarnationist*, 2007

416

DIANE MOTT DAVIDSON

Crunch Time

(New York: William Morrow, 2011)

Series: Goldy Schulz Culinary Series. Book 16
Story type: Cozy Mystery; Series
Subject(s): Mystery; Food; Catering
Major character(s): Goldy Schulz, Detective—Amateur, Caterer; Yolanda Garcia, Friend (of Goldy); Ferdinanda, Aunt (of Yolanda); Ernest McLeod, Detective—Private; Marla, Friend (of Goldy); Arch, Son (of Goldy)
Time period(s): 21st century; 2010s
Locale(s): Colorado, United States

Summary: In *Crunch Time* by Diane Mott Davidson, Colorado caterer Goldy Schulz plays amateur sleuth when arson turns to murder. When Goldy's friend Yolanda is forced out of the home she shares with her aunt Ferdinanda by a suspicious fire, Yolanda and Ferdinanda are taken in by private detective Ernest McLeod. Fire strikes again, destroying Ernest's house—but only after Ernest is killed by a gunshot. Goldy asks the frightened women to stay with her, though she knows her house may now be the arsonist's next target. As another victim falls, Goldy investigates the strange case that involves jewelry theft, illegal puppy sales, and murder. *Crunch Time* is the 16th book in the Goldy Schulz Culinary series.

Where it's reviewed:
Library Journal, Nov. 15, 2010, page 44

Other books by the same author:
Fatally Flaky, 2009
The Cereal Murders, 1994
The Last Suppers, 1994
Dying for Chocolate, 1993
Catering to Nobody, 1992

Other books you might like:
Avery Aames, *The Long Quiche Goodbye*, 2010
Laura Childs, *Death by Darjeeling*, 2001
Cleo Coyle, *On What Grounds*, 2003
Joanne Fluke, *Chocolate Chip Cookie Murder*, 2000
Jenn McKinlay, *Sprinkle with Murder*, 2010

417

TIM DAVYS

Tourquai

(New York: HarperCollins, 2011)

Story type: Alternate Universe
Subject(s): Animals; Toys; Crime
Major character(s): Larry Bloodhound, Toy, Police Officer, Dog; Oswald Vulture, Toy, Bird, Financier, Crime Victim; Falcon Ecu, Toy, Bird, Detective; Phillip Mouse, Mouse, Toy, Detective—Private
Locale(s): Mollisan Town, Fictional Location

Summary: *Tourquai* is the third novel in author Tim Davys's stuffed animal mystery series. Mollisan Town may be inhabited by toys, that doesn't stop the residents from showing some very humanistic qualities—and that includes murder and mayhem. When financial titan Oswald Vulture is found without his head, stuffed dog superintendent Larry Bloodhound and his cohorts, including private investigator Philip Mouse and inspector Falco Ecu, must find the culprit. The list of suspects is ever-growing, as Oswald wasn't the most well-liked toy in the attic, and Larry must sort through them in order to get to the bottom of the crime. Davys is also the author of *Amberville* and *Lanceheim*.

Where it's reviewed:
Library Journal, Jan. 2011, page 82

Other books by the same author:
Lanceheim, 2010
Amberville, 2009

Other books you might like:
Jasper Fforde, *The Big Over Easy: A Nursery Crime*, 2005
Ken Harmon, *The Fat Man*, 2010
Jack O'Connell, *Wireless*, 1993
Akif Pirincci, *Felidae*, 1993
Sam Savage, *Firmin: Adventures of a Metropolitan Lowlife*, 2006

418

DAN DEWEESE

You Don't Love This Man: A Novel (P.S.)

(New York: Harper Perennial, 2011)

Series: P.S. Series. Book 1
Story type: Contemporary
Subject(s): Missing persons; Weddings; Suspense
Major character(s): Paul, Banker, Manager, Father (of Miranda); Miranda, Daughter (of Paul), Bride
Time period(s): 21st century; 2010s
Locale(s): United States

Summary: *You Don't Love This Man: A Novel (P.S.)*, a suspenseful mystery, is the first installment in the P.S. series from debut author Dan Deweese. Paul is having a hard enough time adjusting to the fact that, in a few hours, his 25-year-old daughter, Miranda, is going to walk down the aisle to marry a man twice her age, a man that is one of Paul's closest friends, to deal with any more stress today. Unfortunately, he's just found out that the bank he manages has been robbed by the same thief who executed a robbery 25 years earlier. As if that isn't enough, Miranda has gone missing, throwing Paul and everyone else into a panic. Paul struggles to put together the pieces to this mysterious puzzle to make sense of the robbery, disappearance, and May-December romance that his daughter is involved in. First novel.

419

K.L. DIONNE

Boiling Point

(New York: Jove Books, 2010)

Story type: Disaster
Subject(s): Volcanoes; Science; Mystery
Major character(s): Rebecca Sweet, Scientist, Environmentalist; Philippe Dumas, Scientist, Environmentalist; Max Heat, Scientist, Producer; Sheila Kennedy, Researcher, Scientist
Time period(s): 21st century; 2010s
Locale(s): Santiago, Chile

Summary: *Boiling Point* is a scientific thriller from author K.L. Dionne. The lives of four scientists are intertwined by Chaiten, a Chilean volcano that's been dormant for years. Rebecca Sweet, leader of an environmental advocacy group, is hosting an awareness conference in Santiago. Desperate for some added publicity, she is thrilled when Nobel Prize-winning scientist, Philippe Dumas, agrees to attend. Dumas persuades his scientist pal, Max Heat, to join him in Santiago with suspicions that Chaiten may erupt soon, despite being dormant for nine millennia. Eager to get footage for a TV special, Heat travels to Chile as well. Researcher Shelia Kennedy believes Chaiten's new activity might be an indicator of a serious environmental violation and she's determined to find the evidence she needs to uncover the sinister plot.

Where it's reviewed:
Publishers Weekly, November 1, 2010, page 29

Other books by the same author:
Freezing Point, 2008

Other books you might like:
Michael Crichton, *Congo*, 1980
Douglas Preston, *Blasphemy*, 2008
Douglas Preston, *Tyrannosaur Canyon*, 2005

420

LAURA DISILVERIO

Swift Justice

(New York: Minotaur Books, 2011)

Story type: Contemporary
Subject(s): Detective fiction; Adoption; Abuse
Major character(s): Charlotte "Charlie" Swift, Detective—Private; Gigi Goldman, Detective—Private
Time period(s): 21st century; 2010s
Locale(s): Colorado Springs, Colorado

Summary: Laura DiSilverio's *Swift Justice* follows private detectives Charlotte "Charlie" Swift and her new partner, Gigi Goldman, as they attempt to track down the missing mother of an abandoned baby. Charlie and Gigi couldn't be more different, but the two women utilize their differences to get to the bottom of this increasingly dangerous case. A baby has been left on the doorstep of a woman who has endured years of abuse, and the baby, the private eyes soon learn, is the child of the woman's teenage daughter, whom she put up for adoption when the teen was still a baby. First novel.

Where it's reviewed:
Booklist, September 15, 2010, page 35
Publishers Weekly, August 9, 2010, page 34

Other books you might like:
Maggie Barbieri, *Murder 101*, 2006
Linda Barnes, *A Trouble of Fools*, 1987
Janet Evanovich, *One for the Money*, 1994
Candace Havens, *Charmed and Dangerous*, 2005
Lisa Lutz, *The Spellman Files*, 2007

421

TIM DORSEY

Electric Barracuda

(New York: William Morrow Publishers, 2011)

Series: Serge O. Storms Series. Book 13
Story type: Serial Killer

Mystery

Subject(s): Serial murders; Vacations; Crime
Major character(s): Serge Storms, Serial Killer; The Doberman, Bounty Hunter
Locale(s): Florida, United States

Summary: *Electric Barracuda* is the 13th installment in Tim Dorsey's Serge Storms series. This time, serial killer Serge has the brilliant idea of starting a new web-based business that offers vacationers the opportunity to tour the hideaways of some of Florida's most famous fugitives. In the meantime, the police have finally caught up to the murderer, and so has a bounty hunter named the Doberman. The Doberman has a reality television series, and he knows that netting Serge Storms will skyrocket his falling ratings. Can Serge get out of this one with everything intact?

Where it's reviewed:
Library Journal, Feb. 1, 2011, page 52

Other books by the same author:
Gator A-Go-Go, 2010
Triggerfish Twist, 2002
Orange Crush, 2001
Hammerhead Ranch Motel, 2000
Florida Roadkill, 1999

Other books you might like:
Tom Corcoran, *The Mango Opera*, 1998
Carl Hiaasen, *Tourist Season*, 1986
Bob Morris, *Bahamarama*, 2004
Laurence Shames, *Florida Straits: A Novel*, 1992
Randy Wayne White, *The Man Who Invented Florida*, 1994

422

DAVID DOWNING

Potsdam Station

(New York: Soho Publishing, 2011)

Series: James Russell Series. Book 4
Story type: Historical - World War II
Subject(s): World War II, 1939-1945; Germans; Antisemitism
Major character(s): John Russell, Journalist, Spy, Boyfriend (of Effi), Father (of Paul); Effi Koenen, Girlfriend (of John); Paul Russell, Son (of John)
Time period(s): 20th century; 1930s-1940s
Locale(s): Berlin, Germany

Summary: *Potsdam Station* is and the fourth book in author David Downing's John Russell series of historical novels centered on World War II. As this novel opens, the year is 1945 and Hitler's reign is finally coming to a halt, yet his stronghold on Berlin remains—for now. As bombs fall on the city, John Russell must figure out a way to get communication through to his son Paul and his lover Effi, neither of whom he has seen since 1941. Despite the falling Nazi Empire, John detects a new threat on the horizon in the form of the Soviet Republic. Now he is determined to get Paul and Effi out of Berlin at all costs, even if it means going behind enemy lines himself.

Where it's reviewed:
Publishers Weekly, Feb. 7, 2011, page 36

Other books by the same author:
Sealing their Fate, 2009
Stettin Station, 2009
Silesian Station, 2008
Zoo Station, 2007

Other books you might like:
Charles Cumming, *A Spy by Nature*, 2007
Jeffery Deaver, *Garden of Beasts*, 2004
Alan Furst, *The World at Night*, 1996
Philip Kerr, *March Violets*, 1989
Olen Steinhauer, *The Bridge of Sighs*, 2003

423

MARGARET DUFFY

Corpse in Waiting

(London: Severn House Publishers, 2010)

Series: Gillard and Langley Mysteries Series. Book 14
Story type: Contemporary
Subject(s): Detective fiction; Murder; Organized crime
Major character(s): Patrick Gillard, Detective—Private; Ingrid Langley, Detective—Private, Writer; Alexandra Nightingale, Girlfriend (ex-girlfriend of Patrick)
Time period(s): 21st century; 2010s
Locale(s): Bath, United Kingdom

Summary: In *Corpse in Waiting*, author Margaret Duffy presents the 14th novel in the Gillard and Langley Mysteries, centering on the escapades of a husband-wife crime-solving team. This edition finds Patrick and Ingrid retreating to Bath for a little rest and relaxation, but their holiday takes a dark turn when the two stumble across a decomposing corpse. Determined to find the killer, they delve into the back story of the dead woman, meet her family, get involved with mobsters, and—always—stay on the twisting path of a murderer.

Where it's reviewed:
Booklist, September 1, 2010, page 48
Library Journal, September 1, 2010, page 94
Publishers Weekly, August 2, 2010, page 33

Other books by the same author:
Souvenirs of Murder, 2009
Who Killed Cock Robin?, 1990
Brass Eagle, 1989
Death of a Raven, 1988
A Murder of Crows, 1987

Other books you might like:
Agatha Christie, *Partners in Crime*, 1929
Deborah Crombie, *A Share in Death*, 1993
Christopher Fowler, *Full Dark House*, 2003
Dashiell Hammett, *The Thin Man*, 1934
Barry Maitland, *The Marx Sisters*, 1999

424

CAROLA DUNN

Anthem for Doomed Youth

(New York: Minotaur Books, 2011)

Series: Daisy Dalrymple Series. Book 19
Story type: Historical
Subject(s): Murder; World War I, 1914-1918; Mystery
Major character(s): Alec Fletcher, Detective; Daisy Dalrymple, Detective—Amateur
Time period(s): 20th century; 1920s (1926)
Locale(s): England

Summary: *Anthem for Doomed Youth*, a historical mystery, is the 19th installment in the Daisy Dalrymple series from author Carola Dunn. In 1926, Alec Fletcher, a detective with the Scotland Yard, is called in to investigate the discovery of three corpses outside of London. The three victims, none of whom had identification, were each shot through the heart and buried in shallow graves in Epping Forest. Alec is tasked with finding the connection between the three men and doing his best to keep his supervisor's wife, Daisy Dalrymple, away from the case. Alec fails on both accounts and soon Daisy is in the midst of the investigation, uncovering a shocking connection between the three dead men and World War I.

425

SAM EASTLAND

Shadow Pass

(New York: Bantam Books, 2011)

Series: Inspector Pekkala Series. Book 2
Story type: Historical; Series
Subject(s): Mystery; History; Murder
Major character(s): Pekkala, Detective—Police; Rolan Nagorski, Military Personnel (colonel); Josef Stalin, Historical Figure
Time period(s): 20th century
Locale(s): Solomon Islands

Summary: In *Shadow Pass* by Sam Eastland, the grisly murder of a Soviet weapons inventor forces Josef Stalin to call in Inspector Pekkala—a detective Stalin respects and fears. Formerly an investigator for the Romanov family, Pekkala is shrewd and brilliant. On Stalin's orders, he searches for the man who murdered Colonel Rolan Nagorski—the creator of a powerful weapon known as T-34. Pekkala is granted full access to prominent military officials and sensitive information. As he uncovers the truth about Nagorski's death, Inspector Pekkala puts the Communist regime and his own life at risk. *Shadow Pass* is the second book in the Pekkala series.

Where it's reviewed:
Library Journal, Oct. 15, 2010, page S4

Other books by the same author:
Eye of the Red Tsar, 2010

Other books you might like:
Philip Kerr, *March Violets*, 1989
William Ryan, *The Holy Thief*, 2010
Martin Cruz Smith, *Stalin's Ghost*, 2007
Tom Rob Smith, *Child 44: A Novel*, 2008
Olen Steinhauer, *The Bridge of Sighs*, 2003

426

WESSEL EBERSOHN

The October Killings

(Roggebaai, South Africa: Umuzi, 2009)

Story type: Contemporary
Subject(s): Murder; Detective fiction; Apartheid
Major character(s): Abigail Bukulu, Government Official (Justice Department); Leon Lourens, Police Officer; Bishop, Murderer
Time period(s): 21st century; 2000s
Locale(s): South Africa

Summary: In *The October Killings*, author Wessel Ebersohn tells the story of Abigail Bukulu, an esteemed young member of the South African Justice Department, and the police officer she helps. Every year on the anniversary of the Lesotho attacks, another member of the police force turns up dead. Officer Leon Lourens turns to Abigail for help, and he soon realizes that his charge knows who is behind the annual killings. With Abigail's aid, Leon searches for the man known as Bishop, the ruthless criminal who masterminds the yearly October killings.

Where it's reviewed:
Booklist, Dec. 1, 2010, page 31
Library Journal, Nov. 15, 2010, page 66
Publishers Weekly, Nov. 15, 2010, page 42

Other books by the same author:
Closed Circle, 1990
Klara's Visitors, 1987
Store Up the Anger, 1980
The Centurion, 1979
A Lonely Place to Die, 1979

Other books you might like:
Jonathan Kellerman, *When the Bough Breaks*, 1985
Jassy MacKenzie, *Random Violence*, 2008
James McClure, *The Steam Pig*, 1971
Deon Meyer, *Dead Before Dying*, 2006
Malla Nunn, *A Beautiful Place to Die*, 2009

427

MARTIN EDWARDS

The Hanging Wood

(Scottsdale, Arizona: Poisoned Pen Press, 2011)

Series: Lake District Mystery Series. Book 5
Story type: Police Procedural; Series
Subject(s): Mystery; Detective fiction; Murder
Major character(s): Hanna Scarlett, Detective (chief inspector); Callum Hinds, Teenager (murder victim);

Mystery

Orla Payne, Sister (of Callum)
Time period(s): 21st century; 2010s
Locale(s): England

Summary: In *The Hanging Wood* by Martin Edwards, a woman returns to the Lake District where her then 13-year-old brother vanished two decades ago. Though the authorities at the time believed that Callum Hinds was killed by his uncle (a theory reinforced by the uncle's subsequent suicide in the Hanging Wood), Orla Payne never accepted the explanation. Living near her family's home once again, Orla is more certain than ever that someone else is responsible for Callum's death. Unfortunately, DCI Hannah Scarlett ignores Orla's claims until Orla dies in a suspicious accident. *The Hanging Wood* is the fifth book in the Lake District Mystery series.

Where it's reviewed:
Publishers Weekly, Feb. 7, 2011, page 39

Other books by the same author:
The Serpent Pool, 2010
The Arsenic Labyrinth, 2007
The Cipher Garden, 2005
The Coffin Trail, 2004
All the Lonely People, 1991

Other books you might like:
Stephen Booth, *Black Dog*, 2000
Deborah Crombie, *A Share in Death*, 1993
Reginald Hill, *A Clubbable Woman*, 1970
Susan Hill, *The Various Haunts of Men*, 2007
Louise Penny, *Still Life*, 2006

428

J.T. ELLISON

The Immortals

(Don Mills, Ontario, Canada: Mira, 2010)

Series: Taylor Jackson Series. Book 5
Story type: Police Procedural
Subject(s): Mystery; Murder; Occultism
Major character(s): Taylor Jackson, Detective—Homicide, Police Officer (lieutenant); John Baldwin, FBI Agent, Fiance(e) (of Taylor)
Time period(s): 21st century; 2010s
Locale(s): Nashville, Tennessee

Summary: *The Immortals* is a suspenseful police procedural from best-selling author J.T. Ellison. The book is the fifth installment in the Taylor Jackson series. Taylor Jackson finally gets her lieutenant badge back on Halloween, just in time to investigate the grisly murders of eight Nashville teens. The bodies are found naked and covered with occult symbols in a posh Nashville neighborhood. The public is outraged and horrified by the brutal act of violence, creating a media frenzy that Taylor needs to carefully tread through. Unable to rely on the assistance of her fiance, FBI profiler John Baldwin, who is being investigated for a mishandled case, Taylor must guide the investigation herself, diving headfirst into a world of ritual murders, witchcraft, and mysticism to find the deranged killer.

Where it's reviewed:
Publishers Weekly, August 23, 2010, page 34

Other books by the same author:
The Cold Room, 2010
Judas Kiss, 2009
14, 2008
All the Pretty Girls, 2007

Other books you might like:
Allison Brennan, *Sudden Death*, 2009
Lisa Gardner, *Alone*, 2005
Alex Kava, *A Perfect Evil*, 2001
Karin Slaughter, *Blindsighted*, 2001
Chevy Stevens, *Still Missing*, 2010

429

HALLIE EPHRON

Come and Find Me

(New York: HarperCollins, 2011)

Story type: Techno-Thriller
Subject(s): Computers; Missing persons; Death
Major character(s): Diana Highsmith, Computer Expert, Widow(er); Daniel Highsmith, Spouse (of Diana, deceased)
Time period(s): 21st century; 2000s

Summary: In *Come and Find Me*, author Hallie Ephron tells the story of Diana Highsmith, a former computer hacker mired in grief after the loss of her husband Daniel during a mountain-climbing expedition. Diana spends her days locked up at home, working as a computer-security expert, and her only real attempts at socialization include online chats with clients via a persona she's created named Nadia. For now her virtual existence is just fine, until the disappearance of her sister yanks her back to reality. Now Diana must battle enemies both real and imaginary in order to find her sister and avoid losing yet another person she loves.

Where it's reviewed:
Publishers Weekly, Feb. 7, 2011, page 36

Other books by the same author:
The Everything Guide to Writing Your First Novel, 2010
The Bibliophile's Devotional, 2009
Never Tell a Lie: A Novel of Suspense, 2009
1001 Books for Every Mood, 2008
Writing and Selling Your Mystery Novel, 2005

Other books you might like:
Linwood Barclay, *No Time for Goodbye*, 2007
Harlan Coben, *Promise Me*, 2006
Sophie Hannah, *The Wrong Mother*, 2009
Pam Lewis, *Speak Softly, She Can Hear*, 2005
Laura Lippman, *What the Dead Know*, 2007

430

KATHLEEN ERNST

Old World Murder

(Woodbury, Minnesota: Midnight Ink, 2010)

Series: Chloe Ellefson Mystery Series. Book 1
Story type: Amateur Detective; Cozy Mystery

Subject(s): Mystery; Antiques; Museums
Major character(s): Chloe Ellefson, Museum Curator, Detective—Amateur; Berget Lundquist, Aged Person
Time period(s): 20th century; 1980s (1982)
Locale(s): Wisconsin, United States

Summary: *Old World Murder* is the first book in the Chloe Ellefson Mystery series by award-winning author Kathleen Ernst. It's 1982 and Chloe Ellefson has just started a job as a curator at Old World Wisconsin, an outdoor museum celebrating settlement life during the late 19th century. During Chloe's first day on the job, she's approached by Berget Lundquist, an elderly woman seeking assistance tracking down a family heirloom. The antique in question is a hand-painted Norwegian ale bowl that the Lundquist family donated to the museum two decades earlier. Moments after making her request, Berget is killed in a suspicious car accident, prompting Chloe to start a secret investigation into the whereabouts of the bowl. The deeper Chloe digs into the bowl's history, the more dangerous and deadly her search becomes.

Where it's reviewed:
Booklist, October 1, 2010, page 35
Library Journal, September 1, 2010, page 94
Publishers Weekly, August 9, 2010, page 34
Publishers Weekly, August 9, 2010, page 34

Other books by the same author:
Clues in the Shadows, 2009
The Runaway Friend, 2008
Midnight in Lonesome Hollow, 2007
Secrets in the Hills, 2006
Danger at the Zoo, 2005

Other books you might like:
Simon Brett, *Murder in the Museum*, 2003
Kate Carlisle, *Homicide in Hardcover*, 2009
Jane K. Cleland, *Consigned to Death*, 2006
Sheila Connolly, *Fundraising the Dead*, 2010
Jo Dereske, *Miss Zukas and the Library Murders*, 1994

431

LOREN D. ESTLEMAN

The Left-Handed Dollar

(New York: Forge Books, 2010)

Series: Amos Walker Series. Book 20
Story type: Contemporary
Subject(s): Detective fiction; Friendship; Suspense
Major character(s): Amos Walker, Detective—Private; Barry Stockpole, Journalist, Friend (of Walker), Crime Victim; Joseph Ballista, Organized Crime Figure; Lucille "Lefty Lucy" Lettermore, Lawyer
Time period(s): 21st century; 2010s
Locale(s): Detroit, Michigan

Summary: *The Left-Handed Dollar* is the 20th book in Loren D. Estleman's Amos Walker mystery series. This episode finds Walker's best pal, journalist Barry Stockpole, nearly killed in an apparent bombing by mobsters. Lucille Lettermore is the attorney hired by the accused organized crime figure, and "Lefty Lucy" then hires Walker to clear her client's name. This turn of events puts the PI in an entirely new place, torn between the

demands of his work and his personal affection for his best friend.

Where it's reviewed:
Booklist, December 15, 2010, page 24
Library Journal, December 2010, page 100
New York Times Book Review, December 12, 2010, page 30
Publishers Weekly, October 25, 2010, page 33

Other books by the same author:
American Detective, 2007
The Glass Highway, 1983
The Midnight Man, 1982
Angel Eyes, 1981
Motor City Blue, 1980

Other books you might like:
K.C. Constantine, *The Rocksburg Railroad Murders*, 1972
Jon A. Jackson, *The Diehard*, 1977
Michael Koryta, *Tonight I Said Goodbye*, 2004
Elmore Leonard, *City Primeval: High Noon in Detroit*, 1980
Bill Pronzini, *The Snatch*, 1969

432

LINDA FAIRSTEIN

Silent Mercy

(New York: Dutton, 2011)

Series: Alexandra Cooper Series. Book 13
Story type: Police Procedural
Subject(s): Religion; Mystery; Murder
Major character(s): Alexandra Cooper, Lawyer, Detective; Mike Chapman, Detective
Time period(s): 21st century; 2010s
Locale(s): New York, New York

Summary: *Silent Mercy* is the thirteenth installment in the Alexandra Cooper series. New York prosecutor, Alex Cooper and detective, Mike Chapman are sent to Harlem when the body of a decapitated woman is found burning on the steps of Mount Neboh Baptist Church. A few days later, another mutilated body is found at a cathedral in Little Italy. Despite the different beliefs of the two victims, Cooper and Chapman are certain that a religious motive is at work. Determined to stop another killing, Cooper travels across Manhattan to various houses of worship, trying to find a connection between the murders, but before she can get too far into the investigation, a high-ranking religious leader in the area has her pulled from the case. That's not enough to keep Cooper from snooping around and putting together the pieces, even though the truth puts her at great risk.

Where it's reviewed:
Library Journal, January 2011, page 83

Other books by the same author:
Hell Gate, 2010
The Deadhouse, 2001
Cold Hit, 1999
Likely to Die, 1997
Final Jeopardy, 1996

Other books you might like:
Rose Connors, *Absolute Certainty*, 2002
Perri O'Shaughnessy, *Motion to Suppress*, 1995
Richard North Patterson, *The Lasko Tangent*, 1979
Lisa Scottoline, *Final Appeal*, 1994
Robert K. Tanenbaum, *No Lesser Plea*, 1987

433

DIANE FANNING

Twisted Reason

(Sutton, Surrey, England: Severn House, 2011)

Series: Lucinda Pierce Series. Book 4
Story type: Police Procedural
Subject(s): Detective fiction; Mystery; Alzheimer's disease
Major character(s): Lucinda Pierce, Detective—Homicide
Time period(s): 21st century; 2010s
Locale(s): Virginia, United States

Summary: *Twisted Reason* is the fourth installment in the Lucinda Pierce series. Homicide detective Lucinda Pierce's newest case is hitting awfully close to home. An elderly man, suffering from dementia, disappears without a trace for five months before his body shows up on his son's porch. All early signs point to a heart attack, but some of the circumstances surrounding the death seem unusual to Lucinda. When two other Alzheimer's patients also show up dead—one by drowning and one by head trauma—Lucinda begins to suspect the worst. As Lucinda investigates the three deaths and a slew of other disappearances, she's forced to confront the demons of her past regarding the death of her parents.

Where it's reviewed:
Library Journal, December 2010, page 91
Publishers Weekly, November 15, 2010, page 43

Other books by the same author:
Mistaken Identity, 2010
Punish the Deed, 2009
The Trophy Exchange, 2008
Bite the Moon, 2007
Written in Blood, 2005

Other books you might like:
Kathryn Casey, *Singularity*, 2008
Jodi Compton, *The 37th Hour*, 2003
Dianne Emley, *The First Cut: A Novel*, 2006
J.A. Jance, *Desert Heat*, 1993
Virginia Lanier, *Death in Bloodhound Red*, 1995

434

JASPER FFORDE

One of Our Thursdays Is Missing

(New York: Viking, 2011)

Series: Thursday Next Series. Book 6
Story type: Fantasy; Series
Subject(s): Mystery; Fantasy; Literature

Major character(s): Thursday Next, Detective; Whitby Jett, Businessman (EZ-Read)
Time period(s): 21st century; 2010s
Locale(s): England; BookWorld, Fictional Location

Summary: In *One of Our Thursdays Is Missing* by Jasper Fforde, the BookWorld is shaken by a disagreement among the genres and Thursday Next is the only one who can sort things out. In the BookWorld, each genre—crime, horror, comedy, children's fiction, and others—occupies an assigned territory. Recently, a border dispute has emerged between Women's Fiction and Racy Novel. When the real Thursday (a literary detective) goes missing before negotiations are set to begin, the residents of the BookWorld convince the written Thursday to come out of her book to settle the quarrel. *One of Our Thursdays Is Missing* is the sixth book in the Thursday Next series.

Where it's reviewed:
Library Journal, Feb. 15, 2011, page 99
Publishers Weekly, Jan. 17, 2011, page 26

Other books by the same author:
First Among Sequels, 2007
Something Rotten, 2004
The Well of Lost Plots, 2003
Lost in a Good Book, 2002
The Eyre Affair: A Novel, 2001

Other books you might like:
Douglas Adams, *The Hitchhiker's Guide to the Galaxy*, 1979
Eoin Colfer, *Artemis Fowl*, 2001
China Mieville, *Perdido Street Station*, 2000
Jack O'Connell, *Box Nine*, 1992
Thomas Pynchon, *The Crying of Lot 49*, 1966

435

JOY FIELDING

Now You See Her

(New York: Simon and Schuster, 2011)

Subject(s): Parent-child relations; Missing persons; Divorce
Major character(s): Marcy Taggart, Divorced Person, Mother (of Devon); Devon Taggart, Daughter (of Marcy)
Locale(s): Ireland

Summary: In *Now You See Her*, Fielding tells the story of Marcy Taggart, a 50-year-old, newly divorced woman who is vacationing in Ireland. The trip was supposed to be a celebratory sojourn for her 25th wedding anniversary—that is, until her husband decided he'd much rather keep company with a woman who worked at their country club. Alone and still grieving over the loss of her daughter, Devon, who went missing more than two years ago, Marcy decides to make the most of her time in the Emerald Isle. Then she sees a girl who looks just like Devon, and her vacation turns into a mission to find her daughter once and for all.

Where it's reviewed:
Booklist, Jan. 1, 2011, page 50

Library Journal, Feb. 1, 2011, page 52
Publishers Weekly, Dec. 13, 2010, page 36

Other books by the same author:
The Wild Zone, 2010
Still Life, 2009
Charley's Web, 2008
Heartstopper, 2007
Mad River Road, 2006

Other books you might like:
Mary Higgins Clark, *Where Are the Children?*, 1975
Nicci French, *Catch Me When I Fall*, 2006
Lisa Gardner, *The Survivors Club*, 2001
Judith Kelman, *Prime Evil*, 1986
Pam Lewis, *Speak Softly, She Can Hear*, 2005

436

SHARON FIFFER

Backstage Stuff

(New York: Minotaur Books, 2011)

Series: Jane Wheel Series. Book 7
Story type: Private Detective
Subject(s): Mystery; Plays; Murder
Major character(s): Jane Wheel, Detective—Private, Antiquarian; Tim Lowry, Friend (of Jane)
Time period(s): 21st century; 2010s
Locale(s): United States

Summary: *Backstage Stuff* is the seventh installment in the Jane Wheel series. Jane Wheel is a private investigator, antiques lover, and soon-to-be divorcee. Her best friend, Tim Lowry, knows that Jane needs something to keep her mind off her personal affairs so he hatches a seemingly brilliant plan. Tim has discovered an old murder-mystery play that he wants to direct, despite claims that the script is actually haunted. Tim enlists Jane's help with the production, ignoring a series of worrisome notes in the script about the play's alleged curse. When the play's carpenter mysteriously dies, Tim begins to rethink the curse and Jane wonders who is so against the play's production that they're willing to murder to put an end to it.

Where it's reviewed:
Booklist, December 15, 2010, page 22
Publishers Weekly, November 15, 2010, page 43

Other books by the same author:
Scary Stuff, 2009
Buried Stuff, 2004
The Wrong Stuff, 2003
Dead Guy's Stuff, 2002
Killer Stuff, 2001

Other books you might like:
Barbara Allan, *Antiques Roadkill*, 2006
Jennie Bentley, *Fatal Fixer-Upper*, 2008
Jane K. Cleland, *Consigned to Death*, 2006
Sarah Graves, *The Dead Cat Bounce*, 1998
Julie Hyzy, *Grace Under Pressure*, 2010

437

JOANNE FLUKE

Devil's Food Cake Murder

(New York: Kensington Publishing Corporation, 2011)

Series: Hannah Swensen Series. Book 14
Story type: Contemporary; Series
Subject(s): Mystery; Food; Murder
Major character(s): Hannah Swenson, Baker, Detective—Amateur; Norman Rhodes, Dentist; Bev Thorndike, Dentist, Fiance(e) (of Norman, former); Mike Kingston, Detective—Police; Matthew Walters, Religious (minister); Bob Knudsen, Religious (minister); Claire Knudsen, Spouse (of Bob), Friend (of Swenson)
Time period(s): 21st century; 2010s
Locale(s): Lake Eden, Minnesota

Summary: In *Devil's Food Cake Murder* by Joanne Fluke, bakery owner and amateur sleuth, Hannah Swenson helps her police-detective boyfriend track the killer of a substitute minister. Reverend Matthew Walters agreed to fill in at Lake Eden's Holy Redeemer church while his friend, Reverend Bob Knudsen, is away on his honeymoon. When Walters is shot while eating a piece of chocolate cake, Hannah assists in the investigation. The good news is—they have a witness. The bad news is—the witness is a mynah bird that repeats one cryptic phrase, "The wages of sin is death." *Devil's Food Cake Murder* is the 14th book in the Hannah Swensen series.

Where it's reviewed:
Library Journal, Feb. 1, 2011, page 47

Other books by the same author:
Apple Turnover Murder, 2010
Lemon Meringue Pie Murder, 2003
Blueberry Muffin Murder, 2002
Strawberry Shortcake Murder, 2001
Chocolate Chip Cookie Murder, 2000

Other books you might like:
Avery Aames, *The Long Quiche Goodbye*, 2010
Laura Childs, *Death by Darjeeling*, 2001
Cleo Coyle, *On What Grounds*, 2003
Diane Mott Davidson, *Catering to Nobody*, 1990
Jenn McKinlay, *Sprinkle with Murder*, 2010

438

T.J. FORRESTER

Miracles Inc.

(New York: Simon & Schuster, 2011)

Story type: Religious
Subject(s): Religion; Crime; Murder
Major character(s): Vernon Oliver, Television Personality (televangelist); Miriam MacKenzie, Businesswoman (owner of Miracles, Inc.)

Summary: *Miracles Inc.* is the debut novel by author T.J. Forrester. In this book, the author juxtaposes the downtrodden existence of Death Row inmate Vernon Oliver with his former life of wealth and luxuries. As Vernon waits out his death sentence, he narrates the tale of his success and subsequent downfall as a popular televangelist. His career began at the behest of Miriam MacKenzie, owner of Miracles Inc. Vernon's image as a motorcycle-riding messenger of God soon has Miracles Inc. raking in millions at the expense of others' faith. Yet Vernon's personal life remains in shambles as his wife falls apart, and Vernon finds himself imprisoned for a double murder he didn't commit—or did he? First book.

Where it's reviewed:
Booklist, Feb. 1, 2011, page 28
Publishers Weekly, Oct. 25, 2010, page 26

Other books you might like:
Martin Clark, *The Many Aspects of Mobile Home Living*, 2000
Martin Clark, *Plain Heathen Mischief*, 2004
Harry Dolan, *Bad Things Happen*, 2009
Sara Gruen, *Water for Elephants*, 2007
Michael Lister, *Power in the Blood*, 2006

439

REBECCA FRAYN

Deceptions

(New York: Washington Square Press, 2011)

Story type: Child-in-Peril
Subject(s): Missing persons; Parent-child relations; Interpersonal relations
Major character(s): Julian, Fiance(e) (of Annie); Annie, Fiance(e) (of Julian), Widow(er), Mother (of Rachel and Dan); Dan, Son (of Annie); Rachel, Daughter (of Annie)

Summary: In *Deceptions*, Rebecca Frayn tells the story of Julian and Annie, a recently engaged couple eager to reveal news of their betrothal to Annie's children. Annie hopes that the happy news will begin to heal wounds created by the death of their father several years before. Yet on the day they are to make their announcement, Annie's son Dan doesn't come home. Soon a missing persons investigation is launched, and weeks become months as Dan is nowhere to be found. Julian narrates the story as Annie risks her relationship with her daughter, Rachel, as well as with Julian by refusing to give up hope. When a teenager shows up on the family's doorstep claiming to be Dan, Annie is overwhelmed with joy—but Julian is doubtful of the truthfulness of this stranger's claims. Frayn is also the author of *One Life*.

Other books by the same author:
One Life, 2007

Other books you might like:
Linwood Barclay, *No Time for Goodbye*, 2007
Nicci French, *Secret Smile*, 2004
Tana French, *In the Woods*, 2007
Sophie Hannah, *The Wrong Mother*, 2009
Laura Lippman, *I'd Know You Anywhere*, 2010

440

LEIGHTON GAGE

Every Bitter Thing

(New York: Soho Crime, 2010)

Series: Chief Inspector Mario Silva Mystery Series. Book 4
Story type: Contemporary
Subject(s): Detective fiction; South Americans; Murder
Major character(s): Mario Silva, Detective—Police; Arnaldo Nunes, Sidekick (of Silva)
Time period(s): 21st century; 2010s
Locale(s): Brazil

Summary: Brazilian police inspector Mario Silva and his partner Arnaldo Nunes are on the hunt for a killer. After a brutal murder in which the son of a prominent politician is killed, Silva and Nunes are fast on the case. They soon unearth links to a string of other murders involving high-profile individuals, and the duo sets out to stop a killer from striking again—even if that means crossing the bounds of the law. Leighton Gage's *Every Bitter Thing* is the fourth novel in the Chief Inspector Mario Silva series.

Where it's reviewed:
Booklist, November 1, 2010, page 29
Library Journal, October 15, 2010, page 74
New York Times Book Review, December 12, 2010, page 30
Publishers Weekly, October 11, 2010, page 29

Other books by the same author:
Dying Gasp, 2010
Buried Strangers, 2009
Blood of the Wicked, 2008

Other books you might like:
Andrea Camilleri, *The Shape of Water*, 2002
David Corbett, *Blood of Paradise*, 2007
Luiz Alfredo Garcia-Roza, *The Silence of the Rain*, 2002
Kent Harrington, *Red Jungle: A Novel*, 2004
Martin Limon, *Jade Lady Burning*

441

MATTHEW GALLAWAY

The Metropolis Case

(New York: Crown Publishers, 2010)

Subject(s): Operas; Music; Homosexuality
Major character(s): Martin, Lawyer, Homosexual; Maria, Orphan, Singer; Lucien, Son (of scientist), Singer
Time period(s): 21st century; (2000s); 20th century; (1960s); 19th century
Locale(s): Paris, France; Germany; New York, New York; Philadelphia, Pennsylvania

Summary: *The Metropolis Case* is a novel from debut author Matthew Gallaway. The story connects the lives of three unique characters, each living in a different era and place. In New York City in 2001, Martin is a 40-

year-old homosexual lawyer suffering from HIV and a midlife crisis. Meanwhile, Maria is a musically talented orphan living in Philadelphia in 1960, and Lucien is a scientist's son living in Paris during the mid-19th century. Their three stories are interwoven by their love for the opera, particularly *Tristan and Isolde*. Lucien performs in the role of Tristan in the opera's Germanic premiere; Maria appears as Isolde in the Metropolitan Opera's rendition; and Martin eventually quits his job as a lawyer and pursues his interest in the opera. First novel.

Where it's reviewed:
Library Journal, Sept. 1, 2010, page 98
New York Times, Dec. 28, 2010, page C9

Other books you might like:
Louis Bayard, *The School of Night*, 2011
Ian Caldwell, *The Rule of Four*, 2004
Katherine Neville, *The Eight*, 1988
Arturo Perez-Reverte, *The Flanders Panel*, 1990
Vikram Seth, *An Equal Music*, 1999

442

LISA GARDNER

Love You More

(New York: Bantam Books, 2011)

Series: D.D. Warren Series. Book 5
Story type: Police Procedural; Series
Subject(s): Detective fiction; Murder; Mystery
Major character(s): D.D. Warren, Detective—Police; Tessa Leoni, Police Officer (Massachusetts state trooper); Brian Darby, Spouse (of Tessa); Sophie, Daughter (of Tessa and Brian), 6-Year-Old; Bobby Dodge, Detective—Police, Lover (of D.D., former)
Time period(s): 21st century; 2010s
Locale(s): Boston, Massachusetts

Summary: In *Love You More* by Lisa Gardner, Massachusetts state trooper Tessa Leoni admits that she killed her husband, but insists that she acted in self-defense. When Boston police sergeant D.D. Warren is assigned to the case, she realizes that Tessa's bruises support her claims of abuse but questions the absence of the couple's six-year-old daughter. As the authorities look for little Sophie, Tessa carefully controls the information that she shares and uses her familiarity with police procedure to influence the case. Meanwhile, D.D. learns that former boyfriend Bobby Dodge will also be working the case. *Love You More* is the fifth book in the D.D. Warren series.

Where it's reviewed:
Booklist, January 1, 2011, page 49
Library Journal, January 2011, page 83
Publishers Weekly, January 17, 2011, page 26

Other books by the same author:
Live to Tell, 2010
The Neighbor, 2009
Hide, 2007
Gone, 2006
Alone, 2005

Other books you might like:
Linwood Barclay, *No Time for Goodbye*, 2007
Jodi Compton, *The 37th Hour*, 2003
Gillian Flynn, *Sharp Objects*, 2006
Tess Gerritsen, *Vanish: A Novel*, 2005
Pam Lewis, *Speak Softly, She Can Hear*, 2005

443

JASON GOODWIN

An Evil Eye

(New York: Farrar, Straus, and Giroux, 2011)

Series: Yashim the Eunuch Series. Book 4
Story type: Historical - Exotic; Series
Subject(s): Mystery; Detective fiction; Turkish history
Major character(s): Yashim, Detective; Fevzi Pasha, Military Personnel (admiral)
Time period(s): 19th century; 1840s
Locale(s): Istanbul, Turkey

Summary: In *An Evil Eye* by Jason Goodwin, Yashim, a eunuch, investigates the defection of his mentor, Fevzi Pasha. To Yashim, the Ottoman fleet's admiral, Pasha, seems an unlikely traitor to the empire. Yashim recalls him as a brutal but steadfast follower of the sultan—a man who trained Yashim well in the art of detection. Yashim's investigation into Pasha's background leads him to the sultan's palace—a mysterious world inhabited by family members, servants, and the harem. As the eunuch detective soon realizes, it is sultan's seductive and dangerous household that holds the key to Fevzi Pasha's shocking actions. *An Evil Eye* is the fourth book in the Yashim the Eunuch series.

Where it's reviewed:
Publishers Weekly, Feb. 21, 2011, page 110

Other books by the same author:
The Bellini Card, 2008
The Snake Stone, 2007
The Janissary Tree, 2006
Lords of the Horizons, 1998

Other books you might like:
Boris Akunin, *The Winter Queen*, 2003
Barbara Cleverly, *The Last Kashmiri Rose*, 2001
Donna Leon, *Death at La Fenice*, 1992
Barbara Nadel, *Belshazzar's Daughter*, 2004
Jenny White, *The Sultan's Seal*, 2006

444

HOWARD GORDON

Gideon's War

(New York: Simon and Schuster, 2011)

Story type: Contemporary
Subject(s): Brothers; Terrorism; Suspense
Major character(s): Gideon Davis, Diplomat (negotiator), Brother (of Tillman); Tillman Davis, Terrorist, Brother (of Gideon); Earl Parker, Friend (of Gideon), Hostage; Kate Murphy, Manager (of oil rig)

Time period(s): 21st century; 2010s
Locale(s): Mohan, Oceania

Summary: In *Gideon's War*, screenwriter and author, Howard Gordon crafts a tale of suspense and political intrigue, centered on the relationship between two estranged brothers. Gideon Davis has a renowned reputation as a peacemaker and diplomat, and he is summoned by an old friend, Earl Parker, to bring a rogue government agent back to the United States. That agent is Tillman Davis, and he is Gideon's brother. As Gideon attempts to find his sibling, things go horribly wrong: Earl Parker is held hostage and Tillman is nowhere to be found. Now it's up to Gideon and oil rig supervisor Kate Murphy to save Parker and extradite Tillman—at the risk of their own lives. First novel.

Where it's reviewed:
Booklist, January 1, 2011, page 49
Globe & Mail, January 27, 2011, page R3
Library Journal, December 2010, page 104
Publishers Weekly, November 8, 2010, page 43

Other books you might like:
Vince Flynn, *Transfer of Power*, 1999
Christopher Reich, *Rules of Deception*, 2008
Matthew Reilly, *Ice Station*, 1999
Joel Rosenberg, *The Last Jihad: A Novel*, 2002
Brad Thor, *The Lions of Lucerne*, February 27, 2007

445

STEVEN GORE

Absolute Risk

(Scottsdale, Arizona: Poisoned Pen Press, 2010)

Story type: Contemporary
Subject(s): Politics; Adventure; Detective fiction
Major character(s): Graham Gage, Detective—Private; Hani Ibraham, Professor (for MIT mathematician); Faith, Spouse (of Graham)
Time period(s): 21st century; 2010s
Locale(s): United States

Summary: Political intrigue takes center stage in Steven Gore's *Absolute Risk*. San Francisco private eye Graham Gage is summoned by the government to track down the real story behind the mysterious death of a former agent with the Federal Bureau of Investigation. Gage has no idea that this simple job will lead him into the dangerous underbelly of contemporary politics, taking him on a whirlwind adventure from the United States to China and bringing him face to face with some of the most powerful—and evil—figures in the modern world.

Where it's reviewed:
Library Journal, December 2010, page 91
Publishers Weekly, September 27, 2010, page 38

Other books by the same author:
Final Target, 2010

Other books you might like:
Vince Flynn, *Separation of Power*, 2001
David Hagberg, *White House*, 1999
Brian Haig, *The President's Assassin*, 2005

Mike Lawson, *The Inside Ring*, 2005
Brad Thor, *The Last Patriot: A Thriller*, 2008

446

MICHAEL GREGORIO (Pseudonym of Daniela De Gregorio and Michael G. Jacob)

Unholy Awakening

(New York: Minotaur Books, 2010)

Series: Hanno Stiffeniis Series. Book 4
Story type: Historical
Subject(s): Detective fiction; Germanic peoples; Murder
Major character(s): Hanno Stiffeniis, Police Officer (police magistrate); Angela Enke, Seamstress, Crime Victim; Emma Rimmele, Employer (of Angela)
Time period(s): 19th century
Locale(s): Prussia, Europe

Summary: Set in Prussia during the early 19th century, *Unholy Awakening* follows the crime-solving exploits of magistrate Hanno Stiffeniis, who is still grieving the loss of his son after a plague of illness sweeps the town. When the body of local seamstress Angela Enke is discovered, Hanno finds the perfect escape from his grief. As he sets out to nab the killer, he becomes enmeshed in the life of Angela's boss, the strange yet alluring Emma Rimmele, and struggles with his own personal attraction to her. Meanwhile, the town is in an uproar, fearful that Angela was killed by a vampire and will rise from the dead at any moment. This volume is the fourth novel in the Hanno Stiffeniis series.

Where it's reviewed:
Booklist, September 1, 2010, page 53
The Independent, October 25, 2010, page 14
Library Journal, September 1, 2010, page 94
Publishers Weekly, August 30, 2010, page 32

Other books by the same author:
A Visible Darkness, 2009
Days of Atonement, 2008
Critique of Criminal Reason, 2006

Other books you might like:
Bruce Alexander, *Blind Justice*, 1994
Bernard Cornwell, *Sharpe's Rifles*, 1988
C.S. Harris, *What Angels Fear*, 2005
Deanna Raybourn, *Silent in the Grave*, 2007
Will Thomas, *Some Danger Involved*, 2004

447

LAURA GRIFFIN

Unforgivable

(New York: Pocket Books, 2010)

Series: Tracers Series. Book 3
Story type: Romantic Suspense
Subject(s): Romances (Fiction); Mystery; Suspense
Major character(s): Mia Voss, Consultant (DNA), Crime Victim; Ric Santos, Detective

Time period(s): 21st century; 2010s
Locale(s): United States

Summary: *Unforgivable* is a romantic thriller from best-selling author Laura Griffin. The book is the third installment in the Tracers series. When DNA expert Mia Voss is the victim of a carjacking, she chalks it up as nothing more than a random act of violence. When the threats and crimes against her begin piling up, Mia realizes someone is after her. It seems her only hope of protecting her loved ones is to deliberately sabotage a case and let a crazed killer go free. Detective Ric Santos may have ruined his chances of having a romantic relationship with Mia, but he's not about to let her get hurt. He can tell that she's lying and terrified about something, but the only way he can successfully protect her is if he can earn her trust again.

Where it's reviewed:
Booklist, December 1, 2010, page 36
Publishers Weekly, October 25, 2010, page 35
Romantic Times, December 2010, page 62

Other books by the same author:
Unspeakable, 2010
Untraceable, 2009
Whisper of Warning, 2009
One Wrong Step, 2008
Thread of Fear, 2008

Other books you might like:
Allison Brennan, *Love Me to Death*, 2010
Dianne Emley, *The First Cut: A Novel*, 2006
Michelle Gagnon, *The Tunnels*, 2007
Tami Hoag, *Cry Wolf*, 1993
Wendy Corsi Staub, *Scared to Death*, 2010

448

PAUL GROSSMAN

The Sleepwalkers

(New York: St. Martin's Press, 2010)

Story type: Historical
Subject(s): Detective fiction; Serial murders; Crime
Major character(s): Willi Kraus, Military Personnel (German soldier), Detective
Time period(s): 20th century; 1930s-1940s (1932)
Locale(s): Berlin, Germany

Summary: *The Sleepwalkers*, by Paul Grossman, features Willi Kraus, a Jewish-German soldier and one of the country's most revered detectives. After cracking a case involving a child killer, Kraus finds himself swept up into another case. A woman's body is found in a river. Death and bodies are commonplace in 1932 Berlin, but something is different about this corpse. She is missing her wisdom teeth—which is out of the ordinary for the time period—and her legs look as if the skin was removed and sewn back together again. As Kraus searches for the killer, a missing princess and hypnotist complicate the case.

Where it's reviewed:
Booklist, October 15, 2010, page 35
Kirkus Reviews, September 1, 2010, page 814

Library Journal, July 2010, page 71
Publishers Weekly, July 19, 2010, page 110

Other books you might like:
Rebecca Cantrell, *A Trace of Smoke*, 2009
Jeffery Deaver, *Garden of Beasts*, 2004
Alan Furst, *Red Gold*, 1999
Philip Kerr, *March Violets*, 1989
Olen Steinhauer, *The Bridge of Sighs*, 2003

449

BETH GROUNDWATER

Deadly Currents

(Woodbury, Minnesota: Midnight Ink, 2011)

Story type: Amateur Detective
Subject(s): White water paddling; Rafting (Sports); Sports
Major character(s): Mandy Tanner, Detective—Amateur; Tom King, Businessman (real estate developer)

Summary: *Deadly Currents* is the first book in author Beth Groundwater's outdoor-adventure series. When Mandy Tanner takes a job as a guide for her uncle's white-water-rafting company, she doesn't really expect calm waters, but pulling a dead man from the water is more than she bargained for. The deceased turns out to be Tom King, a well-connected real estate mogul with more enemies than friends, and the list of suspects is endless. Still, Tom's death sends Mandy's uncle's business into a public-relations tailspin. When Mandy's uncle turns up dead as well, she decides to do some amateur sleuthing of her own, and soon she learns that things aren't always as they seem. Groundwater is also the author of *To Hell in a Handbasket*.

Where it's reviewed:
Publishers Weekly, Jan. 10, 2011, page 34

Other books by the same author:
To Hell in a Handbasket, 2009
A Real Basket Case, 2007

Other books you might like:
Margaret Coel, *The Eagle Catcher*, 1995
John Galligan, *Red Sky, Red Dragonfly*, 2001
Victoria Houston, *Dead Angler*, 2000
William Kent Krueger, *Iron Lake*, 1998
Mary Logue, *Blood Country*, 1999

450

PARNELL HALL

The KenKen Killings

(New York: Minotaur Books, 2011)

Series: Puzzle Lady Series. Book 12
Story type: Cozy Mystery
Subject(s): Mystery; Murder; Games
Major character(s): Cora Felton, Detective—Amateur; Melvin, Divorced Person (ex-husband of Cora), Crime Suspect

Time period(s): 21st century; 2010s
Locale(s): United States

Summary: *The KenKen Killings*, a suspenseful cozy mystery, is the 12th installment in the Puzzle Lady Mystery series from author Parnell Hall. When Cora Felton, aka the Puzzle Lady, is bequeathed a check for $10,000 from the late Chester T. Markowitz, a man she doesn't recall but may have been married to, she can't help but cash it, without asking questions. In no time, her seedy ex-husband Melvin arrives in town demanding that he no longer pay alimony since she allegedly remarried. Meanwhile, Cora is called on by the police to crack a KenKen puzzle that was left at the scene of a robbery at a banker's home. When the banker is murdered, more KenKen puzzles begin popping up, sending Cora a clear message and possibly linking the murders to Melvin.

Where it's reviewed:
Publishers Weekly, Nov. 1, 2010, page 30

Other books by the same author:
Caper, 2010
The Puzzle Lady vs. The Sudoku Lady, 2010
A Clue for the Puzzle Lady, 1999
The Baxter Trust, 1989
Detective, 1987

Other books you might like:
M.C. Beaton, *Agatha Raisin and the Quiche of Death*, 1992
Jill Churchill, *Grime and Punishment*, 1989
Rita Lakin, *Getting Old Is Murder*, 2005
Laura Levine, *This Pen for Hire*, 2002
Elaine Viets, *Shop Till You Drop*, 2003

451

KIM HARRINGTON

Clarity

(New York: Point, 2011)

Story type: Young Adult
Subject(s): Mystery; Murder; Supernatural
Major character(s): Clarity "Clare" Fern, 16-Year-Old, Psychic; Gabriel, Teenager, Son (of detective)
Time period(s): 21st century; 2010s
Locale(s): Massachusetts, United States

Summary: *Clarity* is a paranormal mystery for young adult readers from author Kim Harrington. Sixteen-year-old Clarity "Clare" Fern has a supernatural gift to see visions from the past and uncover emotions whenever she touches an object, something that makes her a bit of a tourist attraction in her small Cape Cod town but carries with it great responsibility. When a young girl is murdered, Clare's cheating ex-boyfriend begs her to help with the investigation. At first, Clare is reluctant until her supernaturally gifted brother is pegged as a suspect. Soon, Clare finds herself teaming up with Gabriel, the hot son of a new detective, to uncover the mysteries surrounding the killing in an attempt to track the murderer and clear her brother's name.

452

C.S. HARRIS (Pseudonym of Candace Proctor)

Where Shadows Dance

(New York: Obsidian, 2011)

Series: Sebastian St. Cyr Series. Book 6
Story type: Historical - Regency; Series
Subject(s): Mystery; Murder; History
Major character(s): Sebastian St. Cyr, Detective—Police; Paul Gibson, Doctor (surgeon); Hero Jarvis, Fiance(e) (of Sebastian)
Time period(s): 19th century; 1810s (1812)
Locale(s): London, England

Summary: In *Where Shadows Dance* by C.S. Harris, a London physician calls on Detective Sebastian St. Cyr when he realizes that a cadaver in his laboratory did not die from natural causes. St. Cyr soon learns that the corpse, a diplomat with the foreign office, was stabbed and that he is not to be the only victim in a politically motivated spree. In 1812, the atmosphere in London is tense as Napoleon has extended his reach to Russia. The case becomes personal when the killer sets his sights on St. Cyr's fiance, Hero Jarvis. *Where Shadows Dance* is the sixth book in the Sebastian St. Cyr series.

Where it's reviewed:
Publishers Weekly, Jan. 24, 2011, page 135

Other books by the same author:
What Remains of Heaven, 2009
Where Serpents Sleep, 2008
Why Mermaids Sing, 2007
When Gods Die, 2006
What Angels Fear, 2005

Other books you might like:
Tasha Alexander, *And Only to Deceive*, 2005
Rhys Bowen, *Her Royal Spyness*, 2007
Charles Finch, *A Beautiful Blue Death*, 2007
Deanna Raybourn, *Silent in the Grave*, 2007
Victoria Thompson, *Murder on Astor Place*, 1999

453

CORA HARRISON

Eye of the Law

(Sutton, Surrey, England: Severn House, 2010)

Series: Burren Mystery Series. Book 5
Story type: Historical - Medieval
Subject(s): Ireland; Irish history; Murder
Major character(s): Mara, Spouse (of the King), Lawyer, Professor; Iarla, 20-Year-Old, Crime Victim; Ardal O'Lochlainn, Nobleman
Time period(s): 16th century; 1510s (1510)
Locale(s): Burren, Ireland

Summary: *Eye of the Law*, a medieval mystery, is the fifth installment in the Burren Mystery series from author Cora Harrison. Set in 1510 in Ireland, the book follows the King's pregnant wife, Mara, who serves as a law professor and Burren's brehon, or lawgiver. Twenty-year-old Iarla arrives in Burren from the Aran Islands, claiming that wealthy nobleman Ardal O'Lochlainn is his biological father. He bases his claim on his late mother's deathbed confession, despite Ardal's vehement denial. Mara is called upon to rule in the case, but decides to wait two weeks before releasing a verdict. Meanwhile, Iarla is brutally murdered after being stabbed in the eye, leaving the town to question whether Ardal is capable of killing his potential son or if the spirit of Balor, the one-eyed god, has punished Iarla for lying.

454

ELLEN HART

The Cruel Ever After

(New York: Minotaur Books, 2010)

Series: Jane Lawless Series. Book 18
Story type: Contemporary
Subject(s): Detective fiction; Murder; Restaurants
Major character(s): Jane Lawless, Restaurateur, Detective—Amateur; Chester "Chess" Garity, Spouse (ex-husband of Jane), Antiques Dealer; Melvin Dial, Crime Victim
Time period(s): 21st century; 2010s
Locale(s): Minneapolis, Minnesota

Summary: Jane Lawless is a Minneapolis-based restaurant owner and amateur detective. Her former husband, Chess, is an antiques dealer who finds himself ensnared in the mysterious death of a potential client. When the client turned up dead, Chess was the only one nearby who could've had anything to do with the murder, and now he's being blackmailed by an unknown party. Desperate, he goes to his ex-wife for help, and Jane sets out to find the truth behind the killing. *The Cruel Ever After* is the 18th installment in Ellen Hart's Jane Lawless Mysteries.

Where it's reviewed:
Library Journal, December 2010, page 91
Publishers Weekly, October 25, 2010, page 33

Other books by the same author:
The Mirror and the Mask, 2009
A Killing Cure, 1993
Stage Fright, 1992
Vital Lies, 1991
Hallowed Murder, 1989

Other books you might like:
Mary Kay Andrews, *Savannah Blues*, 2002
Adeena Karasick, *Amuse Bouche*, 2009
Cecile Lamalle, *Appetite for Murder*, 1999
Sandra Scoppettone, *Everything You Have Is Mine*, 1991
Mark Richard Zubro, *Another Dead Teenager*, 1995

455

SETH HARWOOD

Young Junius

(Madison, Wisconsin: Tyrus Books, 2010)

Story type: Contemporary
Subject(s): Housing; Murder; Suspense
Major character(s): Junius, 14-Year-Old
Time period(s): 20th century; 1980s (1987)
Locale(s): Cambridge, Massachusetts

Summary: Seth Harwood's *Young Junius* chronicles a day in the life of a Cambridge, Massachusetts, housing project, where a teenager named Junius is searching for those responsible for his brother's murder. Perspectives shift as more and more characters from the project are introduced, and the risk to Junius has soon grown into a tangible presence. But everyone within the unit is moving toward a destiny they are helpless to stop, culminating in a brutal battle that will change all of them forever.

Where it's reviewed:
Booklist, September 1, 2010, page 47
Publishers Weekly, August 16, 2010, page 32

Other books by the same author:
Jack Wakes Up, 2009

Other books you might like:
Sean Doolittle, *The Cleanup*, 2006
Victor Gischler, *The Deputy*, 2010
Charlie Huston, *Caught Stealing*, 2004
Gary Phillips, *The Jook*, 1999
Don Winslow, *Savages*, 2010

456

MICHAEL HASKINS

Free Range Institution

(Waterville, Maine: Five Star, 2011)

Series: Mick Murphy Key West Mystery Series. Book 2
Story type: Contemporary; Series
Subject(s): Mystery; Journalism; Drugs
Major character(s): Mick Murphy, Journalist; Tita Toledo, Lawyer, Girlfriend (of Mick); Jay Bruehl, Friend (of Mick); Rebecca Connelly, Police Officer (undercover); Thomas Collins, Religious (priest)
Time period(s): 21st century; 2010s
Locale(s): Florida, United States

Summary: In *Free Range Institution* by Michael Haskins, journalist Mick Murphy's afternoon date with his lawyer girlfriend is interrupted by the murder of his friend. When Mick sees Jay Bruehl, an informant, fall from the top of the Hotel Key West, he knows that it is not an accident. Jay had told Mick that members of a Colombian drug ring were meeting at the hotel. Undercover police officer Rebecca Connelly was supposed to be at the meeting, too, but has disappeared. Thomas Collins, a priest, knows where Connelly's body can be found, but the authorities don't believe that he got his information from angels, as Collins claims. *Free Range Institution* is the

Mystery

second book in the Mick Murphy Key West Mystery series.

Where it's reviewed:
Booklist, Jan. 1, 2011, page 48
Publishers Weekly, Dec. 20, 2010, page 37

Other books by the same author:
Chasin' the Wind, 2008

Other books you might like:
Tom Corcoran, *The Mango Opera*, 1998
Tim Dorsey, *Florida Roadkill*, 1999
Carl Hiaasen, *Skin Tight*, 1989
Bob Morris, *Bahamarama*, 2004
Randy Wayne White, *The Man Who Invented Florida*, 1994

457

MO HAYDER

Gone

(New York: Atlantic Monthly Press, 2011)

Series: Jack Caffery Series. Book 5
Story type: Child-in-Peril
Subject(s): Detective fiction; Kidnapping; Crime
Major character(s): Jack Caffery, Detective—Police; Martha Bradley, Kidnap Victim

Summary: *Gone* is the fifth novel in author Mo Hayder's mystery series featuring Detective Inspector Jack Caffery. When 11-year-old Martha Bradley is taken during a car theft, Jack begins to wonder if the target wasn't the car after all, but the girl herself. Soon the carjacker sends hints to the police that he might commit another, far worse crime, and it's up to Jack to find the criminal before it's too late. But can Jack keep everyone else involved in the investigation in check without having them jeopardize his chances of finding Martha. Hayder is also the author of *Birdman*, *Ritual*, *The Treatment*, and *Skin*.

Where it's reviewed:
Booklist, Nov. 15, 2010, page 24
Library Journal, Oct. 1, 2010, page 67
Publishers Weekly, Dec. 20, 2010, page 32

Other books by the same author:
Skin, 2009
Ritual, 2008
Pig Island, 2006
The Treatment, 2001
Birdman, 1999

Other books you might like:
Mark Billingham, *Sleepyhead*, 2001
Liza Marklund, *Paradise*, 2000
Val McDermid, *The Mermaids Singing*, 1995
Denise Mina, *Field of Blood*, 2005
Martyn Waites, *The Mercy Seat*, 2006

458

TONY HAYS

The Beloved Dead

(New York: Forge, 2011)

Story type: Historical
Subject(s): Mystery; England; Royalty
Major character(s): Malgwyn ap Cuneglas, Counselor (to King Arthur), Detective; Arthur, Royalty (King)
Time period(s): 5th century
Locale(s): England

Summary: *The Beloved Dead* is a suspenseful mystery novel set in 5th-century Britain. Malgwyn ap Cuneglas has had a trusting relationship with King Arthur, first as his friend, then as his counselor, so it's no surprise that Malgwyn is the man tasked with retrieving Arthur's bride-to-be from northern England. Despite King Arthur's love for Guinevere, he has chosen another woman to be his wife in an effort to earn the respect and support of his people. Malgwyn is desperate to succeed in his quest, which proves challenging given the many protests against the king and his Christian faith. On Malgwyn's journey, he uncovers a series of violent and brutal sexual assaults and murders on young virgins, prompting him to conduct a thorough investigation to find both the murderer and motive.

Where it's reviewed:
Library Journal, Feb. 1, 2011, page 47
Publishers Weekly, Feb. 14, 2011, page 39

Other books by the same author:
The Divine Sacrifice, 2010
The Killing Way, 2009
The Trouble with Patriots, 2002
Murder in the Latin Quarter, 1993
Murder on the Twelfth Night, 1993

Other books you might like:
Bernard Cornwell, *The Last Kingdom*, 2004
Susanna Gregory, *A Plague on Both Your Houses*, 1998
Cora Harrison, *My Lady Judge*, 2007
C.J. Sansom, *Dissolution*, 2003
Peter Tremayne, *Absolution by Murder*, 1994

459

WILLIAM HEFFERNAN

The Dead Detective

(Brooklyn: Akashic Books, 2010)

Story type: Contemporary
Subject(s): Detective fiction; Teachers; Psychics
Major character(s): Harry Doyle, Detective—Police, Psychic; Darlene Beckett, Crime Victim, Teacher
Time period(s): 21st century; 2010s
Locale(s): Florida, United States

Summary: In William Heffernan's *The Dead Detective*, Harry Doyle isn't a typical hard-nosed police detective. As a child, he and his brother were killed by their mentally unstable mother; Harry was successfully revived, while his sibling died. Now Harry can sense certain messages from the dead—a skill that comes in handy at work. A local schoolteacher, who caused a firestorm of controversy after she slept with a teenaged student, is found brutally murdered, and it's up to Harry to connect with the dead woman and find her killer.

Where it's reviewed:
Booklist, September 15, 2010, page 31
New York Times Book Review, October 3, 2010, page 34
Publishers Weekly, August 2, 2010, page 32

Other books by the same author:
A Time Gone By, 2003
The Dinosaur Club, 1997
Scarred, 1992
Ritual, 1989
Blood Rose, 1988

Other books you might like:
James O. Born, *Field of Fire*, 2007
James W. Hall, *Bones of Coral*, 1991
Jonathon King, *The Blue Edge of Midnight*, 2002
James Swain, *Midnight Rambler: A Novel of Suspense*, 2007
Darryl Wimberley, *A Rock and a Hard Place*, 1999

460

LIBBY FISCHER HELLMANN

Set the Night on Fire
(Chicago, Illinois: Allium Press, 2010)

Story type: Political
Subject(s): Student protests; Mystery; Family
Major character(s): Lila Hilliard, Crime Victim
Time period(s): 21st century; 2010s
Locale(s): Chicago, Illinois

Summary: Lila Hilliard is certain that someone wants her dead. What she can't figure out is why. While visiting her family over the holidays, Lila's home is set on fire, trapping her dad and brother inside. Later, a mysterious man on a motorcycle attacks her. Determined to figure out who is trying to kill her, Lila begins digging into the dark past of her father and is shocked by the secrets she uncovers. Do the threats on her life have to do with her father's involvement in the student protests and tumultuous politics in Chicago during the 1960s? The deeper Lila digs into her father's past, the more terrifying and sinister the secrets become.

Other books by the same author:
Easy Innocence, 2008
A Shot to Die For, 2005
An Image of Death, 2004
A Picture of Guilt, 2003
An Eye for Murder, 2002

Other books you might like:
Frankie Y. Bailey, *You Should Have Died on Monday*, 2007
Reed Farrel Coleman, *The James Deans*, 2005
Laura Lippman, *What the Dead Know*, 2007

Ross Macdonald, *Underground Man*, 1971
Sara Paretsky, *Hardball*, 2009

461

PETER HELTON

Falling More Slowly
(New York: Soho Constable, 2011)

Story type: Police Procedural
Subject(s): Mystery; Weapons; Terrorism
Major character(s): Liam McLusky, Detective
Time period(s): 21st century; 2010s
Locale(s): Bristol, England

Summary: *Falling More Slowly* is a suspenseful police procedural from author Peter Helton. Barely recovered from an injury sustained in the line of duty, Detective Inspector Liam McLusky also has to cope with the backlash of being transferred to a new police team in Bristol that's unwelcoming of the outsider. It doesn't take long for McLusky to receive his first assignment, a major case involving bombings throughout the city. Someone has taken everyday objects, ranging from a champagne bottle to a women's makeup compact, and transformed them into bombs, detonating them at random throughout Bristol and killing innocent victims. McLusky is tasked with tracking down the killer and thwarting his attack, but when everything is a potential weapon, he has no idea where to start looking.

Where it's reviewed:
Booklist, Dec. 1, 2010, page 29
Library Journal, Jan. 2011, page 66
Publishers Weekly, Nov. 29, 2010, page 33

Other books by the same author:
Rainstone Fall, 2008
Slim Chance, 2006
Headcase, 2005

Other books you might like:
Colin Bateman, *Divorcing Jack*, 1995
Mark Billingham, *Lazy Bones*, 2003
John Harvey, *Lonely Hearts*, 1989
Peter James, *Dead Simple*, 2006
Stuart MacBride, *Cold Granite*, 2005

462

SARA J. HENRY

Learning to Swim
(New York: Shaye Areheart Books, 2011)

Story type: Contemporary
Subject(s): Mystery; Detective fiction; Children
Major character(s): Troy Chance, Young Woman, Writer; Paul, Boy
Time period(s): 21st century; 2010s
Locale(s): Vermont, United States

Summary: In *Learning to Swim* by Sara J. Henry, a woman riding a commuter ferry on Lake Champlain is drawn into a strange case of kidnapping. When Troy Chance sees a young child being dumped into the lake from

Mystery

another ferry, she immediately plunges into the frigid water to rescue him. The boy, bound and scared, speaks no English but communicates to Troy that his name is Paul. Fearing for the boy's safety, Troy investigates the case on her own, trying to locate Paul's parents. A writer experienced in researching stories, Troy is stunned as the true horror of Paul's story is revealed. First novel.

Where it's reviewed:
Booklist, December 15, 2010, page 24
Library Journal, October 15, 2010, page S1
Publishers Weekly, November 29, 2010, page 28

Other books you might like:
Jodi Compton, *Sympathy between Humans*, 2005
Hallie Ephron, *Never Tell a Lie: A Novel of Suspense*, 2009
K.J. Erickson, *Third Person Singular*, 2001
Jennifer McMahon, *Promise Not to Tell*, 2006
Jess Walter, *Over Tumbled Graves*, 2001

463

KEIGO HIGASHINO

The Devotion of Suspect X
(New York: Minotaur Books, 2011)

Story type: Contemporary
Subject(s): Mystery; Murder; Deception
Major character(s): Yasuko Hanaoka, Divorced Person, Murderer, Single Mother, Abuse Victim; Ishigami, Neighbor (of Yasuko), Teacher; Togashi, Divorced Person (ex-husband of Yasuko), Crime Victim
Time period(s): 21st century; 2010s
Locale(s): Japan

Summary: *The Devotion of Suspect X* is a suspenseful mystery novel from best-selling Japanese author Keigo Higashino. After enduring an abusive relationship and a painful divorce, Yasuko Hanaoka is finally free of her ex, Togashi, and able to focus on starting a new life with her teenage daughter. When Togashi shows up and tries extorting money from Yasuko, the situation gets heated and violent, resulting in Togashi's death. Yasuko's neighbor, a kind-hearted and lonely math teacher named Ishigami, overhears the commotion and comes to Yasuko's aid, helping her get rid of the body and craft an airtight alibi, but when Togashi's body is discovered, Ishigami becomes the police's prime suspect.

Where it's reviewed:
Booklist, Jan. 1, 2011, page 47
Library Journal, Nov. 15, 2010, page 60
Publishers Weekly, Dec. 6, 2010, page 30
USA Today, Feb. 24, 2011, page 05D

Other books by the same author:
Malice, 2009
Naoko, 2004

Other books you might like:
Karin Fossum, *Don't Look Back*, 2002
Mo Hayder, *Tokyo*, 2004
Jesse Kellerman, *The Executor*, 2010
Natsuo Kirino, *Out*, 2005
Martin Cruz Smith, *Tokyo Station*, 2001

464

OWEN HILL

The Incredible Double
(Oakland: PM Press, 2009)

Story type: Contemporary
Subject(s): Detective fiction; Drugs; Suspense
Major character(s): Clay Blackburn, Scout (book scout), Detective—Amateur; Bailey Dao, FBI Agent (ex-FBI agent), Colleague (of Clay); Marvin, Fortune Hunter, Colleague (of Clay); Dino Centro, Friend (of Clay); Drugstore Wally, Businessman
Time period(s): 21st century; 2010s
Locale(s): Berkeley, California

Summary: Owen Hill's *The Incredible Double* charts the investigative misadventures of a Berkley, California, bookseller and amateur PI. Clay Blackburn is desperate to find some meaning in modern life, and with a trio of companions—a former FBI operative, an opportunist, and a smooth talker—he sets out to unearth that meaning. What he discovers, instead, is a city brimming with crime...and Clay just might be the only man to put an end to it once and for all.

Where it's reviewed:
The Gay & Lesbian Review Worldwide, May-June 2010, page 42

Other books by the same author:
The Chandler Apartments, 2002

Other books you might like:
Lawrence Block, *Burglars Can't Be Choosers*, 1977
Kinky Friedman, *Greenwich Killing Time: A Novel*, 1986
Neil S. Plakcy, *Mahu*, 2005
Dawn Powell, *The Wicked Pavilion*, 1954
Mark Richard Zubro, *Sorry Now?*, 1991

465

CHARLOTTE HINGER

Lethal Lineage
(Scottsdale, Arizona: Poisoned Pen Press, 2011)

Story type: Cozy Mystery
Subject(s): Detective fiction; Law; Crime
Major character(s): Lottie Albright, Lawman (sheriff), Twin (of Josie); Bishop Talesbury, Religious (bishop); Mary Farnsworth, Religious (reverend); Josie Albright, Twin (of Lottie)
Locale(s): Kansas, United States

Summary: *Lethal Lineage* is the second novel in author Charlotte Hinger's mystery series featuring Deputy Sheriff Lottie Albright. As Lottie and her twin sister, Josie, stand in an Episcopal church to witness their newborn niece's baptism, they are taken aback at the Bishop Talesbury's angry homily. Then Rev. Mary Farnsworth turns up dead in the ante-room, and Lottie must go to work to find out what happened. The official story is that Mary had a heart attack, but Lottie isn't so sure. Now she must get to the bottom of this peculiar mystery before it is too late. Hinger is also the author of *Deadly Descent*.

Where it's reviewed:
Publishers Weekly, Jan. 10, 2011, page 34

Other books by the same author:
Deadly Descent, 2009
Come Spring, 1986

Other books you might like:
Judy Clemens, *Till the Cows Come Home*, 2004
Donald Harstad, *Eleven Days: A Novel of the Heartland*, 1998
Margaret Maron, *Bootlegger's Daughter*, 1992
Nancy Pickard, *The Virgin of Small Plains*, 2006
Julia Spencer-Fleming, *In the Bleak Midwinter*, 2002

466

TAMI HOAG

Secrets to the Grave
(New York: Dutton, 2011)

Story type: Police Procedural; Serial Killer
Subject(s): Murder; Mystery; Children
Major character(s): Tony Mendez, Detective; Anne Leone, Teacher (former); Haley, Child, Crime Victim
Time period(s): 21st century; 2010s
Locale(s): Oak Knoll, California

Summary: Bestselling author Tami Hoag's *Secrets to the Grave*, the second thriller in the *Deeper than the Dead* series, follows detective Tony Mendez as he tries to make sense of a vicious murder. The peaceful town of Oak Knoll, California, is thrown into a frenzy when, just days before the trial of the See-No-Evil serial killer, a child calls 911 to report spousal abuse. When police find young Haley, she is clutching the brutally beaten corpse of her mother, Marissa Fordham. Tony quickly realizes that his only hope of solving the crime lies in Haley's testimony. Desperate for assistance with the traumatized girl, Tony calls on child advocate Anne Leone, a newlywed and key witness in the See-No-Evil case. Tony and Anne begin working together to learn more about who Marissa and the secretive life she led. Then they learn the most shocking secret of all: Marissa's existence was a myth. Now Tony and Anne must struggle to discover the source of the danger, as well as its true targets.

Where it's reviewed:
Booklist, December 15, 2010, page 26
Publishers Weekly, November 22, 2010, page 44
The Times of London, January 15, 2011, page 12

Other books by the same author:
The Alibi Man, 2007
Prior Bad Acts, 2006
Kill the Messenger, 2004
Dark Horse, 2002
Ashes to Ashes, 1999

Other books you might like:
Eileen Dreyer, *Bad Medicine*, 1995
Kay Hooper, *Haunting Rachel*, 1998
Linda Howard, *To Die For*, 2005

Iris Johansen, *The Face of Deception*, 1998
Michele Martinez, *Most Wanted*, 2005

467

STEVE HOCKENSMITH

World's Greatest Sleuth!
(New York: Minotaur Books, 2011)

Series: Holmes on the Range Mystery Series. Book 5
Story type: Historical
Subject(s): World's Columbian Exposition, Chicago, Illinois, 1893; Mystery; Murder
Major character(s): Gustav "Old Red" Amlingmeyer, Detective, Brother (of Otto); Otto "Big Red" Amlingmeyer, Brother (of Gustav), Detective
Time period(s): 19th century; 1890s (1893)
Locale(s): Chicago, Illinois

Summary: *World's Greatest Sleuth!*, a humorous historical mystery, is the fifth installment in the Holmes on the Range Mystery series from award-winning author Steve Hockensmith. For the Amlingmeyer brothers, Gustav (aka Old Red) and Otto (aka Big Red), a detective contest at the World's Columbian Exposition in Chicago is the prime opportunity to win $10,000, justify their claims of being the best sleuths in the world, and make their hero, Sherlock Holmes, proud. The brothers have barely arrived from Montana when the competition turns deadly serious. When one of the contest's organizers, Armstrong B. Curtis, is killed, the competing detectives must work together to piece together a real murder investigation.

Where it's reviewed:
Booklist, Dec. 15, 2010, page 26

Other books by the same author:
Dawn of the Dreadfuls, 2010
The Crack in the Lens, 2009
The Black Dove, 2008
On the Wrong Track, 2007
Holmes on the Range, 2006

Other books you might like:
Caleb Carr, *The Alienist*, 1994
Mark Frost, *The List of Seven*, 1993
Joe R. Lansdale, *Savage Season*, 1990
Fidelis Morgan, *Unnatural Fires*, 2000
Will Thomas, *Some Danger Involved*, 2004

468

KEITH HOLLIHAN

The Four Stages of Cruelty
(New York: Macmillan, 2010)

Story type: Contemporary
Subject(s): Mystery; Prisons; Prisoners
Major character(s): Joshua Riff, 19-Year-Old, Convict; Kali Williams, Guard (prison); Jon Crowley, Convict
Time period(s): 21st century; 2010s
Locale(s): Fictional Location

Mystery

Summary: In *The Four Stages of Cruelty* by Keith Hollihan, the inmates and guards of Ditmarsh Penitentiary face a daily struggle between good and evil. Corrections officer Kali Williams has so far resisted the pull of the criminal world that surrounds her, but is eventually drawn to the prison's dark side by a teenaged convict named Joshua Riff. Riff comes to Williams with a fantastic story about an inmate, Jon Crowley, who is creating an illustrated book about a network of tunnels below the prison. Williams discounts his tale until Crowley goes missing. As she searches for Crowley, Williams discovers the secrets hidden beneath Ditmarsh Penitentiary. First novel.

Where it's reviewed:
Publishers Weekly, Oct. 11, 2010, page 26

Other books you might like:
Peter Abrahams, *End of Story*, 2006
Eddie Bunker, *No Beast So Fierce*, 1973
Edward Bunker, *Animal Factory*, 1977
Pete Earley, *The Hot House: Life Inside Leavenworth Prison*, 1992
Kim Wozencraft, *Rush*, 1990

469

JULIE HYZY

Buffalo West Wing
(New York: Berkley Prime Crime, 2011)

Series: White House Chef Mystery Series. Book 4
Story type: Cozy Mystery
Subject(s): Mystery; Presidents (Government); Cooking
Major character(s): Olivia Paras, Cook (executive chef), Detective—Amateur; Parker Hyden, Government Official (U.S. president)
Time period(s): 21st century; 2010s
Locale(s): Washington, District of Columbia

Summary: *Buffalo West Wing* is a suspenseful cozy mystery from bestselling author Julie Hyzy. The book is the fourth installment in the White House Executive Chef Mystery series. With Parker Hyden taking office as the new Commander-in-Chief and his family moving into the White House, executive chef Olivia Paras has her hands full trying to make the new First Family happy and dealing with their arrogant and bossy personal chef. Making matters worse is a skirmish with the new First Lady over a box of take-out chicken. When the wings mysteriously appear for the president's children, Olivia refuses to let the kids have them, much to the First Lady's chagrin. When Olivia's staffers consume the chicken and get violently ill, it becomes apparent that a much greater threat is on the horizon, centering on the President's young children.

Where it's reviewed:
Publishers Weekly, November 22, 2010, page 45

Other books by the same author:
Eggsecutive Orders, 2010
Grace Under Pressure, 2010
Hail to the Chef, 2008
State of the Onion, 2008
Deadly Blessings, 2006

Other books you might like:
Laura Childs, *Death by Darjeeling*, 2001
Laura Childs, *Eggs in Purgatory*, 2008
Diane Mott Davidson, *Catering to Nobody*, 1990
Krista Davis, *The Diva Runs out of Thyme*, 2008
Joanne Fluke, *Chocolate Chip Cookie Murder*, 2000

470

ARNALDUR INDRIDASON

Hypothermia
(New York: Minotaur Books, 2010)

Series: Inspector Sveinsson Series. Book 6
Story type: Contemporary; Police Procedural
Subject(s): Detective fiction; Murder; Family
Major character(s): Erlendur, Detective—Police; Maria, Young Woman, Crime Victim
Time period(s): 21st century; 2010s
Locale(s): Reykjavik, Iceland

Summary: Against the backdrop of Reykjavik, Iceland, police detective Erlendur is investigating the apparent suicide of a troubled young woman named Maria. The more Erlendur learns about Maria, however, the more he suspects that she did not take her own life. Rather, Erlendur believes Maria was murdered as the result of an unusually evil scheme. As more details about Maria's case are revealed, Erlendur examines his own life, the choices he has made, and the misdeeds of his past that remain unresolved. *Hypothermia* is the sixth book in Arnaldur Indridason's Reykjavik Thriller series, which also includes *Arctic Chill* and *The Draining Lake*.

Where it's reviewed:
Booklist, August 1, 2010, page 32
The Independent on Sunday, November 21, 2010, page 65
Publishers Weekly, July 5, 2010, page 26
Sunday Times (London), November 22, 2009, page 44

Other books by the same author:
Arctic Chill, 2009
The Draining Lake, 2008
Voices, 2007
Silence of the Grave, 2006
Jar City, 2005

Other books you might like:
Karin Fossum, *Don't Look Back*, 2002
Stieg Larsson, *The Girl with the Dragon Tattoo*, 2008
Henning Mankell, *Faceless Killers*, 1991
Jo Nesbo, *The Redbreast*, 2007
Maj Sjowall, *The Laughing Policeman*, 1977

471

LISA JACKSON

Devious
(New York: Kensington Publishing, 2011)

Series: Bentz and Montoya Series. Book 7
Story type: Police Procedural

Subject(s): Murder; Detective fiction; Mystery
Major character(s): Rick Bentz, Detective—Homicide;
Reuben Montoya, Detective—Homicide, Boyfriend
(former, of Camille); Camille Renard, Religious
(nun), Girlfriend (former, of Reuben), Crime Victim,
Sister (of Val); Val Houston, Police Officer (former),
Sister (of Camille)
Locale(s): New Orleans, Louisiana

Summary: *Devious* is the seventh novel in Lisa Jackson's
Bentz and Montoya detective series. In this installment,
New Orleans-based homicide detectives, Rick Bentz and
Reuben Montoya, must find who is murdering nuns at
St. Marguerite's Convent. When Montoya's high-school
sweetheart, Camille, turns up as the killer's latest victim,
the case gets personal. Meanwhile, Camille's sister Valerie decides that the investigation is going too slowly for
her taste, and decides to take matters into her own hands.
As a former cop, Valerie has the training to solve the
case, but will that be enough to take down a ruthless
killer?

Where it's reviewed:
Library Journal, Jan. 2011, page 84

Other books by the same author:
Without Mercy, 2010
Risky Business, 2009
Unspoken, 1999
Whispers, 1996
A Twist of Fate, 1983

Other books you might like:
J. T. Ellison, *Judas Kiss*, 2009
Dianne Emley, *The First Cut: A Novel*, 2006
Lisa Gardner, *Alone*, 2005
Lynne Heitman, *Hard Landing*, 2001
Erica Spindler, *Last Known Victim*, 2007

472

QUINTIN JARDINE

A Rush of Blood
(London: Headline, 2010)

Series: Robert Skinner Series. Book 20
Story type: Contemporary
Subject(s): Detective fiction; Murder; Scots (British
people)
Major character(s): Bob Skinner, Detective—Police; To-
mas Zaliukas, Entrepreneur, Crime Victim
Time period(s): 21st century; 2010s
Locale(s): Scotland

Summary: A multitude of crimes and strange coincidences
converge in *A Rush of Blood*, the 20th installment in
Quintin Jardine's Bob Skinner Mysteries series. When
power-mad businessman Tomas Zaliukas is found dead,
Skinner and his team investigate, assuming that suicide
was a more likely scenario than murder. But the more
their investigation reveals, the more Skinner begins to
think that Zaliukas's nefarious wheelings and dealings,
plus his volatile personal life, may have something to do
with the man's savage killing.

Where it's reviewed:
Library Journal, December 2010, page 91

Publishers Weekly, October 18, 2010, page 28
The Scotsman, June 12, 2010, page 7

Other books by the same author:
Fatal Last Words, 2009
Skinner's Round, 1996
Skinner's Trail, 1996
Skinner's Festival, 1995
Skinner's Rules, 1993

Other books you might like:
John Harvey, *Lonely Hearts*, 1989
Val McDermid, *The Mermaids Singing*, 1995
Russel D. McLean, *The Good Son*, 2009
Ian Rankin, *Black and Blue*, 1997
Peter Robinson, *Gallows View*, 1987

473

DARYNDA JONES

First Grave on the Right
(New York: St. Martin's Press, 2011)

Series: Charley Davidson Series. Book 1
Subject(s): Detective fiction; Love; Supernatural
Major character(s): Charlotte "Charley" Davidson, Psychic
(grim reaper), Detective—Private; Angel, Gang
Member
Time period(s): 21st century; 2010s
Locale(s): United States

Summary: Darynda Jones's *First Grave on the Right*, the
first novel in a series, charts the adventures of Charlotte
"Charley" Davidson, a wisecracking private eye with a
decidedly unusual side job. Charley, who has been a
grim reaper since she was a child, ushers recently
departed souls into the afterlife and helps them clear up
any lingering business here on Earth. When three at-
torneys are murdered, they come to Charley for help in
finding their killer. But the hardheaded PI has no idea of
the hurdles she will have to cross—or the bizarre
personalities (human and otherwise) she will have
confront—in order to solve this case. First novel.

Where it's reviewed:
Booklist, Feb. 1, 2011, page 42
Library Journal, Nov. 1, 2010, page 55
Publishers Weekly, Dec. 6, 2010, page 29

Other books you might like:
Robin Becker, *Brains: A Zombie Memoir*, 2010
Shirley Damsgaard, *Witch Way to Murder*, 2005
Casey Daniels, *Don of the Dead*, 2006
Charlaine Harris, *Dead Until Dark*, 2001
Carolyn G. Hart, *Ghost at Work: A Mystery*, 2008

474

ERIN KELLY

The Poison Tree
(New York: Pamela Dorman Books/Viking, 2011)

Subject(s): Brothers and sisters; Family; Murder
Major character(s): Karen Clarke, Student—College; Biba

Mystery

Capel, Friend (of Karen), Sister (of Rex); Rex,
Friend (of Karen), Brother (of Biba)
Time period(s): 20th century; 1990s (1993)
Locale(s): United Kingdom

Summary: Set in England during the early 1990s, Erin
Kelly's *The Poison Tree* follows the lives of three
individuals and the dark secrets that hold them captive.
Karen Clarke is enchanted by theater student Biba Capel,
and, much to Karen's surprise, Biba counts Karen among
her closest friends. She is soon introduced to Biba's
brother, Rex, and the three share a house together. Karen
soon learns more about Biba and Rex's history, and she
is helpless to prevent herself from being sucked into the
vortex of their complex relationship and its tortured past.
First novel.

Where it's reviewed:
The Bookseller, March 12, 2010, page 35
Library Journal, October 15, 2010, page 65
Publishers Weekly, January 3, 2011, page 8
USA Today, February 3, 2011, page 04D
The Washington Times, January 7, 2011, page B07

Other books you might like:
Tana French, *The Likeness*, 2008
Laura Lippman, *I'd Know You Anywhere*, 2010
Cammie McGovern, *Neighborhood Watch*, 2010
Martyn Waites, *Speak No Evil*, 2010
Minette Walters, *The Ice House*, 1992

475

GRAEME KENT

Devil-Devil

(New York: Soho, 2011)

Series: Sister Conchita and Sergeant Kella Series. Book 1
Story type: Historical
Subject(s): Islands; Mystery; Murder
Major character(s): Ben Kella, Police Officer, Leader
(spiritual); Conchita, Religious (nun)
Time period(s): 20th century; 1960s (1960)
Locale(s): Solomon Islands

Summary: *Devil-Devil* is the first book in the Sister Conchita and Sergeant Kella series from author Graeme
Kent. Set in 1960 in the British-governed Solomon
Islands, the book follows the adventures of Ben Kella, a
man who struggles with his dual roles as a police
sergeant and a spiritual peacekeeper of the Lau people.
His conflicting callings lead to wariness from both his
bosses and the island's indigenous people. When he
stumbles upon Sister Conchita, a young American nun,
trying to bury a bullet-ridden skull, he suspects a connection with the uprising of a cult and a missing
American anthropologist, and he reluctantly begins working with the stubborn nun to investigate a series of
murders that seem connected to the strange happenings
on the island.

Where it's reviewed:
Publishers Weekly, Nov. 29, 2010, page 32

Other books you might like:
John Burdett, *Bangkok 8*, 2003
Colin Cotterill, *The Coroner's Lunch*, 2004

Malla Nunn, *A Beautiful Place to Die*, 2009
Xiaolong Qiu, *Death of a Red Heroine*, 2000
Eric Stone, *Living Room of the Dead*, 2005

476

PHILIP KERR

Field Grey

(New York: G. P. Putnam's Sons, 2011)

Series: Bernie Gunther Series. Book 7
Subject(s): Mystery; History; World War II, 1939-1945
Major character(s): Bernie Gunther, Detective—Private
Time period(s): 20th century; 1950s (1954)
Locale(s): Cuba; Germany; New York, New York

Summary: In *Field Gray* by Philip Kerr, a German private
investigator is dragged back into the past when suspicions
about his war activities resurface. It is 1954 and Bernie
Gunther is in Cuba working for an organized-crime boss
when he is picked up by American military authorities.
First imprisoned at Guantanamo, then in New York,
Gunther endures the interrogation and physical punishment of his captors, who want information about his
involvement with the SS. Strong and smart, Gunther
revisits his horrific war experiences but doesn't crack,
even when he is sent to Germany's infamous Landsberg
Prison. *Field Gray* is the seventh book in the Bernie
Gunther series.

Where it's reviewed:
Library Journal, Nov. 15, 2010, page 44
Publishers Weekly, Feb. 21, 2011, page 110

Other books by the same author:
If the Dead Rise Not, 2009
The One From the Other, 2006
A German Requiem, 1991
The Pale Criminal, 1990
March Violets, 1989

Other books you might like:
Robert Harris, *Fatherland*, 1992
Joseph Kanon, *Stardust*, 2009
Jonathan Rabb, *Rosa*, 2005
Martin Cruz Smith, *Havana Bay*, 1999
Olen Steinhauer, *The Bridge of Sighs*, 2003

477

RAYMOND KHOURY

The Templar Salvation

(New York: Dutton, 2010)

Series: Last Templar Series. Book 2
Subject(s): Suspense; Catholicism; Conspiracy
Major character(s): Sean Reilly, Agent (FBI); Mansoor
Zahed, Professor; Conrad of Tripoli, Knight
Time period(s): 13th century; (1200s); 21st century; 2010s
Locale(s): Constantinople; Europe, Vatican City

Summary: In 1203, a series of documents detailing the
formative years of the Christian religion are secreted

away for fear of reprisals against the church. Fast forward to the present, where Iranian teacher Mansoor Zahed is determined to find the elusive documents in hopes of avenging the killing of his family. As his search unfolds, agent Sean Reilly is on a mission of his own: to track down his missing lover, Tess. These three stories converge in *The Templar Salvation*, the second install-ment in Raymond Khoury's Last Templar series.

Where it's reviewed:
Booklist, September 15, 2010, page 36
Library Journal, September 15, 2010, page 60
Publishers Weekly, August 30, 2010, page 27
The Times of London, January 15, 2011, page 12

Other books by the same author:
The Sign, 2009
The Sanctuary, 2007
The Last Templar, 2005

Other books you might like:
James Becker, *The First Apostle*, 2009
Steve Berry, *The Templar Legacy*, 2006
Dan Brown, *The Da Vinci Code*, 2003
Paul Christopher, *The Sword of the Templars*, 2009
James Rollins, *Map of Bones*, 2005

478

TRACY KIELY

Murder on the Bride's Side
(New York: Minotaur Books, 2010)

Series: Elizabeth Parker Series. Book 2
Story type: Contemporary
Subject(s): Detective fiction; Murder; Weddings
Major character(s): Elizabeth Parker, Detective—Amateur; Bridget, Friend (of Elizabeth), Bride; Roni, Crime Victim, Aunt (of Bridget)
Time period(s): 21st century; 2010s
Locale(s): Richmond, Virginia

Summary: Elizabeth Parker is a Jane Austen acolyte and amateur detective who has just attended the wedding of her best friend. But the morning after the nuptials, the aunt of the bride is found murdered. Each member of the wedding party had a motive, but it is Elizabeth who is found to be in possession of the dead woman's jewels. As she tries to figure out who framed her for murder, Elizabeth crosses paths with a series of refined Southern-ers—any of whom could be a killer. Tracy Kiely's *Murder on the Bride's Side* is the second novel in the Elizabeth Parker series.

Where it's reviewed:
Publishers Weekly, July 26, 2010, page 55

Other books by the same author:
Murder at Longbourn, 2009

Other books you might like:
Donna Andrews, *Murder with Peacocks*, 1999
Jane Austen, *Pride and Prejudice*, 1813
Stephanie Barron, *Jane and the Unpleasantness at Scargrave Manor*, 1996
Ellen Crosby, *The Merlot Murders*, 2006
Julie Hyzy, *Grace Under Pressure*, 2010

479

CHRIS KNOPF

Bad Bird
(New York: St. Martin's Press, 2011)

Story type: Legal
Subject(s): Law; Detective fiction; Aircraft accidents
Major character(s): Jackie Swiatkowski, Lawyer

Summary: *Bad Bird* is the second novel of author Chris Knopf's mystery series featuring Jackie Swaitkowski. After watching an airplane explode in mid-air, Jackie knows that there is more to the so-called accident than simple pilot error. Jackie steps up to defend the police's only suspect, the pilot's husband, and that's where the real danger begins. When Jackie retrieves a camera case thrown from the plane seconds before detonation, she finds herself embroiled in a mystery in which she had no idea she'd play such a personal role. Now Jackie is on the run herself, and she must find the real suspect before it is too late. Knopf is also the author of *Short Squeeze*.

Where it's reviewed:
Booklist, Jan. 1, 2011, page 46
Library Journal, Feb. 1, 2011, page 47
Publishers Weekly, Dec. 13, 2010, page 40

Other books by the same author:
Short Squeeze, 2010
Hardstop, 2009
Head Wounds, 2008
The Last Refuge, 2005
Two Time, 2005

Other books you might like:
Harlan Coben, *Promise Me*, 2006
David Handler, *The Cold Blue Blood*, 2001
Susan Isaacs, *Compromising Positions*, 1978
J.A. Konrath, *Whiskey Sour*, 2004
David Rosenfelt, *Open and Shut*, 2002

480

MICHAEL KORYTA

The Cypress House
(New York: Little, Brown, and Company, 2011)

Subject(s): Psychics; Hurricanes; Death
Major character(s): Arlen Wagner, Psychic, Veteran; Rebecca Cady, Hotel Owner (boardinghouse owner); Paul Brickhill, Friend (of Arlen)
Time period(s): 20th century
Locale(s): Florida, United States

Summary: Set just after the First World War, Michael Ko-ryta's *The Cypress House* finds veteran Arlen Wagner dealing with a very unusual gift: he can predict when people will die just by looking in their eyes. While en route to Florida on a train, he senses the imminent deaths of all on board and, when they refuse to believe his as-sertions, he abandons the train and ends up at a boardinghouse run by Rebecca Cady. There the unset-tling danger only mounts as a hurricane threatens to destroy everything in its path.

Where it's reviewed:
The Houston Chronicle, January 23, 2011, page 15
Library Journal, November 1, 2010, page 56
Publishers Weekly, November 29, 2010, page 29
The Tampa Tribune, January 30, 2011, page 8

Other books by the same author:
So Cold the River, 2010
The Silent Hour, 2009
Envy the Night, 2008
Sorrow's Anthem, 2006
Tonight I Said Goodbye, 2004

Other books you might like:
Megan Abbott, *Bury Me Deep*, 2009
John Connolly, *The Reapers*, 2008
Jonathon King, *The Blue Edge of Midnight*, 2002
Peter Matthiessen, *Killing Mr. Watson*, 1990
Sheldon Russell, *The Insane Train*, 2010

481

JOE R. LANSDALE

Devil Red
(New York: Knopf, 2011)

Series: Hap and Leonard Series. Book 8
Story type: Contemporary; Series
Subject(s): Mystery; Murder; Cults
Major character(s): Hap Collins, Detective—Private; Leonard Pine, Detective—Private; Marvin Hanson, Detective—Private; Vanilla Ride, Murderer (assassin)
Time period(s): 21st century; 2010s
Locale(s): Texas, United States

Summary: In *Devil Red* by Joe Lansdale, a private investigator calls on the odd duo of Hap Collins and Leonard Pine to crack a cold case. In East Texas, Hap and Leonard are known for their unique crime-busting talents. But when the partners review the evidence from the two-year-old double murder in question, they realize that the case is especially sinister. One of the victims was a member of a vampire cult; both were heirs to fortunes. When Hap and Leonard notice a devil's head drawn on a tree in one of the crime-scene photos, they dig a little deeper and learn that "Devil Red" has killed before. *Devil Red* is the eighth book in the Hap Collins and Leonard Pine series.

Where it's reviewed:
Library Journal, Jan. 2011, page 85

Other books by the same author:
Vanilla Ride, 2009
Bad Chili, 1997
Two-Bear Mambo, 1995
Mucho Mojo, 1994
Savage Season, 1990

Other books you might like:
James Lee Burke, *Cadillac Jukebox*, 1996
Robert Crais, *The Watchman*, 2007
Ben Rehder, *Buck Fever*, 2002

Rick Riordan, *Big Red Tequila*, 1997
Richard Stark, *Point Blank*, 1962

482

DENNIS LEHANE

Moonlight Mile
(New York: William Morrow, 2010)

Series: Patrick Kenzie/Angela Gennaro Series. Book 6
Story type: Contemporary
Subject(s): Missing persons; Urban life; Detective fiction
Major character(s): Patrick Kenzie, Detective—Private; Angela "Angie" Gennaro, Detective—Private; Amanda McCready, 16-Year-Old (missing person)
Time period(s): 21st century; 2010s
Locale(s): Boston, Massachusetts

Summary: From Dennis Lehane, the bestselling author of *Mystic River* and *Gone, Baby, Gone*, comes the sixth novel in the Patrick Kenzie and Angela Gennaro mystery series. Over a decade ago, Patrick and Angie helped track down Amanda McCready, a missing 4-year-old girl—but then had to return her to a negligent home. When Amanda is grown and disappears again, Patrick and Angie can't help but get involved in the case. What they find leads them back into the dark underbelly of Boston, bringing them face to face with some startling truths—truths that could very well cost them their lives.

Where it's reviewed:
Booklist, October 1, 2010, page 34
Entertainment Weekly, November 12, 2010, page 78
Library Journal, September 15, 2010, page 60
Publishers Weekly, September 20, 2010, page 45
Tampa Tribune, November 28, 2010, page 4

Other books by the same author:
Prayers for Rain, 1999
Gone, Baby, Gone, 1998
Sacred, 1997
Darkness, Take My Hand, 1996
A Drink Before the War, 1994

Other books you might like:
Linda Barnes, *A Trouble of Fools*, 1987
Robert Crais, *The Watchman*, 2007
Laura Lippman, *No Good Deeds*, 2006
Robert B. Parker, *A Catskill Eagle*, 1985
Greg Rucka, *Keeper*, 1996

483

JOHN T. LESCROART

Damage
(New York: Dutton, 2011)

Series: Dismas Hardy Series. Book 16
Story type: Contemporary
Subject(s): Detective fiction; Wealth; Murder
Major character(s): Abe Glitsky, Detective—Police; Dismas Hardy, Lawyer; Ro Curtlee, Wealthy, Crime Suspect

Time period(s): 21st century; 2010s
Locale(s): San Francisco, California

Summary: Police detective Abe Glitsky teams up with attorney Dismas Hardy to try to find evidence linking a wealthy San Franciscan to the murder of an innocent servant. But Ro Curtlee, who has just posted bail for the crime he's accused of, is one step ahead of the law, eliminating those who testified against him and exerting pressure on the rich and powerful. Can Glitsky and Hardy find the truth before they too fall victim to Curtlee's terrifying violence? John T. Lescroart's *Damage* is the 16th novel in the Abe Glitsky/Dismas Hardy series.

Where it's reviewed:
Daily Herald, January 14, 2011, page 39
Library Journal, November 1, 2010, page 57
St. Louis Post-Dispatch, January 9, 2011, page D8

Other books by the same author:
A Plague of Secrets, 2009
Betrayal, 2008
Guilt, 1997
A Certain Justice, 1995
Dead Irish, 1990

Other books you might like:
Jonnie Jacobs, *Shadow of Doubt*, 1996
Steve Martini, *Compelling Evidence*, 1992
Lisa Scottoline, *Everywhere That Mary Went*, 2003
Sheldon Siegel, *Special Circumstances: A Novel*, 2000
Robert K. Tanenbaum, *No Lesser Plea*, 1987

484

KATIA LIEF (Pseudonym of Kate Pepper)

Next Time You See Me
(New York: Avon, 2010)

Story type: Police Procedural
Subject(s): Murder; Mystery; Kidnapping
Major character(s): Karin Schaeffer, Detective, Spouse (of Mac), Mother; Mac MacLeary, Detective, Spouse (of Karin), Kidnap Victim, Father
Time period(s): 21st century; 2010s
Locale(s): United States

Summary: It's been three years since Detective Karin Schaeffer's life was destroyed when a crazed killer murdered her entire family. At the time, Karin was ready to give up on everything, but her partner, Mac MacLeary, gave her a new reason to live. The two fell in love, got married, and had a son. Just when Karin finally begins to feel like the pieces of her life are coming together, everything is shattered again. Mac's parents are murdered and then he vanishes without a trace. Desperate to find and save her husband, Karin is willing to go to whatever lengths necessary, but her shocking investigation reveals dark secrets about the man she thought she loved.

Other books by the same author:
You Are Next, 2010

Other books you might like:
Lisa Gardner, *Alone*, 2005
Lisa Jackson, *Running Scared*, 2010

Alex Kava, *A Perfect Evil*, 2001
Cody McFadyen, *Shadow Man*, 2006
Erica Spindler, *Last Known Victim*, 2007

485

LAURA LIPPMAN

The Girl in the Green Raincoat
(New York: Avon A, 2011)

Series: Tess Monaghan Series. Book 10
Story type: Contemporary
Subject(s): Pregnancy; Missing persons; Detective fiction
Major character(s): Tess Monaghan, Detective—Private; Crow, Boyfriend (of Tess); Mrs. Blossom, Assistant (of Tess); Whitney Talbot, Friend (of Tess)
Time period(s): 21st century; 2010s
Locale(s): Baltimore, Maryland

Summary: Laura Lippman's *The Girl in the Green Raincoat* is the tenth installment in the Tess Monaghan mystery series. This outing finds the private investigator confined to bed rest as she enters the final trimester of her pregnancy. She passes the time watching passersby out her apartment window, and one in particular catches her eye: a woman in a green raincoat walking her dog. But one day the woman doesn't show up, and only her dog, running around without a leash, is left behind. Despite her sensitive condition, Tess grows more and more determined to find out what happened to the girl in the green raincoat.

Where it's reviewed:
Library Journal, January 2011, page 80

Other books by the same author:
Another Thing to Fall, 2008
In Big Trouble, 1999
Butchers Hill, 1998
Baltimore Blues, 1997
Charm City, 1997

Other books you might like:
Linda Barnes, *A Trouble of Fools*, 1987
Sue Grafton, *"A" Is for Alibi*, 1982
Sujata Massey, *The Salaryman's Wife*, 1997
Marcia Muller, *Edwin of the Iron Shoes: A Novel of Suspense*, 1977
Cornell Woolrich, *Rear Window and Other Stories*, 1994

486

ALICE LOWEECEY

Force of Habit
(Woodbury, Minnesota: Midnight Ink, 2011)

Story type: Private Detective
Subject(s): Detective fiction; Stalking; Nuns
Major character(s): Giulia Falcone, Religious (former nun), Detective—Private; Frank Driscoll, Detective—Private, Employer (of Giulia); Blake Parker, Wealthy,

Crime Victim, Client (of Frank & Giulia), Fiance(e)
Time period(s): 21st century; 2010s
Locale(s): United States

Summary: *Force of Habit* is a suspenseful mystery novel from debut author Alice Loweecey. Adjusting to life outside a convent is difficult for Giulia Falcone, formerly Sister Mary Regina Coelis, especially when it involves an undeniable attraction to her boss, Frank Driscoll, and a new job as a private investigator. Her first case seems perfectly suited for her when a stalker uses biblical language to harass sexy millionaire Blake Parker and his fiancee, but Giulia is definitely out of her element as she tries to interrogate Blake's feisty ex-girlfriends about the crime. It's not long until Giulia becomes the stalker's next victim, receiving threatening letters and incriminating photos that jeopardize her new career and her hopes for a romantic future with Frank. First novel.

Where it's reviewed:
Library Journal, Jan. 2011, page 66
Publishers Weekly, Nov. 29, 2010, page 32

Other books you might like:
Linda Barnes, *A Trouble of Fools*, 1987
Eleanor Taylor Bland, *Dead Time*, 1992
Sue Grafton, *"A" Is for Alibi*, 1982
Norman Green, *The Last Gig*, 2009
Sara Paretsky, *Indemnity Only*, 1982

487

MICHAEL DAVID LUKAS

The Oracle of Stamboul
(New York: HarperCollins, 2011)

Story type: Historical
Subject(s): Turkish history; Family relations; Politics
Major character(s): Eleonora Cohen, Girl; Yakob Cohen, Father (of Eleonora), Merchant (carpet); Ruxandra, Stepmother (of Eleonora); Moncef Bey, Friend (of Yakob); Sultan Abdulhamid II, Ruler
Time period(s): 19th century; 1870s-1880s
Locale(s): Romania; Istanbul, Turkey

Summary: In *The Oracle of Stamboul* by Michael David Lukas, the birth of a girl in 1877 Romania fulfills a king's prophecy and alters the future of the Ottoman Empire. Eleonora Cohen, the baby whose arrival is announced by a flock of birds and a celestial alignment, loses her mother at the moment of her birth but enjoys a close relationship with her carpet-trader father, Yakob. At the age of eight, Eleonora accompanies Yakob on a trip to Turkey, where she meets an exotic cast of characters, including Sultan Abdulhamid II. A tragic accident leaves Eleonora in the care of her father's friend, Moncef Bey, in a heady world where she becomes an adviser to the sultan. First novel.

Where it's reviewed:
Booklist, Februrary 1, 2011, page 40
Library Journal, December 2010, page 104
New York Times Book Review, February 27, 2011, page 6(L)
Publishers Weekly, October 11, 2010, page 23

Other books you might like:
Boris Akunin, *The Winter Queen*, 2003
Barbara Cleverly, *The Last Kashmiri Rose*, 2001
Jason Goodwin, *The Janissary Tree*, 2006
M.M. Kaye, *Trade Wind*, 1963
Barbara Nadel, *Belshazzar's Daughter*, 2004

488

LISA LUTZ
DAVID HAYWARD, Co-Author

Heads You Lose
(New York: G. P. Putnam's Sons, 2011)

Story type: Contemporary
Subject(s): Mystery; Writers; Brothers and sisters
Major character(s): Lacey Hansen, Waiter/Waitress (barista), Detective—Amateur; Paul Hansen, Brother (of Lacey); Hart Drexel, Lover (of Lacey, former); Brandy Chester, Stripper
Time period(s): 21st century; 2010s
Locale(s): California, United States

Summary: In *Heads You Lose* by Lisa Lutz and David Hayward, brother-and-sister business partners Lacey and Paul Hansen make an unpleasant discovery on their California property. Because their business consists of growing illegal marijuana, the rapidly decomposing headless body they find poses a major problem. When they move the body to avoid attracting the attention of the authorities, it only resurfaces. Lacey decides to play detective and learns that the mysterious corpse belongs to a former boyfriend. Lutz and Hayward (once romantically involved in the real world) write alternate chapters that increase tension, humor, and the number of victims as the sleuthing siblings search for a killer.

Where it's reviewed:
Publishers Weekly, Feb. 14, 2011, page 36

Other books by the same author:
The Spellmans Strike Again, 2010
Revenge of the Spellmans, 2009
Curse of the Spellmans, 2008
The Spellman Files, 2007

Other books you might like:
T.C. Boyle, *Budding Prospects: A Pastoral*, 1984
Jasper Fforde, *Shades of Grey: A Novel*, 2009
Sue Grafton, *"A" Is for Alibi*, 1982
Christopher Moore, *Practical Demonkeeping*, 1992
Carol O'Connell, *Bone by Bone*, 2009

489

MATT LYNN

Shadow Force
(London: Headline, 2011)

Series: Death Force Series. Book 3
Story type: Contemporary
Subject(s): Pirates; Suspense; Adventure
Major character(s): Ali Yasin, Pirate

Time period(s): 21st century; 2010s
Locale(s): Africa

Summary: Matt Lynn's *Shadow Force* is the third book in the Death Force series, which follows the adventures of a band of bounty hunters. This installment centers on the Force's attempts to bring Somali pirates to justice. The pirates are terrorizing innocent people in the waters off Africa and preventing any vital international trade. The fighters of Shadow Force step in to take Ali Yasin, the head of the pirates, prisoner. They soon learn, however, that Ali is just one link in a long chain of criminals involved in a massive conspiracy—and mounting violence.

Other books by the same author:
Fire Force, 2010
Death Force, 2009

Other books you might like:
Andrew Grant, *Even*, 2009
Stephen Leather, *Hard Landing*, 2004
Andy McNab, *Remote Control*, 1997
John Nichol, *Point of Impact*, 1996
Mark Powell, *Quantum Breach*, 2010

490

JASSY MACKENZIE

Stolen Lives
(New York: Soho, 2011)

Series: Jade de Jong Investigation Series. Book 2
Story type: Private Detective
Subject(s): Mystery; Kidnapping; Detective fiction
Major character(s): Jade de Jong, Detective—Private; Pamela Jordaan, Client (of Jade's), Prostitute (former); David Patel, Police Officer (superintendent)
Time period(s): 21st century; 2010s
Locale(s): South Africa

Summary: *Stolen Lives*, a mystery novel, is the second book in the Jade de Jong Investigation series from author Jassy MacKenzie. Private investigator Jade de Jong is relieved when Pamela Jordaan shows up at her cottage and offers her a job as a bodyguard. Pamela's husband, Terrance, has disappeared and the distraught wife is fearful for her own safety. Desperate for something to keep her mind off her failed romance with married police superintendent, David Patel, Jade jumps at the chance to make some extra cash on what seems like an easy gig. However, when a gunman fires at Jade and Pamela, and David's family falls victim to a crime, Jade begins to connect the incidents to a sinister plot involving human trafficking.

Other books by the same author:
Random Violence, 2010

Other books you might like:
Deon Meyer, *Dead Before Dying*, 2006
Mukoma Wa Ngugi, *Nairobi Heat*, 2009
Mike Nicol, *Payback*, 2010
Margie Orford, *Like Clockwork*, 2006
Michael Stanley, *A Carrion Death*, 2008

491

LOU MANFREDO

Rizzo's Fire
(New York: Minotaur Books, 2011)

Series: Joe Rizzo Series. Book 2
Story type: Police Procedural
Subject(s): Mystery; Murder; Detective fiction
Major character(s): Joe Rizzo, Detective, Police Officer
Time period(s): 21st century; 2010s
Locale(s): New York, New York

Summary: *Rizzo's Fire*, a suspenseful police procedural, is the second book in the Joe Rizzo series from author Lou Manfredo. After 20 years serving on the NYPD, Detective Sergeant Joe Rizzo's career isn't getting any easier. He's recently been paired up with a new partner (a lesbian African-American) and he's been assigned to an unusual murder case. Robert Lauria, a recluse who was recently fired from his job at a shoe store, was dead for ten days before his body was discovered in his apartment. His only known relative, a cousin, barely knew the guy and said he rarely left his home. Rizzo is dumbstruck by the case, trying to understand why someone would strangle the hermit in the middle of the night, but suspects that the killing may somehow be linked to the recent murder of a big-time Broadway producer.

Where it's reviewed:
Booklist, Feb. 1, 2011, page 39
Library Journal, Feb. 1, 2011, page 47
Publishers Weekly, Jan. 3, 2011, page 32

Other books by the same author:
Rizzo's War, 2009

Other books you might like:
Gabriel Cohen, *Red Hook*, 2001
Reed Farrel Coleman, *Walking the Perfect Square*, 2001
Jim Fusilli, *Closing Time*, 2001
Ed McBain, *Cop Hater*, 1956
S.J. Rozan, *China Trade*, 1994

492

MARGARET MARON

Christmas Mourning
(New York: Grand Central Publishing, 2010)

Series: Deborah Knott Series. Book 16
Story type: Contemporary
Subject(s): Murder; Christmas; Detective fiction
Major character(s): Deborah Knott, Judge, Detective—Amateur; Dwight Bryant, Police Officer, Spouse (of Deborah); Mallory Johnson, Crime Victim
Time period(s): 21st century; 2010s
Locale(s): Colleton County, North Carolina

Summary: The holidays are approaching, and North Carolina judge Deborah Knott and her policeman husband Dwight Bryant are planning a massive family celebration. A series of murders, however, threatens to derail the couple's Christmas plans as members of their small Southern town start turning up dead. Now it's up to Deborah and Dwight to find the killer, and their investigation leads them to a long unsolved murder, which may hold the clues necessary to solving this latest string of mysterious deaths. *Christmas Mourning* is the 16th book in Margaret Maron's Deborah Knott mystery series.

Where it's reviewed:
Booklist, October 1, 2010, page 32
Globe & Mail, December 23, 2010, page R4
Publishers Weekly, September 27, 2010, page 39

Other books by the same author:
Sand Sharks, 2009
Up Jumps the Devil, 1996
Shooting at Loons, 1994
Southern Discomfort, 1993
Bootlegger's Daughter, 1992

Other books you might like:
Martin Clark, *The Legal Limit*, 2008
John Hart, *Down River*, 2007
Joan Hess, *Mischief in Maggody: An Ozarks Murder Mystery*, 1988
Sharyn McCrumb, *If Ever I Return, Pretty Peggy-O*, 1990
Katy Munger, *Legwork*, 1997

493

NANCY MARTIN

Our Lady of Immaculate Deception

(New York: Minotaur Books, 2010)

Story type: Amateur Detective
Subject(s): Mystery; Murder; Organized crime
Major character(s): Roxy Abruzzo, Single Mother, Store Owner (salvage shop), Detective—Amateur, Niece (of Mafia don)
Time period(s): 21st century; 2010s
Locale(s): Pittsburgh, Pennsylvania

Summary: *Our Lady of Immaculate Deception*, a humorous mystery, is the first installment in the Roxy Abruzzo series from award-winning author Nancy Martin. Roxy Abruzzo divides her time between being the owner of an architectural salvage shop, an amateur detective, a single mother, and the niece of a Mafia don. Roxy visits the burnt remains of a local millionaire's mansion on a standard salvage run. While there, she discovers a seven-foot Greek garden statue that she swipes in hopes of reselling it for a profit. When the mansion's owner is murdered shortly thereafter and his ailing mother frets about the missing statue, Roxy finds herself on the run from a killer who is hell-bent on retrieving the sculpture.

494

PETER MAY

Blowback

(Scottsdale, Arizona: Poisoned Pen Press, 2011)

Series: Enzo Files Series. Book 5
Story type: Private Detective

Subject(s): Mystery; Murder; French (European people)
Major character(s): Enzo Macleod, Detective; Marc Fraysse, Restaurateur, Crime Victim
Time period(s): 21st century; 2000s-2010s
Locale(s): France

Summary: *Blowback*, a mystery novel, is the fifth installment in the Enzo Files series from award-winning author Peter May. When Marc Fraysse, a renowned French chef, organizes a massive press conference, rumors begin circulating that Fraysse's shocking statement involves losing one of his three Michelin stars. When the media arrives at his isolated French restaurant, they learn that the chef has been murdered without ever sharing his news. Seven years later, his killer is still at large, motivating Enzo Macleod to reopen the case. As he pieces together the mystery of Fraysse's life and death, Macleod finds surprising parallels to his own personal drama that force him to confront his dark past.

Where it's reviewed:
Library Journal, Feb. 1, 2011, page 47

Other books by the same author:
Freeze Frame, 2010
Blacklight Blue, 2008
The Critic, 2007
Extraordinary People, 2006
The Firemaker, 1999

Other books you might like:
Simon Beckett, *The Chemistry of Death*, 2006
Ellen Crosby, *The Merlot Murders*, 2006
Aaron Elkins, *Fellowship of Fear*, 1982
Erin Hart, *Haunted Ground*, 2003
Louise Penny, *Still Life*, 2006

495

CAROL MCCLEARY

The Illusion of Murder

(New York: Forge, 2011)

Series: Nellie Bly Series. Book 2
Story type: Historical; Series
Subject(s): Mystery; History; Murder
Major character(s): Nellie Bly, Historical Figure, Journalist, Detective; Sarah Bernhardt, Historical Figure, Actress, Magician; Frederick Selous, Historical Figure, Explorer, Magician
Time period(s): 19th century; 1880s (1889)
Locale(s): Asia; Egypt; England; United States

Summary: In *The Illusion of Murder*, author Carol McCleary creates a fictional account of the exploits of Victorian journalist and feminist Nellie Bly. It is 1889 and Bly has set out to reenact the global circumnavigation described in Jules Verne's *Around the World in 80 Days*. The adventure turns deadly when Bly witnesses the murder of an Englishman in Egypt. As Bly continues her journey to Asia and North America, she realizes that she is being followed by the killer she observed in northern Africa. Sarah Bernhardt and Frederick Selous aid Bly in her investigation of the mystery. *The Illusion of Murder* is the second book in the Nellie Bly series.

Where it's reviewed:
Library Journal, March 1, 2011, page 60
Publishers Weekly, Feb. 21, 2011, page 116

Other books by the same author:
The Alchemy of Murder, 2010

Other books you might like:
Tasha Alexander, *And Only to Deceive*, 2005
Rhys Bowen, *Murphy's Law*, 2001
Stefanie Pintoff, *In the Shadow of Gotham*, 2009
Victoria Thompson, *Murder on Astor Place*, 1999
Jacqueline Winspear, *Maisie Dobbs*, 2003

496

VAL MCDERMID

The Fever of the Bone

(London: Little, Brown and Company, 2009)

Series: Tony Hill/Carol Jordan Series. Book 6
Story type: Contemporary
Subject(s): Serial murders; Detective fiction; Suspense
Major character(s): Tony Hill, Detective; Jennifer Maidment, Crime Victim, Teenager
Time period(s): 21st century; 2000s
Locale(s): United Kingdom

Summary: The sixth installment in Val McDermid's Tony Hill/Carol Jordan mystery series, *The Fever of the Bone* finds detective Tony Hill confronting his most grueling case yet. When teenager Jennifer Maidment is killed and butchered, Hill struggles to find the person responsible. But with a little investigative work, he comes to realize that Jennifer's murder is just one killing in a long list of proposed deaths committed by an unknown enemy. None of the victims seem to have any connection to one another, further confounding Tony's investigation. But as he works tirelessly to stop the killer from striking again, Tony is going to have to battle his own demons and face his darkest fears.

Where it's reviewed:
The Daily Mail, September 25, 2009, page 69
Publishers Weekly, July 26, 2010, page 48
The Scotsman, October 10, 2009, page 7
The Times of London, February 20, 2010, page 11

Other books by the same author:
Beneath the Bleeding, 2007
The Torment of Others, 2004
The Last Temptation, 2002
The Wire in the Blood, 1997
The Mermaids Singing, 1995

Other books you might like:
Mark Billingham, *Lazy Bones*, 2003
Stuart MacBride, *Cold Granite*, 2005
Denise Mina, *Garnethill*, 1998
Ian Rankin, *Resurrection Men*, 2001
John Sandford, *Rules of Prey*, 1989

497

CRAIG MCDONALD

One True Sentence

(New York: Minotaur Books, 2011)

Series: Hector Lassiter Series. Book 4
Story type: Amateur Detective; Historical
Subject(s): Mystery; Writers; Murder
Major character(s): Hector Lassiter, Writer, Detective—Amateur; Brinke Devlin, Writer, Detective—Amateur, Lover (of Hector)
Time period(s): 20th century; 1920s (1924)
Locale(s): Paris, France

Summary: *One True Sentence* is the fourth installment in the Hector Lassiter series from award-winning author Craig McDonald. The story, set in Paris in 1924, follows aspiring crime writer turned amateur sleuth, Hector Lassiter. When a number of magazine editors are murdered, Gertrude Stein assembles a group of mystery writers to solve the crimes. Hector teams up with sexy novelist, Brinke Devlin, both in the bedroom and on the investigation. As the investigation intensifies, Hector suspects that a group of writers might be responsible for the deaths, causing him to question the motives of everyone around him and fear for his own safety.

Where it's reviewed:
Booklist, Jan. 1, 2011, page 51
Publishers Weekly, Dec. 6, 2010, page 33

Other books by the same author:
Print the Legend, 2010
Toros & Torsos, 2008
Wolf, 2008
Head Games, 2007

Other books you might like:
Ernest Hemingway, *The Sun Also Rises*, 1926
Joseph Kanon, *Stardust*, 2009
Paula McLain, *The Paris Wife*, 2011
Walter Satterthwait, *Masquerade*, 1998
Georges Simenon, *The Crime of Inspector Maigret*, 1932

498

G.A. MCKEVETT (Pseudonym of Sonja Massie)

A Decadent Way to Die

(New York: Kensington, 2011)

Series: Savannah Reid Series. Book 16
Story type: Contemporary
Subject(s): Detective fiction; Dolls; Murder
Major character(s): Savannah Reid, Detective—Private; Helene Strauss, Crime Victim; Tammy Hart, Assistant (of Savannah)
Time period(s): 21st century; 2010s
Locale(s): United States

Summary: G.A. McKevett's *A Decadent Way to Die* is the 16th novel in the Savannah Reid Mysteries series. When Helene Strauss, the elderly inventor of a popular children's doll, is found dead, the list of suspects is long. Very long. Now it's up to private investigator Savannah Reid to wade through the laundry list of possibilities, which includes Helene's ungrateful relatives and questionable employees. But things take an even darker turn when two key figures in the investigation turn up dead, and the pressure is on for Savannah to solve this case before anyone else meets an untimely end.

Where it's reviewed:
Library Journal, December 2010, page 91
Publishers Weekly, December 13, 2010, page 40

Other books by the same author:
Wicked Craving, 2010
Cooked Goose, 1998
Killer Calories, 1997
Bitter Sweets, 1996
Just Desserts, 1995

Other books you might like:
M.C. Beaton, *Agatha Raisin and the Quiche of Death*, 1992
Joanne Fluke, *Chocolate Chip Cookie Murder*, 2000
Sue Ann Jaffarian, *Too Big to Miss: An Odelia Grey Mystery*, 2006
Kathryn Lilley, *Dying to Be Thin*, 2007
Elizabeth Atwood Taylor, *The Cable Car Murder*, 1981

499

JENNIFER MCMAHON

Don't Breathe a Word

(New York: HarperCollins, 2011)

Story type: Child-in-Peril
Subject(s): Mystery; Missing persons; Fantasy
Major character(s): Lisa, Sister (of Sam), 12-Year-Old; Sam, Brother (of Lisa), Boyfriend (of Phoebe); Phoebe, Girlfriend (of Sam)

Summary: In *Don't Breathe a Word*, a novel by author Jennifer McMahon, the author transports the reader back and forth in time as she describes a past and present world involving two siblings. Despite a reality that was less than ideal, 12-year-old Lisa spent most of her time daydreaming of a world where she was Queen of the Fairies. Then Lisa vanishes, and her younger brother Sam hears nothing from her until 15 years later. Then, he and his girlfriend Phoebe are led to a book about a king of the fairies—a tome that Lisa reportedly used to transport herself into a dream world. But things are not always as they seem, and Phoebe and Sam must cope with their own emotional baggage in order to discern fact from fiction and truth from reality.

Other books by the same author:
Dismantled, 2009
Island of Lost Girls, 2008
My Tiki Girl, 2008
Promise Not to Tell, 2007

Other books you might like:
John Connolly, *The Book of Lost Things*, 2006
Keith Donohue, *The Stolen Child*, 2006
Tana French, *The Likeness*, 2008

Ira Levin, *Rosemary's Baby*, 1967
Laura Lippman, *I'd Know You Anywhere*, 2010

500

BRAD MELTZER

The Inner Circle

(New York: Grand Central Publishing, 2011)

Story type: Contemporary; Political
Subject(s): Conspiracy; Politics; Suspense
Major character(s): Beecher White, Clerk (archivist); Clementine Kaye, Friend (of Beecher)
Time period(s): 21st century; 2010s
Locale(s): Washington, District of Columbia

Summary: Brad Meltzer's *The Inner Circle* tells the story of Beecher White, an employee of the National Archives who stumbles upon a conspiracy among the highest echelons of the Washington political scene. When Beecher makes a startling find of a rare book, it opens the door to a mystery that soon sends him on his own increasingly dangerous investigation into the conspiracy and corruption of American politics. He is joined in his adventure by Clementine Kaye, an old friend who has a very personal investment in uncovering the truth behind the cover-up.

Where it's reviewed:
Library Journal, December 2010, page 100
Publishers Weekly, November 22, 2010, page 42
USA Today, January 11, 2011, page 01D

Other books by the same author:
The Zero Game, 2005
The Millionaires, 2002
The First Counsel, 2001
Dead Even, 1999
The Tenth Justice, 1998

Other books you might like:
David Baldacci, *The Camel Club*, 2005
Dan Brown, *The Lost Symbol*, 2009
Lincoln Child, *Relic*, 1995
Daniel Silva, *The Kill Artist*, 2000
Stuart Woods, *Grass Roots*, 1989

501

BRADFORD MORROW

The Diviner's Tale

(Boston: Houghton Mifflin Harcourt, 2011)

Story type: Psychological
Subject(s): Mystery; Psychology; Supernatural
Major character(s): Cassandra Brooks, Teacher (substitute), Psychic (dowser); Laura Bryant, Runaway
Time period(s): 21st century; 2010s
Locale(s): New York, United States

Summary: In *The Diviner's Tale* by Bradford Morrow, a single mother freelances as a dowser to supplement the income she earns as a substitute teacher. Cassandra Brooks discovered her talent for divining when she was just a girl. Now, her powers seem to be growing. While she is dowsing an upstate New York property for a client, she discovers the body of a young woman hanging in a tree. She brings the authorities to the grisly scene but finds that the body is gone. Not long after, the same girl Cassandra saw in her vision walks out of the forest, claiming to be the victim of a kidnapping.

Where it's reviewed:
Library Journal, Oct. 15, 2010, page 68
New York Times Book Review, Feb. 6, 2011, page 22(L)

Other books by the same author:
Come Sunday, 2008
Ariel's Crossing, 2002
Giovanni's Gift, 1997
Trinity Fields, 1995
The Almanac Branch, 1991

Other books you might like:
Laura Benedict, *Isabella Moon*, 2008
Tom Franklin, *Crooked Letter, Crooked Letter*, 2010
Tim Gautreaux, *The Clearing*, 2003
Vicki Lane, *The Day of Small Things*, 2010
Daniel Woodrell, *Winter's Bone: A Novel*, 2006

502

WALTER MOSLEY

When the Thrill Is Gone
(New York: Riverhead Books, 2011)

Series: Leonid McGill Series. Book 3
Story type: Private Detective
Subject(s): Detective fiction; Mystery; Family
Major character(s): Leonid McGill, Detective—Private, Spouse; Crystal Tyler, Wealthy, Client (of Leonid); Harris Vartan, Criminal
Time period(s): 21st century; 2010s
Locale(s): New York, New York

Summary: *When the Thrill Is Gone* is a mystery novel from author Walter Mosley. This book is the third installment in the Leonid McGill series about a savvy private investigator in New York City. In desperate need of cash, Leonid accepts a case from Crystal Tyler, a beautiful woman who suspects her billionaire husband is having an affair and planning to kill her. Although Leonid has his suspicions about Crystal's honesty, he agrees to work with her. Meanwhile, Leonid's own life is in disarray: his wife is cheating on him, his son is a scammer, and his mentor is dying from cancer. When crime boss, Harris Vartan, asks Leonid for a favor, the detective is sent on a wild journey that forces him to confront his own life and shortcomings.

Where it's reviewed:
Booklist, January 1, 2011, page 53
Publishers Weekly, January 3, 2011, page 30

Other books by the same author:
Known to Evil, 2010
The Long Fall, 2009

Fearless Jones, 2001
Always Outnumbered, Always Outgunned, 1997
Devil in a Blue Dress, 1990

Other books you might like:
Lawrence Block, *In the Midst of Death*, 1976
Reed Farrel Coleman, *Walking the Perfect Square*, 2001
Robert Crais, *The Last Detective*, 2003
Gar Anthony Haywood, *Cemetery Road*, 2010
S.J. Rozan, *China Trade*, 1994

503

KATE MOSSE

The Winter Ghosts
(New York: Penguin, 2011)

Story type: Ghost Story
Subject(s): World War I, 1914-1918; French (European people); Mental health
Major character(s): Freddie Watson, Mentally Ill Person, Brother (of George); George Watson, Brother (of Freddie)
Locale(s): French Pyrenees, France

Summary: *The Winter Ghosts* is a novel by author Kate Mosse. Upon learning that his brother George went missing during the Great War, Freddie Watson suffered a mental breakdown and was subsequently institutionalized. Now, a decade later, Freddie is released from the mental hospital. He makes his way to France to find closure for his brother's disappearance, but when a car wreck leaves him stranded in a rural village, he begins to lose hope. Salvation comes to him in the form of a woman named Fabrissa, with whom he spends the night. Yet the following morning, upon awakening, Freddie finds himself in the midst of a centuries-old mystery. Mosse is also the author of *Sepulchre* and *Labyrinth*.

Where it's reviewed:
Library Journal, Dec. 2010, page 105

Other books by the same author:
Sepulchre, 2007
Labyrinth, 2005

Other books you might like:
Rennie Airth, *River of Darkness*, 1999
Pat Barker, *Regeneration*, 1991
Susan Hill, *Strange Meeting*, 1971
Charles Todd, *A Duty to the Dead*, 2009
Jacqueline Winspear, *Maisie Dobbs*, 2003

504

J.J. MURPHY

Murder Your Darlings
(New York: Obsidian, 2011)

Series: Algonquin Round Table Mystery Series. Book 1
Story type: Historical
Subject(s): Mystery; Murder; Writers
Major character(s): Dorothy Parker, Historical Figure,

Mystery

Writer, Detective—Amateur; Billy Faulkner, Historical Figure, Writer, Crime Suspect
Time period(s): 20th century; 1920s
Locale(s): New York, New York

Summary: *Murder Your Darlings* is the first installment in the Algonquin Round Table Mystery series about the legendary lunch group of actors, writers, and critics who met daily at the Algonquin Hotel in the 1920s. In *Murder Your Darlings*, acclaimed writer Dorothy Parker turns into an amateur sleuth after finding a dead body under the round table. Drama critic Leland Mayflower was murdered with a pen, and Southern writer, Billy Faulkner, looks to be guilty. Sure of Billy's innocence, Dorothy recruits her writer pals to do some detective work to find the real killer. First novel.

Where it's reviewed:
Publishers Weekly, November 22, 2010, page 45

Other books you might like:
Rhys Bowen, *Her Royal Spyness*, 2007
Gyles Brandreth, *Oscar Wilde and a Death of No Importance*, 2008
Agatha Christie, *The Secret Adversary*, 1922
Kerry Greenwood, *Murder in Montparnasse*, 2002
Dorothy L. Sayers, *Strong Poison*, 1930

505

TAMAR MYERS

The Headhunter's Daughter

(New York: William Morrow, 2011)

Story type: Historical
Subject(s): Missing persons; Tribalism; Mystery
Major character(s): Amanda Brown, Young Woman, Religious (missionary)
Time period(s): 20th century; 1940s-1950s
Locale(s): Congo

Summary: *The Headhunter's Daughter*, a thought-provoking historical mystery, is the sequel to *The Witch Doctor's Wife* from author Tamar Myers. In 1945, in the jungles of the Belgian Congo, a Bashilele headhunter stumbles across an abandoned infant while on his way to kill an enemy. Despite the baby's Caucasian race, the tribesman takes her back to his village to raise her as his own daughter. Thirteen years later, Amanda Brown, an American missionary in nearby Belle Vue, hears rumors that a white girl is living among the Bashilele headhunters and begins to question the child's origins. As Amanda searches for the truth, she makes a shocking discovery about the girl's identity and her disappearance that rocks the entire community.

Where it's reviewed:
Booklist, Feb. 15, 2011, page 55
Publishers Weekly, Dec. 20, 2010, page 37

Other books by the same author:
The Grass is Always Greener, 2011
Butter Safe than Sorry, 2010
The Witch Doctor's Wife, 2009
Larceny and Old Lace, 1996
Too Many Crooks Spoil the Broth, 1993

Other books you might like:
Alan Bradley, *The Sweetness at the Bottom of the Pie*, 2009
Colin Cotterill, *The Coroner's Lunch*, 2004
Isak Dinesen, *Out of Africa*, 1937
Peter Matthiessen, *At Play in the Fields of the Lord*, 1965
Alexander McCall Smith, *The No. 1 Ladies' Detective Agency*, 1998

506

STEVE O'BRIEN

Bullet Work

(Washington, DC: A & N Publishing, 2011)

Story type: Contemporary
Subject(s): Horse racing; Horses; Mystery
Major character(s): Dan Morgan, Animal Lover (horse owner); AJ Kaine, Animal Lover, Horse Trainer (hot walker)
Time period(s): 21st century; 2010s
Locale(s): United States

Summary: *Bullet Work* is set in the world of horse racing. Opening day is rapidly approaching, causing excitement and anxiety among the owners, vets, trainers, and jockeys in the sport of competitive horse racing. As the launch of another season inches closer, something unthinkable and shocking has happened: a sadistic madman has targeted three horses. One horse has been poisoned, one vanishes without a trace, and another is viciously attacked and wounded. Soon, the stables are being extorted, forced to pay high premiums to protect the horses in their care. When Dan Morgan's filly is targeted, he teams up with hot walker AJ Kaine, an odd young man who holds a powerful secret that could trap the culprit and stop the attacks.

507

GERARD O'DONOVAN

The Priest

(London: Sphere, 2010)

Story type: Contemporary
Subject(s): Detective fiction; Murder; Suspense
Major character(s): Mike Mulcahy, Detective—Police; Siobhan Fallon, Journalist
Time period(s): 21st century; 2010s
Locale(s): Dublin, Ireland

Summary: In *The Priest*, author Gerard O'Donovan chronicles the investigations of Dublin police detective Mike Mulcahy. Mike's latest case has everyone stumped—and more than a little terrified. A man known only as The Priest is prowling the streets of the city and committing the most unholy acts of violence. As the crimes grow ever darker and more perverse, Mike feels desperate to stop them. Teaming up with journalist Siobhan Fallon, Mike sets out to stop The Priest before he can continue his reign of terror on the streets of Dublin. First novel.

Where it's reviewed:
Library Journal, January 2011, page 89
Publishers Weekly, January 24, 2011, page 132
The Times of London, November 13, 2010, page 12

Other books you might like:
Ken Bruen, *The Guards*, 2003
Declan Hughes, *City of Lost Girls*, 2010
Stuart MacBride, *Cold Granite*, 2005
Brian McGilloway, *Borderlands*, 2008
Stuart Neville, *The Ghosts of Belfast*, 2009

508

NICK OLDHAM

Hidden Witness

(Sutton, Surrey, England: Severn House, 2011)

Series: Henry Christie Series. Book 15
Story type: Police Procedural
Subject(s): Mystery; Murder; Organized crime
Major character(s): Henry Christie, Detective (superintendent); Karl Donaldson, FBI Agent, Friend (of Henry's)
Time period(s): 21st century; 2010s
Locale(s): Blackpool, England

Summary: *Hidden Witness*, a suspenseful police procedural, is the fifteenth installment in the Detective Superintendent Henry Christie series from author Nick Oldham. When an old man is run over twice and shot in the head on a Blackpool street, it becomes obvious that this death is no accident. Detective Superintendent Henry Christie is called away from his family vacation to investigate the murder, of which there were two witnesses, one who has also shown up dead. Christie teams up with an old pal, FBI agent Karl Donaldson, when it's discovered that the victim is an Italian mobster with a long line of enemies. Christie and Donaldson's only hope for nabbing the killer is to track down the one remaining witness, but they'll have to hurry if they want to find him alive.

Where it's reviewed:
Booklist, Dec. 15, 2010, page 23
Library Journal, Feb. 1, 2011, page 47
Publishers Weekly, Dec. 20, 2010, page 38

Other books by the same author:
Seizure, 2010
The Last Big Job, 1999
Nightmare City, 1998
One Dead Witness, 1998
A Time for Justice, 1996

Other books you might like:
John Harvey, *Flesh and Blood*, 2004
Peter James, *Dead Simple*, 2006
Denise Mina, *Garnethill*, 1998
Ian Rankin, *Strip Jack*, 1992
Peter Robinson, *Gallows View*, 1987

509

DANIEL PALMER

Delirious

(New York: Kensington, 2011)

Story type: Contemporary
Subject(s): Suspense; Murder; Technology
Major character(s): Charlie Giles, Computer Expert, Crime Suspect; Joe, Mentally Ill Person, Brother (of Charlie)
Time period(s): 21st century; 2010s
Locale(s): United States

Summary: In Daniel Palmer's *Delirious*, Charlie Giles is a man who seems to have it all. A rising star at his very technical job, Charlie is on the verge of great fame and fortune with the development of a revolutionary new product. But a series of hard luck episodes lead to Charlie's firing, and when his coworkers start being methodically killed off, he becomes the chief suspect. As his success crumbles around him, Charlie wonders if this chain of events is really happening—or if it's all in his head. First novel.

Where it's reviewed:
Booklist, October 15, 2010, page 24
Publishers Weekly, December 6, 2010, page 32

Other books you might like:
Michael Crichton, *Disclosure: A Novel*, 1993
Joseph Finder, *Killer Instinct*, 2006
Joseph Finder, *Paranoia*, 2004
John Grisham, *The Firm*, 1991
Keith Raffel, *Dot.dead*

510

MICHAEL PALMER

A Heartbeat Away

(New York: St. Martin's Press, 2011)

Story type: Medical
Subject(s): Suspense; Medicine; Hospitals
Major character(s): President, Government Official; Griffin Rhodes, Scientist, Prisoner

Summary: *A Heartbeat Away* is a medical mystery by author Michael Palmer. In this novel, Palmer tells the story of a homegrown terrorist organization named Genesis, who releases viral agents in the middle of the President's State of the Union address. The President knows how deadly this virus can be: after all, it was he who ordered the manufacturing of it to be used in biological warfare. Worse yet, the only person who can help them is Griffin Rhodes, a scientist whom the President sent to prison. Now the President must free Griffin if an anti-virus is ever to be created—but can Griffin let go of his grudge long enough to save Washington?

Where it's reviewed:
Booklist, December 15, 2010, page 23
Publishers Weekly, December 13, 2010, page 36

Mystery

Other books by the same author:
The Last Surgeon, 2010
The Second Opinion, 2009
The First Patient, 2008
The Fifth Vial, 2007
The Society, 2004

Other books you might like:
Robin Cook, *Vector*, 1999
Tess Gerritsen, *Harvest*, 1996
Leonard Goldberg, *Deadly Medicine*, 1992
Mike Lawson, *House Secrets*, 2009
Alexandra Sokoloff, *The Price*, 2008

511

I.J. PARKER

The Fires of the Gods

(New York: Severn House Publishers, 2011)

Series: Sugawara Akitada Series. Book 8
Story type: Historical
Subject(s): Japanese history, to 1185; Japanese (Asian people); Detective fiction
Major character(s): Sugawara Akitada, Detective— Amateur, Government Official
Time period(s): 11th century
Locale(s): Japan

Summary: *The Fires of the Gods* is the eighth installment of author I.J. Parker's mystery series featuring Sugawara Akitada. In 11th-century Japan, Ministry of Justice Senior Secretary Akitada must track down an arsonist wreaking havoc in the city of Heian-Kyo. But Akitada's job is cut out for him, as it appears that backroom dealings amongst his political rivals have resulted in his demotion to Junior Secretary. When Akitada goes to confront the man behind his downfall, he finds him murdered—and now Akitada is the only suspect. Can Akitada clear his name and stop the arsonist before it is too late?

Where it's reviewed:
Publishers Weekly, Feb. 7, 2011, page 38

Other books by the same author:
The Convict's Sword, 2009
Black Arrow, 2006
The Dragon Scroll, 2005
The Hell Screen, 2003
Rashomon Gate, 2002

Other books you might like:
Ariana Franklin, *Mistress of the Art of Death*, 2007
Sujata Massey, *The Salaryman's Wife*, 1997
Candace M. Robb, *The Apothecary Rose*, 1993
Laura Joh Rowland, *Shinju*, 1994
C.J. Sansom, *Dissolution*, 2003

512

T. JEFFERSON PARKER

The Border Lords

(New York: Dutton, 2011)

Series: Charlie Hood Mystery Series. Book 4
Story type: Contemporary
Subject(s): Suspense; Drugs; Detective fiction
Major character(s): Charlie Hood, Veteran, Police Officer; Sean Ozburn, Agent (ATF)
Time period(s): 21st century; 2010s
Locale(s): California, United States

Summary: Sean Ozburn is an agent with the Department of Alcohol, Tobacco, and Firearms. He has been sent on an undercover mission deep within a California drug cartel. After he disappears, Sean begins sending cryptic videos to his frantic wife. L.A. cop Charlie Hood delves into the mystery surrounding Sean's case, uncovering some startling revelations about the ATF agent and his increasingly dangerous situation. *The Border Lands* is the fourth installment in T. Jefferson Parker's Charlie Hood Mystery series. T. Jefferson Parker is the author of more than a dozen novels and the winner of the Edgar Award.

Where it's reviewed:
Booklist, November 1, 2010, page 29
Daily Herald, February 4, 2011, page 39
Entertainment Weekly, January 7, 2011, page 73
Library Journal, November 1, 2010, page 57
Publishers Weekly, November 8, 2010, page 42

Other books by the same author:
Iron River, 2010
The Renegades, 2009
L.A. Outlaws, 2008
California Girl, 2004
Silent Joe, 2001

Other books you might like:
Michael Connelly, *The Concrete Blonde*, 1994
Robert Crais, *The Watchman*, 2007
Kent Harrington, *Dia de los Muertos*, 1997
Barbara Seranella, *No Human Involved*, 1997
Don Winslow, *Savages*, 2010

513

BRAD PARKS

Eyes of the Innocent

(New York: Minotaur Books, 2011)

Series: Carter Ross Series. Book 2
Story type: Contemporary; Series
Subject(s): Mystery; Crime; Journalism
Major character(s): Carter Ross, Journalist; Akilah Harris, Mother (of deceased boys); Windy Byers, Political Figure (councilman); Tommy Hernandez, Journalist; Tee Jamison, Friend (of Carter); Tina Thompson, Girlfriend (of Carter)

Time period(s): 21st century; 2010s
Locale(s): Newark, New Jersey

Summary: In *Eyes of the Innocent* by Brad Parks, investigative journalist Carter Ross visits the scene of a deadly Newark house fire that may or may not have been accidental. The mother of the two boys who died explains that she was at work at the time of the fire. When a city councilman and court documents disappear, Ross realizes that a faulty heater may not be the root cause of the tragedy. Lauren McMillan, his pretty new intern, proves more helpful than he expected. Old friends, Tommy Hernandez, Tee Jamison, and Tina Thompson help Ross dig deep into a story of crime and corruption. *Eyes of the Innocent* is the second book in the Carter Ross series.

Where it's reviewed:
Booklist, Dec. 1, 2010, page 29
Publishers Weekly, Nov. 1, 2010, page 29

Other books by the same author:
Faces of the Gone, 2010

Other books you might like:
Jan Brogan, *A Confidential Source*, 2005
Bruce DeSilva, *Rogue Island*, 2010
David Ellis, *Line of Vision*, 2001
Bryan Gruley, *Starvation Lake*, 2009
Karen E. Olson, *Sacred Cows*, 2005

514

R.T. RAICHEV

Murder at the Villa Byzantine
(London: Constable & Robinson Limited, 2011)

Series: Antonia Darcy and Major Payne Series. Book 6
Story type: Contemporary; Series
Subject(s): Mystery; Detective fiction; Murder
Major character(s): Hugh Payne, Detective—Private; Antonia Darcy, Writer, Spouse (of Hugh); Melisande Chevret, Actress; Stella Markoff, Friend (of Melisande)
Time period(s): 21st century; 2010s
Locale(s): London, England

Summary: In *Murder at the Villa Byzantine* by R.T. Raichev, a stuffy social event draws Major Hugh Payne, a private investigator, and his spouse, Antonia Darcy, a mystery author, into a case of murder. While attending a party honoring Melisande Chevret, an actress, Hugh and Antonia meet a collection of colorful guests. Not long after the party, one of those guests, Stella Markoff, is beheaded with a sword at London's Villa Byzantine. As Hugh and Antonia investigate the case, they discover Markoff's connections to Bulgarian royalty. *Murder at the Villa Byzantine* is the sixth book in the Antonia Darcy and Major Payne series.

Where it's reviewed:
Publishers Weekly, Jan. 31, 2011, page 32

Other books by the same author:
The Curious Incident at Claridge's, 2010
The Little Victims, 2009
Assassins at Ospreys, 2008

The Death of Corinne, 2007
The Hunt for Sonya Dufrette, 2006

Other books you might like:
Agatha Christie, *Hercule Poirot's Christmas*, 1938
Ann Granger, *Say It with Poison*, 1991
G.M. Malliet, *Death of a Cozy Writer*, 2008
Louise Penny, *Still Life*, 2006
Dorothy L. Sayers, *Clouds of Witness*, 1925

515

IAN RANKIN

The Complaints
(London: Orion Books, 2009)

Subject(s): Crime; Detective fiction; Mystery fiction
Major character(s): Malcolm Fox, Detective—Police (Complaints and Conduct Department); Jamie Breck, Police Officer
Time period(s): 21st century
Locale(s): Edinburgh, United Kingdom

Summary: Ian Rankin's debut novel *The Complaints* is about a group called the Complaints, short for the Complaints and Conduct Department. The group is charged with investigating other cops. Malcolm Fox is part of this elite law enforcement group and is on top of the world in his professional life. His personal life is a different story. His father is ill and in a nursing home, while his sister is in love with an abusive monster that she won't leave. Fox has been put in charge of a new assignment—following Jamie Breck, a dirty cop. This is going to be a tough case since no one can prove that Breck has actually done anything wrong. Fox's investigation leads him to a murder—a murder that is too close for comfort. First Novel.

Where it's reviewed:
Library Journal, Jan. 2011, page 90

Other books by the same author:
Doors Open, 2008
Resurrection Men, 2002
Black and Blue, 1997
Hide and Seek, 1990
Knots and Crosses, 1987

Other books you might like:
Mark Billingham, *Sleepyhead*, 2001
John Harvey, *Lonely Hearts*, 1989
Val McDermid, *Dead Beat*, 1993
Denise Mina, *Garnethill*, 1998
Andrew Taylor, *An Air That Kills*, 1995

516

RUTH RENDELL

Portobello
(New York: Scribner, 2010)

Story type: Literary
Subject(s): Mystery; Suspense; Burglary

Major character(s): Eugene Wren, Recluse; Ella Cotswold, Girlfriend (of Eugene); Lance Platt, Criminal (burglar); Gilbert Gibson, Uncle (of Lance)
Time period(s): 21st century; 2010s
Locale(s): London, England

Summary: *Portobello*, a mystery novel by Ruth Rendell, takes place on Portobello Road in London, where a group of people previously unknown to each other come together in surprising ways. In the neighborhood, Eugene Wren, somewhat of a recluse with an addiction to candy lozenges, is deciding whether or not to marry his girlfriend Ella Cotswold, a physician. Meanwhile, Lance Platt is busy casing the neighborhood, trying to determine which homes would be best to break into; his uncle Gilbert Gibson, a former burglar, is no help now that he has found religion. When someone finds an envelope full of money, he places "Found" signs around the neighborhood, bringing the four people together in a disastrous and violent way.

Where it's reviewed:
Library Journal, July 2010, page 78
New York Times Book Review, October 3, 2010, page 34

Other books by the same author:
The Crocodile Bird, 1993
Going Wrong, 1990
The Bridesmaid, 1989
The Tree of Hands, 1984
A Judgment in Stone, 1977

Other books you might like:
P.D. James, *An Unsuitable Job for a Woman*, 1972
J. Wallis Martin, *A Likeness in Stone*, 1997
Louise Penny, *Still Life*, 2006
Martyn Waites, *Speak No Evil*, 2010
Minette Walters, *Disordered Minds*, 2004

517

MICHAEL ROBERTSON

The Brothers of Baker Street

(New York: Minotaur Books, 2011)

Series: Baker Street Mysteries Series. Book 2
Story type: Legal
Subject(s): Mystery; Letters (Correspondence); Law
Major character(s): Reggie Heath, Brother (of Nigel), Lawyer, Detective—Amateur; Nigel Heath, Brother (of Reggie), Lawyer, Detective—Amateur
Time period(s): 20th century; 1990s (1997)
Locale(s): London, England

Summary: *The Brothers of Baker Street*, a suspenseful mystery novel, is the second book in the Baker Street Mysteries series from author Michael Robertson. Brothers and lawyers, Reggie and Nigel Heath, soon learn that one of the unexpected responsibilities of leasing an office at 221B Baker Street is responding to letters to fictional detective Sherlock Holmes. Despite the trouble they landed in after replying to his missives in *The Baker Street Letters*, Reggie and Nigel are faithful in responding to each letter addressed to Holmes. Besides, it's something to keep them busy when work is slow. But Reggie and Nigel soon have their hands full when they receive a note from someone claiming to be Professor Moriarty's descendant and simultaneously take on a puzzling case defending a cab driver accused of killing two American tourists.

Where it's reviewed:
Booklist, Feb. 1, 2011, page 35
Publishers Weekly, Jan. 3, 2011, page 36

Other books by the same author:
The Baker Street Letters, 2009

Other books you might like:
Sir Arthur Conan Doyle, *A Study in Scarlet*, 1887
Christopher Fowler, *Full Dark House*, 2003
John Gardner, *The Return of Moriarty*, 1974
Steve Hockensmith, *Holmes on the Range*, 2006
Graham Moore, *The Sherlockian*, 2010

518

JEREMY ROBINSON

Threshold

(New York: Thomas Dunne Books, 2011)

Series: Jack Sigler Series. Book 3
Story type: Fantasy
Subject(s): Mythology; Espionage; Fantasy
Major character(s): Jack Sigler, Agent; Hercules, Mythical Creature
Locale(s): Fort Bragg, North Carolina

Summary: In *Threshold*, the third installment of the Jack Sigler series, author Jeremy Robinson blends the mysterious and the mythological as he tells the tale of a group of elite agents and their battle to save the planet. This time, Jack must rush to save his own daughter Fiona after she goes missing during an attack on a military base. The clock is ticking; if Fiona's insulin pump runs out before Jack gets to her, she could die. Now Jack must call upon both real and mythical forces—including the President of the United States and Hercules, the Roman god of strength—to help him save his daughter. Robinson is also the author of *Pulse* and *Instinct*.

Where it's reviewed:
Publishers Weekly, Feb. 21, 2011, page 111

Other books by the same author:
Beneath, 2010
Instinct, 2010
Pulse, 2009
Raising the Past, 2006
The Didymus Contingency, 2005

Other books you might like:
Steve Berry, *The Templar Legacy*, 2006
Lincoln Child, *The Ice Limit*, 2000
Chris Kuzneski, *Sign of the Cross*, 2006
Matthew Reilly, *Ice Station*, 1999
James Rollins, *Sandstorm*, 2004

519

ANDERS ROSLUND
BORGE HELLSTROM, Co-Author

Three Seconds

(London: Quercus, 2010)

Story type: Contemporary
Subject(s): Drugs; Swedes; Suspense
Major character(s): Piet Hoffman, Convict (former; undercover informer); Ewert Grens, Detective—Police
Time period(s): 21st century; 2010s
Locale(s): Sweden

Summary: Anders Roslund and Borge Hellstrom's *Three Seconds* charts the escapades of Piet Hoffman, a former convict now working undercover for the Swedish police. His assignment impels him to become a key player in a prison amphetamine ring, which requires Piet to get arrested, go to prison, and gain the confidence of insider big-shots in order to bring down the ring. But the assignment goes tragically awry, and Piet must join forces with the determined Detective Inspector Ewert Grens. Translated by Kari Dickson, *Three Seconds* won the Swedish Academy of Crime Writers' award for Best Swedish Crime Novel of the Year in 2009.

Where it's reviewed:
Booklist, December 1, 2010, page 33
New York Times, January 6, 2011, page C1
Publishers Weekly, November 29, 2010, page 28
USA Today, January 3, 2011, page 01D

Other books by the same author:
Box 21, 2009

Other books you might like:
Karin Fossum, *Don't Look Back*, 2002
Stieg Larsson, *The Girl with the Dragon Tattoo*, 2008
Henning Mankell, *Faceless Killers*, 1991
Jo Nesbo, *The Redbreast*, 2007
Maj Sjowall, *The Laughing Policeman*, 1977

520

PATRICK ROTHFUSS

The Wise Man's Fear

(New York: Penguin, 2011)

Series: Kingkiller Chronicles Series. Book 2
Story type: Fantasy; Series
Subject(s): Fantasy; Fairies; Assassination
Major character(s): Kvothe, Orphan; Ambrose, Villain; Felurian, Lover (of Kvothe), Mythical Creature (fairy); Chronicler, Writer (scribe)
Time period(s): Indeterminate
Locale(s): Newarre, Alternate Universe

Summary: *The Wise Man's Fear* by Patrick Rothfuss continues the story of Kvothe the Bloodless begun in *The Name of the Wind*. Orphaned at a young age, Kvothe evolves from actor to hero to proprietor of the Waystone Inn, encountering a range of villains and adventures along the way. Having vowed to reveal his fantastic tale to the kingdom's chronicler in just three days, Kvothe fills the second day of his testimony with accounts of his confrontations with Ambrose, Felurian the fairy goddess, and the Adem mercenary forces. *The Wise Man's Fear* is the second book in the Kingkiller Chronicles series.

Where it's reviewed:
Library Journal, February 15, 2011, page 105
Publishers Weekly, January 24, 2011, page 136

Other books by the same author:
The Name of the Wind, 2007

Other books you might like:
Raymond E. Feist, *Magician: Apprentice*, 1982
Scott Lynch, *The Lies of Locke Lamora*, 2006
George R.R. Martin, *A Game of Thrones*, 1996
Dan Simmons, *Hyperion*, 1989

521

LORI ROY

Bent Road

(New York: Dutton, 2011)

Story type: Family Saga
Subject(s): Suspense; Family life; Grief
Major character(s): Arthur Scott, Brother (of Eve and Ruth), Father (of Eve-ee and Elaine), Spouse (of Celia); Ruth, Spouse (of Roy), Sister (of Eve and Arthur); Eve, Sister (of Ruth and Arthur, deceased); Roy, Spouse (of Ruth), Crime Suspect; Celia, Spouse (of Arthur)
Locale(s): Kansas, United States

Summary: *Bent Road* is the debut novel by author Lori Roy. After being absent from his hometown for two decades, Arthur Scott is ready to return home in order to protect his family from the dangers of city living in Detroit. Upon arriving in Kansas, Arthur soon realizes that the memory of his sister Eve, whose death precipitated his leaving, still remains. Further tension develops when a local child goes missing and Arthur's brother-in-law Roy, who was accused of killing Eve so long ago, is named as the suspect. Now the family must make some choices that could lead to serious consequences for their future relationships. First book.

Where it's reviewed:
Library Journal, Feb. 1, 2011, page 56

Other books you might like:
Laura Benedict, *Isabella Moon*, 2008
Gillian Flynn, *Sharp Objects*, 2006
Jennifer McMahon, *Promise Not to Tell*, 2006
Jane Smiley, *A Thousand Acres*, 1991
Donna Tartt, *The Little Friend*, 2002

522

SHELDON RUSSELL

The Insane Train

(New York: Minotaur Books, 2010)

Series: Hook Runyon Series. Book 2
Story type: Historical

Mystery

Subject(s): Mystery; Arson; Murder
Major character(s): Hook Runyon, Railroad Worker, Security Officer
Time period(s): 20th century; 1940s
Locale(s): United States

Summary: *The Insane Train* is the second installment in the Hook Runyon series. After a fatal fire at a California insane asylum, the surviving patients need to be transferred to a facility in Oklahoma. Hook Runyon, a railroad security agent, is put in charge of overseeing the transport. Hook hires four World War II vets to help keep the patients in line, especially since a number of them are highly dangerous criminals. The transport is anything but smooth as the train breaks down, a killer is on the loose, and a beautiful nurse vanishes. Hook, along with his ragtag team of associates, must uncover the dark secrets surrounding the asylum and find the killer before more victims die.

Where it's reviewed:
Booklist, October 1, 2010, page 33
Kirkus Reviews, August 1, 2010, page 705
New York Times Book Review, December 26, 2010, page 26
Publishers Weekly, September 6, 2010, page 26

Other books by the same author:
The Yard Dog, 2009
Dreams to Dust, 2006
Requiem at Dawn, 2000
The Savage Trail, 1998

Other books you might like:
Ace Atkins, *White Shadow*, 2006
Tom Franklin, *Hell at the Breech*, 2003
Dashiell Hammett, *Red Harvest*, 1929
Steve Hockensmith, *Holmes on the Range*, 2006
Peter Quinn, *Hour of the Cat*, 2005

523

MARK RUSSINOVICH

Zero Day

(New York: Thomas Dunne Books, 2011)

Story type: Techno-Thriller
Subject(s): Computers; Technology; Terrorism
Major character(s): Jeff Aiken, Computer Expert

Summary: *Zero Day* is a technological thriller by author Michael Russinovich. After a sinister computer virus nearly crashes a plane and causes medical errors in a hospital, killing several patients, computer-security expert Jeff Aiken is summoned to get to the root of the problem. What Jeff discovers, however, is that an even worse menace looms. The computer virus is just the beginning of a technological attack launched by terrorists backed by Osama bin Laden, and now it's up to Jeff to stop them before the entire cyberworld is brought to its knees. First novel.

Where it's reviewed:
Booklist, Feb. 15, 2011, page 57

Other books you might like:
Mark Alpert, *Final Theory: A Novel*, 2008

Richard A. Clarke, *The Scorpion's Gate*, 2005
Douglas Preston, *Blasphemy*, 2008
Michelle Slatalla, *Flame War: A Cyberthriller*, 1997
Daniel Suarez, *Daemon*, 2009

524

IAN SANSOM

The Bad Book Affair

(New York: Harper, 2010)

Series: Mobile Library Series. Book 4
Story type: Amateur Detective; Satire
Subject(s): Mystery; Libraries; Missing persons
Major character(s): Israel Armstrong, Librarian, Detective—Amateur; Lyndsay Morris, 14-Year-Old, Kidnap Victim, Daughter (of politician)
Time period(s): 21st century; 2010s
Locale(s): Ireland

Summary: *The Bad Book Affair*, a satirical mystery novel, is the fourth installment in the Mobile Library series from author Ian Sanson. Suffering from a recent breakup and on the brink of turning 30, mobile librarian turned amateur sleuth Israel Armstrong finds himself the prime suspect in the disappearance of a politician's daughter. The day after Israel loans out a copy of Philip Roth's *American Pastoral* to 14-year-old Lyndsay Morris, daughter of a Unionist candidate, the young girl vanishes without a trace. Israel is certain that her disappearance is somehow connected to her library selection and he's determined to find out how. Dodging interest from the police and a local news reporter, Israel sets out on his own investigation to find Lyndsay, clear his name, and get back that book before overdue charges are incurred.

525

GERALD SEYMOUR

The Collaborator

(London: Hodder & Stoughton, 2011)

Story type: Psychological Suspense
Subject(s): Crime; Murder; Organized crime
Major character(s): Eddie Deacon, Teacher; Immacolata Borelli, Organized Crime Figure
Locale(s): London, England; Naples, Italy

Summary: In *The Collaborator*, author Gerald Seymour tells the story of Eddie Deacon, a London-based language teacher who thinks his life is going nowhere. Eddie gets a break, though, when he meets Immacolata. Truth be told, Eddie's not sure what a girl like her sees in a bloke like him: she's gorgeous, has an Italian accent to die for, and boy can she cook. When Immacolata suddenly leaves him, Eddie follows her to her native Naples. There, he finds out her true identity as daughter of the Borellis, a ruthless organized-crime family. Immacolata has turned against the family and is being guarded at the Palace of Justice. Unfortunately, no one is guarding Eddie, and he's asked too many questions already. Seymour also is the author of *Dead Ground* and *The Dealer and the Dead*.

Where it's reviewed:
Publishers Weekly, Jan. 10, 2011, page 33

Other books by the same author:
Timebomb, 2008
Dead Ground, 1998
Killing Ground, 1997
The Journeyman Tailor, 1994
Harry's Game, 1975

Other books you might like:
Lynda LaPlante, *Bella Mafia*, 1991
Mario Puzo, *The Godfather*, 1969
Leonardo Sciascia, *To Each His Own*, 1989
Olen Steinhauer, *The Tourist*, 2009
Mark Winegardner, *The Godfather Returns*, 2004

526

ZOE SHARP

Fourth Day

(London: Allison and Busby, 2010)

Series: Charlie Fox Series. Book 8
Story type: Contemporary
Subject(s): Cults; Murder; Suspense
Major character(s): Charlotte "Charlie" Fox, Bodyguard;
Sean Meyer, Colleague (of Charlie); Thomas Witney,
Father (of Liam), Cult Member; Liam Witney, Son
(of Thomas), Cult Member; Randall Bane, Leader (of
cult)
Time period(s): 21st century; 2010s
Locale(s): California, United States

Summary: In Zoe Sharp's *Fourth Day*, bodyguard Charlie
Fox and her right-hand man Sean Meyer are hired to
rescue Thomas Witney from the clutches of a cult. Years
ago, Witney had entered the cult in hopes of finding
proof that the group's leader, Randall Bane, was behind
the death of Witney's son. Now Witney is a full-fledged
member of Bane's flock, and after Charlie and Sean
remove him, he's convinced Bane had nothing to do
with his son's murder. Charlie and Sean must work
together to find the truth behind who killed Liam Witney—but in order to do so, they must figure out the
mystery of Thomas Witney. This volume is the eighth
installment in the Charlie Fox series.

Where it's reviewed:
Booklist, December 15, 2010, page 22
Publishers Weekly, December 20, 2010, page 29

Other books by the same author:
Third Strike, 2009
Second Shot, 2007
First Drop, 2005

Other books you might like:
Lee Child, *Killing Floor*, 1997
Liza Cody, *Dupe*, 1980
Patricia Cornwell, *Postmortem*, 1990
Greg Rucka, *Keeper*, 1996
P.J. Tracy, *Monkeewrench*, 2003

527

JEFFREY SIGER

Prey on Patmos

(Scottsdale, Arizona: Poisoned Pen Press, 2011)

Series: Andreas Kaldis Mystery Series. Book 3
Story type: Religious
Subject(s): Mystery; Religion; Murder
Major character(s): Andreas Kaldis, Inspector, Detective
Time period(s): 21st century; 2010s
Locale(s): Patmos, Greece

Summary: *Prey on Patmos* is the third installment in the
Andreas Kaldis series. Patmos is a small Aegean island
that houses 20 monasteries, making it the center of the
Eastern Orthodox Church. When a monk is murdered in
the town square, Andreas Kaldis, chief inspector for
Greece's special crimes unit, is sent from Athens to
investigate. Being Easter week, the monasteries are
unavailable and unwilling to help in Kaldis's investigation and the local authorities are resistant to share any
information with him. Kaldis has to rely on town gossip
to get the answers he needs—answers that hint at a major
religious and political plot that could have international
ramifications.

Where it's reviewed:
Library Journal, December 2010, page 91
Publishers Weekly, November 1, 2010, page 30

Other books by the same author:
Assassins of Athens, 2010
Murder in Mykonos, 2009

Other books you might like:
Andrea Camilleri, *The Shape of Water*, 2002
Paul Johnston, *A Deeper Shade of Blue*, 2002
Barbara Nadel, *Belshazzar's Daughter*, 2004

528

CLEA SIMON

Dogs Don't Lie

(Scottsdale, Arizona: Poisoned Pen Press, 2011)

Series: Pru Marlowe Pet Noir Series. Book 1
Story type: Contemporary; Series
Subject(s): Mystery; Detective fiction; Murder
Major character(s): Pru Marlowe, Psychic
Time period(s): 21st century; 2010s
Locale(s): United States

Summary: In *Dogs Don't Lie* by Clea Simon, Pru Marlowe brings her unique talent for communicating with
animals to her hometown in the Berkshire Mountains.
With her cat, Wallis, as her most trusted friend, Pru sets
herself up in business as an animal behaviorist. When
one of her clients, Charles, is killed, his pit bull Lily
seems the probable suspect. (The dog is covered in blood
and Charles's body has suffered serious trauma.) Lily is
too upset to give any useful information to Pru, so she
must gather clues from other animals. *Dogs Don't Lie* is
the first book in the Pru Marlowe Pet Noir series.

Where it's reviewed:
Publishers Weekly, Feb. 14, 2011, page 40

Other books by the same author:
Grey Zone, 2010
Probable Claws, 2009
Shades of Grey, 2009
Cattery Row, 2006
Mew is for Murder, 2005

Other books you might like:
Susan Conant, *A New Leash on Death*, 1990
Linda O. Johnston, *Sit, Stay, Slay*, 2005
Lee Charles Kelley, *A Nose for Murder*, 2003
Virginia Lanier, *Death in Bloodhound Red*, 1995
Spencer Quinn, *Dog on It: A Chet and Bernie Mystery*, 2009

529

WILBUR SMITH

Those in Peril

(New York: Pan MacMillan, 2011)

Subject(s): Adventure; Kidnapping; Mother-daughter relations
Major character(s): Hazel Bannock, Heiress, Mother (of Cayla); Hector Cross, Security Officer; Cayla, Daughter (of Hazel), Kidnap Victim
Time period(s): 21st century; 2010s
Locale(s): Indian Ocean

Summary: Wilbur Smith's *Those in Peril* chronicles the adventurous tale of Hazel Bannock, heiress to an oil company fortune, whose daughter is kidnapped by pirates. The pirates demand an outrageous ransom that would bankrupt Bannock Oil, so Hazel turns to the man in charge of her company's security, Hector Cross. Hazel and Hector work together to bring her daughter back safely while ensuring the pirates receive just punishment for their actions.

Where it's reviewed:
Library Journal, Dec. 2010, page 84

Other books by the same author:
Elephant Song, 1991
Hungry as the Sea, 1978
Cry Wolf, 1976
Eagle in the Sky, 1974
Shout at the Devil, 1968

Other books you might like:
Ted Bell, *Hawke*, 2003
Lincoln Child, *The Ice Limit*, 2000
Clive Cussler, *Pacific Vortex!*, 1983
Robert Girardi, *The Pirate's Daughter*, 1997
Stuart Woods, *Run Before the Wind*, 1983

530

SALLY SPENCER

Echoes of the Dead

(Sutton, England: Severn House Publishers, 2011)

Series: Monika Paniatowski Mystery Series. Book 3
Story type: Historical; Mystery
Subject(s): Mystery; Detective fiction; Murder
Major character(s): Monika Pania, Detective (chief inspector); Charlie Woodend, Detective—Police (retired); Lilly Dawson, 13-Year-Old; Fred Howerd, Convict; Tom Hall, Detective (chief inspector); George Baxter, Police Officer (constable); Ralph Bannerman, Police Officer (former)
Time period(s): Multiple Time Periods; 20th century; (1950s); 20th century; 1970s (1973)
Locale(s): Whitebridge, Lancashire

Summary: In *Echoes of the Dead* by Sally Spencer, a convict's dying admission that he did not commit the crime for which he was imprisoned earns DCI Monika Paniatowski a challenging cold case. It was 1951 when a 13-year-old girl was sexually assaulted and killed. At the time, Scotland Yard's Chief Inspector Charlie Woodend and his team arrested the man they believed to be responsible. In 1973, Paniatowski revisits the case to find the real perpetrator and determine what role Woodend—Paniatowski's former supervisor—played in the erroneous conviction. *Echoes of the Dead* is the third book in the Monika Paniatowski Mystery series.

Where it's reviewed:
Booklist, Feb. 15, 2011, page 54
Publishers Weekly, Jan. 31, 2011, page 32

Other books by the same author:
The Ring of Death, 2010
The Dead Hand of History, 2009
The Salton Killings, 1998
Old Father Thames, 1995
Salt of the Earth, 1993

Other books you might like:
Deborah Crombie, *A Share in Death*, 1993
Clare Curzon, *I Give You Five Days*, 1983
Elly Griffiths, *The Crossing Places*, 2010
Ruth Rendell, *No More Dying Then*, 1971
Peter Turnbull, *Fear of Drowning*, 2000

531

JULIA SPENCER-FLEMING

One Was a Soldier

(New York: Minotaur Books, 2011)

Series: Clare Fergusson/Russ Van Alstyne Series. Book 7
Story type: Contemporary; Series
Subject(s): Mystery; Detective fiction; Wars
Major character(s): Clare Fergusson, Religious (priest), Veteran (Iraq war); Russ Van Alstyne, Police Officer (chief); Eric McCrea, Police Officer, Veteran (Iraq war); Will Ellis, Veteran (Iraq war), Amputee; Trip Stillman, Doctor, Veteran (Iraq war); Tally McNabb,

Accountant, Veteran (Iraq war)
Time period(s): 21st century; 2010s
Locale(s): Millers Kill, New York

Summary: In *One Was a Soldier* by Julia Spencer-Fleming, five Iraq War veterans lean on other members of the Millers Kill support group to cope with their complex feelings. Clare Fergusson served as a combat pilot, but has returned to her pastoral position and her relationship with local police chief Russ Van Alstyne. As the other group members—a police officer, a former athlete, a doctor, and a bookkeeper—deal with their pain in different ways, Clare struggles to settle back into her old life. The death of a local veteran tests Clare's investigative skills and her relationship with Russ. *One Was a Soldier* is the seventh book in the Clare Fergusson/Russ Van Alstyne series.

Where it's reviewed:
Booklist, Feb. 1, 2011, page 36

Other books by the same author:
I Shall Not Want, 2008
To Darkness and to Death, 2005
Out of the Deep I Cry, 2004
A Fountain Filled with Blood, 2003
In the Bleak Midwinter, 2002

Other books you might like:
Kate Charles, *A Drink of Deadly Wine*, 1991
Kate Charles, *Evil Intent*, 2005
Deborah Crombie, *A Share in Death*, 1993
Louise Penny, *Still Life*, 2006
Phil Rickman, *The Wine of Angels*, 1998

532

DANA STABENOW

Though Not Dead

(New York: St. Martin's Press, 2011)

Series: Kate Shugak Series. Book 18
Story type: Psychological Suspense
Subject(s): Detective fiction; Crime; Mystery
Major character(s): Kate Shugak, Detective—Private, Niece (of Uncle Sam); Sam Dementieff, Uncle (of Kate)
Locale(s): Alaska, United States

Summary: *Though Not Dead* is the 18th novel in Dana Stabenow's series featuring detective Kate Shugak. This time, Kate is sent into the Alaskan wilderness after her favorite Uncle Sam leaves her a cabin in his will, not to mention a curious mystery for her to solve. Now Kate is on the lookout for clues about Uncle Sam's life, and she finds some interesting information, including the fact that he once knew Dashiell Hammett. Unfortunately, Uncle Sam's history has caught a mysterious stranger's eye as well, and that stranger seems determined to get rid of Kate once and for all.

Where it's reviewed:
Booklist, Dec. 1, 2010, page 32
Library Journal, Dec. 2010, page 91
Publishers Weekly, Oct. 25, 2010, page 32

Other books by the same author:
A Night Too Dark, 2010
A Cold-Blooded Business, 1994
A Cold Day for Murder, 1992
Dead in the Water, 1992
A Fatal Thaw, 1992

Other books you might like:
Nevada Barr, *Winter Study*, 2008
Giles Blunt, *Forty Words for Sorrow*, 2001
Dashiell Hammett, *Red Harvest*, 1929
Sue Henry, *Murder on the Iditarod Trail*, 1991
J.A. Jance, *Desert Heat*, 1993

533

KELLI STANLEY

The Curse-Maker

(New York: Minotaur Books, 2011)

Series: Roman Noir Series. Book 2
Story type: Historical
Subject(s): Roman Empire, 30 BC-476 AD; Murder; Mystery
Major character(s): Arcturus, Doctor, Detective—Amateur
Time period(s): 1st century
Locale(s): England

Summary: *The Curse-Maker* is the second installment in the award-winning Roman Noir series from author Kelli Stanley. Set in Roman Britain, the book follows the adventures of Arcturus, a governor's doctor turned amateur sleuth. Arcturus and his wife travel to Bath for a relaxing getaway, only to uncover a spooky murder with lasting ramifications. The body of Rufus Bibax is found floating in the spring with an inscribed piece of lead in his mouth. Arcturus learns that Bibax was a curse-maker whose haunting hexes repeatedly came true. As a series of grisly murders follows, Arcturus is unsure if a copycat killer is on the loose or another curse is at work.

Where it's reviewed:
Booklist, Jan. 1, 2011, page 48
Publishers Weekly, Nov. 29, 2010, page 32

Other books by the same author:
City of Dragons, 2010
A Long Night for Sleeping, 2008

Other books you might like:
Lindsey Davis, *The Silver Pigs*, 1989
Robert Harris, *Imperium: A Novel of Ancient Rome*, 2006
John Maddox Roberts, *SPQR I: The King's Gambit*, 1990
Steven Saylor, *Roman Blood*, 1991
Simon Scarrow, *Under the Eagle*, 2001

534

WENDY CORSI STAUB

Scared to Death

(New York: Avon, 2010)

Story type: Contemporary
Subject(s): Crime; Women; Suspense

Major character(s): Elsa Cavalon, Mother; Marin Quinn, Mother; Lauren Walsh, Friend (of Marin)
Time period(s): 21st century; 2010s
Locale(s): United States

Summary: In Wendy Corsi Staub's *Scared to Death*, the second novel in a trilogy, the lives of two women become forever entwined by the presence of a madman. Elsa Cavalon and her husband are adopting a child, nearly a year after learning their kidnapped son was murdered long ago. Meanwhile, the former wife of the child's killer, Marin Quinn, struggles to raise her own children and put the past behind her. But the challenges of both these women are only exacerbated when they start receiving threats from a criminal genius who is intent on terrorizing them. But who is he? And why has he targeted these two women who share such a strange, troubling connection?

Where it's reviewed:
Publishers Weekly, November 22, 2010, page 43

Other books by the same author:
Live to Tell, 2010
Dead Before Dark, 2009
Dying Breath, 2008
Don't Scream, 2007
The Final Victim, 2006

Other books you might like:
V.C. Andrews, *Flowers in the Attic*, 1979
Mary Burton, *I'm Watching You*, 2007
Tami Hoag, *Deeper Than the Dead*, 2010
Lisa Jackson, *If She Only Knew*, 2000
Erica Spindler, *Blood Vines*, 2010

535

TAYLOR STEVENS

The Informationist

(New York: Shaye Areheart Books, 2011)

Story type: Contemporary
Subject(s): Mystery; Detective fiction; Missing persons
Major character(s): Vanessa Michael Munroe, Detective—Private; Kate Breeden, Consultant (marketing), Friend (of Vanessa); Miles Bradford, Security Officer; Richard Burbank, Businessman (oilman); Emily Burbank, Daughter (of Richard, adopted); Francisco Beyard, Boyfriend (of Vanessa, former)
Time period(s): 21st century; 2010s
Locale(s): Africa; Texas, United States

Summary: In *The Informationist* by Taylor Stevens, a missing-persons case draws Vanessa Michael Munroe back to the treacherous region of Africa she escaped as a teenager. While living with her missionary parents in Cameroon, Vanessa ran off with a shady gun-runner before giving up her risky lifestyle for a job in the States. Working as an informationist in Texas, Vanessa gathers intelligence for prominent clients. When a wealthy businessman, Richard Burbank, needs help locating his missing daughter in Africa, Vanessa agrees to return. Back in Africa, Vanessa meets up with her ex, Francisco Beyard, and confronts the dangers she left behind. First novel.

Where it's reviewed:
Library Journal, Feb. 1, 2011, page 57

Other books you might like:
Chelsea Cain, *Heartsick*, 2007
Joseph Finder, *Vanished*, 2009
Jamie Freveletti, *Running from the Devil*, 2009
Michael Gruber, *Valley of Bones*, 2005
Stieg Larsson, *The Girl with the Dragon Tattoo*, 2008

536

WALLACE STROBY

Cold Shot to the Heart

(New York: Minotaur Books, 2011)

Story type: Contemporary
Subject(s): Theft; Criminals; Murder
Major character(s): Crissa Stone, Thief; Eddie Santiago, Mercenary; Lou Letteri, Crime Victim
Time period(s): 21st century; 2010s
Locale(s): Fort Lauderdale, Florida

Summary: In *Cold Shot to the Heart*, author Wallace Stroby chronicles the dark adventures of two criminals-for-hire. Crissa Stone commits thefts in exchange for a cut of the booty, but her latest case hits a snag when the card game she was hired to rob turns violent. Now one man is dead, and that man had some very important friends in the world of organized crime. Eddie Santiago is hired by the dead man's family to seek revenge, but when he crosses paths with Crissa, he learns there is more—*much* more—to this case than meets the eye.

Where it's reviewed:
Booklist, November 15, 2010, page 24
Library Journal, December 2010, page 91
Publishers Weekly, November 1, 2010, page 28

Other books by the same author:
Gone Til November, 2010
The Heartbreak Lounge, 2005
The Barbed-Wire Kiss, 2003

Other books you might like:
Michael Connelly, *Void Moon*, 2000
David Corbett, *The Devil's Redhead*, 2002
Jim Fusilli, *Closing Time*, 2001
George V. Higgins, *The Digger's Game*, 1973
James Swain, *Grift Sense*, 2001

537

P.G. STURGES

Shortcut Man

(New York: Scribner, 2011)

Story type: Contemporary
Subject(s): Mystery; Humor; Crime
Major character(s): Dick Henry, Criminal; Artie Benjamin, Producer (porn), Client (of Dick)
Time period(s): 21st century; 2010s
Locale(s): Los Angeles, California

Summary: *Shortcut Man* is a humorous and suspenseful mystery from author P.G. Sturges. In Los Angeles, Dick Henry is the guy everyone goes to when they need things done. Known as the "Shortcut Man," Dick's not above cutting through red tape and disregarding the law in order to please his clients. Most of his work is relatively easy, like getting a negligent tenant to pay his rent or keeping an elderly woman from getting ripped off by contractors, until porn producer Artie Benjamin hires him for a job that hits a little too close to home. Soon, Dick finds himself wrestling with an impossible case as he struggles to keep his career, and himself, alive.

Where it's reviewed:
Booklist, Dec. 1, 2010, page 32
Library Journal, Dec. 2010, page 91
Publishers Weekly, Dec. 6, 2010, page 31

Other books you might like:
Raymond Chandler, *The Big Sleep*, 1939
Robert Crais, *The Monkey's Raincoat*, 1987
Marshall Karp, *The Rabbit Factory: A Novel*, 2006
Dick Lochte, *Sleeping Dog*, 1985
Thomas Perry, *Strip*, 2010

538

FRANK TALLIS

Vienna Twilight

(New York: Random House, 2011)

Series: Max Liebermann Series. Book 5
Story type: Historical; Psychological
Subject(s): Murder; Mystery; Psychology
Major character(s): Oskar Reinhardt, Detective, Friend (of Max); Max Liebermann, Psychologist
Time period(s): 20th century; 1900s (1903)
Locale(s): Vienna, Austria

Summary: *Vienna Twilight* is the fifth installment in the Max Liebermann series from author Frank Tallis. In Vienna, 1903, Detective Inspector Oskar Reinhardt calls on his friend, psychoanalyst Max Liebermann, for assistance with yet another murder investigation. A series of young women have been killed with a hatpin in the midst of having sex. As terror mounts in Vienna, Reinhardt and Liebermann race to track down the murderer before he can strike again. Meanwhile, as Liebermann treats a patient who claims he has a terrifying doppelganger loose in the city, the doctor wonders if there's a connection with the outrageous claims and the brutal murders.

Where it's reviewed:
Booklist, Feb. 1, 2011, page 38
Library Journal, Jan. 2011, page 66
Publishers Weekly, Jan. 17, 2011, page 33

Other books by the same author:
Vienna Secrets, 2009
Fatal Lies, 2008
Vienna Blood, 2006
A Death in Vienna, 2005
Killing Time, 1999

Other books you might like:
Boris Akunin, *The Winter Queen*, 2003

Barbara Cleverly, *The Last Kashmiri Rose*, 2001
Matthew Gallaway, *The Metropolis Case*, 2010
Jed Rubenfeld, *The Interpretation of Murder: A Novel*, 2006
Irvin D. Yalom, *When Nietzsche Wept*, 1992

539

BRAD TAYLOR

One Rough Man

(New York: Dutton, 2011)

Story type: Espionage
Subject(s): Espionage; Mystery; Terrorism
Major character(s): Pike Logan, Agent; Jennifer, Young Woman

Summary: *One Rough Man* is the debut novel of author Brad Taylor. In this thriller, Taylor tells the story of Pike Logan. Pike belongs to an elite force of special agents assigned to protect national security no matter what, even if it means breaking any laws necessary to complete their task. After being sidelined by his own personal disasters, Pike soon returned to the force with a vengeance. But when Pike goes up against a pair of terrorists who have their hands on a deadly weapon, he must team up not with trained agents like himself, but with a mysterious woman named Jennifer. First book.

Where it's reviewed:
Booklist, Dec. 15, 2010, page 24
Library Journal, Feb. 15, 2011, page 100
Publishers Weekly, Dec. 6, 2010, page 29

Other books you might like:
Lee Child, *Killing Floor*, 1997
Vince Flynn, *Transfer of Power*, 1999
Matt Hilton, *Dead Men's Dust*, 2009
Brad Thor, *The Lions of Lucerne*, February 27, 2007
John Weisman, *Rogue Warrior*, 1992

540

LARRY D. THOMPSON

The Trial

(New York: St. Martin's Press, 2011)

Story type: Legal
Subject(s): Mystery; Law; Trials
Major character(s): Luke Vaughn, Lawyer; Samantha Vaughn, Daughter (of Luke); Dr. Alfred Kingsbury, Businessman (pharmaceutical company)
Time period(s): 21st century; 2010s
Locale(s): San Marcos, Texas

Summary: In *The Trial* by Larry Thompson, an attorney who leaves Houston for small-town Texas life is drawn back into the courtroom to save his daughter. When Luke Vaughn's teenage daughter Samantha agrees to participate in a drug trial for a new antibiotic, they have no idea that the decision will put her life in danger. After taking the experimental medication, Samantha learns that she has suffered irreversible liver damage. Luke

Mystery

traces the blame to Alfred Kingsbury, the owner of the pharmaceutical company that manufactures the drug. As he prepares his case, Luke Vaughn uncovers a complex tale of public deception, ethics violations, and murder.

Where it's reviewed:
Booklist, Feb. 1, 2011, page 39
Publishers Weekly, Feb. 14, 2011, page 38

Other books by the same author:
So Help Me God, 2005

Other books you might like:
Reed Arvin, *The Will*, 2000
David Ellis, *Line of Vision*, 2001
William Lashner, *Hostile Witness*, 1995
Robert Traver, *Anatomy of a Murder*, 1958
Scott Turow, *Presumed Innocent*, 1987

541

RICHARD THOMPSON

Big Wheat

(Scottsdale, Arizona: Poisoned Pen Press, 2011)

Story type: Historical
Subject(s): Mystery; History; Serial murders
Major character(s): Windmill Man, Murderer (serial killer); Charlie Krueger, Young Man; Mabel Boysen, Girlfriend (of Charlie); Jim Avery, Worker (machinist)
Time period(s): 20th century; 1910s (1919)
Locale(s): North Dakota, United States

Summary: In *Big Wheat* by Richard Thompson, threshing season arrives in 1919 North Dakota, bringing promise, prosperity, and fear as a psychotic killer hunts the plains. On the night that Charlie Krueger is ditched by his longtime girlfriend, the young man finally leaves his abusive father to seek work with the wheat harvesters. When Charlie sees a dark figure digging in an exposed field, he doesn't realize that the man is burying his beloved Mabel Boysen, or that he will soon be a suspect in her murder. The killer, who calls himself the Windmill Man, sets his sights on Charlie, whom he believes is the only witness to his crime.

Where it's reviewed:
Booklist, Dec. 1, 2010, page 28
Publishers Weekly, Oct. 4, 2010, page 30

Other books by the same author:
Frag Box, 2009
Fiddle Game, 2008

Other books you might like:
Robert Goolrick, *A Reliable Wife: A Novel*, 2009
Hillary Jordan, *Mudbound*, 2008
Sheldon Russell, *The Yard Dog*, 2009
Jane Smiley, *The All-True Travels and Adventures of Lidie Newton*, 1998
John Steinbeck, *East of Eden*, 1952

542

CHARLES TODD (Pseudonym of Caroline Todd and Charles Todd)

A Lonely Death

(New York: William Morrow, 2011)

Series: Ian Rutledge Series. Book 13
Story type: Historical
Subject(s): Detective fiction; Murder; Suspense
Major character(s): Ian Rutledge, Detective—Police
Time period(s): 20th century; 1920s (1920)
Locale(s): Surrey, United Kingdom

Summary: The 13th book in the Inspector Ian Rutledge Mystery series, Charles Todd's *A Lonely Death* focuses on the PI's attempts to find the person responsible for three deaths in a small English village. It is 1920, and Rutledge is determined to unlock the mystery surrounding the killing of the three men, all of whom were veterans of World War I. Shortly after his arrival in the village, another man is killed, putting pressure on Rutledge to solve the crimes before he himself becomes the next victim.

Where it's reviewed:
Booklist, December 15, 2010, page 24
Entertainment Weekly, January 7, 2011, page 73
New York Times Book Review, January 9, 2011, page 22
Publishers Weekly, November 22, 2010, page 45
The Washington Times, January 14, 2011, page B07

Other books by the same author:
The Red Door, 2010
Legacy of the Dead, 2000
Search the Dark, 1999
Wings of Fire, 1998
A Test of Wills, 1996

Other books you might like:
Rennie Airth, *River of Darkness*, 1999
Jill Paton Walsh, *A Presumption of Death*, 2003
Jed Rubenfeld, *The Death Instinct*, 2011
Dorothy L. Sayers, *Whose Body?*, 1923
Jacqueline Winspear, *Maisie Dobbs*, 2003

543

SIMON TOLKIEN

The King of Diamonds

(New York: Minotaur Books, 2010)

Story type: Historical
Subject(s): Mystery; Murder; History
Major character(s): William Trave, Detective, Divorced Person; David Swain, Crime Suspect, Prisoner; Katya Osman, Crime Victim, Girlfriend (former, of David), Niece (of Titus); Titus Osman, Uncle (of Katya), Jeweler
Time period(s): 20th century; 1960s (1960)
Locale(s): Oxford, England

Summary: *The King of Diamonds* is a suspenseful historical mystery novel from author Simon Tolkien. Two years earlier, in 1958, Oxford Detective Inspector William Trave's testimony leads to the murder conviction and life sentence of David Swain, a man who allegedly murdered the new lover of his former flame, Katya Osman. Now, Swain has escaped from prison and Katya's been murdered. All signs point to Swain as the killer, but Trave grows increasingly suspicious of Katya's uncle, Titus Osman, a wealthy and overbearing diamond dealer. Since Trave's ex-wife has taken up with Titus, the detective's suspicions are written off by his colleagues as jealous accusation, but Trave is so convinced of Titus's guilt that he starts a rogue investigation of his own.

Where it's reviewed:
Library Journal, Feb. 1, 2011, page 58
Publishers Weekly, Jan. 3, 2011, page 33

Other books by the same author:
The Inheritance, 2010

Other books you might like:
Margery Allingham, *The Crime at Black Dudley*, 1929
Benjamin Black, *Christine Falls*, 2007
Peter Lovesey, *The Last Detective*, 1991
Ngaio Marsh, *A Man Lay Dead*, 1934
Ruth Rendell, *From Doon with Death*, 1964

544

HOLLY TUCKER

Blood Work: A Tale of Medicine and Murder in the Scientific Revolution

(New York: W.W. Norton, 2011)

Story type: Historical
Subject(s): Mystery; Murder; Science

Summary: Written by Holly Tucker, *Blood Work: A Tale of Medicine and Murder in the Scientific Revolution* is a historical examination of the mysterious events surrounding the first blood transfusion. In 1667, a Parisian physician named Jean Denis performed history's first blood transfusion, transferring lamb's blood into a madman. The scientific feat earned Denis rivals on every side as conservatives called the procedure blasphemous and fellow scientists were outraged that Denis had beaten them to it. Just days later, Denis's patient was murdered and the physician was framed for the crime, thus ending all blood-transfusion attempts for over a century. Tucker takes readers to 17th-century France and examines the mystery of Denis's work and conviction.

545

MARILYN VICTOR
MICHAEL ALLAN MALLORY, Co-Author

Killer Instinct

(Detroit, Michigan: Five Star, 2010)

Series: Snake Jones Mystery Series. Book 2
Story type: Amateur Detective

Subject(s): Animal rights; Wolves; Mystery
Major character(s): Lavender "Snake" Jones, Scientist (zoologist); Gina Brown, Scientist (wolf biologist)
Time period(s): 21st century; 2010s
Locale(s): Minnesota, United States

Summary: *Killer Instinct* is the second installment in the Snake Jones Mystery series featuring the zoologist and her herpetologist husband, Jeff. Across the United States, there's an ongoing debate about the gray wolf and whether or not the federal government should protect the species. In northern Minnesota, near the Minnesota Wolf Institute (MWI), someone decides to settle the debate their own way, killing four wolves and leaving their bodies near the MWI. Finding the animal carcasses sends Snake's old pal, wolf biologist Gina Brown, into a wild rage. When the bodies of humans start piling up, Snake grows concerned that Gina may have taken matters into her own hands.

Other books by the same author:
Death Roll, 2007

Other books you might like:
Nevada Barr, *Winter Study*, 2008
Vicki Delany, *In the Shadow of the Glacier*, 2007
William Kent Krueger, *Iron Lake*, 1998
Dana Stabenow, *A Cold Day for Murder*, 1992

546

NORB VONNEGUT

The Gods of Greenwich

(New York: Thomas Dunne Books, 2011)

Story type: Psychological Suspense
Subject(s): Finance; Business; Suspense
Major character(s): Jimmy Cusack, Financier
Time period(s): 21st century; 2000s (2007)
Locale(s): New York, New York

Summary: *The Gods of Greenwich* is a psychological thriller by author Norb Vonnegut. After watching his hedge fund fall apart courtesy of a shy backer who refuses to invest, financier Jimmy Cusack is certain he will soon face financial ruin. When he is offered a job with Leeser Capital, an investment firm with a less-than-stellar reputation, he decides he must accept in order to protect his family's assets. Soon Jimmy realizes he should have listened to his gut instinct as the firm's crooked dealings and shifty practices come to light. When Jimmy begins facing a danger even worse than bankruptcy, he may be in too deep to get out. Vonnegut is also the author of *Top Producer*.

Where it's reviewed:
Library Journal, March 1, 2011, page 71
Publishers Weekly, Feb. 7, 2011, page 35

Other books by the same author:
Top Producer, 2009

Other books you might like:
Nelson DeMille, *The Gold Coast*, 1990
Joseph Finder, *Paranoia*, 2004
Christopher Reich, *The First Billion*, 2002

Mystery

Peter Spiegelman, *Black Maps*, 2003
Tom Wolfe, *The Bonfire of the Vanities*, 1987

547

LEA WAIT

Shadows of a Down East Summer

(McKinleyville, California: John Daniel and Company, 2011)

Series: Antique Print Mystery Series. Book 5
Story type: Amateur Detective; Cozy Mystery
Subject(s): Antiques; Painting (Art); Diaries
Major character(s): Maggie Summer, Antiques Dealer, Detective—Amateur
Time period(s): 21st century; 2010s
Locale(s): Waymouth, Maine

Summary: *Shadows of a Down East Summer* is the fifth installment in the Antique Print Mysteries series from author Lea Wait. For antique-print dealer and sometimes sleuth, Maggie Summer, a weekend getaway to Waymouth, Maine, with boyfriend Will Brewer sounds like the perfect way to spend a few days, but when a century-old diary ends up in Maggie's hands, she soon finds herself caught in the middle of a murder investigation. The diary, written in 1890 by 18-year-old Anna May Pratt who posed, along with her sister, for one of Homer's paintings, belonged to recently murdered Carolyn Chase. The journal, filled with shocking family secrets and allegations, might be the key to the killing, and if Maggie wants to stop the murderer from striking again, she needs to decipher fact from fiction before it's too late.

Where it's reviewed:
Publishers Weekly, Feb. 21, 2011, page 117

Other books by the same author:
Finest Kind, 2006
Shadows at the Spring Show, 2005
Shadows on the Ivy, 2004
Shadows on the Coast of Maine, 2003
Shadows at the Fair, 2002

Other books you might like:
Sarah Atwell, *Through a Glass, Deadly*, 2008
Laura Childs, *Keepsake Crimes*, 2003
Jane K. Cleland, *Consigned to Death*, 2006
Carolyn G. Hart, *Death on Demand*, 1987
Katherine Hall Page, *The Body in the Belfry*, 1990

548

DAVID J. WALKER

Too Many Clients

(London: Severn House Publishers, 2010)

Series: Kirsten and Dugan Series. Book 4
Story type: Contemporary
Subject(s): Detective fiction; Murder; Suspense
Major character(s): Kirsten, Detective—Private; Dugan, Lawyer, Spouse (of Kirsten); Johnny O'Hern, Crime Victim

Time period(s): 21st century; 2010s
Locale(s): Chicago, Illinois

Summary: Corrupt cop Johnny O'Hern has been murdered. O'Hern's brother hires private detective Kirsten and her attorney husband Dugan to find the killer, but the case is an unsettlingly personal one: Dugan had once hired the dead man for some unethical work with his law practice. Now Kirsten is intent on finding the killer to clear suspicion from her husband and find peace for the victim's family. *Too Many Clients* is the fourth novel in David J. Walker's Wild Onion Ltd. Mysteries series.

Where it's reviewed:
Booklist, October 1, 2010, page 35
Publishers Weekly, September 20, 2010, page 51

Other books by the same author:
All the Dead Fathers, 2005
A Beer at a Bawdy House, 2000
The End of Emerald Woods, 2000
A Ticket to Die For, 1998
Fixed in His Folly, 1995

Other books you might like:
Robert Campbell, *The Junkyard Dog*, 1986
Sean Chercover, *Big City, Bad Blood*, 2007
Michael Harvey, *The Chicago Way*, 2007
Theresa Schwegel, *Officer Down*, 2005
Sheldon Siegel, *Special Circumstances: A Novel*, 2000

549

PERSIA WALKER

Black Orchid Blues

(Brooklyn, New York: Akashic Books, 2011)

Series: Harlem Renaissance Series. Book 3
Story type: Historical; Series
Subject(s): Mystery; Detective fiction; Crime
Major character(s): Queenie Lovetree, Homosexual (drag queen); Lanie Price, Journalist; Sam Delaney, Co-Editor; John Blackie, Detective—Police; Stax Murphy, Criminal (loan shark); Jack-a-Lee Talbot, Homosexual (transvestite)
Time period(s): 20th century; 1920s
Locale(s): New York, New York

Summary: In *Black Orchid Blues* by Persia Walker, a lofty drag queen named Queenie Lovetree is the reigning star at the Cinnamon Club in 1920s Harlem. Seeking some press for her onstage persona, the "Black Orchid," Queenie meets with local columnist Lanie Price. But before Queenie and Lanie can discuss business, Queenie is removed from the club by a man with a cowboy hat and a gun. Afterward, Lanie can't locate Queenie and starts her own investigation into her disappearance. Neither Lanie's editor nor the police chief are pleased with her interference in the case. *Black Orchid Blues* is the third book in the Harlem Renaissance series.

Where it's reviewed:
Publishers Weekly, Feb. 21, 2011, page 116

Other books by the same author:
Darkness and the Devil Behind Me, 2007
Harlem Redux, 2002

Other books you might like:
David Fulmer, *Chasing the Devil's Tail*, 2001
Chester Himes, *For Love of Imabelle*, 1957
Walter Mosley, *Devil in a Blue Dress*, 1990
Barbara Neely, *Blanche on the Lam*, 1992
Jean Toomer, *Cane*, 1923

550

MICHAEL WALLNER

The Russian Affair

(New York: Nan A. Talese, 2011)

Story type: Espionage
Subject(s): Russian history; Espionage; Cold War, 1945-1991
Major character(s): Anna Tsazukhina, Lover (of Alexey), Spouse (of Leonid), Mother (of Petya), Spy; Alexey Bulyagkov, Government Official, Lover (of Anna); Petya, Son (of Anna); Leonid, Spouse (of Anna)
Time period(s): 20th century; 1970s
Locale(s): Moscow, Russia

Summary: Author Michael Wallner uses the background of 1970s Soviet Russia in his novel, *The Russian Affair*. Anna Tsazukhina is a Moscow-based painter who lives with her father, her son, and her military husband. With her spouse, Leonid, often away with the army, Anna must work hard to feed and clothe her family, a task made even harder due to son Petya's infirm condition. Then Anna meets Alexey, a government official who can promise her a better life for her and her family. Unfortunately for Anna nothing in life comes for free; when her affair with Alexey is discovered, she must spy on him for the KGB or risk complete ruin. Wallner is also the author of *April in Paris*.

Where it's reviewed:
Library Journal, March 1, 2011, page 71
Publishers Weekly, Feb. 14, 2011, page 37

Other books by the same author:
April in Paris, 2007

Other books you might like:
John Le Carre, *The Russia House*, 1987
Robert Littell, *Mother Russia*, 1978
Charles McCarry, *The Secret Lovers*, 1977
Edmund P. Murray, *The Peregrine Spy*, 2004
Martin Cruz Smith, *Gorky Park*, 1981

551

JILL PATON WALSH

The Attenbury Emeralds

(New York: Minotaur Books, 2011)

Story type: Historical
Subject(s): Detective fiction; Suspense; Murder
Major character(s): Lord Peter Wimsey, Detective—Private, Spouse (of Harriet); Harriet Vane, Detective—Private, Writer, Spouse (of Peter); Bunter, Servant; Lord Attenbury, Nobleman

Time period(s): 20th century
Locale(s): United Kingdom

Summary: Jill Paton Walsh's finds Lord Peter and his mystery-writer wife reflecting on Wimsey's inaugural case some 30 years prior. Peter, recovering from a breakdown, investigates a wealthy family's missing jewels. Now, one of the surviving family members wants to pawn the emeralds—and Lord Peter and Harriet unearth a whole new mystery surrounding the precious gems.

Where it's reviewed:
Booklist, December 1, 2010, page 29
The Financial Times, September 25, 2010, page 19
The Guardian, October 23, 2010, page 10
Publishers Weekly, November 8, 2010, page 44
The Times of London, October 16, 2010, page 12

Other books by the same author:
Debts of Dishonor, 2006
A Presumption of Death, 2003
Thrones, Dominations, 1998
A Piece of Justice, 1995
The Wyndham Case, 1993

Other books you might like:
Margery Allingham, *The Tiger in the Smoke*, 1952
John Dickson Carr, *Hag's Nook*, 1933
Georgette Heyer, *Duplicate Death*, 1951
Ngaio Marsh, *Vintage Murder*, 1937
Dorothy L. Sayers, *Gaudy Night*, 1935

552

WENDY LYN WATSON

Scoop to Kill

(New York: Signet, 2010)

Series: Mystery a La Mode Series. Book 2
Story type: Contemporary
Subject(s): Detective fiction; Food; Murder
Major character(s): Tallulah "Tally" Jones, Businesswoman, Detective—Amateur; Alice, Niece (of Tally)
Time period(s): 21st century; 2010s
Locale(s): Dallas, Texas

Summary: Wendy Lyn Watson's *Scoop to Kill* is the second book in the Mystery a La Mode series, centering on the sleuthing escapades of Dallas ice cream shop owner Tallulah "Tally" Jones. Tally has been hired to serve ice cream at a local university event, but when a body turns up at the gala, she takes off her apron and picks up the magnifying glass. Tally's investigation leads her deep into the heart of academia, where nothing is as it seems, and she soon finds her loyalties divided and her investigation growing ever more perilous.

Other books by the same author:
I Scream, You Scream, 2009

Other books you might like:
Jessica Beck, *Glazed Murder: A Donut Shop Mystery*, 2010
Diane Mott Davidson, *Catering to Nobody*, 1990
Joanne Fluke, *Chocolate Chip Cookie Murder*, 2000

Mystery

Jenn McKinlay, *Sprinkle with Murder*, 2010
L.J. Washburn, *A Peach of a Murder*, 2006

553

ROBERT PAUL WESTON

Dust City

(New York: Razorbill, 2010)

Story type: Fantasy; Young Adult
Subject(s): Fantasy; Wolves; Fables
Major character(s): Henry Whelp, Teenager, Wolf; Jack, Roommate (of Henry), Thief; Fiona, Wolf
Time period(s): 21st century; 2010s
Locale(s): Dust City, Fictional Location

Summary: *Dust City* is an imaginative fantasy novel for young adult readers from author Robert Paul Weston. Life has been rough for teenage wolf Henry Whelp since his father was convicted and imprisoned for the murder of Little Red Riding Hood. Henry has managed to stay out of sight and out of trouble at the Home for Wayward Wolves, until a mysterious murder takes place. Henry begins to question his father's guilt, pondering the possibility that someone may have framed him for Red's murder. Recruiting help from his roommate Jack and the beautiful Fiona, Henry sets out on a dangerous investigation to Dust City, a dark place ruled by the ominous Water Nixies, to find the truth about his father's alleged crime.

554

RANDY WAYNE WHITE

Night Vision

(New York: G. P. Putnam's Sons, 2011)

Series: Doc Ford Series. Book 18
Story type: Child-in-Peril
Subject(s): Mystery; Murder; Illegal immigrants
Major character(s): Tula Choimha, 13-Year-Old, Religious, Immigrant; Harris, Manager (park), Pornographer, Drug Dealer, Murderer; Doc Ford, Scientist (marine biologist), Agent (CIA)
Time period(s): 21st century; 2010s
Locale(s): Florida, United States

Summary: *Night Vision*, a suspenseful thriller, is the 18th installment in the best-selling Doc Ford series from author Randy Wayne White. A seedy Florida trailer park, sarcastically referred to as Little Guadalajara, is home to a sea of illegal immigrants. The piece of land housing the trailer park is being coveted by unscrupulous property developers who will stop at nothing to get their hands on it. To put their plan in motion, the developers pay off the park's shady manager, Harris, to work as their hired gun. To prove his value, Harris soon murders a resident, but not without being seen by Tula Choimha, a 13-year-old Guatemalan girl with a supernatural gift. Determined to silence Tula for good, Harris sets out to find her before she has a chance to get marine biologist/undercover CIA agent, Doc Brown, involved.

Where it's reviewed:
Library Journal, March 1, 2011, page 70
Publishers Weekly, December 20, 2010, page 29
St. Petersburg Times, February 20, 2011, page 9E

Other books by the same author:
Deep Shadow, 2009
Twelve Mile Limit, 2002
Ten Thousand Islands, 2000
Captiva, 1996
Sanibel Flats, 1990

Other books you might like:
Tom Corcoran, *The Mango Opera*, 1998
James W. Hall, *Under Cover of Daylight*, 1987
Christine Kling, *Surface Tension*, 2002
Bob Morris, *Bahamarama*, 2004
James Swain, *Midnight Rambler: A Novel of Suspense*, 2007

555

TINA WHITTLE

The Dangerous Edge of Things

(Scottsdale, Arizona: Poisoned Pen Press, 2011)

Story type: Amateur Detective
Subject(s): Mystery; Murder; Brothers and sisters
Major character(s): Tai Randolph, Store Owner (gun shop), Detective—Amateur, Crime Suspect; Trey Seaver, Accident Victim, Security Officer
Time period(s): 21st century; 2010s
Locale(s): Atlanta, Georgia

Summary: Not only does Tai Randolph have to deal with the stresses of relocating (from Savannah to Atlanta) and running a new business (a Confederate-themed gun shop she inherited), she's suddenly become a person of interest in a homicide investigation. When Tai finds a corpse in her brother's driveway and her brother is long gone on a trip to the Bahamas, Tai finds herself at the center of the Atlanta PD's investigation. Determined to clear her name, Tai does a little sleuthing of her own, made more difficult by the police attention and the addition of Trey Seaver, a dangerous security agent with emotional baggage, hired to guard Tai no matter what.

Where it's reviewed:
Booklist, December 15, 2010, page 22
Publishers Weekly, December 13, 2010, page 36

Other books you might like:
Lisa Gardner, *The Neighbor*, 2009
Tami Hoag, *Night Sins*, 1995
Cody McFadyen, *Shadow Man*, 2006
Theresa Schwegel, *Officer Down*, 2005
Karin Slaughter, *Triptych*, 2006

556

MICHAEL WILEY

The Bad Kitty Lounge

(New York: Minotaur Books, 2010)

Story type: Private Detective
Subject(s): Mystery; Murder; Detective fiction
Major character(s): Joe Kozmarski, Detective—Private; Greg Samuelson, Client (of Joe), Crime Suspect; Eric Stone, Crime Victim
Time period(s): 21st century; 2010s
Locale(s): Chicago, Illinois

Summary: Chicago private investigator Joe Kozmarski has been hired by Greg Samuelson for what seems like a routine adultery investigation. Greg knows his wife is cheating on him with Eric Stone and wants Joe to get proof. Before Joe has the chance to get his investigation off the ground, Eric's Mercedes is torched, Greg's boss is murdered, and Greg is found suffering from what the police are calling a self-inflicted gunshot wound. All of the evidence points to Greg, a jilted husband trying to get revenge, but Joe isn't so sure. Greg's murdered boss is a nun with a sketchy past, Eric is convinced Greg didn't torch his car, and a civil-rights activist wants to bribe Joe to leave the case alone.

Where it's reviewed:
Booklist, February 1, 2010, page 31
The Florida Times Union, April 11, 2010, page E-6
Library Journal, February 1, 2010, page 51
Publishers Weekly, December 7, 2009, page 37

Other books by the same author:
Romantic Migrations, 2008
The Last Striptease, 2007

Other books you might like:
Robert Campbell, *The Junkyard Dog*, 1986
Sean Chercover, *Big City, Bad Blood*, 2007
Michael Harvey, *The Chicago Way*, 2007
Libby Fischer Hellmann, *Set the Night on Fire*, 2010
Sara Paretsky, *Hardball*, 2009

557

KATE WILHELM

Heaven is High

(New York: St. Martin's Press, 2011)

Series: Barbara Holloway Series. Book 12
Story type: Legal
Subject(s): Emigration and immigration; Law; Illegal immigrants
Major character(s): Barbara Holloway, Lawyer; Martin Owens, Football Player, Spouse (of Binnie); Binnie, Spouse (of Martin), Immigrant

Summary: *Heaven is High* is the 12th novel in author Kate Wilhelm's Barbara Holloway mystery series. In this book, Barbara must help an old friend, retired football player Martin Owens, when his wife faces expulsion from the U.S. Martin's wife Binnie is the daughter of a slave who was taken from her homeland of Belize to Haiti. Now Binnie is a woman without a country, and it's up to Barbara to help find her true heritage. But when Barbara travels to Beliza to find out the truth about Binnie's mother, she wanders into an international plot that could put them all in peril.

Where it's reviewed:
Booklist, Dec. 1, 2010, page 30
Publishers Weekly, Dec. 20, 2010, page 31

Other books by the same author:
Cold Case, 2008
Defense for the Devil, 1999
For the Defense, 1996
The Best Defense, 1994
Death Qualified, 1991

Other books you might like:
Rose Connors, *Absolute Certainty*, 2002
Linda Fairstein, *Final Jeopardy*, 1996
Perri O'Shaughnessy, *Motion to Suppress*, 1995
Richard North Patterson, *The Lasko Tangent*, 1979
Lisa Scottoline, *Final Appeal*, 1994

558

LAURA WILSON

An Empty Death

(New York: Minotaur Books, 2011)

Series: Ted Stratton Series. Book 2
Story type: Historical - World War II
Subject(s): Mystery; World War II, 1939-1945; Deception
Major character(s): Ted Stratton, Detective, Inspector; Duncan Reynolds, Doctor, Crime Victim
Time period(s): 20th century; 1940s (1944)
Locale(s): London, England

Summary: *An Empty Death* is the second installment in the award-winning Ted Stratton series from author Laura Wilson. As World War II wages on, Scotland Yard Detective Inspector Ted Stratton continues to throw himself into his work, desperate for a respite from his war-torn country. His latest case has him baffled as he tries to make sense of the death of Duncan Reynolds, a physician at Middlesex Hospital. Reynolds's body was found near the site of a bombing, but his injuries suggest that he might've been dead before the bomb struck. As Stratton investigates the possible murder, he uncovers a great deal of secrets among the hospital's staff including adulterous affairs, hidden identities, and dangerous obsession.

Where it's reviewed:
Booklist, Feb. 1, 2011, page 36
Library Journal, Jan. 2011, page 66
Publishers Weekly, Jan. 3, 2011, page 33

Other books by the same author:
The Man Who Wasn't There, 2008
Stratton's War, 2007
My Best Friend, 2001
Dying Voices, 2000
A Little Death, 1999

Mystery

Other books you might like:
James R. Benn, *Billy Boyle*, 2006
Jeffery Deaver, *Garden of Beasts*, 2004
David Downing, *Zoo Station*, 2007
Alan Furst, *Red Gold*, 1999
Robert Wilson, *A Small Death in Lisbon*, 2000

559

JACQUELINE WINSPEAR

A Lesson in Secrets

(New York: HarperCollins, 2011)

Series: Maisie Dobbs Series. Book 8
Story type: Historical
Subject(s): Murder; Mystery; England
Major character(s): Maisie Dobbs, Psychologist, Investigator, Nurse (former), Spy
Time period(s): 20th century; 1930s (1932)
Locale(s): Cambridge, England

Summary: *A Lesson in Secrets* is the eighth book in the best-selling Maisie Dobbs historical mystery series by author Jacqueline Winspear. In the summer of 1932, psychologist and investigator, Maisie Dobbs is given a top-secret assignment by the British Secret Service. She goes undercover as a junior philosophy lecturer at a private Cambridge university to observe activities that might seem contrary to the government's best interest. When Greville Liddicote, the college's notorious founder, is murdered, Maisie is ordered to stay out of the investigation. It doesn't take long for Maisie to connect Greville's murder with other peculiar behavior going on with the faculty and students and to note a shocking connection with the Nazi Party's growing power in England.

Where it's reviewed:
Booklist, February 1, 2011, page 36
Library Journal, February 15, 2011, page 106

Other books by the same author:
The Mapping of Love and Death, 2010
Message of Truth, 2006
Pardonable Lies, 2005
Birds of a Feather, 2004
Maisie Dobbs, 2003

Other books you might like:
Rennie Airth, *River of Darkness*, 1999
Rhys Bowen, *Her Royal Spyness*, 2007
Agatha Christie, *The Secret Adversary*, 1922
Caroline Petit, *The Fat Man's Daughter*, 2005
Charles Todd, *A Duty to the Dead*, 2009

560

LOIS WINSTON

Assault with a Deadly Glue Gun

(Woodbury, Minnesota: Midnight Ink, 2011)

Series: Anastasia Pollack Crafting Mystery Series. Book 1

Story type: Cozy Mystery
Subject(s): Mystery; Murder; Art
Major character(s): Anastasia Pollack, Widow(er), Single Mother, Co-Editor (crafts), Crime Suspect, Detective—Amateur
Time period(s): 21st century; 2010s
Locale(s): United States

Summary: *Assault with a Deadly Glue Gun* is the first installment in the Anastasia Pollack Crafting Mystery series. Magazine crafts editor Anastasia Pollack's world is turned upside down when her husband dies in Vegas, leaving her to take care of their two teenage sons and the mounds of debt from his secret gambling addiction. At work, things only get worse when a dead body is discovered in Anastasia's office chair. The corpse in question belongs to fashion editor Marlys Vandenburg, a vindictive woman with a long list of enemies. But when the police investigation reveals that Marlys was having a passionate affair with Anastasia's late husband, Anastasia finds herself as the prime suspect in the case.

Other books by the same author:
Love, Lies and a Double Shot of Deception, 2007
Talk Gertie to Me, 2006

Other books you might like:
Elizabeth Lynn Casey, *Sew Deadly*, 2009
Sarah Graves, *The Dead Cat Bounce*, 1998
Amanda Lee, *The Quick and the Thread*, 2010
Cricket McRae, *Lye in Wait*, 2007
Clare O'Donohue, *The Lover's Knot*, 2008

561

STUART WOODS

Santa Fe Edge

(New York: G.P. Putnam's Sons, 2010)

Series: Ed Eagle Series. Book 4
Story type: Contemporary
Subject(s): Detective fiction; Organized crime; Divorce
Major character(s): Ed Eagle, Lawyer, Detective—Private; Barbara, Spouse (ex-wife of Ed); Susannah, Spouse (of Ed); Tip Hanks, Crime Suspect, Golfer; Todd Bacon, Agent (CIA); Teddy Fay, Fugitive (ex-CIA agent)
Time period(s): 21st century; 2010s
Locale(s): Santa Fe, New Mexico

Summary: Powerhouse lawyer and imposing PI Ed Eagle is a wanted man. His ex-wife, Barbara, has escaped from jail and wants Ed and his new wife, Susannah, dead. Meanwhile, golfer Tip Hanks has been accused of murder and wants Ed to serve as his legal counsel. If these challenges aren't enough to keep Ed on his toes, CIA newcomer Todd Bacon may need Ed's help when he arrives in Santa Fe on the hunt for a rogue CIA agent. *Santa Fe Edge* is the fourth book in Stuart Woods's Ed Eagle series.

Where it's reviewed:
Booklist, July 1, 2010, page 8
Publishers Weekly, July 12, 2010, page 26

Other books by the same author:
Santa Fe Dead, 2008

Short Straw, 2006
Orchid Beach, 1998
Santa Fe Rules, 1992
New York Dead, 1991

Other books you might like:
David Baldacci, *The Camel Club*, 2005
Lincoln Child, *Gideon's Sword*, 2011
John Grisham, *The Firm*, 1991
Robert B. Parker, *The Godwulf Manuscript*, 1973
James Patterson, *Along Came a Spider: A Novel*, 1993

562

RICHARD YANCEY

The Highly Effective Detective Crosses the Line

(New York: St. Martin's Press, 2011)

Series: Highly Effective Detective Series. Book 4
Story type: Private Detective
Subject(s): Detective fiction; Mystery; Law
Major character(s): Teddy Ruzak, Detective—Private; Farrell, Police Officer

Summary: *The Highly Effective Detective Crosses the Line* is the fourth installment in author Richard Yancey's Highly Effective Detective series. In this book, Highly Effective Detective Teddy Ruzak isn't so effective after all, after a mishap leaves him without a practicing detective license. However, that won't stop him from investigating a man at the request of his old friend Farrell. Farrell suspects that his daughter is being stalked by an old boyfriend, and he wants Teddy on the case. Yet the closer Teddy gets to the truth about the guy, the more he is in danger of crossing some very blurred lines. Yancey is also the author of *The Highly Effective Detective Plays the Fool* and *The Highly Effective Detective Goes to the Dogs*.

Where it's reviewed:
Booklist, Dec. 1, 2010, page 30
Publishers Weekly, Nov. 22, 2010, page 44

Other books by the same author:
The Highly Effective Detective Plays the Fool, 2010
The Curse of the Wendigo, 2009
The Monstrumologist, 2009
The Highly Effective Detective Goes to the Dogs, 2008

The Highly Effective Detective, 2006

Other books you might like:
Lawrence Block, *Burglars Can't Be Choosers*, 1977
Alan Bradley, *The Sweetness at the Bottom of the Pie*, 2009
Matthew Dicks, *Unexpectedly, Milo*, 2010
Lee Goldberg, *Mr. Monk Goes to the Firehouse*, 2006
Joan Hess, *Malice in Maggody: An Ozarks Murder Mystery*, 1987

563

THOMAS W. YOUNG

The Mullah's Storm

(New York: G.P. Putnam's Sons, 2010)

Subject(s): Afghanistan Conflict, 2001-; Prisoners of war; Survival
Major character(s): Michael Parson, Military Personnel (pilot); Master Sergeant Gold, Military Personnel (interpreter)
Time period(s): 21st century; 2000s
Locale(s): Afghanistan

Summary: In Thomas W. Young's *The Mullah's Storm*, a plane holding co-pilot Major Michael Parson, Pashto interpreter Master Sergeant Gold, and a radical Islamic mullah is shot down over Afghanistan. The trio must battle the elements of a fierce blizzard pummeling the region, as they attempt to make their way to safety. Unfortunately, the weather isn't the only thing they're fighting. The Taliban is lurking around every corner, the locals are distrustful, and the mullah himself is praying for the chance to flee. First novel.

Where it's reviewed:
Booklist, September 1, 2010, page 51
Publishers Weekly, July 26, 2010, page 43
USA Today, October 21, 2010, page 05D

Other books by the same author:
The Speed of Heat, 2008

Other books you might like:
Alex Berenson, *The Faithful Spy*, 2006
Andrew Britton, *The Invisible*, 2008
Dan Fesperman, *The Warlord's Son*, 2004
Frederick Forsyth, *The Afghan*, 2006
Brad Thor, *The Apostle*, 2009

Mystery

Is Literature Necessary?
by
Natalie Danford

My beloved New York City apartment is on the market. We've lived here for twenty years and renovated several times along the way. (The space is, in broker parlance, "in mint condition," in case you're shopping for an apartment.) Each time that we hired a contractor to sand the floors or paint the walls, we also added bookshelves. We added a wall of bookshelves in the living room, then a double row of shelves up near the ceiling on the opposite wall. We built in another row in the bedroom. I joke that our apartment is decorated in the "early bookshelf" style.

And for good reason—I own a lot of books. Our apartment is also located on the same block as New York's famous Strand bookstore, and sometimes it feels as if I don't leave the house without stopping in and purchasing a book. I sell books to the Strand, too, but somehow the outflow never seems as unending and quick as the inflow. These days, though, as I try to straighten up to show the apartment to prospective buyers and also prepare to move by going through my belongings and tossing some things I didn't even know I had anymore, I'm thinning the supply on my bookshelves. This doesn't mean the shelves are empty, just that the books are now one row deep rather than two, with the extras and oversize volumes piled haphazardly on top.

Meanwhile, our broker constantly reassures potential buyers that they can easily tear out the shelves. It makes me realize how far out of the norm I am with these books everywhere (and perhaps with my belief that books make a home—whenever I visit someone else's home for the first time I make a beeline for the bookshelves. How else to judge a new friend's character?) I think the same thing as I very reluctantly part with books I haven't looked at in twenty years or more, books I didn't even know I still owned: What good are all these books? I mean, I know what good they are for me personally—I read them and enjoy them. A day without at least an hour or so of reading in it is no day at all for me. But does literary fiction (the majority of the books I own) have a purpose? What good is reading fiction? A friend once told me that if I did any other activity—shopping, eating, drinking alcohol—with the consistency and fervor

that I employ for reading novels, she'd hold an intervention for me. I laughed (because it's true), but there was a time in history when the reading of fiction was considered as dangerous as those other pursuits, especially for impressionable young people, and especially for women. In the 1700s and early 1800s, there was a widely held belief that getting involved with made-up stories resulted in weakened moral fiber. Reading fiction was a vice that would lead to unrealistic expectations out of life and inevitable disappointment and then downfall.

In contemporary society, reading is generally seen as "positive." Non-reading friends (yes, I have a few) say to me all the time, "I wish I read as much as you do." (The fact that I cook frequently elicits the same response—preparing your own food with care is another one of those acts that in the modern day has become both rare and regarded as wholesome.) Yet they never articulate why it is they wish they read more, or at all. Surely reading literature serves some purpose. As far as I know, every university in the world teaches literature courses. Reading fiction and learning to analyze it is considered a standard part of an education.

For one thing, having some familiarity with literature is part of cultural literacy. It would be impossible to appreciate most movies and television programs without at least a very basic understanding of narrative and the forms that it can take. It might even be impossible to engage in an adult conversation, because adult conversation (at work, at parties, and elsewhere) is littered with often unconscious references to books. And while reading a history book may be similar to reading a novel in that you are reading a series of events, as I often tell students when I'm teaching a creative writing class, a life is not a story. If it were, being a biographer would be the easiest job in the world—you'd simply write down the events of someone's life and be done with it. But what biographers and novelists do is shape human experience into narrative form, with a beginning, middle, and end, and with some kind of message. If you were unfamiliar with fiction, you probably would be at least a really boring conversationalist who tells pointless stories.

A work of literary fiction does serve the same purpose as a history text in one way: It always reflects the historical period in which it was written (even if it isn't necessarily set in that same period.) If history repeats itself, then it's the responsibility of all of us to inform ourselves about our past, and that means more than merely memorizing the dates of key events. We need to know how people thought, how they dressed, what their attitudes toward each other was like. In reading literary fiction, we also get a sense of how they spoke and how language mutates over time, which is another clue that leads us to human and historical insight.

While overtly "political" novels often fail as entertainment, literature is undeniably political. Anyone who doesn't have a message to send doesn't write a novel, plain and simple. An awkwardly written political novel may come across as a dull, didactic screed, but it is still attempting to make a point. Think of classics such as Harriet Beecher Stowe's *Uncle Tom's Cabin* and its effect on the slavery debate, or Theodore Dreiser's *Sister Carrie*, about a young woman who moves to the city and misplaces her moral compass. Not only does the latter novel tell us what was happening in 1900 when the book was first published; it illustrates the author's moral stance as clearly as if he simply wrote three sentences about his viewpoint on a piece of paper and read them aloud, but with a lot more impact, because we can't help but feel something—even disdain or distance—about the title character and what she does.

Finally, reading literature makes us more understanding people who are better able to relate to others, something to consider in an age when many are more likely to go online and read Facebook status updates than they are to pick up a hefty novel. While it might seem contradictory that a solitary activity such as reading would improve our ability to relate to others, in October 2006 Raymond A. Mar, Keith Oatley, Jacob Hirsch, Jennifer dela Paz, and Jordan Peterson published an article in the *Journal of Research in Personality* titled "Bookworms versus Nerds: Exposure to Fiction versus Non-fiction, Divergent Associations with Social Ability, and the Simulation of Fictional Social Worlds," in which they reported the results of a study they'd conducted that showed that people who read fiction have better social skills (not so for the subjects who read non-fiction). Reading fiction appeared to help readers develop empathy. The researchers concluded that it was the very thing that separates reading fiction from other types of reading—the reader's immersion in a made-up world, complete with emotions and conflicts and characters—that made it special.

Popular Fiction

564

H.G. ADLER

Panorama

(New York: Random House, 2011)

Story type: Historical
Subject(s): Holocaust, 1933-1945; Jews; Adventure
Major character(s): Josef Kramer, Survivor
Time period(s): 20th century
Locale(s): Prague, Czech Republic

Summary: H.G. Adler's *Panorama* chronicles the life and adventures of concentration-camp survivor Josef Kramer, whom readers meet as a youngster and follow him through the often-trying experiences of his life. Josef endures an uneasy coming-of-age while a student at a nightmarish boarding school, followed by the onset of war, which sends him to a concentration camp. Josef survives the ordeal and, after liberation, flees to the United Kingdom, looking back on his life and experiences with the perspective of one who has survived life's most challenging blows. This volume is translated from Czech by Peter Filkins and contains an afterword by Peter Demetz.

Where it's reviewed:
Booklist, December 1, 2010, page 33
New York Times Book Review, January 30, 2011, page 16
Publishers Weekly, October 25, 2010, page 27

Other books by the same author:
The Journey, 2008

Other books you might like:
Travis Holland, *The Archivist's Story*, 2007
Tony Judt, *The Memory Chalet*, 2010
W. G. Sebald, *Austerlitz*, 2001

565

ANDREW FOSTER ALTSCHUL

Deus Ex Machina

(Berkeley: Counterpoint Press, 2011)

Story type: Contemporary
Subject(s): Television; Identity; Psychology

Major character(s): Gloria Hamm, Assistant (dental hygienist), Contestant (reality show participant)
Time period(s): 21st century; 2010s

Summary: Life behind and in front of the cameras is duly examined in Andrew Foster Altschul's *Deus Ex Machina*, which takes place in the popular world of reality television. The show is set on a desert island, where a group of inhabitants must outwit one another to stay on the show, not get voted off, and win the coveted cash prize. Among the participants are a poet, an attorney, a beautician, a military man, and a dental hygienist, who, now that she's on the show, doesn't want to take part. First novel.

Where it's reviewed:
Booklist, December 15, 2010, page 19
Publishers Weekly, December 6, 2010, page 31

Other books by the same author:
Lady Lazarus: A Novel, 2008

Other books you might like:
Jonathan Dee, *The Privileges*, 2010
Rivka Galchen, *Atmospheric Disturbances: A Novel*, 2008
Glen David Gold, *Sunnyside: A Novel*, 2009
Carolyn Parkhurst, *Lost and Found*, 2006

566

JEFFREY ARCHER

And Thereby Hangs a Tale: Short Stories

(New York: St. Martin's Press, 2010)

Story type: Collection
Subject(s): Short stories; Love; Adventure

Summary: Author Jeffrey Archer presents a collection of his best short fiction, featuring powerful accounts of love, adventure, and identity in the book *And Thereby Hangs a Tale: Short Stories*. The volume includes 15 tales—10 of which are based on real-life events. Titles in this volume include "Stuck on You," "Members Only," "Better the Devil You Know," "The Queen's Telegram," "Where There's a Will," "Politically Correct," and "No Room at the Inn." Archer is also the author of *Cat*

O'Nine Tales: And Stories, The Prodigal Daughter, and As the Crow Flies.

Where it's reviewed:
Library Journal, September 15, 2010, page 59
Publishers Weekly, July 26, 2010, page 50

Other books by the same author:
Paths of Glory, 2009
False Impression, 2006
As the Crow Flies, 1991
The Prodigal Daughter, 1982
Kane and Abel, 1979

Other books you might like:
Barbara Taylor Bradford, The Triumph of Katie Byrne, 2001
Ken Follett, World Without End, 2007
James Patterson, Double Cross, 2007

567

REZA ASLAN

Tablet and Pen: Literary Landscapes from the Modern Middle East

(New York: W.W. Norton & Company, 2010)

Story type: Collection; Ethnic
Subject(s): Short stories; Middle East; Literature
Summary: Tablet and Pen: Literary Landscapes from the Modern Middle East is a collection of short stories by Middle Eastern authors such as Arab poet Khalil Gibran and Nobel Prize winner Orhan Pamuk. The editor of the book, Reza Aslan—a writer himself and author of No god but God—has compiled stories that depict the writing styles of several different Middle Eastern languages, including Arabic, Persian, Turkish, and Urdu, and highlights countries such as Morocco, Iran, Turkey, and Pakistan.

Where it's reviewed:
Booklist, November 15, 2010, page 8
Library Journal, October 1, 2010, page 76
Publishers Weekly, October 11, 2010, page 27

Other books by the same author:
How to Win a Cosmic War, 2009
No God But God, 2006

Other books you might like:
Hanan al-Shaykh, Women of Sand and Myrrh, 1992
Rajaa Alsanea, Girls of Riyadh, 2007
Maha Gargash, The Sand Fish: A Novel from Dubai, 2009
Nadine Gordimer, Loot, and Other Stories, 2003

568

KATE ATKINSON

Started Early, Took My Dog

(New York: Little, Brown, and Company, 2011)

Series: Jackson Brodie Series. Book 4
Story type: Mystery

Subject(s): Missing persons; Detective fiction; Actors
Major character(s): Jackson Brodie, Detective—Private; Tracy Waterhouse, Detective—Police (retired); Tilly Squires, Actress
Time period(s): 21st century; 2010s
Locale(s): Leeds, United Kingdom

Summary: Detective Jackson Brodie has come back to his hometown to investigate the case of a young woman looking for her biological parents. As he hits dead end after dead end, retired police detective Tracy Waterhouse suddenly finds herself embroiled in the case of a young child placed in her care. Figuring into these disparate cases is Tilly Squires, an aging actress who is descending into dementia. Kate Atkinson's Started Early, Took My Dog is the fourth installment in a series starring PI Jackson Brodie.

Where it's reviewed:
Booklist, January 1, 2011, page 52
Library Journal, January 2011, page 76
Publishers Weekly, January 17, 2011, page 26

Other books by the same author:
When Will There Be Good News?: A Novel, 2008
One Good Turn, 2006
Emotionally Weird, 2000
Human Croquet, 1997
Case Histories, 1996
Behind the Scenes at the Museum, 1995

Other books you might like:
Gillian Flynn, Sharp Objects, 2006
Tana French, In the Woods, 2007
Laura Lippman, What the Dead Know, 2007

569

PAUL AUSTER

Sunset Park

(New York: Henry Holt and Co., 2010)

Story type: Contemporary
Subject(s): Identity; Family; Friendship
Major character(s): Miles Heller, Streetperson (squatter), Friend (of Bing, Alice, and Ellen), Son (of Morris); Bing, Streetperson (squatter), Friend (of Miles), Leader; Alice, Streetperson (squatter), Writer, Friend (of Miles); Ellen, Streetperson (squatter), Artist, Friend (of Miles); Morris, Father (of Miles), Publisher
Time period(s): 21st century; 2000s (2008)
Locale(s): Brooklyn, New York

Summary: In Sunset Park, author Paul Auster explores how the financial meltdown of 2008 affects a group of young people. Miles Heller has been living and working in Florida when he loses his job and returns to his hometown of Brooklyn. With few friends or family members to rely on for help, Miles decides to squat with a motley group of artists and outcasts in an abandoned Sunset Park building. As he gets to know this ragtag band of troubled individuals, Miles contemplates his life, his choices, and his damaged relationship with his father. Against the backdrop of economic uncertainty and possible financial desolation, Miles and his crew must confront the personal demons that threaten to ruin their lives.

Where it's reviewed:
Details, November 2010, page 52
Library Journal, July 2010, page 68
New York Times Book Review, December 19, 2010, page 18

Other books by the same author:
Invisible, 2009
Man in the Dark, 2008
The Brooklyn Follies, 2006
Travels in the Scriptorium, 2006
Auggie Wren's Christmas Story, 2004

Other books you might like:
Allegra Goodman, *The Cookbook Collector: A Novel*, 2010
Claire Messud, *The Emperor's Children*, 2006
Tom Rachman, *The Imperfectionists: A Novel*, 2010

570

RICK BASS

Nashville Chrome

(Boston: Houghton Mifflin Harcourt, 2010)

Story type: Historical
Subject(s): Country music; Musicians; Family
Major character(s): Maxine Brown, Musician, Sister (of Jim Ed and Bonnie); Jim Ed Brown, Musician, Brother (of Maxine and Bonnie); Bonnie Brown, Musician, Sister (of Maxine and Jim Ed)
Time period(s): 20th century-21st century; 1950s-2010s
Locale(s): Nashville, Tennessee; West Memphis, Tennessee

Summary: Rick Bass's *Nashville Chrome* is an account of the rise and fall of a country music-singing family, who pioneered a new sound in the world of 1950s Nashville. Maxine Brown is now an old woman, looking back on her life and the stardom she achieved with her siblings, Jim Ed and Bonnie. Desperate to relive the standing ovations and adulation, Maxine struggles to understand the precarious nature of fame and the effects it has had on her family.

Where it's reviewed:
Booklist, August 1, 2010, page 26
Entertainment Weekly, October 1, 2010, page 78
Publishers Weekly, July 26, 2010, page 43

Other books by the same author:
The Diezmo, 2006
The Lives of Rocks, 2006
The Hermit's Story, 2003
The Ninemile Wolves, 1992
The Watch, 1989

Other books you might like:
Bill Flanagan, *A & R: A Novel*, 2000
Oscar Hijuelos, *The Mambo Kings Play Songs of Love*, 1989
Arthur Phillips, *The Song is You*, 2009
Annie Proulx, *Heart Songs*, 1988

571

CHARLES BAXTER

Gryphon: New and Selected Stories

(New York: Pantheon Books, 2011)

Subject(s): Self awareness; Identity; Short stories

Summary: In *Gryphon: New and Selected Stories*, acclaimed author Charles Baxter offers an anthology of 23 original short stories threaded sensitively with topics of love, death, identity, and the challenges of daily life. The characters who people these tales each find moments of supreme self-knowledge, in which the roots of their motivations and the choices they have made are revealed. Titles in this volume include "The Old Murderer," "Ghosts," "Royal Blue," and "Poor Devil."

Where it's reviewed:
Booklist, December 1, 2010, page 25
Library Journal, October 15, 2010, page 71
New York Times Book Review, January 16, 2011, page 1
The New Yorker, January 24, 2011, page 75
Publishers Weekly, September 20, 2010, page 44

Other books by the same author:
The Feast of Love, 2000
Believers, 1997
A Relative Stranger, 1990
Through the Safety Net, 1985
Harmony of the World, 1984

Other books you might like:
Lauren Groff, *Delicate Edible Birds: And Other Stories*, 2009
Alice Munro, *Hateship, Friendship, Courtship, Loveship, Marriage*, 2001
Lydia Peelle, *Reasons for and Advantages of Breathing: Stories*, 2009

572

ANDREJ BLATNIK

You Do Understand

(Champaign, Illinois: Dalkey Archive Press, 2010)

Subject(s): Interpersonal relations; Love; Short stories

Summary: In *You Do Understand*, renowned Slovenian author, Andrej Blatnik presents a collection of very short fiction that tackles some of life's most perplexing questions with sparse humor and great insight. From the ups and downs of modern love to the inherent difficulties of effective communication, the tales of this volume take on the distinct challenges of being human in an oftentimes inhuman world. *You Do Understand* was translated from Slovenian by Tamara M. Sobon.

Where it's reviewed:
Library Journal, August 2010, page 76
Publishers Weekly, July 26, 2010, page 48

Other books by the same author:
Writings From an Unbound Europe, 1998

Popular Fiction

Other books you might like:
Michal Ajvaz, *The Other City*, 2009
Hans Fallada, *Every Man Dies Alone*, 2009
Aleksandar Hemon, *Love and Obstacles*, 2009
Tod Wodicka, *All Shall Be Well; and All Shall Be Well; and All Manner of Things Shall Be Well*, 2008

573

PAULA BOMER

Baby and Other Stories

(Middletown, New Jersey: Word Riot Press, 2010)

Subject(s): Family; Mothers; Fathers
Locale(s): United States

Summary: In *Baby and Other Stories*, author Paula Bomer skewers the contemporary American family with ten tales of dissonance and discord. The forgotten fathers, unhappy mothers, and traumatized children who populate these stories find themselves navigating the rough seas of family, desperate for connection, affection, and, in many cases, escape. Titles in this volume include "The Second Son," "A Galloping Infection," and the title tale.

Where it's reviewed:
Booklist, December 1, 2010, page 22
O, The Oprah Magazine, January 2011, page 98
Publishers Weekly, September 27, 2010, page 34

Other books you might like:
Judy Budnitz, *Nice Big American Baby*, 2005
Miranda July, *No One Belongs Here More than You: Stories*, 2007
Eric Puchner, *Music Through the Floor: Stories*, 2005

574

ROSALIND BRACKENBURY

Becoming George Sand

(Boston: Houghton Mifflin Harcourt, 2011)

Subject(s): Love; Self knowledge; Writers
Major character(s): Maria Jameson, Professor; George Sand, Writer; Frederic Chopin, Musician
Time period(s): 21st century; (2010s); 19th century
Locale(s): Edinburgh, Scotland; Majorca, Spain

Summary: Rosalind Brackenbury's *Becoming George Sand* follows the romantic adventures of two women living in two different eras. In the present, Maria Jameson meets a man in a rundown bookstore, and the two begin a passionate affair. Wracked with guilt over an affair that becomes increasingly consuming, Maria turns to the life of writer George Sand. Readers are then taken back in time to Sand's Majorcan escapades with Chopin, illustrating the two women's search for love, belonging, and identity.

Where it's reviewed:
Herizons, Spring 2010, page 39
Publishers Weekly, January 3, 2011, page 32

Other books by the same author:
Windstorm and Flood, 2007
Yellow Swing, 2004
The House in Morocco, 2003
Seas Outside the Reef, 2000
Coming Home the Long Way Round the Mountain, 1993

Other books you might like:
A.S. Byatt, *Possession: A Romance*, 1990
Elizabeth Hay, *A Student of Weather*, 2001
Maggie O'Farrell, *The Hand That First Held Mine*, 2010
Cynthia Ozick, *Heir to the Glimmering World*, 2004
Jane Smiley, *Ordinary Love and Good Will*, 1989

575

KEVIN BROCKMEIER

The Illumination

(New York: Pantheon Books, 2011)

Story type: Contemporary
Subject(s): Grief; Healing; Friendship
Major character(s): Jason Williford, Photojournalist, Widow(er); Chuck Carter, Neighbor (of Jason); Ryan Shifrin, Religious
Time period(s): 21st century; 2010s
Locale(s): United States

Summary: In Kevin Brockmeier's *The Illumination*, a series of characters find their innermost pain revealed physically in the form of brilliant light, and they are no longer able to conceal their suffering from others. Photographer Jason Williford is grieving the sudden loss of his wife and finds serenity helping a wayward teenage girl. Meanwhile, Jason's neighbor, Chuck Carter, steals love letters from Jason and hands them over to a distressed minister. Each of these characters is forced to finally confront the pain they've kept hidden from the world, which is now expressed through a light that cannot be denied.

Where it's reviewed:
Library Journal, November 15, 2010, page 58
Library Journal, October 15, 2010, page S4
Publishers Weekly, October 25, 2010, page 26

Other books by the same author:
The View from the Seventh Layer, 2008
The Brief History of the Dead, 2006
The Truth About Celia, 2003
Things That Fall from the Sky, 2002

Other books you might like:
Dan Chaon, *Await Your Reply: A Novel*, 2009
David Levithan, *The Lover's Dictionary*, 2011
Colum McCann, *Let the Great World Spin*, 2009
Frederick Reiken, *Day for Night*, 2010

576

ELEANOR BROWN

The Weird Sisters

(New York: Penguin, 2011)

Story type: Contemporary
Subject(s): Sisters; Family life; Cancer
Major character(s): Dr. James Andreas, Professor, Spouse (of Mrs. Andreas), Father (of Cordy, Rose, and Bean); Rose Andreas, Sister (of Cordy and Bean), Teacher (math), Daughter (of Dr. and Mrs. Andreas); Mrs. Andreas, Mother (of Cordy, Rose, and Bean), Spouse (of Dr. Andreas), Cancer Patient; Bean Andreas, Daughter (of Dr. and Mrs. Andreas), Sister (of Rose and Cordy); Cordy Andreas, Daughter (of Dr. and Mrs. Andreas), Sister (of rose and bean)

Summary: In *The Weird Sisters*, author Eleanor Brown tells the story of a trio of sisters and their relationships with each other, their family, and the world around them. The daughters of a Shakespearean scholar, Rose, Cordy, and Bean Andreas earned a reputation in the town of Barnwell for being just plain weird—always having their noses buried in books rather than caring about things that normal kids are supposed to care about. Once they grow up, Cordy and Bean move away onto bigger and better things, leaving Rose behind in the comfort of her hometown. But when the sisters' mother is diagnosed with cancer, the sisters return to their childhood home, harboring secrets and wondering if life can ever be the same again.

Where it's reviewed:
Booklist, October 15, 2010, page 35
Library Journal, October 1, 2010, page 65
New York Times, January 17, 2011, page C7
Publishers Weekly, November 15, 2010, page 39
USA Today, January 20, 2011, page 5D

Other books by the same author:
The Vanishing Act of Esme Lennox, 2007
The Thirteenth Tale, 2006
In Her Shoes, 2002
Amy and Isabelle, 1998

Other books you might like:
Deborah Harkness, *A Discovery of Witches*, 2011

577

ELIZABETH BUCHAN

Separate Beds

(New York: Viking, 2011)

Story type: Contemporary
Subject(s): Marriage; Family; Money
Major character(s): Tom, Spouse (of Annie); Annie, Spouse (of Tom)
Time period(s): 21st century
Locale(s): United States

Summary: A financial catastrophe plays a major role in saving a marriage in Elizabeth Buchan's *Separate Beds*.

Though Tom and Annie have grown children and are enjoying a relatively prosperous life, their marriage is far from ideal. When the economic downturn hits, Tom is fired from his job and both the couple's son and Tom's mother are forced to move in with the couple. Suddenly Tom and Annie are forced to make this unorthodox situation work, leading them to unexpected results that bring them back to one another.

Where it's reviewed:
Booklist, December 1, 2010, page 27
Library Journal, November 1, 2010, page 53
Publishers Weekly, October 18, 2010, page 24

Other books by the same author:
The Second Wife, 2006
Everything She Thought She Wanted, 2005
The Good Wife Strikes Back, 2004
Revenge of the Middle-Aged Woman, 2003
Perfect Love, 1999

Other books you might like:
Carol Edgarian, *Three Stages of Amazement*, 2011
Joe Meno, *The Great Perhaps*, 2009
Eric Puchner, *Model Home: A Novel*, 2010
Lynn Schnurnberger, *The Best Laid Plans*, 2011
Jess Walter, *The Financial Lives of the Poets*, 2009

578

DRUSILLA CAMPBELL

The Good Sister

(New York: Grand Central Publishing, 2010)

Story type: Contemporary
Subject(s): Sisters; Mental disorders; Family
Major character(s): Simone Duran, Mentally Ill Person, Sister (of Roxanne); Roxanne, Sister (of Simone)
Time period(s): 21st century; 2010s
Locale(s): California, United States

Summary: Drusilla Campbell's *The Good Sister* tells of the relationship between Roxanne and her troubled sister Simone. The two girls endured a challenging childhood with their narcissistic mother, and, as adults, chose very different paths in life. Roxanne, always looking out for her sister, is helpless when Simone marries a bullying brute who keeps getting her pregnant in hopes of having a son. Meanwhile, Simone falls deeper into the pit of postpartum depression, growing increasingly dependent on her insensitive husband and powerless sister. The downward spiral eventually causes Simone to snap, killing her children and turning once more to her sister for support.

Where it's reviewed:
Publishers Weekly, August 30, 2010, page 31

Other books by the same author:
Bone Lake, 2008
Blood Orange, 2005
The Edge of the Sky, 2004
Wildwood, 2003
Reunion, 1985

Other books you might like:
Emma Donoghue, *Room*, 2010

Popular Fiction

Myla Goldberg, *The False Friend*, 2010
Laura Lippman, *I'd Know You Anywhere*, 2010
Tawni O'Dell, *Back Roads*, 1999

579

MASSIMO CARLOTTO

Bandit Love

(Rome; New York: Europa Editions, 2010)

Series: Alligator Series. Book 5
Story type: Mystery
Subject(s): Detective fiction; Italy; Organized crime
Major character(s): Marco "The Alligator" Buratti, Detective—Private; Beniamino Rossini, Friend (colleague of Buratti); Max la Memoria, Businessman (bar owner); Sylvie, Kidnap Victim, Lover (of Rossini)
Time period(s): 21st century; 2010s
Locale(s): Padua, Italy

Summary: In *Bandit Love*, Massimo Carlotto presents the fifth adventure starring private eye, Marco "The Alligator" Buratti. In this outing, the girlfriend of Buratti's associate Beniamino Rossini has been kidnapped, and the detective sets out to find her. Joining forces with Rossini and bar owner Max la Memoria, Buratti travels across Italy in search of the missing woman. The investigation leads the trio into a world of deceit, corruption, and organized crime. This volume is translated from Italian by Antony Shugaar.

Where it's reviewed:
Booklist, October 15, 2010, page 22
Publishers Weekly, August 23, 2010, page 27

Other books by the same author:
Poisonville, 2009
Death's Dark Abyss, 2006
The Goodbye Kiss, 2006
The Master of Knots, 2004
The Columbian Mule, 2003

Other books you might like:
Niccolo Ammaniti, *I'm Not Scared*, 2004
Andrea Camilleri, *August Heat*, 2009
Amara Lakhous, *Clash of Civilizations over an Elevator in Piazza Vittorio*, 2008
Roberto Saviano, *Gomorrah*, 2007

580

JUSTIN CARTWRIGHT

Other People's Money

(New York: Bloomsbury USA, 2011)

Story type: Contemporary
Subject(s): Finance; Family; Actors
Major character(s): Julian Tubal, Banker; Harry Tubal, Father (of Julian); Artair Macleod, Actor; Fleur, Spouse (ex-wife of Artair)
Time period(s): 21st century; 2010s
Locale(s): United Kingdom

Summary: In *Other People's Money*, Justin Cartwright tells the story of one family and how the effects of the financial crisis cause them to come apart at the seams. Julian Tubal is taking over the private bank once owned by his quickly deteriorating father, and he soon finds the bank in possession of some questionable assets. This leads to a string of events that put Tubal and Co. on the front page of the papers, forcing the family to reevaluate their business, their customers, and their relationships with one another.

Where it's reviewed:
Publishers Weekly, November 29, 2010, page 27

Other books by the same author:
To Heaven by Water, 2009
The Song before It Is Sung, 2007
The Promise of Happiness, 2005
Masai Dreaming, 1993
Look at It This Way, 1990

Other books you might like:
Jonathan Dee, *The Privileges*, 2010
Adam Haslett, *Union Atlantic: A Novel*, 2010
Joe Meno, *The Great Perhaps*, 2009
Eric Puchner, *Model Home: A Novel*, 2010
Jess Walter, *The Financial Lives of the Poets*, 2009

581

JOHN CASEY

Compass Rose

(New York: Alfred A. Knopf, 2010)

Story type: Family Saga
Subject(s): Family sagas; Fishing (Recreation); Interpersonal relations
Major character(s): Elsie Buttrick, Naturalist (natural resources warden); Dick Pierce, Fisherman, Lover (of Elsie); Rose, Daughter (of Elsie and Dick); May Pierce, Spouse (of Dick)
Time period(s): 20th century-21st century; 1990s-2010s
Locale(s): Sawtooth Point, Rhode Island

Summary: In *Compass Rose*, author John Casey revisits the cast of characters he introduced in his 1989 novel, *Spartina*. Elsie Buttrick's family is trying to transform its small estuary community of Sawtooth Point, Rhode Island, into a vacation spot for the rich. Elsie, a wildlife warden, opposes her family's ideology with choices in her professional and her personal life. As the new mother of a baby girl fathered by local fisherman Dick Pierce, Elsie has added to the controversies swirling in Sawtooth Point. But as little Rose grows into a young woman, the relationships in town adapt just as the coastal environment endures change.

Where it's reviewed:
Entertainment Weekly, October 22, 2010, page 118
The Houston Chronicle, November 21, 2010, page 17
New York Times Book Review, November 7, 2010, page 14
Publishers Weekly, July 12, 2010, page 24

Other books by the same author:
The Half-Life of Happiness, 1998

Spartina, 1989
South Country, 1988
Testimony and Demeanor, 1979
An American Romance, 1977

Other books you might like:
Julia Glass, *I See You Everywhere*, 2008
Richard Russo, *Empire Falls*, 2001
Rose Tremain, *Trespass*, 2010

582

LAN SAMANTHA CHANG

All Is Forgotten, Nothing Is Lost
(New York: W. W. Norton and Company, 2010)

Subject(s): Poetry; Writers; College environment
Major character(s): Miranda Sturgis, Writer (poet),
   Teacher; Bernard Blithe, Writer (poet), Student (of
   Miranda); Roman Morris, Writer (poet), Student (of
   Miranda)
Time period(s): 20th century-21st century; 1980s-2010s
Locale(s): United States

Summary: The power of poetry, artistic integrity, and
personal determination collide in Lan Samantha Chang's
All Is Forgotten, Nothing Is Lost. At a prestigious writing school, Miranda Sturgis is a tough but respected
teacher whose passion inspires two male students and
forever influences their lives. Bernard Blithe is a focused,
talented poet who hopes to gain Miranda's professional
and personal affections. Meanwhile, Roman Morris, a
wildly gifted but undisciplined poet, harbors an interest
in Miranda that is more sensual and spiritual that his
classmate's. The two men set out to win Miranda's
heart—even as her presence begins to erode their lives.

Where it's reviewed:
New York Times Book Review, September 26, 2010,
   page 14
Publishers Weekly, July 26, 2010, page 50
The Santa Fe New Mexican, October 8, 2010, page
   PA14

Other books by the same author:
Inheritance, 2004
Hunger, 1998

Other books you might like:
Nicholson Baker, *The Anthologist: A Novel*, 2009
Michael Chabon, *Wonder Boys*, 1995
Francine Prose, *Blue Angel*, 2000

583

TEJU COLE

Open City
(New York: Random House, 2011)

Story type: Contemporary
Subject(s): Africans; Ethnicity; Identity
Major character(s): Julius, Immigrant

Time period(s): 21st century; 2010s
Locale(s): New York, New York

Summary: In Teju Cole's *Open City*, the streets of New
York serve as the backdrop for the reflections of a
Nigerian immigrant. Julius has just graduated with a
degree in psychology, and he spends his days wandering
the boroughs of Manhattan and ruminating on all the
random thoughts that cross his mind. Throughout his
journeying, Julius encounters individuals with whom he
engages in lively conversations about life, politics, art,
and philosophy. First novel.

Where it's reviewed:
Booklist, December 15, 2010, page 20
Library Journal, November 15, 2010, page 58
Publishers Weekly, November 1, 2010, page 25

Other books you might like:
Jhumpa Lahiri, *The Namesake*, 2003
Dinaw Mengestu, *How to Read the Air*, 2010
Joseph O'Neill, *Netherland: A Novel*, 2008
Rose Tremain, *The Road Home*, 2008

584

ROWAN COLEMAN

The Home for Broken Hearts
(New York: Gallery Books, 2010)

Story type: Contemporary
Subject(s): Mother-son relations; Grief; Friendship
Major character(s): Ellen Wood, Widow(er); Charlie, 11-
   Year-Old, Son (of Ellen); Hannah, Sister (of Ellen);
   Sabine, Businesswoman (co-worker of Hannah),
   Boarder (of Ellen); Matt, Journalist, Boarder (of
   Ellen); Allegra Howard, Writer, Boarder (of Ellen)
Time period(s): 21st century; 2010s
Locale(s): London, United Kingdom

Summary: In Rowan Coleman's *The Home for Broken
Hearts*, Ellen Wood is struggling with the sudden death
of her husband and the potential loss of the home she
now shares with her troubled 11-year-old son. To make
ends meet, Ellen begins taking in boarders. Her new
houseguests include a famous romance novelist, a rising-
star journalist, and a German-born colleague of Ellen's
sister. As her relationships with her boarders grow, Ellen
finds the strength to deal with the problems before her
and finds her life altered in the most unexpected ways.

Where it's reviewed:
Booklist, September 1, 2010, page 42
Publishers Weekly, July 26, 2010, page 50

Other books by the same author:
The Accidental Family, 2009
Mommy by Mistake, 2009
Another Mother's Life, 2008
The Accidental Mother, 2007
Growing Up Twice, 2002

Other books you might like:
Elizabeth Berg, *Open House*, 2000
Jane Green, *The Beach House*, 2008
Adriana Trigiani, *Big Cherry Holler*, 2001
Karen White, *Falling Home*, 2002

585

REBECCA CONNELL

The Art of Losing

(London, England: HarperCollins, 2010)

Story type: Contemporary
Subject(s): Grief; Death; Infidelity
Major character(s): Louise, Young Woman, Narrator, Daughter (of deceased Lydia); Nicholas Steiner, Professor, Father, Lover (of Lydia); Lydia, Mother (of Louise), Lover (of Nicholas)
Time period(s): 20th century-21st century; 1980s-2000s
Locale(s): England

Summary: *The Art of Losing* is a novel about love, grief, and forgiveness from debut author Rebecca Connell. In 1989, when Louise was just ten years old, her mother Lydia died tragically. Nearly two decades later, Louise is desperate to find the man responsible for Lydia's death and make him suffer. The person she's hunting, college professor Nicholas Steiner, carried on an adulterous affair with Lydia in the 1980s that ultimately ended in her death. Louise assumes her mom's name and tracks Nicholas down, in hopes of destroying his life. What she doesn't plan for, however, is falling in love with Nicholas' son, a surprising twist of fate that results in Louise moving in with Nicholas' family and learning a great deal about the mother she barely knew. First novel.

Where it's reviewed:
Publishers Weekly, August 23, 2010, page 28

Other books you might like:
Tana French, *Faithful Place: A Novel*, 2010
Penelope Lively, *The Photograph*, 2003
Kate Morton, *The Distant Hours*, 2010

586

MICHAEL CUNNINGHAM

By Nightfall

(New York: Farrar, Straus and Giroux, 2010)

Story type: Contemporary
Subject(s): Marriage; Family; Self knowledge
Major character(s): Peter Harris, Art Dealer, Spouse (of Rebecca); Rebecca Harris, Co-Editor, Spouse (of Peter); Ethan "Mizzy", Brother (of Rebecca)
Time period(s): 21st century; 2010s
Locale(s): New York, New York

Summary: In *By Nightfall*, Pulitzer Prize-winning author Michael Cunningham crafts a penetrating character study of a middle-aged New Yorker facing a crisis of the spirit. Peter Harris is a high-end art dealer married to Rebecca, an art magazine editor. They sleepwalk through their fashionable life in New York's Soho neighborhood. But their well-ordered world shatters when Rebecca's younger brother Mizzy comes to visit. Mizzy is a carefree 23-year-old with a history of drug abuse and no real ties to any sort of responsibility. His arrival on the scene shakes Peter to the core, who is suddenly con-fronted with a wave of truths about himself that have gone unacknowledged for far too long.

Where it's reviewed:
Details, October 2010, page 76
Library Journal, August 2010, page 66
New York Times Book Review, October 3, 2010, page 16
Publishers Weekly, October 25, 2010, page 42

Other books by the same author:
Specimen Days, 2005
The Hours, 1998
Flesh and Blood, 1995
A Home at the End of the World, 1990
Golden States, 1984

Other books you might like:
Andrew Sean Greer, *The Story of a Marriage: A Novel*, 2008
Allan Gurganus, *Plays Well with Others*, 1997
Jane Smiley, *Private Life*, 2010
Rafael Yglesias, *A Happy Marriage: A Novel*, 2009

587

LESLIE DANIELS

Cleaning Nabokov's House

(New York: Simon and Schuster, 2011)

Story type: Contemporary
Subject(s): Self confidence; Prostitution; Writers
Major character(s): Barb Barrett, Madam, Mother; Margie, Agent (literary); Greg, Carpenter
Time period(s): 21st century; 2010s
Locale(s): New York, United States

Summary: Leslie Daniels's *Cleaning Nabokov's House* follows Barb Barrett who, after losing her children in a custody battle, retreats to a house in upstate New York once owned by Vladimir Nabokov. After finding notes that may have been for an uncompleted novel by the great writer, Barb submits the paperwork to experts, who promptly dismiss any claims they were Nabokov's. Desperate for money, Barb then turns her home into a brothel, populating the place with amorous young men who cater to the ladies of the community. Throughout the process, Barb finds a surprising will to go on and fight for custody of her children. First novel.

Where it's reviewed:
Library Journal, December 2010, page 99
Publishers Weekly, December 13, 2010, page 34

Other books you might like:
Steven Carter, *Famous Writers School*, 2006
Karen Joy Fowler, *The Jane Austen Book Club*, 2004
Allegra Goodman, *The Cookbook Collector: A Novel*, 2010
Abraham Verghese, *Cutting for Stone: A Novel*, 2009

588

RANA DASGUPTA

Solo

(London: Fourth Estate, 2009)

Subject(s): Birds; Politics; Love
Time period(s): 20th century
Locale(s): Bulgaria

Summary: In *Solo*, acclaimed author Rana Dasgupta chronicles the emotional odyssey of a blind, unnamed Bulgarian man, who at age 100, lives the life of a hermit. The aged hero remembers a time before he lost his sight, when a band of explorers found a flock of wild parrots who spoke the language of a long-extinct people. Though they attempted to study the birds, the parrots died before they reached the laboratory. Now the old man wonders if his life will take the same course—what if he dies before he says all he has to say? This pondering leads him to a series of revelations about his journey through life.

Where it's reviewed:
Booklist, October 15, 2010, page 22
Library Journal, September 15, 2010, page 57
New York Times Book Review, February 6, 2011, page 15
Publishers Weekly, November 1, 2010, page 25

Other books by the same author:
Tokyo Canceled, 2005

Other books you might like:
Paolo Giordano, *The Solitude of Prime Numbers*, 2010
Stefan Merrill Block, *The Story of Forgetting: A Novel*, 2008
David Mitchell, *The Thousand Autumns of Jacob De Zoet*, 2010

589

TATIANA DE ROSNAY

A Secret Kept

(New York: St. Martin's Press, 2010)

Story type: Contemporary
Subject(s): Brothers and sisters; Family; Identity
Major character(s): Antoine Rey, Architect, Brother (of Melanie); Melanie, Sister (of Antoine)
Time period(s): 21st century; 2010s
Locale(s): Noirmoutier Island, France; Paris, France

Summary: Tatiana de Rosnay's *A Secret Kept* centers on a middle-aged architect named Antoine Rey, who is forced to unlock the mysteries of his family's past and in the process finds his own identity. After his sister Melanie becomes haunted by the emergence of a long-suppressed memory, Antoine looks into the unusual recollection plaguing his sibling—Melanie remembers their mother in a relationship with another woman. This discovery leads Antoine on a quest to understand his family's past while the challenges faced by his family in the present challenge him at every turn. But as his inquiry unfolds, Antoine finds the one thing he never expected: himself.

Where it's reviewed:
Booklist, August 1, 2010, page 33
Library Journal, November 15, 2010, page 34
Publishers Weekly, July 26, 2010, page 46
USA Today, September 16, 2010, page 4D
Vanity Fair, September 2010, page 184

Other books by the same author:
Sarah's Key, 2007

Other books you might like:
Chris Cleave, *Little Bee: A Novel*, 2009
Catherine Texier, *Victorine*, 2004
Jeannette Walls, *Half Broke Horses: A True-Life Novel*, 2009

590

LOUISE DEAN

The Old Romantic

(New York: Riverhead Books, 2011)

Story type: Contemporary
Subject(s): Family; Father-son relations; Humor
Major character(s): Ken, Father (of Nick and Dan); Nick, Son (of Ken), Brother (of Dan); Dan, Brother (of Nick), Son (of Ken)
Time period(s): 21st century; 2010s
Locale(s): United Kingdom

Summary: Louise Dean's *The Old Romantic* charts the attempts of one family to come together when estranged patriarch Ken becomes convinced he has a short time to live. Ken is a crotchety, potty-mouthed old man who has managed to alienate one son and his ex-wife, though his other son, Dave, makes a valiant stab at creating peace within the fractured family unit. The father and sons eventually end up on a journey together, confronting the past in ways none of them could have foreseen and allowing them to find a tentative, though shaky, resolution.

Where it's reviewed:
Booklist, December 1, 2010, page 27
Library Journal, December 2010, page 100

Other books by the same author:
The Idea of Love, 2009
This Human Season, 2007
Becoming Strangers, 2006

Other books you might like:
Kate Christensen, *The Epicure's Lament*, 2004
Howard Jacobson, *The Finkler Question*, 2010
Philip Roth, *Exit Ghost*, 2007
Tod Wodicka, *All Shall Be Well; and All Shall Be Well; and All Manner of Things Shall Be Well*, 2008

591

ROBB FORMAN DEW

Being Polite to Hitler

(New York: Little, Brown, and Company, 2010)

Series: Scofield Trilogy. Book 3
Subject(s): Self knowledge; Women; History

Major character(s): Agnes Scofield, Widow(er), Teacher
Time period(s): 20th century; 1950s-1970s (1953-1973)
Locale(s): Washburn, Ohio

Summary: In *Being Polite to Hitler*, award-winning author Robb Forman Dew presents the third and final installment in a trilogy centered on the denizens of the Scofield family. Set in the small Ohio town of Washburn from the 1950s through the 1970s, this volume follows 70-something Agnes Scofield as she both looks back on the eras she's lived through and deals with the shifting winds of the current times. As the world around her changes, Agnes's perspective of the past is altered as well, and she finds new meaning in the host of unusual circumstances in which she has found herself throughout her life.

Where it's reviewed:
Good Housekeeping, January 2011, page 171
New York Times, January 3, 2011, page C4
New York Times Book Review, January 16, 2011, page 7
People, January 20, 2011, page 47
Publishers Weekly, October 18, 2010, page 24

Other books by the same author:
The Truth of the Matter, 2005
The Evidence Against Her, 2004
Fortunate Lives, 1993
The Time of Her Life, 1984
Dale Loves Sophie to Death, 1982

Other books you might like:
Ian McEwan, *Atonement*, 2002
Kate Morton, *The House at Riverton: A Novel*, 2008
Julie Orringer, *The Invisible Bridge*, 2010

592

ABBY DRAKE

The Secrets Sisters Keep

(New York: Avon A, 2010)

Story type: Family Saga
Subject(s): Sisters; Sibling rivalry; Humor
Major character(s): Ellie Dalton, Historian, Caregiver (to uncle Edward), Sister; Amanda Delaney, Socialite, Wealthy, Sister; Naomi "Babe" Dalton, Actress, Sister; Carleen Dalton, Teacher, Sister; Edward, Uncle (to Ellie, Amanda, Naomi, & Carleen), Guardian (to Ellie, Amanda, Naomi, & Carleen), Homosexual
Time period(s): 21st century; 2010s
Locale(s): Kamp Kasteel, New York

Summary: *The Secrets Sisters Keep* is a humorous family saga from author Abby Drake. The Dalton sisters—Ellie, Amanda, Carleen, and Naomi "Babe"—are gathering together in Kamp Kasteel, New York, to celebrate the 75th birthday of their eccentric, gay Uncle Edward. Shortly before the soiree, Edward vanishes, forcing the sisters to band together and find him, lest he marry his partner, Henry, and write them all out of his will. Coming together is no small feat for these four women who are harboring age-old secrets and unspoken desires. Ellie is fed up with taking care of Edward and longs to leave everything behind and travel to Egypt, Amanda's

admirable Park Avenue existence is crashing around her now that her husband has left her for a younger woman, Babe's has-been actor husband isn't cutting it for her anymore, and Carleen is desperate for her sisters' forgiveness for the tragedy she caused 20 years earlier. The search for Edward forces these women to confront the past and make peace with the future in hopes of restoring their sisterly bond.

Where it's reviewed:
Publishers Weekly, August 30, 2010, page 29

Other books by the same author:
Perfect Little Ladies, 2009
Good Little Wives, 2007

Other books you might like:
Fannie Flagg, *I Still Dream About You: A Novel*, 2010
Elinor Lipman, *The Family Man*, 2009
Stephen McCauley, *The Object of My Affection*, 1987
Cathleen Schine, *The Three Weissmanns of Westport*, 2010

593

SLAVENKA DRAKULIC

A Guided Tour Through the Museum of Communism: Fables from a Mouse, a Parrot, a Bear, a Cat, a Mole, a Pig, a Dog, and a Raven

(New York: Penguin, 2011)

Story type: Contemporary
Subject(s): Communism; Animals; Satire
Time period(s): 21st century; 2010s

Summary: In *A Guided Tour Through the Museum of Communism: Fables from a Mouse, a Parrot, a Bear, a Cat, a Mole, a Pig, a Dog, and a Raven*, author Slavenka Drakulic offers an incisive examination of communism as seen through the eyes of animals. The critters that narrate this eight-part tale each provide a different glimpse into communist life, from its effects on young people to its fall in popularity around the world.

Where it's reviewed:
Publishers Weekly, December 13, 2010, page 35

Other books by the same author:
Frida's Bed, 2008
They Would Never Hurt a Fly, 2004
S: A Novel about the Balkans, 2000
Cafe Europa: Life after Communism, 1997
The Taste of a Man, 1997

Other books you might like:
Ken Kalfus, *A Disorder Peculiar to the Country*, 2006
Milan Kundera, *Ignorance*, 2002
George Orwell, *Animal Farm*, 1954

594

MARK DUNN

Under the Harrow

(San Francisco: MacAdam/Cage, 2010)

Subject(s): Rural life; Satire; Humor
Major character(s): Frederick Trimmers, Lawyer, Narrator
Time period(s): 21st century; 2010s
Locale(s): Dingley Dell, Pennsylvania

Summary: Mark Dunn's *Under the Harrow* is set in the fictional backwoods town of Dingley Dell, Pennsylvania, where a group of outsiders has formed an unorthodox Victorian community. Narrated by the lawyer Frederick Trimmers, this volume follows the denizens of Dingley Dell as they develop their unusual society and customs, deal with runaways, and confront the outside world.

Where it's reviewed:
Booklist, December 1, 2010, page 22
Library Journal, November 15, 2010, page 58
Publishers Weekly, October 18, 2010, page 29

Other books by the same author:
Ibid, 2004
Welcome to Higby, 2002
Ella Minnow Pea, 2001

Other books you might like:
Emma Donoghue, *Room*, 2010
Keith Donohue, *The Stolen Child*, 2006
William Golding, *Lord of the Flies*, 1954

595

KIM EDWARDS

The Lake of Dreams

(New York: Viking, 2011)

Story type: Contemporary
Subject(s): Fathers; Family; Mystery
Major character(s): Lucy Jarrett, Sister (of Blake), Niece (of Art); Keegan Fall, Artist; Blake, Brother (of Lucy); Art, Uncle (of Lucy)
Time period(s): 21st century; 2010s
Locale(s): Lake of Dreams, New York

Summary: Kim Edwards's *The Lake of Dreams* follows Lucy Jarrett, who, in the grip of a midlife crisis, returns to her childhood hometown of Lake of Dreams, New York. What she finds, however, is a place far from the memories of her childhood. Her mother is living in squalor and embarking on a love affair, while her uncle and brother are intent on destroying the community and transforming it into a housing development. After becoming involved with old friend Keegan Fall, Lucy begins to piece together the fragments of her family's past—with startling results .

Where it's reviewed:
Good Housekeeping, January 2011, page 171
Library Journal, October 15, 2010, page 64
Publishers Weekly, October 11, 2010, page 23

Other books by the same author:
The Memory Keeper's Daughter, 2005
The Secrets of a Fire King, 1997

Other books you might like:
Maeve Binchy, *Heart and Soul*, 2009
Lisa Genova, *Still Alice*, 2009
Kate Morton, *The Distant Hours*, 2010

596

JANICE EIDUS

The Last Jewish Virgin: A Novel of Fate

(Pasadena: Red Hen Press, 2010)

Story type: Contemporary
Subject(s): Vampires; Jews; Mother-daughter relations
Major character(s): Lilith Zeremba, Student—College; Colin Abel, Artist; Baron Rock, Vampire; Beth, Mother (of Lilith)
Time period(s): 21st century; 2010s
Locale(s): New York, New York

Summary: Janice Eidus's *The Last Jewish Virgin: A Novel of Fate* tells the story of college student, Lilith Zeremba, who has made a vow to maintain her virginity until she is established as a successful fashion designer. But her resolution is put to the test when she meets two very different men. One is a magnetic young artist name Colin Abel, who is both personally captivating and socially conscious. The other is Baron Rock, who possesses a unique, undeniable charm of his own. There's just one problem with Mr. Rock that Lilith had not foreseen: he's a vampire.

Where it's reviewed:
Booklist, October 1, 2010, page 28
Publishers Weekly, August 30, 2010, page 30

Other books by the same author:
The War of the Rosens, 2007
The Celibacy Club, 1997
Urban Bliss, 1994
Vito Loves Geraldine, 1990
Faithful Rebecca, 1986

Other books you might like:
MaryJanice Davidson, *Undead and Unwed*, 2004
Floyd Kemske, *Human Resources: A Corporate Nightmare*, 1995
Christopher Moore, *Bloodsucking Fiends: A Love Story*, 1995
Mark Sumner, *Vampires of Vermont*, 1999

597

JENNY ERPENBECK

Visitation

(New York: New Directions, 2010)

Story type: Historical
Subject(s): Germans; History; Housing

Time period(s): 19th century-20th century
Locale(s): Brandenburg, Germany

Summary: In *Visitation*, author Jenny Erpenbeck tells the 100-year history of an isolated house in Brandenburg, Germany. Beginning in the 19th century, the novel spans a century of German history, including the Weimar Republic, World War II, the Socialist German Democratic Republic, and reunification. Over the course of *Visitation*, the story's main character, a lakeside cottage, is occupied by 12 distinct residents, each possessing his or her own unique hopes, fears, secrets, and dreams. Erpenbeck tells the life stories of each tenant, including a Jewish girl murdered during the Holocaust, a committed Communist, a Germania Project architect, and two wild and rebellious college students escaping their Western upbringing.

Where it's reviewed:
Library Journal, September 15, 2010, page 58
Publishers Weekly, July 26, 2010, page 48

Other books by the same author:
The Book of Words, 2007
The Old Child and Other Stories, 2005

Other books you might like:
Julie Orringer, *The Invisible Bridge*, 2010
Rachel Seiffert, *The Dark Room*, 2001
Lara Vapnyar, *There Are Jews in My House*, 2003

598

ALISON ESPACH

The Adults

(New York: Scribner, 2011)

Story type: Contemporary
Subject(s): Coming of age; Family; Adolescent interpersonal relations
Major character(s): Emily Vidal, 14-Year-Old; Mark Resnick, Neighbor (of Emily); Mrs. Resnick, Neighbor (of Emily); Mr. Resnick, Neighbor (of Emily)
Time period(s): 21st century; 2010s
Locale(s): United States

Summary: Alison Espach's *The Adults* follows 14-year-old Emily Vidal as she charters the uncertain waters of young adulthood. Not only does Emily learn her parents are getting a divorce, but she also soon finds her father having an affair with Mrs. Resnick, the woman who lives next door. Further complicating Emily's transition to womanhood is the suicide of Mrs. Resnick's husband and Emily's own relationship with the Resnicks' son, Mark. As she makes her way through this series of challenges, young Emily must look within herself to find the strength and humor to make it through. First novel.

Where it's reviewed:
Library Journal, November 15, 2010, page 59
Publishers Weekly, December 13, 2010, page 34

Other books you might like:
Jonathan Franzen, *The Corrections*, 2001
Lily King, *Father of the Rain: A Novel*, 2010
Alice McDermott, *Child of My Heart*, 2002

599

JONATHAN EVISON

West of Here

(New York: Algonquin Books, 2011)

Story type: Literary
Subject(s): Time; Family; Americana
Time period(s): 19th century; (1890s); 21st century; 2000s
Locale(s): Port Bonita, Washington

Summary: In *West of Here*, novelist and social networker extraordinaire Jonathon Evison tells a story that contrasts the lives of the founders of a small Pacific Northwestern town and the founders' descendents, who one hundred years later are still dealing with the repercussions of their ancestors' actions. The differences between the two settings and groups of characters make a bold comment on just how far society has come since the days of frontier life. The novel's narration staggers between the 1890s and 2006. *West of Here* is described as epic in its storytelling and praised for its evocative description of the Pacific Northwest. Jonathan Evison is also the author of the highly praised novel *All About Lulu*.

Where it's reviewed:
Library Journal, October 1, 2010, page 66
Publishers Weekly, November 1, 2010, page 1

Other books by the same author:
All About Lulu, 2008

Other books you might like:
Patricia Ferguson, *Peripheral Vision*, 2008
Maggie O'Farrell, *The Hand That First Held Mine*, 2010
Jonathan Raban, *Surveillance*, 2007
Jonathan Raymond, *The Half Life*, 2004
Amy Sackville, *The Still Point*, 2011

600

SIOBHAN FALLON

You Know When the Men Are Gone

(New York: G.P. Putnam's Sons, 2011)

Story type: Contemporary
Subject(s): Military life; Military bases; Family

Summary: In *You Know When the Men Are Gone*, author Siobhan Fallon presents a collection of short stories revolving around the Army wives at a US military base. The tales of this volume are tied together by the diverse experiences of a group of unforgettable women as they struggle with personal dramas, deployed spouses, and the challenges of life as single parents. Through these stories, Fallon shows readers the courage of the families who are left behind when soldiers go off to war. First book.

Where it's reviewed:
The Denver Post, January 23, 2011, page E10
Library Journal, November 15, 2010, page 65

The New York Times, January 11, 2011, page C6
Publishers Weekly, October 11, 2010, page 23
USA Today, January 18, 2011, page 3D

Other books you might like:
Susan Minot, *Monkeys*, 1986
Lionel Shriver, *So Much for That*, 2010

601

SUSAN FLETCHER

Corrag

(London: Fourth Estate, 2010)

Story type: Historical
Subject(s): Witchcraft; Scots (British people); Family
Major character(s): Corrag, Crime Suspect; Charles Leslie,
   Religious (Catholic loyalist interrogator)
Time period(s): 17th century
Locale(s): Scotland

Summary: In *Corrag*, Susan Fletcher spins a tale of
witchcraft, bravery, and redemption, set in 17th-century
Scotland. The entire MacDonald clan has been brutally
murdered, and an enchanting young woman named Corrag is accused of the crime. Suspected of being a witch,
she is thrown into prison and interrogated by Irish
Catholic loyalist Charles Leslie. As he sets out to find
answers, Charles learns Corrag's fascinating story, from
her relationship with her mother, who was hanged for
being a witch, to her association with the massacred
MacDonalds.

Where it's reviewed:
Library Journal, September 15, 2010, page 58
Publishers Weekly, September 6, 2010, page 23

Other books by the same author:
Oystercatchers, 2007
Eve Green, 2004

Other books you might like:
Kathleen Kent, *The Heretic's Daughter*, 2008
Kathleen Kent, *The Wolves of Andover*, 2010
Karen Maitland, *Company of Liars*, 2008
Hilary Mantel, *Wolf Hall*, 2009
Jennifer Roberson, *Lady of the Glen*, 1996

602

AMINATTA FORNA

The Memory of Love

(London; New York: Bloomsbury, 2011)

Story type: Contemporary
Subject(s): Psychology; Africa; Diaries
Major character(s): Adrian Lockheart, Psychologist; Elias
   Cole, Mentally Ill Person; Agnes, Mentally Ill
   Person; Kai, Doctor
Time period(s): 21st century; 2000s
Locale(s): Sierra Leone

Summary: In Aminatta Forna's *The Memory of Love*,
psychologist Adrian Lockheart has arrived in Sierra Le-

one with a grand ambition: to contemporize the medical
approaches used on the country's mentally ill. But before
long, Adrian is drawn into the lives of the characters that
populate his African hospital. There's Elias Cole, a
former teacher who may or may not be involved in a
criminal activity; Agnes, a patient permanently enveloped
in a fugue state; and a fellow doctor named Kai, who is
battling demons of his own and is considering leaving
Sierra Leone.

Where it's reviewed:
Booklist, November 15, 2010, page 22
New York Times Book Review, January 9, 2011, page 14
Publishers Weekly, September 6, 2010, page 21

Other books by the same author:
Ancestor Stones, 2006
The Devil That Danced on the Water, 2002
Mother of All Myths, 1998

Other books you might like:
Chimamanda Ngozi Adichie, *The Thing Around Your
   Neck*, 2009
Russell Banks, *The Darling*, 2004
Maaza Mengiste, *Beneath the Lion's Gaze*, 2010

603

KAREN JOY FOWLER

What I Didn't See and Other Stories

(Easthampton, Massachusetts: Small Beer Press, 2010)

Subject(s): History; Fantasy; Short stories

Summary: In *What I Didn't See and Other Stories*,
bestselling author Karen Joy Fowler offers a collection
of short fiction that blends elements of traditional
literature, science fiction and fantasy, and historical
narrative. From 19th-century America to present-day
California, the 12 stories of this volume chart the experiences of unforgettable characters as they face the most
defining moments of their lives. Titles in this volume
include "The Pelican Bar," "Booth's Ghost," "Always,"
"Standing Room Only," and "King Rat."

Where it's reviewed:
Library Journal, November 1, 2010, page 59
Publishers Weekly, July 26, 2010, page 49

Other books by the same author:
Wit's End, 2008
The Jane Austen Book Club, 2004
Sister Noon, 2001
The Sweetheart Season, 1996
Sarah Canary, 1991

Other books you might like:
J.G. Ballard, *Kingdom Come*, 2006
Marilyn Krysl, *Dinner with Osama*, 2008
Ursula K. Le Guin, *Changing Planes*, 2003

Popular Fiction

604

JULIA FRANCK

The Blind Side of the Heart

(London: Harvill Secker, 2009)

Story type: Historical - World War II
Subject(s): Family sagas; World War I, 1914-1918; World War II, 1939-1945
Major character(s): Helene, Young Woman; Wilhelm, Spouse (of Helene)
Time period(s): 20th century; 1940s (1945)
Locale(s): Germany

Summary: *The Blind Side of the Heart* is a novel written by Julia Franck and translated by Anthea Bell. The novel begins at a German train station in 1945; Helene is fleeing Germany along with thousands of others, and though she has survived the war with her seven-year-old son, she leaves him on the station platform and never comes back. The book then flashes back to Helene's childhood, growing up during World War I with her distant mother. Helene fell in love once, but her fiance died before their wedding, leading her into a tragic, loveless marriage with a man named Wilhelm, from which came her son. Helene soon could think only of disappearing, which led her to that train station in 1945. The events that follow make up the rest of the novel.

Where it's reviewed:
Booklist, September 15, 2010, page 36
Library Journal, August 2010, page 68
New York Times Book Review, October 17, 2010, page 22
Publishers Weekly, July 19, 2010, page 109
Vogue, October 2010, page 258

Other books you might like:
Tatiana de Rosnay, *Sarah's Key*, 2007
Julie Orringer, *The Invisible Bridge*, 2010
William Styron, *Sophie's Choice*, 1979

605

JAMES FRANCO

Palo Alto: Stories

(New York: Scribner, 2010)

Story type: Collection
Subject(s): Short stories; Adolescence; Bullying
Time period(s): 21st century; 2010s
Locale(s): Palo Alto, California

Summary: In *Palo Alto: Stories*, author, artist, and actor James Franco presents a collection of short fiction exploring the intersecting lives of a group of troubled California teenagers. Palo Alto's idyllic suburban setting belies the challenges that its adolescent residents face. In "American History," a high school student's convincing performance at a school play triggers an act of racial vengeance. In "Lockheed," a girl is shocked from boredom with her summer job when a party turns violent. In "I Could Kill Someone," a student overwhelmed by the harassment he endures each school day purchases a gun to silence his intimidator. First book.

Where it's reviewed:
Booklist, October 15, 2010, page 21
Library Journal, September 15, 2010, page 66
New York Times Book Review, October 24, 2010, page 27
Publishers Weekly, August 30, 2010, page 27
USA Today, October 19, 2010, page 3D

Other books you might like:
Poppy Z. Brite, *The Devil You Know*, 2003
Dave Eggers, *How We Are Hungry*, 2004
Bret Easton Ellis, *The Informers*, 1994
Susan Minot, *Monkeys*, 1986

606

THAISA FRANK

Heidegger's Glasses

(Beverly Hills: Counterpoint Press, 2010)

Story type: Historical - World War II
Subject(s): Writers; Holocaust, 1933-1945; Letters (Correspondence)
Major character(s): Elie, Leader (of Nazi Briefkation), Lover (of Gerhardt); Gerhardt, Leader (of Nazi Briefkation), Lover (of Elie)
Time period(s): 20th century; 1940s
Locale(s): Germany

Summary: In *Heidegger's Glasses*, author Thaisa Frank tells the story behind the little-known Nazi program Nazi Briefkation, which required a select group of concentration-camp inmates to answer letters written to fellow prisoners across Europe. Overseen by secret anti-Nazis Elie and Gerhardt, the prisoners of Nazi Briefkation encounter an unexpected hurdle in their letter writing when they are forced to reply to correspondence written by the brilliant philosopher Martin Heidegger. First novel.

Other books by the same author:
Sleeping in Velvet, 1997
Finding Your Writer's Voice, 1994
A Brief History of Camouflage, 1992
Desire 1, 1982

Other books you might like:
Jenna Blum, *Those Who Save Us*, 2004
Dan Chaon, *Await Your Reply: A Novel*, 2009
Anita Diamant, *Day After Night*, 2009
Travis Holland, *The Archivist's Story*, 2007
Daniel Silva, *A Death in Vienna*, 2004

607

LAURA FURMAN

The Mother Who Stayed

(New York: Free Press, 2011)

Subject(s): Mothers; Family; Short stories

Summary: In *The Mother Who Stayed*, award-winning author Laura Furman offers a collection of short fiction centering on three different families, principally on the relationships of mothers and their children. From the 19th-century journals of a roughhewn farmer's wife to the modern-day challenges of raising teenaged children, these stories encompass various women's experiences as caregivers, nurturers, and role models. Titles in this volume include "The Hospital Room," "Blue Birds Come Today," "The Eye," and "The Thief."

Where it's reviewed:
Booklist, January 1, 2011, page 42
Publishers Weekly, December 20, 2010, page 29

Other books by the same author:
Drinking with the Cook, 2001
Watch Time Fly, 1983
The Shadow Line, 1982
The Glass House, 1980
Tuxedo Park, 1986

Other books you might like:
Susan Minot, *Monkeys*, 1986
Elissa Schappell, *Use Me*, 2000
Marisa Silver, *Alone with You: Stories*, 2010

608

ERIC GANSWORTH

Extra Indians
(Minneapolis: Milkweed Editions, 2010)

Story type: Contemporary
Subject(s): Missing persons; Native Americans; Japanese (Asian people)
Major character(s): Tommy Jack McMorsey, Truck Driver, Veteran; Annie Boans, Scholar
Time period(s): 21st century; 2010s
Locale(s): United States

Summary: In Eric Gansworth's *Extra Indians*, Tommy Jack McMorsey is a truck driver who offers a ride to a Japanese woman embarking on a treasure hunt. But the woman is not prepared for the harsh winter cold, and she disappears into the snowy Midwestern landscape. News outlets are fast on the story, and Tommy Jack finds himself at the center of a media firestorm. The scrutiny brings up a series of issues and secrets from Tommy Jack's past—secrets that intellectual Annie Boans becomes determined to uncover.

Where it's reviewed:
Booklist, October 1, 2010, page 28
Library Journal, September 1, 2010, page 98
Publishers Weekly, August 2, 2010, page 27

Other books by the same author:
Breathing the Monster Alive, 2006
Mending Skins, 2005
Smoke Dancing, 2004
Nickel Eclipse, 2000
Indian Summers, 1998

Other books you might like:
Denis Johnson, *Jesus' Son*, 1992
Barbara Kingsolver, *The Lacuna: A Novel*, 2009

609

ROBERTA GATELY

Lipstick in Afghanistan
(New York: Gallery Books, 2010)

Story type: Contemporary
Subject(s): Nursing; Afghanistan Conflict, 2001-; Friendship
Major character(s): Elsa Murphy, Nurse; Parween, Neighbor (of Elsa); Mike, Military Personnel
Time period(s): 21st century; 2000s
Locale(s): Bamiyan, Afghanistan

Summary: Roberta Gately's *Lipstick in Afghanistan* centers on Elsa Murphy, who arrives in a rural Afghan village following the tragedy of September 11, 2001. Elsa has come to the region to offer medical services to the poverty-stricken villagers and soon finds herself enmeshed in the lives of the locals. She strikes up a friendship with neighbor Parween, who is harboring a deep abhorrence of Taliban forces, and American solider Mike, who helps open Elsa's eyes to the reality of Afghan life—and the secrets of her own heart. First novel.

Where it's reviewed:
Booklist, October 15, 2010, page 33
Library Journal, October 1, 2010, page 66
Publishers Weekly, August 23, 2010, page 25

Other books you might like:
Chris Cleave, *Little Bee: A Novel*, 2009
Siobhan Fallon, *You Know When the Men Are Gone*, 2011
Abraham Verghese, *Cutting for Stone: A Novel*, 2009

610

LISA GENOVA

Left Neglected
(New York: Gallery Books, 2011)

Story type: Contemporary
Subject(s): Neurosciences; Self awareness; Marriage
Major character(s): Sarah Nickerson, Consultant, Spouse (of Bob); Bob Nickerson, Spouse (of Sarah)
Time period(s): 21st century; 2010s
Locale(s): Massachusetts, United States

Summary: Lisa Genova's *Left Neglected* charts the life-changing experiences of a middle-aged wife and mother, who is diagnosed with a rare neurological disorder. Sarah Nickerson and her husband, Bob, lead hardworking but charmed lives in suburban Boston. When a car accident sends Sarah into a coma, she comes to days later and learns she has been diagnosed with Left Neglect, a brain impairment that prevents an individual from seeing the left side of anything in his or her field of vision. Now, armed with this strange condition, Sarah must learn to re-navigate her life and finds something surprising along the way: herself.

Where it's reviewed:
Booklist, December 1, 2010, page 26

Library Journal, November 15, 2010, page 59
Publishers Weekly, October 18, 2010, page 24
USA Today, January 4, 2011, page 4D

Other books by the same author:
Still Alice, 2008

Other books you might like:
Joshua Ferris, *The Unnamed*, 2010
Rivka Galchen, *Atmospheric Disturbances: A Novel*, 2008
Sue Miller, *The Senator's Wife*, 2008
Maggie O'Farrell, *The Hand That First Held Mine*, 2010

611

TED GILLEY

Bliss and Other Short Stories

(Lincoln: University of Nebraska Press, 2010)

Subject(s): Human behavior; Conduct of life; Short stories

Summary: In *Bliss and Other Short Stories*, author Ted Gilley presents a collection of nine stories revolving around characters seeking their unique identities in the larger, daunting world. From the tale of a gay soldier coming to terms with his sexuality to the love song of a Cambodian immigrant struggling to find sexual fulfillment, these stories capture indelible characters at moments of great personal and emotional transformation. *Bliss and Other Short Stories* was awarded the Prairie Schooner Book Prize in Fiction.

Where it's reviewed:
Library Journal, August 2010, page 76

Other books you might like:
Paul Harding, *Tinkers*, 2008
Philipp Meyer, *American Rust: A Novel*, 2009
Ron Rash, *Burning Bright: Stories*, 2010
Wells Tower, *Everything Ravaged, Everything Burned*, 2009

612

DEBRA GINSBERG

The Neighbors Are Watching

(New York: Shaye Areheart Books, 2010)

Story type: Contemporary
Subject(s): Neighborhoods; Father-daughter relations; Missing persons
Major character(s): Diana Jones, Pregnant Teenager; Joe Montana, Father (of Diana); Allison, Stepmother (of Diana), Spouse (of Joe)
Time period(s): 21st century; 2000s
Locale(s): San Diego, California

Summary: Debra Ginsberg's *The Neighbors Are Watching* marries soap opera and psychological thriller in its exploration of the lives affected by the disappearance of a San Diego teen. In the posh neighborhood of Fuller Court, pregnant 17-year-old Diana comes to live with her father, Joe, and his wife, Allison. Diana's appearance in the neighborhood sets the entire subdivision talking and gossiping. But when Diana disappears during the 2007 wildfires, the girl's true impact on the community is felt: everyone in Fuller Court is a suspect.

Where it's reviewed:
Booklist, October 1, 2010, page 30
Library Journal, August 2010, page 68
New York Times Book Review, December 26, 2010, page 26
Publishers Weekly, September 20, 2010, page 45

Other books by the same author:
The Grift, 2008
Blind Submission, 2006
About My Sisters, 2004
Raising Blaze, 2002
Waiting: The True Confessions of a Waitress, 2001

Other books you might like:
Valerie Laken, *Dream House: A Novel*, 2009
Nancy Mauro, *New World Monkeys: A Novel*, 2009
Joe Meno, *The Great Perhaps*, 2009
Eric Puchner, *Model Home: A Novel*, 2010
Jennifer Vanderbes, *Strangers at the Feast: A Novel*, 2010

613

JULIA GLASS

The Widower's Tale

(New York: Pantheon Books, 2010)

Story type: Contemporary
Subject(s): Family; Love; Cults
Major character(s): Percy Glass, Retiree, Father (of Clover), Grandfather (of Robert); Clover, Teacher, Daughter (of Percy); Robert, Student—College, Cult Member, Grandson (of Percy); Ira, Teacher, Homosexual; Celestino, Immigrant, Gardener
Time period(s): 21st century; 2010s
Locale(s): Boston, Massachusetts

Summary: In *The Widower's Tale*, award-winning author Julia Glass tells the story of a family going through a profound transformation. Seventy-year-old patriarch Percy Glass has no idea that renting his barn to a preschool will change his life so completely. His daughter Clover takes a job at the school, while Percy's adored grandson Robert falls in with a cult. Percy himself starts a relationship with a much younger teacher at the preschool as the paths of two men—another teacher and an immigrant gardener—begin to collide with those of Percy and his family.

Where it's reviewed:
Entertainment Weekly, September 3, 2010, page 77
Good Housekeeping, October 2010, page 222
O, The Oprah Magazine, September 2010, page 158
People, September 20, 2010, page 63
Self, October 2010, page 40

Other books by the same author:
I See You Everywhere, 2008

The Whole World Over, 2006
Three Junes, 2002

Other books you might like:
Michael Cunningham, *The Hours*, 1998
Lily King, *Father of the Rain: A Novel*, 2010
Sue Miller, *The Senator's Wife*, 2008

614

MYLA GOLDBERG

The False Friend

(New York: Doubleday, 2010)

Story type: Literary; Psychological
Subject(s): Psychology; Memory; Interpersonal relations
Major character(s): Celia Durst, Young Woman; Djuna, Friend (of Celia); Huck, Boyfriend (of Celia)
Time period(s): 21st century; 2010s
Locale(s): New York, United States

Summary: In *The False Friend* by Myla Goldberg, a woman returns to her childhood home to face the truth about her friend's disappearance. It has been more than 20 years since Celia Durst set off on a walk in the woods with her friend, Djuna. Both 11 years old at the time, Celia and Djuna headed a clique of girls, but competed with each other for dominance. After one spat, Celia and Djuna ventured onto a forbidden route through the woods. When Celia emerged alone, she reported that Djuna had been abducted in a mysterious car. As an adult, Celia admits that Djuna actually stumbled into a hole, but the other girls in the old clique dispute that account as well.

Where it's reviewed:
Library Journal, September 1, 2010, page 99
New York Times Book Review, October 24, 2010,, page 8
Publishers Weekly, August 2, 2010, page 28
Self, November 2010, page 41
USA Today, January 4, 2011, page 4D

Other books by the same author:
Wickett's Remedy, 2005
Time's Magpie, 2004
Bee Season, 2000

Other books you might like:
Emma Donoghue, *Room*, 2010
Tana French, *In the Woods*, 2007
Laura Lippman, *I'd Know You Anywhere*, 2010
Donna Tartt, *The Little Friend*, 2002

615

MARTHA GRIMES

Fadeaway Girl

(New York: Viking, 2011)

Series: Emma Graham Series. Book 4
Subject(s): Kidnapping; Detective fiction; Mystery
Major character(s): Emma Graham, 12-Year-Old, Detec-tive—Amateur; Fay, Kidnap Victim
Time period(s): 21st century; 2010s
Locale(s): La Porte, Maryland

Summary: Twelve-year-old detective Emma Graham is investigating a 20-year-old kidnapping case that involves the disappearance of a wealthy family's infant child. As she delves into the long-forgotten details of the case, Emma unearths startling new evidence that implicates those previously thought innocent. Her investigation eventually leads Emma herself into the path of danger, which will take all her feisty young wits if she's going to make it out alive. Martha Grimes's *Fadeaway Girl* is the fourth novel in a series featuring the investigative adventures of Emma Graham.

Where it's reviewed:
Booklist, December 15, 2010, page 22
Publishers Weekly, December 20, 2010, page 28

Other books by the same author:
The Black Cat, 2010
Dakota, 2008
Belle Ruin, 2005
Cold Flat Junction, 2001
Hotel Paradise, 1996

Other books you might like:
Gillian Flynn, *Dark Places*, 2009
Donna Tartt, *The Little Friend*, 2002
Liza Ward, *Outside Valentine: A Novel*, 2004

616

LINDA LEGARDE GROVER

The Dance Boots

(Athens, Georgia: University of Georgia Press, 2010)

Subject(s): Native Americans; Cultural identity; Family
Major character(s): Artense, Narrator; Shirley, Aunt (of Artense)
Time period(s): 20th century-21st century
Locale(s): Minnesota, United States

Summary: Linda LeGarde Grover's *The Dance Boots* is a series of interconnected stories chronicling the cultural disintegration of the Ojibwe tribe in rural Minnesota. Through the stories of her dying aunt Shirley, Artense relates the tales of several generations within the tribe as they struggle to hold onto their traditions and stand firm in the face of Western influence. *The Dance Boots* was awarded the 2010 Flannery O'Connor Award for Short Fiction.

Where it's reviewed:
Booklist, September 1, 2010, page 41
Publishers Weekly, July 26, 2010, page 49

Other books you might like:
Sherman Alexie, *The Lone Ranger and Tonto Fist Fight in Heaven*, 1993
Louise Erdrich, *Love Medicine*, 1984
Susan Power, *The Grass Dancer*, 1994

617

BENJAMIN HALE

The Evolution of Bruno Littlemore

(New York: Hachette Book Group, 2011)

Story type: Wild Talents
Subject(s): Monkeys; Chimpanzees; Evolution (Biology)
Major character(s): Bruno Littlemore, Chimpanzee; Dr. Lydia Littlemore, Researcher, Rescuer (of Bruno)

Summary: Benjamin Hale's *The Evolution of Bruno Littlemore* is the story of a chimpanzee who develops language skills and evolves until he is almost human—but not quite. Bruno the chimpanzee narrates his own quest as he grows up in a zoo, surrounded by humans and their emotions and desires. Bruno develops these same feelings as well, and after being rescued by a researcher from a laboratory in Chicago, he finds himself falling in love. But will the five percent difference between Bruno's DNA and that of his beloved prove to be too great an obstacle to overcome? First novel.

Where it's reviewed:
Booklist, October 15, 2010, page 30
Library Journal, January 2011, page 83
Publishers Weekly, October 18, 2010, page 23
The Record, January 1, 2011, page F1

Other books you might like:
Robert Cohen, *Inspired Sleep*, 2001
Allegra Goodman, *Intuition*, 2006
J.M. Ledgard, *Giraffe*, 2006
Rafi Zabor, *The Bear Comes Home*, 1997

618

BARBARA HAMBY

Lester Higata's 20th Century

(Iowa City: University of Iowa Press, 2010)

Subject(s): Japanese Americans; Hawaiians; Short stories
Major character(s): Lester Higata, Spouse (of Katherine); Katherine, Spouse (of Lester)
Time period(s): 20th century; 1940s-1990s (1946-1999)
Locale(s): Hawaii, United States

Summary: In *Lester Higata's 20th Century*, author Barbara Hamby recounts the life, loves, and adventures of a Japanese man living in Honolulu. This collection of intersecting short stories opens with Lester Higata's death and gradually winds its way back through time to 1946, when Lester was recuperating from a war injury. The 50+ years documented in this volume profile the evolution of Hawaiian culture as experienced through the eyes of an unforgettable man and his family. *Lester Higata's 20th Century* was awarded the Iowa Short Fiction Award.

Where it's reviewed:
Library Journal, September 1, 2010, page 105
Publishers Weekly, August 9, 2010, page 30

Other books by the same author:
Seriously Funny, 2010

All-Night Lingo Tango, 2009
The Alphabet of Desire, 2006
Babel, 2004
Delirium, 2000

Other books you might like:
Muriel Barbery, *The Elegance of the Hedgehog*, 2008
Robert Olen Butler, *A Good Scent from a Strange Mountain: Stories*, 1992
Paul Harding, *Tinkers*, 2008
Susan Minot, *Monkeys*, 1986
Tara Bray Smith, *West of Then*, 2004

619

BARRY HANNAH

Long, Last, Happy: New and Selected Stories

(New York: Grove Press, 2010)

Story type: Collection
Subject(s): Short stories; Love; Adventure

Summary: *Long, Last, Happy: New and Selected Stories* is a collection of short stories by the late Barry Hannah. Collected after his death in March of 2010, this book includes more than 30 of Hannah's best short stories. The stories are grouped by time period, such as "1986-1993: Bats Out of Hell" and "1993-1996: High Lonesome." Despite the times at which Hannah wrote these stories, they are strung together by a similar theme: desire. The characters in this collection each long for something—love, success, food, adventure—and refuse to settle down until they achieve their goals. This collection features four never-before-published stories, including "Sick Soldier at Your Door" and "Out-tell the Teller."

Where it's reviewed:
The Denver Post, December 5, 2010, page E6
The Houston Chronicle, January 9, 2011, page 13
The New York Times, December 29, 2010, page C3
New York Times Book Review, December 26, 2010, page 12
Publishers Weekly, October 4, 2010, page 27

Other books by the same author:
Bats Out of Hell, 1993
Captain Maximus, 1985
Black Butterfly, 1982
Two Stories, 1982
Airships, 1978

Other books you might like:
Charles Baxter, *Gryphon: New and Selected Stories*, 2011
Alice Munro, *Hateship, Friendship, Courtship, Loveship, Marriage*, 2001
Lydia Peelle, *Reasons for and Advantages of Breathing: Stories*, 2009
Carol Shields, *Collected Stories*, 2005

620

ALAN HEATHCOCK
Volt
(Minneapolis: Graywolf Press, 2011)

Subject(s): Rural life; Violence; Short stories
Locale(s): United States

Summary: Alan Heathcock's *Volt* is a collection a short stories set in remote small towns on the Midwestern plains of the United States. The characters of these eight pieces are struggling with hardships, challenges, and, quite often, violence. From a newly minted female sheriff investigating the disappearance of a child to a man attempting to burn a body of the person he's murdered, these tales are dark portraits of life in a bleak, desolate place. Titles in this volume include "Peacekeeper," "The Daughter," "Smoke," "The Staying Freight," and "Lazarus."

Where it's reviewed:
Library Journal, January 2011, page 91
Publishers Weekly, January 3, 2011, page 31

Other books you might like:
Philipp Meyer, *American Rust: A Novel*, 2009
Ron Rash, *Burning Bright: Stories*, 2010
Justin Taylor, *Everything Here Is the Best Thing Ever*, 2010
Wells Tower, *Everything Ravaged, Everything Burned*, 2009

621

YAEL HEDAYA
Eden
(New York: Metropolitan Books, 2010)

Story type: Contemporary Realism; Ethnic
Subject(s): Rural life; Family life; Israelis
Major character(s): Alona, Spouse (of Mark), Friend (of Dafna); Mark, Spouse (of Alona), Father (of Roni), Lover (of Dafna); Roni, Daughter (of Mark); Dafna, Lover (of Mark), Friend (of Alona)
Locale(s): Israel

Summary: *Eden* is a novel by Israeli author Yael Hedaya, head writer and creator of the HBO series *In Treatment*. The novel takes place in an Israeli farm collective as its residents attempt to live their lives while in constant fear of terrorist attacks. Hedaya follows the characters as the community transforms from paradise to an upper-class society filled with gossip and scandal. Inhabitants include Alona and Mark, a couple headed for divorce as they deal with the ongoing teen drama of Mark's daughter, Roni; and Dafna, Alona's best friend, who is attempting to get pregnant via in vitro fertilization just as she embarks on an illicit affair with Mark. Hedaya is also the author of *Accidents* and Housebroken: Three Novellas.

Where it's reviewed:
Booklist, October 1, 2010, page 27

Library Journal, October 15, 2010, page 65

Other books by the same author:
Accidents, 2005
Accidents, 2005
Housebroken, 2001

Other books you might like:
David Grossman, *To the End of the Land*, 2010
Amos Oz, *Black Box*, 1988
Naomi Ragen, *The Tenth Song*, 2010
Frederick Reiken, *Day for Night*, 2010

622

ALEKSANDAR HEMON
Best European Fiction 2011
(Champaign, Illinois: Dalkey Archive Press, 2010)

Subject(s): Literature; Writers; Short stories

Summary: In *Best European Fiction 2011*, editor Aleksander Hemon presents a collection of short fiction written by both long-established and emerging European authors. From the witty to the dramatic, the political to the personal, the stories of this volume capture the unique voices of today's most important European writers. Those contributing to this volume include William Owen Roberts, Verena Stefan, Enrique Vila-Matas, Kevin Barry, Toomas Vint, Laszlo Krasznahorkai, and Olga Tokarczuk. Author Colum McCann provides a preface to the collection.

Where it's reviewed:
Library Journal, November 15, 2010, page 65
The New York Times, December 30, 2010, page C1
Publishers Weekly, September 6, 2010, page 23

Other books by the same author:
Love and Obstacles, 2009
The Lazarus Project, 2008
Nowhere Man, 2002
The Question of Bruno, 2000

Other books you might like:
Laura Furman, *The Pen/O. Henry Prize Stories 2010*, 2010
Bill Henderson, *The Pushcart Prize XXXV*, 2010
The New Yorker, *20 Under 40: Stories from The New Yorker*, 2010
Richard Russo, *The Best American Short Stories 2010*, 2010

623

SUSAN HENDERSON
Up from the Blue: A Novel
(New York: HarperCollins, 2010)

Story type: Family Saga
Subject(s): Family relations; Mother-daughter relations; Mystery
Major character(s): Tillie Harris, Narrator, Young Woman,

Sister (of Phil); Phil Harris, Young Man, Brother (of Tillie)

Locale(s): District of Columbia, United States

Summary: Susan Henderson's *Up from the Blue: A Novel* explores how a mother's mental illness affects her daughter. Tillie's father, a strict man who spent many years in the military, constantly clashes with her free-spirited mother. All is well until the family moves to Washington, D.C., and Tillie's mother disappears. Tillie turns to her brother, Phil, for comfort. Then one day the siblings discover a secret: Their father is keeping their mother locked in the basement. Years pass and Tillie eventually leaves home to start a life of her own. After the birth of her child, she reaches out to her father, determined to overcome the emotional events of their past.

Where it's reviewed:
Booklist, September 1, 2010, page 47
Library Journal, August 2010, page 69
Publishers Weekly, August 23, 2010, page 27

Other books you might like:
Julianna Baggott, *Girl Talk*, 2001
Mark Childress, *Crazy in Alabama*, 1993
Stephanie Kallos, *Sing Them Home: A Novel*, 2009
Lily King, *Father of the Rain: A Novel*, 2010

624

FRANCES HILL

Deliverance from Evil

(New York: Overlook Press, 2011)

Story type: Historical
Subject(s): Witches; Trials; Marriage
Major character(s): Mary Cheever, Spouse (of George); George Burroughs, Religious, Spouse (of Mary); Peter White, Friend (of George)
Time period(s): 17th century; 1690s
Locale(s): Wells, Maine; Salem, Massachusetts

Summary: The real-life events of the Salem Witch Trials serve as the backdrop for Frances Hill's *Deliverance from Evil*. In rural Maine, Reverend George Burroughs saves Mary Cheever from a Native American attack, and the two eventually wed. But a few hundred miles to the south, in Salem, Massachusetts, rumors of witches are rampant, and George is named as a potential supplicant to the devil. He is arrested, and Mary sets out to prove her husband's innocence and clear his name. She is unprepared, however, for the hysteria gripping Salem Village—and just what it will take to save George.

Where it's reviewed:
Publishers Weekly, January 3, 2011, page 33

Other books by the same author:
Such Men Are Dangerous: The Fanatics of 1692 and 2004, 2004
Hunting for Witches: A Visitor's Guide to the Salem Witch Trials, 2002
The Salem Witch Trials Reader, 2000

A Delusion of Satan: The Full Story of the Salem Witch Trials, 1995
Out of Bounds, 1985

Other books you might like:
Kathleen Kent, *The Heretic's Daughter*, 2008
Karen Maitland, *Company of Liars*, 2008
Mary Sharratt, *Daughters of the Witching Hill*, 2010

625

ALICE HOFFMAN

The Red Garden

(New York: Random House, 2010)

Story type: Collection
Subject(s): History; Pioneers; Rural life

Summary: Author Alice Hoffman's *The Red Garden* is a collection of short stories, all of which center around the settlement of a Massachusetts town named Blackwell and a plot of land known as the Red Garden. The author describes the town as it progresses throughout two centuries, and tells of the people and creatures who inhabit the town. Hoffman does not limit her characterization to that of the human persuasion, instead telling the stories of those in the spirit world and even a group of bears. Hoffman is also the author of *Blackbird House* and *The Story Sisters*.

Where it's reviewed:
Booklist, October 1, 2010, page 30
Library Journal, October 15, 2010, page S3
Publishers Weekly, October 4, 2010, page 25

Other books by the same author:
The Story Sisters: A Novel, 2009
Skylight Confessions, 2007
The Ice Queen, 2005
Here on Earth, 1997
Practical Magic, 1995

Other books you might like:
Sue Miller, *While I Was Gone*, 1999
Anita Shreve, *The Weight of Water*, 1997
Elizabeth Strout, *Olive Kitteridge*, 2008

626

CARA HOFFMAN

So Much Pretty

(New York: Simon and Schuster, 2011)

Story type: Contemporary
Subject(s): Murder; Rural life; Women
Major character(s): Wendy White, Teenager, Crime Victim; Stacy Flynn, Journalist; Alice Piper, 15-Year-Old, Detective—Amateur
Time period(s): 21st century; 2010s
Locale(s): Haeden, New York

Summary: The lives of three very different women converge in Cara Hoffman's *So Much Pretty*. When good-natured teen Wendy White disappears, the small New York community of Haeden is bereft. That sadness turns to grief when, months later, Wendy's body is found.

Journalist Stacy Flynn wants to get to the bottom of the story, but those in Haeden seem to want to blame an outsider and put the case to rest. Meanwhile, 15-year-old Alice Piper isn't about to stand on her laurels. After reading Stacy's story about the murder, she embarks on her own investigation into Wendy's death. First novel.

Where it's reviewed:
Booklist, Feb. 15, 2011, page 56
Library Journal, February 1, 2011, page 54
Publishers Weekly, January 10, 2011, page 30

Other books you might like:
Adam Haslett, *Union Atlantic: A Novel*, 2010
Laura Lippman, *What the Dead Know*, 2007
Allison Lynn, *Now You See It*, 2004
Eric Puchner, *Model Home: A Novel*, 2010

627

ELIZABETH COBBS HOFFMAN
Broken Promises
(New York: Ballantine Books, 2011)

Story type: Historical - American Civil War
Subject(s): Spies; Love; United States history
Major character(s): Charles Francis Adams, Spy; Baxter Sams, Friend (of Charles); Julia Birch, Young Woman
Time period(s): 19th century; 1860s
Locale(s): United Kingdom; United States
Summary: Set during the Civil War, Rebecca Cobbs Hoffman's *Broken Promises* follows Charles Adams, son of late president John Quincy Adams, to Europe as he attempts to glean information about international reaction to the war in the States. As this spy story plays out, Adams's friend Baxter Sams falls in love with Julia Birch, the daughter of Sir Walter Birch, and young Julia is forced to make a decision that could make or break their relationship.

Where it's reviewed:
Library Journal, October 15, 2010, Page S2
Publishers Weekly, January 10, 2011, page 29

Other books by the same author:
All You Need Is Love: The Peace Corps and the Spirit of the 1960s, 1998
The Rich Neighbor Policy: Rockefeller and Kaiser in Brazil, 1992

Other books you might like:
Dara Horn, *All Other Nights: A Novel*, 2009
Jill Lepore, *Blindspot: By a Gentleman in Exile and a Lady in Disguise*, 2008
Jeane Westin, *The Virgin's Daughters: In the Court of Elizabeth I*, 2009

628

SHERI HOLMAN
The Witches on the Road Tonight
(New York: Atlantic Monthly Press, 2011)

Story type: Witchcraft
Subject(s): Family; Fear; Witchcraft

Major character(s): Eddie Alley, Television Personality, Son (of Cora), Father (of Wallis); Cora Alley, Mother (of Eddie), Witch, Grandmother (of Wallis); Wallis Alley, Daughter (of Eddie), Journalist, Granddaughter (of Cora); Jasper, Orphan
Time period(s): Multiple Time Periods; 20th century; (1940s); 21st century; 2010s
Locale(s): New York, New York; Virginia, United States
Summary: *The Witches on the Road Tonight* is a novel about fear, witchcraft, and dark family secrets from bestselling author, Sheri Holman. Eddie Alley grew up in rural Virginia during the Depression, raised by his mother, Cora, who was rumored to be a witch. Desperate to leave his dark childhood behind, Eddie moved to New York City where he established a career as a campy TV presenter of horror films and started a family of his own. But when Eddie takes in Jasper, a homeless boy who interns at the TV station, dark questions about Eddie's past arise, stirring up a powerful interest in Eddie's daughter, Wallis, who longs to know more about her mysterious grandmother.

Where it's reviewed:
Library Journal, January 2011, page 84
Publishers Weekly, November 15, 2010, page 34

Other books by the same author:
The Mammoth Cheese, 2003
The Dress Lodger, 2000
A Stolen Tongue, 1997

Other books you might like:
Brunonia Barry, *The Lace Reader: A Novel*, 2008
Kathleen Kent, *The Heretic's Daughter*, 2008
Elizabeth Kostova, *The Historian*, 2005
Arthur Phillips, *Angelica*, 2007
Rebecca Stott, *Ghostwalk*, 2007

629

REBECCA HUNT
Mr. Chartwell
(New York: Dial Press, 2011)

Story type: Historical
Subject(s): Depression (Mood disorder); Dogs; Fantasy
Major character(s): Esther Hammerhans, Librarian, Widow(er); Winston Churchill, Political Figure; Mr. Chartwell, Dog
Time period(s): 20th century; 1960s (1964)
Locale(s): London, United Kingdom
Summary: In *Mr. Chartwell*, author Rebecca Hunt examines the effects of depression on two very different individuals: statesman Winston Churchill and widowed librarian Esther Hammerhans. Both are leading lives of quiet desperation in London when a large talking dog named Mr. Chartwell shows up on Esther's doorstep. He is the same animal that goaded her husband into suicide months earlier, and now he has come for Esther. During the days, Mr. Chartwell pays visits to Churchill, who is waging his own war with the illness. First novel.

Where it's reviewed:
Booklist, November 1, 2010, page 33
The Financial Times, October 16, 2010, page 15

Library Journal, November 1, 2010, page 55
Publishers Weekly, November 15, 2010, page 35
Spectator, January 1, 2011, page 29

Other books you might like:
Tracy Chevalier, *Remarkable Creatures*, 2009
Michael Cunningham, *The Hours*, 1998
Janice Galloway, *The Trick Is to Keep Breathing*, 1989

630

HOWARD JACOBSON

The Finkler Question

(London; New York: Bloomsbury, 2010)

Story type: Contemporary
Subject(s): Friendship; Love; Jews
Major character(s): Julian Treslove, Producer, Friend (of Sam and Libor); Sam Finkler, Friend (of Julian and Libor), Philosopher, Writer, Television Personality; Libor Sevick, Teacher, Friend (of Julian and Sam)
Time period(s): 21st century; 2010s
Locale(s): London, United Kingdom

Summary: In *The Finkler Question*, celebrated author Howard Jacobson tells a tale of love, loss, and friendship. Julian Treslove is an ex-radio producer for the BBC who has a horrible track record with women. His old friend, Sam Finkler, is a beloved philosopher and public figure. Although the two are polar opposites, they've maintained a tense friendship over the years. One evening, the two friends have dinner with their old teacher, Libor Sevick, and the three men use the opportunity to reflect on happier times in their lives. Later, Julian is brutally attacked on his way home. In the blink of an eye, everything he knows and loves is changed irrevocably.

Where it's reviewed:
Booklist, November 15, 2010, page 21
Entertainment Weekly, November 19, 2010, page 104
Library Journal, November 1, 2010, page 54
The New York Times, October 21, 2010, page C8
The New Yorker, November 8, 2010, page 86

Other books by the same author:
The Act of Love, 2009
Kalooki Nights, 2007
The Making of Henry, 2004
The Very Model of a Man, 1994
Peeping Tom, 1985

Other books you might like:
Saul Bellow, *Herzog*, 1964
Kate Christensen, *The Epicure's Lament*, 2004
Daniel Menaker, *The Treatment*, 1998

631

GISH JEN

World and Town

(New York: Alfred A. Knopf, 2010)

Story type: Contemporary
Subject(s): Chinese Americans; Refugees; Modern Life

Major character(s): Hattie Kong, Widow(er); Carter Hatch, Scientist
Time period(s): 21st century; 2000s (2001)
Locale(s): Riverlake, United States

Summary: Award-winning author Gish Jen presents the moving story of a middle-aged woman struggling to begin anew after suffering two crushing losses. *World and Town* finds Hattie Kong in a new city after enduring the loss of both her husband and her best friend. Settling into Riverlake, she soon encounters a Cambodian family fleeing big city turmoil and a scientist who just happens to be an ex-beau. As Hattie's life intersects with this diverse group, she is forced to confront the reality of the world in which she finds herself: an increasingly hostile place littered with new dangers and fears—but also, somewhere deep below the troubled surface, the possibility of redemption.

Where it's reviewed:
Entertainment Weekly, October 8, 2010, page 78
Good Housekeeping, October 2010, page 222
The Houston Chronicle, November 28, 2010, page 13
New York Times Book Review, November 7, 2010, page 9
The New Yorker, December 6, 2010, page 89

Other books by the same author:
The Love Wife, 2004
Who's Irish?, 1999
Mona in the Promised Land, 1996
Typical American, 1991

Other books you might like:
Julia Glass, *Whole World Over*, 2006
Allegra Goodman, *The Cookbook Collector: A Novel*, 2010
Claire Messud, *The Emperor's Children*, 2006

632

CARSTEN JENSEN

We, the Drowned

(New York: Houghton Mifflin Harcourt, 2011)

Story type: Historical
Subject(s): Danes; Denmark; Sea stories
Major character(s): Laurids Madsen, Sailor
Time period(s): 19th century-20th century; 1840s-1940s (1848-1948)

Summary: In *We, the Drowned*, author Carsten Jensen tells of a family living along the coast of Denmark, in Jensen's hometown of Marstal. Starting with the family patriarch, Laurids Madsen, Jensen relays the tale of the Madsens spanning a hundred years, from 1848 as Denmark wages war with Germany to World War II, as Denmark fights against Nazi occupation. Meanwhile, the Madsens forge a heritage upon the seas, creating a legacy of sailors. As generations of men go off to sea, fighting for riches in faraway lands, their wives and children wait for them, never knowing if they will return.

Where it's reviewed:
Booklist, December 15, 2010, page 20

Library Journal, September 15, 2010, page 60
Publishers Weekly, October 11, 2010, page 23

Other books you might like:
Joshua Ferris, *Then We Came to the End: A Novel*, 2007
Amitav Ghosh, *Sea of Poppies*, 2008
Sena Jeter Naslund, *Ahab's Wife*, 1999

633

MAT JOHNSON

Pym

(New York: Spiegel and Grau, 2011)

Story type: Contemporary
Subject(s): African Americans; Voyages and travels;
  Fantasy
Major character(s): Chris Jaynes, Professor; Garth, Friend
  (of Chris); Angela, Friend (of Chris); Nathaniel,
  Spouse (of Angela)
Time period(s): 21st century; 2010s
Locale(s): Antarctica; United States

Summary: In Mat Johnson's *Pym*, Chris Jaynes is a
university professor who finds an unlikely mission after
unearthing a long-lost manuscript by Edgar Allan Poe.
The story tells of an all-black island near Antarctica, and
what's more shocking than the discovery of the tale is
the notion that Chris believes it is a true story. With a
team of friends and acquaintances, Chris sets sail for the
storied island, but he and his crew are in no way prepared
for the terror and uncertainty that lay ahead.

Where it's reviewed:
Library Journal, January 2011, page 84
Publishers Weekly, November 29, 2010, page 1

Other books by the same author:
Dark Rain, 2010
Incognegro, 2008
*The Great Negro Plot: A Tale of Conspiracy and
  Murder in Eighteenth-Century New York*, 2007
Hunting in Harlem, 2003
Drop, 2000

Other books you might like:
John Colapinto, *About the Author*, 2001
Adam Langer, *The Thieves of Manhattan*, 2010
Margot Livesey, *The House on Fortune Street*, 2008
Alice Randall, *The Wind Done Gone*, 2001
Matthew Sharpe, *Jamestown*, 2007

634

HIROMI KAWAKAMI

Manazuru

(Berkeley: Counterpoint Press, 2010)

Story type: Contemporary
Subject(s): Memory; Marriage; Family
Major character(s): Kei, Mother (of Momo); Momo,
  Daughter (of Kei and Rei), 16-Year-Old; Rei, Spouse
  (estranged husband of Kei), Father (of Momo)

Time period(s): 21st century; 2010s
Locale(s): Manazuru, Japan

Summary: In Hiromi Kawakami's *Manazuru*, Kei and her
16-year-old daughter Momo live with Kei's mother in
Tokyo, where they have managed to eke out a relatively
contented life. But Kei still harbors deep hurt over her
husband Rei's abandonment when Momo was just an
infant. In the resort town of Manazuru, Kei is finally
forced to confront the pain of the past and the long-
buried guilt and bitterness she has been holding. This
volume is translated from the Japanese by Michael
Emmerich.

Where it's reviewed:
Booklist, September 1, 2010, page 44
Publishers Weekly, July 26, 2010, page 49

Other books you might like:
Miyuki Miyabe, *The Devil's Whisper*, 2007
Kenzaburo Oe, *Chugaeri*, 2003

635

DOUGLAS KENNEDY

The Pursuit of Happiness

(New York: Atria, 2010)

Subject(s): Journalism; McCarthyism; Family
Major character(s): Sara Smythe, Writer; Jack Malone,
  Journalist; Eric, Brother (of Sara); Kate, Daughter
  (of Jack)
Time period(s): 20th century-21st century; 1940s-2010s
Locale(s): New York, New York

Summary: In Douglas Kennedy's *The Pursuit of Happiness*, Sara Smythe comes to Manhattan in the 1940s
with the hopes of establishing a career as a writer. While
at a party hosted by her brother, Sara meets Jack Malone, a journalist with the United States Army. This
unexpected encounter forever binds the lives of Sara and
Jack and leads to surprising repercussions not only for
themselves but for future generations. The shadow of
McCarthyism soon makes its way into Sara and Jack's
relationship and stretches all the way into the present,
where Jack's daughter Kate is attempting to find her
own place in the world.

Where it's reviewed:
Library Journal, November 1, 2010, page 5
Publishers Weekly, August 30, 2010, page 30

Other books by the same author:
Leaving the World, 2010
The Woman in the Fifth, 2007
Temptation, 2006
State of the Union, 2005
The Big Picture, 1997

Other books you might like:
Elizabeth Berg, *Dream When You're Feeling Blue: A
  Novel*, 2007
Myla Goldberg, *Wickett's Remedy*, 2005
Michael Lowenthal, *Charity Girl*, 2007
Penny Vincenzi, *An Absolute Scandal*, 2007
Kate Walbert, *Our Kind*, 2004

636

KATHLEEN KENT

The Wolves of Andover

(New York: Little, Brown and Co., 2010)

Story type: Historical
Subject(s): History; Romances (Fiction); Politics
Major character(s): Martha Allen, Young Woman; Thomas Carrier, Worker (hired hand)
Time period(s): 17th century
Locale(s): Massachusetts, United States

Summary: In *The Wolves of Andover* by Kathleen Kent, a young woman finds romance and international intrigue in 17th- century Massachusetts. While working on her cousin's farm, Martha Allen, 23, is attracted to farmhand Thomas Carrier, but it takes a wolf attack to bring the two together. After Thomas comes to Martha's rescue, he learns that his own life is in danger. Suspected of participating in King Charles I's execution, Thomas is the target of a band of hired killers dispatched from England to avenge the monarch's death. *The Wolves of Andover* is the prequel to Kent's 2008 *The Heretic's Daughter*.

Where it's reviewed:
The Houston Chronicle, December 19, 2010, page 13
Marie Claire, November 2010, page 144
The New York Times, November 18, 2010, page C6
New York Times Book Review, December 26, 2010, page 20
People, December 6, 2010, page 61

Other books by the same author:
The Heretic's Daughter, 2008

Other books you might like:
Brunonia Barry, *The Lace Reader: A Novel*, 2008
Sally Gunning, *The Widow's War*, 2006
Katherine Howe, *The Physick Book of Deliverance Dane*, 2009
Mary Sharratt, *Daughters of the Witching Hill*, 2010
Anita Shreve, *The Weight of Water*, 1997

637

JONAS HASSEN KHEMIRI

Montecore: The Silence of the Tiger

(New York: Knopf, 2011)

Story type: Contemporary
Subject(s): Father-son relations; Immigrants; Sweden
Major character(s): Jonas Khemiri, Writer; Abbas Khemiri, Photojournalist, Father (of Jonas); Kadir, Friend (of Abbas)
Time period(s): 21st century; 2010s
Locale(s): Sweden

Summary: In *Montecore: The Silence of the Tiger*, author Jonas Hassen Khemiri provides a fictionalized account of his attempts to reconcile with his father, a famous photographer with the same name. When his father's friend Kadir maintains that the two should work together to write a biography of Jonas's father, Jonas is reluctant...to say the least. Father and son haven't spoken in nearly a decade, and through the correspondence of Jonas and Kadir, the ghosts of the past begin to emerge. This volume is translated from Swedish by Rachel Willson-Broyles.

Where it's reviewed:
Booklist, January 1, 2011, page 42
Library Journal, January 2011, page 84
Publishers Weekly, December 6, 2010, page 30

Other books you might like:
Indra Sinha, *Animal's People*, 2008
Juan Gabriel Vasquez, *The Informers*, 2009

638

KATHE KOJA

Under the Poppy

(Easthampton, Massachusetts: Small Beer Press, 2010)

Story type: Historical
Subject(s): Love; Prostitution; Family
Major character(s): Rupert, Businessman (brothel operator); Istvan, Friend (of Rupert), Brother (of Decca); Decca, Businesswoman (brothel operator), Sister (of Istvan)
Time period(s): 19th century
Locale(s): Europe

Summary: Set in 19th-century Europe, Kathe Koja's *Under the Poppy* chronicles the lives of various characters whose fates intersect at a brothel known as The Poppy. Among the diverse individuals whose destinies cross paths at The Poppy are Rupert and Istvan, two lifelong friends who fall in love with one another. Enter into this mix Istvan's sister Decca, an assortment of puppets, a love triangle, and an impending war, and the result is a unique story of love, identity, and art.

Where it's reviewed:
Library Journal, September 15, 2010, page 60
Publishers Weekly, August 23, 2010, page 28

Other books by the same author:
Extremities, 1998
Kink, 1996
Strange Angels, 1994
Skin, 1993
Bad Brains, 1992
The Cipher, 1991

Other books you might like:
Megan Chance, *Prima Donna*, 2009
Emma Donoghue, *Slammerkin*, 2001
Ann Parker, *Leaden Skies*, 2009
Dan Simmons, *Drood: A Novel*, 2008
Sarah Waters, *Fingersmith*, 2002

639

NICOLE KRAUSS

Great House

(New York: W.W. Norton & Company, 2010)

Story type: Light Fantasy
Subject(s): Writers; World War II, 1939-1945; Authorship
Time period(s): Multiple Time Periods
Locale(s): Chile; Jerusalem, Israel

Summary: A desk is the main focus in Nicole Krauss's *Great House*. More than 25 years ago, an American writer inherited a desk from a Chilean poet who was taken away by Pinochet's secret police and never heard from again. Years later, the novelist receives a knock at her door. A girl, claiming to be the poet's daughter, has arrived to claim the desk. A man in London who has ties to the same desk unearths an awful secret about his dying wife that changes everything he thought he knew. An antiques dealer in Jerusalem is trying to put the pieces of his father's study back together after it was destroyed in 1944 by Nazis. These three people are connected by a desk that unleashes magnificent power over those who possess it.

Where it's reviewed:
The Denver Post, October 17, 2010, page E11
The Houston Chronicle, October 17, 2010, page 17
New York Times Book Review, October 17, 2010, page 1

Other books by the same author:
The History of Love, 2005
Man Walks into a Room, 2002

Other books you might like:
Dan Chaon, *Await Your Reply: A Novel*, 2009
Jayne Anne Phillips, *Lark and Termite: A Novel*, 2009
Frederick Reiken, *Day for Night*, 2010

640

MARK KURLANSKY

Edible Stories: A Novel in Sixteen Parts

(New York: Riverhead Books, 2010)

Subject(s): Food; Human behavior; Cooking

Summary: In *Edible Stories: A Novel in Sixteen Parts*, acclaimed author Mark Kurlansky presents a series of interconnected short stories that create a snapshot of human behavior and the ties that bind. Whether ruminating on the challenges and joys of tofu turkey, hot dogs, and espresso or struggling to keep down a possibly poisonous creme brulee, the characters that people these tales experience profound moments of love, loss, and epiphany.

Where it's reviewed:
Booklist, October 15, 2010, page 19
Library Journal, September 15, 2010, page 67

New York Times Book Review, November 14, 2010, page 8
Publishers Weekly, September 20, 2010, page 45

Other books by the same author:
The Eastern Stars, 2009
The Last Fish Tale, 2008
The Big Oyster, 2006
Boogaloo on Second Avenue, 2005
Cod, 1997

Other books you might like:
Allegra Goodman, *The Cookbook Collector: A Novel*, 2010
Monique Truong, *The Book of Salt*, 2003
Michelle Wildgen, *But Not for Long*, 2009

641

HERVE LE TELLIER

Enough About Love

(New York: Other Press, 2011)

Story type: Contemporary
Subject(s): Love; Infidelity; Marriage
Major character(s): Anna Stein, Doctor; Louise Blum, Lawyer; Yves Janvier, Writer; Dr. Thomas Le Gall, Psychologist
Time period(s): 21st century; 2010s
Locale(s): Paris, France

Summary: The intricacies of love and fidelity are explored in Herve Le Tellier's *Enough About Love*. This volume follows four individuals whose lives intersect while playing the complex game of romance. There's Anna, a married doctor, who embarks on an affair with a carefree writer named Yves. Attorney Louise, meanwhile, is also married but finds herself involved in an affair with Anna's psychotherapist, Thomas. These four characters learn some powerful lessons about affairs of the heart and just how thoroughly they can penetrate one's entire existence. *Enough About Love* is translated by Adriana Hunter.

Where it's reviewed:
Harper's Magazine, February 2011, page 69
Publishers Weekly, December 20, 2010, page 32

Other books by the same author:
The Sextine Chapel, 2011

Other books you might like:
Allegra Goodman, *The Cookbook Collector: A Novel*, 2010
Diane Johnson, *Le Divorce*, 1997
David Levithan, *The Lover's Dictionary*, 2011

642

CAROLINE LEAVITT

Pictures of You: A Novel

(Chapel Hill, North Carolina: Algonquin Books, 2010)

Story type: Mystery
Subject(s): Marriage; Mystery; Accidents
Major character(s): April, Mother (of Sam), Spouse (of

Charlie); Charlie, Father (of Sam), Spouse (of April); Sam, Son (of April and Charlie); Isabelle, Young Woman
Time period(s): 21st century; 2010s
Locale(s): Cape Cod, Massachusetts

Summary: In Caroline Leavitt's *Pictures of You: A Novel*, two women abandon their families for different reasons on a foggy afternoon in Cape Cod. Their lives converge in a terrible car accident that leaves one of them dead. After April is killed, Isabelle is left to deal with the fallout. The young woman soon finds herself drawn to April's grieving husband, Charlie, and her asthmatic son, Sam. Together, they begin to heal. As Isabelle grows closer to the family, Charlie realizes that he may not have known his wife very well after all. Soon, they start to unravel the mystery of where April was going on that fateful afternoon.

Where it's reviewed:
Booklist, November 15, 2010, page 22
Library Journal, September 1, 2010, page 103
O, The Oprah Magazine, January 2011, page 98
Publishers Weekly, August 23, 2010, page 25

Other books by the same author:
Girls in Trouble, 2004
Coming Back to Me, 2001
Live Other Lives, 1995
Into Thin Air, 1993
Family, 1987

Other books you might like:
Antonya Nelson, *Bound*, 2010
Allison Winn Scotch, *The Department of Lost and Found*, 2007
Ayelet Waldman, *Red Hook Road*, 2010

643

BRIAN LEUNG

Take Me Home

(New York: HarperCollins, 2010)

Story type: Historical
Subject(s): Immigrants; Chinese (Asian people); Miners
Major character(s): Adele "Addie" Maine, Sister (of Tom); Wing Lee, Miner; Tom, Brother (of Addie); Muuk, Miner
Time period(s): 19th century; (1880s); 20th century; 1920s
Locale(s): Dire, Wyoming

Summary: Set in the rural coal-mining community of Dire, Wyoming, Brian Leung's *Take Me Home* follows Addie Maine as she returns to the town that holds an abundance of personal pain and terror. Addie's homecoming calls forth memories of her long-ago relationship with local Chinese coal miner Wing Lee, a man with whom she shared a clandestine association—and a dark secret. Now Addie must once again face Wing and the history they share, confronting the long-buried ghosts of a relationship that still haunt her every waking moment.

Where it's reviewed:
The Denver Post, November 7, 2010, page E15
Kirkus Reviews, September 1, 2010, page 815

Library Journal, August 2010, page 70
Publishers Weekly, August 23, 2010, page 27

Other books by the same author:
Lost Men, 2007
World Famous Love Acts, 2004

Other books you might like:
Robert Goolrick, *A Reliable Wife: A Novel*, 2009
Nami Mun, *Miles from Nowhere*, 2008
Robert J. Randisi, *The Sons of Daniel Shaye: Pearl River Junction*, 2006
Ron Rash, *Serena*, 2008
Richard S. Wheeler, *North Star: A Barnaby Skye Novel*, 2009

644

YAN LIANKE

Dream of Ding Village

(New York: Grove Press, 2011)

Story type: Contemporary
Subject(s): AIDS (Disease); China; Family
Major character(s): Shuiyang, Father (of Ding Hui); Ding Hui, Wealthy (blood trader), Son (of Shuiyang)
Time period(s): 20th century; 1990s
Locale(s): Henan, China

Summary: Yan Lianke's *Dream of Ding Village* is set in a fictional rural community in the Henan province of China. It is the 1990s and AIDS is ravaging this small village; at the heart of the village is Ding Hui and his family. Ding Hui has built up a fortune as a peddler of tainted blood, even as one of his sons has already died from AIDS and another is living with it. Soon Hui's father, Shuiyang, intervenes, and sets out to help the villagers of Ding get the assistance they need and rebuild their lives. This volume is translated by Cindy Carter.

Where it's reviewed:
Booklist, January 1, 2011, page 42
Publishers Weekly, September 6, 2010, page 1

Other books by the same author:
Serve the People, 2008

Other books you might like:
Wang Gang, *English*, 2009
Myla Goldberg, *Wickett's Remedy*, 2005
Ma Jian, *Beijing Coma: A Novel*, 2008
Yiyun Li, *The Vagrants: A Novel*, 2009

645

R. ZAMORA LINMARK

Leche

(Minneapolis, Minnesota: Coffee House Press, 2011)

Story type: Contemporary
Subject(s): Travel; Humor; Homosexuality
Major character(s): Vince, Homosexual, Expatriate
Time period(s): 20th century; 1990s (1991)
Locale(s): Manila, Philippines

Summary: It's been 13 years since Vince left his homeland of the Philippines for the beauty of Hawaii. Now, thanks to a contest he's won, the expatriate is returning home as a proud gay man in his early 20s. Vince expects a fun and typical trip, made even better by his free accommodations, but he's met with more than a few surprises, culture shocks, and political implications. Vince, hoping to learn more about his heritage, soon finds himself trying to navigate the lively and quirky city of Manila amid a cast of unusual characters, including the President's actress daughter, a politically driven movie director, and a rebellious nun.

Where it's reviewed:
Library Journal, February 15, 2011, page 100
Publishers Weekly, January 3, 2011, page 2

Other books by the same author:
The Evolution of a Sigh, 2008
Prime-Time Apparitions, 2005
Rolling the R's, 1995

Other books you might like:
Peter Bacho, *Cebu*, 1991
Jessica Hagedorn, *Dogeaters*, 1990
Lucia Orth, *Baby Jesus Pawn Shop*, 2008

646

LAURA LIPPMAN

I'd Know You Anywhere
(New York: HarperCollins, 2010)

Subject(s): Prisoners; Rape; Murder
Major character(s): Eliza Benedict, Crime Victim, Spouse, Mother; Walter Bowman, Kidnapper, Prisoner, Murderer
Time period(s): 21st century; 2010s
Locale(s): District of Columbia, United States

Summary: In Laura Lippman's *I'd Know You Anywhere*, housewife Eliza Benedict moves with her husband, daughter, and son from England back to her hometown of Washington, D.C. One day she receives a letter that shakes her world. It's from Walter Bowman, the man who kidnapped her when she was 15 years old. Eliza remembers the horrific experience, and the memories bring back the pain she's kept hidden deep inside for more than two decades. Bowman, a rapist and murderer, held her hostage but eventually set her free. Others weren't so lucky. Now he's contacted her just weeks before he is set to be put to death for his crimes. At first Eliza feels fear and tries to ignore the letter. But then her curiosity gets the best of her: Why did he let her live all those years ago? She makes the fateful decision to contact him.

Where it's reviewed:
Booklist, May 1, 2010, page 30
New York Times Book Review, September 19, 2010, page 23
O, The Oprah Magazine, September 2010, page 160
People, August 30, 2010, page 45
Publishers Weekly, August 2, 2010, page 31

Other books by the same author:
Life Sentences, 2009
Hardly Knew Her, 2008
What the Dead Know, 2008
The Power of Three, 2005
Every Secret Thing, 2003

Other books you might like:
Kate Atkinson, *When Will There Be Good News?: A Novel*, 2008
Emma Donoghue, *Room*, 2010
Gillian Flynn, *Dark Places*, 2009
Tana French, *Faithful Place: A Novel*, 2010
Stewart O'Nan, *Snow Angels: A Novel*, 1994

647

WILLIAM LYCHACK

The Architect of Flowers
(Boston: Houghton Mifflin Harcourt, 2011)

Subject(s): Interpersonal relations; Conduct of life; Short stories

Summary: William Lychack's *The Architect of Flowers* is a compilation of the author's short fiction and deals primarily with human relationships and the seemingly mundane details of everyday life. The situations that comprise these stories illustrate such events as an elderly woman who teaches a bird to steal and a police officer who is forced to kill a hurt dog. Titles in this volume include "Chickens," "Thin End of the Wedge," "Love Is a Temper," "Like a Demon," and the title tale.

Where it's reviewed:
Library Journal, February 1, 2011, page 58
Publishers Weekly, December 6, 2010, page 29

Other books by the same author:
The Wasp Eater, 2004

Other books you might like:
Stuart Dybek, *The Coast of Chicago*, 1991
Alan Heathcock, *Volt*, 2011
Ron Rash, *Burning Bright: Stories*, 2010
Wells Tower, *Everything Ravaged, Everything Burned*, 2009

648

GREGORY MAGUIRE

The Next Queen of Heaven
(New York: Harper, 2010)

Story type: Contemporary
Subject(s): Mother-daughter relations; Christmas; Humor
Major character(s): Leontina Scales, Religious; Tabitha, Daughter (of Leontina); Jeremy Carr, Director (choir director), Homosexual
Time period(s): 20th century; 1990s (1999)
Locale(s): Thebes, New York

Summary: In *The Next Queen of Heaven*, Gregory Maguire charts the experiences of small-town residents as they stumble toward the year 2000. The denizens of Thebes, New York, are each facing unique, hilarious challenges while preparing for the new millennium. Among them are Leontina Scales, who must deal with a crisis of faith as well as the shenanigans of her determined children; gay choirmaster Jeremy Carr, who is torn between his desires and his dreams; and the performers of a Christmas pageant that doesn't quite go off as planned.

Where it's reviewed:
Booklist, September 15, 2010, page 28
Publishers Weekly, August 23, 2010, page 30

Other books by the same author:
Matchless: A Christmas Story, 2009
Mirror Mirror, 2003
Lost, 2001
Confessions of an Ugly Stepsister, 1999
Wicked: The Life and Times of the Wicked Witch of the West, 1995

Other books you might like:
Lauren Groff, *The Monsters of Templeton*, 2008
Kathleen Kent, *The Heretic's Daughter*, 2008
Valerie Martin, *Trespass*, 2007

649

STEVE MARTIN

An Object of Beauty

(New York: Grand Central Publishing, 2010)

Story type: Contemporary
Subject(s): Art; Social class
Major character(s): Lacey Yeager, Art Dealer
Time period(s): 20th century-21st century; 1990s-2000s
Locale(s): New York, New York

Summary: Actor and writer Steve Martin paints a detailed picture of the New York City art scene during the end of the 20th century in his novel *An Object of Beauty*. Lacey Yeager uses her extreme ambition to climb to the peak of New York City society. She uses her allure to get the best jobs, the most useful friends, and the richest lovers. However, as the country's economy begins to decline, Lacey finds herself scrambling to recapture the success that once came so easily. Martin is also the author of a collection of short stories and a well-received novella titled *Shopgirl*, which was made into a film.

Where it's reviewed:
Entertainment Weekly, November 26, 2010, page 74
The Houston Chronicle, November 21, 2010, page 14
The New York Times, November 29, 2010, page C1
New York Times Book Review, November 28, 2010, page 9
USA Today, December 7, 2010, page 3D

Other books by the same author:
Late for School, 2010
The Pleasure of My Company, 2003
The Pleasure of My Company, 2003
Shopgirl, 2000
Pure Drivel, 1998

Other books you might like:
Kate Christensen, *The Great Man*, 2007
Danielle Ganek, *Lulu Meets God and Doubts Him*, 2007
Allan Gurganus, *Plays Well with Others*, 1997
Claire Messud, *The Emperor's Children*, 2006
Samantha Peale, *The American Painter Emma Dial*, 2009

650

ARMISTEAD MAUPIN

Mary Ann in Autumn

(New York: HarperCollins, 2010)

Series: Tales of the City Series. Book 8
Story type: Literary; Series
Subject(s): Homosexuality; Interpersonal relations; Urban life
Major character(s): Mary Ann Singleton, Television Personality; Michael Tolliver, Gardener, Friend (of Mary Ann); Shawna, Daughter (of Mary Ann), Journalist (sex blogger); Jake Greenleaf, Assistant (to Michael); DeDe Halcyon-Wilson, Socialite; Anna Madrigal, Landlord (of Mary Ann, former)
Time period(s): 21st century; 2010s
Locale(s): San Francisco, California

Summary: Mary Ann Singleton has returned to her network of friends in San Francisco after a 20-year absence. Having left her husband and daughter on the West Coast for a television job in Manhattan, Mary Ann is in need of a friend and turns first to Michael Tolliver. While staying with Michael and his assistant, Jake Greenleaf, she becomes reacquainted with the cast of characters she left behind—DeD Halcyon-Wilson, a socialite; her one-time landlady, Anna Madrigal; and her own daughter, Shawna, who is enjoying success as a sex writer on the Internet. *Mary Ann in Autumn* is the eighth book in the Tales of the City series.

Where it's reviewed:
Booklist, October 15, 2010, page 20
The New York Times, November 18, 2010, page C6
New York Times Book Review, November 14, 2010, page 9
Publishers Weekly, August 30, 2010, page 27
USA Today, November 23, 2010, page 7D

Other books by the same author:
Michael Tolliver Lives, 2007
The Night Listener, 2000
Maybe the Moon, 1992
Back to Barbary Lane, 1991
Tales of the City, 1978

Other books you might like:
Elizabeth Buchan, *Revenge of the Middle-Aged Woman*, 2003
Fannie Flagg, *I Still Dream About You: A Novel*, 2010
Christina Schwarz, *All Is Vanity*, 2002
Carol Shields, *Unless*, 2002

651

JOYCE MAYNARD

The Good Daughters

(New York: William Morrow, 2010)

Subject(s): Friendship; Family; Women
Major character(s): Ruth Plank, Friend (of Dana); Dana Dickerson, Friend (of Ruth)
Time period(s): 20th century-21st century; 1950s-2010s
Locale(s): New Hampshire, United States

Summary: In *The Good Daughters*, best-selling author Joyce Maynard shares the story of the Planks and the Dickersons, two New Hampshire families tied together by the experiences of their youngest daughters. Dana Dickerson and Ruth Plank are born on the same day, in the same hospital, and though their lives takes decidedly different paths, their two families remain inextricably connected. The girls come of age, discover love, and search for their identities in a rapidly changing world. When the truth behind their families' strange association is finally divulged, Dana and Ruth must confront startling realities about their own destinies.

Where it's reviewed:
Entertainment Weekly, August 20, 2010, page 129
People, September 13, 2010, page 69
Star Tribune, November 8, 2010, page 8E
The Tampa Tribune, August 29, 2010, page 7

Other books by the same author:
Labor Day, 2009
The Cloud Chamber, 2005
The Usual Rules, 2003
At Home in the World, 1998
To Die For, 1992

Other books you might like:
Julia Glass, *I See You Everywhere*, 2008
Anne Tyler, *Digging to America*, 2006
Ayelet Waldman, *Red Hook Road*, 2010

652

PAULA MCLAIN

The Paris Wife

(New York: Ballantine Books, 2011)

Story type: Historical
Subject(s): Marriage; Writers; Voyages and travels
Major character(s): Hadley Richardson Hemingway, Spouse (of Ernest); Ernest Hemingway, Spouse (of Hadley), Writer
Time period(s): 20th century
Locale(s): Europe

Summary: Paula McLain's *The Paris Wife* brings to life the often-overlooked adventures of Ernest Hemingway's devoted spouse, Hadley Richardson Hemingway. Injured as a child, Hadley never thought she had many prospects in the way of marriage, but when she meets a charismatic Ernest Hemingway, her entire life changes. The two travel the world together and gather research for Hem-

ingway's novels, though it is Hadley who takes center stage in this story of a woman who, though eventually spurned, provided great love and support to one of the greatest writers of the 20th century.

Where it's reviewed:
Library Journal, November 15, 2010, page 60
Publishers Weekly, December 6, 2010, page 27

Other books by the same author:
A Ticket to Ride, 2008

Other books you might like:
Kate Christensen, *The Great Man*, 2007
Nancy Horan, *Loving Frank: A Novel*, 2007
Susan Vreeland, *Clara and Mr. Tiffany*, 2011

653

SAM MEEKINGS

Under Fishbone Clouds

(New York: Thomas Dunne Books, 2010)

Subject(s): Chinese (Asian people); Chinese history; Marriage
Major character(s): Jinyi, Spouse (of Yuying); Yuying, Spouse (of Jinyi)
Time period(s): 20th century-21st century; 1940s-2000s
Locale(s): China

Summary: China's Cultural Revolution provides the backdrop to Sam Meekings's *Under Fishbone Clouds*. Moving back and forth in time, this volume illustrates the love story between Jinyi and Yuying, shedding light on the personal and professional challenges they endure under Communist rule. But through it all—from the imprisonment of their sons to the couple's enforced separation—Jinyi and Yuying remain true to one another and the ideals of their union, offering a poignant tribute to the power of love. First novel.

Where it's reviewed:
Booklist, October 15, 2010, page 31
Library Journal, November 1, 2010, page 57
The New York Times, December 9, 2010, page C9
New York Times Book Review, December 12, 2010, page 23
Publishers Weekly, August 30, 2010, page 27

Other books you might like:
Lisa Huang Fleischman, *Dream of the Walled City*, 2000
Ma Jian, *Beijing Coma: A Novel*, 2008
Ha Jin, *Waiting*, 1999
Yiyun Li, *The Vagrants: A Novel*, 2009
Anchee Min, *Pearl of China: A Novel*, 2009

654

ELLEN MEEROPOL

House Arrest

(Pasadena: Red Hen Press, 2011)

Story type: Contemporary
Subject(s): Nursing; Friendship; Cults

Popular Fiction

Major character(s): Emily Klein, Nurse; Pippa Glenning,
   Cult Member
Time period(s): 21st century; 2010s
Locale(s): United States

Summary: The friendship between two women and their
respective pain are explored in Ellen Meeropol's *House
Arrest*. Emily Klein is a home health nurse who has been
dispatched to care for Pippa Glenning, a young, pregnant
mother on house arrest after the accidental deaths of her
two children. The women establish a surprising rapport
that inspires each of them to reach into the pain of their
pasts and rely on their strength—and one another—to set
themselves free. First novel.

Where it's reviewed:
Library Journal, January 2011, page 88
Publishers Weekly, November 29, 2010, page 28

Other books you might like:
David Ebershoff, *The 19th Wife*, 2008
Julia Glass, *The Widower's Tale*, 2010
Ayelet Waldman, *Red Hook Road*, 2010

655

DINAW MENGESTU

How to Read the Air

(New York: Riverhead Books, 2010)

Story type: Contemporary
Subject(s): Immigrants; Parent-child relations; Travel
Major character(s): Yosef, Immigrant (Ethiopian); Mariam,
   Immigrant (Ethiopian), Spouse (of Yosef)
Time period(s): 21st century; 2010s
Locale(s): Illinois, United States; Tennessee, United States

Summary: In *How to Read the Air* by Dinaw Mengestu, a
young man recreates a journey made by his immigrant
parents three decades earlier. After his father's death, 30-
year-old Jonas sets out from Peoria, Illinois for Nashville,
Tennessee in a search for clues about his own identity,
the relationship between his parents, Yosef and Mariam,
and their Ethiopian heritage. His own marriage over and
his career on hold in Manhattan, Jonas follows the path
laid by his mother and father, exploring their experiences as immigrants and how their challenges and
explosive relationship impacted his own life as a first-
generation American.

Where it's reviewed:
Library Journal, June 1, 2010, page 82
New York Times Book Review, October 10, 2010, page
   18
Newsweek, October 25, 2010, page 69
O, The Oprah Magazine, October 2010, page 157
Publishers Weekly, August 2, 2010, page 27

Other books by the same author:
The Beautiful Things That Heaven Bears, 2006

Other books you might like:
Jonathan Franzen, *Freedom*, 2010
Jhumpa Lahiri, *The Namesake*, 2003
Maaza Mengiste, *Beneath the Lion's Gaze*, 2010
Rose Tremain, *The Road Home*, 2008

656

A.D. MILLER

Snowdrops

(London: Atlantic, 2011)

Story type: Contemporary
Subject(s): Love; Crime; Russians
Major character(s): Nicholas "Nick" Platt, Lawyer; Masha,
   Lover (of Nick), Sister (of Katya); Katya, Sister (of
   Masha)
Time period(s): 21st century; 2000s
Locale(s): Moscow, Russia

Summary: A.D. Miller's *Snowdrops* follows British attorney Nick Platt as he relocates to Russia and takes a
low-level job. He soon meets two enchanting sisters, one
of whom, Masha, he can't get out of his mind. He finds
himself drawn into her orbit...and into a scheme that
could spell his personal and financial ruin. First novel.

Where it's reviewed:
Booklist, November 1, 2010, page 25
Library Journal, January 2011, page 88
Publishers Weekly, November 1, 2010, page 25
Spectator, January 22, 2011, page 35

Other books you might like:
Arthur Phillips, *Prague*, 2002
Lionel Shriver, *We Need to Talk about Kevin*, 2003
Katharine Weber, *True Confections: A Novel*, 2009

657

GRAHAM MOORE

The Sherlockian

(New York: Twelve, 2010)

Subject(s): Detective fiction; Mystery; History
Major character(s): Arthur Conan Doyle, Writer; Harold
   White, Researcher, Detective—Amateur
Time period(s): 19th century-20th century; 1890s-1900s
Locale(s): London, England

Summary: In *The Sherlockian* by Graham Moore, Sherlock Holmes fans are devastated when author Arthur Conan Doyle kills off the elusive detective in 1893. Readers throughout London fall into a deep depression,
adorning themselves with black armbands and vowing
revenge on Doyle—who never told anybody why he did
it. Years pass and in 1901, Doyle brings back the beloved
Holmes. After Doyle's death, one of his journals goes
missing. Years later, literary researcher Harold White is
invited to join the prominent Sherlock Holmes enthusiast
society called the Baker Street Irregulars. When a
Doylean scholar is found dead, White finds himself in
the middle of a murder investigaton. He vows to find the
killer—and the missing journal—in true Sherlockian
fashion.

Where it's reviewed:
Entertainment Weekly, December 10, 2010, page 17
The Houston Chronicle, December 12, 2010, page 16
The New York Times, December 16, 2010, page C1

New York Times Book Review, December 26, 2010, page 26

Publishers Weekly, October 4, 2010, page 27

Other books you might like:

Matt Bondurant, *The Third Translation*, 2005

Anthony Boucher, *The Case of the Baker Street Irregulars*, 1940

Matthew Gallaway, *The Metropolis Case*, 2010

Michael Gruber, *The Book of Air and Shadows: A Novel*, 2007

658

KATE MORTON

The Distant Hours

(New York: Atria Books, 2010)

Story type: Literary

Subject(s): History; Mystery; Mother-daughter relations

Major character(s): Edie Burchill, Co-Editor; Persephone Blythe, Aged Person, Twin (of Seraphina); Seraphina Blythe, Aged Person, Twin (of Persephone); Juniper, Sister (half-sister of Persephone and Seraphina); Raymond Blythe, Father (of Persephone, Seraphina and Juniper); Meredith, Mother (of Edie); Thomas Cavill, Fiance(e) (of Juniper, former)

Time period(s): 20th century; 1990s (1992)

Locale(s): England

Summary: In *The Distant Hours* by Kate Morton, a London editor receives a letter 50 years after it was mailed to her mother. When Edie Burchill realizes that the correspondence was written by an elderly woman who lives in Milderhurst Castle, she heads to the English countryside to visit the place where her mother spent the war years. At Milderhurst, Edie meets aged twins Persephone and Seraphina (daughters of famed children's author Raymond Blythe) and their half-sibling, Juniper, the author of the letter. As Edie soon learns, the castle holds many secrets, some of which involved her own mother, Meredith.

Where it's reviewed:

Booklist, November 15, 2010, page 25

Entertainment Weekly, December 17, 2010, page 82

Library Journal, November 1, 2010, page 57

Publishers Weekly, September 20, 2010, page 45

Other books by the same author:

Paradise Lane, 2010

Dream Breaker, 2009

The Forgotten Garden: A Novel, 2008

The House at Riverton: A Novel, 2008

The Secret, 2007

Other books you might like:

Debra Dean, *The Madonnas of Leningrad*, 2006

Jennifer Egan, *The Keep*, 2006

Daphne Kalotay, *Russian Winter: A Novel*, 2010

Diane Setterfield, *The Thirteenth Tale*, 2006

659

PETER MOUNTFORD

A Young Man's Guide to Late Capitalism

(Boston: Houghton Mifflin Harcourt, 2011)

Story type: Contemporary

Subject(s): Capitalism; Adventure; Love

Major character(s): Gabriel, Businessman

Time period(s): 21st century; 2000s

Locale(s): La Paz, Bolivia

Summary: In Peter Mountford's *A Young Man's Guide to Late Capitalism*, Gabriel is an up-and-comer at the hedge fund where he works. One of his initial assignments takes him to Bolivia, a task which, if carried out properly, could lead to a huge financial windfall for Gabriel. But the young businessman is about to run into some major obstacles in his attempts to dig out secret information on Bolivia's scandalous soon-to-be president. There's Gabriel's mother, who has personally suffered the effects of Pinochet's reign; a press agent working for the government with whom Gabriel has an affair; and the fact that Gabriel's huge raise would come at the expense of an entire nation. First novel.

Where it's reviewed:

Publishers Weekly, December 6, 2010, page 27

Other books you might like:

Russell Banks, *Rule of the Bone: A Novel*, 1995

Jonathan Evison, *West of Here*, 2011

Benjamin Kunkel, *Indecision*, 2005

660

ES'KIA MPHAHLELE

In Corner B

(New York: Penguin, 2011)

Subject(s): Apartheid; Racism; Short stories

Locale(s): South Africa

Summary: Apartheid is the theme permeating Es'kia Mphahlele's short-story collection *In Corner B*. The characters who populate these tales find their lives ravaged by the affects of racism, class divisions, and political oppression. Titles in this volume include "Nigerian Talking Points," "A Ballad of Oyo," and "Man Must Live." *In Corner B* includes an introduction by Peter N. Thuynsma.

Where it's reviewed:

Booklist, January 1, 2011, page 56

Publishers Weekly, December 20, 2010, page 34

The Wall Street Journal, January 27, 2011, page A19

Other books by the same author:

The Wanderers, 1984

Chirundu, 1979

Other books you might like:

Chimamanda Ngozi Adichie, *Half of a Yellow Sun: A Novel*, 2006

Michael Chapman, *Omnibus of a Century of South African Short Stories*, 2009
Nadine Gordimer, *Loot, and Other Stories*, 2003

661

MANUEL MUNOZ

What You See in the Dark
(Chapel Hill: Algonquin Books of Chapel Hill, 2011)

Subject(s): Movie industry; Love; Murder
Major character(s): Alfred "The Director" Hitchcock, Director; Janet "The Actress" Leigh, Actress; Dan Watson, Lover (of Teresa); Teresa Garza, Lover (of Dan)
Time period(s): 20th century; 1950s
Locale(s): Bakersfield, California
Summary: In *What You See in the Dark*, author Manuel Munoz weaves two stories of murder, centering on the creation of the movie *Psycho*. Alfred Hitchcock and Janet Leigh are working together to make the legendary film, but, meanwhile, there is a real-life horror story playing out nearby. Dan Watson and Teresa Garza are two lovers whose romance is playing out near the set of the movie, but things go horribly wrong, and their relationship ends in murder. The two stories then converge to create an all-encompassing look at crime, creativity, and the thin line between the two. First novel.

Where it's reviewed:
Booklist, February 1, 2011, page 39
Library Journal, December 2010, page 105
Publishers Weekly, January 17, 2011, page 1

Other books by the same author:
The Faith Healer of Olive Avenue, 2007
Zigzagger, 2003

Other books you might like:
Michael Chabon, *The Amazing Adventures of Kavalier & Clay: A Novel*, 2000
Glen David Gold, *Sunnyside: A Novel*, 2009
Joyce Carol Oates, *Blonde: A Novel*, 2000

662

SENA JETER NASLUND

Adam and Eve: A Novel
(New York: HarperCollins, 2010)

Story type: Adventure
Subject(s): Religion; Futuristic society; Extraterrestrial life
Major character(s): Thom Bergmann, Spouse (of Lucy), Scientist (astrophysicist); Lucy, Spouse (of Thom); Pierre Saad, Anthropologist, Friend (of Thom); Adam, Military Personnel (U.S. soldier)
Time period(s): 21st century; 2010s (2017)
Locale(s): Cairo, Egypt; France
Summary: In *Adam and Eve: A Novel* by Sena Jeter Naslund, a widow and a soldier find love in a new Garden of Eden as they try to protect the outside world

from a secret that will test all faiths. Lucy Bergmann is transporting a computer flash drive containing information about her recently deceased husband Thom's search for extraterrestrial life when her plane crashes in the Middle East. In the ancient land near the Tigris and Euphrates rivers, Lucy meets Adam, a disillusioned soldier who guides her out of the wilderness. Meanwhile, Thom's colleague, anthropologist Pierre Saad, holds a secret of his own—a book that exposes the true author of the Book of Genesis.

Where it's reviewed:
Booklist, May 1, 2010, page 4
Good Housekeeping, November 2010, page 190
Library Journal, July 2010, page 77
Publishers Weekly, June 14, 2010, page 31

Other books by the same author:
Abundance, 2008
Four Spirits, 2003
Ahab's Wife, 1999
The Disobedience of Water, 1999
Sherlock in Love, 1993

Other books you might like:
Eva Hoffman, *Appassionata*, 2009
Gish Jen, *World and Town*, 2010
Mona Simpson, *My Hollywood*, 2010

663

MICAH NATHAN

Losing Graceland
(New York: Three Rivers Press, 2011)

Story type: Contemporary
Subject(s): Adventure; College environment; Identity
Major character(s): John Barrow, Aged Person; Ben Fish, 21-Year-Old, Driver (of John)
Time period(s): 21st century; 2010s
Locale(s): Buffalo, New York; Memphis, Tennessee
Summary: Two men head cross country to Elvis Presley's Graceland in hopes of finding salvation in Micah Nathan's *Losing Graceland*. Ben Fish is a recent college graduate dealing with the death of his father and a breakup with his longtime girlfriend. He accepts an offer to drive John Barrow, who thinks he's Elvis, from New York State to Memphis, Tennessee, where John plans to track down his missing granddaughter. Their adventure leads them into some unexpected terrain, where each man must confront the realities of the past, present, and future.

Where it's reviewed:
Booklist, November 15, 2010, page 22
Library Journal, November 1, 2010, page 56
Publishers Weekly, October 4, 2010, page 26

Other books by the same author:
Gods of Aberdeen, 2005

Other books you might like:
Michael Dahlie, *A Gentleman's Guide to Graceful Living*, 2008
Binnie Kirshenbaum, *The Scenic Route*, 2009
Renee Manfredi, *Running Away with Frannie*, 2006

Tod Wodicka, *All Shall Be Well; and All Shall Be Well; and All Manner of Things Shall Be Well*, 2008

664

ANTONYA NELSON

Bound

(New York: Bloomsbury, 2010)

Story type: Contemporary
Subject(s): Childhood; Parenthood; Friendship
Major character(s): Catherine Desplaines, Guardian (of Cattie), Friend (of Misty), Spouse (of Oliver); Cattie, Teenager; Misty, Mother (of Cattie), Friend (of Catherine), Accident Victim; Oliver, Spouse (of Catherine)
Time period(s): 21st century; 2010s
Locale(s): Wichita, Kansas

Summary: Antonya Nelson's *Bound* tells the story of Catherine Desplaines, who is appointed guardian of teenaged Cattie after Catherine's best friend and Cattie's mother, Misty, is killed in a car accident. The arrival of Cattie impels Catherine to reflect on her own childhood, marked by her mother's exacting ways and the terror of a serial killer's presence in the community. As Catherine deals with sudden motherhood, she must also confront the harsh realities of life with her womanizing husband, Oliver, who is spending more and more time with his mistress and seems ready to walk out the door for good.

Where it's reviewed:
The New York Times, October 28, 2010, page D1
New York Times Book Review, October 3, 2010, page 18
O, The Oprah Magazine, October 2010, page 164
People, October 18, 2010, page 51

Other books by the same author:
Nothing Right, 2008
Some Fund, 2006
Living to Tell, 2000
Nobody's Girl, 1998
Talking in Bed, 1996

Other books you might like:
Dan Chaon, *You Remind Me of Me*, 2004
Julia Glass, *I See You Everywhere*, 2008
Kent Haruf, *Plainsong*, 1999
Stephanie Kallos, *Sing Them Home: A Novel*, 2009
Patrick Somerville, *The Cradle: A Novel*, 2009

665

AMELIE NOTHOMB

Hygiene and the Assassin

(Rome; New York: Europa Editions, 2010)

Subject(s): Writers; Cancer; Journalism
Major character(s): Pretextat Tach, Cancer Patient, Writer; Nina, Journalist
Time period(s): 20th century
Locale(s): France

Summary: In *Hygiene and the Assassin*, Amelie Nothomb tells the story of a terminally ill author who allows a determined young journalist into his orbit. Pretextat Tach is a Nobel Prize-winning writer who also happens to be one of the most offensive men on the planet. He's a rude, prejudiced, overweight old codger, but when news of his impending death leaks to the media, he's suddenly the most sought-after interview subject in the country. Nina is the only one of the selected journalists who can stand Tach, mainly because she's thoroughly inspected his life and history. When she confronts the dying writer about the actions of his past, he slowly starts to admire her integrity, thereby transforming his final days into a very unexpected experience.

Where it's reviewed:
Library Journal, September 15, 2010, page 61
Publishers Weekly, September 13, 2010, page 25

Other books by the same author:
Tokyo Fiancee, 2008
The Book of Proper Names, 2004
The Character of Rain, 2002
Fear and Trembling, 2001
Loving Sabotage, 2000

Other books you might like:
Nicholson Baker, *The Anthologist: A Novel*, 2009
Valerie Martin, *The Confessions of Edward Day*, 2009
Philip Roth, *Exit Ghost*, 2007

666

SUSAN HEYBOER O'KEEFE

Frankenstein's Monster

(New York: Three Rivers Press, 2010)

Story type: Horror
Subject(s): Monsters; Horror; Human behavior
Major character(s): Robert Walton, Shipowner, Explorer; Frankenstein, Monster, Narrator; Lily Winterbourne, Niece (of Robert)
Time period(s): 19th century; 1820s (1828)
Locale(s): England

Summary: Written by best-selling author Susan Heyboer O'Keefe, *Frankenstein's Monster* is the suspenseful sequel to Mary Shelley's classic horror novel *Frankenstein*. O'Keefe's follow-up begins right where Shelley's tale left off, with the death of Victor Frankenstein and the vengeful vow of ship captain Robert Walton to destroy Victor's creature. The monster, who narrates this novel, is desperate to outmaneuver Walton's attempts on his life and decides to travel to England to kill the captain's family. Along the way, Frankenstein shockingly discovers both his heart and humanity when he meets Walton's impulsive niece, Lily Winterbourne, and falls madly in love with her.

Where it's reviewed:
Booklist, October 15, 2010, page 32
Library Journal, June 15, 2010, page S2
Publishers Weekly, August 16, 2010, page 30

Other books by the same author:
Hungry Monster ABC, 2007

Baby Day, 2006
Christmas Gifts, 2004
Death by Eggplant, 2004
One Hungry Monster, 1989

Other books you might like:
Peter Ackroyd, *The Casebook of Victor Frankenstein*,
     2008
Geraldine Brooks, *March*, 2004
Elizabeth Kostova, *The Historian*, 2005
Valerie Martin, *Mary Reilly*, 1990
Laurie Sheck, *A Monster's Notes*, 2009

667

STEWART O'NAN

Emily, Alone

(New York: Viking, 2011)

Story type: Contemporary
Subject(s): Aging (Biology); Family; Conduct of life
Major character(s): Emily Maxwell, Aged Person; Arlene,
     Relative (sister-in-law of Emily)
Time period(s): 21st century; 2010s
Locale(s): Pittsburgh, Pennsylvania

Summary: Stewart O'Nan's *Emily, Alone*, the sequel to
Wish You Were Here, centers on elderly Emily Maxwell,
whose comings and goings depend upon her aging sister-
in-law, Arlene. But after Arlene has a stroke and is
incapacitated, Emily is suddenly on her own, forced to
reach out to others in her life. Among them are her
children and grandchildren, and Emily must learn a
whole new way of communicating and connecting with
her family.

Where it's reviewed:
Library Journal, February 1, 2011, page 55
Publishers Weekly, December 13, 2010, page 1

Other books by the same author:
Songs for the Missing, 2008
The Good Wife, 2005
Wish You Were Here, 2002
Everyday People, 2001
Snow Angels: A Novel, 1994

Other books you might like:
Michael Dahlie, *A Gentleman's Guide to Graceful
     Living*, 2008
Julia Glass, *The Widower's Tale*, 2010
Sue Miller, *The Senator's Wife*, 2008

668

TEA OBREHT

The Tiger's Wife

(New York: Random House, 2011)

Subject(s): Detective fiction; Mystery; Death
Major character(s): Natalia, Doctor, Detective—Amateur
Time period(s): 21st century; 2010s
Locale(s): The Balkans

Summary: *The Tiger's Wife*, by Tea Obreht, explores the
life of a young doctor living in the Balkans. When Natalia hears of the strange circumstances surrounding her
grandfather's death, she leaves behind her life as a doctor to try and put the pieces together. She trades her
place at the orphanage for a trip around the world—
which may never end. Natalia knows that her grandfather
died while searching for a man who claimed to be immortal, but she can't figure out what would lead a reason-
able man on a journey such as this. She sets off to find
the elusive "deathless man" and finds herself in the midst
of an adventure.

Where it's reviewed:
Library Journal, January 2011, page 89
Publishers Weekly, January 17, 2011, page 26

Other books you might like:
Jonathan Safran Foer, *Everything Is Illuminated*, 2002
Rivka Galchen, *Atmospheric Disturbances: A Novel*,
     2008
Aleksandar Hemon, *The Lazarus Project*, 2008

669

BRAGI OLAFSSON

The Ambassador

(Rochester, New York: Open Letter, 2010)

Story type: Contemporary
Subject(s): Family; Poetry; Self awareness
Major character(s): Sturla Jon Jonsson, Writer (poet)
Time period(s): 21st century; 2010s
Locale(s): Lithuania

Summary: Bragi Olaffson's *The Ambassador* chronicles
the unusual adventures of a drunken Icelandic poet.
Sturla Jon Jonsson is attending a Lithuanian literary
gathering, which turns out to be an eye-opening series of
confrontations and challenges. Fending off accusations
of plagiarism and the affections of an overzealous
hooker, Sturla slowly comes to realize how he got to this
strange place in life. Through stories of his family and
his history, Sturla discovers the most creative, inventive
story of all: his own. *The Ambassador* is translated from
Icelandic by Lytton Smith.

Where it's reviewed:
Booklist, October 1, 2010, page 27
Publishers Weekly, August 16, 2010, page 32

Other books by the same author:
Pets, 2008

Other books you might like:
Nicholson Baker, *The Anthologist: A Novel*, 2009
Kate Christensen, *The Epicure's Lament*, 2004
J.M. Coetzee, *Diary of a Bad Year*, 2007
Tod Wodicka, *All Shall Be Well; and All Shall Be Well;
     and All Manner of Things Shall Be Well*, 2008

670

E.C. OSONDU

Voice of America

(New York: Harper, 2010)

Subject(s): Africans; Cultural identity; Cultural conflict
Locale(s): Nigeria

Summary: In *Voice of America*, author E.C. Osundo sheds light on the cultural and historical gap that has grown between the United States and Nigeria. Through a collection of 18 short stories, Osundo captures the experiences of refugees, poor villagers, and fractured families as they struggle to scrape by and remain true to their cultural heritage in the face of Western influence. Titles in this volume include "Jimmy Carter's Eyes," "Our First American," "Waiting," "Welcome to America," and the title story.

Where it's reviewed:
Booklist, September 15, 2010, page 30
Library Journal, July 2010, page 80
The New York Times, November 18, 2010, page C6
Publishers Weekly, September 27, 2010, page 35

Other books you might like:
Chimamanda Ngozi Adichie, *The Thing Around Your Neck*, 2009
Uwem Akpan, *Say You're One of Them*, 2008
Buchi Emecheta, *The New Tribe*, 2000

671

ANN PACKER

Swim Back to Me

(New York: Knopf, 2011)

Subject(s): Family; Interpersonal relations; Short stories

Summary: Ann Packer's *Swim Back to Me* contains a collection of the author's short stories as well as two novellas. The tales of this volume follow characters undergoing monumental emotional changes, from the sensitive relationship between two teenagers to a woman coming to terms with her missing husband. Titles in this volume include "Molten," "Dwell Time," "Her First Born," and "Walk for Mankind."

Where it's reviewed:
Library Journal, January 2011, page 92
Publishers Weekly, December 13, 2010, page 34

Other books by the same author:
Songs without Words, 2007
The Dive from Clausen's Pier, 2002
Mendocino and Other Stories, 1994

Other books you might like:
Raymond Carver, *What We Talk about When We Talk about Love: Stories*, 1981
Joyce Carol Oates, *Sourland: Stories*, 2010
Jennifer Weiner, *The Guy Not Taken: Stories*, 2006

672

JEREMY PAGE

Sea Change

(New York: Viking, 2010)

Story type: Contemporary
Subject(s): Grief; Family; Imagination
Major character(s): Guy, Spouse (ex-husband of Judy), Father (of Freya); Judy, Spouse (ex-wife of Guy), Mother (of Freya); Freya, Accident Victim, Daughter (of Guy and Judy)
Time period(s): 21st century; 2010s
Locale(s): East Anglia, United Kingdom

Summary: In Jeremy Page's *Sea Change*, Guy has taken to the seas after the sudden death of his young daughter. Within months of Freya's death, Guy and his wife Judy have divorced, and the newly single, grieving father lives a solitary life aboard his boat. But his fantasies are far from lonely, and Guy keeps himself entertained with dreams of what could have been. As his imaginings become more complex and more entwined with his present state of mind, Guy begins to lose his ability to distinguish fact from fiction. A chance encounter with another family eventually impels Guy to reevaluate his life and form a different perspective on his all-consuming grief.

Where it's reviewed:
The Atlanta Journal Constitution, December 19, 2010, page E4
Library Journal, November 15, 2010, page 61
People, January 10, 2011, page 47
Publishers Weekly, September 27, 2010, page 33
Star Tribune, December 29, 2010, page 2E

Other books by the same author:
Salt, 2008

Other books you might like:
Chris Bohjalian, *Before You Know Kindness*, 2004
Lily King, *Father of the Rain: A Novel*, 2010
Sue Miller, *The Lake Shore Limited*, 2010
Anita Shreve, *The Weight of Water*, 1997

673

JAY PARINI

The Passages of H.M.: A Novel of Herman Melville

(New York: Doubleday, 2010)

Story type: Literary
Subject(s): Literature; Writers; Biographies
Major character(s): Herman Melville, Alcoholic, Spouse (of Lizzie), Writer; Lizzie Melville, Spouse (of Herman); Nathaniel Hawthorne, Writer
Time period(s): 19th century

Summary: In *The Passages of H.M.*, Jay Parini provides a fictionalized account of the family life of Herman Melville, author of *Moby Dick* and *Billy Budd*. The story is told through the eyes of Lizzie Melville, the author's

Popular Fiction

wife, as she struggles with her husband's growing detachment to his family, his devotion to his writing career, and his descent into depression and alcoholism. Meanwhile, Melville's life is highlighted through third-person narrative, revealing his interactions with his mentor, Nathaniel Hawthorne, and his adventures at sea. Parini is also the author of *The Last Station* and *The Patch Boys*.

Where it's reviewed:
Booklist, September 1, 2010, page 55
Entertainment Weekly, November 5, 2010, page 75
Library Journal, September 15, 2010, page 62
New York Times Book Review, November 28, 2010, page 22
Publishers Weekly, August 2, 2010, page 27

Other books by the same author:
The Apprentice Lover, 2002
Benjamin's Crossing, 1996
Bay of Arrows, 1992
The Last Station, 1990
The Patch Boys, 1986

Other books you might like:
Tracy Chevalier, *Remarkable Creatures*, 2009
Sheridan Hay, *The Secret of Lost Things: A Novel*, 2007
Patricia O'Brien, *Harriet and Isabella*, 2008
John Pipkin, *Woodsburner: A Novel*, 2009

674

VICTORIA PATTERSON

This Vacant Paradise

(New York: Counterpoint Press, 2011)

Story type: Contemporary
Subject(s): Family; Money; Marriage
Major character(s): Esther Wilson, Granddaughter (of Eileen), Girlfriend (of Charlie); Eileen, Grandmother (of Esther); Charlie Murphy, Boyfriend (of Esther), Professor
Time period(s): 20th century; 1990s
Locale(s): Orange County, California

Summary: Victoria Patterson's *This Vacant Paradise* is set in 1990s Orange County, California, where Esther Wilson lives with her wealthy grandmother, Eileen. Eileen's motivations for helping her granddaughter are questionable at best; she wants to keep the young woman indebted to her. Desperate to marry and be on her own, Esther reconnects with former beau Charlie Murphy—much to Eileen's outrage. But can Charlie remove the woman he loves from Eileen's financial and emotional grip while reigniting the spark of their relationship? First novel.

Where it's reviewed:
Publishers Weekly, January 24, 2011, page 133

Other books by the same author:
Drift, 2009

Other books you might like:
Chandler Burr, *You or Someone Like You*, 2009
Nell Freudenberger, *The Dissident*, 2006

Christina Schwarz, *All Is Vanity*, 2002
Jane Smiley, *Ten Days in the Hills*, 2007

675

EDITH PEARLMAN

Binocular Vision: New and Selected Stories

(Wilmington, North Carolina: Lookout Books, 2011)

Subject(s): Love; Modern Life; Short stories
Summary: In *Binocular Vision: New and Selected Stories*, celebrated author Edith Pearlman presents a collection of her short fiction, culled from a lifetime of singular work. The 23 stories of this volume offer Pearlman's unique takes on the world, from America to the Middle East, Central America to central Europe, and profile characters on the brink of profound personal change. Titles in this volume include "Vaquita," "The Noncombatant," and "Hanging Fire." Ann Patchett provides an introduction to the collection.

Where it's reviewed:
Booklist, January 1, 2011, page 41
New York Times Book Review, January 16, 2011, page 1
Publishers Weekly, November 15, 2010, page 39

Other books by the same author:
How to Fall, 2005
Love Among the Greats, 2002
Vaquita, 1996

Other books you might like:
Ann Beattie, *Park City: New and Selected Stories*, 1999
Amy Bloom, *A Blind Man Can See How Much I Love You: Stories*, 2000
Antonya Nelson, *Nothing Right*, 2008

676

ALLISON PEARSON

I Think I Love You

(New York: Knopf Publishing, 2011)

Story type: Contemporary
Subject(s): Popular culture; Rock music; Adolescent interpersonal relations
Major character(s): Petra, Fanatic (of David Cassidy), Friend (of Sharon); Sharon, Friend (of Petra); David Cassidy, Musician; Bill Finn, Writer

Summary: In *I Think I Love You*, Allison Pearson tells the story of Petra, a Welsh teenager who idolizes 1970s pop singer David Cassidy. During one of his concerts, Petra and her best friend Sharon bump into a young man named Bill, who writes for a magazine based around Cassidy's comings and goings. Twenty five years later, Petra is picking up the pieces of a failing marriage and grieving her recently deceased mother when amongst her mother's belongings she finds an old letter announcing her as the winner of the Ultimate David Cassidy Quiz. When the media reports on Petra's story, she finds herself on a sojourn 25 years in the making, on her way to Las Vegas to meet David Cassidy as well as the man named Bill whom she met so long ago.

Where it's reviewed:
Booklist, October 15, 2010, page 20
Library Journal, November 1, 2010, page 58
New York Times, February 1, 2011, page C1
Publishers Weekly, October 4, 2010, page 25

Other books by the same author:
I Don't Know How She Does It, 2002

Other books you might like:
Nick Hornby, *High Fidelity*, 1995
Jonathan Tropper, *The Book of Joe*, 2004
Jennifer Weiner, *Best Friends Forever*, 2009

677

JODI PICOULT

Sing You Home
(New York: Atria Books, 2011)

Story type: Contemporary
Subject(s): Marriage; Homosexuality; Law
Major character(s): Zoe Baxter, Therapist (music therapist), Spouse (partner of Vanessa); Vanessa, Spouse (partner of Zoe), Counselor; Max, Spouse (ex-husband of Zoe)
Time period(s): 21st century; 2010s
Locale(s): United States

Summary: In best-selling author Jodi Picoult's *Sing You Home*, Zoe is a music therapist whose marriage falls apart after an attempt at in-vitro fertilization fails. Zoe then finds herself attracted to another woman, Vanessa, a school guidance counselor. Zoe's husband Max, an alcoholic who seeks refuge in the church, refuses to let Zoe and Vanessa use any of the previously frozen embryos to have a child of their own—and a legal battle ensues.

Where it's reviewed:
Booklist, January 1, 2011, page 42
Publishers Weekly, December 6, 2010, page 27

Other books by the same author:
House Rules, 2010
Handle with Care: A Novel, 2009
Change of Heart, 2008
Nineteen Minutes, 2007
Vanishing Acts, 2005

Other books you might like:
Caroline Leavitt, *Girls in Trouble*, 2004
Sue Miller, *The Good Mother*, 1986
Anita Shreve, *Rescue*, 2010

678

HANNAH PITTARD

The Fates Will Find Their Way
(New York: Ecco, 2011)

Subject(s): Missing persons; Adolescent interpersonal relations; Mystery

Major character(s): Nora Lindell, 16-Year-Old (missing person)
Time period(s): 20th century-21st century
Locale(s): United States

Summary: Hannah Pittard's *The Fates Will Find Their Way* charts the repercussions of the disappearance of 16-year-old Nora Lindell. No one is certain what exactly happened to Nora, but theories abound. Those boys, who are now grown men, left in the wake of the girl's vanishing each possess his own ideas of what led to Nora's disappearance, and each man presents his take on the events that transpired that fateful night. First novel.

Where it's reviewed:
Booklist, December 1, 2010, page 24
Library Journal, September 15, 2010, page 62
New York Times Book Review, January 30, 2011, page 7
Publishers Weekly, December 20, 2010, page 31

Other books you might like:
Myla Goldberg, *The False Friend*, 2010
Laura Lippman, *What the Dead Know*, 2007
Stewart O'Nan, *Snow Angels: A Novel*, 1994

679

FRANCINE PROSE

My New American Life
(New York: HarperCollins Publishers, 2011)

Story type: Contemporary
Subject(s): United States; Immigrants; Babysitters
Major character(s): Lula, Immigrant, Babysitter; Stanley, Businessman, Employer (of Lula), Father (of Zeke); Zeke, Student—High School, 12th Grader, Son (of Stanley)
Time period(s): 21st century; 2000s
Locale(s): New Jersey, United States

Summary: *My New American Life* is a humorous novel from Francine Prose. After visiting New York City on a tourist visa, 26-year-old Albanian immigrant, Lula, accepts an easy nannying gig in order to stay in the United States. A Wall Street businessman, Stanley, hires Lula to look after his teenage son, Zeke. Lula makes such a strong impression on Stanley that he finds a lawyer to help her earn her citizenship. Shortly after receiving her papers, Lula finds herself caught in a legal mess when three Albanian men show up at her door and ask her to hide a gun for them.

Where it's reviewed:
Booklist, February 1, 2011, page 31
Library Journal, January 2011, page 90
Publishers Weekly, January 3, 2011, page 28

Other books by the same author:
Goldengrove, 2008
A Changed Man, 2005
Blue Angel, 2000
Guided Tours of Hell, 1997
Hunters and Gatherers, 1995

Other books you might like:
Gish Jen, *Typical American*, 1991

Popular Fiction

Mona Simpson, *My Hollywood*, 2010
Rose Tremain, *The Road Home*, 2008

680

NAOMI RAGEN

The Tenth Song

(New York: St. Martin's Press, 2010)

Story type: Contemporary
Subject(s): Jews; Mother-daughter relations; Self aware-ness
Major character(s): Abigail Samuels, Spouse (of Adam), Mother (of Kayla); Kayla Samuels, Dancer (of Adam and Abigail), Student—College; Adam Samuels, Spouse (of Abigail), Father (of Kayla), Accountant
Time period(s): 21st century; 2010s
Locale(s): Israel; Boston, Massachusetts

Summary: In Naomi Ragen's *The Tenth Song*, the Samuels family seems to have it all: husband Adam is a successful accountant, wife Abigail is a pillar of Boston Jewish society, and daughter Kayla is attending Harvard and engaged to be married. But when evidence emerges of Adam's involvement in terrorist funding, the Samuels' well-ordered life begins to crumble. Kayla heads off to a remote stretch of Israeli desert, and Abigail follows after her. As her daughter becomes charmed by a magnetic Kabbalist leader, Abigail begins her own odyssey of discovery, realizing, for the first time, both the pain and purpose of her life.

Where it's reviewed:
Booklist, September 15, 2010, page 29
Publishers Weekly, August 2, 2010, page 30

Other books by the same author:
The Saturday Wife, 2007
The Covenant, 2004
The Ghost of Hannah Mendes, 1998
The Sacrifice of Tamar, 1994
Jephte's Daughter, 1989

Other books you might like:
Jonathan Dee, *St. Famous*, 1996
Joan Leegant, *Wherever You Go: A Novel*, 2010
Ilana Stanger-Ross, *Sima's Undergarments for Women*, 2009

681

ATIQ RAHIMI

A Thousand Rooms of Dream and Fear

(New York: Other Press, 2011)

Subject(s): Middle East; Friendship; Mothers
Major character(s): Farhad, Student—College; Mahnaz, Widow(er), Mother
Time period(s): 20th century; 1970s (1979)
Locale(s): Kabul, Afghanistan

Summary: The trials of the Afghan people are reflected in the characters of Atiq Rahimi's *A Thousand Rooms of Dream and Fear*. It is 1979, and Kabul college student Farhad misses curfew, is tortured by police, and is left for dead in the streets. He is rescued by widow Mahnaz, and the two embark on an unusual relationship that places them both squarely in the path of the brutal authorities and their penchant for punishment. This volume is translated by Sarah Maguire and Yama Yari.

Where it's reviewed:
Booklist, January 1, 2011, page 44
Publishers Weekly, November 29, 2010, page 30

Other books by the same author:
The Patience Stone, 2010
Earth and Ashes, 2002

Other books you might like:
Maaza Mengiste, *Beneath the Lion's Gaze*, 2010
Daniyal Mueenuddin, *In Other Rooms, Other Wonders*, 2009
Marjane Satrapi, *Persepolis: The Story of a Childhood*, 2003

682

REBECCA RASMUSSEN

The Bird Sisters

(New York: Shaye Areheart Books, 2011)

Subject(s): Sisters; Family; Women
Major character(s): Milly, Sister (of Twiss); Twiss, Sister (of Milly)
Time period(s): 20th century-21st century
Locale(s): Spring Green, Wisconsin

Summary: In *The Bird Sisters*, author Rebecca Rasmussen tells the story of Milly and Twiss, two sisters living in rural Wisconsin. Their father, whom Twiss idolizes, is injured in an accident that curtails his career as an aspiring professional golfer. Milly, meanwhile, dreams of the day she can find true love and escape. The sisters come of age and find themselves inexorably connected to the land in which they live. They finally become old women together and spend their days bird-watching and considering their relationships with the beloved property. First novel.

Where it's reviewed:
Library Journal, October 15, 2010, Page S3
Publishers Weekly, January 3, 2011, page 28

Other books you might like:
Alice Hoffman, *The Story Sisters: A Novel*, 2009
Aryn Kyle, *The God of Animals*, 2007
Elizabeth Strout, *Amy and Isabelle*, 1998

683

JEAN ROLIN

The Explosion of the Radiator Hose, and Other Mishaps, on a Journey from Paris to Kinshasa

(Champaign, Illinois: Dalkey Archive Press, 2011)

Story type: Contemporary
Subject(s): Travel; Automobiles; Africa
Major character(s): Jean Rolin, Traveler
Time period(s): 21st century
Locale(s): Congo; France

Summary: *The Explosion of the Radiator Hose, and Other Mishaps, on a Journey from Paris to Kinshasa* is a humorous and partly autobiographical novel from award-winning author Jean Rolin. The story follows Rolin's adventures and misfortunes as he attempts to cart a dilapidated Audi from France to the Congo. The automobile is intended for a Congolese security guard to be used by his family as a taxi. Unfortunately for Rolin, traveling thousands of miles through Europe and Africa with a car is no small feat. Along the way to fulfilling the unusual request, Rolin encounters unrelenting thieves, even greedier politicians, and unreliable mechanics.

Where it's reviewed:
Publishers Weekly, January 24, 2011, page 129

Other books by the same author:
Christians in Palestine, 2006

Other books you might like:
Jesse Ball, *The Way through Doors*, 2009
Roberto Bolano, *The Savage Detectives*, 2007
Binnie Kirshenbaum, *The Scenic Route*, 2009

684

PHILIP ROTH

Nemesis

(Boston, Massachusetts: Houghton Mifflin Harcourt, 2010)

Story type: Historical - World War II
Subject(s): Health; World War II, 1939-1945; Responsibility
Major character(s): Bucky Cantor, Overseer (playground director)
Time period(s): 20th century; 1940s (1944)
Locale(s): Newark, New Jersey

Summary: Philip Roth's *Nemesis* tells the story of Bucky Cantor, a young man who works as a playground director in 1944 Newark, New Jersey. As summer descends on the community, an outbreak of polio is terrorizing the citizens, and Bucky feels helplessness and desperation in his attempts to stop it. Already struggling with guilt over being unable to serve in the war, Bucky is forced to come to terms with his challenging circumstances—and the vulnerability of the human experience.

Where it's reviewed:
The Denver Post, October 24, 2010, page E11

The New York Times, October 5, 2010, page C1
New York Times Book Review, October 10, 2010, page 1
New York Times Book Review, October 31, 2010, page 6
USA Today, October 7, 2010, page 5D

Other books by the same author:
Exit Ghost, 2007
Everyman, 2006
The Plot Against America, 2004
The Human Stain, 2000
American Pastoral, 1997
The Counterlife, 1986

Other books you might like:
Julia Glass, *The Widower's Tale*, 2010
Elinor Lipman, *Inn at Lake Devine*, 1998
Tom Rachman, *The Imperfectionists: A Novel*, 2010

685

ANURADHA ROY

An Atlas of Impossible Longing

(New York: Free Press, 2011)

Story type: Family Saga
Subject(s): Family; Indians (Asian people); Love
Major character(s): Amulya, Merchant, Grandfather (of Bakul); Bakul, Granddaughter (of Amulya); Mukunda, Orphan
Time period(s): 20th century
Locale(s): Bengal, India

Summary: *An Atlas of Impossible Longing* is a sweeping family saga from author Anuradha Roy. In the small Indian village of Bengal, a multigenerational family lives in isolation, wrestling with their own demons and secrets. Amulya, the family's patriarch, sells fragrances and herbal medicines, but has his hands full overseeing the family's many woes. His mentally ill wife, who is locked away in the attic, spends her days spying on the neighbors. His son, Nirmal, struggles to raise his daughter, Bakul, after her mother died during childbirth. Bakul, for her part, spends her days exploring with Mukunda, an orphan boy taken in by the family, but as Bakul and Mukunda grow older, their affection deepens. The family sends Mukunda away, assuming it's best for everyone, but he is determined to find his way back to Bakul.

Where it's reviewed:
Library Journal, February 15, 2011, page 101
Publishers Weekly, January 17, 2011, page 24

Other books you might like:
Roopa Farooki, *Bitter Sweets*, 2007
Rohinton Mistry, *Family Matters*, 2002
Bharati Mukherjee, *Desirable Daughters*, 2002

686

SALMAN RUSHDIE

Luka and the Fire of Life

(New York: Random House, 2010)

Subject(s): Father-son relations; Voyages and travels; Adventure

Major character(s): Luka, 12-Year-Old; Rashid, Father (of Luka); Bear, Dog; Dog, Bear
Time period(s): Indeterminate Past
Locale(s): Alifbay, Fictional Location

Summary: Award-winning author Salman Rushdie crafts a magical tale of adventure and self-discovery in this sequel to 1991's *Haroun and the Sea of Stories*. *Luka and the Fire of Life* takes place in a kingdom called Alifbay, where young Luka watches helplessly as his father slips into a seemingly permanent sleep. Determined to wake him, Luka embarks on an odyssey of discovery through an enchanted land with his devoted friends Bear the dog and Dog the bear at his side. Scheduled for release in November 2010.

Where it's reviewed:
The Atlanta Journal-Constitution, November 14, 2010, page E5
New York Times Book Review, November 7, 2010, page 27
The New Yorker, January 3, 2011, page 67
Star Tribune, November 24, 2010, page 7E

Other books by the same author:
The Enchantress of Florence, 2008
Shalimar the Clown, 2005
Fury, 2001
The Ground Beneath Her Feet, 1999
The Satanic Verses, 1988

Other books you might like:
Jonathan Safron Foer, *Extremely Loud and Incredibly Close*, 2005
Mark Haddon, *The Curious Incident of the Dog in the Night-Time*, 2003
Yann Martel, *Life of Pi*, 2001

687

KAREN RUSSELL

Swamplandia!

(New York: Random House, 2011)

Story type: Fantasy
Subject(s): Swamps; Alligators; Family relations
Major character(s): Ava Bigtree, 13-Year-Old
Locale(s): Florida, United States

Summary: *Swampladia* is a novel by author Karen Russell. The book features a dilapidated Everglades tourist trap called Swampladia, which is headed by an alligator-wrestling family, the Bigtrees. As Swampladia begins to fail, the Bigtrees disband and scatter in different directions of Florida. Ava, the youngest at 13 years old, has the strength and determination to get her family back, but she must literally go through hell to retrieve them. Russell is also the author of *St. Lucy's Home for Girls Raised by Wolves*.

Where it's reviewed:
The Atlanta Journal-Constitution, February 6, 2011, page E6
Booklist, October 15, 2010, page 31
Library Journal, October 15, 2010, page 69

New York Times Book Review, February 6, 2011, page 1
Publishers Weekly, December 6, 2010, page 29

Other books by the same author:
St. Lucy's Home for Girls Raised by Wolves, 2006

Other books you might like:
Betsy Carter, *Swim to Me*, 2007
Katherine Dunn, *Geek Love*, 1989
Matthew Sharpe, *Jamestown*, 2007

688

AMY SACKVILLE

The Still Point

(Berkeley: Counterpoint, 2011)

Subject(s): Adventurers; Marriage; Family
Major character(s): Edward Mackley, Explorer; Julia, Niece (great-great-niece of Edward), Spouse (of Simon); Simon, Spouse (of Julia)
Time period(s): 19th century-21st century
Locale(s): United Kingdom

Summary: Two stories converge in Amy Sackville's *The Still Point*, both revolving around the life of famed explorer Edward Mackley, who traversed the Arctic in the 19th century. One aspect of this volume chronicles the final days of Mackley's life, spent surrounded by his past glories and dreams of travels never taken. The other perspective is set 100 years later, in which Mackley's great-great-niece Julia and her husband live in the home of Edward's brother. They too are surrounded by the century-old successes of their late relative and must come to terms with the legacy he has left. First novel.

Where it's reviewed:
Booklist, December 15, 2010, page 21
Library Journal, November 15, 2010, page 64
Publishers Weekly, November 1, 2010, page 26

Other books you might like:
A.S. Byatt, *Possession: A Romance*, 1990
Tatiana de Rosnay, *Sarah's Key*, 2007
Sue Miller, *While I Was Gone*, 1999
Maggie O'Farrell, *The Vanishing Act of Esme Lennox*, 2007
Anita Shreve, *The Weight of Water*, 1997

689

RALPH SASSONE

The Intimates

(New York: Farrar, Straus and Giroux, 2011)

Story type: Contemporary
Subject(s): Friendship; Homosexuality; Coming of age
Major character(s): Robbie, Homosexual, Friend (of Maize); Maize, Friend (of Robbie)
Time period(s): 21st century
Locale(s): New York, New York

Summary: In *The Intimates*, author Ralph Sassone tells the story of a friendship that follows two young people through the changing tides of adolescence and young adulthood. Robbie and Maize meet in high school, and though they date for a short period, Robbie is coming to terms with the fact that he is gay. Maize, meanwhile, develops relationships with older men that have a profound effect on her life. The two go their separate ways, but both eventually find their way back to one another, becoming roommates and seeing each other through the hardships and challenges of growing up. First novel.

Where it's reviewed:
Booklist, October 15, 2010, page 33
Publishers Weekly, November 8, 2010, page 41

Other books you might like:
Jonathan Franzen, *Freedom*, 2010
Joshua Henkin, *Matrimony*, 2007
Stephen McCauley, *The Object of My Affection*, 1987

690

MAX SCHAEFER

Children of the Sun
(New York: Soft Skull Press, 2010)

Subject(s): Homosexuality; Neo-Nazis; Identity
Major character(s): Tony Crawford, Teenager (skinhead), Homosexual; James, Writer, Homosexual; Nicky Crane, Leader (of skinhead movement)
Time period(s): 20th century; (1970s); 21st century; 2000s (2003)
Locale(s): London, United Kingdom

Summary: Max Schaefer's *Children of the Sun* tells the interwoven stories of two men united by their interest in Britain's skinhead subculture. In the 1970s, Tony Crawford is a closeted gay teen drawn into the increasingly violent group, while in 2003, James is telling the story of one of the group's founding members, Nicky Crane. The journeys of Tony and James gradually become more and more entwined as Tony comes to terms with his sexuality and James discovers startling neo-Nazi parallels between the movement and his own relationship with his boyfriend. First novel.

Where it's reviewed:
Booklist, September 1, 2010, page 39
Library Journal, August 2010, page 74
Publishers Weekly, July 26, 2010, page 46

Other books you might like:
Joshua Furst, *The Sabotage Cafe*, 2007
Brendan Halpin, *Dear Catastrophe Waitress*, 2007
Pagan Kennedy, *The Exes*, 1998
Dale Peck, *Martin and John: A Novel*, 1993

691

RAFIK SCHAMI

The Calligrapher's Secret
(Northampton, Massachusetts: Interlink Books, 2011)

Subject(s): Marriage; Love; Family
Major character(s): Noura, Seamstress (dressmaker),

Spouse (of Hamid); Hamid Farsi, Artist (calligrapher), Spouse (of Noura); Nasri Albani, Wealthy (philanderer); Salman, Apprentice (of Hamid); Rami Arabi, Father (of Noura)
Time period(s): 20th century; 1930s-1950s (1931-1956)
Locale(s): Damascus, Syria

Summary: In *The Calligrapher's Secret*, author Rafik Schami interweaves the stories of a group of people living in Damascus, Syria, in the middle of the 20th century. There is Hamid Farsi, a respected calligrapher, and his dressmaker wife Noura; Nasri, a ladies' man fixated on Noura; a Christian boy named Salman, who is Hamid's apprentice; and Rami Arabi, father of the beautiful Noura, who is dealing with his own irritation at how the modern world views God. Against the ever-changing backdrop of Damascus, these characters converge in astounding ways, affecting each of them and altering the courses of their lives.

Where it's reviewed:
Publishers Weekly, October 25, 2010, page 28

Other books by the same author:
The Dark Side of Love, 2009
Albert and Lila, 1999
Fatima and the Dream Thief, 1996
Damascus Nights, 1990
A Hand Full of Stars, 1990

Other books you might like:
Radwa Ashour, *Specters*, 2010
Laila Lalami, *Secret Son*, 2009
Adania Shibli, *Touch*, 2010

692

BERNHARD SCHLINK

The Weekend
(New York: Pantheon Books, 2010)

Story type: Contemporary
Subject(s): Terrorism; Friendship; Morality
Major character(s): Jorg, Convict; Christiane, Sister (of Jorg); Marko, Friend (of Jorg)
Time period(s): 21st century; 2010s
Locale(s): Europe

Summary: Award-winning author Bernhard Schlink tells a tale of zealotry and the price of fanatical devotion in *The Weekend*. Christiane has invited all of her brother Jorg's friends for an unusual reunion. Jorg is a convicted terrorist just released from prison, and Christiane is worried for his well-being now that he is back in society. She hopes to rally support from his old allies, but instead she meets opposition in Marko, who is determined to have Jorg continue in his role as leader of their old terrorist faction. *The Weekend* is translated from the original German by Shaun Whiteside.

Where it's reviewed:
Library Journal, August 2010, page 74
New York Times Book Review, October 17, 2010, page 12
The New Yorker, December 6, 2010, page 89
Publishers Weekly, July 5, 2010, page 24

Other books by the same author:
Homecoming: A Novel, 2008
Self's Deception, 2007
Self's Punishment, 2005
Flights of Love, 2001
The Reader, 1997

Other books you might like:
Russell Banks, *The Darling*, 2004
Massimo Carlotto, *The Goodbye Kiss*, 2006
John Cheever, *Falconer*, 1977

693

PAMELA SCHOENEWALDT

When We Were Strangers

(New York: HarperCollins, 2011)

Story type: Historical
Subject(s): Immigrants; Italy; Women
Major character(s): Irma Vitale, Immigrant
Time period(s): 19th century
Locale(s): Italy; Chicago, Illinois

Summary: Pamela Schoenewaldt's *When We Were Strangers* tells the story of a poverty-stricken Italian woman named Irma Vitale. Before her mother dies, the older woman advises Irma to stay in their small Italian village, but Irma is desperate to be free of her overly affectionate father. She manages to immigrate to the United States, and, along the way, encounters a string of strangers who help her forge her way in this bizarre new world. First novel.

Where it's reviewed:
Booklist, December 1, 2010, page 34
Publishers Weekly, October 11, 2010, page 23

Other books you might like:
Amy Bloom, *Away: A Novel*, 2007
Julie Orringer, *The Invisible Bridge*, 2010
Salvatore Scibona, *The End*, 2008

694

DAVID SEDARIS

Squirrel Seeks Chipmunk: A Modest Bestiary

(New York: Little, Brown and Company, 2010)

Story type: Collection
Subject(s): Fables; Animals; Humor

Summary: Beloved essayist David Sedaris regales readers with a series of funny and powerful fables focusing on various animal characters. The short stories of *Squirrel Seeks Chipmunk: A Modest Bestiary* find lovable critters caught up in all sorts of puzzling, challenging, and oftentimes hilarious situations: a cat grumbles his way through compulsory 12-step meetings; a squirrel and chipmunk discover true love with one another; and a trio of animals find solace in complaining to each other about

the powers-that-be. *Squirrel Seeks Chipmunk* includes illustrations by Ian Falconer.

Other books by the same author:
When You Are Engulfed in Flames, 2008
Dress Your Family in Corduroy and Denim, 2004
Me Talk Pretty One Day, 2001
Naked, 1998

Other books you might like:
Jasper Fforde, *The Big Over Easy: A Nursery Crime*, 2005
Kenneth Grahame, *The Wind in the Willows*, 1908
David Rakoff, *Half Empty*, 2010
David Sedaris, *When You Are Engulfed in Flames*, 2008
Bill Willingham, *Fables: 1001 Nights of Snowfall*, 2006

695

JENNY SHANK

The Ringer

(Sag Harbor, New York: Permanent Press, 2011)

Story type: Contemporary
Subject(s): Baseball; Murder; Grief
Major character(s): Ed O'Fallon, Police Officer; Patricia Maestas, Widow(er), Mother
Time period(s): 21st century; 2010s
Locale(s): Denver, Colorado

Summary: In Jenny Shank's *The Ringer*, the lives of two individuals converge in ways that reveal the injustices of the legal system and the vagaries of guilt and forgiveness. Ed O'Fallon is a policeman who shoots and kills a Latino man during a drug raid. The event sends Ed into a spiral of guilt and self-recrimination. Meanwhile, the dead man's widow, Patricia Maestas is ravaged by grief and trying to stay focused on her adolescent son, who loves baseball. Ed's own children are baseball fanatics as well, leading both Patricia and Ed to a place of mercy and strength. First novel.

Where it's reviewed:
Library Journal, February 1, 2011, page 64
Publishers Weekly, January 3, 2011, page 34

Other books you might like:
Valerie Laken, *Dream House: A Novel*, 2009
Jennifer Vanderbes, *Strangers at the Feast: A Novel*, 2010
Jeannette Walls, *Half Broke Horses: A True-Life Novel*, 2009

696

ELENA MAULI SHAPIRO

13, rue Therese

(New York: Little, Brown, and Company, 2011)

Subject(s): Women; Love; World War I, 1914-1918
Major character(s): Trevor Stratton, Scholar; Louise Brunet, Young Woman; Josianne, Secretary

Time period(s): 21st century; (2010s); 20th century; 1910s (1914-1918)

Locale(s): Paris, France

Summary: In Elena Mauli Shapiro's *13, rue Therese*, Trevor Stratton is an American man employed by a college in Paris. There he comes across a box of mementos left behind by a World War I-era woman named Louise Brunet. As he becomes increasingly fascinated with the box and the objects inside, Trevor crafts an imaginative story of Louise's life and adventures. The box, however, was no accidental find. One of Trevor's colleagues, Josianne, put the box in his possession in an attempt to test his romantic imaginings. First novel.

Where it's reviewed:
Booklist, January 1, 2011, page 56
Library Journal, November 15, 2010, page 64
Publishers Weekly, December 13, 2010, page 37

Other books you might like:
Tatiana de Rosnay, *Sarah's Key*, 2007
Julie Orringer, *The Invisible Bridge*, 2010
Tom Rachman, *The Imperfectionists: A Novel*, 2010

697

JANICE SHAPIRO

Bummer, and Other Stories

(Berkeley: Soft Skull Press, 2010)

Story type: Contemporary
Subject(s): Women; Love; Identity
Time period(s): 21st century

Summary: In *Bummer, and Other Stories*, author Janice Shapiro presents a collection of tales chronicling the experiences of women who must face difficult life decisions. From a punk-rock twentysomething to a frazzled middle-aged housewife, the characters that people these stories find themselves in potentially life-altering situations, inspiring them to rely on their intellect and emotion to reach agreeable resolutions. Titles in this volume include "Death and Disaster," "In Its Place," "Night and Day," and "1966."

Where it's reviewed:
Publishers Weekly, September 20, 2010, page 46

Other books you might like:
Junot Diaz, *Drown*, 1996
Maile Meloy, *Both Ways Is the Only Way I Want It*, 2009
Joe Meno, *Hairstyles of the Damned*, 2004

698

ADRIENNE SHARP

The True Memoirs of Little K

(New York: Farrar, Straus and Giroux, 2010)

Subject(s): History; Ballet; Russian history
Major character(s): Mathilde "Little K" Kschessinska, Narrator, Dancer (ballerina), Lover (of Nikolai); Ni-

kolai Romanov, Historical Figure, Political Figure (Russian czar)

Time period(s): 20th century
Locale(s): Russia

Summary: *The True Memoirs of Little K* is a historical novel from author Adrienne Sharp. Based on factual information, the book recounts the life of Mathilde Kschessinska, former prima ballerina for the Russian Imperial Ballet. At the age of 99, Mathilde—or Little K as she's known—decides to tell her life story in a memoir. She recounts her childhood in Russia, her great dancing skills, and her teenage love affair with Nikolai Romanov, which lasted until he became czar. Although they were pulled apart, Little K and Nikolai stayed in love. Little K moved on to seduce Nikolai's cousins, but ultimately her heart and loyalty remained with the czar. However, when the government toppled, Little K's commitment was put to the ultimate test.

Where it's reviewed:
Booklist, October 15, 2010, page 25
Library Journal, September 15, 2010, page 63
The New York Times, November 18, 2010, page C6
O, The Oprah Magazine, November 2010, page 143
Publishers Weekly, July 19, 2010, page 109

Other books by the same author:
First Love, 2005
The Sleeping Beauty, 2005
White Swan, Black Swan, 2001

Other books you might like:
Muriel Barbery, *The Elegance of the Hedgehog*, 2008
David Benioff, *City of Thieves: A Novel*, 2008
Debra Dean, *The Madonnas of Leningrad*, 2006
William Newton, *The Mistress of Abha*, 2010
Marilynne Robinson, *Gilead*, 2004

699

JIM SHEPARD

You Think That's Bad: Stories

(New York: Knopf, 2011)

Story type: Collection
Subject(s): Friendship; Romances (Fiction); Love

Summary: *You Think That's Bad: Stories* is a collection of short stories written by Jim Shepard. The characters in these pieces have found themselves in troubling predicaments; for example, a man falls in love with his brother's girlfriend, another man is required to keep secrets from his wife, but is allowed to tell his wife's secrets to his coworkers, and a woman travels the world to try to rid herself from the agony she feels over the loss of her sister. People of all different cultures and backgrounds appear throughout the pages of this collection. Shepard is also the author of *Like You'd Understand, Anyway*.

Where it's reviewed:
Library Journal, December 2010, page 110
Publishers Weekly, December 6, 2010, page 28

Other books by the same author:
Like You'd Understand Anyway, 2007
Love and Hydrogen, 2004

Project X, 2004
Nosferatu, 1998
Batting against Castro, 1996

Other books you might like:
Paula Bomer, *Baby and Other Stories*, 2010
Miranda July, *No One Belongs Here More than You: Stories*, 2007
Jon Raymond, *Livability*, 2008
Justin Taylor, *Everything Here Is the Best Thing Ever*, 2010

700

T.M. SHINE

Nothing Happens Until It Happens to You: A Novel without Pay, Perks, or Privileges

(New York: Crown, 2010)

Story type: Contemporary
Subject(s): Unemployment; Self perception; Family
Major character(s): Jeffrey Reiner, Unemployed; Alex, Neighbor (of Jeffrey)
Time period(s): 21st century; 2010s
Locale(s): Florida, United States
Summary: In T.M. Shine's *Nothing Happens Until It Happens to You: A Novel without Pay, Perks, or Privileges*, copywriter, Jeffrey Reiner has lost his longtime job, thrusting him into a mid-life crisis that threatens to fracture his entire family. Jeffrey is both thrilled and devastated at the loss of his newspaper job, but he gradually adjusts to the unemployed life. Soon he has settled into the laid-back existence of a slacker, picking up odd jobs, commiserating with those in the same position, and visiting bars during the daylight hours. But when his family starts to take note of his inactivity, Jeffrey realizes he may have to take some bold action to hold his family—and his life—together. First novel.

Where it's reviewed:
Booklist, August 1, 2010, page 26
Library Journal, June 15, 2010, page S2
Publishers Weekly, July 26, 2010, page 45

Other books by the same author:
Timeline, 2001
Fathers Aren't Supposed to Die, 2000

Other books you might like:
Michael Dahlie, *A Gentleman's Guide to Graceful Living*, 2008
Adam Haslett, *Union Atlantic: A Novel*, 2010
Ken Kalfus, *A Disorder Peculiar to the Country*, 2006
Jess Walter, *The Financial Lives of the Poets*, 2009

701

ANITA SHREVE

Rescue

(New York: Little, Brown and Company, 2010)

Story type: Contemporary
Subject(s): Family; Alcoholism; Mothers

Major character(s): Peter Webster, Worker (paramedic), Spouse (of Sheila), Father (of Rowan); Sheila Arsenault, Alcoholic, Spouse (of Peter), Mother (of Rowan); Rowan, Daughter (of Peter and Sheila)
Time period(s): 20th century-21st century; 1990s-2010s
Locale(s): Vermont, United States

Summary: In *Rescue*, bestselling author Anita Shreve crafts an emotional family drama centering on paramedic Peter Webster, his estranged wife Sheila, and their troubled daughter Rowan. After Peter rescued Sheila from a drunk-driving accident she caused, the two fell in love, married, and had Rowan. But years have passed, and Sheila, who has never confronted her drinking, has now disappeared from Peter and Rowan's life. Rowan, however, has developed serious issues of her own, and in order to combat them, Peter reaches out to the one person he hopes can help her: her mother.

Where it's reviewed:
Library Journal, October 1, 2010, page 70
The New York Times, November 18, 2010, page C6
USA Today, December 16, 2010, page 9B

Other books by the same author:
A Change in Altitude, 2009
Testimony, 2008
Body Surfing, 2007
A Wedding in December, 2005
Light on Snow, 2004

Other books you might like:
Caroline Leavitt, *Girls in Trouble*, 2004
Jodi Picoult, *Handle with Care: A Novel*, 2009
Allison Winn Scotch, *The Department of Lost and Found*, 2007

702

CHRISTINA SNEED

Portraits of a Few of the People I've Made Cry: Stories

(Amherst, Massachusetts: University of Massachusetts Press, 2010)

Subject(s): Love; Aging (Biology); Short stories

Summary: The agony and ecstasy of love serve as the major themes for the tales that comprise Christine Sneed's *Portraits of a Few of the People I've Made Cry: Stories*. The ten pieces of this volume capture love in a variety of forms: from affairs between lovers of diverse ages to relationships fueled by pain and remorse, from the effects of grief to the turmoil of revisiting the past. Winner of the Grace Paley Prize for Short Fiction, this volume includes the titles "Quality of Life," "Twelve + Twelve," and the title tale.

Where it's reviewed:
Booklist, November 15, 2010, page 23
Publishers Weekly, October 4, 2010, page 29

Other books you might like:
Mary Gaitskill, *Don't Cry: Stories*, 2009
Shirley Ann Grau, *Nine Women*, 1986
Lauren Groff, *Delicate Edible Birds: And Other Stories*, 2009

Lorrie Moore, *Birds of America*, 1998
Suzanne Rivecca, *Death Is Not an Option*, 2010

703

DANIELLE STEEL

Legacy: A Novel

(New York: Delacorte Press, 2010)

Story type: Romance
Subject(s): Family history; Genealogy; History
Major character(s): Brigitte Nicholson, Young Woman; Marc Henri, Professor; Marquise de Margerac/ Wachiwi, Indian
Time period(s): 21st century; (2010s); 18th century
Locale(s): Paris, France; Boston, Massachusetts; Sioux Falls, South Dakota; Salt Lake City, Utah

Summary: In *Legacy*, bestselling author Danielle Steel crafts a tale of romance and adventure, focusing on two couples from different eras. Brigitte Nicholson, bereft after losing both her job and her longtime beau, delves into a genealogy project that reveals some surprising information about her family's past. She finds that her Native American ancestor, Wachiwi, was somehow involved with a French nobleman. This discovery leads Brigitte on a globetrotting quest to find the truth about her family. She eventually lands in Paris, where a handsome Sorbonne professor catches her eye. Meanwhile, the story of Wachiwi unfolds, chronicling the beautiful young woman's epic adventure during the French Revolution.

Where it's reviewed:
Booklist, July 1, 2010, page 8
Publishers Weekly, August 2, 2010, page 30

Other books by the same author:
Big Girl, 2010
Family Ties, 2010
A Good Woman, 2009
Matters of the Heart, 2009
One Day at a Time, 2009
Southern Lights, 2009

Other books you might like:
Gina Holmes, *Crossing Oceans*, 2010
Julia London, *One Season of Sunshine*, 2010
Susan Mallery, *Almost Perfect*, 2010
JoAnn Ross, *The Homecoming*, 2010
Susan Wiggs, *Table for Five*, 2005

704

SCARLETT THOMAS

Our Tragic Universe

(Orlando, Florida: Houghton Mifflin Harcourt, 2010)

Story type: Contemporary; Mystical
Subject(s): Astrology; Psychics; Interpersonal relations
Major character(s): Meg Carpenter, Writer, Young Woman, Girlfriend

Time period(s): 21st century; 2010s
Locale(s): Dartmouth, United Kingdom

Summary: Aspiring writer Meg Carpenter has it rough. She promised a novel but has yet to deliver. She promised to be a good girlfriend but is fed up with her boyfriend's lack of enthusiasm about their relationship. And she promised to stay connected with family and friends, but her cell phone is out of minutes and she can't afford to buy more. In Scarlett Thomas's *Our Tragic Universe*, Meg finds that she'll do just about anything for cash—including review a new-age book about the secret to living forever. She knows little to nothing about astrology, physics, cosmology, or predicting the future, so she throws herself into years' worth of research to better the chances of her review being informative and making sense to her publisher. As she studies and reads the book, titled *The Science of Living Forever*, she discovers more about herself, her life, and her relationships with others than she ever imagined. The ultimate question remains to be answered, however: Would she really want to live forever? Would anyone?

Where it's reviewed:
Entertainment Weekly, September 3, 2010, page 77
Library Journal, July 2010, page 79
New York Times Book Review, September 19, 2010, page 15
Publishers Weekly, July 26, 2010, page 42

Other books by the same author:
The End of Mr. Y, 2006
PopCo, 2005
Going Out, 2004
In Your Face, 1999
Seaside, 1999

Other books you might like:
Aimee Bender, *An Invisible Sign of My Own*, 2000
Peter Carey, *Parrot and Olivier in America*, 2010
Liz Jensen, *My Dirty Little Book of Stolen Time*, 2006

705

STACY TINTOCALIS

The Tiki King: Stories

(Athens, Ohio: Swallow Press, 2010)

Subject(s): Interpersonal relations; Family; Short stories

Summary: In *The Tiki King: Stories*, Stacy Tintocalis presents a compilation of short stories featuring a diverse assortment of characters faced with life-changing decisions—decisions that could ultimately lead to disastrous consequences. Stories in this volume include that of a boy harboring resentment toward his father, who is fanatical about going back to his boyhood home, and the tale of a divorcee who gains a few moments of much-needed solace with the company of his ex's dog.

Where it's reviewed:
Publishers Weekly, July 26, 2010, page 47

Other books you might like:
Daniel Alarcon, *Lost City Radio*, 2007
Anthony Doerr, *Memory Wall: Stories*, 2010

Lydia Peelle, *Reasons for and Advantages of Breathing: Stories*, 2009

Matthew Pitt, *Attention Please Now*, 2010

706

COLM TOIBIN

The Empty Family: Stories
(New York: Scribner, 2011)

Story type: Collection
Subject(s): Family; Short stories; Homosexuality
Summary: In *The Empty Family: Stories*, author Colm Toibin presents nine short stories featuring unconventional familial situations. Of the protagonists in the collection, some have left behind their families in an effort to forge a new, faraway life, while others return home after years of absence. One narrative follows a Pakistani man as he struggles to start over in a foreign town. Another details the life of an Irish woman's uneasy return to Dublin after a significant absence. Many of the works in *The Empty Family* also deal with issues of homosexuality and associated feelings of division, rejection, or prejudice.

Where it's reviewed:
Booklist, November 15, 2010, page 21
The Houston Chronicle, January 2, 2011, page 14
Library Journal, November 15, 2010, page 65
New York Times Book Review, January 16, 2011, page 1
Publishers Weekly, October 11, 2010, page 24

Other books by the same author:
Brooklyn, 2009
Mothers and Sons, 2007
The Master, 2004
The Blackwater Lightship, 2000
The Story of the Night, 1997

Other books you might like:
James Joyce, *Dubliners*, 1914
David Leavitt, *Collected Stories*, 2003
Maile Meloy, *Both Ways Is the Only Way I Want It*, 2009
William Trevor, *Cheating at Canasta: Stories*, 2007

707

ROSE TREMAIN

Trespass
(London: Chatto & Windus, 2010)

Story type: Contemporary
Subject(s): Brothers and sisters; Family; Alcoholism
Major character(s): Audrun, Sister (of Aramon); Aramon, Brother (of Audrun), Alcoholic; Anthony Verey, Antiques Dealer, Brother (of Veronica); Veronica, Sister (of Anthony), Lover (of Kitty); Kitty, Lover (of Veronica)
Time period(s): 21st century; 2010s
Locale(s): France

Summary: Rose Tremain's *Trespass* tells the story of two sets of siblings whose lives take powerful, unexpected turns in the French countryside. Audrun lives with her alcoholic brother, Aramon, in a small but beautiful country house. Aramon is determined to sell the property, leading to painful confrontations with his sister, who would be out of a home should he sell the place. Meanwhile, Veronica's life is turned upside-down by the appearance of her brother, Anthony, who maneuvers his way into her world and comes between Veronica and her lover, Kitty.

Where it's reviewed:
Library Journal, August 2010, page 75
New York Times Book Review, October 24, 2010, page 23
The New Yorker, November 1, 2010, page 109

Other books by the same author:
The Road Home, 2007
Music and Silence, 2000
The Way I Found Her, 1998
Restoration, 1989
The Swimming Pool Season, 1985

Other books you might like:
Kate Christensen, *The Epicure's Lament*, 2004
Adam Haslett, *Union Atlantic: A Novel*, 2010
Valerie Laken, *Dream House: A Novel*, 2009
Joe Meno, *The Great Perhaps*, 2009
Eric Puchner, *Model Home: A Novel*, 2010

708

CHIKA UNIGWE

On Black Sisters Street
(London, England: Jonathan Cape, 2011)

Story type: Contemporary; Mystery
Subject(s): Africans; Prostitution; Murder
Major character(s): Sisi, Prostitute, Roommate; Ama, Prostitute, Roommate; Efe, Prostitute, Roommate; Joyce, Prostitute, Roommate
Time period(s): 21st century; 2010s
Locale(s): Antwerp, Belgium

Summary: Sisi, Ama, Efe, and Joyce each left her African homeland for false promises of wealth and happiness in Europe. Where they've ended up is the red light district in Belgium, controlled by a terrifying pimp and desperate for escape. Despite sharing an apartment, each woman lives an isolated existence, harboring private secrets of the past and dreams for the future. When one of them is murdered, the other three women need to come together and open their lives and hearts in hopes of finding the killer. The truth about their painful pasts, real identities, and shameful secrets come to light, revealing the sinister path that led each of them to a lifestyle of regret.

Where it's reviewed:
Library Journal, February 1, 2011, page 58
Publishers Weekly, January 10, 2011, page 27

Other books you might like:
Chimamanda Ngozi Adichie, *Half of a Yellow Sun: A Novel*, 2006
Dinaw Mengestu, *How to Read the Air*, 2010
Rose Tremain, *The Road Home*, 2008

709

SANDRO VERONESI

Quiet Chaos
(New York: Ecco, 2011)

Story type: Contemporary
Subject(s): Grief; Family; Love
Major character(s): Pietro Paladini, Businessman; Lara, Spouse (of Pietro); Eleonora, Young Woman
Time period(s): 21st century; 2010s
Locale(s): Italy

Summary: In Sandro Veronesi's *Quiet Chaos*, an Italian businessman named Pietro Paladini finds his life massively reordered after he rescues a woman from drowning. At the precise instant the rescue occurs, Pietro's wife, Lara, dies, sending Pietro into a full examination of his life and motivations. As he takes a quieter view of life and its inherent difficulties, he encounters trouble at work and even more trouble in the form of Eleonora, the young woman he saved.

Where it's reviewed:
Publishers Weekly, January 10, 2011, page 28

Other books by the same author:
The Force of the Past, 2003

Other books you might like:
Lynne Sharon Schwartz, *The Fatigue Artist: A Novel*
Leah Stewart, *Husband and Wife: A Novel*, 2010
Meg Wolitzer, *The Wife*, 2003

710

MARY VOLMER

Crown of Dust
(New York: Soho Press, 2010)

Story type: Historical
Subject(s): California Gold Rush, 1849; Frontier life; Women
Major character(s): Alex, Runaway; Emaline, Innkeeper
Time period(s): 19th century
Locale(s): Motherlode, California

Summary: Mary Volmer's *Crown of Dust* charts the experiences of a young female runaway named Alex, who dresses as a man in order to strike it rich in the California gold country of the 19th century. Once she reaches the settlement of Motherlode, Alex is taken in by innkeeper Emaline, and the two develop an unexpected friendship. With Emaline's protection, Alex is able to hide her identity and search for gold. When she at last discovers a valuable find, Alex falls under scrutiny from the locals, jeopardizing both her masquerade and her future. First novel.

Where it's reviewed:
Booklist, October 15, 2010, page 28
Library Journal, September 15, 2010, page 66
New York Times Book Review, December 26, 2010, page 20
Publishers Weekly, September 6, 2010, page 22

Other books by the same author:
Motherlode, 2005

Other books you might like:
Isabel Allende, *Daughter of Fortune*, 1999
Sarah Blake, *The Postmistress*, 2010
Glen David Gold, *Carter Beats the Devil*, 2001
John Jakes, *California Gold*, 1989
Jane Smiley, *Private Life*, 2010

711

SUSAN VREELAND

Clara and Mr. Tiffany
(New York: Random House, 2011)

Subject(s): Artists; Working conditions; Women
Major character(s): Clara Driscoll, Artist; Louis Comfort Tiffany, Artist, Employer (of Clara)
Time period(s): 19th century
Locale(s): New York, New York

Summary: In *Clara and Mr. Tiffany*, author Susan Vreeland presents a fictionalized version of the life of the woman who crafted the first Tiffany glass lamp. Clara Driscoll toils in the workshop of famed artisan Louis Comfort Tiffany while dealing with the ups and downs of her love life. She finds an outlet in the creative work of Tiffany's studio, where she makes the colorful lamp that would become the trademark of Tiffany glass. Meanwhile, she gains a powerful awareness of the plight of the working class, becoming a hero to the women who work for her.

Where it's reviewed:
Booklist, November 15, 2010, page 26
Good Housekeeping, January 2011, page 171
Library Journal, November 1, 2010, page 58
Publishers Weekly, September 27, 2010, page 33
USA Today, February 1, 2011, page 2D

Other books by the same author:
Luncheon of the Boating Party, 2007
The Forest Lover, 2004
Life Studies: Stories, 2004
The Passion of Artemisia, 2002
Girl in Hyacinth Blue, 1999
What Love Sees, 1996

Other books you might like:
T.C. Boyle, *The Women*, 2009
Tracy Chevalier, *The Lady and the Unicorn*, 2004
C.S. Harris, *What Angels Fear*, 2005
Nancy Horan, *Loving Frank: A Novel*, 2007
Jed Rubenfeld, *The Interpretation of Murder: A Novel*, 2006

Popular Fiction

712

CAROL WALLACE

Leaving Van Gogh

(New York: Spiegel & Grau, 2011)

Story type: Historical
Subject(s): Artists; Mental disorders; History
Major character(s): Vincent van Gogh, Artist, Mentally Ill Person, Historical Figure; Paul Gachet, Doctor
Time period(s): 19th century; 1890s (1890)
Locale(s): Auvres, France

Summary: *Leaving Van Gogh* is a historical novel from author Carol Wallace. Relying on historical research, Wallace tells the story of Vincent van Gogh's final months through the eyes of his physician, Paul Gachet. In the spring of 1890, after Vincent decides to travel to Auvres, France, to paint and relax, his younger brother, Theo, approaches Paul, a doctor specializing in mental illness, about accompanying Vincent for the summer. Paul, intrigued by Vincent's incredible talent and troubling emotional ailments, agrees. As Vincent slips further into a dark mental and emotional abyss, Paul struggles to diagnose the artist's illness and works feverishly to remedy him before it's too late.

Where it's reviewed:
Library Journal, January 2011, page 91
Publishers Weekly, January 17, 2011, page 24

Other books by the same author:
That Doggone Calf, 2009
Bub, Snow, and the Burly Bear Scare, 2003
Chomps, Fela, and Gray Cat (That's Me!), 2001
The Flying Flea, Callie, and Me, 1999
That Furball Puppy and Me, 1999

Other books you might like:
Tracy Chevalier, *Girl with a Pearl Earring*, 1999
Laurel Corona, *The Four Seasons: A Novel of Vivaldi's Venice*, 2008
Sarah Dunant, *The Birth of Venus*, 2003
Nancy Horan, *Loving Frank: A Novel*, 2007

713

FRANCES WASHBURN

The Sacred White Turkey

(Lincoln: University of Nebraska Press, 2010)

Subject(s): Native Americans; Shamanism; Women
Major character(s): Hazel Latour, Witch (medicine woman), Grandmother (of Stella); Stella, Granddaughter (of Hazel), 12-Year-Old; George Wanbli, Shaman
Time period(s): 20th century; 1960s
Locale(s): United States

Summary: Frances Washburn's *The Sacred White Turkey* tells the story of a Lakota medicine woman named Hazel Latour, who lives with her adolescent granddaughter Stella on a remote farm. On Easter Sunday, Hazel and Stella are surprised at the sudden appearance of a snow-white turkey, who takes up residence in their chicken coop. News of the turkey's arrival soon spreads to Hazel and Stella's neighbors, including Hazel's nemesis George Wanbli. Meanwhile, the two women have very different views on just what the turkey represents, illustrating the differences between generations, cultures, and family members.

Where it's reviewed:
Booklist, August 1, 2010, page 27
Publishers Weekly, July 26, 2010, page 48

Other books you might like:
Sherman Alexie, *The Lone Ranger and Tonto Fist Fight in Heaven*, 1993
Louise Erdrich, *Love Medicine*, 1984
Susan Power, *The Grass Dancer*, 1994

714

STANLEY GORDON WEST

Blind Your Ponies

(Chapel Hills, North Carolina: Algonquin Books, 2011)

Story type: Contemporary - Innocent
Subject(s): Rural life; Sports; Romances (Fiction)
Major character(s): Sam Pickett, Coach (basketball); Olaf Gustafson, Student—Exchange, Basketball Player; Tom Stonebreaker, Student—High School, Basketball Player; Peter Strong, Student—High School, Basketball Player
Locale(s): Willow Creek, Montana

Summary: In *Blind Your Ponies*, author Stanley Gorden West tells the story of a small-town high school basketball team and their quest for a championship that no one thought would ever come. After more than 90 losses under his belt, Coach Sam Pickett has just about had it. Then Olaf Gustafson, a visiting student from Norway, comes along: at nearly seven feet tall, Olaf seems like a saving grace for the floundering team. Olaf is joined by Tom Stonebreaker and Peter Strong, two new recruits who show a ton of promise, and soon winning looks like an actual possibility. In the meantime, the residents of the tiny town band together to help the team along, learning a little bit about themselves in the process.

Where it's reviewed:
Booklist, November 15, 2010, page 21
Publishers Weekly, October 18, 2010, page 25

Other books by the same author:
Amos, 1983

Other books you might like:
Jonathan Evison, *West of Here*, 2011
Jeannette Walls, *Half Broke Horses: A True-Life Novel*, 2009

715

DEBORAH WILLIS

Vanishing and Other Stories

(New York: Harper Perennial, 2010)

Subject(s): Interpersonal relations; Family; Short stories

Summary: Deborah Willis's *Vanishing and Other Stories* is a collection of tales about individuals who are forced to confront relationship problems with friends, family members, and loved ones. These fragile ties that bind are different for each character, from the affections of an absent father to the heartbreak of a woman whose mother is afflicted with Alzheimer's. Each story, however, has one common thread: a passionate quest for meaning, forgiveness, and redemption.

Where it's reviewed:
Booklist, August 1, 2010, page 28
Publishers Weekly, July 26, 2010, page 48

Other books you might like:
Judy Budnitz, *Nice Big American Baby*, 2005
Miranda July, *No One Belongs Here More than You: Stories*, 2007
Maile Meloy, *Both Ways Is the Only Way I Want It*, 2009
Lydia Peelle, *Reasons for and Advantages of Breathing: Stories*, 2009

716

ANDREW WINER

The Marriage Artist: A Novel

(New York: Henry Holt and Co., 2010)

Story type: Arts; Religious
Subject(s): Love; Art; Father-son relations
Major character(s): Daniel Lichtmann, Artist, Widow(er); Benjamin Wind, Artist
Time period(s): Multiple Time Periods
Locale(s): Vienna, Austria

Summary: Andrew Winer's *The Marriage Artist: A Novel* traces three generations of characters. Art critic Daniel Lichtmann tries to pick up the pieces after the death of his wife, who committed suicide, but was not alone at the time: The body of Benjamin Wind, her alleged lover and an acquaintance of Daniel, was found right next to her. Not only has he lost his wife, but also his prodigy. Little does Daniel know, the course of his life was determined many years earlier in Vienna. A child from a Jewish family who gave up on their religion finds that he has the ability to build beautiful ketubots[97]Jewish marriage contracts. After learning of this gift, he must choose between family and pursuing his love of art.

Where it's reviewed:
Booklist, September 15, 2010, page 28
Library Journal, August 2010, page 75
Publishers Weekly, July 12, 2010, page 24

Other books by the same author:
The Color Midnight Made, 2002

Other books you might like:
Mary Gordon, *Men and Angels*, 1985
Nicole Krauss, *The History of Love*, 2005
Frederick Reiken, *Day for Night*, 2010
Markus Zusak, *The Book Thief*, 2006

717

MEG WOLITZER

The Uncoupling

(New York: Riverhead Books, 2011)

Story type: Contemporary
Subject(s): Men; Women; Sexual behavior
Time period(s): 21st century; 2010s
Locale(s): Stellar Plains, New Jersey

Summary: In the town of Stellar Plains, New Jersey, strange things are happening among the women. A carefree new drama teacher has chosen the play Lysistrata for an upcoming school production. The play, written by Aristophanes, is about a community of women who stop having sex with their partners in an attempt to end a war. Almost instantly, a strange spell seems to be cast over the women of Stellar Plains, causing them to lose all desire for passion and intimacy. As the women grow perplexed by their newfound lack of interest, the men go absolutely insane with frustration, and everyone is forced to reevaluate their relationships and sexuality.

Where it's reviewed:
Library Journal, February 1, 2011, page 58
Publishers Weekly, January 10, 2011, page 27

Other books by the same author:
The Ten-Year Nap, 2008
The Position, 2005
The Wife, 2003
Surrender, Dorothy, 1999
Friends for Life, 1994

Other books you might like:
Allegra Goodman, *The Cookbook Collector: A Novel*, 2010
Gish Jen, *World and Town*, 2010
Tom Rachman, *The Imperfectionists: A Novel*, 2010

718

SUMMER WOOD

Wrecker

(New York: Bloomsbury USA, 2011)

Subject(s): Foster children; Family; Coming of age
Major character(s): Wrecker, Foster Child
Time period(s): 20th century
Locale(s): Humboldt County, California

Summary: Summer Wood's *Wrecker* charts the adventures of the title hero, a boy who finds himself a victim in the nation's poorly constructed foster care program. After his mother is sent to prison, Wrecker becomes just another number in the system, shuttled from foster home to foster home until he goes to live with relatives in the distant terrain of Humboldt County, California. Once filled with anger, Wrecker is slowly transformed by life in this beautiful place, and the people he meets challenge his long-held notions of what constitutes a family.

Where it's reviewed:
Library Journal, February 1, 2011, page 58

Publishers Weekly, November 15, 2010, page 36

Other books by the same author:
Arroyo, 2001

Other books you might like:
Peter Carey, *His Illegal Self*, 2008
Emma Donoghue, *Room*, 2010
Daniel Woodrell, *Winter's Bone: A Novel*, 2006

719

SUSI WYSS

The Civilized World

(New York: Henry Holt and Co., 2011)

Story type: Contemporary
Subject(s): Women; Forgiveness; Africa
Major character(s): Adjoa, Twin (of Kojo); Kojo, Twin (of Adjoa); Janice, Worker (aid worker), Employer (of Adjoa)
Time period(s): 21st century; 2010s
Locale(s): Africa

Summary: Susi Wyss's *The Civilized World* is a novel told through a series of short stories. The pieces of this volume are set in Africa and revolve around five women and their attempts to find freedom and happiness. Among them are Adjoa, who dreams of one day opening her own hair salon, and Janice, who is looking for a place to settle down and discover her identity. The tales of this collection converge to create an affecting, at times shattering portrait of modern Africa and the people who populate it. First novel.

Where it's reviewed:
Library Journal, December 2010, page 110
Publishers Weekly, December 20, 2010, page 27

Other books you might like:
Ama Ata Aidoo, *Changes: A Love Story*, 1993
Buchi Emecheta, *The Joys of Motherhood: A Novel*, 1979
Shirley Ann Grau, *Nine Women*, 1986
Margot Livesey, *The House on Fortune Street*, 2008

720

QIU XIAOLONG

Years of Red Dust: Stories of Shanghai

(New York: St. Martin's Press, 2010)

Subject(s): China; Chinese (Asian people); Chinese history
Time period(s): 20th century-21st century
Locale(s): Shanghai, China

Summary: The evolution of contemporary China is reflected in the tales of Qiu Xiaolong's *Years of Red Dust: Stories of Shanghai*. Each short story in this collection takes place on or around a single street known as Red Dust Lane in the city of Shanghai. From this angle, the challenges and triumphs of modern China are experienced: from the Communist Revolution to the Cultural Revolution, from the influence and death of Chairman Mao to the protests in Tiananmen Square. *Years of Red Dust* offers an intimately personal glimpse at the making of one of the world's most powerful countries.

Where it's reviewed:
New York Times Book Review, October 17, 2010, page 21
Publishers Weekly, August 23, 2010, page 27

Other books by the same author:
Red Mandarin Dress, 2007
A Case of Two Cities, 2006
When Red Is Black, 2004
Lines Around China, 2003
A Loyal Character Dancer, 2002

Other books you might like:
Wang Gang, *English*, 2009
Ma Jian, *Beijing Coma: A Novel*, 2008
Yiyun Li, *The Vagrants: A Novel*, 2009

721

RUIYAN XU

The Lost and Forgotten Languages of Shanghai

(New York: St. Martin's Press, 2010)

Story type: Contemporary
Subject(s): Speech; Love; Chinese (Asian people)
Major character(s): Li Jing, Businessman, Accident Victim; Rosalyn Neal, Doctor, Divorced Person; Meiling, Spouse (of Li)
Time period(s): 20th century; 1990s (1999)
Locale(s): Shanghai, China

Summary: In *The Lost and Forgotten Languages of Shanghai*, Ruiyan Xu tells the story of a Chinese businessman who is unable to speak his native language after suffering a traumatic brain injury. Li Jing can suddenly communicate in only English, a language he has not spoken since moving back to China when still a young boy. His lack of language causes a rift with his wife, Meiling, who is struggling to run his business and raise their son in his absence. Meanwhile, American doctor, Rosalyn Neal is summoned to help Li, but their connection has unexpected consequences for doctor, patient, and the patient's harried wife. First novel.

Where it's reviewed:
Booklist, September 1, 2010, page 44
Library Journal, August 2010, page 76
Publishers Weekly, August 2, 2010, page 28

Other books you might like:
Hans Fallada, *Every Man Dies Alone*, 2009
Nell Freudenberger, *The Dissident*, 2006
Ha Jin, *A Free Life: A Novel*, 2007

722

MIKE YOUNG

Look! Look! Feathers

(Middletown, New Jersey: Word Riot Press, 2010)

Story type: Contemporary
Subject(s): Modern Life; Internet; Short stories
Time period(s): 21st century; 2010s
Locale(s): California, United States; Oregon, United States

Summary: In *Look! Look! Feathers*, Mike Young presents a collection of short fiction set against the backdrop of modern life and all its foibles. The stories that comprise this volume follow a variety of characters through unusual contemporary situations, from a youngster who feels his hand is magically linked to the Internet to a widowed man who learns his online romance is not with a woman his own age—but a teenager. Titles in this volume include "Snow You Know and Snow You Don't," "No Such Thing as a Wild Horse," and "Mosquito Fog."

Where it's reviewed:
Publishers Weekly, November 8, 2010, page 44

Other books by the same author:
We Are All Good If They Try Hard Enough, 2010

Other books you might like:
Paula Bomer, *Baby and Other Stories*, 2010
Judy Budnitz, *Nice Big American Baby*, 2005
Julie Orringer, *How to Breathe Underwater*, 2003

The Year in Science Fiction: 2010
by
Don D'Ammassa

There has been considerable discussion in recent years about whether or not science fiction as a genre has outlived its time. Supplanted in great part by fantasy in recent years, it occupies much less shelf space in bookstores than it did in the 1970s and 1980s. Recent advances in science have made many of the standard devices of the genre obsolete or anachronistic. Colonization of other planets sounds good in theory but in practice it is difficult to imagine a practical method by which large groups of humans could be transplanted elsewhere, and even worlds with acceptable ranges of climate would present biological difficulties that may be insuperable. We no longer believe that John Smith and his friends will build a working spaceship in their spare time, time travel has been largely relegated to fantasy, science and engineering are no longer though to be the ultimate solution to all problems, and advanced mental powers such as telepathy and teleportation now seem remote possibilities.

Modern science fiction fans seem to have fragmented into special readerships. In the past it was not unusual for an individual author to routinely write alternate history, military adventure, other worlds romance, dystopian futures, and time travel stories. Today writers are much less likely to venture away from a single theme once they have found a niche. Harry Turtledove is associated with alternate history—which some claim isn't even science fiction; David Weber and David Drake write mostly military stories; Iain Banks, Peter F. Hamilton, and Alastair Reynolds deal in far future space operas on a grand scale; Julie E. Czerneda and C.J. Cherryh write other worlds romances; Kim Stanley Robinson's books deal with ecological disaster; and Jack McDevitt writes mysteries set on other worlds. None of these are absolutes, obviously, but the drift toward specialization is widespread and undeniable, in part because a successful book leads publishers to ask for more of the same. The probability that an individual novel is part of a series has risen dramatically and now approaches the level of fantasy fiction.

The erosion of the short story market continues as well. Although there are probably just as many short stories published today either on line or by small press publishers as there were when a dozen or more pulp fiction magazines appeared regularly, the fact remains that most new SF stories do not get the exposure to a general readership that was once possible. The number of professional magazines has dwindled to a handful and some of these, notably *The Magazine of Fantasy & Science Fiction*, have reduced their frequency. Original anthologies continue to appear with some regularity and occasionally produce some genuinely first-rate work, but the tendency to group these collections around single themes often results in comparatively lifeless books targeted toward a subset of readers. Shared universe anthologies have virtually disappeared, although media tie-in novels, most notably Star Wars, Star Trek, and Warhammer, remain popular with their respective fan bases. Reprint anthologies have had a slight resurgence thanks to editors such as John Joseph Adams, but without the broad base of new stories to draw from, they are often lackluster or are merely reassemblies of stories anthologized in the past.

Part of the recent decline is probably self inflicted. Faced with daily reminders of the rise of terrorism, the deterioration of the environment, the polarization of political movements, and the realization that technology renders every place in the world unsafe from attack, the reading public cannot be blamed if it prefers to delve into magical worlds where good always triumphs over evil rather than a description of a potentially new disaster, or the unfortunate future consequences of contemporary trends. It is no coincidence that the dystopian satire has virtually disappeared from the genre. We're all too aware of the problems around us without being reminded of them in our leisure time.

That said, there are clear indications that all the news isn't bad for science fiction. There are new voices rising even as the old ones fade. The last few years have seen the emergence of Paolo Bacigalupi, Cherie Priest, John Scalzi, Cory Doctorow, and others who have brought innovative narrative methods, original plots, fascinating new settings and situations, and clever variations of old themes to the genre. While not as wildly optimistic as their predecessors, they see the silver lining as well as the cloud. New voices help bring new readers and refresh the imaginations of the old guard.

So how did 2010 measure up? It was a somewhat mixed bag with some books looking backward, some holding the course, and some moving toward new territory. The most notable book in the first category is *Detour to Otherness* by Henry Kuttner and C.L. Moore, a restrospective collection of stories by a husband and wife writing team active during the 1940s and 1950s. There has been considerable effort to make the work of some of the best authors of years past available in new collections in recent years by Baen Books, NESFA Press, Haffner Press, and others. Kuttner and Moore were best known for their short fiction and this new volume includes a good sampling of it. *Betrayer of Worlds* by Larry Niven and Edward M. Lerner is not quite the same case because it's a brand new novel, but it is part of an extension and elaboration of the Known Space series that Niven wrote during the 1960s and 1970s, many of which are classic genre stories. *The Best of Larry Niven* also contains vintage stories as well as more recent ones.

Two newer writers had major novels this year. Lauren Beukes is a South African writer whose international science fiction debut *Moxyland*—the novel had previously been published in her home country—mixes tropes by incorporating cyberpunk devices with a dystopian future on the verge of ecological disaster. It also suggests that one of the underpinnings of the genre is mistaken, that technological progress is not necessarily a good thing. Cherie Priest started her career writing outstanding novels of the supernatural, but turned to steampunk with *Boneshaker* in 2009, to which this year's *Dreadnought* is an even better sequel. During an alternate version of the American Civil War a young woman takes a perilous journey to the West Coast to see her estranged father.

Space opera was well represented as well. Iain Banks returned to the Culture Universe in *Surface Detail*, a future so remote that common technology seems almost magical. A murdered woman is restored to life by an artificial intelligence so that she can track down those responsible for her death. Jack McDevitt's take on space opera is entirely different. In *Echo*, the latest Alex Benedict adventure, the space traveling antiques hunter stumbles across an artifact whose implications lead him and his assistant on a perilous search from one world to another to unearth the secret of an alien encounter that had disastrous consequences. Unlike Banks, McDevitt narrows his focus to a single linear plot and spends little time elaborating on the setting or technology.

After a considerable gap of years during which she wrote only fantasy, Lois McMaster Bujold returned to the popular Vorkosigian saga for *Cryoburn*. The series began as quasi-military adventure but turned increasingly to intrigue, mystery, and political maneuverings in the last few titles. This new book continues that trend. The protagonist has changed professions from soldier to diplomat, and finds himself kidnapped and mystified by the efforts of an illegal cryonics enterprise.

Time travel stories were quite prominent this year, chiefly because of the appearance of *Blackout* and *All Clear*, a two-part novel by Connie Willis. A team of time travelers visits blitz era London to conduct historical research. Although theoretically time is immutable, it appears that their presence may have changed the course of history in minor ways. The first title ends with a cliffhanger and the story resumes in *All Clear*. Trapped by their malfunctioning equipment, frightened by evidence that they may be changing the future, the stranded time travelers must survive in the midst of a war that might

no longer progress as they believed it would. 2010 also saw the appearance of the final book in the Company series by Kage Baker, who recently passed away. *Not Less Than Gods* is another of her unique efforts involving an organization that can move through time, though with restrictions, and which in this case is trying to affect the outcome of the Crimean War. Baker mixed steampunk with espionage in what will certainly be viewed as one of the high points of this series.

Planetary romances are essentially adventure stories set wholly or in large part on an alien world. They are one of the staples of the genre but are often characterized as little more than a Star Trek adventure story, which they occasionally resemble. Michael Flynn's *Up Jim River* proves that they can be more than that, a nuanced look at complex characters as they travel across an imaginary landscape. Timothy Zahn's *The Domino Pattern*, the latest Frank Compton novel, posits a unique form of star travel, a kind of railroad through an alternate version of space. This time they are essentially en route throughout the story, which involves a sort of locked room murder mystery and a temporary truce with his recurring enemy, the mind dominating Modhri. Allen Steele brought his saga of the planet Coyote to an apparent close in *Coyote Destiny*, which series is in part loosely based on American history. The colonists have managed to overcome efforts by the authorities on Earth to establish control of Coyote, and in fact there has been a considerable lapse since there was any communication between the two. Efforts to re-establish contact are hampered by the existence of a confederation of alien races that has effectively blockaded humanity's home world.

Obviously not all of the year's outstanding fiction was upbeat. Ian McDonald explores a mildly dystopian future Turkey in *The Dervish House*. McDonald is probably the field's most convincing creator of near future societies, incorporating current trends and extrapolating new ones, without causing his imagined new societies to become unrecognizable. This complex story, which follows the lives of six ordinary but very different people, is one of his best. More optimistic about the future, but with reservations, is Alexander Jablokov's first novel in a decade, *Brain Thief*, which may also be his best. It's a blend of mystery thriller and speculation involving space probes, artificial intelligence, missing persons, and other scientific advances.

As always, the most comprehensive overview of the year's short fiction can be found in *The Year's Best Science Fiction: Volume 27* edited by Gardner Dozois. Dozois also provides an extensive and informative overview of various aspects of the genre, from publishing to media. The best single author collection of the year was *The Best of Kim Stanley Robinson*.

Recommended Titles

Novels were more dominant than usual among the best books published this year, although this was offset somewhat by "best of" collections. There is increasing evidence that space opera is making a comeback, though the flavor is much different than it was in the past, and that steampunk—stories set in alternate versions of the 19th Century—has displaced cyberpunk as the trendy sub-genre. Time travel has also enjoyed some renewed popularity, although this might be specific to a very few recent works rather than indicative of an actual trend. Note that some 2010 titles were covered in the previous volume in this series.

Surface Detail by Iain Banks

Not Less Than Gods by Kage Baker

Moxyland by Lauren Beukes

Cryoburn by Lois McMaster Bujold

The Year's Best Science Fiction Volume 27 edited by Gardner Dozois

Up Jim River by Michael Flynn

Brain Thief by Alexander Jablokov

Detour to Otherness by Henry Kuttner and C.L. Moore

Echo by Jack McDevitt

Dervish House by Ian McDonald

The Best of Larry Niven by Larry Niven

Betrayer of Worlds by Larry Niven and Edward M. Lerner

Dreadnought by Cherie Priest

The Best of Kim Stanley Robinson by Kim Stanley Robinson

Coyote Destiny by Allen Steele

Blackout by Connie Willis

All Clear by Connie Willis

The Domino Pattern by Timothy Zahn

Science Fiction

723

DAN ABNETT
CHRISTIAN DUNN, Co-Editor

Sabbat Worlds

(Memphis, Tennessee: Games Workshop, 2010)

Story type: Collection
Subject(s): Science fiction; Short stories

Summary: In *Sabbat Worlds*, editors Dan Abnett and Christian Dunn present a collection of stories centered on the realm's ongoing battle. The collection includes works by authors Dan Abnett, Aaron Dembski-Bowden, Graham McNeill, Sandy Mitchell, and others.

Other books by the same author:
The Lost, 2010
Prospero Burns, 2010
Blood Pact, 2009
The Story of Martha, 2008
Titanicus, 2008

Other books you might like:
Ben Counter, *Daemon World*, 2009
Mike Lee, *Fallen Angels*, 2009
Steve Parker, *Gunheads*, 2009
Rob Sanders, *Redemption Corps*, 2010
James Swallow, *Red Fury*, 2008

724

JOHN JOSEPH ADAMS

Brave New Worlds: Dystopian Stories

(San Francisco: Night Shade Books, 2010)

Subject(s): Dystopias; Futuristic society; Short stories

Summary: In *Brave New Worlds: Dystopian Stories*, editor John Joseph Adams presents a compilation of stories set in marginalized, near-future societies. The 33 short stories of this volume encompass the gamut of dystopian experience, from overzealous government control to the stifling effects of technology. Authors contributing to this volume include Ursula K. Le Guin, Shirley Jackson, Kurt Vonnegut, Joseph Paul Haines, J.G. Ballard, Matt

Williamson, and Vylar Kaftan. *Brave New Worlds* contains a list of further recommended reading.

Where it's reviewed:
Publishers Weekly, December 20, 2010, page 39

Other books by the same author:
The Living Dead 2, 2010
By Blood We Live, 2009
Federations, 2009
The Living Dead, 2008
Wastelands, 2008

Other books you might like:
Ray Bradbury, *Fahrenheit 451*, 1953
Aldous Huxley, *Brave New World*, 1932
Rebecca Ore, *Outlaw School*, 2000
George Orwell, *1984*, 1949
Scott Westerfeld, *Uglies*, 2005

725

ANN AGUIRRE

Kill Box

(New York: Ace Books, 2010)

Series: Sirantha Jax Series. Book 4
Subject(s): Adventure; Extraterrestrial life; Spanish colonies
Major character(s): Sirantha Jax, Adventurer (jumper)
Time period(s): Indeterminate Future

Summary: Sirantha Jax was an ambassador with all the power in the world. Now she's desperate to return to her adventurous ways, so she reverts to her old job of "jumper," transporting herself between outer-space worlds in order to protect the innocent from harm. Her first case back on the job requires her to help a band of courageous colonists from flesh-hungry extraterrestrials who will not be deterred by anything—or anyone—in their quest for human flesh. *Kill Box* is the fourth book in Ann Aguirre's Sirantha Jax series.

Other books by the same author:
Blue Diablo, 2009
Doubleblind, 2009
Skin Game, 2009
Wanderlust, 2008
Grimspace, 2007

Other books you might like:
C.J. Cherryh, *The Book of Morgaine*, 1979
Julie E. Czerneda, *A Thousand Words for Stranger*, 1997
Melissa Scott, *Dreaming Metal*, 1997
Karen Traviss, *Judge*, 2008
S.L. Viehl, *Dream Called Time*, 2010

726

JERRY AHERN
SHARON AHERN, Co-Author

Written in Time

(Riverdale, New York: Baen, 2010)

Subject(s): Time travel; Adventure; Fantasy
Major character(s): Jack Naile, Writer, Time Traveler
Time period(s): 21st century; (2010s); 20th century; 1900s (1903)
Locale(s): Nevada, United States

Summary: Jerry and Sharon Ahearn's *Written in Time* is a time-travel fantasy featuring Jack Naile, a writer who receives a mysterious photo in the mail. The photo was taken just after the turn of the century in a small Nevada town, and it inexplicably contains an image of Jack. After a little investigation, Jack finds doppelgangers of himself and his family living in that era. Now the only way to learn more about this strange phenomenon is for Jack to travel back to 1903 Nevada, where he will have to confront the ghosts of past he never knew he had.

Other books by the same author:
Countdown, 1993
Death Watch, 1993
No Survivors, 1990
The Killing Wedge, 1988
The Nightmare Begins, 1981

Other books you might like:
Robert Adams, *Castaways in Time*, 1979
Robert Chilson, *The Shores of Kansas*, 1976
L. Sprague de Camp, *Rivers of Time*, 1993
David Drake, *Time Safari*, 1982
John Jakes, *Black in Time*, 1970

727

KATHERINE ALLRED

Close Contact

(New York: EOS, 2010)

Series: Alien Affairs Series. Book 2
Story type: Romance; Series
Subject(s): Science fiction; Romances (Fiction); Extraterrestrial life
Major character(s): Echo Adams, Genetically Altered Being
Time period(s): Indeterminate Future
Locale(s): Earth; Madrea, Planet—Imaginary

Summary: In *Close Contact*, by Katherine Allred, Echo Adams is a Genetically Engineered Person (GEP) who is comfortable in her career with the Galactic Federation where she serves as a social ambassador to visiting aliens. Like other GEPs, Echo possesses enhanced psychic talents. The Bureau of Alien Affairs realizes that Echo's skills are exceptional and recruits her as an agent in their organization. Leaving her fun-loving lifestyle behind, Echo travels to the dull planet Madrea to begin her first assignment—tracking down a missing crystal that holds an extraterrestrial being. *Close Contact* is the second book in the Alien Affairs series.

Other books by the same author:
Close Encounters, 2009
Second Time Around, 2008
For Love of Charley, 2007
What Price Paradise, 2007
The Sweet Gum Tree, 2005

Other books you might like:
Catherine Asaro, *Sunrise Alley*, 2004
Robert A. Heinlein, *Friday*, 1982
James H. Schmitz, *Trigger & Friends*, 2001
Melissa Scott, *Trouble and Her Friends*, 1994
Karen Traviss, *The World Before*, 2005

728

POUL ANDERSON

Sir Dominic Flandry: The Last Knight of Terra

(Riverdale, New York: Baen Books, 2010)

Series: Technic Civilization Saga. Book 6
Story type: Space Opera
Subject(s): Science fiction; Extraterrestrial life; Adventure
Major character(s): Dominic Flandry, Military Personnel (captain), Knight
Time period(s): Indeterminate Future
Locale(s): Terran Empire, Fictional Location

Summary: In *Sir Dominic Flandry: The Last Knight of Terra* by Poul Anderson, the Terran Empire awaits the coming "Long Night," when their civilization will be overrun by invading brutish forces. Leading the defense is Captain Dominic Flandry, who has recently been granted knighthood in recognition of his duty to the empire. The title does little to impress the Merseians, the enemy forces that recognize Flandry as the main obstacle in their plot to overthrow the Terran Empire. As Landry realizes that war is unavoidable, he anticipates a subsequent era of enlightenment. *Sir Dominic Flandry* is the sixth book in the Technic Civilization series.

Other books by the same author:
Starfarers, 1998
The Shield of Time, 1990
Time Patrolman, 1983
Tau Zero, 1970
Strangers from Earth, 1961

Other books you might like:
Harry Harrison, *The Stainless Steel Rat Returns*, 2010
Keith Laumer, *Relief in the Ruins*, 1986

Murray Leinster, *The Med Service*, 1983
Mike Resnick, *Santiago: A Myth of the Far Future*, 1986
Timothy Zahn, *Night Train to Rigel*, 2005

729

SCOTT ANDREWS

Children's Crusade

(London: Abaddon Books, 2010)

Series: Afterblight Chronicles. Book 8
Subject(s): Children; Orphans; Adventure
Major character(s): Jane Crowther, Teacher
Time period(s): Indeterminate Future
Locale(s): United Kingdom

Summary: In *Children's Crusade*, author Scott Andrews presents the eighth novel in The Afterblight Chronicles series. The apocalyptic event known as the Cull has left Earth in tatters, and countless number of children throughout England have been orphaned. To further complicate matters, someone or something is rounding up orphans left and right, and schoolteacher Jane Crowther becomes determined to stop the kidnappings at any cost.

Other books by the same author:
Operation Motherland, 2009
School's Out, 2007

Other books you might like:
Jeff Carlson, *Plague War*, 2008
Stephen King, *The Stand*, 1978
Rebecca Levene, *Kill or Cure*, 2007
S.M. Stirling, *Dies the Fire*, 2004
Roger Zelazny, *Damnation Alley*, 1969

730

CHRISTOPHER ANVIL

The Power of Illusion

(New York: Baen, 2010)

Subject(s): Fantasy; Adventure; Humor

Summary: In *The Power of Illusion*, author Christopher Anvil offers a collection of original short stories that blends humor and science fiction. Containing 21 short tales and a novella, this volume brings together the best of Anvil's unique canon of short fiction, which celebrates the wit and fantasy of the science-fiction genre. Titles in this collection include "A Taste of Poison," "The Day the Machines Stopped," "Key to the Crime," "High Road to the East," and "A Tourist Named Death."

Other books by the same author:
Rx for Chaos, 2009
War Games, 2008
The Trouble with Humans, 2007
The Trouble with Aliens, 2006
Pandora's Legions, 2002

Other books you might like:

John Brunner, *The Best of John Brunner*, 1988
Gordon R. Dickson, *Beginnings*, 1988
Robert A. Heinlein, *Off the Main Sequence: The Other Science Fiction Stories of Robert A. Heinlein*, 2005
Murray Leinster, *First Contacts: The Essential Murray Leinster*, 1998
Frederik Pohl, *Platinum Pohl*, 2005

731

IAIN M. BANKS

Surface Detail

(London: Orbit, 2010)

Series: The Culture Series. Book 9
Subject(s): Adventure; Revenge; Hell
Major character(s): Lededje Y'breq, Slave (former sex slave)
Time period(s): Indeterminate Future
Locale(s): Outer Space

Summary: Lededje Y'breq was killed at the hands of a dirty politician, but she has now been brought back to life and is out for revenge. As her quest for vengeance plays out, the Culture authorities are trying to decide what to do about Hell. Do they leave the underworld in place as a punishment? Or do they simply let evildoers die without passing into its flames? These two stories come crashing together in the most unexpected ways in *Surface Detail*, the ninth novel in Iain M. Banks's Culture series.

Where it's reviewed:
Booklist, December 15,2010, page 29

Other books by the same author:
Matter, 2008
The Algebraist, 2004
Inversions, 2000
Look to Windward, 2000
Excession, 1996

Other books you might like:
Kevin J. Anderson, *Scattered Suns*, 2005
Gregory Benford, *Great Sky River*, 1987
Peter F. Hamilton, *The Evolutionary Void*, 2010
Alastair Reynolds, *The Prefect*, 2007
Vernor Vinge, *A Deepness in the Sky*, 1999

732

GREG BEAR

Hull Zero Three

(New York: Orbit, 2010)

Story type: Space Opera
Subject(s): Science fiction; Suspense; Space flight
Major character(s): Teacher, Space Explorer
Time period(s): Indeterminate Future
Locale(s): Outer Space

Summary: In *Hull Zero Three*, a spacecraft on a mission to find new worlds suffers a midflight crisis that

Science Fiction

endangers its crew. When one of the space travelers, "Teacher," is freed from a state of suspended animation, he finds that his ship is overrun by strange creatures. Teacher seeks shelter from the monsters and the dangerous cold in the craft's many winding passageways and finds that he is not the only crew member who has awakened from the Dreamtime. As Teacher and his new group of allies struggle to survive the threats on board, they try to figure out what caused the ship's catastrophic failure.

Where it's reviewed:
Booklist, October 1, 2010, page 38
Locus, November 2010, page 18
Publishers Weekly, October 18, 2010, page 30

Other books by the same author:
Quantico, 2007
Women in Deep Time, 2003
Darwin's Radio, 1999
Dinosaur Summer, 1998
The Forge of God, 1987

Other books you might like:
Brian W. Aldiss, *Non-Stop*, 1976
Paul Chafe, *Genesis*, 2007
Robert A. Heinlein, *Orphans of the Sky*, 1963
Brian Stableford, *Dark Ararat*, 2002
Gene Wolfe, *On Blue's Waters*, 1999

733

LAUREN BEUKES

Moxyland

(Nottingham, United Kingdom: Angry Robot, 2009)

Subject(s): Technology; Dystopias; Internet
Major character(s): Toby, Teenager; Kendra, Photographer; Lerato, Computer Expert; Tendeka, Activist
Time period(s): Indeterminate Future
Locale(s): Cape Town, South Africa

Summary: Lauren Beukes's *Moxyland* is set in Cape Town, South Africa, in the not-too-distant future. This future is marked by global corporate dominance, government corruption, and powerful technology that renders computers and online life just as valuable as physical life. In this increasingly dangerous society, four individuals are about to take a stand against the oppression of the authorities and the suffocating impact of the Internet.

Other books by the same author:
Zoo City, 2010
Maverick, 2004

Other books you might like:
John Brunner, *The Sheep Look Up*, 1972
Alan Dean Foster, *Montezuma Strip*, 1995
Gwyneth Jones, *White Queen*, 1993
Ian McDonald, *Chaga*, 1996
Maureen F. McHugh, *China Mountain Zhang*, 1992

734

JOHN BIRMINGHAM

After America

(New York: Del Rey, 2010)

Story type: Contemporary
Subject(s): Disasters; Adventure; Immigrants
Major character(s): Julianne Balwyn, Smuggler; Rhino, Smuggler; Miguel Pieraro, Rancher, Immigrant
Time period(s): 21st century; 2000s (2003)
Locale(s): Earth

Summary: John's Birmingham's *After America* is the sequel to 2009's *Without Warning*. In this science-fiction adventure, a mysterious energetic element has passed over the Earth, leaving destruction and mayhem in its wake. Now the people of the world are quickly splintering, and life on Earth has become a terrifying, trying ordeal. Among the hordes of people thrown into turmoil are two thieves, an embattled immigrant, and a special agent.

Other books by the same author:
Without Warning, 2010
Final Impact, 2007
Designated Targets, 2005
Weapons of Choice, 2004

Other books you might like:
Steven Barnes, *Lion's Blood: A Novel of Slavery and Freedom in an Alternate America*, 2002
Neal Barrett Jr., *Through Darkest America*, 1986
Kim Stanley Robinson, *The Years of Rice and Salt*, 2002
S.M. Stirling, *A Meeting at Corvallis*, 2006
Robert Charles Wilson, *Darwinia*, 1998

735

THOMAS BLACKTHORNE

Edge

(Nottingham, United Kingdom: Angry Robot, 2010)

Subject(s): Weapons; Futuristic society; Missing persons
Major character(s): Josh Cumberland, Agent (former special forces agent)
Time period(s): Indeterminate Future
Locale(s): United Kingdom

Summary: Thomas Blackthorne's *Edge* is set in a futuristic Great Britain, where reality television has become a brutal bloodbath—and the country's most popular pastime. TV programs are now largely real-time knife fights, a fact that causes a young boy with a phobia of weapons to run away from home. Josh Cumberland is a former special agent hired by the boy's father to track the child down, but before he can do that, Josh will have to infiltrate the culture's fascination with knives and other weaponry. First novel.

Other books you might like:
John Brunner, *The Shockwave Rider*, 1975
William C. Dietz, *Alien Bounty*, 1990

Mike McQuay, *The Deadliest Game in Town*, 1982
Richard K. Morgan, *Market Forces*, 2004
Robert Sheckley, *Hunter/Victim*, 1988

736

DARIN BRADLEY

Noise

(New York: Spectra, 2010)

Subject(s): Fantasy; Television; Apocalypse
Major character(s): Hiram, Friend (of Levi); Levi, Friend (of Hiram)
Time period(s): 21st century; 2010s
Locale(s): Slade, Texas

Summary: Darin Bradley's *Noise* tells the story of Hiram and Levi, two friends living in a world plagued by the threat of annihilation. In the switch from analog to digital television, unknown forces have hijacked the airwaves, and their cryptic messages demand decoding. When Hiram and Levi piece together what these messages are saying, they are thrust into the dark heart of a mystery that, if not solved, could destroy humankind as they know it. First novel.

Other books you might like:
Jeff Carlson, *Plague Zone*, 2009
Arthur C. Clarke, *The Hammer of God*, 1993
Ron Goulart, *After Things Fell Apart*, 1970
Stephen King, *The Stand*, 1978
Jerry Pournelle, *Lucifer's Hammer*, 1977

737

ERIC BROWN

Engineman

(London: Solaris, 2010)

Subject(s): Spacetime; Adventure; Space exploration
Major character(s): Ralph Mirren, Pilot (former engineman); Ella Fernandez, Artist
Time period(s): Indeterminate Future
Locale(s): Outer Space

Summary: In *Engineman*, author Eric Brown tells the story of Ralph Mirren, who once held the title position but has since been fired. After the discovery of wormholes that permitted instantaneous intergalactic travel, the need for enginemen was eradicated. But now Ralph is faced with a tempting new prospect. He is given the chance to traverse through one of the wormholes himself—but he has no idea the adventure that awaits him on the other side.

Other books by the same author:
Guardians of the Phoenix, 2010
Cosmopath, 2009
Kethani, 2008
Helix, 2007
The Fall of Tartarusq, 2005

Other books you might like:
Michael Bishop, *A Funeral for the Eyes of Fire*, 1975
Mike Brotherton, *Spider Star*, 2008
Arthur C. Clarke, *Rendezvous with Rama*, 1973
Jack McDevitt, *Omega*, 2003
Robert J. Sawyer, *Starplex*, 1996

738

ERIC BROWN

Guardians of the Phoenix

(London: Solaris, 2010)

Subject(s): Apocalypse; Adventure; Voyages and travels
Major character(s): Pierre, Survivor
Time period(s): Indeterminate Future
Locale(s): Paris, France

Summary: Eric Brown's *Guardians of the Phoenix* is set on Earth in the wake of a near-catastrophic apocalypse. The environment is in tatters, and few humans have lived through the ecological meltdown. One of these humans is Pierre, who lives in the ruins of Paris and is quickly running out of water. Now he must decide whether to further risk his life by joining a band of travelers heading south in order to find drinkable water.

Other books by the same author:
Engineman, 2010
Cosmopath, 2009
Kethani, 2008
Helix, 2007
New York Dreams, 2004

Other books you might like:
J.G. Ballard, *The Burning World*, 1964
Charles Einstein, *The Day New York Went Dry*, 1964
Mary Rosenblum, *The Drylands*, 1993
Kate Wilhelm, *Juniper Time*, 1979

739

LOIS MCMASTER BUJOLD

Cryoburn

(Riverdale, New York: Baen, 2010)

Series: Vorkosigan Series. Book 20
Subject(s): Adventure; Death; Diplomacy
Major character(s): Miles Vorkosigan, Diplomat; Jin Sato, Young Woman
Time period(s): Indeterminate Future
Locale(s): Kibou-daini, Planet—Imaginary

Summary: Lois McMaster Bujold's *Cryoburn* is the 20th installment in The Vorkosigan Saga science-fiction series. This outing centers on diplomat Miles Vorkosigan as he arrives on the planet Kibou-daini, where he is nearly abducted by local thugs who want him to stop his investigations into the planet's attempts to defy death. In the wake of the near-kidnapping, he is cared for by Jin Sato, who herself has a sordid history with the thugs who dominate Kibou-daini. With Jin's help, Miles is able to further probe the planet's cryo lobbies—causing the threat of great harm to them both.

Science Fiction

Where it's reviewed:
Library Journal, October 15, 2010, page 72
Locus, October 2010, page 25
Publishers Weekly, September 6, 2010, page 29

Other books by the same author:
Diplomatic Immunity, 2002
A Civil Campaign, 1999
Cetaganda, 1996
Memory, 1996
Ethan of Athos, 1986

Other books you might like:
Roger MacBride Allen, *The Cause of Death*, 2006
Iain M. Banks, *Matter*, 2008
C.J. Cherryh, *The Chanur Saga*, 2000
Peter F. Hamilton, *The Neutronium Alchemist*, 1997
Joan D. Vinge, *Dreamfall*, 1996

740

MARCELLA BURNARD

Enemy Within

(New York: Berkley, 2010)

Story type: Romance
Subject(s): Space flight; Adventure; Love
Major character(s): Ari Idylle, Pilot (spaceship captain);
   Cullin Seaghdh, Pilot (spaceship captain)
Time period(s): Indeterminate Future
Locale(s): Outer Space

Summary: In *Enemy Within*, author Marcella Burnard crafts a tale of romance and science fiction, set on a starship sailing through outer space. Captain Ari Idylle has recently been released from enslavement at the hands of her alien captors. When Cullin Seaghdh joins the command of her father's ship, Ari is both infuriated and intrigued by the handsome stranger. Together Ari and Cullin face a series of dangers as they make their way through space—not the least of which is their mounting attraction to one another. First novel.

Where it's reviewed:
Booklist, November 15, 2010, page 26
Publishers Weekly, September 20, 2010, page 54

Other books you might like:
Catherine Asaro, *Alpha*, 2006
Lois McMaster Bujold, *A Civil Campaign*, 1999
Denise Lopes Heald, *Mistwalker*, 1994
Elizabeth Moon, *Victory Conditions*, 2008
Melissa Scott, *The Empress of Earth*, 1987

741

KATHRYN CRAMER
DAVID HARTWELL, Co-Editor

Year's Best SF 15

(New York: Harper Voyager, 2010)

Subject(s): Adventure; Space colonies; Short stories

Summary: Editors, David G. Hartwell and Kathryn Cramer present an anthology of science-fiction works set in the distant future. The 24 short stories of this volume follow various characters through a series of intergalactic adventures, all set on far-off planets or in the outermost reaches of space. Authors contributing to this volume include Bruce Sterling, Robert Charles Wilson, Vandana Singh, Peter M. Ball, and Mary Robinette Kowal. The editors provide an introduction to this collection.

Where it's reviewed:
Locus, June 2010, page 15

Other books by the same author:
Year's Best SF 14, 2009
The Hard SF Renaissance, 2002
Centaurus, 1999
The Ascent of Wonder, 1994
Christmas Forever, 1993

Other books you might like:
Stephen Baxter, *Phase Space*, 2002
Nancy Kress, *Nano Comes to Clifford Falls and Other Stories*, 2008
Alastair Reynolds, *Galactic North*, 2006
Robert Charles Wilson, *The Perseids: And Other Stories*, 2000
Gene Wolfe, *The Best of Gene Wolfe: A Definitive Retrospective of His Finest Short Fiction*, 2009

742

HANK DAVIS

The Best of the Bolos: Their Finest Hours

(Riverdale, New York: Baen, 2010)

Story type: Alternate Intelligence; Collection
Subject(s): Short stories; Science fiction; Robots

Summary: *The Best of the Bolos: Their Finest Hours*, edited by Hank Davis, is a collection of short-fiction stories written about the Bolo, a massive tank created to think for itself and protect and serve humans during times of war. The Bolo was created by science-fiction author Keith Laumer, a former captain in the US Air Force. In this collection, other science-fiction writers incorporate the Bolo into their own work. This collection includes "Lost Legion" by Stephen Sterling, "A Time to Kill" by David Weber, and "Operation Desert Fox" by Mercedes Lackey and Larry Dixon.

Other books you might like:
Leo Frankowski, *A Boy and His Tank*, 1999
William H. Keith, *Bolo Brigade*, 1997
Keith Laumer, *Bolo: The Annals of the Dinochrome Brigade*, 1976
David Weber, *Bolo!*, 2005
Timothy Zahn, *The Cobra Trilogy*, 2004

743

AARON DEMBSKI-BOWDEN

The First Heretic

(Nottingham, United Kingdom: Games Workshop, 2010)

Series: Horus Heresy Series. Book 16
Subject(s): Adventure; Wars; Heretics
Time period(s): 41st century
Locale(s): Warhammer, Alternate Universe

Summary: The Emperor has been punished, and the Word Bearers are anything but thrilled with their leader's sentence. In search of an outlet for their rage, the warriors unleash their anger on the front line, but slowly come to the realization of the one thing that would bring all the Word Bearers exactly what they desire. And they will stop at nothing to achieve it—even if it means becoming a band of heretics. Aaron Dembski-Bowden's *The First Heretic* is the 16th novel in The Horus Heresy Series.

Other books by the same author:
Helsreach, 2010
Cadian Blood, 2009

Other books you might like:
Dan Abnett, *Titanicus*, 2008
Ben Counter, *Horus Heresy: Battle for the Abyss*, 2008
Nick Kyme, *Firedrake*, 2010
Mike Lee, *Fallen Angels*, 2009
Steve Lyons, *Dead Man Walking*, 2010

744

TROY DENNING

Vortex

(New York: Random House, 2010)

Series: Star Wars: Fate of the Jedi Series. Book 6
Story type: Series
Subject(s): Science fiction; Adventure; Space colonies
Major character(s): Luke Skywalker, Warrior, Father (of Ben); Ben, Son (of Luke); Abeloth, Supernatural Being; Natasi Daala, Leader (Galactic Alliance Chief of State); Vestara Khai, Apprentice (Sith)
Time period(s): Indeterminate Future
Locale(s): Pydyr, Fictional Location; Coruscant, Planet—Imaginary

Summary: In *Star Wars: Fate of the Jedi: Vortex* by Troy Denning, a fragile alliance between Luke Skywalker and the Sith is shattered when they succeed in eliminating the horrifying Abeloth. Now, Luke and his son Ben find themselves once again at odds with the Sith, just as they learn that the galaxy is facing another menace. While dodging the Sith, Luke and Ben travel with Sith warrior-in-training Vestara Khai, trying to muster enough force to defend the galaxy. With the Skywalkers stranded on Pydyr and their allies stranded on Coruscant, devastation seems inevitable. *Vortex* is the sixth book in the Star Wars: Fate of the Jedi series.

Where it's reviewed:
Booklist, November 1, 2010, page 36

Library Journal, October 15, 2010, page 72

Other books by the same author:
Abyss, 2009
Tattooine Ghost, 2003
The Sorcerer, 2002
The Siege, 2001
Star by Star, 2001

Other books you might like:
Paul S. Kemp, *Star Wars: Crosscurrent*, 2010
Karen Miller, *Star Wars: Clone Wars Gambit: Siege*, 2010
Joe Schreiber, *Star Wars: Red Harvest*, 2010
Michael A. Stackpole, *Star Wars: New Jedi Order: Dark Tide II: Ruin*, 2000
Sean Stewart, *Star Wars: Yoda: Dark Rendezvous*, 2004

745

WILLIAM C. DIETZ

Bones of Empire

(New York: Ace Books, 2010)

Subject(s): Adventure; Space colonies; Fantasy
Major character(s): Jack Cato, Police Officer; The Emperor, Shape-Shifter
Time period(s): Indeterminate Future
Locale(s): Outer Space

Summary: William C. Dietz's *Bones of Empire* is the second installment in the science-fiction series that began with *At Empire's Edge*. This outing once again centers on police officer Jack Cato, who now comes face to face with the Emperor of the Uman Empire. Cato then makes a stunning revelation: the Emperor is a shape-shifter. As he sets out to stay on the elusive Emperor's tail, Cato must decipher what this newfound information means for the destiny of the galaxy.

Other books by the same author:
At Empire's Edge, 2009
When Duty Calls, 2008
When All Seems Lost, 2007
Logos Run, 2006
Runner, 2005

Other books you might like:
Gregory Benford, *Find the Changeling*, 1980
Avram Davidson, *The Enemy of My Enemy*, 1966
Joe Haldeman, *Camouflage*, 2004
Doris Piserchia, *The Fluger*, 1980
Roger Zelazny, *Eye of Cat*, 1982

746

GARDNER DOZOIS

The Year's Best Science Fiction: 27th Annual Collection

(New York: St. Martin's Press, 2010)

Subject(s): Fantasy; Space exploration; Short stories

Summary: In *The Year's Best Science Fiction: 27th Annual Collection*, award-winning editor Gardner Dozois presents a collection of sci-fi short stories that encompasses the wide berth of modern science-fiction styles and genres. From space travel to extraterrestrial life, this volume offers an inventive new take on the classic science-fiction short story. Authors contributing to this volume include Ian McDonald, Nancy Kress, Robert Charles Wilson, Nicola Griffith, and John Barnes.

Where it's reviewed:
Locus, August 2010, page 18

Other books by the same author:
Strange Days, 2001
Geodesic Dreams, 1992
Slow Dancing Through Time, 1990
Strangers, 1978
The Visible Man, 1977

Other books you might like:
John Barnes, *Apostrophes and Apocalypses*, 1998
Kathryn Cramer, *Year's Best SF 15*, 2010
Nicola Griffith, *Slow River*, 1995
Nancy Kress, *Beaker's Dozen*, 1998
James Van Pelt, *The Radio Magician and Other Stories*, 2009

747

DAVID DRAKE

What Distant Deeps

(New York: Baen Books, 2010)

Story type: Alternate Universe; Space Opera
Subject(s): Space colonies; Science fiction; Adventure
Major character(s): Daniel Leary, Military Personnel (captain); Adele Mundy, Friend (of Leary), Spy
Time period(s): Indeterminate Future
Locale(s): Outer Space

Summary: *What Distant Deeps* is a science fiction novel by David Drake. In the novel, Captain Daniel Leary and his friend Adele Mundy, a spy, continue to work for the Republic of Cinnabar's freedom from the Alliance of Free Stars; Cinnabar's people have been struggling, and the Republic is failing after heavy taxation and wars with high casualties have made trade virtually impossible. Daniel and Adele are eventually sent to the edges of known space to rest after years of war; however, they discover that the people living in the outer reaches have developed plans of their own: to bring down both the Republic of Cinnabar and the Alliance and get the entire galaxy under their command. It's up to Daniel and Adele to stop them and prevent all of civilization from collapsing.

Where it's reviewed:
Booklist, September 15, 2010, page 38
Library Journal, September 15, 2010, page 64

Other books by the same author:
Patriots, 2009
When the Tide Rises, 2008
The Way to Glory, 2005

The Reaches, 2004
Seas of Venus, 2002

Other books you might like:
Gordon R. Dickson, *Soldier, Ask Not*, 1967
Joe Haldeman, *The Forever War*, 1974
Mike Resnick, *Starship: Mutiny*, 2005
Mike Shepherd, *Kris Longknife: Mutineer*, 2004
David Weber, *Ashes of Victory*, 2000

748

DAVID DRAKE

Complete Hammer's Slammers, Volume 3

(San Francisco: Night Shade Books, 2010)

Story type: Collection
Subject(s): Science fiction; Military life; Short stories

Summary: *The Complete Hammer's Slammers, Volume 3* collects the two concluding novels in David Drake's Hammer's Slammers series, *The Sharp End* and *Paying the Piper*. Originally published in the 1970s, Drake's military science-fiction stories chronicle the adventures of a futuristic mercenary tank contingent and its commanding officer, Colonel Alois Hammer. This volume also includes "The Darkness," a novella by Drake. Science-fiction writer Barry Malzberg provides the introduction.

Other books by the same author:
Patriots, 2009
When the Tide Rises, 2008
The Way to Glory, 2005
The Reaches, 2004
Seas of Venus, 2002

Other books you might like:
David Feintuch, *Prisoner's Hope*, 1995
Leo Frankowski, *A Boy and His Tank*, 1999
Robert Frezza, *A Small Colonial War*, 1990
Keith Laumer, *Bolo: The Annals of the Dinochrome Brigade*, 1976
Jerry Pournelle, *Fires of Freedom*, 2009

749

DAVE DUNCAN

Pock's World

(Calgary: EDGE Science Fiction and Fantasy, 2010)

Subject(s): Extraterrestrial life; Adventure; Voyages and travels
Major character(s): Father Andre, Religious; Athena Fimble, Political Figure; Millie Backet, Worker (bureaucrat); Linn Lazuline, Wealthy; Ratty Turnsole, Journalist
Time period(s): Indeterminate Future
Locale(s): Pock's World, Planet—Imaginary

Summary: In *Pock's World*, author Dave Duncan tells the story of five people sent to investigate a possible alien infestation on a human-populated planet. Determined priest Father Andre, political figure Athena Fimble, paper-pusher Millie Backet, wealthy Linn Lazuline, and journalist Ratty Turnsole are dispatched to Pock's World to find the truth behind the rumors. What they discover, however, is beyond what any of them could have possibly imagined.

Other books by the same author:
The Alchemist's Pursuit, 2009
Hero!, 1991
Strings, 1989
West of January, 1989
Shadow, 1987

Other books you might like:
Michael Bishop, *Beneath the Shattered Moons*, 1976
John Brunner, *The Altar on Asconel*, 1965
Philip K. Dick, *The Game-Players of Titan*, 1963
Alan Dean Foster, *The Deluge Drivers*, 1987
Gene Wolfe, *The Fifth Head of Cerberus*, 1972

750

CHRISTIAN DUNN

Fear the Alien

(Memphis: Games Workshop, 2010)

Story type: Alternate Universe
Subject(s): Extraterrestrial life; Monsters; Wars

Summary: *Fear the Alien*, edited by Christian Dunn, is a science-fiction and fantasy short-story collection in the Warhammer series. The pieces in this collection discuss the possible outcomes of wars between humans, aliens, and other monsters. The aliens have always been the most feared, but the humans and their protectors, the Space Marines, are also aware of the other possible threats: orcs, tyranids, necrons, taus, and eldars. The Space Marines and the people they serve desperately want to rid the world of these dangerous races, but both groups know that entering war with these creatures may be fatal.

Other books by the same author:
Legends of the Space Marines, 2010

Other books you might like:
Dan Abnett, *Sabbat Martyr*, 2003
Ben Counter, *Grey Knights*, 2004
Graham McNeill, *Warriors of Ultramar*, 2003
Sandy Mitchell, *Caves of Ice*, 2004
Gav Thorpe, *The Last Chancers*, 2006

751

ERIC FLINT

1635: The Eastern Front

(New York: Baen, 2010)

Series: Assiti Shards Series. Book 8
Subject(s): Time travel; Thirty Years War, 1618-1648; United States

Major character(s): Mike Stearns, Warrior; Gustavus Adolphus, Royalty (King of Sweden)
Time period(s): 17th century; 1630s (1635)
Locale(s): Europe

Summary: *1635: The Eastern Front* is the eighth installment in Eric Flint's Assiti Shards series. This outing brings readers back to the Thirty Years War, which is tearing across Europe and destroying the continent. Now a new power is emerging in the war: the United States of Europe, headed by the king of Sweden. But Gustavus Adolphus isn't the only powerful player in this new faction. A strange, supernatural occurrence has caused visitors from 20th-century West Virginia to arrive in Europe and pick up arms.

Other books by the same author:
Worlds, 2009
1634: The Baltic War, 2007
1634: The Cannon Law, 2006
1824: The Arkansas War, 2006
1812: The Rivers of War, 2005
Crown of Slaves, 2003
1633, 2002
1632, 2000

Other books you might like:
Phyllis Eisenstein, *Shadow of Earth*, 1979
Leo Frankowski, *Conrad's Time Machine*, 2002
Kim Stanley Robinson, *The Years of Rice and Salt*, 2002
William Sanders, *Journey to Fusang*, 1988
S.M. Stirling, *Island in the Sea of Time*, 1998

752

ALAN DEAN FOSTER

The Human Blend

(New York: Del Rey Books, 2010)

Subject(s): Alternative worlds; Futuristic society; Murder
Major character(s): Whispr, Genetically Altered Being, Murderer; Jiminy Cricket, Genetically Altered Being, Murderer; Dr. Ingrid Seastrom, Doctor
Locale(s): Savannah, Georgia

Summary: *The Human Blend* by Alan Dean Foster is a mystery that takes place in a futuristic society. Whispr and Jiminy, two ruffians with genetically altered body parts, have discovered what they think is pay dirt after killing a tourist with artificial limbs. They abandon their original plan—to sell the tourist's robotic limbs—when they come across a mysterious silver thread that they are sure is worth a lot of money. Yet as soon as they steal the device, misfortune befalls them. Jiminy has vanished, and Whispr is seriously injured. Now Whispr must team up with Dr. Ingrid Seastrom, a Harvard-educated natural human, to figure out what the silver thread is and who wants it from him. Foster is also the author of the Pip and Flinx series.

Where it's reviewed:
Library Journal, June 15, 2010, page S6

Other books by the same author:
Flinx Transcendent: A Pip and Flinx Adventure, 2009

The Candle of Distant Earth, 2006
Drowning World, 2003
The Approaching Storm, 2002
Diuturnity's Dawn, 2002

Other books you might like:
Terry Bisson, *Johnny Mnemonic*, 1995
Lee Killough, *Dragon's Teeth*, 1990
Nancy Kress, *Oaths and Miracles*, 1996
Mike McQuay, *Hot Time in Old Town*, 1981
Richard K. Morgan, *Woken Furies*, 2005

753

DAVID R. GEORGE III

Rough Beasts of Empire

(New York: Simon and Schuster, 2010)

Series: Star Trek: Typhon Pact Series. Book 3
Subject(s): Adventure; Space colonies; Space flight
Major character(s): Spock, Supernatural Being (half-human, half-Vulcan); Benjamin Sisko, Military Personnel (Starfleet officer)
Time period(s): Indeterminate Future
Locale(s): Outer Space

Summary: David R. George III's *Rough Beasts of Empire* is the third novel in the Star Trek: Typhon Pact series. This outing finds Spock struggling to unite the Romulans and the Vulcans, but his best efforts only further divide the warring civilizations. As he continues his attempts to bring peace, Benjamin Sisko is called back to Starfleet for one last assignment. But this final mission requires more time and energy than Sisko had counted on, and now he must face a major decision: go home to his beloved family and risk further danger to the galaxy—or stay on board Starfleet and risk danger to himself and his colleagues.

Other books by the same author:
The Star to Every Wandering, 2007
Provenance of Shadows, 2006
The Serpents Among the Ruins, 2003
Twilight, 2002

Other books you might like:
Christopher L. Bennett, *The Buried Age*, 2007
Margaret Wander Bonanno, *Burning Dreams*, 2006
Greg Cox, *Star Trek: To Reign in Hell: The Exile of Khan Noonien Singh*, 2006
J.M. Dillard, *Resistance*, 2007
S.D. Perry, *Rising Son*, 2003

754

WALTER GREATSHELL

Mad Skills

(New York: Ace Books, 2010)

Subject(s): Accidents; Technology; Adventure
Major character(s): Maddy Grant, Accident Victim

Time period(s): Indeterminate
Locale(s): Harmony, United States

Summary: In Walter Greatshell's *Mad Skills*, Maddy Grant is involved in a near-fatal accident that sends her into a months-long coma. Upon waking, she finds herself in the Braintree Institute, where doctors are experimenting with a new treatment option for her brain injury. They have embedded a piece of revolutionary equipment in her brain, allowing her to be cured. But as Maddy reemerges and enters the community once more, she finds her emotions are going haywire—and someone seems to be controlling her every move.

Where it's reviewed:
Publishers Weekly, November 29, 2010, page 35

Other books by the same author:
Xombies: Apocalypticon, 2010
Xombies, 2004

Other books you might like:
Ben Bova, *The Multiple Man: A Novel of Suspense*, 1976
Algis Budrys, *Who?*, 1958
D.G. Compton, *The Unsleeping Eye*, 1974
Christopher Hodder-Williams, *The Egg-Shaped Thing*, 1967
Daniel Keyes, *Flowers for Algernon*, 1966

755

EDMOND HAMILTON

The Universe Wreckers: The Collected Edmond Hamilton, Volume 3

(Royal Oak, Michigan: Haffner Press, 2010)

Story type: Collection
Subject(s): Science fiction; Short stories

Summary: In *The Universe Wreckers: The Collected Edmond Hamilton, Volume 3*, editor Stephen Haffner presents the third compilation of fiction by science-fiction master Edmond Hamilton. The volume features works previously published in the publications *Weird Tales*, *Amazing Stories*, *Air Wonder Stories*, and *Astounding Stories*. The collection includes "Cities in the Air," "The Life-Masters," "The Space Visitors," "Evans of the Earth Guard," "The Plant Revolt," "The Universe Wreckers," "The Death Lord," "Pigmy Island," "Second Satellite," "World Atavism," and "The Man Who Saw the Future." Author Eric Leif Davin provides the introduction.

Other books by the same author:
The Star Stealers, 2009
What's It Like Out There?, 1974
The Closed Worlds, 1968
The Haunted Stars, 1960
The Star Kings, 1949

Other books you might like:
Roger MacBride Allen, *The Shattered Sphere*, 1994
John W. Campbell, *Black Star Passes*, 1930
Peter F. Hamilton, *The Reality Dysfunction*, 1996

E.E. 'Doc' Smith, *Galactic Patrol*, 1998
Jack Williamson, *The Queen of the Legion*, 1983

756

HARRY HARRISON

The Stainless Steel Rat Returns

(New York: Tor, 2010)

Series: Stainless Steel Rat Series. Book 12
Subject(s): Space colonies; Adventure; Satire
Major character(s): Slippery Jim DiGriz, Retiree; Angelina, Spouse (of Slippery Jim)
Time period(s): 35th century
Locale(s): Moneyplenty, Planet—Imaginary

Summary: In *The Stainless Steel Rat Returns*, author Harry Harrison brings his beloved anti-hero out of retirement for one last intergalactic adventure. Set in the 35th century, this story follows Slippery Jim DiGriz as he relishes his golden years with wife Angelina. But when Jim's uncouth relatives show up on planet Moneyplenty, he is thrust into a new mission that, if not properly accomplished, could spell the end of his happy retirement. This volume is the 12th installment in The Stainless Steel Rat series.

Where it's reviewed:
Booklist, July 1, 2010, page 44
Library Journal, June 15,2010, page 66
Publishers Weekly, June 14, 2010, page 39

Other books by the same author:
Fifty in Fifty, 2001
Return to Eden, 1988
Planet of No Return, 1981
Skyfall, 1976
The Stainless Steel Rat, 1961

Other books you might like:
Poul Anderson, *Sir Dominic Flandry: The Last Knight of Terra*, 2010
Alan Dean Foster, *Flinx Transcendent: A Pip and Flinx Adventure*, 2009
Keith Laumer, *Reward for Retief*, 1989
Murray Leinster, *Med Ship*, 2002
Mike Resnick, *A Gathering of Widowmakers*, 2005

757

ANDY HOARE

Hunt for Voldorius

(Nottingham, United Kingdom: Games Workshop, 2010)

Series: Warhammer 40,000: Space Marine Battles Series. Book 3
Subject(s): Adventure; Demons; Fantasy
Major character(s): Kor'sarro Khan, Military Personnel (Space Marine Captain); Voldorius, Demon
Time period(s): 41st century; 40000s
Locale(s): Warhammer, Alternate Universe

Summary: Kor'sarro Khan is a Space Marine captain with an epic mission on his hands. He must track down and destroy the demon Voldorius. Over the course of ten years, Khan hunts the evil monster terrorizing the world, leading to a landmark battle that changes the young marine's life forever. Andy Hoare's *Hunt for Voldorius* is the third installment in the Warhammer 40,000: Space Marine Battles series.

Other books by the same author:
Star of Damocles, 2007
Rogue Star, 2006

Other books you might like:
Dan Abnett, *Traitor General*, 2004
Matthew Farrer, *Legacy*, 2004
Jonathan Green, *Crusade for Armageddon*, 2003
Simon Spurrier, *Fire Warrior*, 2003
James Swallow, *Faith and Fire*, 2006

758

TANYA HUFF

The Truth of Valor

(New York: DAW, 2010)

Series: Confederation Series. Book 5
Subject(s): Ships; Adventure; Kidnapping
Major character(s): Torin Kerr, Military Personnel (former marine); Craig Ryder, Worker (salvage operator), Boyfriend (of Torin)
Time period(s): Indeterminate Future
Summary: Tanya Huff's *The Truth of Valor* is the fifth novel in the Confederation of Valor science-fiction adventures. Torin Kerr has just left the Marines and is trying to start life anew aboard the ship called Promise. With her boyfriend Craig Ryder at her side, Torin is looking to establish a new career and put the past behind her. But when Craig is kidnapped, Torin springs into action, relying on her Marine training to get back her beloved—and unearth the secret behind his abduction.

Other books by the same author:
The Enchantment Emporium, 2009
Valor's Trial, 2008
The Heart of Valor, 2007
The Better Part of Valor, 2002
Valor's Choice, 2000

Other books you might like:
Lois McMaster Bujold, *Diplomatic Immunity*, 2002
William C. Dietz, *By Force of Arms*, 2000
R.M. Meluch, *The Queen's Squadron*, 1992
Elizabeth Moon, *Once a Hero*, 1997
Mike Resnick, *Starship: Flagship*, 2009

759

KERRIE HUGHES
MARTIN H. GREENBERG, Co-Editor

Love and Rockets

(New York: Penguin, 2010)

Story type: Romance; Space Opera
Subject(s): Love; Romances (Fiction); Extraterrestrial life

Science Fiction

Summary: *Love and Rockets*, edited by Martin H. Greenberg and Kerrie Hughes, is a science-fiction and fantasy short-story collection that focuses on intergalactic love. The stories in this collection feature couples of mixed races—mostly alien and human. These couples fall in love on alien planets, in space ships, in the midst of chaotic space colonies, and even at the space station. Despite their extremely different backgrounds, these couples all realize that love is worth the fight and that happy endings are not always sure things. This collection includes "Second Shift" by Brenda Cooper, "Wanted" by Anita Ensal, and "Dance of Life" by Jody Lynn Nye.

Other books by the same author:
The Dimension Next Door, 2008
Alien Abductions, 1999
Animal Brigade 3000, 1994
Christmas on Ganymede and Other Stories, 1990
Cosmic Critiques, 1990

Other books you might like:
Brenda Cooper, *Wings of Creation*, 2009
Nina Kiriki Hoffman, *Time Travelers, Ghosts, and Other Visitors*, 2003
Jay Lake, *Rocket Science*, 2005
Jody Lynn Nye, *Strong Arm Tactics*, 2005
Kristine Kathryn Rusch, *The Retrieval Artist*, 2002

760

ELIZABETH ANNE HULL

Gateways

(New York: Tor, 2010)

Subject(s): Fantasy; Space exploration; Short stories

Summary: Acclaimed science-fiction expert Elizabeth Anne Hull offers an anthology of short science-fiction stories. *Gateways* includes tales that range from the dramatic to the witty, from the conventional to the creative. The authors contributing to this collection make up a veritable Who's Who of legendary sci-fi authors, including Neil Gaiman, Greg Bear, Ben Bova, Cory Doctorow, and Gene Wolfe.

Other books you might like:
Brian W. Aldiss, *Common Clay: 20 Odd Stories*, 1996
Joe Haldeman, *Dealing in Futures*, 1985
Larry Niven, *Stars and Gods*, 2010
Frederik Pohl, *Platinum Pohl*, 2005
Connie Willis, *Impossible Things*, 1994

761

MARIANNA JAMESON
BILL EVANS, Co-Author

Frozen Fire

(New York: Forge Books, 2010)

Story type: Contemporary
Subject(s): Ecology; Adventure; Fantasy

Major character(s): Dennis Cavendish, Businessman; Garner Blaylock, Activist
Time period(s): 21st century; 2010s
Locale(s): Taino, Caribbean

Summary: In *Frozen Fire*, authors Bill Evans and Marianna Jameson craft a fantasy thriller set on the fictional island of Taino, where a powerful businessman has discovered a precious natural gas that could save Earth from ecological catastrophe. Dennis Cavendish has erected an undersea home with his army of sexually enslaved females, and he is out to mine the valuable gas—with no concern to the possible environmental damage of such action. Into the fold comes environmental activist Garner Blaylock, who is determined to stop Cavendish at any cost.

Where it's reviewed:
Publishers Weekly, August 31, 2009, page 53

Other books by the same author:
Category 7, 2007

Other books you might like:
Michael Crichton, *State of Fear*, 2004
Dakota James, *Greenhouse*, 1984
Judith Moffett, *The Ragged World: A Novel of the Hefn on Earth*, 1991
Kim Stanley Robinson, *Forty Signs of Rain*, 2004
Bruce Sterling, *Heavy Weather*, 1994

762

MICHEL JEURY

Chronolysis

(Encino, California: Black Coat Press, 2010)

Story type: Futuristic
Subject(s): Science fiction; Drugs; Alternative worlds
Major character(s): Daniel Diersant, Explorer (psychronaut); Harry Krupp Hitler I, Nobleman (Emperor of the Undetermined)
Time period(s): Indeterminate Future
Locale(s): Alternate Universe

Summary: Originally published in France in the 1970s, Michel Jeury's *Chronolysis* is recognized as a science-fiction classic. The time-bending plot focuses on a group of "psychronauts," human subjects treated with chronolytic drugs that can alter time. Future, past, and present intersect and collide as the diverse cast of characters travels through a series of alternate universes, experiencing events that have not yet transpired or reliving other events again and again. This edition includes a brief biography of the author, as well as a short story by Jeury published here for the first time. American science-fiction author, Theodore Sturgeon provides the foreword.

Other books you might like:
Pierre Barbet, *The Joan of Arc Replay*, 1978
Rene Barjavel, *Future Times Three*, 1970
Stephen Baxter, *Timelike Infinity*, 1993
John Brunner, *Dreaming Earth*, 1963
Fritz Leiber, *The Big Time*, 1961

763

LES JOHNSON
TRAVIS S. TAYLOR, Co-Author

Back to the Moon

(Riverdale, New York: Baen, 2010)

Subject(s): Space flight; Adventure; Fantasy
Major character(s): Bill Stetson, Astronaut; Paul Gesling, Pilot; Gary Childers, Wealthy
Time period(s): Indeterminate Future
Locale(s): Outer Space

Summary: In *Back to the Moon*, authors Travis S. Taylor and Les Johnson tell the story of a group's attempt to travel to the moon on a luxury commercial voyage. The fates of the three men are wrapped up in the epic journey: astronaut Bill Stetson, charged with overseeing the excursion; Paul Gesling, the main pilot for the ship; and Gary Childers, owner of the company that possesses the spacecraft. Can these three men make it to the moon safely, without endangering themselves, their fellow passengers—or the world?

Other books by the same author:
One Good Soldier, 2009
The Tau Ceti Agenda, 2008
One Day on Mars, 2007
The Quantum Connection, 2005
Warp Speed, 2004

Other books you might like:
Ben Bova, *Moonwar*, 1998
Arthur C. Clarke, *A Fall of Moondust*, 1961
Robert A. Heinlein, *The Moon Is a Harsh Mistress*, 1966
Allen Steele, *Lunar Descent*, 1991
Jeff Sutton, *First on the Moon*, 1958

764

RUDY JOSEPHS

The Edge

(New York: Simon & Schuster Children's Publishing, 2010)

Series: Star Trek: Starfleet Academy Series. Book 2
Story type: Series; Young Adult
Subject(s): Science fiction; Adventure; Schools
Major character(s): James T. Kirk, Student (Starfleet Academy cadet)
Time period(s): 23rd century; 2200s (2255)
Locale(s): San Francisco, California

Summary: In the young adult novel *The Edge*, James T. Kirk is a young man—a freshman cadet at the Starfleet Academy in California. The new cadet is prepared to leave behind his delinquent life in Iowa and study hard to survive the academy's rigorous program. While he struggles to adjust to the lowly life of a plebe, he acquaints himself with the classmates who will become his allies and his adversaries. One fellow cadet seems to excel with ease, and Kirk suspects that he is getting help from one of the female students. *The Edge* is the second book in the Star Trek: Starfleet Academy series.

Other books by the same author:
Big Apple Takedown, 2010
The Marine, 2010

Other books you might like:
Peter David, *Once Burned: The Captain's Table, Book 5*, 1998
David Mack, *Zero Sum Game*, 2010
Dean Wesley Smith, *A Hard Rain*, 2002
Jeri Taylor, *Mosaic*, 1996

765

DREW KARPYSHYN

Retribution

(New York: Del Rey, 2010)

Series: Mass Effect Series. Book 3
Subject(s): Adventure; Space exploration; Extraterrestrial life
Major character(s): Paul Grayson, Military Personnel (former Cerberus operative); Kahlee Sanders, Director; David Anderson, Hero; The Illusive Man, Leader (of Cerberus)
Time period(s): Indeterminate Future
Locale(s): Outer Space

Summary: The Reapers are a band of human-like spacecrafts with a sinister mission: they seek to cull the universe's species and use them toward their own evil ends. The Illusive Man is out to battle the Reapers at any cost, even if that means conducting experiments on someone embedded with Reaper technology. That someone is Paul Grayson, whose subsequent disappearance sets in motion an intergalactic adventure. Based on the video game Mass Effect, Drew Karpyshyn's *Retribution* is the third novel in a series.

Other books by the same author:
Rule of Two, 2008
Revelation, 2007
Path of Destruction, 2006
Temple Hill, 2001
Throne of Bhaal, 2001

Other books you might like:
William C. Dietz, *At Empire's Edge*, 2009
Steven L. Kent, *The Clone Republic*, 2006
Richard K. Morgan, *Black Man*, 2007
Christopher Rowley, *The Bloodstained Man*, 2011
Timothy Zahn, *Blackcollar*, 2006

766

MARILYN KAYE

Now You See Me

(New York: Kingfisher, 2010)

Series: Gifted Series. Book 5
Story type: Young Adult
Subject(s): Magic; Adventure; Spies
Major character(s): Tracey, Student—High School;

Amanda, Student—High School; Jenna, Friend (of Tracey)
Time period(s): 21st century; 2010s
Locale(s): United States

Summary: Tracey is a high-school student with a very unusual power: she can make herself invisible. This talent comes in handy when a series of strange events plague Tracey and other members of her school's "gifted" class, a group of magically talented youngsters. After a spy is thought to be in the ranks of the Gifted, and Tracey's friend Jenna is framed for a crime she had no part of, Tracey uses her unique power to find the truth. Marilyn Kaye's *Now You See Me* is the fifth book in the Gifted series.

Other books by the same author:
Finders Keepers, 2010
Better Late Than Never, 2009
Here Today, Gone Tomorrow, 2009
Play, 2002
Rewind, 2002

Other books you might like:
Wilhelmina Baird, *Chaos Come Again*, 1996
Lester Del Rey, *Pstalemate*, 1971
Alexander Key, *The Forgotten Door*, 1965
Robert Silverberg, *Dying Inside*, 1972
Kate Wilhelm, *City of Cain*, 1974

767

STEVEN L. KENT

The Clone Empire
(New York: Ace Books, 2010)

Series: Clone Series. Book 6
Subject(s): Cloning; Adventure; Space colonies
Major character(s): Wayson Harris, Clone, Military Personnel
Time period(s): Indeterminate Future
Locale(s): Outer Space

Summary: In *The Clone Empire*, Steven L. Kent presents the sixth volume in the Clone series, continuing the escapades of Clone solider Wayson Harris. Harris and his men have managed to live through an epic war, but now they are captives being used for deadly target practice. The only option for escape lies in reconnecting with the Clone Empire and fighting with a vengeance against those who enslave Harris and his crew.

Other books by the same author:
The Clone Betrayal, 2009
The Clone Elite, 2008
The Clone Alliance, 2007
The Clone Republic, 2006
Rogue Clone, 2006

Other books you might like:
C.J. Cherryh, *Betrayer*, 2010
William C. Dietz, *Bodyguard*, 1994
Alan Dean Foster, *Icerigger*, 1974
Joe Haldeman, *Forever Peace*, 1997
S.L. Viehl, *Afterburn*, 2005

768

JAMES KNAPP

The Silent Army
(New York: Roc, 2010)

Series: Revivors Series. Book 2
Subject(s): Zombies; Adventure; Horror
Major character(s): Nico Wachalowski, Agent (federal); Samuel Fawkes, Reanimated Dead (zombie leader)
Time period(s): Indeterminate Future
Locale(s): Earth

Summary: The second novel in James Knapp's Revivors series, *The Silent Army* finds federal agent Nico Wachalowski attempting to prevent a full-fledged zombie attack on the innocent people of the world. Samuel Fawkes is determined to assemble and revive his own private army of the undead, but Nico will do everything in his power to prevent his enemy's dark plan. There's just one problem. Nico may have to slay the woman he loves in order to stop Samuel.

Other books by the same author:
State of Decay, 2010

Other books you might like:
Kevin J. Anderson, *Resurrection, Inc.*, 1988
Ian McDonald, *Terminal Cafe*, 1994
David A. McIntee, *White Darkness*, 1993
Cherie Priest, *Boneshaker*, 2009
Lucius Shepard, *Green Eyes*, 1984

769

E.E. KNIGHT

March in Country
(New York: Roc, 2010)

Series: Vampire Earth Series. Book 9
Subject(s): Vampires; Adventure; Voyages and travels
Major character(s): David Valentine, Military Personnel
Time period(s): Indeterminate Future
Locale(s): United States

Summary: In *March in Country*, author E.E. Knight offers the ninth installment in the Vampire Earth series. This volume finds Major David Valentine reassembling his crew for a mission to track down aid before the Kurian vampires take control. Their adventure leads them into the heart of America as they attempt to save themselves—and the world—from total vampire domination.

Other books by the same author:
Winter Duty, 2009
Fall with Honor, 2008
Valentine's Resolve, 2007
Valentine's Exile, 2006
Choice of the Cat, 2004

Other books you might like:
William R. Burkett, *Sleeping Planet*, 1965
William C. Dietz, *Deathday*, 2001
David Gerrold, *A Matter for Men*, 1983

Robert A. Heinlein, *The Puppet Masters*, 1990
Larry Niven, *Footfall*, 1985

770

GINI KOCH

Alien Tango

(New York: DAW, 2010)

Subject(s): Adventure; Extraterrestrial life; Humor
Major character(s): Kitty Katt, Leader (Centaurian Division commander); Jeff Martini, Leader (Centaurian Division commander), Boyfriend (of Kitty)
Time period(s): Indeterminate Future
Locale(s): United States

Summary: Gini Koch's *Alien Tango* blends humor and science fiction to continue the adventures of Centaurian Division commander Kitty Katt, first begun in 2010's *Touched by an Alien*. Now safely ensconced in their shelter under the desert, Kitty and her comrade/boyfriend Jeff Martini are about to embark on a series of new battles that take them across the country to Florida. En route, they deal with a string of enemies, from terrorists to alien killers. And then there are the most formidable enemies of all: Jeff's family, who are about to meet Kitty Katt for the first time.

Where it's reviewed:
Booklist, December 1, 2010, page 36

Other books by the same author:
Touched by an Alien, 2010

Other books you might like:
Greg Bear, *Queen of Angels*, 1990
Randall Garrett, *Unwise Child*, 1962
Lynn S. Hightower, *Alien Blues*, 1992
Lee Killough, *Deadly Silents*, 1981
Robert J. Sawyer, *Illegal Alien*, 1997

771

MARY ROBINETTE KOWAL

The Hugo Awards Showcase: 2010 Volume

(Rockville, Maryland: Prime, 2010)

Story type: Collection
Subject(s): Science fiction; Short stories
Summary: In *The Hugo Award Showcase*, editor Mary Robinette Kowal presents a collection of short stories selected from the winners of the 2009 Hugo Awards. Chosen by the World Science Fiction Convention, the winning entries represent the best in science-fiction and fantasy writing. This collection includes "The Erdmann Nexus" by Nancy Kress—an eerie tale set in a nursing home; "26 Monkeys, Also the Abyss" by Kij Johnson, which deals with a group of vanished primates; and "Pride and Prometheus" by John Kessel, which blends the works of Jane Austen and Mary Shelley. Kowal provides the introduction.

Other books by the same author:
Chill, 2010

Dust, 2007
Undertow, 2007
Carnival, 2006
Hammered, 2005

Other books you might like:
Paul Di Filippo, *Neutrino Drag*, 2004
Nancy Kress, *The Aliens of Earth*, 1993
Larry Niven, *Stars and Gods*, 2010
Kristine Kathryn Rusch, *Recovering Apollo 8 and Other Stories*, 2010
Michael Swanwick, *The Best of Michael Swanwick*, 2008

772

HENRY KUTTNER
C.L. MOORE, Co-Author

Detour to Otherness

(Royal Oak, Michigan: Haffner Press, 2010)

Story type: Collection
Subject(s): Science fiction; Short stories

Summary: In *Detour to Otherness*, editor Stephen Haffner collects science-fiction stories by Henry Kuttner and C.L. Moore. Included are stories that appeared in *Bypass to Otherness* (1961)—"Cold War," "Call Him Demon," "The Dark Angel," "The Piper's Son," "Absalom," "The Little Things," "Nothing but Gingerbread Left," and "Housing Problem;" and *Return to Otherness* (1962)— "See You Later," "This Is the House," "The Proud Robot," "Gallegher Plus," "The Ego Machine," "Android," "The Sky Is Falling," and "Juke-Box." The volume also features eight previously unpublished stories—"Open Secret," "All Is Illusion," "Rite of Passage," "Baby Face," "Happy Ending," "The Children's Hour," "Dream's End," and "Near Miss."

Other books by the same author:
Secret of the Earth Star and Others, 1991
The Startling Worlds of Henry Kuttner, 1987
Mutant, 1963
Return to Otherness, 1962
Ahead of Time, 1953

Other books you might like:
Philip K. Dick, *Human Is?*, 2007
Damon Knight, *One Side Laughing: Stories Unlike Other Stories*, 1991
Murray Leinster, *First Contacts: The Essential Murray Leinster*, 1998
Eric Frank Russell, *Major Ingredients*, 2000
Robert Sheckley, *Dimensions of Sheckley*, 2002

773

NICK KYME

Firedrake

(Nottingham, United Kingdom: Games Workshop, 2010)

Series: Tome of Fire Trilogy. Book 2
Subject(s): Adventure; Hostages; Magic

Science Fiction

Major character(s): Da'Kir, Librarian; Chaplain Elysius, Hostage
Time period(s): Indeterminate Future
Locale(s): Outer Space

Summary: *Firedrake* is the second book in Nick Kyme's Tome of Fire series. This outing continues the adventures of Da'Kir, who has just been promoted to the status of librarian. Meanwhile, Chaplain Elysius is being held hostage by the Dark Eldar, and the Firedrakes set out on a mission to rescue him. But the Chaplain holds some dangerous secrets—secrets that could spell trouble for the future of the world—and the Firedrakes are in a race against time to ensure the Dark Eldar doesn't gain access to the Chaplain's knowledge.

Other books by the same author:
Grimblades, 2010
Honourkeeper, 2009
Salamander, 2009
Oathbreaker, 2008
Back from the Dead, 2006

Other books you might like:
Aaron Dembski-Bowden, *The First Heretic*, 2010
Graham McNeill, *Chapter's Due*, 2010
Steve Parker, *Rynn's World*, 2010
James Swallow, *Nemesis*, 2010
Henry Zou, *Emperor's Mercy*, 2009

774

LORA LEIGH

Styx's Storm

(New York: Berkley, 2010)

Series: Breeds Series. Book 22
Subject(s): Romances (Fiction); Fantasy; Love
Major character(s): Styx Mackenzie, Supernatural Being (Wolf Breed); Storme Montague, Young Woman
Time period(s): Indeterminate Future

Summary: The 22nd novel in Lora Leigh's Breeds series, *Styx's Storm* finds beautiful Storme Montague on the run from the Breeds who harbor a violent resentment against her father. Styx, a Wolf Breed, is charged with finding—and seducing—Storme in order to get the young woman and her much-sought-after secrets. But as soon as Styx and Storme meet, the fire between them is evident, and it can only be quenched by following their hearts' mutual desire.

Other books by the same author:
Bengal's Heart, 2009
Coyote's Mate, 2009
Mercury's War, 2008
Dawn's Awakening, 2007
Megan's Mark, 2006

Other books you might like:
Stephen Baxter, *Manifold Time*, 2000
Michael G. Coney, *Cat Karina*, 1982
Andre Norton, *Breed to Come*, 1972
Marta Randall, *Dangerous Games*, 1980
S. Andrew Swann, *Fearful Symmetries*, 1999

775

REBECCA LEVENE

Ghost Dance

(London, England: Abaddon Books, 2010)

Series: Infernal Game Series. Book 2
Subject(s): Murder; Supernatural; Fantasy
Major character(s): Morgan, Agent (Hermetic Division), Investigator; Alex, Psychic, Agent (CIA)
Time period(s): 21st century; 2010s
Locale(s): England; United States

Summary: *Ghost Dance* is a chilling, terrifying, and captivating fantasy novel from author Rebecca Levene. The Hermetic Division sends Morgan on a mission to track down the murderer of John Dee, a leading expert on Elizabethan chemistry. The killer possesses superhuman abilities and works for Mossad. In the United States, the CIA hires Alex, a spiritual medium, to investigate the Croatans, a cult that can control animals. When Morgan travels to the US in search of something very valuable to John Dee, she and Alex meet. Together they must work together to uncover Dee's prized possession before it falls into the hands of the wrong person.

Other books by the same author:
Cold Warriors, 2010
Anno Mortis, 2009
Kill or Cure, 2007
End of the Line, 2005
Bad Timing, 2004

Other books you might like:
Piers Anthony, *Blue Adept*, 1981
Andre Norton, *Janus*, 2002
Rudy Rucker, *Hylozoic*, 2009
S.M. Stirling, *The High King of Montival*, 2010
Lawrence Watt-Evans, *Out of This World*, 1994

776

MIKE LUPICA

Hero

(New York: Philomel Books, 2010)

Story type: Young Adult
Subject(s): Fathers; Death; Magic
Major character(s): Zach Harriman, 14-Year-Old; Kate, Girlfriend (of Zach); Mr. Herbert, Aged Person
Time period(s): 21st century; 2010s
Locale(s): United States

Summary: In *Hero*, Mike Lupica tells the story of Zach Harriman, a 14-year-old boy facing a dangerous investigation and a life-changing decision. After his government-agent father is killed, Zach looks into his death and makes a shocking discovery: his dad had special magical powers. What's more is that Zach has seemingly inherited these abilities. Now the teen must decide whether to just let himself be a kid—or follow in his father's footsteps to use his power for the good of the world...and jeopardize his safety.

Where it's reviewed:
Booklist, October 1, 2010, page 86
Publishers Weekly, October 25, 2010, page 49
School Library Journal, December 2010, page 118

Other books by the same author:
The Batboy, 2010
Million-Dollar Throw, 2010
The Big Field, 2009
Safe at Home, 2009
Two-Minute Drill, 2009

Other books you might like:
Michael Bishop, *Count Geiger's Blues*, 1992
Arthur Byron Cover, *Born in Fire*, 2002
Greg Cox, *Friend or Foe?*, 2001
Nancy Holder, *Hauntings*, 2003
Stephen Leigh, *Aces Abroad*, 1988

777

STEVE LYONS

Dead Man Walking

(Nottingham, United Kingdom: Games Workshop, 2010)

Subject(s): Adventure; Fantasy; Wars
Major character(s): Gunthar Soreson, Overseer; Arex, Girlfriend (of Gunthar)
Time period(s): 41st century
Locale(s): Warhammer, Alternate Universe

Summary: The Death Korps of Krieg is the most evil and feared army in the Warhammer Universe. When they conquer and enslave his community, miner Gunthar Soreson is determined to fight back—something he's never done before. Gunthar undergoes training to take on the Death Korps and retrieve the love of his life, who is trapped within the city walls. Steve Lyon's *Dead Man Walking* is an installment in the Wahammer 40000: Imperial Guard series.

Other books by the same author:
Ice Guard, 2008
Death World, 2006
The Stealers of Dreams, 2005
Salvation, 1999
The Witch Hunters, 1998

Other books you might like:
Dan Abnett, *Legion*, 2008
Nick Kyme, *Salamander*, 2009
Graham McNeill, *Storm of Iron*, 2002
James Swallow, *Nemesis*, 2010
Gav Thorpe, *Annihilation Squad*, 2004

778

DAVID MACK

Zero Sum Game

(New York: Simon and Schuster, 2010)

Series: Star Trek: Typhon Pact Series. Book 1
Story type: Series; Space Opera

Subject(s): Science fiction; Space exploration; Adventure
Major character(s): Dr. Julian Bashir, Agent (Starfleet Intelligence); Sarina Douglas, Agent (Starfleet Intelligence); Ezri Dax, Spaceship Captain (U.S.S. Aventine)
Time period(s): Indeterminate Future
Locale(s): U.S.S. Aventine, At Sea; Outer Space

Summary: In *Zero Sum Game* by David Mack, two genetically engineered operatives take on a mission to stop a dangerous Starfleet enemy from implementing a new Federation technology. Agents Sarina Douglas and Dr. Julian Bashir seek out the Breen, the strange species that has stolen Starfleet's prototype slipstream drive, to demolish the device before the Breen can put it into service. Aboard the *U.S.S. Aventine*, Captain Ezri Dax is charged with retrieving Douglas and Bashir, but an enemy Typhon Pact Fleet is doing its best to foil Dax's mission. *Zero Sum Game* is the first book in the Star Trek: Typhon Pact series.

Other books by the same author:
Promises Broken, 2009
Gods of Night, 2008
Mere Mortals, 2008
Reap the Whirlwind, 2007
Harbinger, 2005

Other books you might like:
Rudy Josephs, *The Edge*, 2010
Jeffrey Lang, *Cohesion: String Theory, Book 1*, 2005
Michael A. Martin, *Seize the Fire*, 2010
Dave Stern, *Daedalus*, 2004
Geoffrey Thorne, *Sword of Damocles*, 2007

779

MICHAEL A. MARTIN

Seize the Fire

(New York: Simon and Schuster, 2010)

Series: Star Trek: Typhon Pact Series. Book 2
Story type: Series; Space Opera
Subject(s): Science fiction; Space exploration; Adventure
Major character(s): Riker, Spaceship Captain (U.S.S. Titan); Tuvok, Military Personnel (Commander, U.S.S. Titan)
Time period(s): Indeterminate Future
Locale(s): U.S.S. Titan, At Sea; Outer Space

Summary: In *Seize the Fire* by Michael Martin, an environmental catastrophe that devastates a vital warrior-breeding installation sets off a battle between the Federation and the Gorn Hegemony. In the aftermath of the destruction of their hatchery, the Gorn set to work on reviving an ancient method for synthesizing new worlds. On board the U.S.S. Titan, captains Riker and Tuvok also search the universe for the archaic technology, knowing that the mission puts the lives of their crew in danger. Tuvok also recognizes that the terra-forming technology they seek may pose a bigger threat than the Gorn. *Seize the Fire* is the second book in the Star Trek: Typhon Pact series.

Other books by the same author:
The Needs of the Many, 2010

Science Fiction

Other books you might like:
Kirsten Beyer, *Full Circle*, 2009
Diane Carey, *Star Trek: Voyager: Fire Ship: Captain's Table, Book 4*, 1998
Rudy Josephs, *The Edge*, 2010
David Mack, *Zero Sum Game*, 2010
Olivia Woods, *Fearful Symmetry*, 2008

780

MICHAEL J. MARTINECK

Cinco de Mayo

(Calgary: EDGE Science Fiction and Fantasy, 2010)

Subject(s): Memory; Fantasy; Adventure
Time period(s): Indeterminate Future
Locale(s): Earth

Summary: Michael J. Martineck's *Cinco de Mayo* is set on Earth after a strange, world-changing occurrence has rocked the planet. After several seconds of intense pain experienced by everyone around the world, a feeling of universal bliss sets in...followed by startling revelations. The people of Earth now have access to painful memories—memories not their own. Suddenly, denizens of the entire world know everything there is to know about one another. But why has this happened? And how? And what does it mean for the future of humankind?

Other books by the same author:
The Misspellers, 2002

Other books you might like:
Poul Anderson, *Brain Wave*, 1954
Gregory Benford, *Cosm*, 1998
Karel Capek, *The Absolute at Large*, 1927
Robert J. Sawyer, *Flashforward*, 1999
John Wyndham, *The Day of the Triffids*, 1951

781

ANNE MCCAFFREY
ELIZABETH ANN SCARBOROUGH, Co-Author

Catacombs

(New York: Del Rey, 2010)

Series: Tales of the Barque Cats Series. Book 2
Subject(s): Domestic cats; Adventure; Space flight
Major character(s): Chester, Cat; Jubal, 10-Year-Old; Pshaw-Ra, Cat
Time period(s): Indeterminate Future
Locale(s): Earth; Outer Space

Summary: Feline, Chester and his psychic boy sidekick, Jubal set out to save the world from a power-hungry cat. The Barque cats have been labeled a health risk by authorities on Earth, so the felines team up and jump on board Pshaw-Ra's spaceship, destined for a kitty-dominated planet. But Pshaw-Ra has sinister plans to take over Earth, and Chester and Jubal are the only ones who can stop him. *Catacombs* is the second novel in

Anne McCaffrey and Elizabeth Ann Scarborough's Tales of the Barque Cats series.

Where it's reviewed:
Booklist, December 1, 2010, page 36
Library Journal, October 15, 2010, page 73
Publishers Weekly, October 4, 2010, page 31

Other books by the same author:
Freedom's Ransom, 2003
A Gift of Dragons, 2002
Pegasus in Space, 2000
Acorna, 1997
Dragonseye, 1997

Other books you might like:
C.J. Cherryh, *The Pride of Chanur*, 1981
Ron Goulart, *Tin Angel*, 1973
Tara K. Harper, *Cataract*, 1995
Andre Norton, *The Beast Master*, 1959
James H. Schmitz, *The Demon Breed*, 1968

782

TODD J. MCCAFFREY

Dragongirl

(New York: Del Rey-Ballantine Books, 2010)

Subject(s): Dragons; Science fiction; Adventure
Major character(s): Fiona, Young Woman (dragon-rider), Leader; Talenth, Dragon
Time period(s): Indeterminate
Locale(s): Pern, Planet—Imaginary

Summary: An installment in the voluminous Dragonriders of Pern series, Todd J. McCaffrey's *Dragongirl* follows the adventure-filled life of dragon-rider Fiona. The daring young woman—rider of the lauded gold dragon—has just come back from a far-off realm where hurt dragons and their riders can heal peacefully, away from the threat of the dangerous Thread. But now Fiona has returned, and a series of surprising events soon places her in command of the entire realm. Not only must she win over a reluctant citizenry, but also she must save the population—human and dragon alike—from the ever-increasing threat of more deadly Thread.

Where it's reviewed:
Library Journal, July 2010, page 74

Other books by the same author:
Dragonheart, 2008
Dragonsblood, 2005

Other books you might like:
Michael Bishop, *Stolen Faces*, 1977
C.J. Cherryh, *Angel with the Sword*, 1985
Julie E. Czerneda, *Survival*, 2004
Alan Dean Foster, *Cachalot*, 1980
Murray Leinster, *The Forgotten Planet*, 1954

783

JACK MCDEVITT

Echo

(New York: Ace Books, 2010)

Series: Alex Benedict Series. Book 5
Subject(s): Antiques; Extraterrestrial life; Space exploration
Major character(s): Alex Benedict, Antiques Dealer; Chase Kolpath, Colleague (partner of Alex); Sunset Tuttle, Adventurer
Time period(s): Indeterminate Future
Locale(s): Outer Space

Summary: Antiques specialist Alex Benedict comes across a stone tablet that may contain stunning information about the existence of alien life. When intergalactic adventurer Sunset Tuttle died, he left the tablet with his lover, who has, in turn, brought the relic to Alex and his partner Chase Kolpath. Intrigued by what this artifact's coded message has to say about the possibility of extraterrestrial life forms, Alex and Chase join forces to find the truth behind Sunset Tuttle's stone tablet. *Echo* is the fifth volume in Jack McDevitt's Alex Benedict series.

Where it's reviewed:
Library Journal, October 15, 2010, page 73
Locus, November 2010, page 23
Publishers Weekly, September 27, 2010, page 42

Other books by the same author:
Time Travelers Never Die, 2009
The Devil's Eye, 2008
Cauldron, 2007
Odyssey, 2006
Outbound, 2006

Other books you might like:
John Brunner, *The Dramaturges of Yan*, 1972
Gordon R. Dickson, *Mission to Universe*, 1965
Alan Dean Foster, *Flinx's Folly*, 2003
Frederik Pohl, *Stopping at Slowyear*, 1991
Kristine Kathryn Rusch, *Buried Deep*, 2005

784

KAREN MILLER

Star Wars: Clone Wars Gambit: Siege

(New York: LucasBooks, 2010)

Series: Star Wars: Clone Wars Gambit Series. Book 5
Story type: Futuristic; Space Opera
Subject(s): Adventure; Weapons; Feuds
Major character(s): Anakin Skywalker, Warrior; Obi-Wan Kenobi, Warrior
Time period(s): Indeterminate Future

Summary: The fifth novel in a series, Karen Miller's *Star Wars: Clone Wars Gambit: Siege* continues the otherworldly adventures of the Jedi. This time around, Anakin Skywalker and Obi-Wan Kenobi have infiltrated the distant planet of Lanteeb, where Lok Durd's henchmen are developing a weapon of mass destruction. Durd's army is fast on the trail of the Jedi warriors, and Anakin and Obi-Wan know they will have to act quickly if they are going to save the inhabitants of Lanteeb—and the entire world—from destruction.

Other books by the same author:
The Prodigal Mage, 2010
The Reluctant Mage, 2010
Hammer of God, 2009
The Riven Kingdom, 2008
The Innocent Mage, 2007

Other books you might like:
Elaine Cunningham, *Dark Journey*, 2002
Troy Denning, *Abyss*, 2009
Paul S. Kemp, *Star Wars: Crosscurrent*, 2010
James Luceno, *Dark Lord: The Rise of Darth Vader*, 2005
Steve Perry, *Shadows of the Empire*, 1996

785

L.E. MODESITT JR.

Empress of Eternity

(New York: Tor, 2010)

Story type: Futuristic
Subject(s): Canals; Technology; Revolutions
Major character(s): Maertyn, Scientist; Maarlyna, Scientist; Eltyn, Scientist; Faelyna, Scientist; Duhyle, Scientist; Helkira, Scientist
Time period(s): Multiple Time Periods

Summary: In *Empress of Eternity*, author L.E. Modesitt, Jr., presents a century-spanning tale of scientists living in three different eras struggling to figure out the secrets of a monolithic canal that divides Earth. Six scientists each tries to crack the code of the fabled structure, how it came to be, and what it means for the future of humankind, all while dealing with the drama, turmoil, and danger of life in their respective civilizations.

Where it's reviewed:
Analog, March 2011, page 106
Booklist, November 15, 2010, page 27
Library Journal, November 15,2010, page 62

Other books by the same author:
The Eternity Artifact, 2005
Ecolitan Prime, 2003
The Ethos Effect, 2003
Archform: Beauty, 2002
Adiamante, 1996

Other books you might like:
Isaac Asimov, *The End of Eternity*, 1955
Gregory Benford, *Timescape*, 1980
Gordon R. Dickson, *Time Storm*, 1977
Fritz Leiber, *The Big Time*, 1961
Jamil Nasir, *The Higher Space*, 1996

Science Fiction

786

LARRY NIVEN
EDWARD M. LERNER, Co-Author

Betrayer of Worlds
(New York: Tor, 2010)

Series: Ringworld Series. Book 8
Subject(s): Adventure; Fantasy; Space colonies
Major character(s): Louis Wu, Adventurer; Achilles, Political Figure; Nessus, Alien; Ol't'ro, Supernatural Being
Time period(s): Indeterminate Future
Locale(s): Outer Space

Summary: In *Betrayer of Worlds*, authors Larry Niven and Edward Lerner present the fourth novel in the Ringworld series. This outing finds a band of fighters, including adventurer Louis Wu, taking on a new threat to the future of civilization. Along the way, Wu, along with Achilles, Nessus, and Ol't'ro, must face down his most deadly adversary yet—and risk his life in the process.

Where it's reviewed:
Locus, December 2010, page 23

Other books by the same author:
Stars and Gods, 2010
The Draco Tavern, 2006
Ringworld's Children, 2004
Scatterbrain, 2003
Tales of Known Space, 1975

Other books you might like:
Kevin J. Anderson, *Hidden Empire*, 2002
Poul Anderson, *Star Ways*, 1956
Gregory Benford, *Beyond Infinity*, 2004
Peter F. Hamilton, *Judas Unchained*, 2006
Alastair Reynolds, *House of Suns*, 2009

787

LARRY NIVEN

The Best of Larry Niven
(Burton, Michigan: Subterranean, 2010)

Story type: Collection
Subject(s): Science fiction; Short stories

Summary: *The Best of Larry Niven* collects 27 short stories by award-winning author Larry Niven, first published between 1965 and 2000. Covering a range of genres from fantasy and science fiction to mystery and nonfiction, the collection reveals Niven's versatility and longevity as an author. Featured stories include "Not Long Before the End," "Man of Steel, Woman of Kleenex," "The Deadlier Weapon," "All the Myriad Ways," "Flash Crowd," and others. A headnote by Niven prefaces each story. Author Jerry Pournelle provides the introduction.

Where it's reviewed:
Booklist, November 1, 2010, page 36
Locus, December 2010, page 23
Publishers Weekly, October 4, 2010, page 32

Other books by the same author:
Stars and Gods, 2010
The Draco Tavern, 2006
Ringworld's Children, 2004
Scatterbrain, 2003
Tales of Known Space, 1975

Other books you might like:
Poul Anderson, *Call Me Joe*, 2009
Stephen Baxter, *Traces*, 1998
Greg Bear, *The Collected Stories of Greg Bear*, 2002
Gregory Benford, *Immersion and Other Short Novels*, 2002
Arthur C. Clarke, *The Collected Stories of Arthur C. Clarke*, 2001

788

PEARL NORTH

The Boy from Ilysies
(New York: Tor Teen, 2010)

Subject(s): Cultural conflict; Fantasy; Food
Major character(s): Po, 15-Year-Old
Time period(s): Indeterminate Future
Locale(s): Libyrinth, Fictional Location

Summary: Fifteen-year-old Po was raised on Ilysies, a culture where women are dominant to men, and has now come to the community of Libyrinth, which operates under much different cultural norms. Suddenly confronted with a new set of values, Po must reexamine all he has been taught, prompting him to search for a long-lost artifact known as the Endymion Rose, which could restore peace to the warring cultures and help end a long-enduring food shortage. Pearl North's *The Boy from Ilysies* is the sequel to 2009's *Libyrinth*.

Other books by the same author:
Libyrinth, 2009

Other books you might like:
Jim Aikin, *The Wall at the Edge of the World*, 1993
Benjamin Appel, *The Death Master (The Funhouse)*, 1959
Orson Scott Card, *Empire*, 2007
Louise Marley, *The Maquisarde*, 2002
Fred Saberhagen, *Love Conquers All*, 1974

789

PHILIP PALMER

Version 43
(New York: Orbit, 2010)

Subject(s): Crime; Adventure; Fantasy
Major character(s): Version 43/44, Cyborg
Time period(s): Indeterminate Future
Locale(s): Belladonna, Planet—Imaginary

Summary: Philip Palmer's *Version 43* tells the story of a cyborg good-guy charged with eradicating the rampant crime plaguing the planet Belladonna. Version 43, as he is known, investigates murders, corruption, and position in Bompasso City, and he is used to the nefarious goings-on of the bustling berg. But when a band of intergalactic adversaries declares war, Version 43 will be forced to face the most daunting challenge of his career.

Other books by the same author:
Red Claw, 2009
Debatable Space, 2008

Other books you might like:
Neal Barrett Jr., *The Karma Corps*, 1984
Alfred Bester, *The Stars My Destination*, 1956
Philip K. Dick, *The Unteleported Man*, 1964
Sean Williams, *The Resurrected Man*, 1998
Walter Jon Williams, *Knight Moves*, 1985

790

GRAHAM SHARP PAUL

The Battle for Commitment Planet
(New York: Del Rey, 2010)

Series: Helfort's War Series. Book 4
Subject(s): Adventure; Love; Space colonies
Major character(s): Helfort, Military Personnel; Anna Cheung, Girlfriend (of Helfort), Captive
Time period(s): Indeterminate Future
Locale(s): Hammer Worlds, Alternate Universe

Summary: Graham Sharp Paul's *The Battle for Commitment Planet* is the fourth novel in the Helfort's War series. This outing finds Helfort, a solider of the Federation, faced with a decision that could spell doom for both himself and the woman he loves. The evildoers of the Hammer Worlds want Helfort to turn himself in, and if he doesn't, they have brutal plans in store for their captive, Helfort's girlfriend, Anna Cheung. Now Helfort must decide how to both rescue Anna and evade his own capture and inevitable demise at the hands of the Hammer Worlds.

Other books by the same author:
The Battle of Devastation Reef, 2009
The Battle of the Hammer Worlds, 2008
The Battle at the Moons of Hell, 2007

Other books you might like:
John Dalmas, *The Lizard War*, 1989
William C. Dietz, *The Final Battle*, 1995
David Feintuch, *Midshipman's Hope*, 1994
Mike Shepherd, *Kris Longknife: Redoubtable*, 2010
David Weber, *Off Armageddon Reef*, 2006

791

CHERIE PRIEST

Clementine
(Burton, Michigan: Subterranean Press, 2010)

Subject(s): Alternative worlds; Space flight; Fantasy
Major character(s): Maria Isabella Boyd, Spy; Croggon Hainey, Pirate

Time period(s): 19th century
Locale(s): United States

Summary: Cherie Priest's *Clementine* is a steampunk thriller set in an alternative 19th century. Here Maria Isabella Boyd, onetime actress turned Confederate double agent, embarks on a mission aboard the spaceship known as Clementine. But Clementine is a highly sought after vessel, and the ship's former owner, ex-slave Croggon Hainey, wants it back in his possession. Soon Maria and Croggon are forced to combat a mutual enemy as they race against time to save the fate of Clementine—and the world.

Other books by the same author:
Dreadnought, 2010
Boneshaker, 2009
Fathom, 2008
Nor Flesh Nor Feathers, 2007
Wings to the Kingdom, 2006

Other books you might like:
Stephen Baxter, *Anti-Ice*, 1993
Paul Di Filippo, *The Steampunk Trilogy*, 1995
K.W. Jeter, *Infernal Devices: A Mad Victorian Fantasy*, 1987
Keith Laumer, *Imperium*, 2005
Bruce Sterling, *The Difference Engine*, 1991

792

JEAN RABE
MARTIN H. GREENBERG, Co-Editor

Steampunk'd
(New York: DAW, 2010)

Story type: Alternate History; Collection
Subject(s): Industrial Revolution, ca. 1750-1900; Robotics; Science fiction
Time period(s): 19th century-20th century; 1830-1900

Summary: *Steampunk'd*, edited by Jean Rabe and Martin H. Greenberg, is a short-story collection that blends science fiction, horror, and fantasy elements in an industrial setting. The stories in this book take place between 1830 and 1900 in various locations throughout the world, from England to South Africa to America. At this time, electricity had not yet been invented, so all machines and robots—and humans with robotic limbs—ran on steam energy. The stories in this collection include "Chance Corrigan and the Tick-Tock King of the Nile," "The Battle of Cumberland Gap," "Scourge of the Spoils," and "Echoer."

Other books by the same author:
The Finest Challenge, 2006
The Finest Choice, 2005
The Finest Creation, 2004
Downfall, 2000
The Day of the Tempest, 1997

Other books you might like:
Paul Di Filippo, *The Steampunk Trilogy*, 1995
Harry Harrison, *A Transatlantic Tunnel, Hurrah!*, 1972
Michael Moorcock, *The Warlord of the Air*, 1971

Cherie Priest, *Dreadnought*, 2010
Bruce Sterling, *The Difference Engine*, 1991

H. Nearing, *The Sinister Researches of C.P. Ransome*, 1954

793

CRIS RAMSAY

Brain Box Blues

(New York: Ace Books, 2010)

Subject(s): Fantasy; Rural life; Adventure
Major character(s): Jack Carter, Police Officer (sheriff)
Time period(s): 21st century; 2010s
Locale(s): Eureka, Oregon

Summary: In *Brain Box Blues*, author Cris Ramsay presents a novel based on the popular SyFy network television show *Eureka*. Set in a small town in the Pacific Northwest, this volume follows Sheriff Jack Carter as he attempts to save the town's residents from a strange device that can record and retain human thought. Known as the Brain Box, the bizarre device wreaks havoc on the minds of Eureka residents, and it takes all Carter's cunning and skill to combat this formidable foe.

Other books by the same author:
Substitution Method, 2010

Other books you might like:
Michael Greatrex Coney, *Friends Come in Boxes*, 1973
Dennis Danvers, *Circuit of Heaven*, 1998
Michael J. Martineck, *Cinco de Mayo*, 2010
Bob Shaw, *Other Days, Other Eyes*, 1972
Ian Watson, *The Flies of Memory*, 1990

794

CRIS RAMSAY

Substitution Method

(New York: Ace Books, 2010)

Story type: Contemporary
Subject(s): Rural life; Technology; Adventure
Major character(s): Jack Carter, Police Officer (sheriff)
Time period(s): 21st century; 2010s
Locale(s): Eureka, Oregon

Summary: The town of Eureka, Oregon, is a community like no other: all of its denizens are geniuses. But as the town produces more and more cutting-edge technology, that technology poses an increasing threat to the citizenry. Sheriff Jack Carter stands at the threshold of public safety and responsibility, determined to keep the town safe from its latest chaotic happening. Cris Ramsay's *Substitution Method* is based on the television series *Eureka*.

Other books by the same author:
Brain Box Blues, 2010

Other books you might like:
Alan Dean Foster, *Codgerspace*, 1992
Ron Goulart, *The Enormous Hourglass*, 1976
Isidore Haiblum, *Out of Sync*, 1990
Edward Hoch, *The Transvection Machine*, 1971

795

MIKE RESNICK

Blasphemy

(Urbana, Illinois: Golden Gryphon Press, 2010)

Subject(s): Religion; Faith; Short stories

Summary: Award-winning author Mike Resnick presents a collection of original short fiction revolving around the themes of authoritarianism and the human need to believe. *Blasphemy* is made up of two novellas and five short stories and tackles the consequences of faith with the author's trademark style and insight. Titles in this volume include "Genesis: The Rejected Canon," "Walpurgis III," and "The Branch."

Other books by the same author:
Starship: Flagship, 2009
New Dreams for Old, 2006
A Miracle of Rare Design, 2004
The Return of Santiago, 2003
The Outpost, 2001

Other books you might like:
L. Sprague de Camp, *Aristotle and the Gun and Other Stories*, 2002
Harry Harrison, *Fifty in Fifty*, 2001
Keith Laumer, *Alien Minds*, 1991
Murray Leinster, *First Contacts: The Essential Murray Leinster*, 1998
Jack Vance, *The Narrow Land*, 1982

796

J.D. ROBB

Indulgence in Death

(New York: G.P. Putnam's Sons, 2010)

Series: Eve Dallas Series. Book 32
Subject(s): Mystery fiction; Serial murders; Law enforcement
Major character(s): Eve Dallas, Detective—Police (Lieutenant), Spouse (of Roarke); Roarke, Spouse (of Eve); Delia Peabody, Detective—Police; Jamal Houston, Chauffeur; Ava Crampton, Prostitute; Luc Delaflote, Cook (celebrity chef); Adrianne Jonas, Businesswoman
Time period(s): 21st century; 2050s (2059)
Locale(s): New York, New York

Summary: In *Indulgence in Death* by J.D. Robb, Eve Dallas is a lieutenant with New York's Police and Security Department in the mid-21st century. Returning from a trip to Ireland, Eve goes back to work immediately on a gruesome case of serial murder. The high-society victims include chauffeur Jamal Houston, high-class call girl Ava Crampton, famous chef Luc Delaflote, and socialite Adrianne Jones. The killer's choice of peculiar weapons includes a crossbow, bayonet, harpoon, and bullwhip.

Eve brings her husband, Roarke, and Detective Delia Peabody onto the case to find the twisted murderer before he kills again. *Indulgence in Death* is the 32nd book in the Eve Dallas series.

Where it's reviewed:
Booklist, October 1, 2010, page 33
Publishers Weekly, September 6, 2010, page 22

Other books by the same author:
Fantasy in Death, 2010
Kindred in Death, 2009
Promises in Death, 2009
Salvation in Death, 2008
Strangers in Death, 2008

Other books you might like:
Eric Brown, *New York Blues*, 2001
Lee Killough, *The Doppelganger Gambit*, 1979
Paul Levinson, *The Consciousness Plague*, 2002
Richard K. Morgan, *Altered Carbon*, 2002
Lawrence Watt-Evans, *Nightside City*, 1989

797

JACK ROGAN

The Ocean Dark

(New York: Ballantine Books, 2010)

Story type: Contemporary
Subject(s): Monsters; Adventure; Brothers
Major character(s): Josh Hart, Agent (FBI); Gabe Rio, Brother (of Miguel), Criminal; Miguel Rio, Brother (of Gabe), Criminal
Time period(s): 21st century; 2010s
Locale(s): Caribbean

Summary: Jack Rogan's *The Ocean Dark* is set on a far-off Caribbean island, where a ship of illegal arms has docked to conduct its nefarious business. The ship is run by brothers, Miguel and Gabe Rio, but there is also an undercover FBI operative, Josh Hart, on board, ready to arrest the fugitive siblings. Hart, however, soon learns there is something far more sinister going down than the trading of illegal guns—and it involves inhuman creatures hungry for the souls of mankind.

Other books you might like:
Steve Alten, *Meg: A Novel of Deep Terror*, 1997
Peter Benchley, *White Shark*, 1994
Lincoln Child, *Relic*, 1995
James Rollins, *Ice Hunt*, 2003
Charles Wilson, *Extinct*, 1997

798

KAREN A. ROMANKO

Retro Spec: Tales of Fantasy and Nostalgia

(Raven Electrick Ink, 2010)

Story type: Alternate History; Collection
Subject(s): Fantasy; Alternative worlds; Short stories
Summary: *Retro Spec: Tales of Fantasy and Nostalgia*, edited by Karen A. Romanko, is a short-story collection

that blends not only genres, but also time periods. The stories in this collection fall within the realms of science fiction, fantasy, and horror. They take place during World War II, the fall of the Berlin Wall, and even at the time of Chernobyl. Aliens invade Earth, ghosts haunt their loved ones, and women make the very first trip into outer space in this collection. Twenty-six authors contributed to this collection, including David D. Levine, Marge Simon, Jude-Marie Green, and G. O. Clark.

Other books you might like:
Charles Dickinson, *A Shortcut in Time*, 2003
George Alec Effinger, *The Nick of Time*, 1985
Jack Finney, *Time and Again*, 1970
Joe Haldeman, *The Accidental Time Machine*, 2007
Robert A. Heinlein, *The Door into Summer*, 1957

799

CHRISTOPHER ROWLEY

Money Shot

(New York: Tor, 2010)

Series: Netherworld Trilogy. Book 3
Subject(s): Adventure; Murder; Memory
Major character(s): Rook Venner, Detective—Police; Plesur, Model (Pleasure Model)
Time period(s): Indeterminate Future

Summary: At one point, police detective Rook Venner had a thriving career with the local police department, but a murder case has caused him to go on the run with the beautiful woman who apparently witnessed the brutal event. The memory of the murder, however, is implanted deep within her brain, and the authorities have dispatched a band of robotic warriors to cull this data—and they will stop at nothing to get the truth they so desperately seek. *Money Shot* is the third book in Christopher Rowley's Netherworld Trilogy.

Other books by the same author:
The Bloodstained Man, 2010
Pleasure Model, 2010
To a Highland Nation, 1993
The Vang: The Battlemaster, 1990
The War for Eternity, 1983

Other books you might like:
Tobias S. Buckell, *Halo: The Cole Protocol*, 2008
William C. Dietz, *Halo: The Flood*, 2003
Nick Kyme, *Back from the Dead*, 2006
Eric S. Nylund, *Halo: Ghosts of Onyx*, 2006
Karen Traviss, *Aspho Fields*, 2008

800

KRISTINE KATHRYN RUSCH

Recovering Apollo 8 and Other Stories

(Urbana, Illinois: Golden Gryphon Press, 2010)

Story type: Alternate History; Collection
Subject(s): Extraterrestrial life; Space exploration; Discovery and exploration

Summary: *Recovering Apollo 8 and Other Stories* is a collection of short stories and one novella written by Kristine Kathryn Rusch. This collection blends genres such as science fiction, history, and horror. The stories in this book focus on the seemingly never-ending battle between humans and aliens for not only Earth, but also the entire galaxy. The characters in these stories fight witches, aliens, and warlords for their loves, families, and country. This collection includes "The Strangeness of the Day," "The End of the World," and "Craters." Rusch is also the author of many romance, mystery, and science-fiction titles including *The Black Queen*, *X-Men*, and *Star Wars: The New Rebellion*.

Where it's reviewed:
Locus, July 2010, page 19

Other books by the same author:
Diving into the Wreck, 2009
Duplicate Effort, 2009
Recovery Man, 2007
Paloma, 2006
The Retrieval Artist, 2002

Other books you might like:
Greg Bear, *The Collected Stories of Greg Bear*, 2002
Nina Kiriki Hoffman, *Legacy of Fire*, 1990
Larry Niven, *Stars and Gods*, 2010
Joanna Russ, *The Hidden Side of the Moon*, 1987
Robert Charles Wilson, *The Perseids: And Other Stories*, 2000

801

PAMELA SARGENT

Seed Seeker

(New York: Tor, 2010)

Subject(s): Space colonies; Adolescent interpersonal relations; Adventure
Major character(s): Bian, Teenager; Safrah, Teenager
Time period(s): Indeterminate Future
Locale(s): Home, Planet—Imaginary

Summary: Pamela Sargent's *Seed Seeker*, the third novel in a series, is set on a distant planet colonized by humans. Two teen girls, Bian and Safrah, live on the planet called Home, and when they see a strange light in the sky, they are convinced that Ship, the vessel that created them, is returning. Both girls have very different responses to the potential event, which produces a colony-wide war between the different villages on Home.

Where it's reviewed:
Booklist, December 15, 2010, page 29
Locus, December 2010, page 25
Publishers Weekly, September 13, 2010, page 28

Other books by the same author:
Farseed, 2007
Thumbprints, 2004
Child of Venus, 2001
Climb the Wind, 1999
Cloned Lives, 1976

Other books you might like:
Greg Bear, *Moving Mars*, 1993
Michael Bishop, *Beneath the Shattered Moons*, 1976
Larry Niven, *The Legacy of Heorot*, 1987
Kim Stanley Robinson, *Red Mars*, 1993
Allen Steele, *Coyote*, 2002

802

KEN SCHOLES

Diving Mimes, Weeping Czars and Other Unusual Suspects

(Kent, Washington: Fairwood Press, 2010)

Subject(s): Fantasy; Apocalypse; Short stories

Summary: In the short-story collection, *Diving Mimes, Weeping Czars and Other Unusual Suspects*, author Ken Scholes marries humor, fantasy, and science fiction with a series of offbeat tales. The unusual entries of this volume encompass a number of whimsical adventures, from a flamboyant minister and his devoted flock fumbling through America in the wake of the apocalypse to the relationship problems plaguing the world's superheroes. With their eccentricity and humor, these lighthearted tales offer a fresh perspective on the sci-fi genre.

Other books by the same author:
Antiphon, 2010
Canticle, 2009
Lamentation, 2009
Long Walks, Last Flights, and Other Strange Journeys, 2008
Last Flight of the Goddess, 2006

Other books you might like:
Paul Di Filippo, *Harsh Oases*, 2009
Harlan Ellison, *The Troublemakers: Stories by Harlan Ellison*, 2001
John Kessel, *The Pure Product*, 1997
Ursula K. Le Guin, *Changing Planes*, 2003
Joanna Russ, *The Zanzibar Cat*, 1983

803

JOE SCHREIBER

Star Wars: Red Harvest

(New York: LucasBooks, 2010)

Subject(s): Zombies; Horror; Flowers
Major character(s): Hestizo Trace, Warrior (Jedi); Darth Scabrous, Leader (Sith Lord)
Time period(s): Indeterminate Future
Locale(s): Alternate Universe

Summary: Joe Schreiber's *Star Wars: Red Harvest* finds sinister Darth Scabrous enacting a dark plot capable of destroying the entire Empire. Determined to become immortal, he sends his henchman to pilfer the most precious ingredient necessary to his plans: a rare black orchid. But the orchid's keeper, Hestizo Trace, is certain that Darth's attempts at eternal life will be met with failure, and she just may be proven right when Scabrous's magical formula unleashes a band of bloodthirsty zombies.

Other books by the same author:
The Unholy Cause, 2010
Death Troopers, 2009
No Doors, No Windows, 2009
Chasing the Dead, 2006

Other books you might like:
Troy Denning, *Star by Star*, 2001
Greg Keyes, *Edge of Victory I: Conquest*, 2001
Matthew Woodring Stover, *Star Wars: The New Jedi Order: Traitor (Book 13)*, 2002
Karen Traviss, *Order 66*, 2008
Sean Williams, *The Force Unleashed*, 2008

804

MIKE SHEPHERD

Kris Longknife: Redoubtable

(New York: Ace Books, 2010)

Series: Kris Longknife Series. Book 8
Subject(s): Adventure; Pirates; Wars
Major character(s): Kris Longknife, Military Personnel; Vicki Peterwald, Military Personnel
Time period(s): Indeterminate Future
Locale(s): Outer Space

Summary: Soldier Kris Longknife is on a new assignment to protect the world from pirates, who are conducting businesses outside the Rim in an attempt to evade authorities. Kris and her crew wage war on hoards of savage pirates, and during their escapades, happen upon a planet that's been conquered by the Peterwald Security Firm. And Peterwald has its own interests in keeping the pirates alive. But Kris is on a mission, and she isn't about to let the political interests of a nefarious planet deter her. Mike Shepherd's *Kris Longknife: Redoubtable* is the eighth novel in the Kris Longknife series.

Other books by the same author:
Kris Longknife: Undaunted, 2009
Kris Longknife: Intrepid, 2008
Kris Longknife: Audacious, 2007
Kris Longknife: Resolute, 2006
Kris Longknife: Deserter, 2005

Other books you might like:
Jack Campbell, *The Lost Fleet: Dauntless*, 2006
Elizabeth Moon, *Change of Command*, 1999
Graham Sharp Paul, *The Battle of Devastation Reef*, 2009
Mike Resnick, *Starship: Mercenary*, 2007
Karen Traviss, *Star Wars 501st*, 2009

805

JAMES ROBERT SMITH

The Flock

(New York: Forge Books, 2010)

Story type: Contemporary
Subject(s): Ecology; Dinosaurs; Adventure
Major character(s): Vance Holcomb, Activist, Wealthy
Time period(s): 21st century; 2010s
Locale(s): Florida, United States

Summary: James Robert Smith's *The Flock* follows the exploits of a powerful media company out to conquer and gentrify an isolated Florida swampland—and eliminate the dinosaur-like birds that inhabit it. The Berg Brothers are major media figures who decide a stretch of land in the Florida swamps is the perfect place to erect the ideal American town. But the creatures who live there are ready to fight these invaders at all costs, and they're aided in their efforts by wealthy environmental activist Vance Holcomb. First novel.

Other books you might like:
Greg Bear, *Dinosaur Summer*, 1998
James Blish, *The Night Shapes*, 1962
L. Sprague de Camp, *Rivers of Time*, 1993
Sir Arthur Conan Doyle, *The Lost World*, 1912
John Taine, *The Greatest Adventure*, 1929

806

JAMES SWALLOW

Nemesis

(Nottingham, United Kingdom: Games Workshop, 2010)

Series: Horus Heresy Series. Book 15
Subject(s): Wars; Assassination; Violence
Time period(s): 41st century
Locale(s): Warhammer, Alternate Universe

Summary: The 15th book in The Horus Heresy series, James Swallow's *Nemesis* is set in the Warhammer Universe, where the Dropsite Massacre has left scores dead and the Imperial factions desperate for a resolution. To bring about this end, they let loose a band of killers unlike anything the world has ever seen—resulting in a shocking turn of events in an already bloody battle.

Other books by the same author:
Black Tide, 2010
Nightfall, 2009
Red Fury, 2008
The Flight of the Eisenstein, 2007
Faith and Fire, 2006

Other books you might like:
Dan Abnett, *Prospero Burns*, 2010
Aaron Dembski-Bowden, *Helsreach*, 2010
Graham McNeill, *A Thousand Sons*, 2010
Anthony Reynolds, *Dark Creed*, 2010
Henry Zou, *Flesh and Iron*, 2010

807

PATRICK SWENSON

The Best of Talebones

(Kent, Washington: Fairwood Press, 2010)

Subject(s): Fantasy; Adventure; Short stories

Summary: In *The Best of Talebones*, editor Patrick Swenson compiles a collection of short sci-fi fiction taken from the pages of *Talebones* magazine. This anthology of stories contains 42 tales of fantasy, adventure, and intergalactic intrigue, written by both established authors and emerging voices in the field.

Where it's reviewed:
Locus, November 2010, page 21

Other books you might like:
Jack Cady, *Ghosts of Yesterday*, 2003
Nina Kiriki Hoffman, *Courting Disasters and Other Strange Affinities: Short Stories*, 1991
Jay Lake, *Rocket Science*, 2005
William F. Nolan, *Wild Galaxy*, 2005
Ray Vukcevich, *Boarding Instructions*, 2010

808

SHERI S. TEPPER

The Waters Rising

(New York: Harper Voyager, 2010)

Subject(s): Ecology; Adventure; Apocalypse
Major character(s): Xulai, Young Woman; Great Bear, Overseer (protector of Xulai); Precious Wind, Overseer (protector of Xulai)
Time period(s): Indeterminate Future
Locale(s): Norland, Fictional Location

Summary: In *The Waters Rising*, author Sheri S. Tepper tells the story of Xulai, a young woman living in a post-apocalyptic world. The threat to the planet, however, is not over yet: the oceans are beginning to rise at an alarming level. The world's only hope lies in Xulai, who witnesses a ghost from a previous era that assigns her a noble and treacherous mission. Can Xulai and her protectors stop the rising water levels before it's too late?

Where it's reviewed:
Publishers Weekly, July 26, 2010, page 58

Other books by the same author:
The Margarets, 2008
The Companions, 2003
The Fresco, 2000
The Family Tree, 1997
Gibbons Decline and Fall, 1997

Other books you might like:
Brian W. Aldiss, *Hothouse*, 1962
Philip Jose Farmer, *Dark Is the Sun*, 1979
Mick Farren, *The Song of Phaid the Gambler*, 1981
Steven Gould, *Blind Waves*, 2000
Brian Stableford, *Serpent's Blood*, 1996

809

KAREN TRAVISS

Anvil Gate

(New York: Del Rey-Ballantine Books, 2010)

Series: Gears of War Series. Book 3
Story type: Dystopian; Military
Subject(s): Wars; Adventure; Fantasy
Major character(s): Marcus Fenix, Warrior
Time period(s): Indeterminate Future
Locale(s): Jacinto, Planet—Imaginary

Summary: Karen Traviss's *Gears of War: Anvil Gate* is the third installment in the Gears of War series. On a far-off futuristic planet, the Locust Horde has finally been defeated. Just as the survivors are cleaning up the wreckage and trying to move on, however, another threat beckons. The force known as The Lambent has come to wreak havoc, and Marcus Fenix and the Gears will have to join forces with the Stranded in order to destroy this new enemy.

Other books by the same author:
501st, 2009
Jacinto's Remnant, 2009
Aspho Fields, 2008
Judge, 2008
Ally, 2007

Other books you might like:
Tobias S. Buckell, *Halo: The Cole Protocol*, 2008
William C. Dietz, *Halo: The Flood*, 2003
Robert A. Heinlein, *Starship Troopers*, 1959
Eric S. Nylund, *Halo: The Fall of Reach*, 2001
Joseph Staten, *Halo: Contact Harvest*, 2007

810

JOHN TREVILLIAN

The A-Men

(Leicester, United Kingdom: Troubador Publishing, 2010)

Subject(s): Adventure; Fantasy; Technology
Major character(s): Jack, Hero
Time period(s): Indeterminate Future
Locale(s): Earth; Outer Space

Summary: In *The A-Men*, author John Trevillian tells the story of a band of renegade outcasts who become mighty superheroes protecting the planet from corruption. Jack has no clue who he is or how he ended up on the mean streets of Dead City. All he knows is that the dastardly authorities are after him, and he has to stay one step ahead of them or risk being caught. His only chance is to join up with The A-Men and take on the evildoers once and for all. First novel.

Other books you might like:
John Brunner, *The Shockwave Rider*, 1975
Peter F. Hamilton, *Mindstar Rising*, 1993
L.E. Modesitt, *Archform: Beauty*, 2002
Pamela Sargent, *The Sudden Star*, 1979
A.E. Van Vogt, *The Mind Cage*, 1957

811

HARRY TURTLEDOVE

Atlantis and Other Places

(New York: Roc, 2010)

Story type: Alternate History
Subject(s): Fantasy; History; Short stories

Summary: Harry Turtledove's *Atlantis and Other Places* is a compilation of the author's short stories. In this book, Turtledove examines a series of hypothetical scenarios. Turtledove explores a range of real-life events and crafts tales around what the world would have been like had these events turned out differently. Titles in this volume include "Audubon in Atlantis," "Bedfellows," "The Horse of Bronze," and "Uncle Alf."

Where it's reviewed:
Booklist, September 1, 2010, page 41

Other books by the same author:
West and East, 2010
Hitler's War, 2009
The Breath of God, 2008
Gladiator, 2007
The Disunited States of America, 2006

Other books you might like:
Philip K. Dick, *The Man in the High Castle*, 1962
James P. Hogan, *The Proteus Operation*, 1985
Ward Moore, *Bring the Jubilee*, 1953
Keith Roberts, *Pavane*, 1968
Howard Waldrop, *Them Bones*, 1984

812

HARRY TURTLEDOVE

West and East

(New York: Del Rey, 2010)

Series: War that Came Early Series. Book 2
Story type: Alternate History
Subject(s): World War II, 1939-1945; Adventure; History
Major character(s): Alistair Walsh, Military Personnel; Chaim Weinberg, Military Personnel; Sergeant Fujita, Military Personnel
Time period(s): 20th century; 1930s-1940s
Locale(s): Europe

Summary: *West and East* is the second novel in The War That Came Early series by acclaimed author Harry Turtledove. This volume continues the adventures begun in *Hitler's War*, centering on the escapades of various troops as they wage battle on Germany. Among them are Sergeant Alistair Walsh, soldier Chaim Weinberg, and Sergeant Fujita, whose separate adventures lead them to a unification that takes on the most brutal dictator the world has ever known.

Where it's reviewed:
Publishers Weekly, June 14, 2010, page 37

Other books by the same author:
Atlantis and Other Places, 2010

Hitler's War, 2009
The Breath of God, 2008
Gladiator, 2007
The Disunited States of America, 2006

Other books you might like:
Brian W. Aldiss, *The Year Before Yesterday: A Novel in Three Acts*, 1987
Ben Bova, *Triumph*, 1993
Newt Gingrich, *1945*, 1995
Christopher Priest, *The Separation*, 2002
David Westheimer, *Downfall*, 1971

813

MARK L. VAN NAME

Jump Gate Twist

(Riverdale, New York: Baen, 2010)

Subject(s): Extraterrestrial life; Transportation; Short stories
Major character(s): Jon Moore, Warrior; Lobo, Object (assault vehicle)
Time period(s): Indeterminate Future

Summary: *Jump Gate Twist* is a collection of novellas and short stories written by Mark L. Van Name. Each installment offers another adventure in the continuing series of Jon and Lobo, an extraterrestrial and his mode of transportation, respectively, who are trying to get back to Jon's home planet. Titles in this volume include "My Sister, My Self," "Slanted Jack," and "One Jump Ahead."

Other books by the same author:
Children No More, 2010
Overthrowing Heaven, 2009
Slanted Jack, 2008
One Jump Ahead, 2007

Other books you might like:
Edmond Hamilton, *The Star-Stealers: The Complete Adventures of the Interstellar Patrol, the Collected Edmond Hamilton, Volume Two*, 2009
Keith Laumer, *Bolo: The Annals of the Dinochrome Brigade*, 1976
Andre Norton, *The Solar Queen*, 2003
Steve White, *Eagle Against the Stars*, 2000
Timothy Zahn, *The Domino Pattern*, 2009

814

MARK L. VAN NAME

Children No More

(New York: Baen Books, 2010)

Series: Jon and Lobo Series. Book 4
Story type: Space Opera
Subject(s): Science fiction; Adventure; Space exploration
Major character(s): Jon Moore, Warrior; Alissa Lim, Friend (of Jon); Lobo, Object (assault vehicle)
Time period(s): Indeterminate Future
Locale(s): Outer Space

Summary: *Children No More* is the fourth book in the Jon and Lobo futuristic science fiction series by Mark L. Van Name. Jon Moore was trained to be a soldier when he was still a child, and though he works independently now, he believes that no child should suffer the same fate. His old comrade, Alissa Lin, tells him of a group of children that has been captured, and they are being held on a remote planet with the intention of being turned into soldiers. Alissa asks for Jon's help in rescuing them, and he agrees, not realizing what he is getting into. Things continue to get more complicated for Jon, Alissa, and his intelligent ship Lobo, as they find themselves fighting a group of rebels, a mysterious government, and a powerful con man in a race to save the child soldiers.

Where it's reviewed:
Library Journal, July 2010, page 75

Other books by the same author:
Jump Gate Twist, 2010
Overthrowing Heaven, 2009
Slanted Jack, 2008
One Jump Ahead, 2007

Other books you might like:
C.J. Cherryh, *Exile's Gate*, 1988
Ray Cummings, *Brigands of the Moon*, 1931
Edmond Hamilton, *The Star-Stealers: The Complete Adventures of the Interstellar Patrol, the Collected Edmond Hamilton, Volume Two*, 2009
Murray Leinster, *Med Ship*, 2002
Andre Norton, *Masks of the Outcasts*, 2005

815

PATRICK A. VANNER

Ragnarok

(Riverdale, New York: Baen Books, 2010)

Series: Xan-Sskarn War Series. Book 1
Story type: Series; Space Opera
Subject(s): Science fiction; Military life; Extraterrestrial life
Major character(s): Alexandria McLaughlin, Military Personnel (starship captain); Stewart Optika, Military Personnel (Marine officer)
Time period(s): 22nd century; 2100s (2198)
Locale(s): Earth; Solar System

Summary: In *Ragnarok*, the 22nd century finds the Earth in an ongoing battle against reptilian alien invaders known as the Xan-Sskarn. Having depleted their own resources, the destructive Xan-Sskarn are in a desperate hunt for a source of fresh water. Though Earth has suffered severe damage in the attacks, human forces have so far waged a successful defense. Two of the planet's toughest fighters, Alexandria McLaughlin and Stewart Optika, must work together to fend off the ferocious reptiles as they try to identify the conspirator within their own ranks. *Ragnarok* is the first book in the Xan-Sskarn War series. First novel.

Where it's reviewed:
Publishers Weekly, July 12, 2010, page 33

Other books you might like:
Roger MacBride Allen, *Allies and Aliens*, 1995
Jack Campbell, *Victorious*, 2010
Mike Resnick, *Starship: Rebel*, 2008
Mike Shepherd, *Kris Longknife: Redoubtable*, 2010
David Weber, *By Heresies Distressed*, 2009

816

S.L. VIEHL

Dream Called Time

(New York: Roc, 2010)

Series: Stardoc Series. Book 10
Subject(s): Spacetime; Adventure; Extraterrestrial life
Major character(s): Cherijo, Adventurer
Time period(s): Indeterminate Future
Locale(s): Outer Space

Summary: The tenth novel in the Stardoc series, S.L. Viehl's *Dream Called Time* finds Cherijo stumbling upon a startling new discovery: an extraterrestrial ship that has emerged from a hole in the time-space continuum. Intrigued, she investigates the ship, only to learn the aliens are in possession of a new and possibly dangerous technology. Can Cherijo avoid being ensnared in another dimension by the alien's powerful technological means? Or can she escape and make it home safely to her family?

Other books by the same author:
Crystal Healer, 2010
Omega Games, 2008
Plague of Memory, 2007
Afterburn, 2005
Bio Rescue, 2004

Other books you might like:
Elizabeth Bear, *The Chains That You Refuse*, 2006
Lois McMaster Bujold, *Dreamweaver's Dilemma*, 1996
C.J. Cherryh, *Chanur's Legacy*, 1992
Elizabeth Moon, *Command Decision*, 2007
Karen Traviss, *City of Pearl*, 2004

817

DAVID WEBER

Out of the Dark

(New York: Tor Books, 2010)

Story type: Invasion of Earth
Subject(s): Space colonies; Adventure; Armed forces
Major character(s): Stephen Buchevsky, Military Personnel (Master Sergeant); Dave Dvorak, Military Personnel (Marine)
Time period(s): Indeterminate Future
Locale(s): American South; Europe

Summary: To some, human beings may not seem like threatening creatures; to others, humans are a force to be reckoned with. In *Out of the Dark*, Earth is in danger. Being seen as a threat by a committee known as the Galactic Hegemony, Earth and its inhabitants will be eradicated by a race of murderous carnivores known as the Shongairi. As much of the population begins to die out, a few strong souls fight for their home. Now, two soldiers must try to protect the survivors and find a way to save the planet from the alien invaders.

Where it's reviewed:
Publishers Weekly, August 2, 2010, page 34

Other books by the same author:
By Heresies Distressed, 2009
By Schism Rent Asunder, 2008
Old Soldiers, 2005
The Shadow of Saganami, 2004
Empire from the Ashes, 2003

Other books you might like:
Chris Bunch, *Firemask*, 2000
William C. Dietz, *Legion of the Damned*, 1993
David Drake, *Fireships*, 1996
Sandra McDonald, *The Outback Stars*, 2007
John Scalzi, *Old Man's War*, 2005

818

K.D. WENTWORTH

L. Ron Hubbard Presents Writers of the Future, Volume 26

(Los Angeles, California: Galaxy Press, 2010)

Story type: Collection
Subject(s): Science fiction; Short stories

Summary: In *L. Ron Hubbard Presents Writers of the Future, Volume 26*, editor, K.D. Wentworth collects the work of new science-fiction writers and illustrators recognized through Writers and Illustrators of the Future contests. The collection includes "Living Rooms" by Laurie Tom, "The Black Side of Memory" by Lael Sala-ets, "Seeing Double" by Tom Crosshill, "Not in the Flesh" by Adam Colston, "Written in Light" by Jeff Young, and "Digital Rights" by Brent Knowles. Among the featured illustrators are Irena Kovalenko, Jordan Cornthwaite, Olivia Pelaez, Cassandra Shaffer, Rachael Jade Sweeney, and Jingxuan Hu.

Other books by the same author:
Stars Over Stars, 2002
Black on Black, 1999
House of Moons, 1995
The Imperium Gam, 1994
Moonspeaker, 1994

Other books you might like:
Christopher Anvil, *The Power of Illusion*, 2010
Algis Budrys, *The Unexpected Dimension*, 1960
Paul Di Filippo, *Harsh Oases*, 2009
Nancy Kress, *Beaker's Dozen*, 1998
Pamela Sargent, *Thumbprints*, 2004

819

LYNDA WILLIAMS

Avim's Oath

(Calgary: EDGE Science Fiction and Fantasy, 2010)

Series: Okal Rel Saga Series. Book 6
Subject(s): Royalty; Adventure; Fantasy
Major character(s): Amel, Royalty (prince); Erien, Royalty (prince); Alivda, Royalty (princess)
Time period(s): Indeterminate Future

Summary: In the wake of the Queen's death, Prince Amel and his brother, Prince Erien, are about to be pushed into a battle neither desires. But someone needs to be king, and Amel and Erien's respective wives are each determined to see her husband take the throne. Now the princes must battle both their consciences and one another as they engage in an epic struggle to win power. *Avim's Oath* is the sixth book in Lynda Williams's Okal Rel Saga.

Other books by the same author:
Far Arena, 2009
Pretenders, 2008
Righteous Anger, 2007
The Courtesan Prince, 2005
Throne Price, 2003

Other books you might like:
Catherine Asaro, *Diamond Star*, 2009
C.J. Cherryh, *Conspirator*, 2009
Julie E. Czerneda, *To Trade the Stars*, 2002
Karen Traviss, *Crossing the Line*, 2004
S.L. Viehl, *Crystal Healer*, 2010

820

SEAN WILLIAMS

Star Wars: The Old Republic: Fatal Alliance

(New York: LucasBooks, 2010)

Series: Star Wars: The Old Republic Series. Book 1
Story type: Series
Subject(s): Feuds; Space colonies; Fantasy
Major character(s): Tassaa Bareesh, Leader (of the Hutts)
Time period(s): Indeterminate Future

Summary: The first novel in a series, Sean Williams's *Star Wars: The Old Republic: Fatal Alliance* opens with Hutt leader Tassaa Bareesh auctioning off a rare relic that holds monumental power throughout the galaxy. News of the obscure find has reached the furthest ends of the universe, and everyone wants to nab the coveted treasure. Jedis, Siths, and Mandalorians each hatch their own schemes to get their hands on the artifact and harness its extraordinary powers.

Where it's reviewed:
Booklist, May 15, 2010, page 7
Library Journal, July 2010, page 75

Other books by the same author:
The Force Unleashed, 2010
The Grand Conjunction, 2009
Earth Ascendant, 2008
Saturn Returns, 2007
Metal Fatigue, 1999

Other books you might like:
Troy Denning, *Vortex*, 2010
Drew Karpyshyn, *Dynasty of Evil*, 2009
James Luceno, *The Unifying Force*, 2003
Karen Miller, *Stealth*, 2010
Karen Traviss, *Bloodlines*, 2006

821

MICHAEL Z. WILLIAMSON

Do Unto Others

(Riverdale, New York: Baen, 2010)

Story type: Space Opera
Subject(s): Adventure; Science fiction; Space exploration
Major character(s): Bryant Prescott, Engineer; Caron Prescott, Daughter (of Bryant); Alex Marlow, Security Officer
Time period(s): Indeterminate Future
Locale(s): Govannon, Fictional Location

Summary: *Do Unto Others* by Michael Z. Williamson is a science fiction novel that takes place in the future, where man has left Earth and is free to explore and colonize other planets. The Prescott family was the first to develop the technology that allowed the colonization of other planets, as well as the development of environments for the rich, such as indoor ski slopes, casinos, rides, and cable cars that travel over volcanoes. As a result, the Prescotts, led by Bryant Prescott and his daughter Caron, are the wealthiest family in the galaxy, and as such, need personal security guards to protect them. Though Caron is initially resistant to such protection, she finds they are necessary on the planet Govannon, where the family's enemies decide to make a move and attempt to kidnap her; though Caron is up against an army, her personal guards are equipped with nuclear weapons, and they are not afraid to use them.

Other books by the same author:
Contract with Chaos, 2009
Better to Beg Forgiveness, 2007
The Weapon, 2005
Freehold, 2004

Other books you might like:
Lois McMaster Bujold, *Cetaganda*, 1996
Gordon R. Dickson, *Naked to the Stars*, 1982
Joe Haldeman, *The Forever War*, 1974
David Weber, *The Shadow of Saganami*, 2004

822

CONNIE WILLIS

All Clear

(New York: Spectra, 2010)

Story type: Time Travel
Subject(s): Time travel; World War II, 1939-1945; History
Major character(s): Michael Davies, Historian; Merope Ward, Historian; Polly Churchill, Historian; Mr. Dunworthy, Historian; Colin Templer, 17-Year-Old, Assistant (to Mr. Dunworthy)
Time period(s): Multiple Time Periods; 21st century; (2060s); 20th century; 1940s (1940)
Locale(s): London, England; Oxford, England

Summary: In *All Clear*, Connie Willis returns to the time-traveling band of historians she introduced in *Blackout*. When Michael Davis, Merope Ward, and Polly Churchill departed Oxford in 2060 for 1940 London, the team intended to study wartime events as innocuous observers. Now the trio is unable to return to the present, and their presence seems to be having subtle but noticeable changes on future events. Back at Oxford, the team's director, Mr. Dunworthy, and his assistant, Colin Templer, try desperately to save the time-traveling historians before they rewrite history. Colin's crush on Polly gives their task an extra sense of urgency.

Where it's reviewed:
Locus, December 2010, page 62

Other books by the same author:
Blackout, 2010
Passage, 2001
To Say Nothing of the Dog, 1997
Doomsday Book, 1992
Lincoln's Dreams, 1987

Other books you might like:
Michael Crichton, *Timeline*, 1999
Joshua Dann, *Timeshare*, 1997
Kathleen Ann Goonan, *The Bones of Time*, 1996
Robert A. Heinlein, *The Door into Summer*, 1957
Lisa Mason, *Summer of Love*, 1994

823

BRIAN YANSKY

Alien Invasion and Other Inconveniences

(Somerville, Massachusetts: Candlewick Press, 2010)

Story type: Invasion of Earth; Young Adult
Subject(s): Science; Extraterrestrial life; Telepathy
Major character(s): Jesse, Teenager
Time period(s): 21st century; 2010s
Locale(s): Texas, United States

Summary: In *Alien Invasion and Other Inconveniences*, a high-school student is thrown into an intergalactic battle for survival when extraterrestrials overtake Earth in just a few seconds. The majority of the planet's inhabitants succumb instantly to the assault, but Jesse—who was sitting in class during the invasion—and others who possess similar psychic talents, are spared. Although Jesse has survived the initial invasion, he has lost his family and friends and has been forced into service to one of the alien commanders. Gradually, Jesse hones his telepathic skills and establishes relationships with his fellow survivors.

Other books you might like:
Bruce Coville, *Aliens Ate My Homework*, 1993
David Lubar, *My Rotten Life*, 2009
Daniel Manus Pinkwater, *The Snarkout Boys and the Avocado of Death*, 1982
Pamela F. Service, *A Question of Destiny*, 1986
Alfred Slote, *The Trouble on Janus*, 1985

Science Fiction

Inspirational Fiction in 2011
by
Angie Kiesling for FaithfulReader.com

A genre that can trace its roots back to the late 1970s with gentle prairie romances, inspirational fiction—like a famous ad slogan once said—"has come a long way, baby." The sweet, predictable plots and stereotyped characters of yesteryear have made room for multilayered stories and complex characters who deal with issues that once pushed the boundaries of the taboo: illicit sex, alcoholism, mental illness, out-of-wedlock pregnancy, broken marriages, pornography addiction, imaginary worlds, ghosts, monsters, and yes, even vampires. And if current trends hold true, the inspirational fiction genre looks poised to pioneer increasingly edgy territory in years to come.

Sure Sellers

Faced with the fiscal realities of a prolonged recession, publishers continue to focus their resources on proven sellers—the heavy-hitters of their author lists—find ways to "repurpose" bestsellers (and authors) from decades past, and saturate the market with anthologies such as Steeple Hill's ubiquitous 3-in-1 romance compilations in the Love Inspired, Love Inspired Suspense, and Love Inspired Historical imprints. No doubt about it, publishers have found that stand-alone books don't sell as well as they used to. The success of trilogies and series, whether they fall in the romance, suspense/thriller, historical, mystery, or contemporary genres, guarantees that readers will see plenty more in the coming months as publishers find ways to cultivate author loyalty and create new author "brands."

The explosion of the Amish romance subgenre shows no signs of slowing down and in fact is so impressive the category now commands its own shelf or section in many bookstores. Readers of inspirational fiction can't seem to get enough of the simple life portrayed through winsome Amish characters. And, as with protagonists of other categories, the issues these heroines face grow edgier with every new publishing season.

First Novels on the Rise

While big-name authors still dominate the market, the publication of new literary voices seems to be on the upswing, with writers such as Jennifer Erin Valent, who won the 2010 Christy Award for First Novel (*Fireflies in December*), creating a literary stir and a fast following. Always on the lookout for the next generation of bestselling authors, publishers have to walk a tightrope balancing act of signing book deals with moneymakers—the authors whose very names on book covers guarantee sales—and trawling for breakout writers with fresh literary styles that will garner both current and future sales.

Among the first-time novelists this spring are Meg Moseley (*When Sparrows Fall*), Sherry Kyle (*Delivered with Love*), Rosslyn Elliott (*Fairer Than Morning*), Tessa Stockton (*The Unforgivable*), Elizabeth Camden (*The Lady of Bolton Hill*), Ginny L. Yttrup (*Words*), Mesu Andrews (*Love amid the Ashes*), and Leonard Sweet (*The Seraph Seal*, see section below).

"Repurposed" Authors

In a nod to the "repurposing" tactic, perhaps the biggest news of winter/spring 2011 is the release of bestselling author Lee Strobel's debut fiction work, *The Ambition: A Novel* (Zondervan). Known for his incisive apologetic books, chief among them *The Case for Christ*, Strobel waded into the fiction waters after his daughter Alison Strobel made a name for herself with novels such as *Reinventing Rachel*, *The Weight of Shadows*, and *The Heart of Memory*.

This is not the first time inspirational publishers have tried to turn a bestselling nonfiction author into a novelist, and it surely won't be the last, but in the case of Strobel the transition actually seems to work. His background as an investigative journalist for the *Chicago Tribune* gives him the credibility to tell this "gripping insider's tale of power, politics, and payoffs set in a gleaming suburban megachurch, a big-city newspaper struggling for survival, and the shadowy corridors of political intrigue."

Another nonfiction heavy-hitter whose first novel debuted this year is Leonard Sweet, the E. Stanley Jones Professor of Evangelism at Drew Theological School in

Madison, New Jersey, and author of more than 25 spirituality/apologetic books. Co-authored with Lori Wagner, *The Seraph Seal* uses the four horsemen of the apocalypse to symbolize the four Gospels, four transcendentals, and four forces of the universe (air, water, earth, and fire).

Together, Sweet and Wagner weave a fast-paced, end-times tale of good vs. evil and the promise of a new dawn for humanity. Set in 2048, the story takes off when cultural history professor Paul Binder receives a mysterious letter that leads him to examine a lost second-century Diatessaron manuscript. Ancient prophecies, cryptic letters, and strange events set him on a course to uncover the missing clues that could lead humanity into a new age. The book's description brings echoes of Dan Brown, another teacher-turned-author whose novels *The Da Vinci Code* and *Angels & Demons* became publishing phenomena and eventual movies.

Chick Lit Waning

One other trend worth noting is the cooling off of the inspirational Chick Lit category, a genre that sprang to life on the heels of the wildly successful *Bridget Jones's Diary* and *Sex and the City* books in the mid-1990s general market, but which took several years to catch on in the inspirational aisles. While new titles are still popping up, such as *Who Is My Shelter?* (March), book 4 in the Yada Yada House of Hope series by Neta Jackson, and *Perfectly Invisible: A Universally Misunderstood Novel* (Young Adult/July) by Kristin Billerbeck, the inspirational fiction market is no longer saturated with books of this genre.

Recommended Titles

The Priest's Graveyard by Ted Dekker (suspense)

Chasing Sunsets: A Cedar Key Novel by Eva Marie Everson (contemporary)

The Blessed: A Novel by Ann H. Gabhart (Amish)

Undercurrent by Michelle Griep (speculative)

Who Is My Shelter? by Neta Jackson (chick lit)

The Daughter's Walk: A Novel by Jane Kirkpatrick (historical)

Blue Skies Tomorrow by Sarah Sundin (historical romance)

The Seraph Seal by Leonard Sweet and Lori Wagner (mystery)

Inspirational Fiction

824

MESU ANDREWS

Love Amid the Ashes: A Novel

(Grand Rapids, Michigan: Revell, 2011)

Story type: Inspirational
Subject(s): Bible stories; Diseases; Good and evil
Major character(s): Job, Biblical Figure, Spouse (of Dinah); Dinah, Spouse (of Job)

Summary: In *Love Amid the Ashes*, author Mesu Andrews retells the classic Old Testament story of Job. Job had great wealth, a loving family, and outstanding status in his community until everything fell down around him. Now as Job sits upon an ash heap in the town dump, only one woman, Dinah, his wife, is left to fight for him. A longtime caregiver for her grandfather Isaac, Dinah has married Job out of obligation to Isaac's dying wish. When Job loses everything, Dinah's own faith is shaken. Can this husband and wife stand together in the ultimate test of faith in God? First novel.

Other books you might like:
Tosca Lee, *Havah: The Story of Eve: A Novel*, 2008
Janette Oke, *Acts of Faith Series*, 2009
Linda Rios-Brook, *The Deliver*, 2009
Jill Eileen Smith, *Wives of King David Series*, 2009
Diana Wallis Taylor, *Journey to the Well*, 2008

825

TAMMY BARLEY

Faith's Reward

(Kensington, Pennsylvania: Whitaker House, 2011)

Series: Sierra Chronicles. Book 3
Story type: Historical
Subject(s): Ranch life; History; Suspense
Major character(s): Jessica Bennett, Spouse (to Jake), Rancher; Jake Bennett, Spouse (of Jessica), Rancher
Time period(s): 19th century; 1860s (1865)
Locale(s): California, United States

Summary: *Faith's Reward*, a historical inspirational novel, is the third installment in the Sierra Chronicles series from author Tammy Barley. It's been a rough year for Jake and Jessica Bennett. Although they've been blessed with a pregnancy, things on their western ranch have gone from bad to worse. The summer drought nearly killed their cattle and now a fierce winter threatens to freeze them to death. Worse yet, Jake has gotten pneumonia. Come springtime, Jake has healed and the ranch is thriving, but Jessica's inheritance has mysteriously disappeared from her bank account and a series of murders has the couple fearing for their lives. Jessica must confront the danger head-on, putting herself and her unborn child at risk, to save not only her family, but the lives of countless others.

Other books by the same author:
Hope's Promise: A Novel, 2010
Love's Rescue: A Novel, 2009

Other books you might like:
Lynn Austin, *While We're Far Apart*, 2010
Karen Kingsbury, *Leaving*, 2011
DiAnn Mills, *The Fire in Ember*, 2011
Delia Parr, *Hearts Awakening*, 2010
Lauraine Snelling, *No Distance Too Far*, 2010

826

TERRI BLACKSTOCK

Vicious Cycle

(Grand Rapids, Michigan: Zondervan, 2011)

Series: Intervention Series. Book 2
Story type: Mystery
Subject(s): Crime; Addiction; Drug abuse
Major character(s): Lance Covington, Son (of Barbara), 15-Year-Old; Jordan, Pregnant Teenager, Addict; Barbara Covington, Mother (of Lance); Kent Harlan, Lawyer

Summary: *Vicious Cycle* is the second novel in author Terri Blackstock's Intervention series. After successfully convincing his sister to get treatment, teenager Lance Covington once again sees the signs of addiction in a new school friend. Soon he is able to convince his friend, Jordan, to seek treatment for her meth addiction, if not just for her sake then for the sake of her unborn baby. When Jordan checks out of rehab early, Lance is afraid she'll return to her former life. Then he comes across a newborn baby dumped in the back of a car, and he's sure that the baby belongs to Jordan. Lance goes to the police to seek help for both the baby and Jordan, but finds himself under arrest for abduction. Can Lance's mother, Barbara, rescue him with the help of family friend Kent Harlan? Furthermore, can all of them help Jordan see the error of her ways?

Other books by the same author:
Predator: A Novel, 2010
Double Minds: A Novel, 2009
Cape Refuge Series, 2002-2005
Restoration Series, 2005-2008

Other books you might like:
Randy Alcorn, *The Chasm: A Journey to the Edge of Life*, 2011
Brandilyn Collins, *Deceit*, 2010
Irene Hannon, *Fatal Judgment*, 2011
Kathy Herman, *False Pretenses*, 2011
Jerry B. Jenkins, *The Brotherhood*, 2011

827

ANDREA BOESHAAR

Unexpected Love

(Lake Mary, Florida: Realms, 2011)

Series: Seasons of Redemption Series. Book 3
Story type: Romance; Series
Subject(s): Christian life; Romances (Fiction); Nursing
Major character(s): Lorenna Fields, Nurse; Mr. Blackeyes, Patient (hospital)
Time period(s): 19th century; 1860s (1866)
Locale(s): Chicago, Illinois

Summary: In *Unexpected Love* by Andrea Boeshaar, Lorenna Fields works as a nurse at Lakeview Hospital in Chicago. It is 1866 and Nurse Fields values her career, always keeping her relationships with her patients professional. But when an amnesiac man with dark eyes is brought to Lakeview after a shipping accident, Lorenna is enchanted and begins referring to the new patient as "Mr. Blackeyes." As she tends to Mr. Blackeyes's medical and spiritual needs, Lorenna knows that when he recovers she may lose him to a past he can't remember. *Unexpected Love* is the third book in the Seasons of Redemption series.

Other books by the same author:
Undaunted Faith, 2011
Uncertain Heart, 2010
Unwilling Warrior, 2010

Other books you might like:
Mindy Starns Clark, *The Amish Midwife*, 2011
DiAnn Mills, *The Fire in Ember*, 2011
Golden Keyes Parsons, *Where Hearts Are Free*, 2010
Tracie Peterson, *Embers of Love*, 2010
Martha Rogers, *Caroline's Choice*, 2011

828

MICHELE ANDREA BOWEN

More Church Folk

(New York: Grand Central Publishing, 2010)

Story type: Religious
Subject(s): Religion; Religious life; Deception
Major character(s): Theophilus Simmons, Religious (reverend), Father; Eddie Tate, Religious (reverend), Friend (of Theophilus)
Time period(s): 20th century; 1980s (1986)
Locale(s): United States

Summary: *More Church Folk*, a humorous inspirational novel, is the sequel to the best-selling novel, *Church Folk*, from author Michele Andrea Bowen. Picking up 23 years after its predecessor left off, *More Church Folk* sees the religious leaders of the Gospel United Church preparing for another conference. Best friends, Theophilus Simmons and Eddie Tate, successful reverends in St. Louis and Chicago respectively, are getting frustrated with the way the church leadership is governing their congregations. They hope things will change after the upcoming bishop election, but with four deceptive and wealthy con men trying to buy their spots on their church governance board, things are looking grim for the future of the Gospel United Church.

Where it's reviewed:
Booklist, June 1, 2010, page 31
Library Journal, June 15, 2010, page 52

Other books by the same author:
Up at College, 2009
Holy Ghost Corner, 2008
Second Sunday, 2003
Church Folk, 2002

Other books you might like:
ReShonda Tate Billingsley, *Let the Church Say Amen*, 2004
ReShonda Tate Billingsley, *Holy Rollers*, 2010
E. Lynn Harris, *In My Father's House: A Novel*, 2010
Kimberla Lawson Roby, *Love, Honor and Betray*, 2011
Kimberla Lawson Roby, *Be Careful What You Pray For*, 2010

829

MARGARET BROWNLEY

A Vision of Lucy

(Nashville, Tennessee: Thomas Nelson, 2011)

Series: Rocky Creek Romance Series. Book 3
Story type: Romance; Series
Subject(s): Christian life; Romances (Fiction); History
Major character(s): Lucy Bradshaw, Photographer; David Wolf, Friend (of Lucy)
Time period(s): 19th century; 1880s
Locale(s): Rocky Creek, Texas

Summary: In *A Vision of Lucy* by Margaret Brownley, Lucy Bradshaw wants a career as a photographer, but as a young woman in 19th-century Texas she meets resistance from the community and her father. Though Lucy's late mother was an artist, her father refuses to give her photography the same respect. With determination and faith, Lucy tries to prove herself through her work. When a business relationship with loner David Wolf turns to romance, both Lucy and David learn how to forgive the transgressions of the past. *A Vision of Lucy* is the third book in the Rocky Creek Romance series.

Other books by the same author:
A Suitor for Jenny, 2010
A Lady Like Sarah, 2009

Other books you might like:
Mona Hodgson, *Two Brides Too Many: A Novel*, 2010
Dorothy Love, *Beyond All Measure*, 2011
Allison K. Pittman, *Lilies in Moonlight: A Novel*, 2011
Catherine Richmond, *Spring for Susannah*, 2011
Kathleen Y'Barbo, *The Inconvenient Marriage of Charlotte Beck: A Novel*, 2011

830

ROGER BRUNER
KRISTI RAE BRUNER, Co-Author

Found in Translation: An Unforgettable Mission Trip Where Faith, Obedience, and Forgiveness Intersect

(Uhrichsville, Ohio: Barbour Publishers, 2011)

Series: Altered Hearts Series. Book 1
Story type: Young Adult
Subject(s): Missionaries; Missions (Religion); Christianity
Major character(s): Kim Hartlinger, 18-Year-Old, Wealthy, Religious
Time period(s): 21st century; 2010s
Locale(s): Mexico

Summary: The first book in the Altered Hearts series, *Found in Translation: An Unforgettable Mission Trip Where Faith, Obedience, and Forgiveness Intersect* is an inspirational novel for young adult readers from authors Kristi Rae Bruner and Roger Bruner. Wealthy and spoiled to the core, 18-year-old Kim Hartlinger isn't really the missionary type—especially if mission work involves building houses in a remote Mexican village without plumbing or electricity. By the time Kim realizes what she's inadvertently signed herself up for, she's a long way from home with no idea what to do. She can swallow her pride and pick up a hammer, or she can get out of Mexico on the first available flight. Staying on the trip means roughing it, but there's also a chance that lives will be changed, including Kim's own.

Other books by the same author:
I Started a Joke, 2005

Other books you might like:
Jim Britts, *To Save a Life*, 2009

831

VICTORIA BYLIN

The Outlaw's Return

(New York: Steeple Hill Books, 2011)

Story type: Romance; Western
Subject(s): Romances (Fiction); Western fiction; Christianity
Major character(s): J.T. Quinn, Gunfighter; Mary Larue, Restaurateur, Religious, Guardian
Time period(s): 19th century; 1870s (1876)
Locale(s): Denver, Colorado

Summary: It's been two years since gunslinger J.T. Quinn last saw Mary Larue, the beautiful actress with the voice of an angel who was the only woman he ever truly gave his heart to. Determined to win her back, J.T. travels to Denver only to find that Mary is a changed woman. She's a restaurant owner, a respected member of the community, a loving guardian to her younger siblings, and a devout Christian. J.T. fears that a scruffy outlaw like himself could never be good enough to win Mary's heart now, but when she and her family are put in danger, he risks his life to save his love and finds redemption in the process.

Other books by the same author:
Kansas Courtship, 2010
Wyoming Lawmen, 2010
The Maverick Preacher, 2009
The Bounty Hunter's Bride, 2008
Abbie's Outlaw, 2005

Other books you might like:
Lyn Cote, *Her Healing Ways*, 2010
Mandy Goff, *The Blackmailed Bride*, 2011
Kelly Eileen Hake, *Rugged and Relentless*, 2011
Laurie Kingery, *The Doctor Takes a Wife*, 2011
DiAnn Mills, *A Woman Called Sage*, 2010

832

AMANDA CABOT

Tomorrow's Garden

(Grand Rapids, Michigan: Revell, 2011)

Series: Texas Dreams Trilogy. Book 3
Story type: Historical; Series
Subject(s): Christian life; History; Romances (Fiction)
Major character(s): Harriet Kirk, Teacher; Lawrence Wood, Lawman (Texas Ranger)
Time period(s): 19th century; 1850s (1857)
Locale(s): Ladreville, Texas

Summary: In *Tomorrow's Garden* by Amanda Cabot, a young woman sets out to make a new start for her and her siblings in 1857 Texas. Eager to escape her troubled past, Harriet Kirk comes to Ladreville to work as a school teacher—a career that will keep her busy and help her provide for her family. But Lawrence Wood presents a distraction. The good-looking former Texas Ranger gradually charms his way into Harriet's life. Though Lawrence gives Harriet hope, she wonders if she can trust her heart with another man. *Tomorrow's Garden* is the third book in the Texas Dreams trilogy.

Other books by the same author:
Scattered Petals, 2010
Paper Roses, 2009

Other books you might like:
Cathy Marie Hake, *Serendipity*, 2010
Julie Klassen, *Girl in the Gatehouse*, 2011
Siri Mitchell, *A Heart Most Worthy*, 2011
Delia Parr, *Hidden Affections*, 2011
Tracie Peterson, *Hearts Aglow*, 2011

833

ELIZABETH CAMDEN

The Lady of Bolton Hill

(Minneapolis, Minnesota: Bethany House, 2011)

Story type: Historical
Subject(s): Christian life; Romances (Fiction); History
Major character(s): Clara Endicott, Journalist; Daniel Tremain, Businessman
Time period(s): 19th century; 1870s (1879)
Locale(s): Baltimore, Maryland

Summary: In *The Lady of Bolton Hill* by Elizabeth Camden, Clara Endicott's journalism career takes her to London where she exposes the plight of the city's underclass. When she comes home to Baltimore in 1879, Clara reconnects with a man from her past. As a girl, Clara knew Daniel Tremain as a lowly factory worker. Now, her long-ago romantic interest is a businessman. Clara is intrigued by Daniel, but begins to realize that his success may have compromised his moral integrity. As Clara tries to show Daniel God's grace in his life, Daniel struggles to protect Clara from a dangerous threat.

Other books you might like:
Laurie Alice Eakes, *Lady in the Mist*, 2011
Deeanne Gist, *Maid to Match*, 2010
Dorothy Love, *Beyond All Measure*, 2011
Nancy Moser, *An Unlikely Suitor*, 2011
Catherine Richmond, *Spring for Susannah*, 2011

834

JULIE CAROBINI

Fade to Blue

(Nashville: B&H Books, 2011)

Series: Otter Bay Series. Book 3
Story type: Contemporary; Series
Subject(s): Christian life; Community relations; Romances (Fiction)
Major character(s): Suz Mitchell, Single Mother; Jeremiah, Son (of Suz); Len, Spouse (former, of Suz); Seth, Boyfriend (former, of Suz)
Time period(s): 21st century; 2010s
Locale(s): California, United States

Summary: In *Fade to Blue* by Julie Carobini, a single parent moves to a coastal California community seeking a

new start for her son and her own career. While Suz Mitchell's ex-husband is in prison, she sets off with their son, Jeremiah, for Otter Bay where she hopes to pursue a career in art. When she accepts a position at Hearst Castle as a restorer, she has no idea that an old flame is also on staff there. Suz loves her new job and her beautiful surroundings, but Seth's presence forces Suz to rethink her future plans. *Fade to Blue* is the third book in the Otter Bay series.

Other books by the same author:
A Shore Thing: An Otter Bay Novel, 2010
Sweet Waters: An Otter Bay Novel, 2009
Truffles by the Sea, 2008
Chocolate Beach, 2007

Other books you might like:
Terri Blackstock, *Vicious Cycle*, 2011
Kathy Herman, *False Pretenses*, 2011
Neta Jackson, *Who Is My Shelter?*, 2010
Karen Kingsbury, *Leaving*, 2011
Karen Kingsbury, *Take Four*, 2010

835

ROBIN CAROLL

In the Shadow of Evil

(Nashville, Tennessee: B & H Publishing, 2011)

Story type: Mystery
Subject(s): Romances (Fiction); Suspense; Mystery fiction
Major character(s): Maddox Bishop, Detective—Homicide; Layla Taylor, Crime Suspect
Locale(s): Louisiana, United States

Summary: *In the Shadow of Evil* is an inspirational mystery by author Robin Caroll. Detective Maddox Bishop has had his guard up against loving another human being for nearly 20 years, ever since walking into his own house to find his mother's dead body. He's poured his heart into his work, trying to avenge the death of other homicide victims through the criminal-justice system. Then he encounters Layla Taylor, a contractor suspected of arson. Maddox is unsure if Layla is guilty of this crime, until her life is put in danger. Now he must work to protect this woman, to whom he is finding himself more and more attracted. But can he protect his heart, too?

Other books by the same author:
Dead Air, 2010
Deliver Us From Evil: A Novel, 2010
Fear No Evil, 2010
Blackmail, 2009
Bayou Justice, 2007

Other books you might like:
Terri Blackstock, *Intervention Series*, 2009
Mindy Starns Clark, *Secrets of Harmony Grove*, 2010
Lynette Eason, *Women of Justice Series*, 2010
Sibella Giorello, *The Rivers Run Dry*, 2009
Susan May Warren, *Double Trouble*, 2010

836

COLLEEN COBLE

The Lightkeeper's Ball

(Nashville, Tennessee: Thomas Nelson, 2011)

Series: Mercy Falls Series. Book 3
Story type: Historical; Series
Subject(s): Christian life; History; Romances (Fiction)
Major character(s): Olivia Stewart, Socialite; Eleanor Stewart, Sister (of Olivia); Harrison Bennett, Fiance(e) (of Eleanor)
Time period(s): 20th century; 1910s (1910)
Locale(s): Mercy Falls, California; New York, New York

Summary: In *The Lightkeeper's Ball* by Colleen Coble, Olivia Stewart escapes 1910 New York and the prospects of an arranged marriage to investigate the death of her sister Eleanor. Eleanor had been living in Mercy Falls, California, engaged to Harrison Bennett. Though Olivia considers Harrison as a suspect, she reassesses her opinion when, at their first meeting, Harrison saves her life. When circumstances compel Olivia and Harrison to spend two nights unchaperoned, they decide that an engagement is the only way to avoid scandal. But as Olivia plays Harrison's fiancee, she realizes that she wants to be his wife. *The Lightkeeper's Ball* is the third book in the Mercy Falls series.

Other books by the same author:
The Lightkeeper's Bride, 2010
Lonestar Homecoming, 2010
Cry in the Night, 2009
Lonestar Secrets, 2009
Without a Trace, 2007

Other books you might like:
Colleen Coble, *Abomination*, 2008
Colleen Coble, *Distant Echoes*, 2005
Thomas Kinkade, *The Wedding Promise*, 2011
Judith Miller, *A Bond Never Broken*, 2011
Martha Rogers, *Caroline's Choice*, 2011

837

BRANDILYN COLLINS

Over the Edge

(Nashville, Tennessee: B&H Publishing Group, 2011)

Story type: Contemporary
Subject(s): Christian life; Medical care; Diseases
Major character(s): Dr. Brock McNeil, Researcher; Janessa McNeil McNeil, Spouse (of Brock)
Time period(s): 21st century; 2010s
Locale(s): United States

Summary: In *Over the Edge* by Brandilyn Collins, Dr. Brock McNeil, an authority on tick-borne sickness, denies the existence of Chronic Lyme Disease. As he prepares to make his controversial findings public, his wife, Janessa, is deliberately infected with the disease by an unknown assailant. Despite the debilitating symptoms Janessa develops, Brock refuses to reconsider his position. As Brock and Janessa's daughter becomes the attacker's next target, Janessa struggles with her physical condition and the emotional strain of her husband's behavior. Meanwhile, Janessa's assailant makes it clear that he will take any measures necessary to bring the issue of Lyme disease to the attention of the public, the media, the medical community, and the insurance industry.

Other books by the same author:
Deceit, 2010
Exposure, 2009
Hidden Faces Series, 2004-2006
Kanner Lake Series, 2006-2008
The Rayne Tour, 2009-2010

Other books you might like:
Terri Blackstock, *Predator: A Novel*, 2010
Ted Dekker, *The Priest's Graveyard*, 2011
Rene Gutteridge, *Possession*, 2010
Vicki Hinze, *Forget Me Not*, 2010
Bodie Thoene, *Against the Wind*, 2011

838

BRANDILYN COLLINS

Deceit

(Grand Rapids, Michigan: Zondervan, 2010)

Story type: Amateur Detective; Mystery
Subject(s): Murder; Mystery; Suspense
Major character(s): Joanne Weeks, Detective—Amateur; Melissa Harkhoff, Foster Child, Young Woman; Baxter Jackson, Businessman, Widow(er), Crime Suspect, Religious
Time period(s): 21st century; 2010s
Locale(s): California, United States

Summary: *Deceit* is a suspenseful Christian mystery about murder, deception, and justice, from best-selling author Brandilyn Collins. It has been seven years since Joanne Weeks's best friend, Linda Jackson, disappeared. Joanne has always suspected that Linda was murdered by her husband, Baxter, but has never been able to prove it. Now, Baxter's second wife has died in a mysterious accident, and Joanne is more convinced of his guilt than ever. Unfortunately, she's the only one who thinks the beloved town member and church elder is a murderer. Determined to prove her theory, Joanne sets out to find Melissa Harkhoff, a young woman who was a foster child in the Jackson's home at the time of Linda's disappearance. As Joanne's investigation begins, she encounters a series of odd events, including a stranger stepping in front of her car on a rainy night and a possible home break-in, which lead Joanne to believe someone is desperate to stop her from uncovering the truth.

Where it's reviewed:
Booklist, July 1, 2010, page 35

Other books by the same author:
Over the Edge, 2011
Dark Pursuit, 2010
Exposure, 2010
Final Touch, 2010
Always Watching, 2009

Other books you might like:
Terri Blackstock, *Vicious Cycle*, 2011
Steven James, *The Bishop*, 2010
Jerry B. Jenkins, *The Last Operative*, 2010

839

MARY CONNEALY

Sharpshooter in Petticoats

(Uhrichsville, Ohio: Barbour Publishers, 2011)

Series: Sophie's Daughters Series. Book 3
Story type: Historical
Subject(s): Ranch life; Romances (Fiction); History
Major character(s): Mandy McClellan Gray, Single Mother, Widow(er); Tom Linscott, Rancher
Time period(s): 19th century; 1880s (1884)
Locale(s): United States

Summary: *Sharpshooter in Petticoats*, a historical inspirational romance, is the third installment in the Sophie's Daughters series from award-winning author Mary Connealy. For widow and single mother Mandy McClellan Gray, life is busier and better than it ever was when she was married. She's made a cozy home for her three children in the mountains and her bank account is full of enough gold to keep them taken care of. Unfortunately, a gang of outlaws is after Mandy, trapping her and her family in their remote mountain house. Cranky rancher Tom Linscott is desperate to save Mandy, even if she's too stubborn to receive his help, but when he brings her back to his house, trouble comes knocking at his door.

Other books by the same author:
Doctor in Petticoats, 2010
Lassoed in Texas Trilogy, 2010
Wildflower Bride, 2010
Wrangler in Petticoats, 2010

Other books you might like:
Mary Connealy, *Cowboy Christmas*, 2009
Susan Page Davis, *The Blacksmith's Bravery*, 2011
Cathy Marie Hake, *Serendipity*, 2010
Vickie McDonough, *Second Chance Brides*, 2010
Kim Vogel Sawyer, *Courting Miss Amsel*, 2011

840

MARY CONNEALY

Deep Trouble

(Uhrichsville, Ohio: Barbour Publishing, 2011)

Story type: Historical
Subject(s): Christian life; History; Romances (Fiction)
Major character(s): Gabe Lasley, Wanderer; Shannon Dysart, Adventurer
Time period(s): 19th century; 1880s (1881)
Locale(s): United States

Summary: In *Deep Trouble* by Mary Connealy, Shannon Dysart holds the map that can lead her to a city of gold and redeem her father's tarnished name. It is 1881 and independent-minded Shannon has embarked on her Arizona adventure alone. Then she meets Gabe Lasley who is on a journey of his own as he tries to outrun a band of dangerous pursuers. Though Gabe has no interest in companionship, an unusual series of circumstances brings the pair together. Shannon is so determined to find the elusive treasure that she puts their lives at risk. Meanwhile, Gabe weighs his desire for wealth against the cost of allowing Shannon into his life.

Other books by the same author:
Sharpshooter in Petticoats, 2011
Doctor in Petticoats, 2010
Wrangler in Petticoats, 2010
Montana Rose, 2009
Petticoat Ranch, 2009

Other books you might like:
Cathy Marie Hake, *Serendipity*, 2010
Julie Klassen, *Girl in the Gatehouse*, 2011
Vickie McDonough, *Finally a Bride*, 2011
Kim Vogel Sawyer, *Courting Miss Amsel*, 2011
Karen Witemeyer, *Head in the Clouds*, 2010

841

KATHRYN CUSHMAN

Another Dawn

(Bloomington, Minnesota: Bethany House Publishing, 2011)

Story type: Coming-of-Age
Subject(s): Children; Medical care; Diseases
Major character(s): Grace Graham, Mother (of Dylan); Dylan, 4-Year-Old, Son (of Grace)
Locale(s): Shoal Creek, Tennessee

Summary: In *Another Dawn*, author Kathryn Cushman tells the story of Grace Graham, a young woman whose natural lifestyle includes the refusal of giving her young son vaccinations. Grace is summoned home to Shoal Creek, Tennessee to care for her father, who is recovering from knee surgery. Grace is reluctant to return because of the tenuous relationship she shares with her father, but her sister insists that her presence is needed. When the children of Shoal Creek, including Grace's son Dylan, contract measles, Rachel begins to wonder if she could in fact be to blame. Cushman is also the author of *Leaving Yesterday* and *Waiting for Daybreak*.

Other books by the same author:
Angel Song, 2010
Leaving Yesterday, 2009
Waiting for Daybreak, 2008
A Promise to Remember, 2007

Other books you might like:
Kathy Herman, *False Pretenses*, 2011
Karen Kingsbury, *Unlocked: A Love Story*, 2010
Gayle Roper, *A Rose Revealed*, 2011
Lisa Samson, *Quaker Summer*, 2007

842

KAYE DACUS

The Art of Romance

(Uhrichsville, Ohio: Barbour Publishing, 2011)

Series: Matchmakers Series. Book 2
Story type: Romance; Series
Subject(s): Christian life; Romances (Fiction); Identity
Major character(s): Dylan Bradley, Artist (illustrator); Caylor Evans, Writer (novelist)
Time period(s): 21st century; 2010s
Locale(s): Nashville, Tennessee

Summary: In *The Art of Romance* by Kaye Dacus, Dylan Bradley, an artist, relocates to Nashville to live in the guest house on his grandparents' property. Caylor Evans, a writer, also lives in the city with her grandmother. Dylan and Caylor's female relatives happen to be friends and try to arrange a romance between the two. But both hide a secret that could jeopardize any hope for a relationship. Dylan's past career credits include a stint illustrating hot romance novels as Patrick Callaghan; Caylor used to write racy romances as Melanie Mason. *The Art of Romance* is the second book in The Matchmakers series.

Other books by the same author:
A Case for Love, 2010
Love Remains, 2010
Ransome's Crossing, 2010
Ransome's Honor, 2009
Stand-in Groom, 2009

Other books you might like:
Kristin Billerbeck, *A Billion Reasons Why*, 2011
Susan Page Davis, *The Crimson Cipher*, 2010
Christine Lynxwiler, *The Stars Remember*, 2011
Janice A. Thompson, *Stars Collide*, 2011
Susan May Warren, *My Foolish Heart*, 2011

843

MARGARET DALEY

Trail of Lies

(Don Mills, Ontario, Canada: Harlequin, 2011)

Story type: Romance
Subject(s): Christian life; Romances (Fiction); Suspense
Major character(s): Melora Hudson, Widow(er); Daniel Boone Riley, Lawman (Texas Ranger)
Time period(s): 21st century; 2010s
Locale(s): Texas, United States

Summary: In *Trail of Lies* by Margaret Daley, Melora Hudson's perfect life was shattered when her husband vanished two years ago. But now Melora knows that her family's perfection was the perception of others, not the reality of their secretive existence. When Melora's husband's body is discovered, and his death finally confirmed, Melora knows that she and her daughter will now be the targets of her rich husband's colleagues. She holds information that they do not want revealed—information that must be buried with the dead. As law-

man Daniel Boone Riley works to solve the case, he realizes that he is becoming personally involved with Melora.

Other books by the same author:
What Sarah Saw, 2009
Don't Look Back, 2008
A Texas Thanksgiving, 2008
Hearts on the Line, 2006
When Dreams Come True, 2006

Other books you might like:
Lynette Eason, *Threat of Exposure*, 2011
Valerie Hansen, *Face of Danger*, 2011
Ramona Richards, *House of Secrets*, 2011
Roxanne Rustand, *Murder at Granite Falls*, 2011
Susan May Warren, *Mission: Out of Control*, 2011

844

C.J. DARLINGTON

Bound by Guilt

(Carol Stream, Illinois: Tyndale House Publishers, 2011)

Story type: Child-in-Peril
Subject(s): Foster children; Theft; Books
Major character(s): Roxi Gold, Foster Child, 16-Year-Old; Abby Dawson, Police Officer

Summary: *Bound by Guilt* is an inspirational novel by author C.J. Darlington. At 16, Roxi Gold has already been in the foster-care system for the majority of her life. She's been shipped from foster home to foster home, and at times she thinks it can't get any worse. The worst comes, however, when she is sent to live with a family of career burglars who live in a recreational vehicle. They travel from town to town swiping books from rare book stores, and Roxi is scared that if she doesn't go along with the plan, she'll be sent back into the system again. Can fate set Roxi on the right path again?

Other books by the same author:
Thicker Than Blood, 2009

Other books you might like:
Terri Blackstock, *Intervention Series*, 2009

845

SUSAN PAGE DAVIS

Alaska Weddings

(Uhrichsville, Ohio: Barbour Publishers, 2011)

Story type: Family Saga; Romance
Subject(s): Romances (Fiction); Wilderness areas; Family
Major character(s): Cheryl Holland, Widow(er), Mother; Robyn Holland, Animal Trainer, Daughter (of Cheryl); Rick Barker, Veterinarian; Aven Holland, Military Personnel (Coast Guard officer), Son (of Cheryl)
Time period(s): 21st century; 2010s
Locale(s): Alaska, United States

Inspirational

Summary: Life in the last great frontier is full of danger, surprise, and love for the Holland family in *Alaska Weddings*. Widowed matriarch Cheryl Holland was certain she'd never find love again, but when a mysterious wildlife scientist takes a job at Cheryl's clinic, she's caught off guard by their instant attraction and chemistry. Meanwhile, Cheryl's daughter Robyn is desperate to save her sled-dog kennel despite recent financial difficulties, and veterinarian Rick Barker seems like the perfect guy to help. But when her best dogs are stolen, Robyn and Rick are forced to rely on God like never before. For Coast Guard officer Aven Holland a new romance seems like an exciting proposition, but he and Caddie Lyle have too many dark secrets lurking in their past that might quell their love before it begins.

Other books by the same author:
Wyoming Weddings, 2011

Other books you might like:
Irene Brand, *Love Finds You Under the Mistletoe*, 2010
Lynn A. Coleman, *Harbor Hopes*, 2010
Janice Hanna, *Jersey Sweets*, 2010
Aaron McCarver, *Tennessee Brides*, 2011
Amy Wallace, *Healing Promises*, 2008

846

SUSAN PAGE DAVIS

Love Finds You in Prince Edward Island, Canada

(Minneapolis, Minnesota: Ellie Claire Gift & Paper Corporation, 2011)

Story type: Historical
Subject(s): Christian life; History; Romances (Fiction)
Major character(s): Molly Orland, Young Woman; Peter Stark, Steward
Time period(s): 19th century; 1860s (1860)
Locale(s): Prince Edward Island, Canada

Summary: In *Love Finds You in Prince Edward Island, Canada* by Susan Page Davis, the 1860 visit of the Prince of Wales to Prince Edward Island could change the future of islander Molly Orland. For Molly, a member of the working class, the prince's stay offers no hope for an invitation to the royal ball; it does provide the opportunity for extra maid's work—and extra wages. A royal steward, Peter Stark, is smitten with Molly—an affection that is much more sincere than the prince's advances. As Peter and Molly's relationship grows they learn sensitive information that could redeem the Orlands but scandalize the royal family.

Other books by the same author:
The Blacksmith's Bravery, 2010
The Crimson Cipher, 2010
The Gunsmith's Gallantry, 2010
Hearts in Crosshairs, 2009
Just Cause, 2008

Other books you might like:
Irene Brand, *Love Finds You Under the Mistletoe*, 2010
Kelly Eileen Hake, *Rugged and Relentless*, 2011

Janice Hanna, *Love Finds You in Camelot, Tennessee*, 2011
Mona Hodgson, *Too Rich for a Bride: A Novel*, 2011
Allison K. Pittman, *Lilies in Moonlight: A Novel*, 2011

847

TED DEKKER

The Priest's Graveyard

(New York: Center Street, 2011)

Story type: Contemporary
Subject(s): Suspense; Vigilantes; Drugs
Major character(s): Danny Hansen, Religious (priest); Renee Gilmore, Vigilante
Time period(s): 21st century; 2010s
Locale(s): United States

Summary: In *The Priest's Graveyard* by Ted Dekker, Danny Hansen leaves his native Bosnia and comes to the United States carrying the violent memories of the wartime horrors he witnessed. In America, Danny becomes a priest who pursues those who ignore the law of God. Renee Gilmore is on another search. The victim of a cruel man who ruined her life, Renee vows to exact revenge against that man. Both Danny and Renee are convinced that their causes are just, even though they are willing to justify certain wrongs to achieve their end goals. When Danny and Renee meet, their separate quests intertwine with devastating results.

Other books by the same author:
The Bride Collector, 2011
BoneMan's Daughters, 2010
Burn, 2010
Immanuel's Veins, 2010
Kiss, 2009
Obsessed, 2006

Other books you might like:
Erin Healy, *The Promises She Keeps*, 2011
Stephen R. Lawhead, *The Skin Map*, 2010
Robert Liparulo, *Timescape*, 2009
Robert Liparulo, *Whirlwind*, 2009
James L. Rubart, *Book of Days*, 2011

848

LAURIE ALICE EAKES

Lady in the Mist

(Grand Rapids, Michigan: Revell, 2011)

Series: Midwives Series. Book 1
Story type: Historical; Romance
Subject(s): Romances (Fiction); History; Medical care
Major character(s): Tabitha Eckles, Midwife; Dominick Cherrett, Nobleman, Servant
Time period(s): 19th century; 1800s (1809)
Locale(s): Virginia, United States

Summary: Set in Virginia in the early 19th century, *Lady in the Mist* follows Tabitha Eckles, a lonely woman marked by personal tragedy, who has thrown herself into her taxing job as a midwife. In the midst of political turmoil between America and England, Tabitha is shocked to meet Dominick Cherrett, a British nobleman working as an indentured servant for the town's mayor. The two cross paths on an isolated beach and reluctantly form an alliance that begins as friendship but develops toward love. The pair meets their fair share of obstacles as they're thrown into the midst of public scandal, kidnappings, and a possible murder mystery, all the while grappling with their growing feelings for one another and their personal issues with God.

Other books by the same author:
Jersey Brides, 2011
When the Snow Flies, 2010
The Glassblower, 2009
Better Than Gold, 2008
The Widow's Secret, 2002

Other books you might like:
Margaret Brownley, *A Suitor for Jenny*, 2010
Cara Lynn James, *Love on Assignment*, 2011
Siri Mitchell, *She Walks in Beauty*, 2010
Delia Parr, *Hidden Affections*, 2011
Susan May Warren, *Nightingale*, 2010

849

LYNETTE EASON

Missing

(New York: Steeple Hill, 2011)

Story type: Romantic Suspense
Subject(s): Kidnapping; Suspense; Romances (Fiction)
Major character(s): Lacey Gibson, Single Mother; Mason Stone, Lawman (U.S. marshal), Father
Time period(s): 21st century; 2010s
Locale(s): United States

Summary: *Missing* is a romance novel from author Lynette Eason. When Lacey Gibson's teenage daughter vanishes without a trace, the single mother is devastated and determined to find her child, no matter the cost. Unsure of what to do, Lacey chooses to confront the former love of her life, U.S. Marshall Mason Stone, a man she hasn't seen in sixteen years and the unknowing father of her child. Mason is shocked to learn that not only is he a father, but his daughter has gone missing. As Mason and Lacey race to locate the people responsible for their daughter's disappearance, they begin to wonder if their love can be recovered as well.

Other books by the same author:
Protective Custody, 2010
Too Close to Home, 2010
A Silent Fury, 2009
A Silent Terror, 2009
Holiday Illusion, 2008

Other books you might like:
Irene Hannon, *Fatal Judgment*, 2011
Rachelle McCalla, *Danger on Her Doorstep*, 2011
Shirlee McCoy, *Running Blind*, 2010
Lisa May Warren, *Point of No Return*, 2011
Lenora Worth, *Body of Evidence*, 2011

850

LYNETTE EASON

A Killer Among Us: A Novel

(Grand Rapids, Michigan: Revell, 2011)

Series: Women of Justice Series. Book 3
Story type: Mystery; Series
Subject(s): Christian life; Mystery; Murder
Major character(s): Kit Kenyon, Police Officer (hostage negotiator); Noah Lambert, Detective—Police
Time period(s): 21st century; 2010s
Locale(s): United States

Summary: In *A Killer among Us* by Lynette Eason, detective Noah Lambert and hostage negotiator Kit Kenyon team up to track a serial killer. Though they've only been partners on the police force for a short time, they use their combined skills to learn the identity of the murderer who has already claimed several victims. As Noah and Kit build their case they realize that they have also become targets. Meanwhile, the partners' professional relationship is complicated by their mutual romantic attraction. *A Killer among Us* is the third book in the Women of Justice series.

Other books by the same author:
Missing, 2011
Don't Look Back, 2010
Too Close to Home, 2010
A Silent Pursuit, 2009
A Silent Terror, 2009

Other books you might like:
Robin Caroll, *In the Shadow of Evil*, 2011
Brandilyn Collins, *Over the Edge*, 2011
Kristen Heitzmann, *Indelible*, 2011
Ronie Kendig, *Wolfsbane*, 2011
DiAnn Mills, *Pursuit of Justice*, 2010

851

ROSSLYN ELLIOTT

Fairer Than Morning

(Nashville, Tennessee: Thomas Nelson Publishers, 2011)

Series: Saddler's Legacy Series. Book 1
Story type: Romance; Series
Subject(s): Christian life; Romances (Fiction); History
Major character(s): Ann Miller, Young Woman; Will Hanby, Apprentice (saddle maker)
Time period(s): 19th century; 1820s (1826)
Locale(s): Ohio, United States; Pittsburgh, Pennsylvania

Summary: In *Fairer than Morning* by Rosslyn Elliott, Ann Miller moves to Pittsburgh in 1826 with her minister father and sisters. Ann suspects that her father may be keeping a dangerous secret, but can't guess what it might be. In their new city, the Millers live next door to a saddle maker, whose indentured worker, Will Hanby, is dealing with personal torments of his own. Mistreated by his employer, Will finds a pleasant distraction in Ann's attention. With newfound resolve, Will risks his own safety to help the escaped slaves who have made their way to Pennsylvania. *Fairer than Morning* is the first book in the Saddler's Legacy series. First novel.

Other books you might like:
Laura Frantz, *The Colonel's Lady: A Novel*, 2011
Cara Lynn James, *Love on Assignment*, 2011
Dorothy Love, *Beyond All Measure*, 2011
DiAnn Mills, *The Fire in Ember*, 2011

852

MARY ELLIS

Abigail's New Hope

(Eugene, Oregon: Harvest House Publishers, 2011)

Series: Wayne County Series. Book 1
Story type: Romance; Series
Subject(s): Christian life; Amish; Romances (Fiction)
Major character(s): Abigail Graber, Midwife; Catherine, Sister (of Abigail); Daniel Graber, Spouse (of Abigail); Isaiah, Cousin (of Daniel)
Time period(s): 21st century; 2010s
Locale(s): Wayne County, Ohio

Summary: In *Abigail's New Hope* by Mary Ellis, Abigail Graber, an Amish midwife, is unable to save the life of a woman in childbirth and is subsequently imprisoned for her role in the mother's death. With Abigail's husband, Daniel, left alone to tend his fields, Abigail's sister Catherine comes to take care of the children. While there, Catherine befriends Daniel's deaf cousin, Isaiah. Because of his hearing impairment, Isaiah is believed to be mentally handicapped as well. But Catherine and Isaiah develop of means of communication that opens both their lives to new possibilities. *Abigail's New Hope* is the first book in the Wayne County series.

Other books by the same author:
Never Far From Home, 2010
Sarah's Christmas Miracle, 2010
The Way to a Man's Heart, 2010
A Widow's Hope, 2009

Other books you might like:
Wanda E. Brunstetter, *The Journey*, 2011
Jerry S. Eicher, *Ella's Wish*, 2011
Kathleen Fuller, *What the Heart Sees: A Collection of Amish Romances*, 2011
Kelly Long, *Lily's Wedding Quilt*, 2011
Marta Perry, *Sarah's Gift*, 2011

853

SARA EVANS
RACHEL HAUCK, Co-Author

Softly and Tenderly

(Nashville, Tennessee: Thomas Nelson Publishing, 2011)

Series: Jade Benson Series. Book 2
Story type: Religious
Subject(s): Christian life; Addiction; Death
Major character(s): Jade Benson, Spouse (of Max); Max,
Spouse (of Jade); Rice, Friend (of Jade), Accident Victim

Summary: *Softly and Tenderly* is the second installment in the Jade Benson series of Inspirational novels by Sara Evans and Rachel Hauck. Jade has already faced her share of tragedy, having coped with her husband's addiction and her mother's cancer. Now she must help her mother-in-law deal with her husband's unfaithfulness as she deals with her own diagnosis of infertility. When Jade's best friend, Rice, is killed in an airplane accident, Jade begins to wonder if it is more than she can bear. Then her husband Max confesses that he is the father of Rice's young son, and he wants custody. Can Jade's strong faith in the Lord help keep her afloat in a sea of never-ending tragedy?

Other books by the same author:
The Sweet By and By, 2010
You'll Always Be My Baby, 2006

Other books you might like:
Kristin Billerbeck, *A Billion Reasons Why*, 2011
Rachel Hauck, *Dining with Joy*, 2010
Neta Jackson, *Who Is My Shelter?*, 2010
Karen White, *Falling Home*, 2002
Karen Witemeyer, *Head in the Clouds*, 2010

854

EVA MARIE EVERSON

Chasing Sunsets

(Grand Rapids, Michigan: Revell, 2011)

Series: Return to Cedar Key Series. Book 1
Story type: Contemporary; Series
Subject(s): Christian life; Divorce; Self knowledge
Major character(s): Kimberly Tucker, Divorced Person
Time period(s): 21st century; 2010s
Locale(s): Florida, United States

Summary: In *Chasing Sunsets* by Eva Marie Everson, a divorced mother searches for answers and peace of mind on the island where she spent her childhood summers. Kimberly Tucker is bitter, angry, and weary. Her ex has happily made a new start, leaving her to care for their young sons. But when the boys visit their father over summer vacation, Kimberly retreats to Cedar Key Island—a comforting refuge off the Florida coast. On Cedar Key, Kim reconnects with a former flame and renews her own spirit with the help of God's grace. *Chasing Sunsets* is the first book in the Return to Cedar Key series.

Other books by the same author:
This Fine Life: A Novel, 2010
Things Left Unspoken: A Novel, 2009
The Potluck Catering Club Series, 2008-2011
The Potluck Club Series, 2005-2006
Shadow of Dreams Series, 2002-2003

Other books you might like:
Sandra D. Bricker, *Always the Baker, Never the Bride*, 2010
Maureen Lang, *Springtime of the Spirit*, 2011
Elizabeth Musser, *The Sweetest Thing*, 2011

Gayle Roper, *Shadows on the Sand: A Seaside Mystery*, 2011

Susan May Warren, *My Foolish Heart*, 2011

855

ANN H. GABHART

Angel Sister

(Grand Rapids, Michigan: Revell, 2011)

Story type: Historical
Subject(s): Family; Faith; History
Major character(s): Kate Merritt, 14-Year-Old
Time period(s): 20th century; 1930s (1936)
Locale(s): Rosey Corner, Kentucky

Summary: Set in Kentucky during the summer of 1936, *Angel Sister* follows Kate Merritt, middle child and family caregiver, as she strives to keep her family together during a trying time. Kate's father's struggle with post-traumatic stress disorder has given way to full-fledged alcoholism, while her mother withdrawals emotionally to avoid the stress of their financial woes. Kate's sisters seem unaware of the family's dire situation, leaving Kate to tend to everyone's needs on her own. When Kate finds an abandoned and hungry 5-year-old girl on the steps of a local church, she brings her home, unaware that this child will change everything for the Merritt family and their small town of Rosey Corner.

Other books by the same author:
The Seeker: A Novel, 2010
The Believer: A Novel, 2009
The Outsider: A Novel, 2008

Other books you might like:
Heather Gudenkauf, *These Things Hidden*, 2011
Heather Newton, *Under the Mercy Trees*, 2011
Michael Phillips, *Angel Heart*, 2011
Ann Tatlock, *Promises to Keep*, 2011

856

SHARON GILLENWATER

Megan's Hero

(Grand Rapids, Michigan: Revell, 2011)

Series: Callahans of Texas Series. Book 3
Story type: Romance; Series
Subject(s): Christian life; Romances (Fiction); Western fiction
Major character(s): Megan Smith, Young Woman; Will Callahan, Rancher
Time period(s): 21st century; 2010s
Locale(s): Texas, United States

Summary: In *Megan's Hero* by Sharon Gillenwater, Megan Smith—single and pregnant—is stranded on a road in Texas during a sudden storm. After barely surviving the tornado, Megan is rescued by Will Callahan, who brings her home to his family's ranch. In the welcoming atmosphere of the Callahan ranch, Megan begins to fall for Will. Though the attraction seems mutual, Megan doubts that her pregnancy and dismal financial status make her desirable to Will. Though the local gossips believe that Megan is only after the Callahan clan's money, Will tries to make her understand that his love for her is genuine.

Other books by the same author:
Emily's Chance: A Novel, 2010
Jenna's Cowboy: A Novel, 2010
Standing Tall, 2005
Highland Call, 1999
Texas Tender, 1997

Other books you might like:
Margaret Brownley, *A Lady Like Sarah*, 2009
Mary Connealy, *Cowboy Christmas*, 2009
Denise Hunter, *A Cowboy's Touch*, 2011
Karen Witemeyer, *To Win Her Heart*, 2011
Kathleen Y'Barbo, *The Inconvenient Marriage of Charlotte Beck: A Novel*, 2011

857

DEEANNE GIST

The Trouble with Brides

(Bloomington, Minnesota: Bethany House Publishing, 2011)

Story type: Collection; Romance
Subject(s): Marriage; Weddings; Romances (Fiction)

Summary: *The Trouble with Brides* is a collection of three inspirational romance novels by author Deeanne Gist. In *A Bride Most Begrudging*, Gist tells the story of Lady Constance Morrow, a noblewoman who has been kidnapped and taken from England to America. There, she meets Drew O'Connor, who wants Constance as his bride—but is he up for the challenge? *Courting Trouble* is the story of Essie Spreckelmeyer, a 30-year-old spinster who decides to take fate into her own hands and find herself a man. In *Deep in the Heart of Trouble*, Gist continues Essie's story as she begins to win the heart of Tony Morgan, a worker in her father's oil company who is unsure if Essie is nuts or the woman of his dreams. In each novel, Gist shows how independent female characters put their faith in God to maintain their strength.

Other books by the same author:
Beguiled, 2010
Maid to Match, 2010
A Bride in the Bargain, 2009
The Measure of a Lady, 2006
A Bride Most Begrudging, 2005

Other books you might like:
Maggie Brendan, *The Jewel of His Heart: A Novel*, 2009
Colleen Coble, *The Lightkeeper's Bride*, 2010
Lori Copeland, *Walker's Wedding*, 2010
Laura Frantz, *Courting Morrow Little: A Novel*, 2010
Karen Witemeyer, *A Tailor-Made Bride*, 2010

Inspirational

858

LOUISE M. GOUGE

At the Captain's Command

(Don Mills, Ontario, Canada: Harlequin, 2011)

Story type: Historical
Subject(s): Christian life; History; Romances (Fiction)
Major character(s): Thomas Moberly, Military Personnel (Captain, British Navy); Dinah Templeton, Southern Belle; James Templeton, Brother (of Dinah)
Time period(s): 18th century; 1780s
Locale(s): United States

Summary: In *At the Captain's Command* by Louise M.Gouge, Thomas Moberly and Dinah Templeton come from different worlds. A captain in the British navy and the son of nobility, Thomas Moberly is nonetheless enchanted by the Southern Belle from Florida. As war looms in the colonies, the loyalty of James Templeton, Dinah's brother, comes into question. Dinah makes her feelings for Thomas known, but she eventually must decide if she will forfeit family duty for the man she loves.

Other books by the same author:
The Captain's Lady, 2010
Love Thine Enemy, 2009
Then Came Hope, 2007
Son of Perdition, 2006
Hannah Rose, 2004

Other books you might like:
Winnie Griggs, *The Proper Wife*, 2011
Valerie Hansen, *The Doctor's Newfound Family*, 2010
Jillian Hart, *Patchwork Bride*, 2010
Laurie Kingery, *Mail-Order Cowboy*, 2010
Anna Schmidt, *A Convenient Wife*, 2010

859

SHEILA M. GROSS

Delilah

(Deer Park, New York: Urban Books, 2011)

Story type: Romance
Subject(s): Religion; Christian life; Real estate
Major character(s): Samson Judges, Religious (pastor), Fiance(e) (of Julia); Julia Rivers, Fiance(e) (of Samson); Delilah Baker, Worker (of William); William Trusts, Real Estate Agent

Summary: In *Delilah*, author Sheila M. Gross retells the Biblical story of Samson and Delilah with a modern twist and flair. Samson Judges has it all: a loving family, a beautiful fiancee named Julia Rivers, and a faithful congregation at the Peaceful Rest Missionary Church, where he is pastor. Yet Samson also has some sin in his heart, particularly in the form of his desire for Delilah Baker. Delilah works for William Trusts, a local real-estate developer who wants the land of Samson's church for himself. William will stop at nothing to get the land,

and that includes using Delilah as a pawn. As Samson fights temptation, Delilah struggles with the love she feels for a man she cannot have. Will either of them find strength in God?

Other books by the same author:
Roses Are Thorns, Violets Are True, 2007

Other books you might like:
Stacy Hawkins Adams, *Dreams That Won't Let Go: A Novel*, 2010
Wanda B. Campbell, *Right Package, Wrong Baggage*, 2010
Sherryle Kiser Jackson, *Soon After*, 2010
Sheila E. Lipsey, *My Son's Ex-Wife*, 2010
Vanessa Miller, *Forgiven*, 2010

860

MARCIA GRUVER

Raider's Heart

(Uhrichsville, Ohio: Barbour Publishers, 2011)

Story type: Historical; Romance
Subject(s): Southern United States; Love; Romances (Fiction)
Major character(s): Duncan McRae, Thief, Kidnapper, Brother (of Hooper); Hooper McRae, Thief, Kidnapper, Brother (of Duncan); Dawsey Wilkes, Kidnap Victim
Time period(s): 19th century; 1870s
Locale(s): North Carolina, United States

Summary: *Raider's Heart*, a historical inspirational romance, is part of the Backwoods Brides series from author Marcia Gruver. Set in the backwoods of North Carolina, the tale follows bandit brothers, Duncan and Hooper McRae, different as can be except for their taste in women. Duncan is the gentle and kind brother, who can barely stand a life of thievery, while Hooper is violent and adventurous, always willing to take a risk for a good find. An impromptu burglary results in the kidnapping of sweet-natured and well-bred Dawsey Wilkes, a woman who has been raised in a far different family than the McRaes but who wins the brothers' hearts just the same. Duncan and Hooper soon find themselves competing for Dawsey's affections in a love triangle that uncovers deep family secrets and God's bigger purpose for the Wilkes and McRae clans.

Other books by the same author:
Chasing Charity, 2009
Diamond Duo, 2008

Other books you might like:
Jamie Carie, *The Snowflake*, 2010
Kelly Eileen Hake, *Rugged and Relentless*, 2011
Denise Hunter, *Seaside Letters*, 2009
Delia Parr, *Love's First Bloom*, 2010
Tracie Peterson, *Hearts Aglow*, 2011

861

LISA HARRIS

Blood Covenant

(Grand Rapids, Michigan: Zondervan, 2011)

Series: Mission Hope Series. Book 2
Story type: Religious
Subject(s): Rebellion; Africa; Refugees
Major character(s): Dr. Paige Ryan, Doctor, Volunteer;
    Nick Gilbert, Pilot, Volunteer
Time period(s): 21st century; 2010s
Locale(s): Africa

Summary: *Blood Covenant*, a suspenseful inspirational novel, is the second installment in the Mission Hope series from author Lisa Harris. When a battle begins in the Republic of Dhambizao between rebel soldiers and the government, immediate assistance is needed to evacuate thousands of innocent civilians and set up a refugee camp. Dr. Paige Ryan, a worker with Volunteers of Hope International, and Nick Gilbert, a pilot for Compassion Air, are among the volunteers who offer to bring in supplies and set up a safe site. Between overcrowding and factions forming, things are spiraling out of control in the camp. When a group of American climbers are attacked by the rebel soldiers and brought to the camp, it's discovered that one of them is carrying an infectious disease. Paige and Nick need vaccinations quick before an outbreak, but the vile army of rebels is blocking the only road and they refuse to move until their demands are met.

Other books by the same author:
Blood Ransom, 2010
The Chef's Deadly Dish, 2009
Baker's Fatal Dozen, 2008
Final Deposit, 2008
Recipe for Murder, 2008

Other books you might like:
Jan Karon, *In the Company of Others*, 2010

862

LIZ CURTIS HIGGS

Mine Is the Night

(Colorado Springs, Colorado: WaterBrook Press, 2011)

Story type: Historical
Subject(s): Christian life; Scotland; Social class
Major character(s): Elisabeth Kerr, Seamstress, Widow(er);
    Marjory Kerr, Relative (of Elisabeth, mother-in-law)
Time period(s): 18th century; 1740s
Locale(s): Scotland

Summary: In *Mine is the Night* by Liz Curtis Higgs, a woman and her daughter-in-law move to Selkirk, Scotland in the 1740s after their lives are shattered by tragedy. Marjory Kerr has lost her husband and sons and arrives in Selkirk hoping that a relative there will offer some much-needed support. With her is Elisabeth Kerr, the wife of her deceased son. A skilled seamstress, Elisabeth is eager to make a new start but realizes that both

women face daunting odds. Accused of being traitors, Elisabeth and Marjory have been stung by betrayal, but hope that Selkirk holds the promise of redemption.

Other books by the same author:
Here Burns My Candle: A Novel, 2010
Bookends, 2005
Mixed Signals, 2005
Lowlands of Scotland Series, 2003-2004

Other books you might like:
Deeanne Gist, *Beguiled*, 2010
Julie Klassen, *Girl in the Gatehouse*, 2011
Michael Phillips, *Angel Heart*, 2011
Ann Tatlock, *Promises to Keep*, 2011
Linda Windsor, *Healer*, 2010

863

LAURA V. HILTON

Patchwork Dreams

(New Kensington, Pennsylvania: Whitaker House, 2011)

Series: Amish of Seymour County Series. Book 1
Story type: Romance; Series
Subject(s): Amish; Christian life; Romances (Fiction)
Major character(s): Becky Troyer, Young Woman; Jacob
    Miller, Worker (farmhand)
Time period(s): 21st century; 2010s
Locale(s): Seymour, Missouri

Summary: In *Patchwork Dreams* by Laura V. Hilton, a young Amish girl's "rumspringa" experience leaves her husbandless and pregnant. When Becky Troyer comes home to Seymour, Missouri, her community there shuns her despite her public confession and declaration of renewed faith. As a single mother, Becky knows that the only man who might want her for a wife is a widower with children. But Jacob Miller, a young man sent from his Pennsylvania Amish community to Seymour, is attracted to Becky despite her status. Eventually, Jacob must choose between Becky and the girlfriend he left behind in Pennsylvania. *Patchwork Dreams* is the first book in the Amish of Seymour County series.

Other books you might like:
Linda Byler, *Big Decisions*, 2011
Barbara Cameron, *A Time to Love*, 2010
Mindy Starns Clark, *The Amish Nanny*, 2011
Amy Clipston, *A Place of Peace*, 2010
Cindy Woodsmall, *Plain Wisdom: An Invitation into an
    Amish Home and the Hearts of Two Women*, 2011

864

VICKI HINZE

Deadly Ties

(Colorado Springs, Colorado: Multnomah Books, 2011)

Series: Crossroads Crisis Center Series. Book 2
Story type: Romantic Suspense
Subject(s): Romances (Fiction); Faith; Abuse
Major character(s): Lisa Harper, Abuse Victim, Daughter

Inspirational

(of Annie); Annie, Mother (of Lisa), Abuse Victim; Dutch Hauk, Spouse (of Annie), Stepfather (of Lisa), Criminal; Mark Taylor, Military Personnel (special ops)

Time period(s): 21st century; 2010s
Locale(s): United States

Summary: *Deadly Ties*, a suspenseful inspirational romance, is the second installment in the Crossroads Crisis Center series from award-winning author Vicki Hinze. As a child, Lisa Harper's father died, leaving her lonely and desperate mother Annie to quickly remarry a man named Dutch Hauk. In no time, Dutch's abusive and violent nature appeared, his hatred for Lisa knowing no bounds. In an effort to spare her daughter's life, Annie sent Lisa away to live with a trustworthy pal. Now, as an adult, Lisa is given a second chance to build a relationship, and a home, with her mother, but Dutch has other plans. His nefarious friends are plotting a horrendous fate for Lisa and Annie as soon as they're located. The only person Lisa can turn to is Mark Taylor, a former special ops officer whose secret love for Lisa will propel him to take any risk to ensure her safety.

Other books by the same author:
Forget Me Not, 2010
Kill Zone, 2009
Her Perfect Life, 2006
Double Dare, 2005
Acts of Honor, 1999

Other books you might like:
Terri Blackstock, *Vicious Cycle*, 2011
Jamie Carie, *Angel's Den*, 2010
Robin Caroll, *Deliver Us From Evil: A Novel*, 2010
Ronie Kendig, *Dead Reckoning*, 2010
Richard L. Mabry, *Code Blue*, 2010

865

DON HOESEL

The Alarmists

(Minneapolis, Minnesota: Bethany House, 2011)

Story type: End of the World
Subject(s): Suspense; End of the world; Fear
Major character(s): Jameson Richards, Professor (sociology), Researcher; General Michaels, Military Personnel (general), Scientist; Jeremy Maxwell, Wealthy, Manufacturer (weapons)
Time period(s): 21st century; 2010s
Locale(s): Washington, District of Columbia

Summary: *The Alarmists* is a suspenseful inspirational novel from author Don Hoesel. As the world draws nearer to December 21, 2012, the day the Mayan calendar predicts the world will come to an end, panic and hysteria are beginning to creep into the general population. Sociology professor Jameson Richards is intent on researching the impact the build-up, and certain letdown, has on society when the date passes without incident. He's teamed up with General Michaels, a Pentagon scientist monitoring potential terrorists, for the assignment and together they uncover a shocking secret about billionaire and weapons manufacturer, Jeremy

Maxwell. It seems that Maxwell is trying to capitalize on the world's trepidation, but his plan could lead to a major military conflict in the Middle East if Richards and Michaels can't expose his plan and stop him first.

Other books by the same author:
Hunter's Moon, 2010
Elisha's Bones, 2009

Other books you might like:
Ted Dekker, *The Priest's Graveyard*, 2011
Alton Gansky, *The Mayan Apocalypse*, 2010
Robert Liparulo, *Frenzy*, 2010
Mark Mynheir, *The Corruptible: A Ray Quinn Mystery*, 2011
Robert L. Wise, *Shrouded in Silence*, 2011

866

DENISE HUNTER

A Cowboy's Touch

(Nashville, Tennessee: Thomas Nelson Publishers, 2011)

Story type: Romance
Subject(s): Western fiction; Romances (Fiction); Cowhands
Major character(s): Abigail Jones, Journalist; Wade Ryan, Cowboy/Cowgirl

Summary: In *A Cowboy's Touch*, author Denise Hunter tells the story of Abigail Jones, a journalist who is finally taking some much-needed time off. She travels to her aunt's ranch to help out for a while, and there she meets Wade Ryan, a neighboring rancher. When Wade, a widower, suddenly finds himself without a nanny for his daughter, Abigail steps up to the plate and volunteers to fill in for a little while. The more time she spends with Wade and his daughter, though, the more they feel like family. Now Abigail has a major life decision to make: is she ready to give up her career for the love of a lifetime?

Other books by the same author:
Driftwood Lane: A Nantucket Love Story, 2010
Seaside Letters, 2009
Sweetwater Gap, 2008
Surrender Bay, 2007
Saving Grace, 2005

Other books you might like:
Colleen Coble, *Lonestar Series*, 2008
Mary Connealy, *Sophie's Daughters Series*, 2010
Susan Page Davis, *Ladies' Shooting Club Series*, 2009
Sara Evans, *The Sweet By and By*, 2009
Vickie McDonough, *Texas Boardinghouse Brides Series*, 2010

867

STEVEN JAMES

The Bishop

(Grand Rapids, Michigan: Revell, 2010)

Series: Patrick Bowers Files Series. Book 4
Story type: Contemporary

Subject(s): Murder; Christian life; Detective fiction
Major character(s): Patrick Bowers, Criminologist
Time period(s): 21st century; 2010s
Locale(s): United States

Summary: *The Bishop* is the fourth novel in Steven James's Patrick Bowers Files series. This installment finds Patrick, a criminologist with the FBI, investigating the savage murder of a primate researcher. The researcher, who was the daughter of a high-ranking politician, was tied up before the killer unleashed a horde of rabid lab animals on her. Now, Patrick must find a ruthless psychopath—even as his private life deals him some crushing blows.

Where it's reviewed:
Booklist, Nov 15, 2010, page 13
Booklist, August 1, 2010, page 30

Other books by the same author:
The Knight, 2010
The Pawn, 2009
The Rook, 2009

Other books you might like:
Terri Blackstock, *Predator: A Novel*, 2010
Julie Cave, *The Shadowed Mind*, 2010
Brandilyn Collins, *Deceit*, 2010
Irene Hannon, *Fatal Judgment*, 2011
Randy Singer, *Fatal Convictions*, 2010

868

JERRY B. JENKINS

The Brotherhood

(Carol Stream, Illinois: Tyndale House Publishers, 2011)

Series: Precinct 11 Series. Book 1
Story type: Police Procedural
Subject(s): Christian life; Gangs; Law
Major character(s): Boone Drake, Police Officer
Time period(s): 21st century; 2010s
Locale(s): Chicago, Illinois

Summary: *The Brotherhood* is an installment from author Jerry B. Jenkins's Precinct 11 series. In this book, Jenkins tells the story of Officer Boone Drake, an up-and-coming cop in the Chicago Police Department whose life seems to be right on track. He's got a burgeoning career, a loving wife, a wonderful son, and a new home. When his wife and child are killed in a fire, he begins to wonder why God has forsaken him, and instead turns away from his faith. Then his job brings him face to face with a dreadful organized-crime boss, and he learns to forgive not only God, but also himself.

Other books by the same author:
The Last Operative, 2010
Riven, 2009
Demon's Bluff, 2007
Underground Zealot Series, 2004-2006

Other books you might like:
Randy Alcorn, *The Chasm: A Journey to the Edge of Life*, 2011
Tim LaHaye, *Edge of Apocalypse*, 2010
Josh D. McDowell, *The Witness*, 2010

Joel Rosenberg, *The Twelfth Imam: A Novel*, 2010
Randy Singer, *Fatal Convictions*, 2010

869

JENNY B. JONES

Save the Date

(Nashville, Tennessee: Thomas Nelson, 2010)

Story type: Romance
Subject(s): Romances (Fiction); Faith; Marriage
Major character(s): Alex Sinclair, Football Player (ex-NFL), Entrepreneur, Political Figure; Lucy Wiltshire, Young Woman, Social Worker
Time period(s): 21st century; 2010s
Locale(s): United States

Summary: Alex Sinclair and Lucy Wiltshire couldn't be more different: he's a former NFL star with a successful business and a dream of being a congressman, and she's an independent woman who runs a transitional shelter and lives paycheck to paycheck. When this unlikely pair meets and is photographed together at a gala, a romance is suggested in the tabloids and the public goes crazy for these alleged lovebirds. Alex sees an opportunity to improve his public image and get the votes needed for his Congress bid: in exchange for cash, Lucy will pose as his fiancee. The plan seems mutually beneficial and strictly business until it becomes evident that God has another plan for these two.

Other books by the same author:
Finding God, 2009
Just Between You and Me: A Novel of Losing Fear and Finding God, 2009

Other books you might like:
Kristin Billerbeck, *A Billion Reasons Why*, 2011
Sandra D. Bricker, *Always the Baker, Never the Bride*, 2010
Rachel Hauck, *Love Starts with Elle*, 2008
Trish Perry, *Perfect Blend*, 2010
Janice A. Thompson, *Stars Collide*, 2011

870

RONIE KENDIG

Digitalis

(Uhrichsville, Ohio: Barbour Publishers, 2011)

Series: Discarded Heroes Series. Book 2
Story type: Romance
Subject(s): Armed forces; Romances (Fiction); Suspense
Major character(s): Colton "Cowboy" Neely, Military Personnel, Single Father; Piper Blum, Saleswoman
Time period(s): 21st century; 2010s
Locale(s): Texas, United States

Summary: *Digitalis*, a suspenseful inspirational romance, is the second installment in the Discarded Heroes series from author Ronie Kendig. Colton "Cowboy" Neely is trying to settle into a normal life on his parents' Texas ranch, but the single father and former Marine is suffer-

Inspirational

ing from painful and debilitating flashbacks of his time in active duty. As part of an elite black ops group known as Nightshade, Colton has been granted the time he needs to heal before another mission requires his attention. A casual shopping trip leads him to Piper Blum, a mysterious and beautiful woman with a secret past. Colton begins falling for Piper until a dangerous mission causes their pasts to collide.

Other books by the same author:
Dead Reckoning, 2010
Nightshade, 2010

Other books you might like:
Colleen Coble, *Abomination*, 2007
Brandilyn Collins, *Brink of Death*, 2004
Vicki Hinze, *Deadly Ties*, 2011
Mel Odom, *Paid in Blood*, 2006
Bodie Thoene, *The Gathering Storm*, 2010

871

JILLIAN KENT

Secrets of the Heart

(Lake Mary, Florida: Realms, 2011)

Series: Ravensmoore Chronicles Series. Book 1
Story type: Historical
Subject(s): Christian life; History; Romances (Fiction)
Major character(s): Madeline Whittington, Noblewoman; Devlin Greyson, Nobleman
Time period(s): 19th century; 1810s (1817)
Locale(s): England

Summary: In *Secrets of the Heart* by Jillian Kent, Madeline Whittington has lost her father, the Earl of Richfield, as well as her desire to participate in 1817 English society. After months of mourning, Madeline finds her perception of the world altered when she aids a patient who has escaped from the nearby Ashcroft Insane Asylum. Meanwhile, Devlin Greyson suffers the loss of his older brother and subsequently assumes the title, Earl of Ravensmoore. But Devlin had planned on a career as a physician, not the life of a nobleman. Madeline and Devlin seek God's guidance as they try to balance personal conviction with family loyalty. *Secrets of the Heart* is the first book in the Ravensmoore Chronicles series. First novel.

Other books you might like:
Andrea Boeshaar, *Undaunted Faith*, 2011
Mike Dellosso, *Darkness Follows*, 2011
Linda Rios-Brook, *The Redeemer*, 2011
Martha Rogers, *Summer Dream*, 2011
Perry Stone, *How to Interpret Dreams and Visions: Understanding God's warnings and guidance*, 2011

872

KAREN KINGSBURY

Leaving

(Grand Rapids, Michigan: Zondervan, 2011)

Series: Bailey Flanigan Series. Book 1
Story type: Romance; Series

Subject(s): Christian life; Romances (Fiction); Actors
Major character(s): Bailey Flanigan, Actress; Brandon Paul, Actor; Matt Keagan, Football Player; Cody Coleman, Veteran (Iraq War); Landon Blake, Fire Fighter
Time period(s): 21st century; 2010s
Locale(s): Bloomington, Indiana; New York, New York

Summary: In *Leaving* by Karen Kingsbury, Bailey Flanigan's appearance in the movie *Unlocked* has earned her an audition—and a callback—for a Broadway show. When Bailey moves from Bloomington, Indiana to New York City, she leaves behind her close-knit family and friends but brings her romantic troubles along. Her *Unlocked* co-star, Brandon Paul, has made his interest known, as has pro-football player Matt Keagan. But Bailey's heart still belongs to Cody Coleman, an Iraq War veteran who ended their relationship to deal with his mother's drug addiction. *Leaving* is the first book in the Bailey Flanigan series.

Other books by the same author:
Take Four, 2010
Unlocked: A Love Story, 2010
Redemption, 2009
Shades of Blue, 2009
A Thousand Tomorrows, 2007

Other books you might like:
Tammy Barley, *Faith's Reward*, 2011
Suzanne Woods Fisher, *The Waiting: A Novel*, 2010
Dee Henderson, *Kidnapped*, 2008
Ann Tatlock, *Promises to Keep*, 2011

873

JANE KIRKPATRICK

The Daughter's Walk: A Novel

(Colorado Springs, Colorado: WaterBrook Press, 2011)

Story type: Historical
Subject(s): Christian life; History; Mother-daughter relations
Major character(s): Clara Estby, 19-Year-Old; Helga Estby, Mother (of Clara)
Time period(s): 19th century; 1890s (1896)
Locale(s): NewYork, New York; Spokane, Washington

Summary: In *The Daughter's Walk* by Jane Kirkpatrick, the 1896 fashion industry has introduced short dresses that are designed to be more practical. To promote the idea, a $10,000 award is offered to a woman who can walk across country wearing one. Motivated by her family's dire financial situation, Helga Etsby sets out from Spokane, Washington on a 3500-mile trek to New York City. Clara Etsby, 19, accompanies her mother on the seven-month trip. The walk changes Clara forever. Though her mother goes home to the family's Washington farm, Clara continues her travels, changes her name, and forges a career at the turn of the 20th century.

Other books by the same author:
An Absence So Great: A Novel, 2010
A Flickering Light, 2009
A Mending at the Edge, 2008

A Sweetness to the Soul, 2008
A Clearing in the Wild, 2006

Other books you might like:
Richard Paul Evans, *Miles to Go*, 2011
Ann H. Gabhart, *Angel Sister*, 2011
Linda Lawrence Hunt, *Bold Spirit: Helga Estby's
  Forgotten Walk Across Victorian America*, 2005
Michael Phillips, *Angel Harp: A Novel*, 2011
Bodie Thoene, *Against the Wind*, 2011

874

SHERRY KYLE

Delivered with Love

(Nashville, Tennessee: Abingdon Press, 2011)

Story type: Romance
Subject(s): Christian life; Romances (Fiction); Family
  relations
Major character(s): Claire James, Young Woman, Waiter/
  Waitress; Michael Thompson, Real Estate Agent
Time period(s): 21st century; 2010s
Locale(s): Capitola, California; Los Angeles, California

Summary: In *Delivered with Love* by Sherry Kyle, Claire
James inherits her mother's old car when she dies and
embarks on a journey into the past. When Claire finds a
love letter among the contents of the car's glove
compartment, she is determined to find the author. The
loss of her job and a place to stay prompt Claire to travel
to Capitola, California to make a new start and find the
man who was in love with her mother over 30 years ago.
Michael Thompson is enjoying a quiet life as a father
and real estate agent until Claire arrives in town to reveal
secrets from the past. First novel.

Other books you might like:
Amanda Cabot, *Scattered Petals*, 2010
Melody Carlson, *Love Finds You in Sisters, Oregon*,
  2009
Colleen Coble, *The Lightkeeper's Bride*, 2010
Rene Gutteridge, *Never the Bride*, 2009
Karen Kingsbury, *Leaving*, 2011

875

C.S. LAKIN

The Map Across Time

(Chattanooga, Tennessee: AMG Publishers, 2011)

Series: Gates of Heaven Series. Book 2
Story type: Fantasy
Subject(s): Fairy tales; Christianity; Royalty
Major character(s): Adin, Twin (of Aletha), Royalty
  (prince of Sherbourne); Aletha, Twin (of Adin),
  Royalty (princess of Sherbourne)
Locale(s): Sherbourne, Fictional Location

Summary: *The Map Across Time* is the second novel in
C.S. Lakin's inspirational fantasy series The Gates of
Heaven. In this novel, Adin and Aletha, prince and
princess of Sherbourne, must watch as their father falls

into a deep depression as the result of their mother's
recent death. The fate of all of Sherbourne relies on their
father, the King, and the twin siblings are afraid that
their beloved kingdom will soon fall. Then they come
across a map that leads them through time. Can this
sacred map help Adin and Aletha save their father and
their country? Lakin is also the author of *The Wolf of
Tebron*.

Other books by the same author:
Someone to Blame, 2010
The Wolf of Tebron, 2010

Other books you might like:
C.S. Lewis, *Chronicles of Narnia*, 1950
J.R.R. Tolkien, *The Lord of the Rings Trilogy*, 1954

876

JULIE LESSMAN

A Hope Undaunted

(Grand Rapids, Michigan: Revell, 2010)

Series: Winds of Change Series. Book 1
Story type: Historical; Romance
Subject(s): Romances (Fiction); History; Women
Major character(s): Katie O'Connor, Young Woman,
  Lawyer; Jack Worthington, Wealthy, Young Man,
  Boyfriend (of Katie); Luke McGee, Young Man,
  Lawyer
Time period(s): 20th century; 1920s (1929)
Locale(s): Boston, Massachusetts

Summary: *A Hope Undaunted*, a historical inspirational
romance, is the first installment in the Winds of Change
series from author Julie Lessman. Despite being a young
woman in the 1920s, an era that strongly encourages
females to be submissive housewives, Katie O'Connor
has the fierce determination and ambition of a modern
woman. Her passionate romance with the wealthy, handsome, and well-bred Jack Worthington and a recent law
degree set Katie up for the life she's always dreamed of.
But when her father forces her to spend the summer of
1929 volunteering at the Boston Children's Aid Society
with childhood nemesis Luke McGee of all people,
Katie's well-laid plans begin to unravel as her heart is
tugged in a different direction.

Where it's reviewed:
Publishers Weekly, July 5, 2010, page 28

Other books by the same author:
A Passion Denied, 2009
A Passion Most Pure, 2008
A Passion Redeemed, 2008

Other books you might like:
Delia Parr, *Hidden Affections*, 2011

877

ELIZABETH LUDWIG
JANELLE MOWERY, Co-Author

Died in the Wool

(Uhrichsville, Ohio: Heartsong Presents, 2011)

Series: Mayhem Mystery Series. Book 2
Story type: Mystery

Subject(s): Mystery; Murder; Libraries
Major character(s): Monah Trenary, Librarian, Crime Suspect; Casey Alexander, Detective, Friend (of Monah); Mike Brockman, Police Officer, Detective
Time period(s): 21st century; 2010s
Locale(s): Pine Mills, Massachusetts

Summary: *Died in the Wool*, a humorous and suspenseful inspirational mystery, is the second installment in the Massachusetts Mayhem Mystery series from authors Elizabeth Ludwig and Janelle Mowery. In the city of Pine Mills, dedicated librarian Monah Trenary would do just about anything to secure more funding for her library, but murder is going a tad too far. Or is it? When her rival for the funds is killed, Monah finds herself as a prime suspect in the case. As more bodies begin stacking up, police detective Mike Brockman isn't sure what to believe. Fortunately, Monah has the help of superior sleuth Casey Alexander on her side to clear her name and track down the real killer.

Other books by the same author:
Inn Plain Sight, 2011
Where the Truth Lies, 2008

Other books you might like:
Frances Devine, *Miss Aggie's Gone Missing*, 2008
K.D. Hays, *Worth Its Weight in Old*, 2008
Cynthia Hickey, *Chocolate-Covered Crime*, 2011
Cynthia Hickey, *Fudge-Laced Felonies*, 2008
Anita Higman, *Another Stab at Life*, 2010

878

RICHARD L. MABRY

Diagnosis: Death

(Nashville, Tennessee: Abingdon Press, 2011)

Series: Prescription for Trouble Series. Book 3
Story type: Medical; Series
Subject(s): Christian life; Medicine; Suspense
Major character(s): Dr. Elena Gardner, Doctor
Time period(s): 21st century; 2010s
Locale(s): Texas, United States

Summary: In *Diagnosis: Death* by Richard L. Mabry, a physician's grief over the loss of her husband is compounded by suspicions that she may have played a role in his death. Elena Gardener is at her husband's side when he is removed from life support, but later, when she is questioned about the series of events, her memory seems sketchy. Elena begins receiving menacing phone calls, and when another patient dies under similar circumstances, she transfers to another hospital. When the calls persist and a yet another death occurs, even her colleagues wonder if Elena is a mercy killer. *Diagnosis: Death* is the third book in the Prescription for Trouble series.

Other books by the same author:
Code Blue, 2010
Medical Error, 2010

Other books you might like:
Candace Calvert, *Code Triage*, 2010
Kathy Herman, *False Pretenses*, 2011

Mark Mynheir, *The Corruptible: A Ray Quinn Mystery*, 2011
Amy N. Wallace, *Enduring Justice*, 2009
Lis Wiehl, *Face of Betrayal*, 2009

879

KATHI MACIAS

People of the Book

(Birmingham, Alabama: New Hope Publishers, 2011)

Story type: Contemporary
Subject(s): Christian life; Islam; Religion
Major character(s): Farah, Teenager; Kareem, Brother (of Farah)
Time period(s): 21st century; 2010s
Locale(s): Riyadh, Saudi Arabia

Summary: In *People of the Book* by Kathi Macias, the Ramadan journey of a young Muslim girl in Saudi Arabia takes an unexpected turn. Farah is devoted to Islam, but as she seeks a closer relationship with Allah during the month of fasting, she is shocked when Jesus (the Muslim prophet Isa) summons her in a dream. Farah's cousin is also familiar with Jesus and has learned through a Muslim Internet group that others of their faith believe that Isa is truly God's son. Both girls find that their religious views bring them into conflict with members of their families.

Other books by the same author:
More Than Conquerors, 2010
No Greater Love, 2010
Red Ink, 2010
My Son, John, 2009
Toni Matthews Mystery Series, 2001-2002

Other books you might like:
Tessa Afshar, *Pearl in the Sand*, 2010
Lynn Austin, *Though Waters Roar*, 2009
T.L. Higley, *Petra: City in Stone*, 2010
Jeff Nesbit, *Peace*, 2010
Don Reid, *One Lane Bridge*, 2010

880

GAIL GAYMER MARTIN

A Dad of His Own

(New York: Steeple Hill Books, 2011)

Story type: Romance
Subject(s): Family; Children; Diseases
Major character(s): Ethan Fox, Businessman (board member, Dreams Come True Foundation); Lexie Carlson, Mother (of Cooper); Cooper Carlson, Son (of Lexie)

Summary: As a board member for the Dreams Come True Foundation, Ethan Fox has been able to grant many sick and terminally ill children their wishes. When he meets Lexie Carlson and her son, Cooper, he knows that Jonas Brother concerts and Caribbean vacations just won't do—what Cooper really needs is a father. The more time

Ethan spends with Cooper and Lexie, the more he'd love to grant Cooper's wish. Unfortunately, Ethan's been hurt before, and he's afraid loving Lexie will break him. Can the Lord help these three deserving people come together as a family after all?

Other books by the same author:
Bride in Training, 2010
The Christmas Kite, 2008
Loving Treasures, 2002

Other books you might like:
Janet Dean, *Wanted: A Family Love*, 2011
Linda Goodnight, *A Place to Belong*, 2011
Deb Kastner, *A Colorado Match*, 2011
Lisa Manley, *Family to the Rescue*, 2011
Kathryn Springer, *The Prodigal Comes Home*, 2011

881

BOOKER T. MATTISON

Snitch: A Novel

(Grand Rapids, Michigan: Revell, 2011)

Story type: Psychological Suspense
Subject(s): Suspense; Murder; Faith
Major character(s): Andre Bolden, Driver (bus), Writer, Father
Time period(s): 21st century; 2010s
Locale(s): Jersey City, New Jersey

Summary: *Snitch: A Novel* is a suspenseful inspirational novel from author Booker T. Mattison. The unspoken laws of Jersey City are widely understood and revered by everyone who lives there. Topping the list is the commitment to silence, especially in light of a crime, as snitching is severely frowned upon in the community. Bus driver and aspiring writer, Andre Bolden's loyalty is put to the test when he witnesses a murder during his bus route, and the killer spots him. Suddenly Andre finds himself torn between being faithful to his job and his own conscience, and protecting his family and loved ones from the fierce danger that's sure to accompany his testimony.

Other books by the same author:
Unsigned Hype: A Novel, 2009

Other books you might like:
Randy Alcorn, *Edge of Eternity*, 1998
Ted Dekker, *Blink of an Eye*, 2008
Erin Healy, *Never Let You Go*, 2010
Jerry B. Jenkins, *The Last Operative*, 2010
Robert Liparulo, *Timescape*, 2009

882

AARON MCCARVER
DIANE ASHLEY, Co-Author

Tennessee Brides

(Uhrichsville, Ohio: Barbour Publishers, 2011)

Story type: Historical; Romance
Subject(s): Romances (Fiction); History; Racism
Major character(s): Rebekah Taylor, Fiance(e) (of Asher Landon); Asher Landon, Student—College, Fiance(e) (of Rebekah), Military Personnel (soldier); Iris Landon, Adventurer, Child-Care Giver; Amelia Montgomery, Agent (underground railroad)
Time period(s): 19th century
Locale(s): Tennessee, United States

Summary: *Tennessee Brides*, a historical inspirational romance novel, is part of the Romancing America series from authors Aaron McCarvey and Diane Ashley. Three women face challenges and surprises in 19th-century Tennessee in this uplifting book. After years of waiting to marry Asher Landon, Rebekah Taylor now has to contend with the war with Britain for her beau's heart and hand. Iris Landon finds herself nannying two Cherokee orphans in a small Tennessee town where racism and prejudice run rampant, threatening her safety and future. Amelia Montgomery unwittingly becomes an active participant in the Underground Railroad, making her a prime target for Confederate troops. Can these three women untangle the mess of their lives and still find their happily ever after?

Other books by the same author:
The Mockingbird's Call, 2010
A Bouquet for Iris, 2009
Under the Tulip Poplar, 2009
Beyond the Quiet Hills, 1997
Over the Misty Mountains, 1997

Other books you might like:
Susan Page Davis, *Alaska Weddings*, 2011
Linda Ford, *Dakota Child*, 2009
Cheryl St. John, *The Preacher's Wife*, 2009
Amber Miller Stockton, *Michigan Brides*, 2010
Stephanie Grace Whitson, *Sixteen Brides*, 2010

883

VICKIE MCDONOUGH

Finally a Bride

(Uhrichsville, Ohio: Barbour Publishing, 2011)

Series: Texas Boardinghouse Brides Series. Book 3
Story type: Romance; Series
Subject(s): Christian life; Romances (Fiction); Western fiction
Major character(s): Jody Chapman, Religious (preacher); Jacqueline Hamilton, Journalist; Carly Payton, Convict (former); Garrett Corbett, Cowboy/Cowgirl; Christine Taylor, Widow(er); Rand Kessler, Cowboy/Cowgirl
Time period(s): 19th century; 1890s (1896)
Locale(s): Lookout, Texas

Summary: In *Finally a Bride* by Vickie McDonough, Jody Chapman moves back to Lookout, Texas, in 1896, hoping that service as the town's preacher will reconcile his past indiscretions. Though local journalist Jacqueline Davis suspects that Chapman is hiding something, she can't ignore the romantic feelings growing between them. Carly Payton is also back in Lookout, settling into the boardinghouse after completing her jail sentence. Garrett Corbett is in the market for a bride, and though

Inspirational

he finds Carly physically attractive, he is troubled by her criminal history. *Finally a Bride* is the third book in the Texas Boardinghouse Brides series.

Other books by the same author:
The Anonymous Bride, 2010
Second Chance Brides, 2010
Straight for the Heart, 2009
A Wagonload of Trouble, 2009
Sooner or Later, 2005

Other books you might like:
Mary Connealy, *Sharpshooter in Petticoats*, 2011
Lori Copeland, *A Kiss for Cade*, 2009
Laura Frantz, *Courting Morrow Little: A Novel*, 2010
Kelly Eileen Hake, *The Bride Blunder*, 2009
Stephanie Grace Whitson, *Sixteen Brides*, 2010

884

HENRY MCLAUGHLIN

Journey to Riverbend

(Carol Stream, Illinois: Tyndale House Publishers, 2011)

Story type: Romance
Subject(s): Christian life; Death; Family
Major character(s): Michael Archer, Religious (preacher); Rachel Stone, Young Woman; Sam Carstairs, Businessman, Father (of Ben); Ben Carstairs, Son (of Sam), Convict
Time period(s): 19th century; 1870s (1878)
Locale(s): Riverbend, United States

Summary: *Journey to Riverbend* by Henry McLaughlin is the story of Michael Archer, a 19th-century preacher with a promise to keep. When Ben Carstairs is hanged for a crime he didn't commit, Michael vows to at least help Ben with one final wish—to have his body reunited with his family. The only problem is, Sam Carstairs—a hardhearted entrepreneur on the Western frontier—wants nothing to do with his son in life or in death. Michael travels to Riverbend to try to reason with the businessman, and there the preacher meets and falls for Rachel Stone. When Michael receives word that Sam has been abducted while returning from a business trip, he and Rachel must work to find a man who might need saving in more ways than one.

Other books you might like:
Nicole Baart, *Beneath the Night Tree*, 2010
Kathy Herman, *The Right Call*, 2010
Karen Kingsbury, *Take Three*, 2010

885

DANA MENTINK

Turbulence

(New York: Steeple Hill Books, 2011)

Series: Steeple Hill Love Inspired Suspense. Book 3
Story type: Romantic Suspense
Subject(s): Romances (Fiction); Suspense; Airplanes
Major character(s): Maddie Lambert, Daughter, Fiance(e) (former, of Paul); Dr. Paul Ford, Doctor, Fiance(e) (former, of Maddie)
Time period(s): 21st century; 2010s
Locale(s): United States

Summary: *Turbulence*, a suspenseful inspirational romance, is part of the Love Inspired Suspense series from author Dana Mentnik. Maddie Lambert's wealthy and powerful father is desperately in need of a heart transplant and Maddie is determined to get the organ to him on time. Flying alongside her ex-fiance, Dr. Paul Ford, a man she blames for the family tragedy, Maddie is accompanying the heart to her father's hospital, but it would seem someone is intent on keeping the transplant from ever happening. The plane goes down in a dangerous and isolated area, leaving Maddie and Paul to fight for survival. Maddie's forced to overcome her feelings of betrayal and trust Paul completely if she hopes to reach her father before it's too late.

Other books by the same author:
Betrayal in the Badlands, 2010
Endless Night, 2010
Flashover, 2009
Race to Rescue, 2009
Fog Over Finny's Nose, 2008

Other books you might like:
Christy Barritt, *Keeping Guard*, 2011
Lauren Nichols, *Marked for Murder*, 2010
Viriginia Smith, *A Deadly Game*, 2011
Hope White, *Hidden in Shadows*, 2010
Lenora Worth, *Body of Evidence*, 2011

886

SIRI MITCHELL

A Heart Most Worthy

(Bloomington, Minnesota: Bethany House Publishing, 2011)

Story type: Romance
Subject(s): Immigrants; Family; Italian Americans
Major character(s): Luciana, Seamstress, Immigrant (from Italy); Julietta, Immigrant (from Italy), Seamstress; Annamaria, Seamstress, Immigrant (from Italy)
Time period(s): 20th century; 1910s (1918)
Locale(s): Boston, Massachusetts

Summary: *A Heart Most Worthy* is a inspirational romance by author Siri Mitchell. Annamaria, Julietta, and Luciana are all young women, each of whom has immigrated from Italy and each with her own share of secrets. Annamaria is in love with the son of a local grocer who her devoutly Catholic family will never accept. Julietta longs to rid herself of her Southern Italian accent and truly become an American. Luciana is the daughter of the Count of Roma who fled for her life after her father's murder. Now the three young women must work together at Madame Forza's dress shop in the posh part of Boston, even though every night they return home to the Italian ghetto of North Boston. Can their continued faith in God keep them going long enough to achieve their dreams?

Other books by the same author:
She Walks in Beauty, 2010
Love's Pursuit, 2009

A Constant Heart, 2008
The Cubicle Next Door, 2006
Chateau of Echoes, 2005

Other books you might like:
Deeanne Gist, *The Trouble with Brides*, 2011
Julie Klassen, *The Silent Governess*, 2010
Julie Lessman, *A Hope Undaunted*, 2010
Nancy Moser, *Masquerade*, 2010
Karen Witemeyer, *A Tailor-Made Bride*, 2010

`887`

JOYCE MAGNIN MOCCERO

Griselda Takes Flight

(Nashville, Tennessee: Abingdon Press, 2011)

Series: Bright's Pond Series. Book 3
Story type: Contemporary; Series
Subject(s): Christian life; Sisters; Interpersonal relations
Major character(s): Griselda Sparrow, Young Woman; Agnes Sparrow, Sister (of Griselda); Cliff, Pilot; Stella Kincaid, Neighbor (of Griselda); Ivy Slocum, Neighbor (of Griselda); Mildred Blessing, Police Officer (chief)
Time period(s): 21st century; 2010s
Locale(s): Bright's Pond, Pennsylvania

Summary: In *Griselda Takes Flight* by Joyce Magnin, Griselda Sparrow is learning to spread her wings now that her seriously overweight sister, Agnes, is in the care of a nursing home. Griselda's flying lessons with Cliff, a good-looking pilot, keep her busy. And as always, the town of Bright's Pond and its cast of quirky characters offer plenty of distractions. At the moment, the main focus of Bright's Pond's attention is the case of Stella Kincaid's wealthy, comatose brother and the woman who claims to be his fiancee. Police Chief Mildred Blessing's investigation digs up some surprising revelations. *Griselda Takes Flight* is the third book in the Bright's Pond series.

Other books by the same author:
Charlotte Figg Takes Over Paradise, 2010
The Prayers of Agnes Sparrow, 2009

Other books you might like:
Judy Christie, *The Glory of Green*, 2011
Mindy Starns Clark, *Under the Cajun Moon*, 2009
Gail Fraser, *Lumby on the Air*, 2010
Dave Jackson, *Harry Bentley's Second Chance*, 2008
Lisa Wingate, *Larkspur Cove*, 2011

`888`

KATHLEEN MORGAN

A Heart Divided: A Novel

(Grand Rapids, Michigan: Revell, 2011)

Series: Heart of the Rockies Series. Book 1
Story type: Historical; Series
Subject(s): Christian life; History; Romances (Fiction)

Major character(s): Sarah Caldwell, Young Woman; Cord Wainwright, Rancher
Time period(s): 19th century; 1870s (1878)
Locale(s): Colorado, United States

Summary: In *A Heart Divided* by Kathleen Morgan, a long-standing family feud between the Caldwells and Wainwrights of the Rocky Mountains reaches a climax in 1878. Sarah Caldwell's father convinces her to divert the attention of one of the Wainwrights' ranch hands so that the Caldwell men can break in. But the young man that Sarah successfully distracts is Cord Wainwright, who is not amused by the Caldwells' latest prank. Since the local lawman is out of town, Cord takes Sarah into custody himself. Sarah's initial outrage gradually gives way to affection for her captor. *A Heart Divided* is the first book in the Heart of the Rockies series.

Other books by the same author:
As High as the Heavens, 2008
A Fire Within, 2007
Wings of Morning, 2006
Child of the Mist, 2005
Giver of Roses, 2005

Other books you might like:
Cara Lynn James, *Love By the Book*, 2011
Vickie McDonough, *The Anonymous Bride*, 2010
Catherine Palmer, *The Gunman's Bride*, 2011
Tracie Peterson, *Dawn's Prelude*, 2009
Martha Rogers, *Caroline's Choice*, 2011

`889`

MEG MOSELEY

When Sparrows Fall: A Novel

(Colorado Springs, Colorado: Multnomah Books, 2011)

Story type: Romance
Subject(s): Christian life; Romances (Fiction); Family relations
Major character(s): Miranda Hanford, Widow(er), Mother (of six children); Mason Chandler, Religious (pastor); Jack Hanford, Relative (brother-in-law of Miranda); Timothy, Son (of Miranda)
Time period(s): 21st century; 2010s
Locale(s): United States

Summary: In *When Sparrows Fall* by Meg Moseley, a widowed mother fights to protect her family from the secrets of the past. In the wake of her husband's death, Miranda Hanford works hard to raise her six children alone and finds strength in her local church community. But when the congregation plans to move, Miranda learns that events from her past may be revealed. A sudden injury incapacitates Miranda and she is forced to call in her brother-in-law, Jack, to help. Jack has had little contact with Miranda and her children, but is easily drawn into the family. A college professor, Jack tries to broaden Miranda's protective parenting style. First novel.

Other books you might like:
Hillary McFarland, *Quivering Daughters*, 2010

890

NANCY MOSER

An Unlikely Suitor

(Bloomington, Minnesota: Bethany House Publishing, 2011)

Story type: Romance
Subject(s): Social class; Friendship; Love
Major character(s): Rowena Langdon, Socialite, Wealthy, Friend (of Lucy and Sofia); Lucy Scarpelli, Seamstress, Sister (of Sofia), Friend (of Rowena); Sofia Scarpelli, Seamstress, Sister (of Lucy), Friend (of Rowena)
Time period(s): 19th century; 1890s (1895)
Locale(s): Newport, Rhode Island

Summary: *An Unlikely Suitor* is an inspirational romance by author Nancy Moser. Rowena Langdon and Lucy Scarpelli are from two different worlds: Rowena is a rich socialite, and Lucy is a seamstress who must work to help support her family. Yet they form an improbable bond as Lucy creates Rowena's attire, and Rowena soon invites her new friend to her family's mansion in Newport. Along with her young sister Sofia, Lucy soon finds herself enthralled by a life she could have never imagined. Soon all three young women find themselves in the midst of romances as unlikely as their friendships seemed.

Other books by the same author:
Masquerade, 2010
How Do I Love Thee?, 2009
John 3:16, 2008
The Sister Circle, 2008
Solemnly Swear, 2008
Crossroads, 2006
Mozart's Sister, 2006

Other books you might like:
Kristin Billerbeck, *A Billion Reasons Why*, 2011
Kaye Dacus, *Love Remains*, 2010
Karen Kingsbury, *Shades of Blue*, 2009
Trish Perry, *Unforgettable*, 2011
Francine Rivers, *Her Mother's Hope*, 2010

891

JANELLE MOWERY

When All My Dreams Come True

(Eugene, Oregon: Harvest House Publishers, 2011)

Story type: Romance; Western
Subject(s): Western fiction; Romances (Fiction); Ranch life
Major character(s): Bobbie McIntyre, Rancher, Cowboy/Cowgirl; Jace Kincaid, Rancher, Employer (of Bobbie)
Time period(s): 19th century; 1870s (1872)
Locale(s): Colorado, United States

Summary: *When All My Dreams Come True*, a Western inspirational romance, is part of the Colorado Runaway series from author Janelle Mowery. Growing up on a ranch without a female influence, Bobbie McIntyre's only skill and passion is wrangling. She dreams of owning a ranch of her own someday, but for now working for another rancher will have to do. Jace Kincaid is shocked when the beautiful and feisty young lady shows up at his ranch looking for work, but he can't ignore her adeptness so he hires her on the spot. With such a handsome and friendly new boss, Bobbie begins to find her focus shifting from the cattle to matters of the heart. But when a series of cows begin disappearing, Bobbie is considered a suspect, putting her and Jace's potential romance to the ultimate test.

Other books by the same author:
Love Finds You in Silver City, Idaho, 2010
Where the Truth Lies, 2008

Other books you might like:
Amanda Cabot, *Tomorrow's Garden*, 2011
Colleen Coble, *The Lightkeeper's Bride*, 2010
Yvonne Harris, *The Vigilante's Bride*, 2010
Vickie McDonough, *Second Chance Brides*, 2010

892

ELIZABETH MUSSER

The Sweetest Thing

(Bloomington, Minnesota: Bethany House Publishing, 2011)

Story type: Historical
Subject(s): Christian life; Social class; Schools
Major character(s): Perri Singleton, Student (prep school); Mary "Dobbs" Dillard, Daughter (of preacher)
Time period(s): 20th century; 1930s
Locale(s): Atlanta, Georgia

Summary: In *The Sweetest Thing* by Elizabeth Musser, Perri Singleton's life of privilege is initially spared the effects of the Great Depression. At the prestigious Washington Seminary in Atlanta, Perri and her classmates enjoy parties, dates, and trips to town while the nation's less fortunate suffer. When Mary "Dobbs" Dillard, a preacher's daughter, arrives at the school from an urban Chicago neighborhood, her background and divergent point of view prompt Perri to reconsider the way she conducts her own life. When the Singleton family faces a crisis, Perri relies on her faith in God and her friendship with Mary for strength.

Other books by the same author:
Words Unspoken, 2009
Searching for Eternity, 2007
The Dwelling Place, 2005
The Swan House, 2001
Two Testaments, 1997

Other books you might like:
Lynn Austin, *Though Waters Roar*, 2009
Jane Kirkpatrick, *The Daughter's Walk: A Novel*, 2011
Julie Klassen, *The Silent Governess*, 2010
Francine Rivers, *Her Daughter's Dream*, 2010
Ann Tatlock, *Promises to Keep*, 2011

893

KENDRA NORMAN-BELLAMY

Upon This Rock

(Deer Park, New York: Urban Books, 2011)

Series: Shelton Heights Series. Book 4
Story type: Romance
Subject(s): Romances (Fiction); African Americans; Crime
Major character(s): Deon "Rocky" Rockford, Convict (former)
Time period(s): 21st century; 2010s
Locale(s): Shelton Heights, United States

Summary: *Upon this Rock* is the fourth book from the Shelton Heights series by author Kendra Norman-Bellamy. Deon "Rocky" Rockford is finally out of prison after nearly three decades, and he comes out a saved man thanks to prayer. Yet living life on the straight and narrow proves difficult for a man who has been in jail for 25 years, and Rocky begins to wonder if maybe he was better off behind bars. As he moves to the community of Shelton Heights and begins to cope with his new life, he learns that his faith in God must be stronger than ever as he makes it in the outside world. Norman-Bellamy is also the author of *The Lyon's Den* and *In Greene Pastures*.

Other books by the same author:
Fifteen Years, 2010
The Morning After, 2010
Song of Solomon, 2010
One Prayer Away, 2006
A Love So Strong, 2004

Other books you might like:
Cheryl Faye, *Who Said It Would Be Easy?: A Story of Faith*, 2011
Zaria Garrison, *Losing It*, 2010
Teresa McClain-Watson, *Murder Through the Grapevine*, 2010
Vanessa Miller, *Long Time Coming*, 2010
Kimberla Lawson Roby, *Be Careful What You Pray For*, 2010

894

DELIA PARR

Hidden Affections

(Minneapolis, Minnesota: Bethany House, 2011)

Story type: Historical
Subject(s): Christian life; History; Divorce
Major character(s): Annabelle Tyler, Divorced Person; Harrison Graymoor, Bachelor
Time period(s): 19th century
Locale(s): Philadelphia, Pennsylvania

Summary: In *Hidden Affections* by Delia Parr, Annabelle Tyler's position in 19th-century Philadelphia society is complicated by her husband's infidelity—and their subsequent divorce. Annabelle is determined to make her own way, but Harrison Graymoor throws Annabelle off course again. Through a series of strange circumstances, Annabelle and Harrison become man and wife—but in name only. Before Graymoor can have their marriage annulled, the nuptials are announced in the Philadelphia newspapers. As the reluctant bride and groom sort out their true feelings, Annabelle's ex comes back into her life and Graymoor deals with secrets from his own past.

Other books by the same author:
Hearts Awakening, 2010
Love's First Bloom, 2010
A Place Called Trinity, 2002
The Promise of Flowers, 2000
Home Ties Trilogy, 2006-2008

Other books you might like:
Margaret Brownley, *A Vision of Lucy*, 2011
Ann H. Gabhart, *Angel Sister*, 2011
Shelley Shepard Gray, *The Caregiver*, 2011
Mona Hodgson, *Two Brides Too Many: A Novel*, 2010
Julie Lessman, *A Hope Undaunted*, 2010

895

TRISH PERRY

Tea for Two

(Eugene, Oregon: Harvest House Publishers, 2011)

Series: Tea with Millicent Series. Book 2
Story type: Romance; Series
Subject(s): Christian life; Romances (Fiction); Faith
Major character(s): Tina Milano, Counselor; Zack Cooper, Farmer, Single Father; Millicent, Restaurateur (tea shop owner)
Time period(s): 21st century; 2010s
Locale(s): Middleburg, Virginia

Summary: In *Tea for Two* by Trish Perry, the residents of Middleburg visit Milly's Tea Shop for tea and treats served up with the proprietor's motherly advice. Tina Milano, a counselor, is a regular at Milly's, as is Zack Cooper, a farmer who supplies the shop's produce. Zack is the single parent of two teenagers who have grown increasingly unruly. At Milly's suggestion, Zack consults Tina about his parental problems. During their meetings at the tea shop, Tina and Zack's relationship gradually grows into a romance that seems blessed by God. *Tea for Two* is the second book in the Tea with Millicent series.

Other books by the same author:
Unforgettable, 2011
The Perfect Blend, 2010
Sunset Beach, 2009
Beach Dreams, 2008
The Guy I'm Not Dating, 2006

Other books you might like:
Sara Evans, *The Sweet By and By*, 2009
Rachel Hauck, *Dining with Joy*, 2010
Beth Patillo, *The Dashwood Sisters Tell All*, 2011
Trish Perry, *Unforgettable*, 2011
Linda Evans Shepherd, *Bake Until Golden: A Novel*, 2011

896

TRACIE PETERSON

Hope Rekindled

(Minneapolis, Minnesota: Bethany House, 2011)

Series: Striking a Match Series. Book 3
Story type: Historical; Series
Subject(s): Christian life; History; Marriage
Major character(s): Deborah Vandermark, Fiance(e) (of Christopher), Doctor; Christopher, Doctor, Fiance(e) (Deborah)
Time period(s): 19th century
Locale(s): Kansas City, Kansas; Texas, United States

Summary: In *Hope Rekindled* by Tracie Peterson, a family crisis threatens the approaching marriage of Deborah Vandermark and her fiance. Deborah is training to be a doctor, like her husband-to-be, and is happily anticipating their wedding when Christopher is called away. In Kansas City, Christopher learns that he has become guardian of his five younger brothers and sisters. Though he is certain of Deborah's love for him, he is unsure how receptive she will be to the prospect of instant motherhood. Back in Texas, Deborah deals with a threat that could destroy her family's logging business. *Hope Rekindled* is the third book in the Striking a Match series.

Other books by the same author:
Hearts Aglow, 2011
Embers of Love, 2010
Twilight's Serenade, 2010
A Surrendered Heart, 2009
A Promise to Believe In, 2008

Other books you might like:
Amanda Cabot, *Tomorrow's Garden*, 2011
Colleen Coble, *The Lightkeeper's Bride*, 2010
Judith Pella, *A Hope Beyond*, 1997
Kim Vogel Sawyer, *Courting Miss Amsel*, 2011
Lauraine Snelling, *A Heart for Home*, 2011

897

ALLIE PLEITER

Yukon Wedding

(Don Mills, Ontario, Canada: Harlequin, 2011)

Story type: Historical
Subject(s): Christian life; History; Romances (Fiction)
Major character(s): Lana Bristow, Widow(er); Mack Tanner, Friend (of Lana's late husband)
Time period(s): 19th century; 1890s (1898)
Locale(s): Treasure Creek, Alaska

Summary: In *Yukon Wedding* by Allie Pleiter, a young mother vows to stay in the gold-rush community of Treasure Creek, Alaska, after the death of her husband. Though Lana Bristow came to Treasure Creek as a city girl, she has grown to love Alaska and wants to raise her son there. Mack Tanner was Lana's husband's business partner when he died and now feels that he should marry Lana so that she and her son can stay. Despite her resentment toward Mack, Lana considers his proposal. As the

two embark on their practical marriage, they find their hearts opening to true romance.

Other books by the same author:
Bluegrass Blessings, 2009
Bluegrass Courtship, 2009
Bluegrass Hero, 2008
Masked by Moonlight, 2008
My So-Called Love Life, 2006

Other books you might like:
Dorothy Clark, *The Law and Miss Mary*, 2009
Winnie Griggs, *The Christmas Journey*, 2009
Laurie Kingery, *The Sheriff's Sweetheart*, 2011
Pamela Nissen, *Rocky Mountain Redemption*, 2011
Renee Ryan, *The Lawman Claims His Bride*, 2011

898

DEBORAH RANEY

Forever After

(Nashville, Tennessee: Howard Books, 2011)

Series: Hanover Falls Series. Book 2
Story type: Contemporary; Series
Subject(s): Christian life; Fires; Rescue work
Major character(s): Lucas Vermontez, Fire Fighter; Jenna Morgan, Widow(er)
Time period(s): 21st century; 2010s
Locale(s): Hanover Falls, Missouri

Summary: In *Forever After* by Deborah Raney, the aftermath of the deadly fire at Grove Street Homeless Shelter finds the residents of Hanover Falls, Missouri struggling to deal with grief and anger. Jenna Morgan lost her husband Zach in the blaze, but realizes that their relationship was not a happy one. She and Zach's friend Lucas Vermontez, another firefighter who was seriously injured in the fire, offer one another support. Though Jenna tries to be a suitable widow and Zach tries to remain loyal to his dead friend, neither can deny the romantic feelings growing between them. *Forever After* is the second book in the Hanover Falls series.

Other books by the same author:
Almost Forever, 2010
Beneath a Southern Sky, 2010
Above All Things, 2009
Insight, 2009
A Vow to Cherish, 2006

Other books you might like:
Lynette Eason, *Don't Look Back*, 2010
Kristen Heitzmann, *Indelible*, 2011
Denise Hunter, *Seaside Letters*, 2009
Karen Kingsbury, *Unlocked: A Love Story*, 2010
Robert Whitlow, *Greater Love*, 2010

899

MARTHA ROGERS

Caroline's Choice

(Lake Mary, Florida: Realms, 2011)

Series: Winds Across the Prairie Series. Book 4
Story type: Historical; Series

Subject(s): Christian life; Romances (Fiction); History
Major character(s): Caroline Frankston, Young Woman; Matthew Haynes, Friend (of Caroline)
Time period(s): 20th century; 1900s (1907)
Locale(s): Barton Creek, United States; Oklahoma City, United States

Summary: In *Caroline's Choice* by Martha Rogers, 26-year-old Caroline Frankston sets out from the tiny community of Barton Creek to begin a new life in Oklahoma City. Despite Caroline's long-held affection for Matthew Haynes, she accepts his romantic reluctance and moves on. As she eagerly acclimates herself to the excitement of life in the city, Matthew finally recognizes how important Caroline is to him. When he learns that Caroline is traveling back to Barton Creek by rail for a visit, he hopes to declare his love but his plan is ruined by a train wreck. *Caroline's Choice* is the fourth book in the Winds across the Prairie series.

Other books by the same author:
Finding Becky, 2010
Morning for Dove, 2010
Becoming Lucy, 2009

Other books you might like:
Colleen Coble, *The Lightkeeper's Bride*, 2010
Mary Connealy, *Wrangler in Petticoats*, 2010
Pamela Griffin, *Love Finds You in Hope, Kansas*, 2010
Cathy Marie Hake, *Serendipity*, 2010
Tracie Peterson, *Hearts Aglow*, 2011

900

JAMES L. RUBART

Book of Days

(Nashville, Tennessee: B&H Publishing Group, 2011)

Story type: Mystery
Subject(s): Books; Mystery; Suspense
Major character(s): Cameron Vaux, Widow(er); Ann Bannister, Television Personality; Taylor Stone, Guide
Time period(s): 21st century; 2010s
Locale(s): Oregon, United States

Summary: *Book of Days* is a suspenseful inspirational novel from author James L. Rubart. Despite being so young, Cameron Vaux is beginning to lose memories of his late wife, killed only two years prior in a car accident. Cameron's dad predicted this would happen and assures Cameron that the only way to preserve his memory is to find the book of days that allegedly contains a record of every person's past and future. Cameron doubts the book's existence but sets off on a wild journey to find it anyways. The clues lead him to a small Oregon town where he teams up with the mysterious Taylor Stone and TV personality,\ Ann Bannister, both of whom have their doubts about the book and a slew of secrets. The unlikely trio must come together to find the book before it ends up in the hands of New Age guru Jason Judah who will stop at nothing to possess it.

Other books by the same author:
Rooms: A Novel, 2010

Other books you might like:
Terri Blackstock, *Predator: A Novel*, 2010

Ted Dekker, *The Priest's Graveyard*, 2011
Bill Myers, *The God Hater: A Novel*, 2010
Robin Parrish, *Offworld*, 2009
Joel Rosenberg, *The Twelfth Imam: A Novel*, 2010

901

KIM VOGEL SAWYER

Courting Miss Amsel

(Minneapolis, Minnesota: Bethany House, 2011)

Story type: Historical; Romance
Subject(s): Teachers; Rural life; History
Major character(s): Edythe Amsel, Teacher, Young Woman; Joel Townsend, Young Man, Guardian (to nephews)
Time period(s): 19th century; 1880s (1882)
Locale(s): Walnut Hill, Nebraska

Summary: *Courting Miss Amsel* is a historical inspirational romance from best-selling author Kim Vogel Sawyer. Edythe Amsel receives her first teaching assignment in a tiny schoolhouse in a small Nebraska town. The assignment is perfectly suited for the smart and independent young educator, but it isn't long until her eccentric teaching methods, which involve hands-on activities that foster creativity, stir up trouble around town. Joel Townsend, guardian to his two nephews, is captivated by the new teacher's beauty and intellect and he's grateful that his adopted sons will have a female influence in their life. But when Miss Amsel takes the class to hear Susan Anthony speak on the women's suffrage movement, there is an outcry among the townspeople that causes even Joel to question Miss Amsel's trustworthiness with his children and with his heart.

Other books by the same author:
A Hopeful Heart, 2010
In Every Heartbeat, 2010
Beginnings, 2009
Where Willows Grow, 2007
Waiting for Summer's Return, 2006

Other books you might like:
Wanda E. Brunstetter, *Brides of Lehigh Canal Series*, 2010
Shelley Shephard Gray, *The Caregiver*, 2011
Beverly Lewis, *The Rose Trilogy*, 2010
Tracie Peterson, *Striking a Match Series*, 2010
Lauraine Snelling, *Home to Blessing Series*, 2009

902

LORNA SEILSTAD

A Great Catch: A Novel

(Grand Rapids, Michigan: Revell, 2011)

Series: Lake Manawa Summers Series. Book 2
Story type: Historical; Series
Subject(s): Christian life; History; Romances (Fiction)
Major character(s): Emily Graham, Suffragette; Carter Stockton, Baseball Player, Graduate (college)

Time period(s): 20th century; 1900s
Locale(s): Lake Manawa, Iowa

Summary: In *A Great Catch* by Lorna Seilstad, a young woman rebels against the conventions of society as her female relatives try to marry her off. It is the turn of the 20th century at Iowa's Lake Manawa Resort and Emily Graham, 22, is interested in winning the vote for women, not husband-hunting. But college graduate and baseball player, Carter Stockton just may change her mind. As he soaks up his last carefree days at Lake Manawa before joining his father's business, Carter falls in love with spirited and stubborn Emily. *A Great Catch* is the second book in the Lake Manawa Summers series.

Other books by the same author:
Making Waves: A Novel, 2010

Other books you might like:
Deeanne Gist, *Beguiled*, 2010
Denise Hunter, *A Cowboy's Touch*, 2011
Julie Lessman, *A Passion Denied*, 2009
Tracie Peterson, *Dawn's Prelude*, 2009
Sarah Sundin, *A Memory Between Us*, 2010

903

LESLIE J. SHERROD

Secret Place

(Deer Park, New York: Urban Books, 2011)

Story type: Psychological Suspense
Subject(s): Mental disorders; Murder; Suspense
Major character(s): Charisma Joel, Spouse (of Gideon); Gideon, Spouse (of Charisma), Doctor (psychiatrist), Mentally Ill Person
Time period(s): 21st century; 2010s

Summary: *Secret Place* is an inspirational novel by author Leslie J. Sherrod. In it, Sherrod explores the stigma of mental illness within the black community. Charisma is the daughter of a mother who suffers from a debilitating mental illness, a secret which has long-threatened to tear her family apart. Charisma sees freedom in marrying Gideon, a psychiatrist who can provide for her the life she has long desired. Soon Charisma is living the dream of a doctor's wife, with a lovely house and a beautiful daughter. When she begins to see familiar signs of mental illness in her husband, however, she wonders if she can ever find the help she needs with this secret.

Other books by the same author:
Like Sheep Gone Astray, 2006

Other books you might like:
Shana Burton, *Flaws and All*, 2010
Rhonda McKnight, *An Inconvenient Friend*, 2019
Likita Lynette Nichols, *Crossroads*, 2011
Kim Cash Tate, *Faithful*, 2010
T.N. Williams, *Peace of Me*, 2010

904

ANN SHOREY

The Dawn of a Dream

(Grand Rapids, Michigan: Revell, 2011)

Series: At Home in Beldon Grove Series. Book 3
Story type: Historical; Series
Subject(s): Christian life; History; Marriage
Major character(s): Luellen O'Connell, Young Woman
Time period(s): 19th century; 1840s
Locale(s): Beldon Grove, Illinois

Summary: In *The Dawn of a Dream* by Ann Shorey, a young wife in 1830s St. Lawrenceville, Missouri, is shocked when her husband walks out on their one-month-old marriage. Luellen O'Connell's situation is further complicated by her spouse's revelation that he is already married. Despite her grief and shame, Luellen decides to pursue her long-time dream of becoming a schoolteacher. Through personal determination and faith, Luellen faces the uncertainties of the future as she tries to escape pain of the past. *The Dawn of a Dream* is the third book in the At Home in Beldon Grove series.

Other books by the same author:
The Promise of Morning, 2010
The Edge of Light, 2009

Other books you might like:
Shelley Shephard Gray, *The Caregiver*, 2011
Kelly Eileen Hake, *Rugged and Relentless*, 2011
Liz Curtis Higgs, *Mine Is the Night*, 2011
Kim Vogel Sawyer, *Courting Miss Amsel*, 2011
Beth Wiseman, *Plain Proposal*, 2011

905

SUSAN SLEEMAN

Behind the Badge

(Don Mills, Ontario, Canada: Harlequin, 2011)

Story type: Romance
Subject(s): Christian life; Romances (Fiction); Suspense
Major character(s): Sydney Tucker, Police Officer; Russ Morgan, Police Officer (chief)
Time period(s): 21st century; 2010s
Locale(s): Logan Lake, United States

Summary: In *Behind the Badge* by Susan Sleeman, a vengeful murderer is targeting Logan Lake's newest police officer and her sister. Sydney Tucker's involvement in a drug arrest has attracted the attention of a killer who will do anything to retrieve the evidence that he believes Sydney possesses. Although Sydney, in fact, doesn't have the evidence, the killer threatens to track down her sister. As the killer closes in on Sydney, he tries to destroy the people most important in her life. Police chief Russ Morgan does his best to protect the women, but when his relationship with Lucy grows beyond friendship, he also becomes a target.

Other books by the same author:
High-Stakes Inheritance, 2010
Nipped in the Bud, 2010

Other books you might like:
Leigh Bale, *The Forest Ranger's Promise*, 2011
Debby Giusti, *The Officer's Secret*, 2011
Ruth Logan Herne, *Small-Town Hearts*, 2011
Liz Johnson, *Code of Justice*, 2011
Regina Scott, *The Irresistible Earl*, 2011

906

JILL EILEEN SMITH

Bathsheba: A Novel

(Grand Rapids, Michigan: Revell, 2011)

Story type: Historical
Subject(s): Bible stories; Christian life; Royalty
Major character(s): Bathsheba, Biblical Figure, Spouse (of Uriah), Lover (of King David); King David, Lover (of Bathsheba), Royalty (king of Israel), Biblical Figure; Uriah, Warrior, Spouse (of Bathsheba)
Time period(s): 11th century; 1000s (1000)
Locale(s): Israel

Summary: In *Bathsheba: A Novel*, author Jill Eileen Smith retells the Biblical story of King David and Bathsheba. With her husband, Uriah the Hittite, away at war, Bathsheba is lonely and vulnerable. It is then that King David, grieving over the loss of his wife, spies her bathing and sets out to seduce her. Soon Bathsheba learns that she is with child, and is devastated by the scandal it creates. Will God ever forgive her for her transgressions? This novel is part of the Wives of King David series, which also includes *Abigail* and *Michal*.

Other books by the same author:
Abigail: A Novel, 2010
Michal, 2009

Other books you might like:
Orson Scott Card, *Rachel and Leah: Women of Genesis*, 2005
Ginger Garrett, *Chosen: The Lost Diaries of Queen Esther*, 2005
Tosca Lee, *Havah: The Story of Eve: A Novel*, 2008
Janette Oke, *Acts of Faith Series*, 2009
Diana Wallis Taylor, *Journey to the Well*, 2008

907

LAURAINE SNELLING

A Heart for Home

(Bloomington, Minnesota: Bethany House Publishing, 2011)

Series: Home to Blessing Series. Book 3
Story type: Romance
Subject(s): Native American reservations; United States history, 1865-1901; Pioneers
Major character(s): Dr. Astrid Bjorkland, Doctor, Girlfriend (former, of Joshua); Joshua Landsverk, Boyfriend (former, of Astrid)
Time period(s): 20th century; 1900s
Locale(s): South Dakota, United States

Summary: *A Heart for Home* is a novel from author Lauraine Snelling's Home to Blessing series, which follows a community of pioneers as they forge a town called Blessing out of the South Dakota frontier. In this novel, Dr. Astrid Bjorkland goes to the nearby reservation of the Rosebud Indians to attempt to stop a illness that is spreading throughout the tribe. While the tribal leaders at first balk at her assistance, they begin to accept her help when the ill recover. One person who does not accept Astrid's work, however, is her former beau, Joshua Landsverk. Can Astrid prove to Joshua that her caring for the Rosebuds is all part of God's plan?

Other books by the same author:
No Distance Too Far, 2010
A Measure of Mercy, 2009
Red River of the North Series, 2006
Saturday Morning, 2005

Other books you might like:
Amy Clipston, *Kauffman Amish Bakery Series*, 2009
Suzanne Woods Fisher, *Lancaster County Secrets Series*, 2010
Beverly Lewis, *Courtship of Nellie Fisher Series*, 2007
Marta Perry, *Pleasant Valley Series*, 2009
Tracie Peterson, *Striking a Match Series*, 2010

908

LAURAINE SNELLING

On Hummingbird Wings: A Novel

(New York: FaithWords, 2011)

Story type: Family Saga
Subject(s): Faith; Gardening; Mother-daughter relations
Major character(s): Gillian Ormsby, Businesswoman, Caregiver (to mother)
Time period(s): 21st century; 2010s
Locale(s): California, United States

Summary: *On Hummingbird Wings: A Novel* is an inspirational novel from best-selling author Lauraine Snelling. For corporate exec Gillian Ormsby, leaving behind the bright lights of Manhattan to return to her quiet California home to take care of her mother is the least of her desires. But when Gillian's older sister insists that their mother, who has always suffered from hypochondria, is truly ill, Gillian has no choice but to return. Upon arriving, Gillian is dismayed to see that her mother's garden is in total disarray and her mother, although diagnosed as healthy by doctors, is wasting away in bed. With a little help from a handsome neighbor, Gillian begins to carefully tend to both her ailing mother and the dying garden, in hopes of bringing them both into new life.

Other books by the same author:
A Heart for Home, 2011
No Distance Too Far, 2010
A Measure of Mercy, 2009
One Perfect Day: A Novel, 2008
Breaking Free: A Novel, 2007

Other books you might like:
Kathryn Cushman, *Another Dawn*, 2011

Kristen Heitzmann, *Indelible*, 2011
Jane Kirkpatrick, *The Daughter's Walk: A Novel*, 2011
Beverly Lewis, *The Thorn*, 2010
Michael Phillips, *Angel Harp: A Novel*, 2011

909

CARLA STEWART

Broken Wings: A Novel

(New York: FaithWords, 2011)

Story type: Contemporary
Subject(s): Christian life; Volunteerism; Friendship
Major character(s): Gabe Steiner, Aged Person; Mitzi Steiner, Spouse (of Gabe), Volunteer (hospital); Brooke Woodson, Patient (hospital)
Time period(s): 21st century; 2010s
Locale(s): Tulsa, Oklahoma

Summary: In *Broken Wings*, an elderly woman faces the implications of her husband's advancing dementia. Mitzi and Gabe Steiner have been married for 60 years, and for 20 of those years they enjoyed life in the limelight as a popular singing act. Now Gabe has Alzheimer's and Mitzi is uncertain what lies ahead for her. While volunteering at a Tulsa hospital, Mitzi meets Brooke Woodson, a patient who is facing her own personal crisis. Brooke is engaged to an ambitious attorney who has serious anger-management issues. Guided by her new-found friendship with Mitzi and her faith in God, Brooke searches for a way to deal with her troubled relationship.

Other books by the same author:
Chasing Lilacs: A Novel, 2010

Other books you might like:
Mike Duran, *The Resurrection*, 2011
Gina Holmes, *Crossing Oceans*, 2010
Kevin Alan Milne, *The Final Note: A Novel*, 2011
Sheila Walsh, *Sweet Sanctuary*, 2011
Marybeth Whalen, *She Makes It Look Easy: A Novel*, 2011

910

TESSA STOCKTON

The Unforgivable

(Beaverton, Oregon: Risen Books, 2011)

Series: Wounds of South America Series. Book 1
Story type: Historical; Series
Subject(s): Christian life; History; Politics
Major character(s): Carlos Cornella, Criminal (war)
Time period(s): 20th century; 1970s
Locale(s): Argentina

Summary: In *The Unforgivable* by Tessa Stockton, Argentina is being torn apart by a state-sponsored campaign of terrorism against its own citizens. During the "Dirty War" of the 1970s and 80s, thousands of Argentineans are tortured or killed; some simply disappear forever. In this fictionalized account, Carlos Cornella emerges as one of the era's cruelest war criminals. He is known as a murderer and a monster, yet even Cornella seems to be worthy of forgiveness in the eyes of God and in the hearts of those who know him. *The Unforgivable* is the first book in the Wounds of South America series. First novel.

Other books you might like:
Brandt Dodson, *Seventy Times Seven*, 2006
Paul Robertson, *According to Their Deeds*, 2009
Paul Robertson, *The Heir*, 2007

911

KAY MARSHALL STROM

The Triumph of Grace

(Nashville, Tennessee: Abingdon Press, 2011)

Series: Grace in Africa Series. Book 3
Story type: Historical
Subject(s): Slavery; Faith; History
Major character(s): Grace Winslow, Royalty (African princess), Slave; Cabeto, Spouse (of Grace), Slave
Time period(s): 18th century; 1780s
Locale(s): England; United States

Summary: *The Triumph of Grace*, an inspirational historical novel, is the third and final installment in the Grace in Africa series from author Kay Marshall Strom. Desperate to locate her husband, Cabeto, Grace risks everything to travel across the sea to America. Learning that Cabeto is on a plantation in South Carolina, Grace disguises herself as a sailor and sneaks onto a ship carrying slaves to the United States. Her true identity is quickly discovered and, as punishment, she's locked away on the ship. Upon arriving in America, Grace is purchased as a slave by John Hull, but her story of faith, commitment, and perseverance wins John over and he commits to helping her find Cabeto once and for all.

Other books by the same author:
The Voyage of Promise, 2010
The Call of Zulina, 2009

Other books you might like:
Lisa Tawn Bergren, *Claim: A Novel of Colorado*, 2010
Lisa Tawn Bergren, *Sing: A Novel of Colorado*, 2010
Wanda E. Brunstetter, *Kelly's Chance*, 2010
Francine Rivers, *Her Daughter's Dream*, 2010
Marylu Tyndall, *Surrender the Heart*, 2010

912

LEONARD SWEET
LORI WAGNER, Co-Author

The Seraph Seal

(Nashville, Tennessee: Thomas Nelson, 2011)

Story type: End of the World
Subject(s): Good and evil; Apocalypse; Religion
Major character(s): Paul Binder, Professor (cultural history)
Time period(s): 21st century; 2040s (2048)

Summary: Based on the four horsemen mentioned in the book of Revelation, *The Seraph Seal* tells the tale of Earth in the not-so-distant future facing total destruction. It's 2048 and the planet is rapidly deteriorating after centuries of poor treatment. When cultural history professor Paul Binder receives a mysterious letter, he's drawn to an ancient Diatessaron manuscript that holds secrets about the world's future. His studies, laced with mysterious prophecies and ancient religious symbolism, lead him on a dangerous mission to find the lost clues that might save the world from destruction.

Other books you might like:
C.S. Lewis, *Chronicles of Narnia*, 1950
J.R.R. Tolkien, *The Lord of the Rings Trilogy*, 1954

913

DIANA WALLIS TAYLOR

Martha: A Novel

(Grand Rapids, Michigan: Revell, 2011)

Story type: Religious
Subject(s): Bible stories; Christianity; History
Major character(s): Martha, Biblical Figure
Time period(s): 1st century

Summary: In *Martha*, author Diana Wallis Taylor presents a fictionalized account of the life of Martha of Bethany. Though Martha is well known from the Bible as the dutiful, responsible sister of Mary and Lazarus, Taylor fleshes out this crucial New Testament figure to present the portrait of a true godly woman. Expanding on scriptural accounts, the author chronicles the events of Martha's tumultuous life. Martha loses loved ones, becomes romantically involved with a Roman soldier, and oversees her family's household. All the while, she remains faithful to the call of God.

Other books by the same author:
Journey to the Well, 2009
Smoke Before the Wind, 2009
Wings of the Wind, 2006

Other books you might like:
Davis Bunn, *The Centurion's Wife*, 2009
Janette Oke, *The Damascus Way*, 2011
Jill Eileen Smith, *Abigail: A Novel*, 2010
Jill Eileen Smith, *Bathsheba: A Novel*, 2011
Jill Eileen Smith, *Michal*, 2009

914

MARYLU TYNDALL

Surrender the Night

(Uhrichsville, Ohio: Barbour Books, 2011)

Story type: Romance
Subject(s): United States history, 1865-1901; Christian life; Romances (Fiction)
Major character(s): Rose McGuire, Farmer; Alex Reed, Military Personnel (naval lieutenant)

Time period(s): 19th century; 1810s (1812-1815)
Locale(s): Baltimore, Maryland

Summary: *Surrender the Night* is the second novel in author Marylu Tyndall's Surrender to Destiny series. This novel takes place during the War of 1812, as Maryland farmer Rose McGuire is rescued by a Lieutenant Alex Reed of the British Navy after an attack by enemy troops. Because Alex was wounded during the attack, Rose feels it is her duty to keep him safe as his injuries mend—after all, he was the man who saved her. As Alex heals, Rose and he find themselves drawn to one another. Unfortunately, with their countries at war, they must decide how much they are willing to put on the line for love. Tyndall is also the author of *Surrender the Heart*.

Other books by the same author:
Surrender the Heart, 2010
The Falcon and the Sparrow, 2008
Charles Towne Belles Trilogy, 2009-2010
Legacy of the King's Pirates Series, 2006-2007

Other books you might like:
Mindy Starns Clark, *Secrets of Harmony Grove*, 2010
Kaye Dacus, *Ransome's Crossing*, 2010
Laura Frantz, *Courting Morrow Little: A Novel*, 2010
Deeanne Gist, *Beguiled*, 2010
Cathy Marie Hake, *Serendipity*, 2010

915

DEBRA ULLRICK

The Unexpected Bride

(Don Mills, Ontario, Canada: Harlequin, 2011)

Story type: Romance
Subject(s): Christian life; Romances (Fiction); History
Major character(s): Haydon Bowen, Widow(er); Rainelle Devonwood, Mail Order Bride
Time period(s): 19th century; 1870s
Locale(s): Idaho Territories, United States

Summary: In *The Unexpected Bride* by Debra Ullrick, Rainelle Devonwood boards a stagecoach for the Idaho Territories in the 1870s to marry a man she's never met. Desperate to escape the control of her brother, Rainelle sets aside her position in society and advertises herself as a mail-order bride. But Haydon Bowen, the man waiting at the end of her journey, was hurt once by love and has vowed never to let it happen again. It was Haydon's brother who replied to Rainelle's ad on Haydon's behalf. Rainelle is eager to start a new life but first must convince her reluctant groom not to send her back.

Other books by the same author:
Deja Vu Bride, 2009

Other books you might like:
Dorothy Clark, *Gold Rush Baby*, 2011
Janet Dean, *The Substitute Bride*, 2010
Laura Kingery, *The Sheriff's Sweetheart*, 2011
Regina Scott, *The Irresistible Earl*, 2011
Karen Witemeyer, *To Win Her Heart*, 2011

Inspirational

916

ERICA VETSCH

Idaho Brides

(Uhrichsville, Ohio: Barbour Publishing, 2011)

Story type: Romance; Series
Subject(s): Christian life; Romances (Fiction); History
Major character(s): Alec McConnell, Cowboy/Cowgirl; Trace McConnell, Lawman; Cal McConnell, Rebel (maverick); Clara Bainbridge, Girlfriend (of Alec); Lily Whitman, Girlfriend (of Trace); Maggie Davis, Police Officer (U.S. Marshal)
Time period(s): 19th century; 1880s
Locale(s): Idaho, United States

Summary: In *Idaho Brides* by Erica Vetsch, three brothers in 19th-century Idaho look for love as they try to escape the influence of their abusive father. Alec, Trace, and Cal McConnell had a difficult childhood and now face the prejudice of a community that associates the young men with their father's alcoholic behavior. But Alec is in love with Clara Bainbridge—the daughter of a local rancher who is also Alec's boss. Trace is determined to win Lily Whitman's affection by helping her find her missing niece. Cal is smitten with Maggie Davis—until he learns that she is a U.S. Marshal who has come to bring him to justice.

Other books by the same author:
Clara and the Cowboy, 2010
The Engineered Engagement, 2010
Lily and the Lawman, 2010
The Marriage Masquerade, 2010
The Bartered Bride, 2009

Other books you might like:
Susan Page Davis, *Alaska Weddings*, 2011
Terry Fowler, *Kentucky Weddings*, 2011
Kathleen E. Kovach, *Oregon Weddings*, 2011
Aaron McCarver, *Tennessee Brides*, 2011
Janet Spaeth, *Minnesota Brides*, 2011

917

DAN WALSH

The Deepest Waters

(Grand Rapids, Michigan: Revell, 2011)

Story type: Historical
Subject(s): Christian life; History; Romances (Fiction)
Major character(s): John Foster, Traveler; Laura Foster, Spouse (of John)
Time period(s): 19th century; 1850s (1857)
Locale(s): Atlantic Ocean, At Sea

Summary: In *The Deepest Waters* by Dan Walsh, a newlywed couple en route to New York in 1857 is separated when a violent storm destroys their vessel. When the *SS Vandevere* goes down in a hurricane, John and Laura Foster follow protocol. Laura joins the other female survivors on a sailing ship sent to rescue them; John remains in the water, clinging to floating debris with the other men. As Laura makes her way to safety,

she holds tight to the hope that John might survive the ordeal. Walsh's novel is based on the events surrounding the sinking of the *SS Central America*.

Other books by the same author:
The Homecoming: A Novel, 2010
The Unfinished Gift: A Novel, 2009

Other books you might like:
Lynn Austin, *While We're Far Apart*, 2010
Jan Karon, *In the Company of Others*, 2010
Julie Klassen, *The Silent Governess*, 2010
Nicholas Sparks, *Safe Haven*, 2010
Jason F. Wright, *The Seventeen Second Miracle*, 2010

918

MERRILLEE WHREN

Hometown Dad

(New York: Steeple Hill, 2011)

Story type: Romance
Subject(s): Romances (Fiction); Single parent family; Faith
Major character(s): Melanie Drake, Single Mother; Nathan Keller, Banker, Coach
Time period(s): 21st century; 2010s
Locale(s): United States

Summary: *Hometown Dad*, an inspirational romance novel, is part of the Love Inspired series from author Merrillee Whren. Single mom Melanie Drake has her hands full trying to raise two rambunctious little boys on her own. She desperately longs for a partner to help shoulder the parenting responsibilities and tend to her heart, but unfortunately she doesn't have many prospects. That is, until Nathan Keller enters her life. Nathan is a successful banker, respected member of the town, and an excellent baseball coach to Melanie's two sons. As the boys grow closer to their handsome coach, Melanie finds herself falling for him as well, despite her belief that he's out of her league. Soon, she discovers the entire town is standing on the sidelines cheering on their potential romance, rooting for a hometown love story.

Other books by the same author:
Hometown Promise, 2010
Hometown Proposal, 2010
Love Walked In, 2007
The Heart's Homecoming, 2005

Other books you might like:
Carolyne Aarsen, *The Baby Promise*, 2010
Renee Andrews, *Her Valentine Family*, 2011
Irene Hannon, *Child of Grace*, 2011
Glynna Kaye, *Second Chance Courtship*, 2011
Brenda Minton, *The Cowboy Family*, 2010

919

LISA WINGATE

Larkspur Cove

(Minneapolis, Minnesota: Bethany House, 2011)

Story type: Romance
Subject(s): Romances (Fiction); Divorce; Faith

Major character(s): Andrea Henderson, Single Mother, Divorced Person, Social Worker; Mart McClendon, Lawman (game warden)
Time period(s): 21st century; 2010s
Locale(s): Moses Lake, Texas

Summary: After a painful divorce, Andrea Henderson and her son have uprooted their lives and are starting afresh in the small town of Moses Lake, Texas, a place filled with happy childhood memories for Andrea. Desperate to put the past behind her and find new purpose in life, Andrea begins a new career as a social worker while her son gets into trouble in his quest to fit in. His latest escapade leads Andrea to game warden Mart McClendon, a mysterious man with a tragic past. When a little girl is spotted with the town hermit, Andrea and Matt join together to find her true identity, growing precariously close to one another in the process and uncovering secrets from their own pasts.

Other books by the same author:
Beyond Summer, 2010
Never Say Never, 2010
Word Gets Around, 2009
Talk of the Town, 2008
Tending Roses, 2003

Other books you might like:
Kathryn Cushman, *Another Dawn*, 2011
Neta Jackson, *Who Is My Shelter?*, 2010
Kim Vogel Sawyer, *In Every Heartbeat*, 2010
Karen White, *Falling Home*, 2002
Lisa Wingate, *Never Say Never*, 2010

920

BETH WISEMAN

Plain Proposal

(Nashville, Tennessee: Thomas Nelson Publishers, 2011)

Story type: Romance
Subject(s): Amish; Family; Father-son relations
Major character(s): Miriam Raber, Fiance(e) (of Saul); Saul Fisher, Fiance(e) (of Miriam)
Locale(s): Lancaster, Pennsylvania

Summary: *Plain Proposal* is an installment from Beth Wiseman's Daughters of the Promise series. In this book, Wiseman tells the story of Miriam Raber and Saul Fisher, an Amish couple with plans to marry. However, Miriam and Saul both carry the weight of secrets. Saul has long hidden his father's alcoholism from the rest of their community in Lancaster. When an opportunity for a career presents itself, Saul wonders if taking it might be too selfish—after all, it will then be left to his brothers to continue hiding his father's secret. Meanwhile, Miriam struggles with the possibility that Saul and she might leave their family and friends behind for an unknown life. Can their belief in the Lord help this couple make the right decisions?

Other books by the same author:
Plain Paradise, 2010
Seek Me With All Your Heart, 2010
Plain Promise, 2009

Plain Pursuit, 2009
Plain Perfect, 2008

Other books you might like:
Patricia Davids, *An Amish Christmas*, 2010
Jerry S. Eicher, *A Wedding Quilt for Ella*, 2011
Suzanne Woods Fisher, *The Search*, 2011
Tricia Goyer, *Beside Still Waters*, 2011
Shelley Shephard Gray, *The Caregiver*, 2011

921

KAREN WITEMEYER

To Win Her Heart

(Grand Rapids, Michigan: Bethany House Publishing, 2011)

Story type: Romance
Subject(s): Rural life; Christian life; Scandals
Major character(s): Eden Spencer, Librarian; Levi Grant, Blacksmith, Convict (ex)
Locale(s): Spencer, Texas

Summary: *To Win Her Heart* is an inspirational romance by author Karen Witemeyer. Librarian Eden Spencer has decided that she is done with men after having her heart broken one too many times. Then she meets Levi Grant, a newcomer to town who exudes honor and sincerity. Levi has arrived in Spencer, Texas, to start a new life as the town blacksmith, but he harbors a past filled with secrets that Eden might not be able to handle. Both Eden and Levi have plenty of faith in God, but can they put enough faith in one another to find the love they so desperately need? Witemeyer is also the author of *Tailor-Made Bride* and *Head in the Clouds*.

Other books by the same author:
Head in the Clouds, 2010
A Tailor-Made Bride, 2010

Other books you might like:
Amanda Cabot, *Scattered Petals*, 2010
Mary Connealy, *Out of Control*, 2011
Mona Hodgson, *Two Brides Too Many: A Novel*, 2010
Delia Parr, *Hidden Affections*, 2011
Stephanie Grace Whitson, *Sixteen Brides*, 2010

922

KIMBERLEY WOODHOUSE
KAYLA WOODHOUSE, Co-Author

No Safe Haven

(Nashville, Tennessee: B & H Publishing, 2011)

Story type: Mystery
Subject(s): Diseases; Accidents; Aircraft accidents
Major character(s): Jenna Tikaani-Gray, Mother (of Andi); Andi Tikaani-Gray, Daughter (of Jenna); Cole, Traveler
Locale(s): Alaska, United States

Summary: Andi Tikaani-Gray and her mother, Jenna, have had a long, hard road: Andi has a rare affliction that affects her nerves, and her father, Jenna's husband, recently died in a car accident. Yet they are overjoyed to receive word that treatment for Andi's condition may be possible. When their plane crashes in the mountains of Alaska, however, they not only must decide if they have the will to survive, but also if they can trust their fellow passenger, a mysterious man named Cole.

Other books by the same author:
Welcome Home: Our Family's Journey to Extreme Joy, 2009

Other books you might like:
Robin Caroll, *Fear No Evil*, 2010
Robin Caroll, *In the Shadow of Evil*, 2011
C.J. Darlington, *Bound by Guilt*, 2011
Sibella Giorello, *The Mountains Bow Down*, 2011
Lis Weihl, *Heart of Ice*, 2011

923

GINNY L. YTTRUP

Words

(Nashville, Tennessee: B&H Publishing Group, 2011)

Story type: Contemporary
Subject(s): Christian life; Faith; Speech
Major character(s): Kaylee Wren, 10-Year-Old, Abuse Victim; Unnamed Character, Villain (Kaylee's abuser); Sierra Dawn, Artist
Time period(s): 21st century; 2010s
Locale(s): California, United States

Summary: In *Words* by Ginny L. Yttrup, a ten-year-old girl abandoned by her addict mother faces a life of abuse with her mother's ex-boyfriend. In response to the shocking events, Kaylee Wren stops speaking but retains a unique relationship with words through a dictionary that belonged to her mother. As Kaylee develops tactics to survive her keeper's cruel treatment, she escapes by expanding her unspoken vocabulary. Sierra Dawn, an artist who is still struggling with the death of her baby girl over a decade ago, eventually becomes Kaylee's rescuer. Together, Sierra and Kaylee face the future with newfound friendship and faith in God. First novel.

Other books you might like:
Melody Carlson, *Hometown Ties*, 2010

Erin Healy, *The Promises She Keeps*, 2011
Patricia Hickman, *The Pirate Queen: A Novel*, 2010
Francine Rivers, *Her Daughter's Dream*, 2010
Becky Tirabassi, *Sacred Obsession*, 2006

924

PENNY ZELLER

Kaydie

(Kensington, Pennsylvania: Whitaker House, 2011)

Series: Montana Skies Series. Book 2
Story type: Romance; Series
Subject(s): Christian life; Romances (Fiction); Western fiction
Major character(s): Kaydie Kraemer, Widow(er); Jonah Dickenson, Worker (ranchhand); McKenzie Sawyer, Sister (of Kaydie); Zach Sawyer, Spouse (of Kaydie); Cedric Van Aulst, Friend (of Kaydie)
Time period(s): 21st century; 2010s
Locale(s): Montana, United States

Summary: In *Kaydie* by Penny Zeller, Kaydie Kraemer is living with her sister and brother-in-law, McKenzie and Zach Sawyer, on their Montana ranch after her husband Darius dies. Though she is pregnant with Darius's child, Kaydie can't deny her relief that her cruel husband is dead. On the ranch, Kaydie meets Jonah Dickenson, one of Zach's employees. Jonah has no interest in romantic relationships until Kaydie comes into his life. But when a man from Kaydie's past arrives with a surprising proposal, she must rely on her faith to guide her decision. *Kaydie* is the second book in Zeller's Montana Skies series.

Other books by the same author:
McKenzie, 2010

Other books you might like:
Marcia Gruver, *Raider's Heart*, 2011
Loree Lough, *Beautiful Bandit*, 2010
Sharlene MacLaren, *Sarah My Beloved*, 2007
Nancy Moser, *An Unlikely Suitor*, 2011
Tracie Peterson, *A Promise for Tomorrow*

Romance Fiction in Review
by
Kristin Ramsdell

"Romance has been elegantly defined as the offspring of fiction and love."
—Benjamin Disraeli

"Turbulence is a life force. It is opportunity. Let's love turbulence and use it for change."
—Ramsay Clark

Whether it's natural disasters, political and civil unrest, or changes in technology, we are living in tumultuous times; and while it is highly doubtful that Clark was singling out technology or had popular romance or the romance fiction industry in mind when he made the observation above, there is little question that it applies to the current state of affairs. For years now, technology has been making inroads into our lives, affecting everything from the way we handle the routines and business of our daily activities to the way we communicate with each other and entertain ourselves. Those of us in the writing world now collaborate with other authors online, interact with our editors online, submit manuscripts and receive galleys online, and even have our work published online; and those of us in the library world are dealing with the explosion of e-formats (and the attendant rights and standardization issues) and the complexities of acquiring them and making them accessible to an increasingly tech-savvy clientele. For most of us these changes are exciting, and so far we've navigated them rather well.

But if recent events and the current buzz are any indication, there is more turbulence to come and it will change the landscape in fascinating ways. For example, by now we're used to the fact that many publishers release new titles in print and e-book and audio formats at the same time and that some houses are releasing their backlists in e-book format; but the fact that most mainline romance publishers are establishing e-only imprints and, in some cases (e.g. Dorchester), have discontinued their mass market print programs and switched to e-only formats is a potential game-changer. Add to this Google's mission to digitize "the world," publishers' and authors' ongoing concerns about digital rights, the growth of self-publishing and self-marketing, and the exponentially increasing impact of online companies such as Amazon on brick-and-mortar stores (e.g., Borders' recent bankruptcy filing) and it's easy to see why things are in turmoil.

There's no doubt about it: Change is difficult, uncomfortable, and disconcerting; but it's an opportunity—and it's here. So here's to turbulence, here's to change, and here's to our ability to use it to our advantage! Carpe diem.

A Genre Overview

With its usual grace and flair, the Romance genre is managing to weather the ups and downs of the current choppy environment, skillfully retaining its traditional readership with tried-and-true subgenres and formats, while bravely venturing into uncharted waters to experiment with new technologies, speculative themes, and innovative marketing ideas.

As usual, some trends and changes are specific to individual subgenres, but there are also some that are common to the genre as a whole. This year it is technology and the lightning-speed changes it is precipitating across the entire publishing industry that has everyone wondering what is coming next. E-book sales skyrocketed in 2010, while print declined ("E-book Sales Up 164% as Other Trade Segments Fall"; *Publishers Weekly* 16 February 2011), and "Digital Up, Print Down at Harlequin" by Jim Milliot, *Publishers Weekly* 2 March 2011); titles are being released routinely in both electronic and formats; backlists are being made available in e-format; e-only imprints are multiplying; marketing is becoming instantaneous (and often uncontrolled) via twitter, Facebook, and other forms of social networking; new devices for reading electronically are popping up every day; and publishers are frantically trying to figure out how to use the resulting chaos to their advantage. In addition, a growing number of publishers are making their advance review galleys available online via firms such as NetGalley, a practice that has gotten a mixed reception among romance reviewers.

Another trend that is affecting all of romance is the fascination with, what I will call for lack of a better term, community books. Series of stories linked by a community of some kind, usually a small town or rural area, are all the rage; they are most popular in Contemporary and Historical romance subgenres but can be found in most of the others as well. *Cross Your Heart*, the latest in Michele Bardsley's paranormal Broken Heart series, is one example of many.

Closely linked to, and encompassing, the community trend is the genre's continuing love affair with linked books. Related by place, family, or other aspect, books in trilogies, quartets, or other groupings have been popular for some time, and as more publishers and writers climb on to the bandwagon, they are likely to remain so. In an interesting related development, some writers are introducing their print series of linked books with short prequels or novellas that are only available online. Some of these, of course, will eventually make it into print, but the idea is novel and is a definite indication of what many of us already know—that romance readers are quickly embracing the current tech trends.

Also making use of the community idea, but with a twist, is the spate of Amish books currently flooding the entire publishing market. Although religious practice and the Amish lifestyle are inherent in these stories and some do fall within the Inspirational Romance bounds, many, such as Marta Perry's suspenseful *Murder in Plain Sight*, do not, choosing instead to use the Amish culture primarily as a setting for romances of other types.

As in the past, the sensuality levels for the genre run the gamut, remaining relatively high as a whole and in a few cases even verging on erotica; on the other hand, the number of sweet romances available and their continuing, possibly growing, appeal attest to the fact that not every book has to be sexy to be popular. Not unexpectedly, this trend has not gone unnoticed by Harlequin, which plans to launch Harlequin Heartwarming, a program that features titles from its backlist rewritten to "remove sex scenes and minimize sexual tension, in April 2011. At the moment, the program is scheduled to run for four months.

Humor of all types, from the gently funny to the laugh-out-loud hilarious, continues to add sparkle and a sense of fun to romances in all, even the most unexpected, subgenres. Lately it appears that humor (light or dark, studied or whimsical, subtle or overt) is simply becoming part of the fabric of the genre; and though there remain many romances out there without a shred of humor, there are not so many as there once were.

Finally, genreblending continues to blur the lines among the various subgenres as mystery, suspense, and various paranormal and fantasy elements migrate into romances of all types, creating intriguing, delightfully complex stories—and causing all kinds of problems for those who need to categorize them!

Subgenres in Detail

As usual, Contemporary Romances, both category series and single titles, continue to dominate the genre. While due in large part to the sheer number of titles released in Harlequin's popular category lines, single titles are published by all the romance houses and are a growing, important part of the mix. Limited only by the requirement that the story be set in the present, Contemporary Romances are incredibly diverse and come in all flavors, with stories ranging from funny, wacky romps (e.g., Cathie Linz's *Luck Be a Lady*, Ruth Saberton's *Katy Carter Wants a Hero*) to heartwarming stories that tackle more serious issues (e.g., Susan Mallery's *Almost Perfect*, Jodi Thomas's *Somewhere along the Way*) to action-packed adventures (e.g., Carly Phillips' *Love Me if you Dare*). As mentioned earlier, small towns and their environs are the settings *du jour*, and *The Homecoming* by JoAnn Ross, *Home Again* by Mariah Stewart, and the Mallery and Thomas titles mentioned above are examples of the many that successfully use these cozy settings. Ranches, particularly those "out West, are also popular settings (e.g., Tina Welling's *Cowboys Never Cry*, Kat Martin's *Against the Wind*) in both Contemporary as well as Historical romances. Of course cities, with all their fast-paced glitter are not neglected, but they are not quite so prevalent as in previous years. Characters of all varieties populate the pages of the current romance crop, but firefighters and cowboys continue to be fan favorites (e.g., *Burning Up* by Susan Andersen, *Mark: Secret Cowboy* by Pamela Britton), while lawyers and cooks are making their mark as well (*Icebreaker* by Deirdre Martin, *You're All I Need* by Karen White-Owens, *The Love Goddess' Cooking School* by Melissa Senate). As always, Contemporary romances are quick to reflect current trends: Teresa Medeiros's use of Twitter in *Goodnight Tweetheart* is one recent example.

Typically second in size to the Contemporary subgenre, Historicals continue their rise in popularity as they charm readers with a wide variety of romantic adventures from past eras. Any time prior to World War II is currently considered within the "historical boundaries, but the current period of choice continues to be Regency England by a large margin. (Note: Although the actual Regency period is the brief time (1811–1820) during which the man who would become George IV in 1820 officially became Regent for the incapacitated George III, many writers have expanded the time frame to include the decades on either side of the decade because of the similarities in style and custom.) However, trendy though it is, the Regency Period is not the only popular setting; and the Victorian, Georgian, and to a lesser extent the Medieval, eras are enjoying an increase in interest among readers. Likewise, the nineteenth century American West, popular a number of years earlier, is experiencing a surge in popularity.

Paranormals, Futuristics, Fantasies, and most of the Alternative Reality subgenres continue to shine, enchanting fans with magical, speculative tales that are some of the most creative in the genre. Vampires still enthrall readers, although their popularity is currently being shared by a wide variety of other paranormal beings, such as assorted shapeshifters, demons, elves, dragons, witches, faeries, angels, etc. Guardians of various types continue to be popular (e.g., *Demon Blood* in Meljean Brook's Guardian series, *Tempted by Fate* in Kate Perry's Guardians of Destiny series), and mythical gods and goddesses continue to interfere in mortal affairs (e.g., *Entwined* in Elisabeth Naughton's Eternal Guardians series, *Sins of the Heart* in Eve Silver's Otherkin series). Water also seems to hold a particular fascination for writers and readers, *Immortal Sea* by Virginia Kantra and *Water Bound* by Christine Feehan being two recent examples. Although many of these books tend to be serious, gritty, violent, and intense, some, such as Vicki Lewis Thompson's *A Werewolf in Manhattan*, Lynsay Sands' *Hungry for You*, and *Spun by Sorcery* in Barbara Bretton's Sugar Maple Chronicles series take a decidedly lighter, humorous, or even homey path.

As always, Romantic Suspense continues to thrill and terrify readers with an eclectic array of chilling adventures. Serial killers stalking unwary—or sometimes wary—victims are everywhere (e.g., *The Search* by Nora Roberts, *Don't Cry* by Beverly Barton); police officers and other law enforcement professionals vie with investigators and detectives of the private variety for hero status; and settings range from cities to small towns, and can keep the action in one place or sweep their characters around the world. As expected, most of these stories are serious and intense; however, some, such as Penny McCall's *Worth the Trip*, are infused with humor, while others, such as *Ghost Shadow* by Heather Graham, have a paranormal touch. Finally, whereas most of these stores are Contemporary Romantic Suspense, suspenseful romantic mysteries set in the past, such as Allegra Gray's spy thriller, *Nothing but Deception* or Deanna Raybourn's *Dark Road to Darjeeling*, are becoming an increasingly popular trend. Multicultural Romances, those stories that feature characters of varying cultural and ethnic backgrounds, continue to be popular. Whether these stories are published as parts of dedicated imprints, such as Kensington's Dafina or Harlequin's various Kimani lines, or as part of a publisher's regular romance line, these romances are attracting readers of all backgrounds, not just those featured in the stories. As usual, romances featuring the African American community are the most numerous, and *Operation Prince Charming* by Phyllis Bourne, *Butterfly* by Rochelle Alers, and *You're All I Need* by Karen White-Owens are only a few of the titles in this current volume.

Inspirational Romances continue to inspire their readers with a wide variety of sweet, faith-based Christian stories from both mainstream and religious presses. While never straying from their core religious tenets, these stories are surprisingly diverse and include both contemporary and historical settings, as well as mystery (*Licensed for Trouble* by Susan May Warren), paranormal (*Almost Heaven* by Chris Fabry), and multicultural (*Ray of Hope* by Vanessa Davis Griggs) elements. Cooks

will especially enjoy Rachel Hauck's *Dining with Joy*, complete with recipes. In addition, while these are not always Inspirational Romances, the many romances featuring the Amish culture and way of life are also of interest to this group of readers, as well as attracting non-Inspirational fans to this romance niche.

Finally, as mentioned earlier, linked books in all romance subgenres continue to flood the market. Some, such as Anne Stuart's dark, erotic, historical House of Rohan series, have been released back-to-back in successive months, while others, such as Nora Roberts's light-hearted contemporary Bride Quartet series, which is concluded by *Happy Ever After*, are spaced more widely. In addition, some are finite series, such as Bride Quartet just mentioned, whereas others, such as Michele Bardsley's Broken Heart series (*Cross Your Heart* is the latest addition) and Debbie Macomber's Cedar Cove series, which added its tenth book with *1022 Evergreen Place*, are continuing, with no apparent end in sight.

Statistics Note

As of this writing the romance statistics for 2010 are not yet available; the 2009 figures were discussed in the previous essay and for even more information, check out the statistics page at the site of Romance Writers of America (http://www.rwa.org/cs/the_romance_genre/romance_literature_statistics). With any luck the 2010 statistics should be tallied and available in time for the next volume of *What Do I Read Next?*.

Conferences, Grants, Awards, and Other Romance News of Interest

Every year numerous romance-related conferences, gatherings, and workshops take place across the country, and even around the world; but the most important of these, at least for American writers, is the annual conference of the Romance Writers of America (RWA). Usually held in July, this year to conference breaks with tradition (for scheduling reasons I won't go into) and is slated to be held June 28–July 1 in New York City. Primarily a working conference for romance writers, this event provides an opportunity for members to connect with each other and various industry professionals, attend numerous workshops and presentations, and honor their own at the star-studded Rita Awards Ceremony the last night of the conference. Among the speakers for the conference are Madeline Hunter, who will give the keynote address; Sherrilyn Kenyon, who will speak at the Awards Luncheon; and Meg Cabot, who will host the Rita Awards Ceremony.

As usual, the RWA conference will be preceded by Librarians' Day, a day-long event specifically targeting the local library community. Fast-paced, informative, and invariably entertaining, the day is filled with presentations by writers, editors, and librarians on a host of current, useful topics. Among this year's speakers are Robyn Carr, Jayne Ann Krentz, Lara Adrian, Wendy Crutcher, John Charles, Judi McCoy, Deanna Raybourn, and Leah Hultenschmidt. Julia Quinn will be the luncheon speaker. For more information and registration forms, see http://www.rwa.org/cs/rwa_annual_conference/librarians_day/librarians_day_overview.

Academics will also be interested that this year's conference of the International Association for the Study of Popular Romance (IASPR) will be held in New York City, just prior to RWA's conference. For more information, see the organization's website (iaspr.org). Also of interest of academics, August 2010 saw the launch of the *Journal of Popular Romance Studies* (ISSN 2159-4473), published by the International Association for the Study of Popular Romance (IASPR). Breaking new academic ground, this online, peer-reviewed journal presents "scholarship on representations of romantic love in popular media, now and in the past, from anywhere in the world" and is available at http://jprstudies.org/.

Every year since 1995 RWA has honored a librarian who has shown outstanding support of the genre with the Librarian of the Year Award. This year's recipient is Wendy Crutcher, materials evaluator for OC (Orange County) Public Libraries in California. The award will be presented at RWA's Awards Luncheon on June 30th.

This year the Academic Grant committee selected two research grant proposals for funding: Joanna Gregson and Jennifer Lois's for research on their proposed book, *Craft and Career: The Gendered Culture of Romance Writers*, and Heather Schell for her study, *Harlequins in Translation: The Turkish Experience of the American Romance Novel*.

Finally, readers were saddened by the July death of long-time favorite Historical Romance Writer Elizabeth Thornton (Mary Forrest George). Born in Scotland but living in Canada, she had 27 Historical romances to her credit and was an international best-selling author.

Future Trends

If Shakespeare was right and it's true that "past is prologue", we should have only to look over our shoulders to see what's coming next for Romance. Right? Well, not always, but because past and current trends are often harbingers of the future, at least it's a good place to start.

It almost goes without saying that technology will continue to impact the genre. The tech genie is out of the bottle and the rapidity with which new devices, protocols, and applications are being developed and adopted by all of us only points to changes of increasing magnitude down the road. Based on what is happening now, we might expect the following:

1. E-books will become more popular as the e-readers (e.g., iPad, Nook, kindle) improve in quality, more content becomes available, and devices and formats are standardized.

2. Publishers who do not have e-only imprints may establish them (especially if the early adopters have been successful), and more publishers (and possibly authors on their own) will make their backlists, especially out-of-print titles, available digitally.

3. There may be fewer publishers as some fail to adapt or find a way to stay profitable. With the ease of online self-publishing, the larger return on the book price, and the fact that much of the marketing of current romances is in the hands of the authors already, some writers may choose to strike out on their own.

4. Linked books, especially those revolving around small towns or other close-knit communities, will continue their rapid growth in popularity, and this trend will not be limited to any one subgenre, although it may be more popular in Contemporary or Inspirational romances.

5. In general, all the subgenres will continue to do well. Contemporaries will lead, of course, thanks to the popular contemporary series lines and the trend toward cozy, community-based romance. Historicals will continue to shine, and some writers will add various suspense and paranormal elements. Most aspects of the Alternative Realities group (Paranormal, Fantasy, Time Travel, Futuristic) will continue to make inroads, although Paranormal and Urban Fantasy will be especially important.

6. Romances will still be steamy, although the steady climb toward hotter and hotter sex is abating (at least in Romance, not necessarily Erotica); and it seems as though there may be a trend toward gentler, less sexually explicit stories.

7. Finally, academic interest in the genre, so very long in coming, is increasing and should continue to do so, finally providing the genre with the scholarly cache so necessary to any field of study that wants to be taken seriously.

Despite the tendency of the future to build on the past, things do not always play out as expected and events can turn on a dime. Obviously, none of these predictions mentioned above may happen—or they may. But whatever happens, Romance, one of the most flexible, innovative, and accommodative of all the fiction genres, will take it in stride—and make it better. At the very least, 2011 should be a fascinating year. Romance in Review

The traditional review sources, *Booklist* (www.ala.org/ala/aboutala/offices/publishing/booklist_publications/booklist/booklist.cfm), *Library Journal* (www.libraryjournal.com), and *Publishers Weekly* (www.publishersweekly.com), continue their coverage of the romance genre, as do a handful of newspapers across the country. *Library Journal* publishes a regular bimonthly romance review column with occasional additional mini-columns; *Booklist* has a separate romance fiction category in each issue, as do the other genres; and *Publishers Weekly* recently inaugurated a romance review section, as well. All three provide online review coverage that vary in amount and delivery method, and is becoming increasingly important. Many of these journal and newspaper reviews are picked up by various indexing services, such as EbscoHosts' Academic Search Premier, InfoTrac's Expanded Academic ASAP, or bookseller's websites, such as Amazon.com. and Barnes & Noble.

Without a doubt, coverage of the romance genre by mainstream sources has improved over the years; nevertheless, the most comprehensive coverage still is provided by the genre-specific publications, with *RT Book Reviews* (www.romantictimes.com) being by far the most complete. (Familiarly just called *RT*, this publication has changed names several times over the years.) Many of these print publications have a web presence, and *RT*'s, which includes reviews and other materials, is easy to use and exceptionally useful (www.rtbookreviews.com). Another veteran print publication that has gone through a number of ups and downs but can still be useful is *Affaire de Coeur* (www.affairedecoeur.com). Strictly online romance reviews sites continue to grow in popularity; and whereas most of them, like any web source—or any review, for that matter—need to be considered critically, they are becoming more important all the time and should not be ignored. All about Romance (www.likesbooks.com/), Romance Reviews Today (www.romrevtoday.com), The Romance Reader (www.theromancereader.com), Romance in Color (www.romanceincolor.com), and PNR (www.paranormalromance.org) are only several of the many general and genre-specific sites currently available. Online lists, such as RRA-L (Romance Readers Anonymous) (est. 1992), remain useful forums for romance readers to discuss the genre and share their views and recommendations. Log on to http://groups.yahoo.com/group/rra-l to subscribe. Fiction-L is another list of interest to readers and librarians that, while not specifically devoted to romance, does focus on the genre on a regular basis (www.webrary.org/rs/flbklistmenu.html). Blogs, wikis, and similar sites are increasing exponentially and can also be a source of opinions, if not formal reviews, and a host of additional information and commentary. New sites pop up daily and if you find bloggers whose opinions you respect, they can be gold mines. Finally, those interested in the academic side of the genre may be interested in the Romance Scholar listserv (mailman.depaul.edu/mailman/listinfo/romancescholar), as well as the Romance Wiki (www.romancewiki.com), an active site useful to readers, writers, and scholars alike. Many of these sites/organizations also have a presence on Facebook, can be followed via Twitter, and/or are available via RSS feed. As technology changes and expands, romance is sure to have a presence. (Note: Romancing the Blog, a popular and well-regarded blog that a number of popular writers contributed to, went on hiatus at the end of 2009. Although it had planned to come back later this year, as of this writing, according to the website it is offline for the foreseeable future. The name, however,

has been appropriated by various romance authors for their personal blogs.) Recommendations for Romance

Reading tastes vary greatly. What makes a book appeal to one person may make another reject it. By the same token, two people may like the same book for totally different reasons. Obviously, reading is a highly subjective and personal undertaking. For this reason, the recommended readings attached to each entry have tried to cast as broad a net as was reasonably possible. Suggested titles have been chosen on the basis of similarity to the main entry in one or more of the following areas: historical time period, geographic setting, theme, character types, plot pattern or premise, writing style, or overall mood or "feel." All suggestions may not appeal to the same person, but it is to be hoped that at least one would appeal to most.

Because romance reading tastes do vary so widely and readers (and writers) often apply vastly differing criteria in determining what makes a romance good, bad, or exceptional, I cannot claim that the following list of recommendations consists solely of the "best" romance novels of the year. (In fact many of these received no awards or special recognition at all.) It is simply a selection of books that the romance contributors, John Charles, Shelley Mosley, Sandra Van Winkle, and I found particularly interesting; perhaps some of these will appeal to you, too.

Butterfly by Rochelle Alers

Deadly Intent by Kylie Brant

Promise Canyon by Robyn Carr

Midnight Crystal by Jayne Castle

Whisper of Scandal by Nicola Cornick

Barely a Lady by Eileen Dreyer

Water Bound by Christine Feehan

Night Myst by Yasmine Galenorm

Marry Me by Jo Goodman

Mesmerizing Stranger by Jennifer Greene

Pleasures of a Notorious Gentleman by Lorraine Heath

A Kiss at Midnight by Eloisa James

Dracula My Love by Syrie James

A Hellion in Her Bed by Sabrina Jeffries

Immortal Sea by Virginia Kantra

When Harry Met Molly by Kieran Kramer

Wicked Surrender by Jade Lee

Butterfly Swords by Jeannie Lin

Luck Be a Lady by Cathie Linz

Almost Perfect by Susan Mallery

Goodnight Tweetheart by Teresa Medeiros

To Tempt a Saint by Kate Moore

Killer Heat by Brenda Novak

Heart Journey by Robin D. Owens

The Search by Nora Roberts

Sins of the Heart by Eve Silver

The Mischief of Mistletoe by Lauren Willig

For Further Reference

Publisher Websites and Book Clubs

In addition to going to the general websites of online book suppliers such as Amazon.com and traditional bookstores such as Barnes & Noble, readers can now order books in print and/or e-book, and in some cases downloadable audio, formats directly from a number of individual publishers' websites. Many of these websites also feature reviews, information on any subscription book clubs the publisher has, and ways for readers to connect with each other. Several of these, (e.g., Avalon, Five Star) target the library market and have standing order plans available. Services vary from website to website; several of the more popular are listed below. Publishers

Avalon Books: www.avalonbooks.com/

Barbour Publishing (Heartsong Presents): www. barbourbooks.com (See Heartsong Presents book club information below)

Ellora's Cave: www.jasminejade.com/default. aspx?skinid=11

Five Star: www.gale.cengage.com/fivestar/

HarperCollins/Avon Books: www.avonromance.com

Dorchester Publishing (Leisure and Love Spell): www. dorchesterpub.com (Click on the Romance link) Note: As of September 2010 Dorchester announced the company will no longer publish print mass-market titles and will focus on e-books and trade

Harlequin Books (Harlequin, Silhouette, Spice, MIRA, Red Dress Ink, Luna, HQN, Steeple Hill, Kimani Press, Worldwide Library): www.eharlequin.com

Kensington Books (Zebra, Dafina, Brava, Strapless, Aphrodisia, Urban Soul, Pinnacle): www.kensingtonbooks. com (Choose Books or Advanced Search to get to the romance imprint links)

Medallion Press: www.medallionpress.com

Penguin Group (Berkley, Putnam, Signet, NAL, Jove, Plume, Dutton, Onyx): us.penguingroup.com (Choose Romance under the Special Interests menu in the left-hand column)

Red Sage Publishing: www.eredsage.com

Simon and Schuster (Pocket): www.simonsays.com (Choose Categories and then choose the link for Romance)

Sourcebooks, Inc. (Sourcebooks Casablanca): www. sourcebooks.com (Choose Browse Books in the left hand column, then Fiction, and then Romance)

Tom Doherty Associates: (Tor Paranormal Romance) us. macmillan.com/TorForge.aspx (Choose Books and then Romance on the dropdown menu) Selected Book Clubs and Mail Order Services

Dorchester Book Clubs: Because of the firm's new format directions, as well as other issues, this book club is currently undergoing changes. Check the webpage for more information. http://www. dorchesterpub.com/store/book-club.aspx?

Harlequin Romance Book Clubs: Provides books in the Harlequin and Silhouette series on a monthly subscription basis. Check the website for series descriptions and price information. http://www.bookclubdeals.com/ index.php?action=2&idm=54

Harlequin Romance Ebook Clubs: Provides Harlequin and Silhouette series romances in eBook format on a monthly subscription basis. Check the website for more information. http://www.bookclubdeals.com/ index.php?action=2&idm=902

Heartsong Presents: Provides contemporary and historical Christian romances, published by Barbour Publishing Company on a subscription basis. Check the website for titles, price, and subscription information. http://www.heartsongpresents.com

Rhapsody Book Club: Rhapsody provides romances from a variety of sources on a subscription basis. Check the website, phone, or write for more information. http://www.rhapsodybookclub.com Note: All of these book clubs, not just the Harlequin ones, are also accessible via the bookclubdeals.com website: http:// www.bookclubdeals.com/index.php?action=4 Conferences

Numerous conferences are held each year for writers and readers of romance fiction. Two of the more important national ones are listed below:

The Annual RT Book Lovers Convention is sponsored by *Romantic Times Book Club Magazine*. The 28th Annual RT Book Lovers Convention was held on April 6–10, 2011, in Los Angeles, California. The 29th Annual Book Lovers Convention is scheduled to be held April 11–15, 2012, in Chicago, Illinois. This lively convention focuses primarily on fans and readers, and the Romantic Times organization also sponsors a number of romance-related tours for readers and writers.

The RWA Annual Conference is sponsored by Romance Writers of America and usually held in July. As mentioned previously, the 2010 Conference was held July 28–31, 2010, in Orlando, Florida. (Originally the 2010 conference was to be held in Nashville, Tennessee, but because of serious local flooding it was moved to Orlando.) The 2011 conference is scheduled for June 28&nadsh;July 1 in New York City. This "working" conference is aimed at romance writers, editors, librarians, and other romance professionals, rather than fans and readers.

For a more complete listing, particularly of regional or local conferences designed primarily for romance writers, consult the *Romance Writers' Report*, a monthly publication of The Romance Writers of America, or visit their website (www.rwanational.org).

Popular Romances

925

ROCHELLE ALERS

Butterfly

(Washington, D.C.: Kimani Press, 2010)

Story type: Contemporary
Subject(s): Romances (Fiction); African Americans; Plastic surgery
Major character(s): Seneca Houston, Model; Luis Navarro, Designer (fashion); Dr. Eliot Rollins, Doctor (plastic surgeon)
Time period(s): 21st century; 2010s
Locale(s): United States

Summary: In *Butterfly* by Rochelle Alers, a beautiful model searches for true happiness amidst the demands of her relatives and the public. At the age of 33, Seneca Houston has enjoyed a glamorous life on the fashion runways of the world. Despite the fame and financial comfort her career has brought her, Butterfly—as designer Luis Navarro calls her—wants the one thing she could not have—a family. Contemplating retirement, Seneca retreats to her agent's opulent home where she meets plastic surgeon Eliot Rollins. As Rollins is entranced by Seneca's beauty and personality, Seneca realizes the impact her career has had on those around her.

Where it's reviewed:
Romantic Times, August 2010, page 53

Other books by the same author:
Because of You, 2010
Breakaway, 2010
Sweet Dreams, 2010
Twice the Temptation, 2010
Sweet Deception, 2009

Other books you might like:
Sally Beauman, *Destiny*, 1987
Ginna Gray, *The Prodigal Daughter*, 2000
Sandra Kitt, *Family Affairs*, 1999
Francis Ray, *Any Rich Man Will Do*, 2005
Erica Spindler, *Red*, 1995

926

SUSAN ANDERSEN

Burning Up

(Don Mills, Ontario, Canada: HQN Books, 2010)

Story type: Contemporary
Subject(s): Romances (Fiction); Rescue work; Scandals
Major character(s): Macy O'James, Singer; Gabriel Donovan, Fire Fighter
Time period(s): 21st century; 2010s
Locale(s): Sugarville, Washington

Summary: In *Burning Up* by Susan Andersen, a successful recording artist returns to her hometown to take care of an ailing relative and face the community's long-held resentment. Back in Sugarville, Washington, Macy O'James meets fireman Gabriel Donovan at the local boarding house. Although he's heard stories about Macy's many transgressions, he can't help being drawn to her. Though Gabriel is good-looking, Macy doesn't think she could fall for such a respectable guy—but that doesn't stop the fireman from trying to win her over. As Macy resists Gabriel's attempts to tame her behavior, the two find common ground in their mutual physical attraction.

Where it's reviewed:
Library Journal, August 2010, page 60

Other books by the same author:
Bending the Rules, 2009
Cutting Loose, 2008
Coming Undone, 2007
Just for Kicks, 2006
Skintight, 2005

Other books you might like:
Connie Brockway, *Hot Dish*, 2006
Victoria Dahl, *Lead Me On*, 2010
Christina Dodd, *Tongue in Chic*, 2007
Susan Lyons, *Sex Drive*, 2009
Lisa Plumley, *Let's Misbehave*, 2007

927

KATE ANGELL

Sweet Spot

(New York: Dorchester Publishing, 2010)

Series: Richmond Rogues Series. Book 5
Story type: Contemporary; Series
Subject(s): Sports; Baseball; Romances (Fiction)
Major character(s): Cat May, Businesswoman; James "Law" Lawless, Baseball Player
Time period(s): 21st century; 2010s
Locale(s): Richmond, Virginia

Summary: In *Sweet Spot* by Kate Angell, up-and-coming businesswoman Cat May sets out to make a name for herself in her new position at an investment company. Pro baseball player James "Law" Lawless is interested in investing in a Richmond club. Cat would love to have Law as a client, but she can't accompany him to the club without resurrecting a bad memory from her past. *Sweet Spot* is the fifth book in the Richmond Rogues series.

Other books by the same author:
Sliding Home, 2009
Strike Zone, 2008
Curveball, 2007
Squeeze Play, 2006
Crazy for You, 2005

Other books you might like:
Gemma Bruce, *The Man for Me*, 2008
Lori Foster, *Back in Black*, 2010
Lisa Renee Jones, *Hot Target*, 2010
Deirdre Martin, *Power Play*, 2008
Jill Shalvis, *Slow Heat*, 2010

928

KRISTI ASTOR (Pseudonym of Kristina Cook)

A Midnight Clear

(New York: Zebra, 2010)

Story type: Holiday Themes
Subject(s): Romances (Fiction); Painting (Art); Christmas
Major character(s): Troy Davenport, Artist; Miranda Granger, Socialite
Time period(s): 21st century; 2010s

Summary: *A Midnight Clear* is a novel by author Katherine Cook, writing under her pseudonym Kristi Astor. After attempting to paint a beautiful mystery woman, Troy Davenport loses sight of her. Tony soon has a stroke of luck, however, when he sees her name in a society column. Miranda Granger, the woman he longs to paint, will be vacationing at the Grandview Hotel over the Christmas holiday, and now Tony will too. Miranda has a long history of making the wrong choices with men, and this time she is determined not to let her heart rule over her head. Can Troy win over this icy socialite in time for Christmas?

Where it's reviewed:
Booklist, November 1, 2010, page 34
Romantic Times, November 2010, page 46

Other books you might like:
Jane Goodger, *A Christmas Scandal*, 2009
Deborah Hale, *Highland Rogue*, 2004
Michelle Styles, *A Christmas Wedding Wager*, 2007
Sherry Thomas, *Not Quite a Husband*, 2009
Susan Wiggs, *Halfway to Heaven*, 2001

929

MARY BALOGH
COLLEEN GLEASON, Co-Author
SUSAN KRINARD, Co-Author
JANET MULLANY, Co-Author

Bespelling Jane Austen

(Don Mills, Ontario: Harlequin, 2010)

Story type: Paranormal
Subject(s): Literature; Vampires; Witches

Summary: *Bespelling Jane Austen* is a collection of short stories based around the settings and characters of Jane Austen's works. In the story "Almost Persuaded" by Mary Balogh, two lovers from past lives—Jane Everett and Capt. Robert Mitford—reconnect and realize that they are meant to be for eternity. Colleen Gleason's "Northanger Castle" mashes up the famous abbey from Jane Austen's novel of the same name as vampire novel enthusiast Caroline Merrill suspects her new boyfriend of being one of the undead. In Susan Krinard's "Blood and Prejudice," New Yorkers Liz Bennett and Mr. Darcy search for a cure for the vampires that have begun plaguing the city. The final story, "Little to Hex Her," by Janet Mullany, follows Emma, a witch who runs a dating service.

Where it's reviewed:
Library Journal, October 15, 2010, page 62
Romantic Times, October 2010, page 41

Other books you might like:
Jo Beverley, *Chalice of Roses*, 2010
Angie Fox, *My Zombie Valentine*, 2010
Eloisa James, *Talk of the Ton*, 2005
Stephanie Laurens, *It Happened One Night*, 2008
Cathy Maxwell, *Four Dukes and a Devil*, 2009

930

MAYA BANKS

No Place to Run

(New York: Berkley Sensation, 2010)

Series: KGI Series. Book 2
Story type: Romantic Suspense
Subject(s): Suspense; Romances (Fiction); Pregnancy
Major character(s): Sam Kelly, Military Personnel; Sophie Lundgren, Crime Victim
Time period(s): 21st century; 2010s
Locale(s): United States

Summary: *No Place to Run* is the second installment in the KGI series about the Kelly brothers, a group of trained operatives hired for private and government covert missions. Sam Kelly and Sophie Lundgren had a brief, but incredibly passionate affair when Sam was working on a mission in Mexico. Sophie vanished as quickly as she first appeared, leaving Sam to dream and fantasize about her for months. Five months later, Sophie is back with a shocking surprise for Sam. Not only is she pregnant with his child, but her life is also in danger and the evil men looking for her might want to kill Sam as well.

Where it's reviewed:
Romantic Times, December 2010, page 62

Other books by the same author:
The Darkest Hour, 2010
Golden Eyes, 2010
Linger, 2010
Sweet Temptation, 2010
Wild, 2010

Other books you might like:
Nina Bruhns, *If Looks Could Chill*, 2009
Leslie Parrish, *Fade to Black*, 2009
Leslie Parrish, *Pitch Black*, 2009
Christy Reece, *Last Chance*, 2010

931

MICHELE BARDSLEY

Cross Your Heart

(New York: Signet, 2010)

Series: Broken Heart Vampires Series. Book 7
Subject(s): Vampires; Love; Rural life
Major character(s): Elizabeth Bretton, Vampire, Heiress; Tez Jones, Cat (were-jaguar)
Time period(s): 21st century; 2010s
Locale(s): Broken Heart, Oklahoma

Summary: In *Cross Your Heart*, author Michele Bardsley presents the seventh installment in the Broken Heart Vampires series. This episode features Elizabeth Bretton, an heiress-turned-vampire who lives in her family's ancestral manor. When Elizabeth finds a secret room in the house, she comes face to face with an evil phantom intent on killing her. Further complicating matters is the appearance of Tez Jones, an unusual breed of were-cat, who finds an unlikely alliance—and love—with the vamp Elizabeth.

Where it's reviewed:
Booklist, September 1, 2010, page 56
Library Journal, August 2010, page 59

Other books by the same author:
Come Hell or High Water, 2010
Over My Dead Body, 2009
Because Your Vampire Said So, 2008
Wait Till Your Vampire Gets Home, 2008
Don't Talk Back to Your Vampire, 2007

Other books you might like:
Sharon Ashwood, *Scorched*, 2009

Dakota Cassidy, *Kiss & Hell*, 2009
Cindy Miles, *MacGowan's Ghost*, 2009

932

BEVERLY BARTON (Pseudonym of Beverly Beaver)

Don't Cry

(New York: Zebra Books, 2010)

Story type: Romantic Suspense; Serial Killer
Subject(s): Serial murders; Detective fiction; Love
Major character(s): Audrey Sherrod, Counselor; J.D. Cass, Agent (Tennessee Bureau of Investigation), Father (of Zoe); Zoe, Daughter (of J.D.)
Time period(s): 21st century; 2010s
Locale(s): Chattanooga, Tennessee

Summary: Beverly Barton's *Don't Cry* follows therapist and police assistant Audrey Sherrod as she helps authorities track down a serial killer. Sherrod is called in to help investigate when officials find the bodies of women who have been killed holding long-dead infants. J.D. Cass, a special agent with the Tennessee Bureau of Investigation, is sent to work with Audrey on the especially disturbing case. The two butt heads from the start, but when Audrey meets J.D.'s daughter Zoe, they begin to see past their differences. Then, as the investigation becomes more dangerous and even darker, Audrey and J.D. find that they can't help but have feelings for one another.

Where it's reviewed:
Publishers Weekly, July 5, 2010, page 42
Romantic Times, September 2010, page 76

Other books by the same author:
Dead by Midnight, 2010
Silent Killer, 2009
Cold Hearted, 2008
Dying for You, 2008
A Time to Die, 2007

Other books you might like:
Carla Cassidy, *Broken Pieces*, 2008
Karen Rose, *Nothing to Fear*, 2005
Karen Rose, *Scream for Me*, 2008
Jenna Ryan, *A Voice in the Dark*, 2010
Anne Stuart, *Silver Falls*, 2009

933

MARY BLAYNEY

Courtesan's Kiss

(New York: Bantam Books, 2010)

Story type: Historical
Subject(s): Romances (Fiction); History; Love
Major character(s): Mia Castellano, Young Woman (courtesan); David Pennistan, Nobleman
Time period(s): 19th century; 1810s (1819)
Locale(s): England

Summary: In *Courtesan's Kiss*, a young woman defies the conventions of her 19th-century English village and

Romances [side tab]

pursues the life of a courtesan. After Mia Castellano's fiance ends their engagement, she becomes an outcast in the town. Undeterred by her precarious social standing, Mia decides that she will make her own living and take any lover she wishes. At the request of his brother, Lord David Pennistan arrives to save Mia from ruin and persuades her to accompany him to the Pennistan estate. Mia proves to be an exasperating travel companion, but David soon learns he can't resist the would-be courtesan's charms.

Where it's reviewed:
Romantic Times, July 2010, page 45

Other books by the same author:
Stranger's Kiss, 2009
Lover's Kiss, 2008
Traitor's Kiss, 2008
The Captain's Mermaid, 2004
The Pleasure of His Company, 2003

Other books you might like:
Kathryn Caskie, *A Lady's Guide to Rakes*, 2005
Loretta Lynda Chase, *Your Scandalous Ways*, 2008
Nicola Cornick, *The Virtuous Cyprian*, 1998
Lisa Kleypas, *Someone to Watch over Me*, 1999
Kat Martin, *Secret Ways*, 2003

934

PHYLLIS BOURNE (Pseudonym of Phyllis Bourne Williams)

Operation Prince Charming

(New York: Love Spell, 2010)

Subject(s): Manners and customs; Love; Interpersonal relations
Major character(s): Ali Spencer, Teacher; Hunter Coleman, Detective; Erica, Fiance(e) (of Hunter)
Time period(s): 21st century; 2010s
Locale(s): Nashville, Tennessee

Summary: Phyllis Bourne's *Operation Prince Charming* charts the romance that develops between a rough-around-the-edges detective and the proprietress of a charm school. Hunter Coleman is forced by his fiancee to attend Ali Spencer's classes at the Spencer School of Etiquette. The heat between Hunter and Ali is evident from the moment their eyes meet, but Ali knows she must maintain her professionalism. It isn't long, however, before their mutual desire pulls them both in, jeopardizing Ali's career and Hunter's relationship with his fiancee.

Where it's reviewed:
Romantic Times, August 2010, page 80

Other books by the same author:
A Moment on the Lips, 2006

Other books you might like:
Meg Cabot, *Every Boy's Got One*, 2005
Marie Geraci, *The Boyfriend of the Month Club*, 2010
Sophie Kinsella, *Remember Me?*, 2008
Sally Koslow, *With Friends Like These*, 2010
Ruth Saberton, *Katy Carter Wants a Hero*, 2010

935

CELESTE BRADLEY

Scoundrel in My Dreams

(New York: St. Martin's Press, 2010)

Series: Runaway Bride Series. Book 2
Story type: Regency
Subject(s): Children; Romances (Fiction); Sisters
Major character(s): John "Jack" Redgrave, Nobleman, Father (of Melody); Amaryllis, Sister (of Laurel); Laurel, Sister (of Amaryllis), Mother (of Melody); Melody, Daughter (of Laurel and Jack)

Summary: *Scoundrel in My Dreams* is a novel from author Celeste Bradley's romance series, The Runaway Brides. A toddler is left on the doorstep of Lord John "Jack" Redgrave's men's club, and Jack is certain to whom it belongs: him. He is also quite sure who the mother is: his long-time romantic conquest, Amaryllis Clarke. Jack has loved Amaryllis for a long time, but after finally luring her into his bed she turned down his wedding proposition the following day. Soon he learns that the woman he slept with, however, was not his love Amaryllis but her sister, Laurel. Now Laurel must try to get her daughter Melody back from the man who took her virginity, as Jack comes to grips with his real feelings for Laurel and the fact that she might be the one he loves after all. Bradley is also the author of *Rogue in my Arms* and *Devil in My Bed*.

Where it's reviewed:
Romantic Times, October 2010, page 36

Other books by the same author:
Devil in My Bed, 2010
Rogue in My Arms, 2010
Desperately Seeking a Duke, 2008
Duke Most Wanted, 2008
The Duke Next Door, 2008

Other books you might like:
Anna Campbell, *My Reckless Surrender*, 2010
Patricia Grasso, *Tempting the Prince*, 2007
Brenda Joyce, *An Impossible Attraction*, 2010
Lavinia Kent, *A Talent for Sin*, 2009
Kat Martin, *Reese's Bride*, 2009

936

KYLIE BRANT (Pseudonym of Kim Bahnsen)

Deadly Intent

(New York: Berkley Sensation, 2010)

Series: Mindhunters Series. Book 4
Story type: Child-in-Peril; Romantic Suspense
Subject(s): Kidnapping; Romances (Fiction); Suspense
Major character(s): Macy Reid, Investigator, Kidnap Victim; Kellan Burke, Investigator
Time period(s): 21st century; 2010s
Locale(s): Denver, Colorado

Summary: *Deadly Intent* is part of the Mindhunters series. When the 11-year-old daughter of a wealthy Denver businessman is kidnapped for the second time, forensic linguist Macy Reid is assigned to the case. After all, she's the woman who rescued the little girl during her first kidnapping. Macy was also the victim of a kidnapping herself as a child, giving her special insight into the crime. As Macy dives into the investigation, she soon discovers that the biggest challenge comes in the form of Kellan Burke, the sexy and acerbic investigator whose blatant disregard for rules drives Macy crazy. Kellan might be the key to unlocking the case...and opening Macy's heart, as well.

Where it's reviewed:
Romantic Times, November 2010, page 68

Other books by the same author:
Deadly Dreams, 2011
Terms of Attraction, 2009
Waking Evil, 2009
Waking Nightmare, 2009
Waking the Dead, 2009

Other books you might like:
Nina Bruhns, *If Looks Could Chill*, 2009
Darlene Gardner, *The Hero's Sin*, 2009
Gemma Halliday, *The Perfect Shot*, 2010
Jenna Ryan, *A Voice in the Dark*, 2010

937

MARILYN BRANT   (Pseudonym of Marilyn B. Weigel)

Friday Mornings at Nine
(New York: Kensington, 2010)

Story type: Contemporary
Subject(s): Love; Marriage; Friendship
Major character(s): Bridget, Friend (of Tamara and Jennifer); Tamara, Friend (of Bridget and Jennifer); Jennifer, Friend (of Tamara and Bridget); David, Boyfriend (former boyfriend of Jennifer); Luke, Dentist, Employer (of Bridget); Aaron, Neighbor (of Tamara)
Time period(s): 21st century; 2010s
Locale(s): United States

Summary: Three friends are trapped in loveless marriages in Marilyn Brant's *Friday Mornings at Nine*. Every week, Bridget, Tamara, and Jennifer meet at the Indigo Moon Cafe to talk about the states of their respective marriages. But things take an unexpected turn when each woman confesses to a crush on another man, opening the door to possibilities of infidelity and throwing each marriage further into question.

Where it's reviewed:
Publishers Weekly, August 9, 2010, page 29
Romantic Times, October 2010, page 52

Other books by the same author:
According to Jane, 2009

Other books you might like:
Patricia Gaffney, *The Saving Graces*, 1999
Beth Kendrick, *Nearlyweds*, 2006
Tanya Michaels, *The Good Kind of Crazy*, 2006
Jane Porter, *Easy on the Eyes*, 2009

Barbara Samuel, *The Goddesses of Kitchen Avenue*, 2004

938

BARBARA BRETTON

Spun by Sorcery
(New York: Berkley Trade, 2010)

Series: Sugar Maple Chronicles Series. Book 3
Story type: Fantasy; Mystery
Subject(s): Magic; Vampires; Werewolves
Major character(s): Chloe Hobbs, Businesswoman (owner of a yarn shop), Girlfriend (of Luke), Friend (of Janice); Luke MacKenzie, Police Officer (chief), Boyfriend (of Chloe); Janice, Friend (of Chloe)
Time period(s): 21st century; 2010s
Locale(s): Sugar Maple, Vermont

Summary: In Barbara Bretton's *Spun by Sorcery*, Chloe Hobbs and her boyfriend, Luke MacKenzie, are ready to settle down. She owns a successful yarn shop, he's the chief of police, and they just bought a place in Sugar Maple, Vermont. Sugar Maple is unlike other places; it's home to vampires, werewolves, shape-shifters, and sorcerers—like Chloe. When the entire town of Sugar Maple suddenly disappears, Chloe and Luke are determined to figure out who is responsible for removing the town and all of its people and supernatural creatures from the map. Luckily, Chloe's friend Janice knows exactly where to start their search. This is the third book in the Sugar Maple Chronicles series.

Where it's reviewed:
Romantic Times, November 2010, page 82

Other books by the same author:
Someone Like You, 2010
Laced with Magic, 2009
Casting Spells, 2008
Just Desserts, 2008
Just Like Heaven, 2007

Other books you might like:
Annette Blair, *Bedeviled Angel*, 2010
Tracy Madison, *A Taste of Magic*, 2009
Deb Stover, *The Gift*, 2009
Helen Scott Taylor, *The Magic Knot*, 2009
C.L. Wilson, *Queen of Song and Souls*, 2009

939

TERRI BRISBIN   (Pseudonym of Theresa S. Brisbin)

A Storm of Pleasure
(New York: Brava, 2010)

Series: Storm Trilogy. Book 2
Story type: Historical - Medieval
Subject(s): Love; Family; Prophecy
Major character(s): Katla Svensdottir, Young Woman; Gavin of Durness, Psychic
Time period(s): 11th century; 1090s (1098)
Locale(s): Scotland

Summary: In medieval Scotland, Katla Svensdottir is prepared to do what it takes to get her brother cleared of treason. She soon realizes that the only way to prevent her brother's execution is to seduce Gavin, a seer whom Katla is sure can offer solid proof of her brother's innocence. But Katla never plans on falling in love with the aloof Gavin, and Gavin doesn't count on the overwhelming charms of beautiful Katla. *A Storm of Pleasure* is the second book in Terri Brisbin's Storm Trilogy.

Where it's reviewed:
Booklist, November 15, 2010, page 26
Library Journal, December 15, 2010, page 90
Romantic Times, October 2010, page 45

Other books by the same author:
The Mercenary's Bride, 2010
The Conqueror's Lady, 2009
A Storm of Passion, 2009
Possessed by the Highlander, 2008
Surrender to the Highlander, 2008

Other books you might like:
Shari Anton, *Midnight Magic*, 2005
Sandy Blair, *A Man in a Kilt*, 2004
Catherine Coulter, *The Penwyth Curse*, 2003
Mary Reed McCall, *Beyond Temptation*, 2005
Tina St. John, *Heart of the Hunter*, 2004

940

PAMELA BRITTON

Mark: Secret Cowboy

(Don Mills, Ontario, Canada: Harlequin, 2010)

Story type: Contemporary; Series
Subject(s): Romances (Fiction); Western fiction; Family
Major character(s): Mark Hansen, Rodeo Rider; Nicki Sable, Young Woman
Time period(s): 21st century; 2010s
Locale(s): Wyoming, United States

Summary: In *Mark: Secret Cowboy* by Pamela Britton, rodeo rider Mark Hansen takes on the powerful Cody family as he tries to win the heart of Nicki Sable. Though Nicki is a close friend of the Codys, she is attracted to Mark's rugged cowboy looks and strong character. When Mark discovers some sensitive information, he must decide how to use it. If he reveals the secret, he could ruin the despised Codys and advance his own social standing. If he keeps the information to himself, he will retain his lowly rodeo rider status but improve his chances with Nicki.

Where it's reviewed:
Romantic Times, September 2010, page 105

Other books by the same author:
Slow Burn, 2009
The Wrangler, 2009
On the Move, 2008
To the Limit, 2007
Total Control, 2007

Other books you might like:
Jan Hambright, *The High Country Rancher*, 2009

Rita Herron, *Platinum Cowboy*, 2009
R.C. Ryan, *Montana Destiny*, 2010
Bobbi Smith, *Wanted: The Texan*, 2008

941

MELJEAN BROOK

Demon Blood

(New York: Berkley, 2010)

Series: Guardians Series. Book 6
Subject(s): Vampires; Angels; Demons
Major character(s): Rosalia, Guardian (angel); Deacon, Vampire
Time period(s): Indeterminate
Locale(s): Asia; Europe; North America

Summary: Before her days as a guardian, Rosalia learned that she could never be too careful around men—especially male demons. In *Demon Blood*, the sixth book in The Guardians series, Rosalia finds it difficult to fight her attraction to one of the most dangerous male creatures in the world. Although down on his luck, Deacon still possesses the power to slay any demon—or guardian—that crosses his path. As a vampire who recently deceived his family, Deacon is on his own until Rosalia finds him and requests his help. Rosalia, an angel-like creature, wishes to protect vampires and guardians, but the only way to do that is to destroy demons. Alone, Rosalia cannot accomplish this feat, but with a powerful vampire on her side, she knows she has a chance. If Deacon agrees to help Rosalia, he may be able to win back the respect of his community and get revenge on the demon who caused them to turn their backs on him in the first place.

Where it's reviewed:
Romantic Times, July 2010, page 97

Other books by the same author:
Demon Forged, 2009
Demon Bound, 2008
Demon Angel, 2007
Demon Moon, 2007
Demon Night, 2007

Other books you might like:
Kresley Cole, *Kiss of a Demon King*, 2009
Christine Feehan, *Dark Magic*, 2000
Susan Krinard, *Come the Night*, 2008
Lora Leigh, *Wicked Sacrifice*, 2009
Lucy Monroe, *Moon Craving*, 2010

942

CAROLYN BROWN

Honky Tonk Christmas

(Naperville, Illinois: Sourcebooks Casablanca, 2010)

Story type: Contemporary; Western
Subject(s): Romances (Fiction); Country music; Bars (Drinking establishments)
Major character(s): Sharlene Waverly, Saloon Keeper/

Owner; Holt Jackson, Carpenter
Time period(s): 21st century; 2010s
Locale(s): Texas, United States

Summary: As the most recent owner of the Honky Tonk, a lively country-western bar in Texas, Sharlene Waverly has a fair share of work to do if she wants to get the joint remodeled and reopened before Christmas. It's no surprise that she hires Holt Jackson, the best contractor in the area, to fix the place up, but Sharlene doesn't expect to be so attracted to the man. Holt, meanwhile, is trying hard to keep things professional because he desperately needs the work, but the passion and sexual attraction between he and Sharlene is too much for either of them to bear.

Where it's reviewed:
Romantic Times, November 2010, page 77

Other books by the same author:
If He's Dangerous, 2011
If He's Wild, 2010
If He's Sinful, 2009
If He's Wicked, 2009
Highland Sinner, 2008

Other books you might like:
Donna Fletcher, *The Highlander's Bride*, 2007
Monica McCarty, *Highlander Untamed*, 2007
Amanda Scott, *Knight's Treasure*, 2007
Amanda Scott, *Seduced by a Rogue*, 2010

943

CAROLYN BROWN

My Give a Damn's Busted

(Naperville, Illinois: Sourcebooks Casablanca, 2010)

Series: Honky Tonk Series. Book 3
Story type: Western
Subject(s): Bars (Drinking establishments); Romances (Fiction); Western fiction
Major character(s): Larissa Morley, Businesswoman, Saloon Keeper/Owner; Hank Wells, Cowboy/Cowgirl
Time period(s): 21st century; 2010s
Locale(s): Texas, United States

Summary: *My Give a Damn's Busted* is the third installment in the Honky Tonk series. The Honky Tonk, a small country-western bar in Texas, has changed owners once again. Larissa Morley, a strong-willed woman with a secretive past, is the fourth proprietor of the joint, after each of the previous owners found love and passed the Honky Tonk down to another. Hank Wells, a cowboy with a few mysteries of his own, is visiting Palo Pinto County for the summer, staying at his father's massive ranch, with a secret plan to buy the Honky Tonk. Larissa and Hank clash in more ways than one, but soon the Honky Tonk isn't the only thing at risk...their hearts are in a precarious position as well!

Where it's reviewed:
Romantic Times, October 2010, page 86

Other books by the same author:
Love Drunk Cowboy, 2011
Walkin' on Clouds, 2011

Hell, Yeah, 2010
Honky Tonk Christmas, 2010
I Love This Bar, 2010

Other books you might like:
B.J. Daniels, *Montana Royalty*, 2008
Geralyn Dawson, *Her Outlaw*, 2007
Delores Fossen, *Branded by the Sheriff*, 2009
Georgina Gentry, *To Love a Texan*, 2007
R.C. Ryan, *Montana Destiny*, 2010

944

CAROLYN BROWN

Come High Water

(New York: Avalon Books, 2010)

Series: Broken Heart Vampires Series. Book 3
Story type: Historical; Series
Subject(s): Romances (Fiction); History; Hotels and motels
Major character(s): Bridget O'Shea, Single Mother, 19-Year-Old; Catherine, Sister (of Bridget); Alice, Sister (of Bridget); Wyatt Ferguson, Traveler
Time period(s): 20th century; 1920s (1920)
Locale(s): Huttig, Arkansas

Summary: In *Come High Water*, a divorced single mother struggles to keep the Black Swan Inn in business in 1920 Huttig, Arkansas. With her parents deceased and her sisters married and gone, 19-year-old Bridget O'Shea cares for her daughter, Ella, as she runs the inn alone. When she needs to recruit some help, she visits the local train station where she's sure to find soldiers returning from the war and eager to find work. Wyatt Ferguson hadn't intended to stay in Huttig, but with his sweetheart promised to another man, a six-week stay at the Black Swan seems a welcome distraction. *Come High Water* is the third book in the Black Swan series.

Where it's reviewed:
Booklist, June 1, 2010, page 43

Other books by the same author:
Hell, Yeah, 2010
I Love this Bar, 2010
My Give a Damn's Busted, 2010
Lucky in Love, 2009
One Lucky Cowboy, 2009

Other books you might like:
Susan Crandall, *Back Roads*, 2003
LaVyrle Spencer, *Morning Glory*, 1989
Sherryl Woods, *Flowers on Main*, 2009
Sherryl Woods, *The Inn at Eagle Point*, 2009
Sherryl Woods, *Seaview Inn*, 2008

945

GRACE BURROWES

The Heir

(Naperville, Illinois: Sourcebooks Casablanca, 2010)

Story type: Historical - Regency
Subject(s): Romances (Fiction); Royalty; England

Romances

Major character(s): Gayle Windham, Bachelor, Nobleman (earl of Westhaven), Employer (of Anna); Anna Seaton, Housekeeper
Time period(s): 19th century; 1810s
Locale(s): London, England

Summary: *The Heir* is a historical romance novel from award-winning author Grace Burrowes. Gayle Windham, the Earl of Westhaven, is so eager to avoid marriage pressure from his father that he decides to stay in London all summer instead of traveling to the country like the rest of high society. Windham's home runs smoothly, until a beautiful new housekeeper arrives and changes everything. Anna Seaton is not only gorgeous, but also intelligent, sophisticated, and educated. Windham can't figure out why this proper woman would choose a life of servitude, but he's determined to find out. As the pair fall into a sensual romance, Windham tries to convince Anna to become his wife, but her secretive past threatens to destroy them both.

Where it's reviewed:
Romantic Times, December 2010, page 38

Other books you might like:
Elizabeth Boyle, *This Rake of Mine*, 2005
Gaelen Foley, *My Wicked Marquess*, 2009
Laura Lee Ghurke, *And Then He Kissed Her*, 2007
Susan Gee Heino, *Mistress by Mistake*, 2009
Lavinia Kent, *Bound by Temptation*, 2010

946

PAMELA CALLOW

Damaged

(Don Mills, Ontario, Canada: Mira, 2010)

Subject(s): Murder; Suspense; Romances (Fiction)
Major character(s): Kate Lange, Lawyer, Detective—Amateur; Marian MacAdam, Grandmother (of Lisa); Lisa, Teenager, Crime Victim; Randall Barrett, Lawyer
Time period(s): 21st century; 2010s
Locale(s): Halifax, Nova Scotia

Summary: Pamela Callow's *Damaged* chronicles a dangerous case taken on by Halifax lawyer Kate Lange. Kate is visited by a concerned grandmother who is seeking custody of her teenage granddaughter, Lisa. But the case takes a sudden dark turn when Lisa is found murdered. Now Kate finds herself enmeshed in her own unusual investigation—an investigation that brings her face to face with Lisa's mother, who is a powerful judge, and Kate's ex-boyfriend, who is the police detective working on his own investigation of Lisa's death. First novel.

Where it's reviewed:
Publishers Weekly, March 29, 2010, page 44
Romantic Times, June 2010, page 88

Other books by the same author:
Indefensible, 2010

Other books you might like:
Margaret Carroll, *A Dark Love*, 2009
Brenda Novak, *Trust Me*, 2008
Marilyn Pappano, *Intimate Enemy*, 2008

Debra Webb, *Anywhere She Runs*, 2010
Debra Webb, *Everywhere She Turns*, 2009

947

CANDACE CALVERT

Code Triage

(Carol Stream, Illinois: Tyndale House Publishers, 2010)

Series: Mercy Hospital Series. Book 3
Subject(s): Romances (Fiction); Christian life; Physicians
Major character(s): Dr. Leigh Stathos, Doctor (emergency room), Spouse (of Nick); Nick Stathos, Police Officer, Spouse (of Leigh)
Time period(s): 21st century; 2010s
Locale(s): San Francisco, California

Summary: *Code Triage* is the third novel in the Mercy Hospital series by Candace Calvert. In the novel, emergency room doctor Leigh Stathos is still reeling from the news of her husband's infidelity. A week before her divorce is finalized, Leigh throws herself into her work. Leigh's husband, Nick Stathos, is a police officer in San Francisco, and he is absolutely determined to put a stop to the divorce. Leigh is determined to put the past behind her, but she is horrified when she comes face to face with the woman who cheated with her husband. Leigh has little time to think about this when Mercy Hospital is put under lockdown after a violent episode. Now, Leigh and Nick are forced to confront their real feelings for each other.

Where it's reviewed:
Romantic Times, November 2010, page 61

Other books by the same author:
Disaster Status, 2010
Critical Care, 2009

Other books you might like:
Margaret Daley, *Once upon a Family*, 2007
S.Q. Eads, *Angels in Cowboy Boots*, 2010
Linda Goodnight, *A Very Special Delivery*, 2006
Janet Tronstad, *Dr. Right*, 2010
Kim Watters, *On the Wings of Love*, 2010

948

LIZ CARLYLE (Pseudonym of Susan Woodhouse)

One Touch of Scandal

(New York: HarperCollins, 2010)

Story type: Historical; Series
Subject(s): Romances (Fiction); History; Social class
Major character(s): Grace Gauthier, Governess; Ethan Holding, Employer (of Grace); Rance Welham, Friend (of Grace); Adrian Forsythe, Nobleman; Royden Napier, Police Officer
Time period(s): 19th century; 1840s
Locale(s): London, England

Summary: In *One Touch of Scandal*, a young woman wanted for murder in Victorian London seeks the aid of a family friend. Governess Grace Gauthier is betrothed to the father of her charges, Ethan Holding. When her betrothed is murdered, Grace flees the authorities and searches for Rance Welham, an associate of her father's. Though she can't find Welham, one of his friends, Lord Ruthveyn, offers his assistance. A psychic, Ruthveyn can see into the future but can't foretell what will happen to Grace as the police further implicate her in Holding's death. *One Touch of Scandal* is the first book in a Victorian supernatural trilogy.

Where it's reviewed:
Booklist, September 15, 2010, page 50
Romantic Times, October 2010, page 38

Other books by the same author:
Tempted All Night, 2009
Wicked All Day, 2009
Never Romance a Rake, 2008
Never Deceive a Duke, 2007
Never Lie to a Lady, 2007

Other books you might like:
Connie Brockway, *So Enchanting*, 2009
Elizabeth Hoyt, *The Raven Prince*, 2006
Barbara Metzger, *Truly Yours*, 2007
Mary Jo Putney, *Loving a Lost Lord*, 2009
Elizabeth Thornton, *The Scot and I*, 2009

949

ROBYN CARR

Promise Canyon
(New York: Mira, 2011)

Series: Virgin River Series. Book 11
Story type: Contemporary
Subject(s): Love; Rural life; Interpersonal relations
Major character(s): Clay Tahoma, Technician (veterinary technician); Lilly Yazhi, Young Woman
Time period(s): 21st century; 2010s
Locale(s): Virgin River, California

Summary: Clay Tahoma has arrived in Virgin River, California, to work in the town veterinary offices. He soon meets local woman Lilly Yazhi and is immediately smitten. As the two explore the possibility of a relationship, the town is thrown into chaos when a wealthy member of the community dies, leaving millions of dollars to the city. Suddenly the true natures of some of Virgin Falls's residents are revealed, and Clay and Lilly's new relationship is put to the test. *Promise Canyon* is the 11th novel in Robyn Carr's Virgin River series.

Where it's reviewed:
Romantic Times, January 2011, page 83

Other books by the same author:
Harvest Moon, 2011
Wild Man Creek, 2011
Angel's Peak, 2010
Moonlight Road, 2010
A Summer in Sonoma, 2010

Other books you might like:
J.S. Hawley, *Come with Me*, 2007
Candice Poarch, *Lighthouse Magic*, 2003

Candice Poarch, *Loving Delilah*, 2004
Deborah Smith, *The Crossroads Cafe*, 2006

950

KATHRYN CASKIE

The Duke's Night of Sin
(New York: Avon, 2010)

Story type: Regency
Subject(s): Romances (Fiction); Royalty; Humor
Major character(s): Lady Siusan Sinclair, Noblewoman; Sebastian Beaufort, Nobleman (The Duke of Exeter)

Summary: Lady Siusan Sinclair is desperately trying to stay out of trouble, but when she encounters Sebastian Beaufort, the Duke of Exeter, in a dark room during a ball, she can't help but misbehave. In an effort to avoid the duke learning her identity, she takes off for northern England to become a teacher. Still, Sebastian is determined to find out who the mysterious lover in the library was. Will Siusan and Sebastian ever meet again?

Where it's reviewed:
Booklist, December 1, 2010, page 34
Romantic Times, December 2010, page 33

Other books by the same author:
The Most Wicked of Sins, 2009
How to Propose to a Prince, 2008
To Sin with a Stranger, 2008
How to Engage an Earl, 2007
How to Seduce a Duke, 2006

Other books you might like:
Christina Dodd, *Some Enchanted Evening*, 2004
Suzanne Enoch, *London's Perfect Scoundrel*, 2003
Candice Hern, *Lady Be Bad*, 2007
Sabrina Jeffries, *The Truth About Lord Stoneville*, 2010
Julia London, *Highlander in Disguise*, 2005

951

JAYNE CASTLE (Pseudonym of Jayne Anne Krentz)

Midnight Crystal
(New York: Jove, 2010)

Series: Dreamlight Trilogy. Book 3
Story type: Paranormal
Subject(s): Romances (Fiction); Futuristic society; Alternative worlds
Major character(s): Adam Winters, Hunter (ghost hunter); Marlowe Jones, Psychic
Time period(s): Indeterminate Future
Locale(s): Harmony, Fictional Location

Summary: In *Midnight Crystal* by Jayne Castle, the futuristic world of Harmony is characterized by an underworld of ghost hunters and dreamlight readers. Leader of the Ghost Hunter Guild is Adam Winters. Adam is struggling not only with his new leadership position, but also an ancient curse that plagues his family. A hidden artifact could release Adam from his grim

Romances

destiny, but only a skilled dreamlight reader can find what he needs. When Marlowe Jones arrives in town on a motorcycle, Adam thinks that she might be the answer to his prayers. But Adam soon learns that Marlowe is a member of the Arcane clan—the long-time enemy of the Winters family. *Midnight Crystal* is the third book in the Dreamlight trilogy.

Where it's reviewed:
Booklist, August 1, 2010, page 34
Library Journal, August 1, 2010, page 59
Romantic Times, September 2010, page 92

Other books by the same author:
Obsidian Prey, 2009
Dark Light, 2008
Silver Master, 2007
Ghost Hunter, 2006
After Glow, 2004

Other books you might like:
Susan Grant, *Moonstruck*, 2008
Eve Kenin, *Driven*, 2007
Liz Maverick, *Crimson and Steam*, 2010
Gena Showalter, *Seduce the Darkness*, 2009

952

JUDY CHRISTIE

Goodness Gracious Green

(Nashville: Abingdon Press, 2010)

Series: Green Series. Book 2
Story type: Contemporary
Subject(s): Love; Faith; Rural life
Major character(s): Lois Barker, Journalist; Chris, Neighbor (of Lois)
Time period(s): 21st century; 2010s
Locale(s): Green, Louisiana

Summary: Lois Barker has settled comfortably into small-town life in Green, Louisiana. Her position as owner of the town paper is running smoothly, her relationship with her boyfriend is solid, and she enjoys her quiet life in the rural South. But Lois's newfound contentment is put to the test when a series of challenges is laid out before her, including a bite from the mayor's feisty dog and the reemergence of the newspaper's former owners, who want the business back from Lois. Judy Christie's *Goodness Gracious Green* is the second novel in the Green series.

Other books you might like:
Joyce Magnin, *Charlotte Figg Takes over Paradise*, 2010
Beth Pattillo, *Heavens to Betsy*, 2005
Deborah Shelley, *Talk about Love*, 1999
Lisa Wingate, *Never Say Never*, 2010

953

ANN CHRISTOPHER (Pseudonym of Sally Young Moore)

Deadly Pursuit

(New York: Kensington, 2010)

Story type: Contemporary
Subject(s): Love; African Americans; Suspense
Major character(s): Jack Parker, Agent (DEA); Amara Clarke, Lawyer; Kareem Gregory, Drug Dealer
Time period(s): 21st century; 2010s
Locale(s): United States

Summary: In Ann Christopher's *Deadly Pursuit*, Jack Parker is a sexy DEA operative who comes to the rescue of attorney Amara Clarke during a carjacking. After Jack's heroism hits the newsstands, his mortal enemy, drug lord Kareem Gregory, sets out to find Jack. Fearful for Amara's safety, Jack takes Amara and the two hit the road in hopes of thwarting Kareem's henchman. Along the way, Jack and Amara encounter danger and violence—and a mutual desire that consumes them both.

Where it's reviewed:
Publishers Weekly, September 20, 2010, page 55
Romantic Times, November 2010, page 68

Other books by the same author:
Redemption's Kiss, 2010
Seduced on the Red Carpet, 2010
Campaign for Seduction, 2009
Road to Seduction, 2009
Tender Secrets, 2008

Other books you might like:
Rochelle Alers, *Breakaway*, 2010
Rochelle Alers, *Hidden Agenda*, 1997
Marcia King-Gamble, *Come Back to Me*, 2004
Selena Montgomery, *Secrets and Lies*, 2007

954

TIFFANY CLARE

The Surrender of a Lady

(New York: St. Martin's Press, 2010)

Story type: Historical
Subject(s): Love; Gambling; Prostitution
Major character(s): Elena Ravenscliffe, Noblewoman, Prostitute; Griffin Summerfield, Rescuer (of Elena)
Time period(s): 19th century; 1840s
Locale(s): Greece

Summary: In Tiffany Clare's *The Surrender of a Lady*, Lady Elena Ravenscliffe is sold into prostitution and forced to serve clients in a 19th-century Greek brothel. When she is rescued by Griffin Summerfield, the first man she ever loved, all the old feelings come bubbling to the surface, and it isn't long before neither Elena nor Griffin can deny the burning passion they share. First novel.

Where it's reviewed:
Booklist, October 15, 2010, page 107
Romantic Times, October 2010, page 40

Other books by the same author:
The Seduction of His Wife, 2011

Other books you might like:
Renee Bernard, *Revenge Wears Rubies*, 2010
Lisa Kleypas, *Lady Sophia's Lover*, 2002
Stephanie Laurens, *The Elusive Bride*, 2010
Christine Merrill, *A Wicked Liaison*, 2009
Emma Wildes, *Lessons from a Scarlet Lady*, 2010

955

EVANGELINE COLLINS (Pseudonym of Nicole Collins)

Seven Nights to Forever

(New York: Berkley, 2010)

Story type: Historical - Regency
Subject(s): Prostitution; Love; Marriage
Major character(s): Rose Marlowe, Prostitute (courtesan); James Archer, Merchant, Wealthy
Time period(s): 19th century
Locale(s): United Kingdom

Summary: Evangeline Collins's Regency-set romance *Seven Nights to Forever* tells the story of Rose Marlowe, who lives a quiet country life with her younger brother. For one week a month, however, Rose becomes a high-paid courtesan at a renowned brothel, using the money she makes to support herself and her sibling and repay the debts her late father had accumulated. One night she meets a handsome married man named James Archer, and their fateful night together turns into a week. Their attraction is authentic and all-consuming, but following through with it could spell disaster in their well-ordered lives.

Where it's reviewed:
Booklist, October 15, 2010, page 26
Publishers Weekly, September 13, 2010, page 29
Romantic Times, November 2010, page 38

Other books by the same author:
Her Ladyship's Companion, 2009

Other books you might like:
Mary Balogh, *The Secret Pearl*, 1991
Anna Campbell, *Tempt the Devil*, 2008
Loretta Lynda Chase, *Your Scandalous Ways*, 2008
Gaelen Foley, *The Duke*, 2000
Lisa Kleypas, *Someone to Watch over Me*, 1999

956

NICOLA CORNICK

Whisper of Scandal

(Toronto; New York: Harlequin, 2010)

Series: Scandalous Women of the Ton Trilogy. Book 1
Story type: Historical - Regency
Subject(s): Love; Adventure; Marriage
Major character(s): Joanna Ware, Widow(er); Alex, Nobleman

Time period(s): 19th century; 1810s
Locale(s): London, United Kingdom

Summary: In Regency-era England, Lady Joanna Ware is struggling to uphold the reputation of her late husband, a philandering explorer who made numerous expeditions to the Arctic. But one man, the nobleman Alex, knows the truth about Joanna's husband, and he isn't about to believe her tall tales. When the two are named guardians of a child Joanna's husband fathered out of wedlock, they set off to Russia to claim the child. Along the way, Joanna and Alex are stunned to find themselves drawn to one another and into the mutual passion they share. *Whisper of Scandal* is the first installment in Nicola Cornick's Scandalous Women of the Ton trilogy.

Where it's reviewed:
Booklist, September 15, 2010, page 53
Publishers Weekly, August 23, 2010, page 35
Romantic Times, October 2010, page 44

Other books by the same author:
The Confessions of a Duchess, 2009
Kidnapped: His Innocent Mistress, 2009
The Scandals of an Innocent, 2009
The Undoing of a Lady, 2009
Unmasked, 208

Other books you might like:
Jo Beverley, *To Rescue a Rogue*, 2006
Liz Carlyle, *Never Lie to a Lady*, 2007
Sabrina Jeffries, *Beware a Scot's Revenge*, 2007
Stephanie Laurens, *The Elusive Bride*, 2010
Mary Jo Putney, *Loving a Lost Lord*, 2009

957

CATHERINE COULTER

The Valcourt Heiress

(New York: G.P. Putnam's Sons, 2010)

Series: Medieval Song Series. Book 7
Story type: Historical - Medieval
Subject(s): Romances (Fiction); History; Middle Ages
Major character(s): Garron, Knight; Arthur, Brother (of Garron); Merry, Young Woman; Black Demon, Villain
Time period(s): Multiple Time Periods
Locale(s): England

Summary: In *The Valcourt Heiress* by Catherine Coulter, Garron of Kersey survives his service in the Crusades only to find that his family's estate has been devastated. Though he had planned on assuming his rightful title of Baron Wareham, his holdings now include the remains of Wareham Castle. The servants that have stayed recount the castle's siege by a treasure-hunting attacker known as the Black Demon. Though the castle did not reveal its riches, it is now home to a strange young girl, Merry, who is educated beyond her station. As Garron searches for the Black Demon, he embarks on a romantic relationship with Merry. *The Valcourt Heiress* is the seventh book in the Medieval Song series.

Where it's reviewed:
Booklist, October 1, 2010, page 38
Romantic Times, November 2010, page 40

Romances

Other books by the same author:
Whiplash, 2010
Knockout, 2009
Tailspin, 2008
Wizard's Daughter, 2008
Double Take, 2007

Other books you might like:
Shari Anton, *Twilight Magic*, 2006
Sandy Blair, *A Rogue in a Kilt*, 2004
Karyn Monk, *Once a Warrior*, 1997
Amanda Quick, *Desire*, 1993
Tina St. John, *Heart of the Hunter*, 2004

958

JENNIFER CRUSIE

Maybe This Time

(New York: St. Martin's Press, 2010)

Subject(s): Haunted houses; Humor; Love
Major character(s): Andie Miller, Young Woman (ex-wife of North); North Archer, Young Man (ex-husband of Andie)
Time period(s): 21st century; 2010s
Locale(s): United States

Summary: Bestselling author Jennifer Crusie presents a lighthearted tale of love and romance in *Maybe This Time*. Andie Miller is making plans to marry her beloved fiance when her ex-husband, North, comes barreling back into the picture. North, who is slated to inherit two unruly children from a long-lost cousin, needs Andie's help finding a suitable nanny before the kids arrive. Andie agrees to help out, but when she meets the children, she discovers their house is not only in a state of massive disarray, but it also appears to be haunted. What ensues is a comical adventure in which all manner of unforgettable characters attempt to exorcise the demons of the house as Andie and North begin to rethink the demise of their relationship.

Where it's reviewed:
Booklist, July 1, 2010, page 32
Library Journal, July 2010, page 69
Publishers Weekly, July 5, 2010, page 25
Romantic Times, September 2010, page 84

Other books by the same author:
Wild Ride, 2010
Dogs and Goddesses, 2009
Agnes and the Hitman, 2007
The Unfortunate Miss Fortunes, 2007
Don't Look Down, 2006
Bet Me, 2004
Charlie All Night, 2004
Faking It, 2002
Welcome to Temptation, 2000
Crazy for You, 1999

Other books you might like:
Elizabeth Bevarly, *Ready and Willing*, 2008
Patricia Coughlin, *The Lost Enchantress*, 2010
Mindy L. Klasky, *When Good Wishes Go Bad*, 2010

Jenna McKnight, *Love in the Fast Lane*, 2007
Heather Webber, *Truly, Madly*, 2010

959

VICTORIA DAHL

A Little Bit Wild

(New York: Zebra, 2010)

Story type: Historical - Regency
Subject(s): Love; Marriage; Sexuality
Major character(s): Marisa York, Noblewoman; Jude Bertrand, Heir
Time period(s): 19th century
Locale(s): United Kingdom

Summary: Set in Regency England, Victoria Dahl's *A Little Bit Wild* tells the story of young noblewoman Marisa York, whose interest in sensuality led to the loss of her virginity by an unworthy suitor. Fearful of the disgrace she could face, Marisa's family marries her off to the wealthy but physically unappealing Jude Bertrand. Marisa is far from thrilled about the arrangement, but the more she gets to know her new husband, the more desire she feels for him. Can Marisa and Jude find love and avoid the scandal that could erupt if news of Marisa's past emerges?

Where it's reviewed:
Romantic Times, August 2010, page 45

Other books by the same author:
Lead Me on, 2010
One Week as Lovers, 2009
Start Me Up, 2009
Talk Me Down, 2009
A Rake's Guide to Pleasure, 2008

Other books you might like:
Victoria Alexander, *The Virgin's Secret*, 2009
Mary Balogh, *First Comes Marriage*, 2009
Celeste Bradley, *Duke Most Wanted*, 2008
Tessa Dare, *Three Nights with a Scoundrel*, 2010
Olivia Drake, *Seducing the Heiress*, 2009

960

JANET DAILEY

Santa in Montana

(New York: Zebra Books/Kensington Publishing, 2010)

Story type: Holiday Themes
Subject(s): Holidays; Christmas; Romances (Fiction)
Major character(s): Chase Calder, Father (of Cat), Matchmaker; Cat Calder, Widow(er), Daughter (of Chase)
Time period(s): 21st century; 2010s
Locale(s): Montana, United States

Summary: *Santa in Montana* is a Christmas-themed romance novel from best-selling author Janet Dailey. The Calder family's Christmas get-together is coming up and father Chase Calder is planning a secret surprise to turn this holiday season into one the family won't soon forget. When it comes to his widowed daughter, Cat, Chase is determined to find her the best Christmas gift of all: love. He thinks it's time for Cat to find a new man and this holiday season might be the perfect opportunity to set her up. Cat's new mystery man isn't the only surprise facing the Calder family this winter. They'll have to deal with an unexpected visitor with a few mysteries of their own.

Where it's reviewed:
Library Journal, October 15, 2010, page 60

Other books by the same author:
Bannon Brothers: Trust, 2011
American Destiny, 2009
Santa in a Stetson, 2009
Searching for Santa, 2008
A Capitol Holiday, 2001

Other books you might like:
Marcia Evanick, *A Berry Merry Christmas*, 2004
Carol Finch, *One Starry Christmas*, 2004
Joan Johnston, *Lone Star Christmas*, 1997
Shirley Jump, *Marry-Me Christmas*, 2008
Mary McBride, *A Western Family Christmas*, 2001

961

TESSA DARE   (Pseudonym of Eve Ortega)

Three Nights with a Scoundrel
(New York: Ballantine Books, 2010)

Series: Stud Club Trilogy. Book 3
Story type: Historical - Regency
Subject(s): Love; Revenge; Family
Major character(s): Julian Bellamy, Friend (of Leo); Lily Chatwick, Sister (of Leo); Leo Chatwick, Crime Victim, Friend (of Julian), Brother (of Lily)
Time period(s): 19th century; 1810s
Locale(s): London, United Kingdom

Summary: The third and final novel in Tessa Dare's Stud Club Trilogy, *Three Nights with a Scoundrel* tells the story of Julian Bellamy, a young man who blames himself for the death of his best friend, Leo. Leo's sister, Lily Chatwick, does not blame Julian and watches helplessly as he sets out to exact a brutal revenge on those responsible for Leo's death. To thwart his plans for vengeance, Lily attempts to woo Julian into marriage, never suspecting that the two will fall in love in the process.

Where it's reviewed:
Booklist, August 1, 2010, page 35
Romantic Times, August 2010, page 40

Other books by the same author:
One Dance with a Duke, 2010
Twice Tempted by a Rogue, 2010
Goddess of the Hunt, 2009
A Lady of Persuasion, 2009
Surrender of a Siren, 2009

Other books you might like:
Mary Balogh, *First Comes Marriage*, 2009
Liz Carlyle, *Never Romance a Rake*, 2008

Madeline Hunter, *The Rules of Seduction*, 2006
Julia London, *The Dangers of Deceiving a Viscount*, 2007
Sophia Nash, *Secrets of a Scandalous Bride*, 2010

962

TESSA DARE   (Pseudonym of Eve Ortega)

Twice Tempted by a Rogue
(New York: Ballantine Books, 2010)

Series: Stud Club Trilogy. Book 2
Story type: Historical - Regency
Subject(s): Love; Adventure; Battle of Waterloo, 1815
Major character(s): Rhys St. Maur, Military Personnel; Meredith Maddox, Innkeeper
Time period(s): 19th century; 1810s
Locale(s): Devonshire, United Kingdom

Summary: Rhys St. Maur has returned from war and is stifled by grief over the loss of his best friend during a bloody battle. Back in Devonshire, he meets innkeeper Meredith Maddox, who is focused on her work and has no time for romance. But soon she cannot deny her attraction to the handsome Rhys, and the two have embarked upon a love affair that could set them both free from the pain of their respective pasts. *Twice Tempted by a Rogue* is the second book in Tessa Dare's Stud Club trilogy.

Where it's reviewed:
Romantic Times, July 2010, page 40

Other books by the same author:
One Dance with a Duke, 2010
Goddess of the Hunt, 2009
A Lady of Persuasion, 2009
Surrender of a Siren, 2009

Other books you might like:
Pamela Britton, *Seduced*, 2003
Gaelen Foley, *Her Only Desire*, 2007
Sabrina Jeffries, *Beware a Scot's Revenge*, 2007
Kasey Michaels, *A Gentleman by Any Other Name*, 2006

963

DEE DAVIS   (Pseudonym of Dee Davis Oberwetter)

Dangerous Desires
(New York: Forever, 2010)

Story type: Contemporary
Subject(s): Love; Adventure; Kidnapping
Major character(s): Drake, Agent (special forces); Madeline Reynard, Kidnap Victim
Time period(s): 21st century; 2010s
Locale(s): Colombia

Summary: Dee Davis's *Dangerous Desires* finds special forces agent Drake attempting to make his way out of the jungles of Colombia, where he has rescued the beautiful Madeline Reynard from a dangerous crime lord. But Madeline is not willing to go easily, not after spending so much time in captivity. She's going to fight Drake every step of the way. But how long can Madeline fight the mounting attraction between the two of them?

Where it's reviewed:
Romantic Times, July 2010, page 81

Other books by the same author:
Dark Deceptions, 2010
Desperate Deeds, 2010
Chain Reaction, 2007
A Match Made on Madison, 2007
Eye of the Storm, 2006

Other books you might like:
Cherry Adair, *Hide and Seek*, 2001
Cherry Adair, *Kiss and Tell*, 2000
Suzanne Brockmann, *Over the Edge*, 2001
Cindy Gerard, *To the Brink*, 2006
Cindy Gerard, *Whisper No Lies*, 2009

964

JO DAVIS

Ride the Fire

(New York: Signet, 2010)

Series: The Firefighters of Station Five Series. Book 5
Story type: Contemporary
Subject(s): Fires; Alcoholism; Love
Major character(s): Sean Tanner, Fire Fighter, Widow(er);
   Eve Marshall, Fire Fighter
Time period(s): 21st century; 2010s
Locale(s): United States

Summary: The fifth installment in Jo Davis's The Firefighters of Station Five series, *Ride the Fire*, tells the story of Captain Sean Tanner, who turned to the bottle after the sudden death of his wife and children. Now Sean is out of treatment and ready to be a part of Station Five again, but first, he's going to have to make amends for the wrongs of the past and prove himself as a capable fireman. When he meets fellow firefighter Eve Marshall, feelings he thought were long dead begin to stir, and Sean sees a second chance at happiness.

Where it's reviewed:
Romantic Times, December 2010, page 64

Other books by the same author:
I Spy a Dark Obsession, 2011
I Spy a Naughty Game, 2010
I Spy a Wicked Sin, 2010
Line of Fire, 2010
Hidden Fire, 2009

Other books you might like:
Cherry Adair, *White Heat*, 2007
Suzanne Brockmann, *Bodyguard*, 1999
Jasmine Cresswell, *Decoy*, 2004
Cindy Gerard, *Into the Dark*, 2007

965

LILA DIPASQUA

The Princess in His Bed

(New York: Berkley, 2010)

Story type: Historical
Subject(s): Love; Sexuality; History
Time period(s): 17th century
Locale(s): France

Summary: Lila DiPasqua's *The Princess in His Bed* is a collection of three novellas centering on fairy tale-like scenarios and lovelorn heroes and heroines. Against the backdrop of 17th-century France, each of the main characters that people these tales charts a course down the rocky road of love, finding challenges—and unexpected redemption—in the arms of their respective lovers.

Where it's reviewed:
Romantic Times, November 2010, page 45

Other books by the same author:
Awakened by a Kiss, 2010

Other books you might like:
Cherry Adair, *Black Magic*, 2010
Jennifer Armintrout, *Veil of Shadows*, 2009
Susan Grant, *Sureblood*, 2010
Karen Kelly, *The Falcon Prince*, 2010
Christina Skye, *Bound by Dreams*, 2009

966

CHRISTINA DODD

Chains of Fire

(New York: Penguin, 2010)

Series: Chosen Ones Series. Book 4
Story type: Fantasy; Series
Subject(s): Romances (Fiction); Fantasy; Good and evil
Major character(s): Samuel Faa, Lawyer, Psychic; Isabelle
   Mason, Heiress, Healer
Time period(s): 21st century; 2010s
Locale(s): Switzerland

Summary: In *Chains of Fire* by Christina Dodd, Samuel Faa and Isabelle Mason are Chosen Ones, an elite group bestowed with supernatural powers. Samuel, a Gypsy attorney, can control the minds of others. Isabelle, a rich socialite, has psychic healing skills. Though the two have a love-hate relationship, they must set aside their animosity as they embark on their assignment to release the Gypsy travel funds. In Switzerland, while they are buried beneath an icy avalanche, Samuel and Isabelle realize that the feelings they have hidden are about to emerge again. *Chains of Fire* is the fourth book in the Chosen Ones series.

Where it's reviewed:
Romantic Times, September 2010, page 93

Other books by the same author:
Chains of Ice, 2010
In Bed with the Duke, 2010

Danger in a Red Dress, 2009
Storm of Shadows, 2009
Storm of Visions, 2009

Other books you might like:
Christine Feehan, *Dark Curse*, 2008
Christine Feehan, *Murder Game*, 2008
Yasmine Galenorn, *Night Myst*, 2010
Jill Jones, *Circle of the Lily*, 1998
Eve Kenin, *Hidden*, 2008

967

KIT DONNER

The Vengeful Bridegroom

(New York: Zebra Books, 2010)

Story type: Historical
Subject(s): Romances (Fiction); History; Revenge
Major character(s): Madelene Colgate, Young Woman;
   Gabriel Westcott, Spouse (of Madelene)
Time period(s): 19th century; 1810s (1812)
Locale(s): London, England

Summary: In *The Vengeful Bridegroom* by Kit Donner, the
fate of a family's fortune lies in a daughter's ability to
find a groom. Madelene Colgate knows that she must get
married within three days in order to protect her family's
finances. Gabriel Westcott's appearance seems an answer
to her prayers. Eager to marry and good-looking, Gabriel
withholds his real motive until after the ceremony. An
adversary of the Colgate clan, Westcott wants only to
disgrace Madelene and her family. But as he gets to
know his lovely new bride he learns that he may have
gotten much more than he bargained for.

Other books by the same author:
The Notorious Bridegroom, 2009

Other books you might like:
Elizabeth Boyle, *Stealing the Bride*, 2003
Nicola Cornick, *The Scandals of an Innocent*, 2009
Jacquie D'Alessandro, *The Bride Thief*, 2002
Stephanie Laurens, *A Rogue's Proposal*, 1999
Sonia Simone, *Stealing Midnight*, 1996

968

SUSAN DONOVAN

Not That Kind of Girl

(New York: St. Martin's Press, 2010)

Story type: Contemporary
Subject(s): Love; Dogs; Interpersonal relations
Major character(s): Roxanne "Roxie" Bloom, Writer
   (blogger); Eli Gallagher, Trainer (dog trainer)
Time period(s): 21st century; 2010s
Locale(s): United States

Summary: Susan Donovan's *Not That Kind of Girl* charts
the romance between a man-hating blogger and a handsome dog trainer. Roxanne Bloom has had her heart
shattered one too many times, prompting her to start a

Web site devoted to man-bashing. When her dog Lilith
starts misbehaving (mostly toward men), Roxie reluctantly hires dog trainer Eli Gallagher to help tame the
pooch. But the closer Roxie and Eli get, the more Roxie
realizes that maybe *she* is the one who is being tamed by
this sensitive, sexy man.

Where it's reviewed:
Romantic Times, December 2010, page 74

Other books by the same author:
The Night She Got Lucky, 2010
Ain't Too Proud to Beg, 2009
The Girl Most Likely To..., 2008
The Kept Woman, 2006
He Loves Lucy, 2005

Other books you might like:
Toni Blake, *Sugar Creek*, 2010
Victoria Dahl, *Start Me Up*, 2009
Marie Farrarella, *Plain Jane and the Playboy*, 2009
Marilyn Pappano, *Intimate Enemy*, 2008

969

EILEEN DREYER

Barely a Lady

(New York: Forever, 2010)

Series: Drake's Rakes Series. Book 1
Story type: Historical
Subject(s): Love; Marriage; Battle of Waterloo, 1815
Major character(s): Olivia Grace, Spouse (ex-wife of
   Jack); Jack Wyndham, Spouse (ex-husband of
   Grace), Military Personnel
Time period(s): 19th century
Locale(s): United Kingdom

Summary: Olivia Grace's life changes forever when she
finds her former husband, Jack Wyndham, injured on the
battlefields of Waterloo. Strangely, Jack is wearing the
uniform of a French soldier, but even more troubling is
his total lack of memory. As Olivia nurses her ex-
husband back to health, she puts on the charade that the
two are still married in hopes of jogging his memory.
But the further the charade goes along, the more genuine
the feelings become for Olivia—and for Jack, who's
experiencing them for the first time. *Barely a Lady* is the
first book in Eileen Dreyer's Drake's Rakes series.

Where it's reviewed:
Booklist, July 2010, page 41
Library Journal, June 15, 2010, page 48
Romantic Times, July 2010, page 42

Other books by the same author:
Never a Gentleman, 2011
Sinners and Saints, 2005
Head Games, 2004
With a Vengeance, 2003
Brain Dead, 1998

Other books you might like:
Mary Balogh, *A Secret Affair*, 2010
Jo Beverley, *Lady Beware*, 2007
Gaelen Foley, *My Dangerous Duke*, 2010

Romances

Georgette Heyer, *An Infamous Army*, 1938
Eloisa James, *Duchess in Love*, 2002

970

TERRI DULONG

Casting Around

(New York: Kensington, 2010)

Story type: Contemporary
Subject(s): Love; Stepmothers; Family
Major character(s): Monica Brooks, Store Owner (owner of yarn shop), Spouse (of Adam), Stepmother (of Clarissa Jo); Adam Brooks, Spouse (of Monica), Father (of Clarissa Jo); Clarissa Jo, Daughter (of Adam), Stepdaughter (of Monica)
Time period(s): 21st century; 2010s
Locale(s): Cedar Key, Florida

Summary: Terri DuLong's *Casting Around* is the sequel to *Spinning Forward* and continues the adventures of yarn shop owner Monica Brooks. Monica has adjusted to life in Cedar Key, Florida, and come to embrace her job as proprietress of the local yarn supply store. But when her husband's daughter arrives on their doorstep, Monica faces the biggest challenge of her life: motherhood.

Where it's reviewed:
Romantic Times, December 2010, page 54

Other books by the same author:
Spinning Forward, 2009
Daughters of the Mill, 2004
Lost Souls of the Witches' Castle, 2002

Other books you might like:
Heidi Betts, *Knock Me for a Loop*, 2010
Kate Jacobs, *The Friday Night Knitting Club: A Novel*, 2007
Debbie Macomber, *Summer on Blossom Street*, 2009
Christie Ridgway, *Dirty Sexy Knitting*, 2009
Lori Wilde, *The Sweethearts' Knitting Club*, 2009

971

SUZANNE ENOCH

Rules of an Engagement

(New York: Avon, 2010)

Series: Adventurers Club Series. Book 3
Story type: Historical
Subject(s): Love; Adventure; Social class
Major character(s): Bradshaw Carroway, Sea Captain; Zephyr Ponsley, Noblewoman
Time period(s): 19th century
Locale(s): United Kingdom

Summary: In Suzanne Enoch's *Rules of an Engagement*, ship captain Bradshaw Carroway is less than thrilled about his latest job: shuttling a group of posh upper-crust society folk across the sea. There is, however, one bright spot in this bleak gig, and her name is Zephyr Ponsley. Zephyr is smart and sophisticated but totally naive when it comes to affairs of the heart. Fortunately,

Bradshaw is willing to take things slow and romance this beautiful young woman the way she deserves. This volume is the third novel in the Adventurers' Club series.

Where it's reviewed:
Romantic Times, November 2010, page 40

Other books by the same author:
A Lady's Guide to Improper Behavior, 2010
Always a Scoundrel, 2009
The Care and Taming of a Rogue, 2009
After the Kiss, 2008
Before the Scandal: The Notorious Gentlemen, 2008

Other books you might like:
Victoria Alexander, *Secrets of a Proper Lady*, 2007
Laura Lee Ghurke, *And Then He Kissed Her*, 2007
Karen Hawkins, *The Abduction of Julia*, 2000
Sabrina Jeffries, *Never Seduce a Scoundrel*, 2006
Stephanie Laurens, *The Lady Chosen*, 2003

972

ELIZABETH ESSEX

The Pursuit of Pleasure

(New York: Brava, 2010)

Story type: Historical - Georgian
Subject(s): Love; Marriage; Spies
Major character(s): Lizzie Paxton, Young Woman; Jameson Marlowe, Military Personnel
Time period(s): 18th century
Locale(s): United Kingdom

Summary: Elizabeth Essex's *The Pursuit of Pleasure* is set in Georgian-era England, where Lizzie Paxton agrees to marry a man who is about to fake his own death. Military captain Jameson Marlowe needs to infiltrate a group of weapons smugglers, and the only way he can successfully accomplish this is to stage his own demise. To make the scene more plausible, he needs a young widow to grieve for him, and Lizzie fits the bill. There's just one problem: Lizzie and Jameson are enchanted by one another and can soon no longer hide their true feelings. First novel.

Where it's reviewed:
Booklist, December 1, 2010, page 35
Romantic Times, December 2010, page 36

Other books you might like:
Elizabeth Boyle, *One Night of Passion*, 2002
Sylvia Day, *The Stranger I Married*, 2007
Michelle Marcos, *When a Lady Misbehaves*, 2007
Amanda Quick, *Seduction*, 1990
Julia Ross, *The Seduction*, 2002

973

CHRIS FABRY

Almost Heaven

(Carol Stream, Illinois: Tyndale House Publishers, 2010)

Subject(s): Christian life; Music; Musicians
Major character(s): Billy Allman, Musician; Malachi, Angel

Time period(s): 21st century; 2010s
Locale(s): Dogwood, West Virginia

Summary: In *Almost Heaven* by Chris Fabry, Billy Allman is astonishingly intelligent and a wonderful musician, but he has almost no social skills to speak of and lives in the hills of West Virginia, virtually ostracized from his community. He plays the mandolin as a testament to his love for God, though he finds that everything else in his life tends to go wrong. Billy chooses to build a radio station out of his home, using spare parts he has found throughout his life. Even as people in the town continue to ridicule him, an angel, Malachi, is sent by God to observe him. It becomes clear to Malachi just how important Billy's music will be to those who hear it.

Where it's reviewed:
Romantic Times, November 2010, page 58

Other books by the same author:
June Bug, 2009
The Winner's Manual: For the Game of Life, 2009
Dogwood, 2008
Blind Spot, 2007
Over the Wall, 2007

Other books you might like:
Debbie Macomber, *Shirley, Goodness, and Mercy*, 1999
Jeffrey Overstreet, *Raven's Ladder: A Novel*, 2010
Jonathan Rogers, *The Charlatan's Boy*, 2010
Sharon Carter Rogers, *Drift*, 2010
Anne Elisabeth Stenge, *Heartless*, 2010

974

CHRISTINE FEEHAN

Water Bound

(New York: Jove, 2010)

Series: Sisters of the Heart Series. Book 1
Story type: Fantasy
Subject(s): Magic; Memory disorders; Love
Major character(s): Rikki, Young Woman; Lev Prakenskii, Amnesiac

Summary: Rikki is a beautiful young woman who possesses magical powers. She leads a life of solace and fulfillment with a band of equally-gifted, adopted "sisters." But Rikki's peaceful existence is shattered when she dives into the sea to save Lev Prakenskii, a handsome stranger with no memory of the past. When Rikki pulls Lev from the water, he explains his last memory is of falling in. As the two set out to uncover the mystery of Lev's identity, they can't help but be attracted to one another—despite the danger it may present. *Water Bound* is the first book in Christine Feehan's Sisters of the Heart series.

Where it's reviewed:
Library Journal, August 2010, page 59
Romantic Times, August 2010, page 88

Other books by the same author:
Ruthless Game, 2011
Dark Peril, 2010
Street Game, 2010

Wild Fire, 2010
Dark Slayer, 2009

Other books you might like:
Virginia Kantra, *Sea Fever*, 2008
Jayne Ann Krentz, *Sizzle and Burn*, 2008
Cait London, *At the Edge*, 2007
Loucinda McGary, *The Wild Irish Sea*, 2010
Nora Roberts, *Blue Smoke*, 2005

975

SHERRY LYNN FERGUSON

Major Lord David

(New York: Avalon Books, 2010)

Story type: Historical - Regency
Subject(s): Love; Marriage; Identity
Major character(s): David Trent, Nobleman; Wilhelmina "Billie" Caswell, Daughter (of David's neighbor)
Time period(s): 19th century
Locale(s): United Kingdom

Summary: Sherry Lynn Ferguson's *Major Lord David* is set in Regency England and follows the love that develops between honorable nobleman David Trent and his neighbor's daughter, the beautiful Billie Caswell. One night at a masked ball, David kisses an irresistible young woman, having no idea the woman is actually Billie. When news of the kiss spreads, he proposes marriage, but Billie refuses. Though she loves David with all her heart, she must convince him to fall in love with her before she will entertain the idea of marriage.

Where it's reviewed:
Booklist, September 15, 2010, page 46

Other books by the same author:
Quiet Meg, 2008
The Honorable Marksley, 2007

Other books you might like:
Blair Bancroft, *The Major Meets His Match*, 2003
Susannah Carleton, *The Marriage Campaign*, 2003
Megan Frampton, *A Singular Lady*, 2005
Barbara Metzger, *Miss Westlake's Windfall*, 2001
Rhonda Woodward, *Lady Emma's Dilemma*, 2005

976

GAELEN FOLEY

My Dangerous Duke

(New York: Avon, 2010)

Story type: Historical - Regency
Subject(s): Romances (Fiction); History; Sexuality
Major character(s): Rohan Kilburn, Nobleman (Duke of Warrington); Kate Madsen, Young Woman
Time period(s): 19th century; 1800s
Locale(s): London, England

Summary: *My Dangerous Duke* is a Regency romance novel by Gaelen Foley. In the novel, Rohan Kilburn, the Duke of Warrington, is a member of the Inferno Club. The men in the club are a secretive group of aristocrats who fight to protect the king and England. The Warrington men are historically cursed in love, so Rohan has decided to devote his entire life to the Inferno Club. Then Kate Madsen is brought to him by the other men as a type of "sacrificial virgin" in an attempt to calm his temper; however, Kate is too headstrong to agree to any such arrangement. Soon, Rohan realizes that his feelings for her go beyond lust, and that despite his better intentions, he is falling in love with her.

Where it's reviewed:
Romantic Times, July 2010, page 40

Other books by the same author:
My Irresistible Earl, 2011
My Wicked Marquess, 2009
Her Every Pleasure, 2008
Her Only Desire, 2007
Her Secret Fantasy, 2007

Other books you might like:
Elizabeth Boyle, *This Rake of Mine*, 2005
Eileen Dreyer, *Barely a Lady*, 2010
Katherine Greyle, *No Place for a Lady*, 2003
Cathy Maxwell, *A Seduction at Christmas*, 2008
Mary Jo Putney, *Never Less than a Lady*, 2010

977

DELORES FOSSEN

Wild Stallion

(Toronto: Harlequin, 2010)

Story type: Ranch Life
Subject(s): Western fiction; Romances (Fiction); Kidnapping
Major character(s): Bailey Hodges, Mother; Jackson Malone, Rancher, Father (adoptive)

Summary: *Wild Stallion* is a Harlequin romance by author Delores Fossen. Lonely and forlorn Bailey Hodges is thrilled when she finds out she is pregnant: finally, she can share her love with a little baby. However, the moment her baby boy is born, he is stolen in a horrific confrontation. Now Bailey must fight to find her kidnapped child, and that means going up against the most ruthless man around, Jackson Malone. Jackson has adopted Bailey's son under the guise that Bailey was dead, and Bailey is in for the fight of her life to get him back. But when Jackson turns out to be more protective and gentle than she could have ever imagined, Bailey finally sees hope for her future. Unfortunately, an even worse threat lurks near. Can Jackson protect his newfound family before it is too late?

Where it's reviewed:
Romantic Times, December 2010, page 86

Other books by the same author:
The Baby's Guardian, 2010
Daddy Devastating, 2010
The Mommy Mystery, 2010
Savior in the Saddle, 2010
She's Positive, 2009

Other books you might like:
Carolyn Davidson, *Maggie's Beau*, 2001

Jill Gregory, *Once an Outlaw*, 2001
Charlene Sands, *Taming the Texan*, 2008
Bobbi Smith, *Wanted: The Texan*, 2008
Jodi Thomas, *Tall, Dark, and Texan*, 2008

978

LORI FOSTER
SUSAN DONOVAN, Co-Author
VICTORIA DAHL, Co-Author

The Guy Next Door

(Don Mills, Ontario: Harlequin, 2010)

Story type: Collection
Subject(s): Short stories; Romances (Fiction); Interpersonal relations

Summary: *The Guy Next Door* is a collection of three short stories written by popular romance authors, Lori Foster, Susan Donovan, and Victoria Dahl. In Foster's "Ready, Set, Jett," she tells the story of Natalie Alexander, a teacher who wants nothing more than a casual affair with her neighbor, Jett Sutter. But when Jett wants more than just a fun romance, Natalie realizes she signed up for more than she bargained for. In "Gail's Gone Wild," by Donovan, university professor Gail Chapman takes her daughter on a vacation to Key West for some fun in the sun. There she meets Jesse Batista, a handsome writer who is booked in the hotel room next door. Dahl's "Just One Taste" tells the story of a romance between Eric Donovan, owner of a local brewery, and erotic store owner Beth Cantrell. All three short stories focus on the relationships and romances of strong, independent women as they fall for the guy next door.

Where it's reviewed:
Publishers Weekly, January 3, 2011, page 38

Other books you might like:
Victoria Dahl, *Start Me Up*, 2009
Louisa Edwards, *Can't Stand the Heat*, 2009
Sue Margolis, *Forget Me Knot*, 2009
Carol Snow, *Just Like Me, Only Better*, 2010

979

CAROLINE FYFFE

Montana Dawn

(Wayne, Pennsylvania: Leisure Books, 2010)

Story type: Western
Subject(s): Romances (Fiction); Western fiction; Grief
Major character(s): Luke McCutcheon, Rancher; Faith Brown, Single Mother, Widow(er)
Time period(s): 19th century; 1880-1890 (1883)
Locale(s): Montana, United States

Summary: In Caroline Fyffe's *Montana Dawn*, Luke McCutcheon finds Faith Brown in the midst of giving labor on a wagon trail in Montana. Though he doesn't know her, he helps deliver the baby and then takes her into his care. As they ride the trail, Luke and Faith learn about each other's past. Luke has let one too many chances at love slip away, while Faith fell in love fast and was crushed by the death of her new husband. Now, Luke's only responsibilities are for himself, and Faith is poor and left alone to care for her newborn child. Can they learn to love and trust each other enough to start a new family? Is this their last chance at true love and a happy ending?

Where it's reviewed:
Romantic Times, August 2010, page 46

Other books by the same author:
Where the Wind Blows, 2009

Other books you might like:
Leigh Greenwood, *Daisy*, 1996
Lorraine Heath, *Never Marry a Cowboy*, 2001
Jill Marie Landis, *Summer Moon*, 2001
Maggie Osborne, *Prairie Moon*, 2002
Jodi Thomas, *The Lone Texan*, 2009

980

TINA GABRIELLE

A Perfect Scandal

(New York: Zebra, 2010)

Story type: Historical - Regency
Subject(s): Love; Artists; Marriage
Major character(s): Isabelle Cameron, Artist; Markus Hawksley, Businessman
Time period(s): 19th century
Locale(s): London, United Kingdom

Summary: In Tina Gabrielle's *A Perfect Scandal*, Lady Isabelle Cameron is about to enter into an arranged marriage she wants no part of. Isabelle's dream is to study art, not give in to the pressures of Regency-era London. When her childhood crush, Marcus Hawksley, reenters her life, she sees the perfect escape from her impending nuptials and sets out to ruin her reputation with Marcus. The plan goes off without a hitch, and soon Isabelle and Marcus are engaged to be married. But what happens when these two friends find a genuine passion that cannot be denied?

Where it's reviewed:
Romantic Times, October 2010, page 45

Other books by the same author:
Lady of Scandal, 2009

Other books you might like:
Anne Gracie, *To Catch a Bride*, 2009
Lisa Kleypas, *Married by Morning*, 2010
Kat Martin, *Rule's Bride*, 2010
Gail Ranstrom, *Unlacing Lilly*, 2008

981

ALICE GAINES

Miss Foster's Folly

(Carina Press, 2010)

Story type: Historical
Subject(s): Romances (Fiction); British history, 1815-1914; Marriage

Major character(s): Juliet Foster, Spinster, Wealthy; David Winslow, Nobleman (marquess), Bachelor
Time period(s): 19th century; 1880s (1886)
Locale(s): England; New York, New York

Summary: *Miss Foster's Folly* is a historical romance novel from author Alice Gaines. It's 1886 and, at the age of 32, Juliet Foster has just become the wealthiest bachelorette in Manhattan. Her unpleasant and controlling father has died, leaving his millions to Juliet. Free to live any life she wants, Juliet sets out on a steamy adventure across London to find as many lovers as possible. As the Marquess of Derrington, David Winslow is determined to find a wife. If he hopes to break his family's curse, he must marry a woman as strong-willed and independent as himself. After one night with Juliet, David wants to make an honest woman out of her, but she's not interested in anything besides a passionate affair. Can David change Juliet's mind about marriage and tame her once and for all?

Where it's reviewed:
Romantic Times, September 2010, page 44

Other books by the same author:
My Lady's Pleasure, 2010
Can't Hide Love, 2009
Child of Balance, 2009
Dr. Feelgood, 2009
To Touch a Woman, 2009

Other books you might like:
Susan Gee Heino, *Mistress by Mistake*, 2009
Lavinia Kent, *A Talent for Sin*, 2009
Kat Martin, *Reese's Bride*, 2009
Kat Martin, *Rule's Bride*, 2010

982

SHANA GALEN

The Making of a Gentleman

(Naperville, Illinois: Sourcebooks Casablanca, 2010)

Series: Sons of the Revolution Trilogy. Book 2
Story type: Historical - French Revolution
Subject(s): Love; Teachers; Prisoners
Major character(s): Felicity Bennett, Governess; Armand Harcourt, Prisoner (former prisoner)
Time period(s): 18th century; 1780s
Locale(s): France

Summary: Felicity Bennett is a beautiful governess recruited to help a man recently released from prison. Armand Harcourt can no longer speak after spending the last 12 years as a prisoner of the French Revolution. With Felicity's help, however, Armand may just learn to speak—and love—again. Shana Galen's *The Making of a Gentleman* is the second book in the Sons of the Revolution series.

Where it's reviewed:
Publishers Weekly, August 9, 2010, page 36
Romantic Times, October 2010, page 44

Other books by the same author:
The Making of a Rogue, 2011
The Making of a Duchess, 2010

Romances

Blackthorne's Bride, 2007
Good Groom Hunting, 2007
No Man's Bride, 2006

Other books you might like:
Mary Balogh, *Simply Love*, 2006
Jo Beverley, *To Rescue a Rogue*, 2006
Christina Dodd, *Move Heaven and Earth*, 1995
Laura Kinsale, *Flowers from the Storm*, 1992
Mary Jo Putney, *Thunder and Roses*, 1993

983

YASMINE GALENORN

Night Myst

(New York: Jove, 2010)

Series: Indigo Court Series. Book 1
Subject(s): Sexuality; Vampires; Fairies
Major character(s): Cicely Waters, Witch; Myst, Vampire
Time period(s): 21st century; 2010s
Locale(s): New Forest, Washington

Summary: *Night Myst* is the first book in the Indigo Court series by Yasmine Galenorn. The book takes place in New Forest, Washington, where centuries ago, a group of vampires attempted to turn the Dark Fae. They hoped to gain some of their magic and power, but instead, created an entirely new and incredibly powerful demonic race. Myst, who is now the Vampiric Fae Queen of the Indigo Court, is planning to start a deadly supernatural war. Cicely Waters is a witch who left New Forest years ago but is forced to come back with this turn of events. She has the ability to control the power of the wind and is the one who has been prophesied to stop the supernatural war. In addition, only she can save the man she loves, a Fae, from Myst's clutches.

Where it's reviewed:
Romantic Times, July 2010, page 105

Other books by the same author:
Blood Wyne, 2011
Bone Magic, 2010
Harvest Hunting, 2010
Demon Mistress, 2009
Night Huntress, 2009
Dragon Wytch, 2008
Changeling, 2007
Darkling, 2007

Other books you might like:
Anya Bast, *Wicked Enchantment*, 2010
Anya Bast, *Witch Fire*, 2007
Jeaniene Frost, *At Grave's End: A Night Huntress Novel*, 2008
Sherrilyn Kenyon, *Stroke of Midnight*, 2004
Sherrilyn Kenyon, *Unleash the Night*, 2006

984

DIANE GASTON (Pseudonym of Diane Perkins)

Chivalrous Captain, Rebel Mistress

(Toronto; New York: Harlequin, 2010)

Story type: Historical - Regency
Subject(s): Love; Battle of Waterloo, 1815; Marriage
Major character(s): Allan Landon, Military Personnel; Marian Pallant, Young Woman
Time period(s): 19th century; 1810s
Locale(s): London, United Kingdom

Summary: In Diane Gaston's *Chivalrous Captain, Rebel Mistress*, Captain Allan Landon is a handsome redcoat fighting the Battle of Waterloo when, during the bloodshed, he stumbles upon an injured boy. He soon finds that this is no boy, it's the beautiful Marian Pallant, and he sets out to protect her at all costs. The two are eventually separated by the demands of war, but when they are reunited in London, the sparks once again fly—and Allan is faced with the biggest decision of his life.

Where it's reviewed:
Booklist, September 15, 2010, page 53
Romantic Times, September 2010, page 45

Other books by the same author:
Gallant Officer, Forbidden Lady, 2009
Scandalizing the Ton, 2008
The Vanishing Viscountess, 2008
Innocence and Impropriety, 2007
A Reputable Rake, 2006

Other books you might like:
Louise Allen, *The Viscount's Betrothal*, 2010
Jo Beverley, *The Rogue's Return*, 2006
Candice Hern, *Lady Be Bad*, 2007
Julia Justiss, *The Proper Wife*, 2001
Carole Mortimer, *Lady Arabella's Scandalous Marriage*, 2010

985

NANCY GIDEON

Chased by Moonlight

(New York: Pocket Books, 2010)

Series: Moonlight Series. Book 2
Story type: Romantic Suspense
Subject(s): Romances (Fiction); Supernatural; Mystery
Major character(s): Charlotte Caissie, Detective, Lover (of Max); Max Savoie, Shape-Shifter, Crime Suspect, Lover (of Charlotte)
Time period(s): 21st century; 2010s
Locale(s): United States

Summary: *Chased by Moonlight* is a supernatural romance novel from award-winning author Nancy Gideon. For Detective Charlotte Caissie, the lines between her private and professional lives just got incredibly blurry. Her sexy shape-shifting lover, Max Savoie, has been accused of murder and it's up to Charlotte to prove his innocence. In order to focus on the case, Charlotte needs space from

Max, but trying to deny their attraction and passion is proving more difficult than either imagined. Max's dark past is filled with secrecy and mystery, but he's desperate to uncover the truth about whom he really is. As Max searches for answers, he fears that his real identity might push Charlotte away forever.

Where it's reviewed:
Romantic Times, July 2010, page 98

Other books by the same author:
Captured by Moonlight, 2010
Masked by Moonlight, 2010
Warrior for One Night, 2007
Warrior's Second Chance, 2006
Warrior without Rules, 2005

Other books you might like:
Sherrilyn Kenyon, *Stroke of Midnight*, 2004
Sherrilyn Kenyon, *Unleash the Night*, 2006
J.D. Robb, *Naked in Death*, 1995
Rebecca York, *Crimson Moon*, 2005
Rebecca York, *Killing Moon*, 2003

986

JO GOODMAN (Pseudonym of Joanne Dobrzanski)

Marry Me

(New York: Zebra, 2010)

Story type: Western
Subject(s): Love; Family; Identity
Major character(s): Dr. Coleridge "Cole" Monroe, Doctor; Rhyne Abbott, Young Woman; Judah Abbott, Father (of Rhyne)
Time period(s): 19th century; 1880s (1884)
Locale(s): Reidsville, Colorado

Summary: In 1884 Colorado, Dr. Coleridge Monroe has come to establish a medical practice in the small mountain town of Reidsville. There he meets the town killjoy, a crotchety old man with a soft-spoken son named Runt. But Cole soon learns that Runt Abbott is not a boy at all, but a beautiful young woman. And there is an immediate attraction between the two, awakening feelings Rhyne Abbott never knew she possessed. Jo Goodman's *Marry Me* is the sequel to *Never Love a Lawman*.

Where it's reviewed:
Booklist, September 15, 2010, page 48
Library Journal, December 2010, page 97
Publishers Weekly, September 27, 2010, page 43
Romantic Times, December 2010, page 42

Other books by the same author:
Never Love a Lawman, 2009
The Price of Desire, 2008
If His Kiss Is Wicked, 2007
One Forbidden Evening, 2006
A Season to Be Sinful, 2005

Other books you might like:
C.H. Admirand, *The Rancher's Heart*, 2007
Lorraine Heath, *Hard Lovin' Man*, 2003

Maggie Osborne, *The Seduction of Samantha Kincade*, 1995
Maggie Osborne, *Silver Lining*, 2000
Patricia Potter, *Defiant*, 1995

987

ANNE GRACIE

The Accidental Wedding

(New York: Berkley Books, 2010)

Story type: Historical
Subject(s): Rural life; Memory disorders; Romances (Fiction)
Major character(s): Nash Renfrew, Diplomat; Maddy Woodford, Caregiver (of Nash)
Time period(s): 21st century; 2010s
Locale(s): England

Summary: Nash Renfrew wants two things in life: to be successful and to find a mate. As a diplomat for England, he's already achieved the first goal and is trying to move on to the second when he meets a terrible accident. He awakes in a country cottage with a beautiful woman named Maddy Woodford taking care of him and no memory of his previous life. Yet, as he learns more about whom he was before the accident, he begins to wonder if he didn't have his priorities mixed up, and if he might be where he was supposed to end up all along.

Where it's reviewed:
Romantic Times, October 2010, page 45

Other books by the same author:
To Catch a Bride, 2009
His Captive Lady, 2008
The Stolen Princess, 2008
The Perfect Kiss, 2007
The Perfect Stranger, 2006

Other books you might like:
Jo Beverley, *The Rogue's Return*, 2006
Julia Justiss, *The Proper Wife*, 2001
Edith Layton, *To Wed a Stranger*, 2003
Barbara Metzger, *The Bargain Bride*, 2009
Diane Perkins, *The Marriage Bargain*, 2005

988

HEATHER GRAHAM

Ghost Shadow

(Don Mills, Ontario: Mira, 2010)

Subject(s): Romances (Fiction); Mystery; Murder
Major character(s): Katie O'Hara, Businesswoman; David Beckett, Museum Curator
Time period(s): 21st century; 2010s
Locale(s): Florida, United States

Summary: In *Ghost Shadow*, a novel by Heather Graham, Katie O'Hara is the successful owner of a karaoke business who has just decided to purchase and reopen an old wax museum. The museum closed ten years ago when a

Romances

woman was found murdered in one of the exhibits; she just happened to be the fiancee of David Beckett, one of the owners of the wax museum, and was discovered by him. The crime was never solved, and Beckett left town under suspicion. When Katie attempts to purchase the museum, however, he comes back to halt the sale; then, another murder victim is found in a second museum. Katie has the unique ability to communicate with ghosts, and finds herself drawn into the mystery, even as she begins to receive warnings from the other side. In addition, she feels an irresistible attraction to David, unable to believe that he is a murderer.

Where it's reviewed:
Romantic Times, July 2010, page 97

Other books by the same author:
Ghost Moon, 2010
Ghost Night, 2010
Dust to Dust, 2009
Nightwalker, 2009

Other books you might like:
Jayne Ann Krentz, *Sizzle and Burn*, 2008
Holly Lisle, *Midnight Rain*, 2004
Cait London, *At the Edge*, 2007
Cait London, *For Her Eyes Only*, 2008
Cait London, *A Stranger's Touch*, 2008

989

HEATHER GRAHAM   (Pseudonym of Heather Graham Pozzessere)

Night of the Vampires

(Don Mills, Ontario, Canada: HQN, 2010)

Story type: Historical - American Civil War; Vampire Story
Subject(s): Vampires; United States Civil War, 1861-1865; Romances (Fiction)
Major character(s): Cole Granger, Lawman (sheriff), Military Personnel (soldier), Vampire Hunter; Megan Fox, Vampire Hunter
Time period(s): 19th century; 1860s
Locale(s): United States

Summary: *Night of the Vampires* is a supernatural romance novel set during the Civil War. Cole Granger is a soldier and Texas sheriff, risking his life to bring order and peace to his nation. Unfortunately, there's another war going on that's far more sinister than the battle between the Confederacy and the Union. A legion of vampires has unleashed their wrath on America and it's up to Cole and his friends to stop them. Megan Fox is determined to uncover the truth about a dark family secret that's somehow connected to the Virginia vampire riots. The only way Megan can get the answers she needs is by joining forces with Cole, despite their mutual mistrust and undeniable chemistry. As Megan and Cole get nearer to the truth, their hearts grow closer together, but Megan's dark past threatens to pull them apart forever.

Other books by the same author:
Heart of Evil, 2011
Phantom Evil, 2011

Ghost Moon, 2010
Ghost Night, 2010
Ghost Shadow, 2010

Other books you might like:
Meljean Brook, *Demon Moon*, 2007
Emma Holly, *Hot Spell*, 2005
Sherrilyn Kenyon, *Unleash the Night*, 2006
Liz Maverick, *Crimson City*, 2005
Pamela Palmer, *The Dark Gate*, 2007

990

HEATHER GRAHAM   (Pseudonym of Heather Graham Pozzessere)

The Keepers

(Toronto, Ontario, Canada: Harlequin, 2010)

Story type: Vampire Story
Subject(s): Vampires; Supernatural; Murder
Major character(s): Jagger DeFarge, Vampire, Detective; Fiona MacDonald, Police Officer (keeper)
Time period(s): 21st century; 2010s
Locale(s): New Orleans, Louisiana

Summary: *The Keepers* is a supernatural romance novel from author Heather Graham. In the haunted and divided city of New Orleans, Fiona MacDonald and her sisters utilize their supernatural skills and strength to serve as keepers, an extraordinary group responsible for policing the otherworldly creatures that roam their city. Fiona is responsible for overseeing the vampires to ensure that peace remains between them and the shape-shifters. When a body drained of blood is discovered, vampire detective Jagger DeFarge must join forces with Fiona to find the murderer. As the killings continue, it becomes increasingly obvious that a rogue vampire is on the loose threatening to destroy the city's peace. When the killer plots to make Fiona his next victim, Jagger must decide between his own species and the woman who has captured his heart.

Where it's reviewed:
Romantic Times, October 2010, page 105

Other books by the same author:
Heart of Evil, 2011
Phantom Evil, 2011
Ghost Moon, 2010
Ghost Night, 2010
Ghost Shadow, 2010

Other books you might like:
Amanda Ashley, *After Sundown*, 2003
Christine Feehan, *Dark Symphony*, 2003
Shiloh Walker, *Hunter's Need*, 2009
Christine Warren, *Born to be Wild*, 2010

991

AMANDA GRANGE
SHARON LATHAN, Co-Author
CAROLYN EBERHART, Co-Author

A Darcy Christmas

(Naperville, Illinois: Sourcebooks Landmark, 2010)

Story type: Historical
Subject(s): Love; Family; Christmas
Major character(s): Fitzwilliam Darcy, Hero; Lizzie Bennet, Heroine
Time period(s): 19th century
Locale(s): United Kingdom

Summary: In *A Darcy Christmas*, acclaimed romance authors Amanda Grange, Sharon Lathan, and Carolyn Eberhart present three novellas set during the holiday season and inspired by Jane Austen's classic *Pride and Prejudice.* "Mr. Darcy's Christmas Carol" offers an alternate perspective on Charles Dickens's classic story, while "A Darcy Christmas" finds Darcy and Lizzie dreaming of future holidays together. Grange's "Christmas Present" finds the couple traveling to the Bingley household for a holiday celebration, where a surprise awaits them.

Other books you might like:
Sandra Heath, *A Regency Christmas*, 2002
Sandra Heath, *A Regency Christmas Feast: Five Stories*, 1996
Carla Kelly, *A Regency Christmas Present*, 1999
Barbara Metzger, *Regency Christmas Courtship*, 2005
Elizabeth Rolls, *Mistletoe Kisses*, 2006

992

DONNA GRANT

Wicked Highlander

(New York: St. Martin's Press, 2010)

Series: Dark Sword Series. Book 3
Story type: Fantasy
Subject(s): Magic; Immortality; Love
Major character(s): Quinn MacLeod, Warrior; Marcail, Young Woman; Deirdre, Mythical Creature (druid; enemy of Quinn)
Time period(s): 17th century
Locale(s): Scotland

Summary: Donna Grant's *Wicked Highlander* is the third novel in the Dark Sword series. This outing centers on the romance between immortal Quinn MacLeod and the Druid-raised beauty Marcail. When the two meet, Quinn finds his notorious anger quieted by Marcail's powerful presence, but the lovers are about to face down Quinn's mortal enemy, Deirdre. Deirdre has laid plans to entangle Quinn and Marcail in her deceitful web, and their love will face a series of deadly challenges.

Where it's reviewed:
Romantic Times, November 2010, page 38

Other books by the same author:

Forbidden Highlander, 2010
Highland Dawn, 2010
Dangerous Highlander, 2009
Highland Nights, 2009
Highland Mist, 2006

Other books you might like:
Victoria Alexander, *What a Lady Wants*, 2007
Jo Beverley, *Devilish*, 2000
Donna Grant, *Dangerous Highlander*, 2010
Amanda Scott, *Seduced by a Rogue*, 2010

993

ALLEGRA GRAY (Pseudonym of Allegra Johnston)

Nothing but Deception

(New York: Zebra Books/Kensington Publishing, 2010)

Story type: Historical; Romantic Suspense
Subject(s): British history, 1714-1815; Romances (Fiction); Deception
Major character(s): Beatrice Pullingham, Widow(er), Lady; Jean-Philippe Durand, Artist
Time period(s): 19th century; 1810s (1815)
Locale(s): England

Summary: *Nothing but Deception* is a steamy historical romance novel from author Allegra Gray. Despite being a breathtaking beauty, Lady Beatrice Pullingham has never known love, much less great passion, but all of that is about to change with the arrival of a mysterious and sexy French painter. Jean-Philippe Durand has come to England in search of his real father, but after one glimpse of Beatrice, he knows he must paint her. Beatrice agrees to pose for Jean-Philippe, unaware that she's going to learn the true role of an artistic muse. As the pair begins to fall madly in love, Jean-Philippe grows suspicious that Beatrice is keeping a secret from him...a secret that could destroy their love and lives forever.

Where it's reviewed:
Romantic Times, August 2010, page 46

Other books by the same author:
Nothing but Scandal, 2009

Other books you might like:
Celeste Bradley, *One Night with a Spy*, 2006
Celeste Bradley, *The Spy*, 2004
Jane Feather, *A Husband's Wicked Ways*, 2009
Stephanie Laurens, *The Lady Chosen*, 2003
Jenna Petersen, *From London with Love*, 2006

994

JENNIFER GREENE (Pseudonym of Alison Hart)

Mesmerizing Stranger

(Toronto; New York: Harlequin, 2010)

Story type: Contemporary
Subject(s): Love; Cruise ships; Murder
Major character(s): Harm Connolly, Businessman; Cate Campbell, Cook

Romances (side tab)

Time period(s): 21st century; 2010s

Summary: Jennifer Greene's *Mesmerizing Stranger* is set onboard a cruise ship, where businessman Harm Connolly has booked passage for a little pampering and retreat from the workaday world. When he meets the ship's chef, however, all hope of a non-eventful vacation is lost. Chef Cate Campbell is sexy, talented, and whip-smart, and she's seen Harm's kind before; she knows how to deal with passengers like him. But when one of Harm's colleagues is killed aboard the ship, he and Cate will have to work together to stop a killer.

Where it's reviewed:
Romantic Times, September 2010, page 111

Other books by the same author:
Secretive Stranger, 2010
Blame It On Paris, 2008
Blame It On Cupid, 2007
The Soon-to-be-Disinherited Wife, 2006
Sparkle, 2006

Other books you might like:
Michele Albert, *Hide in Plain Sight*, 2006
Linda Winstead Jones, *Truly, Madly, Dangerously*, 2005
Virginia Kantra, *Stolen Memory*, 2005
Elizabeth Lowell, *Death Echo*, 2010
Sydney Ryan, *High-Heeled Alibi*, 2006

995

VANESSA DAVIS GRIGGS

Ray of Hope

(New York: Dafina, 2010)

Story type: Contemporary
Subject(s): Family; Faith; Christian life
Major character(s): Ma Ray Nichols, Grandmother (of Sahara and Crystal); Sahara, Granddaughter (of Ma Ray), 17-Year-Old; Crystal, Granddaughter (of Ma Ray), 15-Year-Old
Time period(s): 21st century; 2010s
Locale(s): United States

Summary: Vanessa Davis Griggs charts the family drama that evolves over the course of one fateful summer in *Ray of Hope*. Ma Ray Nichols takes in her two street-wise grandchildren in hopes of giving them a break from big-city life. She soon realizes the challenges the summer will hold, testing her relationships with 17-year-old Sahara and 15-year-old Crystal and forcing her to examine her relationships with her family and with her faith.

Where it's reviewed:
Booklist, December 1, 2010, page 27

Other books by the same author:
Strongholds, 2010
The Truth Is the Light, 2010
Goodness and Mercy, 2009
Practicing What You Preach, 2009
If Memory Serves, 2008

Other books you might like:
Rhonda Bowen, *Man Enough for Me*, 2011

Harry Lee Kraus, *The Six-Liter Club*, 2010
Vanessa Miller, *A Love for Tomorrow*, 2010
Pat Simmons, *Still Guilty*, 2010
Michelle Stimpson, *Last Temptation*, 2010

996

GEMMA HALLIDAY

The Perfect Shot

(Seattle: CreateSpace, 2010)

Story type: Contemporary
Subject(s): Love; Suspense; Photography
Major character(s): Cameron "Cam" Dakota, Photographer; Trace Brody, Actor
Time period(s): 21st century; 2010s
Locale(s): Los Angeles, California

Summary: Gemma Halliday's *The Perfect Shot* finds paparazzi photographer Cameron "Cam" Dakota trailing a handsome, A-list actor named Trace Brody. Trace is about to be married in a no-holds-barred wedding extravaganza, and Cam is determined to get the most intimate photos of the big event. But when she witnesses Trace apparently being assaulted at gunpoint, Cam is thrust into the dangerous web of a dark mystery—a mystery she must unravel if she herself doesn't want to end up in the city morgue.

Where it's reviewed:
Romantic Times, September 2010, page 76

Other books by the same author:
Mayhem in High Heels, 2009
Scandal Sheet, 2009
Alibi in High Heels, 2008
Killer in High Heels, 2007
Undercover in High Heels, 2007

Other books you might like:
Nina Bruhns, *If Looks Could Chill*, 2009
Linda Howard, *Burn*, 2009
Christy Reece, *No Chance*, 2010
Stephanie Tyler, *Hard to Hold*, 2009

997

DARCI HANNAH

The Exile of Sara Stevenson: A Historical Novel

(New York: Ballantine Books, 2010)

Subject(s): Time travel; Romances (Fiction); Letters (Correspondence)
Major character(s): Sara Stevenson, Young Woman (pregnant), Lover (of Thomas Crichton), Friend (of William Campbell), Daughter (of Robert Stevenson), Exile; Thomas Crichton, Young Man, Sailor, Lover (of Sara Stevenson); William Campbell, Widow(er), Lighthouse Keeper, Friend (of Sara Stevenson); Robert Stevenson, Father (of Sara Stevenson), Designer (of lighthouses)

Time period(s): 19th century; 1810-1820 (1814)
Locale(s): Edinburgh, Scotland

Summary: In Darci Hannah's *The Exile of Sara Stevenson: A Historic Novel*, young lovers Sara Stevenson and Thomas Crichton hatch a plan to secretly marry. When Thomas, a sailor, fails to show, Sara is left alone and pregnant. After her father, lighthouse designer Robert Stevenson, finds out about her predicament, he exiles her to a lighthouse on Cape Wrath in northwest Scotland. There Sara befriends William Campbell, the lighthouse keeper, who is haunted by his past. William helps Sara correspond with an Oxford antiquarian who has ties to Thomas. As time passes, Sara and William grow much closer, and their friendship develops into feelings of romantic love. Will Sara forget about Thomas and start a new life with William?

Where it's reviewed:
Kirkus Reviews, March 1, 2010, page 223
Library Journal, May 1, 2010, page 65
Publishers Weekly, May 24, 2010, page 32
Romantic Times, November 2010, page 47

Other books you might like:
Anna Campbell, *My Reckless Surrender*, 2010
Jennifer Crusie, *Maybe This Time*, 2010
Juliet Gael, *Romancing Miss Bronte*, 2010
Kat Martin, *Reese's Bride*, 2009

998

MEGAN HART

Precious and Fragile Things

(New York: Mira, 2011)

Story type: Contemporary
Subject(s): Love; Kidnapping; Mothers
Major character(s): Gilly Solomon, Kidnap Victim, Mother; Todd, Kidnapper (of Gilly)
Time period(s): 21st century; 2010s
Locale(s): United States

Summary: In Megan Hart's *Precious and Fragile Things*, Gilly Solomon is a young mother on the verge of a breakdown. When she is carjacked and subsequently held captive, part of her is relieved to have a little respite from her harried life. Gilly slowly gets to know her captor, Todd, who is not the monster she first thought he was. A connection develops between the two, and Gilly's life and emotions are thrown into turmoil by her feelings for the man holding her hostage.

Where it's reviewed:
Publishers Weekly, October 25, 2010, page 28

Other books by the same author:
Collide, 2011
Naked, 2010
Switch, 2010
All You Can Eat, 2009
Deeper, 2009

Other books you might like:
Linda Howard, *Burn*, 2009
Ana Leigh, *Holding Out for a Hero*, 2009

Gail Ranstrom, *Unlacing Lilly*, 2008
Christy Reece, *No Chance*, 2010

999

RACHEL HAUCK

Dining with Joy

(Nashville, Tennessee: Thomas Nelson Publishers, 2010)

Story type: Inspirational
Subject(s): Cooking; Romances (Fiction); Christian life
Major character(s): Joy Ballard, Television Personality; Luke Davis, Cook

Summary: *Dining with Joy* is an inspirational romance written by Rachel Hauck. When Joy Ballard's father, a television cook, passes away, she must take over his cooking show—after all, the show must go on. The only problem is, Joy doesn't know how to cook. Although she is initially successful with instead turning the show into a comedy featuring her cooking foibles, her new executive producer wants her to go back to her father's format so that the show can be shopped to a major network. Enter Luke Davis, a top chef from New York who just might be the perfect ingredient Joy needs to save her show. But can Joy keep from falling for Luke?

Where it's reviewed:
Romantic Times, December 2010, page 45

Other books by the same author:
Love Starts with Elle, 2008
Sweet Caroline, 2008
Diva Nashvegas, 2007
Lambert's Peace, 2006
Lost in Nashvegas, 2006

Other books you might like:
Judy Christie, *Goodness Gracious Green*, 2010
Beth Pattillo, *Heavens to Betsy*, 2005
Cerella D. Sechrist, *Love Finds You in Hershey, Pennsylvania*, 2010
Susan May Warren, *Licensed for Trouble*, 2010
Lisa Wingate, *Never Say Never*, 2010

1000

ALEXANDRA HAWKINS

Till Dawn with the Devil

(New York: St. Martin's Press, 2010)

Story type: Historical
Subject(s): Love; Death; Grief
Major character(s): Gabriel "Reign" Housely, Widow(er); Sophia, Noblewoman
Time period(s): 19th century; 1820s
Locale(s): London, United Kingdom

Summary: *Till Dawn with the Devil* is an installment in Alexandra Hawkins's Lords of Vice series. This outing is set in 1820s England and revolves around Gabriel "Reign" Housely, a British nobleman grieving the loss of his wife several years prior. When he meets beautiful but shy Lady Sophia, the wall he's built around his heart begins to crack and crumble. But Reign has secrets... secrets that could very well destroy any possible future with Sophia.

Where it's reviewed:
Romantic Times, August 2010, page 42

Other books by the same author:
All Night with a Rogue, 2010

Other books you might like:
Celeste Bradley, *Duke Most Wanted*, 2008
Jane Feather, *A Husband's Wicked Ways*, 2009
Eloisa James, *A Kiss at Midnight*, 2010
Sophia James, *One Unashamed Night*, 2010
Caroline Linden, *For Your Arms Only*, 2009

1001

JENNIFER HAYMORE
A Season of Seduction
(New York: Hachette, 2010)

Series: Tristan Family Series. Book 3
Story type: Historical; Series
Subject(s): Romances (Fiction); History; Christmas
Major character(s): Rebecca, Noblewoman, Widow(er); Jack Fulton, Bachelor
Time period(s): 19th century; 1820s (1827)
Locale(s): London, England

Summary: In *A Season of Seduction* by Jennifer Haymore, a young widow prepares for Christmas by searching for a suitable new lover. Having lost one husband, Lady Rebecca has no interest in marrying again, but she does need a man who's willing to fulfill her physical needs. Confirmed bachelor Jack Fulton seems to fit Rebecca's requirements. But this time, Jack is looking for more than a physical relationship. As Christmas approaches, he knows that his days are numbered unless he can convince the lovely Lady Rebecca to become his wife. *A Season of Seduction* is the third book in the Tristan Family series.

Where it's reviewed:
Romantic Times, October 2010, page 38

Other books by the same author:
A Touch of Scandal, 2010
A Hint of Wicked, 2009

Other books you might like:
Jo Beverley, *To Rescue a Rogue*, 2006
Liz Carlyle, *Never Lie to a Lady*, 2007
Candice Hern, *Her Scandalous Affair*, 2004
Sabrina Jeffries, *Never Seduce a Scoundrel*, 2006
Stephanie Laurens, *A Rake's Vow*, 1998

1002

LORRAINE HEATH (Pseudonym of Jan Nowasky)
Pleasures of a Notorious Gentleman
(New York: Avon, 2010)

Series: London's Greatest Lovers Series. Book 2
Story type: Historical

Subject(s): Love; Marriage; Crimean War, 1853-1856
Major character(s): Mercy Dawson, Nurse; Stephen Lyons, Military Personnel (soldier)
Time period(s): 19th century; 1850s
Locale(s): United Kingdom

Summary: Nurse Mercy Dawson arrives on the doorstep of the Duke of Ainsley holding the baby she conceived with the duke's soldier brother Stephen. She has no idea, however, that Stephen is still alive after fighting in the Crimean War, and the handsome soldier is determined not to disgrace the beautiful Mercy any further. The two wed and discover a mutual passion that changes their lives forever. *Pleasures of a Notorious Gentleman* is the second novel in Lorraine Heath's London's Greatest Lovers series.

Where it's reviewed:
Romantic Times, December 2010, page 33

Other books by the same author:
Passions of a Wicked Earl, 2010
Between the Devil and Desire, 2009
Midnight Pleasures with a Scoundrel, 2009
Surrender to the Devil, 2009
In Bed with the Devil, 2008

Other books you might like:
Tessa Dare, *Twice Tempted by a Rogue*, 2010
Lisa Kleypas, *Love in the Afternoon*, 2010
Kat Martin, *Reese's Bride*, 2009
Raye Morgan, *The Prince's Secret Bride*, 2008

1003

RITA HERRON
Unbreakable Bond
(Toronto; New York: Harlequin, 2010)

Story type: Contemporary
Subject(s): Love; Adventure; Missing persons
Major character(s): Nina Nash, Mother; Slade Blackburn, Detective
Time period(s): 21st century; 2010s
Locale(s): United States

Summary: Rita Herron's *Unbreakable Bond* tells the story of Nina Nash, a young mother who is still reeling from the disappearance of her daughter years prior. Enter Slade Blackburn, a sexy detective who decides it's time to ramp up the search and finally find Nina's daughter. But as Slade and Nina work together, they realize they are being targeted, and someone wants them to mind their own business. Meanwhile, their relationship slowly evolves into a passionate love that neither can deny.

Where it's reviewed:
Romantic Times, July 2010, page 108

Other books by the same author:
Forbidden Passion, 2010
Rawhide Ranger, 2010
Insatiable Desire, 2008
Say You Love Me, 2007
Return to Falcon Ridge, 2006

Other books you might like:
Carla Cassidy, *Scene of the Crime: Bridgewater, Texas*, 2009
Pam Jenoff, *Almost Home*, 2009
Andrea Kane, *Drawn in Blood*, 2009
Elizabeth Lowell, *Blue Smoke and Murder*, 2008
Debra Webb, *Colby Velocity*, 2010

1004

SANDRA HILL

The Viking Takes a Knight
(New York: Avon Books, 2010)

Series: Viking I Series. Book 9
Story type: Historical; Series
Subject(s): Romances (Fiction); History; Vikings
Major character(s): John, Knight; Ingrith, Viking (princess)
Time period(s): 10th century; 970s
Locale(s): Northumbria, Fictional Location

Summary: In *The Viking Takes a Knight* by Sandra Hill, John of Hawk's Lair, a knight with a penchant for beekeeping, finds his ordered life disrupted by the arrival of a Viking princess. When Ingrith comes to John's castle seeking protection for a band of orphans being targeted by a Saxon leader, the reclusive knight wants nothing to do with her. When he reluctantly takes them in, John's castle is overrun by the noisy group of children—and the overbearing Ingrith. Gradually, the bachelor beekeeper and the Viking princess discover a mutual attraction that transcends their dissimilarities. *The Viking Takes a Knight* is the ninth book in the Viking I series.

Where it's reviewed:
Romantic Times, September 2010, page 44

Other books by the same author:
Dark Viking, 2010
Viking in Love, 2010
So Into You, 2009
Viking Heat, 2009
Viking Unchained, 2008

Other books you might like:
Alice Borchardt, *Devoted*, 1995
Diana Groe, *Erinsong*, 2006
Johanna Lindsey, *Until Forever*, 1995
Josie Litton, *Dream of Me*, 2001
Susan Squires, *Danelaw*, 2003

1005

SANDRA HILL

Dark Viking
(New York: Berkley Books, 2010)

Story type: Historical; Time Travel
Subject(s): United States. Navy; Vikings; Time travel
Major character(s): Rita Sawyer, Military Personnel (Navy WEAL); Steven of Norstead, Viking

Time period(s): 8th century-11th century

Summary: Naval officer Rita Sawyer recently has become a member of a new, innovative task force called the WEALS—a female version of the Navy SEALs. After a particularly risky maneuver, Rita blacks out. When she wakes up, she finds herself transported back in time to the Middle Ages. Even more shocking, she is a captive of a Viking tribe whose chief seems to take a liking to her. Can Rita find her way back home, or is the familiarity she feels toward Chief Steven of Norstead a sign that she is exactly where she is supposed to be?

Where it's reviewed:
Romantic Times, October 2010, page 42

Other books by the same author:
Viking in Love, 2010
Viking Heat, 2009
Viking Unchained, 2008
Down and Dirty, 2007
Rough and Ready, 2006

Other books you might like:
Dakota Cassidy, *Kiss & Hell*, 2009
MaryJanice Davidson, *Undead and Unwelcome*, 2009
Angie Fox, *The Accidental Demon Slayer*, 2008
Judi McCoy, *Almost a Goddess*, 2006
Vicki Lewis Thompson, *Blonde with a Wand*, 2010

1006

EMMA HOLLY

Devil at Midnight
(New York: Berkley Books, 2010)

Story type: Ghost Story; Vampire Story
Subject(s): Ghosts; Time travel; History
Major character(s): Grace Michaels, Young Woman, Abuse Victim, Spirit; Christian Durand, Mercenary; Nim Wei, Vampire
Time period(s): Multiple Time Periods

Summary: In *Devil at Midnight*, Emma Holly tells the story of a spirit named Grace Michaels. Grace was murdered by her father in the mid-20th century, yet she is serving time in the spirit world in 1460. There, she must guide a swarthy mercenary captain named Christian away from the clutches of Nim Wei, queen of the vampires. But as Christian's men fall prey to all of Nim Wei's tricks, he finds himself struggling between his physical desire and what is in his heart. Holly is also the author of *Angel at Dawn*, *Master of Smoke*, and *Saving Midnight*.

Where it's reviewed:
Romantic Times, November 2010, page 44

Other books by the same author:
Breaking Midnight, 2009
Kissing Midnight, 2009
Saving Midnight, 2009
Courting Midnight, 2005
Hunting Midnight, 2003

Other books you might like:
Shana Abe, *The Time Weaver*, 2010

Romances

Lynn Kurland, *A Garden in the Rain*, 2003
Karen Marie Moning, *The Highlander's Touch*, 2000
Constance O'Day-Flannery, *Time After Time*, 2001
Susan Squires, *The Mists of Time*, 2010

1007

EMMA HOLLY

Angel at Dawn

(New York: Berkley, 2011)

Story type: Historical
Subject(s): Movie industry; Vampires; Love
Major character(s): Christian Durand, Vampire; Grace Gladwell, Writer
Time period(s): 20th century; 1950s
Locale(s): Hollywood, California

Summary: In *Angel at Dawn*, best-selling author Emma Holly tells a tale of romance and vampires set against the glittering backdrop of 1950s Hollywood. Christian Durand is a nearly 500-year-old vamp who is summoned to Tinseltown to star in the movies being created by his maker, who is now a film director. When Christian encounters aspiring screenwriter Grace Gladwell, his heart shatters: she is the reincarnation of the first woman he ever loved. As their paths fatefully cross more and more often, Christian must finally give in to his passion for Grace—and all the dangers that lie therein. *Angel at Dawn* is an installment in the Novels of the Upyr series.

Where it's reviewed:
Publishers Weekly, November 15, 2010, page 45

Other books by the same author:
Devil at Midnight, 2010
Breaking Midnight, 2009
Kissing Midnight, 2009
Saving Midnight, 2009
Courting Midnight, 2005

Other books you might like:
Meljean Brook, *Demon Angel*, 2007
Kathleen Nance, *Dragon Unmasked*, 2010
Joy Nash, *Silver Silence*, 2009
Gena Showalter, *Awaken Me Darkly*, 2005
Nalini Singh, *Angels' Blood*, 2009

1008

CHERYL HOLT

Dreams of Desire

(New York: Berkley Books, 2010)

Story type: Regency
Subject(s): Magic; Romances (Fiction); Royalty
Major character(s): Lily Lambert, Governess (to Melinda and Melissa); Melinda Middleton, Twin (of Melissa), Daughter (of Earl of Penworth), Ward (of Lily); Melissa Middleton, Ward (of Lily), Twin (of Melinda), Daughter (of Earl of Penworth); John Middleton, Nobleman, Father (of Melissa and Melinda), Employer (of Lily); Philip Dubois, Magician
Locale(s): England; Scotland

Summary: Lily Lambert has just accepted a position with the Earl of Penworth as the governess for his twin daughters, Melissa and Melinda. Lily enlists the help of the magical Philip Dubois, who gives her a potion that will help her attract a husband so that she can quit her job. Yet John Middleton, the Earl of Penworth and her boss, is the one falling in love with her. Holt is also the author of *Mountain Dreams*, *Love Lessons*, and *Taste of Temptation*.

Where it's reviewed:
Romantic Times, December 2010, page 37

Other books by the same author:
Double Fantasy, 2008
My True Love, 2008
Mountain of Dreams, 2007
Secret Fantasy, 2007
Total Surrender, 2007

Other books you might like:
Annie Burrows, *A Countess by Christmas*, 2010
Sophie Jordan, *Wicked Nights with a Lover*, 2010
Stephanie Laurens, *A Secret Love*, 2000
Julie London, *The Year of Living Dangerously*, 2010
Maggie MacKeever, *The Tyburn Waltz*, 2010

1009

LINDA HOWARD

Veil of Night

(New York: Ballantine Books, 2010)

Subject(s): Murder; Romances (Fiction); Weddings
Major character(s): Jaclyn Wilde, Planner (wedding planner); Eric Wilder, Detective—Police; Carrie Edwards, Crime Victim
Time period(s): 21st century; 2010s
Locale(s): United States

Summary: In *Veil of Night*, bestselling author Linda Howard crafts a tale of murder and intrigue surrounding wedding planner Jaclyn Wilde and the police detective who can't resist her. After working with temperamental and detestable bride Carrie Edwards, Jaclyn isn't altogether shocked when Carrie is found murdered. Detective Eric Wilder, with whom Jaclyn once had a fling, is called in to investigate. As the list of suspects grows, Eric knows Jaclyn is one of many who despised Carrie Edwards, which means he must keep a professional distance until the crime is solved.

Where it's reviewed:
Romantic Times, September 2010, page 74

Other books by the same author:
Prey, 2011
Burn, 2009
Ice, 2009
Death Angel, 2008
Up Close and Dangerous, 2007

Other books you might like:
Stephanie Bond, *Finding Your Mojo*, 2006
Christie Craig, *Weddings Can Be Murder*, 2008
Jasmine Cresswell, *No Sin Too Great*, 1996
Jennifer Crusie, *Tell Me Lies*, 1999
Jayne Ann Krentz, *Eclipse Bay*, 2000

1010

ELIZABETH HOYT (Pseudonym of Nancy M. Finney)

Wicked Intentions

(New York: Grand Central Publishing, 2010)

Series: Maiden Lane Series. Book 1
Story type: Historical; Series
Subject(s): Romances (Fiction); History; England
Major character(s): Lazarus Huntington, Nobleman;
    Temperance Dews, Widow(er)
Time period(s): 18th century; 1730s (1737)
Locale(s): London, England
Summary: In *Wicked Intentions* by Elizabeth Hoyt, a
nobleman hunting for a murderer in London's dangerous
backstreets enlists the help of a widow who runs an
orphanage in the St. Giles slum. Lazarus Huntington,
Lord Caire, is well known for his sexual exploits, but
when he asks Temperance Dews to be his guide, his
intentions are strictly professional. In return for her
services, Temperance strikes a bargain with Huntington
that will secure the financial future of the foundling
home. But as they navigate the dark world of St. Giles
together, Temperance and Lazarus gradually surrender to
their growing physical attraction. *Wicked Intentions* is
the first book in the Maiden Lane series.

Where it's reviewed:
Booklist, August 2010, page 35
Publishers Weekly, June 21, 2010, page 37
Romantic Times, August 2010, page 40

Other books by the same author:
Notorious Pleasures, 2011
The Ice Princess, 2010
To Beguile a Beast, 2009
To Desire a Devil, 2009
To Seduce a Sinner, 2008
To Taste Temptation, 2008
The Leopard Prince, 2007
The Raven Bride, 2006

Other books you might like:
Brenda Hiatt, *Rogue's Honor*, 2001
Eloisa James, *Desperate Duchesses*, 2007
Kate Moore, *To Save the Devil*, 2010
Kate Moore, *To Tempt a Saint*, 2010
Rachelle Morgan, *A Scandalous Lady*, 2003

1011

JILLIAN HUNTER (Pseudonym of Maria Hoag)

A Duke's Temptation

(New York: Signet, 2010)

Series: Bridal Pleasures Series. Book 1
Story type: Historical - Regency

Subject(s): Love; Marriage; Writers
Major character(s): Lily Boscastle, Noblewoman; Samuel
    Charles Aubrey St. Aldwyn, Writer
Time period(s): 19th century
Locale(s): London, United Kingdom

Summary: Lily Boscastle is anticipating a little fun before
she and her fiance formally announce their engagement.
Her pursuit of a wild time leads her to a masquerade ball
peopled with the biggest literary figures of the day, and
Lily is thrilled to be in such company. There she meets
the Duke of Gravenhurst, Samuel Charles Aubrey St.
Aldwyn. The Duke is a man with a secret—a secret that,
if revealed, could spell trouble for Lily's impending
marriage. *A Duke's Temptation* is the first book in Jillian
Hunter's Bridal Pleasures series.

Where it's reviewed:
Booklist, November 1, 2010, page 34
Romantic Times, November 2010, page 42

Other books by the same author:
The Wicked Duke Takes a Wife, 2009
A Wicked Lord at the Wedding, 2009
Wicked as Sin, 2008
The Sinful Nights of a Nobleman, 2006
The Wicked Games of a Gentleman, 2006

Other books you might like:
Celeste Bradley, *The Spy*, 2004
Jacquie D'Alessandro, *Tempted at Midnight*, 2009
Shana Galen, *Blackthorne's Bride*, 2007
Sabrina Jeffries, *Don't Bargain with the Devil*, 2009
Julia London, *A Courtesan's Scandal*, 2009

1012

BRENDA JACKSON

Star of His Heart

(Don Mills, Ontario, Canada: Kimani Press, 2010)

Story type: Contemporary
Subject(s): Romances (Fiction); African Americans; Ac-
tors
Major character(s): Ethan Chambers, Actor; Rachel Welle-
sley, Artist (makeup)
Time period(s): 21st century; 2010s
Locale(s): Hollywood, California

Summary: In *Star of His Heart* by Brenda Jackson, a
makeup artist becomes a reluctant leading lady in a TV
star's love life. For Rachel Wellesley, landing the job of
cosmetologist on the medical show *Paging the Doctor* is
sure to give a big boost to her career. But she is
unprepared for the attention she gains from the press and
the show's star, handsome Ethan Chambers. When Ethan
joins the cast of *Paging the Doctor*, he is definitely not
looking to start a relationship. But when Ethan meets
Rachel, who prefers to stay behind the scenes, he begins
to reconsider his single lifestyle.

Where it's reviewed:
Romantic Times, August 2010, page 108

Other books by the same author:
A Silken Thread, 2011
Bachelor Unleashed, 2010

Romances

Hidden Pleasures, 2010
In Too Deep, 2010
What a Westmoreland Wants, 2010

Other books you might like:
Rochelle Alers, *Butterfly*, 2010
Gwynne Forster, *Once in a Lifetime*, 2002
Shirley Hailstock, *My Lover, My Friend*, 2006
Sandra Kitt, *Between Friends*, 1998
Francis Ray, *It Had to Be You*, 2010

1013

ALLYSON JAMES (Pseudonym of Jennifer Ashley)

Firewalker

(New York: Berkley, 2010)

Series: Stormwalker Series. Book 2
Story type: Contemporary
Subject(s): Love; Good and evil; Fantasy
Major character(s): Janet Begay, Supernatural Being (half hell-goddess), Hotel Owner; Mick, Boyfriend (of Janet), Shape-Shifter; Nash Jones, Police Officer (sheriff)
Time period(s): 21st century; 2010s
Locale(s): Hopi County, Arizona

Summary: The second book in Allyson James's Stormwalker series, *Firewalker* finds hotel owner Janet Begay possessed by a force of evil more powerful than anything the world has ever known. Her dragon shape-shifter beau Mick is determined to help her at any cost, and when a dead body is found in the hotel, all fingers seem to point to Janet. Can Mick delve into the forces of darkness to help Janet prove her innocence?

Where it's reviewed:
Publishers Weekly, September 2010, page 54
Romantic Times, November 2010, page 86

Other books by the same author:
Stormwalker, 2010
Mortal Seductions, 2009
Mortal Temptations, 2009
The Dragon Master, 2008
The Black Dragon, 2007

Other books you might like:
Sharon Ashwood, *Ravenous*, 2009
Annette Blair, *Naked Dragon*, 2010
Christina Dodd, *Scent of Darkness*, 2007
Karen Marie Moning, *Darkfever*, 2006
Eileen Rendahl, *Don't Kill the Messenger*, 2010

1014

ELOISA JAMES

A Kiss at Midnight

(New York: Avon, 2010)

Story type: Historical - Regency
Subject(s): Love; Family; Royalty

Major character(s): Katherine Daltry, Spinster; Gabriel, Royalty (prince)
Time period(s): 19th century
Locale(s): United Kingdom

Summary: Eloisa James's *A Kiss at Midnight* offers a unique twist on the classic Cinderella story. This volume is set in Regency England, where Katherine Daltry lives a trying life as servant to her mean-spirited stepmother and stepsister. When she is required to attend a local ball in place of her stepsister, Katherine meets Prince Gabriel. Though the cards are stacked against them, the two feel the heat of passion the moment their eyes meet, and Gabriel sets out to make Katherine his princess.

Where it's reviewed:
Library Journal, August 1, 2010, page 60
Publishers Weekly, June 21, 2010, page 37
Romantic Times, August 2010, page 40

Other books by the same author:
A Duke of Her Own, 2009
This Duchess of Mine, 2009
Duchess by Night, 2008
When the Duke Returns, 2008
An Affair before Christmas, 2007

Other books you might like:
Elizabeth Boyle, *Love Letters from a Duke*, 2007
Christina Dodd, *Scandalous Again*, 2003
Teresa Medeiros, *A Kiss to Remember*, 2001
Maya Rodale, *The Heir and the Spare*, 2007

1015

JUDITH JAMES

Libertine's Kiss

(Don Mills, Ontario: Harlequin, 2010)

Story type: Historical
Subject(s): English Civil War, 1642-1649; England; Romances (Fiction)
Major character(s): Elizabeth, Caregiver (of William); William de Veres, Nobleman, Writer (poet)
Time period(s): 17th century
Locale(s): England

Summary: *Libertine's Kiss* is a historical romance novel by author Judith James, set at the time of the English Civil War. William de Veres is a gentleman serving under the court of King Charles I. After being harbored by a young woman named Elizabeth while fleeing Oliver Cromwell's men, he returns to England and is later declared the Earl Rivers, the king's poet. Now that the Civil War has ended and order is restored in the monarchy of England, Elizabeth has arrived at the court to ask that the damage Cromwell's men did to her, which includes the seizure of her family's land, be compensated. Can William convince the king to help the woman who acted so kindly when he needed her?

Where it's reviewed:
Booklist, September 15, 2010, page 42

Other books by the same author:
Broken Wing, 2008

Other books you might like:
Denise Domning, *Lady in Waiting*, 1998
Amanda McCabe, *A Notorious Woman*, 2007
Lauren Royal, *Amber*, 2001
Jeane Westin, *Lady Anne's Dangerous Man*, 2006

1016

SOPHIA JAMES

One Unashamed Night

(Toronto; New York: Harlequin, 2010)

Story type: Historical - Regency
Subject(s): Love; Blindness; Voyages and travels
Major character(s): Taris Wellingham, Nobleman;
   Beatrice-Maude Bassingstoke, Spinster
Time period(s): 19th century
Locale(s): United Kingdom

Summary: In Sophia James's *One Unashamed Night*, Lord Taris Wellingham is struggling with his rapidly advancing blindness. When he meets Beatrice-Maude Bassingstoke, he is drawn to the reserved spinster, but both know that a relationship would be out of the question. Fate, however, has different plans, and when Taris and Beatice-Maude are forced to spend a single night together, their lives—and hearts—are forever changed.

Where it's reviewed:
Romantic Times, August 2010, page 47

Other books by the same author:
The Border Lord, 2009
Mistletoe Magic, 2009
Masquerading Mistress, 2008
High Seas to High Society, 2007
Fallen Angel, 2005

Other books you might like:
Terri Brisbin, *A Storm of Passion*, 2009
Alexandra Hawkins, *Till Dawn with the Devil*, 2010
Alissa Johnson, *Destined to Last*, 2010
Stephanie Laurens, *Temptation and Surrender*, 2009
Kat Martin, *Heart of Courage*, 2009

1017

SYRIE JAMES

Dracula My Love

(New York: Avon, 2010)

Story type: Vampire Story
Subject(s): Vampires; Romances (Fiction); Literature
Major character(s): Mina Harker, Spouse (of Jonathan);
   Jonathan Harker, Spouse (of Mina); Dracula,
   Vampire

Summary: *Dracula My Love* is a horror-romance novel by author Syrie James, based on the novel *Dracula* by Bram Stoker. This story speaks from the point of view of Mina Harker, a small character in Stoker's original piece. Mina loves Jonathan, her betrothed and later her husband, but is torn by her lust for the Dark Prince himself, Nicolae

Dracula. She plots to have her cake and eat it too: she will remain the wife of Jonathan while she is alive, but when she is made immortal she will turn to Dracula for companionship. Meanwhile, the requisite characters of Stoker's novel fill in the back story.

Where it's reviewed:
Library Journal, July 2010, page 72
Publishers Weekly, June 21, 2010, page 30

Other books by the same author:
The Secret Diaries of Charlotte Bronte, 2009
The Lost Memoirs of Jane Austen, 2007

Other books you might like:
Colleen Gleason, *The Rest Falls Away*, 2007
Kim Lennox, *So Still the Night*, 2009
Teresa Medeiros, *After Midnight*, 2005
Deanna Raybourn, *The Dead Travel Fast*, 2010
Kathryn Smith, *Taken by the Night*, 2007

1018

SABRINA JEFFRIES (Pseudonym of Deborah Gonzales)

A Hellion in Her Bed

(New York: Pocket Star Books, 2010)

Story type: Family Saga
Subject(s): Gambling; Grandmothers; Marriage
Major character(s): Lord Jarret Sharpe, Manager (of
   brewery); Annabel Lake, Businesswoman

Summary: *A Hellion in Her Bed* is a romance novel by author Sabrina Jeffries. Lord Jarret Sharpe has never met odds that he didn't like, but the bet he has made with his grandmother seems like a gamble even for him. Lord Sharpe's grandmother, the family matriarch, has made a deal with her grandson that if he successfully manages the family for a year, he is exempt from her requirement that all her grandchildren marry or be disowned. If Lord Sharpe wins this bet, he will not only obtain his rightful inheritance but will also get to keep the brewery. Yet when he meets the lovely Annabel Lake, who owns a competing brewery, he wonders if he bet on more than he bargained for.

Where it's reviewed:
Booklist, September 15, 2010, page 46
Romantic Times, October 2010, page 38

Other books by the same author:
The Truth about Lord Stoneville, 2010
Don't Bargain with the Devil, 2009
Wed Him before You Bed Him, 2009
Let Sleeping Rogues Lie, 2008
Beware a Scot's Revenge, 2007

Other books you might like:
Claudia Dain, *The Courtesan's Wager*, 2009
Suzanne Enoch, *Reforming a Rake*, 2000
Karen Hawkins, *How to Treat a Lady*, 2003
Julia London, *A Courtesan's Scandal*, 2009
Tracy Anne Warren, *The Husband Trap*, 2006

Romances

1019

BEVERLY JENKINS

Midnight

(New York: Avon, 2010)

Story type: Historical - American Revolution
Subject(s): Love; African Americans; Spies
Major character(s): Faith Kingston, Spy; Nicholas Grey, Young Man
Time period(s): 18th century; 1770s (1775)
Locale(s): Boston, Massachusetts

Summary: Set in 18th-century Boston, Beverly Jenkins's *Midnight* tells the story of a rebel spy and the dashing stranger she falls for. No one knows that Faith Kingston is really the notorious spy Lady Midnight, fighting for the States' freedom from British rule. Meanwhile, Nicholas Grey has come back to Boston in search of retribution against the man he thinks killed his father. That man is none other than Faith's own father—but when Nicholas and Faith meet, their mutual desire is palpable. Will their love spell the end of their respective missions?

Where it's reviewed:
Romantic Times, December 2010, page 36

Other books by the same author:
A Second Helping, 2010
Bring on the Blessings, 2009
Captured, 2009
Jewel, 2008
Deadly Sexy, 2007

Other books you might like:
Anita Richmond Bunkley, *Starlight Passage*, 1996
Kimberly Cates, *The Raider's Bride*, 1994
Miranda Jarrett, *Gift of the Heart*, 1996
Susan Kay Law, *Traitorous Hearts*, 1994
Kerrelyn Sparks, *For Love or Country*, 2002

1020

KATHRYN JOHNSON

The Gentleman Poet

(New York: Avon, 2010)

Story type: Historical
Subject(s): Shipwrecks; Shakespeare, William; Literature
Major character(s): Elizabeth Persons, Cook, Servant; William Strachey, Historian, Writer

Summary: *The Gentleman Poet*, by Kathryn Johnson, is an adaptation of the story behind the story in William Shakespeare's play *The Tempest*. Orphan, Elizabeth Persons has been enlisted as a servant aboard a ship owned by the Virginia Company, but when that ship is wrecked en route to the New World, Elizabeth finds herself in an even more important role. She becomes the chef and caretaker for the men who have survived, one of whom is William Strachey, a historian and poet. As Elizabeth grows into her newfound position, she also begins falling for her assistant cook. When William

writes a play to encourage their romance, Elizabeth begins to suspect that there is more to this historian than meets the eye. Could he in fact be The Bard himself?

Where it's reviewed:
Romantic Times, September 2010, page 48

Other books you might like:
Jennifer Ashley, *The Queen's Handmaiden*, 2007
Philippa Gregory, *The Other Boleyn Girl*, 2002
Barbara Kyle, *The Queen's Captive*, 2010
Anne O'Brien, *The Virgin Widow*, 2010
Tori Phillips, *Lady of the Knight*, 1999

1021

LISA RENEE JONES

Hot Target

(Toronto, Ontario, Canada: Harlequin, 2010)

Story type: Romantic Suspense
Subject(s): Romances (Fiction); Safety; Sports
Major character(s): Luke Winter, Baseball Player (pitcher); Katie Lyons, Security Officer
Time period(s): 21st century; 2010s
Locale(s): United States

Summary: *Hot Target* is a suspenseful romance novel from author Lisa Renee Jones. Luke Winter is a major-league baseball hotshot, regularly stalked by obsessed fans and crazed women, but a new series of threats has Luke questioning his safety. Although he's reluctant at first, Luke finally comes around when the team suggests that he hire a private security detail. Katie Lyons is thrilled when her small business lands the job, even though she hates arrogant athletes. The most obvious tactic to protect Luke is for Katie to pretend to be his new girlfriend in order to stay close to him at all times. Unfortunately, it isn't long until Katie and Luke develop a real romantic relationship, endangering their hearts and lives when they get lost in the passion.

Where it's reviewed:
Romantic Times, August 2010, page 103

Other books by the same author:
Love Drunk Cowboy, 2011
Walkin' on Clouds, 2011
Hell, Yeah, 2010
I Love This Bar, 2010
My Give a Damn's Busted, 2010

Other books you might like:
Toni Blake, *Sugar Creek*, 2010
Jan Hambright, *The High Country Rancher*, 2009
Rita Herron, *Platinum Cowboy*, 2009
R.C. Ryan, *Montana Destiny*, 2010

1022

BRENDA JOYCE

The Promise

(Toronto; New York: Harlequin, 2010)

Series: De Warenne Dynasty Series. Book 13
Story type: Historical

Subject(s): Love; Marriage; Family
Major character(s): Alexi de Warenne, Spouse (of Elysse), Adventurer; Elysse de Warenne, Spouse (of Alexi)
Time period(s): 19th century; 1830s
Locale(s): United Kingdom

Summary: In *The Promise*, best-selling author Brenda Joyce charts the relationship between a husband and wife whose relationship is headed for disaster. Intrepid explorer Alexi de Warenne marries the beautiful noblewoman Elysse, with whom he has been friends since the two were children. After returning from a long voyage at sea, he is stunned to find Elysse the victim of malicious gossip around town—gossip suggesting Alexi had abandoned her. Now that he's back, Elysse sets out to win her husband's heart, and the husband and wife discover a passion they never knew possible. This volume is the 13th installment in the de Warenne Dynasty series.

Where it's reviewed:
Romantic Times, October 2010, page 38

Other books by the same author:
Deadly Vows, 2011
An Impossible Attraction, 2010
Dark Lover, 2009
Dark Victory, 2009
Dark Embrace, 2008

Other books you might like:
Jennifer Crusie, *Maybe This Time*, 2010
Victoria Holt, *On the Night of the Seventh Moon*, 1972
Kat Martin, *Reese's Bride*, 2009
Kat Martin, *Rule's Bride*, 2010

1023

JULIA JUSTISS (Pseudonym of Janet Justiss)

The Smuggler and the Society Bride

(Don Mills, Ontario: Harlequin, 2010)

Story type: Regency
Subject(s): Social class; Romances (Fiction); English (British people)
Major character(s): Honoria Carlow, Noblewoman (exiled); Gabriel Hawksworth, Smuggler
Locale(s): England

Summary: *The Smuggler and the Society Bride* is a Regency romance by author Julia Justiss. Lady Honoria Carlow is persona non grata in British high society, having made too many mistakes to remain in the court. Now exiled to Cornwall, Honoria meets the swarthy Gabriel Hawksworth, a smuggler. Gabriel is dangerous and untrustworthy, but he is the only person who believes in Honoria. Can she convince him to give up his wild ways and make her an honest woman once and for all? Justiss is also the author of *The Wedding Gamble*, *The Untamed Heiress*, and *Scandalous Proposal*.

Where it's reviewed:
Romantic Times, August 2010, page 46

Other books by the same author:
From Waif to Gentleman's Wife, 2009

A Most Unconventional Match, 2008
Rogue's Lady, 2007
The Untamed Heiress, 2006
The Courtesan, 2005

Other books you might like:
Louise Allen, *The Earl's Intended Wife*, 2006
Jo Beverley, *The Rogue's Return*, 2006
Diane Gaston, *Gallant Officer, Forbidden Lady*, 2009
Karen Hawkins, *Confessions of a Scoundrel*, 2003
Edith Layton, *The Devil's Bargain*, 2002

1024

VIRGINIA KANTRA

Immortal Sea

(New York: Berkley Books, 2010)

Story type: Alternate World
Subject(s): Fantasy; Romances (Fiction); Human-animal relationships
Major character(s): Dr. Elizabeth Rodriguez, Mother (of Zack and Liz), Lover (of Morgan), Widow(er); Morgan, Shape-Shifter (Selkie); Zack Rodriguez, Son (of Elizabeth and Morgan); Liz Rodriguez, Daughter (of Elizabeth)

Summary: *The Immortal Sea* is an installment from author Virginia Kantra's Children of the Sea series. When Dr. Elizabeth Rodriguez moves to World's End Island, a remote island off the coast of Maine, she hopes that she can finally heal from her husband's untimely death. However, she unexpectedly puts herself into a position to reunite with a long-lost love named Morgan. Morgan and Elizabeth shared a night of passion 16 years ago, and Morgan is the father of Elizabeth's son Zack. Yet Morgan is not human; he is a Selkie, a shape-shifting species that can assume a human's shape. Can Elizabeth accept Morgan in time for her son to get to know his real father, and in time for her to fall in love?

Where it's reviewed:
Romantic Times, September 2010, page 92

Other books by the same author:
Sea Lord, 2009
Sea Fever, 2008
Sea Witch, 2008
Home Before Midnight, 2006
Close Up, 2005

Other books you might like:
Shana Abe, *The Last Mermaid*, 2004
Alyssa Day, *Atlantis Redeemed*, 2010
Christine Feehan, *Water Bound*, 2010
Dawn Thompson, *Lord of the Deep*, 2007
Gayle Ann Williams, *Tsunami Blue*, 2010

1025

DONNA KAUFFMAN

Simon Says...

(Toronto; New York: Harlequin, 2010)

Story type: Contemporary
Subject(s): Love; Adventure; Theft

Romances

Major character(s): Sophie Maplethorpe, Manager (hotel); Simon Lassiter, Agent (security)
Time period(s): 21st century; 2010s
Locale(s): United States
Summary: Donna Kauffman's *Simon Says...* charts the steamy romance between a hotel manager and an international security agent. When Sophie Maplethorpe enters one of the rooms in her hotel, she has no idea she has just walked into a potential crime scene. Simon Lassiter is about to retrieve a stolen gemstone and nab those responsible for its theft. The sparks fly immediately between Sophie and Simon, and despite Simon's best efforts to curtail a romance, the two soon find themselves in the throes of an undeniable passion.

Where it's reviewed:
Booklist, July 2010, page 107

Other books by the same author:
The Black Sheep and the Princess, 2010
Here Comes Trouble, 2010
Some Like It Scot, 2010
The Great Scot, 2009
Dear Prince Charming, 2008

Other books you might like:
Julie Kenner, *Starstruck*, 2009
Michelle Rowen, *Hot Spell*, 2009
Jill Shalvis, *The Heat Is On*, 2010
Isabel Sharpe, *Wild Side*, 2001
Hope Tarr, *Twelve Nights*, 2009

1026

DONNA KAUFFMAN
CYNTHIA EDEN, Co-Author
SUSAN FOX (Pseudonym of Susan Lyons), Co-Author

The Naughty List

(New York: Kensington, 2010)

Story type: Holiday Themes
Subject(s): Christmas; Holidays; Romances (Fiction)
Summary: *The Naughty List* is a collection of holiday-themed romances by authors Donna Kauffman, Cynthia Eden, and Susan Fox. In "Naughty but Nice," Kauffman tells the story of tough, go-getting mogul Griffin, whose entire business domain is set to expand and make him rich beyond his wildest dreams. Yet when beautiful, innocent Melody comes into his life, he realizes that maybe he was concentrating on the wrong dreams after all. In Eden's "All I Want for Christmas," toymaker Christie finds herself involved in a sexy affair with Jonas, a policeman working as Santa for the holidays. In "Tattoos and Mistletoe," Fox tells the story of two former classmates, Charlie and LJ. LJ held a torch for Charlie all during high school. Now that Charlie's back in town, she can't deny that she's eating her heart out over turning him down years ago. Can these three stories set the scene for the best Christmas ever?

Where it's reviewed:
Romantic Times, October 2010, page 89

Other books you might like:
Lauren Dane, *Chased*, 2007

Lauren Dane, *Coming Undone*, 2010
Lori Foster, *Perfect for the Beach*, 2004
Donna Kauffman, *Bad Boys on Board*, 2003
Stephanie Rowe, *Date Me, Baby, One More Time*, 2006

1027

CHRISTIE KELLEY

Scandal of the Season

(New York: Zebra Books, 2010)

Story type: Holiday Themes
Subject(s): Romances (Fiction); Christmas; Holidays
Major character(s): Lord Anthony "Viscount Somerton" Westfield, Nobleman, Spy; Victoria Seaton, Lover (of Lord Anthony)
Locale(s): England
Summary: *Scandal of the Season* is a romance novel by author Christie Kelley. The party of the year is fast approaching, and all of English nobility is slated to be there. That also means this Christmas party is the perfect opportunity for Lord Anthony Westfield, the Viscount Somerton, to do some spying on the country's lords and ladies. Unfortunately, to conduct such business he must first lead a convincing double life—and that's where Victoria Seaton fits in. After having a passionate affair with her ten years before, Lord Westfield both discovered and revealed some shocking aspects of his life to Victoria. Now he sees that she would play the perfect role as his mistress for the holidays. Can he convince her to forgive him in time for the party? Kelley is also the author of *A Week of Pleasure* and *Something Scandalous*.

Where it's reviewed:
Romantic Times, October 2010, page 46

Other books by the same author:
Something Scandalous, 2010
Every Time We Kiss, 2009
Every Night I'm Yours, 2008

Other books you might like:
Diane Farr, *Under a Lucky Star*, 2004
Gaelen Foley, *My Wicked Marquess*, 2009
Eloisa James, *Desperate Duchesses*, 2007
Lavinia Kent, *A Talent for Sin*, 2009
Kat Martin, *Royal's Bride*, 2009

1028

ERIN KELLISON (Pseudonym of Clarissa Ellison)

Shadow Fall

(Wayne: Leisure Books, 2010)

Series: Shadow Series. Book 2
Story type: Fantasy; Werewolf Story
Subject(s): Angels; Werewolves; Ballet
Major character(s): Custo Santovari, Angel; Annabella, Dancer
Time period(s): 21st century; 2010s
Locale(s): Manhattan, New York

Summary: In Erin Kellison's *Shadow Fall*, Custo Santovari doesn't believe he's ready or deserving of the afterlife Heaven has to offer him, so he willingly leaves. Soon, the angel is falling from the sky and suddenly, he's in Manhattan again. Leaving Heaven has its consequences, of course. He now has to find and help a ballerina named Annabella, who is being hunted by a dark creature. The wolf watches her while she performs and fills her head with horrifying, yet wondrous, images. If Custo cannot reach Annabelle, the beast will surely consume her. As he protected his best friend, Adam, from an untimely and violent death, he must do the same for Annabella. This is the second book in the Shadows series.

Where it's reviewed:
Romantic Times, August 2010, page 94

Other books by the same author:
Shadow Bound, 2011

Other books you might like:
Kresley Cole, *A Hunger Like No Other*, 2006
Sherrilyn Kenyon, *Born of Night*, 1996
Joy Nash, *Immortals: The Crossing*, 2008
Elisabeth Naughton, *Marked*, 2010
Nalini Singh, *Angels' Blood*, 2009

1029

JOANNE KENNEDY

One Fine Cowboy

(Naperville, Illinois: Sourcebooks Casablanca, 2010)

Story type: Contemporary
Subject(s): Romances (Fiction); Animal rights; Western fiction
Major character(s): Charlie Banks, Student—Graduate; Nate Shawcross, Cowboy/Cowgirl
Time period(s): 21st century; 2010s
Locale(s): Wyoming, United States

Summary: In *One Fine Cowboy* by Joanne Kennedy, Charlie Banks is a graduate student from New Jersey who has come to Wyoming to meet a "horse whisperer." She is a member of an animal rights group and is doubtful about the way horses are treated on a ranch. Once there she meets Nate Shawcross, and she begins to change her mind about the treatment the horses receive. She also learns of an incident in Nate's past—his ex-girlfriend set up a con in order to get people to come to the ranch so she could steal their money; she recently left town. Charlie is quickly developing feelings for Nate, and she decides that she is going to help him deal with his ex so he can put the past behind him.

Where it's reviewed:
Booklist, September 15, 2010, page 46
Publishers Weekly, July 5, 2010, page 32

Other books by the same author:
Cowboy Trouble, 2010

Other books you might like:
Donna Alward, *Marriage at Circle M*, 2007
Catherine Anderson, *Sun Kissed*, 2007
Sadie Callahan, *Lone Star Woman*, 2009

Tracy Garrett, *Touched by Love*, 2008
Joanna Wayne, *24 Karat Ammunition*, 2007

1030

KATHRYNE KENNEDY

The Fire Lord's Lover

(Naperville, Illinois: Sourcebooks Casablanca, 2010)

Series: The Elven Lords Series. Book 1
Story type: Fantasy
Subject(s): Love; Marriage; Magic
Major character(s): Dominic Raikes, Son (of the Fire Lord); Cassandra, Assassin, Spouse (of Dominic)
Time period(s): Indeterminate Past

Summary: In an enchanted kingdom rife with elves and faeries, Dominic Raikes is the powerful son of the much-feared Fire Lord. Through an arranged marriage, he is slated to wed Lady Cassandra, a beautiful young woman he doesn't know has clandestinely been trained as an assassin—and she is out to kill him. But as their marriage brings them closer together, Dominic and Cassandra realize they may just be fighting on the same side, awakening desires in them both for vengeance, freedom... and one another. *The Fire Lord's Lover* is the first book in Kathryne Kennedy's The Elven Lords series.

Where it's reviewed:
Romantic Times, July 2010, page 44

Other books by the same author:
Enchanting the Beast, 2009
My Unfair Lady, 2009
Double Enchantment, 2008
Enchanting the Lady, 2008
Beneath the Thirteen Moons, 2005

Other books you might like:
Kathleen Korbel, *Dangerous Temptation*, 2006
Kathleen Korbel, *Dark Seduction*, 2008
Kathleen Korbel, *Deadly Redemption*, 2008
Susan Krinard, *The Forest Lord*, 2002
Susan Krinard, *Lord of Legends*

1031

JANETTE KENNY

In a Cowboy's Arms

(New York: Zebra Books, 2010)

Story type: Romantic Suspense
Subject(s): Missing persons; Romances (Fiction); Suspense
Major character(s): Dade Logan, Lawman (sheriff); Maggie, Bride (to be), Friend
Time period(s): 21st century; 2010s
Locale(s): Colorado, United States

Summary: *In a Cowboy's Arms* is a steamy romance novel from author Janette Kenny. Sheriff Dade Logan has spent 20 years searching for his sister, Daisy, and he's thrilled at the prospect of finally seeing her. Unfortunately, their

Romances

long-awaited reunion doesn't happen at all. Instead, Dade finds himself confronted by Daisy's longtime friend, Maggie, a beautiful woman running away from her upcoming wedding. Dade is desperate to find his sister and Maggie might be the final piece of the puzzle. They team up to track down information about Daisy's whereabouts, regardless of what it takes. As the investigation heats up, so does their passion for one another, but their newfound romance is endangered when their search leads them into the path of a ruthless bounty hunter.

Where it's reviewed:
Romantic Times, December 2010, page 42

Other books by the same author:
The Illegitimate Tycoon, 2011
Captured and Crowned, 2010
Innocent in the Italian's Possession, 2010
Pirate Tycoon, Forbidden Baby, 2009
Proud, Revenge, Passionate Wedlock, 2009

Other books you might like:
Geralyn Dawson, *Her Outlaw*, 2007
Georgina Gentry, *To Love a Texan*, 2007
Leigh Greenwood, *Texas Tender*, 2006
Linda Lael Miller, *A Wanted Man*, 2007
R.C. Ryan, *Montana Destiny*, 2010

1032

LAVINIA KENT (Pseudonym of Lavinia Klein)

Taken by Desire
(New York: Avon, 2010)

Story type: Historical
Subject(s): Marriage; Love; Social class
Major character(s): Anna Steele, Spouse (of Alexander); Alexander Struthers, Spouse (of Anna), Businessman

Summary: *Taken by Desire* is a historical romance by author Lavinia Kent. In this book, Kent tells the story of Anna Steele and Alexander Struthers, two lovers who could not resist falling to temptation and breaking societal norms. When their affair is discovered, however, they must either marry or risk being shunned by everyone they know. Anna and Alexander must both deal with one another's dark secrets, which include Anna's battle against relatives trying to steal her inheritance money, and some business transactions of Alexander's that aren't entirely on the up-and-up. Soon they discover, however, that the only way they'll get through this mess is to trust one another implicitly. Kent is also the author of *Bound by Temptation* and *A Talent for Sin*.

Where it's reviewed:
Romantic Times, December 2010, page 41

Other books by the same author:
Bound by Temptation, 2010
A Talent for Sin, 2009

Other books you might like:
Suzanne Enoch, *Always a Scoundrel*, 2009
Anne Gracie, *To Catch a Bride*, 2009
Lisa Kleypas, *Tempt Me at Twilight*, 2009
Raye Morgan, *The Prince's Secret Bride*, 2008

1033

BETH KERY

Explosive
(New York: Heat, 2010)

Story type: Romantic Suspense
Subject(s): Erotica; Romances (Fiction); Suspense
Major character(s): Dr. Sophie Gable, Doctor; Thomas Nicasio, Advisor (investment), Military Personnel (former Navy explosives specialist)
Time period(s): 21st century; 2010s
Locale(s): Illinois, United States

Summary: *Explosive* is an erotic romance novel from bestselling author Beth Kery. Dr. Sophie Gable is looking forward to a relaxing vacation spent at her parents' lake cottage, but her quiet getaway is turned upside down by a surprise visit from an unexpected guest. Thomas Nicasio, a Navy explosives specialist turned financial advisor, works in the same office building as Sophie and, although the pair are intensely attracted to one another, they're essentially strangers. Thomas shows up on Sophie's doorstep, desperate to be with her. As the pair falls into a heated romance, Sophie realizes something much more sinister is at work in Thomas' life, and his haunted past might come back to hurt them both.

Where it's reviewed:
Romantic Times, December 2010, page 99

Other books by the same author:
Fleet Blade, 2010
Release, 2010
Subtle Touch, 2010
Velvet Cataclysm, 2010
Fire Angel, 2009

Other books you might like:
Maya Banks, *Sweet Persuasion*, 2009
Jo Davis, *When Alex Was Bad*, 2009
Lilli Feisty, *Bound to Please*, 2009
Lora Leigh, *Renegade*, 2010

1034

LISA KLEYPAS

Christmas Eve at Friday Harbor
(New York: St. Martin's Press, 2010)

Subject(s): Christmas; Family; Love
Major character(s): Mark Nolan, Brother (of Victoria), Foster Parent (of Holly); Holly, 6-Year-Old, Daughter (of Victoria), Foster Child (of Mark); Maggie Collins, Manager (of Toy Shop)
Time period(s): 21st century; 2010s

Summary: In *Christmas Eve at Friday Harbor*, Mark Nolan finds himself a new father as his niece becomes an orphan. When Mark's sister Victoria passes away, she leaves behind a six-year-old daughter named Holly. Mark is an inexperienced caretaker, and to compound the situation, Holly's trauma has taken away her ability to speak. Parallel to Mark's story is Maggie Collins, recently widowed toy store owner who holds on to her vast imagination and belief in magic, yet struggles with feeling alone. When Maggie meets Holly, she instantly recognizes that the young girl is in dire need of hope, love, and a little holiday magic. Will the Christmas spirit draw this trio together and help them find comfort in one another?

Where it's reviewed:
Library Journal, October 15, 2010, page 60
Publishers Weekly, September 6, 2010, page 24
Romantic Times, November 2010, page 77

Other books by the same author:
Love in the Afternoon, 2010
Married by Morning, 2010
Smooth Talking Stranger, 2009
Tempt Me at Twilight, 2009
A Wallflower Christmas, 2008

Other books you might like:
Marcia Evanick, *A Berry Merry Christmas*, 2004
Marcia Evanick, *Mistletoe Bay*, 2007
Shirley Jump, *Marry-Me Christmas*, 2008
Fern Michaels, *Comfort and Joy*, 2007
Susan Wiggs, *Lakeshore Christmas*, 2009

1035

ANGELA KNIGHT

Master of Smoke

(New York: Berkley, 2011)

Series: Mageverse Series. Book 10
Story type: Paranormal
Subject(s): Adventure; Love; Werewolves
Major character(s): Eva Roman, Werewolf; David/Smoke, Supernatural Being
Time period(s): Indeterminate

Summary: Eva Roman has just been transformed into a werewolf. After the mysterious attack, she is suddenly able to shift into one herself, throwing her entire life into turmoil. She soon rescues another innocent from the same fate, an irresistibly handsome man named David. But David is no innocent—he's a supernatural being whose real name is Smoke, and he is being pursued by the ruthless leader of a band of werewolf killers. *Master of Smoke* is the tenth book in Angela Knight's Mageverse series.

Where it's reviewed:
Publishers Weekly, November 22, 2010, page 47

Other books by the same author:
Master of Fire, 2010
Master of Dragons, 2007
Master of Swords, 2006
Master of Wolves, 2006
Master of the Moon, 2005

Other books you might like:
Susan Krinard, *Lord of Legends*
Lora Leigh, *Wicked Sacrifice*, 2009
Kim Lenox, *Darker than Night*, 2010
Lucy Monroe, *Moon Craving*, 2010
Alexis Morgan, *Dark Defender*, 2006

1036

BETINA KRAHN
JACQUIE D'ALESSANDRO, Co-Author
HOPE TARR, Co-Author

A Harlequin Christmas Carol

(Toronto; New York: Harlequin, 2010)

Story type: Historical
Subject(s): Love; Family; Christmas
Time period(s): 19th century

Summary: The three novellas that comprise *A Harlequin Christmas Carol* are set during the festivities of the holiday season. Acclaimed romance authors Betina Krahn, Jacquie D'Alessandro, and Hope Tarr each contribute a love story to this collection, which centers on beautiful young heroines finding the men of their dreams as the drama and joy of the Christmas season unfolds around them.

Where it's reviewed:
Romantic Times, December 2010, page 39

Other books you might like:
Nicola Cornick, *Christmas Wedding Belles*, 2007
Carla Kelly, *A Regency Christmas Present*, 1999
Allison Lane, *Regency Christmas Magic*, 2004
Elizabeth Rolls, *Mistletoe Kisses*, 2006
Michelle Styles, *A Christmas Wedding Wager*, 2007

1037

KIERAN KRAMER

Dukes to the Left of Me, Princes to the Right

(New York: St. Martin's Press, 2010)

Series: Impossible Bachelors Series. Book 2
Story type: Regency
Subject(s): Marriage; Royalty; Social class
Major character(s): Poppy Smith-Barnes, Socialite; Nicholas Staunton, Nobleman (duke of Drummond)
Locale(s): England

Summary: *Dukes to the Left of Me, Princes to the Right* is a Regency romance by author Kieran Kramer, and is the second novel in her Impossible Bachelors series. Everyone's life should be as hard as that of Poppy Smith-Barnes. In an effort to stave off other suitors, Poppy invents a fiance named the Duke of Drummond. Little does she realize, however, that the Duke of Drummond really exists, and when Nicholas Staunton—the real duke—comes bearing a ring, she is flabbergasted. Nicholas has secrets of his own, though. He is a spy for the British government and must maintain an adequate cover in order to avoid being discovered. Poppy and Nicholas agree to a "fake" engagement, but little do they realize how real their feelings for each other will soon become.

Where it's reviewed:
Booklist, November 1, 2010, page 34
Library Journal, December 1, 2010, page 96
Romantic Times, December 2010, page 34

Other books by the same author:
When Harry Met Molly, 2010

Other books you might like:
Celeste Bradley, *Desperately Seeking a Duke*, 2008
Kathryn Caskie, *How to Seduce a Duke*, 2006
Cara Elliott, *To Sin with a Scoundrel*, 2010
Julia London, *The Hazards of Hunting a Duke*, 2006
Sarah MacLean, *Nine Rules to Break When Romancing a Rake*, 2010

1038

KIERAN KRAMER

When Harry Met Molly

(New York: St. Martin's Press, 2010)

Story type: Regency
Subject(s): Romances (Fiction); Marriage; Social class
Major character(s): Lady Molly Fairbanks, Socialite, Fiance(e) (former, of Cedric); Cedric Alliston, Fiance(e) (former, of Molly); Fiona, Lover (of Harry and Cedric); Lord Harry Traemore, Bachelor
Locale(s): England

Summary: *When Harry Met Molly* is a Regency romance by author Kieran Kramer, and is the first novel in her Impossible Bachelors series. After being jilted by her betrothed, the wimpy Cedric Alliston, for Lord Harry Traemore's mistress, Lady Molly Fairbanks has sworn to get even. Harry has the perfect plot for revenge, too—Molly will pose as his new mistress, making him a shoo-in for the "Most Delectable Companion" competition among his fellow bachelors. There's only one problem: Harry and Molly hate each other, and have done so for a long time. Can the duo look past their loathing long enough to get even with their former lovers?

Where it's reviewed:
Booklist, October 15, 2010, page 26
Romantic Times, November 2010, page 38

Other books you might like:
Elizabeth Boyle, *His Mistress by Morning*, 2006
Loretta Chase, *Miss Wonderful*, 2004
Susan Gee Heino, *Mistress by Mistake*, 2009
Alissa Johnson, *Tempting Fate*, 2009
Olivia Parker, *At the Bride Hunt Ball*, 2008

1039

STEPHANIE LAURENS

The Reckless Bride

(New York: Avon, 2010)

Series: Black Corbra Quartet. Book 4
Story type: Historical

Subject(s): Romances (Fiction); British history, 1815-1914; Suspense
Major character(s): Rafe Carstairs, Military Personnel; Loretta, Young Woman
Time period(s): 19th century; 1820s (1822)
Locale(s): England; India

Summary: *The Reckless Bride* is the fourth and final installment in the Black Cobra quartet. It's 1822 and four former British officers work together to reveal the true identity of a treacherous traitor known as the Black Cobra. Captain Rafe Carstairs and his three associates depart from India for England, each traveling on separate ships to deliver a letter identifying the Black Cobra. Determined to avoid Black Cobra assassins, Rafe takes an unexpected route to England and along the way rescues an elderly woman from an attack. Lady Esme hires Rafe to guard her and her beautiful niece Loretta during her own journey back to England. Rafe is focused on his mission and Loretta is determined not to fall in love, but the undeniable attraction between them makes them both forget their primary objectives.

Where it's reviewed:
Romantic Times, November 2010, page 39

Other books by the same author:
The Brazen Bride, 2010
The Elusive Bride, 2010
Mastered by Love, 2009
Temptation and Surrender, 2009
The Untamed Bride, 2009

Other books you might like:
Liz Carlyle, *Never Lie to a Lady*, 2007
Gaelen Foley, *Her Only Desire*, 2007
Karen Hawkins, *Her Master and Commander*, 2006
Lynn Kerstan, *Dangerous Deceptions*, 2004
Christine Merrill, *A Wicked Liaison*, 2009

1040

JADE LEE (Pseudonym of Katherine Ann Gill)

Wicked Surrender

(New York: Berkley, 2010)

Story type: Historical - Regency
Subject(s): Love; Marriage; Theater
Major character(s): Scheherazade "Scher" Martin, Businessman (theater owner); Brandon Cates, Rake
Time period(s): 19th century
Locale(s): London, United Kingdom

Summary: In *Wicked Surrender*, author Jade Lee tells the romantic tale of an actress's daughter and a rakish nobleman. Scheherazade "Scher" Martin owns a small theater in Regency-era London, where she crosses paths with notorious rogue Brandon Cates. But Scher isn't interested in a one-time fling; she'd much rather find a man with whom to settle down. After accepting a marriage proposal from Brandon's cousin, Scher thinks she's finally found the happiness she has craved for so long. But she soon realizes that she can't stop thinking about Brandon, who has awakened cravings of a different sort....

Where it's reviewed:
Booklist, September 15, 2010, page 53
Romantic Times, September 2010, page 42

Other books by the same author:
The Concubine, 2009
Dragonbound, 2009
Getting Physical, 2009
The Dragon Earl, 2008
Dragonborn, 2008

Other books you might like:
Elizabeth Boyle, *No Marriage of Convenience*, 2000
Cara Elliott, *To Sin with a Scoundrel*, 2010
Madeline Hunter, *The Rules of Seduction*, 2006
Nicole Jordan, *To Tame a Dangerous Lord*, 2010
Christine Wells, *Scandal's Daughter*, 2007

1041

JULIE LESSMAN

Love's First Bloom

(Bloomington, Minnesota: Bethany House, 2010)

Story type: Historical; Religious
Subject(s): Romances (Fiction); Faith; History
Major character(s): Katie O'Connor, Young Woman; Luke McGee, Friend (of Katie); Jack, Boyfriend (of Katie)
Time period(s): 20th century; 1920s
Locale(s): Boston, Massachusetts

Summary: *A Hope Undaunted: A Novel* is a historical romance novel from author Julie Lessman. Despite the fact that it's the 1920s, Katie O'Connor has ambitions for her life that include more than marriage and family. Eager to have it all, intelligent and spirited Katie wants a successful career in law and a happy marriage to a handsome man. Her boyfriend Jack, a sexy and wealthy man with great connections, seems to be the perfect candidate for a husband; but a summer spent with a childhood foe changes everything for Katie. Although she vowed to herself to loathe Luke McGee for all time, Katie finds her heart changing after spending a few months with her former childhood nemesis. With her heart being pulled in two different directions, Katie has to decide between the carefully planned future she constructed in her mind and a life of love that her heart is tugging her toward.

Where it's reviewed:
Romantic Times, September 2010, page 71

Other books by the same author:
A Passion Denied, 2009
A Passion Most Pure, 2008
A Passion Redeemed, 2008

Other books you might like:
Lynn Austin, *Until We Reach Home*, 2008
Deeanne Gist, *The Measure of a Lady*, 2006
Susan Meissner, *The Shape of Mercy*, 2008
Ruth Axtell Morren, *The Making of a Gentleman*, 2008
Jan Watson, *Still House Pond*, 2010

1042

KATIA LIEF (Pseudonym of Kate Pepper)

You Are Next

(New York: Avon, 2010)

Story type: Psychological Suspense
Subject(s): Mystery; Detective fiction; Serial murders
Major character(s): Karin Schaeffer, Detective (former); Martin Price, Serial Killer (the Domino Killer)

Summary: *You Are Next* is a psychological thriller and the debut novel of author Katia Lief. As the only survivor of a serial killer's reign of terror, former detective Karin Schaeffer has been torn apart. Everyone she has ever loved and held dear has been murdered by the Domino Killer, and now she is left behind to pick up the pieces. When the Domino Killer, aka Martin Price, escapes from prison, he comes back to finish what he started. After all, he's best known for never leaving a job unfinished. But this time, Karin isn't going down without a fight. First book.

Where it's reviewed:
Romantic Times, October 2010, page 84

Other books by the same author:
Next Time You See Me, 2010

Other books you might like:
Brenda Novak, *Trust Me*, 2008
Kelsey Roberts, *The Night in Question*, 2009
Jenna Ryan, *A Voice in the Dark*, 2010
Hope Tarr, *Every Breath You Take...*, 2009
Kay Thomas, *Better than Bulletproof*, 2009

1043

JEANNIE LIN

Butterfly Swords

(Don Mills, Ontario, Canada: Harlequin, 2010)

Story type: Historical
Subject(s): China; Adventure; Love
Major character(s): Ai Li, Noblewoman
Time period(s): 7th century-10th century; 600s-900s (618-907)
Locale(s): China

Summary: China's Golden Age is brought to life in Jeannie Lin's *Butterfly Swords*. Ai Li unearths evidence of a violent plan to destroy her family, and she flees in the nick of time with only her trusty butterfly swords. On the run and on the verge of collapse, Ai Li is saved by a handsome warrior. Together they set off across the empire in hopes of reclaiming their respective reputations—and exploring their all-consuming love for one another. *Butterfly Swords* was awarded the 2009 Golden Heart for Historical Romance.

Where it's reviewed:
Romantic Times, October 2010, page 44

Other books you might like:
Cameron Dokey, *Wild Orchid: A Retelling of 'The Ballad of Mulan'*, 2009

Romances

Jade Lee, *Hungry Tigress*, 2005
Jade Lee, *White Tigress*, 2005
Mary Jo Putney, *The Bartered Bride*, 2002
Mary Jo Putney, *The China Bride*, 2000

1044

CATHIE LINZ (Pseudonym of Cathie L. Baumgardner)

Luck Be a Lady
(New York: Berkley, 2010)

Story type: Humor
Subject(s): Romances (Fiction); Humor; Grief
Major character(s): Megan West, Librarian; Logan Doyle, Detective
Time period(s): 21st century; 2010s
Locale(s): Las Vegas, Nevada

Summary: In Cathie Linz's *Luck Be a Lady*, librarian Megan West travels to Las Vegas for a cousin's wedding and uncovers secrets she never believed her family members were capable of keeping from her. Megan can handle that she was never told of a particular family member's marriage. What she can't seem to wrap her head around, however, is the fact that her mother is still alive. For years, Megan believed she'd passed away—and her family, who knew otherwise, had never muttered a word to her about it. To get the answers she so desperately needs, Megan sets off on the mother of all road trips with Detective Logan Doyle. Along the way, Megan discovers secrets about her family and herself.

Where it's reviewed:
Romantic Times, October 2010, page 88

Other books by the same author:
Mad, Bad, and Blonde, 2010
Big Girls Don't Cry, 2009
Smart Girls Think Twice, 2009
Bad Girls Don't, 2006
Good Girls Do, 2006

Other books you might like:
Christie Craig, *Divorced, Desperate and Deceived*, 2009
Curtiss Ann Matlock, *Cold Tea on a Hot Day*, 2001
Kasey Michaels, *Can't Take My Eyes Off of You*, 2000
Christie Ridgway, *Wish You Were Here*, 2000
Deborah Shelley, *Marriage 101*, 2008

1045

JULIA LONDON (Pseudonym of Dinah Dinwiddie)

The Year of Living Scandalously
(New York: Pocket, 2010)

Series: Secrets of Hadley Green Series. Book 1
Story type: Historical - Regency
Subject(s): Love; Identity; Mystery
Major character(s): Keira Hannigan, Young Woman; Declan O'Connor, Nobleman
Time period(s): 19th century
Locale(s): Hadley Green, United Kingdom

Summary: In the Regency-era village of Hadley Green, Keira Hannigan has arrived at a local estate to help clear up some long unfinished business, posing as her noblewoman cousin in order to get the deeds at hand accomplished as quickly as possible. When Declan O'Connor arrives, he sees through Keira's ruse, knowing full well she is not the Countess of Ashwood. But he is immediately taken with beautiful Keira and helps her solve a mystery that has gripped the entire village in terror—and, along the way, the two give in to the fire of their mutual desire for one another. *The Year of Living Scandalously* is the first novel in Julia London's Secrets of Hadley Green series.

Where it's reviewed:
Booklist, November 15, 2010, page 27
Romantic Times, November 2010, page 40

Other books by the same author:
One Season of Sunshine, 2010
A Courtesan's Scandal, 2009
Highland Scandal, 2009
Summer of Two Wishes, 2009
The Book of Scandal, 2008

Other books you might like:
Connie Brockway, *The Golden Season*, 2010
Christina Dodd, *That Scandalous Evening*, 1998
Candice Hern, *Lady Be Bad*, 2007
Madeline Hunter, *Secrets of Surrender*, 2008
Sophia Nash, *Love with the Perfect Scoundrel*, 2009

1046

SUSAN LYONS

Sex on the Slopes
(New York: Berkley Books, 2010)

Story type: Contemporary
Subject(s): Skiing; Sexual behavior; Romances (Fiction)
Major character(s): Maddie Daniels, Sister (of the groom); Logan, Friend (of the groom); Andi Radcliffe, Planner (of weddings); Brianna George, Television Personality (talk show host), Friend (of the groom); Jared Stone, Fire Fighter

Summary: *Sex on the Slopes* is a romance novel by author Susan Lyons. The book revolves around three women: Andi Radcliffe, Brianna George, and Maddie Daniels. As the three arrive at a popular ski resort for a wedding, they encounter opportunities for excitement, relaxation and, most of all, romance. When a fire at her chalet forces wedding planner Andi out into the cold clad in nothing but her lingerie, she meets handsome firefighter Jared Stone. Even though they share an undeniable sexual attraction, Andi isn't sure that Jared, a widower, is ready for the longtime commitment she wants. Brianna, the groom's supervisor, has always been about the job at hand. When an attractive ski instructor catches her eye, her attention is swayed away from her career long enough to put it at risk. The groom's younger sister, Maddie, cannot wait to show his roguish friend Logan how much she's grown up. Will Logan be the bad boy that Maddie remembers? Lyons is also the author of *Calendar of Love, Champagne Rules*, and *Men on Fire*.

Where it's reviewed:
Romantic Times, December 2010, page 99

Other books by the same author:
Alex, 2010
Jillian, 2010
Sex on the Beach, 2010
Calendar of Love, 2009
Carrie, 2009

Other books you might like:
Maya Banks, *Sweet Persuasion*, 2009
Jo Davis, *When Alex Was Bad*, 2009
Lilli Feisty, *Bound to Please*, 2009
Lora Leigh, *Guilty Pleasure*, 2010
Sheri Whitefeather, *Private Dancer*, 2010

1047

KATIE MACALISTER
VICKI LEWIS THOMPSON, Co-Author
CONNIE BROCKWAY, Co-Author

Cupid Cats
(New York: Signet, 2010)

Story type: Anthology
Subject(s): Animals; Romances (Fiction); Short stories

Summary: *Cupid Cats* is a collection of three short stories by authors Connie Brockway, Kate McAllister, and Vicki Lewis Thompson. The stories all revolve around an animal shelter called Cupid Cats, where furry felines help lend a hand in matchmaking for their human caregivers. In Brockway's "Cat Scratch Fever," a social misfit who owns the shelter is matched with a widower unsure if he can give his heart away to another. "A Cat's Game," by Thompson, tells the story of a mystical cat who brings former lovers back together. McAlister's "Unleashed" is a paranormal romance about the love between a half-human, half-jaguar and the wildlife officer who hunts it.

Where it's reviewed:
Romantic Times, July 2010, page 99

Other books you might like:
Jennifer Greene, *Baby, It's Cold Outside*, 2010
Tracy Kelleher, *Write It Up!*, 2006
Cathie Linz, *Catch of the Day*, 2006
Julia London, *Hot Ticket*, 2006
Vicki Lewis Thompson, *A Fare to Remember*, 2006

1048

SARAH MACLEAN (Pseudonym of Sarah Trabucchi)

Ten Ways to Be Adored When Landing a Lord
(New York: Avon, 2010)

Story type: Historical - Regency
Subject(s): Love; Ships; Family
Major character(s): Isabel Townsend, Noblewoman;

Nicholas St. John, Nobleman
Time period(s): 19th century
Locale(s): United Kingdom

Summary: Sarah MacLean's *Ten Ways to Be Adored When Landing a Lord* revolves around the red-hot romance between an impoverished noblewoman and a highly sought-after bachelor. Lady Isabel Townsend is drifting at sea in the aftermath of her father's death, struggling to keep her younger sibling's title and reputation intact. Meanwhile, Nicholas St. John has come onboard hoping to escape the onslaught of single ladies who have eyed him as potential marriage material. The sparks fly immediately between Isabel and Nicholas, opening the doors to a passion neither knew they could ever possess.

Where it's reviewed:
Romantic Times, November 2010, page 38

Other books by the same author:
Nine Rules to Break When Romancing a Rake, 2010

Other books you might like:
Elizabeth Boyle, *Stealing the Bride*, 2003
Loretta Chase, *Mr. Impossible*, 2005
Tessa Dare, *Goddess of the Hunt*, 2009
Karen Hawkins, *How to Treat a Lady*, 2003
Olivia Parker, *At the Bride Hunt Ball*, 2008

1049

DEBBIE MACOMBER

1022 Evergreen Place
(Don Mills, Ontario, Canada: Mira Books, 2010)

Series: Cedar Cove Series. Book 10
Story type: Contemporary
Subject(s): Interpersonal relations; Dating (Social customs); Romances (Fiction)
Major character(s): Mary Jo Wyse, Single Mother, Mother (of Noelle); Noelle, Baby, Daughter (of Mary Jo); David Rhodes, Father (of Noelle), Lover (former, of Mary Jo); Mack McAfee, Neighbor (of Mary Jo)
Time period(s): 21st century; 2010s
Locale(s): Cedar Cove, Washington

Summary: *1022 Evergreen Place* is the tenth installment in Debbie Macomber's Cedar Cove series. Mary Jo Wyse has had a hard time finding the right man. Her relationship with David Rhodes, the father of her young daughter, ended badly, and she's cautious about new relationships altogether. Now, she finds herself falling in love with neighbor Mack McAfee. When Mary Jo and Mack stumble across a stack of old love letters from World War II, it could be just the trick for Mary Jo to get over her relationship phobias. Macomber is also the author of *A Cedar Cove Christmas* and *92 Pacific Boulevard*.

Where it's reviewed:
Romantic Times, September 2010, page 52

Other books by the same author:
Hannah's List, 2010
The Manning Grooms, 2010
Orchard Valley Brides, 2010
Orchard Valley Grooms, 2010

Romances

92 Pacific Boulevard, 2009

Other books you might like:
Susan Andersen, *Burning Up*, 2010
Toni Blake, *Sugar Creek*, 2010
Robyn Carr, *A Summer in Sonoma*, 2010
Susan Donovan, *Not That Kind of Girl*, 2010
Linda Goodnight, *Winning the Single Mom's Heart*, 2008

1050

SUSAN MALLERY

Almost Perfect

(Don Mills, Ontario: Harlequin, 2010)

Series: Fool's Gold Series. Book 2
Story type: Contemporary
Subject(s): Romances (Fiction); Love; Single parent family
Major character(s): Liz Sutton, Single Mother; Ethan Hendrix, Boyfriend (ex, of Liz)
Time period(s): 21st century; 2010s
Locale(s): Fool's Gold, California

Summary: In *Almost Perfect*, a romance novel by Susan Mallery, Liz Sutton and Ethan Hendrix dated secretly in high school. He was the most popular boy in school, and he helped her through some difficult times; that is, until he humiliated and betrayed her in front of everyone, and she left town. Though she tried a few times, she never managed to tell Ethan that she was pregnant with his child. Now a few years later, Liz returns to Fool's Gold, California, intending to finally tell Ethan about his son. Despite her lingering resentment, it is difficult for Liz and Ethan to deny their attraction to each other; however, she doesn't know if she will ever be able to trust him again.

Where it's reviewed:
Romantic Times, July 2010, page 90

Other books by the same author:
The Best of Friends, 2010
Chasing Perfect, 2010
Finding Perfect, 2010
High-Powered, Hot-Blooded, 2009
Hot on Her Heels, 2009

Other books you might like:
Robyn Carr, *Second Chance Pass*, 2008
Barbara Freethy, *On Shadow Beach*, 2010
Jill Marie Landis, *Lover's Lane*, 2003
Linda Lael Miller, *Montana Creeds: Tyler*, 2009
Sherryl Woods, *The Inn at Eagle Point*, 2009

1051

SUSAN MALLERY (Pseudonym of Susan Macias Redmond)

The Best of Friends

(New York: Pocket Star, 2010)

Story type: Contemporary
Subject(s): Love; Family; Friendship

Major character(s): Jayne Scott, Servant; Rebecca Worden, Friend (of Jayne); David Worden, Brother (of Rebecca)
Time period(s): 21st century; 2010s
Locale(s): Los Angeles, California

Summary: Susan Mallery's *The Best of Friends* follows former pals Jayne Scott and Rebecca Worden as they are brought back together after years of separation. Jayne now works for Rebecca's family, and with Rebecca's arrival comes a massive shake-up within the family unit. On Rebecca's heels comes her brother David, who always had a special place in Jayne's heart. Now, as the Wordens deal with the ghosts of an unresolved past, Jayne finds herself once again drawn to David—but she just might lose her best friend in the process.

Other books by the same author:
Already Home, 2011
Almost Perfect, 2010
Chasing Perfect, 2010
Finding Perfect, 2010
Hot on Her Heels, 2009

Other books you might like:
Barbara Delinsky, *Heart of the Night*, 1989
Barbara Delinsky, *The Passions of Chelsea Kane*, 1992
Kristin Hannah, *Between Sisters*, 2003
Leslie LaFoy, *Jackson's Way*, 2001
Emilie Richards, *Fox River*, 2001

1052

JILL MANSELL

Take a Chance on Me

(London: Headline Review, 2010)

Story type: Contemporary; Romance
Subject(s): Sisters; Love; Friendship
Major character(s): Cleo Quinn, Young Woman, Sister (of Abbie), Girlfriend (of Will); Johnny LaVenture, Young Man, Artist (sculptor); Abbie, Sister (of Cleo), Spouse (of Tom); Will, Boyfriend (of Cleo); Tom, Spouse (of Abbie)
Time period(s): 21st century; 2010s
Locale(s): Channings Hill, Fictional Location

Summary: To Cleo Quinn, life is just about perfect in the love department. She has a wonderful boyfriend, Will, and her sister and best friend, Abbie, is happily married and content. Cleo's world is shaken a bit, however, when Johnny LaVenture moves back to town. As an irksome child, Johnny constantly competed with Cleo for attention and admiration. Now that he's back, it seems he hasn't changed, and Cleo decides to avoid him altogether. Channing's Hill is a small town, though, and Cleo's job requires her to travel to each end and back. As Cleo grapples with the circumstances of her sworn enemy's return, Abbie begins to struggle with the changes in her increasingly distant husband, Tom, and she fears that their marriage might be in jeopardy. *Take a Chance on Me* by Jill Mansell showcases the two sisters as they struggle with the men in their lives.

Where it's reviewed:
Romantic Times, October 2010, page 88

Other books you might like:
Lisa Cach, *Have Glass Slippers, Will Travel*, 2005
Jennifer Greene, *Blame It on Chocolate*, 2006
Kristan Higgins, *Catch of the Day*, 2007
Naomi Neale, *Method Man*, 2007
Jane Porter, *The Frog Prince*, 2005

1053

ASHLEY MARCH

Seducing the Duchess

(New York: Signet, 2010)

Story type: Regency
Subject(s): Divorce; Romances (Fiction); Love
Major character(s): Phillip Burgess, Nobleman (duke of Rutherford), Spouse (of Charlotte); Charlotte Burgess, Noblewoman (duchess of Rutherford), Spouse (of Phillip); Lady Joanna Grey, Fiance(e) (former, of Phillip)

Summary: *Seducing the Duchess* is a romance novel by author Ashley March. The marriage of Phillip Burgess, Duke of Rutherford, and his wife Charlotte, the Duchess, is in trouble. Phillip knows it's his own fault, and he'll do anything to repair the damage that he caused to make his wife stray. It may be too late, however, as Charlotte has been begging him for a divorce for some time now. Then Phillip has a plan: grant his wife the divorce she thinks she so desperately wants so that he may pursue Lady Joanna Grey, to whom he was formerly betrothed prior to his marriage. Little does Charlotte realize that this is just a scam to win back her affections. Will Phillip be able to successfully seduce the Duchess?

Where it's reviewed:
Romantic Times, October 2010, page 42
Romantic Times, October 2010, page 42

Other books you might like:
Suzanne Enoch, *Always a Scoundrel*, 2009
Anne Gracie, *To Catch a Bride*, 2009
Susan Johnson, *Sexy As Hell*, 2009
Melody Thomas, *Beauty and the Duke*, 2009

1054

DEIRDRE MARTIN

Icebreaker

(New York: Berkley Books, 2010)

Series: New York Blades Series. Book 10
Story type: Legal
Subject(s): Hockey; Romances (Fiction); Sports
Major character(s): Adam Perry, Hockey Player; Sinead O'Brien, Lawyer
Locale(s): New York, New York

Summary: *Icebreaker* is a romance novel by Deirdre Martin, and is the tenth novel in her New York Blades hockey-romance series. After hockey player Adam Perry makes a devastating hit on an opponent during a match, he finds himself facing assault charges despite the legal-

ity of the play. In order to face the charges of a ruthless D.A. head on, Adam hires hard-hitting attorney Sinead O'Brien. Can O'Brien restore Adam's hopes of rejoining the Blades hockey team and leading them to a Stanley Cup victory, or will their undeniable chemistry derail any chance of Adam being cleared of the charges? Martin is also the author of *The Penalty Box* and *Body Check*.

Where it's reviewed:
Romantic Times, February 2011, page 70

Other books by the same author:
Straight Up, 2010
With a Twist, 2009
Just a Taste, 2008
Power Play, 2008
Chasing Stanley, 2007

Other books you might like:
Gemma Bruce, *The Man for Me*, 2008
Lori Foster, *Back in Black*, 2010
Lisa Renee Jones, *Hot Target*, 2010
Jill Shalvis, *Slow Heat*, 2010

1055

KAT MARTIN (Pseudonym of Kathleen Kelly Martin)

Against the Wind

(Don Mills, Ontario, Canada: MIRA, 2010)

Series: Raines of Wind Canyon Series. Book 1
Story type: Contemporary; Series
Subject(s): Suspense; Single parent family; Romances (Fiction)
Major character(s): Jackson Raines, Rancher; Sarah Allen, Widow(er); Holly, Daughter (of Sarah)
Time period(s): 21st century; 2010s
Locale(s): Wind Canyon, Wyoming

Summary: In *Against the Wind* by Kat Martin, a widow flees Los Angeles after her violent husband is killed. With her young daughter, Holly, in tow, Sarah Allen returns to Wind Canyon, Wyoming. Car trouble en route brings Sarah and the high-school boyfriend she treated cruelly together again. As Sarah learns, Jackson Raines has become a successful rancher who would have been a better catch than the husband she chose. Though Jackson knows he should still be angry with Sarah, he finds himself falling in love with her again. *Against the Wind* is the first book in the Raines of Wind Canyon series.

Where it's reviewed:
Romantic Times, January 2011, page 74

Other books by the same author:
Reese's Bride, 2010
Rule's Bride, 2010
Heart of Courage, 2009
Royal's Bride, 2009
Heart of Fire, 2008

Other books you might like:
Susan Andersen, *Burning Up*, 2010
Toni Blake, *Sugar Creek*, 2010
Carolyn Brown, *The Dove*, 2008

Romances

Margaret Carroll, *A Dark Love*, 2009
Victoria Dahl, *Start Me Up*, 2009

1056

CATHY MAXWELL

His Christmas Pleasure

(New York: Avon, 2010)

Story type: Holiday Themes; Regency
Subject(s): Marriage; Romances (Fiction); Interpersonal relations
Major character(s): Freddy, Lover (former, of Abigail); Abigail Montross, Socialite, Spouse (of Andres); Baron Andres de Vasconia, Nobleman, Spouse (of Abigail)

Summary: *His Christmas Pleasure* is a holiday-themed Regency romance by author Cathy Maxwell. Abigail Montross is 25 years old, considered in her social circle to be well over the hill for marriage. Yet Abigail believes her love, Freddy, will soon propose. As it turns out, Abigail is right and Freddy does propose—to her cousin! Desperate to have her daughter married off, Abigail's father arranges a marriage between her and a man twice her age with 13 children. In an effort to satisfy her father's wishes yet still marry, Abigail elopes with Baron Andres de Vasconia. But can she cure her new husband of his roguish ways in time for the holidays?

Where it's reviewed:
Romantic Times, December 2010, page 34

Other books by the same author:
The Marriage Ring, 2010
The Earl Claims His Wife, 2009
In the Highlander's Bed, 2008
A Seduction at Christmas, 2008
Bedding the Heiress, 2007

Other books you might like:
Mary Balogh, *A Christmas Bride*, 1997
Eloisa James, *An Affair Before Christmas*, 2007
Julia London, *Highland Scandal*, 2009
Sophia Nash, *Love with the Perfect Scoundrel*, 2009
Tracy Anne Warren, *The Wife Trap*, 2006

1057

PENNY MCCALL (Pseudonym of Penny McCusker)

Worth the Trip

(New York: Berkley, 2010)

Story type: Contemporary
Subject(s): Love; Prisoners; Father-daughter relations
Major character(s): Norah MacArthur, Psychologist; Trip Jones, Agent (FBI)
Time period(s): 21st century; 2010s
Locale(s): United States

Summary: Penny McCall's *Worth the Trip* finds psychologist Norah MacArthur's father released from prison, sending the young woman into personal turmoil. Fearful

for her safety, Norah is wondering how she will be able to live her life knowing her father is on the loose. Meanwhile, FBI agent Trip Jones is dispatched to protect Norah. He has no idea, however, how this one assignment will change his life—and his heart—forever.

Where it's reviewed:
Romantic Times, November 2010, page 69

Other books by the same author:
The Bliss Factor, 2010
Packing Heat, 2009
Ace Is Wild, 2008
All Jacked Up, 2007
Tag, You're It, 2007

Other books you might like:
Michele Albert, *One Way Out*, 2005
Christina Dodd, *Trouble in High Heels*, 2006
Julie James, *Something About You*, 2010
Elisabeth Naughton, *Stolen Fury*, 2009
Roxanne St. Claire, *French Twist*, 2004

1058

MONICA MCCARTY

The Hawk

(New York: Random House, 2010)

Series: Highland Guard Series. Book 2
Story type: Historical; Series
Subject(s): Romances (Fiction); History; Scotland
Major character(s): Erik MacSorley, Sea Captain; Elyne de "Ellie" Burgh, Noblewoman
Time period(s): 14th century; 1300s (1307)
Locale(s): Ireland; Scotland

Summary: In *The Hawk*, the Highland Guard struggles to win freedom for Scotland as one indomitable sailor rises to the challenge. Erik MacSorley, known as "The Hawk," refuses to be defeated by an enemy, a rough sea, or a female. When he rescues a woman from Irish waters, he at first fails to recognize the threat she poses. Claiming to be a nursemaid, the woman is in reality Lady Elyne de Burgh, the daughter of an Irish nobleman. Resistant to Erik's overt advances, Lady Elyne possesses political knowledge that could endanger the Highland Guard's cause. *The Hawk* is the second book in the Highland Guard series.

Where it's reviewed:
Romantic Times, September 2010, page 40

Other books by the same author:
The Ranger, 2011
The Chief, 2010
Highland Outlaw, 2009
Highland Scoundrel, 2009

Other books you might like:
Terri Brisbin, *The Maid of Lorne*, 2006
Diana Cosby, *His Captive*, 2007
Juliana Garnett, *The Laird*, 2002
Kathleen Givens, *On a Highland Shore*, 2006
Susan King, *Laird of the Wind*, 1998

1059

ANNETTE MCCLEAVE

Surrender to Darkness

(New York: Signet, 2011)

Series: Soul Gatherers Series. Book 3
Story type: Paranormal
Subject(s): Adventure; Demons; Love
Major character(s): Jamie Murdoch, Warrior (demon fighter); Kiyoko Ashida, Warrior (demon fighter)
Time period(s): 21st century; 2010s
Locale(s): Japan

Summary: Annette McCleave's *Surrender to Darkness* is the third novel in the Soul Gatherers series. This outing focuses on the romance that develops between two warriors, both of whom take on the forces of evil in an effort to protect the world from demons. Jamie Murdoch is a fiery demon-slayer who is sent to Japan to look for a long-lost weapon that could help him in his demon fighting. He soon crosses paths with Kiyoko Ashida, a beautiful, dying, young woman who has devoted her life to battling evil. She too has a connection to the ancient relic Jamie seeks, and it seems to be the only thing keeping her alive—until she encounters Jamie's scorching touch.

Where it's reviewed:
Publishers Weekly, November 22, 2010, page 47

Other books by the same author:
Bound by Darkness, 2010
Drawn into Darkness, 2009

Other books you might like:
Jennifer Ashley, *Immortals: The Calling*, 2007
Cynthia Eden, *Immortal Danger*, 2009
Christine Feehan, *Dark Legend*, 2002
Jacquelyn Frank, *Gideon*, 2007
Susan Krinard, *Come the Night*, 2008

1060

CHEYENNE MCCRAY

Vampires Not Invited

(New York: St. Martin's Press, 2010)

Story type: Vampire Story
Subject(s): Supernatural; Vampires; Romances (Fiction)
Major character(s): Nyx, Detective—Private; Volod, Vampire
Locale(s): New York, New York

Summary: *Vampires Not Invited* is a novel from author Cheyenne McCray's Night Tracker series. When private detective "Night Tracker" Nyx, a half-human, half-elf, accepts her newest assignment, she's somewhat surprised to find it focusing on the Sprites of New York City. These mischievous creatures are known for causing trouble, to be sure, but Nyx has vampires to catch. That's when she realizes that the recent rash of Spritely naughtiness is simply a ruse devised by Volod, the Master Vampire, to distract Nyx from her target. But Nyx is too smart for Volod, and she's determined to take down every vamp in

the city once and for all. McCray is also the author of *Demons Not Included* and *No Werewolves Allowed*.

Where it's reviewed:
Romantic Times, December 2010, page 81

Other books by the same author:
Kade, 2010
No Werewolves Allowed, 2010
Demons Not Included, 2009
Luke, 2009
The Second Betrayal, 2009

Other books you might like:
Yasmine Galenorn, *Bone Magic*, 2010
A.J. Menden, *Phenomenal Girl 5*, 2008
Gena Showalter, *The Darkest Whisper*, 2009
Shiloh Walker, *Hunter's Need*, 2009

1061

LOUCINDA MCGARY

The Wild Irish Sea

(Naperville, Illinois: Sourcebooks, Incorporated, 2010)

Story type: Contemporary
Subject(s): Romances (Fiction); Ireland; Suspense
Major character(s): Kevin Hennessey, Police Officer (former); Amber O'Neill, Traveler
Time period(s): 21st century; 2010s
Locale(s): Ireland

Summary: In *The Wild Irish Sea*, a woman's attempt to save her brother leads her to the home of a former policeman. Amber O'Neill has followed the trail left by her troubled brother to Ireland's treacherous coastline. Caught in a storm, she makes her way to a nearby village where she meets Kevin Hennessey. Intrigued by Amber's story, Hennessey wants to help her find her brother, but he is on the run himself from memories he can't face. Enchanted by the atmosphere of the village and the power of the sea, Kevin and Amber find themselves united by a mysterious bond.

Where it's reviewed:
Romantic Times, August 2010, page 87

Other books by the same author:
The Treasures of Venice, 2009
The Wild Sight, 2008

Other books you might like:
Christine Feehan, *Turbulent Sea*, 2008
Christine Feehan, *Water Bound*, 2010
Virginia Kantra, *Sea Fever*, 2008
Virginia Kantra, *Sea Witch*, 2008
Deborah Smith, *Alice at Heart*, 2002

1062

LINDSAY MCKENNA (Pseudonym of Eileen Nauman)

Deadly Identity

(Don Mills, Ontario, Canada: HQN, 2010)

Story type: Romantic Suspense
Subject(s): Romances (Fiction); Identity; Love

Romances

Major character(s): Rachel Carson, Child-Care Giver, Abuse Victim; Cade Garner, Guardian, Lawman (sheriff), Employer (of Rachel)
Time period(s): 21st century; 2010s
Locale(s): Jackson Hole, Wyoming

Summary: *Deadly Identity* is a suspenseful romance novel from author Lindsay McKenna. Rachel Carson made a fateful choice that resulted in a life of fear and hidden identities. On the run from her past, Rachel has settled down in Jackson Hole, Wyoming. She knows her dreams of finding love or having a baby will never come to fruition, but at least she's safe. Or so she thinks. Sheriff Cade Gardner's life was turned upside down when he became the legal guardian of a baby girl named Jenny. Desperate for assistance, he hires Rachel to work as a nanny for young Jenny. Rachel is a wonderful caregiver, but Cade suspects she's hiding a dark secret. He longs to protect the beautiful nanny, but first, he must uncover the truth.

Where it's reviewed:
Romantic Times, December 2010, page 64

Other books by the same author:
The Adversary, 2010
Guardian, 2010
His Woman in Command, 2010
Reunion, 2010
Shadows from the Past, 2009

Other books you might like:
Margaret Carroll, *A Dark Love*, 2009
Jennifer Crusie, *Maybe This Time*, 2010
Victoria Dahl, *Lead Me On*, 2010
Brenda Novak, *Trust Me*, 2008
Marilyn Pappano, *Intimate Enemy*, 2008

1063

LEE MCKENZIE

Firefighter Daddy

(Toronto; New York: Harlequin, 2010)

Story type: Contemporary
Subject(s): Love; Single parent family; Teachers
Major character(s): Mitch Donovan, Fire Fighter, Single Father, Widow(er); Rory Borland, Teacher
Time period(s): 21st century; 2010s
Locale(s): San Francisco, California

Summary: In Lee McKenzie's *Firefighter Daddy*, Mitch Donovan is a widower and firefighter struggling to raise his daughter on his own. His daughter's teacher, Rory Borland, is devoted to her profession and doesn't have time for romance. When Mitch and Rory meet, their lives are thrown into chaos. Neither had planned on a mutual attraction, but it isn't long before they realize they cannot deny the demands of their hearts.

Where it's reviewed:
Romantic Times, July 2010, page 107

Other books by the same author:
The Man for Maggie, 2007
With this Ring, 2007

Other books you might like:
Jo Davis, *Trial by Fire*, 2008
Anna DeStefano, *The Firefighter's Secret Baby*, 2010
Trish Milburn, *A Firefighter in the Family*, 2008
Alison Roberts, *The Firefighter's Baby*, 2005
Kathryn Shay, *After the Fire*, 2003

1064

LUANN MCLANE
SUSANNA CARR, Co-Author
JANICE MAYNARD, Co-Author

Wicked Wonderland

(New York: NAL Trade, 2010)

Story type: Contemporary
Subject(s): Love; Erotica; Christmas
Time period(s): 21st century; 2010s

Summary: In *Wicked Wonderland*, best-selling authors, LuAnn McLane, Susanna Carr, and Janice Maynard, each contribute an erotic novella centered around the events of the holidays. McLane's "Hot Whisper" is set in a small town, where a young woman finds lodging with a sexy stranger. In Carr's "Hot for the Holidays," a business Christmas party turns longtime enemies into something very unexpected. Maynard's "Hot Arctic Nights" takes place at an Alaskan bed and breakfast, where the innkeeper and a new guest embark upon a steamy, sensual romance as the snow blankets the earth.

Where it's reviewed:
Romantic Times, November 2010, page 79

Other books you might like:
Jacquie D'Alessandro, *A Blazing Little Christmas*, 2007
Lori Foster, *Santa Baby*, 2006
Jennifer Greene, *Baby, It's Cold Outside*, 2010
Julia London, *Hot Ticket*, 2006

1065

TERESA MEDEIROS

Goodnight Tweetheart

(New York: Gallery Books, 2010)

Story type: Contemporary Realism
Subject(s): Information science; Technology; Communications
Major character(s): Abby Donovan, Writer; MarkBaynard, Young Man
Time period(s): 21st century; 2000s

Summary: *Goodnight Tweetheart* is a romance novel by Teresa Medeiros. Several years ago, Abby Donovan was a best-selling author who nearly won the Pulitzer. Now working on her second novel, she finds herself stuck on Chapter Six and well over deadline. When her publicist suggests she sign up for a Twitter account, Abby hopes she will somehow tap into some type of creativity by writing every day. In the meantime, she begins to form an online relationship with a follower named "MarkBaynard." The more she exchanges messages with this online persona, the closer she feels—but is he really the person he says he is? Medeiros is also the author of *The Devil Wears Plaid* and *The Bride and the Beast*.

Where it's reviewed:
Kirkus Reviews, December 1, 2010, page 1182

Other books by the same author:
Some Like It Wild, 2009
Some Like It Wicked, 2008
After Midnight, 2005
Yours Until Dawn, 2004
One Night of Summer, 2003

Other books you might like:
Beth Harbison, *Thin, Rich, Pretty*, 2010
Jane Porter, *Easy on the Eyes*, 2009
Melissa Senate, *The Love Goddess' Cooking School*, 2010
Susan Shapiro, *Speed Shrinking*, 2009

1066

FERN MICHAELS

Cross Roads

(New York: Kensington Publishing Corp, 2010)

Series: Sisterhood Series. Book 18
Story type: Political
Subject(s): Women; Crime; Suspense
Major character(s): Myra Rutledge, Wealthy, Vigilante; Annie Ryland de Silva, Noblewoman (countess), Vigilante; Nikki Quinn, Lawyer, Vigilante; Lizzie Fox Cricket, Vigilante, Lawyer; Alexis Thorn, Vigilante; Kathryn Lucas, Vigilante; Isabelle Flanders, Architect, Vigilante; Yoko Akia, Vigilante

Summary: *Cross Roads* is a novel from best-selling author Fern Michael's series, "The Sisterhood." Myra, Annie, Nikki, Isabelle, Kathryn, Yoko, Maggie, Alexis, and Lizzie all belong to a group known as the Sisterhood, an assemblage of female vigilantes paid to find justice. After being granted a pardon from the president in the previous novel, *Game Over*, the Sisterhood has dispersed and everyone has gone their separate ways. But when one of their own has her private plane hijacked, the Sisterhood must decide if they will come together for one more assignment.

Where it's reviewed:
Romantic Times, October 2010, page 50

Other books by the same author:
Deadly Deals, 2010
Exclusive, 2010
Game Over, 2010
Razor Sharp, 2009
The Scoop, 2009

Other books you might like:
Laura Griffin, *One Last Breath*, 2007
Jayne Ann Krentz, *Light in Shadow*, 2002
Carla Neggers, *Cold River*, 2009
Brenda Novak, *The Perfect Murder*, 2009
Colleen Thompson, *Head On*, 2007

1067

COURTNEY MILAN

Trial by Desire

(Toronto; New York: Harlequin, 2010)

Story type: Historical - Regency
Subject(s): Love; Marriage; Interpersonal relations
Major character(s): Katherine "Kate" Carhart, Spouse (of Ned); Ned Carhart, Spouse (of Kate)
Time period(s): 19th century
Locale(s): United Kingdom

Summary: Courtney Milan's *Trial by Desire* finds noblewoman Kate Carhart in a loveless marriage to Ned. Determined to woo her reluctant husband, Kate sets out to win Ned's aloof heart, but when he abruptly leaves the country, she is devastated. Years go by, and Ned returns a much different man than when he left. Kate's old feelings are reawakened, and this husband and wife set out to find the love that has been heatedly ignited for the first time.

Where it's reviewed:
Booklist, September 15, 2010, page 50
Romantic Times, October 2010, page 36

Other books by the same author:
Proof by Seduction, 2010

Other books you might like:
Adele Ashworth, *Duke of Sin*, 2004
Lisa Kleypas, *Tempt Me at Twilight*, 2009
Julianne MacLean, *Surrender to a Scoundrel*, 2007
Kathryn Smith, *When Marrying a Scoundrel*, 2010
Sherry Thomas, *Private Arrangements*, 2008

1068

JULIE MILLER

Man with the Muscle

(New York: Harlequin, 2010)

Story type: Romantic Suspense
Subject(s): Romances (Fiction); Gangs; Law
Major character(s): Audrey Kline, Lawyer; Alex Taylor, Agent (SWAT), Bodyguard
Time period(s): 21st century; 2010s
Locale(s): United States

Summary: *Man with the Muscle* is a suspenseful romance novel from Julie Miller. Audrey Kline's job has put her in harm's way. As the assistant district attorney, she's working hard to convict a dangerous gang leader, making her a prime target for the gang's revenge. The threats are so serious that Audrey needs to find someone to protect her. SWAT officer Alex Taylor has the skill and experience necessary to protect Audrey from harm, but once he meets the sexy and smart lawyer, he realizes Audrey isn't the only one in danger. His heart runs the risk of being overtaken by the passion he feels for his beautiful new client.

Where it's reviewed:
Romantic Times, December 2010, page 86

Romances

Other books by the same author:
Protecting Plain Jane, 2011
Takedown, 2010
Beauty and the Badge, 2009
Out of Control, 2009
Pulling the Trigger, 2009

Other books you might like:
Jaci Burton, *Riding on Instinct*, 2009
Julie James, *Something About You*, 2010
Elizabeth Jennings, *Shadows at Midnight*, 2010
Lora Leigh, *Black Jack*, 2010
Lora Leigh, *Renegade*, 2010

1069

KATE MOORE

To Save the Devil

(New York: Penguin, 2010)

Series: Sons of Sin Series. Book 2
Story type: Historical; Series
Subject(s): Romances (Fiction); History; Family
Major character(s): Will Jones, Spy (former); Helen of Troy, Young Woman (brothel resident); Archibald March, Villain
Time period(s): 19th century; 1820s (1820)
Locale(s): London, England

Summary: In *To Save the Devil* by Kate Moore, the son of a courtesan searches for his missing brother and finds a beguiling young woman in a London brothel. When William Jones follows his brother's trail to Archibald March, he is distracted from his mission by a virginal young woman being auctioned off to the highest bidder. William escapes with Helen of Troy, as the woman is known, only to find her back at March's house on his return trip. Since William and Helen are both targeting the same man for different reasons, they unite in their quest, finding romance along the way. *To Save the Devil* is the second book in the Sons of Sin series.

Where it's reviewed:
Library Journal, October 15, 2010, page 52

Other books by the same author:
To Tempt a Saint, 2010
Sexy Lexy, 2005
A Prince among Men, 1997
An Improper Widow, 1996
Winterburn's Rose, 1996

Other books you might like:
Brenda Hiatt, *Rogue's Honor*, 2001
Elizabeth Hoyt, *Wicked Intentions*, 2010
Sabrina Jeffries, *Dance of Seduction*, 2003
Rachelle Morgan, *A Scandalous Lady*, 2003
Deborah Raleigh, *Bedding the Baron*, 2008

1070

KATE MOORE

To Tempt a Saint

(New York: Berkley Sensation, 2010)

Series: Sons of Sin Series. Book 1
Story type: Historical; Series
Subject(s): Romances (Fiction); History; Marriage
Major character(s): Alexander Jones, Nobleman; Cleo Spencer, Heiress
Time period(s): 19th century; 1810s (1816)
Locale(s): London, England

Summary: In *To Tempt a Saint* by Kate Moore, the son of a courtesan proves himself a hero but struggles to make a place for himself in London society. Knighted for his rescue of the prince regent, Alexander Jones knows that he must marry a noblewoman if he is to be received by the nobility. Cleo Spencer is heiress to a fortune, but she must take a husband to inherit her wealth. Alexander and Cleo marry for practical reasons, neither recognizing the true love growing between them. *To Tempt a Saint* is the first book in the Sons of Sin series.

Where it's reviewed:
Booklist, September 15, 2009, page 52
Library Journal, December 15, 2009, page 91
Romantic Times, January 2010, page 44

Other books by the same author:
To Save the Devil, 2010
Sexy Lexy, 2005
A Prince among Men, 1997
An Improper Widow, 1996
Winterburn's Rose, 1996

Other books you might like:
Brenda Hiatt, *Rogue's Honor*, 2001
Elizabeth Hoyt, *Wicked Intentions*, 2010
Sabrina Jeffries, *Dance of Seduction*, 2003
Rachelle Morgan, *A Scandalous Lady*, 2003
Deborah Raleigh, *Bedding the Baron*, 2008

1071

MARGARET MOORE (Pseudonym of Margaret Wilkins)

Highland Rogue, London Miss

(Toronto; New York: Harlequin, 2010)

Story type: Historical - Regency
Subject(s): Marriage; Love; Social class
Major character(s): Quintus MacLachlann, Rake; Esme, Young Woman (sham wife of Quintus)
Time period(s): 19th century
Locale(s): Edinburgh, Scotland

Summary: In *Highland Rogue, London Miss*, author Margaret Moore charts the relationship that evolves from a fake marriage arrangement in Regency-era Scotland. Quintus MacLachlann is a notorious rake, and he's thrilled at the opportunity to pose as husband to the beautiful Esme. Their goal is to break into Edinburgh society, but things become all too real when a mutual attraction develops between Quintus and Esme, jeopardizing their arrangement and their plans to permeate the upper crust.

Where it's reviewed:
Romantic Times, August 2010, page 45

Other books by the same author:
The Viscount's Kiss, 2009
Knave's Honor, 2008
Hers to Desire, 2006
The Willing Bride, 2005
The Notorious Knight, 2010

Other books you might like:
Jennifer Ashley, *The Madness of Lord Ian Mackenzie*, 2009
Janet Chapman, *Wedding the Highlander*, 2003
Kathleen Givens, *On a Highland Shore*, 2006
Karen Ranney, *A Highland Duchess*, 2010
Michele Sinclair, *Desiring the Highlander*, 2009

1072

KIRA MORGAN (Pseudonym of Glynnis Campbell)

Captured by Desire

(New York: Forever, 2010)

Story type: Historical
Subject(s): Scotland; Scots (British people); Love
Major character(s): Florie Gilder, Young Woman; Rane MacAllister, Viking; Mavis Fraser, Noblewoman
Time period(s): 16th century; 1560s (1568)
Locale(s): Scotland

Summary: Kira Morgan's *Captured by Desire* takes place in 16th-century Scotland, where beautiful Florie Gilder has come to the Selkirk Fair in hopes of finding her birth father. Through a series of unfortunate run-ins, she crosses a powerful noblewoman named Lady Mavis, and soon Mavis sets out to exact a brutal revenge on Florie. On the run from Lady Mavis, Florie encounters dashing Rane MacAllister, who protects her from the noblewoman's ruthless pursuit. In the process, Florie and Rane find a romance beyond their wildest imaginings. First novel.

Where it's reviewed:
Romantic Times, August 2010, page 46

Other books you might like:
Julie Garwood, *Shadow Music*, 2007
Jen Holling, *My Shadow Warrior*, 2005
Hannah Howell, *Highland Sinner*, 2008
Michele Sinclair, *Desiring the Highlander*, 2009
Mary Wine, *To Conquer a Highlander*, 2010

1073

ELISABETH NAUGHTON

Entwined

(New York: Dorchester Publishing, 2010)

Story type: Alternate World; Fantasy
Subject(s): Mythology; Knights; Immortality

Major character(s): Callia, Healer; Zander, Warrior (Argonaut)

Summary: Zander is an Argonaut who has volunteered to marry the king's daughter, a task even he is surprised to accept. When he arrives to have a final physical exam by the king's doctor before the wedding, he finds himself face to face with his one true love, Callia. Callia is now the king's personal healer and must ensure that Zander is virile enough to bear future royalty. After his examination, both Callia and Zander realize that the flame between them hasn't died. Unfortunately, Zander is now betrothed to one of the most powerful women in the country. Can Callia suppress her love, or will she shirk her royalty duty?

Where it's reviewed:
Romantic Times, August 2010, page 92

Other books by the same author:
Marked, 2010
Stolen Fury, 2009
Stolen Heat, 2009
Stolen Seduction, 2009

Other books you might like:
Jennifer Ashley, *Immortals: The Gathering*, 2007
Kresley Cole, *Kiss of a Demon King*, 2009
Christine Feehan, *Dark Magic*, 2000
Sherrilyn Kenyon, *Born of Ice*, 2009
Eve Silver, *Sins of the Soul*, 2010

1074

CARLA NEGGERS

The Whisper

(Don Mills, Ontario, Canada: MIRA, 2010)

Series: BPD-FBI Series. Book 4
Story type: Mystery; Series
Subject(s): Mystery; Murder; Crime
Major character(s): Sophie Malone, Archaeologist; Cyrus "Scoop" Wisdom, Detective—Police
Time period(s): 21st century; 2010s
Locale(s): Ireland; Boston, Massachusetts

Summary: In *The Whisper*, a missing collection of Celtic artifacts draws an archaeologist and a detective into a mysterious case of murder. Sophie Malone first discovered the cache of gold in a cave in Ireland. Alone in the cave, surrounded by a whispering presence, Sophie was attacked and the artifacts went missing. Back in the United States, Sophie follows the treasure's trail to Boston, where detective Cyrus Wisdom is on the hunt for the man who tried to kill him. Sophie and Cyrus's paths cross when another cop becomes the victim of a ritual killing. *The Whisper* is the fourth book in the BPD-FBI series.

Where it's reviewed:
Romantic Times, July 2010, page 81

Other books by the same author:
Cold Dawn, 2010
Cold River, 2009
The Mist, 2009

Romances

The Angel, 2008
Cold Pursuit, 2008

Other books you might like:
Beverly Barton, *The Fifth Victim*, 2003
Kylie Brant, *Waking Evil*, 2009
Carla Cassidy, *Are You Afraid?*, 2006
Heather Graham, *Ghost Shadow*, 2010
Colleen Thompson, *Touch of Evil*, 2010

1075

MIRANDA NEVILLE

The Dangerous Viscount

(New York: HarperCollins, 2010)

Series: Burgandy Club Series. Book 2
Story type: Historical; Series
Subject(s): Romances (Fiction); History; Marriage
Major character(s): Diana Fanshawe, Noblewoman; Lord Blakeney, Nobleman; Sebastian, Nobleman (Viscount Iverley)
Time period(s): 19th century; 1810s (1819)
Locale(s): England

Summary: In *The Dangerous Viscount* by Miranda Neville, a noblewoman must choose between a man who will make a suitable husband and another who is an irresistible scoundrel. Lady Diana Fanshawe is aware of the disdain 19th-century London society holds for her troubled family. To assume her rightful place in society, Diana must marry appropriately, and Lord Blakeney seems a prime—if unlovable—candidate. When Sebastian, Viscount Iverley boldly kisses her, she knows that she could surrender herself to him, body and soul. The problem is, the Viscount has no interest in marriage or Diana. *The Dangerous Viscount* is the second book in the Burgundy Club series.

Where it's reviewed:
Romantic Times, October 2010, page 46

Other books by the same author:
The Wild Marquis, 2010
Never Resist Temptation, 2009

Other books you might like:
Nicole Jordan, *To Romance a Charming Rogue*, 2009
Lavinia Kent, *A Talent for Sin*, 2009
Lisa Kleypas, *Married by Morning*, 2010
Gail Ranstrom, *Unlacing Lilly*, 2008

1076

BRENDA NOVAK

Killer Heat

(Don Mills, Ontario, Canada: Mira, 2010)

Story type: Romantic Suspense
Subject(s): Detective fiction; Serial murders; Romances (Fiction)
Major character(s): Jonah Young, Security Officer (private); Francesca Moretti, Detective—Private

Time period(s): 21st century; 2010s
Locale(s): Skull Valley, Arizona

Summary: *Killer Heat* is a steamy romance novel from Brenda Novak. When the bodies of seven murdered women are discovered in Skull Valley, Arizona, the Yavapai County Sheriff's Office seeks the help of private security agent, Jonah Young. Unfortunately for Jonah, working on the case means working alongside private detective, Francesca Moretti, a woman he has a long and complicated past with. Ten years ago, Jonah betrayed Francesca and she still carries a massive grudge against him, but she doesn't have a choice about their working situation. Francesca was hired to find a woman who ended up murdered in the same way as the victims in Jonah's case. Now they must team up to find the person responsible before the killer finds them.

Where it's reviewed:
Romantic Times, October 2010, page 76

Other books by the same author:
Inside, 2011
Body Heat, 2010
White Heat, 2010
The Perfect Liar, 2009
The Perfect Murder, 2009

Other books you might like:
Christy Reece, *Last Chance*, 2010
Christy Reece, *No Chance*, 2010
Kelsey Roberts, *The Night in Question*, 2009
Jenna Ryan, *A Voice in the Dark*, 2010
Stephanie Tyler, *Hard to Hold*, 2009

1077

CONSTANCE O'BANYON (Pseudonym of Evelyn Gee)

Wolf Runner

(New York: Dorchester Publishing, 2010)

Story type: Historical - American West
Subject(s): Native Americans; United States history; Indigenous peoples
Major character(s): Cheyenne, Granddaughter (of Ivy Gatlin), Indian (half-Native American); Wolf Runner, Indian (Native American); Ivy Gatlin, Grandmother (of Cheyenne)
Locale(s): New Mexico, United States

Summary: *Wolf Runner* is a historical romance written by Constance O'Banyon. Living amongst the white people as a person of mixed heritage, Cheyenne has always longed to connect with her Native American cultural roots. Yet life in her town in New Mexico has not allowed her to do so, and instead she has been treated as a pariah by those who see her as different. When her ailing grandmother sends for an old family friend to escort Cheyenne to meet her grandfather, Cheyenne is stunned. Her escort is Wolf Runner, and Cheyenne is instantly drawn to him. Wolf Runner is also half-White, half-Native American, yet he exudes confidence and strength. Can he teach Cheyenne to be confident as well?

Where it's reviewed:
Romantic Times, August 2010, page 44

Other books by the same author:
Wind Warrior, 2010
Comanche Moon Rising, 2009
Enchantress, 2009
Daughter of Egypt, 2008
Desert Prince, 2008

Other books you might like:
Elaine Barbieri, *Hawk's Prize*, 2006
Veronica Blake, *Black Horse*, 2009
Carol Ann Didier, *Navajo Night*, 2009
Cassie Edwards, *Savage Dawn*, 2009
Georgina Gentry, *Diablo*, 2010

1078

LORIE O'CLARE

Play Dirty

(New York: St. Martin's Press, 2010)

Story type: Contemporary
Subject(s): Love; Marriage; Suspense
Major character(s): Haley King, Witness (to a murder), Spouse (of Greg); Greg King, Bounty Hunter, Spouse (of Haley)
Time period(s): 21st century; 2010s
Locale(s): United States

Summary: In *Play Dirty*, author Lori O'Clare tells the story of a husband and wife who are given a second chance at love. Haley King was forced to secretly enter the Witness Protection Program, leaving behind her sexy bounty hunter husband Greg. Heartbroken, Greg has tried to move on with his life in the aftermath of his wife's sudden disappearance. Now Haley is back, and she needs his help. Can these two reconcile the pain of the past with the dangers of their current predicament, which finds Haley the target of dangerous assassins?

Where it's reviewed:
Romantic Times, October 2010, page 78

Other books by the same author:
Black Passion, 2010
Black Seduction, 2010
Feather Torn, 2010
Strong, Sleek and Sinful, 2010
Vision Fulfilled, 2010

Other books you might like:
Margaret Carroll, *A Dark Love*, 2009
Pamela Clare, *Naked Edge*, 2010
Jo Davis, *Hidden Fire*, 2009
Marilyn Pappano, *Intimate Enemy*, 2008

1079

DELIA PARR

Love's First Bloom

(Ada, Michigan: Bethany House Publishing, 2010)

Story type: Inspirational
Subject(s): Murder; Christian life; Identity

Major character(s): Ruth Livingstone, Young Woman; Jake Spencer, Journalist
Time period(s): 19th century
Locale(s): Toms River, New Jersey

Summary: *Love's First Bloom* is an inspirational romance novel by author Delia Parr. The story revolves around Ruth Livingstone, the daughter of a reverend who surprises her one day by presenting her with a child and shipping her off to New Jersey with a brand new identity. There, Ruth must pretend she is a widow and the child's mother as her father fights murder charges in their hometown. She soon meets Jake Spencer, a handsome man to whom she feels instantly drawn. Jake has a secret, though—he is a reporter who is seeking Ruth to tell her story in the penny press. Will Jake and Ruth ever learn of each other's secret identity?

Where it's reviewed:
Romantic Times, September 2010, page 66

Other books by the same author:
Heart's Awakening, 2010
Carry the Light, 2008
Refining Emma, 2008
A Hearth in Candlewood, 2007
Abide with Me, 2006

Other books you might like:
Tamera Alexander, *Beyond This Moment*, 2009
Lynn Austin, *Until We Reach Home*, 2008
Kaye Dacus, *Ransome's Crossing*, 2010
Robin Lee Hatcher, *Dear Lady*, 2000
Marylu Tyndall, *Surrender the Heart*, 2010

1080

KATE PEARCE (Pseudonym of Catherine Duggan)

Kiss of the Rose

(New York: Signet, 2010)

Series: Tudor Vampire Series. Book 1
Story type: Historical; Vampire Story
Subject(s): British history, 1066-1688; Vampires; Alternative worlds
Major character(s): Rosalind Llewellyn, Vampire Hunter; Sir Christopher Ellis, Vampire Hunter; Henry Tudor VIII, Royalty (king of England)
Time period(s): 16th century
Locale(s): England

Summary: *Kiss of the Rose* is the first novel in the Tudor Vampire series, written by author Catherine Duggan under the pseudonym Kate Pearce. This series tells an alternative point of view to the story of the Tudor Dynasty, and how Henry Tudor took the crown from Richard III after striking a deal with the Druids and enslaving a clan of vampire hunters named the Llewellyns. In this book, Henry VIII has taken the crown. But when murder victims begin turning up, all evidence pointing to Henry VIII, one vampire slayer named Rosalind must band together with a Druid slayer named Sir Christopher Ellis to protect the kingdom.

Where it's reviewed:
Romantic Times, August 2010, page 46

Romances

Other books by the same author:
Simply Insatiable, 2010
Simply Shameless, 2009
Simply Wicked, 2009
Simply Sexual, 2008
Simply Sinful, 2008

Other books you might like:
Denise Domning, *Lady in White*, 1999
Colleen Gleason, *The Rest Falls Away*, 2007
Kim Lenox, *Night Falls Darkly*, 2008
Teresa Medeiros, *The Vampire Who Loved Me*, 2006
Kathryn Smith, *Be Mine Tonight*, 2006

1081

KATE PERRY (Pseudonym of Katia Zolfaghari)

Tempted by Fate
(New York: Forever, 2010)

Series: Guardians of Destiny Series. Book 3
Story type: Contemporary
Subject(s): Love; Serial murders; Suspense
Major character(s): Rick Ramirez, Detective—Police; Willow Tarata, Guardian (of The Book of Wood)
Time period(s): 21st century; 2010s
Locale(s): San Francisco, California
Summary: The third novel in The Guardians of Destiny series, Kate Perry's *Tempted by Fate* follows the romantic adventures of Willow Tarata, a Guardian who is after those responsible for killing her mother. Meanwhile, San Francisco police detective Rick Ramirez needs Willow's help in finding a serial killer, who may be responsible for her mother's death. Sparks fly immediately between Rick and Willow, but the two must learn to work together—and deal with their mutual desire—before a killer strikes again.

Where it's reviewed:
Library Journal, December 2010, page 97
Romantic Times, December 2010, page 78

Other books by the same author:
Chosen by Desire, 2009
Marked by Passion, 2009
Project Date, 2007
Project Daddy, 2006

Other books you might like:
Maureen Child, *Eternally*, 2006
Kresley Cole, *Dark Desires After Dusk*, 2008
Angela Knight, *Master of the Night*, 2004
Jennifer Lyon, *Blood Magic*, 2009
Mary Jo Putney, *Kiss of Fate*, 2004

1082

MARTA PERRY

Murder in Plain Sight
(Don Mills, Ontario, Canada: HQN Books, 2010)

Subject(s): Amish; Murder; Detective fiction
Major character(s): Jessica Langdon, Lawyer; Trey Morgan, Businessman
Time period(s): 21st century; 2010s
Locale(s): Lancaster County, Pennsylvania
Summary: A small Amish community in Lancaster, Pennsylvania, is devastated when an Amish teenager is accused of murdering a young woman. Now, lawyer Jessica Langdon is determined to defend the young boy despite threats from the community. Armed with only a basic knowledge of the Amish lifestyle, Jessica needs to know more to defend her client. She soon enlists the help of Trey Morgan, a local businessman with ties to the Amish community. Unsure if she can trust Trey, Jessica searches for the truth and quickly makes some shocking discoveries.

Where it's reviewed:
Romantic Times, December 2010, page 63

Other books by the same author:
Vanish in Plain Sight, 2011
Anna's Return, 2010
The Guardian's Honor, 2010
Heart of the Matter, 2010
Rachel's Garden, 2010

Other books you might like:
Wanda E. Brunstetter, *Looking for a Miracle*, 2006
Wanda E. Brunstetter, *A Sister's Secret*, 2007
Wanda E. Brunstetter, *The Storekeeper's Daughter*, 2005

1083

JENNA PETERSEN

The Unclaimed Duchess
(New York: Avon, 2010)

Story type: Regency
Subject(s): Royalty; Social class; Romances (Fiction)
Major character(s): Anne Danvers, Noblewoman (duchess of Waverly); Rhys Carlisle, Nobleman (duke of Waverly)
Locale(s): England
Summary: *The Unclaimed Duchess* is a romance novel by author Jenna Petersen. Lady Anne Danvers has been lucky since birth, having been born into a family of noblemen and noblewomen. Her lifelong good fortune includes never having to search for a husband, as she has been engaged since birth to Rhys Carlisle, Duke of Waverly, one of the most sought-after heirs in all of England. Yet when Rhys takes off immediately after their wedding, Anne begins to wonder if being a duchess isn't all it's cracked up to be. Still she's determined to win back the title, and the man, that are rightfully hers. Petersen is also the author of *Seduction is Forever*, *Desire Never Dies*, and *From London with Love*.

Where it's reviewed:
Romantic Times, September 2010, page 42

Other books by the same author:
Her Notorious Viscount, 2009
What the Duke Desires, 2009
Lessons from a Courtesan, 2008
Desire Never Dies, 2007
Seduction Is Forever, 2007

Other books you might like:
Gaelen Foley, *My Wicked Marquess*, 2009
Susan Gee Heino, *Mistress by Mistake*, 2009
Julie Anne Long, *Since the Surrender*, 2009
Lisa Valdez, *Patience*, 2010

1084

CARLY PHILLIPS (Pseudonym of Karen Drogin)

Love Me if You Dare

(Don Mills, Ontario, Canada: HQN, 2010)

Story type: Romantic Suspense
Subject(s): Romances (Fiction); Law enforcement;
    Suspense
Major character(s): Rafe Mancuso, Police Officer,
    Bachelor; Sara Rios, Police Officer
Time period(s): 21st century; 2010s
Locale(s): New York, New York

Summary: *Love Me if You Dare* is a steamy romance novel from best-selling author Carly Phillips. Rafe Mancuso suddenly becomes a New York City hero when the hostage negotiator takes a bullet to save the life of his former partner Sara Rios. The sexy NYPD officer is quickly named the city's most eligible bachelor by the Bachelor Blog and gossip swirls about the nature of Rafe and Sara's relationship. Desperate for a break from the media attention, Rafe escapes to a private lake cottage, leaving Sara to fend for herself in the limelight. As Sara's injuries heal and she waits to testify at an upcoming trial, the only thought preoccupying her mind is of Rafe. Sara sets out to track him down and discover if there's any truth to the rumors.

Where it's reviewed:
Romantic Times, September 2010, page 85

Other books by the same author:
Kiss Me If You Can, 2010
Lucky Break, 2009
Lucky Streak, 2009
Hot Property, 2008
Lucky Charm, 2008

Other books you might like:
Victoria Dahl, *Start Me Up*, 2009
Sue Margolis, *Forget Me Knot*, 2009
Marilyn Pappano, *Intimate Enemy*, 2008

1085

LISA PLUMLEY

Mail-Order Groom

(New York: Harlequin, 2010)

Story type: Historical - American West
Subject(s): Western fiction; Romances (Fiction); Identity
Major character(s): Savannah Reed, Actress (former);
    Adam Corwin, Detective, Lawman
Time period(s): 19th century; 1880s (1884)
Locale(s): Morrow Creek, Arizona

Summary: *Mail-Order Groom* is a romantic, historical novel from best-selling author Lisa Plumley. After enduring a major scandal on the New York stage, lively actress Savannah Reed heads west to Morrow Creek for a quieter life as the telegraph operator. Her job leads her to a new man, just not the one she's expecting. Eagerly awaiting her mail-order groom, Savannah is shocked to find him shot and clinging to life on her doorstep. She nurses him back to health, unaware that the man she's falling in love with isn't her groom after all. Former U.S. Marshal Adam Corwin is now a detective, tracking the man Savannah is planning to marry. One look at Savannah's sexy smile has Adam out of sorts and totally unsure about how he's going to break the news that her mail-order groom is an outlaw and her life is in danger. Although, if Savannah is looking for a new husband, Adam just might be willing to take the job.

Where it's reviewed:
Romantic Times, December 2010, page 37

Other books by the same author:
The Bride Raffle, 2011
Holiday Affair, 2010
My Favorite Witch, 2009
Home for the Holidays, 2008
Let's Misbehave, 2007

Other books you might like:
Georgina Gentry, *To Tame a Texan*, 2003
Leigh Greenwood, *The Independent Bride*, 2004
Leigh Greenwood, *The Reluctant Bride*, 2005
Linda Lael Miller, *A Wanted Man*, 2007

1086

JANE PORTER

She's Gone Country

(New York: 5 Spot, 2010)

Story type: Contemporary
Subject(s): Love; Family; Divorce
Major character(s): Shey Darcy, Model, Mother, Divorced
    Person; Dane Kelly, Rodeo Rider, Divorced Person
Time period(s): 21st century; 2010s
Locale(s): Texas, United States

Summary: In Jane Porter's *She's Gone Country*, Shey Darcy returns to her small Texas hometown with her three teenaged sons. After living the high life as a New York model, Shey finds it hard adjusting to the rural environment, especially with the presence of her strict minister mother. Further complicating matters is Dane Kelly, an old flame of Shey's, who is rekindling the fires of her long-dormant heart.

Where it's reviewed:
Library Journal, July 1, 2010, page 78
Publishers Weekly, June 28, 2010, page 109
Romantic Times, October 2010, page 87

Other books by the same author:
Duty, Desire, and the Desert King, 2009
Easy on the Eyes, 2009
King of the Desert, Captive Bride, 2008

Romances

Mrs. Perfect, 2008
The Sheik's Chosen Queen, 2008

Other books you might like:
Patricia Gaffney, *Flight Lessons*, 2002
Beth Kendrick, *Second Time Around*, 2010
Tanya Michaels, *The Good Kind of Crazy*, 2006
Allison Rushby, *The Dairy Queen*, 2006
Barbara Samuel, *No Place Like Home*, 2002

1087

TARA TAYLOR QUINN

The Fourth Victim

(New York: Mira, 2010)

Story type: Contemporary
Subject(s): Love; Suspense; Adventure
Major character(s): Clay Thatcher, Agent (FBI); Kelly Chapman, Psychologist
Time period(s): 21st century; 2010s
Locale(s): United States

Summary: In *The Fourth Victim*, best-selling author Tara Taylor Quinn tells the story of a determined FBI agent and the case that captures his heart. Clay Thatcher is on the hunt for Kelly Chapman, a psychologist and trial witness who mysteriously vanished. But the deeper Clay gets into his investigation, the more he realizes this is no ordinary missing-persons case: both his head and his heart are captivated by a woman he's never even met—and, if he doesn't get to her in time, may never have the chance to meet.

Where it's reviewed:
Library Journal, December 2010, page 97
Romantic Times, December 2010, page 62

Other books by the same author:
The First Wife, 2010
The Second Lie, 2010
The Third Secret, 2010
A Daughter's Trust, 2009
Sophie's Secret, 2009

Other books you might like:
Beverly Barton, *Close Enough to Kill*, 2006
Suzanne Brockmann, *Breaking Point*, 2005
Brenda Novak, *The Perfect Liar*, 2009
Brenda Novak, *The Perfect Murder*, 2009
Lorie O'Clare, *Tall, Dark and Deadly*, 2009

1088

GAIL RANSTROM

A Rake by Midnight

(Toronto; New York: Harlequin, 2010)

Story type: Historical - Regency
Subject(s): Love; Crime; Interpersonal relations
Major character(s): Eugenia "Gina" O'Rourke, Young Woman; James Hunter, Rescuer (of Gina)
Time period(s): 19th century

Locale(s): United Kingdom

Summary: Gail Ranstrom's *A Rake by Midnight* tells the story of Eugenia "Gina" O'Rourke, a young woman who is nearly raped and killed by a group of thugs. Fortunately, help arrives in the form of sexy James Hunter, who is immediately smitten with the beautiful Gina. He vows to protect her at all costs, but Gina is embarrassed by the circumstances of her attack. Can James convince Gina that his feelings are real—and far more than that of a protector for his charge?

Where it's reviewed:
Romantic Times, October 2010, page 48

Other books by the same author:
Unlacing Lilly, 2008
Lord Libertine, 2007
The Courtesan's Courtship, 2006
Indiscretions, 2006
The Missing Heir, 2005

Other books you might like:
Pamela Britton, *Seduced*, 2003
Nicola Cornick, *Lord of Scandal*, 2007
Diane Gaston, *A Reputable Rake*, 2006
Amanda McCabe, *To Deceive a Duke*, 2010
Kathryn Smith, *A Game of Scandal*, 2002

1089

DEANNA RAYBOURN

Dark Road to Darjeeling

(New York: Mira, 2010)

Series: Lady Julia Grey Series. Book 4
Subject(s): Pregnancy; Indian history; Detective fiction
Major character(s): Julia Grey, Detective—Amateur, Spouse (of Nicholas), Friend (of Jane); Nicholas Brisbane, Friend (of Jane), Detective—Amateur, Spouse (of Julia); Jane, Friend (of Julia and Nicholas)
Time period(s): 19th century
Locale(s): Darjeeling, India

Summary: Lady Julia Grey and husband Nicholas Brisbane learn that their longtime friend, Jane, is facing difficult times. Jane's husband has recently died, leaving her pregnant and entirely on her own. However, her troubles, it seems, are just beginning. Someone wants Jane dead, and it's up to her old friends Julia and Nicholas to stop the culprit and protect the expectant widow. *Dark Road to Darjeeling* is the fourth installment in Deanna Raybourn's Lady Julia Grey series.

Where it's reviewed:
Booklist, October 15, 2010, page 23
Library Journal, September 1, 2010, page 104
Publishers Weekly, August 16, 2010, page 30
Romantic Times, October 2010, page 82

Other books by the same author:
The Dead Travel Fast, 2010
Silent on the Moor, 2009
Silent in the Sanctuary, 2008
Silent in the Grave, 2007

Other books you might like:
Tasha Alexander, *A Poisoned Season*, 2007
Rhys Bowen, *Murphy's Law*, 2001
Carol K. Carr, *India Black*, 2011
Anne Perry, *The Cater Street Hangman*, 1979
Elizabeth Peters, *Crocodile on the Sandbank*, 1975

1090

LISA MARIE RICE

Into the Crossfire

(New York: Avon Red, 2010)

Story type: Romantic Suspense
Subject(s): Romances (Fiction); Sexuality; Terrorism
Major character(s): Sam Reston, Businessman, Military Personnel (former Navy SEAL); Nicole Pearce, Businesswoman
Time period(s): 21st century; 2010s
Locale(s): United States

Summary: *Into the Crossfire* is a Protectors romantic suspense novel by Lisa Marie Rice. In this novel, Sam Reston is a former Navy SEAL who now lives a fairly secretive, unpredictable and sometimes dangerous life, with no room in it for anyone else. Then the stunning Nicole Pearce moves in next door. She has just started a new business and is trying to take care of her ill father. Sam and Nicole immediately recognize their attraction for each other, but when their relationship suddenly puts Nicole in danger, Sam realizes he will do anything to protect her.

Where it's reviewed:
Romantic Times, October 2010, page 118

Other books by the same author:
Hotter than Wildfire, 2011
Dangerous Passion, 2009
A Fine Specimen, 2009
Dangerous Secrets, 2008
Dangerous Lover, 2007

Other books you might like:
Jaci Burton, *Riding on Instinct*, 2009
Julie James, *Something About You*, 2010
Lora Leigh, *Black Jack*, 2010
Lora Leigh, *Renegade*, 2010

1091

PATRICIA RICE

The Wicked Wyckerly

(New York: Signet, 2010)

Series: Rebellious Sons Series. Book 1
Story type: Historical - Regency
Subject(s): Marriage; Love; Inheritance and succession
Major character(s): John Fitzhugh "Fitz" Wyckerly, Nobleman; Abigail "Abby" Merriweather, Farmer
Time period(s): 19th century; 1810s
Locale(s): United Kingdom

Summary: John Fitzhugh Wyckerly is on the hunt for a wife. The recent inheritor of a title and a dilapidated manor house, Fitz needs a spouse with money, and quickly. With his illegitimate daughter in tow, he sets out for the London social scene, but first he makes a stop at Abigail Merriweather's farm. Abby is immediately put on edge by Fitz's presence, yet she just can't deny her attraction to the flirtatious rake. She is not, however, the kind of woman Fitz is looking for—or is she? *The Wicked Wyckerly* is the first novel in Patricia Rice's Rebellious Sons series.

Where it's reviewed:
Romantic Times, July 2010, page 44

Other books by the same author:
Mystic Warrior, 2009
Mystic Rider, 2008
Mystic Guardian, 2007
Magic Man, 2006
Much Ado about Magic, 2005

Other books you might like:
Candace Camp, *Promise Me Tomorrow*, 2000
Suzanne Enoch, *Rules of an Engagement*, 2010
Lisa Kleypas, *Secrets of a Summer Night*, 2004
Kieran Kramer, *When Harry Met Molly*, 2010
Stephanie Laurens, *The Reckless Earl*, 2010

1092

NORA ROBERTS

The Search

(New York: Putnam, 2010)

Story type: Mystery
Subject(s): Mystery; Serial murders; Romances (Fiction)
Major character(s): Fiona Bristow, Animal Trainer; Simon Doyle, Artist
Time period(s): 21st century; 2010s
Locale(s): Orcas Island, Washington

Summary: *The Search* by Nora Roberts takes place on Orcas Island off the Seattle coast; search-and-rescue dog trainer Fiona Bristow moved to the island eight years earlier, after a serial killer murdered her police officer fiance and almost took her life as well. The book begins when Simon Doyle, an artisan cabinetmaker, moves to the island. Though the two initially avoid each other, they begin spending time together because Simon has a new puppy and Fiona is working on training her dogs. A romance begins between Simon and Fiona, but when a series of murders begin to occur on the island, it seems as if the serial murderer who almost killed Fiona eight years ago might have someone after her again.

Where it's reviewed:
Booklist, April 1, 2010, page 5
Library Journal, April 15, 2010, page 37
Publishers Weekly, March 22, 2010, page 46
Romantic Times, July 2010, page 81

Other books by the same author:
Savor the Moment, 2010
The Search, 2010
Bed of Roses, 2009

Romances

Black Hills, 2009
Vision in White, 2009
The Pagan Stone, 2008

Other books you might like:
Cherry Adair, *On Thin Ice*, 2004
Catherine Coulter, *The Cove*, 1996
Linda Howard, *Open Season*, 2001
Jayne Ann Krentz, *Eclipse Bay*, 2000
Elizabeth Lowell, *Midnight in Ruby Bayou*, 2000

1093

NORA ROBERTS

Happy Ever After

(New York: Berkley, 2010)

Series: Bride Quartet Series. Book 4
Story type: Contemporary
Subject(s): Weddings; Marriage; Love
Major character(s): Parker "Legs" Brown, Planner (wedding planner); Malcolm "Mal" Kavanaugh, Mechanic, Biker
Time period(s): 21st century; 2010s
Locale(s): Connecticut, United States

Summary: Parker "Legs" Brown has formed a thriving wedding planning business with her three best girlfriends. Unlike her happy clients, Parker has had more than her fair share of drama in the romance department. Her luck takes an unexpected turn when she meets sexy mechanic Malcolm Kavanaugh. A biker with a heart of gold, Mike sets out to demolish Parker's emotional walls and win her heart. *Happy Ever After* is the fourth and final book in Nora Roberts's Bride Quartet series.

Where it's reviewed:
Booklist, September 15, 2010, page 42
Library Journal, October 15, 2010, page 62
Publishers Weekly, September 6, 2010, page 29
Romantic Times, November 2010, page 76

Other books by the same author:
Savor the Moment, 2010
The Search, 2010
Bed of Roses, 2009
Black Hills, 2009
Vision in White, 2009

Other books you might like:
Rachel Gibson, *Nothing but Trouble*, 2010
Kristan Higgins, *The Next Best Thing*, 2010
Deirdre Martin, *Just a Taste*, 2008
Susan Elizabeth Phillips, *Match Me If You Can*, 2005
Christie Ridgway, *Crush on You*, 2010

1094

ELISABETH ROSE (Pseudonym of Elisabeth Hoorwig)

Instant Family

(New York: Avalon Books, 2010)

Story type: Contemporary
Subject(s): Family; Single parent family; Love
Major character(s): Chloe Gardiner, Single Parent; Alex Bergman, Single Parent
Time period(s): 21st century; 2010s
Locale(s): United States

Summary: Elisabeth Rose's *Instant Family* chronicles the relationship between two single parents who are drawn together through their children and attempt to make a relationship work. Chloe has cared for her younger siblings since their parents were killed years earlier. Divorcee Alex meets Chloe when her brother vandalizes Alex's home. The attraction between the two parents is instantaneous, but the challenges of single parenting—and Alex's fiery daughter—become roadblocks to the formation of a successful relationship.

Where it's reviewed:
Booklist, October 15, 2010, page 26

Other books by the same author:
Outback Hero, 2009
Stuck, 2009
Coming Home, 2008
Strings Attached, 2008
The Right Chord, 2007

Other books you might like:
Zelda Benjamin, *Chocolate Secrets*, 2008
Carolyn Hughey, *Cupid's Web*, 2007
Annette Mahon, *The Secret Admirer*, 2001
Deborah Shelley, *Marriage 101*, 2008
Kim Watters, *Stake Your Claim*, 2003

1095

JOANN ROSS

The Homecoming

(New York: Penguin Group, 2010)

Series: Shelter Bay Series. Book 1
Story type: Contemporary; Series
Subject(s): Romances (Fiction); Sheriffs; Single parent family
Major character(s): Sax Douchett, Military Personnel (former Navy SEAL); Kara Conway, Police Officer (sheriff), Single Mother
Time period(s): 21st century; 2010s
Locale(s): Shelter Bay, Oregon

Summary: In JoAnn Ross's *The Homecoming*, former Navy SEAL Sax Douchett comes home to Shelter Bay, Oregon, for much needed relaxation after serving in the war. Sax is looking forward to making a new start, but he is surprised that his friends consider him a hero. Soon, memories from the past resurface and Sax encounters an old friend, Kara Conway—who is now Shelter Bay's sheriff. As Sax spends more time with Kara and her little boy, shocking revelations rock the community of Shelter Bay and jeopardize Sax and Kara's future. *The Homecoming* is the first book in the Shelter Bay series.

Where it's reviewed:
Booklist, July 2010, page 41
Library Journal, June 15, 2010, page 50
Romantic Times, July 2010, page 90

Other books by the same author:
Shattered, 2009
Crossfire, 2008
Freefall, 2008
No Safe Place, 2007
Impulse, 2006

Other books you might like:
Christine Feehan, *The Twilight Before Christmas*, 2003
Barbara Freethy, *In Shelter Cove*, 2010
Barbara Freethy, *On Shadow Beach*, 2010
Jill Marie Landis, *Heartbreak Hotel*, 2005
Mariah Stewart, *Home Again*, 2010

1096

CASSIE RYAN (Pseudonym of Tina Gerow)

Seducing the Succubus

(New York: Berkley, 2010)

Series: Sisters of Darkness Series. Book 1
Subject(s): Supernatural; Love; Adventure
Major character(s): Jezebeth, Demon (succubus); Noah Halston, Writer; Lilith, Royalty (queen)
Time period(s): 21st century; 2010s
Locale(s): United States

Summary: Succubus Jezebeth is resigned to her fate: destroying men in the name of her dark goddess, Lilith. Meanwhile, author Noah Halston's life has been saved by Lilith, and he must return the favor by doing her bidding. This entails rounding up Jezebeth and taking her to the goddess, but there's just one snag in the plan. Noah and Jezebeth are immediately attracted to one another, and it isn't long before their mutual desire impels them to question their allegiance to Lilith. *Seducing the Succubus* is the first novel in the Sisters of Darkness series by Cassie Ryan.

Where it's reviewed:
Romantic Times, October 2010, page 96

Other books by the same author:
Trio of Seduction, 2009
Vision of Seduction, 2008
Ceremony of Seduction, 2007

Other books you might like:
Lila DiPasqua, *The Princess in His Bed*, 2010
Charlotte Featherstone, *Sinful*, 2010
Megan Hart, *Naked*, 2010
Lora Leigh, *Styx's Storm*, 2010
Sophie Renwick, *Velvet Heaven*, 2010

1097

JENNA RYAN (Pseudonym of Jacqueline Goff)

Shadow Protector

(Don Mills, Ontario: Harlequin, 2010)

Story type: Serial Killer
Subject(s): Mystery; Rural life; Murder
Major character(s): Sera Hudson, Survivor (of serial killer); The Blindfold Killer, Serial Killer; Logan, Lawman (sheriff)

Summary: *Shadow Protector* is a Harlequin romance by author Jenna Ryan. Sera Hudson isn't the first stranger to come to Blue Mountain, but unlike most she harbors a dark secret. She's hiding from a serial murderer called the Blindfold Killer, who is eager to shut Sera, his only survivor, up for good. When the killer gets too close for comfort, Sera must turn to the local lawman for protection. Now it's up to Logan, the town sheriff, to guard Sera and take this murderer down. Ryan is also the author of *Cast in Wax, Cloak and Dagger,* and *Southern Cross.*

Where it's reviewed:
Romantic Times, September 2010, page 106

Other books by the same author:
Darkwood Manor, 2011
A Perfect Stranger, 2010
Kissing the Key Witness, 2009
Dangerously Attractive, 2008
Cold Case Cowboy, 2007

Other books you might like:
Margaret Carroll, *A Dark Love*, 2009
B.J. Daniels, *Montana Royalty*, 2008
Delores Fossen, *Branded by the Sheriff*, 2009
Leslie Parrish, *Black at Heart*, 2009

1098

RUTH SABERTON

Katy Carter Wants a Hero

(New York: Orion Publishing, 2010)

Story type: Contemporary Realism
Subject(s): Writers; Teachers; Humor
Major character(s): Katy Carter, Teacher (English), Writer; James, Fiance(e) (ex, of Katy)
Time period(s): 21st century; 2010s

Summary: *Katy Carter Wants a Hero* is a romance novel by author Ruth Saberton. Katy Carter is an English teacher during the day, but whenever she gets a spare moment she is trying to write a novel of her very own. The only trouble is, she can't exactly write about romance when she doesn't have any in her own life. After being unceremoniously dumped by her fiance James, Katy finds herself wrapped up in a series of mishaps and calamities—all for the sake of finding a Prince Charming of her own. First novel.

Where it's reviewed:
Romantic Times, December 2010, page 28

Other books you might like:
Jill Kargman, *Arm Candy: A Novel*, 2010
Beth Kendrick, *Second Time Around*, 2010
Sophie Kinsella, *Confessions of a Shopaholic*, 2001
Jill Mansell, *Millie's Fling*, 2009
Teresa Medeiros, *Goodnight Tweetheart*, 2010

Romances

1099

SHARON SALA

Torn Apart

(Don Mills, Ontario, Canada: MIRA, 2010)

Series: Storm Front Series. Book 2
Story type: Contemporary; Series
Subject(s): Romances (Fiction); Suspense; Kidnapping
Major character(s): Katie Earle, Mother; Bobby Earle, Son (of Katie); J.R., Spouse (of Katie, estranged)
Time period(s): 21st century; 2010s
Locale(s): Bordelaise, Louisiana

Summary: In *Torn Apart* by Sharon Sala, a boy is abducted during a tornado's rampage through Bordelaise, Louisiana. Katie Earle knows that her son Bobby is not a victim of the storm and immediately suspects her estranged husband of kidnapping him. When J.R. Earle convinces his wife that he is innocent, the couple decides to work together, despite their animosity, to find their son. Knowing that the kidnapper will try to use the chaos created by the storm to steal away with Bobby, Katie and J.R. face a desperate race against time. *Torn Apart* is the second book in the Storm Front series.

Where it's reviewed:
Library Journal, June 15, 2010, page 50
Romantic Times, July 2010, page 83

Other books by the same author:
Blood Stains, 2011
Blown Away, 2010
Deadlier than the Male, 2010
Swept Aside, 2010
The Warrior, 2009

Other books you might like:
Rochelle Alers, *Hidden Agenda*, 1997
Linda Howard, *Cry No More*, 2003
Marcia King-Gamble, *Come Back to Me*, 2004
Patricia Lewin, *Out of Reach*, 2004
Dinah McCall, *The Perfect Lie*, 2003

1100

LYNSAY SANDS

Hungry for You

(New York: Avon, 2010)

Series: Argeneau Vampire Series. Book 14
Story type: Vampire Story
Subject(s): Vampires; Romances (Fiction); Restaurants
Major character(s): Cale Valens, Vampire; Alexandra Willan, Restaurateur, Human
Time period(s): 21st century; 2010s
Locale(s): Canada

Summary: *Hungry for You* is a suspenseful romance novel from best-selling author Lynsay Sands. The book is the 14th installment in the Argeneau Vampire series. Cale Valens, a millenia-old vampire from the ancient Argeneau coven, has lost hope that he'll ever find love, despite the constant encouragement and pressure from his friends and family who are determined to find him the perfect mate. Alexandra Willan, on the other hand, has far more pressing matters to tend to than finding love. Weeks before her restaurant is slated to open, she loses her chef. She's thrilled to find a replacement so quick, especially one who comes so highly recommended and is so devilishly handsome. Cooking isn't one of Cale's skills, especially since he hasn't a regular meal in 2,000 years, but one look at Alexandra has him experiencing a new kind of hunger that he's determined to fill.

Where it's reviewed:
Romantic Times, December 2010, page 77

Other books by the same author:
Breathless Descent, 2011
High Octane, 2011
Jump Start, 2011
Captive of the Beast, 2009
Lone Star Surrender, 2009

Other books you might like:
Gemma Bruce, *The Man for Me*, 2008
Lori Foster, *Back in Black*, 2010
Deirdre Martin, *Power Play*, 2008
Jill Shalvis, *Slow Heat*, 2010

1101

MELISSA SENATE

The Love Goddess' Cooking School

(New York: Gallery Books, 2010)

Story type: Humor
Subject(s): Romances (Fiction); Cooking; Teaching
Major character(s): Holly Maguire, Young Woman, Teacher (cooking)
Time period(s): 21st century; 2010s
Locale(s): Blue Crab Island, Maine

Summary: *The Love Goddess' Cooking School* is a humorous romance novel from best-selling author Melissa Senate. As a child, Holly Maguire spent summers on Blue Crab Island, Maine, visiting with her grandmother, a romantic Italian fortune-teller with an unparalleled gift for cooking. As an adult, Holly returns to Blue Crab Island, eager to escape her own failed romances and unfulfilled dreams. When her grandmother passes away, leaving her Italian-cooking school to Holly, Holly decides to give teaching a try. So what if she can barely boil water? She only has four students in her class, anyways: her childhood friend, a single father, a serial dater, and a 12-year-old girl. As the class continues to meet week after week, Holly and her classmates learn a thing or two about cooking, friendship, and love.

Where it's reviewed:
Romantic Times, November 2010, page 50

Other books by the same author:
The Secret of Joy, 2009
Questions to Ask before Marrying, 2008
Love You to Death, 2007
The Breakup Club, 2006
Whose Wedding Is It Anyway?, 2004

Other books you might like:
Patricia Gaffney, *Flight Lessons*, 2002
Nadine Haobsh, *Confessions of a Beauty Addict*, 2009
Beth Kendrick, *My Favorite Mistake*, 2004
Jane Porter, *Flirting with Forty*, 2006
Barbara Samuel, *The Goddesses of Kitchen Avenue*, 2004

[1102]

JILL SHALVIS (Pseudonym of Jill Sheldon)

Simply Irresistible

(New York: Hachette Book Group, 2010)

Story type: Contemporary
Subject(s): Romances (Fiction); Mother-daughter relations; Sisters
Major character(s): Maddie Moore, Abuse Victim; Jax Cullen, Carpenter
Locale(s): Lucky Harbor, Wisconsin

Summary: *Simply Irresistible* is a novel from author Jill Shalvis's Lucky Harbor series. Maddie Moore is on a mission to transform her image. After enduring a tumultuous relationship and losing her job, Maddie heads to Lucky Harbor, Wisconsin, to help her half-sisters renovate the inn their mother has left them. There, Maddie meets Jax Cullen. Jax seems to be able to do it all: he's an expert carpenter, he's the town's mayor, and he's not bad on the eyes at all. Can Jax also help Maddie get over her anxiety over commitment and learn to trust men again? Shalvis is also the author of *The Sweetest Thing*, *The Trouble with Paradise*, and *Animal Magnetism*.

Where it's reviewed:
Romantic Times, October 2010, page 87

Other books by the same author:
Animal Magnetism, 2011
Instant Temptation, 2010
Slow Heat, 2010
Double Play, 2009
Instant Gratification, 2009

Other books you might like:
Sarah Abbot, *Destiny Bay*, 2008
Louisa Edwards, *Can't Stand the Heat*, 2009
Linda Goodnight, *Winning the Single Mom's Heart*, 2008
Kimberly Raye, *Slippery When Wet*, 2008

[1103]

JILL SHALVIS (Pseudonym of Jill Sheldon)

Animal Magnetism

(New York: Berkley Books, 2010)

Story type: Contemporary - Innocent
Subject(s): Rural life; Romances (Fiction); Animal rights
Major character(s): Lilah Young, Animal Lover (rescue and shelter owner); Brady Miller, Pilot, Brother (foster, of Adam and Dell); Dell, Brother (foster, of Adam and Brady); Adam, Brother (foster, of Dell and Brady)
Locale(s): Sunshine, Idaho

Summary: *Animal Magnetism* is a romance novel by author Jill Shalvis. In it, Shalvis tells the story of Lilah Young, who operates a kennel and animal rescue in rural Sunshine, Idaho. Young is happier spending her days with animals rather than people, and her time is too packed with work and distance-education classes to worry about finding a boyfriend. Fate intervenes, however, when she smashes into the back of Brady Miller's truck. In town to visit his foster brothers, Adam and Dell, Brady insists that he is simply visiting and not looking to make Sunshine a permanent home. Yet as sparks fly between Brady and Lilah, both of them must come to terms with the fact that romance and commitment may be in the cards for them after all. Shalvis is also the author of *Simply Irresistible* and *The Sweetest Thing*.

Where it's reviewed:
Publishers Weekly, December 13, 2010, page 43

Other books by the same author:
Simply Irresistible, 2010
Slow Heat, 2010
Double Play, 2009
Instant Gratification, 2009
Instant Temptation, 201

Other books you might like:
Kathy Love, *Wanting What You Get*, 2004
Lisa Plumley, *Perfect Together*, 2003
Stephanie Rowe, *Date Me, Baby, One More Time*, 2006
Stephanie Rowe, *He Loves Me, He Loves Me Hot*, 2007

[1104]

KATHRYN SHAY

The Perfect Family

(Valley Falls, New York: Bold Strokes Books, 2010)

Story type: Contemporary
Subject(s): Homosexuality; Love; Family
Major character(s): Jamie Davidson, 17-Year-Old, Homosexual; Mike Davidson, Father (of Jamie and Brian); Maggie Davidson, Mother (of Jamie and Brian); Brian Davidson, Brother (of Jamie)
Time period(s): 21st century; 2010s
Locale(s): United States

Summary: Kathryn Shay's *The Perfect Family* chronicles the emotional aftermath of a 17-year-old's coming out to his family. When Jamie Davidson discloses his homosexuality to his parents and brother, he is relieved, but he soon finds that his declaration has had painful effects on each of them. As Jamie attempts to reconcile his newfound sexuality with his family's feelings, his father struggles with his faith, his mother tries to safeguard Jamie against bullying, and his brother deals with problems at school.

Where it's reviewed:
Romantic Times, September 2010, page 52

Romances

Other books by the same author:
Back to Luke, 2009
A Man She Couldn't Forget, 2009
Taking the Heat, 2008
Tell Me No Lies, 2006
Ties That Bind, 2006

Other books you might like:
Louisa Edwards, *Can't Stand the Heat*, 2009
Louisa Edwards, *Just One Taste*, 2010
Louisa Edwards, *On the Steamy Side*, 2010
Sue Margolis, *Forget Me Knot*, 2009

1105

KANDY SHEPHERD

Home Is Where the Bark Is

(New York: Berkley Sensation, 2010)

Story type: Contemporary
Subject(s): Romances (Fiction); Mystery; Dogs
Major character(s): Serena Oakley, Businesswoman (doggy day care owner); Nick Whalen, Detective—Private
Time period(s): 21st century; 2010s
Locale(s): San Francisco, California

Summary: In *Home Is Where the Bark Is*, a former supermodel who left the world of fashion to open a day care for dogs falls for a new client and his tiny Yorkshire. Although Serena Oakley is immediately attracted to Nick Whalen when he walks through the door of Paws-A-While, she suspects he's hiding something. In truth, Nick is a private detective who borrowed the Yorkie as cover for his investigation into the rash of identity thefts that center on Serena's business. When Serena also becomes a victim, Nick loses his prime suspect but gains an ally and a romantic interest.

Where it's reviewed:
Romantic Times, July 2010, page 92

Other books by the same author:
Love Is a Four-legged Word, 2009

Other books you might like:
Elizabeth Bevarly, *Her Man Friday*, 1999
Catherine Coulter, *Born to Be Wild*, 2006
Christina Dodd, *Trouble in High Heels*, 2006
Julia Harper, *Hot*, 2008
Susan Sey, *Money Honey*, 2010

1106

EVE SILVER

Sins of the Heart

(Toronto; New York: Harlequin, 2010)

Subject(s): Love; Supernatural; Adventure
Major character(s): Dagan Krayl, Supernatural Being (soul reaper); Roxy Tam, Warrior
Time period(s): 21st century; 2010s

Summary: Two unlikely souls come together to fight the forces of evil in Eve Silver's *Sins of the Heart*. In the Underworld, Dagan Krayl gathers the souls of the dead, but when his brother is brutally killed, his entire view of the Underworld is transformed. Now Dagan wants to find those responsible for the murder in hopes of resurrecting his brother. Roxy Tam is a warrior in the battle against evil, and it is her duty to stop Dagan's ruthless mission. As sparks fly between the two, Dagan is forced to reevaluate his plans and ally himself with Roxy, who has won him completely—heart and soul.

Where it's reviewed:
Library Journal, August 2010, page 60
Romantic Times, August 2010, page 88

Other books by the same author:
Seduced by a Stranger, 2009
Sins of the Flesh, 2009
Sins of the Soul, 2009
Demon's Hunger, 2008
His Wicked Sins, 2008

Other books you might like:
Sherrilyn Kenyon, *The Dream-Hunter*, 2007
L.J. McDonald, *The Battle Sylph*, 2010
L.J. McDonald, *The Shattered Sylph*, 2010
Gena Showalter, *The Darkest Kiss*, 2008
Gena Showalter, *The Darkest Pleasure*, 2008

1107

NALINI SINGH
MELJEAN BROOK, Co-Author
VIRGINIA KANTRA, Co-Author
ANGELA KNIGHT, Co-Author

Burning Up

(New York: Berkley Books, 2010)

Story type: Collection
Subject(s): Fantasy; Romances (Fiction); Science fiction

Summary: *Burning Up* is a collection of short stories that mix romance with fantasy, science fiction, and even horror themes. In "Whisper of Sin," Nalini Singh offers an installment from her Psy-Changeling series, which revolves around a community of shape-shifters and the humans they are sworn to protect. "Blood and Roses" features a vampire knight who is held captive by a witch and who secretly holds the key to keeping the witch's sister safe. "Shifting Sea" by Virginia Kantra is an installment from her Children of the Sea series, which follows humans as they interact and fall in love with members of the finfolk clan. Finally, "Here There Be Monsters" is a steampunk short story from author Meljean Brook.

Where it's reviewed:
Romantic Times, August 2010, page 94

Other books you might like:
Meljean Brook, *Demon Blood*, 2010
Virginia Kantra, *Immortal Sea*, 2010
Angela Knight, *Master of Fire*, 2010
Nalini Singh, *Blaze of Memory*, 2009
Nalini Singh, *Bonds of Justice*, 2010

1108

KERRELYN SPARKS

Eat, Prey, Love

(New York: Avon, 2010)

Story type: Romantic Suspense
Subject(s): Supernatural; Vampires; Werewolves
Major character(s): Carlos Panterra, Shape-Shifter, Were-wolf (panther), Guardian (of orphans); Caitlyn Whelan, Human
Time period(s): 21st century; 2010s
Locale(s): United States

Summary: *Eat, Prey, Love* is a supernatural romance novel from best-selling author Kerrelyn Sparks. After assuming guardianship over young orphans, shape-shifting were-panther Carlos Panterra is eager to find a mate to help him raise the children and further the race. Caitlyn Whelan is beautiful, smart, and sexy and seems to be his perfect match in every way but one: she's a mortal. Not only is she a mortal, but her father also works for the CIA department responsible for eliminating supernatural beings like Carlos. When Caitlyn is offered the chance to work alongside Carlos, she takes the job without a second thought because she's determined to prove that she's the right woman for him, regardless of how danger-ous he is.

Where it's reviewed:
Romantic Times, October 2010, page 94

Other books by the same author:
The Vampire and the Virgin, 2010
Forbidden Nights with a Vampire, 2009
Secret Life of a Vampire, 2009
Holiday Pleasures, 2008
The Undead Next Door, 2008

Other books you might like:
Lori Handeland, *Blue Moon*, 2004
Sherrilyn Kenyon, *Unleash the Night*, 2006
Lynsay Sands, *Bite Me If You Can*, 2007
Lynsay Sands, *Single White Vampire*, 2003
Rachel Vincent, *The Stray*, 2007

1109

ROXANNE ST. CLAIRE

Edge of Sight

(New York: Forever, 2010)

Series: Guardian Angelinos Series. Book 1
Story type: Contemporary
Subject(s): Love; Suspense; Family
Major character(s): Samantha "Sam" Fairchild, Student; Zach Angelino, Agent (special forces); Vivi Ange-lino, Sister (of Zach), Friend (of Sam)
Time period(s): 21st century; 2010s
Locale(s): Boston, Massachusetts

Summary: Roxanne St. Claire's *Edge of Sight* follows the chilling adventures of law school student Sam Fairchild, who bears witness to a murder and is subsequently refused protection by the police department. She soon crosses paths with old pal Vivi Angelino and Vivi's brother, Zach, whom Sam used to date before he left her heartbroken. But now that time has passed, the spark between Sam and Zach is reignited—even as they find themselves targets at the centers of a dangerous conspiracy. This volume is the first installment in The Guardian Angelinos series.

Where it's reviewed:
Publishers Weekly, September 27, 2010, page 43
Romantic Times, November 2010, page 68

Other books by the same author:
Face of Danger, 2011
Shiver of Fear, 2011
Hunt Her Down, 2009
Make Her Pay, 2009
Now You Die, 2008

Other books you might like:
Cherry Adair, *Hide and Seek*, 2001
Allison Brennan, *Sudden Death*, 2009
Suzanne Brockmann, *Bodyguard*, 1999
Patricia Potter, *Behind the Shadows*, 2008
Patricia Potter, *Catch a Shadow*, 2008

1110

MARIAH STEWART

Home Again

(New York: Ballantine Books, 2010)

Series: Chesapeake Diaries Series. Book 2
Story type: Contemporary
Subject(s): Romances (Fiction); Acting; Divorce
Major character(s): Dallas McGregor, Actress, Divorced Person, Single Mother; Emilio Baird, Producer, Divorced Person; Cody, Son (of Dallas & Emilio)
Time period(s): 21st century; 2010s
Locale(s): Los Angeles, California; St. Dennis, Maryland

Summary: *Home Again* is the second installment in the Chesapeake Diaries series. Dallas MacGregor is living a charmed life as one of Hollywood's A-list celebrities. Although she's nearly divorced from her producer husband, Emilio Baird, Dallas's career is soaring and she's the happy mother to a young son, Cody. When a sex scandal involving Emilio is uncovered, Dallas becomes a prime target for tabloid gossip. Desperate to escape and to protect Cody from the fallout of Emilio's lifestyle, Dallas returns to her childhood home in St. Dennis, Maryland. The laid-back lifestyle and a rekindled romance with her high-school sweetheart have Dallas questioning whether the Hollywood dream is what she wants anymore. When Cody goes missing and Emilio races to Maryland, tabloids in tow, Dallas must decide between two different lifestyles and two very different men.

Where it's reviewed:
Romantic Times, September 2010, page 86

Other books by the same author:
Coming Home, 2010
Acts of Mercy, 2009

Romances

Cry Mercy, 2009
Forgotten, 2008
Mercy Street, 2008

Other books you might like:
Kristin Hannah, *On Mystic Lake*, 1999
Kristin Hannah, *Summer Island*, 2001
Barbara Samuel, *A Piece of Heaven*, 2003
Susan Wiggs, *Fireside*, 2009
Susan Wiggs, *Snowfall at Willow Lake*, 2008

1111

MICHELLE STIMPSON

Last Temptation

(New York: Dafina Publishing, 2010)

Story type: Inspirational
Subject(s): Marriage; Christian life; African Americans
Major character(s): Peaches Miller, Fiance(e) (of Quinn); Quinn, Fiance(e) (of Peaches)
Time period(s): 21st century; 2010s

Summary: *Last Temptation* is an inspirational Christian romance by author Michelle Stimpson. When Peaches Miller's fiance, Quinn, earns a promotion that will move him to a different city, Peaches is reluctant to follow him. After all, she is an independent woman and has a great job of her own. Meanwhile, her son is struggling with a learning disability, and her ex-husband has reappeared. Can Peaches, through her Christian faith, strike a balance between love and autonomy? Stimpson is also the author of *Divas of Damascus Road* and *Boaz Brown*.

Where it's reviewed:
Romantic Times, November 2010, page 50

Other books by the same author:
The Good Stuff, 2009
Trouble in My Way, 2008
Divas of Damascus Road, 2006
Boaz Brown, 2005

Other books you might like:
ReShonda Tate Billingsley, *Holy Rollers*, 2010
Michele Andrea Bowen, *More Church Folk*, 2010
Harry Lee Kraus, *The Six-Liter Club*, 2010
Vanessa Miller, *A Love for Tomorrow*, 2010
Pat Simmons, *Still Guilty*, 2010

1112

ANNE STUART (Pseudonym of Anne Kristine Stuart Ohlrogge)

Breathless

(Don Mills, Ontario, Canada: MIRA, 2010)

Series: House of Rohan Series. Book 3
Story type: Historical; Series
Subject(s): Romances (Fiction); Social class; History
Major character(s): Miranda Rohan, Young Woman; Lucien de Malheur, Spouse (of Miranda)
Time period(s): 19th century

Locale(s): England

Summary: In *Breathless*, Miranda Rohan knows that her spectacular social fall is irreversible. Suddenly liberated from the conventions of London society that have governed her life, Miranda becomes carefree and careless. She meets Lucien de Malheur, a mysterious stranger who proposes marriage despite her tainted name. Though he is called the Scorpion, Miranda seems oblivious to the danger he poses until after they are wed. Lucien is an enemy of the Rohan clan who married Miranda to ruin her family, but he may have underestimated his beautiful bride's temper. *Breathless* is the third book in the House of Rohan series.

Where it's reviewed:
Romantic Times, October 2010, page 36

Other books by the same author:
Reckless, 2010
Ruthless, 2010
Silver Falls, 2009
Fire and Ice, 2008
Ice Storm, 2007

Other books you might like:
Jo Beverley, *Lady Beware*, 2007
Suzanne Enoch, *Always a Scoundrel*, 2009
Suzanne Enoch, *Reforming a Rake*, 2000
Edith Layton, *The Devil's Bargain*, 2002
Barbara Metzger, *The Duel*, 2005

1113

ANNE STUART (Pseudonym of Anne Kristine Stuart Ohlrogge)

Ruthless

(New York: Mira, 2010)

Series: House of Rohan Series. Book 1
Story type: Historical
Subject(s): Love; Sexuality; Family
Major character(s): Elinor Harriman, Noblewoman; Viscount Rohan, Rake
Time period(s): 18th century; 1760s (1760)
Locale(s): Paris, France

Summary: Viscount Rohan is a man driven by desires of the flesh. Elinor Harriman is a poverty-stricken noblewoman whose mother flees to the carnal events hosted by Rohan. When Elinor goes to find her, she encounters the sexy Viscount for the first time. Can Elinor tame this sexual beast? Can Viscount mend his ways and charm this beautiful young woman? Author Anne Stuart finds out in *Ruthless*, the first novel in The House of Rohan series.

Where it's reviewed:
Library Journal, August 2010, page 61
Publishers Weekly, June 21, 2010, page 37
Romantic Times, August 2010, page 42

Other books by the same author:
Breathless, 2010
Reckless, 2010
Silver Falls, 2009
Fire and Ice, 2008
Ice Storm, 2007

Other books you might like:
Jo Beverley, *Something Wicked*, 1997
Jane Feather, *A Husband's Wicked Ways*, 2009
Alexandra Hawkins, *Till Dawn with the Devil*, 2010
Elizabeth Hoyt, *Wicked Intentions*, 2010
Jennifer St. Giles, *Darkest Dreams*, 2006

1114

ANNE STUART

Reckless

(New York: Mira, 2010)

Series: House of Rohan Series. Book 2
Story type: Historical
Subject(s): Love; Marriage; Family
Major character(s): Charlotte Spenser, Spinster; Adrian
   Alistair Rohan, Rake
Time period(s): 19th century
Locale(s): United Kingdom

Summary: Charlotte Spenser's future looks bleak...until
she meets sexy rake Adrian Alistair Rohan. Adrian,
however, only wants Charlotte for physical pleasures, a
concept Charlotte rejects from the outset. Yet she can't
stop thinking about this notorious troublemaker, and she
sets out to win his heart, no matter the cost to her
reputation. *Reckless* is the second book in Anne Stuart's
House of Rohan series.

Where it's reviewed:
Romantic Times, September 2010, page 42

Other books by the same author:
Breathless, 2010
Ruthless, 2010
Silver Falls, 2009
Fire and Ice, 2008
Ice Storm, 2007

Other books you might like:
Gaelen Foley, *My Dangerous Duke*, 2010
Beth Kery, *Daring Time*, 2009
Lisa Valdez, *Patience*, 2010
Tracy Anne Warren, *Seduced by His Touch*, 2009

1115

JOANNE SUNDELL

Hearts Persuaded

(Detroit, Michigan: Five Star, 2010)

Series: Quaker and Confederate Series. Book 2
Story type: Historical; Series
Subject(s): Romances (Fiction); History; Civil war
Major character(s): Levi Clement, Quaker; Comfort
   Clarke, Spouse (of Levi); Willa Mae Tyler, Military
   Personnel (Confederate soldier); Surry Lion, Slave
   (escaped); Penny, Sister (of Surry)
Time period(s): 19th century; 1860s (1862)
Locale(s): Loudoun County, Virginia

Summary: In *Hearts Persuaded*, the Civil War complicates
the lives of a Quaker man and his family. Levi Clement
married Comfort Clarke (also a Quaker) out of a sense
of duty to his father. But Levi's heart belongs to Willa
Mae Tyler, a woman embittered by the loss of her brothers who were killed at the hands of the Union soldiers.
Despite a pregnancy which she has revealed to no one,
Willa Mae assumes the role of Confederate soldier to
avenge the deaths of her brothers. *Hearts Persuaded* is
the second book in the Quaker and the Confederate
series.

Other books by the same author:
Hearts Divided, 2010
Meggie's Remains, 2009
The Parlor House Daughter, 2009
A...My Name's Amelia, 2007
Matchmaker, Matchmaker, 2006

Other books you might like:
Joanna Hampton, *Woven Dreams*, 2000
Alexis Harrington, *Allie's Moon*, 2000
Lorraine Heath, *Always to Remember*, 1996
Martha Kirkland, *The Magnolia Tree*, 1998
Patricia Rice, *Wayward Angel*, 1997

1116

HOPE TARR

The Tutor

(Toronto; New York: Harlequin, 2010)

Story type: Historical
Subject(s): Love; Sexuality; Marriage
Major character(s): Bea Lindsey, Noblewoman; Ralph
   Sylvester, Rogue
Time period(s): 19th century
Locale(s): United Kingdom

Summary: In Hope Tarr's *The Tutor*, Lady Bea Lindsey is
engaged to be married, but she is fearful of the wedding
night. After all, Bea is a proper lady and has no experience in sexual matters. Enter Ralph Sylvester, a handsome stranger who agrees to teach Bea the fine art of
lovemaking. But Ralph has one stipulation that must be
met: she must hand herself over to him, body and soul,
for one week. That week, it turns out, changes both their
lives and fortunes forever.

Where it's reviewed:
Romantic Times, July 2010, page 107

Other books by the same author:
Every Breath You Take..., 2010
Twelve Nights, 2009
Bound to Please, 2008
The Haunting, 2007
Strokes of Midnight, 2007

Other books you might like:
Karen Anders, *The Bare Facts*, 2002
Kira Anders, *Whispers in the Dark*, 2002
Lori Borrill, *Private Confessions*, 2010
Julie Kenner, *Starstruck*, 2009
Joanne Rock, *Double Play*, 2010

Romances

1117

LESLIE TENTLER

Midnight Caller

(Don Mills, Ontario, Canada: Mira, 2010)

Series: Chasing Evil Series. Book 1
Story type: Romantic Suspense; Serial Killer
Subject(s): Serial murders; Stalking; Romances (Fiction)
Major character(s): Dr. Rain Sommers, Psychologist, Radio Personality, Orphan; Trevor Rivette, FBI Agent
Time period(s): 21st century; 2010s
Locale(s): New Orleans, Louisiana

Summary: *Midnight Caller* is the first installment in the Chasing Evil series. Dr. Rain Sommers is a psychologist and host of the late-night radio show, Midnight Confessions. When Rain was a baby, her mother, a legendary goth singer, was murdered by her father, a suicidal guitarist. Now, a caller on Rain's show has a terrifying obsession with Rain and her mother's murder. Meanwhile, a vicious serial killer, known as the Vampire, has been murdering women across the country and has set his sights on New Orleans, and possibly Rain. FBI agent Trevor Rivette fears that the Vampire and the obsessed caller are the same person and that Rain is his next target. First novel.

Where it's reviewed:
Publishers Weekly, December 13, 2010, page 39

Other books you might like:
Erin McCarthy, *The Taking*, 2010
Leslie Parrish, *Pitch Black*, 2009
Jenna Ryan, *A Voice in the Dark*, 2010

1118

JODI THOMAS

Somewhere Along the Way

(New York: Berkley Books, 2010)

Series: Harmony Trilogy. Book 2
Story type: Contemporary - Innocent
Subject(s): Rural life; Family relations; Community relations
Major character(s): Reagan Truman, Young Woman, Waiter/Waitress; Gabe Leary, Recluse
Locale(s): Harmony, Texas

Summary: *Somewhere Along the Way* is the second novel in author Jodi Thomas's Harmony series, which revolves around the recently orphaned Reagan Truman and her relocation to the town of Harmony to live with her Uncle Jeremiah. In this novel, Reagan is beginning to feel at home in Harmony and even has a new job at the local diner. When her co-worker Edith doesn't come into work, Reagan must pick up her slack and deliver a dinner to the reclusive Gabe Leary. Soon, Reagan and Gabe form a tentative friendship, and when Reagan's life is put in danger, Gabe is thrust into the role of her hero—a role that warrants him much unwanted attention.

Where it's reviewed:
Romantic Times, November 2010, page 76

Other books by the same author:
The Lone Texan, 2009
Tall, Dark, and Texan, 2008
Twisted Creek, 2008
Texas Rain, 2006
The Texan's Reward, 2005

Other books you might like:
Carolyn Brown, *Honky Tonk Christmas*, 2010
Sadie Callahan, *Lone Star Woman*, 2009
Joanne Kennedy, *One Fine Cowboy*, 2010
R.C. Ryan, *Montana Glory*, 2010

1119

MARIN THOMAS

Dexter: Honorable Cowboy

(Toronto; New York: Harlequin, 2010)

Story type: Contemporary
Subject(s): Ranch life; Love; Single parent family
Major character(s): Josie Charles, Single Mother; Dexter Cody, Cowboy/Cowgirl
Time period(s): 21st century; 2010s
Locale(s): United States

Summary: Marin Thomas's *Dexter: Honorable Cowboy* centers on the relationship between a sexy rancher and a beautiful single mother. Josie Charles has just returned with her young son to her hometown, where she crosses paths with the twin brother of her son's father. Dexter Cody always admired Josie from afar, but he now finds it impossible to resist her. He's also ready to be the father and provider his brother is unable to be. But can he convince Josie to give him a shot—and just maybe win her heart in the process?

Where it's reviewed:
Romantic Times, July 2010, page 107

Other books by the same author:
A Cowboy's Promise, 2009
Samantha's Cowboy, 2009
The Cowboy and the Angel, 2008
Ryan's Renovation, 2007
Daddy by Choice, 2005

Other books you might like:
Pamela Britton, *The Wrangler*, 2009
Kathleen Eagle, *The Last True Cowboy*, 1998
Cathy McDavid, *Dusty: Wild Cowboy*, 2010
Patricia Thayer, *The Cowboy's Adopted Daughter*, 2010
Jeannie Watt, *The Brother Returns*, 2008

1120

CARLENE THOMPSON

Nowhere to Hide

(New York: St. Martin's Press, 2010)

Story type: Contemporary
Subject(s): Love; Suspense; Murder

Major character(s): Marissa Gray, Journalist; Gretchen, Crime Victim, Friend (of Marissa); Catherine, Sister (of Marissa)
Time period(s): 21st century; 2010s
Locale(s): Aurora Falls, United States

Summary: In Carlene Thompson's *Nowhere to Hide*, Marissa Gray has returned to her hometown of Aurora Falls—and to the painful memories surrounding the unsolved murder of her best friend, Gretchen. Once Marissa settles back into small-town life, she learns that the ghosts of the past are still very much alive in Aurora Falls, and someone is intent on keeping her from learning the truth of Gretchen's death, even all these years later. When Gretchen's friends start being murdered, Marissa is in the race of her life to find a killer before she too becomes just another obituary in the local newspaper.

Where it's reviewed:
Romantic Times, December 2010, page 63

Other books by the same author:
You Can Run..., 2009
If You Ever Tell, 2008
Last Seen Alive, 2007
Last Whisper, 2006
Share No Secrets, 2005

Other books you might like:
Sarah Abbot, *Destiny Bay*, 2008
Jessica Bird, *An Unforgettable Lady*, 2010
Shannon K. Butcher, *Love You to Death*, 2009
Julie James, *Something About You*, 2010

1121

VICKI LEWIS THOMPSON

A Werewolf in Manhattan
(New York: Signet, 2011)

Series: Wild About You Series. Book 1
Story type: Paranormal
Subject(s): Werewolves; Love; Family
Major character(s): Emma Gavin, Writer; Aidan Wallace, Werewolf
Time period(s): 21st century; 2010s
Locale(s): New York, New York

Summary: Emma Gavin is a horror-fiction writer famous for her werewolf novels. Her knowledge of the subject, however, inspires werewolf Aidan Wallace to follow Emma as she embarks upon a book tour. When Emma is nearly attacked by a werewolf, Aidan steps in to save her. Soon he cannot deny his feelings for her, thereby dividing his loyalties between his pack and the woman he loves. Vicki Lewis Thompson's *A Werewolf in Manhattan* is the first novel in the Wild About You series.

Where it's reviewed:
Publishers Weekly, November 15, 2010, page 45

Other books by the same author:
Blonde with a Wand, 2010
Chick with a Charm, 2010
Casual Hex, 2009

Wild and Hexy, 2008
Overhexed, 2007

Other books you might like:
Kathleen Bacus, *Fiance at Her Fingertips*, 2008
Dakota Cassidy, *The Accidental Werewolf*, 2008
Shelly Laurenston, *Beast Behaving Badly*, 2010
Ronda Thompson, *Confessions of a Werewolf Supermodel*, 2007
Minda Webber, *The Daughters Grimm*, 2008

1122

ELIZABETH THORNTON (Pseudonym of Mary George)

A Bewitching Bride
(New York: Berkley, 2010)

Story type: Historical
Subject(s): Love; Marriage; Psychics
Major character(s): Gavin Hepburn, Psychic; Kate Cameron, Young Woman
Time period(s): 19th century
Locale(s): United Kingdom

Summary: In Elizabeth Thornton's *A Bewitching Bride*, psychically gifted Gavin Hepburn knows beautiful Kate Cameron is in trouble. After he rescues her, the two hide out together, but their evening alone with one another sends ripples through Regency society. Gavin and Kate are forced to marry, even as Kate tries to escape the clutches of a madman who is intent on killing her.

Where it's reviewed:
Romantic Times, November 2010, page 40

Other books by the same author:
The Runaway McBride, 2009
The Scot and I, 2009
The Pleasure Trap, 2007
The Bachelor Trap, 2006
The Marriage Trap, 2005

Other books you might like:
Connie Brockway, *So Enchanting*, 2009
Catherine Coulter, *Wizard's Daughter*, 2007
Robyn DeHart, *Deliciously Wicked*, 2006
Mary Jo Putney, *Kiss of Fate*, 2004
Amanda Quick, *Wait Until Midnight*, 2005

1123

STEPHANIE TYLER

Promises in the Dark
(New York: Dell, 2010)

Series: Shadow Force Series. Book 2
Story type: Contemporary
Subject(s): Love; Adventure; Terrorism
Major character(s): Zane Scott, Military Personnel (Navy SEAL); Dr. Olivia Strohm, Doctor
Time period(s): 21st century; 2010s
Locale(s): Sierra Leone

Summary: The second book in Stephanie Tyler's Shadow Force series, *Promises in the Dark* is the story of Navy

Romances

SEAL Zane Scott, who finds love and adventure with Dr. Olivia Strohm. Though the two have never met, Zane is enchanted by stories of Olivia, and he sets out to save her from terrorists in Sierra Leone. The sparks fly instantaneously between the two, but in order to rescue her and bring her to safety, Zane will have to tame Olivia's wild heart.

Where it's reviewed:
Romantic Times, December 2010, page 62

Other books by the same author:
Hold on Tight, 2010
Lie with Me, 2010
Hard to Hold, 2009
Too Hot to Hold, 2009
Beyond His Control, 2008

Other books you might like:
Jennifer Crusie, *Maybe This Time*, 2010
Victoria Holt, *On the Night of the Seventh Moon*, 1972
Kat Martin, *Reese's Bride*, 2009
Kat Martin, *Rule's Bride*, 2010

1124

STEPHANIE TYLER

Lie with Me

(New York: Dell, 2010)

Series: Shadow Force Series. Book 1
Story type: Romantic Suspense
Subject(s): Kidnapping; Romances (Fiction); Suspense
Major character(s): Cameron Moore, Military Personnel; Skylar Slavin, Writer, Kidnap Victim
Time period(s): 21st century; 2010s
Locale(s): United States

Summary: *Lie with Me* is the first installment in the Shadow Force series. Delta Force operative Cameron Moore is rescued by the CIA after being framed for a double murder. Unfortunately for Cam, his freedom comes at a price: he must carry out questionable black ops missions for the CIA. Determined to win his freedom once and for all, Cam develops what seems like a foolproof plan: kidnap the daughter of his CIA wrangler. The "victim" in question is Skylar Slavin, a smart and sexy best-selling novelist, who seems like an easy target...until Cam falls in love with her. When Skylar's life is put at risk by real kidnappers, Cam becomes determined to save her, regardless of the cost.

Where it's reviewed:
Romantic Times, November 2010, page 69

Other books by the same author:
Hold on Tight, 2010
Promises in the Dark, 2010
Hard to Hold, 2009
Too Hot to Hold, 2009
Beyond His Control, 2008

Other books you might like:
Nina Bruhns, *If Looks Could Chill*, 2009
Leslie Parrish, *Fade to Black*, 2009
Leslie Parrish, *Pitch Black*, 2009
Christy Reece, *Last Chance*, 2010

1125

SHILOH WALKER

Veil of Shadows

(New York: Berkley Books, 2010)

Story type: Fantasy
Subject(s): Fantasy; Alternative worlds; Demons
Major character(s): Xan, Military Personnel (soldier); Laisyn Carr, Military Personnel (captain)

Summary: *Veil of Shadows* is the second book in author Shiloh Walker's Veil series, which also includes *Through the Veil*. In the space between human Earth and the demon world of Anqar lies a secret dimension known as Ishtan. For years, Anqaran warlords have invaded Ishtan in a quest to capture women for breeding purposes. Now, the people of Ishtan must find a way to drive out the demons roaming free around their world. In this installment, the gates of Ishtan have fallen, finally separating the world from the demon realm. A platoon of rebel soldiers is all that is left to defend Ishtan. When a soldier named Xan comes seemingly from nowhere, Captain Laisyn Carr cannot deny her attraction. Yet before she gives her heart to this newcomer, she must first decide if he has the best interests of Ishtan in mind, or if he is yet another foe from the demon realm.

Where it's reviewed:
Romantic Times, September 2010, page 61

Other books by the same author:
The First Book of Grimm, 2010
Hearts and Wishes, 2010
Nebulous, 2010
Under Your Spell, 2010
Never as It Seems, 201

Other books you might like:
Dakota Cassidy, *Kiss & Hell*, 2009
Maureen Child, *Vanished*, 2009
Pamela Palmer, *Dark Deceiver*, 2008
J.D. Warren, *Crate and Peril*, 2008

1126

KAKI WARNER (Pseudonym of Kathleen Warner)

Chasing the Sun

(New York: Berkley Trade, 2011)

Series: Blood Rose Trilogy. Book 3
Story type: Historical - American West
Subject(s): Single parent family; Love; Western fiction
Major character(s): Jack Wilkins, Wanderer; Daisy Etheridge, Singer, Single Mother
Time period(s): 19th century; 1870s (1873)
Locale(s): New Mexico, United States

Summary: The third and final installment in Kaki Warner's Blood Rose Trilogy, *Chasing the Sun* is set in 19th-century New Mexico, where aspiring singer Daisy Etheridge is struggling to adjust to life as a single mother. Meanwhile, restless wanderer Jack Wilkins has returned home in an attempt to woo back the only woman he's ever loved. But when Daisy and Jack cross paths, the memories of a fateful night they once shared come surging back into the present—and Jack realizes he has become a father.

Where it's reviewed:
Publishers Weekly, November 29, 2010, page 35

Other books by the same author:
Open Country, 2010
Pieces of Sky, 2010

Other books you might like:
Georgina Gentry, *To Tame a Texan*, 2003
Leigh Greenwood, *Rose*, 1993
Lorraine Heath, *A Rogue in Texas*, 1999
Maggie Osborne, *Prairie Moon*, 2002
Jodi Thomas, *The Lone Texan*, 2009

1127

CHRISTINE WARREN

Prince Charming Doesn't Live Here

(New York: Macmillan, 2010)

Series: Others Series. Book 10
Story type: Paranormal; Series
Subject(s): Romances (Fiction); Law; Fantasy
Major character(s): Danice Carter, Lawyer; McIntyre Callahan, Detective—Private, Mythical Creature (fairy); Rosemary, Young Woman
Time period(s): 21st century; 2010s
Locale(s): New York, New York

Summary: In *Prince Charming Doesn't Live Here*, an ambitious New York attorney takes an assignment that could make her career. To Danice Carter, the request made by one of her firm's partners seems easy—persuade his pregnant granddaughter Rosemary to file a paternity suit against her unborn baby's father. First, Danice must locate Rosemary. Private investigator McIntyre Callahan is also on the hunt for Rosemary, but he has an advantage over Danice. Part human and part fae, Callahan can follow Rosemary to the mysterious world of The Others where the expectant mother may be in danger. *Prince Charming Doesn't Live Here* is the 10th book in the Others series.

Where it's reviewed:
Romantic Times, November 2010, page 82

Other books by the same author:
Born to Be Wild, 2010
Big Bad Wolf, 2009
You're So Vein, 2009
One Bite with a Stranger, 2008
Walk on the Wild Side, 2008

Other books you might like:
Sherrilyn Kenyon, *Fantasy Lover*, 2002
Judi McCoy, *Almost a Goddess*, 2006
Michelle Rowen, *Bitten & Smitten*, 2006
Helen Scott Taylor, *The Magic Knot*, 2009
Heather Webber, *Truly, Madly*, 2010

1128

NANCY WARREN

My Fake Fiancee

(Toronto; New York: Harlequin, 2010)

Story type: Contemporary
Subject(s): Love; Cooks; Catering
Major character(s): David Wolfe, Businessman; Chelsea Hammond, Caterer
Time period(s): 21st century; 2010s
Locale(s): United States

Summary: In Nancy Warren's *My Fake Fiancee*, businessman David Wolfe is desperate for a promotion and is willing to pretend he's engaged in order to secure a vice president position. Chelsea Hammond is a caterer who could put David's impressive kitchen to good use with her start-up catering business, and she agrees to pose as his fiancee in return for the kitchen. It isn't long, however, before things start heating up *outside* the kitchen, and David and Chelsea are dealing with their red-hot mutual attraction.

Where it's reviewed:
Booklist, July 2010, page 107

Other books by the same author:
Under the Influence, 2010
The One I Want, 2008
Turn Left at Sanity, 2008
Speed Dating, 2007
Private Relations, 2005

Other books you might like:
Leslie Kelly, *Naturally Naughty*, 2002
Debbi Rawlins, *Texas Blaze*, 2009
Jill Shalvis, *Room Service*, 2006
Vicki Lewis Thompson, *Claimed!*, 2010
Lori Wilde, *Zero Control*, 2009

1129

SUSAN MAY WARREN

Licensed for Trouble

(Carol Stream, Illinois: Tyndale House Publishers, 2010)

Series: PJ Sugar Series. Book 3
Story type: Cozy Mystery; Inspirational
Subject(s): Christian life; Detective fiction; Mystery
Major character(s): PJ Sugar, Detective—Private; Jeremy Kane, Detective—Private; Max Smith, Handyman
Time period(s): 21st century; 2010s

Summary: *Licensed for Trouble* is the third novel in the PJ Sugar series by Susan May Warren. This time, PJ has just found out that a local mansion was bequeathed to her. The estate is in shambles, so she calls upon a enigmatic handyman to help her with the repairs. Unfortunately PJ is low on dough, so he strikes a deal with her—help him solve a mystery and he'll do the work for free. This is the perfect opportunity for PJ to hone her private-investigator skills, but with her PI

Romances

license test looming near and a budding romance with Jeremy in the works, how will she find the time?

Where it's reviewed:
Romantic Times, August 2010, page 65

Other books by the same author:
Double Trouble, 2010
Nothing but Trouble, 2009
Wiser than Serpents, 2008
Happily Ever After, 2007
Tying the Knot, 2007

Other books you might like:
Judy Christie, *Goodness Gracious Green*, 2010
Rachel Hauck, *Dining with Joy*, 2010
Debbie Macomber, *Shirley, Goodness, and Mercy*, 1999
Beth Pattillo, *Heavens to Betsy*, 2005
Lisa Wingate, *Never Say Never*, 2010

1130

DEBRA WEBB

Colby Core

(Don Mills, Ontario, Canada: Harlequin, 2010)

Series: Colby Agency Series. Book 42
Story type: Contemporary; Series
Subject(s): Romances (Fiction); Christmas; Suspense
Major character(s): Tessa Woods, Captive; Riley Porter, Agent (undercover)
Time period(s): 21st century; 2010s
Locale(s): United States

Summary: In *Colby Core* by Debra Webb, the Colby Agency, an elite unit of undercover operatives, dispatches Riley Porter to find a woman who has been missing for years. A former Navy SEAL, Porter is a skilled agent, but he is shocked when he encounters the human traffickers who have been holding Tessa Woods, her child, and other prisoners. Despite the grueling conditions of her captivity, Tessa has remained strong and willing to do whatever it takes to protect her fellow captives. Though Porter assures Tessa that he can rescue them all, she is hesitant to trust him. *Colby Core* is the 42nd book in the Colby Agency series.

Where it's reviewed:
Romantic Times, December 2010, page 86

Other books by the same author:
Anywhere She Runs, 2010
Colby Brass, 2010
Colby Justice, 2010
Colby Lockdown, 2010
Everywhere She Turns, 2009

Other books you might like:
Carla Cassidy, *Profile Durango*, 2009
B.J. Daniels, *Montana Royalty*, 2008
Delores Fossen, *Branded by the Sheriff*, 2009
R.C. Ryan, *Montana Destiny*, 2010

1131

HEATHER WEBBER

Deeply, Desperately

(New York: St. Martin's, 2010)

Series: Lucy Valentine Series. Book 2
Story type: Fantasy; Series
Subject(s): Romances (Fiction); Supernatural; Fantasy
Major character(s): Lucy Valentine, Psychic, Matchmaker; Sean Donahue, Detective—Private, Neighbor (of Lucy)
Time period(s): 21st century; 2010s
Locale(s): Boston, Massachusetts

Summary: In *Deeply, Desperately*, Lucy Valentine seems like a misfit in her family's psychic-matchmaking firm. In a mishap, Lucy lost her matchmaking powers but gained a talent for locating lost items—and people. Rather than finding new mates for her clients, Lucy tries to reunite them with loves from the past. When one of her cases draws Lucy into a murder investigation, she calls on Sean Donahue, private detective and neighbor, for help. As Lucy and Sean work to find a killer, Lucy realizes she may have found a romantic match of her own. *Deeply, Desperately* is the second book in the Lucy Valentine series.

Where it's reviewed:
Romantic Times, August 2010, page 92

Other books by the same author:
Truly, Madly, 2010
Digging Up Trouble, 2006
A Hoe Lot of Trouble, 2004

Other books you might like:
Patti Berg, *Looking for a Hero*, 1998
Patricia Coughlin, *The Lost Enchantress*, 2010
Mindy L. Klasky, *How Not to Make a Wish*, 2009
Jenna McKnight, *Love in the Fast Lane*, 2007

1132

TINA WELLING

Cowboys Never Cry

(New York: New American Library, 2010)

Story type: Contemporary
Subject(s): Romances (Fiction); Ranch life; Cowhands
Major character(s): Cassie Danner, Widow(er); Robbin McKeag, Actor
Time period(s): 21st century; 2010s
Locale(s): Wyoming, United States

Summary: In *Cowboys Never Cry* by Tina Welling, a widow and a celebrity struggling with substance abuse and mental illness forge an unlikely relationship on a Wyoming dude ranch. Cassie Danner's husband has been dead for three years, the victim of a mountain-climbing accident. When she takes a job as a cook on a dude ranch—another in a long list of temporary positions—Cassie meets the owner's son, actor Robbin McKeag, a recovering alcoholic with psychological problems. As Cassie struggles to find her place on the ranch and Robbin tries to re-energize his career, they gradually recognize their mutual attraction.

Where it's reviewed:
Romantic Times, October 2010, page 86

Other books by the same author:
Crybaby Ranch, 2009
Fairy Tale Blues, 2009

Other books you might like:
Jan Hambright, *The High Country Rancher*, 2009
Rita Herron, *Platinum Cowboy*, 2009
R.C. Ryan, *Montana Destiny*, 2010
Bobbi Smith, *Wanted: The Texan*, 2008

1133

KAREN WHIDDON

Profile for Seduction

(Toronto; New York: Harlequin, 2010)

Story type: Contemporary
Subject(s): Love; Serial murders; Suspense
Major character(s): Lea Cordasic, Agent (FBI); Marc Kenyon, Police Officer
Time period(s): 21st century; 2010s
Locale(s): Texas, United States

Summary: Karen Whiddon's *Profile for Seduction* centers on the steamy relationship between a beautiful FBI agent and a sexy Texas lawman. Lea Cordasic had been instrumental in putting away the notorious Cowtown Killer, but he's now on the loose and coming after her. Her only hope for survival rests in the brawny arms of Texas police officer Marc Kenyon, who has never forgotten the ravishing Lea after she was terrorized by the Cowtown Killer before putting him behind bars. Sparks fly between the two, and they are soon in a race against the clock to save themselves—and any hopes of a relationship—from a dangerous madman.

Where it's reviewed:
Romantic Times, October 2010, page 110

Other books by the same author:
Lone Wolf, 2011
The Perfect Soldier, 2009
Wild Wolf, 2009
The Black Sheep P.I., 2008
Dance of the Wolf, 2008

Other books you might like:
Toni Blake, *Sugar Creek*, 2010
Delores Fossen, *Branded by the Sheriff*, 2009
Lindsay McKenna, *Deadly Intention*, 2010
Brenda Novak, *Trust Me*, 2008
Debra Webb, *Anywhere She Runs*, 2010

1134

KAREN WHITE-OWENS

You're All I Need

(New York: Dafina Books, 2010)

Story type: Legal
Subject(s): Interracial dating; African Americans; Race relations
Major character(s): Tia Edwards, Lawyer, Lover (of Christophe); Christophe Jensen, Lawyer, Lover (of Tia)

Summary: *You're All I Need* is a romance novel by author Karen White-Owens. When up-and-coming attorney Tia Edwards is asked by her supervising partner to act as a tour guide for Christophe Jensen, she's surprised to find herself attracted to him. He's a visiting attorney from France and he is white, someone she would never normally choose for herself. Despite their initial chemistry, Tia and Christophe maintain a professional distance from one another; until, that is, Tia learns that her own boyfriend has been unfaithful. Christophe proves to be a saving grace, and passion develops between them that soon grows into love. But when Christophe is called back to France, Tia must make a decision that will not only test her faith in their relationship, but also the cultural and racial divide between them.

Where it's reviewed:
Romantic Times, October 2010, page 89

Other books by the same author:
I Can Make You Love Me, 2009
The Way You Aren't, 2007
Now Until Forever, 2006
Someone to Love, 2006
Love Changes Everything, 2005

Other books you might like:
Gwynne Forster, *Against the Wind*, 2006
J.D. Mason, *This Fire Down in My Soul*, 2007
Francis Ray, *Like the First Time*, 2004
Chilufiya Safaa, *The Art of Love*, 2007

1135

LORI WILDE (Pseudonym of Laurie Vanzura)

The First Love Cookie Club

(New York: Avon, 2010)

Story type: Contemporary
Subject(s): Love; Single parent family; Writers
Major character(s): Sarah "Sadie Cool" Collier, Writer; Travis Walker, Single Father
Time period(s): 21st century; 2010s
Locale(s): Twilight, Texas

Summary: In *The First Love Cookie Club*, Lori Wilde tells the story of Sarah Collier, a successful children's author who returns to her hometown to visit an ailing fan. Sarah's memories of Twilight, Texas, are filled with images of her years as a chubby teen pining for Travis Walker, so she is stunned to find that Travis is the father of her sick fan. When she learns Travis is now single, all

Sarah's teenaged dreams come back to her in an instant, and she sets out to win the heart of the man she never got over.

Where it's reviewed:
Romantic Times, December 2010, page 77

Other books by the same author:
The Welcome Home Garden Club, 2011
His Final Seduction, 2010
Sweet Surrender, 2010
The True Love Quilting Club, 2010
The Sweethearts' Knitting Club, 2009

Other books you might like:
Robyn Carr, *A Virgin River Christmas*, 2008
Marcia Evanick, *A Berry Merry Christmas*, 2004
Lisa Kleypas, *Christmas Eve at Friday Harbor*, 2010
Linda Lael Miller, *Montana Creeds: Dylan*, 2009
Susan Wiggs, *Lakeshore Christmas*, 2009

1136

EMMA WILDES (Pseudonym of Katherine Smith)

His Sinful Secret
(New York: Penguin, 2010)

Series: Notorious Bachelors Series. Book 3
Story type: Historical; Series
Subject(s): Romances (Fiction); Love; Marriage
Major character(s): Michael Hepburn, Nobleman; Julianne Sutton, Fiance(e) (of Michael Hepburn)
Time period(s): 19th century
Locale(s): England

Summary: In *His Sinful Secret*, the sudden death of nobleman Harry Hepburn leaves his bride-to-be with an uncertain future. Harry's brother Michael, a confirmed bachelor and spy for the Crown, must fulfill his family duty by marrying Julianne Sutton and assuming the title of Marquess of Longhaven. Though his new wife is charming and beautiful, Michael is preoccupied with his work and threats against his life. As he tries to protect Julianne from his perilous lifestyle, he learns that his young bride is hiding details about her own past. *His Sinful Secret* is the third book in the Notorious Bachelors series.

Where it's reviewed:
Booklist, October 15, 2010, page 26
Romantic Times, November 2010, page 42

Other books by the same author:
Lessons from a Scarlet Lady, 2010
My Lord Scandal, 2010
Our Wicked Mistake, 2010
An Indecent Proposition, 2009
Seducing the Highlander, 2009

Other books you might like:
Mary Blayney, *Traitor's Kiss*, 2008
Jacquie D'Alessandro, *Sleepless at Midnight*, 2007
Stephanie Laurens, *What Price Love?: A Cynster Novel*, 2006
Amanda Quick, *Scandal*, 1991
Elizabeth Thornton, *The Bachelor Trap*, 2006

1137

EMMA WILDES (Pseudonym of Katherine Smith)

My Lord Scandal
(New York: Penguin, 2010)

Series: Notorious Bachelors Series. Book 1
Story type: Historical; Series
Subject(s): Romances (Fiction); History; Love
Major character(s): Alexander St. James, Nobleman; Amelia Hathaway, Noblewoman
Time period(s): 19th century
Locale(s): England

Summary: In *My Lord Scandal*, a feud between families brings the scoundrel Alexander St. James to the Hathaway home to reclaim a lost family possession. At first Alexander thinks that the house is vacant, but in his search he finds the lovely—and scantily dressed—Lady Amelia in her bed chamber. Instead of retrieving his grandmother's heirloom, St. James kisses Amelia and leaves empty-handed. Though shocked by the mysterious intruder's actions, Lady Amelia is smitten with Alexander even after she discovers his identity and his notorious reputation. *My Lord Scandal* is the first book in the Notorious Bachelors series.

Where it's reviewed:
Romantic Times, September 2010, page 45

Other books by the same author:
Lessons from a Scarlet Lady, 2010
Seducing the Highlander, 2010
An Indecent Proposition, 2009

Other books you might like:
Claudia Dain, *The Courtesan's Wager*, 2009
Susan Gee Heino, *Mistress by Mistake*, 2009
Madeline Hunter, *The Rules of Seduction*, 2006
Michelle Marcos, *When a Lady Misbehaves*, 2007
Christine Wells, *Scandal's Daughter*, 2007

1138

EMMA WILDES (Pseudonym of Katherine Smith)

Our Wicked Mistake
(New York: Penguin, 2010)

Series: Notorious Bachelors Series. Book 2
Story type: Historical; Series
Subject(s): Romances (Fiction); History; Scandals
Major character(s): Madeline May, Widow(er); Luke Daudet, Nobleman
Time period(s): 19th century
Locale(s): England

Summary: In *Our Wicked Mistake*, a young widow takes desperate measures to protect her privacy and reputation. During Madeline May's marriage, her husband, Colin, kept a diary containing explicit information about their relationship—information Madeline would not like to be made public. Luke Daudet is the one man capable of retrieving the diary, but not without serious complications. Madeline and Luke have a sexual history that would prove ruinous if revealed. If Daudet recovers

Colin's diary, Madeline's marital secrets may be protected, but her virtue may be in greater danger than before. *Our Wicked Mistake* is the second book in the Notorious Bachelors series.

Where it's reviewed:
Romantic Times, October 2010, page 40

Other books by the same author:
Lessons from a Scarlet Lady, 2010
My Lord Scandal, 2010
Seducing the Highlander, 2010
An Indecent Proposition, 2009

Other books you might like:
Suzanne Enoch, *Before the Scandal: The Notorious Gentlemen*, 2008
Madeline Hunter, *The Rules of Seduction*, 2006
Nicole Jordan, *To Tame a Dangerous Lord*, 2010
Amanda Quick, *Seduction*, 1990
Julia Ross, *The Seduction*, 2002

1139

MICHELLE WILLINGHAM

Surrender to an Irish Warrior

(Toronto; New York: Harlequin, 2010)

Story type: Historical - Medieval
Subject(s): Love; Ireland; Irish (European people)
Major character(s): Trahern MacEgan, Warrior; Morren O'Reilly, Young Woman
Time period(s): 12th century; 1100s
Locale(s): Ireland

Summary: Michelle Willingham's *Surrender to an Irish Warrior* is set in 1100s Ireland, where sexy warrior Trahern MacEgan has sworn off love after having his heart effectively shattered. When Morren O'Reilly enters his life, however, Trahern experiences feelings he thought were a thing of the past. This disgraced beauty may just have the power to open his heart and allow him to love again. But can Morren overcome her own pain and give herself permission to surrender to this handsome Irish warrior?

Where it's reviewed:
Romantic Times, October 2010, page 47

Other books by the same author:
The Accidental Countess, 2010
The Accidental Princess, 2010
Taming Her Irish Warrior, 2009
Her Warrior King, 2008
Her Warrior Slave, 2008

Other books you might like:
May Stella Burke, *The Conqueror's Lady*, 1930
Glynnis Campbell, *My Champion*, 2000
Margaret Mallory, *Knight of Desire*, 2009
Joanne Rock, *The Captive*, 2010
Tina St. John, *Lord of Vengeance*, 1999

1140

GAYLE WILSON
AMANDA MCCABE, Co-Author
CAROLE MORTIMER, Co-Author

Regency Christmas Proposals

(Toronto; New York: Harlequin, 2010)

Story type: Historical - Regency
Subject(s): Love; Christmas; Marriage
Time period(s): 19th century
Locale(s): United Kingdom

Summary: Authors Gayle Wilson, Amanda McCabe, and Carole Mortimer each present a holiday-themed novella of romance and intrigue. *Regency Christmas Proposals* contains three short novels, each set during Christmases in Regency England. Featuring strong heroines and sexy heroes, these tales prove that love is the greatest gift of all.

Where it's reviewed:
Romantic Times, November 2010, page 44

Other books you might like:
Anne Burrows, *One Candlelight Christmas*, 2008
Nicola Cornick, *Christmas Wedding Belles*, 2007
Sandra Heath, *A Regency Christmas*, 2002
Barbara Metzger, *Regency Christmas Courtship*, 2005
Elizabeth Rolls, *Mistletoe Kisses*, 2006

1141

MARY WINE

Bedding the Enemy

(New York: Brava, 2010)

Story type: Historical
Subject(s): Love; Marriage; Family
Major character(s): Keir McQuade, Laird; Helena Knyvett, Noblewoman
Time period(s): 16th century-17th century; 1580s-1600s
Locale(s): United Kingdom

Summary: Mary Wine's *Bedding the Enemy* is the story of a newly minted laird and his romance with a repressed noblewoman. Set in Elizabethan England, this tale follows Keir McQuade to the royal court, where he hopes to meet a refined woman to make his wife. There he crosses paths with Helena Knyvett, a quiet beauty who lives under the tyranny of her brother's thumb. Keir and Helena's attraction is intense, but in order for the two to be together, they will have to confront the roadblocks in their lives—and in their hearts.

Where it's reviewed:
Booklist, August 2010, page 44

Other books by the same author:
Highland Hellcat, 2010
In the Warrior's Bed, 2010
To Conquer a Highlander, 2010
In Bed with a Stranger, 2009
Let Me Love You, 2008

Other books you might like:
Margaret Mallory, *Knight of Pleasure*, 2009
Monica McCarty, *Highland Warrior*, 2009
Karen Marie Moning, *To Tame a Highland Warrior*, 2000
Bertrice Small, *The Border Lord and the Lady*, 2009
Sue-Ellen Welfonder, *Devil in a Kilt*, 2001

1142

VERONICA WOLFF

Devil's Highlander

(New York: Berkley, 2010)

Series: Clan MacAlpin Series. Book 1
Story type: Fantasy
Subject(s): Scotland; Scottish history; Fantasy
Major character(s): Cormac MacAlpin, Nobleman; Marjorie Keith, Caregiver
Locale(s): Scotland

Summary: *Devil's Highlander* is the first installment in author Veronica Wolff's Clan MacAlpin series, which revolves around a family of Scottish nobility who return to their family's castle after the conclusion of the Scottish Civil Wars. In this installment, brother Cormac MacAlpin is approached by a former love interest, Marjorie Keith, to help locate a lost child. Cormac sees this as an opportunity to redeem himself after losing his twin brother years ago. Will Marjorie and Cormac rekindle a romance, or is Cormac too mired in his long-standing guilt?

Where it's reviewed:
Romantic Times, August 2010, page 47

Other books by the same author:
Lord of the Highlands, 2009
Warrior of the Highlands, 2009
Master of the Highlands, 2008
Sword of the Highlands, 2008

Other books you might like:
Diana Gabaldon, *Outlander*, 1991
Donna Grant, *Dangerous Highlander*, 2010
Melissa Mayhue, *A Highlander's Homecoming*, 2010
Karen Marie Moning, *The Highlander's Touch*, 2000
Lynsay Sands, *Taming the Highland Bride*, 2010

1143

SHERRYL WOODS

A Chesapeake Shores Christmas

(New York: Mira, 2010)

Series: Chesapeake Shores Series. Book 4
Story type: Contemporary
Subject(s): Love; Marriage; Family
Major character(s): Megan O'Brien, Divorced Person; Mick O'Brien, Divorced Person; Connor O'Brien, Son (of Megan and Mick)

Time period(s): 21st century; 2010s
Locale(s): Chesapeake Shores, United States

Summary: Megan and Mick O'Brien are a divorced couple who have long went their separate ways. But now that their children are grown and life has quieted down, they find themselves drawn back to one another and toward reconciliation. The idea doesn't sit well with all members of the family, however. Megan is unsure if Mick's sometimes-volatile temper can be truly tolerated, and the couple's son Connor is dead set against the reunion. Meanwhile, a secret from Mick's past emerges, threatening any future hopes of love and remarriage. *A Chesapeake Shores Christmas* is the fourth installment in Sherryl Woods's Chesapeake Shores series.

Where it's reviewed:
Booklist, October 1, 2010, page 37
Library Journal, October 15, 2010, page 61
Romantic Times, October 2010, page 87

Other books by the same author:
Home in Carolina, 2010
Honeysuckle Summer, 2010
Sweet Tea at Sunrise, 2010
Flowers on Main, 2009
Harbor Lights, 2009

Other books you might like:
Becky Cochrane, *A Coventry Christmas*, 2006
Marcia Evanick, *Mistletoe Bay*, 2007
Teresa Hill, *Twelve Days*, 2000
Debbie Macomber, *The Christmas Basket*, 2002

1144

REBECCA YORK (Pseudonym of Ruth Glick)

Guarding Grace

(Toronto; New York: Harlequin, 2010)

Subject(s): Adventure; Love; Suspense
Major character(s): Grace Cunningham, Witness (to a murder); Brady Lockwood, Brother (of murder victim)
Time period(s): 21st century; 2010s
Locale(s): United States

Summary: Rebecca York's *Guarding Grace* tells of the romantic adventure embarked upon by a woman who witnessed a murder and the brother of the victim. Grace Cunningham knows she's next in line to meet an untimely end if she doesn't surrender to the protection of handsome Brady Lockwood. But Grace has a secret that could spell doom for she and Brady's attempts to escape her would-be assassins—and a possible end to the love affair she and Brady have begun.

Where it's reviewed:
Romantic Times, July 2010, page 108

Other books by the same author:
Day of the Dragon, 2010
Dragon Moon, 2009
New Moon, 2007
Shadow of the Moon, 2006
Killing Moon, 2003

Other books you might like:
Beverly Barton, *Silent Killer*, 2009
Lisa Jackson, *Chosen to Die*, 2009
Brenda Novak, *The Perfect Couple*, 2009
Aimee Thurlo, *Alpha Warrior*, 2010
Debra Webb, *First Night*, 2009

1145

REBECCA YORK (Pseudonym of Ruth Glick)

Day of the Dragon
(New York: Penguin, 2010)

Story type: Paranormal
Subject(s): Romances (Fiction); Suspense; Archaeology
Major character(s): Madison Dartmoor, Archaeologist
Time period(s): 21st century; 2010s
Locale(s): Las Vegas, Nevada

Summary: In *Day of the Dragon* by Rebecca York, an archaeologist makes a discovery that puts her life in danger. At a Las Vegas conference, Madison Dartmoor realizes the importance of her latest find when she is abducted after a lecture. The man who tries to come to her rescue appears to be human, but he has the ability to transform himself into a mythical creature. When Madison learns his true identity and the magnitude of her discovery, she will be forever changed.

Where it's reviewed:
Romantic Times, December 2010, page 76

Other books by the same author: page 76

Other books by the same author:
Guarding Grace, 2010
Powerhouse, 2010
Dragon Moon, 2009
Eternal Moon, 2009
More than a Man, 2009

Other books you might like:
Jennifer Ashley, *Immortals: The Calling*, 2007
D.D. Barant, *Dying Bites: The Bloodhound Files*, 2009
Pamela Palmer, *Desire Untamed*, 2009
Pamela Palmer, *Obsession Untamed*, 2009
Robin T. Popp, *Immortals*, 2007

Romances

Series Index

This index alphabetically lists series to which books featured in the entries belong. Beneath each series name, book titles are listed alphabetically with author names and genre codes. The genre codes are as follows: *c* Popular Fiction, *f* Fantasy, *h* Horror, *i* Inspirational, *m* Mystery, *r* Romance, *s* Science Fiction, and *t* Historical. Numbers refer to the entries that feature each title.

Time Period Index

This index chronologically lists the time settings in which the featured books take place. Main headings refer to a century; where no specific time is given, the headings MULTIPLE TIME PERIODS, INDETERMINATE PAST, INDETERMINATE FUTURE, and INDETERMINATE are used. The 15th through 27th centuries are broken down into decades when possible. (Note: 1800s, for example, refers to the first decade of the 19th century.) Featured titles are listed alphabetically beneath time headings, with author names and genre codes. The genre codes are as follows: *c* Popular Fiction, *f* Fantasy, *h* Horror, *i* Inspirational, *m* Mystery, *r* Romance, *s* Science Fiction, and *t* Historical. Numbers refer to the entries that feature each title.

40000s

INDETERMINATE FUTURE

INDETERMINATE

Geographic Index

This index provides access to all featured books by geographic settings—such as countries, continents, oceans, and planets. States and provinces are indicated for the United States and Canada. Also interfiled are headings for fictional place names (Spaceships, Imaginary Planets, etc.). Sections are further broken down by city or the specific name of the imaginary locale. Book titles are listed alphabetically under headings, with author names and genre codes. The genre codes are as follows: *c* Popular Fiction, *f* Fantasy, *h* Horror, *i* Inspirational, *m* Mystery, *r* Romance, *s* Science Fiction, and *t* Historical. Numbers refer to the entries that feature each title.

SCOTLAND

SIERRA LEONE

SOLAR SYSTEM

SOLOMON ISLANDS

SOUTH AFRICA

SOUTH AMERICA

SPAIN

SUDAN

SWEDEN

SWITZERLAND

SYRIA

THE BALKANS

TRINIDAD AND TOBAGO

TURKEY

UNITED KINGDOM

Morrow Creek
Mail-Order Groom - Lisa Plumley   *r*   1085

Skull Valley
Killer Heat - Brenda Novak   *r*   1076

ARKANSAS

Huttig
Come High Water - Carolyn Brown   *r*   944

CALIFORNIA
The Border Lords - T. Jefferson Parker   *m*   512
Coronets and Steel - Sherwood Smith   *f*   87
Deceit - Brandilyn Collins   *i*   838
Fade to Blue - Julie Carobini   *i*   834
Faith's Reward - Tammy Barley   *i*   825
Fourth Day - Zoe Sharp   *m*   526
The Good Sister - Drusilla Campbell   *c*   578
Heads You Lose - Lisa Lutz   *m*   488
Look! Look! Feathers - Mike Young   *c*   722
On Hummingbird Wings: A Novel - Lauraine
   Snelling   *i*   908
Words - Ginny L. Yttrup   *i*   923

Bakersfield
What You See in the Dark - Manuel
   Munoz   *c*   661

Berkeley
The Incredible Double - Owen Hill   *m*   464

Capitola
Delivered with Love - Sherry Kyle   *i*   874

Delilah
Siren - John Everson   *h*   281

Fool's Gold
Almost Perfect - Susan Mallery   *r*   1050

Hollywood
Angel at Dawn - Emma Holly   *r*   1007
*The Life and Opinions of Maf the Dog, and of His
   Friend Marilyn Monroe* - Andrew
   O'Hagan   *t*   221
Sloane Hall - Libby Sternberg   *t*   249
Star of His Heart - Brenda Jackson   *r*   1012

Humboldt County
Wrecker - Summer Wood   *c*   718

Los Angeles
The Best of Friends - Susan Mallery   *r*   1051
Delivered with Love - Sherry Kyle   *i*   874
Guilt by Association - Marcia Clark   *m*   399
Home Again - Mariah Stewart   *r*   1110
Kill the Dead - Richard Kadrey   *h*   308
Kind of Blue - Miles Corwin   *m*   410
The Perfect Shot - Gemma Halliday   *r*   996
Sandman Slim - Richard Kadrey   *h*   307
The Sentry - Robert Crais   *m*   412
Shortcut Man - P.G. Sturges   *m*   537
When Pleasure Rules - J.K. Beck   *h*   271
The Fifth Witness - Michael Connelly   *m*   406

Mercy Falls
The Lightkeeper's Ball - Colleen Coble   *i*   836

Motherlode
Crown of Dust - Mary Volmer   *c*   710

Oak Knoll
Secrets to the Grave - Tami Hoag   *m*   466

Oakland
Something for Nothing - David Anthony   *m*   369

Orange County
This Vacant Paradise - Victoria Patterson   *c*   674

Palo Alto
Palo Alto: Stories - James Franco   *c*   605

San Diego
The Neighbors Are Watching - Debra
   Ginsberg   *c*   612
The Wish List - Gabi Stevens   *f*   90

San Francisco
Altar of Bones - Philip Carter   *m*   394
Code Triage - Candace Calvert   *r*   947
Damage - John T. Lescroart   *m*   483
The Edge - Rudy Josephs   *s*   764
Firefighter Daddy - Lee McKenzie   *r*   1063
Home Is Where the Bark Is - Kandy
   Shepherd   *r*   1105
The Lies that Bind - Kate Carlisle   *m*   392
The Loving Dead - Amelia Beamer   *h*   268
Mary Ann in Autumn - Armistead Maupin   *c*   650
Tempted by Fate - Kate Perry   *r*   1081

Virgin River
Promise Canyon - Robyn Carr   *r*   949

COLORADO
Crunch Time - Diane Mott Davidson   *m*   416
A Heart Divided: A Novel - Kathleen
   Morgan   *i*   888
In a Cowboy's Arms - Janette Kenny   *r*   1031
When All My Dreams Come True - Janelle
   Mowery   *i*   891

Colorado Springs
Swift Justice - Laura Disilverio   *m*   420

Denver
Deadly Intent - Kylie Brant   *r*   936
The Outlaw's Return - Victoria Bylin   *i*   831
The Ringer - Jenny Shank   *c*   695

Reidsville
Marry Me - Jo Goodman   *r*   986

CONNECTICUT
Happy Ever After - Nora Roberts   *r*   1093

Mystick Falls
Death by Diamonds - Annette Blair   *f*   11

DELAWARE
Port Mortuary - Patricia Cornwell   *m*   409

DISTRICT OF COLUMBIA
I'd Know You Anywhere - Laura Lippman   *c*   646
Up from the Blue: A Novel - Susan
   Henderson   *c*   623

Washington
The Alarmists - Don Hoesel   *i*   865
Buffalo West Wing - Julie Hyzy   *m*   469
The First Assassin - John J. Miller   *t*   208
The Inner Circle - Brad Meltzer   *m*   500
The School of Night - Louis Bayard   *m*   376

The Second Life of John Wilkes Booth - Barnaby
   Conrad   *t*   131

FLORIDA
The Bone Yard - Jefferson Bass   *m*   375
Chasing Sunsets - Eva Marie Everson   *i*   854
The Cypress House - Michael Koryta   *m*   480
The Dead Detective - William Heffernan   *m*   459
Electric Barracuda - Tim Dorsey   *m*   421
The Flock - James Robert Smith   *s*   805
Free Range Institution - Michael Haskins   *m*   456
Ghost Shadow - Heather Graham   *r*   988
Night Vision - Randy Wayne White   *m*   554
*Nothing Happens Until It Happens to You: A Novel
   without Pay, Perks, or Privileges* - T.M.
   Shine   *c*   700
Swamplandia! - Karen Russell   *c*   687

Cedar Key
Casting Around - Terri DuLong   *r*   970

Fort Lauderdale
Cold Shot to the Heart - Wallace Stroby   *m*   536

GEORGIA
The Gendarme - Mark T. Mustian   *t*   215

Atlanta
The Dangerous Edge of Things - Tina
   Whittle   *m*   555
The Darkest Edge of Dawn - Kelly Gay   *h*   286
The Sweetest Thing - Elizabeth Musser   *i*   892

Elderberry
Miss Dimple Disappears - Mignon F.
   Ballard   *t*   112

Savannah
The Human Blend - Alan Dean Foster   *s*   752

Threestep
The Cailiffs of Baghdad, Georgia - Mary Helen
   Stefaniak   *t*   248

HAWAII
Lester Higata's 20th Century - Barbara
   Hamby   *c*   618

IDAHO
Idaho Brides - Erica Vetsch   *i*   916

Sunshine
Animal Magnetism - Jill Shalvis   *r*   1103

ILLINOIS
Dust - Joan Frances Turner   *h*   359
Explosive - Beth Kery   *r*   1033
How to Read the Air - Dinaw Mengestu   *c*   655

Beldon Grove
The Dawn of a Dream - Ann Shorey   *i*   904

Chicago
The Bad Kitty Lounge - Michael Wiley   *m*   556
The Brotherhood - Jerry B. Jenkins   *i*   868
Other Eyes - Barbara D'Amato   *m*   415
Set the Night on Fire - Libby Fischer
   Hellmann   *m*   460
Side Jobs: Stories from the Dresden Files - Jim
   Butcher   *f*   18
Too Many Clients - David J. Walker   *m*   548

Genre Index

This index lists the books featured as main entries in *What Do I Read Next?* by genre and story type within each genre. Beneath each of the nine genres, the story types appear alphabetically, and titles appear alphabetically under story type headings. The name of the primary author, genre code and the book entry number also appear with each title. The genre codes are as follows: *c* Popular Fiction, *f* Fantasy, *h* Horror, *i* Inspirational, *m* Mystery, *r* Romance, *s* Science Fiction, and *t* Historical. For definitions of the story types, see the "Key to Genre Terms" following the Introduction.

FANTASY FICTION

Adventure

The Farwalker's Quest - Joni Sensel   *f*   82

The King's Bastard - Rowena Cory Daniells   *f*   27

Rogue Angel: Phantom Prospect - Alex Archer   *f*   6

Rogue Angel: The Dragon's Mark - Alex Archer   *f*   5

Alternate History

At the Queen's Command - Michael A. Stackpole   *f*   89

The Cardinal's Blades - Pierre Pevel   *f*   76

Much Fall of Blood - Dave Freer   *f*   35

Alternate World

Against All Things Ending - Stephen R. Donaldson   *f*   30

Banners in the Wind - Juliet E. McKenna   *f*   67

Boarding Instructions - Ray Vukcevich   *f*   99

Cinkarion: The Heart of Fire - J.A. Cullum   *f*   24

Corvus - Paul Kearney   *f*   50

A Cup of Normal - Devon Monk   *f*   72

Dragon Soul - Danielle Bennett   *f*   9

Grimblades - Nick Kyme   *f*   52

The Half-Made World - Felix Gilman   *f*   37

Hawkwood and the Kings - Paul Kearney   *f*   49

Imager's Intrigue - L.E. Modesitt   *f*   71

Naamah's Curse - Jacqueline Carey   *f*   19

Path of the Sun - Violette Malan   *f*   63

The Questing Road - Lyn McConchie   *f*   64

Shadow's Son - Jon Sprunk   *f*   88

Stormlord Rising - Glenda Larke   *f*   57

Temple of the Serpent - C.L. Werner   *f*   101

The Uncrowned King - Rowena Cory Daniells   *f*   26

Weight of Stone - Laura Anne Gilman   *f*   38

Ancient Evil Unleashed

The Warded Man - Peter V. Brett   *f*   14

Collection

Boarding Instructions - Ray Vukcevich   *f*   99

Dark and Stormy Knights - P.N. Elrod   *f*   31

Coming-of-Age

The Warded Man - Peter V. Brett   *f*   14

Contemporary

Archangel's Kiss - Nalini Singh   *f*   85

Rogue Angel: Tribal Ways - Alex Archer   *f*   4

Family Saga

From Hell with Love - Simon R. Green   *f*   39

Futuristic

Salute the Dark - Adrian Tchaikovsky   *f*   98

Who Fears Death - Nnedi Okorafor   *f*   75

Historical

A Star Shall Fall - Marie Brennan   *f*   13

Historical - American West

The Native Star - M.K. Hobson   *f*   44

Historical - Victorian

The Horns of Ruin - Tim Akers   *f*   1

Horror

Bullet - Laurell K. Hamilton   *f*   41

Circle of Skulls - James P. Davis   *f*   29

Legend

Stuff of Legends - Ian Gibson   *f*   36

Magic Conflict

A Star Shall Fall - Marie Brennan   *f*   13

Mystery

Hunted by the Others - Jess Haines   *f*   40

A Wild Light - Marjorie M. Liu   *f*   58

Mystical

The Warded Man - Peter V. Brett   *f*   14

Occult

The Horns of Ruin - Tim Akers   *f*   1

Paranormal

Coronets and Steel - Sherwood Smith   *f*   87

The Wish List - Gabi Stevens   *f*   90

Political

Imager's Intrigue - L.E. Modesitt   *f*   71

Quest

Sword of Justice - Chris Wraight   *f*   103

Romance

Bullet - Laurell K. Hamilton   *f*   41

In the Darkest Night - Patti O'Shea   *f*   74

Shades of Milk and Honey - Mary Robinette Kowal   *f*   51

A Wild Light - Marjorie M. Liu   *f*   58

Science Fantasy

Dragonfly Falling - Adrian Tchaikovsky   *f*   96

Series

Against All Things Ending - Stephen R. Donaldson   *f*   30

HISTORICAL FICTION

INSPIRATIONAL FICTION

POPULAR FICTION

Contemporary - Innocent

Contemporary Realism

Ethnic

Family Saga

Fantasy

Historical

Historical - American Civil War

Historical - World War II

Horror

Light Fantasy

Literary

Mystery

Mystical

Psychological

Religious

Romance

Series

Wild Talents

Witchcraft

POPULAR ROMANCES

Alternate World

The Princess in His Bed - Lila DiPasqua   *r*   965

The Promise - Brenda Joyce   *r*   1022

Reckless - Anne Stuart   *r*   1114

The Reckless Bride - Stephanie Laurens   *r*   1039

Rules of an Engagement - Suzanne Enoch   *r*   971

Ruthless - Anne Stuart   *r*   1113

A Season of Seduction - Jennifer Haymore   *r*   1001

The Surrender of a Lady - Tiffany Clare   *r*   954

Taken by Desire - Lavinia Kent   *r*   1032

Till Dawn with the Devil - Alexandra Hawkins   *r*   1000

To Save the Devil - Kate Moore   *r*   1069

To Tempt a Saint - Kate Moore   *r*   1070

The Tutor - Hope Tarr   *r*   1116

The Vengeful Bridegroom - Kit Donner   *r*   967

The Viking Takes a Knight - Sandra Hill   *r*   1004

Wicked Intentions - Elizabeth Hoyt   *r*   1010

Historical - American Civil War

Night of the Vampires - Heather Graham   *r*   989

Historical - American Revolution

Midnight - Beverly Jenkins   *r*   1019

Historical - American West

Chasing the Sun - Kaki Warner   *r*   1126

Mail-Order Groom - Lisa Plumley   *r*   1085

Wolf Runner - Constance O'Banyon   *r*   1077

Historical - French Revolution

The Making of a Gentleman - Shana Galen   *r*   982

Historical - Georgian

The Pursuit of Pleasure - Elizabeth Essex   *r*   972

Historical - Medieval

A Storm of Pleasure - Terri Brisbin   *r*   939

Surrender to an Irish Warrior - Michelle Willingham   *r*   1139

The Valcourt Heiress - Catherine Coulter   *r*   957

Historical - Regency

Chivalrous Captain, Rebel Mistress - Diane Gaston   *r*   984

A Duke's Temptation - Jillian Hunter   *r*   1011

The Heir - Grace Burrowes   *r*   945

Highland Rogue, London Miss - Margaret Moore   *r*   1071

A Kiss at Midnight - Eloisa James   *r*   1014

A Little Bit Wild - Victoria Dahl   *r*   959

Major Lord David - Sherry Lynn Ferguson   *r*   975

My Dangerous Duke - Gaelen Foley   *r*   976

One Unashamed Night - Sophia James   *r*   1016

A Perfect Scandal - Tina Gabrielle   *r*   980

A Rake by Midnight - Gail Ranstrom   *r*   1088

Regency Christmas Proposals - Gayle Wilson   *r*   1140

Seven Nights to Forever - Evangeline Collins   *r*   955

Ten Ways to Be Adored When Landing a Lord - Sarah MacLean   *r*   1048

Three Nights with a Scoundrel - Tessa Dare   *r*   961

Trial by Desire - Courtney Milan   *r*   1067

Twice Tempted by a Rogue - Tessa Dare   *r*   962

Whisper of Scandal - Nicola Cornick   *r*   956

Wicked Surrender - Jade Lee   *r*   1040

The Wicked Wyckerly - Patricia Rice   *r*   1091

The Year of Living Scandalously - Julia London   *r*   1045

Holiday Themes

His Christmas Pleasure - Cathy Maxwell   *r*   1056

A Midnight Clear - Kristi Astor   *r*   928

The Naughty List - Donna Kauffman   *r*   1026

Santa in Montana - Janet Dailey   *r*   960

Scandal of the Season - Christie Kelley   *r*   1027

Humor

The Love Goddess' Cooking School - Melissa Senate   *r*   1101

Luck Be a Lady - Cathie Linz   *r*   1044

Inspirational

Dining with Joy - Rachel Hauck   *r*   999

Last Temptation - Michelle Stimpson   *r*   1111

Licensed for Trouble - Susan May Warren   *r*   1129

Love's First Bloom - Delia Parr   *r*   1079

Legal

Icebreaker - Deirdre Martin   *r*   1054

You're All I Need - Karen White-Owens   *r*   1134

Mystery

The Search - Nora Roberts   *r*   1092

Spun by Sorcery - Barbara Bretton   *r*   938

The Whisper - Carla Neggers   *r*   1074

Paranormal

Bespelling Jane Austen - Mary Balogh   *r*   929

Day of the Dragon - Rebecca York   *r*   1145

Master of Smoke - Angela Knight   *r*   1035

Midnight Crystal - Jayne Castle   *r*   951

Prince Charming Doesn't Live Here - Christine Warren   *r*   1127

Surrender to Darkness - Annette McCleave   *r*   1059

A Werewolf in Manhattan - Vicki Lewis Thompson   *r*   1121

Political

Cross Roads - Fern Michaels   *r*   1066

Psychological Suspense

You Are Next - Katia Lief   *r*   1042

Ranch Life

Wild Stallion - Delores Fossen   *r*   977

Regency

Dreams of Desire - Cheryl Holt   *r*   1008

The Duke's Night of Sin - Kathryn Caskie   *r*   950

Dukes to the Left of Me, Princes to the Right - Kieran Kramer   *r*   1037

His Christmas Pleasure - Cathy Maxwell   *r*   1056

Scoundrel in My Dreams - Celeste Bradley   *r*   935

Seducing the Duchess - Ashley March   *r*   1053

The Smuggler and the Society Bride - Julia Justiss   *r*   1023

The Unclaimed Duchess - Jenna Petersen   *r*   1083

When Harry Met Molly - Kieran Kramer   *r*   1038

Religious

Love's First Bloom - Julie Lessman   *r*   1041

Romance

Take a Chance on Me - Jill Mansell   *r*   1052

Romantic Suspense

Chased by Moonlight - Nancy Gideon   *r*   985

Deadly Identity - Lindsay McKenna   *r*   1062

Deadly Intent - Kylie Brant   *r*   936

Series

Close Contact - Katherine Allred   *s*   727

The Edge - Rudy Josephs   *s*   764

Ragnarok - Patrick A. Vanner   *s*   815

Seize the Fire - Michael A. Martin   *s*   779

Star Wars: The Old Republic: Fatal Alliance - Sean
    Williams   *s*   820

Vortex - Troy Denning   *s*   744

Zero Sum Game - David Mack   *s*   778

Space Opera

Children No More - Mark L. Van Name   *s*   814

Do Unto Others - Michael Z. Williamson   *s*   821

Hull Zero Three - Greg Bear   *s*   732

Love and Rockets - Kerrie Hughes   *s*   759

Ragnarok - Patrick A. Vanner   *s*   815

Seize the Fire - Michael A. Martin   *s*   779

Sir Dominic Flandry: The Last Knight of Terra -
    Poul Anderson   *s*   728

Star Wars: Clone Wars Gambit: Siege - Karen
    Miller   *s*   784

What Distant Deeps - David Drake   *s*   747

Zero Sum Game - David Mack   *s*   778

Time Travel

All Clear - Connie Willis   *s*   822

Young Adult

Alien Invasion and Other Inconveniences - Brian
    Yansky   *s*   823

The Edge - Rudy Josephs   *s*   764

Hero - Mike Lupica   *s*   776

Now You See Me - Marilyn Kaye   *s*   766

Genre Index

Subject Index

This index lists subjects which are covered in the featured titles. Beneath each subject heading, titles are arranged alphabetically with the author names, genre codes, and entry numbers also indicated. The genre codes are as follows: *c* Popular Fiction, *f* Fantasy, *h* Horror, *i* Inspirational, *m* Mystery, *r* Romance, *s* Science Fiction, and *t* Historical.

Subject Index

Devil

Diaries

Dinosaurs

Diplomacy

Disasters

Discovery and exploration

Diseases

Divorce

Dogs

Dolls

Domestic cats

Dragons

Dreams

Drug abuse

Drugs

Druids

Subject Index

Family history

Family life

Family relations

Family Saga

Family sagas

Fantasy

Law enforcement

Indulgence in Death - J.D. Robb   *s*   796
Kind of Blue - Miles Corwin   *m*   410
Love Me if You Dare - Carly Phillips   *r*   1084
The Night Season - Chelsea Cain   *m*   390

Legends

Stuff of Legends - Ian Gibson   *f*   36

Letters (Correspondence)

The Brothers of Baker Street - Michael
   Robertson   *m*   517
The Exile of Sara Stevenson: A Historical Novel -
   Darci Hannah   *r*   997
Fundraising the Dead - Sheila Connolly   *m*   407
Heidegger's Glasses - Thaisa Frank   *c*   606

Libraries

The Bad Book Affair - Ian Sansom   *m*   524
Died in the Wool - Elizabeth Ludwig   *i*   877

Literature

Android Karenina - Leo Tolstoy   *h*   357
Bespelling Jane Austen - Mary Balogh   *r*   929
Best European Fiction 2011 - Aleksandar
   Hemon   *c*   622
Dracula My Love - Syrie James   *r*   1017
Emily Hudson - Melissa Jones   *t*   184
Emma and the Werewolves - Adam Rann   *h*   339
The Gentleman Poet - Kathryn Johnson   *r*   1020
Jane Slayre - Charlotte Bronte   *h*   276
Little Vampire Women - Lynn Messina   *h*   328
Mr. Darcy's Obsession - Abigail Reynolds   *t*   231
One of Our Thursdays Is Missing - Jasper
   Fforde   *m*   434
The Passages of H.M.: A Novel of Herman Melville
   - Jay Parini   *c*   673
*Tablet and Pen: Literary Landscapes from the Mod-
   ern Middle East* - Reza Aslan   *c*   567
Wuthering Bites - Sarah Gray   *h*   293

Love

13, rue Therese - Elena Mauli Shapiro   *c*   696
21 Aldgate - Patricia Friedberg   *t*   158
Afterlight - Elle Jasper   *h*   306
Almost Perfect - Susan Mallery   *r*   1050
And Thereby Hangs a Tale: Short Stories - Jeffrey
   Archer   *c*   566
Angel at Dawn - Emma Holly   *r*   1007
An Atlas of Impossible Longing - Anuradha
   Roy   *c*   685
Barely a Lady - Eileen Dreyer   *r*   969
The Battle for Commitment Planet - Graham Sharp
   Paul   *s*   790
Becoming George Sand - Rosalind
   Brackenbury   *c*   574
Bedding the Enemy - Mary Wine   *r*   1141
The Bells - Richard Harvell   *t*   170
The Best of Friends - Susan Mallery   *r*   1051
A Bewitching Bride - Elizabeth Thornton   *r*   1122
Beyond the Shore - Connie Monk   *t*   211
Binocular Vision: New and Selected Stories - Edith
   Pearlman   *c*   675
Blood Pressure - Terence Taylor   *h*   354
Broken Promises - Elizabeth Cobbs
   Hoffman   *c*   627
Bummer, and Other Stories - Janice
   Shapiro   *c*   697
Butterfly Swords - Jeannie Lin   *r*   1043

The Calligrapher's Secret - Rafik Schami   *c*   691
Captured by Desire - Kira Morgan   *r*   1072
Casting Around - Terri DuLong   *r*   970
Chaos Bites - Lori Handeland   *h*   299
Chasing the Sun - Kaki Warner   *r*   1126
A Chesapeake Shores Christmas - Sherryl
   Woods   *r*   1143
Chivalrous Captain, Rebel Mistress - Diane
   Gaston   *r*   984
Christmas Eve at Friday Harbor - Lisa
   Kleypas   *r*   1034
Courtesan's Kiss - Mary Blayney   *r*   933
Cross Your Heart - Michele Bardsley   *r*   931
Dangerous Desires - Dee Davis   *r*   963
A Darcy Christmas - Amanda Grange   *r*   991
Deadly Identity - Lindsay McKenna   *r*   1062
Deadly Pursuit - Ann Christopher   *r*   953
Deceptions: A Jamestown Novel - Marilyn J.
   Clay   *r*   130
Dexter: Honorable Cowboy - Marin
   Thomas   *r*   1119
Don't Cry - Beverly Barton   *r*   932
A Duke's Temptation - Jillian Hunter   *r*   1011
Edge of Sight - Roxanne St. Claire   *r*   1109
Enemy Within - Marcella Burnard   *s*   740
Enough About Love - Herve Le Tellier   *c*   641
Esperanza - Trish J. MacGregor   *h*   322
The Finkler Question - Howard Jacobson   *c*   630
The Fire Lord's Lover - Kathryne
   Kennedy   *r*   1030
Firefighter Daddy - Lee McKenzie   *r*   1063
Firewalker - Allyson James   *r*   1013
First Grave on the Right - Darynda Jones   *m*   473
The First Love Cookie Club - Lori Wilde   *r*   1135
The Fourth Victim - Tara Taylor Quinn   *r*   1087
Friday Mornings at Nine - Marilyn Brant   *r*   937
Goodness Gracious Green - Judy Christie   *r*   952
Guarding Grace - Rebecca York   *r*   1144
Happy Ever After - Nora Roberts   *r*   1093
A Harlequin Christmas Carol - Betina
   Krahn   *r*   1036
Highland Rogue, London Miss - Margaret
   Moore   *r*   1071
His Sinful Secret - Emma Wildes   *r*   1136
In the Darkest Night - Patti O'Shea   *f*   74
Instant Family - Elisabeth Rose   *r*   1094
Juliet - Anne Fortier   *t*   156
A Kiss at Midnight - Eloisa James   *r*   1014
Lady of the Butterflies - Fiona Mountain   *t*   212
A Little Bit Wild - Victoria Dahl   *r*   959
Long, Last, Happy: New and Selected Stories -
   Barry Hannah   *c*   619
The Lost and Forgotten Languages of Shanghai -
   Ruiyan Xu   *c*   721
Love and Rockets - Kerrie Hughes   *s*   759
Love Me to Death - Allison Brennan   *m*   387
Major Lord David - Sherry Lynn
   Ferguson   *r*   975
The Making of a Gentleman - Shana
   Galen   *r*   982
Marked by the Moon - Lori Handeland   *h*   298
The Marriage Artist: A Novel - Andrew
   Winer   *c*   716
Marry Me - Jo Goodman   *r*   986
Master of Smoke - Angela Knight   *r*   1035
Maybe This Time - Jennifer Crusie   *r*   958
Mesmerizing Stranger - Jennifer Greene   *r*   994
Midnight - Beverly Jenkins   *r*   1019
More Than Words - Judith Miller   *t*   209
My Fake Fiancee - Nancy Warren   *r*   1128
My Lord Scandal - Emma Wildes   *r*   1137
Not That Kind of Girl - Susan Donovan   *r*   968
Nowhere to Hide - Carlene Thompson   *r*   1120

One Unashamed Night - Sophia James   *r*   1016
Operation Prince Charming - Phyllis
   Bourne   *r*   934
The Perfect Family - Kathryn Shay   *r*   1104
A Perfect Scandal - Tina Gabrielle   *r*   980
The Perfect Shot - Gemma Halliday   *r*   996
Play Dirty - Lorie O'Clare   *r*   1078
Pleasures of a Notorious Gentleman - Lorraine
   Heath   *r*   1002
*Portraits of a Few of the People I've Made Cry:
   Stories* - Christina Sneed   *c*   702
Precious and Fragile Things - Megan
   Hart   *r*   998
The Princess in His Bed - Lila DiPasqua   *r*   965
Profile for Seduction - Karen Whiddon   *r*   1133
The Promise - Brenda Joyce   *r*   1022
Promise Canyon - Robyn Carr   *r*   949
Promises in the Dark - Stephanie Tyler   *r*   1123
The Pursuit of Pleasure - Elizabeth Essex   *r*   972
Queen Hereafter: A Novel of Margaret of Scotland
   - Susan Fraser King   *t*   189
Quiet Chaos - Sandro Veronesi   *c*   709
Raider's Heart - Marcia Gruver   *i*   860
A Rake by Midnight - Gail Ranstrom   *r*   1088
Reckless - Anne Stuart   *r*   1114
Regency Christmas Proposals - Gayle
   Wilson   *r*   1140
Ride the Fire - Jo Davis   *r*   964
Roy & Lillie - Loren D. Estleman   *t*   151
Rules of an Engagement - Suzanne Enoch   *r*   971
Ruthless - Anne Stuart   *r*   1113
Seducing the Duchess - Ashley March   *r*   1053
Seducing the Succubus - Cassie Ryan   *r*   1096
Seer of Sevenwaters - Juliet Marillier   *t*   202
Seven Nights to Forever - Evangeline
   Collins   *r*   955
Shades of Milk and Honey - Mary Robinette
   Kowal   *f*   51
She's Gone Country - Jane Porter   *r*   1086
Simon Says... - Donna Kauffman   *r*   1025
Sins of the Heart - Eve Silver   *r*   1106
Sloane Hall - Libby Sternberg   *t*   249
Snowdrops - A.D. Miller   *c*   656
Solo - Rana Dasgupta   *c*   588
A Storm of Pleasure - Terri Brisbin   *r*   939
Styx's Storm - Lora Leigh   *s*   774
The Surrender of a Lady - Tiffany Clare   *r*   954
Surrender to an Irish Warrior - Michelle
   Willingham   *r*   1139
Surrender to Darkness - Annette
   McCleave   *r*   1059
Take a Chance on Me - Jill Mansell   *r*   1052
Taken by Desire - Lavinia Kent   *r*   1032
Tempted by Fate - Kate Perry   *r*   1081
Ten Ways to Be Adored When Landing a Lord -
   Sarah MacLean   *r*   1048
Three Nights with a Scoundrel - Tessa
   Dare   *r*   961
Till Dawn with the Devil - Alexandra
   Hawkins   *r*   1000
Touching Darkness - Jaime Rush   *h*   341
Tracato - Joel Shepherd   *f*   83
Trial by Desire - Courtney Milan   *r*   1067
The Tutor - Hope Tarr   *r*   1116
Twice Tempted by a Rogue - Tessa Dare   *r*   962
Twilight Forever Rising - Lena Meydan   *h*   329
Unbreakable Bond - Rita Herron   *r*   1003
Under the Poppy - Kathe Koja   *c*   638
An Unlikely Suitor - Nancy Moser   *i*   890
The Wake of Forgiveness - Bruce Machart   *t*   199
Water Bound - Christine Feehan   *r*   974
A Werewolf in Manhattan - Vicki Lewis
   Thompson   *r*   1121

Museums

Music

Musicians

Muslims

Mystery

Romanies

Royalty

Rural life

Russian history

Russian Revolution, 1917-1921

Russians

Safety

Satire

Scandals

Schools

Science

Science fiction

The Best of Larry Niven - Larry Niven *s* 787
The Best of the Bolos: Their Finest Hours - Hank Davis *s* 742
The Black Guard - Hideyuki Kikuchi *h* 313
Burning Up - Nalini Singh *r* 1107
Children No More - Mark L. Van Name *s* 814
Chronolysis - Michel Jeury *s* 762
Close Contact - Katherine Allred *s* 727
Complete Hammer's Slammers, Volume 3 - David Drake *s* 748
Detour to Otherness - Henry Kuttner *s* 772
Do Unto Others - Michael Z. Williamson *s* 821
Dragonfly Falling - Adrian Tchaikovsky *f* 96
Dragongirl - Todd J. McCaffrey *s* 782
The Edge - Rudy Josephs *s* 764
Feed - Mira Grant *h* 292
The High King of Montival - S.M. Stirling *f* 92
The Hugo Awards Showcase - Mary Robinette Kowal *s* 771
Hull Zero Three - Greg Bear *s* 732
L. Ron Hubbard Presents Writers of the Future, Volume 26 - K.D. Wentworth *s* 818
Nocturnal Emissions - Jeffrey Thomas *h* 355
Ragnarok - Patrick A. Vanner *s* 815
Sabbat Worlds - Dan Abnett *s* 723
Seize the Fire - Michael A. Martin *s* 779
Sir Dominic Flandry: The Last Knight of Terra - Poul Anderson *s* 728
Steampunk'd - Jean Rabe *s* 792
The Universe Wreckers: The Collected Edmond Hamilton, Volume 3 - Edmond Hamilton *s* 755
Vortex - Troy Denning *s* 744
What Distant Deeps - David Drake *s* 747
Zero Sum Game - David Mack *s* 778

Scotland

Captured by Desire - Kira Morgan *r* 1072
Devil's Highlander - Veronica Wolff *r* 1142
The Hawk - Monica McCarty *r* 1058
The Melody Girls - Anne Douglas *t* 144
Mine Is the Night - Liz Curtis Higgs *i* 862
Murder on the Moor - C.S. Challinor *m* 395
Queen Hereafter: A Novel of Margaret of Scotland - Susan Fraser King *t* 189
The Unbelievers - Alastair Sim *t* 242

Scots (British people)

Blood on Silk - Marie Treanor *h* 358
Captured by Desire - Kira Morgan *r* 1072
Corrag - Susan Fletcher *c* 601
A Pig of Cold Poison - Pat McIntosh *t* 206
A Rush of Blood - Quintin Jardine *m* 472

Scottish history

Devil's Highlander - Veronica Wolff *r* 1142

Sea stories

A Battle Won - S. Thomas Russell *t* 234
Blown off Course - David Donachie *t* 142
For Love of Country - William C. Hammond *t* 169
The Pirate Devlin - Mark Keating *t* 187
Victory - Julian Stockwin *t* 250
We, the Drowned - Carsten Jensen *c* 632

Self awareness

The Ambassador - Bragi Olafsson *c* 669
Gryphon: New and Selected Stories - Charles Baxter *c* 571
Left Neglected - Lisa Genova *c* 610
The Tenth Song - Naomi Ragen *c* 680

Self confidence

Cleaning Nabokov's House - Leslie Daniels *c* 587

Self knowledge

Becoming George Sand - Rosalind Brackenbury *c* 574
Being Polite to Hitler - Robb Forman Dew *c* 591
By Nightfall - Michael Cunningham *c* 586
Chasing Sunsets - Eva Marie Everson *i* 854

Self perception

Nothing Happens Until It Happens to You: A Novel without Pay, Perks, or Privileges - T.M. Shine *c* 700

Serial murders

Big Wheat - Richard Thompson *m* 541
Bloodline - Mark Billingham *m* 379
The Countess - Rebecca Johns *t* 183
The Demon's Parchment - Jeri Westerson *t* 261
Don't Cry - Beverly Barton *r* 932
Electric Barracuda - Tim Dorsey *m* 421
The Fever of the Bone - Val McDermid *m* 496
Indulgence in Death - J.D. Robb *s* 796
Killer Heat - Brenda Novak *r* 1076
Midnight Caller - Leslie Tentler *r* 1117
Palace of Justice - Susanne Alleyn *m* 367
Profile for Seduction - Karen Whiddon *r* 1133
The Search - Nora Roberts *r* 1092
Senseless - Mary Burton *m* 389
The Sleepwalkers - Paul Grossman *m* 448
Tempted by Fate - Kate Perry *r* 1081
Trail of Blood - Lisa Black *m* 381
You Are Next - Katia Lief *r* 1042

Sexual behavior

Sex on the Slopes - Susan Lyons *r* 1046
The Uncoupling - Meg Wolitzer *c* 717

Sexuality

Blanket of White - Amy Grech *h* 294
Into the Crossfire - Lisa Marie Rice *r* 1090
A Little Bit Wild - Victoria Dahl *r* 959
My Dangerous Duke - Gaelen Foley *r* 976
Night Myst - Yasmine Galenorn *r* 983
The Princess in His Bed - Lila DiPasqua *r* 965
Ruthless - Anne Stuart *r* 1113
The Tutor - Hope Tarr *r* 1116

Shakespeare, William

The Gentleman Poet - Kathryn Johnson *r* 1020
The Lunatic, the Lover, and the Poet - Myrlin A. Hermes *t* 171

Shamanism

The Sacred White Turkey - Frances Washburn *c* 713

Sharks

Rogue Angel: Phantom Prospect - Alex Archer *f* 6

Sheriffs

The Homecoming - JoAnn Ross *r* 1095

Ships

A Battle Won - S. Thomas Russell *t* 234
For Love of Country - William C. Hammond *t* 169
Gentleman Captain - J.D. Davies *t* 134
The Jungle - Clive Cussler *m* 414
Ten Ways to Be Adored When Landing a Lord - Sarah MacLean *r* 1048
The Truth of Valor - Tanya Huff *s* 758

Shipwrecks

The Gentleman Poet - Kathryn Johnson *r* 1020
Rogue Angel: Phantom Prospect - Alex Archer *f* 6

Short stories

And Thereby Hangs a Tale: Short Stories - Jeffrey Archer *c* 566
The Architect of Flowers - William Lychack *c* 647
Atlantis and Other Places - Harry Turtledove *s* 811
Battles and Quests - Anthony Horowitz *f* 45
Beasts and Monsters - Anthony Horowitz *f* 46
Best European Fiction 2011 - Aleksandar Hemon *c* 622
The Best of Larry Niven - Larry Niven *s* 787
The Best of Talebones - Patrick Swenson *s* 807
The Best of the Bolos: Their Finest Hours - Hank Davis *s* 742
The Best of Tomes of the Dead - Matthew Smith *h* 347
Binocular Vision: New and Selected Stories - Edith Pearlman *c* 675
Blanket of White - Amy Grech *h* 294
Blasphemy - Mike Resnick *s* 795
Bliss and Other Short Stories - Ted Gilley *c* 611
Blood Lite II: Overbite - Kevin J. Anderson *h* 265
Boarding Instructions - Ray Vukcevich *f* 99
The Book of the Living Dead - John Richard Stephens *h* 349
Brave New Worlds: Dystopian Stories - John Joseph Adams *s* 724
Complete Hammer's Slammers, Volume 3 - David Drake *s* 748
Cupid Cats - Katie MacAlister *r* 1047
Death's Excellent Vacation - Toni L.P. Kelner *h* 310
Detour to Otherness - Henry Kuttner *s* 772
Diving Mimes, Weeping Czars and Other Unusual Suspects - Ken Scholes *s* 802
The Empty Family: Stories - Colm Toibin *c* 706
The End of the Line - Jonathan Oliver *h* 335
Fangs - Otto Penzler *h* 336
Finding the Way and Other Tales of Valdemar - Mercedes Lackey *f* 53
Full Dark, No Stars - Stephen King *h* 315
Gateways - Elizabeth Anne Hull *s* 760
Gryphon: New and Selected Stories - Charles Baxter *c* 571
The Guy Next Door - Lori Foster *r* 978
Haunted Legends - Nick Mamatas *h* 323

Icebreaker - Deirdre Martin *r* 1054
Live Wire - Harlan Coben *m* 404
Sweet Spot - Kate Angell *r* 927

Squid

Kraken - China Mieville *f* 70

Stalking

Force of Habit - Alice Loweecey *m* 486
Midnight Caller - Leslie Tentler *r* 1117

Stepmothers

Casting Around - Terri DuLong *r* 970

Student protests

Set the Night on Fire - Libby Fischer
   Hellmann *m* 460

Students

The Killing Kind - Bryan Smith *h* 346

Success

Empire: The Novel of Imperial Rome - Steven
   Saylor *t* 239

Suicide

Lady Lazarus: A Novel - Andrew Foster
   Altschul *f* 2

Supernatural

Blood Law - Jeannie Holmes *h* 305
Blood of the Mantis - Adrian Tchaikovsky *f* 97
Bonds of Justice - Nalini Singh *f* 86
Chased by Moonlight - Nancy Gideon *r* 985
Circle of Skulls - James P. Davis *f* 29
Clarity - Kim Harrington *m* 451
Dark and Stormy Knights - P.N. Elrod *f* 31
Deeply, Desperately - Heather Webber *r* 1131
The Diviner's Tale - Bradford Morrow *m* 501
Eat, Prey, Love - Kerrelyn Sparks *r* 1108
Esperanza - Trish J. MacGregor *h* 322
Fatal Error - F. Paul Wilson *h* 364
First Grave on the Right - Darynda Jones *m* 473
Ghost Dance - Rebecca Levene *s* 775
Ghoul Strike! - Andrew Newbound *h* 333
Haunted Legends - Nick Mamatas *h* 323
Hunted by the Others - Jess Haines *f* 40
Imager's Intrigue - L.E. Modesitt *f* 71
The Keepers - Heather Graham *r* 990
Mr. Monster - Dan Wells *h* 362
Music of the Distant Stars - Alys Clare *t* 129
Seducing the Succubus - Cassie Ryan *r* 1096
Sins of the Heart - Eve Silver *r* 1106
Something Wicked - Michelle Rowen *h* 340
The Suburb Beyond the Stars - M.T.
   Anderson *f* 3
Touching Darkness - Jaime Rush *h* 341
Trio of Sorcery - Mercedes Lackey *h* 316
Vampires Not Invited - Cheyenne
   McCray *r* 1060
When Blood Calls - J.K. Beck *h* 269
When Pleasure Rules - J.K. Beck *h* 271

Survival

Apocalypse of the Dead - Joe McKinney *h* 324
The Mullah's Storm - Thomas W. Young *m* 563

Suspense

An Act of Treason - Jack Coughlin *m* 411
Against the Wind - Kat Martin *r* 1055
The Alarmists - Don Hoesel *i* 865
Altar of Bones - Philip Carter *m* 394
The Attenbury Emeralds - Jill Paton
   Walsh *m* 551
Behind the Badge - Susan Sleeman *i* 905
Bent Road - Lori Roy *m* 521
Blockade Billy - Stephen King *h* 314
Bloodline - Mark Billingham *m* 379
The Bone Yard - Jefferson Bass *m* 375
Book of Days - James L. Rubart *i* 900
The Border Lords - T. Jefferson Parker *m* 512
Colby Core - Debra Webb *r* 1130
Cross Roads - Fern Michaels *r* 1066
A Cup of Jo - Sandra Balzo *m* 373
Damaged - Pamela Callow *r* 946
Dangerous to Know - Tasha Alexander *t* 108
Day of the Dragon - Rebecca York *r* 1145
Deadly Intent - Kylie Brant *r* 936
Deadly Pursuit - Ann Christopher *r* 953
Deceit - Brandilyn Collins *i* 838
Delirious - Daniel Palmer *m* 509
Diagnosis: Death - Richard L. Mabry *i* 878
Digitalis - Ronie Kendig *i* 870
Edge of Sight - Roxanne St. Claire *r* 1109
Explosive - Beth Kery *r* 1033
Faith's Reward - Tammy Barley *i* 825
The Fever of the Bone - Val McDermid *m* 496
Fourth Day - Zoe Sharp *m* 526
The Fourth Victim - Tara Taylor Quinn *r* 1087
A Gathering of Crows - Brian Keene *h* 309
Gideon's War - Howard Gordon *m* 444
The Gods of Greenwich - Norb Vonnegut *m* 546
Guarding Grace - Rebecca York *r* 1144
A Heartbeat Away - Michael Palmer *m* 510
A Host of Shadows - Harry Shannon *h* 344
Hull Zero Three - Greg Bear *s* 732
I'll Walk Alone - Mary Higgins Clark *m* 400
In a Cowboy's Arms - Janette Kenny *r* 1031
In the Shadow of Evil - Robin Caroll *i* 835
The Incredible Double - Owen Hill *m* 464
The Inner Circle - Brad Meltzer *m* 500
The Jungle - Clive Cussler *m* 414
The Killing Kind - Bryan Smith *h* 346
The Left-Handed Dollar - Loren D.
   Estleman *m* 431
Lie with Me - Stephanie Tyler *r* 1124
A Lonely Death - Charles Todd *m* 542
Love Me if You Dare - Carly Phillips *r* 1084
Love Me to Death - Allison Brennan *m* 387
The Mischief of the Mistletoe - Lauren
   Willig *t* 263
Missing - Lynette Eason *i* 849
Mobbed - Carol Higgins Clark *m* 398
Monsters - Paul Melniczek *h* 327
A Night of Long Knives - Rebecca Cantrell *t* 126
No Place to Run - Maya Banks *r* 930
No Such Things As Dragons - Philip Reeve *f* 78
Nowhere to Hide - Carlene Thompson *r* 1120
The Painted Darkness - Brian James
   Freeman *h* 283
The Perfect Shot - Gemma Halliday *r* 996
Play Dirty - Lorie O'Clare *r* 1078
Portobello - Ruth Rendell *m* 516
The Priest - Gerard O'Donovan *m* 507
The Priest's Graveyard - Ted Dekker *i* 847
Profile for Seduction - Karen Whiddon *r* 1133
The Reckless Bride - Stephanie Laurens *r* 1039
Scared to Death - Wendy Corsi Staub *m* 534
Secret Place - Leslie J. Sherrod *i* 903

The Sentry - Robert Crais *m* 412
Shadow Force - Matt Lynn *m* 489
Siren - John Everson *h* 281
Snitch: A Novel - Booker T. Mattison *i* 881
The Sweet Relief of Missing Children - Sarah
   Braunstein *m* 386
The Templar Salvation - Raymond
   Khoury *m* 477
Tempted by Fate - Kate Perry *r* 1081
Three Seconds - Anders Roslund *m* 519
Too Many Clients - David J. Walker *m* 548
Torn Apart - Sharon Sala *r* 1099
Trail of Blood - Lisa Black *m* 381
Trail of Lies - Margaret Daley *i* 843
The Trinity Six - Charles Cumming *m* 413
Turbulence - Dana Mentink *i* 885
Unforgivable - Laura Griffin *r* 447
The Wild Irish Sea - Loucinda McGary *r* 1061
The Wizard of Ooze - R.L. Stine *h* 350
You Don't Love This Man: A Novel (P.S.) - Dan
   Deweese *m* 418
Young Junius - Seth Harwood *m* 455

Swamps

Swamplandia! - Karen Russell *c* 687

Sweden

Daniel - Henning Mankell *t* 201
Montecore: The Silence of the Tiger - Jonas Hassen
   Khemiri *c* 637

Swedes

Three Seconds - Anders Roslund *m* 519

Teacher-student relations

The Cailiffs of Baghdad, Georgia - Mary Helen
   Stefaniak *t* 248

Teachers

Courting Miss Amsel - Kim Vogel Sawyer *i* 901
The Dead Detective - William Heffernan *m* 459
Firefighter Daddy - Lee McKenzie *r* 1063
The Irresistible Henry House - Lisa
   Grunwald *t* 166
Katy Carter Wants a Hero - Ruth
   Saberton *r* 1098
The Making of a Gentleman - Shana
   Galen *r* 982
Third Degree - Maggie Barbieri *m* 374

Teaching

The Love Goddess' Cooking School - Melissa
   Senate *r* 1101

Technology

The A-Men - John Trevillian *s* 810
Delirious - Daniel Palmer *m* 509
Empress of Eternity - L.E. Modesitt Jr. *s* 785
Goodnight Tweetheart - Teresa Medeiros *r* 1065
The Half-Made World - Felix Gilman *f* 37
Mad Skills - Walter Greatshell *s* 754
Moxyland - Lauren Beukes *s* 733
Salute the Dark - Adrian Tchaikovsky *f* 98
The Strange Affair of Spring Heeled Jack - Mark
   Hodder *h* 304
Substitution Method - Cris Ramsay *s* 794
Zero Day - Mark Russinovich *m* 523

Character Name Index

This index alphabetically lists the major characters in each featured title. Each character name is followed by a description of the character. Citations also provide titles of the books featuring the character, listed alphabetically if there is more than one title; author names and genre codes. The genre codes are as follows: *c* Popular Fiction, *f* Fantasy, *h* Horror, *i* Inspirational, *m* Mystery, *r* Romance, *s* Science Fiction, and *t* Historical. Numbers refer to the entries that feature each title.

A

Aaron (Neighbor)
Friday Mornings at Nine - Marilyn Brant   *r*   937

Abbie (Sister; Spouse)
Take a Chance on Me - Jill Mansell   *r*   1052

Abbott, Judah (Father)
Marry Me - Jo Goodman   *r*   986

Abbott, Rhyne (Young Woman)
Marry Me - Jo Goodman   *r*   986

Abdulhamid, Sultan II (Ruler)
The Oracle of Stamboul - Michael David Lukas   *m*   487

Abel, Colin (Artist)
The Last Jewish Virgin: A Novel of Fate - Janice Eidus   *c*   596

Abeloth (Supernatural Being)
Vortex - Troy Denning   *s*   744

Abercrombie, Nathan (5th Grader; Supernatural Being; Spy)
The Big Stink - David Lubar   *h*   317

Abigail (Friend)
The Big Stink - David Lubar   *h*   317

Abruzzo, Roxy (Single Mother; Store Owner; Detective—Amateur; Niece)
Our Lady of Immaculate Deception - Nancy Martin   *m*   493

Abuzeid, Mahmoud Bey (Businessman; Spouse; Father)
Lyrics Alley - Leila Aboulela   *t*   104

Abuzeid, Nabilah (Spouse; Young Woman)
Lyrics Alley - Leila Aboulela   *t*   104

Abuzeid, Nur (Son; Accident Victim)
Lyrics Alley - Leila Aboulela   *t*   104

Abuzeid, Waheeba (Spouse; Religious)
Lyrics Alley - Leila Aboulela   *t*   104

Achilles (Political Figure)
Betrayer of Worlds - Larry Niven   *s*   786

Adam (Brother)
Animal Magnetism - Jill Shalvis   *r*   1103
Deceptions: A Jamestown Novel - Marilyn J. Clay   *t*   130

Adam (Military Personnel)
Adam and Eve: A Novel - Sena Jeter Naslund   *c*   662

Adams, Charles Francis (Spy)
Broken Promises - Elizabeth Cobbs Hoffman   *c*   627

Adams, Echo (Genetically Altered Being)
Close Contact - Katherine Allred   *s*   727

Adams, George (Inspector)
Devoured - D.E. Meredith   *t*   207

Adele (Royalty)
The Greyfriar - Susan Griffith   *h*   295

Adin (Twin; Royalty)
The Map Across Time - C.S. Lakin   *i*   875

Adjoa (Twin)
The Civilized World - Susi Wyss   *c*   719

Adler, Damian (Son)
The God of the Hive - Laurie R. King   *t*   188

Adolphus, Gustavus (Royalty)
1635: The Eastern Front - Eric Flint   *s*   751

Aethelred (Royalty; Spouse)
The Forever Queen - Helen Hollick   *t*   176

Agamemnon (Royalty)
The Armour of Achilles - Glyn Iliffe   *t*   178

Agnes (Mentally Ill Person)
The Memory of Love - Aminatta Forna   *c*   602

Aiken, Jeff (Computer Expert)
Zero Day - Mark Russinovich   *m*   523

Akehurst, Sam (Police Officer)
The Age of Zeus - James Lovegrove   *f*   61

Akia, Yoko (Vigilante)
Cross Roads - Fern Michaels   *r*   1066

Akitada, Sugawara (Detective—Amateur; Government Official)
The Fires of the Gods - I.J. Parker   *m*   511

Akitada, Sugawara (Government Official; Detective—Amateur)
The Masuda Affair - I.J. Parker   *t*   223

al-Hasan, Caliph Rashid (Leader; Young Man)
The Lion of Cairo - Scott Oden   *t*   222

Alatriste, Diego (Pirate; Mercenary)
Pirates of the Levant - Arturo Perez-Reverte   *t*   225

Alatriste, Inigo (Son; Mercenary; Pirate)
Pirates of the Levant - Arturo Perez-Reverte   *t*   225

Albani, Nasri (Wealthy)
The Calligrapher's Secret - Rafik Schami   *c*   691

Albright, Josie (Twin)
Lethal Lineage - Charlotte Hinger   *m*   465

Albright, Lottie (Lawman; Twin)
Lethal Lineage - Charlotte Hinger   *m*   465

Alden, Earl (Spouse)
Cold Wind - C.J. Box   *m*   384

Alden, Missy (Mother)
Cold Wind - C.J. Box   *m*   384

Alder (Stepbrother)
The Bird of the River - Kage Baker   *f*   8

Aletha (Twin; Royalty)
The Map Across Time - C.S. Lakin   *i*   875

Alex (Neighbor)
Nothing Happens Until It Happens to You: A Novel without Pay, Perks, or Privileges - T.M. Shine   *c*   700

Alex (Nobleman)
Whisper of Scandal - Nicola Cornick   *r*   956

Alex (Psychic; Agent)
Ghost Dance - Rebecca Levene   *s*   775

Alex (Runaway)
Crown of Dust - Mary Volmer   *c*   710

Alexa (Daughter)
Dark Fire - Chris D'Lacey   *f*   25

Alexander (Warrior; Student; 13-Year-Old; Son; Heir)
The Golden Mean: A Novel of Aristotle and Alexander the Great - Annabel Lyon   *t*   197

Alexander, Casey (Detective; Friend)
Died in the Wool - Elizabeth Ludwig   *i*   877

Alice (Niece)
Scoop to Kill - Wendy Lyn Watson   *m*   552

Alice (Sister)
Come High Water - Carolyn Brown   *r*   944

Alice (Streetperson; Writer; Friend)
Sunset Park - Paul Auster   *c*   569

Alienor (Royalty)
The Sixth Surrender - Hana Samek Norton   *t*   217

Alivda (Royalty)
Avim's Oath - Lynda Williams   *s*   819

Allen, Hannah (Daughter)
The Quickening Maze - Adam Foulds   *t*   157

Allen, Martha (Young Woman)
The Wolves of Andover - Kathleen Kent   *c*   636

Allen, Dr. Matthew (Businessman; Doctor)
The Quickening Maze - Adam Foulds   *t*   157

Austen, Jane (Writer; Sister)
Jane and the Madness of Lord Byron - Stephanie Barron *t* 114

Austen, Reverend (Father)
Jane and the Damned - Janet Mullany *t* 213

Avery, Jim (Worker)
Big Wheat - Richard Thompson *m* 541

Avery, Linden (Young Woman)
Against All Things Ending - Stephen R. Donaldson *f* 30

B

Backet, Millie (Worker)
Pock's World - Dave Duncan *s* 749

Bacon, Todd (Agent)
Santa Fe Edge - Stuart Woods *m* 561

Bailey, Maggie (16-Year-Old)
All My Sins - Linda Sole *t* 245

Bainbridge, Clara (Girlfriend)
Idaho Brides - Erica Vetsch *i* 916

Baird, Emilio (Producer; Divorced Person)
Home Again - Mariah Stewart *r* 1110

Baker, Delilah (Worker)
Delilah - Sheila M. Gross *i* 859

Bakul (Granddaughter)
An Atlas of Impossible Longing - Anuradha Roy *c* 685

Baldwin, John (FBI Agent; Fiance(e))
The Immortals - J.T. Ellison *m* 428

Ballard, Joy (Television Personality)
Dining with Joy - Rachel Hauck *r* 999

Ballista (Military Personnel)
King of Kings - Harry Sidebottom *t* 241

Ballista, Joseph (Organized Crime Figure)
The Left-Handed Dollar - Loren D. Estleman *m* 431

Balthasar (Spouse)
Lightborn - Alison Sinclair *f* 84

Balwyn, Julianne (Smuggler)
After America - John Birmingham *s* 734

Bane, Randall (Leader)
Fourth Day - Zoe Sharp *m* 526

Banks, Charlie (Student—Graduate)
One Fine Cowboy - Joanne Kennedy *r* 1029

Bannerman, Ralph (Police Officer)
Echoes of the Dead - Sally Spencer *m* 530

Bannister, Ann (Television Personality)
Book of Days - James L. Rubart *i* 900

Bannock, Hazel (Heiress; Mother)
Those in Peril - Wilbur Smith *m* 529

Bannon, Kate (Agent)
Agent X - Noah Boyd *m* 385

Bao (Companion)
Naamah's Curse - Jacqueline Carey *f* 19

Barak, Jack (Sidekick; Investigator)
Heartstone - C.J. Sansom *t* 237

Barbara (Historical Figure; Noblewoman; Spouse)
The Second Duchess - Elizabeth Loupas *t* 196

Barbara (Spouse)
Santa Fe Edge - Stuart Woods *m* 561

Barclay, Ralph (Military Personnel)
Blown off Course - David Donachie *t* 142

Bareesh, Tassaa (Leader)
Star Wars: The Old Republic: Fatal Alliance - Sean Williams *s* 820

Barker, Lois (Journalist)
Goodness Gracious Green - Judy Christie *r* 952

Barker, Rick (Veterinarian)
Alaska Weddings - Susan Page Davis *i* 845

Barlow, Julian (Werewolf)
Marked by the Moon - Lori Handeland *h* 298

Barrett, Barb (Madam; Mother)
Cleaning Nabokov's House - Leslie Daniels *c* 587

Barrett, Randall (Lawyer)
Damaged - Pamela Callow *r* 946

Barrett, Randall (Lawyer; Crime Suspect)
Indefensible - Pamela Callow *m* 391

Barrow, John (Aged Person)
Losing Graceland - Micah Nathan *c* 663

Bashir, Dr. Julian (Agent)
Zero Sum Game - David Mack *s* 778

Bassingstoke, Beatrice-Maude (Spinster)
One Unashamed Night - Sophia James *r* 1016

Batholdy, Elizabeth (Noblewoman)
Much Fall of Blood - Dave Freer *f* 35

Bathory, Erzsebet (Noblewoman; Serial Killer)
The Countess - Rebecca Johns *t* 183

Bathsheba (Biblical Figure; Spouse; Lover)
Bathsheba: A Novel - Jill Eileen Smith *i* 906

Baudelaire, Varik (Fiance(e); Vampire; Detective)
Blood Law - Jeannie Holmes *h* 305

Baum, Fred (Architect)
The Tale of Oat Cake Crag - Susan Wittig Albert *t* 106

Baxter, George (Police Officer)
Echoes of the Dead - Sally Spencer *m* 530

Baxter, Zoe (Therapist; Spouse)
Sing You Home - Jodi Picoult *c* 677

Bea (Friend)
Almost to Die For - Tate Hallaway *h* 296

Bean, Roy (Judge)
Roy & Lillie - Loren D. Estleman *t* 151

Bear (Dog)
Luka and the Fire of Life - Salman Rushdie *c* 686

Beaufort, Margaret (Widow(er))
The Red Queen - Philippa Gregory *t* 164

Beaufort, Sebastian (Nobleman)
The Duke's Night of Sin - Kathryn Caskie *r* 950

Beauhall, Sarah (Warrior; Lesbian)
Black Blade Blues - J.A. Pitts *f* 77

Beckett, Darlene (Crime Victim; Teacher)
The Dead Detective - William Heffernan *m* 459

Beckett, David (Museum Curator)
Ghost Shadow - Heather Graham *r* 988

Begay, Janet (Supernatural Being; Hotel Owner)
Firewalker - Allyson James *r* 1013

Bellamy, Julian (Friend)
Three Nights with a Scoundrel - Tessa Dare *r* 961

Belle (Slave)
The Kitchen House - Kathleen Grissom *t* 165

Beloved (Hunter; Murderer)
The Last Hunt - Bruce Coville *f* 23

Ben (Son)
Vortex - Troy Denning *s* 744

Benedict, Alex (Antiques Dealer)
Echo - Jack McDevitt *s* 783

Benedict, Eliza (Crime Victim; Spouse; Mother)
I'd Know You Anywhere - Laura Lippman *c* 646

Benedikt (Vampire)
Confessions of a Vampire's Girlfriend - Katie MacAlister *h* 321
In the Company of Vampires - Katie MacAlister *h* 320

Bengler, Hans (Scientist)
Daniel - Henning Mankell *t* 201

Benjamin, Artie (Producer; Client)
Shortcut Man - P.G. Sturges *m* 537

Bennet, Elizabeth (Hunter)
Pride and Prejudice and Zombies: Dawn of the Dreadfuls - Steve Hockensmith *h* 303

Bennet, Lizzie (Heroine)
A Darcy Christmas - Amanda Grange *r* 991

Bennett (Student—College)
In Every Heartbeat - Kim Vogel Sawyer *t* 238

Bennett, Charles (Spouse)
Forbidden Places - Penny Vincenzi *t* 257

Bennett, Elizabeth (Gentlewoman)
Mr. Darcy's Obsession - Abigail Reynolds *t* 231

Bennett, Felicity (Governess)
The Making of a Gentleman - Shana Galen *r* 982

Bennett, Harrison (Fiance(e))
The Lightkeeper's Ball - Colleen Coble *i* 836

Bennett, Jake (Spouse; Rancher)
Faith's Reward - Tammy Barley *i* 825

Bennett, Jane (Sister)
Mr. Darcy's Obsession - Abigail Reynolds *t* 231

Bennett, Jessica (Spouse; Rancher)
Faith's Reward - Tammy Barley *i* 825

Bennett, Lydia (Sister)
Mr. Darcy's Obsession - Abigail Reynolds *t* 231

Benson, Jade (Spouse)
Softly and Tenderly - Sara Evans *i* 853

Bent, Jane (Friend)
Crazy - William Peter Blatty *t* 120

Bentz, Rick (Detective—Homicide)
Devious - Lisa Jackson *m* 471

Berger (Aged Person)
Mischief Night - Paul Melniczek *h* 326

Bergeron, Alison (Professor; Detective—Amateur)
Third Degree - Maggie Barbieri *m* 374

Bergman, Alex (Single Parent)
Instant Family - Elisabeth Rose *r* 1094

Bergmann, Thom (Spouse; Scientist)
Adam and Eve: A Novel - Sena Jeter Naslund *c* 662

Bernfeld, Loe (Socialite)
A Curable Romantic - Joseph Skibell *t* 243

Bernhardt, Sarah (Historical Figure; Actress; Magician)
The Illusion of Murder - Carol McCleary *m* 495

Bertrand, Jude (Heir)
A Little Bit Wild - Victoria Dahl *r* 959

Bessingham, Katherine (Noblewoman)
Devoured - D.E. Meredith *t* 207

Beth (Mother)
The Last Jewish Virgin: A Novel of Fate - Janice Eidus *c* 596

F

G

Gladwell, Grace (Writer)
Angel at Dawn - Emma Holly   *r*   1007

Glanville, Eleanor (Scientist)
Lady of the Butterflies - Fiona Mountain   *t*   212

Glanville, Humphrey (Criminal)
Lifeblood - Tom Becker   *h*   272

Glanville, Richard (Spouse)
Lady of the Butterflies - Fiona Mountain   *t*   212

Glass, Percy (Retiree; Father; Grandfather)
The Widower's Tale - Julia Glass   *c*   613

Glenning, Pippa (Cult Member)
House Arrest - Ellen Meeropol   *c*   654

Glitsky, Abe (Detective—Police)
Damage - John T. Lescroart   *m*   483

Gloom (Police Officer; Angel)
Demon Strike - Andrew Newbound   *h*   334

Gold, Master Sergeant (Military Personnel)
The Mullah's Storm - Thomas W. Young   *m*   563

Gold, Roxi (Foster Child; 16-Year-Old)
Bound by Guilt - C.J. Darlington   *i*   844

Goldman, Gigi (Detective—Private)
Swift Justice - Laura Disilverio   *m*   420

Gonzales, Marco (Friend)
The Wizard of Ooze - R.L. Stine   *h*   350

Gorda, George "Lord Byron" (Writer)
Jane and the Madness of Lord Byron - Stephanie Barron   *t*   114

Goss (Murderer)
Kraken - China Mieville   *f*   70

Graber, Abigail (Midwife)
Abigail's New Hope - Mary Ellis   *i*   852

Graber, Daniel (Spouse)
Abigail's New Hope - Mary Ellis   *i*   852

Grace, Olivia (Spouse)
Barely a Lady - Eileen Dreyer   *r*   969

Graham, Emily (Suffragette)
A Great Catch: A Novel - Lorna Seilstad   *i*   902

Graham, Emma (12-Year-Old; Detective—Amateur)
Fadeaway Girl - Martha Grimes   *c*   615

Graham, Grace (Mother)
Another Dawn - Kathryn Cushman   *i*   841

Granger, Cole (Lawman; Military Personnel; Vampire Hunter)
Night of the Vampires - Heather Graham   *r*   989

Granger, Miranda (Socialite)
A Midnight Clear - Kristi Astor   *r*   928

Grant, Levi (Blacksmith; Convict)
To Win Her Heart - Karen Witemeyer   *i*   921

Grant, Maddy (Accident Victim)
Mad Skills - Walter Greatshell   *s*   754

Grantham, George Granny (Coach)
Blockade Billy - Stephen King   *h*   314

Graves, Rex (Lawyer; Detective—Amateur)
Murder on the Moor - C.S. Challinor   *m*   395

Gray, Mandy McClellan (Single Mother; Widow(er))
Sharpshooter in Petticoats - Mary Connealy   *i*   839

Gray, Marissa (Journalist)
Nowhere to Hide - Carlene Thompson   *r*   1120

Graymoor, Harrison (Bachelor)
Hidden Affections - Delia Parr   *i*   894

Grayson, Paul (Military Personnel)
Retribution - Drew Karpyshyn   *s*   765

Great Bear (Overseer)
The Waters Rising - Sheri S. Tepper   *s*   808

Great Khan (Relative)
Naamah's Curse - Jacqueline Carey   *f*   19

Greenleaf, Jake (Assistant)
Mary Ann in Autumn - Armistead Maupin   *c*   650

Greg (Carpenter)
Cleaning Nabokov's House - Leslie Daniels   *c*   587

Gregory (Friend)
The Suburb Beyond the Stars - M.T. Anderson   *f*   3

Gregory, Kareem (Drug Dealer)
Deadly Pursuit - Ann Christopher   *r*   953

Gregos (Detective; Crime Victim)
Still Waters - Marilyn Todd   *t*   255

Greifinger, Hans (Immigrant; Father)
A Call from Jersey - P.F. Kluge   *t*   191

Greifinger, Heinz (Son; Brother)
A Call from Jersey - P.F. Kluge   *t*   191

Grens, Ewert (Detective—Police)
Three Seconds - Anders Roslund   *m*   519

Gretchen (Crime Victim; Friend)
Nowhere to Hide - Carlene Thompson   *r*   1120

Grey, Lady Joanna (Fiance(e))
Seducing the Duchess - Ashley March   *r*   1053

Grey, Julia (Detective—Amateur; Spouse; Friend)
Dark Road to Darjeeling - Deanna Raybourn   *r*   1089

Grey, Miranda (Musician; Psychic)
Queen of Shadows - Dianne Sylvan   *h*   353

Grey, Nicholas (Young Man)
Midnight - Beverly Jenkins   *r*   1019

Greyson, Devlin (Nobleman)
Secrets of the Heart - Jillian Kent   *i*   871

Griffin, George (Son; Brother; Writer)
A Call from Jersey - P.F. Kluge   *t*   191

Guest, Crispin (Detective; Knight)
The Demon's Parchment - Jeri Westerson   *t*   261

Gunther, Bernie (Detective—Private)
Field Grey - Philip Kerr   *m*   476

Gupta, Michael (Adoptee)
The Omega Theory - Mark Alpert   *m*   368

Gustafson, Olaf (Student—Exchange; Basketball Player)
Blind Your Ponies - Stanley Gordon West   *c*   714

Guy (Spouse; Father)
Sea Change - Jeremy Page   *c*   672

H

Habib, Munir (Crime Victim)
Fatal Error - F. Paul Wilson   *h*   364

Hainey, Croggon (Pirate)
Clementine - Cherie Priest   *s*   791

Halcyon-Wilson, DeDe (Socialite)
Mary Ann in Autumn - Armistead Maupin   *c*   650

Haley (Child; Crime Victim)
Secrets to the Grave - Tami Hoag   *m*   466

Hall, Jim (Agent; Traitor)
An Act of Treason - Jack Coughlin   *m*   411

Hall, Tom (Detective)
Echoes of the Dead - Sally Spencer   *m*   530

Haller, Mickey (Lawyer)
The Fifth Witness - Michael Connelly   *m*   406

Halston, Noah (Writer)
Seducing the Succubus - Cassie Ryan   *r*   1096

Hamilton, Alex (Spouse; Father)
Shadow on the Land - Anne Doughty   *t*   143

Hamilton, Emily (Spouse; Mother)
Shadow on the Land - Anne Doughty   *t*   143

Hamilton, Jacqueline (Journalist)
Finally a Bride - Vickie McDonough   *i*   883

Hamilton, Jane (Nurse; Daughter; Sister)
Shadow on the Land - Anne Doughty   *t*   143

Hamilton, Johnny (Military Personnel; Son; Brother)
Shadow on the Land - Anne Doughty   *t*   143

Hamilton, Lizzie (Military Personnel; Daughter; Sister)
Shadow on the Land - Anne Doughty   *t*   143

Hamlet (Royalty)
The Lunatic, the Lover, and the Poet - Myrlin A. Hermes   *t*   171

Hamm, Gloria (Assistant; Contestant)
Deus Ex Machina - Andrew Foster Altschul   *c*   565

Hammond, Chelsea (Caterer)
My Fake Fiancee - Nancy Warren   *r*   1128

Hammond, Kim (Prostitute; Crime Victim)
Trail of Blood - Lisa Black   *m*   381

Hanaoka, Yasuko (Divorced Person; Murderer; Single Mother; Abuse Victim)
The Devotion of Suspect X - Keigo Higashino   *m*   463

Hanby, Will (Apprentice)
Fairer Than Morning - Rosslyn Elliott   *i*   851

Hanford, Jack (Relative)
When Sparrows Fall: A Novel - Meg Moseley   *i*   889

Hanford, Miranda (Widow(er); Mother)
When Sparrows Fall: A Novel - Meg Moseley   *i*   889

Hank (Sidekick)
The Darkest Edge of Dawn - Kelly Gay   *h*   286

Hanks, Tip (Crime Suspect; Golfer)
Santa Fe Edge - Stuart Woods   *m*   561

Hannah (Sister)
The Home for Broken Hearts - Rowan Coleman   *c*   584

Hannigan, Keira (Young Woman)
The Year of Living Scandalously - Julia London   *r*   1045

Hansen, Danny (Religious)
The Priest's Graveyard - Ted Dekker   *i*   847

Hansen, Lacey (Waiter/Waitress; Detective—Amateur)
Heads You Lose - Lisa Lutz   *m*   488

Hansen, Mark (Rodeo Rider)
Mark: Secret Cowboy - Pamela Britton   *r*   940

Hansen, Paul (Brother)
Heads You Lose - Lisa Lutz   *m*   488

Hanson, Marvin (Detective—Private)
Devil Red - Joe R. Lansdale   *m*   481

Harbinger, Evelyn (Witch)
Petty Magic: Being the Memoirs and Confessions of Miss Evelyn Harbinger, Temptress and Troublemaker - Camille DeAngelis   *t*   137

Harcourt, Armand (Prisoner)
The Making of a Gentleman - Shana
    Galen *r* 982

Hardcastle, Ernest (Detective—Police)
Hardcastle's Soldiers - Graham Ison *t* 179

Hardy, Dismas (Lawyer)
Damage - John T. Lescroart *m* 483

Hargreaves, Colin (Spouse)
Dangerous to Know - Tasha Alexander *t* 108

Hargreaves, Emily (Noblewoman;
    Detective—Amateur; Spouse)
Dangerous to Know - Tasha Alexander *t* 108

Harker, Jonathan (Spouse)
Dracula My Love - Syrie James *r* 1017

Harker, Mina (Spouse)
Dracula My Love - Syrie James *r* 1017

Harkhoff, Melissa (Foster Child; Young Woman)
Deceit - Brandilyn Collins *i* 838

Harlan, Kent (Lawyer)
Vicious Cycle - Terri Blackstock *i* 826

Harp, Will (Doctor)
Red Rain - Bruce Murkoff *t* 214

Harper, Lisa (Abuse Victim; Daughter)
Deadly Ties - Vicki Hinze *i* 864

Harriman, Elinor (Noblewoman)
Ruthless - Anne Stuart *r* 1113

Harriman, Zach (14-Year-Old)
Hero - Mike Lupica *s* 776

Harris (Manager; Pornographer; Drug Dealer;
    Murderer)
Night Vision - Randy Wayne White *m* 554

Harris, Akilah (Mother)
Eyes of the Innocent - Brad Parks *m* 513

Harris, Peter (Art Dealer; Spouse)
By Nightfall - Michael Cunningham *c* 586

Harris, Phil (Young Man; Brother)
Up from the Blue: A Novel - Susan
    Henderson *c* 623

Harris, Rebecca (Editor; Spouse)
By Nightfall - Michael Cunningham *c* 586

Harris, Tillie (Narrator; Young Woman; Sister)
Up from the Blue: A Novel - Susan
    Henderson *c* 623

Harris, Wayson (Clone; Military Personnel)
The Clone Empire - Steven L. Kent *s* 767

Harrow, Billy (Museum Curator; Scientist)
Kraken - China Mieville *f* 70

Hart, Josh (Agent)
The Ocean Dark - Jack Rogan *s* 797

Hart, Tammy (Assistant)
A Decadent Way to Die - G.A. McKevett *m* 498

Harten, Colin (Young Man)
Well of Sorrows - Benjamin Tate *f* 95

Hartlinger, Kim (18-Year-Old; Wealthy; Religious)
*Found in Translation: An Unforgettable Mission
    Trip Where Faith, Obedience, and Forgiveness
    Intersect* - Roger Bruner *i* 830

Hatch, Carter (Scientist)
World and Town - Gish Jen *c* 631

Hathaway, Amelia (Noblewoman)
My Lord Scandal - Emma Wildes *r* 1137

Hatton, Adolphus (Scientist)
Devoured - D.E. Meredith *t* 207

Hauk, Dutch (Spouse; Stepfather; Criminal)
Deadly Ties - Vicki Hinze *i* 864

Hawkes, Declan (Spy; Friend)
The Palace of Impossible Dreams - Jennifer
    Fallon *f* 33

Hawksley, Markus (Businessman)
A Perfect Scandal - Tina Gabrielle *r* 980

Hawksmith, Elizabeth Anne (Witch; Orphan)
The Witch's Daughter - Paula Brackston *t* 122

Hawksworth, Gabriel (Smuggler)
The Smuggler and the Society Bride - Julia
    Justiss *r* 1023

Hawthorne, Nathaniel (Writer)
The Passages of H.M.: A Novel of Herman Melville
    - Jay Parini *c* 673

Hayden, Charles (Military Personnel)
A Battle Won - S. Thomas Russell *t* 234

Haynes, Matthew (Friend)
Caroline's Choice - Martha Rogers *i* 899

Hazel (Mythical Creature)
The Called - Warren Rochelle *f* 79

Hearne, Telmaine (Heroine)
Lightborn - Alison Sinclair *f* 84

Heat, Max (Scientist; Producer)
Boiling Point - K.L. Dionne *m* 419

Heath, Nigel (Brother; Lawyer;
    Detective—Amateur)
The Brothers of Baker Street - Michael
    Robertson *m* 517

Heath, Reggie (Brother; Lawyer;
    Detective—Amateur)
The Brothers of Baker Street - Michael
    Robertson *m* 517

Heathcliff (Vampire; Orphan)
Wuthering Bites - Sarah Gray *h* 293

Heelis, Will (Fiance(e))
The Tale of Oat Cake Crag - Susan Wittig
    Albert *t* 106

Helen of Troy (Young Woman)
To Save the Devil - Kate Moore *r* 1069

Helene (Young Woman)
The Blind Side of the Heart - Julia Franck *c* 604

Helevetian, Anne-Marie (Friend)
For Love of Country - William C.
    Hammond *t* 169

Helfort (Military Personnel)
The Battle for Commitment Planet - Graham Sharp
    Paul *s* 790

Helios (Royalty; Prisoner; Son; Prisoner; Historical
    Figure)
Lily of the Nile - Stephanie Dray *t* 147

Helkira (Scientist)
Empress of Eternity - L.E. Modesitt Jr. *s* 785

Heller, Miles (Streetperson; Friend; Son)
Sunset Park - Paul Auster *c* 569

Hemingway, Dixie (Animal Lover; Babysitter;
    Detective—Amateur)
Cat Sitter Among the Pigeons - Blaize
    Clement *m* 403

Hemingway, Ernest (Spouse; Writer)
The Paris Wife - Paula McLain *c* 652

Hemingway, Ernest (Writer; Detective—Amateur)
Hemingway Cutthroat - Michael Atkinson *t* 110

Hemingway, Hadley Richardson (Spouse)
The Paris Wife - Paula McLain *c* 652

Henderson, Andrea (Single Mother; Divorced
    Person; Social Worker)
Larkspur Cove - Lisa Wingate *i* 919

Hendrix, Ethan (Boyfriend)
Almost Perfect - Susan Mallery *r* 1050

Hennessey, Kevin (Police Officer)
The Wild Irish Sea - Loucinda McGary *r* 1061

Henri, Marc (Professor)
Legacy: A Novel - Danielle Steel *c* 703

Henry (Artist; Spouse; Father)
The Painted Darkness - Brian James
    Freeman *h* 283

Henry (Royalty)
Pale Rose of England - Sandra Worth *t* 264

Henry (Royalty; Historical Figure)
Secrets of the Tudor Court: By Royal Decree - Kate
    Emerson *t* 148

Henry (Royalty; Spouse; Father; Mentally Ill
    Person)
*The Queen of Last Hopes: The Story of Margaret of
    Anjou* - Susan Higginbotham *t* 173

Henry (Uncle)
All That Lives Must Die - Eric Nylund *f* 73

Henry, Dick (Criminal)
Shortcut Man - P.G. Sturges *m* 537

Henry VII (Son)
The Red Queen - Philippa Gregory *t* 164

Hepburn, Gavin (Psychic)
A Bewitching Bride - Elizabeth Thornton *r* 1122

Hepburn, Michael (Nobleman)
His Sinful Secret - Emma Wildes *r* 1136

Hepplewhite, Queenie (Servant)
Royal Blood - Rhys Bowen *t* 121

Mr. Herbert (Aged Person)
Hero - Mike Lupica *s* 776

Hercules (Mythical Creature)
Threshold - Jeremy Robinson *m* 518

Hernandez, Tommy (Journalist)
Eyes of the Innocent - Brad Parks *m* 513

Higata, Lester (Spouse)
Lester Higata's 20th Century - Barbara
    Hamby *c* 618

Highsmith, Daniel (Spouse)
Come and Find Me - Hallie Ephron *m* 429

Highsmith, Diana (Computer Expert; Widow(er))
Come and Find Me - Hallie Ephron *m* 429

Hill, Tony (Detective)
The Fever of the Bone - Val McDermid *m* 496

Hilliard, Lila (Crime Victim)
Set the Night on Fire - Libby Fischer
    Hellmann *m* 460

Hillock, Avis (Sister)
The Sisters from Hardscrabble Bay - Beverly
    Jensen *t* 182

Hillock, Idella (Sister)
The Sisters from Hardscrabble Bay - Beverly
    Jensen *t* 182

Hinds, Callum (Teenager)
The Hanging Wood - Martin Edwards *m* 427

Hinds, Coley (13-Year-Old)
Red Rain - Bruce Murkoff *t* 214

Hiram (Friend)
Noise - Darin Bradley *s* 736

Hitchcock, Alfred "The Director" (Director)
What You See in the Dark - Manuel
    Munoz *c* 661

Hitler, Harry Krupp I (Nobleman)
Chronolysis - Michel Jeury *s* 762

I

J

K

Lady Adriane (Noblewoman)
The Lunatic, the Lover, and the Poet - Myrlin A.
  Hermes   *t*   171

Lady Macbeth (Widow(er))
Queen Hereafter: A Novel of Margaret of Scotland
  - Susan Fraser King   *t*   189

Laissa (Sidekick)
Kings of the North - Cecelia Holland   *t*   175

Lake, Annabel (Businesswoman)
A Hellion in Her Bed - Sabrina Jeffries   *r*   1018

Lambert, Lily (Governess)
Dreams of Desire - Cheryl Holt   *r*   1008

Lambert, Maddie (Daughter; Fiance(e))
Turbulence - Dana Mentink   *i*   885

Lambert, Noah (Detective—Police)
A Killer Among Us: A Novel - Lynette
  Eason   *i*   850

Landon, Allan (Military Personnel)
Chivalrous Captain, Rebel Mistress - Diane
  Gaston   *r*   984

Landon, Asher (Student—College; Fiance(e); Military Personnel)
Tennessee Brides - Aaron McCarver   *i*   882

Landon, Iris (Adventurer; Child-Care Giver)
Tennessee Brides - Aaron McCarver   *i*   882

Landsverk, Joshua (Boyfriend)
A Heart for Home - Lauraine Snelling   *i*   907

Lang, Petra (Young Woman)
When Wicked Craves - J.K. Beck   *h*   270

Langdon, Jessica (Lawyer)
Murder in Plain Sight - Marta Perry   *r*   1082

Langdon, Rowena (Socialite; Wealthy; Friend)
An Unlikely Suitor - Nancy Moser   *i*   890

Lange, Kate (Lawyer; Detective—Amateur)
Damaged - Pamela Callow   *r*   946
Indefensible - Pamela Callow   *m*   391

Langley, Ingrid (Detective—Private; Writer)
Corpse in Waiting - Margaret Duffy   *m*   423

Langtry, Lillie (Actress)
Roy & Lillie - Loren D. Estleman   *t*   151

Lara (Spouse)
Quiet Chaos - Sandro Veronesi   *c*   709

Larue, Mary (Restaurateur; Religious; Guardian)
The Outlaw's Return - Victoria Bylin   *i*   831

Lasalle, Guerin de (Mercenary; Bridegroom)
The Sixth Surrender - Hana Samek Norton   *t*   217

Lasley, Gabe (Wanderer)
Deep Trouble - Mary Connealy   *i*   840

Lassair (Healer; Young Woman)
Music of the Distant Stars - Alys Clare   *t*   129

Lassiter, Hector (Writer; Detective—Amateur)
One True Sentence - Craig McDonald   *m*   497

Lassiter, Simon (Agent)
Simon Says... - Donna Kauffman   *r*   1025

Latham, Archibald (Government Official; Knight)
India Black - Carol K. Carr   *m*   393

Latouche, Henri de (Lover)
The Last Rendezvous - Anne Plantagenet   *t*   228

Latour, Hazel (Witch; Grandmother)
The Sacred White Turkey - Frances
  Washburn   *c*   713

Laurel (Sister; Mother)
Scoundrel in My Dreams - Celeste
  Bradley   *r*   935

Laurence (Religious)
Romeo and Juliet and Vampires - Claudia
  Gabel   *h*   284

Laurence, Laurie (Friend)
Little Women and Werewolves - Porter
  Grand   *h*   291

Laurence, Theodore "Laurie" (Human; Young
Man)
Little Vampire Women - Lynn Messina   *h*   328

Laurence, Will (Military Personnel)
Tongues of Serpents - Naomi Novik   *t*   218

LaVenture, Johnny (Young Man; Artist)
Take a Chance on Me - Jill Mansell   *r*   1052

Lavinia (7-Year-Old; Servant)
The Kitchen House - Kathleen Grissom   *t*   165

Lawless, James "Law" (Baseball Player)
Sweet Spot - Kate Angell   *r*   927

Lawless, Jane (Restaurateur; Detective—Amateur)
The Cruel Ever After - Ellen Hart   *m*   454

Lazuline, Linn (Wealthy)
Pock's World - Dave Duncan   *s*   749

Le Gall, Dr. Thomas (Psychologist)
Enough About Love - Herve Le Tellier   *c*   641

Leary, Daniel (Military Personnel)
What Distant Deeps - David Drake   *s*   747

Leary, Gabe (Recluse)
Somewhere Along the Way - Jodi Thomas   *r*   1118

LeBlanc, Dr. Madeleine (Psychologist)
A Twisted Ladder - Rhodi Hawk   *h*   300

LeBlanc, Marc (Brother)
A Twisted Ladder - Rhodi Hawk   *h*   300

Ledger, Joe (Military Personnel)
The Dragon Factory - Jonathan Maberry   *h*   319

Leduc, Aimee (Investigator; Detective—Private)
Murder in Passy - Cara Black   *m*   380

Lee, Robert E. (Historical Figure; Military Personnel)
The Second Life of John Wilkes Booth - Barnaby
  Conrad   *t*   131

Lee, Wing (Miner)
Take Me Home - Brian Leung   *c*   643

Leesha (Healer)
The Warded Man - Peter V. Brett   *f*   14

Legris, Victor (Store Owner; Detective—Amateur)
The Montmartre Investigation - Claude
  Izner   *t*   180

Leif the Icelander (Sidekick)
Kings of the North - Cecelia Holland   *t*   175

Leigh, Janet "The Actress" (Actress)
What You See in the Dark - Manuel
  Munoz   *c*   661

Leightner, Jack (Detective—Homicide)
The Ninth Step - Gabriel Cohen   *m*   405

Len (Spouse)
Fade to Blue - Julie Carobini   *i*   834

Lennon, John (Historical Figure)
The Irresistible Henry House - Lisa
  Grunwald   *t*   166

Lenox, Charles (Detective; Government Official)
A Stranger in Mayfair - Charles Finch   *t*   153

Leon (Friend)
Kraken - China Mieville   *f*   70

Leone, Anne (Teacher)
Secrets to the Grave - Tami Hoag   *m*   466

Leoni, Tessa (Police Officer)
Love You More - Lisa Gardner   *m*   442

Leonid (Spouse)
The Russian Affair - Michael Wallner   *m*   550

Leonora (12-Year-Old; Kidnap Victim)
The Sweet Relief of Missing Children - Sarah
  Braunstein   *m*   386

Lerato (Computer Expert)
Moxyland - Lauren Beukes   *s*   733

Leslie, Charles (Religious)
Corrag - Susan Fletcher   *c*   601

Letteri, Lou (Crime Victim)
Cold Shot to the Heart - Wallace Stroby   *m*   536

Lettermore, Lucille "Lefty Lucy" (Lawyer)
The Left-Handed Dollar - Loren D.
  Estleman   *m*   431

Levi (Friend)
Noise - Darin Bradley   *s*   736

Levine, Ash (Detective—Police)
Kind of Blue - Miles Corwin   *m*   410

Mr. Levitt (Serial Killer)
The Zombies of Lake Woebegoten - Harrison
  Geillor   *h*   287

Lewrie, Alan (Sea Captain; Military Personnel;
Widow(er))
The Invasion Year - Dewey Lambdin   *t*   192

Li, Ai (Noblewoman)
Butterfly Swords - Jeannie Lin   *r*   1043

Libby (Student—College)
In Every Heartbeat - Kim Vogel Sawyer   *t*   238

Lichtmann, Daniel (Artist; Widow(er))
The Marriage Artist: A Novel - Andrew
  Winer   *c*   716

Liebermann, Max (Psychologist)
Vienna Twilight - Frank Tallis   *m*   538

Ligeia (Mythical Creature)
Siren - John Everson   *h*   281

Lijuan (Angel)
Archangel's Kiss - Nalini Singh   *f*   85

Lilith (Royalty)
Seducing the Succubus - Cassie Ryan   *r*   1096

Lilly, Ray (Thief; Clerk)
Game of Cages - Harry Connolly   *f*   21

Lily (Detective)
A Legacy of Daemons - Camille
  Bacon-Smith   *f*   7

Lim, Alissa (Friend)
Children No More - Mark L. Van Name   *s*   814

Lincoln, Abraham (Historical Figure)
The First Assassin - John J. Miller   *t*   208

Lincoln, Abraham (Hunter; Historical Figure)
Abraham Lincoln: Vampire Hunter - Seth
  Grahame-Smith   *h*   290

Lindell, Nora (16-Year-Old)
The Fates Will Find Their Way - Hannah
  Pittard   *c*   678

Lindsay, James (Fiance(e); Military Personnel)
Emily Hudson - Melissa Jones   *t*   184

Lindsey, Bea (Noblewoman)
The Tutor - Hope Tarr   *r*   1116

Linnaeus, Carl (Historical Figure; Scientist)
The Curious Death of Peter Artedi: A Mystery in
  the History of Science - Theodore W.
  Pietsch   *t*   227

Linscott, Tom (Rancher)
Sharpshooter in Petticoats - Mary
  Connealy   *i*   839

Linton, Edgar (Neighbor; Wealthy)
Wuthering Bites - Sarah Gray   *h*   293

Peterwald, Vicki (Military Personnel)
Kris Longknife: Redoubtable - Mike Shepherd   *s*   804

Petey (Student—College; Religious)
In Every Heartbeat - Kim Vogel Sawyer   *t*   238

Petra (Fanatic; Friend)
I Think I Love You - Allison Pearson   *c*   676

Petronius (Friend)
Nemesis - Lindsey Davis   *t*   135

Petrule, Lizzy (Young Woman; Slave)
The Shattered Sylph - L.J. McDonald   *f*   65

Petya (Son)
The Russian Affair - Michael Wallner   *m*   550

Philip (Vampire)
Memories of Envy - Barb Hendee   *h*   301

Philippa (Passenger)
The Bloodstained Throne - Simon Beaufort   *t*   115

Phoebe (Girlfriend)
Don't Breathe a Word - Jennifer McMahon   *m*   499

Phoenix, Elizabeth "Liz" (Warrior)
Chaos Bites - Lori Handeland   *h*   299

Pickering, Dawn (Mother)
Fatal Error - F. Paul Wilson   *h*   364

Pickett, Joe (Government Official)
Cold Wind - C.J. Box   *m*   384

Pickett, Sam (Coach)
Blind Your Ponies - Stanley Gordon West   *c*   714

Pieraro, Miguel (Rancher; Immigrant)
After America - John Birmingham   *s*   734

Pierce, Dick (Fisherman; Lover)
Compass Rose - John Casey   *c*   581

Pierce, Lucinda (Detective—Homicide)
Twisted Reason - Diane Fanning   *m*   433

Pierce, May (Spouse)
Compass Rose - John Casey   *c*   581

Pierre (Survivor)
Guardians of the Phoenix - Eric Brown   *s*   738

Pignot, Joseph (Assistant)
The Montmartre Investigation - Claude Izner   *t*   180

Pike, Joe (Military Personnel; Detective)
The Sentry - Robert Crais   *m*   412

Pili (Son)
The Crocodile's Last Embrace - Suzanne Arruda   *t*   109

Pinarius, Lucius (Father)
Empire: The Novel of Imperial Rome - Steven Saylor   *t*   239

Pinarius, Lucius (Son)
Empire: The Novel of Imperial Rome - Steven Saylor   *t*   239

Pinckney, Charles (Historical Figure)
Tempest at Dawn - James D. Best   *t*   119

Pine, Leonard (Detective—Private)
Devil Red - Joe R. Lansdale   *m*   481

Piper, Alice (15-Year-Old; Detective—Amateur)
So Much Pretty - Cara Hoffman   *c*   626

Piro (13-Year-Old; Daughter; Royalty; Sister)
The Uncrowned King - Rowena Cory Daniells   *f*   26

Piro (Slave)
The Usurper - Rowena Cory Daniells   *f*   28

Plank, Ruth (Friend)
The Good Daughters - Joyce Maynard   *c*   651

Plantagenet, Richard (Nobleman; Historical Figure)
Pale Rose of England - Sandra Worth   *t*   264

Platt, Lance (Criminal)
Portobello - Ruth Rendell   *m*   516

Platt, Nicholas "Nick" (Lawyer)
Snowdrops - A.D. Miller   *c*   656

Plesur (Model)
Money Shot - Christopher Rowley   *s*   799

Po (15-Year-Old)
The Boy from Ilysies - Pearl North   *s*   788

Pocahontas (Diplomat)
Deceptions: A Jamestown Novel - Marilyn J. Clay   *t*   130

Poe, Riley (Artist; Sister)
Afterlight - Elle Jasper   *h*   306

Pollack, Anastasia (Widow(er); Single Mother; Editor; Crime Suspect; Detective—Amateur)
Assault with a Deadly Glue Gun - Lois Winston   *m*   560

Pollocke, Grace MacDonald (Artist; Friend)
Original Sins: A Novel of Slavery & Freedom - Peg Kingman   *t*   190

Ponsley, Zephyr (Noblewoman)
Rules of an Engagement - Suzanne Enoch   *r*   971

Porter, Jessica "Jessie" Anne (Reanimated Dead; 15-Year-Old)
Dust - Joan Frances Turner   *h*   359

Porter, Riley (Agent)
Colby Core - Debra Webb   *r*   1130

Portia (Slave)
The First Assassin - John J. Miller   *t*   208

Post, Eliot (Twin; 15-Year-Old)
All That Lives Must Die - Eric Nylund   *f*   73

Post, Fiona (15-Year-Old; Twin)
All That Lives Must Die - Eric Nylund   *f*   73

Potter, Beatrix (Writer; Detective—Amateur)
The Tale of Oat Cake Crag - Susan Wittig Albert   *t*   106

Powell (Werewolf)
Overwinter: A Werewolf Tale - David Wellington   *h*   361

Prakenskii, Lev (Amnesiac)
Water Bound - Christine Feehan   *r*   974

Pratt, Eleanor "Nell" (Antiquarian; Detective—Amateur)
Fundraising the Dead - Sheila Connolly   *m*   407

Precious Wind (Overseer)
The Waters Rising - Sheri S. Tepper   *s*   808

Prescott, Bryant (Engineer)
Do Unto Others - Michael Z. Williamson   *s*   821

Prescott, Caron (Daughter)
Do Unto Others - Michael Z. Williamson   *s*   821

Prescott, Josie (Antiques Dealer)
Deadly Threads - Jane K. Cleland   *m*   402

President (Government Official)
A Heartbeat Away - Michael Palmer   *m*   510

Price, Fanny (Wealthy; Heiress; Crime Victim)
Murder at Mansfield Park - Lynn Shepherd   *t*   240

Price, Fanny (Young Woman)
Mansfield Park and Mummies: Monster Mayhem, Matrimony, Ancient Curses, True Love, and Other Dire Delights - Vera Nazarian   *h*   332

Price, Lanie (Journalist)
Black Orchid Blues - Persia Walker   *m*   549

Price, Martin (Serial Killer)
You Are Next - Katia Lief   *r*   1042

Prince Manfred (Diplomat)
Much Fall of Blood - Dave Freer   *f*   35

Prince Radu (Royalty)
Romeo and Juliet and Vampires - Claudia Gabel   *h*   284

Prince Starigan (Royalty)
Darkling Fields of Arvon - Mark Sebanc   *f*   81

Prince Vlad (Nobleman)
Much Fall of Blood - Dave Freer   *f*   35

Prince Wilhelm (Leader)
Grimblades - Nick Kyme   *f*   52

Princess Beatrice (Archaeologist)
The Bards of Bone Plain - Patricia A. McKillip   *f*   68

Prospero (Sorcerer; Hostage)
Prospero in Hell - L. Jagi Lamplighter   *f*   56

Prudence (Cousin)
The Suburb Beyond the Stars - M.T. Anderson   *f*   3

Pshaw-Ra (Cat)
Catacombs - Anne McCaffrey   *s*   781

Pullingham, Beatrice (Widow(er); Lady)
Nothing but Deception - Allegra Gray   *r*   993

Putnam, Chess (Agent)
Unholy Magic - Stacia Kane   *f*   48

Puttock, Simon (Investigator)
The Oath - Michael Jecks   *t*   181

Q

Qu, Panterra (Teenager)
Bearers of the Black Staff - Terry Brooks   *f*   16

Quanah (Indian; Chieftain)
Comanche Sundown - Jan Reid   *t*   229

Queen Elizabeth I (Royalty)
Rival to the Queen - Carolly Erickson   *t*   149

Queen Isabella (Spouse; Lover)
The Oath - Michael Jecks   *t*   181

Quinn (Fiance(e))
Last Temptation - Michelle Stimpson   *r*   1111

Quinn, Cleo (Young Woman; Sister; Girlfriend)
Take a Chance on Me - Jill Mansell   *r*   1052

Quinn, J.T. (Gunfighter)
The Outlaw's Return - Victoria Bylin   *i*   831

Quinn, Marin (Mother)
Scared to Death - Wendy Corsi Staub   *m*   534

Quinn, Nikki (Lawyer; Vigilante)
Cross Roads - Fern Michaels   *r*   1066

Quinton, Matthew (21-Year-Old; Gentleman; Sea Captain)
Gentleman Captain - J.D. Davies   *t*   134

R

Raber, Miriam (Fiance(e))
Plain Proposal - Beth Wiseman   *i*   920

Rachel (Daughter)
Deceptions - Rebecca Frayn   *m*   439

Radcliffe, Andi (Planner)
Sex on the Slopes - Susan Lyons   *r*   1046

Rock, Baron (Vampire)
The Last Jewish Virgin: A Novel of Fate - Janice Eidus   *c*   596

Rockford, Deon "Rocky" (Convict)
Upon This Rock - Kendra Norman-Bellamy   *i*   893

Rodney (Bully)
The Big Stink - David Lubar   *h*   317

Rodriguez, Dr. Elizabeth (Mother; Lover; Widow(er))
Immortal Sea - Virginia Kantra   *r*   1024

Rodriguez, Liz (Daughter)
Immortal Sea - Virginia Kantra   *r*   1024

Rodriguez, Zack (Son)
Immortal Sea - Virginia Kantra   *r*   1024

Rogan, Sean (Detective—Private)
Love Me to Death - Allison Brennan   *m*   387

Roger (Knight; Friend)
The Bloodstained Throne - Simon Beaufort   *t*   115

Rohan, Adrian Alistair (Rake)
Reckless - Anne Stuart   *r*   1114

Rohan, Miranda (Young Woman)
Breathless - Anne Stuart   *r*   1112

Rohan, Viscount (Rake)
Ruthless - Anne Stuart   *r*   1113

Rohm, Ernst (Worker)
A Night of Long Knives - Rebecca Cantrell   *t*   126

Rojer (Musician)
The Warded Man - Peter V. Brett   *f*   14

Rokhlenu (Werewolf; Prisoner)
The Wolf Age - James Enge   *f*   32

Rolen (Royalty; Father)
The Uncrowned King - Rowena Cory Daniells   *f*   26

Rolin, Jean (Traveler)
The Explosion of the Radiator Hose, and Other Mishaps, on a Journey from Paris to Kinshasa - Jean Rolin   *c*   683

Rollins, Dr. Eliot (Doctor)
Butterfly - Rochelle Alers   *r*   925

Roman, Eva (Werewolf)
Master of Smoke - Angela Knight   *r*   1035

Romanov, Nikolai (Historical Figure; Political Figure)
The True Memoirs of Little K - Adrienne Sharp   *c*   698

Romanowski, Nate (Friend)
Cold Wind - C.J. Box   *m*   384

Romero, Max (Detective—Police)
A Darker Night - P.J. Brooke   *m*   388

Romulus (Twin)
The Road to Rome - Ben Kane   *t*   185

Roni (Crime Victim; Aunt)
Murder on the Bride's Side - Tracy Kiely   *m*   478

Roni (Daughter)
Eden - Yael Hedaya   *c*   621

Rook (Military Personnel)
Dragon Soul - Danielle Bennett   *f*   9

Rook, Charles P. (Military Personnel)
The First Assassin - John J. Miller   *t*   208

Rosalia (Guardian)
Demon Blood - Meljean Brook   *r*   941

Rose (Daughter)
Compass Rose - John Casey   *c*   581

Rosemary (Young Woman)
Prince Charming Doesn't Live Here - Christine Warren   *r*   1127

Rosen, Viktor (Musician; Teacher)
A Lily of the Field - John Lawton   *t*   193

Ross, Carter (Journalist)
Eyes of the Innocent - Brad Parks   *m*   513

Rossini, Beniamino (Friend)
Bandit Love - Massimo Carlotto   *c*   579

Roudette (Assassin)
Red Hood's Revenge - Jim C. Hines   *f*   43

Roumande, Albert (Assistant)
Devoured - D.E. Meredith   *t*   207

Rowan (Daughter)
Rescue - Anita Shreve   *c*   701

Roxanne (Sister)
The Good Sister - Drusilla Campbell   *c*   578

Roxie (Murderer)
The Killing Kind - Bryan Smith   *h*   346

Roy (Spouse; Crime Suspect)
Bent Road - Lori Roy   *m*   521

Royce, Alec (Vampire)
Hunted by the Others - Jess Haines   *f*   40

Runyon, Hook (Railroad Worker; Security Officer)
The Insane Train - Sheldon Russell   *m*   522

Rupert (Businessman)
Under the Poppy - Kathe Koja   *c*   638

Ruso, Gaius Petreius (Doctor; Detective)
Caveat Emptor - Ruth Downie   *t*   145

Russell (Mythical Creature)
The Called - Warren Rochelle   *f*   79

Russell, John (Journalist; Spy; Boyfriend; Father)
Potsdam Station - David Downing   *m*   422

Russell, Mary (Detective—Private; Spouse)
The God of the Hive - Laurie R. King   *t*   188

Russell, Paul (Son)
Potsdam Station - David Downing   *m*   422

Rusty (Young Man)
Mischief Night - Paul Melniczek   *h*   326

Ruth (Daughter)
Dead Man's Chest - Kerry Greenwood   *t*   163

Ruth (Spouse; Sister)
Bent Road - Lori Roy   *m*   521

Rutledge, Ian (Detective—Police)
A Lonely Death - Charles Todd   *m*   542

Rutledge, Myra (Wealthy; Vigilante)
Cross Roads - Fern Michaels   *r*   1066

Ruxandra (Stepmother)
The Oracle of Stamboul - Michael David Lukas   *m*   487

Ruzak, Teddy (Detective—Private)
The Highly Effective Detective Crosses the Line - Richard Yancey   *m*   562

Ryan, Jack Jr. (Agent; Cousin)
Dead or Alive - Tom Clancy   *m*   397

Ryan, Dr. Paige (Doctor; Volunteer)
Blood Covenant - Lisa Harris   *i*   861

Ryan, Wade (Cowboy/Cowgirl)
A Cowboy's Touch - Denise Hunter   *i*   866

Ryder, Craig (Worker; Boyfriend)
The Truth of Valor - Tanya Huff   *s*   758

Ryland de Silva, Annie (Noblewoman; Vigilante)
Cross Roads - Fern Michaels   *r*   1066

Ryman, Peter (Political Figure)
Feed - Mira Grant   *h*   292

S

Saad, Pierre (Anthropologist; Friend)
Adam and Eve: A Novel - Sena Jeter Naslund   *c*   662

Sabian, Alexandra "Alex" (Vampire; Detective)
Blood Law - Jeannie Holmes   *h*   305

Sabine (Businesswoman; Boarder)
The Home for Broken Hearts - Rowan Coleman   *c*   584

Sable, Nicki (Young Woman)
Mark: Secret Cowboy - Pamela Britton   *r*   940

Safrah (Teenager)
Seed Seeker - Pamela Sargent   *s*   801

Sahara (Granddaughter; 17-Year-Old)
Ray of Hope - Vanessa Davis Griggs   *r*   995

Salman (Apprentice)
The Calligrapher's Secret - Rafik Schami   *c*   691

Saloman (Vampire)
Blood on Silk - Marie Treanor   *h*   358

Saltonstall, Dudley (Military Personnel)
The Fort: A Novel of the Revolutionary War - Bernard Cornwell   *t*   133

Sam (Brother; Boyfriend)
Don't Breathe a Word - Jennifer McMahon   *m*   499

Sam (Son)
Pictures of You: A Novel - Caroline Leavitt   *c*   642

Samhanach (Demon)
The Samhanach - Lisa Morton   *h*   331

Sammelsohn, Jakob (Doctor)
A Curable Romantic - Joseph Skibell   *t*   243

Sampson, Lily (Archaeologist; Detective—Amateur)
Scorpion's Bite - Aileen G. Baron   *t*   113

Sams, Baxter (Friend)
Broken Promises - Elizabeth Cobbs Hoffman   *c*   627

Samuels, Abigail (Spouse; Mother)
The Tenth Song - Naomi Ragen   *c*   680

Samuels, Adam (Spouse; Father; Accountant)
The Tenth Song - Naomi Ragen   *c*   680

Samuels, Kayla (Dancer; Student—College)
The Tenth Song - Naomi Ragen   *c*   680

Samuelson, Greg (Client; Crime Suspect)
The Bad Kitty Lounge - Michael Wiley   *m*   556

Sand, George (Writer)
Becoming George Sand - Rosalind Brackenbury   *c*   574

Sanders, Kahlee (Director)
Retribution - Drew Karpyshyn   *s*   765

Santiago, Eddie (Mercenary)
Cold Shot to the Heart - Wallace Stroby   *m*   536

Santos, Ric (Detective)
Unforgivable - Laura Griffin   *m*   447

Santovari, Custo (Angel)
Shadow Fall - Erin Kellison   *r*   1028

Sapa, Paha (Indian; Psychic)
Black Hills - Dan Simmons   *h*   345

Sara (Friend)
Hunted by the Others - Jess Haines   *f*   40

Sarah (Spouse)
Siren - John Everson   *h*   281

Vidal, Emily (14-Year-Old)
The Adults - Alison Espach   *c*   598

Vince (Homosexual; Expatriate)
Leche - R. Zamora Linmark   *c*   645

Mr. Vincent (Artist)
Shades of Milk and Honey - Mary Robinette
    Kowal   *f*   51

Vitale, Irma (Immigrant)
When We Were Strangers - Pamela
    Schoenewaldt   *c*   693

Vitalis (Passenger)
The Bloodstained Throne - Simon
    Beaufort   *t*   115

Vivian (Mother)
Antiques Knock-Off - Barbara Allan   *m*   366

Vladimir (Royalty)
At the Queen's Command - Michael A.
    Stackpole   *f*   89

Vogel, Hannah (Journalist; Mother)
A Night of Long Knives - Rebecca Cantrell   *t*   126

Voldorius (Demon)
Hunt for Voldorius - Andy Hoare   *s*   757

Volod (Vampire)
Vampires Not Invited - Cheyenne
    McCray   *r*   1060

Voltaire (Historical Figure; Philosopher)
Voltaire's Calligrapher - Pablo De Santis   *t*   136

von Steuben, Baron Friederich (Friend)
*Valley Forge: George Washington and the Crucible
    of Victory* - William R. Forstchen   *t*   155

von Ulrich, Walter (Spy)
Fall of Giants - Ken Follett   *t*   154

Vorkosigan, Miles (Diplomat)
Cryoburn - Lois McMaster Bujold   *s*   739

Voss, Mia (Consultant; Crime Victim)
Unforgivable - Laura Griffin   *m*   447

Voytek, Meret (10-Year-Old; Musician)
A Lily of the Field - John Lawton   *t*   193

Vulture, Oswald (Toy; Bird; Financier; Crime
    Victim)
Tourquai - Tim Davys   *m*   417

W

Wachalowski, Nico (Agent)
The Silent Army - James Knapp   *s*   768

Wagner, Arlen (Psychic; Veteran)
The Cypress House - Michael Koryta   *m*   480

Wainwright, Brooklyn (Expert;
    Detective—Amateur)
The Lies that Bind - Kate Carlisle   *m*   392

Wainwright, Cord (Rancher)
A Heart Divided: A Novel - Kathleen
    Morgan   *i*   888

Walker, Amos (Detective—Private)
The Left-Handed Dollar - Loren D.
    Estleman   *m*   431

Walker, Travis (Single Father)
The First Love Cookie Club - Lori Wilde   *r*   1135

Wallace, Aidan (Werewolf)
A Werewolf in Manhattan - Vicki Lewis
    Thompson   *r*   1121

Walsh, Alistair (Military Personnel)
West and East - Harry Turtledove   *s*   812

Walsh, Lauren (Friend)
Scared to Death - Wendy Corsi Staub   *m*   534

Walters, Matthew (Religious)
Devil's Food Cake Murder - Joanne
    Fluke   *m*   437

Walton, Robert (Shipowner; Explorer)
Frankenstein's Monster - Susan Heyboer
    O'Keefe   *c*   666

Wanbli, George (Shaman)
The Sacred White Turkey - Frances
    Washburn   *c*   713

Ward, Georginea "Sister Georgia" (Religious)
Stranger Here Below - Joyce Hinnefeld   *t*   174

Ward, Merope (Historian)
All Clear - Connie Willis   *s*   822

Ward, Susan (Journalist)
The Night Season - Chelsea Cain   *m*   390

Ware, Joanna (Widow(er))
Whisper of Scandal - Nicola Cornick   *r*   956

Warren, D.D. (Detective—Police)
Love You More - Lisa Gardner   *m*   442

Warren, Rod (Musician; Lover)
The Melody Girls - Anne Douglas   *t*   144

Washington, George (Historical Figure)
Tempest at Dawn - James D. Best   *t*   119

Washington, George (Political Figure; Military
    Personnel)
*Valley Forge: George Washington and the Crucible
    of Victory* - William R. Forstchen   *t*   155

Waterhouse, Tracy (Detective—Police)
Started Early, Took My Dog - Kate
    Atkinson   *c*   568

Waters, Cicely (Witch)
Night Myst - Yasmine Galenorn   *r*   983

Wati (Spirit; Labor Leader)
Kraken - China Mieville   *f*   70

Watson (Doctor)
Sherlock Holmes and the Ghosts of Bly - Donald
    Thomas   *t*   252

Watson, Dan (Lover)
What You See in the Dark - Manuel
    Munoz   *c*   661

Watson, Freddie (Mentally Ill Person; Brother)
The Winter Ghosts - Kate Mosse   *m*   503

Watson, George (Brother)
The Winter Ghosts - Kate Mosse   *m*   503

Watson, Nick (Detective—Police)
Immortal Quest: The Trouble with Mages - Alexan-
    dra Mackenzie   *f*   62

Waverly, Sharlene (Saloon Keeper/Owner)
Honky Tonk Christmas - Carolyn Brown   *r*   942

Waynest, Shiarra (Detective—Private; Girlfriend)
Hunted by the Others - Jess Haines   *f*   40

Webster, Peter (Worker; Spouse; Father)
Rescue - Anita Shreve   *c*   701

Weeks, Joanne (Detective—Amateur)
Deceit - Brandilyn Collins   *i*   838

Weil, Gideon (Archaeologist; Crime Suspect)
Scorpion's Bite - Aileen G. Baron   *t*   113

Weinberg, Chaim (Military Personnel)
West and East - Harry Turtledove   *s*   812

Welham, Rance (Friend)
One Touch of Scandal - Liz Carlyle   *r*   948

Wellesley, Rachel (Artist)
Star of His Heart - Brenda Jackson   *r*   1012

Wellingham, Taris (Nobleman)
One Unashamed Night - Sophia James   *r*   1016

Wells, Hank (Cowboy/Cowgirl)
My Give a Damn's Busted - Carolyn
    Brown   *r*   943

Wells, John (Spy)
The Secret Soldier - Alex Berenson   *m*   378

West, Marlena (Agent)
Tempting the Fire - Sydney Croft   *h*   278

West, Megan (Librarian)
Luck Be a Lady - Cathie Linz   *r*   1044

Westcott, Gabriel (Spouse)
The Vengeful Bridegroom - Kit Donner   *r*   967

**Westfield, Lord Anthony "Viscount Somerton-
    "** (Nobleman; Spy)
Scandal of the Season - Christie Kelley   *r*   1027

Miss Weston (Administrator)
All That Lives Must Die - Eric Nylund   *f*   73

Whalen, Nick (Detective—Private)
Home Is Where the Bark Is - Kandy
    Shepherd   *r*   1105

Wheel, Jane (Detective—Private; Antiquarian)
Backstage Stuff - Sharon Fiffer   *m*   436

Wheeler, Kay (Widow(er))
Tulagi Hotel - Heikki Hietala   *t*   172

Whelan, Caitlin (Human)
Eat, Prey, Love - Kerrelyn Sparks   *r*   1108

Whelp, Henry (Teenager; Wolf)
Dust City - Robert Paul Weston   *m*   553

Whispr (Genetically Altered Being; Murderer)
The Human Blend - Alan Dean Foster   *s*   752

White, Beecher (Clerk)
The Inner Circle - Brad Meltzer   *m*   500

White, Harold (Researcher; Detective—Amateur)
The Sherlockian - Graham Moore   *c*   657

White, Peter (Friend)
Deliverance from Evil - Frances Hill   *c*   624

White, Wendy (Teenager; Crime Victim)
So Much Pretty - Cara Hoffman   *c*   626

Whitlock, Jeremy (Investigator)
Lucky Stiff - Deborah Coonts   *m*   408

Whitman, Lily (Girlfriend)
Idaho Brides - Erica Vetsch   *i*   916

Whittington, Madeline (Noblewoman)
Secrets of the Heart - Jillian Kent   *i*   871

Wicked Witch of the West (Witch)
*The Undead World of Oz: L. Frank Baum's The
    Wonderful Wizard of Oz Complete with Zombies
    and Monsters* - L. Frank Baum   *h*   267

Wilde, Jaclyn (Planner)
Veil of Night - Linda Howard   *r*   1009

Wilder, Eric (Detective—Police)
Veil of Night - Linda Howard   *r*   1009

Wilhelm (Spouse)
The Blind Side of the Heart - Julia Franck   *c*   604

Wilkes, Dawsey (Kidnap Victim)
Raider's Heart - Marcia Gruver   *i*   860

Wilkins, Jack (Wanderer)
Chasing the Sun - Kaki Warner   *r*   1126

Will (Boyfriend)
Take a Chance on Me - Jill Mansell   *r*   1052

Willan, Alexandra (Restaurateur; Human)
Hungry for You - Lynsay Sands   *r*   1100

William (Cousin; Writer)
Emily Hudson - Melissa Jones   *t*   184

Character Name Index

Character Description Index

This index alphabetically lists descriptions of the major characters in featured titles. The descriptions may be occupations (police officer, lawyer, etc.) or may describe persona (amnesiac, runaway, teenager, etc.). For each description, character names are listed alphabetically. Also provided are book titles, author names, genre codes and entry numbers. The genre codes are as follows: *c* Popular Fiction, *f* Fantasy, *h* Horror, *i* Inspirational, *m* Mystery, *r* Romance, *s* Science Fiction, and *t* Historical

10-YEAR-OLD

Jubal
Catacombs - Anne McCaffrey   *s* 781

Voytek, Meret
A Lily of the Field - John Lawton   *t* 193

Wren, Kaylee
Words - Ginny L. Yttrup   *i* 923

11-YEAR-OLD

Cailiff, Gladys
The Cailiffs of Baghdad, Georgia - Mary Helen Stefaniak   *t* 248

Charlie
The Home for Broken Hearts - Rowan Coleman   *c* 584

Daniels, Barbie
The Hole in the Wall - Lisa Rowe Fraustino   *f* 34

Daniels, Sebastian "Sebby"
The Hole in the Wall - Lisa Rowe Fraustino   *f* 34

Jama
Black Mamba Boy - Nadifa Mohamed   *t* 210

12-YEAR-OLD

Ariel
The Farwalker's Quest - Joni Sensel   *f* 82

Graham, Emma
Fadeaway Girl - Martha Grimes   *c* 615

Leonora
The Sweet Relief of Missing Children - Sarah Braunstein   *m* 386

Lisa
Don't Breathe a Word - Jennifer McMahon   *m* 499

Luka
Luka and the Fire of Life - Salman Rushdie   *c* 686

Malarra, Alannah
Demon Strike - Andrew Newbound   *h* 334
Ghoul Strike! - Andrew Newbound   *h* 333

Stella
The Sacred White Turkey - Frances Washburn   *c* 713

12TH GRADER

Zeke
My New American Life - Francine Prose   *c* 679

13-YEAR-OLD

Alexander
The Golden Mean: A Novel of Aristotle and Alexander the Great - Annabel Lyon   *t* 197

Bigtree, Ava
Swamplandia! - Karen Russell   *c* 687

Choimha, Tula
Night Vision - Randy Wayne White   *m* 554

Dawson, Lilly
Echoes of the Dead - Sally Spencer   *m* 530

Hinds, Coley
Red Rain - Bruce Murkoff   *t* 214

Magpie
Intrigues - Mercedes Lackey   *f* 54

Piro
The Uncrowned King - Rowena Cory Daniells   *f* 26

Williams, Billy
Fall of Giants - Ken Follett   *t* 154

14-YEAR-OLD

Harriman, Zach
Hero - Mike Lupica   *s* 776

Ivy
Ivy's Ever After - Dawn Lairamore   *f* 55

Junius
Young Junius - Seth Harwood   *m* 455

Merritt, Kate
Angel Sister - Ann H. Gabhart   *i* 855

Morris, Lyndsay
The Bad Book Affair - Ian Sansom   *m* 524

Vidal, Emily
The Adults - Alison Espach   *c* 598

15-YEAR-OLD

Capulet, Juliet
Romeo and Juliet and Vampires - Claudia Gabel   *h* 284

Covington, Lance
Vicious Cycle - Terri Blackstock   *i* 826

Crystal
Ray of Hope - Vanessa Davis Griggs   *r* 995

Densmore, Susan
Guilt by Association - Marcia Clark   *m* 399

Elliot
Stuff of Legends - Ian Gibson   *f* 36

Piper, Alice
So Much Pretty - Cara Hoffman   *c* 626

Po
The Boy from Ilysies - Pearl North   *s* 788

Porter, Jessica "Jessie" Anne
Dust - Joan Frances Turner   *h* 359

Post, Eliot
All That Lives Must Die - Eric Nylund   *f* 73

Post, Fiona
All That Lives Must Die - Eric Nylund   *f* 73

Wolf, Waiting
The Owl Hunt - Richard S. Wheeler   *t* 262

16-YEAR-OLD

Bailey, Maggie
All My Sins - Linda Sole   *t* 245

Digger
Star Crossed - Elizabeth C. Bunce   *f* 17

Fern, Clarity "Clare"
Clarity - Kim Harrington   *m* 451

Gold, Roxi
Bound by Guilt - C.J. Darlington   *i* 844

Lindell, Nora
The Fates Will Find Their Way - Hannah Pittard   *c* 678

Locke, Shelby
Never Cry Werewolf - Heather Davis   *h* 279

Maria
Wolf's Cross - S.A. Swann   *h* 352

McCready, Amanda
Moonlight Mile - Dennis Lehane   *m* 482

Momo
Manazuru - Hiromi Kawakami   *c* 634

Parker, Anastasija "Ana" Ramses
Almost to Die For - Tate Hallaway   *h* 296

Paul
The Sweet Relief of Missing Children - Sarah Braunstein   *m* 386

17-YEAR-OLD

Chandler, Alan
The Ragtime Fool - Larry Karp   *t* 186

Davidson, Jamie
The Perfect Family - Kathryn Shay *r* 1104

Ivanova, Valentina
The Jewel of St. Petersburg - Kate
  Furnivall *t* 159

Rev, Dalton
You Killed Wesley Payne - Sean
  Beaudoin *m* 377

Sahara
Ray of Hope - Vanessa Davis Griggs *r* 995

Templer, Colin
All Clear - Connie Willis *s* 822

18-YEAR-OLD

Hartlinger, Kim
*Found in Translation: An Unforgettable Mission
  Trip Where Faith, Obedience, and Forgiveness
  Intersect* - Roger Bruner *i* 830

19-YEAR-OLD

Estby, Clara
The Daughter's Walk: A Novel - Jane
  Kirkpatrick *i* 873

Hudson, Emily
Emily Hudson - Melissa Jones *t* 184

O'Shea, Bridget
Come High Water - Carolyn Brown *r* 944

Riff, Joshua
The Four Stages of Cruelty - Keith
  Hollihan *m* 468

20-YEAR-OLD

Iarla
Eye of the Law - Cora Harrison *m* 453

21-YEAR-OLD

Fish, Ben
Losing Graceland - Micah Nathan *c* 663

Quinton, Matthew
Gentleman Captain - J.D. Davies *t* 134

4-YEAR-OLD

Dylan
Another Dawn - Kathryn Cushman *i* 841

5TH GRADER

Abercrombie, Nathan
The Big Stink - David Lubar *h* 317

6-YEAR-OLD

Holly
Christmas Eve at Friday Harbor - Lisa
  Kleypas *r* 1034

Sophie
Love You More - Lisa Gardner *m* 442

7-YEAR-OLD

Lavinia
The Kitchen House - Kathleen Grissom *t* 165

8-YEAR-OLD

Marsh, Margaret
God on the Rocks - Jane Gardam *t* 160

ABUSE VICTIM

Annie
Deadly Ties - Vicki Hinze *i* 864

Carson, Rachel
Deadly Identity - Lindsay McKenna *r* 1062

Hanaoka, Yasuko
The Devotion of Suspect X - Keigo
  Higashino *m* 463

Harper, Lisa
Deadly Ties - Vicki Hinze *i* 864

Michaels, Grace
Devil at Midnight - Emma Holly *r* 1006

Moore, Maddie
Simply Irresistible - Jill Shalvis *r* 1102

Wren, Kaylee
Words - Ginny L. Yttrup *i* 923

ACCIDENT VICTIM

Abuzeid, Nur
Lyrics Alley - Leila Aboulela *t* 104

Felix
Seer of Sevenwaters - Juliet Marillier *t* 202

Freya
Sea Change - Jeremy Page *c* 672

Grant, Maddy
Mad Skills - Walter Greatshell *s* 754

Jing, Li
The Lost and Forgotten Languages of Shanghai -
  Ruiyan Xu *c* 721

Misty
Bound - Antonya Nelson *c* 664

Rice
Softly and Tenderly - Sara Evans *i* 853

Seaver, Trey
The Dangerous Edge of Things - Tina
  Whittle *m* 555

ACCOUNTANT

McNabb, Tally
One Was a Soldier - Julia
  Spencer-Fleming *m* 531

Montgomery, Kristin
The Wish List - Gabi Stevens *f* 90

Samuels, Adam
The Tenth Song - Naomi Ragen *c* 680

ACTIVIST

Blaylock, Garner
Frozen Fire - Marianna Jameson *s* 761

Holcomb, Vance
The Flock - James Robert Smith *s* 805

Tendeka
Moxyland - Lauren Beukes *s* 733

ACTOR

Booth, John Wilkes
The Second Life of John Wilkes Booth - Barnaby
  Conrad *t* 131

Brody, Trace
The Perfect Shot - Gemma Halliday *r* 996

Chambers, Ethan
Star of His Heart - Brenda Jackson *r* 1012

Gibson, Dan "Danny"
A Pig of Cold Poison - Pat McIntosh *t* 206

Macleod, Artair
Other People's Money - Justin Cartwright *c* 580

McKeag, Robbin
Cowboys Never Cry - Tina Welling *r* 1132

Paul, Brandon
Leaving - Karen Kingsbury *i* 872

ACTRESS

Bernhardt, Sarah
The Illusion of Murder - Carol McCleary *m* 495

Bothwell, Nanty
A Pig of Cold Poison - Pat McIntosh *t* 206

Brooks, Glenna
To Have and To Kill: A Wedding Cake Mystery -
  Mary Jane Clark *m* 401

Carnahan, Mercy
In Search of Mercy - Michael Ayoob *m* 372

Chevret, Melisande
Murder at the Villa Byzantine - R.T.
  Raichev *m* 514

Dalton, Naomi "Babe"
The Secrets Sisters Keep - Abby Drake *c* 592

Delong, Dominique
Death by Diamonds - Annette Blair *f* 11

Donovan, Piper
To Have and To Kill: A Wedding Cake Mystery -
  Mary Jane Clark *m* 401

Flanigan, Bailey
Leaving - Karen Kingsbury *i* 872

Langtry, Lillie
Roy & Lillie - Loren D. Estleman *t* 151

Leigh, Janet "The Actress"
What You See in the Dark - Manuel
  Munoz *c* 661

McGregor, Dallas
Home Again - Mariah Stewart *r* 1110

Monroe, Marilyn
*The Life and Opinions of Maf the Dog, and of His
  Friend Marilyn Monroe* - Andrew
  O'Hagan *t* 221

Reed, Savannah
Mail-Order Groom - Lisa Plumley *r* 1085

Sloane, Pauline
Sloane Hall - Libby Sternberg *t* 249

Squires, Tilly
Started Early, Took My Dog - Kate
  Atkinson *c* 568

ADDICT

Jordan
Vicious Cycle - Terri Blackstock *i* 826

ADMINISTRATOR

Miss Weston
All That Lives Must Die - Eric Nylund *f* 73

ADOPTEE

Gupta, Michael
The Omega Theory - Mark Alpert *m* 368

ADVENTURER

Cameron, Jade del
The Crocodile's Last Embrace - Suzanne
  Arruda *t* 109

Cherijo
Dream Called Time - S.L. Viehl *s* 816

de Warenne, Alexi
The Promise - Brenda Joyce   *r* 1022
Dysart, Shannon
Deep Trouble - Mary Connealy   *i* 840
Jax, Sirantha
Kill Box - Ann Aguirre   *s* 725
Landon, Iris
Tennessee Brides - Aaron McCarver   *i* 882
Tuttle, Sunset
Echo - Jack McDevitt   *s* 783
Wu, Louis
Betrayer of Worlds - Larry Niven   *s* 786

ADVISOR

Nicasio, Thomas
Explosive - Beth Kery   *r* 1033

AGED PERSON

Barrow, John
Losing Graceland - Micah Nathan   *c* 663
Berger
Mischief Night - Paul Melniczek   *h* 326
Blythe, Persephone
The Distant Hours - Kate Morton   *c* 658
Blythe, Seraphina
The Distant Hours - Kate Morton   *c* 658
Conn, Emmett
The Gendarme - Mark T. Mustian   *t* 215
Mr. Herbert
Hero - Mike Lupica   *s* 776
Lundquist, Berget
Old World Murder - Kathleen Ernst   *m* 430
Maxwell, Emily
Emily, Alone - Stewart O'Nan   *c* 667
Steiner, Gabe
Broken Wings: A Novel - Carla Stewart   *i* 909

AGENT

Alex
Ghost Dance - Rebecca Levene   *s* 775
Angelino, Zach
Edge of Sight - Roxanne St. Claire   *r* 1109
Bacon, Todd
Santa Fe Edge - Stuart Woods   *m* 561
Bannon, Kate
Agent X - Noah Boyd   *m* 385
Bashir, Dr. Julian
Zero Sum Game - David Mack   *s* 778
Bolitar, Myron
Live Wire - Harlan Coben   *m* 404
Carson, Lauren
An Act of Treason - Jack Coughlin   *m* 411
Cass, J.D.
Don't Cry - Beverly Barton   *r* 932
Cordasic, Lea
Profile for Seduction - Karen Whiddon   *r* 1133
Creedmoor, John
The Half-Made World - Felix Gilman   *f* 37
Crew, Gideon
Gideon's Sword - Lincoln Child   *m* 396
Cumberland, Josh
Edge - Thomas Blackthorne   *s* 735
Douglas, Sarina
Zero Sum Game - David Mack   *s* 778

Drake
Dangerous Desires - Dee Davis   *r* 963
Ford, Doc
Night Vision - Randy Wayne White   *m* 554
Hall, Jim
An Act of Treason - Jack Coughlin   *m* 411
Hart, Josh
The Ocean Dark - Jack Rogan   *s* 797
Jones, Trip
Worth the Trip - Penny McCall   *r* 1057
Kahne, Sela
Tempting the Fire - Sydney Croft   *h* 278
Lassiter, Simon
Simon Says... - Donna Kauffman   *r* 1025
Livingston, Tess
Esperanza - Trish J. MacGregor   *h* 322
Logan, Pike
One Rough Man - Brad Taylor   *m* 539
Margie
Cleaning Nabokov's House - Leslie
   Daniels   *c* 587
Miyuki
The Other Side - Hideyuki Kikuchi   *h* 312
Montgomery, Amelia
Tennessee Brides - Aaron McCarver   *i* 882
Morgan
Ghost Dance - Rebecca Levene   *s* 775
Otes, Baron
Valley of Dry Bones - Priscilla Royal   *t* 233
Ozburn, Sean
The Border Lords - T. Jefferson Parker   *m* 512
Parker, Jack
Deadly Pursuit - Ann Christopher   *r* 953
Porter, Riley
Colby Core - Debra Webb   *r* 1130
Putnam, Chess
Unholy Magic - Stacia Kane   *f* 48
Reilly, Sean
The Templar Salvation - Raymond
   Khoury   *m* 477
Ryan, Jack Jr.
Dead or Alive - Tom Clancy   *m* 397
Sigler, Jack
Threshold - Jeremy Robinson   *m* 518
Taylor, Alex
Man with the Muscle - Julie Miller   *r* 1068
Thatcher, Clay
The Fourth Victim - Tara Taylor Quinn   *r* 1087
Vail, Steve
Agent X - Noah Boyd   *m* 385
Wachalowski, Nico
The Silent Army - James Knapp   *s* 768
West, Marlena
Tempting the Fire - Sydney Croft   *h* 278

ALCOHOLIC

Aramon
Trespass - Rose Tremain   *c* 707
Arsenault, Sheila
Rescue - Anita Shreve   *c* 701
Kashon, Lou
In Search of Mercy - Michael Ayoob   *m* 372
Melville, Herman
*The Passages of H.M.: A Novel of Herman
   Melville* - Jay Parini   *c* 673

ALIEN

Nessus
Betrayer of Worlds - Larry Niven   *s* 786

AMNESIAC

Felix
Seer of Sevenwaters - Juliet Marillier   *t* 202
Prakenskii, Lev
Water Bound - Christine Feehan   *r* 974

AMPUTEE

Ellis, Will
One Was a Soldier - Julia
   Spencer-Fleming   *m* 531

ANGEL

Deveraux, Elena
Archangel's Kiss - Nalini Singh   *f* 85
Gloom
Demon Strike - Andrew Newbound   *h* 334
Jinn
Circle of Skulls - James P. Davis   *f* 29
Lijuan
Archangel's Kiss - Nalini Singh   *f* 85
Malachi
Almost Heaven - Chris Fabry   *r* 973
Raphael
Archangel's Kiss - Nalini Singh   *f* 85
Santovari, Custo
Shadow Fall - Erin Kellison   *r* 1028
Swift, Flhi
Demon Strike - Andrew Newbound   *h* 334
Yell
Demon Strike - Andrew Newbound   *h* 334

ANIMAL LOVER

Hemingway, Dixie
Cat Sitter Among the Pigeons - Blaize
   Clement   *m* 403
Kaine, AJ
Bullet Work - Steve O'Brien   *m* 506
Morgan, Dan
Bullet Work - Steve O'Brien   *m* 506
Young, Lilah
Animal Magnetism - Jill Shalvis   *r* 1103

ANIMAL TRAINER

Bristow, Fiona
The Search - Nora Roberts   *r* 1092
Holland, Robyn
Alaska Weddings - Susan Page Davis   *i* 845

ANTHROPOLOGIST

Saad, Pierre
Adam and Eve: A Novel - Sena Jeter
   Naslund   *c* 662

ANTIQUARIAN

Pratt, Eleanor "Nell"
Fundraising the Dead - Sheila Connolly   *m* 407
Styles, Bernard
The School of Night - Louis Bayard   *m* 376
Wheel, Jane
Backstage Stuff - Sharon Fiffer   *m* 436

ANTIQUES DEALER

Benedict, Alex
Echo - Jack McDevitt   *s* 783

Borne, Brandy
Antiques Knock-Off - Barbara Allan   *m* 366

Garity, Chester "Chess"
The Cruel Ever After - Ellen Hart   *m* 454

Jordan, Riley
Deadly Threads - Jane K. Cleland   *m* 402

Justin
Petty Magic: Being the Memoirs and Confessions of Miss Evelyn Harbinger, Temptress and Troublemaker - Camille DeAngelis   *t* 137

Prescott, Josie
Deadly Threads - Jane K. Cleland   *m* 402

Summer, Maggie
Shadows of a Down East Summer - Lea Wait   *m* 547

Verey, Anthony
Trespass - Rose Tremain   *c* 707

APPRENTICE

Hanby, Will
Fairer Than Morning - Rosslyn Elliott   *i* 851

Jerzy
Weight of Stone - Laura Anne Gilman   *f* 38

Khai, Vestara
Vortex - Troy Denning   *s* 744

Salman
The Calligrapher's Secret - Rafik Schami   *c* 691

Tucker, Jack
The Demon's Parchment - Jeri Westerson   *t* 261

ARCHAEOLOGIST

Creed, Annja
Rogue Angel: Phantom Prospect - Alex Archer   *f* 6
Rogue Angel: The Dragon's Mark - Alex Archer   *f* 5
Rogue Angel: Tribal Ways - Alex Archer   *f* 4

Dartmoor, Madison
Day of the Dragon - Rebecca York   *r* 1145

Eriksen, Blue
Other Eyes - Barbara D'Amato   *m* 415

Hodge, Geena
The Chamber of Ten - Christopher Golden   *h* 288

Malone, Sophie
The Whisper - Carla Neggers   *r* 1074

Princess Beatrice
The Bards of Bone Plain - Patricia A. McKillip   *f* 68

Sampson, Lily
Scorpion's Bite - Aileen G. Baron   *t* 113

Weil, Gideon
Scorpion's Bite - Aileen G. Baron   *t* 113

ARCHITECT

Baum, Fred
The Tale of Oat Cake Crag - Susan Wittig Albert   *t* 106

Flanders, Isabelle
Cross Roads - Fern Michaels   *r* 1066

Rey, Antoine
A Secret Kept - Tatiana de Rosnay   *c* 589

ART DEALER

Harris, Peter
By Nightfall - Michael Cunningham   *c* 586

Yeager, Lacey
An Object of Beauty - Steve Martin   *c* 649

ARTIST

Abel, Colin
The Last Jewish Virgin: A Novel of Fate - Janice Eidus   *c* 596

Bradley, Dylan
The Art of Romance - Kaye Dacus   *i* 842

Cameron, Isabelle
A Perfect Scandal - Tina Gabrielle   *r* 980

Davenport, Troy
A Midnight Clear - Kristi Astor   *r* 928

Dawn, Sierra
Words - Ginny L. Yttrup   *i* 923

Doyle, Simon
The Search - Nora Roberts   *r* 1092

Driscoll, Clara
Clara and Mr. Tiffany - Susan Vreeland   *c* 711

Durand, Jean-Philippe
Nothing but Deception - Allegra Gray   *r* 993

Ellen
Sunset Park - Paul Auster   *c* 569

Fall, Keegan
The Lake of Dreams - Kim Edwards   *c* 595

Farsi, Hamid
The Calligrapher's Secret - Rafik Schami   *c* 691

Fernandez, Ella
Engineman - Eric Brown   *s* 737

Franklyn, Georgie
Beyond the Shore - Connie Monk   *t* 211

Henry
The Painted Darkness - Brian James Freeman   *h* 283

Jansen, Amazing Grace "Maze"
Stranger Here Below - Joyce Hinnefeld   *t* 174

LaVenture, Johnny
Take a Chance on Me - Jill Mansell   *r* 1052

Lichtmann, Daniel
The Marriage Artist: A Novel - Andrew Winer   *c* 716

Maze, Paul
21 Aldgate - Patricia Friedberg   *t* 158

Poe, Riley
Afterlight - Elle Jasper   *h* 306

Pollocke, Grace MacDonald
Original Sins: A Novel of Slavery & Freedom - Peg Kingman   *t* 190

Skolnik, Andre
A Lily of the Field - John Lawton   *t* 193

Tiffany, Louis Comfort
Clara and Mr. Tiffany - Susan Vreeland   *c* 711

van Gogh, Vincent
Leaving Van Gogh - Carol Wallace   *c* 712

Mr. Vincent
Shades of Milk and Honey - Mary Robinette Kowal   *f* 51

Wellesley, Rachel
Star of His Heart - Brenda Jackson   *r* 1012

Wind, Benjamin
The Marriage Artist: A Novel - Andrew Winer   *c* 716

ASSASSIN

Cassandra
The Fire Lord's Lover - Kathryne Kennedy   *r* 1030

Krelan
The Bird of the River - Kage Baker   *f* 8

Roudette
Red Hood's Revenge - Jim C. Hines   *f* 43

ASSISTANT

Mrs. Blossom
The Girl in the Green Raincoat - Laura Lippman   *m* 485

Dale, Clarissa
The School of Night - Louis Bayard   *m* 376

Dalessius
Voltaire's Calligrapher - Pablo De Santis   *t* 136

Greenleaf, Jake
Mary Ann in Autumn - Armistead Maupin   *c* 650

Hamm, Gloria
Deus Ex Machina - Andrew Foster Altschul   *c* 565

Hart, Tammy
A Decadent Way to Die - G.A. McKevett   *m* 498

Olivia
Touching Darkness - Jaime Rush   *h* 341

Pignot, Joseph
The Montmartre Investigation - Claude Izner   *t* 180

Roumande, Albert
Devoured - D.E. Meredith   *t* 207

Templer, Colin
All Clear - Connie Willis   *s* 822

ASTRONAUT

Stetson, Bill
Back to the Moon - Les Johnson   *s* 763

AUNT

Dimity
Aunt Dimity and the Family Tree - Nancy Atherton   *m* 371

Ferdinanda
Crunch Time - Diane Mott Davidson   *m* 416

Gardiner, Aunt
Mr. Darcy's Obsession - Abigail Reynolds   *t* 231

Mrs. Norris
Mansfield Park and Mummies: Monster Mayhem, Matrimony, Ancient Curses, True Love, and Other Dire Delights - Vera Nazarian   *h* 332

Roni
Murder on the Bride's Side - Tracy Kiely   *m* 478

Shirley
The Dance Boots - Linda LeGarde Grover   *c* 616

BABY

Faith
Chaos Bites - Lori Handeland   *h* 299

Noelle
1022 Evergreen Place - Debbie Macomber   *r* 1049

BABYSITTER

Hemingway, Dixie
Cat Sitter Among the Pigeons - Blaize Clement   *m* 403

Lula
My New American Life - Francine Prose   *c* 679

BACHELOR

Crawford, Henry
Mansfield Park and Mummies: Monster Mayhem, Matrimony, Ancient Curses, True Love, and Other Dire Delights - Vera Nazarian   *h* 332

Fulton, Jack
A Season of Seduction - Jennifer Haymore   *r* 1001

Graymoor, Harrison
Hidden Affections - Delia Parr   *i* 894

Mancuso, Rafe
Love Me if You Dare - Carly Phillips   *r* 1084

Traemore, Lord Harry
When Harry Met Molly - Kieran Kramer   *r* 1038

Windham, Gayle
The Heir - Grace Burrowes   *r* 945

Winslow, David
Miss Foster's Folly - Alice Gaines   *r* 981

BAKER

Donovan, Piper
To Have and To Kill: A Wedding Cake Mystery - Mary Jane Clark   *m* 401

Swenson, Hannah
Devil's Food Cake Murder - Joanne Fluke   *m* 437

BANKER

Bondurant, Mitchell
The Fifth Witness - Michael Connelly   *m* 406

Keller, Nathan
Hometown Dad - Merrillee Whren   *i* 918

Paul
You Don't Love This Man: A Novel (P.S.) - Dan Deweese   *m* 418

Tubal, Julian
Other People's Money - Justin Cartwright   *c* 580

BASEBALL PLAYER

Blakely, Billy
Blockade Billy - Stephen King   *h* 314

Lawless, James "Law"
Sweet Spot - Kate Angell   *r* 927

Stockton, Carter
A Great Catch: A Novel - Lorna Seilstad   *i* 902

Winter, Luke
Hot Target - Lisa Renee Jones   *r* 1021

BASKETBALL PLAYER

Gustafson, Olaf
Blind Your Ponies - Stanley Gordon West   *c* 714

Stonebreaker, Tom
Blind Your Ponies - Stanley Gordon West   *c* 714

Strong, Peter
Blind Your Ponies - Stanley Gordon West   *c* 714

BEAR

Dog
Luka and the Fire of Life - Salman Rushdie   *c* 686

BIBLICAL FIGURE

Bathsheba
Bathsheba: A Novel - Jill Eileen Smith   *i* 906

Job
Love Amid the Ashes: A Novel - Mesu Andrews   *i* 824

King David
Bathsheba: A Novel - Jill Eileen Smith   *i* 906

Martha
Martha: A Novel - Diana Wallis Taylor   *i* 913

BIKER

Kavanaugh, Malcolm "Mal"
Happy Ever After - Nora Roberts   *r* 1093

BIRD

Ecu, Falcon
Tourquai - Tim Davys   *m* 417

Vulture, Oswald
Tourquai - Tim Davys   *m* 417

BLACKSMITH

Grant, Levi
To Win Her Heart - Karen Witemeyer   *i* 921

BOARDER

Howard, Allegra
The Home for Broken Hearts - Rowan Coleman   *c* 584

Matt
The Home for Broken Hearts - Rowan Coleman   *c* 584

Sabine
The Home for Broken Hearts - Rowan Coleman   *c* 584

BODYGUARD

Erik
Much Fall of Blood - Dave Freer   *f* 35

Fox, Charlotte "Charlie"
Fourth Day - Zoe Sharp   *m* 526

O'Malley, Ry
Altar of Bones - Philip Carter   *m* 394

Stark, James
Kill the Dead - Richard Kadrey   *h* 308

Taylor, Alex
Man with the Muscle - Julie Miller   *r* 1068

BOUNTY HUNTER

King, Greg
Play Dirty - Lorie O'Clare   *r* 1078

Stone, Evangeline
As Lie the Dead - Kelly Meding   *f* 69

Strong, Anna
Chosen - Jeanne C. Stein   *h* 348

The Doberman
Electric Barracuda - Tim Dorsey   *m* 421

BOY

Ansel
No Such Things As Dragons - Philip Reeve   *f* 78

Brian
The Suburb Beyond the Stars - M.T. Anderson   *f* 3

Devanna
Tiger Hills: A Novel - Sarita Mandanna   *t* 200

Magpie
Intrigues - Mercedes Lackey   *f* 54

Paul
Learning to Swim - Sara J. Henry   *m* 462

BOYFRIEND

Beyard, Francisco
The Informationist - Taylor Stevens   *m* 535

Crawford, Bobby
Third Degree - Maggie Barbieri   *m* 374

Crow
The Girl in the Green Raincoat - Laura Lippman   *m* 485

David
Friday Mornings at Nine - Marilyn Brant   *r* 937

Drood, Eddie
From Hell with Love - Simon R. Green   *f* 39

Featherstone, Sam
The Crocodile's Last Embrace - Suzanne Arruda   *t* 109

Hendrix, Ethan
Almost Perfect - Susan Mallery   *r* 1050

Huck
The False Friend - Myla Goldberg   *c* 614

Jack
Love's First Bloom - Julie Lessman   *r* 1041

Landsverk, Joshua
A Heart for Home - Lauraine Snelling   *i* 907

MacKenzie, Luke
Spun by Sorcery - Barbara Bretton   *r* 938

Martini, Jeff
Alien Tango - Gini Koch   *s* 770

Mick
Firewalker - Allyson James   *r* 1013

Montoya, Reuben
Devious - Lisa Jackson   *m* 471

Morbier
Murder in Passy - Cara Black   *m* 380

Murphy, Charlie
This Vacant Paradise - Victoria Patterson   *c* 674

Pavlik, Jake
A Cup of Jo - Sandra Balzo   *m* 373

Russell, John
Potsdam Station - David Downing   *m* 422

Ryder, Craig
The Truth of Valor - Tanya Huff   *s* 758

Sam
Don't Breathe a Word - Jennifer McMahon   *m* 499

Scott
Mobbed - Carol Higgins Clark   *m* 398

Seth
Fade to Blue - Julie Carobini   *i* 834

Will
Take a Chance on Me - Jill Mansell   *r* 1052

Worthington, Jack
A Hope Undaunted - Julie Lessman   *i* 876

BRIDE

Bridget
Murder on the Bride's Side - Tracy Kiely   *m* 478

Charnais, Juliana de
The Sixth Surrender - Hana Samek Norton   *t* 217

Maggie
In a Cowboy's Arms - Janette Kenny   *r* 1031
Miranda
You Don't Love This Man: A Novel (P.S.) - Dan Deweese   *m* 418

BRIDEGROOM

Lasalle, Guerin de
The Sixth Surrender - Hana Samek Norton   *t* 217

BROTHER

Adam
Animal Magnetism - Jill Shalvis   *r* 1103
Deceptions: A Jamestown Novel - Marilyn J. Clay   *t* 130
Amlingmeyer, Gustav "Old Red"
World's Greatest Sleuth! - Steve Hockensmith   *m* 467
Amlingmeyer, Otto "Big Red"
World's Greatest Sleuth! - Steve Hockensmith   *m* 467
Aramon
Trespass - Rose Tremain   *c* 707
Arthur
The Valcourt Heiress - Catherine Coulter   *r* 957
Austen, Harry
Jane and the Madness of Lord Byron - Stephanie Barron   *t* 114
bin Abdul-Aziz, Abdullah
The Secret Soldier - Alex Berenson   *m* 378
bin Abdul-Aziz, Saaed
The Secret Soldier - Alex Berenson   *m* 378
Blake
The Lake of Dreams - Kim Edwards   *c* 595
Brown, Jim Ed
Nashville Chrome - Rick Bass   *c* 570
Bryen
The Uncrowned King - Rowena Cory Daniells   *f* 26
Cailiff, Force
The Cailiffs of Baghdad, Georgia - Mary Helen Stefaniak   *t* 248
Chagetai
Khan: Empire of Silver - Conn Iggulden   *t* 177
Chatwick, Leo
Three Nights with a Scoundrel - Tessa Dare   *r* 961
Clarence
The Virgin Widow - Anne O'Brien   *t* 219
Cutler, Caleb
For Love of Country - William C. Hammond   *t* 169
Dan
The Old Romantic - Louise Dean   *c* 590
Darcy, Mr. Fitzwilliam
Mr. Darcy's Little Sister - C. Allyn Pierson   *t* 226
David
In the Company of Vampires - Katie MacAlister   *h* 320
Davidson, Brian
The Perfect Family - Kathryn Shay   *r* 1104
Davis, Gideon
Gideon's War - Howard Gordon   *m* 444
Davis, Tillman
Gideon's War - Howard Gordon   *m* 444

Dell
Animal Magnetism - Jill Shalvis   *r* 1103
Eric
The Pursuit of Happiness - Douglas Kennedy   *c* 635
Ethan "Mizzy"
By Nightfall - Michael Cunningham   *c* 586
Fyn
The Usurper - Rowena Cory Daniells   *f* 28
Greifinger, Heinz
A Call from Jersey - P.F. Kluge   *t* 191
Griffin, George
A Call from Jersey - P.F. Kluge   *t* 191
Hamilton, Johnny
Shadow on the Land - Anne Doughty   *t* 143
Hansen, Paul
Heads You Lose - Lisa Lutz   *m* 488
Harris, Phil
Up from the Blue: A Novel - Susan Henderson   *c* 623
Heath, Nigel
The Brothers of Baker Street - Michael Robertson   *m* 517
Heath, Reggie
The Brothers of Baker Street - Michael Robertson   *m* 517
Istvan
Under the Poppy - Kathe Koja   *c* 638
Joe
Delirious - Daniel Palmer   *m* 509
Kamrasi, Nathan
Cinkarion: The Heart of Fire - J.A. Cullum   *f* 24
Kareem
People of the Book - Kathi Macias   *i* 879
LeBlanc, Marc
A Twisted Ladder - Rhodi Hawk   *h* 300
Lockwood, Brady
Guarding Grace - Rebecca York   *r* 1144
McRae, Duncan
Raider's Heart - Marcia Gruver   *i* 860
McRae, Hooper
Raider's Heart - Marcia Gruver   *i* 860
Miller, Brady
Animal Magnetism - Jill Shalvis   *r* 1103
Nick
The Old Romantic - Louise Dean   *c* 590
Nolan, Mark
Christmas Eve at Friday Harbor - Lisa Kleypas   *r* 1034
Parr, William
Secrets of the Tudor Court: By Royal Decree - Kate Emerson   *t* 148
Peshkov, Grigori
Fall of Giants - Ken Follett   *t* 154
Peshkov, Lev
Fall of Giants - Ken Follett   *t* 154
Rex
The Poison Tree - Erin Kelly   *m* 474
Rey, Antoine
A Secret Kept - Tatiana de Rosnay   *c* 589
Richard
The Virgin Widow - Anne O'Brien   *t* 219
Rio, Gabe
The Ocean Dark - Jack Rogan   *s* 797
Rio, Miguel
The Ocean Dark - Jack Rogan   *s* 797

Sam
Don't Breathe a Word - Jennifer McMahon   *m* 499
Scott, Arthur
Bent Road - Lori Roy   *m* 521
Seth
Afterlight - Elle Jasper   *h* 306
Templeton, James
At the Captain's Command - Louise M. Gouge   *i* 858
Tennyson, Alfred
The Quickening Maze - Adam Foulds   *t* 157
Tennyson, Septimus
The Quickening Maze - Adam Foulds   *t* 157
Thom
Dragon Soul - Danielle Bennett   *f* 9
Tom
Take Me Home - Brian Leung   *c* 643
Verey, Anthony
Trespass - Rose Tremain   *c* 707
Watson, Freddie
The Winter Ghosts - Kate Mosse   *m* 503
Watson, George
The Winter Ghosts - Kate Mosse   *m* 503
Williams, Billy
Fall of Giants - Ken Follett   *t* 154
Worden, David
The Best of Friends - Susan Mallery   *r* 1051

BULLY

Ridley
The Big Stink - David Lubar   *h* 317
Rodney
The Big Stink - David Lubar   *h* 317

BUSINESSMAN

Abuzeid, Mahmoud Bey
Lyrics Alley - Leila Aboulela   *t* 104
Allen, Dr. Matthew
The Quickening Maze - Adam Foulds   *t* 157
Burbank, Richard
The Informationist - Taylor Stevens   *m* 535
Carstairs, Sam
Journey to Riverbend - Henry McLaughlin   *i* 884
Cavendish, Dennis
Frozen Fire - Marianna Jameson   *s* 761
Connolly, Harm
Mesmerizing Stranger - Jennifer Greene   *r* 994
Drugstore Wally
The Incredible Double - Owen Hill   *m* 464
Fox, Ethan
A Dad of His Own - Gail Gaymer Martin   *i* 880
Gabriel
A Young Man's Guide to Late Capitalism - Peter Mountford   *c* 659
Hawksley, Markus
A Perfect Scandal - Tina Gabrielle   *r* 980
Holt, William
Blackstone and the Wolf of Wall Street - Sally Spencer   *t* 247
Jackson, Baxter
Deceit - Brandilyn Collins   *i* 838
Jett, Whitby
One of Our Thursdays Is Missing - Jasper Fforde   *m* 434

Keller, Nathan
Hometown Dad - Merrillee Whren *i* 918

Pickett, Sam
Blind Your Ponies - Stanley Gordon West *c* 714

COLLEAGUE

Dao, Bailey
The Incredible Double - Owen Hill *m* 464

Kolpath, Chase
Echo - Jack McDevitt *s* 783

Marvin
The Incredible Double - Owen Hill *m* 464

Meyer, Sean
Fourth Day - Zoe Sharp *m* 526

COLLECTOR

Asper, Julius
Caveat Emptor - Ruth Downie *t* 145

COMPANION

Bao
Naamah's Curse - Jacqueline Carey *f* 19

Eva
Queen Hereafter: A Novel of Margaret of Scotland
  - Susan Fraser King *t* 189

Olafson, Julie
The Zombies of Lake Woebegotten - Harrison
  Geillor *h* 287

COMPUTER EXPERT

Aiken, Jeff
Zero Day - Mark Russinovich *m* 523

Giles, Charlie
Delirious - Daniel Palmer *m* 509

Highsmith, Diana
Come and Find Me - Hallie Ephron *m* 429

Lerato
Moxyland - Lauren Beukes *s* 733

CONSULTANT

Breeden, Kate
The Informationist - Taylor Stevens *m* 535

Nickerson, Sarah
Left Neglected - Lisa Genova *c* 610

Voss, Mia
Unforgivable - Laura Griffin *m* 447

CONTESTANT

Hamm, Gloria
Deus Ex Machina - Andrew Foster
  Altschul *c* 565

CONVICT

Carstairs, Ben
Journey to Riverbend - Henry McLaughlin *i* 884

Crowley, Jon
The Four Stages of Cruelty - Keith
  Hollihan *m* 468

Grant, Levi
To Win Her Heart - Karen Witemeyer *i* 921

Hoffman, Piet
Three Seconds - Anders Roslund *m* 519

Howerd, Fred
Echoes of the Dead - Sally Spencer *m* 530

Jorg
The Weekend - Bernhard Schlink *c* 692

Payton, Carly
Finally a Bride - Vickie McDonough *i* 883

Riff, Joshua
The Four Stages of Cruelty - Keith
  Hollihan *m* 468

Rockford, Deon "Rocky"
Upon This Rock - Kendra
  Norman-Bellamy *i* 893

COOK

Campbell, Cate
Mesmerizing Stranger - Jennifer Greene *r* 994

Davis, Luke
Dining with Joy - Rachel Hauck *r* 999

Delaflote, Luc
Indulgence in Death - J.D. Robb *s* 796

Paras, Olivia
Buffalo West Wing - Julie Hyzy *m* 469

Persons, Elizabeth
The Gentleman Poet - Kathryn Johnson *r* 1020

COUNSELOR

Cuneglas, Malgwyn ap
The Beloved Dead - Tony Hays *m* 458

Milano, Tina
Tea for Two - Trish Perry *i* 895

Sherrod, Audrey
Don't Cry - Beverly Barton *r* 932

Vanessa
Sing You Home - Jodi Picoult *c* 677

COURTIER

Parr, William
Secrets of the Tudor Court: By Royal Decree -
  Kate Emerson *t* 148

COUSIN

Caruso, Brian
Dead or Alive - Tom Clancy *m* 397

Caruso, Dominick
Dead or Alive - Tom Clancy *m* 397

Edmund
*Mansfield Park and Mummies: Monster Mayhem,
  Matrimony, Ancient Curses, True Love, and
  Other Dire Delights* - Vera Nazarian *h* 332

Isaiah
Abigail's New Hope - Mary Ellis *i* 852

Knollys, Lettice
Rival to the Queen - Carolly Erickson *t* 149

Machu
Tiger Hills: A Novel - Sarita Mandanna *t* 200

Prudence
The Suburb Beyond the Stars - M.T.
  Anderson *f* 3

Ryan, Jack Jr.
Dead or Alive - Tom Clancy *m* 397

Tybalt
Romeo and Juliet and Vampires - Claudia
  Gabel *h* 284

William
Emily Hudson - Melissa Jones *t* 184

COWBOY/COWGIRL

Cody, Dexter
Dexter: Honorable Cowboy - Marin
  Thomas *r* 1119

Corbett, Garrett
Finally a Bride - Vickie McDonough *i* 883

Ikard, Bose
Comanche Sundown - Jan Reid *t* 229

Kessler, Rand
Finally a Bride - Vickie McDonough *i* 883

McConnell, Alec
Idaho Brides - Erica Vetsch *i* 916

McIntyre, Bobbie
When All My Dreams Come True - Janelle
  Mowery *i* 891

Ryan, Wade
A Cowboy's Touch - Denise Hunter *i* 866

Shawcross, Nate
One Fine Cowboy - Joanne Kennedy *r* 1029

Wells, Hank
My Give a Damn's Busted - Carolyn
  Brown *r* 943

CRIME SUSPECT

Barrett, Randall
Indefensible - Pamela Callow *m* 391

Bothwell, Nanty
A Pig of Cold Poison - Pat McIntosh *t* 206

Corrag
Corrag - Susan Fletcher *c* 601

Curtlee, Ro
Damage - John T. Lescroart *m* 483

d'Este, Alfonso
The Second Duchess - Elizabeth Loupas *t* 196

Dragos, Lucius "Luke"
When Blood Calls - J.K. Beck *h* 269

Faulkner, Billy
Murder Your Darlings - J.J. Murphy *m* 504

Giles, Charlie
Delirious - Daniel Palmer *m* 509

Hanks, Tip
Santa Fe Edge - Stuart Woods *m* 561

Jackson, Baxter
Deceit - Brandilyn Collins *i* 838

Melvin
The KenKen Killings - Parnell Hall *m* 450

Morbier
Murder in Passy - Cara Black *m* 380

O'Fallon, Patrick
False Patriots - Charles O'Brien *t* 220

Pollack, Anastasia
Assault with a Deadly Glue Gun - Lois
  Winston *m* 560

Randolph, Tai
The Dangerous Edge of Things - Tina
  Whittle *m* 555

Rayburn, Eva
Senseless - Mary Burton *m* 389

Roy
Bent Road - Lori Roy *m* 521

Samuelson, Greg
The Bad Kitty Lounge - Michael Wiley *m* 556

Savoie, Max
Chased by Moonlight - Nancy Gideon *r* 985

Swain, David
The King of Diamonds - Simon Tolkien   *m* 543

Taylor, Layla
In the Shadow of Evil - Robin Caroll   *i* 835

Trenary, Monah
Died in the Wool - Elizabeth Ludwig   *i* 877

Weil, Gideon
Scorpion's Bite - Aileen G. Baron   *t* 113

CRIME VICTIM

Asper, Julius
Caveat Emptor - Ruth Downie   *t* 145

Beckett, Darlene
The Dead Detective - William Heffernan   *m* 459

Benedict, Eliza
I'd Know You Anywhere - Laura Lippman   *c* 646

Chatwick, Leo
Three Nights with a Scoundrel - Tessa Dare   *r* 961

de Saint-Martin, Paul
False Patriots - Charles O'Brien   *t* 220

Dial, Melvin
The Cruel Ever After - Ellen Hart   *m* 454

Duke of Dornoch
The Unbelievers - Alastair Sim   *t* 242

Edwards, Carrie
Veil of Night - Linda Howard   *r* 1009

Ellery, "High-Low" Jack
A Drop of the Hard Stuff - Lawrence Block   *m* 382

Enke, Angela
Unholy Awakening - Michael Gregorio   *m* 446

Evanson, Marjorie
An Impartial Witness - Charles Todd   *t* 253

Fontaine, Layla
The Lies that Bind - Kate Carlisle   *m* 392

Fraysse, Marc
Blowback - Peter May   *m* 494

Gibson, Dan "Danny"
A Pig of Cold Poison - Pat McIntosh   *t* 206

Gregos
Still Waters - Marilyn Todd   *t* 255

Gretchen
Nowhere to Hide - Carlene Thompson   *r* 1120

Habib, Munir
Fatal Error - F. Paul Wilson   *h* 364

Haley
Secrets to the Grave - Tami Hoag   *m* 466

Hammond, Kim
Trail of Blood - Lisa Black   *m* 381

Hilliard, Lila
Set the Night on Fire - Libby Fischer Hellmann   *m* 460

Iarla
Eye of the Law - Cora Harrison   *m* 453

Johnson, Mallory
Christmas Mourning - Margaret Maron   *m* 492

Kincaid, Lucy
Love Me to Death - Allison Brennan   *m* 387

Letteri, Lou
Cold Shot to the Heart - Wallace Stroby   *m* 536

Lisa
Damaged - Pamela Callow   *r* 946

Lundgren, Sophie
No Place to Run - Maya Banks   *r* 930

Maidment, Jennifer
The Fever of the Bone - Val McDermid   *m* 496

Maria
Hypothermia - Arnaldur Indridason   *m* 470

Miller, James
Trail of Blood - Lisa Black   *m* 381

O'Hern, Johnny
Too Many Clients - David J. Walker   *m* 548

Osman, Katya
The King of Diamonds - Simon Tolkien   *m* 543

Paco
A Darker Night - P.J. Brooke   *m* 388

Parker, Blake
Force of Habit - Alice Loweecey   *m* 486

Payne, Macy
You Killed Wesley Payne - Sean Beaudoin   *m* 377

Pazos, Jose Robles
Hemingway Cutthroat - Michael Atkinson   *t* 110

Penn-Williams, JoLynne
A Cup of Jo - Sandra Balzo   *m* 373

Price, Fanny
Murder at Mansfield Park - Lynn Shepherd   *t* 240

Rayburn, Eva
Senseless - Mary Burton   *m* 389

Renard, Camille
Devious - Lisa Jackson   *m* 471

Reynolds, Duncan
An Empty Death - Laura Wilson   *m* 558

Roni
Murder on the Bride's Side - Tracy Kiely   *m* 478

Scott, Bunny
The Darling Dahlias and the Cucumber Tree - Susan Wittig Albert   *t* 107

Stockpole, Barry
The Left-Handed Dollar - Loren D. Estleman   *m* 431

Stone, Eric
The Bad Kitty Lounge - Michael Wiley   *m* 556

Strauss, Helene
A Decadent Way to Die - G.A. McKevett   *m* 498

Temple, Victoria
Sherlock Holmes and the Ghosts of Bly - Donald Thomas   *t* 252

Togashi
The Devotion of Suspect X - Keigo Higashino   *m* 463

Trevalyan, Max
Peril at Somner House - Joanna Challis   *t* 127

Vanderzell, Elise
Indefensible - Pamela Callow   *m* 391

Verpa, Sextus
Roman Games - Bruce Macbain   *t* 198

Voss, Mia
Unforgivable - Laura Griffin   *m* 447

Vulture, Oswald
Tourquai - Tim Davys   *m* 417

White, Wendy
So Much Pretty - Cara Hoffman   *c* 626

Williams, Merrin
Horns: A Novel - Joe Hill   *h* 302

Xavierre
Murder in Passy - Cara Black   *m* 380

Zaliukas, Tomas
A Rush of Blood - Quintin Jardine   *m* 472

CRIMINAL

Booth, John Wilkes
The Second Life of John Wilkes Booth - Barnaby Conrad   *t* 131

Cornella, Carlos
The Unforgivable - Tessa Stockton   *i* 910

Glanville, Humphrey
Lifeblood - Tom Becker   *h* 272

Hauk, Dutch
Deadly Ties - Vicki Hinze   *i* 864

Henry, Dick
Shortcut Man - P.G. Sturges   *m* 537

Murphy, Stax
Black Orchid Blues - Persia Walker   *m* 549

Platt, Lance
Portobello - Ruth Rendell   *m* 516

Rio, Gabe
The Ocean Dark - Jack Rogan   *s* 797

Rio, Miguel
The Ocean Dark - Jack Rogan   *s* 797

The Tattoo
Kraken - China Mieville   *f* 70

Vartan, Harris
When the Thrill Is Gone - Walter Mosley   *m* 502

CRIMINOLOGIST

Bowers, Patrick
The Bishop - Steven James   *i* 867

CULT MEMBER

Forge, Eva
The Horns of Ruin - Tim Akers   *f* 1

Glenning, Pippa
House Arrest - Ellen Meeropol   *c* 654

Parnell, Dane
Kraken - China Mieville   *f* 70

Robert
The Widower's Tale - Julia Glass   *c* 613

Witney, Liam
Fourth Day - Zoe Sharp   *m* 526

Witney, Thomas
Fourth Day - Zoe Sharp   *m* 526

CYBORG

Version 43/44
Version 43 - Philip Palmer   *s* 789

DANCER

Annabella
Shadow Fall - Erin Kellison   *r* 1028

Kschessinska, Mathilde "Little K"
The True Memoirs of Little K - Adrienne Sharp   *c* 698

Samuels, Kayla
The Tenth Song - Naomi Ragen   *c* 680

DAUGHTER

Alexa
Dark Fire - Chris D'Lacey   *f* 25

Allen, Hannah
The Quickening Maze - Adam Foulds   *t* 157

Alley, Wallis
The Witches on the Road Tonight - Sheri Holman   *c* 628

Caissie, Charlotte
Chased by Moonlight - Nancy Gideon *r* 985

Chapman, Mike
Silent Mercy - Linda Fairstein *m* 432

Christie, Henry
Hidden Witness - Nick Oldham *m* 508

Cole, Elvis
The Sentry - Robert Crais *m* 412

Coleman, Hunter
Operation Prince Charming - Phyllis
   Bourne *r* 934

Cooper, Alexandra
Silent Mercy - Linda Fairstein *m* 432

Corwin, Adam
Mail-Order Groom - Lisa Plumley *r* 1085

Crawford, Bobby
Third Degree - Maggie Barbieri *m* 374

Crosby
Past Tense - Catherine Aird *m* 365

Cuneglas, Malgwyn ap
The Beloved Dead - Tony Hays *m* 458

Davis, Evan
A Legacy of Daemons - Camille
   Bacon-Smith *f* 7

DeFarge, Jagger
The Keepers - Heather Graham *r* 990

Dimity
Aunt Dimity and the Family Tree - Nancy
   Atherton *m* 371

Doyle, Logan
Luck Be a Lady - Cathie Linz *r* 1044

Ecu, Falcon
Tourquai - Tim Davys *m* 417

Falco, Marcus Didius
Nemesis - Lindsey Davis *t* 135

Fitzhugh, Reginald "Turnip"
The Mischief of the Mistletoe - Lauren
   Willig *t* 263

Fletcher, Alec
Anthem for Doomed Youth - Carola Dunn *m* 424

Frazer, Harry
Blood Justice - David Burton *h* 277

Garrison, Deacon
Senseless - Mary Burton *m* 389

Gregos
Still Waters - Marilyn Todd *t* 255

Guest, Crispin
The Demon's Parchment - Jeri Westerson *t* 261

Hall, Tom
Echoes of the Dead - Sally Spencer *m* 530

Hill, Tony
The Fever of the Bone - Val McDermid *m* 496

Kaldis, Andreas
Prey on Patmos - Jeffrey Siger *m* 527

Kraus, Willi
The Sleepwalkers - Paul Grossman *m* 448

Lenox, Charles
A Stranger in Mayfair - Charles Finch *t* 153

Lily
A Legacy of Daemons - Camille
   Bacon-Smith *f* 7

Lysander
Still Waters - Marilyn Todd *t* 255

MacLean, Theresa
Trail of Blood - Lisa Black *m* 381

MacLeary, Mac
Next Time You See Me - Katia Lief *m* 484

Macleod, Enzo
Blowback - Peter May *m* 494

Madigan, Charlie
The Darkest Edge of Dawn - Kelly Gay *h* 286

McLusky, Liam
Falling More Slowly - Peter Helton *m* 461

Mendez, Tony
Secrets to the Grave - Tami Hoag *m* 466

Next, Thursday
One of Our Thursdays Is Missing - Jasper
   Fforde *m* 434

Nicolaos
The Pericles Commission - Gary Corby *t* 132

Pania, Monika
Echoes of the Dead - Sally Spencer *m* 530

Pike, Joe
The Sentry - Robert Crais *m* 412

Ravel, Aristide
Palace of Justice - Susanne Alleyn *m* 367

Reinhardt, Oskar
Vienna Twilight - Frank Tallis *m* 538

Rizzo, Joe
Rizzo's Fire - Lou Manfredo *m* 491

Ruso, Gaius Petreius
Caveat Emptor - Ruth Downie *t* 145

Sabian, Alexandra "Alex"
Blood Law - Jeannie Holmes *h* 305

Santos, Ric
Unforgivable - Laura Griffin *m* 447

Scarlett, Hanna
The Hanging Wood - Martin Edwards *m* 427

Scarpetta, Kay
Port Mortuary - Patricia Cornwell *m* 409

Schaeffer, Karin
Next Time You See Me - Katia Lief *m* 484
You Are Next - Katia Lief *r* 1042

Sloan
Past Tense - Catherine Aird *m* 365

Stratton, Ted
An Empty Death - Laura Wilson *m* 558

Trave, William
The King of Diamonds - Simon Tolkien *m* 543

Yashim
An Evil Eye - Jason Goodwin *m* 443

DETECTIVE—AMATEUR

Abruzzo, Roxy
Our Lady of Immaculate Deception - Nancy
   Martin *m* 493

Akitada, Sugawara
The Fires of the Gods - I.J. Parker *m* 511
The Masuda Affair - I.J. Parker *t* 223

Annie
Miss Dimple Disappears - Mignon F.
   Ballard *t* 112

Arcturus
The Curse-Maker - Kelli Stanley *m* 533

Armstrong, Israel
The Bad Book Affair - Ian Sansom *m* 524

Bergeron, Alison
Third Degree - Maggie Barbieri *m* 374

Blackburn, Clay
The Incredible Double - Owen Hill *m* 464

Bolitar, Myron
Live Wire - Harlan Coben *m* 404

Bolzjak, Dexter
In Search of Mercy - Michael Ayoob *m* 372

Brisbane, Nicholas
Dark Road to Darjeeling - Deanna
   Raybourn *r* 1089

Campbell, Brun
The Ragtime Fool - Larry Karp *t* 186

Carr, Charlie
Miss Dimple Disappears - Mignon F.
   Ballard *t* 112

Cartier, Anne
False Patriots - Charles O'Brien *t* 220

Corbett, Hugh
The Waxman Murders - Paul Doherty *t* 141

Crawford, Bess
An Impartial Witness - Charles Todd *t* 253

Crawford, Mary
Murder at Mansfield Park - Lynn
   Shepherd *t* 240

Dalessius
Voltaire's Calligrapher - Pablo De Santis *t* 136

Dalrymple, Daisy
Anthem for Doomed Youth - Carola Dunn *m* 424

Devlin, Brinke
One True Sentence - Craig McDonald *m* 497

Donovan, Piper
To Have and To Kill: A Wedding Cake Mystery -
   Mary Jane Clark *m* 401

Ellefson, Chloe
Old World Murder - Kathleen Ernst *m* 430

Felton, Cora
The KenKen Killings - Parnell Hall *m* 450

Graham, Emma
Fadeaway Girl - Martha Grimes *c* 615

Graves, Rex
Murder on the Moor - C.S. Challinor *m* 395

Grey, Julia
Dark Road to Darjeeling - Deanna
   Raybourn *r* 1089

Hansen, Lacey
Heads You Lose - Lisa Lutz *m* 488

Hargreaves, Emily
Dangerous to Know - Tasha Alexander *t* 108

Heath, Nigel
The Brothers of Baker Street - Michael
   Robertson *m* 517

Heath, Reggie
The Brothers of Baker Street - Michael
   Robertson *m* 517

Hemingway, Dixie
Cat Sitter Among the Pigeons - Blaize
   Clement *m* 403

Hemingway, Ernest
Hemingway Cutthroat - Michael Atkinson *t* 110

Iliona
Still Waters - Marilyn Todd *t* 255

Jones, Tallulah "Tally"
Scoop to Kill - Wendy Lyn Watson *m* 552

Knott, Deborah
Christmas Mourning - Margaret Maron *m* 492

Lange, Kate
Damaged - Pamela Callow *r* 946
Indefensible - Pamela Callow *m* 391

DETECTIVE—HOMICIDE

DETECTIVE—POLICE

DETECTIVE—PRIVATE

Fisher, Phryne
Dead Man's Chest - Kerry Greenwood   *t* 163

Gage, Graham
Absolute Risk - Steven Gore   *m* 445

Gennaro, Angela "Angie"
Moonlight Mile - Dennis Lehane   *m* 482

Gillard, Patrick
Corpse in Waiting - Margaret Duffy   *m* 423

Goldman, Gigi
Swift Justice - Laura Disilverio   *m* 420

Gunther, Bernie
Field Grey - Philip Kerr   *m* 476

Hanson, Marvin
Devil Red - Joe R. Lansdale   *m* 481

Holmes, Sherlock
The God of the Hive - Laurie R. King   *t* 188
Sherlock Holmes and the Ghosts of Bly - Donald Thomas   *t* 252

Jong, Jade de
Stolen Lives - Jassy MacKenzie   *m* 490

Kane, Jeremy
Licensed for Trouble - Susan May Warren   *r* 1129

Kenzie, Patrick
Moonlight Mile - Dennis Lehane   *m* 482

Kirsten
Too Many Clients - David J. Walker   *m* 548

Kozmarski, Joe
The Bad Kitty Lounge - Michael Wiley   *m* 556

Langley, Ingrid
Corpse in Waiting - Margaret Duffy   *m* 423

Leduc, Aimee
Murder in Passy - Cara Black   *m* 380

Lupo, Nick
Wolf's Bluff - W.D. Gagliani   *h* 285

McGill, Leonid
When the Thrill Is Gone - Walter Mosley   *m* 502

McLeod, Ernest
Crunch Time - Diane Mott Davidson   *m* 416

Monaghan, Tess
The Girl in the Green Raincoat - Laura Lippman   *m* 485

Moretti, Francesca
Killer Heat - Brenda Novak   *r* 1076

Mouse, Phillip
Tourquai - Tim Davys   *m* 417

Munroe, Vanessa Michael
The Informationist - Taylor Stevens   *m* 535

Murphy, Molly
Bless the Bride - Rhys Bowen   *m* 383

Nyx
Vampires Not Invited - Cheyenne McCray   *r* 1060

Payne, Hugh
Murder at the Villa Byzantine - R.T. Raichev   *m* 514

Pine, Leonard
Devil Red - Joe R. Lansdale   *m* 481

Reid, Savannah
A Decadent Way to Die - G.A. McKevett   *m* 498

Reilly, Regan
Mobbed - Carol Higgins Clark   *m* 398

Richter, Matt
Nekropolis - Tim Waggoner   *h* 360

Rogan, Sean
Love Me to Death - Allison Brennan   *m* 387

Russell, Mary
The God of the Hive - Laurie R. King   *t* 188

Ruzak, Teddy
The Highly Effective Detective Crosses the Line - Richard Yancey   *m* 562

Scudder, Matthew
A Drop of the Hard Stuff - Lawrence Block   *m* 382

Shugak, Kate
Though Not Dead - Dana Stabenow   *m* 532

Sugar, PJ
Licensed for Trouble - Susan May Warren   *r* 1129

Swift, Charlotte "Charlie"
Swift Justice - Laura Disilverio   *m* 420

Vane, Harriet
The Attenbury Emeralds - Jill Paton Walsh   *m* 551

Walker, Amos
The Left-Handed Dollar - Loren D. Estleman   *m* 431

Waynest, Shiarra
Hunted by the Others - Jess Haines   *f* 40

Whalen, Nick
Home Is Where the Bark Is - Kandy Shepherd   *r* 1105

Wheel, Jane
Backstage Stuff - Sharon Fiffer   *m* 436

Wimsey, Lord Peter
The Attenbury Emeralds - Jill Paton Walsh   *m* 551

DIPLOMAT

Davis, Gideon
Gideon's War - Howard Gordon   *m* 444

Pocahontas
Deceptions: A Jamestown Novel - Marilyn J. Clay   *t* 130

Prince Manfred
Much Fall of Blood - Dave Freer   *f* 35

Renfrew, Nash
The Accidental Wedding - Anne Gracie   *r* 987

Vorkosigan, Miles
Cryoburn - Lois McMaster Bujold   *s* 739

DIRECTOR

Carr, Jeremy
The Next Queen of Heaven - Gregory Maguire   *c* 648

Hitchcock, Alfred "The Director"
What You See in the Dark - Manuel Munoz   *c* 661

Sanders, Kahlee
Retribution - Drew Karpyshyn   *s* 765

DIVORCED PERSON

Baird, Emilio
Home Again - Mariah Stewart   *r* 1110

Darcy, Shey
She's Gone Country - Jane Porter   *r* 1086

Hanaoka, Yasuko
The Devotion of Suspect X - Keigo Higashino   *m* 463

Henderson, Andrea
Larkspur Cove - Lisa Wingate   *i* 919

Kelly, Dane
She's Gone Country - Jane Porter   *r* 1086

McGregor, Dallas
Home Again - Mariah Stewart   *r* 1110

Melvin
The KenKen Killings - Parnell Hall   *m* 450

Neal, Rosalyn
The Lost and Forgotten Languages of Shanghai - Ruiyan Xu   *c* 721

O'Brien, Megan
A Chesapeake Shores Christmas - Sherryl Woods   *r* 1143

O'Brien, Mick
A Chesapeake Shores Christmas - Sherryl Woods   *r* 1143

Taggart, Marcy
Now You See Her - Joy Fielding   *m* 435

Togashi
The Devotion of Suspect X - Keigo Higashino   *m* 463

Trave, William
The King of Diamonds - Simon Tolkien   *m* 543

Tucker, Kimberly
Chasing Sunsets - Eva Marie Everson   *i* 854

Tyler, Annabelle
Hidden Affections - Delia Parr   *i* 894

DOCTOR

Allen, Dr. Matthew
The Quickening Maze - Adam Foulds   *t* 157

Arcturus
The Curse-Maker - Kelli Stanley   *m* 533

Bjorkland, Dr. Astrid
A Heart for Home - Lauraine Snelling   *i* 907

Christopher
Hope Rekindled - Tracie Peterson   *i* 896

Ford, Dr. Paul
Turbulence - Dana Mentink   *i* 885

Gable, Dr. Sophie
Explosive - Beth Kery   *r* 1033

Gachet, Paul
Leaving Van Gogh - Carol Wallace   *c* 712

Gardner, Dr. Elena
Diagnosis: Death - Richard L. Mabry   *i* 878

Gibson, Paul
Where Shadows Dance - C.S. Harris   *m* 452

Gideon
Secret Place - Leslie J. Sherrod   *i* 903

Harp, Will
Red Rain - Bruce Murkoff   *t* 214

Jacob
The Demon's Parchment - Jeri Westerson   *t* 261

Kai
The Memory of Love - Aminatta Forna   *c* 602

Monroe, Dr. Coleridge "Cole"
Marry Me - Jo Goodman   *r* 986

Natalia
The Tiger's Wife - Tea Obreht   *c* 668

Neal, Rosalyn
The Lost and Forgotten Languages of Shanghai - Ruiyan Xu   *c* 721

Dr. Ravell
The Doctor and the Diva - Adrienne McDonnell   *t* 205

Reynolds, Duncan
An Empty Death - Laura Wilson   *m* 558

Austen, Reverend
Jane and the Damned - Janet Mullany *t* 213

Blythe, Raymond
The Distant Hours - Kate Morton *c* 658

Bolden, Andre
Snitch: A Novel - Booker T. Mattison *i* 881

Brad
A Legacy of Daemons - Camille Bacon-Smith *f* 7

Brooks, Adam
Casting Around - Terri DuLong *r* 970

Calder, Chase
Santa in Montana - Janet Dailey *r* 960

Carstairs, Sam
Journey to Riverbend - Henry McLaughlin *i* 884

Cass, J.D.
Don't Cry - Beverly Barton *r* 932

Charlie
Pictures of You: A Novel - Caroline Leavitt *c* 642

Cohen, Yakob
The Oracle of Stamboul - Michael David Lukas *m* 487

Daddy Blank
A Twisted Ladder - Rhodi Hawk *h* 300

Davidson, Mike
The Perfect Family - Kathryn Shay *r* 1104

Geminus
Nemesis - Lindsey Davis *t* 135

Glass, Percy
The Widower's Tale - Julia Glass *c* 613

Greifinger, Hans
A Call from Jersey - P.F. Kluge *t* 191

Guy
Sea Change - Jeremy Page *c* 672

Hamilton, Alex
Shadow on the Land - Anne Doughty *t* 143

Henry
The Painted Darkness - Brian James Freeman *h* 283
The Queen of Last Hopes: The Story of Margaret of Anjou - Susan Higginbotham *t* 173

Ken
The Old Romantic - Louise Dean *c* 590

Khemiri, Abbas
Montecore: The Silence of the Tiger - Jonas Hassen Khemiri *c* 637

King Philip
The Golden Mean: A Novel of Aristotle and Alexander the Great - Annabel Lyon *t* 197

MacLeary, Mac
Next Time You See Me - Katia Lief *m* 484

Malone, Jackson
Wild Stallion - Delores Fossen *r* 977

Mark
Eden - Yael Hedaya *c* 621

Martin
Watermark: A Novel of the Middle Ages - Vanitha Sankaran *t* 236

Middleton, John
Dreams of Desire - Cheryl Holt *r* 1008

Montana, Joe
The Neighbors Are Watching - Debra Ginsberg *c* 612

Morath, Brandt
Lady Lazarus: A Novel - Andrew Foster Altschul *f* 2

Morgan, Charlie
How to Be an American Housewife - Margaret Dilloway *t* 140

Morris
Sunset Park - Paul Auster *c* 569

Paul
You Don't Love This Man: A Novel (P.S.) - Dan Deweese *m* 418

Pinarius, Lucius
Empire: The Novel of Imperial Rome - Steven Saylor *t* 239

Rain, David
Dark Fire - Chris D'Lacey *f* 25

Rashid
Luka and the Fire of Life - Salman Rushdie *c* 686

Redgrave, John "Jack"
Scoundrel in My Dreams - Celeste Bradley *r* 935

Rei
Manazuru - Hiromi Kawakami *c* 634

Rhennthyl
Imager's Intrigue - L.E. Modesitt *f* 71

Rhodes, David
1022 Evergreen Place - Debbie Macomber *r* 1049

Rolen
The Uncrowned King - Rowena Cory Daniells *f* 26

Russell, John
Potsdam Station - David Downing *m* 422

Samuels, Adam
The Tenth Song - Naomi Ragen *c* 680

Scott, Arthur
Bent Road - Lori Roy *m* 521

Shuiyang
Dream of Ding Village - Yan Lianke *c* 644

Simmons, Theophilus
More Church Folk - Michele Andrea Bowen *i* 828

Skywalker, Luke
Vortex - Troy Denning *s* 744

Stanley
My New American Life - Francine Prose *c* 679

Steiner, Nicholas
The Art of Losing - Rebecca Connell *c* 585

Stevenson, Robert
The Exile of Sara Stevenson: A Historical Novel - Darci Hannah *r* 997

Stone, Mason
Missing - Lynette Eason *i* 849

Swift, David
The Omega Theory - Mark Alpert *m* 368

Taro
How to Be an American Housewife - Margaret Dilloway *t* 140

Tubal, Harry
Other People's Money - Justin Cartwright *c* 580

Webster, Peter
Rescue - Anita Shreve *c* 701

Willis, William Sr.
Aunt Dimity and the Family Tree - Nancy Atherton *m* 371

Witney, Thomas
Fourth Day - Zoe Sharp *m* 526

FBI AGENT

Andrews, John
The Dragon Factory - Jonathan Maberry *h* 319

Baldwin, John
The Immortals - J.T. Ellison *m* 428

Dao, Bailey
The Incredible Double - Owen Hill *m* 464

Donaldson, Karl
Hidden Witness - Nick Oldham *m* 508

Rivette, Trevor
Midnight Caller - Leslie Tentler *r* 1117

FIANCE(E)

Alliston, Cedric
When Harry Met Molly - Kieran Kramer *r* 1038

Annie
Deceptions - Rebecca Frayn *m* 439

Baldwin, John
The Immortals - J.T. Ellison *m* 428

Baudelaire, Varik
Blood Law - Jeannie Holmes *h* 305

Bennett, Harrison
The Lightkeeper's Ball - Colleen Coble *i* 836

Cavill, Thomas
The Distant Hours - Kate Morton *c* 658

Christopher
Hope Rekindled - Tracie Peterson *i* 896

Chung, Lin
Dead Man's Chest - Kerry Greenwood *t* 163

Colton, Noah
Deceptions: A Jamestown Novel - Marilyn J. Clay *t* 130

Erica
Operation Prince Charming - Phyllis Bourne *r* 934

Fairbanks, Lady Molly
When Harry Met Molly - Kieran Kramer *r* 1038

Fisher, Saul
Plain Proposal - Beth Wiseman *i* 920

Ford, Dr. Paul
Turbulence - Dana Mentink *i* 885

Grey, Lady Joanna
Seducing the Duchess - Ashley March *r* 1053

Heelis, Will
The Tale of Oat Cake Crag - Susan Wittig Albert *t* 106

James
Katy Carter Wants a Hero - Ruth Saberton *r* 1098

Jarvis, Hero
Where Shadows Dance - C.S. Harris *m* 452

Judges, Samson
Delilah - Sheila M. Gross *i* 859

Julian
Deceptions - Rebecca Frayn *m* 439

Lambert, Maddie
Turbulence - Dana Mentink *i* 885

Landon, Asher
Tennessee Brides - Aaron McCarver *i* 882

Lindsay, James
Emily Hudson - Melissa Jones *t* 184

FUGITIVE

GANG MEMBER

GARDENER

Celestino
The Widower's Tale - Julia Glass　*c* 613

Tolliver, Michael
Mary Ann in Autumn - Armistead Maupin　*c* 650

GENETICALLY ALTERED BEING

Adams, Echo
Close Contact - Katherine Allred　*s* 727

Cricket, Jiminy
The Human Blend - Alan Dean Foster　*s* 752

Whispr
The Human Blend - Alan Dean Foster　*s* 752

GENTLEMAN

Darcy, Fitzwilliam
Mr. Darcy's Obsession - Abigail Reynolds　*t* 231

Quinton, Matthew
Gentleman Captain - J.D. Davies　*t* 134

Smith, William
Jane and the Damned - Janet Mullany　*t* 213

GENTLEWOMAN

Bennett, Elizabeth
Mr. Darcy's Obsession - Abigail Reynolds　*t* 231

GIRL

Auda
Watermark: A Novel of the Middle Ages - Vanitha
　Sankaran　*t* 236

Cohen, Eleonora
The Oracle of Stamboul - Michael David
　Lukas　*m* 487

Devi
Tiger Hills: A Novel - Sarita Mandanna　*t* 200

Dorothy
*The Undead World of Oz: L. Frank Baum's The
　Wonderful Wizard of Oz Complete with Zombies
　and Monsters* - L. Frank Baum　*h* 267

GIRLFRIEND

Arex
Dead Man Walking - Steve Lyons　*s* 777

Bainbridge, Clara
Idaho Brides - Erica Vetsch　*i* 916

Bjorkland, Dr. Astrid
A Heart for Home - Lauraine Snelling　*i* 907

Boysen, Mabel
Big Wheat - Richard Thompson　*m* 541

Carpenter, Meg
Our Tragic Universe - Scarlett Thomas　*c* 704

Carson, Lauren
An Act of Treason - Jack Coughlin　*m* 411

Cheung, Anna
The Battle for Commitment Planet - Graham
　Sharp Paul　*s* 790

Cotswold, Ella
Portobello - Ruth Rendell　*m* 516

D'Arcy, Helen
Murder on the Moor - C.S. Challinor　*m* 395

Ellen
A Taint in the Blood - S.M. Stirling　*f* 91

Hobbs, Chloe
Spun by Sorcery - Barbara Bretton　*r* 938

Kate
Hero - Mike Lupica　*s* 776

Koenen, Effi
Potsdam Station - David Downing　*m* 422

Metcalf, Molly
From Hell with Love - Simon R. Green　*f* 39

Nancy
The Blasphemer - Nigel Farndale　*t* 152

Nightingale, Alexandra
Corpse in Waiting - Margaret Duffy　*m* 423

Osman, Katya
The King of Diamonds - Simon Tolkien　*m* 543

Phoebe
Don't Breathe a Word - Jennifer
　McMahon　*m* 499

Quinn, Cleo
Take a Chance on Me - Jill Mansell　*r* 1052

Renard, Camille
Devious - Lisa Jackson　*m* 471

Thompson, Tina
Eyes of the Innocent - Brad Parks　*m* 513

Tila
The Ragged Man - Tom Lloyd　*f* 59

Toledo, Tita
Free Range Institution - Michael Haskins　*m* 456

Waynest, Shiarra
Hunted by the Others - Jess Haines　*f* 40

Whitman, Lily
Idaho Brides - Erica Vetsch　*i* 916

Williams, Merrin
Horns: A Novel - Joe Hill　*h* 302

Wilson, Esther
This Vacant Paradise - Victoria Patterson　*c* 674

Xavierre
Murder in Passy - Cara Black　*m* 380

GLADIATOR

Stark, James
Sandman Slim - Richard Kadrey　*h* 307

GODFATHER

Morbier
Murder in Passy - Cara Black　*m* 380

GOLFER

Hanks, Tip
Santa Fe Edge - Stuart Woods　*m* 561

GOVERNESS

Bennett, Felicity
The Making of a Gentleman - Shana
　Galen　*r* 982

Gauthier, Grace
One Touch of Scandal - Liz Carlyle　*r* 948

Lambert, Lily
Dreams of Desire - Cheryl Holt　*r* 1008

Slayre, Jane
Jane Slayre - Charlotte Bronte　*h* 276

Temple, Victoria
Sherlock Holmes and the Ghosts of Bly - Donald
　Thomas　*t* 252

GOVERNMENT OFFICIAL

Akitada, Sugawara
The Fires of the Gods - I.J. Parker　*m* 511
The Masuda Affair - I.J. Parker　*t* 223

Bukulu, Abigail
The October Killings - Wessel Ebersohn　*m* 426

Bulyagkov, Alexey
The Russian Affair - Michael Wallner　*m* 550

Hyden, Parker
Buffalo West Wing - Julie Hyzy　*m* 469

Latham, Archibald
India Black - Carol K. Carr　*m* 393

Lenox, Charles
A Stranger in Mayfair - Charles Finch　*t* 153

Pickett, Joe
Cold Wind - C.J. Box　*m* 384

President
A Heartbeat Away - Michael Palmer　*m* 510

GRADUATE

Stockton, Carter
A Great Catch: A Novel - Lorna Seilstad　*i* 902

GRANDDAUGHTER

Alley, Wallis
The Witches on the Road Tonight - Sheri
　Holman　*c* 628

Bakul
An Atlas of Impossible Longing - Anuradha
　Roy　*c* 685

Cheyenne
Wolf Runner - Constance O'Banyon　*r* 1077

Crystal
Ray of Hope - Vanessa Davis Griggs　*r* 995

Emaline
Come Again No More: A Novel - Jack
　Todd　*t* 254

Sahara
Ray of Hope - Vanessa Davis Griggs　*r* 995

Stella
The Sacred White Turkey - Frances
　Washburn　*c* 713

Sue
How to Be an American Housewife - Margaret
　Dilloway　*t* 140

Wilson, Esther
This Vacant Paradise - Victoria Patterson　*c* 674

GRANDFATHER

Amulya
An Atlas of Impossible Longing - Anuradha
　Roy　*c* 685

Glass, Percy
The Widower's Tale - Julia Glass　*c* 613

Kennedy, Andrew
The Blasphemer - Nigel Farndale　*t* 152

Taro
How to Be an American Housewife - Margaret
　Dilloway　*t* 140

GRANDMOTHER

Alley, Cora
The Witches on the Road Tonight - Sheri
　Holman　*c* 628

Chloe
A Twisted Ladder - Rhodi Hawk　*h* 300

Eileen
This Vacant Paradise - Victoria Patterson　*c* 674

Gatlin, Ivy
Wolf Runner - Constance O'Banyon　*r* 1077

Latour, Hazel
The Sacred White Turkey - Frances Washburn *c* 713

MacAdam, Marian
Damaged - Pamela Callow *r* 946

Nichols, Ma Ray
Ray of Hope - Vanessa Davis Griggs *r* 995

GRANDSON
Robert
The Widower's Tale - Julia Glass *c* 613

GUARD
Taki, Renzaburo
The Black Guard - Hideyuki Kikuchi *h* 313

Williams, Kali
The Four Stages of Cruelty - Keith Hollihan *m* 468

GUARDIAN
Desplaines, Catherine
Bound - Antonya Nelson *c* 664

Edward
The Secrets Sisters Keep - Abby Drake *c* 592

Garner, Cade
Deadly Identity - Lindsay McKenna *r* 1062

Kess
Stuff of Legends - Ian Gibson *f* 36

Larue, Mary
The Outlaw's Return - Victoria Bylin *i* 831

Panterra, Carlos
Eat, Prey, Love - Kerrelyn Sparks *r* 1108

Rosalia
Demon Blood - Meljean Brook *r* 941

Tarata, Willow
Tempted by Fate - Kate Perry *r* 1081

Townsend, Joel
Courting Miss Amsel - Kim Vogel Sawyer *i* 901

GUIDE
Stone, Taylor
Book of Days - James L. Rubart *i* 900

GUNFIGHTER
Quinn, J.T.
The Outlaw's Return - Victoria Bylin *i* 831

GYPSY
Paco
A Darker Night - P.J. Brooke *m* 388

HANDICAPPED
Auda
Watermark: A Novel of the Middle Ages - Vanitha Sankaran *t* 236

HANDYMAN
Smith, Max
Licensed for Trouble - Susan May Warren *r* 1129

HEALER
Callia
Entwined - Elisabeth Naughton *r* 1073

Lassair
Music of the Distant Stars - Alys Clare *t* 129

Leesha
The Warded Man - Peter V. Brett *f* 14

Mason, Isabelle
Chains of Fire - Christina Dodd *r* 966

HEIR
Alexander
The Golden Mean: A Novel of Aristotle and Alexander the Great - Annabel Lyon *t* 197

Bertrand, Jude
A Little Bit Wild - Victoria Dahl *r* 959

Bryen
The Uncrowned King - Rowena Cory Daniells *f* 26

Edward
The Queen of Last Hopes: The Story of Margaret of Anjou - Susan Higginbotham *t* 173

Kainam
Weight of Stone - Laura Anne Gilman *f* 38

Ogedai
Khan: Empire of Silver - Conn Iggulden *t* 177

HEIRESS
Bannock, Hazel
Those in Peril - Wilbur Smith *m* 529

Bretton, Elizabeth
Cross Your Heart - Michele Bardsley *r* 931

Mason, Isabelle
Chains of Fire - Christina Dodd *r* 966

Price, Fanny
Murder at Mansfield Park - Lynn Shepherd *t* 240

Spencer, Cleo
To Tempt a Saint - Kate Moore *r* 1070

HERO
Anderson, David
Retribution - Drew Karpyshyn *s* 765

Arlen
The Warded Man - Peter V. Brett *f* 14

Darcy, Fitzwilliam
A Darcy Christmas - Amanda Grange *r* 991

Jack
The A-Men - John Trevillian *s* 810

Jordan "Jordan the Red"
Stuff of Legends - Ian Gibson *f* 36

HEROINE
Bennet, Lizzie
A Darcy Christmas - Amanda Grange *r* 991

Hearne, Telmaine
Lightborn - Alison Sinclair *f* 84

HISTORIAN
Blesh, Rudi
The Ragtime Fool - Larry Karp *t* 186

Churchill, Polly
All Clear - Connie Willis *s* 822

Dalton, Ellie
The Secrets Sisters Keep - Abby Drake *c* 592

Davies, Michael
All Clear - Connie Willis *s* 822

Mr. Dunworthy
All Clear - Connie Willis *s* 822

Ritter, Tennyson
The Wish List - Gabi Stevens *f* 90

Strachey, William
The Gentleman Poet - Kathryn Johnson *r* 1020

Swift, David
The Omega Theory - Mark Alpert *m* 368

Ward, Merope
All Clear - Connie Willis *s* 822

HISTORICAL FIGURE
Artedi, Peter
The Curious Death of Peter Artedi: A Mystery in the History of Science - Theodore W. Pietsch *t* 227

Austen, Jane
Jane and the Damned - Janet Mullany *t* 213

Barbara
The Second Duchess - Elizabeth Loupas *t* 196

Bernhardt, Sarah
The Illusion of Murder - Carol McCleary *m* 495

Bly, Nellie
The Illusion of Murder - Carol McCleary *m* 495

Bonaparte, Napoleon
Victory - Julian Stockwin *t* 250

Booth, John Wilkes
The Second Life of John Wilkes Booth - Barnaby Conrad *t* 131

Butler, Pierce
Tempest at Dawn - James D. Best *t* 119

d'Este, Alfonso
The Second Duchess - Elizabeth Loupas *t* 196

Desbordes-Valmore, Marceline
The Last Rendezvous - Anne Plantagenet *t* 228

Disney, Walt
The Irresistible Henry House - Lisa Grunwald *t* 166

Faulkner, Billy
Murder Your Darlings - J.J. Murphy *m* 504

Freud, Sigmund
A Curable Romantic - Joseph Skibell *t* 243

Helios
Lily of the Nile - Stephanie Dray *t* 147

Henry
Secrets of the Tudor Court: By Royal Decree - Kate Emerson *t* 148

James
Pale Rose of England - Sandra Worth *t* 264

Jefferson, Thomas
Tempest at Dawn - James D. Best *t* 119

Jones, John Paul
For Love of Country - William C. Hammond *t* 169

Lee, Robert E.
The Second Life of John Wilkes Booth - Barnaby Conrad *t* 131

Lennon, John
The Irresistible Henry House - Lisa Grunwald *t* 166

Lincoln, Abraham
Abraham Lincoln: Vampire Hunter - Seth Grahame-Smith *h* 290
The First Assassin - John J. Miller *t* 208

Linnaeus, Carl
The Curious Death of Peter Artedi: A Mystery in the History of Science - Theodore W. Pietsch *t* 227

Madison, James
Tempest at Dawn - James D. Best *t* 119

Parker, Dorothy
Murder Your Darlings - J.J. Murphy *m* 504

Parr, William
Secrets of the Tudor Court: By Royal Decree - Kate Emerson *t* 148

Pinckney, Charles
Tempest at Dawn - James D. Best *t* 119

Plantagenet, Richard
Pale Rose of England - Sandra Worth *t* 264

Romanov, Nikolai
The True Memoirs of Little K - Adrienne Sharp *c* 698

Selene
Lily of the Nile - Stephanie Dray *t* 147

Selous, Frederick
The Illusion of Murder - Carol McCleary *m* 495

Shelley, Mary
Out of the Shadows - Joanne Rendell *t* 230

Sherman, Roger
Tempest at Dawn - James D. Best *t* 119

Spock, Dr. Benjamin
The Irresistible Henry House - Lisa Grunwald *t* 166

Stalin, Josef
Shadow Pass - Sam Eastland *m* 425

Valmore, Prosper
The Last Rendezvous - Anne Plantagenet *t* 228

van Gogh, Vincent
Leaving Van Gogh - Carol Wallace *c* 712

Voltaire
Voltaire's Calligrapher - Pablo De Santis *t* 136

Washington, George
Tempest at Dawn - James D. Best *t* 119

HOCKEY PLAYER

Perry, Adam
Icebreaker - Deirdre Martin *r* 1054

HOMOSEXUAL

Carr, Jeremy
The Next Queen of Heaven - Gregory Maguire *c* 648

Crawford, Tony
Children of the Sun - Max Schaefer *c* 690

Davidson, Jamie
The Perfect Family - Kathryn Shay *r* 1104

Edward
The Secrets Sisters Keep - Abby Drake *c* 592

Ira
The Widower's Tale - Julia Glass *c* 613

James
Children of the Sun - Max Schaefer *c* 690

Lovetree, Queenie
Black Orchid Blues - Persia Walker *m* 549

Martin
The Metropolis Case - Matthew Gallaway *m* 441

Robbie
The Intimates - Ralph Sassone *c* 689

Talbot, Jack-a-Lee
Black Orchid Blues - Persia Walker *m* 549

Vince
Leche - R. Zamora Linmark *c* 645

HORSE TRAINER

Desmond, Val
Something for Nothing - David Anthony *m* 369

Kaine, AJ
Bullet Work - Steve O'Brien *m* 506

HOSTAGE

Chaplain Elysius
Firedrake - Nick Kyme *s* 773

Parker, Earl
Gideon's War - Howard Gordon *m* 444

Prospero
Prospero in Hell - L. Jagi Lamplighter *f* 56

HOTEL OWNER

Begay, Janet
Firewalker - Allyson James *r* 1013

Cady, Rebecca
The Cypress House - Michael Koryta *m* 480

HOUSEKEEPER

Seaton, Anna
The Heir - Grace Burrowes *r* 945

Williams, Ethel
Fall of Giants - Ken Follett *t* 154

HUMAN

Bookchild, Rossamund
Factotum - D.M. Cornish *f* 22

Cara
The Last Hunt - Bruce Coville *f* 23

Earnshaw, Catherine
Wuthering Bites - Sarah Gray *h* 293

Laurence, Theodore "Laurie"
Little Vampire Women - Lynn Messina *h* 328

Taki
The Other Side - Hideyuki Kikuchi *h* 312
The Scarlet Clan - Hideyuki Kikuchi *h* 311

Whelan, Caitlyn
Eat, Prey, Love - Kerrelyn Sparks *r* 1108

Willan, Alexandra
Hungry for You - Lynsay Sands *r* 1100

HUNTER

Arlen "Warded Man" -
The Desert Spear - Peter V. Brett *f* 15

Beloved
The Last Hunt - Bruce Coville *f* 23

Bennet, Elizabeth
Pride and Prejudice and Zombies: Dawn of the Dreadfuls - Steve Hockensmith *h* 303

Europe
Factotum - D.M. Cornish *f* 22

Jardir, Ahmann
The Desert Spear - Peter V. Brett *f* 15

Katherine
Shakespeare Undead - Lori Handeland *h* 297

Kiss, Maxine
A Wild Light - Marjorie M. Liu *f* 58

Lincoln, Abraham
Abraham Lincoln: Vampire Hunter - Seth Grahame-Smith *h* 290

Winters, Adam
Midnight Crystal - Jayne Castle *r* 951

IMMIGRANT

Annamaria
A Heart Most Worthy - Siri Mitchell *i* 886

Binnie
Heaven is High - Kate Wilhelm *m* 557

Celestino
The Widower's Tale - Julia Glass *c* 613

Choimha, Tula
Night Vision - Randy Wayne White *m* 554

Greifinger, Hans
A Call from Jersey - P.F. Kluge *t* 191

Julietta
A Heart Most Worthy - Siri Mitchell *i* 886

Julius
Open City - Teju Cole *c* 583

Luciana
A Heart Most Worthy - Siri Mitchell *i* 886

Lula
My New American Life - Francine Prose *c* 679

Mariam
How to Read the Air - Dinaw Mengestu *c* 655

Pieraro, Miguel
After America - John Birmingham *s* 734

Vitale, Irma
When We Were Strangers - Pamela Schoenewaldt *c* 693

Yosef
How to Read the Air - Dinaw Mengestu *c* 655

INDIAN

Cheyenne
Wolf Runner - Constance O'Banyon *r* 1077

de Margerac/Wachiwi, Marquise
Legacy: A Novel - Danielle Steel *c* 703

Dirk
The Owl Hunt - Richard S. Wheeler *t* 262

Quanah
Comanche Sundown - Jan Reid *t* 229

Sapa, Paha
Black Hills - Dan Simmons *h* 345

Wolf, Waiting
The Owl Hunt - Richard S. Wheeler *t* 262

Wolf Runner
Wolf Runner - Constance O'Banyon *r* 1077

INNKEEPER

Emaline
Crown of Dust - Mary Volmer *c* 710

Maddox, Meredith
Twice Tempted by a Rogue - Tessa Dare *r* 962

INSECT

Maker, Stenwold
Salute the Dark - Adrian Tchaikovsky *f* 98

INSPECTOR

Adams, George
Devoured - D.E. Meredith *t* 207

Kaldis, Andreas
Prey on Patmos - Jeffrey Siger   *m* 527

Stratton, Ted
An Empty Death - Laura Wilson   *m* 558

Swift, Flhi
Demon Strike - Andrew Newbound   *h* 334

Troy, Frederick
A Lily of the Field - John Lawton   *t* 193

INTERIOR DECORATOR

Moreland, Alexandra "Zan"
I'll Walk Alone - Mary Higgins Clark   *m* 400

INVENTOR

Zamenhof, Dr. Ludovik Leyzer
A Curable Romantic - Joseph Skibell   *t* 243

INVESTIGATOR

Barak, Jack
Heartstone - C.J. Sansom   *t* 237

Blackstone, Sam
Blackstone and the Wolf of Wall Street - Sally
    Spencer   *t* 247

Burke, Kellan
Deadly Intent - Kylie Brant   *r* 936

de Furnshill, Baldwin
The Oath - Michael Jecks   *t* 181

Dobbs, Maisie
A Lesson in Secrets - Jacqueline
    Winspear   *m* 559

Gabriella
Bloodborn - Nathan Long   *f* 60

Leduc, Aimee
Murder in Passy - Cara Black   *m* 380

Morgan
Ghost Dance - Rebecca Levene   *s* 775

Puttock, Simon
The Oath - Michael Jecks   *t* 181

Reid, Macy
Deadly Intent - Kylie Brant   *r* 936

Seymour, Sandor
A Dead Man in Malta - Michael Pearce   *t* 224

Shardlake, Matthew
Heartstone - C.J. Sansom   *t* 237

Ulrika
Bloodborn - Nathan Long   *f* 60

Whitlock, Jeremy
Lucky Stiff - Deborah Coonts   *m* 408

JEWELER

Osman, Titus
The King of Diamonds - Simon Tolkien   *m* 543

JOURNALIST

Alley, Wallis
The Witches on the Road Tonight - Sheri
    Holman   *c* 628

Barker, Lois
Goodness Gracious Green - Judy Christie   *r* 952

Bly, Nellie
The Illusion of Murder - Carol McCleary   *m* 495

Cameron, Jade del
The Crocodile's Last Embrace - Suzanne
    Arruda   *t* 109

Desroches, Leo
Fall from Grace - Wayne Arthurson   *m* 370

Endicott, Clara
The Lady of Bolton Hill - Elizabeth
    Camden   *i* 833

Fallon, Siobhan
The Priest - Gerard O'Donovan   *m* 507

Flynn, Stacy
So Much Pretty - Cara Hoffman   *c* 626

Gray, Marissa
Nowhere to Hide - Carlene Thompson   *r* 1120

Hamilton, Jacqueline
Finally a Bride - Vickie McDonough   *i* 883

Hernandez, Tommy
Eyes of the Innocent - Brad Parks   *m* 513

Jones, Abigail
A Cowboy's Touch - Denise Hunter   *i* 866

Lacy, Elizabeth "Lizzy"
The Darling Dahlias and the Cucumber Tree -
    Susan Wittig Albert   *t* 107

Malone, Jack
The Pursuit of Happiness - Douglas
    Kennedy   *c* 635

Mason, Georgia
Feed - Mira Grant   *h* 292

Mason, Shaun
Feed - Mira Grant   *h* 292

Matt
The Home for Broken Hearts - Rowan
    Coleman   *c* 584

Murphy, Mick
Free Range Institution - Michael Haskins   *m* 456

Nina
Hygiene and the Assassin - Amelie
    Nothomb   *c* 665

Price, Lanie
Black Orchid Blues - Persia Walker   *m* 549

Ross, Carter
Eyes of the Innocent - Brad Parks   *m* 513

Russell, John
Potsdam Station - David Downing   *m* 422

Shawna
Mary Ann in Autumn - Armistead Maupin   *c* 650

Spencer, Jake
Love's First Bloom - Delia Parr   *r* 1079

Stockpole, Barry
The Left-Handed Dollar - Loren D.
    Estleman   *m* 431

Turnsole, Ratty
Pock's World - Dave Duncan   *s* 749

Vogel, Hannah
A Night of Long Knives - Rebecca Cantrell   *t* 126

Ward, Susan
The Night Season - Chelsea Cain   *m* 390

JUDGE

Bean, Roy
Roy & Lillie - Loren D. Estleman   *t* 151

Knott, Deborah
Christmas Mourning - Margaret Maron   *m* 492

KIDNAP VICTIM

Anton
A Night of Long Knives - Rebecca Cantrell   *t* 126

Bradley, Martha
Gone - Mo Hayder   *m* 457

Cayla
Those in Peril - Wilbur Smith   *m* 529

Ellen
A Taint in the Blood - S.M. Stirling   *f* 91

Fay
Fadeaway Girl - Martha Grimes   *c* 615

Holt, William
Blackstone and the Wolf of Wall Street - Sally
    Spencer   *t* 247

Leonora
The Sweet Relief of Missing Children - Sarah
    Braunstein   *m* 386

MacLeary, Mac
Next Time You See Me - Katia Lief   *m* 484

Morris, Lyndsay
The Bad Book Affair - Ian Sansom   *m* 524

Reid, Macy
Deadly Intent - Kylie Brant   *r* 936

Reynard, Madeline
Dangerous Desires - Dee Davis   *r* 963

Slavin, Skylar
Lie with Me - Stephanie Tyler   *r* 1124

Solomon, Gilly
Precious and Fragile Things - Megan
    Hart   *r* 998

Sylvie
Bandit Love - Massimo Carlotto   *c* 579

Wilkes, Dawsey
Raider's Heart - Marcia Gruver   *i* 860

KIDNAPPER

Bowman, Walter
I'd Know You Anywhere - Laura Lippman   *c* 646

McRae, Duncan
Raider's Heart - Marcia Gruver   *i* 860

McRae, Hooper
Raider's Heart - Marcia Gruver   *i* 860

Todd
Precious and Fragile Things - Megan
    Hart   *r* 998

KNIGHT

Conrad of Tripoli
The Templar Salvation - Raymond
    Khoury   *m* 477

Daye, October "Toby"
An Artificial Night - Seanan McGuire   *f* 66

de Furnshill, Baldwin
The Oath - Michael Jecks   *t* 181

Flandry, Dominic
Sir Dominic Flandry: The Last Knight of Terra -
    Poul Anderson   *s* 728

Garron
The Valcourt Heiress - Catherine Coulter   *r* 957

Guest, Crispin
The Demon's Parchment - Jeri Westerson   *t* 261

John
The Viking Takes a Knight - Sandra Hill   *r* 1004

Latham, Archibald
India Black - Carol K. Carr   *m* 393

Mappestone, Geoffrey
The Bloodstained Throne - Simon
    Beaufort   *t* 115

Mortimer, Roger
The Oath - Michael Jecks   *t* 181

Bishop, Elizabeth
The More I Owe You: A Novel - Michael
Sledge *t* 244

de Macedo Soares, Lota
The More I Owe You: A Novel - Michael
Sledge *t* 244

LIBRARIAN

Armstrong, Israel
The Bad Book Affair - Ian Sansom *m* 524

Da'Kir
Firedrake - Nick Kyme *s* 773

Esther Hammerhans
Mr. Chartwell - Rebecca Hunt *c* 629

Spencer, Eden
To Win Her Heart - Karen Witemeyer *i* 921

Trenary, Monah
Died in the Wool - Elizabeth Ludwig *i* 877

West, Megan
Luck Be a Lady - Cathie Linz *r* 1044

LIGHTHOUSE KEEPER

Campbell, William
The Exile of Sara Stevenson: A Historical Novel -
Darci Hannah *r* 997

LION

Cowardly Lion
*The Undead World of Oz: L. Frank Baum's The
Wonderful Wizard of Oz Complete with Zombies
and Monsters* - L. Frank Baum *h* 267

LOVER

Bathsheba
Bathsheba: A Novel - Jill Eileen Smith *i* 906

Brooke, Elizabeth "Bess"
Secrets of the Tudor Court: By Royal Decree -
Kate Emerson *t* 148

Bulyagkov, Alexey
The Russian Affair - Michael Wallner *m* 550

Caissie, Charlotte
Chased by Moonlight - Nancy Gideon *r* 985

Cooperon, Grant
A Wild Light - Marjorie M. Liu *f* 58

Coudert, Blanche
For the King - Catherine Delors *t* 138

Covenant, Thomas
Against All Things Ending - Stephen R.
Donaldson *f* 30

Crichton, Thomas
The Exile of Sara Stevenson: A Historical Novel -
Darci Hannah *r* 997

Dafna
Eden - Yael Hedaya *c* 621

Devlin, Brinke
One True Sentence - Craig McDonald *m* 497

Dodge, Bobby
Love You More - Lisa Gardner *m* 442

Drexel, Hart
Heads You Lose - Lisa Lutz *m* 488

Dudley, Robert
Rival to the Queen - Carolly Erickson *t* 149

Duft, Amalia
The Bells - Richard Harvell *t* 170

Edwards, Tia
You're All I Need - Karen White-Owens *r* 1134

Elie
Heidegger's Glasses - Thaisa Frank *c* 606

Errollyn
Tracato - Joel Shepherd *f* 83

Felurian
The Wise Man's Fear - Patrick Rothfuss *m* 520

Fiona
When Harry Met Molly - Kieran Kramer *r* 1038

Freddy
His Christmas Pleasure - Cathy Maxwell *r* 1056

Froben, Moses
The Bells - Richard Harvell *t* 170

Garza, Teresa
What You See in the Dark - Manuel
Munoz *c* 661

Gerhardt
Heidegger's Glasses - Thaisa Frank *c* 606

Jensen, Christophe
You're All I Need - Karen White-Owens *r* 1134

King David
Bathsheba: A Novel - Jill Eileen Smith *i* 906

Kitty
Trespass - Rose Tremain *c* 707

Knollys, Lettice
Rival to the Queen - Carolly Erickson *t* 149

Kschessinska, Mathilde "Little K"
The True Memoirs of Little K - Adrienne
Sharp *c* 698

Latouche, Henri de
The Last Rendezvous - Anne Plantagenet *t* 228

Lydia
The Art of Losing - Rebecca Connell *c* 585

Mark
Eden - Yael Hedaya *c* 621

Masha
Snowdrops - A.D. Miller *c* 656

Mortimer, Roger
The Oath - Michael Jecks *t* 181

Nico
The Chamber of Ten - Christopher Golden *h* 288

Parr, William
Secrets of the Tudor Court: By Royal Decree -
Kate Emerson *t* 148

Perrers, Alice
The King's Mistress: A Novel - Emma
Campion *t* 125

Pierce, Dick
Compass Rose - John Casey *c* 581

Queen Isabella
The Oath - Michael Jecks *t* 181

Raphael
Archangel's Kiss - Nalini Singh *f* 85

Rhodes, David
1022 Evergreen Place - Debbie
Macomber *r* 1049

Rodriguez, Dr. Elizabeth
Immortal Sea - Virginia Kantra *r* 1024

Savoie, Max
Chased by Moonlight - Nancy Gideon *r* 985

Seaton, Victoria
Scandal of the Season - Christie Kelley *r* 1027

Sena
The Last Page - Anthony Huso *f* 47

Steiner, Nicholas
The Art of Losing - Rebecca Connell *c* 585

Stevenson, Sara
The Exile of Sara Stevenson: A Historical Novel -
Darci Hannah *r* 997

Sylvie
Bandit Love - Massimo Carlotto *c* 579

Tasha
The Montmartre Investigation - Claude
Izner *t* 180

Taylor, Nora
All That We Are - Elizabeth Lord *t* 195

Tsazukhina, Anna
The Russian Affair - Michael Wallner *m* 550

Veronica
Trespass - Rose Tremain *c* 707

Warren, Rod
The Melody Girls - Anne Douglas *t* 144

Watson, Dan
What You See in the Dark - Manuel
Munoz *c* 661

MADAM

Barrett, Barb
Cleaning Nabokov's House - Leslie
Daniels *c* 587

Black, India
India Black - Carol K. Carr *m* 393

MAGICIAN

Bernhardt, Sarah
The Illusion of Murder - Carol McCleary *m* 495

Digger
Star Crossed - Elizabeth C. Bunce *f* 17

Dubois, Philip
Dreams of Desire - Cheryl Holt *r* 1008

Kamrasi, Saranith
Cinkarion: The Heart of Fire - J.A. Cullum *f* 24

Selous, Frederick
The Illusion of Murder - Carol McCleary *m* 495

Stoltzfus, Levi
A Gathering of Crows - Brian Keene *h* 309

MAIL ORDER BRIDE

Devonwood, Rainelle
The Unexpected Bride - Debra Ullrick *i* 915

MANAGER

Collins, Maggie
Christmas Eve at Friday Harbor - Lisa
Kleypas *r* 1034

Harris
Night Vision - Randy Wayne White *m* 554

Maplethorpe, Sophie
Simon Says... - Donna Kauffman *r* 1025

Murphy, Kate
Gideon's War - Howard Gordon *m* 444

Paul
You Don't Love This Man: A Novel (P.S.) - Dan
Deweese *m* 418

Sharpe, Lord Jarret
A Hellion in Her Bed - Sabrina Jeffries *r* 1018

MANUFACTURER

Maxwell, Jeremy
The Alarmists - Don Hoesel *i* 865

MATCHMAKER

Calder, Chase
Santa in Montana - Janet Dailey   *r* 960
Ricci, Angelina
The Bite Before Christmas - Heidi Betts   *h* 273
Valentine, Lucy
Deeply, Desperately - Heather Webber   *r* 1131
Woodhouse, Emma
Emma and the Werewolves - Adam Rann   *h* 339

MECHANIC

Kavanaugh, Malcolm "Mal"
Happy Ever After - Nora Roberts   *r* 1093

MENTALLY ILL PERSON

Agnes
The Memory of Love - Aminatta Forna   *c* 602
Clare, John
The Quickening Maze - Adam Foulds   *t* 157
Cole, Elias
The Memory of Love - Aminatta Forna   *c* 602
Duran, Simone
The Good Sister - Drusilla Campbell   *c* 578
General
The Half-Made World - Felix Gilman   *f* 37
Gideon
Secret Place - Leslie J. Sherrod   *i* 903
Henry
The Queen of Last Hopes: The Story of Margaret of Anjou - Susan Higginbotham   *t* 173
Joe
Delirious - Daniel Palmer   *m* 509
Temple, Victoria
Sherlock Holmes and the Ghosts of Bly - Donald Thomas   *t* 252
Tennyson, Septimus
The Quickening Maze - Adam Foulds   *t* 157
van Gogh, Vincent
Leaving Van Gogh - Carol Wallace   *c* 712
Watson, Freddie
The Winter Ghosts - Kate Mosse   *m* 503

MERCENARY

Alatriste, Diego
Pirates of the Levant - Arturo Perez-Reverte   *t* 225
Alatriste, Inigo
Pirates of the Levant - Arturo Perez-Reverte   *t* 225
Cabrillo, Juan
The Jungle - Clive Cussler   *m* 414
Dhulyn
Path of the Sun - Violette Malan   *f* 63
Durand, Christian
Devil at Midnight - Emma Holly   *r* 1006
Lasalle, Guerin de
The Sixth Surrender - Hana Samek Norton   *t* 217
Parno
Path of the Sun - Violette Malan   *f* 63
Santiago, Eddie
Cold Shot to the Heart - Wallace Stroby   *m* 536

MERCHANT

Amulya
An Atlas of Impossible Longing - Anuradha Roy   *c* 685

Archer, James
Seven Nights to Forever - Evangeline Collins   *r* 955
Cohen, Yakob
The Oracle of Stamboul - Michael David Lukas   *m* 487

MIDWIFE

Eckles, Tabitha
Lady in the Mist - Laurie Alice Eakes   *i* 848
Graber, Abigail
Abigail's New Hope - Mary Ellis   *i* 852

MILITARY PERSONNEL

Adam
Adam and Eve: A Novel - Sena Jeter Naslund   *c* 662
Anonymous
Day by Day Armageddon: Beyond Exile - J.L. Bourne   *h* 275
Ballista
King of Kings - Harry Sidebottom   *t* 241
Barclay, Ralph
Blown off Course - David Donachie   *t* 142
Boyle, Billy
Rag and Bone - James R. Benn   *t* 117
Buchevsky, Stephen
Out of the Dark - David Weber   *s* 817
Carr, Laisyn
Veil of Shadows - Shiloh Walker   *r* 1125
Carstairs, Rafe
The Reckless Bride - Stephanie Laurens   *r* 1039
Coxon, John
The Pirate Devlin - Mark Keating   *t* 187
Douchett, Sax
The Homecoming - JoAnn Ross   *r* 1095
Dvorak, Dave
Out of the Dark - David Weber   *s* 817
Eisenhower, Dwight
Rag and Bone - James R. Benn   *t* 117
Eperitus
The Armour of Achilles - Glyn Iliffe   *t* 178
Evanson, Meriwether
An Impartial Witness - Charles Todd   *t* 253
Flandry, Dominic
Sir Dominic Flandry: The Last Knight of Terra - Poul Anderson   *s* 728
Fujita, Sergeant
West and East - Harry Turtledove   *s* 812
Gold, Master Sergeant
The Mullah's Storm - Thomas W. Young   *m* 563
Granger, Cole
Night of the Vampires - Heather Graham   *r* 989
Grayson, Paul
Retribution - Drew Karpyshyn   *s* 765
Hamilton, Johnny
Shadow on the Land - Anne Doughty   *t* 143
Hamilton, Lizzie
Shadow on the Land - Anne Doughty   *t* 143
Harris, Wayson
The Clone Empire - Steven L. Kent   *s* 767
Hayden, Charles
A Battle Won - S. Thomas Russell   *t* 234
Helfort
The Battle for Commitment Planet - Graham Sharp Paul   *s* 790

Holland, Aven
Alaska Weddings - Susan Page Davis   *i* 845
Ironfoot
The Office of Shadow - Matthew Sturges   *f* 94
Jones, John Paul
For Love of Country - William C. Hammond   *t* 169
Kelly, Sam
No Place to Run - Maya Banks   *r* 930
Kennedy, Andrew
The Blasphemer - Nigel Farndale   *t* 152
Kerr, Torin
The Truth of Valor - Tanya Huff   *s* 758
Khan, Kor'sarro
Hunt for Voldorius - Andy Hoare   *s* 757
Kraus, Willi
The Sleepwalkers - Paul Grossman   *m* 448
Kydd, Thomas
Victory - Julian Stockwin   *t* 250
Landon, Allan
Chivalrous Captain, Rebel Mistress - Diane Gaston   *r* 984
Landon, Asher
Tennessee Brides - Aaron McCarver   *i* 882
Laurence, Will
Tongues of Serpents - Naomi Novik   *t* 218
Leary, Daniel
What Distant Deeps - David Drake   *s* 747
Ledger, Joe
The Dragon Factory - Jonathan Maberry   *h* 319
Lee, Robert E.
The Second Life of John Wilkes Booth - Barnaby Conrad   *t* 131
Lewrie, Alan
The Invasion Year - Dewey Lambdin   *t* 192
Lindsay, James
Emily Hudson - Melissa Jones   *t* 184
Longknife, Kris
Kris Longknife: Redoubtable - Mike Shepherd   *s* 804
Lovell, Solomon
The Fort: A Novel of the Revolutionary War - Bernard Cornwell   *t* 133
Lyons, Stephen
Pleasures of a Notorious Gentleman - Lorraine Heath   *r* 1002
Marlowe, Jameson
The Pursuit of Pleasure - Elizabeth Essex   *r* 972
McCormack, Chance
Tempting the Fire - Sydney Croft   *h* 278
McKoy, "Geronimo Joe"
Those Who Dare - Phil Ward   *t* 258
McLaughlin, Alexandria
Ragnarok - Patrick A. Vanner   *s* 815
Michaels, General
The Alarmists - Don Hoesel   *i* 865
Mike
Lipstick in Afghanistan - Roberta Gately   *c* 609
Moberly, Thomas
At the Captain's Command - Louise M. Gouge   *i* 858
Moore, Cameron
Lie with Me - Stephanie Tyler   *r* 1124
Nagorski, Rolan
Shadow Pass - Sam Eastland   *m* 425

Neely, Colton "Cowboy"
Digitalis - Ronie Kendig   *i* 870

Nelson, Horatio
Victory - Julian Stockwin   *t* 250

Nicasio, Thomas
Explosive - Beth Kery   *r* 1033

Niven, David
Those Who Dare - Phil Ward   *t* 258

Odysseus
The Armour of Achilles - Glyn Iliffe   *t* 178

Optika, Stewart
Ragnarok - Patrick A. Vanner   *s* 815

Parson, Michael
The Mullah's Storm - Thomas W. Young   *m* 563

Pasha, Fevzi
An Evil Eye - Jason Goodwin   *m* 443

Pearce, John
Blown off Course - David Donachie   *t* 142

Peterwald, Vicki
Kris Longknife: Redoubtable - Mike Shepherd   *s* 804

Pike, Joe
The Sentry - Robert Crais   *m* 412

Randal, John
Those Who Dare - Phil Ward   *t* 258

Rawson, Daniel
Under Siege - Edward Marston   *t* 203

Reed, Alex
Surrender the Night - Marylu Tyndall   *i* 914

Reston, Sam
Into the Crossfire - Lisa Marie Rice   *r* 1090

Revere, Paul
The Fort: A Novel of the Revolutionary War - Bernard Cornwell   *t* 133

Rictus
Corvus - Paul Kearney   *f* 50

Rook
Dragon Soul - Danielle Bennett   *f* 9

Rook, Charles P.
The First Assassin - John J. Miller   *t* 208

Saltonstall, Dudley
The Fort: A Novel of the Revolutionary War - Bernard Cornwell   *t* 133

Sawyer, Rita
Dark Viking - Sandra Hill   *r* 1005

Scott, Zane
Promises in the Dark - Stephanie Tyler   *r* 1123

Sisko, Benjamin
Rough Beasts of Empire - David R. George III   *s* 753

St. Maur, Rhys
Twice Tempted by a Rogue - Tessa Dare   *r* 962

Strake, Owen
At the Queen's Command - Michael A. Stackpole   *f* 89

Swanson, Kyle
An Act of Treason - Jack Coughlin   *m* 411

Taylor, Mark
Deadly Ties - Vicki Hinze   *i* 864

Thom
Dragon Soul - Danielle Bennett   *f* 9

Tuvok
Seize the Fire - Michael A. Martin   *s* 779

Tyler, Willa Mae
Hearts Persuaded - Joanne Sundell   *r* 1115

Valentine, David
March in Country - E.E. Knight   *s* 769

Walsh, Alistair
West and East - Harry Turtledove   *s* 812

Washington, George
Valley Forge: George Washington and the Crucible of Victory - William R. Forstchen   *t* 155

Weinberg, Chaim
West and East - Harry Turtledove   *s* 812

Wyndham, Jack
Barely a Lady - Eileen Dreyer   *r* 969

Xan
Veil of Shadows - Shiloh Walker   *r* 1125

MINER

Lee, Wing
Take Me Home - Brian Leung   *c* 643

Muuk
Take Me Home - Brian Leung   *c* 643

Williams, Billy
Fall of Giants - Ken Follett   *t* 154

MODEL

Darcy, Shey
She's Gone Country - Jane Porter   *r* 1086

Houston, Seneca
Butterfly - Rochelle Alers   *r* 925

Plesur
Money Shot - Christopher Rowley   *s* 799

MONSTER

Bookchild, Rossamund
Factotum - D.M. Cornish   *f* 22

Frankenstein
Frankenstein's Monster - Susan Heyboer O'Keefe   *c* 666

Spring Heeled Jack
The Strange Affair of Spring Heeled Jack - Mark Hodder   *h* 304

MOTHER

Alden, Missy
Cold Wind - C.J. Box   *m* 384

Alley, Cora
The Witches on the Road Tonight - Sheri Holman   *c* 628

Mrs. Andreas
The Weird Sisters - Eleanor Brown   *c* 576

Annie
Deadly Ties - Vicki Hinze   *i* 864
Deceptions - Rebecca Frayn   *m* 439

April
Pictures of You: A Novel - Caroline Leavitt   *c* 642

Arsenault, Sheila
Rescue - Anita Shreve   *c* 701

Bannock, Hazel
Those in Peril - Wilbur Smith   *m* 529

Barrett, Barb
Cleaning Nabokov's House - Leslie Daniels   *c* 587

Benedict, Eliza
I'd Know You Anywhere - Laura Lippman   *c* 646

Beth
The Last Jewish Virgin: A Novel of Fate - Janice Eidus   *c* 596

Carlson, Lexie
A Dad of His Own - Gail Gaymer Martin   *i* 880

Cavalon, Elsa
Scared to Death - Wendy Corsi Staub   *m* 534

Covington, Barbara
Vicious Cycle - Terri Blackstock   *i* 826

Darcy, Shey
She's Gone Country - Jane Porter   *r* 1086

Davidson, Maggie
The Perfect Family - Kathryn Shay   *r* 1104

Earle, Katie
Torn Apart - Sharon Sala   *r* 1099

Emma
The Forever Queen - Helen Hollick   *t* 176

Estby, Helga
The Daughter's Walk: A Novel - Jane Kirkpatrick   *i* 873

Graham, Grace
Another Dawn - Kathryn Cushman   *i* 841

Hamilton, Emily
Shadow on the Land - Anne Doughty   *t* 143

Hanford, Miranda
When Sparrows Fall: A Novel - Meg Moseley   *i* 889

Harris, Akilah
Eyes of the Innocent - Brad Parks   *m* 513

Hodges, Bailey
Wild Stallion - Delores Fossen   *r* 977

Holland, Cheryl
Alaska Weddings - Susan Page Davis   *i* 845

Jin Li Tam
Antiphon - Ken Scholes   *f* 80

Judy
Sea Change - Jeremy Page   *c* 672

Kei
Manazuru - Hiromi Kawakami   *c* 634

Kroft, Justine
Blood Justice - David Burton   *h* 277

Laurel
Scoundrel in My Dreams - Celeste Bradley   *r* 935

Lydia
The Art of Losing - Rebecca Connell   *c* 585

Maestas, Patricia
The Ringer - Jenny Shank   *c* 695

Mahnaz
A Thousand Rooms of Dream and Fear - Atiq Rahimi   *c* 681

March, Margaret "Marmee"
Little Vampire Women - Lynn Messina   *h* 328

Margaret
The Queen of Last Hopes: The Story of Margaret of Anjou - Susan Higginbotham   *t* 173

Meredith
The Distant Hours - Kate Morton   *c* 658

Misty
Bound - Antonya Nelson   *c* 664

Morath, Penny "Power"
Lady Lazarus: A Novel - Andrew Foster Altschul   *f* 2

Nash, Nina
Unbreakable Bond - Rita Herron   *r* 1003

Pickering, Dawn
Fatal Error - F. Paul Wilson   *h* 364

Quinn, Marin
Scared to Death - Wendy Corsi Staub   *m* 534

Kincaid, Stella
Griselda Takes Flight - Joyce Magnin
Moccero   *i* 887

Linton, Edgar
Wuthering Bites - Sarah Gray   *h* 293

Mrs. Mason
Dead Man's Chest - Kerry Greenwood   *t* 163

McAfee, Mack
1022 Evergreen Place - Debbie
Macomber   *r* 1049

Parween
Lipstick in Afghanistan - Roberta Gately   *c* 609

Mrs. Resnick
The Adults - Alison Espach   *c* 598

Mr. Resnick
The Adults - Alison Espach   *c* 598

Resnick, Mark
The Adults - Alison Espach   *c* 598

Slocum, Ivy
Griselda Takes Flight - Joyce Magnin
Moccero   *i* 887

Tinker
Dead Man's Chest - Kerry Greenwood   *t* 163

NIECE

Abruzzo, Roxy
Our Lady of Immaculate Deception - Nancy
Martin   *m* 493

Alice
Scoop to Kill - Wendy Lyn Watson   *m* 552

Jarrett, Lucy
The Lake of Dreams - Kim Edwards   *c* 595

Julia
The Still Point - Amy Sackville   *c* 688

Osman, Katya
The King of Diamonds - Simon Tolkien   *m* 543

Shugak, Kate
Though Not Dead - Dana Stabenow   *m* 532

Winterbourne, Lily
Frankenstein's Monster - Susan Heyboer
O'Keefe   *c* 666

NOBLEMAN

Alex
Whisper of Scandal - Nicola Cornick   *r* 956

Lord Attenbury
The Attenbury Emeralds - Jill Paton
Walsh   *m* 551

Beaufort, Sebastian
The Duke's Night of Sin - Kathryn Caskie   *r* 950

Lord Blakeney
The Dangerous Viscount - Miranda
Neville   *r* 1075

Burgess, Phillip
Seducing the Duchess - Ashley March   *r* 1053

Carlisle, Rhys
The Unclaimed Duchess - Jenna Petersen   *r* 1083

Cherrett, Dominick
Lady in the Mist - Laurie Alice Eakes   *i* 848

Count Vesna
The Ragged Man - Tom Lloyd   *f* 59

d'Este, Alfonso
The Second Duchess - Elizabeth Loupas   *r* 196

Daudet, Luke
Our Wicked Mistake - Emma Wildes   *r* 1138

de Vasconia, Baron Andres
His Christmas Pleasure - Cathy Maxwell   *r* 1056

de Veres, William
Libertine's Kiss - Judith James   *r* 1015

Dunbury, Lord Avery
The Crocodile's Last Embrace - Suzanne
Arruda   *t* 109

Forsythe, Adrian
One Touch of Scandal - Liz Carlyle   *r* 948

Greyson, Devlin
Secrets of the Heart - Jillian Kent   *i* 871

Hepburn, Michael
His Sinful Secret - Emma Wildes   *r* 1136

Hitler, Harry Krupp I
Chronolysis - Michel Jeury   *s* 762

Huntington, Lazarus
Wicked Intentions - Elizabeth Hoyt   *r* 1010

Jones, Alexander
To Tempt a Saint - Kate Moore   *r* 1070

Kilburn, Rohan
My Dangerous Duke - Gaelen Foley   *r* 976

MacAlpin, Cormac
Devil's Highlander - Veronica Wolff   *r* 1142

Middleton, John
Dreams of Desire - Cheryl Holt   *r* 1008

Neville, Richard
The Virgin Widow - Anne O'Brien   *t* 219

O'Connor, Declan
The Year of Living Scandalously - Julia
London   *r* 1045

O'Lochlainn, Ardal
Eye of the Law - Cora Harrison   *m* 453

Pennistan, David
Courtesan's Kiss - Mary Blayney   *r* 933

Plantagenet, Richard
Pale Rose of England - Sandra Worth   *t* 264

Prince Vlad
Much Fall of Blood - Dave Freer   *f* 35

Redgrave, John "Jack"
Scoundrel in My Dreams - Celeste
Bradley   *r* 935

Sebastian
The Dangerous Viscount - Miranda
Neville   *r* 1075

St. James, Alexander
My Lord Scandal - Emma Wildes   *r* 1137

St. John, Nicholas
Ten Ways to Be Adored When Landing a Lord -
Sarah MacLean   *r* 1048

Staunton, Nicholas
Dukes to the Left of Me, Princes to the Right -
Kieran Kramer   *r* 1037

Trent, David
Major Lord David - Sherry Lynn
Ferguson   *r* 975

Trevalyan, Max
Peril at Somner House - Joanna Challis   *t* 127

Wellingham, Taris
One Unashamed Night - Sophia James   *r* 1016

Westfield, Lord Anthony "Viscount Somerton"
Scandal of the Season - Christie Kelley   *r* 1027

Windham, Gayle
The Heir - Grace Burrowes   *r* 945

Winslow, David
Miss Foster's Folly - Alice Gaines   *r* 981

Wyckerly, John Fitzhugh "Fitz"
The Wicked Wyckerly - Patricia Rice   *r* 1091

NOBLEWOMAN

Barbara
The Second Duchess - Elizabeth Loupas   *t* 196

Batholdy, Elizabeth
Much Fall of Blood - Dave Freer   *f* 35

Bathory, Erzsebet
The Countess - Rebecca Johns   *t* 183

Bessingham, Katherine
Devoured - D.E. Meredith   *t* 207

Boscastle, Lily
A Duke's Temptation - Jillian Hunter   *r* 1011

Brooke, Elizabeth "Bess"
Secrets of the Tudor Court: By Royal Decree -
Kate Emerson   *t* 148

Burgess, Charlotte
Seducing the Duchess - Ashley March   *r* 1053

Burgh, Elyne de "Ellie"
The Hawk - Monica McCarty   *r* 1058

Carlow, Honoria
The Smuggler and the Society Bride - Julia
Justiss   *r* 1023

Danvers, Anne
The Unclaimed Duchess - Jenna Petersen   *r* 1083

Eleanor of Aquitaine
*The Captive Queen: A Novel of Eleanor of Aquita-
ine* - Alison Weir   *t* 259

Fanshawe, Diana
The Dangerous Viscount - Miranda
Neville   *r* 1075

Fitzherbert, Maud
Fall of Giants - Ken Follett   *t* 154

Fraser, Mavis
Captured by Desire - Kira Morgan   *r* 1072

Hargreaves, Emily
Dangerous to Know - Tasha Alexander   *t* 108

Harriman, Elinor
Ruthless - Anne Stuart   *r* 1113

Hathaway, Amelia
My Lord Scandal - Emma Wildes   *r* 1137

Knyvett, Helena
Bedding the Enemy - Mary Wine   *r* 1141

Lady Adriane
The Lunatic, the Lover, and the Poet - Myrlin A.
Hermes   *t* 171

Li, Ai
Butterfly Swords - Jeannie Lin   *r* 1043

Lindsey, Bea
The Tutor - Hope Tarr   *r* 1116

Ponsley, Zephyr
Rules of an Engagement - Suzanne Enoch   *r* 971

Rannoch, Georgiana "Georgie"
Royal Blood - Rhys Bowen   *t* 121

Ravenscliffe, Elena
The Surrender of a Lady - Tiffany Clare   *r* 954

Rebecca
A Season of Seduction - Jennifer
Haymore   *r* 1001

Ryland de Silva, Annie
Cross Roads - Fern Michaels   *r* 1066

Seaborn, Jane
Those Who Dare - Phil Ward   *t* 258

Sinclair, Lady Siusan
The Duke's Night of Sin - Kathryn Caskie   *r* 950

Sophia
Till Dawn with the Devil - Alexandra
   Hawkins   *r* 1000
Townsend, Isabel
Ten Ways to Be Adored When Landing a Lord -
   Sarah MacLean   *r* 1048
Whittington, Madeline
Secrets of the Heart - Jillian Kent   *i* 871
York, Marisa
A Little Bit Wild - Victoria Dahl   *r* 959

NOMAD

Martin
Black and Orange - Benjamin Kane
   Ethridge   *h* 280
Teresa
Black and Orange - Benjamin Kane
   Ethridge   *h* 280

NURSE

Crawford, Bess
An Impartial Witness - Charles Todd   *t* 253
Dawson, Mercy
Pleasures of a Notorious Gentleman - Lorraine
   Heath   *r* 1002
Dobbs, Maisie
A Lesson in Secrets - Jacqueline
   Winspear   *m* 559
Fields, Lorenna
Unexpected Love - Andrea Boeshaar   *i* 827
Hamilton, Jane
Shadow on the Land - Anne Doughty   *t* 143
Klein, Emily
House Arrest - Ellen Meeropol   *c* 654
Lydia
God on the Rocks - Jane Gardam   *t* 160
Murphy, Elsa
Lipstick in Afghanistan - Roberta Gately   *c* 609

OBJECT

Lobo
Children No More - Mark L. Van Name   *s* 814
Jump Gate Twist - Mark L. Van Name   *s* 813

ORGANIZED CRIME FIGURE

Ballista, Joseph
The Left-Handed Dollar - Loren D.
   Estleman   *m* 431
Borelli, Immacolata
The Collaborator - Gerald Seymour   *m* 525

ORPHAN

Bookchild, Rossamund
Factotum - D.M. Cornish   *f* 22
Daniel
Daniel - Henning Mankell   *t* 201
Digger
Star Crossed - Elizabeth C. Bunce   *f* 17
Hawksmith, Elizabeth Anne
The Witch's Daughter - Paula Brackston   *t* 122
Heathcliff
Wuthering Bites - Sarah Gray   *h* 293
House, Henry
The Irresistible Henry House - Lisa
   Grunwald   *t* 166

Hudson, Emily
Emily Hudson - Melissa Jones   *t* 184
Jasper
The Witches on the Road Tonight - Sheri
   Holman   *c* 628
Kate
Plain Kate - Erin Bow   *f* 12
Kvothe
The Wise Man's Fear - Patrick Rothfuss   *m* 520
Magpie
Intrigues - Mercedes Lackey   *f* 54
Maria
The Metropolis Case - Matthew
   Gallaway   *m* 441
Mukunda
An Atlas of Impossible Longing - Anuradha
   Roy   *c* 685
Slayre, Jane
Jane Slayre - Charlotte Bronte   *h* 276
Sommers, Dr. Rain
Midnight Caller - Leslie Tentler   *r* 1117
Tucker, Jack
The Demon's Parchment - Jeri Westerson   *t* 261

OUTCAST

Kate
Plain Kate - Erin Bow   *f* 12
Perrish, Ignatius
Horns: A Novel - Joe Hill   *h* 302
Shale
Stormlord Rising - Glenda Larke   *f* 57

OVERSEER

Cantor, Bucky
Nemesis - Philip Roth   *c* 684
Dupre, Eli
Afterlight - Elle Jasper   *h* 306
Great Bear
The Waters Rising - Sheri S. Tepper   *s* 808
Precious Wind
The Waters Rising - Sheri S. Tepper   *s* 808
Soreson, Gunthar
Dead Man Walking - Steve Lyons   *s* 777

PASSENGER

Juhel
The Bloodstained Throne - Simon
   Beaufort   *t* 115
Paisnel
The Bloodstained Throne - Simon
   Beaufort   *t* 115
Philippa
The Bloodstained Throne - Simon
   Beaufort   *t* 115
Vitalis
The Bloodstained Throne - Simon
   Beaufort   *t* 115

PATIENT

Mr. Blackeyes
Unexpected Love - Andrea Boeshaar   *i* 827
Woodson, Brooke
Broken Wings: A Novel - Carla Stewart   *i* 909

PHILOSOPHER

Aristotle
*The Golden Mean: A Novel of Aristotle and Alex-
   ander the Great* - Annabel Lyon   *t* 197
Finkler, Sam
The Finkler Question - Howard Jacobson   *c* 630
Voltaire
Voltaire's Calligrapher - Pablo De Santis   *t* 136

PHOTOGRAPHER

Bradshaw, Lucy
A Vision of Lucy - Margaret Brownley   *i* 829
Dakota, Cameron "Cam"
The Perfect Shot - Gemma Halliday   *r* 996
Kendra
Moxyland - Lauren Beukes   *s* 733

PHOTOJOURNALIST

Khemiri, Abbas
Montecore: The Silence of the Tiger - Jonas Has-
   sen Khemiri   *c* 637
Williford, Jason
The Illumination - Kevin Brockmeier   *c* 575

PILOT

Anderson, Martin
Something for Nothing - David Anthony   *m* 369
Cliff
Griselda Takes Flight - Joyce Magnin
   Moccero   *i* 887
Gesling, Paul
Back to the Moon - Les Johnson   *s* 763
Gilbert, Nick
Blood Covenant - Lisa Harris   *i* 861
Idylle, Ari
Enemy Within - Marcella Burnard   *s* 740
Miller, Brady
Animal Magnetism - Jill Shalvis   *r* 1103
Mirren, Ralph
Engineman - Eric Brown   *s* 737
Seaghdh, Cullin
Enemy Within - Marcella Burnard   *s* 740

PIRATE

Alatriste, Diego
Pirates of the Levant - Arturo
   Perez-Reverte   *t* 225
Alatriste, Inigo
Pirates of the Levant - Arturo
   Perez-Reverte   *t* 225
Devlin, Patrick
The Pirate Devlin - Mark Keating   *t* 187
Hainey, Croggon
Clementine - Cherie Priest   *s* 791
Yasin, Ali
Shadow Force - Matt Lynn   *m* 489

PLANNER

Brown, Parker "Legs"
Happy Ever After - Nora Roberts   *r* 1093
Patton, Hayley
Mobbed - Carol Higgins Clark   *m* 398
Radcliffe, Andi
Sex on the Slopes - Susan Lyons   *r* 1046

Wilde, Jaclyn
Veil of Night - Linda Howard   *r* 1009

POLICE OFFICER

Akehurst, Sam
The Age of Zeus - James Lovegrove   *f* 61

Bannerman, Ralph
Echoes of the Dead - Sally Spencer   *m* 530

Baxter, George
Echoes of the Dead - Sally Spencer   *m* 530

Blessing, Mildred
Griselda Takes Flight - Joyce Magnin
   Moccero   *i* 887

Bloodhound, Larry
Tourquai - Tim Davys   *m* 417

Breck, Jamie
The Complaints - Ian Rankin   *m* 515

Brockman, Mike
Died in the Wool - Elizabeth Ludwig   *i* 877

Bryant, Dwight
Christmas Mourning - Margaret Maron   *m* 492

Carter, Jack
Brain Box Blues - Cris Ramsay   *s* 793
Substitution Method - Cris Ramsay   *s* 794

Cassato, Tony
Antiques Knock-Off - Barbara Allan   *m* 366

Cato, Jack
Bones of Empire - William C. Dietz   *s* 745

Chung, Lin
Dead Man's Chest - Kerry Greenwood   *t* 163

Connelly, Rebecca
Free Range Institution - Michael Haskins   *m* 456

Conway, Kara
The Homecoming - JoAnn Ross   *r* 1095

Davis, Maggie
Idaho Brides - Erica Vetsch   *i* 916

Dawson, Abby
Bound by Guilt - C.J. Darlington   *i* 844

Drake, Boone
The Brotherhood - Jerry B. Jenkins   *i* 868

Farrell
The Highly Effective Detective Crosses the Line -
   Richard Yancey   *m* 562

Fouche
For the King - Catherine Delors   *t* 138

Gloom
Demon Strike - Andrew Newbound   *h* 334

Hennessey, Kevin
The Wild Irish Sea - Loucinda McGary   *r* 1061

Hood, Charlie
The Border Lords - T. Jefferson Parker   *m* 512

Houston, Val
Devious - Lisa Jackson   *m* 471

Hunter, Ellis
Deadly Threads - Jane K. Cleland   *m* 402

Jackson, Taylor
The Immortals - J.T. Ellison   *m* 428

Jones, Nash
Firewalker - Allyson James   *r* 1013

Kella, Ben
Devil-Devil - Graeme Kent   *m* 475

Kenyon, Kit
A Killer Among Us: A Novel - Lynette
   Eason   *i* 850

Kenyon, Marc
Profile for Seduction - Karen Whiddon   *r* 1133

Leoni, Tessa
Love You More - Lisa Gardner   *m* 442

Lourens, Leon
The October Killings - Wessel Ebersohn   *m* 426

Lysander
Still Waters - Marilyn Todd   *t* 255

MacDonald, Fiona
The Keepers - Heather Graham   *r* 990

MacKenzie, Luke
Spun by Sorcery - Barbara Bretton   *r* 938

Mancuso, Rafe
Love Me if You Dare - Carly Phillips   *r* 1084

McCrea, Eric
One Was a Soldier - Julia
   Spencer-Fleming   *m* 531

Miquel, Roch
For the King - Catherine Delors   *t* 138

Morbier
Murder in Passy - Cara Black   *m* 380

Morgan, Russ
Behind the Badge - Susan Sleeman   *i* 905

Napier, Royden
One Touch of Scandal - Liz Carlyle   *r* 948

O'Fallon, Ed
The Ringer - Jenny Shank   *c* 695

Patel, David
Stolen Lives - Jassy MacKenzie   *m* 490

Pavlik, Jake
A Cup of Jo - Sandra Balzo   *m* 373

Rios, Sara
Love Me if You Dare - Carly Phillips   *r* 1084

Rizzo, Joe
Rizzo's Fire - Lou Manfredo   *m* 491

Shannon, Max
Bonds of Justice - Nalini Singh   *f* 86

Stathos, Nick
Code Triage - Candace Calvert   *r* 947

Stiffeniis, Hanno
Unholy Awakening - Michael Gregorio   *m* 446

Sullivan, Daniel
Bless the Bride - Rhys Bowen   *m* 383

Tucker, Sydney
Behind the Badge - Susan Sleeman   *i* 905

Van Alstyne, Russ
One Was a Soldier - Julia
   Spencer-Fleming   *m* 531

Williams, Warren
Chosen - Jeanne C. Stein   *h* 348

Yell
Demon Strike - Andrew Newbound   *h* 334

POLITICAL FIGURE

Achilles
Betrayer of Worlds - Larry Niven   *s* 786

Arkin, Viktor
The Jewel of St. Petersburg - Kate
   Furnivall   *t* 159

Byers, Windy
Eyes of the Innocent - Brad Parks   *m* 513

Churchill, Winston
Mr. Chartwell - Rebecca Hunt   *c* 629

de Saint-Martin, Paul
False Patriots - Charles O'Brien   *t* 220

Dewar, Gus
Fall of Giants - Ken Follett   *t* 154

Fimble, Athena
Pock's World - Dave Duncan   *s* 749

Morris
Tears of the Mountain - John Addiego   *t* 105

Pericles
The Pericles Commission - Gary Corby   *t* 132

Romanov, Nikolai
The True Memoirs of Little K - Adrienne
   Sharp   *c* 698

Ryman, Peter
Feed - Mira Grant   *h* 292

Secundus, Plinius "Pliny"
Roman Games - Bruce Macbain   *t* 198

Sinclair, Alex
Save the Date - Jenny B. Jones   *i* 869

Washington, George
*Valley Forge: George Washington and the Crucible
   of Victory* - William R. Forstchen   *t* 155

PORNOGRAPHER

Harris
Night Vision - Randy Wayne White   *m* 554

POSTAL WORKER

Fernie, Lorna
The Melody Girls - Anne Douglas   *t* 144

PREGNANT TEENAGER

Jones, Diana
The Neighbors Are Watching - Debra
   Ginsberg   *c* 612

Jordan
Vicious Cycle - Terri Blackstock   *i* 826

PRISONER

Ambrosius, Morlock
The Wolf Age - James Enge   *f* 32

Bowman, Walter
I'd Know You Anywhere - Laura Lippman   *c* 646

Friemel, Rudi
The Wedding in Auschwitz - Erich Hackl   *t* 167

Harcourt, Armand
The Making of a Gentleman - Shana
   Galen   *r* 982

Helios
Lily of the Nile - Stephanie Dray   *t* 147
Lily of the Nile - Stephanie Dray   *t* 147

Rayburn, Eva
Senseless - Mary Burton   *m* 389

Rhodes, Griffin
A Heartbeat Away - Michael Palmer   *m* 510

Rokhlenu
The Wolf Age - James Enge   *f* 32

Selene
Lily of the Nile - Stephanie Dray   *t* 147

Swain, David
The King of Diamonds - Simon Tolkien   *m* 543

Worthy, Lilith
The Crocodile's Last Embrace - Suzanne
   Arruda   *t* 109

PRODUCER

Baird, Emilio
Home Again - Mariah Stewart   *r* 1110

Benjamin, Artie
Shortcut Man - P.G. Sturges   *m* 537

Heat, Max
Boiling Point - K.L. Dionne   *m* 419

Treslove, Julian
The Finkler Question - Howard Jacobson   *c* 630

PROFESSOR

Andreas, Dr. James
The Weird Sisters - Eleanor Brown   *c* 576

Applewood, Elijah
Tears of the Mountain - John Addiego   *t* 105

Bergeron, Alison
Third Degree - Maggie Barbieri   *m* 374

Binder, Paul
The Seraph Seal - Leonard Sweet   *i* 912

Eriksen, Blue
Other Eyes - Barbara D'Amato   *m* 415

Fitzgerald, Clara
Out of the Shadows - Joanne Rendell   *t* 230

Henri, Marc
Legacy: A Novel - Danielle Steel   *c* 703

Ibraham, Hani
Absolute Risk - Steven Gore   *m* 445

Jameson, Maria
Becoming George Sand - Rosalind
   Brackenbury   *c* 574

Jaynes, Chris
Pym - Mat Johnson   *c* 633

Mara
Eye of the Law - Cora Harrison   *m* 453

Murphy, Charlie
This Vacant Paradise - Victoria Patterson   *c* 674

Richards, Jameson
The Alarmists - Don Hoesel   *i* 865

Ritter, Ian
Esperanza - Trish J. MacGregor   *h* 322

Steiner, Nicholas
The Art of Losing - Rebecca Connell   *c* 585

Zahed, Mansoor
The Templar Salvation - Raymond
   Khoury   *m* 477

PROSTITUTE

Ama
On Black Sisters Street - Chika Unigwe   *c* 708

Black, India
India Black - Carol K. Carr   *m* 393

Crampton, Ava
Indulgence in Death - J.D. Robb   *s* 796

Efe
On Black Sisters Street - Chika Unigwe   *c* 708

Hammond, Kim
Trail of Blood - Lisa Black   *m* 381

Jordaan, Pamela
Stolen Lives - Jassy MacKenzie   *m* 490

Joyce
On Black Sisters Street - Chika Unigwe   *c* 708

Marlowe, Rose
Seven Nights to Forever - Evangeline
   Collins   *r* 955

Ravenscliffe, Elena
The Surrender of a Lady - Tiffany Clare   *r* 954

Sisi
On Black Sisters Street - Chika Unigwe   *c* 708

PSYCHIC

Alex
Ghost Dance - Rebecca Levene   *s* 775

Braden, Nicholas
Touching Darkness - Jaime Rush   *h* 341

Brooks, Cassandra
The Diviner's Tale - Bradford Morrow   *m* 501

Cutler, Madeira
Death by Diamonds - Annette Blair   *f* 11

Davidson, Charlotte "Charley"
First Grave on the Right - Darynda Jones   *m* 473

Doyle, Harry
The Dead Detective - William Heffernan   *m* 459

Faa, Samuel
Chains of Fire - Christina Dodd   *r* 966

Fern, Clarity "Clare"
Clarity - Kim Harrington   *m* 451

Gavin of Durness
A Storm of Pleasure - Terri Brisbin   *r* 939

Ghetti, Francesca
Confessions of a Vampire's Girlfriend - Katie
   MacAlister   *h* 321
In the Company of Vampires - Katie
   MacAlister   *h* 320

Grey, Miranda
Queen of Shadows - Dianne Sylvan   *h* 353

Hepburn, Gavin
A Bewitching Bride - Elizabeth Thornton   *r* 1122

Jones, Marlowe
Midnight Crystal - Jayne Castle   *r* 951

Malarra, Alannah
Demon Strike - Andrew Newbound   *h* 334
Ghoul Strike! - Andrew Newbound   *h* 333

Marlowe, Pru
Dogs Don't Lie - Clea Simon   *m* 528

Nico
The Chamber of Ten - Christopher Golden   *h* 288

Sapa, Paha
Black Hills - Dan Simmons   *h* 345

Shepard, Lori
Aunt Dimity and the Family Tree - Nancy
   Atherton   *m* 371

Thanquol
Temple of the Serpent - C.L. Werner   *f* 101

Valentine, Lucy
Deeply, Desperately - Heather Webber   *r* 1131

Wagner, Arlen
The Cypress House - Michael Koryta   *m* 480

PSYCHOLOGIST

Alverhuysen, Dr. Liv
The Half-Made World - Felix Gilman   *f* 37

Chapman, Kelly
The Fourth Victim - Tara Taylor Quinn   *r* 1087

Dobbs, Maisie
A Lesson in Secrets - Jacqueline
   Winspear   *m* 559

Freud, Sigmund
A Curable Romantic - Joseph Skibell   *t* 243

Le Gall, Dr. Thomas
Enough About Love - Herve Le Tellier   *c* 641

LeBlanc, Dr. Madeleine
A Twisted Ladder - Rhodi Hawk   *h* 300

Liebermann, Max
Vienna Twilight - Frank Tallis   *m* 538

Lockheart, Adrian
The Memory of Love - Aminatta Forna   *c* 602

MacArthur, Norah
Worth the Trip - Penny McCall   *r* 1057

Sommers, Dr. Rain
Midnight Caller - Leslie Tentler   *r* 1117

PUBLIC RELATIONS

O'Toole, Lucky
Lucky Stiff - Deborah Coonts   *m* 408

PUBLISHER

Morris
Sunset Park - Paul Auster   *c* 569

QUAKER

Clement, Levi
Hearts Persuaded - Joanne Sundell   *r* 1115

RADIO PERSONALITY

Sommers, Dr. Rain
Midnight Caller - Leslie Tentler   *r* 1117

RAILROAD WORKER

Runyon, Hook
The Insane Train - Sheldon Russell   *m* 522

RAKE

Cates, Brandon
Wicked Surrender - Jade Lee   *r* 1040

MacLachlann, Quintus
Highland Rogue, London Miss - Margaret
   Moore   *r* 1071

Rohan, Adrian Alistair
Reckless - Anne Stuart   *r* 1114

Rohan, Viscount
Ruthless - Anne Stuart   *r* 1113

RANCHER

Bennett, Jake
Faith's Reward - Tammy Barley   *i* 825

Bennett, Jessica
Faith's Reward - Tammy Barley   *i* 825

Callahan, Will
Megan's Hero - Sharon Gillenwater   *i* 856

Kincaid, Jace
When All My Dreams Come True - Janelle
   Mowery   *i* 891

Linscott, Tom
Sharpshooter in Petticoats - Mary
   Connealy   *i* 839

Malone, Jackson
Wild Stallion - Delores Fossen   *r* 977

McCutcheon, Luke
Montana Dawn - Caroline Fyffe   *r* 979

McIntyre, Bobbie
When All My Dreams Come True - Janelle
   Mowery   *i* 891

Paint, Eli
Come Again No More: A Novel - Jack
   Todd   *t* 254

Pieraro, Miguel
After America - John Birmingham   *s* 734

Raines, Jackson
Against the Wind - Kat Martin   *r* 1055

Wainwright, Cord
A Heart Divided: A Novel - Kathleen Morgan   *i* 888

REAL ESTATE AGENT

Thompson, Michael
Delivered with Love - Sherry Kyle   *i* 874

Trusts, William
Delilah - Sheila M. Gross   *i* 859

REANIMATED DEAD

Fawkes, Samuel
The Silent Army - James Knapp   *s* 768

Porter, Jessica "Jessie" Anne
Dust - Joan Frances Turner   *h* 359

Richter, Matt
Nekropolis - Tim Waggoner   *h* 360

REBEL

McConnell, Cal
Idaho Brides - Erica Vetsch   *i* 916

RECLUSE

Leary, Gabe
Somewhere Along the Way - Jodi Thomas   *r* 1118

Wren, Eugene
Portobello - Ruth Rendell   *m* 516

REFUGEE

Mahault
Weight of Stone - Laura Anne Gilman   *f* 38

RELATIVE

Arlene
Emily, Alone - Stewart O'Nan   *c* 667

Great Khan
Naamah's Curse - Jacqueline Carey   *f* 19

Hanford, Jack
When Sparrows Fall: A Novel - Meg Moseley   *i* 889

Kerr, Marjory
Mine Is the Night - Liz Curtis Higgs   *i* 862

Tomei, Giulietta
Juliet - Anne Fortier   *t* 156

RELIGIOUS

Abuzeid, Waheeba
Lyrics Alley - Leila Aboulela   *t* 104

Archer, Michael
Journey to Riverbend - Henry McLaughlin   *i* 884

Bronwyn
The Sister Wife - Diane Noble   *t* 216

Brothers, Thomas
The God of the Hive - Laurie R. King   *t* 188

Brown, Amanda
The Headhunter's Daughter - Tamar Myers   *m* 505

Burroughs, George
Deliverance from Evil - Frances Hill   *c* 624

Chandler, Mason
When Sparrows Fall: A Novel - Meg Moseley   *i* 889

Chapman, Jody
Finally a Bride - Vickie McDonough   *i* 883

Charnais, Juliana de
The Sixth Surrender - Hana Samek Norton   *t* 217

Choimha, Tula
Night Vision - Randy Wayne White   *m* 554

Collins, Thomas
Free Range Institution - Michael Haskins   *m* 456

Conchita
Devil-Devil - Graeme Kent   *m* 475

Edsel, Father
The Zombies of Lake Woebegotten - Harrison Geillor   *h* 287

Eleanor
Valley of Dry Bones - Priscilla Royal   *t* 233

Falcone, Giulia
Force of Habit - Alice Loweecey   *m* 486

Farnsworth, Mary
Lethal Lineage - Charlotte Hinger   *m* 465

Father Andre
Pock's World - Dave Duncan   *s* 749

Fergusson, Clare
One Was a Soldier - Julia Spencer-Fleming   *m* 531

Fidelma, Sister
The Dove of Death - Peter Tremayne   *t* 256

Gabriel
The Sister Wife - Diane Noble   *t* 216

Hansen, Danny
The Priest's Graveyard - Ted Dekker   *i* 847

Hartlinger, Kim
Found in Translation: An Unforgettable Mission Trip Where Faith, Obedience, and Forgiveness Intersect - Roger Bruner   *i* 830

Iliona
Still Waters - Marilyn Todd   *t* 255

Inkfist, Daniel
The Zombies of Lake Woebegotten - Harrison Geillor   *h* 287

Ischi, Fernand
A Jew Must Die - Jacques Chessex   *t* 128

Jackson, Baxter
Deceit - Brandilyn Collins   *i* 838

Jacob
The Demon's Parchment - Jeri Westerson   *t* 261

Josef
Wolf's Cross - S.A. Swann   *h* 352

Judges, Samson
Delilah - Sheila M. Gross   *i* 859

Knudsen, Bob
Devil's Food Cake Murder - Joanne Fluke   *m* 437

Larue, Mary
The Outlaw's Return - Victoria Bylin   *i* 831

Laurence
Romeo and Juliet and Vampires - Claudia Gabel   *h* 284

Leslie, Charles
Corrag - Susan Fletcher   *c* 601

Mary Rose
The Sister Wife - Diane Noble   *t* 216

O'Brien, Aiden
I'll Walk Alone - Mary Higgins Clark   *m* 400

Petey
In Every Heartbeat - Kim Vogel Sawyer   *t* 238

Renard, Camille
Devious - Lisa Jackson   *m* 471

Richelieu
The Cardinal's Blades - Pierre Pevel   *f* 76

Scales, Leontina
The Next Queen of Heaven - Gregory Maguire   *c* 648

Shifrin, Ryan
The Illumination - Kevin Brockmeier   *c* 575

Sibeal
Seer of Sevenwaters - Juliet Marillier   *t* 202

Simmons, Theophilus
More Church Folk - Michele Andrea Bowen   *i* 828

Talesbury, Bishop
Lethal Lineage - Charlotte Hinger   *m* 465

Tate, Eddie
More Church Folk - Michele Andrea Bowen   *i* 828

Thomas
Valley of Dry Bones - Priscilla Royal   *t* 233

Walters, Matthew
Devil's Food Cake Murder - Joanne Fluke   *m* 437

Ward, Georginea "Sister Georgia"
Stranger Here Below - Joyce Hinnefeld   *t* 174

REPAIRMAN

Jack
Fatal Error - F. Paul Wilson   *h* 364

RESCUER

Hunter, James
A Rake by Midnight - Gail Ranstrom   *r* 1088

Littlemore, Dr. Lydia
The Evolution of Bruno Littlemore - Benjamin Hale   *c* 617

Mills, Logan
Tempting the Fire - Sydney Croft   *h* 278

Summerfield, Griffin
The Surrender of a Lady - Tiffany Clare   *r* 954

RESEARCHER

Brockton, Dr. Bill
The Bone Yard - Jefferson Bass   *m* 375

Fitzgerald, Clara
Out of the Shadows - Joanne Rendell   *t* 230

Gaddis, Sam
The Trinity Six - Charles Cumming   *m* 413

Kennedy, Sheila
Boiling Point - K.L. Dionne   *m* 419

Littlemore, Dr. Lydia
The Evolution of Bruno Littlemore - Benjamin Hale   *c* 617

McNeil, Dr. Brock
Over the Edge - Brandilyn Collins   *i* 837

Richards, Jameson
The Alarmists - Don Hoesel   *i* 865

St. Claire, Angie
The Bone Yard - Jefferson Bass   *m* 375

White, Harold
The Sherlockian - Graham Moore   *c* 657

RESTAURATEUR

Fraysse, Marc
Blowback - Peter May   *m* 494

Larue, Mary
The Outlaw's Return - Victoria Bylin   *i* 831

Lawless, Jane
The Cruel Ever After - Ellen Hart   *m* 454

Millicent
Tea for Two - Trish Perry   *i* 895

Willan, Alexandra
Hungry for You - Lynsay Sands   *r* 1100

RETIREE

DiGriz, Slippery Jim
The Stainless Steel Rat Returns - Harry
Harrison   *s* 756

Glass, Percy
The Widower's Tale - Julia Glass   *c* 613

Jordan "Jordan the Red"
Stuff of Legends - Ian Gibson   *f* 36

Moore, Ed
Apocalypse of the Dead - Joe McKinney   *h* 324

Willis, William Sr.
Aunt Dimity and the Family Tree - Nancy
Atherton   *m* 371

RODEO RIDER

Hansen, Mark
Mark: Secret Cowboy - Pamela Britton   *r* 940

Kelly, Dane
She's Gone Country - Jane Porter   *r* 1086

ROGUE

Sylvester, Ralph
The Tutor - Hope Tarr   *r* 1116

ROOMMATE

Ama
On Black Sisters Street - Chika Unigwe   *c* 708

Efe
On Black Sisters Street - Chika Unigwe   *c* 708

Jack
Dust City - Robert Paul Weston   *m* 553

Joyce
On Black Sisters Street - Chika Unigwe   *c* 708

Kate
The Loving Dead - Amelia Beamer   *h* 268

Michael
The Loving Dead - Amelia Beamer   *h* 268

Sisi
On Black Sisters Street - Chika Unigwe   *c* 708

ROYALTY

Adele
The Greyfriar - Susan Griffith   *h* 295

Adin
The Map Across Time - C.S. Lakin   *i* 875

Adolphus, Gustavus
1635: The Eastern Front - Eric Flint   *s* 751

Aethelred
The Forever Queen - Helen Hollick   *t* 176

Agamemnon
The Armour of Achilles - Glyn Iliffe   *t* 178

Aletha
The Map Across Time - C.S. Lakin   *i* 875

Alienor
The Sixth Surrender - Hana Samek Norton   *t* 217

Alivda
Avim's Oath - Lynda Williams   *s* 819

Amel
Avim's Oath - Lynda Williams   *s* 819

Arthur
The Beloved Dead - Tony Hays   *m* 458

bin Abdul-Aziz, Abdullah
The Secret Soldier - Alex Berenson   *m* 378

Bryen
The Uncrowned King - Rowena Cory
Daniells   *f* 26
The Usurper - Rowena Cory Daniells   *f* 28

Cnut
The Forever Queen - Helen Hollick   *t* 176

Danielle
Red Hood's Revenge - Jim C. Hines   *f* 43

Dudley, Robert
Rival to the Queen - Carolly Erickson   *t* 149

Edward
The King's Mistress: A Novel - Emma
Campion   *t* 125
*The Queen of Last Hopes: The Story of Margaret of
Anjou* - Susan Higginbotham   *t* 173
The Virgin Widow - Anne O'Brien   *t* 219

Emma
The Forever Queen - Helen Hollick   *t* 176

Erien
Avim's Oath - Lynda Williams   *s* 819

Gabriel
A Kiss at Midnight - Eloisa James   *r* 1014

Hamlet
The Lunatic, the Lover, and the Poet - Myrlin A.
Hermes   *t* 171

Helios
Lily of the Nile - Stephanie Dray   *t* 147

Henry
Pale Rose of England - Sandra Worth   *t* 264
*The Queen of Last Hopes: The Story of Margaret of
Anjou* - Susan Higginbotham   *t* 173
Secrets of the Tudor Court: By Royal Decree -
Kate Emerson   *t* 148

Howl, Caliph
The Last Page - Anthony Huso   *f* 47

Isabella
The King's Mistress: A Novel - Emma
Campion   *t* 125

Ivy
Ivy's Ever After - Dawn Lairamore   *f* 55

James
Pale Rose of England - Sandra Worth   *t* 264

Jin Li Tam
Antiphon - Ken Scholes   *f* 80

Kamiskwa
At the Queen's Command - Michael A.
Stackpole   *f* 89

Kamrasi, Saranith
Cinkarion: The Heart of Fire - J.A. Cullum   *f* 24

King David
Bathsheba: A Novel - Jill Eileen Smith   *i* 906

King Emin
The Ragged Man - Tom Lloyd   *f* 59

King Henry II
*The Captive Queen: A Novel of Eleanor of Aquita-
ine* - Alison Weir   *t* 259

King Louis VII
*The Captive Queen: A Novel of Eleanor of Aquita-
ine* - Alison Weir   *t* 259

King Philip
*The Golden Mean: A Novel of Aristotle and Alex-
ander the Great* - Annabel Lyon   *t* 197

Lilith
Seducing the Succubus - Cassie Ryan   *r* 1096

Malcolm
Queen Hereafter: A Novel of Margaret of Scotland
- Susan Fraser King   *t* 189

Margaret
Queen Hereafter: A Novel of Margaret of Scotland
- Susan Fraser King   *t* 189
*The Queen of Last Hopes: The Story of Margaret of
Anjou* - Susan Higginbotham   *t* 173

Piro
The Uncrowned King - Rowena Cory
Daniells   *f* 26

Prince Radu
Romeo and Juliet and Vampires - Claudia
Gabel   *h* 284

Prince Starigan
Darkling Fields of Arvon - Mark Sebanc   *f* 81

Queen Elizabeth I
Rival to the Queen - Carolly Erickson   *t* 149

Rolen
The Uncrowned King - Rowena Cory
Daniells   *f* 26

Sasha
Tracato - Joel Shepherd   *f* 83

Selene
Lily of the Nile - Stephanie Dray   *t* 147

Snow
Red Hood's Revenge - Jim C. Hines   *f* 43

Talia
Red Hood's Revenge - Jim C. Hines   *f* 43

Tudor, Henry VIII
Kiss of the Rose - Kate Pearce   *r* 1080

Tutankhamun
Tutankhamun: The Book of Shadows - Nick
Drake   *t* 146

Victoria
Queen Victoria, Demon Hunter - A.E.
Moorat   *h* 330

Vladimir
At the Queen's Command - Michael A.
Stackpole   *f* 89

Winslow, Grace
The Triumph of Grace - Kay Marshall
Strom   *i* 911

Ysvorod, Alec
Coronets and Steel - Sherwood Smith   *f* 87

RULER

Abdulhamid, Sultan II
The Oracle of Stamboul - Michael David
Lukas   *m* 487

RUNAWAY

Alex
Crown of Dust - Mary Volmer   *c* 710

Bryant, Laura
The Diviner's Tale - Bradford Morrow   *m* 501

Judith
The Sweet Relief of Missing Children - Sarah
Braunstein   *m* 386

Paul
The Sweet Relief of Missing Children - Sarah
Braunstein   *m* 386

SAILOR

Crichton, Thomas
The Exile of Sara Stevenson: A Historical Novel - Darci Hannah *r* 997

Madsen, Laurids
We, the Drowned - Carsten Jensen *c* 632

SALESMAN

Finley, Allen
More Than Words - Judith Miller *t* 209

SALESWOMAN

Blum, Piper
Digitalis - Ronie Kendig *i* 870

SALOON KEEPER/OWNER

Morley, Larissa
My Give a Damn's Busted - Carolyn Brown *r* 943

Waverly, Sharlene
Honky Tonk Christmas - Carolyn Brown *r* 942

SCHOLAR

Boans, Annie
Extra Indians - Eric Gansworth *c* 608

Cavendish, Henry
The School of Night - Louis Bayard *m* 376

Holdsworth, John
The Anatomy of Ghosts - Andrew Taylor *t* 251

Stratton, Trevor
13, rue Therese - Elena Mauli Shapiro *c* 696

SCIENTIST

Artedi, Peter
The Curious Death of Peter Artedi: A Mystery in the History of Science - Theodore W. Pietsch *t* 227

Bengler, Hans
Daniel - Henning Mankell *t* 201

Bergmann, Thom
Adam and Eve: A Novel - Sena Jeter Naslund *c* 662

Broderig, Benjamin
Devoured - D.E. Meredith *t* 207

Brown, Gina
Killer Instinct - Marilyn Victor *m* 545

Duhyle
Empress of Eternity - L.E. Modesitt Jr. *s* 785

Dumas, Philippe
Boiling Point - K.L. Dionne *m* 419

Eltyn
Empress of Eternity - L.E. Modesitt Jr. *s* 785

Faelyna
Empress of Eternity - L.E. Modesitt Jr. *s* 785

Ford, Doc
Night Vision - Randy Wayne White *m* 554

Glanville, Eleanor
Lady of the Butterflies - Fiona Mountain *t* 212

Harrow, Billy
Kraken - China Mieville *f* 70

Hatch, Carter
World and Town - Gish Jen *c* 631

Hatton, Adolphus
Devoured - D.E. Meredith *t* 207

Heat, Max
Boiling Point - K.L. Dionne *m* 419

Helkira
Empress of Eternity - L.E. Modesitt Jr. *s* 785

Jones, Lavender "Snake"
Killer Instinct - Marilyn Victor *m* 545

Kennedy, Sheila
Boiling Point - K.L. Dionne *m* 419

Linnaeus, Carl
The Curious Death of Peter Artedi: A Mystery in the History of Science - Theodore W. Pietsch *t* 227

Lochum, Dr. Archibald
30 Pieces of Silver - Carolyn McCray *t* 204

Maarlyna
Empress of Eternity - L.E. Modesitt Jr. *s* 785

MacLean, Theresa
Trail of Blood - Lisa Black *m* 381

Maertyn
Empress of Eternity - L.E. Modesitt Jr. *s* 785

Michaels, General
The Alarmists - Don Hoesel *i* 865

Monroe, Dr. Rebecca
30 Pieces of Silver - Carolyn McCray *t* 204

Reynolds, Monique
The Omega Theory - Mark Alpert *m* 368

Rhodes, Griffin
A Heartbeat Away - Michael Palmer *m* 510

Sweet, Rebecca
Boiling Point - K.L. Dionne *m* 419

Swift, David
The Omega Theory - Mark Alpert *m* 368

Szabo, Karel
A Lily of the Field - John Lawton *t* 193

SCOUT

Blackburn, Clay
The Incredible Double - Owen Hill *m* 464

Woods, Nathaniel
At the Queen's Command - Michael A. Stackpole *f* 89

SEA CAPTAIN

Blessing, Mickey
Red Rain - Bruce Murkoff *t* 214

Carroway, Bradshaw
Rules of an Engagement - Suzanne Enoch *r* 971

Cutler, Caleb
For Love of Country - William C. Hammond *t* 169

Cutler, Richard
For Love of Country - William C. Hammond *t* 169

Lewrie, Alan
The Invasion Year - Dewey Lambdin *t* 192

MacSorley, Erik
The Hawk - Monica McCarty *r* 1058

Murchad
The Dove of Death - Peter Tremayne *t* 256

Quinton, Matthew
Gentleman Captain - J.D. Davies *t* 134

SEAMSTRESS

Annamaria
A Heart Most Worthy - Siri Mitchell *i* 886

Enke, Angela
Unholy Awakening - Michael Gregorio *m* 446

Julietta
A Heart Most Worthy - Siri Mitchell *i* 886

Kerr, Elisabeth
Mine Is the Night - Liz Curtis Higgs *i* 862

Luciana
A Heart Most Worthy - Siri Mitchell *i* 886

Noura
The Calligrapher's Secret - Rafik Schami *c* 691

Scarpelli, Lucy
An Unlikely Suitor - Nancy Moser *i* 890

Scarpelli, Sofia
An Unlikely Suitor - Nancy Moser *i* 890

SECRETARY

Josianne
13, rue Therese - Elena Mauli Shapiro *c* 696

Lacy, Elizabeth "Lizzy"
The Darling Dahlias and the Cucumber Tree - Susan Wittig Albert *t* 107

Simon, Clara
21 Aldgate - Patricia Friedberg *t* 158

SECURITY OFFICER

Bradford, Miles
The Informationist - Taylor Stevens *m* 535

Cross, Hector
Those in Peril - Wilbur Smith *m* 529

Lyons, Katie
Hot Target - Lisa Renee Jones *r* 1021

Marlow, Alex
Do Unto Others - Michael Z. Williamson *s* 821

Runyon, Hook
The Insane Train - Sheldon Russell *m* 522

Seaver, Trey
The Dangerous Edge of Things - Tina Whittle *m* 555

Young, Jonah
Killer Heat - Brenda Novak *r* 1076

SERIAL KILLER

Bathory, Erzsebet
The Countess - Rebecca Johns *t* 183

Mr. Levitt
The Zombies of Lake Woebegotten - Harrison Geillor *h* 287

Lowell, Gretchen
The Night Season - Chelsea Cain *m* 390

Price, Martin
You Are Next - Katia Lief *r* 1042

Storms, Serge
Electric Barracuda - Tim Dorsey *m* 421

The Blindfold Killer
Shadow Protector - Jenna Ryan *r* 1097

SERVANT

Ansel
No Such Things As Dragons - Philip Reeve *f* 78

Bunter
The Attenbury Emeralds - Jill Paton Walsh *m* 551

Cherrett, Dominick
Lady in the Mist - Laurie Alice Eakes *i* 848

Dot
Dead Man's Chest - Kerry Greenwood *t* 163

Hepplewhite, Queenie
Royal Blood - Rhys Bowen *t* 121

Lavinia
The Kitchen House - Kathleen Grissom *t* 165

Maria
Wolf's Cross - S.A. Swann *h* 352

Moirin
Naamah's Curse - Jacqueline Carey *f* 19

Persons, Elizabeth
The Gentleman Poet - Kathryn Johnson *r* 1020

Scott, Jayne
The Best of Friends - Susan Mallery *r* 1051

Tora
The Masuda Affair - I.J. Parker *t* 223

SHAMAN

Sawyer
Chaos Bites - Lori Handeland *h* 299

Wanbli, George
The Sacred White Turkey - Frances
    Washburn *c* 713

SHAPE-SHIFTER

David
In the Company of Vampires - Katie
    MacAlister *h* 320

Dominica
Esperanza - Trish J. MacGregor *h* 322

Mick
Firewalker - Allyson James *r* 1013

Morgan
Immortal Sea - Virginia Kantra *r* 1024

Panterra, Carlos
Eat, Prey, Love - Kerrelyn Sparks *r* 1108

Savoie, Max
Chased by Moonlight - Nancy Gideon *r* 985

Sawyer
Chaos Bites - Lori Handeland *h* 299

The Emperor
Bones of Empire - William C. Dietz *s* 745

SHIPOWNER

Cabrillo, Juan
The Jungle - Clive Cussler *m* 414

Walton, Robert
Frankenstein's Monster - Susan Heyboer
    O'Keefe *c* 666

SIDEKICK

Barak, Jack
Heartstone - C.J. Sansom *t* 237

Cowardly Lion
*The Undead World of Oz: L. Frank Baum's The
    Wonderful Wizard of Oz Complete with Zombies
    and Monsters* - L. Frank Baum *h* 267

Hank
The Darkest Edge of Dawn - Kelly Gay *h* 286

Laissa
Kings of the North - Cecelia Holland *t* 175

Leif the Icelander
Kings of the North - Cecelia Holland *t* 175

Marriott, Charles
Hardcastle's Soldiers - Graham Ison *t* 179

Nunes, Arnaldo
Every Bitter Thing - Leighton Gage *m* 440

Scarecrow
*The Undead World of Oz: L. Frank Baum's The
    Wonderful Wizard of Oz Complete with Zombies
    and Monsters* - L. Frank Baum *h* 267

Swinburne, Algernon
The Strange Affair of Spring Heeled Jack - Mark
    Hodder *h* 304

Tin Man
*The Undead World of Oz: L. Frank Baum's The
    Wonderful Wizard of Oz Complete with Zombies
    and Monsters* - L. Frank Baum *h* 267

Wortley
Ghoul Strike! - Andrew Newbound *h* 333

SINGER

Bolade, Patience
The Girls with Games of Blood - Alex
    Bledsoe *h* 274

Erika
The Doctor and the Diva - Adrienne
    McDonnell *t* 205

Etheridge, Daisy
Chasing the Sun - Kaki Warner *r* 1126

Froben, Moses
The Bells - Richard Harvell *t* 170

Lucien
The Metropolis Case - Matthew
    Gallaway *m* 441

Maria
The Metropolis Case - Matthew
    Gallaway *m* 441

O'James, Macy
Burning Up - Susan Andersen *r* 926

Sinatra, Frank
*The Life and Opinions of Maf the Dog, and of His
    Friend Marilyn Monroe* - Andrew
    O'Hagan *t* 221

SINGLE FATHER

Cooper, Zack
Tea for Two - Trish Perry *i* 895

Donovan, Mitch
Firefighter Daddy - Lee McKenzie *r* 1063

Neely, Colton "Cowboy"
Digitalis - Ronie Kendig *i* 870

Robert
All That We Are - Elizabeth Lord *t* 195

Walker, Travis
The First Love Cookie Club - Lori Wilde *r* 1135

SINGLE MOTHER

Abruzzo, Roxy
Our Lady of Immaculate Deception - Nancy
    Martin *m* 493

Brown, Faith
Montana Dawn - Caroline Fyffe *r* 979

Charles, Josie
Dexter: Honorable Cowboy - Marin
    Thomas *r* 1119

Conway, Kara
The Homecoming - JoAnn Ross *r* 1095

Drake, Melanie
Hometown Dad - Merrillee Whren *i* 918

Etheridge, Daisy
Chasing the Sun - Kaki Warner *r* 1126

Gibson, Lacey
Missing - Lynette Eason *i* 849

Gray, Mandy McClellan
Sharpshooter in Petticoats - Mary
    Connealy *i* 839

Hanaoka, Yasuko
The Devotion of Suspect X - Keigo
    Higashino *m* 463

Henderson, Andrea
Larkspur Cove - Lisa Wingate *i* 919

McCafferty, Merran
The Samhanach - Lisa Morton *h* 331

McGregor, Dallas
Home Again - Mariah Stewart *r* 1110

Mitchell, Suz
Fade to Blue - Julie Carobini *i* 834

O'Shea, Bridget
Come High Water - Carolyn Brown *r* 944

Pollack, Anastasia
Assault with a Deadly Glue Gun - Lois
    Winston *m* 560

Sutton, Liz
Almost Perfect - Susan Mallery *r* 1050

Wyse, Mary Jo
1022 Evergreen Place - Debbie
    Macomber *r* 1049

SINGLE PARENT

Bergman, Alex
Instant Family - Elisabeth Rose *r* 1094

Gardiner, Chloe
Instant Family - Elisabeth Rose *r* 1094

SISTER

Abbie
Take a Chance on Me - Jill Mansell *r* 1052

Alice
Come High Water - Carolyn Brown *r* 944

Amaryllis
Scoundrel in My Dreams - Celeste
    Bradley *r* 935

Andreas, Bean
The Weird Sisters - Eleanor Brown *c* 576

Andreas, Cordy
The Weird Sisters - Eleanor Brown *c* 576

Andreas, Rose
The Weird Sisters - Eleanor Brown *c* 576

Angelino, Vivi
Edge of Sight - Roxanne St. Claire *r* 1109

Audrun
Trespass - Rose Tremain *c* 707

Austen, Cassandra
Jane and the Damned - Janet Mullany *t* 213

Austen, Jane
Jane and the Madness of Lord Byron - Stephanie
    Barron *t* 114

Bennett, Jane
Mr. Darcy's Obsession - Abigail Reynolds *t* 231

Bennett, Lydia
Mr. Darcy's Obsession - Abigail Reynolds *t* 231

Bolade, Prudence
The Girls with Games of Blood - Alex
    Bledsoe *h* 274

Brown, Bonnie
Nashville Chrome - Rick Bass *c* 570

Brown, Maxine
Nashville Chrome - Rick Bass *c* 570

Cailiff, May
The Cailiffs of Baghdad, Georgia - Mary Helen Stefaniak *t* 248

Capel, Biba
The Poison Tree - Erin Kelly *m* 474

Catherine
Abigail's New Hope - Mary Ellis *i* 852
Come High Water - Carolyn Brown *r* 944
Nowhere to Hide - Carlene Thompson *r* 1120

Cathy
Shadow on the Land - Anne Doughty *t* 143

Chatwick, Lily
Three Nights with a Scoundrel - Tessa Dare *r* 961

Christiane
The Weekend - Bernhard Schlink *c* 692

Dalton, Carleen
The Secrets Sisters Keep - Abby Drake *c* 592

Dalton, Ellie
The Secrets Sisters Keep - Abby Drake *c* 592

Dalton, Naomi "Babe"
The Secrets Sisters Keep - Abby Drake *c* 592

Daniels, Maddie
Sex on the Slopes - Susan Lyons *r* 1046

Darcy, Georgina
Mr. Darcy's Little Sister - C. Allyn Pierson *t* 226

Decca
Under the Poppy - Kathe Koja *c* 638

Delaney, Amanda
The Secrets Sisters Keep - Abby Drake *c* 592

Duran, Simone
The Good Sister - Drusilla Campbell *c* 578

Ellsworth, Jane
Shades of Milk and Honey - Mary Robinette Kowal *f* 51

Ellsworth, Melody
Shades of Milk and Honey - Mary Robinette Kowal *f* 51

Eve
Bent Road - Lori Roy *m* 521

Florence
Forbidden Places - Penny Vincenzi *t* 257

Hamilton, Jane
Shadow on the Land - Anne Doughty *t* 143

Hamilton, Lizzie
Shadow on the Land - Anne Doughty *t* 143

Hannah
The Home for Broken Hearts - Rowan Coleman *c* 584

Harris, Tillie
Up from the Blue: A Novel - Susan Henderson *c* 623

Hillock, Avis
The Sisters from Hardscrabble Bay - Beverly Jensen *t* 182

Hillock, Idella
The Sisters from Hardscrabble Bay - Beverly Jensen *t* 182

Houston, Val
Devious - Lisa Jackson *m* 471

Jarrett, Lucy
The Lake of Dreams - Kim Edwards *c* 595

Juniper
The Distant Hours - Kate Morton *c* 658

Kamrasi, Saranith
Cinkarion: The Heart of Fire - J.A. Cullum *f* 24

Katya
The Jewel of St. Petersburg - Kate Furnivall *t* 159
Snowdrops - A.D. Miller *c* 656

Laurel
Scoundrel in My Dreams - Celeste Bradley *r* 935

Lisa
Don't Breathe a Word - Jennifer McMahon *m* 499

Maine, Adele "Addie"
Take Me Home - Brian Leung *c* 643

March, Amy
Little Women and Werewolves - Porter Grand *h* 291

March, Beth
Little Women and Werewolves - Porter Grand *h* 291

March, Jo
Little Women and Werewolves - Porter Grand *h* 291

March, Meg
Little Women and Werewolves - Porter Grand *h* 291

Masha
Snowdrops - A.D. Miller *c* 656

Maurier, Angela du
Peril at Somner House - Joanna Challis *t* 127

McRae, Anna
Sugar and Spice - Ruth Hamilton *t* 168

Melanie
A Secret Kept - Tatiana de Rosnay *c* 589

Milly
The Bird Sisters - Rebecca Rasmussen *c* 682

Payne, Orla
The Hanging Wood - Martin Edwards *m* 427

Penny
Hearts Persuaded - Joanne Sundell *r* 1115

Piro
The Uncrowned King - Rowena Cory Daniells *f* 26

Poe, Riley
Afterlight - Elle Jasper *h* 306

Quinn, Cleo
Take a Chance on Me - Jill Mansell *r* 1052

Renard, Camille
Devious - Lisa Jackson *m* 471

Roxanne
The Good Sister - Drusilla Campbell *c* 578

Ruth
Bent Road - Lori Roy *m* 521

Sawyer, McKenzie
Kaydie - Penny Zeller *i* 924

Scarpelli, Lucy
An Unlikely Suitor - Nancy Moser *i* 890

Scarpelli, Sofia
An Unlikely Suitor - Nancy Moser *i* 890

Sparrow, Agnes
Griselda Takes Flight - Joyce Magnin Moccero *i* 887

Stewart, Eleanor
The Lightkeeper's Ball - Colleen Coble *i* 836

Taylor, Maggie
All That We Are - Elizabeth Lord *t* 195

Taylor, Nora
All That We Are - Elizabeth Lord *t* 195

Twiss
The Bird Sisters - Rebecca Rasmussen *c* 682

Veronica
Trespass - Rose Tremain *c* 707

Williams, Ethel
Fall of Giants - Ken Follett *t* 154

SLAVE

Arimnestos
Killer of Men - Christian Cameron *t* 124

Arkady
The Palace of Impossible Dreams - Jennifer Fallon *f* 33

Belle
The Kitchen House - Kathleen Grissom *t* 165

Cabeto
The Triumph of Grace - Kay Marshall Strom *i* 911

Drakis
Song of the Dragon - Tracy Hickman *f* 42

Ikard, Bose
Comanche Sundown - Jan Reid *t* 229

Jerzy
Weight of Stone - Laura Anne Gilman *f* 38

Kratos
God of War - Matthew Stover *f* 93

Lion, Surry
Hearts Persuaded - Joanne Sundell *r* 1115

Lyngdoh, Anibaddh
Original Sins: A Novel of Slavery & Freedom - Peg Kingman *t* 190

Petrule, Lizzy
The Shattered Sylph - L.J. McDonald *f* 65

Piro
The Usurper - Rowena Cory Daniells *f* 28

Portia
The First Assassin - John J. Miller *t* 208

Terelle
Stormlord Rising - Glenda Larke *f* 57

Winslow, Grace
The Triumph of Grace - Kay Marshall Strom *i* 911

Y'breq, Lededje
Surface Detail - Iain M. Banks *s* 731

SMUGGLER

Balwyn, Julianne
After America - John Birmingham *s* 734

Hawksworth, Gabriel
The Smuggler and the Society Bride - Julia Justiss *r* 1023

Rhino
After America - John Birmingham *s* 734

SOCIAL WORKER

Henderson, Andrea
Larkspur Cove - Lisa Wingate *i* 919

Wiltshire, Lucy
Save the Date - Jenny B. Jones *i* 869

SOCIALITE

Bernfeld, Loe
A Curable Romantic - Joseph Skibell *t* 243

Delaney, Amanda
The Secrets Sisters Keep - Abby Drake *c* 592

Fairbanks, Lady Molly
When Harry Met Molly - Kieran Kramer *r* 1038

Granger, Miranda
A Midnight Clear - Kristi Astor *r* 928

Halcyon-Wilson, DeDe
Mary Ann in Autumn - Armistead Maupin *c* 650

Langdon, Rowena
An Unlikely Suitor - Nancy Moser *i* 890

Montross, Abigail
His Christmas Pleasure - Cathy Maxwell *r* 1056

Smith-Barnes, Poppy
Dukes to the Left of Me, Princes to the Right - Kieran Kramer *r* 1037

Stangbourne, Lydia
The Invasion Year - Dewey Lambdin *t* 192

Stewart, Olivia
The Lightkeeper's Ball - Colleen Coble *i* 836

SON

Abuzeid, Nur
Lyrics Alley - Leila Aboulela *t* 104

Adler, Damian
The God of the Hive - Laurie R. King *t* 188

Alatriste, Inigo
Pirates of the Levant - Arturo Perez-Reverte *t* 225

Alexander
The Golden Mean: A Novel of Aristotle and Alexander the Great - Annabel Lyon *t* 197

Alley, Eddie
The Witches on the Road Tonight - Sheri Holman *c* 628

Anton
A Night of Long Knives - Rebecca Cantrell *t* 126

Arch
Crunch Time - Diane Mott Davidson *m* 416

Ben
Vortex - Troy Denning *s* 744

Bryen
The Uncrowned King - Rowena Cory Daniells *f* 26

Carlson, Cooper
A Dad of His Own - Gail Gaymer Martin *i* 880

Carstairs, Ben
Journey to Riverbend - Henry McLaughlin *i* 884

Charlie
The Home for Broken Hearts - Rowan Coleman *c* 584

Cody
Home Again - Mariah Stewart *r* 1110

Covington, Lance
Vicious Cycle - Terri Blackstock *i* 826

Dan
Deceptions - Rebecca Frayn *m* 439
The Old Romantic - Louise Dean *c* 590

Davis, Evan
A Legacy of Daemons - Camille Bacon-Smith *f* 7

Dillon
The Painted Darkness - Brian James Freeman *h* 283

Dylan
Another Dawn - Kathryn Cushman *i* 841

Earle, Bobby
Torn Apart - Sharon Sala *r* 1099

Edward
The Queen of Last Hopes: The Story of Margaret of Anjou - Susan Higginbotham *t* 173

Fyn
The King's Bastard - Rowena Cory Daniells *f* 27

Gabriel
Clarity - Kim Harrington *m* 451

Greifinger, Heinz
A Call from Jersey - P.F. Kluge *t* 191

Griffin, George
A Call from Jersey - P.F. Kluge *t* 191

Hamilton, Johnny
Shadow on the Land - Anne Doughty *t* 143

Helios
Lily of the Nile - Stephanie Dray *t* 147

Heller, Miles
Sunset Park - Paul Auster *c* 569

Henry VII
The Red Queen - Philippa Gregory *t* 164

Holland, Aven
Alaska Weddings - Susan Page Davis *i* 845

Hui, Ding
Dream of Ding Village - Yan Lianke *c* 644

Jakob
Antiphon - Ken Scholes *f* 80

Jeremiah
Against All Things Ending - Stephen R. Donaldson *f* 30
Fade to Blue - Julie Carobini *i* 834

John
The Captive Queen: A Novel of Eleanor of Aquitaine - Alison Weir *t* 259

Lucien
The Metropolis Case - Matthew Gallaway *m* 441

Matthew
I'll Walk Alone - Mary Higgins Clark *m* 400

Nick
The Old Romantic - Louise Dean *c* 590

Nicolaos
The Pericles Commission - Gary Corby *t* 132

O'Brien, Connor
A Chesapeake Shores Christmas - Sherryl Woods *r* 1143

Ogedai
Khan: Empire of Silver - Conn Iggulden *t* 177

Petya
The Russian Affair - Michael Wallner *m* 550

Pili
The Crocodile's Last Embrace - Suzanne Arruda *t* 109

Pinarius, Lucius
Empire: The Novel of Imperial Rome - Steven Saylor *t* 239

Raikes, Dominic
The Fire Lord's Lover - Kathryne Kennedy *r* 1030

Richard
The Captive Queen: A Novel of Eleanor of Aquitaine - Alison Weir *t* 259

Rodriguez, Zack
Immortal Sea - Virginia Kantra *r* 1024

Russell, Paul
Potsdam Station - David Downing *m* 422

Sam
Pictures of You: A Novel - Caroline Leavitt *c* 642

Timothy
When Sparrows Fall: A Novel - Meg Moseley *i* 889

Witney, Liam
Fourth Day - Zoe Sharp *m* 526

Zeke
My New American Life - Francine Prose *c* 679

SORCERER

Ambrosius, Morlock
The Wolf Age - James Enge *f* 32

Little, Catherine
Game of Cages - Harry Connolly *f* 21

Mayart, Giuseppe
The Black Guard - Hideyuki Kikuchi *h* 313

Prospero
Prospero in Hell - L. Jagi Lamplighter *f* 56

Sawyer
Chaos Bites - Lori Handeland *h* 299

SORCERESS

Bruna
The Warded Man - Peter V. Brett *f* 14

Onyesonwu
Who Fears Death - Nnedi Okorafor *f* 75

SOUTHERN BELLE

Templeton, Dinah
At the Captain's Command - Louise M. Gouge *i* 858

SPACE EXPLORER

Teacher
Hull Zero Three - Greg Bear *s* 732

SPACESHIP CAPTAIN

Dax, Ezri
Zero Sum Game - David Mack *s* 778

Riker
Seize the Fire - Michael A. Martin *s* 779

SPINSTER

Bassingstoke, Beatrice-Maude
One Unashamed Night - Sophia James *r* 1016

Daltry, Katherine
A Kiss at Midnight - Eloisa James *r* 1014

Foster, Juliet
Miss Foster's Folly - Alice Gaines *r* 981

Spenser, Charlotte
Reckless - Anne Stuart *r* 1114

SPIRIT

Dimity
Aunt Dimity and the Family Tree - Nancy Atherton *m* 371

Dominica
Esperanza - Trish J. MacGregor *h* 322

Ita
A Curable Romantic - Joseph Skibell *t* 243

Kit
Shadow's Son - Jon Sprunk *f* 88

Michaels, Grace
Devil at Midnight - Emma Holly *r* 1006

Wati
Kraken - China Mieville *f* 70

SPOUSE

Abbie
Take a Chance on Me - Jill Mansell *r* 1052

Abuzeid, Mahmoud Bey
Lyrics Alley - Leila Aboulela *t* 104

Abuzeid, Nabilah
Lyrics Alley - Leila Aboulela *t* 104

Abuzeid, Waheeba
Lyrics Alley - Leila Aboulela *t* 104

Aethelred
The Forever Queen - Helen Hollick *t* 176

Alden, Earl
Cold Wind - C.J. Box *m* 384

Allison
The Neighbors Are Watching - Debra Ginsberg *c* 612

Alona
Eden - Yael Hedaya *c* 621

Mrs. Andreas
The Weird Sisters - Eleanor Brown *c* 576

Andreas, Dr. James
The Weird Sisters - Eleanor Brown *c* 576

Angelina
The Stainless Steel Rat Returns - Harry Harrison *s* 756

Annie
Separate Beds - Elizabeth Buchan *c* 577

April
Pictures of You: A Novel - Caroline Leavitt *c* 642

Arsenault, Sheila
Rescue - Anita Shreve *c* 701

Ashfield, Edmund
Lady of the Butterflies - Fiona Mountain *t* 212

Balthasar
Lightborn - Alison Sinclair *f* 84

Barbara
Santa Fe Edge - Stuart Woods *m* 561
The Second Duchess - Elizabeth Loupas *t* 196

Bathsheba
Bathsheba: A Novel - Jill Eileen Smith *i* 906

Baxter, Zoe
Sing You Home - Jodi Picoult *c* 677

Benedict, Eliza
I'd Know You Anywhere - Laura Lippman *c* 646

Bennett, Charles
Forbidden Places - Penny Vincenzi *t* 257

Bennett, Jake
Faith's Reward - Tammy Barley *i* 825

Bennett, Jessica
Faith's Reward - Tammy Barley *i* 825

Benson, Jade
Softly and Tenderly - Sara Evans *i* 853

Bergmann, Thom
Adam and Eve: A Novel - Sena Jeter Naslund *c* 662

Binnie
Heaven is High - Kate Wilhelm *m* 557

Brisbane, Nicholas
Dark Road to Darjeeling - Deanna Raybourn *r* 1089

Bronwyn
The Sister Wife - Diane Noble *t* 216

Brooks, Adam
Casting Around - Terri DuLong *r* 970

Brooks, Monica
Casting Around - Terri DuLong *r* 970

Bryant, Dwight
Christmas Mourning - Margaret Maron *m* 492

Burgess, Charlotte
Seducing the Duchess - Ashley March *r* 1053

Burgess, Phillip
Seducing the Duchess - Ashley March *r* 1053

Burroughs, George
Deliverance from Evil - Frances Hill *c* 624

Cabeto
The Triumph of Grace - Kay Marshall Strom *i* 911

Carhart, Katherine "Kate"
Trial by Desire - Courtney Milan *r* 1067

Carhart, Ned
Trial by Desire - Courtney Milan *r* 1067

Carol
The Gendarme - Mark T. Mustian *t* 215

Cassandra
The Fire Lord's Lover - Kathryne Kennedy *r* 1030

Celia
Bent Road - Lori Roy *m* 521

Charlie
Pictures of You: A Novel - Caroline Leavitt *c* 642

Cheever, Mary
Deliverance from Evil - Frances Hill *c* 624

Clarke, Comfort
Hearts Persuaded - Joanne Sundell *r* 1115

Cnut
The Forever Queen - Helen Hollick *t* 176

d'Este, Alfonso
The Second Duchess - Elizabeth Loupas *t* 196

Dallas, Eve
Indulgence in Death - J.D. Robb *s* 796

Darby, Brian
Love You More - Lisa Gardner *m* 442

Darcy, Antonia
Murder at the Villa Byzantine - R.T. Raichev *m* 514

de Vasconia, Baron Andres
His Christmas Pleasure - Cathy Maxwell *r* 1056

de Warenne, Alexi
The Promise - Brenda Joyce *r* 1022

de Warenne, Elysse
The Promise - Brenda Joyce *r* 1022

Desplaines, Catherine
Bound - Antonya Nelson *c* 664

Dinah
Love Amid the Ashes: A Novel - Mesu Andrews *i* 824

Dugan
Too Many Clients - David J. Walker *m* 548

Dunbury, Lady Avery
The Crocodile's Last Embrace - Suzanne Arruda *t* 109

DuPree, Rachel
The Personal History of Rachel DuPree: A Novel - Ann Weisgarber *t* 260

Eadulf, Brother
The Dove of Death - Peter Tremayne *t* 256

Eleanor of Aquitaine
The Captive Queen: A Novel of Eleanor of Aquitaine - Alison Weir *t* 259
The Captive Queen: A Novel of Eleanor of Aquitaine - Alison Weir *t* 259

Emily
Blown off Course - David Donachie *t* 142

Emma
The Forever Queen - Helen Hollick *t* 176

Evan
Siren - John Everson *h* 281

Evanson, Marjorie
An Impartial Witness - Charles Todd *t* 253

Faith
Absolute Risk - Steven Gore *m* 445

Farsi, Hamid
The Calligrapher's Secret - Rafik Schami *c* 691

Fleur
Other People's Money - Justin Cartwright *c* 580

Foster, Laura
The Deepest Waters - Dan Walsh *i* 917

Gabriel
The Sister Wife - Diane Noble *t* 216

Garity, Chester "Chess"
The Cruel Ever After - Ellen Hart *m* 454

Gideon
Secret Place - Leslie J. Sherrod *i* 903

Glanville, Richard
Lady of the Butterflies - Fiona Mountain *t* 212

Graber, Daniel
Abigail's New Hope - Mary Ellis *i* 852

Grace, Olivia
Barely a Lady - Eileen Dreyer *r* 969

Grey, Julia
Dark Road to Darjeeling - Deanna Raybourn *r* 1089

Guy
Sea Change - Jeremy Page *c* 672

Hamilton, Alex
Shadow on the Land - Anne Doughty *t* 143

Hamilton, Emily
Shadow on the Land - Anne Doughty *t* 143

Hargreaves, Colin
Dangerous to Know - Tasha Alexander *t* 108

Hargreaves, Emily
Dangerous to Know - Tasha Alexander *t* 108

Harker, Jonathan
Dracula My Love - Syrie James *r* 1017

Harker, Mina
Dracula My Love - Syrie James *r* 1017

Harris, Peter
By Nightfall - Michael Cunningham *c* 586

Harris, Rebecca
By Nightfall - Michael Cunningham *c* 586

Hauk, Dutch
Deadly Ties - Vicki Hinze *i* 864

Susannah
Santa Fe Edge - Stuart Woods   *m* 561

Swift, David
The Omega Theory - Mark Alpert   *m* 368

Tom
Separate Beds - Elizabeth Buchan   *c* 577
Take a Chance on Me - Jill Mansell   *r* 1052

Tsazukhina, Anna
The Russian Affair - Michael Wallner   *m* 550

Uriah
Bathsheba: A Novel - Jill Eileen Smith   *i* 906

Valmore, Prosper
The Last Rendezvous - Anne Plantagenet   *t* 228

Vane, Harriet
The Attenbury Emeralds - Jill Paton
Walsh   *m* 551

Vanessa
Sing You Home - Jodi Picoult   *c* 677

Webster, Peter
Rescue - Anita Shreve   *c* 701

Westcott, Gabriel
The Vengeful Bridegroom - Kit Donner   *r* 967

Wilhelm
The Blind Side of the Heart - Julia Franck   *c* 604

Wimsey, Lord Peter
The Attenbury Emeralds - Jill Paton
Walsh   *m* 551

Worthy, David
The Crocodile's Last Embrace - Suzanne
Arruda   *t* 109

Wyndham, Jack
Barely a Lady - Eileen Dreyer   *r* 969

Yuying
Under Fishbone Clouds - Sam Meekings   *c* 653

SPY

Abercrombie, Nathan
The Big Stink - David Lubar   *h* 317

Adams, Charles Francis
Broken Promises - Elizabeth Cobbs
Hoffman   *c* 627

Anacrites
Nemesis - Lindsey Davis   *t* 135

Boyd, Maria Isabella
Clementine - Cherie Priest   *s* 791

Corbett, Hugh
The Waxman Murders - Paul Doherty   *t* 141

Dobbs, Maisie
A Lesson in Secrets - Jacqueline
Winspear   *m* 559

Eva
Queen Hereafter: A Novel of Margaret of Scotland
 - Susan Fraser King   *t* 189

Mr. French
India Black - Carol K. Carr   *m* 393

Gaffan, Brett
The Secret Soldier - Alex Berenson   *m* 378

Hawkes, Declan
The Palace of Impossible Dreams - Jennifer
Fallon   *f* 33

Jones, Will
To Save the Devil - Kate Moore   *r* 1069

Kingston, Faith
Midnight - Beverly Jenkins   *r* 1019

Mundy, Adele
What Distant Deeps - David Drake   *s* 747

Russell, John
Potsdam Station - David Downing   *m* 422

Sena
The Last Page - Anthony Huso   *f* 47

Silverdun
The Office of Shadow - Matthew Sturges   *f* 94

Tsazukhina, Anna
The Russian Affair - Michael Wallner   *m* 550

von Ulrich, Walter
Fall of Giants - Ken Follett   *t* 154

Wells, John
The Secret Soldier - Alex Berenson   *m* 378

Westfield, Lord Anthony "Viscount Somerton"
Scandal of the Season - Christie Kelley   *r* 1027

STEPBROTHER

Alder
The Bird of the River - Kage Baker   *f* 8

STEPDAUGHTER

Clarissa Jo
Casting Around - Terri DuLong   *r* 970

STEPFATHER

Hauk, Dutch
Deadly Ties - Vicki Hinze   *i* 864

STEPMOTHER

Allison
The Neighbors Are Watching - Debra
Ginsberg   *c* 612

Brooks, Monica
Casting Around - Terri DuLong   *r* 970

Muriel
Beyond the Shore - Connie Monk   *t* 211

Ruxandra
The Oracle of Stamboul - Michael David
Lukas   *m* 487

STEPSISTER

Eliss
The Bird of the River - Kage Baker   *f* 8

STEWARD

Stark, Peter
Love Finds You in Prince Edward Island, Canada
 - Susan Page Davis   *i* 846

STORE OWNER

Abruzzo, Roxy
Our Lady of Immaculate Deception - Nancy
Martin   *m* 493

Brooks, Monica
Casting Around - Terri DuLong   *r* 970

Cutler, Madeira
Death by Diamonds - Annette Blair   *f* 11

Legris, Victor
The Montmartre Investigation - Claude
Izner   *t* 180

Randolph, Tai
The Dangerous Edge of Things - Tina
Whittle   *m* 555

STREETPERSON

Alice
Sunset Park - Paul Auster   *c* 569

Bing
Sunset Park - Paul Auster   *c* 569

Ellen
Sunset Park - Paul Auster   *c* 569

Heller, Miles
Sunset Park - Paul Auster   *c* 569

Tucker, Jack
The Demon's Parchment - Jeri Westerson   *t* 261

STRIPPER

Chester, Brandy
Heads You Lose - Lisa Lutz   *m* 488

STUDENT

Alexander
*The Golden Mean: A Novel of Aristotle and Alex-
ander the Great* - Annabel Lyon   *t* 197

Blithe, Bernard
All Is Forgotten, Nothing Is Lost - Lan Samantha
Chang   *c* 582

Cle, Phelan
The Bards of Bone Plain - Patricia A.
McKillip   *f* 68

Fairchild, Samantha "Sam"
Edge of Sight - Roxanne St. Claire   *r* 1109

Kirk, James T.
The Edge - Rudy Josephs   *s* 764

Morris, Roman
All Is Forgotten, Nothing Is Lost - Lan Samantha
Chang   *c* 582

O'Fallon, Patrick
False Patriots - Charles O'Brien   *t* 220

Singleton, Perri
The Sweetest Thing - Elizabeth Musser   *i* 892

Wolf, Waiting
The Owl Hunt - Richard S. Wheeler   *t* 262

STUDENT—COLLEGE

Bennett
In Every Heartbeat - Kim Vogel Sawyer   *t* 238

Clarke, Karen
The Poison Tree - Erin Kelly   *m* 474

Farhad
A Thousand Rooms of Dream and Fear - Atiq
Rahimi   *c* 681

Landon, Asher
Tennessee Brides - Aaron McCarver   *i* 882

Libby
In Every Heartbeat - Kim Vogel Sawyer   *t* 238

Oldershaw, Frank
The Anatomy of Ghosts - Andrew Taylor   *t* 251

Petey
In Every Heartbeat - Kim Vogel Sawyer   *t* 238

Robert
The Widower's Tale - Julia Glass   *c* 613

Samuels, Kayla
The Tenth Song - Naomi Ragen   *c* 680

Zeremba, Lilith
The Last Jewish Virgin: A Novel of Fate - Janice
Eidus   *c* 596

STUDENT—EXCHANGE

Gustafson, Olaf
Blind Your Ponies - Stanley Gordon West   *c* 714

STUDENT—GRADUATE

Banks, Charlie
One Fine Cowboy - Joanne Kennedy   *r* 1029

Murray, Kim
Coronets and Steel - Sherwood Smith   *f* 87

Silk, Elizabeth
Blood on Silk - Marie Treanor   *h* 358

STUDENT—HIGH SCHOOL

Amanda
Now You See Me - Marilyn Kaye   *s* 766

Payne, Macy
You Killed Wesley Payne - Sean
   Beaudoin   *m* 377

Rev, Dalton
You Killed Wesley Payne - Sean
   Beaudoin   *m* 377

Stonebreaker, Tom
Blind Your Ponies - Stanley Gordon West   *c* 714

Strong, Peter
Blind Your Ponies - Stanley Gordon West   *c* 714

Tracey
Now You See Me - Marilyn Kaye   *s* 766

Zeke
My New American Life - Francine Prose   *c* 679

SUFFRAGETTE

Graham, Emily
A Great Catch: A Novel - Lorna Seilstad   *i* 902

SUPERNATURAL BEING

Abeloth
Vortex - Troy Denning   *s* 744

Abercrombie, Nathan
The Big Stink - David Lubar   *h* 317

Arnold
Hunted by the Others - Jess Haines   *f* 40

Begay, Janet
Firewalker - Allyson James   *r* 1013

Blake, Anita
Bullet - Laurell K. Hamilton   *f* 41

David/Smoke
Master of Smoke - Angela Knight   *r* 1035

Davis, Evan
A Legacy of Daemons - Camille
   Bacon-Smith   *f* 7

Daye, October "Toby"
An Artificial Night - Seanan McGuire   *f* 66

Krayl, Dagan
Sins of the Heart - Eve Silver   *r* 1106

Loki
In the Company of Vampires - Katie
   MacAlister   *h* 320

Mackenzie, Styx
Styx's Storm - Lora Leigh   *s* 774

Ol't'ro
Betrayer of Worlds - Larry Niven   *s* 786

Ril
The Shattered Sylph - L.J. McDonald   *f* 65

Riley, Eden
Something Wicked - Michelle Rowen   *h* 340

Spock
Rough Beasts of Empire - David R. George
   III   *s* 753

SURVIVOR

Hudson, Sera
Shadow Protector - Jenna Ryan   *r* 1097

Kramer, Josef
Panorama - H.G. Adler   *c* 564

Pierre
Guardians of the Phoenix - Eric Brown   *s* 738

TEACHER

Amsel, Edythe
Courting Miss Amsel - Kim Vogel Sawyer   *i* 901

Andreas, Rose
The Weird Sisters - Eleanor Brown   *c* 576

Aristotle
*The Golden Mean: A Novel of Aristotle and Alex-
   ander the Great* - Annabel Lyon   *t* 197

Beckett, Darlene
The Dead Detective - William Heffernan   *m* 459

Borland, Rory
Firefighter Daddy - Lee McKenzie   *r* 1063

Brooks, Cassandra
The Diviner's Tale - Bradford Morrow   *m* 501

Carr, Charlie
Miss Dimple Disappears - Mignon F.
   Ballard   *t* 112

Carter, Katy
Katy Carter Wants a Hero - Ruth
   Saberton   *r* 1098

Cartier, Anne
False Patriots - Charles O'Brien   *t* 220

Cathy
Shadow on the Land - Anne Doughty   *t* 143

Clover
The Widower's Tale - Julia Glass   *c* 613

Crowther, Jane
Children's Crusade - Scott Andrews   *s* 729

Dalton, Carleen
The Secrets Sisters Keep - Abby Drake   *c* 592

Deacon, Eddie
The Collaborator - Gerald Seymour   *m* 525

Dempsey, Arabella
The Mischief of the Mistletoe - Lauren
   Willig   *t* 263

Dirk
The Owl Hunt - Richard S. Wheeler   *t* 262

Ira
The Widower's Tale - Julia Glass   *c* 613

Ishigami
The Devotion of Suspect X - Keigo
   Higashino   *m* 463

Kessligh
Tracato - Joel Shepherd   *f* 83

Kirk, Harriet
Tomorrow's Garden - Amanda Cabot   *i* 832

Leone, Anne
Secrets to the Grave - Tami Hoag   *m* 466

Mr. Ma
All That Lives Must Die - Eric Nylund   *f* 73

Maguire, Holly
The Love Goddess' Cooking School - Melissa
   Senate   *r* 1101

Rosen, Viktor
A Lily of the Field - John Lawton   *t* 193

Scofield, Agnes
Being Polite to Hitler - Robb Forman
   Dew   *c* 591

Sevick, Libor
The Finkler Question - Howard Jacobson   *c* 630

Spencer, Ali
Operation Prince Charming - Phyllis
   Bourne   *r* 934

Spivey, Miss Grace
The Cailiffs of Baghdad, Georgia - Mary Helen
   Stefaniak   *t* 248

Sturgis, Miranda
All Is Forgotten, Nothing Is Lost - Lan Samantha
   Chang   *c* 582

TECHNICIAN

Tahoma, Clay
Promise Canyon - Robyn Carr   *r* 949

TEENAGER

Bian
Seed Seeker - Pamela Sargent   *s* 801

Cara
The Last Hunt - Bruce Coville   *f* 23

Cattie
Bound - Antonya Nelson   *c* 664

Cleaver, John Wayne
Mr. Monster - Dan Wells   *h* 362

Crawford, Tony
Children of the Sun - Max Schaefer   *c* 690

Earnshaw, Catherine
Wuthering Bites - Sarah Gray   *h* 293

Farah
People of the Book - Kathi Macias   *i* 879

Gabriel
Clarity - Kim Harrington   *m* 451

Hinds, Callum
The Hanging Wood - Martin Edwards   *m* 427

Jesse
Alien Invasion and Other Inconveniences - Brian
   Yansky   *s* 823

Judith
The Sweet Relief of Missing Children - Sarah
   Braunstein   *m* 386

Lisa
Damaged - Pamela Callow   *r* 946

Liss, Prue
Bearers of the Black Staff - Terry Brooks   *f* 16

Maidment, Jennifer
The Fever of the Bone - Val McDermid   *m* 496

Qu, Panterra
Bearers of the Black Staff - Terry Brooks   *f* 16

Safrah
Seed Seeker - Pamela Sargent   *s* 801

Sharpe, Cassel
White Cat - Holly Black   *f* 10

Starling, Jonathan
Lifeblood - Tom Becker   *h* 272

Toby
Moxyland - Lauren Beukes   *s* 733

Whelp, Henry
Dust City - Robert Paul Weston   *m* 553

White, Wendy
So Much Pretty - Cara Hoffman   *c* 626

Clevon, Eleisha
Memories of Envy - Barb Hendee *h* 301

Deacon
Demon Blood - Meljean Brook *r* 941

DeFarge, Jagger
The Keepers - Heather Graham *r* 990

Dracula
Dracula My Love - Syrie James *r* 1017

Durand, Christian
Angel at Dawn - Emma Holly *r* 1007

Ericson, Darel
Twilight Forever Rising - Lena Meydan *h* 329

Gabriella
Bloodborn - Nathan Long *f* 60

Gireaux, Simone
Blood Justice - David Burton *h* 277

Heathcliff
Wuthering Bites - Sarah Gray *h* 293

Jean-Claude
Bullet - Laurell K. Hamilton *f* 41

Knightley, George
Emma and the Vampires - Jane Austen *h* 266

March, Amy
Little Vampire Women - Lynn Messina *h* 328

March, Beth
Little Vampire Women - Lynn Messina *h* 328

March, Jo
Little Vampire Women - Lynn Messina *h* 328

March, Margaret "Marmee"
Little Vampire Women - Lynn Messina *h* 328

March, Meg
Little Vampire Women - Lynn Messina *h* 328

Michael
Dying Light - D. Scott Meek *h* 325

Monteguev, Nicholas
When Wicked Craves - J.K. Beck *h* 270

Myst
Night Myst - Yasmine Galenorn *r* 983

Nim Wei
Devil at Midnight - Emma Holly *r* 1006

Parker, Anastasija "Ana" Ramses
Almost to Die For - Tate Hallaway *h* 296

Philip
Memories of Envy - Barb Hendee *h* 301

Reed, John
Jane Slayre - Charlotte Bronte *h* 276

Rock, Baron
The Last Jewish Virgin: A Novel of Fate - Janice Eidus *c* 596

Royce, Alec
Hunted by the Others - Jess Haines *f* 40

Sabian, Alexandra "Alex"
Blood Law - Jeannie Holmes *h* 305

Saloman
Blood on Silk - Marie Treanor *h* 358

Shakespeare, William "Will"
Shakespeare Undead - Lori Handeland *h* 297

Sinakov, Stephan
Blood Justice - David Burton *h* 277

Smith, William
Jane and the Damned - Janet Mullany *t* 213

Solomon, David
Queen of Shadows - Dianne Sylvan *h* 353

Stratford, Simone
Memories of Envy - Barb Hendee *h* 301

Strong, Anna
Chosen - Jeanne C. Stein *h* 348

Ulrika
Bloodborn - Nathan Long *f* 60

Valens, Cale
Hungry for You - Lynsay Sands *r* 1100

Volod
Vampires Not Invited - Cheyenne McCray *r* 1060

Zginski, Rudolfo Vladimir
The Girls with Games of Blood - Alex Bledsoe *h* 274

VAMPIRE HUNTER

Deveraux, Elena
Archangel's Kiss - Nalini Singh *f* 85

Ellis, Sir Christopher
Kiss of the Rose - Kate Pearce *r* 1080

Fox, Megan
Night of the Vampires - Heather Graham *r* 989

Granger, Cole
Night of the Vampires - Heather Graham *r* 989

Llewellyn, Rosalind
Kiss of the Rose - Kate Pearce *r* 1080

Montague, Romeo
Romeo and Juliet and Vampires - Claudia Gabel *h* 284

Nikolai
Almost to Die For - Tate Hallaway *h* 296

VETERAN

Coleman, Cody
Leaving - Karen Kingsbury *i* 872

Conn, Emmett
The Gendarme - Mark T. Mustian *t* 215

Ellis, Will
One Was a Soldier - Julia Spencer-Fleming *m* 531

Fergusson, Clare
One Was a Soldier - Julia Spencer-Fleming *m* 531

Hood, Charlie
The Border Lords - T. Jefferson Parker *m* 512

McCrea, Eric
One Was a Soldier - Julia Spencer-Fleming *m* 531

McGuire, Jack
Tulagi Hotel - Heikki Hietala *t* 172

McMorsey, Tommy Jack
Extra Indians - Eric Gansworth *c* 608

McNabb, Tally
One Was a Soldier - Julia Spencer-Fleming *m* 531

Stillman, Trip
One Was a Soldier - Julia Spencer-Fleming *m* 531

Wagner, Arlen
The Cypress House - Michael Koryta *m* 480

VETERINARIAN

Barker, Rick
Alaska Weddings - Susan Page Davis *i* 845

VIGILANTE

Akia, Yoko
Cross Roads - Fern Michaels *r* 1066

Cricket, Lizzie Fox
Cross Roads - Fern Michaels *r* 1066

Flanders, Isabelle
Cross Roads - Fern Michaels *r* 1066

Gilmore, Renee
The Priest's Graveyard - Ted Dekker *i* 847

Lucas, Kathryn
Cross Roads - Fern Michaels *r* 1066

Quinn, Nikki
Cross Roads - Fern Michaels *r* 1066

Rutledge, Myra
Cross Roads - Fern Michaels *r* 1066

Ryland de Silva, Annie
Cross Roads - Fern Michaels *r* 1066

Thorn, Alexis
Cross Roads - Fern Michaels *r* 1066

VIKING

Cnut
The Forever Queen - Helen Hollick *t* 176

Corbanson, Raef
Kings of the North - Cecelia Holland *t* 175

Ingrith
The Viking Takes a Knight - Sandra Hill *r* 1004

MacAllister, Rane
Captured by Desire - Kira Morgan *r* 1072

Oakenshield, Thorfinn
Vision in the Forest - Michael Goldman *t* 162

Steven of Norstead
Dark Viking - Sandra Hill *r* 1005

VILLAIN

Ambrose
The Wise Man's Fear - Patrick Rothfuss *m* 520

Black Demon
The Valcourt Heiress - Catherine Coulter *r* 957

Despiser
Against All Things Ending - Stephen R. Donaldson *f* 30

du Malphias, Guy
At the Queen's Command - Michael A. Stackpole *f* 89

March, Archibald
To Save the Devil - Kate Moore *r* 1069

Michael, Blind
An Artificial Night - Seanan McGuire *f* 66

Unnamed Character
Words - Ginny L. Yttrup *i* 923

VOLUNTEER

Gilbert, Nick
Blood Covenant - Lisa Harris *i* 861

Katherine
City of Tranquil Light - Bo Caldwell *t* 123

Kiehn, Will
City of Tranquil Light - Bo Caldwell *t* 123

Pazos, Jose Robles
Hemingway Cutthroat - Michael Atkinson *t* 110

Ryan, Dr. Paige
Blood Covenant - Lisa Harris *i* 861

Steiner, Mitzi
Broken Wings: A Novel - Carla Stewart   *i* 909

WAITER/WAITRESS

Hansen, Lacey
Heads You Lose - Lisa Lutz   *m* 488

James, Claire
Delivered with Love - Sherry Kyle   *i* 874

Truman, Reagan
Somewhere Along the Way - Jodi Thomas   *r* 1118

WANDERER

Lasley, Gabe
Deep Trouble - Mary Connealy   *i* 840

Nairn
The Bards of Bone Plain - Patricia A. McKillip   *f* 68

Wilkins, Jack
Chasing the Sun - Kaki Warner   *r* 1126

WARD

Middleton, Melinda
Dreams of Desire - Cheryl Holt   *r* 1008

Middleton, Melissa
Dreams of Desire - Cheryl Holt   *r* 1008

WARLOCK

Masters, Gideon
The Witch's Daughter - Paula Brackston   *t* 122

Stanton, Dreadnought
The Native Star - M.K. Hobson   *f* 44

WARRIOR

Alexander
The Golden Mean: A Novel of Aristotle and Alexander the Great - Annabel Lyon   *t* 197

Ament, Sider
Bearers of the Black Staff - Terry Brooks   *f* 16

Arlen "Warded Man"
The Desert Spear - Peter V. Brett   *f* 15

Ashida, Kiyoko
Surrender to Darkness - Annette McCleave   *r* 1059

Beauhall, Sarah
Black Blade Blues - J.A. Pitts   *f* 77

Chagetai
Khan: Empire of Silver - Conn Iggulden   *t* 177

Drakis
Song of the Dragon - Tracy Hickman   *f* 42

Fenix, Marcus
Anvil Gate - Karen Traviss   *s* 809

Forge, Eva
The Horns of Ruin - Tim Akers   *f* 1

Hooper, Kali
Engines of the Apocalypse - Mike Wild   *f* 102

Jardir, Ahmann
The Desert Spear - Peter V. Brett   *f* 15

Jinn
Circle of Skulls - James P. Davis   *f* 29

Kenobi, Obi-Wan
Star Wars: Clone Wars Gambit: Siege - Karen Miller   *s* 784

Kratos
God of War - Matthew Stover   *f* 93

MacEgan, Trahern
Surrender to an Irish Warrior - Michelle Willingham   *r* 1139

Mackenzie, Rudi
The High King of Montival - S.M. Stirling   *f* 92

MacLeod, Quinn
Wicked Highlander - Donna Grant   *r* 992

Moore, Jon
Children No More - Mark L. Van Name   *s* 814
Jump Gate Twist - Mark L. Van Name   *s* 813

Murdoch, Jamie
Surrender to Darkness - Annette McCleave   *r* 1059

Parnell, Dane
Kraken - China Mieville   *f* 70

Phoenix, Elizabeth "Liz"
Chaos Bites - Lori Handeland   *h* 299

Schwarzhelm, Ludwig
Sword of Justice - Chris Wraight   *f* 103

Skywalker, Anakin
Star Wars: Clone Wars Gambit: Siege - Karen Miller   *s* 784

Skywalker, Luke
Vortex - Troy Denning   *s* 744

Stearns, Mike
1635: The Eastern Front - Eric Flint   *s* 751

Tam, Roxy
Sins of the Heart - Eve Silver   *r* 1106

The Dragon
Rogue Angel: The Dragon's Mark - Alex Archer   *f* 5

The Greyfriar
The Greyfriar - Susan Griffith   *h* 295

Trace, Hestizo
Star Wars: Red Harvest - Joe Schreiber   *s* 803

Uriah
Bathsheba: A Novel - Jill Eileen Smith   *i* 906

Zander
Entwined - Elisabeth Naughton   *r* 1073

WEALTHY

Albani, Nasri
The Calligrapher's Secret - Rafik Schami   *c* 691

Archer, James
Seven Nights to Forever - Evangeline Collins   *r* 955

Blackstone, Mrs. Dahlia
The Darling Dahlias and the Cucumber Tree - Susan Wittig Albert   *t* 107

Childers, Gary
Back to the Moon - Les Johnson   *s* 763

Curtlee, Ro
Damage - John T. Lescroart   *m* 483

Delaney, Amanda
The Secrets Sisters Keep - Abby Drake   *c* 592

Duke of Dornoch
The Unbelievers - Alastair Sim   *t* 242

Foster, Juliet
Miss Foster's Folly - Alice Gaines   *r* 981

Hartlinger, Kim
Found in Translation: An Unforgettable Mission Trip Where Faith, Obedience, and Forgiveness Intersect - Roger Bruner   *i* 830

Holcomb, Vance
The Flock - James Robert Smith   *s* 805

Holt, William
Blackstone and the Wolf of Wall Street - Sally Spencer   *t* 247

Hui, Ding
Dream of Ding Village - Yan Lianke   *c* 644

Knightley, George
Emma and the Werewolves - Adam Rann   *h* 339

Langdon, Rowena
An Unlikely Suitor - Nancy Moser   *i* 890

Lazuline, Linn
Pock's World - Dave Duncan   *s* 749

Linton, Edgar
Wuthering Bites - Sarah Gray   *h* 293

Maxwell, Jeremy
The Alarmists - Don Hoesel   *i* 865

Parker, Blake
Force of Habit - Alice Loweecey   *m* 486

Price, Fanny
Murder at Mansfield Park - Lynn Shepherd   *t* 240

Rutledge, Myra
Cross Roads - Fern Michaels   *r* 1066

Tyler, Crystal
When the Thrill Is Gone - Walter Mosley   *m* 502

Willis, William Sr.
Aunt Dimity and the Family Tree - Nancy Atherton   *m* 371

Worthington, Jack
A Hope Undaunted - Julie Lessman   *i* 876

WEREWOLF

Barlow, Julian
Marked by the Moon - Lori Handeland   *h* 298

Breze, Adrian
A Taint in the Blood - S.M. Stirling   *f* 91

Bridges, Austin III
Never Cry Werewolf - Heather Davis   *h* 279

Carnegie, Elias
Lifeblood - Tom Becker   *h* 272

Chaz
Hunted by the Others - Jess Haines   *f* 40

Clark, Cheyenne "Chey"
Overwinter: A Werewolf Tale - David Wellington   *h* 361

Darien
Wolf's Cross - S.A. Swann   *h* 352

Knightley, George
Emma and the Werewolves - Adam Rann   *h* 339

Lupo, Nick
Wolf's Bluff - W.D. Gagliani   *h* 285

Maria
Wolf's Cross - S.A. Swann   *h* 352

Panterra, Carlos
Eat, Prey, Love - Kerrelyn Sparks   *r* 1108

Powell
Overwinter: A Werewolf Tale - David Wellington   *h* 361

Rand, Vincent
When Pleasure Rules - J.K. Beck   *h* 271

Rochester, Bertha
Jane Slayre - Charlotte Bronte   *h* 276

Rokhlenu
The Wolf Age - James Enge   *f* 32

Roman, Eva
Master of Smoke - Angela Knight   *r* 1035

YOUNG MAN

Raimi, Capac
Procession of the Dead - Darren Shan *h* 343

Rusty
Mischief Night - Paul Melniczek *h* 326

Talbot, Lawrence
The Wolfman - Jonathan Maberry *h* 318

Townsend, Joel
Courting Miss Amsel - Kim Vogel Sawyer *i* 901

Worthington, Jack
A Hope Undaunted - Julie Lessman *i* 876

YOUNG WOMAN

Abbott, Rhyne
Marry Me - Jo Goodman *r* 986

Abuzeid, Nabilah
Lyrics Alley - Leila Aboulela *t* 104

Allen, Martha
The Wolves of Andover - Kathleen Kent *c* 636

Amsel, Edythe
Courting Miss Amsel - Kim Vogel Sawyer *i* 901

Araxie
The Gendarme - Mark T. Mustian *t* 215

Avery, Linden
Against All Things Ending - Stephen R. Donaldson *f* 30

Birch, Julia
Broken Promises - Elizabeth Cobbs Hoffman *c* 627

Bradford, Rebekah
Rebekah's Journey: An Historical Novel - Ann Bell *t* 116

Brooke, Elizabeth "Bess"
Secrets of the Tudor Court: By Royal Decree - Kate Emerson *t* 148

Brown, Amanda
The Headhunter's Daughter - Tamar Myers *m* 505

Brunet, Louise
13, rue Therese - Elena Mauli Shapiro *c* 696

Caldwell, Sarah
A Heart Divided: A Novel - Kathleen Morgan *i* 888

Cameron, Kate
A Bewitching Bride - Elizabeth Thornton *r* 1122

Carpenter, Meg
Our Tragic Universe - Scarlett Thomas *c* 704

Castellano, Mia
Courtesan's Kiss - Mary Blayney *r* 933

Chance, Troy
Learning to Swim - Sara J. Henry *m* 462

Colgate, Madelene
The Vengeful Bridegroom - Kit Donner *r* 967

Darcy, Georgina
Mr. Darcy's Little Sister - C. Allyn Pierson *t* 226

Durst, Celia
The False Friend - Myla Goldberg *c* 614

Eleonora
Quiet Chaos - Sandro Veronesi *c* 709

Esme
Highland Rogue, London Miss - Margaret Moore *r* 1071

Farran
In the Darkest Night - Patti O'Shea *f* 74

Fiona
Dragongirl - Todd J. McCaffrey *s* 782

Frankston, Caroline
Caroline's Choice - Martha Rogers *i* 899

Gilder, Florie
Captured by Desire - Kira Morgan *r* 1072

Hannigan, Keira
The Year of Living Scandalously - Julia London *r* 1045

Harkhoff, Melissa
Deceit - Brandilyn Collins *i* 838

Harris, Tillie
Up from the Blue: A Novel - Susan Henderson *c* 623

Helen of Troy
To Save the Devil - Kate Moore *r* 1069

Helene
The Blind Side of the Heart - Julia Franck *c* 604

Isabelle
Pictures of You: A Novel - Caroline Leavitt *c* 642

Jacobs, Julie
Juliet - Anne Fortier *t* 156

James, Claire
Delivered with Love - Sherry Kyle *i* 874

Jennifer
One Rough Man - Brad Taylor *m* 539

Joie
Blood Pressure - Terence Taylor *h* 354

Lang, Petra
When Wicked Craves - J.K. Beck *h* 270

Lassair
Music of the Distant Stars - Alys Clare *t* 129

Livingstone, Ruth
Love's First Bloom - Delia Parr *r* 1079

Loretta
The Reckless Bride - Stephanie Laurens *r* 1039

Louise
The Art of Losing - Rebecca Connell *c* 585

Madsen, Kate
My Dangerous Duke - Gaelen Foley *r* 976

Maguire, Holly
The Love Goddess' Cooking School - Melissa Senate *r* 1101

Marcail
Wicked Highlander - Donna Grant *r* 992

March, Amy
Little Vampire Women - Lynn Messina *h* 328

March, Beth
Little Vampire Women - Lynn Messina *h* 328

March, Jo
Little Vampire Women - Lynn Messina *h* 328

March, Meg
Little Vampire Women - Lynn Messina *h* 328

Maria
Hypothermia - Arnaldur Indridason *m* 470

Merry
The Valcourt Heiress - Catherine Coulter *r* 957

Michaels, Grace
Devil at Midnight - Emma Holly *r* 1006

Miller, Andie
Maybe This Time - Jennifer Crusie *r* 958

Miller, Ann
Fairer Than Morning - Rosslyn Elliott *i* 851

Montague, Storme
Styx's Storm - Lora Leigh *s* 774

Nicholson, Brigitte
Legacy: A Novel - Danielle Steel *c* 703

O'Connell, Luellen
The Dawn of a Dream - Ann Shorey *i* 904

O'Connor, Katie
A Hope Undaunted - Julie Lessman *i* 876
Love's First Bloom - Julie Lessman *r* 1041

O'Reilly, Morren
Surrender to an Irish Warrior - Michelle Willingham *r* 1139

O'Rourke, Eugenia "Gina"
A Rake by Midnight - Gail Ranstrom *r* 1088

Orland, Molly
Love Finds You in Prince Edward Island, Canada - Susan Page Davis *i* 846

Pallant, Marian
Chivalrous Captain, Rebel Mistress - Diane Gaston *r* 984

Parke, Catherine
Deceptions: A Jamestown Novel - Marilyn J. Clay *i* 130

Paxton, Lizzie
The Pursuit of Pleasure - Elizabeth Essex *r* 972

Petrule, Lizzy
The Shattered Sylph - L.J. McDonald *f* 65

Price, Fanny
Mansfield Park and Mummies: Monster Mayhem, Matrimony, Ancient Curses, True Love, and Other Dire Delights - Vera Nazarian *h* 332

Quinn, Cleo
Take a Chance on Me - Jill Mansell *r* 1052

Rayne, Dru
The Sentry - Robert Crais *m* 412

Rikki
Water Bound - Christine Feehan *r* 974

Rohan, Miranda
Breathless - Anne Stuart *r* 1112

Rosemary
Prince Charming Doesn't Live Here - Christine Warren *r* 1127

Sable, Nicki
Mark: Secret Cowboy - Pamela Britton *r* 940

Sato, Jin
Cryoburn - Lois McMaster Bujold *s* 739

Sibeal
Seer of Sevenwaters - Juliet Marillier *t* 202

Smith, Megan
Megan's Hero - Sharon Gillenwater *i* 856

Sparrow, Griselda
Griselda Takes Flight - Joyce Magnin Moccero *i* 887

Stangbourne, Lydia
The Invasion Year - Dewey Lambdin *t* 192

Stevenson, Sara
The Exile of Sara Stevenson: A Historical Novel - Darci Hannah *t* 997

Stone, Rachel
Journey to Riverbend - Henry McLaughlin *i* 884

Svensdottir, Katla
A Storm of Pleasure - Terri Brisbin *r* 939

Troyer, Becky
Patchwork Dreams - Laura V. Hilton *i* 863

Truman, Reagan
Somewhere Along the Way - Jodi Thomas *r* 1118

Wiltshire, Lucy
Save the Date - Jenny B. Jones *i* 869

Woodhouse, Emma
Emma and the Vampires - Jane Austen   h 266

Xulai
The Waters Rising - Sheri S. Tepper   s 808

Yazhi, Lilly
Promise Canyon - Robyn Carr   r 949

Author Index

This index is an alphabetical listing of the authors of books featured in entries and those listed within entries under the rubrics "Other books by the same author" and "Other books you might like." For each author, the titles of books described or listed in this edition and their entry numbers appear. Bold numbers indicate a featured main entry; light-face numbers refer to books recommended for further reading.

Author Index

Author Index

Author Index

E

Eads, S.Q.
Angels in Cowboy Boots 947

Eager, Edward
Magic by the Lake 3

Eagle, Kathleen
The Last True Cowboy 1119

Eakes, Laurie Alice
Better Than Gold 848
The Glassblower 848
Jersey Brides 848
Lady in the Mist 833, **848**
When the Snow Flies 848
The Widow's Secret 848

Earl, Robert
Ancient Blood 52

Earley, Pete
The Hot House: Life Inside Leavenworth Prison 468

Eason, Lynette
Don't Look Back 898, 850
Holiday Illusion 849
A Killer Among Us: A Novel **850**
Missing **849**, 850
Protective Custody 849
A Silent Fury 849
A Silent Pursuit 850
A Silent Terror 849, 850
Threat of Exposure 843
Too Close to Home 849, 850
Women of Justice Series 835

Eastland, Sam
Eye of the Red Tsar 425
Shadow Pass 235, **425**

Eberhart, Carolyn
A Darcy Christmas **991**

Ebershoff, David
The 19th Wife 654
Pasadena 105

Ebersohn, Wessel
The Centurion 426
Closed Circle 426
Klara's Visitors 426
A Lonely Place to Die 426
The October Killings **426**
Store Up the Anger 426

Eckstut, Arielle
Pride and Promiscuity 213

Eden, Cynthia
Immortal Danger 1059
The Naughty List **1026**

Edgarian, Carol
Rise the Euphrates 215
Three Stages of Amazement 577

Edwards, Anne
Haunted Summer 230

Edwards, Cassie
Savage Dawn 1077

Edwards, Kim
The Lake of Dreams **595**
The Memory Keeper's Daughter 595
The Secrets of a Fire King 595

Edwards, Louisa
Can't Stand the Heat 978, 1102, 1104
Just One Taste 1104
On the Steamy Side 1104

Edwards, Martin
All the Lonely People 427
The Arsenic Labyrinth 427
The Cipher Garden 427
The Coffin Trail 427
The Hanging Wood **427**
The Serpent Pool 427

Eekhout, Greg Van
Norse Code 77

Effinger, George Alec
The Nick of Time 798

Egan, Jennifer
The Keep 658

Eggers, Dave
How We Are Hungry 605

Eicher, Jerry S.
Ella's Wish 852
A Wedding Quilt for Ella 920

Eidus, Janice
The Celibacy Club 596
Faithful Rebecca 596
The Last Jewish Virgin: A Novel of Fate **596**
Urban Bliss 596
Vito Loves Geraldine 596
The War of the Rosens 596

Einstein, Charles
The Day New York Went Dry 738

Eisenstein, Phyllis
Shadow of Earth 751

Elkins, Aaron
Fellowship of Fear 494

Elliott, Cara
To Sin with a Scoundrel 1037, 1040

Elliott, Kate
Traitor's Gate 54

Elliott, Rosslyn
Fairer Than Morning **851**

Ellis, Bret Easton
The Informers 605

Ellis, David
Line of Vision 399, 513, 540

Ellis, Mary
Abigail's New Hope **852**
Never Far From Home 852
Sarah's Christmas Miracle 852
The Way to a Man's Heart 852
A Widow's Hope 852

Ellison, Harlan
Deathbird Stories 99
The Troublemakers: Stories by Harlan Ellison 802

Ellison, J. T.
Judas Kiss 390, 471

Ellison, J.T.
14 428
All the Pretty Girls 389, 428
The Cold Room 428
The Immortals **428**
Judas Kiss 428

Ellory, R.J.
A Quiet Belief in Angels 120

Elphinstone, Margaret
Voyageurs 116

Elrod, P.N.
The Adventures of Myhr 64
Cold Streets 31, 277, 336

Dance of Death 31
Dark and Stormy Knights **31**
The Dark Sleep 31
Lady Crymsyn 31, 360
Quincey Morris, Vampire 297, 303, 330
Song in the Dark 31

Emecheta, Buchi
The Joys of Motherhood: A Novel 719
The New Tribe 670

Emerson, Kate
Secrets of the Tudor Court: Between Two Queens 148
Secrets of the Tudor Court: By Royal Decree **148**
Secrets of the Tudor Court: The Pleasure Palace 148

Emley, Dianne
The First Cut: A Novel 387, 433, 447, 471

Endore, Guy
The Werewolf of Paris 318

Enge, James
Blood of Ambrose 32
This Crooked Way 32
The Wolf Age 1, **32**, 50

Enoch, Suzanne
After the Kiss 971
Always a Scoundrel 971, 1032, 1053, 1112
Before the Scandal: The Notorious Gentlemen 971, 1138
The Care and Taming of a Rogue 971
A Lady's Guide to Improper Behavior 971
London's Perfect Scoundrel 950
Reforming a Rake 1018, 1112
Rules of an Engagement **971**, 1091

Ephron, Hallie
1001 Books for Every Mood 429
The Bibliophile's Devotional 429
Come and Find Me **429**
The Everything Guide to Writing Your First Novel 429
Never Tell a Lie: A Novel of Suspense 238, 429, 462
Writing and Selling Your Mystery Novel 429

Eprile, Tony
The Persistence of Memory 201

Epstein, Jennifer Cody
The Painter from Shanghai 228

Erdrich, Louise
Love Medicine 616, 713
The Master Butchers Singing Club 191

Erickson, Carolly
The Hidden Diary of Marie Antoinette 149, 220
The Last Wife of Henry VIII 149
The Memoirs of Mary Queen of Scots 149, 189
Rival to the Queen **149**, 212
The Secret Life of Josephine 149
The Tsarina's Daughter 149

Erickson, K.J.
Third Person Singular 462

Ernst, Kathleen
Clues in the Shadows 430

Danger at the Zoo 430
Midnight in Lonesome Hollow 430
Old World Murder **430**
The Runaway Friend 430
Secrets in the Hills 430

Erpenbeck, Jenny
The Book of Words 597
The Old Child and Other Stories 597
Visitation **597**

Erwin, Sherri Browning
Jane Slayre **276**

Espach, Alison
The Adults **598**

Essex, Elizabeth
The Pursuit of Pleasure **972**

Essex, Karen
Dracula in Love **150**
Kleopatra 150
Leonardo's Swans 150
Pharaoh 150
Stealing Athena 150

Estep, Jennifer
Karma Girl 48

Estleman, Loren D.
American Detective 431
Angel Eyes 431
Bloody Season 151
The Branch and the Scaffold 151
The Glass Highway 431
The Left-Handed Dollar **431**
The Master Executioner 151
The Midnight Man 431
Motor City Blue 431
Roy & Lillie 151
Sudden Country 151
The Undertaker's Wife 151

Etchison, Dennis
The Death Artist 355
Fine Cuts 344

Ethridge, Benjamin Kane
Black and Orange **280**, 326, 331

Evanick, Marcia
A Berry Merry Christmas 960, 1034, 1135
Mistletoe Bay 1034, 1143

Evanovich, Janet
One for the Money 408, 420
Wicked Appetite 398

Evans, Bill
Frozen Fire **761**

Evans, Erin M.
The God Catcher 29

Evans, Richard Paul
Miles to Go 873

Evans, Sara
Softly and Tenderly **853**
The Sweet By and By 853, 866, 895
You'll Always Be My Baby 853

Everson, Eva Marie
Chasing Sunsets **854**
The Potluck Catering Club Series 854
The Potluck Club Series 854
Shadow of Dreams Series 854
Things Left Unspoken: A Novel 854
This Fine Life: A Novel 854

Everson, John
The 13th 281

Author Index

Author Index

Author Index

Author Index

Author Index

Author Index

Author Index

Title Index

This index alphabetically lists all titles featured in entries and those listed within entries under "Other books by the same author" and "Other books you might like." Each title is followed by the author's name and the number of the entry where the book is described or listed. Bold numbers indicate featured main entries; light-face numbers refer to books recommended for further reading.

Title Index

Title Index

Title Index

Title Index

Title Index

Title Index

Title Index

Title Index

O

Title Index

Title Index

Ride the Fire
Davis, Jo **964**

Ride the Wind: The Story of Cynthia Ann Parker and the Last Days of the Comanche
Robson, Lucia St. Clair 229

Riding on Instinct
Burton, Jaci 1068, 1090

Rifkind's Challenge
Abbey, Lynn 57, 58

The Right Call
Herman, Kathy 884

The Right Chord
Rose, Elisabeth 1094

Right Package, Wrong Baggage
Campbell, Wanda B. 859

The Right to Sing the Blues
Lutz, John 186

Righteous Anger
Williams, Lynda 819

The Righteous Blade
Nicholls, Stan 96

The Ring of Death
Spencer, Sally 530

The Ringer
Shank, Jenny **695**

Ringstones
Sarban 13

Ringworld's Children
Niven, Larry 786, 787

Rise the Euphrates
Edgarian, Carol 215

The Rising
Keene, Brian 275, 289, 292, 359

Rising Son
Perry, S.D. 753

Risky Business
Jackson, Lisa 471

Ritual
Hayder, Mo 457

Ritual
Heffernan, William 459

The Ritual Bath
Kellerman, Faye 410

Ritual in the Dark
Wilson, Colin 304

Rival to the Queen
Erickson, Carolly **149** , 212

Riven
Jenkins, Jerry B. 868

The Riven Kingdom
Miller, Karen 784

River of Blue Fire
Williams, Tad 37

River of Darkness
Airth, Rennie 503, 542, 559

Rivers of Time
de Camp, L. Sprague 726, 805

The Rivers Run Dry
Giorello, Sibella 835

Rizzo's Fire
Manfredo, Lou **491**

Rizzo's War
Manfredo, Lou 491

The Road Home
Tremain, Rose 583, 655, 679, 707, 708

The Road to Jerusalem
Guillou, Jan 222

The Road to Rome
Kane, Ben 185

Road to Seduction
Christopher, Ann 953

The Road to the Sands
Douglas, Anne 144

A Rock and a Hard Place
Wimberley, Darryl 459

Rocket Science
Lake, Jay 759, 807

The Rocksburg Railroad Murders
Constantine, K.C. 431

Rocky Mountain Redemption
Nissen, Pamela 897

Rogue Angel: Phantom Prospect
Archer, Alex **6**

Rogue Angel: The Dragon's Mark
Archer, Alex **5**

Rogue Angel: Tribal Ways
Archer, Alex **4**

Rogue Clone
Kent, Steven L. 767

A Rogue in a Kilt
Blair, Sandy 957

Rogue in My Arms
Bradley, Celeste 935

A Rogue in Texas
Heath, Lorraine 1126

Rogue Island
DeSilva, Bruce 513

Rogue Star
Hoare, Andy 757

Rogue Warrior
Weisman, John 539

Rogue's Honor
Hiatt, Brenda 1010, 1069, 1070

Rogue's Lady
Justiss, Julia 1023

A Rogue's Proposal
Laurens, Stephanie 967

The Rogue's Return
Beverley, Jo 984, 987, 1023

Rolling the R's
Linmark, R. Zamora 645

Rolling Thunder
Berent, Mark 411

Roma
Saylor, Steven 239

Roman Blood
Saylor, Steven 533

Roman Games
Macbain, Bruce 135, **198** , 255

Romancing Miss Bronte
Gael, Juliet 997

Romantic Migrations
Wiley, Michael 556

Romeo and Juliet and Vampires
Gabel, Claudia **284** , 290, 293, 297, 303, 328, 330

Roofworld
Fowler, Christopher 335

The Rook
James, Steven 867

Room
Donoghue, Emma 578, 594, 614, 646, 718

Room Service
Shalvis, Jill 1128

Rooms: A Novel
Rubart, James L. 900

Rosa
Rabb, Jonathan 476

Rose
Greenwood, Leigh 1126

A Rose in Winter
Sole, Linda 245

The Rose of Sebastopol
McMahon, Katherine 152, 253

A Rose Revealed
Roper, Gayle 841

The Rose Trilogy
Lewis, Beverly 901

Rose White, Rose Red
Vivian, Daisy 246

Rosemary and Rue: An October Daye Novel
McGuire, Seanan 48, 66, 286

Rosemary's Baby
Levin, Ira 499

Roses Are Thorns, Violets Are True
Gross, Sheila M. 859

Rotten to the Core
Connolly, Sheila 407

Rough and Ready
Hill, Sandra 1005

Rough Beasts of Empire
George, David R. III **753**

Roy & Lillie
Estleman, Loren D. **151**

Royal Blood
Bowen, Rhys 108, **121** , 183, 263

Royal Flush
Bowen, Rhys 121

A Royal Pain
Bowen, Rhys 121

Royal's Bride
Martin, Kat 1027, 1055

Rubicon
Saylor, Steven 239

Rugged and Relentless
Hake, Kelly Eileen 831, 846, 860, 904

The Rule of Four
Caldwell, Ian 376, 441

Rule of the Bone: A Novel
Banks, Russell 659

Rule of Two
Karpyshyn, Drew 765

Rule's Bride
Martin, Kat 980, 981, 1022, 1123, 1055

Rules of an Engagement
Enoch, Suzanne **971** , 1091

Rules of Deception
Reich, Christopher 444

The Rules of Gentility
Mullany, Janet 213

Rules of Prey
Sandford, John 496

The Rules of Seduction
Hunter, Madeline 961, 1040, 1137, 1138

Run Before the Wind
Woods, Stuart 529

The Runaway Friend
Ernst, Kathleen 430

The Runaway McBride
Thornton, Elizabeth 1122

The Runes of the Earth
Donaldson, Stephen R. 30

The Runes of the Earth
Donaldson, Stephen R. 24

Runner
Dietz, William C. 745

Running Away with Frannie
Manfredi, Renee 663

Running Blind
McCoy, Shirlee 849

Running from the Devil
Freveletti, Jamie 535

Running Scared
Jackson, Lisa 484

Rush
Wozencraft, Kim 468

A Rush of Blood
Jardine, Quintin **472**

The Russia House
Le Carre, John 550

The Russian Affair
Wallner, Michael **550**

Russian Winter: A Novel
Kalotay, Daphne 658

Ruthless
Stuart, Anne 1112, **1113** , 1114

Ruthless Game
Feehan, Christine 974

Rx for Chaos
Anvil, Christopher 730

Ryan's Renovation
Thomas, Marin 1119

Rynn's World
Parker, Steve 773

S

S: A Novel about the Balkans
Drakulic, Slavenka 593

Sabbat Martyr
Abnett, Dan 750

Sabbat Worlds
Abnett, Dan **723**

Sabella, or the Blood Stone
Lee, Tanith 325

The Sabotage Cafe
Furst, Joshua 690

Sacred
Lehane, Dennis 404, 482

Sacred Cows
Olson, Karen E. 513

Sacred Ground
Lackey, Mercedes 316

Sacred Obsession
Tirabassi, Becky 923

Sacred Stone
Cussler, Clive 414

The Sacred White Turkey
Washburn, Frances **713**

Title Index

Title Index

Title Index

Title Index